Advertising
Excellence

McGraw-Hill Series in Marketing

Advertising Excellence

COURTLAND L. BOVÉE

C. ALLEN PAUL DISTINGUISHED CHAIR, GROSSMONT COLLEGE

JOHN V. THILL

CHIEF EXECUTIVE OFFICER, COMMUNICATION SPECIALISTS OF AMERICA

GEORGE P. DOVEL

PRESIDENT, DOVEL GROUP

MARIAN BURK WOOD

PRESIDENT, WOOD AND WOOD ADVERTISING

McGRAW-HILL, INC.

New York   St. Louis   San Francisco   Auckland   Bogotá   Caracas   Lisbon
London   Madrid   Mexico City   Milan   Montreal   New Delhi
San Juan   Singapore   Sydney   Tokyo   Toronto

Advertising Excellence

This book is printed on acid-free paper.

4 5 6 7 8 9 0 VNH VNH 9 0 9 8 7 6

ISBN 0-07-006847-X

This book was set in Century Oldstyle by Better Graphics, Inc.
The editors were Bonnie K. Binkert and Ira C. Roberts;
the design supervisor was Joseph A. Piliero;
the text was designed by Joan Greenfield;
the cover illustration was by Roy Weimann.
the production supervisor was Annette Mayeski.
The photo editor was Susan Holtz.
Von Hoffmann Press, Inc., was printer and binder.

Library of Congress Cataloging-in-Publication Data

Advertising excellence / Courtland L. Bovée . . . [et al.].
    p.   cm. — (McGraw-Hill series in marketing)
    Includes bibliographical references and index.
    ISBN 0-07-006847-X
    1. Advertising.   I. Bovée, Courtland L.   II. Series
    HF5804.A38   1995
    659.1—dc20   94-12495

International Edition

Contents in Brief

Contents

Part I
Understanding
Advertising
Today

Chief
Executive
Officer

Vice President,
Finance

Vice President,
Marketing

Vice President,
Production

Marketing
Manager

Sales
Manager

Advertising
Manager

JELLY-FLOP

Contents

Make A Difference In The Lives Of Seniors And Homeless Pets.

The Purina Pets For People Program helps unite homeless shelter dogs and cats with senior citizens, free of charge through participating humane shelters. And during the month of October, every time you buy Purina pet food, you are helping make possible cash donations ($1 million annually nationwide) to the program.

Studies show that seniors who own pets receive life enriching benefits such as lowered blood pressure and less stress. They make fewer visits to the doctor and have a greater sense of well-being.

Kmart wholeheartedly supports community efforts like Pets For People. And Kmart and Purina thank you for your support.

If you know a senior who would benefit from the companionship of a pet, or if you would like the name of the participating shelter nearest you, call 1800-345-5678. And help kiss loneliness goodbye.

VIDEO EXERCISES

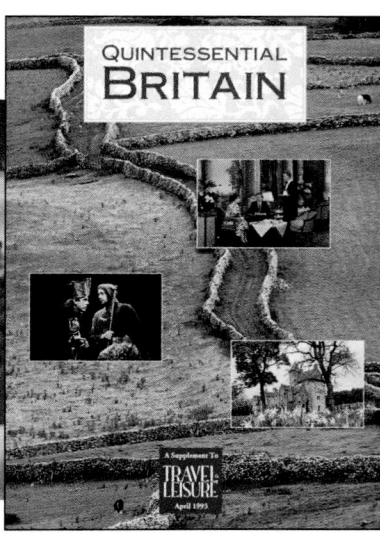

Contents

Looking for customers who fit a certain profile

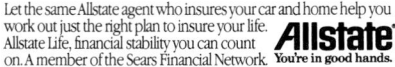
Contents

7 OBJECTIVES, STRATEGY, AND PLANS *162*

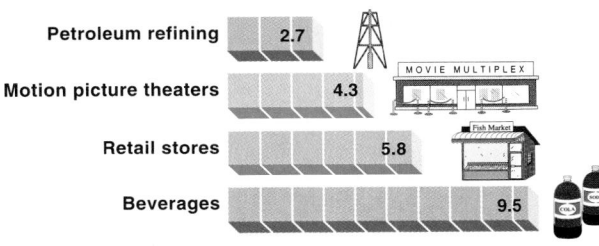

Contents

VIDEO EXERCISES

Contents

Part III
The Creative
Process

Contents

XV

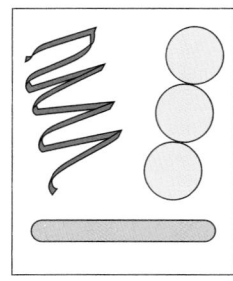

Informal balance

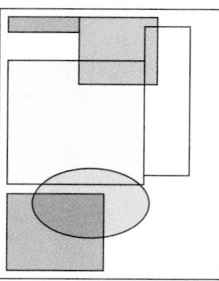

Out of balance

Contents

xvi

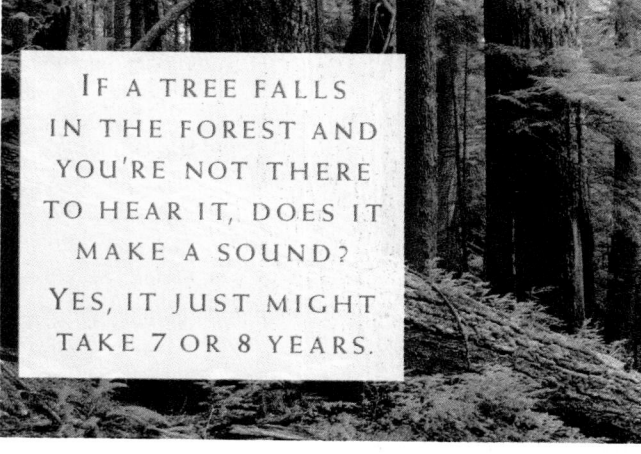

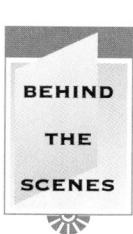

BEHIND
THE
SCENES

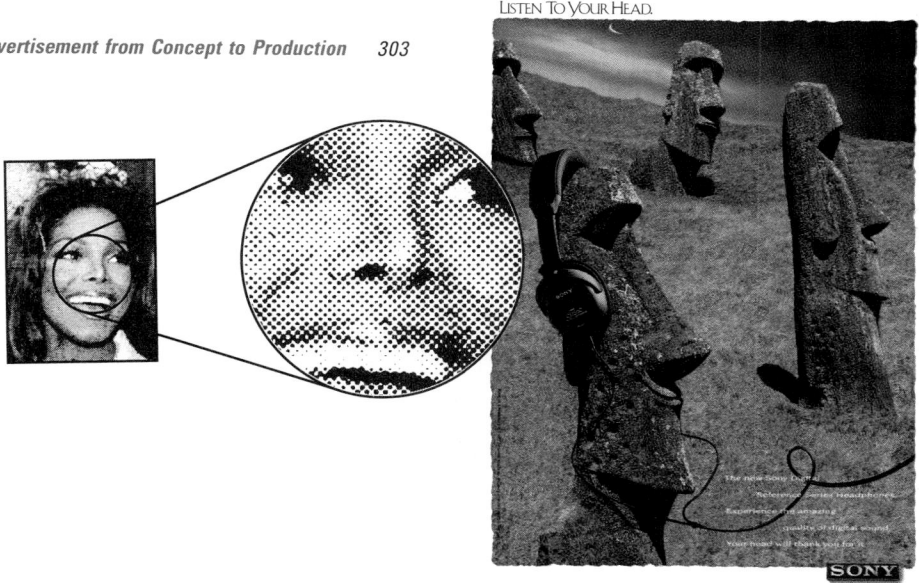

Contents

xvii

Contents

Part IV
Media Choices

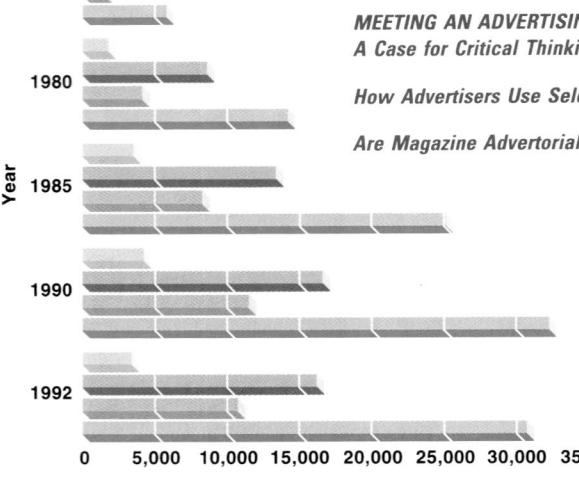

Contents

Oldies **7.7%**

CHR/Top 40 **7.2%**

News/Talk **5.9%**

MOR/Standards **4.4%**

AOR **3.7%**

Spanish **3.5%**

Soft Rock **3.4%**

Urban/Black **3.4%**

Easy Listening **2.2%**

Classic Rock **1.9%**

Jazz **0.6%**

Classical **0.5%**

Variety/All Other **1.2%**

KFMB-TV ch 8
PHONE: 619-571-8888   FAX: 619-569-4203
7677 Engineer Road
San Diego, CA 92111

Contents

We're in the NYNEX Yellow Pages.

VIDEO
V
EXERCISES

Glatt anstadt.

Part V
Putting the
Campaign
Together

ETHICS
IN
ADVERTISING

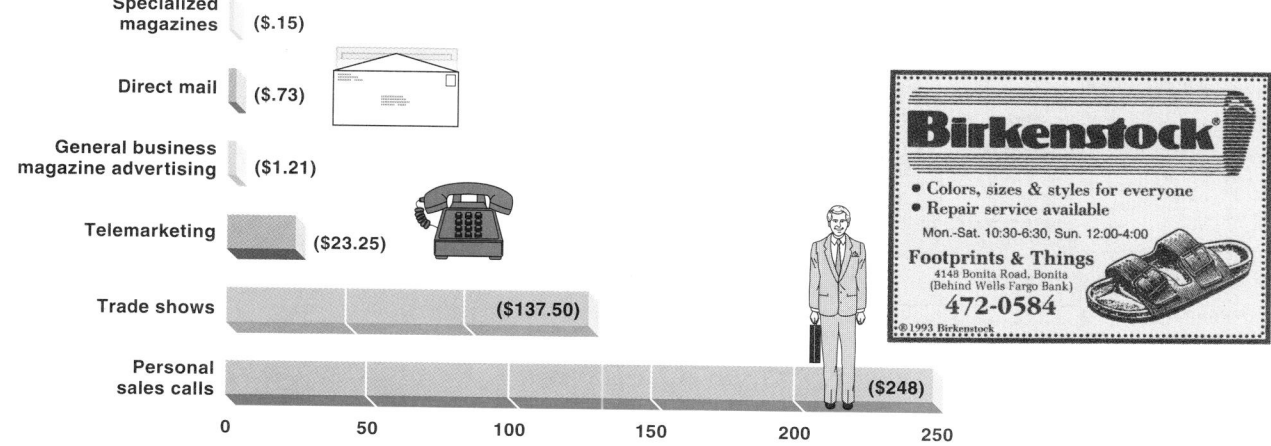

VIDEO

V

EXERCISES

Preface

Preparing Students for the New Realities in Advertising

Advertising used to be such a comfortable and predictable business. Companies could launch a national brand on network television, back it up with print advertising in a handful of national magazines, and they were in business. Technology was simple, and media choices were few and straightforward.

Not any more. Many parts of the country have dozens of broadcast and cable channels, and hundreds more may be on the way. The national magazine market has splintered into hundreds of focused publications. Hungry competitors cross national boundaries in search of new markets. On-line computer-based information services link consumers and businesses around the world, providing advertising options unheard of even a few years ago. Automated kiosks play the dual roles of advertising media and salesperson. Production technologies have made it possible to create full-color print advertising on desktop computers, and digital video editing and special effects give television advertisers capabilities the industry is just beginning to grasp. We can only speculate about other advertising options that future developments in the information superhighway might eventually bring.

Advertising's view of its audience is undergoing significant changes as well. While researchers and practitioners continue to argue the merits of globalized marketing in general and globalized advertising in particular, an intriguing phenomenon has emerged. Advertisers are discovering not only that there are significant cultural differences from country to country but that pockets of cultural uniqueness exist inside many countries. The United States is a prime example of this, with its long and continuing tradition of receiving immigrants from all over the globe. As a result of this growing recognition of cultural diversity in the marketplace, more and more advertisers are searching for effective ways to identify and target specific cultural segments. Advertising to African-Americans is perhaps the most visible example of this in the United States, but microcultures exist in the various Hispanic-American and Asian-American segments, as well as in segments of consumers who trace their roots back to Western and Eastern Europe.

To address this important and exciting development in advertising, we've expanded on the usual coverage of international advertising to include intercultural advertising as well. The two subjects are covered in depth in one chapter as a way to highlight the similarities between crossing cultural borders and crossing national borders, plus they are both discussed at appropriate points throughout the text.

Finally, advertising's perspective on itself is changing, too. Advertisers realize they can no longer afford to execute marketing communication programs in isolation from one another. The trend toward integrated marketing communication (IMC) is the most visible response to this realization.

What do all these changes mean for the student about to move into the field of advertising? First, this is definitely an exciting and chaotic time to be in advertising. Second, yesterday's approach to teaching advertising may not be the right approach for tomorrow's advertising environment. That's why you'll see coverage of emerging technology, new media, intercultural advertising, and other evolving concepts throughout *Advertising Excellence*. This new text provides the most up-to-date coverage possible so instructors have the tools they need to prepare students for the advertising challenges of today *and* tomorrow.

Building on a Solid Foundation

There is some irony in all this focus on new developments, however. As advertising expands and changes with every new technology or insight into audience behavior, a solid understanding of the fundamentals becomes that much more important. Consider interactive, multimedia advertising. There's no real history for this sort of advertising, so we don't have the models and guidelines we have for television, radio, and print. Those of us who get involved in this new advertising are going to have to learn as we go along. The advertising professionals who start with a solid knowledge of consumer and organizational behavior, marketing concepts, design principles, and communication theory are much better prepared to take full advantage of these new and emerging options.

While keeping a sharp eye on the future, *Advertising Excellence* doesn't compromise students' need for a strong foundation in fundamental concepts. Whether it's the history of advertising in Chapter 1 or discussions of buyer behavior in Chapter 4, strategy and planning in Chapter 7, design principles in Chapter 10, media planning in Chapter 13, sales promotion in Chapter 17, or local media in Chapter 19, *Advertising Excellence* emphasizes the need to understand basic principles. Students will be better prepared for the future with an understanding of where advertising has been and where it is today.

Here's a quick sample of some of the content that distinguishes *Advertising Excellence:*

- In-depth coverage of a complete integrated advertising campaign (Chapter 20, on GMC Truck).
- An entire chapter devoted to local advertising, an arena where many students will spend all or part of their advertising careers, and one that is typically given scant attention in advertising texts.
- Unique coverage of the increasingly important field of intercultural advertising.
- Coverage of emerging technologies such as interactive media (including direct-response television, automated kiosks, on-line computer-based information services, videotext), computerized design tools, morphing and other digital special effects, digital video editing, virtual reality, computer-assisted interviews, holograms, ink-jet personalization, selective binding, direct broadcast satellite television, digital cable radio, PR planning software, and multimedia presentations.
- Hundreds of examples that illustrate strategic and tactical concepts used by a wide variety of advertisers. These examples include numerous instances of nonprofit, business-to-business, and international advertising.
- An extensive selection of ads, most of which are award winners. The ads are balanced by industry, media, and geographic scope—including local, national, and international ads from more than 20 countries.

Providing Organized, Coherent Coverage

We realize that one of the biggest challenges in teaching advertising is to sequence and connect the multitude of topics in a way that builds comprehension and minimizes confusion. Our approach to IMC is a good example of how we've addressed this challenge in *Advertising Excellence*. To begin with, we don't wait until late in the book to introduce IMC as a special advertising technique. We define it right up front in Chapter 1 as a strategic philosophy of communication. We then build on that at relevant points throughout the text to give students a cohesive picture. The discussion of audience cognitive processes in Chapter 4 (Audience Analysis and Buyer Behavior) emphasizes that one of IMC's most important benefits is the clarity of message it delivers to the audience. Chapter 7 (Objectives, Strategy, and Plans) follows up with a discussion of how an IMC approach influences the planning process.

The coverage of media beginning with Chapter 13 then points out that an integrated approach to media selection is a key part of IMC as well. Similarly, Chapters 17, 18, and 19 demonstrate how IMC affects decisions in sales promotion, public relations, and local media. Finally, Chapter 20, which presents an entire advertising campaign in detail, shows how GMC Truck put IMC to use in a successful communication program. Rather than offering an isolated dose of IMC theory, *Advertising Excellence* provides a cohesive, cumulative discussion that ties in with material throughout the course.

Exploring Today's Most Important Ethical Issues

Unlike some texts, *Advertising Excellence* draws a clear distinction between ethical dilemmas and ethical lapses, which helps students understand the difference between unresolved ethical questions and behavior that's simply unethical. This text covers ethics in three ways: in a dedicated section in Chapter 3, in 12 Ethics in Advertising boxes, and in shorter examples placed throughout the book. Here's a sampling of the ethical dilemmas we highlight:

- *The Use and Abuse of Infomercials* Examines the current controversy over the potential for deception in program-length advertisements that try to look like news programs or talk shows.

- *Advertising to Kids: Right or Wrong?* Explores the issue of directing advertising at children and the effect that such advertising may have on household purchase behavior.

- *How Healthy Is Medical Advertising?* Discusses the role advertising has in the pharmaceutical industry and raises the question of whether it's proper to let advertising influence important healthcare decisions.

- *When Creative Visuals Become Deceptive Visuals* Looks at the line between attractive product presentation and deceptive presentation. As special-effects technology becomes more widespread, this issue will grow in importance.

- *Is That Really News?* Discusses the role of news releases in print and broadcast journalism. Students learn why the inherent difficulty of editing video news releases leads to much of this footage airing exactly as it's submitted by PR firms. This box is one of several discussions of the relationship between advertisers and the media.

Every Ethics in Advertising box ends with two "What's Your Opinion?" questions that encourage students to think about the issue presented and to draw their own conclusions. These questions can form the basis of class discussions, homework assignments, or student projects.

On the subject of ethics and social responsibility, *Advertising Excellence* has no examples of alcohol promotions. We certainly support companies' rights to promote legal products, but considering that many students taking this course are not of legal drinking age and that alcoholism among college students is a continuing social concern, we believe that an emphasis on alcoholic products in a textbook is inappropriate. *Advertising Excellence* also avoids tobacco examples (other than those cases in which tobacco products are the subject of ethical dilemmas). The trade literature offers thousands of other great advertising examples that students can relate to, and we've taken advantage of those.

Fostering a Successful Learning Experience

Advertising Excellence presents both fundamental and emerging trends in a lively and engaging style that reflects our enthusiasm for the profession. Students not only read about advertising, they get to experience it firsthand through the many involvement activities we present. A quick look at the pedagogy in *Advertising Excellence* reveals a much richer set of exercises and learning experiences than is offered by any other text in the field. In addition to learning objectives, key term definitions, chapter summaries, and other traditional features, we provide role-playing case studies, experiential exercises on a wide range of topics, decision-making opportunities on ethical dilemmas, and numerous possibilities for class discussion. This unmatched collection of teaching tools makes the classroom experience much more interesting for students and frees instructors from the burden of creating all of their own exercises.

FACING AN ADVERTISING CHALLENGE
These unique case studies put the student in the advertisers' shoes to explore a number of decisions related to the chapter material. Each chapter opens with a short slice-of-life vignette that draws students into the chapter by vividly portraying an advertising challenge faced by a real executive. Each chapter concludes with a section entitled Meeting an Advertising Challenge: A Case for Critical Thinking, which describes the actions taken by the featured executive and analyzes the results in light of the concepts presented in the chapter. Then the student takes over, playing a role in the executive's organization by making advertising decisions in four carefully chosen scenarios. The 20 advertising challenges include such intriguing cases as these:

- The U.S. Postal Service using qualitative research to explore the relationships between customers and letter carriers and to build on that knowledge in a new ad campaign
- Saturn striving to build an image as a new kind of U.S. car company
- The Deutsch advertising agency trying to parlay hot creative talents into a major national business
- Cessna Aircraft working to catch the attention of corporate CEOs for the introduction of a new executive jet
- The Swedish retailer Ikea using local advertising to build awareness and traffic for new stores in the United States

SHARPEN YOUR ADVERTISING SKILLS
These assignments offer students the opportunity to practice or analyze a particular advertising skill covered in the chapter. Examples include choosing the visual

imagery for a U.S. television commercial being adapted for the Singapore market, defining an advertising appeal for videophones, and selecting media for promoting snack cakes. By grappling with real-life advertising problems such as these, students develop a much stronger grasp of the material presented in the text. The exercises include both decision-making and communication components, two of the most important skills students will need in their careers.

WHICH AD PULLED BETTER?
These unique exercises let students test their advertising judgment by predicting which of two ads in a pair scored higher in well-known readership tests. The Instructor's Manual provides the answers, along with an analysis of each ad's performance. *Advertising Excellence* offers eight Which Ad Pulled Better? exercises; they appear in Chapters 4, 5, 7, 8, 10, and 11.

HIGHLIGHT BOXES
In addition to the 12 Ethics in Advertising boxes, 27 highlight boxes throughout the text show the steps needed to apply a variety of advertising techniques. These cover a wide range of topics, including using specialized agencies to reach ethnic audiences, deciding whether to use advertising that might offend some members of the audience, recognizing the importance of word-of-mouth communication, addressing the nonrational side of decision making, minimizing waste in advertising budgets, dealing with the question of humor and effectiveness, and using interactive television.

BEHIND THE SCENES
Two comprehensive real-life stories of advertising production take students through the entire process from concept through production, highlighting the decisions that need to be made and the technologies that can be applied to the production process. The first, following Chapter 11, illustrates the creative challenges Ammirati & Puris had to overcome in producing a print ad for Compaq Computer. The second, following Chapter 12, takes students onto the leading edge of technology as it explores the use of virtual reality in a television spot that Ayer Chicago created for Leaf's Jolly Rancher candy.

VIDEO EXERCISES
Video provides a powerful and engaging learning experience, and *Advertising Excellence* ties a package of relevant, professional video programs to the text with unique video exercises. At the end of each part, we offer a synopsis of the video program. Additionally, material in the text provides exercises for analysis, application, ethical judgment, decision making, and teamwork—the same key skills that students will need to apply on the job.

IMPORTANT ADDITIONAL FEATURES TO HELP STUDENTS LEARN
This text includes other useful student-oriented features:

- Learning objectives in every chapter guide the learning effort.
- The glossary provides easy reference for all key terms in the book.
- Advertising checklists in 11 chapters provide quick reference guidelines on such subjects as evaluating an agency, addressing legal issues with endorsements, planning advertising research projects, choosing globalization or localization, producing great copy, designing effective ads, and using yellow pages advertising.
- Key term lists with page references at the end of each chapter help students review learning progress.
- Appendixes provide a sample marketing plan, a sample advertising plan, and extensive coverage of advertising careers.

- Ten Questions for Discussion at the end of each chapter offer five questions for review and five for analysis and application.

What are the benefits of having so many instructional features? Students grasp concepts and terminology more completely because they have the opportunity to learn in several ways: experience, analysis, review, and application. Also, the instructor's preparation time is reduced because discussion questions, activities, and homework possibilities are all here and ready to be used. Instructors won't have to spend their limited time searching out ways to involve students in the course. Finally, the pedagogy is sufficient for instructors to teach the course term after term without exhausting the text's rich resources. By not limiting chapter pedagogy to just simple review questions, *Advertising Excellence* contains enough material to keep the course fresh and interesting for both instructors and students.

Relying on Extensive, Up-to-Date Research

Advertising Excellence provides up-to-date coverage, in terms of both examples and emerging concepts. The thoroughness of the research is evidenced by the number and currency of the endnotes—more than 1,200 sources from academic and trade books and journals. To illustrate every concept, we collected a number of possible examples and then carefully selected the one or two instances that best illustrated the material. For every article and book reference you see in the notes, many more were reviewed and not included. The extensive ad program, the result of a worldwide search conducted over many months, is further evidence of the care put into the preparation of this text.

Catching Students' Attention with Lively Writing

From the beginning of this project, we placed an emphasis on lively, interesting prose that invites students to read. Without sacrificing academic integrity, *Advertising Excellence* communicates and informs with a light touch. Even in a text as carefully and thoroughly researched as this one, it's possible to make the study of advertising enjoyable. Advertising is a lively, energetic business, and we think students should get that feeling throughout the course.

Enhancing Learning with an Attractive, Effective Design

The visual appeal of a textbook has a lot to do with the success of the student's learning efforts. Every element of *Advertising Excellence* is part of an integrated instructional design. Every exhibit includes a complete caption and is closely integrated with the related text. All international and intercultural ads include translations where needed. Advertisements and photos were carefully chosen to support the text, rather than simply to entertain the reader. The open, attractive layout complements the lively writing to ensure a high level of interest and retention.

Supporting the Instructional Process

Obviously, the textbook is only a part of the overall instructional package. To meet the challenges of large classes, heavy teaching loads, and limited preparation time, instructors need a complete program of pedagogical resources and support features. Here are the ways in which *Advertising Excellence* supports the instructional process.

- *Instructor's Resource Manual.* Each chapter in the Instructor's Manual contains annotated learning objectives, key terms, the chapter outline, lecture notes (with references to specific overhead transparencies), and answers to all questions and exercises. We've provided the information instructors need, without slowing them down with extra supplements of questionable value.

- *Acetate Transparency Program.* This set of 100 transparencies presents selected exhibits from the text, plus dozens of new ads for in-class discussion. Each transparency is supported by a cover sheet that outlines the learning objectives for that transparency, the major points that should be emphasized, and several discussion questions specific to each transparency, along with answers.

- *Commercial Reel.* This videotape features 100 successful television commercials that demonstrate a variety of advertising concepts, along with commentary by the authors.

- *Videodisk.* A unique feature among advertising texts, the videodisk provides quick access to all overhead transparencies and selected commercials.

- *Test Bank.* This manual is organized by text chapters and includes a mix of true/false, multiple choice, fill-in, and short cases with multiple-choice questions for each chapter. The questions are coded by level of difficulty, question type, and text page. The test bank has been carefully screened by reviewers to ensure that questions and answers are correct, relevant, and appropriate for this course. The test bank is available both in hard copy and on disk (both IBM and Macintosh formats).

- *Testing Services.* Two major programs are available:
    Computerized Test Bank. A powerful microcomputer program allows the instructor to create customized tests using the questions from the test bank, self-prepared items, or a combination. This versatile program incorporates a broad range of test-making capabilities, including editing and scrambling of questions to create alternative versions of a test. This program is available for both Apple and IBM computers.
    Customized Test Service. Through its Customized Test Service, McGraw-Hill will supply adopters of *Advertising Excellence* with custom-made tests consisting of items selected from the test bank. The test questions can be renumbered in any order. Instructors will receive an original test, ready for reproduction, and a separate answer key. Tests can be ordered by mail or by phone, using a toll-free number.

- *Classroom Management Software.* This program helps with grading and recordkeeping.

Acknowledgments

Advertising Excellence is the product of the concerted efforts of a number of people. A heartfelt thanks to our many friends, acquaintances, and business associates who contributed directly or indirectly to this textbook.

We extend our deep gratitude to Jackie Estrada for her noteworthy talents and dedication. (CLB and JVT)

My thanks to Hewlett-Packard and to Dovel Group clients for the opportunity to work on interesting and successful marketing programs, and to Brandi Coburn and Lynn Mead for consistently top-quality work. Special thanks to Joy Aldrich, Sandy Brown, Brandon Geary, Linda Haynes, Phil Herring, Jeff Idler, Bill Toliver, and the other talented pros at Herring Newman in Seattle. There's nothing better than doing great work with great people. (GPD)

There's no substitute for hands-on experience, so thank you to Citicorp, Chase Manhattan Bank, and the National Retail Federation for the opportunity to address exciting business challenges. And a round of applause for Wally Wood, whose in-depth knowledge of magazine advertising and local advertising has contributed to the success of Wood & Wood Advertising. (MBW)

Our thanks to Terry Anderson, whose communication abilities and organizational skills ensured the clarity and completeness of this project. She aided us admirably throughout the preparation of this textbook.

For the extensive program of domestic and international ads in *Advertising Excellence,* we are indebted to the persistent, creative efforts of photo editor Susan Holtz. Thanks to her, we were able to provide the largest array of international ads of any advertising text.

The insightful comments and helpful ideas of the individuals who reviewed the manuscript were invaluable. Thanks to Edd Applegate, Middle Tennessee State University; Christopher Cakebread, Boston University; Barbara Coe, University of North Texas; Scott de Francesco, New York University; Denis Elbert, University of North Dakota; Harold Hoy, Pennsylvania State University—Elizabethtown College; J. W. Kilpatrick, California State University, Sacramento; Don F. Kirchner, California State University, Northridge; John Phillips, University of San Francisco; Jack Raskopf, Texas Christian University; Ed Riordan, Wayne State University; William Sandberg, University of South Carolina; Cliff Shaluta, Western Kentucky University; Carolyn F. Siegel, Eastern Kentucky University; Tommy Smith, University of Southern Mississippi; Harlan Spotts, Northeastern University; Debra Stephens, Villanova University; and Jay Weiner, University of Texas—Arlington.

We also want to extend our warmest appreciation to the very devoted professionals at McGraw-Hill. They include Gary Burke, Bonnie Binkert, Dundee Holt, Dan Loch, Safra Nimrod, and the outstanding McGraw-Hill sales representatives. Finally, we thank editor Ira Roberts for his dedication and expertise, and we are grateful to Judy Duguid, Joan Greenfield, and Joe Piliero for their superb work.

Courtland L. Bovée

John V. Thill

George P. Dovel

Marian Burk Wood

*Advertising
Excellence*

Understanding Advertising Today

The Foundations of Advertising

After studying this chapter, you will be able to

1. Describe the relationship among advertisers, agencies, media, and suppliers

2. List and classify the types of advertising

3. Explain the functions of advertising

4. Discuss the importance of the marketing concept for advertising and identify the elements of the marketing mix

5. Discuss how the communication process and integrated marketing communications relate to advertising

6. Explain how technological advances during and after the Industrial Revolution expanded advertising

7. Highlight the key challenges and opportunities facing today's advertisers

BE COMFORTABLE WITH WHO YOU ARE.

Hush Puppies

Facing an Advertising Challenge at Levi Strauss & Company

PUTTING THE COLOR BACK INTO A FADING MARKET

How do you turn blue into green? Just ask Levi Strauss & Company. Founded in 1853 as a maker of sturdy britches for gold miners, the San Francisco–based firm has built a $5.6 billion global business by advertising the fashion and function of blue jeans. Blue jeans were red hot during the 1970s and 1980s, so sales and profits soared. In its peak year, the entire U.S. jeans industry sold roughly 500 million pairs. Then the jeans fad faded, and the company faced some tough times as chief executive officer (CEO) Robert D. Haas fought to protect the business his great-great-grand-uncle Levi Strauss had established.

First Haas looked at the U.S. market for blue jeans. He saw that the average age of the population was steadily increasing and that the birth rate was in decline, so far fewer teenagers would be wriggling into jeans in the future. The baby boomers who had originally worn jeans in the 1960s had not only aged but had also gained weight. That meant these customers now needed looser-fitting clothing. Meanwhile, teens and twenty-somethings were going back to basics, seeking casual pants that reflected their sense of fashion. Finally, preteens looked like a growing market eager to don jeans.

To move Levi Strauss ahead, Haas asked his experts to analyze the needs of these groups and then develop products for each. For the baby boomers, they came up with the Dockers line of casual clothing. This line was as comfortable as jeans but featured updated styles and a looser fit. For young people aged 14 to 24, the experts relaunched one of Levi Strauss's original models, the slim 501 button-fly blue jean. And for the pre-teen group, they adapted the newly popular oversize look to create the Big Jeans line.

As these new products were being developed, Haas looked at the competitive situation. An active advertiser, Levi Strauss held the largest share of the jeans market, but Lee and Wrangler were not far behind. These two competitors had successfully used a western image to sell to cowboys and city slickers alike. Haas also noticed that newer jeans makers like Pepe and Cross Colours were taking aim at specific ethnic groups. What's more, the company's rivals were beckoning to jeans wearers of all ages and backgrounds via television, radio, newspaper, magazine, and billboard advertising.

Although Levi Strauss was ready to launch new products geared to the diverse needs of its changing marketplace, it also had to contend with competitors who were aiming at many of the same customers. If you were Robert Haas, how would you use advertising to let people know about your new products? Where would you advertise? And what would you say to convince people to try the new products?[1] ∎

CHAPTER OVERVIEW As Levi Strauss's CEO understands, you have to know what to communicate, who to communicate with, and how to communicate if you want to get ahead in the high-stakes apparel business. So it's no surprise that Robert Haas and his competitors are keenly aware of the power and persuasion of advertising. In this chapter, your journey through the dynamic world of advertising begins with an overview of contemporary advertising. First, you'll meet the four players in the advertising process and learn the definitions, types, and functions of advertising. Next, you'll explore advertising as one element of marketing, examine the communication process, trace the communication phases in advertising, and learn about integrated marketing communications. Then you'll follow the evolution of advertising and learn about the technological advances that have fueled the growth of advertising. Finally, you'll get a look at the key challenges and opportunities faced by today's advertisers, and you'll see how this book follows the flow of the advertising planning process.

Advertising: Many Faces, Many Places

Advertising is virtually everywhere in daily life, and its forms and roles are both contested and admired. Some see advertising as both the mirror and the maker of culture: its words and images reflect the present and the past even as they contribute new sounds and symbols that shape the future. Others say advertising is purely an economic activity with one purpose: to sell. Whatever your view (and you can read about many views of advertising in Chapter 3), many advertisers and agencies believe that advertising creates "magic in the marketplace."[2]

Levi Strauss, like most advertisers, wants to create magic in the marketplace by reaching you where you live, work, play, and buy—not once, but many times—to convince you to buy its products. Evidence of this growth in advertising is all around us: in the mail, in newspapers, in magazines, on television, on the radio, at the movies, on buses and trains, on matchbook covers, on billboards, even on parking meters. During an average day, people in the United States are likely to be exposed to thousands of advertising messages in one form or another.[3]

The explosive growth of advertising continues throughout the world, spreading to Eastern Europe (see Exhibit 1.1) and to Africa as well as to the People's Republic of China, home to more than 1 billion consumers. Foreign brands are becoming available in many Chinese cities, and these brands are using the magic of advertising to tell their story. Chinese television carries commercials for Tang orange drink, billboards feature Ponds facial cream and Vaseline Intensive Care hand lotion, and store windows display the latest Sanyo laser disk players. Johnson & Johnson and other global firms now manufacture in China, and brand-conscious Chinese consumers eagerly snap up these and other well-known products, fueling a business boom.[4] To understand this worldwide growth, it's important to look at what advertising is and how it's used.

Inside the World of Advertising

Advertising is the paid, nonpersonal communication of information about products or ideas by an identified sponsor through the mass media in an effort to persuade or influence behavior. Advertising is *nonpersonal* because it's directed to groups of people rather than to specific individuals. Even when advertising seems to be directed only at you, it's an illusion created by a computer that selects you as part of the target audience and then personalizes the message with your name or address.

Advertising *communicates information about products or ideas,* whether it's the features of a new videocassette recorder or the benefits of voting for a particular candidate. An *identified sponsor* such as a company selling a product or a nonprofit group seeking donations pays for the ad message to be placed in the *mass media,* communication channels that reach many people at once. The information (and the entire context of the advertising message) is intended to *persuade or influence* people to buy a particular product, vote for a specific candidate, or donate money to a worthy cause (see Exhibit 1.2). Sometimes the message is intended to persuade people *against* acting in a certain way, which is the point of ads that highlight the dangers of smoking or drug abuse.

Most television commercials, newspaper ads, billboards, and other advertisements are group efforts representing the work of four distinct players in the advertising process: advertisers, advertising agencies, the media, and suppliers. **Advertisers** are people or organizations that seek to sell products or influence people through advertising. They may be for-profit companies such as Levi Strauss or nonprofit organizations such as the American Cancer Society. Or they may be government agencies, such as the U.S. National Park Service and the Belgian Tourist Office.

Advertisers generally hire **advertising agencies,** independent organizations that specialize in developing and implementing advertising on behalf of advertisers. The advertising agencies in turn select the **media,** the channels through which advertisers' messages are carried to their intended audiences; in some cases, advertisers use only one **medium,** a single channel. The two largest categories of media are print and electronic, but a wide range of other media also carry advertising messages, including local yellow pages directories and direct mail. And in the process of creating and executing persuasive messages, advertisers and advertising agencies also use the services of various **suppliers,** individuals or organizations that provide specialized services such as photography, printing, and video production.

MICHAEL JORDAN LEAPING THROUGH THE AIR TO MAKE A BASKET. (Classical music background).
V.O.: AIR Jordan. It's all in the imagination.

EXHIBIT 1.2
Advertising Informs and Influences

By showing the performance of Nike Air Flight Shoes, Nike tries to persuade consumers to buy its basketball shoes. The Michigan Department of Public Health billboard advertises to give information that will persuade people not to smoke.

TYPES OF ADVERTISING

As you can see from this brief overview, not all advertising is alike. Ads differ depending on who the message is intended for, where the ad is shown, which media are used, and what the advertiser wants to accomplish. So it's helpful to classify advertising according to target audience, geographic area, media used, and purpose (see Exhibit 1.3).

EXHIBIT 1.3 How to Classify Advertising

Advertising can be classified in four ways: by target audience, geographic area, media used, and purpose.

By Target Audience	By Geographic Area	By Media Used	By Purpose
Consumer	International	Print	Product or nonproduct
Business	National	Newspaper	Commercial or noncommercial
Industrial	Regional	Magazine	Primary demand or selective demand
Trade	Local	Electronic	Direct action or indirect action
Professional		Radio	
Agricultural		Television	
		Out-of-home	
		Outdoor (posters, bulletins, spectaculars)	
		Transit (buses, trains, terminals, and stations)	
		Direct mail	
		Directories	
		Other media	

By Target Audience

One way to classify advertising is according to the group it targets. Whether it's in print, on television, or on billboards, every advertisement is aimed at a specific group of people, known as its **target audience.** Because advertisers try to match the message and the media to the target audience, we're usually aware only of ads directed to us as members of a particular audience. Ads are generally addressed to one of two broad audience categories: consumers or businesses.

Consumer Advertising. Much of the advertising around us is aimed at **consumers,** the individuals and families who buy goods and services for personal or family use. Known as **consumer advertising,** this type of advertising can be targeted to the buyer of a product or to the user (see Exhibit 1.4). For example, Toys "R" Us aims its consumer advertising for toys at the parents who buy such products, not at the children who play with them. But Levi Strauss aims its consumer advertising for Dockers and for 501 jeans at users, the people who will wear those products.

Business Advertising. In contrast to the messages aimed at people who buy for household use, **business advertising** (also known as *business-to-business advertising*) directs messages toward people who buy or use products in businesses, not-for-profit organizations, and government agencies (see Exhibit 1.5). Most business advertising appears in business and professional publications or in direct-mail pieces sent to buyers or users in organizations. However, business advertising sometimes appears in consumer-oriented media such as television or newspapers;

EXHIBIT 1.4
How Johnson & Johnson Targets Consumers

This Johnson & Johnson magazine ad for No More Germies antibacterial soap is an example of consumer advertising aimed at parents, who buy such products, rather than children, who use the products.

EXHIBIT 1.5
How Johnson & Johnson Targets Businesses

This Johnson & Johnson ad is an example of business advertising, because it's aimed at the people who buy first-aid kits for their companies.

Federal Express was one of the earliest to reach a business audience by using television, which is generally considered a medium for consumer advertising.[5]

Within the broad category of business advertising are four distinct classifications. **Industrial advertising** targets people who buy or use the materials and services needed to conduct business or to manufacture other products. For example, Pitney Bowes uses industrial advertising to interest businesses in buying its postage meters for weighing and adding postage to outgoing mail; Armstrong uses industrial advertising to sell floor coverings and insulation to construction firms that incorporate these products into their buildings.

Trade advertising targets intermediaries such as wholesalers and retailers that buy goods for resale to customers. Most trade advertising is placed by producers that want their goods or services distributed by the intermediary, but some businesses advertise products to be used by the intermediaries themselves. For example, Duracell might advertise in a trade magazine such as *Hardware Age* to persuade hardware store owners to stock more Duracell batteries for their customers, whereas Sensormatic might advertise in the same magazine to convince store owners to use its antitheft devices on expensive merchandise.

Professional advertising is directed toward licensed professional practitioners such as lawyers, accountants, doctors, dentists, and engineers. This category of advertising may be used to persuade professionals to buy a particular product useful in their work or to recommend that product to their patients or clients. Another category of business advertising targets the agricultural industry. **Agricultural advertising** is used to sell products such as tractors and insecticides.

By Geographic Area

A second way to classify advertising is by geographic area. Advertising can be confined to a single neighborhood or can include the entire world. When an organization crosses national borders to advertise in more than one country, it's placing **international advertising.** For example, Pepsi-Cola uses international advertising in dozens of countries across North and South America, Europe, the Middle East, Asia, and the Pacific. International advertisers who choose television can use MTV (seen in 37 countries) and CNN (seen in 94 countries) and other channels to reach out to a global audience of millions.[6]

When an organization advertises in more than one region of a single country, it's using **national advertising.** McDonald's, AT&T, Xerox, and American Airlines are all considered national advertisers in the United States because they use network television, national magazines, and other media to reach large numbers of people in multiple markets across the country. In the United States, national advertisers account for much of the money spent on advertising (see Exhibit 1.6). In parts of Europe, in Japan, and in other areas, television and newspapers are national in scope, so advertisers using those media are automatically national advertisers and can use one ad to reach the entire country.[7]

Advertising in a specific region without covering the entire country is **regional advertising.** For example, Horizon Air uses regional advertising when it targets the Pacific Northwest area of the United States. Regional advertisers generally use local newspapers, local radio, or local television to reach several geographically linked markets within a region. Compared with regional advertising, the scope of **local advertising** is much narrower, concentrating on a more confined area such as a city. Much of the local advertising you see is **retail advertising,** placed by retailers, including supermarkets and department stores, that want to reach consumers. For this reason, the terms *local advertising* and *retail advertising* are sometimes used interchangeably. However, others also use local advertising, including accountants, doctors, and candidates for public office (see Chapter 19).

By Media

A third way to classify advertising is according to the medium or media used. Popular forms of media advertising include newspaper, magazine, radio, television, outdoor (such as posters), and transit (such as on or inside buses). Because of its

EXHIBIT 1.6 The Largest U.S. National Advertisers

National advertisers invest a significant amount in advertising aimed at target audiences throughout a given country. In the United States, the total amount of money spent by the top 10 national advertisers in 1992 exceeded $11 billion.

Rank	Advertiser	Ad Spending
1	Procter & Gamble Co.	$2,165.6
2	Philip Morris Cos.	2,024.1
3	General Motors Corp.	1,333.6
4	Sears, Roebuck & Co.	1,204.6
5	PepsiCo	928.6
6	Ford Motor Co.	794.5
7	Warner-Lambert Co.	757.5
8	Chrysler Corp.	756.6
9	McDonald's Corp.	743.6
10	Nestlé SA	733.4

Note: Dollars are in millions. 1992 data.

Reprinted with permission from the September 29, 1993 issue of *Advertising Age.* Copyright, Crain Communications Inc. 1993.

(Song): You're pure, you're natural, you're one of a kind. You're my Ivory baby. You're pure, you're soft, you're just the right touch. You're my Ivory baby.

V.O.: Unlike soaps with heavy perfumes and greasy cremes, Ivory is pure. It doesn't need anything else to baby, even a baby's skin.

(Song): You're my Ivory baby.

V.O.: Baby your skin with Ivory.

EXHIBIT 1.7
Procter & Gamble's Television Advertising for Ivory Soap

Out of an annual advertising budget of more than $2 billion, Procter & Gamble spends nearly $1 billion on television commercials. Ivory soap uses national television advertising in the United States to reinforce its image of gentle cleansing.

ability to reach huge audiences across large geographic regions, television is one of the most powerful advertising media and is often the primary medium used by national advertisers such as Procter & Gamble (see Exhibit 1.7).[8] And specialized types of television advertising have become more attractive as cable television, satellite television, interactive television, and other forms of television have drawn larger audiences. Many organizations also advertise through direct mail or in the yellow pages and other directories; the list of media options grows longer as newer media such as in-store radio become commonplace.

By Purpose

A fourth way to classify advertising is by purpose. Just as advertisers are a varied lot, so too are the reasons they use advertising. A company may advertise to build its reputation; a retailer, to attract customers; a manufacturer, to sell its brands; and a nonprofit organization, to find donors. Each advertiser has its own goals, but the purpose behind each message can be classified according to four dimensions: product versus nonproduct, commercial versus noncommercial, primary demand versus selective demand, and direct action versus indirect action.

Product versus Nonproduct Advertising. A **product** is a good or service for which customers will exchange something of value (usually money). The purpose of **product advertising** is to sell the advertiser's goods or services. **Goods** are physical products such as pencils and candy bars; **services** are intangible products that offer financial, legal, medical, recreational, or other customer benefits. So, product advertising may try to sell either a tangible good (such as Levi Strauss jeans) or an intangible service (such as H&R Block tax preparation). The flip side of product advertising is **nonproduct advertising,** also called *institutional* or *corporate advertising,* in which the advertiser is trying to polish its image or influence public opinion about an issue. The aim of nonproduct advertising is to get the audience to think about who's sponsoring the ad or the issue discussed, not about buying the advertiser's products.

Commercial versus Noncommercial Advertising. Much of the advertising around us is *commercial advertising,* placed by a business that expects to make a profit. In contrast, nonprofit and political organizations use *noncommercial advertising* to promote causes or candidates rather than profit-making products. Even though noncommercial advertising sometimes asks for donations, the organizations sponsoring such ads are looking to cover the costs of offering charitable services or producing cultural events, not to make a profit.

Primary-Demand versus Selective-Demand Advertising. The purpose of *primary-demand advertising* is to stimulate demand for a particular product category, not for

Advertising Sports Teams as Products

If you're unhappy with a product, how long do you wait before switching to a rival? That's the dilemma many sports fans face as they watch once-proud local teams skid lower and lower in league standings. From a marketing viewpoint, fans are customers, and professional sports teams are profit-making products that must entice customers to buy tickets and team merchandise if they're to thrive—or even survive. But when the product's not doing well, it's only a matter of time until customers stop buying and take their business elsewhere. What's a team to do?

More troubled teams are trying to turn the tide through advertising. The New York Islanders, a once-spectacular hockey team under new management after several years of dismal performance, started advertising in 1992 to lure back fans who were staying away in record numbers. With a headline that sounded much like the "new and improved" message usually trumpeted by shampoos and canned foods, Jerome Grossman, the team's president, announced the start of "The New Ice Age." The newspaper advertising campaign pledged that the Islanders would do better in the upcoming season. Grossman also sent season-ticket holders a direct-mail package with the same apologetic but forward-looking message: "You've shown amazing passion and perseverance over the years. And we're committed to living up to your loyalty."

Recognizing that many Islanders fans were upset over paying to see a losing team, Grossman decided to adjust ticket prices. He froze many ticket prices and lowered prices on about 20 percent of the seats in the Nassau Coliseum, where the team plays. Then he advertised the new pricing policy and encouraged attendance by pointing out that it would cost fans less to give the team another try.

Over in the National Football League, the Minnesota Vikings have confronted their problems head-on in a series of ads designed to regain credibility among disillusioned fans. One television commercial showed a receptionist for the team talking with fans about unpopular players who were recently released. "Mr. Walker is pursuing other interests," the receptionist answers when asked the whereabouts of former Vikings running back Hershel Walker. Questioned about another player, she responds, "We booted his butt, too." The ads openly admitted that the Vikings needed improvement and went on to reassure

The Atlanta Braves organization markets team merchandise through a direct-mail package sent to fans on its mailing list.

fans that changes were already under way. By using frank ads that didn't gloss over the Vikings' problems, management acknowledged the fans' frustration and showed that the team was working hard to keep fans interested (and hope alive) for another season.

Even successful teams such as the Atlanta Braves advertise to keep fan fervor at a fever pitch as a way of fueling demand for tickets and merchandise (two pages from the Braves' catalog are shown here). What better time to sell next season's tickets or to offer official team jackets than right after a winning season? And for players and fans of losing teams, well, there's always next year.

Apply Your Knowledge

1. Sports teams communicating with their target audiences (fans) need feedback to know whether their messages have been received and understood. What kinds of feedback might the New York Islanders watch for?
2. The Minnesota Vikings use consumer advertising to reach out to fans, but the team also deals with a variety of businesses. What kind(s) of business advertising might the team do and for what purpose?

---

any one brand. This type of advertising is generally placed by associations that represent many manufacturers or service firms, such as the National Honey Board (which wants to encourage honey usage) or the New Hampshire Office of Travel and Tourism Development (which wants to attract tourists to New Hampshire). Once primary-demand advertising has paved the way, *selective-demand advertising* is used by individual producers to build demand for their own brands. (However, when a company introduces an innovative product that creates its own category, it may start with primary-demand advertising to build overall demand.) So the Italian Confectionery Industries Association uses primary-demand advertising to whet the public's appetite for sweets made in Italy, and Perugina uses selective-demand advertising to convince consumers to buy its candies, cookies, and cakes.

(SFX): wind

V.O.: Sundown, 18 degrees and windy. Because of what some folks wake up to in the morning, North Face and Hoechst Cela-

nese set out to create a sleeping bag that would hang tough no matter what the weather. And they did it. With Polarguard. An insulating fiber that'll keep a body warm and

dry even up here. And that's a real comfort to those of us that make high demands of our accommodations. Hoechst Celanese. The Name Behind The Names You Know.

EXHIBIT 1.8
Direct-Action versus Indirect-Action Advertising

Polarguard is a registered trademark of Hoechst Celanese Corporation for continuous filament fiber. The North Face name is a registered trademark of The North Face Company. The Hoechst name and logo are registered trademarks of Hoechst AG.

It's easy for Holiday Inn to gauge response to the German magazine advertisement on the right: it simply counts the number of coupons received. In contrast, Hoechst Celanese doesn't expect any immediate response from the television commercial above, which is intended to boost awareness of its brand name.

Who can understand it better, that you need

RESPITE
from everyday life?

Direct-Action versus Indirect-Action Advertising. When advertising is geared toward getting the audience to respond immediately, it's called *direct-action advertising.* Messages that include a toll-free phone number, a coupon, or a limited-time offer are forms of direct-action advertising. The advertiser can quickly see whether the ad is working by counting the responses. On the other hand, when advertising is used simply to build the audience's awareness of a product, it's *indirect-action advertising.* This type of advertising works over the long haul to boost a product's image, explain product benefits, or show where the product may be purchased (see Exhibit 1.8).

FUNCTIONS OF ADVERTISING

Of course, advertising isn't an end but a means to an end—a tool that advertisers can use to reach their goals. The functions of advertising vary depending on the advertiser and its particular objectives, which usually include one or more of the following:

- *To differentiate products from their competitors.* Campbell Soup uses advertising to identify its soups, tomato juice, and other products as part of the Campbell's family, which reinforces a sense of quality and taste that distinguish those products from rival products.

- *To communicate product information.* When Campbell's advertises its soups, it focuses on the ways consumers can use these products, the taste they can expect, and the convenience.

- *To urge product use.* If you've never tried Campbell's soup, cents-off coupons and mouth-watering recipes in ads may give you the push you need. Once you've tried the soup and liked it, Campbell's advertising serves as a reminder that you should use it again—and again.

- *To expand product distribution.* If you see an ad for Campbell's tomato soup and your local store doesn't carry it, you might ask the manager to stock it. The more customers who are stimulated by advertising to request a product, the more stores will have to carry it. (Trade advertising also aims to build distribution by advertising to wholesalers and retailers.)

- *To increase brand preference and loyalty.* Campbell's Soup has many competitors, so it uses advertising to give you a reason to prefer Campbell's over other brands and to stay with Campbell's when you buy soup.

- *To reduce overall sales costs.* If Campbell's tried to sell its soups door to door, the cost would be astronomical. But if it takes out a full-page color ad in *Family Circle* for $73,000, it can reach 6 million subscribers for pennies each.[9]

Nonprofit organizations and government agencies use advertising for many of the same reasons. Although such organizations aren't seeking a profit or making sales the same way businesses do, they can use advertising to build an identity in the public's mind, to communicate information, and to do all the other things that advertising does so well.

Advertising and Marketing

Advertising isn't developed or delivered in a vacuum; it's one element—a key element—in the process of marketing. Businesses, individuals, governments, and nonprofit organizations all develop products to satisfy **customers,** the people or organizations that purchase a product, and advertising helps persuade customers to select one product rather than another. However, marketing isn't just selling. According to the American Marketing Association, **marketing** is the conception, pricing, promotion, and distribution of ideas, goods, and services that satisfy the needs of individuals and organizations.[10]

Advertising plays an important but relatively limited role in marketing. It can be used to promote a product's many advantages, but it doesn't determine which features will satisfy people's needs, where products should be distributed, or what price should be charged. Such marketing issues must be resolved before any advertising appears; in effect, the marketing process provides the framework in which advertising is created.

THE MARKETING CONCEPT

Today, manufacturers and service firms can produce more goods and services more efficiently than ever before, which means that supply is often greater than demand. Because people have so many product choices, an organization must give customers real reasons for choosing its products over competing products. Otherwise, the organization's profits will suffer as customers flock to rival products. The key to being successful in such a situation is to apply the **marketing concept,** focusing on meeting customer needs and coordinating marketing efforts throughout the organization while working for long-term profits. Here's a closer look at the three main components that make up the marketing concept:

- *Meeting customer needs.* Everyone in an organization, from top managers to receptionists, needs to be involved in the two-step process of satisfying customers: (1) understanding what customers expect and (2) meeting those expectations better than competitors. Of course, some customer wants and needs are obvious. For example, drivers need safe cars, and many customers want comfort or style. But other customer expectations are less obvious, such as a performance guarantee or prompt attention on the telephone. In addition, some customer needs can change over time; for example, because baby-boomer customers had gained weight, Levi Strauss needed to make roomier jeans. It's the conscious dedication to understanding and meeting needs (through product features and benefits) that leads to satisfied customers.

- *Coordinating marketing efforts across the organization.* Marketing is only one of the functions involved in meeting customer needs. Research and development, manufacturing, finance, and other functions are also important, so coordinating these functions with marketing efforts greatly increases an organization's chances of success. When coordination between functions is missing, the results can be disastrous. One study revealed that when marketing and R&D functions did not work closely together, 68 percent of the product development projects failed.[11]

- *Working for long-term profits.* Businesses, governments, and nonprofit organizations all have to think about long-term financial responsibility. Businesses must be profitable (and nonprofit organizations must avoid financial ruin) if they expect to remain operational and meet customer needs year after year. Organizations such as Procter & Gamble and Caterpillar have made major investments in functions that support customer satisfaction, such as marketing research (to find out what customers want), product design (to make what customers want), manufacturing facilities (to produce what customers want with efficiency and quality), promotion (to let customers know where they can get what they want), and customer service facilities (to satisfy any other customer needs). These investments ultimately pay off because customers continue buying the products that best meet their needs, which fuels sales and profits over the long term.[12]

THE MARKETING MIX

Building a business that meets customer needs means working with the four elements that make up the **marketing mix:** product, price, distribution, and promotion (see Exhibit 1.9). As powerful as any single element can be, it's the unique blend you create by changing and juggling all four that leads to customer satisfaction. Thus, promotion (which includes advertising) must be balanced with the product design, the price, and the method of distribution to create the overall marketing mix that customers consider when they choose a product.

- *Product.* The most essential element in the marketing mix is the product. Much more than a collection of features, the product is a "bundle of value" that meets customer expectations. For example, WordPerfect word-processing software is more than a box of disks; it also includes an instruction manual, access to a customer service hotline, and other components. Advertising these extra features and benefits helps customers choose products that fit their needs. To translate the product characteristics into something concrete that can be used to distinguish one product from another, many organizations advertise a distinctive **brand,** a name, a word, a phrase, a symbol, or a combination of these elements. A **brand name** is the portion of a brand that can be expressed

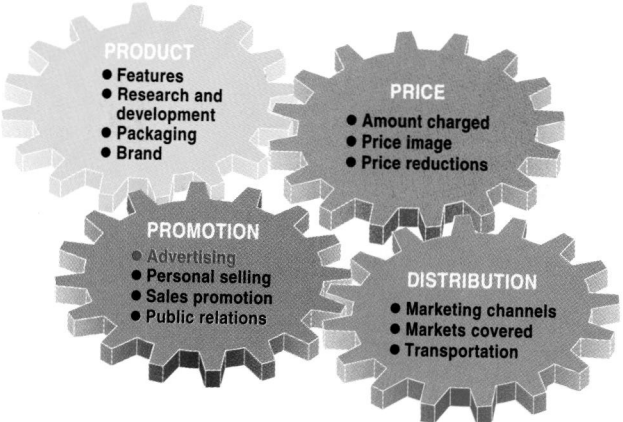

EXHIBIT 1.9
Advertising and the Marketing Mix

Product, price, distribution, and promotion are the four elements that make up the marketing mix. The four main categories of promotion are advertising, personal selling, sales promotion, and public relations.

verbally (including letters, words, or numbers), and a **brand mark** is the portion of a brand that cannot be expressed verbally (including graphic designs or symbols).

- *Price.* **Price** is the value, usually in monetary terms, that sellers ask for their products. A product's price has to cover all the costs involved in its production, distribution, and promotion, as well as any expected profit. Moreover, price can support a product's image, take sales away from competitors, or induce people to change the timing of their purchases. For example, advertising a relatively high price for Porsche cars helps build an exclusive image for that product, and advertising a relatively low price for the Mazda Miata helps create an image of good value. Wal-Mart promotes its low prices on name brands to grab sales from department store rivals. And movie theaters often shift their heavy weekend attendance by advertising lower prices during the slower weekday periods.

- *Distribution.* The process of moving products from the producer to the customer is **distribution.** Distribution is usually accomplished through *marketing channels* (e.g., from manufacturer to wholesaler to retailer to customer). Managing product transportation and storage, processing orders, and keeping track of inventory are also distribution activities. Whether a product is established or being introduced to a new market, advertising is a good way to tell customers where to try and buy. For example, when Sunbeam advertises its electric blankets, it includes a toll-free number to call for store information; Westin Hotels includes in its ads a list of the cities where it has hotels and resorts.

- *Promotion.* **Promotion** covers the variety of techniques used to communicate with customers and potential customers—and this is where advertising comes in. Along with personal selling, public relations, and sales promotion, advertising is one of the four main categories of promotion. **Personal selling** is face-to-face sales contact in which a salesperson tries to persuade someone to buy a product; it plays a big role in major purchases such as automobiles and airplanes. **Public relations** is the relationship between a business and the media, including press conferences to announce political candidacies, media announcements to support fund-raising events, and press releases to bolster a company's image. **Sales promotion** is increasingly important for many organizations today; coupons and rebates are just two sales promotion techniques that advertisers use to reach customers. And, of course, advertising is the nonpersonal communication of information about products to customers.

Advertising and Communication

Advertising is first and foremost a process of communication. At its simplest, the advertiser has a message to communicate, and it wants a response such as higher

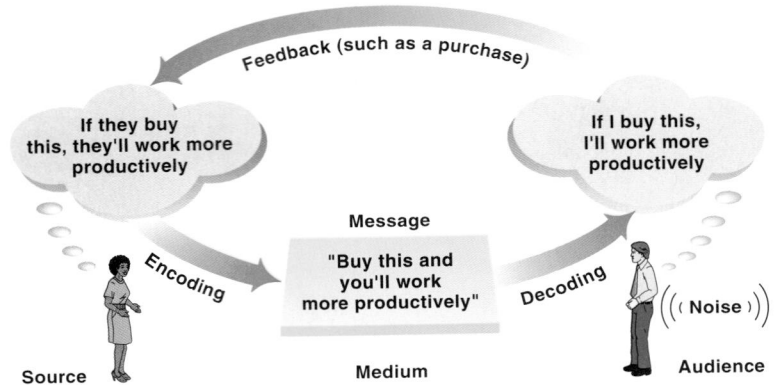

EXHIBIT 1.10

The Communication Process in Advertising

The communication process is complex, and feedback in the form of purchases or other audience action is essential if advertisers are to determine whether their messages have been received and interpreted as intended.

sales or more votes. Whether the message involves words or pictures, education or persuasion, it's important to understand the communication process.

THE COMMUNICATION PROCESS

The process of getting an idea from one person to another is extremely complex. To simplify this complicated situation, think of the communication process in advertising as a circular route between the source and the audience (see Exhibit 1.10). The advertiser that generates the idea is the *source* of the communication. The idea to be communicated is the *message,* and the source *encodes* that message, translating it into symbols such as words or images that can be understood by the *audience,* the person(s) intended to receive the encoded message. The *medium* carries the encoded message to the audience. Typical advertising media include newspapers, magazines, radio, television, signs, packaging, and direct-mail materials. The audience plays a vital role in the communication process, because when people receive the message, they must interpret the meaning, a process called *decoding.*

Reaching an audience may sound simple, but it isn't: as an advertiser, you have to identify and analyze your audience so that you can encode your message in a way your audience will understand and so that you can choose the media most likely to reach your audience. Once people in the audience have received and decoded the message, they respond in some way, and this *feedback* lets the source know how the message was interpreted. Anything that interferes with successful communication is *noise.* Obvious examples of noise are audio or visual interruptions such as a blocked view of the message or a baby crying during a commercial. Other examples include miscommunication that results from cultural, language, or experiential differences. All too often, competing ads may contribute to noise, leading to complaints about **clutter,** the ever-increasing number of ads competing for audience attention. Noise and clutter can distort the message, so it's important to consider how the message moves through every step in the communication process.

COMMUNICATION PHASES IN ADVERTISING

In advertising, communication has a specific purpose: to send a message that will inform and persuade customers to take some action (whether it's buying a product, voting for a candidate, or volunteering time for a worthy cause). The process of sending promotional messages (such as advertisements) to various audiences is called **marketing communication.** When successful, marketing communication moves customers along a continuum from awareness to satisfaction in six phases that involve the communication process just described.

- *Phase 1: Awareness.* Make sure your audience is aware of your products. This is particularly critical when you introduce a new product or when you start selling a product in a new market.

- *Phase 2: Comprehension.* In your marketing communication, make sure that potential customers understand your product's features and benefits. This phase can be challenging when you're advertising a complex product such as a genetically engineered medicine.

- *Phase 3: Acceptance.* Prospective customers must decide whether your product can meet their needs. Although they may reject your product for a variety of reasons, if your advertising message helps them realize that your product can meet their needs, they'll consider how it compares with other products.

- *Phase 4: Preference.* Buyers choose a favorite among the products they believe meet their needs. However, just because people prefer your product doesn't mean they'll buy it. Advertising must offer a compelling reason for people to buy your product (see Exhibit 1.11). For example, ads for Butterball turkeys discuss taste, but they also offer a money-back guarantee to persuade customers to take the next step and buy.

- *Phase 5: Ownership.* The element of your advertising known as the **call to action** motivates people to actually buy your product or to vote for your candidate. In a Johnson & Johnson ad for Acuvue disposable contact lens products, for instance, the phrase "To receive a free trial pair, simply visit your eyecare professional for an exam and see if Acuvue is right for you" is the call to action designed to move customers into the ownership phase. Of course, ownership is the feedback advertisers hope to receive when they communicate with an audience.

- *Phase 6: Reinforcement.* Use advertising to bolster your customers' sense of satisfaction about the action or purchase. This phase starts a new cycle in the communication process because you're sending another message to your audience and looking for feedback such as more purchases.

This continuum is sometimes called the **hierarchy of effects model** because it reflects the audience's stages of reaction to your advertising. Members of your audience progress through the six phases at their own pace, so at any point, some potential customers may be in the awareness phase while others are in the acceptance phase or the satisfaction phase. By understanding how people react to your advertising in each phase, you can pinpoint any communication problems or emphasize messages that encourage people to move from one phase into the next. For example, if you find that many people accept and prefer your product but few people actually buy, you can look for any clues to miscommunication or noise that

EXHIBIT 1.11
Advertising to Build Product Preference

Although consumers in India can choose among many wristwatch brands, Bentex builds preference for its brand through magazine ads that offer specific reasons for buying Bentex.

interferes with your message. Then you can work toward a solution (such as trying a new call to action or using a new medium) to more effectively encourage people to move into the ownership phase.

INTEGRATED MARKETING COMMUNICATIONS

As both markets and marketing have grown more complex in recent years, many advertisers have found themselves with fragmented and confusing marketing communication programs. When you consider all the ways that audiences can receive marketing messages, the potential for confusion isn't surprising. Say you're in the market for a sports car and have your eye on a new Ford Probe. You might see a national television ad, a local television ad, a national magazine ad, a local newspaper ad, or some combination of the four. Plus, you'll talk to a salesperson at the dealership and possibly read product review articles in both newspapers and magazines. On top of all that, you might receive a promotional brochure in the mail from Ford. Now what if all these sources of information told you slightly different stories about the Probe? It's easy to see how Ford and its dealers could spend a huge amount on promotion and wind up with nothing but confused consumers to show for it.

Moreover, most medium and large companies have multiple product divisions, sometimes with their own advertising agencies, creating even more potential for confusion. Executives at Eaton Corporation once found four unrelated ads from four Eaton divisions in the same issue of a magazine. Until recently, computer maker Hewlett-Packard had more than 50 distinct toll-free numbers for customers to call.[13] With examples like these, it's easy to see how marketing can cost more and deliver less than it should.

The solution to this fragmentation is to apply the concept of **integrated marketing communications (IMC),** a strategy of coordinating and integrating all of a company's marketing efforts as well as its promotional communications (through all the diverse channels of communication) to convey a consistent, unified message and image. At its simplest, IMC works to ensure that an advertiser speaks with a single voice in the most consistent, cost-effective manner possible. A more comprehensive vision of IMC includes collecting and analyzing data about current and potential customers before designing integrated marketing communication strategies for specific audiences.[14]

Properly implemented, IMC promises to increase marketing and promotional effectiveness and decrease marketing costs. However, despite the benefits, most advertisers find IMC difficult to implement. The biggest problem stems from the way various elements of communication have been managed in most organizations and in the agencies that support them. For example, consider the separate responsibilities and communication tasks involved when the advertiser's sales department takes care of personal selling, when an advertising agency prepares print and electronic ads, and when a public relations specialist promotes a company's products to the news media. Various company managers oversee these processes and have long-established methods of managing their portions of the marketing mix. Moving to an IMC approach requires new ways of organizing, planning, and managing all marketing functions, and years of habit have created resistance to change.[15] Outside advertising agencies are also caught in the commotion as each type of agency tries to sort out its role in an integrated strategy.[16] As difficult as it may be to implement, the potential benefits of IMC are so valuable that the concept is fast becoming standard for everyone in the advertising and marketing professions.

The Evolution of Advertising

Although much of what we know about advertising and how it works has been learned relatively recently, advertising is hardly a new phenomenon. Even a hundred years ago, advertising was an integral if sometimes unwelcome part of daily life (see Exhibit 1.12). Although some observers at the turn of the century believed advertising to be "a true mirror of life," others complained of being bombarded with ads every minute of the day. National advertising of brand-name products is a relatively new phenomenon, whereas the roots of advertising begin in antiquity.[17] Over the centuries, the evolution of advertising has been closely tied to social, economic, and technological changes that have affected the media and the message.

THE EARLY DAYS

Before public education, few people could read, so for centuries, tradespeople attracted attention with public criers and pictorial signs. In ancient Egypt, as in other countries, criers would entice buyers with flowery descriptions of the cargoes from newly arrived ships, which included rugs, spices, and other items. Like shopkeepers of later periods and other lands, early Greek and Roman merchants used signs to advertise their products, but because many people couldn't read, the signs used symbols or pictures rather than words. In England in the Middle Ages, customers could find weavers by the sign of the spinning wheel or bootmakers by the sign of the golden boot.[18]

In the late 1400s, handbills (lettered by scribes) appeared in England and were akin to today's want ads. They were tacked up by lecturers, clergymen, teachers, and other professionals offering their services.[19] But it wasn't until Johann Gutenberg invented movable type and the printing press in Germany in the mid-1400s that printed materials could be mass-produced. Advertisers began to use quickly printed shop-bills and flyers to reach thousands of people in farflung areas. By the mid-1700s, printed posters and signs were appearing all over England, predecessors to today's billboards.[20] Then the technology of the Industrial Revolution changed both the pattern and the economics of production and consumption, further fueling the growth of advertising.

THE INDUSTRIAL REVOLUTION

Before the Industrial Revolution, most people lived on farms, and households were relatively self-sufficient, growing and making what they needed. Businesses were small family operations that produced items in modest amounts and sought out buyers in the village marketplace. But when power-driven equipment and large-scale factories were introduced in England in the mid-1700s, both households and businesses felt the effect.[21]

Many people left the farms to work in urban factories and relied less on their own production and more on affordable mass-produced goods. Businesses could turn out more and varied items at a faster rate and a lower cost than ever before, and customer demand was growing. However, the gap widened between producer and consumer as people moved away from their villages and craftspeople had less personal contact with their customers. To bridge this gap and to stimulate the demand they needed to sell the larger quantities they were producing, businesses turned to advertising to quickly and easily reach many potential customers.[22]

THE AGE OF TECHNOLOGY

During and after the Industrial Revolution, technological advances changed both the speed and form of communication. The invention of photography gave advertisers a new way of showcasing their products. The telegraph, telephone, typewriter, phonograph, and motion pictures opened up new avenues for personal and business communication. Newspapers and magazines reached into the urban areas and beyond to bring news and ads to thousands of people. However, once the powerful technologies of radio and television became commonplace, the face of advertising changed forever as print and electronic media expanded the use and impact of advertising.

Print Media

A medium as old as paper, print includes both newspapers and magazines. Today's newspapers and magazines offer advertisers the flexibility of targeting audiences in an area as small as a single ZIP code or as large as an entire nation. Of the two major print media, newspapers are the oldest.

Newspapers. London newspapers of the 1700s carried text-only advertisements for patent medicines, books, and other products. Newspapers were usually published once or twice a week, but daily newspapers were soon established. With better rail and mail service, newspapers were able to increase their circulation and carry ads into surrounding communities. In the United States, commercial newspaper ads of the 1700s offered slaves for sale as well as textiles, books, and real estate. Benjamin Franklin's *Pennsylvania Gazette* built the largest circulation and the largest advertising volume of any newspaper in the colonies. By the early 1800s, the United States boasted more newspapers than the United Kingdom.[23]

Newspapers began paying agents to sell space to advertisers, a practice that started an entirely new business, the advertising agency. Volney B. Palmer, thought by historians to be the first advertising agent in the United States, set up an agency in 1841 to sell newspaper advertising space. When Palmer persuaded a firm to buy space, the newspaper paid him a percentage of the revenues. This was the usual arrangement, advertisers paying newspapers for the space they bought from agents. But George P. Rowell and John L. Hooper did things a little differently. As agents in the 1840s, they bought advertising space cheaply from newspapers and then resold it at a profit to advertisers. This system of paying the media for space and time and then billing advertisers is still followed by U.S. agencies.[24]

S. M. Pettingill learned the trade from Palmer and then struck out on his own, adding another service: he offered to write advertisers' ads. Writing ads soon evolved into an integral function of the advertising agency. At the same time, the agencies started controlling the artistic side of print advertising, specifying type styles and creating artwork for ads. By the turn of the century, more agencies were conducting research studies to help clients target their audiences and reach their targets through the media. Many advertisers and media firms soon established their own research departments, and independent research firms began to appear.[25]

Today, U.S. newspapers generally serve a specific geographic area such as a local community. *USA Today* bucked that trend when it was launched in 1982 as a colorful national newspaper with jazzy graphics and brief but punchy articles. After *USA Today* led the way, many U.S. newspapers added color printing capabilities, allowing advertisers to show their products more realistically and to use snazzier art to snag the reader's attention.

Magazines. Magazine advertising grew more slowly than newspaper advertising because many magazine publishers initially turned up their noses at advertising revenues. Although English and U.S. advertisers of the 1800s looked hungrily at the magazines' national audiences, the better magazines took themselves too seriously to stoop to advertising's commercialism. One or two slipped ads into their back pages, but magazines mostly made money from subscriptions. Later, better printing technology and the ability to print photographs and detailed illustrations made magazine ads even more attractive to advertisers.[26]

After the Civil War, *Atlantic Monthly* and other U.S. magazines began carrying more ads. Advertising agency pioneer J. Walter Thompson prodded *Harper's* and other magazines to print ads for foods, soaps, and even patent medicines, whose dubious images were enhanced by their association with reputable publications. In the late 1800s, *The People's Literary Companion* was created specifically to push soap powder sold by mail, and using advertising revenues to subsidize subscription costs, the magazine quickly built a circulation over 500,000.[27]

By the dawn of the twentieth century, advertising had become a social and economic fixture in the United States and the United Kingdom. Magazines (and newspapers) were filled with ads for all kinds of products as "salesmanship in print" helped bridge the gap between producer and customer. However, critics blasted the ethics of advertising patent medicines and other questionable products,

and they decried the puffery and empty prose some advertisers used. Technological advances soon allowed magazine ads to be printed in color, which was more expensive than black and white but which attracted readers' attention (see Exhibit 1.13). Today, most magazines are national (such as *Time*), but you'll also find regional magazines (such as *Southern Living*) and local magazines (such as *Detroit Monthly*).[28]

Electronic Media

As successful as the print media were in expanding advertising's reach, their results have been dwarfed by the reach of the twentieth-century electronic media, radio and television. Although both radio and television started as home-based media, radio has become a take-along medium that goes with people wherever they go.[29]

Radio. Experimental radio stations dotted both sides of the Atlantic Ocean before World War I, but the first commercial stations didn't go on the air in the United States until 1920. The first radio commercial in the United States was carried in 1922 by AT&T's station WEAF in New York, when a real estate developer bought 10 minutes of radio time to advertise New York City property. From the start, critics wanted broadcast advertising banned, but U.S. officials opted to keep the airwaves open to commercials.[30]

Within two years, radio expanded from being a local medium to being a national medium, primarily because of the **network,** a group of stations that broadcast simultaneously in many markets. Early radio networks linked stations regionally and nationally. AT&T, the Columbia Broadcasting System (CBS), and other network operators promised that an advertiser's message would be broadcast simultaneously in many cities, thus extending the reach of radio advertising. In 1926 AT&T sold its network of radio stations to the National Broadcasting Company (now known as NBC).[31]

To blunt criticism, early radio advertising was subtle; advertisers linked their product names to entertainers or shows for a soft sell. Entertainers like the Ipana

Troubadours (sponsored by a toothpaste) barely talked about their product name-sakes; the hosts of shows like the "Fleischmann Yeast Hour" only briefly mentioned their sponsors. By 1933 more than 25 percent of all U.S. stations were owned by newspapers, which used radio to promote their own papers. This dual media role helped newspapers weather the Depression years of the 1930s when newspaper ad revenues plummeted but radio ad revenues rose.[32]

Advertisers and agencies, not networks, controlled much of network radio programming until the early 1940s; they created show ideas, hired entertainers, and leased broadcast facilities to send their programs to network affiliates. During World War II, radio kept listeners informed about the battles abroad, and ad revenues grew. By 1947, 97 percent of all stations were affiliated with networks. In the early 1950s, once television had demonstrated its potential as an advertising medium, observers believed that radio would fade. But radio is today a vibrant medium, with roughly 5,000 AM and 4,000 FM radio stations operating in the United States, and it's used by local, regional, and national advertisers.[33]

Television. Another twentieth-century phenomenon, television has become the most powerful and successful ad medium ever because it can reach more people more quickly than any other medium. Inventors experimented with television broadcasting before 1940, but the first commercial station wasn't established until 1941. After World War II, television became increasingly popular as people bought television sets and corporations staked out profitable station territories. An early community antenna television system that started in Pennsylvania in 1948 was the forerunner of the cable systems that would pop up throughout the country during the 1970s and 1980s.[34]

Like radio, television began as a local medium, but television networks soon linked stations to form a national medium. NBC moved aggressively into television, while rival CBS, flush with radio success, moved more slowly. By 1954 NBC and CBS were the network leaders, trailed by ABC and DuMont (a network that folded in 1955). Television commercials were banned in Great Britain until 1955, but in the United States, national advertisers followed the pattern of radio, controlling programming in television's early years. But as the 1950s came to a close, the networks took over their own programming, and they offered advertisers the opportunity to sponsor parts of shows rather than underwriting the entire cost of a single show.[35]

As the 1960s began, more than 90 percent of all U.S. households owned a television set. In 1972 Home Box Office (HBO) began operation as a pay cable station, and within three years, the station was beaming programs across the United States and Canada via communications satellite. Today network cable (such as MTV and CNN) and local cable (such as public access channels) are widely available, and independent stations are again becoming popular. More than 99 percent of all U.S. households now own a television set, and 65 percent receive cable in some form. Cable television ad revenues are smaller than network television ad revenues, but they're growing more rapidly.[36]

Talk about clutter: the number of television commercials has nearly doubled since 1975. These days, if you watched everything shown on network television in an average day, you'd see almost 1,000 commercials. More than 90 percent of all commercials were 30 seconds long in 1975, but today just over half last 30 seconds, and 15-second commercials account for nearly 40 percent of all commercials. At the other end of the spectrum is the **infomercial,** a longer commercial that mixes information, entertainment, and a sales pitch in a programlike format.[37]

Today's Challenges and Opportunities

Advertising continues to grow in both importance and complexity. As the twenty-first century approaches, we are seeing changes in the technology, in the creative

Not so long ago, the extended television commercials known as infomercials were relegated to pitching slice-and-dice kitchen gadgets and self-improvement tapes during late-night hours on high-numbered cable channels. Now infomercials are moving into the mainstream as advertisers such as Volvo, Avon, and Club Med experiment with the format. With more than $1 billion worth of products sold every year through infomercials, the debate over the uses and abuses of such commercials is becoming more heated. Critics say that infomercials fool viewers by mimicking regular program formats, which blurs the line between entertainment and selling. However, advertisers argue that viewers can discriminate between ads and programs.

One reason more advertisers are using infomercials is because they can say more in 30 minutes than in 30 seconds. As Bob Austin, a Volvo spokesperson, observes, "The story of auto safety is very difficult to do in 30 seconds." That's why Volvo has used 30-minute infomercials to demonstrate and explain its cars' many safety features. What's more, producing a 30-minute commercial costs little more than making a 30-second commercial. And considering the din of short ads crowding the dials, long commercials may actually help advertisers stand out.

Another trend fueling interest in infomercials is availability of broadcast time. Most broadcast stations have dropped long-standing bans on infomercials, so advertisers now have a wider choice of stations and can reach larger audiences. Instead of banishing infomercials to the wee hours of the morning, some stations are airing them at more desirable times (but not, as yet, during prime evening hours). Finally, many advertisers like infomercials because they can easily measure response by counting the number of orders or inquiries received.

At the same time, however, critics are concerned that some of these commercials cross ethical boundaries to masquerade as entertainment by simulating talk shows or news announcements. They charge that viewers can be misled into believing they're watching a program that's independent of the sponsor. As a result, viewers may not realize that these commercials are

To encourage response, AT&T flashes a toll-free number at the end of its infomercials.

offering information provided by advertisers who are not impartial and who want only to persuade viewers to buy their products. Moreover, viewers may not be aware that the person endorsing a product in an infomercial has been paid to do so or that he or she shares in the product's profits.

In response to these ethical concerns, the National Infomercial Marketing Association (a trade group) has established voluntary guidelines for member companies. The group urges advertisers (1) to begin and end every infomercial with a "paid advertisement" announcement (alerting viewers to any financial connection between the advertiser and the endorser) and (2) to be able to prove their product's claims. These guidelines mirror some of the steps already taken by federal regulators who have acted to stop the unethical abuse of infomercial advertising. Even so, some people believe further action is necessary. So to avoid any possibility of taking advantage of viewers who tune in during an infomercial and who might think they're watching an objective program, some consumer groups are demanding that disclaimers air throughout the commercials.

What's Your Opinion?
1. Is it ethical to sell products by making commercials that appear to be talk-show programs?
2. Should television stations agree to air infomercials that do not continuously show disclaimers announcing their ad status? Why or why not?

---

process, in the media choices, and even in the audience. Challenges and opportunities for today's advertisers include better targeting, enhanced creativity, new media horizons, and results-driven advertising.

BETTER LOCAL AND GLOBAL TARGETING

More advertisers are reaching out to many smaller markets through *micromarketing*, which offers an opportunity to focus only on those people interested in their products. The information that fuels micromarketing is growing, and much of it is already available. For example, supermarket scanners record your purchases so that advertisers can see how their products are selling and to whom; detailed mailing lists pinpoint your address as well as your interests and family status. With insight and the computing power to analyze this information, advertisers will be better able to locate and communicate with customers and potential customers by tailoring both message and medium to each individual. People who don't need that product won't see or hear the advertising, but those who do need it will—so advertising won't be wasted, and costs will go down even as effectiveness goes up.

For those advertisers whose markets are truly global, the challenge is not to focus more narrowly, but to use a consistent and cost-effective approach to reaching audiences in many countries. These advertisers want to build their images around the world, but they don't want to develop entirely new advertising for every market. Instead, the challenge is to contain costs by creatively adapting their advertising for local conditions and using the appropriate media to send messages across and within national borders. For example, Coca-Cola's advertising is (by design) much the same in 170 countries. The company does vary the media, but the ads in each country are quite similar to those done in other countries, which cost-effectively reinforces the company's international image.[38]

ENHANCED CREATIVITY THROUGH TECHNOLOGY

From holograms to the computer-manipulated art used in print and electronic media, the creative side of advertising is reaping the benefits of new technology to give advertisers the opportunity to break through clutter and capture attention. For example, the line between entertainment and advertising is blurring as advertisers link computers, videotape, and film to mix fiction and reality. Coca-Cola television commercials feature computer-generated characters, vintage film clips, and contemporary music personalities, intriguing viewers and breaking through the clutter. Now imagine seeing your name on an ad—that's another creative enhancement that will become more common as advertisers harness new technology in pursuit of micromarketing. For example, Buick asked *Newsweek* and *Time,* among other magazines, to use advanced printing technology to add individual subscribers' names to Buick car ads. This creative approach helped Buick capture the attention of these potential car buyers.[39]

NEW MEDIA HORIZONS

New advertising media are all around, opening new opportunities for advertisers to grab our attention at home or away. At home, Prodigy is an online computer service that mixes information with advertising so that ads scroll across the bottom of the computer screen while you read *Consumer Reports* or check the weather.[40] In France, the state-owned phone company has placed small computers called Minitels in 2 million homes, allowing subscribers to bank, shop, make travel plans, and access a wide range of information services from home—which opens yet another medium for promoting products. Commercials on network, cable, independent, syndicated, and satellite television are beamed into homes, and some channels are only for shopping. In its infancy, interactive television marries the television with a response device to allow viewers to request specific commercials and then order products or receive coupons from advertisers.[41]

The new media options pose opportunities as well as challenges. Videocassette recorders, now in 70 percent of all U.S. homes, give viewers the ability to zip through the commercials on recorded programs, making advertisers unhappy. However, more advertisers are taking advantage of the popularity of videotaped-movie rentals by paying to have commercials inserted at the beginning of these tapes.[42] Finally, advertisers are learning how to use the opportunities provided by **place-based advertising** (also known as *in-your-face* advertising), a form of advertising that reaches the target audience when they're away from home and where they can't help but notice the message. Much of this kind of advertising is in-store, such as video screens at the checkout counter, but it also pops up in unexpected places (such as airplanes), bringing ads to people wherever they are (see Exhibit 1.14).[43]

RESULTS-DRIVEN ADVERTISING

If there's one word that sums up advertising's direction in the 1990s and beyond, it's *accountability*. Ads can be intriguing, exciting, even suspenseful, but if they don't achieve the advertisers' goals, they're not good—making the drive for results a major challenge. "When I write an ad, I don't want you to tell me that you find it 'creative,'" advertising pioneer David Ogilvy told a group of national advertisers not long ago. "I want you to find it so persuasive that you buy the product—or buy it more often."[44] Ogilvy's comment cuts to the heart of the question of whether creativity sells products. Many agency people compete fiercely for creativity awards, which boost morale and build professional reputations. But clients are more interested in one bottom-line question: Do the ads *sell?* Reebok, for example, pulled its creatively offbeat "U.B.U." and "physics behind the physiques" ads when they didn't help sales. A European study suggests that the most popular television ads break through clutter, but they don't necessarily influence purchases. So creativity is only one part of the advertising equation, and advertisers and agencies must continue to work toward combining the message and the media to most effectively influence each target audience (see Exhibit 1.15).[45]

EXHIBIT 1.14
Place-Based Advertising

Place-based advertising is specifically designed to reach people when and where they will notice the ad messages. Travelers watching television programs in airport terminals, for example, will see some commercials that air only in airports. This type of advertising is designed to help advertisers reach people who fly.

The Advertising Planning Process

These diverse challenges and opportunities add to the complexity of advertising planning, which is a distinct process within the marketing function. The advertising planning process consists of eight steps: (1) analyzing the current situation, (2) defining the audience, (3) developing marketing goals and a marketing plan, (4) developing advertising goals and an advertising plan based on the marketing plan, (5) agreeing on the advertising budget, (6) developing and executing creative

EXHIBIT 1.15
Results-Driven Advertising

To successfully launch Apple Computer's PowerBook line of notebook computers, BBDO/Los Angeles developed an ad campaign that stressed the product's simple-to-operate convenience. Not only was the campaign creatively exciting, but it also helped build PowerBook's first-year sales to $1 billion.

EXHIBIT 1.16
The Advertising Planning Process

Advertisers move through an eight-step process as they plan, execute, and evaluate their advertising programs. Once they've determined the results of their ad campaigns, advertisers can use this information to reexamine their current situation and make any needed changes.

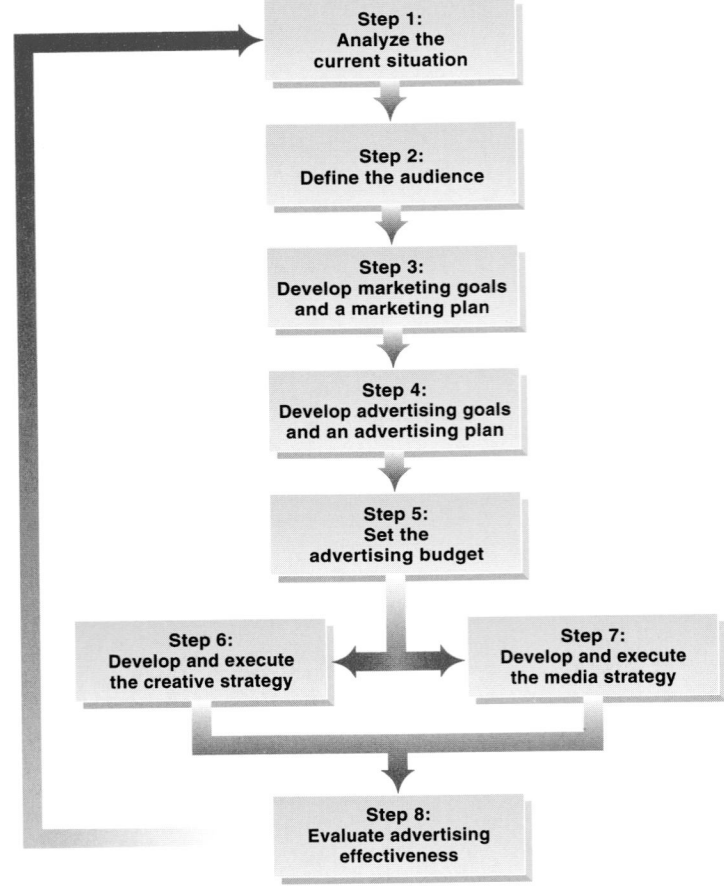

Step 1:
Analyze the current situation

Step 2:
Define the audience

Step 3:
Develop marketing goals and a marketing plan

Step 4:
Develop advertising goals and an advertising plan

Step 5:
Set the advertising budget

Step 6:
Develop and execute the creative strategy

Step 7:
Develop and execute the media strategy

Step 8:
Evaluate advertising effectiveness

strategy, (7) developing and executing media strategy, and (8) evaluating advertising effectiveness (see Exhibit 1.16). As you can see, advertising has to fit within the overall marketing framework used to achieve organizational goals. Each **campaign,** an advertising program designed to promote a specific product during a specific period, has to be coordinated with other tools such as public relations and sales promotion to create a seamless and effective foundation for integrated marketing communications.

The advertising planning process is a useful blueprint for determining where you are now and where you want to be in the future, for learning more about your audience, and for measuring the effectiveness of your messages and media. By the time you reach the last step, you should have the information you need to see whether the advertising was successful or whether you must go back to earlier steps and make changes. You may take some steps out of order or return to earlier steps, but you can't plan and implement an effective advertising program without moving through each step at one point or another.

This book follows the outline of the advertising planning process and examines the steps in creating results-driven advertising. In Part I, you'll explore how advertisers and agencies work together, and you'll learn about the forces within the advertising environment that can affect your situation. Part II describes how audience definition and research relate to goals, strategy, and planning. In Parts III and IV, you'll examine the creative process and media choices. And in Part V, you'll see how to put the entire campaign together, integrating all the promotional tools into a cohesive, coordinated framework designed to get the results you want.

Summary

In the United States and around the world, advertising takes many forms and reaches people where they live, work, play, and buy. Advertisers are people or organizations that seek to sell products or influence people through advertising. Advertisers hire advertising agencies, independent organizations that specialize in developing and implementing advertising on behalf of their clients. The advertising agencies then select the best media to carry advertisers' messages to their intended audiences. Both advertisers and agencies may use suppliers (individuals or organizations that provide specialized services such as photography or video production) to create and execute advertising messages.

Advertising can be classified according to target audience (consumer or business), geographic area (international, national, regional, or local), media used (newspaper, magazine, radio, television, or other media), and purpose (product versus nonproduct, commercial versus noncommercial, primary demand versus selective demand, and direct action versus indirect action). The functions of advertising include (1) differentiating products, (2) communicating product information, (3) urging product use, (4) expanding distribution, (5) boosting brand preference and loyalty, and (6) reducing sales costs.

The marketing concept is the idea of meeting customer needs by integrating marketing with every part of the organization and working for long-term profits. The four elements of the marketing mix (product, price, distribution, and promotion) are the basic tools used to implement the marketing concept and to satisfy customers. Advertising as part of promotion can offer information about how the organization's product meets customer needs. The communication process is central to the way advertising reaches its audience, and it starts with an idea that originates at the source. The message is encoded into words or images that can be understood by the audience, and the medium carries the message to the audience. Once people receive the message, they decode it to interpret its meaning and offer feedback to the source. Integrated marketing communications is a strategy of coordinating and integrating all of a company's marketing efforts as well as its promotional communications (through all the diverse channels of communication) to convey a consistent, unified message and image to the target audience.

Advertising has been evolving since antiquity. When changes in technology brought about the Industrial Revolution, people left the farms to work in large factories in urban areas. Manufacturers could turn out products more quickly and more cheaply than before, and they turned to advertising to stimulate demand and replace the personal contact they once had with customers. The development of the printing press and movable type stimulated the growth of the print media, including newspapers and magazines. Technologies such as radio and television expanded the reach and speed of advertising, allowing advertisers to move beyond local areas into national and international arenas. The challenges and opportunities of advertising today and tomorrow include better local and global targeting, enhanced creativity, new media horizons, and results-driven advertising.

APPLYING WHAT YOU'VE LEARNED

Taking what you learn in an advertising course and applying it to the real world can sometimes be a challenge. Practicing your new skills on a real organization's advertising situation is a good way to prepare, and each chapter in this book gives you that opportunity. You'll read about the organization's situation at the beginning of the chapter, in a vignette called "Facing an Advertising Challenge at . . ." For example, at the beginning of this chapter, you read about the challenge that jeans maker Levi Strauss faced in communicating the benefits of its new products to customers and prospects. After reading the vignette, you can think about the organization's advertising problem as you read the chapter and learn about various concepts.

At the end of each chapter is an innovative activity titled "Meeting an Advertising Challenge at . . .: A Case for Critical Thinking." In each case, you play the role of an advertising executive at the organization introduced in the vignette, facing the situation you'd encounter on the job in that organization. The case starts by explaining what the company actually did and whether it worked. Then the case presents a series of scenarios, each with three possible courses of action, and asks you to select the best alternative. If you don't like any of the alternatives, you may devise your own solution if your instructor allows. These scenarios let you explore various advertising ideas and ask you to apply the concepts and techniques you learn about in the chapter. The organization chosen for each case uses the same principles you're learning about.

The cases were designed not as tests but as a means to stimulate your thinking about various advertising concepts. In fact, some of the questions have more than one acceptable answer, and some have no completely satisfactory answers. The point is to consider the concepts you learn about and to apply your own judgment.

Now you're ready for your first case (see pages 26–27). Because you've just started learning about advertising, this case is a little different from the rest. It relies on your general knowledge about how advertising operates and on your experience as an employee or a volunteer to give you the insight needed to answer the questions. You'll probably be surprised to discover how much you already know about advertising.

Key Terms

advertisers 4
advertising 4
advertising agencies 4
agricultural advertising 7
brand 12
brand mark 13
brand name 12
business advertising 6
call to action 15
campaign 24
clutter 14
consumer advertising 6
consumers 6
customers 11
distribution 13
goods 8
hierarchy of effects model 15
industrial advertising 7
infomercial 20
integrated marketing communications (IMC) 16
international advertising 7
local advertising 7
marketing 11
marketing communication 14
marketing concept 12
marketing mix 12
media 4
medium 4
national advertising 7
network 19
nonproduct advertising 8
personal selling 13
place-based advertising 22
price 13
product 8
product advertising 8
professional advertising 7

Meeting an Advertising Challenge at Levi Strauss & Company

A CASE FOR CRITICAL THINKING

A brave new world of jeans marketing faced Levi Strauss after the sales boom of the 1970s and 1980s ended. CEO Robert Haas knew that he could still wring some sales out of the traditional jeans lines. But he also realized that future growth meant creating new products for the needs of a changing marketplace. For the baby-boomer generation, whose figures and incomes had both filled out, Levi Strauss developed the Dockers line of stylish and casual clothing with a looser fit. For the preteen crowd, the marketing experts created Big Jeans, a line of oversize jeans. And for young people aged 14 to 24, the experts put the spotlight back on the model 501 button-front jean.

Now Haas and his advertising experts worked on introducing the new products. Reaching out to baby boomers, they decided to advertise the wide range of colors and fashion profiles that could be dressed up or down. The message emphasized fit with flair rather than brand image, because the Levi Strauss name was already well known to this generation of jeans buyers. The jeans maker backed this message with a $10 million advertising campaign in print and electronic media, and soon the Dockers line became a runaway hit. By the early 1990s, Dockers products accounted for 37 percent of Levi

Strauss's sales, and in 1993 the firm started a new line, Dockers Authentics, designed for men 21 to 35 years old.

Although boomers and young men were a key audience, Haas also targeted the teen and young adult market. For young people ages 14 to 24—and for young men in particular—Levi Strauss advertised its traditional 501 button-front blue jean. This jean's button fly made a unique style statement in a zip-up world, and the advertising played it up. The television ads were fast-paced and playful with a heavy dose of reality, a refreshing change from the gloss and glitz of designer-jeans ads, and 501 sales skyrocketed.

Next, the company's advertising specialists turned their attention to the launch of the Big Jeans line for 9- to 14-year-olds. They advertised this line extensively on television, using Nickelodeon, MTV, and youth-oriented Fox Broadcasting programs. By showing preteens that Levi Strauss understood their particular needs and interests, the company was also building brandname recognition that would most likely carry over when these youngsters grew into teen sizes and wanted more sophisticated styles.

Despite the successes that Levi Strauss has had with these audiences, Haas isn't sitting back just yet. He has to fend off rivals who want to cash in

on the nonjeans trend that the Dockers line started, and he must also show women that Levi Strauss isn't just for men. So don't look for Haas to slow down anytime soon.

Your Mission: You've been hired as a special assistant to Steve Goldstein, director of consumer marketing for Levi Strauss's jeans division. He's asked you to meet with the ad agency, Foote, Cone & Belding in San Francisco, to consider various approaches to advertising and media. Use your knowledge of advertising and the communication process to respond to the following advertising challenges.

1. You're planning an ad campaign to launch a new line, Levi's Loose denims for men over 25. This audience grew up in 501 jeans but now needs slightly more room in the seat and the leg. You want to convince these men that they don't have to sacrifice fashion for fit. Which of these magazine ads would do the best job of selling Levi's Loose?

a. Show athletic twenty-something men clad in Levi's Loose jeans playing volleyball on a beach; emphasize freedom of movement as well as style.

b. Show a rock star in Levi's Loose jeans; stress that the jeans are so

Questions

FOR REVIEW

1. What is the marketing mix, and how does advertising fit into it?

2. How can advertising be classified by target audience and by geographic area?

3. What are the functions of advertising?

4. What is integrated marketing communications, and what are its benefits?

5. How did the Industrial Revolution affect the evolution of advertising?

FOR ANALYSIS AND APPLICATION

6. How might Bank of America use enhanced creativity to help break through clutter in television advertising?

7. Do you think advertising evolved for economic or for social reasons? Why?

8. How does the communication process apply to a magazine ad placed by Xerox for its small office copiers? Identify the audience, the medium, and any possible noise that might distract the audience from the message.

9. How might a nonprofit organization such as the Girl Scouts

stylish that they're chosen by celebrities who want a comfortable fit.

c. Zero in on the jeans' denim fabric and the reinforced stress points; explain that Levi's Loose are rugged enough to withstand any activity.

2. The agency suggests trying direct-action advertising to promote 501 jeans. Which of these ideas might be most effective in generating sales?

a. Mail a coupon to mothers of teenage children, offering a $10 discount with the purchase of two pairs of 501 jeans.

b. Advertise 501 jeans on billboards near middle and high schools and show a toll-free number to call for the name of the nearest store.

c. Advertise in college newspapers, offering to take $5 off the price of a pair of 501 jeans when students trade in any old or outgrown jeans.

3. Lately you've noticed more jeans ads on television, and you're concerned that the clutter will distract your audience and derail the communication process. How can you make your commercials stand out?

a. Use black and white except for the jeans, which will be shown in color.

b. Make the commercials silent, and flash the company name at the end.

c. Create the commercial as a series of still pictures with no motion, and show the company name in the lower left-hand corner all the time.

A LOOSE INTERPRETATION OF THE ORIGINAL

4. Although the teen market is nearly stagnant, the Hispanic-American market is growing. Research shows that Hispanic families buy 12 percent of all jeans sold in the United States, despite making up only 9 percent of the U.S. population. Moreover, the Levi Strauss name is familiar to this audience. To reach this market, the agency proposes that you run commercials on Spanish-language television and explain the product benefits. Which of the following themes and advertising approaches do you think would do the best job of persuading the target audience to buy your products?

a. "Everybody lives Levi's." In a "something for everyone" approach, emphasize that Levi Strauss is right for every size, age,

and lifestyle. The ads will show people of all ages and body shapes wearing your products, and they will tout every benefit, including fit, style, color, and comfort.

b. "Live the Levi's life." Show the glamour of the brand. The ads should show people clad in Levi Strauss clothing entering exclusive clubs and traveling to exotic places, as if to say, "If you want to live the good life, buy Levi Strauss."

c. "Levi Strauss jeans always fit well." The message is: at work or at play, Levi Straus jeans give the fit and function you need. Whether you're on the job or relaxing, you can depend on Levi Strauss clothing to look and feel good.[46] ∎

of America use direct-action advertising to build membership? How might it use indirect-action advertising?

10. Other than newspapers, magazines, radio, or television, what "new media" might Nintendo use to get an advertising message about a new game cartridge to a target audience of teenagers?

Sharpen Your Advertising Skills

Congratulations! You've just been appointed publisher of *Reader's Digest.* You publish the magazine in 16 languages, and you want to get more advertisers to use non-U.S. editions for international advertising. General Motors already uses

9 *Reader's Digest* editions and recently expanded to all 16 in an effort to reach car buyers throughout the world. Can you convince others to do the same?

Decision: You have two key decisions to make as you think about how you might advertise to attract more *Reader's Digest* ads: (1) Should you use primary or selective advertising? (2) Should you use direct-action or indirect-action advertising? Think about your product, your audience, and your goals as you make these decisions.

Communication: Once you know what you want your advertising to do, write a brief (one-page) memo to your direct-mail agency, John Emmerling, explaining your decisions. Identify the product and the audience so that the agency can begin developing an effective direct-mail advertising campaign. How could you measure your results?

The Advertiser-Agency Partnership

After studying this chapter, you will be able to

1. Explain why some advertisers use independent advertising agencies and some use in-house agencies

2. Identify the advertising manager's duties

3. Discuss an advertising agency's four major functions

4. Distinguish between full-service, limited-service, and specialized advertising agencies

5. Explain how agencies are paid

6. List and describe the steps in an account review

7. Outline the issues involved in client conflicts

ANNOUNCING THE BOZELL SUMMER INTERNSHIP.

As an unpaid creative intern for the Minneapolis office of Bozell Advertising, you'll do a lot of free thinking. All while earning invaluable experience working side-by-side with highly paid professionals. To apply, send 5 to 10 nonreturnable samples of your best print work to: Lisa Clearlite, Bozell. Butler Square, 100 North 6th St. Minneapolis, MN 55403 (Specify whether you're a copywriter or an art director.) The deadline is May 29, 1992. The Bozell creative department summer internship. Applicants are already lining up.

Facing an Advertising Challenge at Deutsch, Inc.

A YOUNG AGENCY GROWS UP

David Deutsch Associates was the name above the door when Donald (Donny) Deutsch joined his father's advertising firm in 1983. The younger Deutsch was 25, and his only previous advertising experience was two years in the New York office of Ogilvy & Mather. At David Deutsch Associates, Deutsch worked briefly in the part of the agency that manages client projects. Then he switched to writing ads, which quickly became his strength. The agency, founded by his father in 1969, was known for its skill in producing effective yet understated print advertising, and David Deutsch still served as chairman. But Donny Deutsch envisioned a larger, more aggressive agency; he wanted the firm to be an industry leader in handling a variety of assignments in all media.

Throughout the 1980s, the agency flourished as Deutsch, appointed creative director, guided a talented young team of experts who developed the ideas, wrote the words, and directed the artwork for clients' ads. In contrast to its formerly staid reputation, the Deutsch agency became known for putting its own quirky spin on feisty but effective advertising. By 1990 the agency, renamed Deutsch, Inc., had grown from $12 million to more than $60 million in annual revenues. Its client roster included British Knights, a maker of athletic shoes; Ikea, a Swedish-based furniture chain expanding in the United States; Oneida Silversmiths, makers of flatware; the Pontiac dealers in metropolitan New York; and Samsung Electronics.

Although the agency had an enviable creative record and a solid client list, Deutsch believed the firm was being pigeonholed as a "hot" but small creative agency. He was eager to expand beyond 92 employees, to push billings over the $100 million mark, and to quickly make a bigger name for Deutsch as a multifaceted agency capable of handling larger advertisers' accounts. So the agency took on a new assignment: to sell itself. "This is the hardest assignment we've ever had," said Deutsch. "But we don't want to wait until we win some big award to get noticed. The best way to let everyone know that we have something exciting to offer is to go out and sell the agency like any other product."

As Donny Deutsch, competing with young, aggressive agencies that were also celebrated for their creative flair, how would you sell Deutsch to advertisers? How would you demonstrate that your agency could manage the many details of developing and running ad campaigns for larger accounts? And how would you show that the agency had graduated to the big time without losing the youthful irreverence that had made its ads stand out?[1] ∎

CHAPTER OVERVIEW As Donny Deutsch and his clients know, making an ad campaign involves a partnership between two key players: the advertiser and the agency. In this chapter, you'll explore the vital role each plays in the advertising process. You'll also learn more about the advertiser-agency partnership, including how to start a new advertising relationship, how to work with an agency, and how to change the advertiser-agency relationship.

The Advertiser: The Visible Partner

The most visible player in the advertising process is the advertiser. Of course, that's by design: it's the advertiser's name or product you're supposed to remember when you see a splashy television commercial, spot a magazine ad, or hear a catchy radio ad (see Exhibit 2.1). As discussed in Chapter 1, advertisers may be international, national, regional, or local; they may be global corporations like PepsiCo, small businesses like Vermont Bicycle Touring, nonprofit organizations like the Houston Grand Opera, or government services like the U.S. Marines.

All this advertising adds up: every year, U.S. advertisers spend more than $140 billion on advertising, which works out to over $570 per person. In your local area, you're exposed to any number of diverse advertisers, ranging from one-person law offices that advertise only in the yellow pages to big public utilities that advertise in newspapers and on billboards. In fact, the *Standard Directory of Advertisers* (known as the "Advertiser Red Book") lists roughly 25,000 advertisers in the United States alone and includes their budgets and their advertising agencies.[2]

The advertiser's desire to sell something or to influence opinions and behavior is what drives the entire advertising process—and thus the work of the advertising

EXHIBIT 2.1
The Advertiser's Name Goes Front and Center

The Sony brand name is prominently featured in this colorful magazine ad promoting My First Sony Electric Sketch Pad. What's not in this ad is the name of the agency that created it: Slater Hanft Martin.

agency. Once an advertiser agrees to use the services of an ad agency, the advertiser becomes that agency's **client.** One of the most basic choices an advertiser must make is signing up as a client with an outside agency or setting up an agency inside its own organization.

CHOOSING AN INDEPENDENT OR AN IN-HOUSE AGENCY

When you think about advertising agencies, the names that come to mind probably include J. Walter Thompson, Saatchi & Saatchi, and other well-known agencies. These agencies are independent—separate from advertisers; they operate autonomously. Nearly 98 percent of all media spending for advertising is handled by independent agencies. In contrast, an **in-house advertising agency** is owned and operated by the advertiser; it's inside the advertiser's organization. In-house agencies aren't well known, and yet their part in the advertising process is critical for their owners because an in-house agency handles some or all of the functions an outside agency would otherwise manage.

Using an Independent Agency

Advertisers hire independent agencies for a variety of reasons. Not every organization can afford to have on staff all the specialists it needs for dealing with the technical aspects of creating, producing, and placing ads. Hiring an independent advertising agency can be a cost-effective way to gain access to a group of trained professionals, much like hiring a law firm.[3] Most independent agencies offer expertise in every aspect of advertising, from advertising research and planning to evaluation. By going outside for these services, the advertiser can enhance or complement the knowledge and experience of its own product specialists. Independent agencies like Deutsch, Inc. work with many products, advertisers, and industries, so they generally have a good idea of what works, what doesn't, and why. Such expertise can mean the difference between success and failure, and it can also save advertisers time and money.[4]

Because independent agencies are continually exposed to a variety of products and advertising problems, they're often more objective about an advertiser's products than in-house agencies. In time, an in-house agency may become too inwardly focused, whereas an independent agency gets a well-rounded view of the market and can therefore put the advertiser's products and concerns into perspective when developing an advertising campaign. Some observers also think that independent agencies offer more talent and creativity than in-house agencies because, they believe, skilled professionals gravitate to the lively, sometimes zany atmosphere of outside agencies and crave the variety of projects such agencies handle. By comparison, an in-house agency might seem relatively staid and corporate; some advertising specialists might even find the in-house environment stagnant or limiting because the agency deals with only one advertiser's problems and resources.[5]

Using an In-House Agency

Although many advertisers opt to hire independent agencies, others prefer the control, responsiveness, and cost structure of an in-house agency. If you're an advertiser with an in-house agency, you gain complete control over all agency functions. Your agency focuses only on your organization's needs and goals, so its staff develops a more thorough understanding of your products and your industry, which is especially important when you deal with highly technical products or processes. The in-house agency isn't looking to profit from handling your business, so your cost may be lower. For example, as discussed later in the chapter, your in-house agency can earn commissions to offset your media costs. Finally, because the in-house agency is physically close to the rest of your organization, its staff can more quickly and easily coordinate efforts with other departments.[6]

No advertiser is too small or too large to use an in-house agency (see Exhibit 2.2). When Thomas Burnham founded Ho-Lee-Chow, a Michigan-based franchise specializing in home delivery of Chinese food, he established an in-house agency to create the newspaper and billboard advertising that supported new store openings. As his chain expands, Burnham may hire an independent agency, but for now, the in-house agency does it all, from store fliers to billboard ads to coupons. John Hewitt, founder of the Jackson Hewitt chain of tax-preparation offices, tried two independent agencies before setting up an in-house agency. He wanted to lower costs, but more important, he wanted his agency to know his business inside and out. Says Hewitt, "An ad agency might have 30 to 40 clients. They don't have the time to understand us as well as we do."[7]

At the other end of the spectrum, some global companies with giant advertising budgets have set up in-house agencies for media buying and other services. Among these companies are Procter & Gamble and Campbell Soup. RJR Nabisco's in-house agency handles print and outdoor media advertising as well. A few international companies have gone further, establishing full-service in-house agencies that also serve other advertisers. In Germany, Daimler-Benz owns the full-service in-house agency Debis Marketing Services; in Switzerland, pharmaceutical giant Ciba-Geigy owns the full-service in-house agency AllComm. Both integrate a variety of communications specialties and have clients other than their parents.[8]

Whether an advertiser uses an independent or an in-house agency, it still needs an advertising department. To better understand how the advertiser's advertising department operates, look at how the tasks are organized, what advertising managers do, and how they're accountable for their results.

ORGANIZING THE ADVERTISING DEPARTMENT

The head of the advertising department is the **advertising manager** (or the *advertising director*), who reports to the advertiser's marketing manager (or the marketing director)—position titles vary from organization to organization. The structure of the advertising department can also vary. In a **centralized advertising department,** one group plans, controls, and coordinates all advertising efforts (see Exhibit 2.3). A centralized advertising department may also be part of a centralized marketing services department that handles a range of marketing functions.

In small businesses or in organizations where top management actively supervises the advertising function, a centralized approach can provide a single, sharp focus and, in many cases, can result in cost savings. For example, in a local flower shop, the owner may also handle the advertising function. Centralization allows the

EXHIBIT 2.2
How West Bend Uses Its In-House Ad Agency

West Bend's in-house advertising agency creates its print advertising, such as this magazine ad for an electric wok. This allows the company to have full control over the message and the way it is conveyed to the target audience.

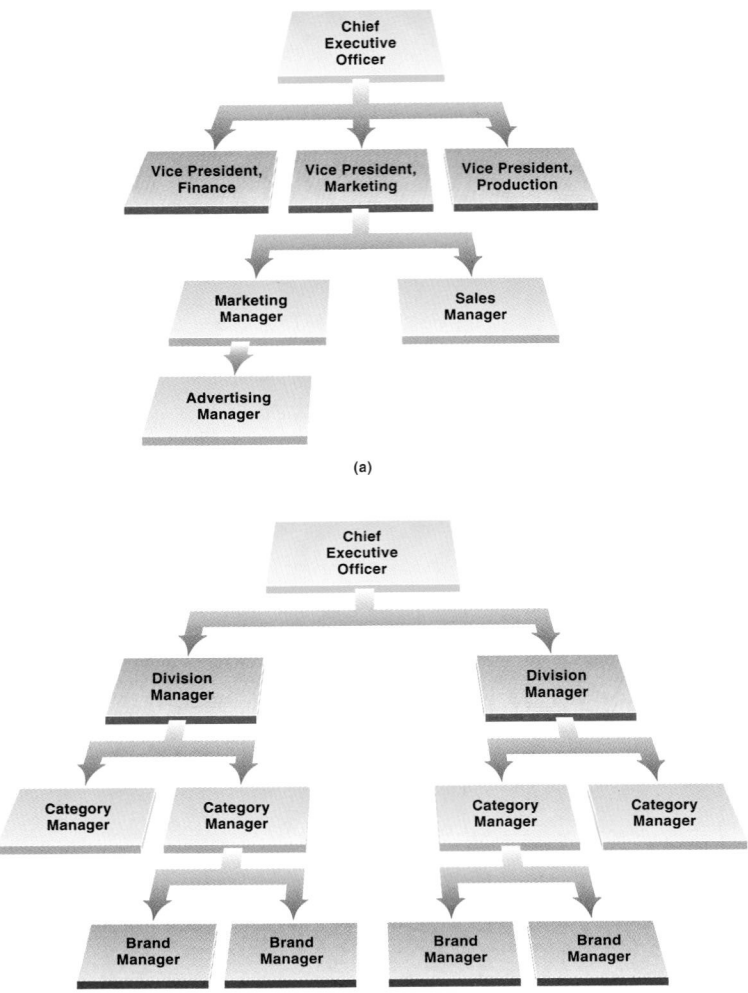

(a)

(b)

EXHIBIT 2.3

Centralized and Decentralized Advertising Departments

If your advertising department is centralized (a), you'll assign one advertising manager to handle all the advertising functions for the organization. However, if your advertising department is decentralized (b), the brand managers will only handle the advertising for their respective products.

organization to tightly control the advertising budget and to operate with only one group of specialists. Because all advertising is developed by one person or group, the advertiser may save money through economies of scale while ensuring that the various messages and materials complement rather than conflict with each other.[9]

On the other hand, when large organizations such as multinational corporations expand or diversify their products, markets, or customer base, they may find a centralized approach unwieldy. To manage this diversity more efficiently, top managers may set up a **decentralized advertising department** for each division or business. This is the approach used by Nestlé and other consumer product giants that sell hundreds of products in one country or a variety of products all over the world (see Exhibit 2.4).

Under decentralization, each division has its own advertising department, its own manufacturing department, and all the other functional departments needed to serve its customers. Many organizations assign each product or brand to a **brand manager**, who is responsible for sales and profits and for supervision of advertising as well as other functions (with the help of one or more assistant brand managers).[10] In some corporations, such as Procter & Gamble, the brand manager reports to a **category manager,** who coordinates the efforts of all the brand managers handling a related group of products. In turn, the category manager reports to the division manager, who has ultimate responsibility for that division's sales and profits. Divisional managers can make decisions without waiting for higher-level approvals, so advertising programs can be quickly planned and implemented, an advantage when competitors make an unexpected move or when market conditions change quickly.[11]

(SFX): Jaunty music
SUPER: DAVID JELLAMY.
SUPER: DAVID JELLAMY'S JELLINGTONS.
SUPER: ROWNTREE'S.

SUPER: JELLY-FLOP.
SUPER: JUST AS JELLICIOUS IN POTS.
SUPER: BOTTIJELLI.
SUPER: ROWNTREE'S.

SUPER: TOM AND JELLY.
SUPER: TOM.
V.O.: If it's not Rowntree's Jelly, throw a wobbly.

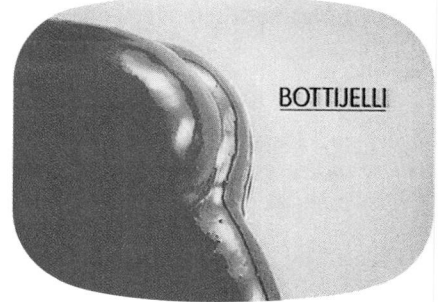

EXHIBIT 2.4
Decentralized Advertising at Nestlé

At Nestlé each division is responsible for advertising its own brands. As a result, the Nestlé managers who hired Ogilvy & Mather/London to create this commercial for Rowntree's Jelly were allowed the freedom to gear the message to their specific target audience.

General Motors, for example, is moving from centralization to decentralization. After years of directing all advertising from the corporate level, General Motors recently gave its individual vehicle divisions more responsibility for their own advertising efforts. In North America, for example, Philip Guarascio, general manager of marketing and advertising (and a former agency executive), works with the general managers in charge of each division's car and truck brands to devise efficient and effective advertising strategies. In addition, he coordinates the activities of the various advertising agencies serving the divisions, and he supervises global media placement. However, the final responsibility for advertising is now at the divisional level.[12]

What the Advertising Manager Does

Philip Guarascio's role at GM illustrates some of the responsibilities that advertising managers assume. Because he relies on independent agencies, he and his staff do not personally create, produce, or place GM's ads, and this is typical of advertising managers in large corporations. Guarascio's responsibilities do include planning and budgeting company advertising, handling administrative tasks, and coordinating GM's outside advertising agencies.

- *Planning and budgeting advertising.* At the heart of the advertising process is planning: setting goals, developing a course of action to meet those goals, ensuring that the ads are executed as planned, and checking the results. (Advertising planning is examined in depth in Chapter 7.) Advertising managers also prepare budgets that detail how much money is needed and how the money will be spent; these budgets are generally approved by top managers who have the final word on the organization's money matters.

- *Creating and producing ads.* In organizations with in-house agencies, the advertising manager (working with people in the advertising department) is responsible for creating and producing ads. This part of the advertising process involves creative strategy, art direction, and production (which are examined in Chapters 9 through 12). When working with an independent agency, the advertising manager reviews and approves the agency's work on creating and producing the ads.

- *Handling administration.* In addition to organizing, staffing, and supervising the advertising department, the advertising manager handles a wide array of administrative tasks such as obtaining management and legal approvals for ads, monitoring the agency's activities and bills, and ensuring that ads run as planned and on time.[13]

- *Coordinating advertising efforts.* One of the advertising manager's most important responsibilities is coordinating advertising efforts with other marketing functions and with other departments such as finance and production. For

EXHIBIT 2.5
Measuring Progress toward Advertising Goals

When Chase Manhattan Bank managers want to measure progress toward the goal of signing more college students for Visa and MasterCard credit cards, they can count the number of calls received on the toll-free hotline or check how many credit applications have been received.

example, the advertising manager coordinates ad campaigns with the production and marketing departments to be sure that the advertised products will be available and that salespeople have samples of them. In the course of planning and executing the advertising campaign, the advertising manager also ensures that the efforts of the advertising agency support company goals by approving the materials and methods, supervising the work, and evaluating the results.

The Advertising Manager's Accountability

Strip away the glitter and glamour of advertising, and the advertising manager is left with one overriding responsibility: to achieve results. Large or small, an advertiser wants to be sure that the time, money, and effort spent on advertising get results. Whether the goal is to boost sales, sway voters, or cut drug abuse, the advertising manager is accountable for how well the organization's advertising resources are used. Of course, it's not easy to prove that good results are due to the effects of advertising, or even that advertising has any impact.[14]

More than ever, the combination of tighter advertising budgets and increased global competition puts advertising managers on the firing line to justify their ad spending and to make progress toward goals. Advertisers are less concerned with winning advertising awards than with improving sales or reaching whatever goals they've set for advertising (see Exhibit 2.5). The Joe Isuzu commercials of the late 1980s were much admired for their freshness and ingenuity. While the commercials ran, Isuzu's truck sales accelerated, but its car sales stalled. So Isuzu launched a new, Joe-less ad campaign that challenged rival Toyota's cars head-to-head.[15]

The Advertising Agency: The Invisible Partner

Advertising agencies play a key but invisible role in the advertising process by translating the advertisers' goals—for higher sales, more votes, or more donations—into creative messages that are placed with the media to reach the target audience. Independent agencies serve a variety of advertisers and see a wide range of marketing problems, so they build a storehouse of knowledge, experiences, and ideas they can use to help all their clients.

The *Standard Directory of Advertising Agencies* (the "Agency Red Book") lists the locations, managers, billings, and client names of thousands of U.S. agencies. Nearly 10,000 agencies operate in the United States, and thousands more operate in other countries. You'll find agencies in most major cities, including New York, London, even Beijing, the capital of the world's most populous market. The action, though, isn't confined to big cities: many agencies in smaller communities serve local advertisers such as charities, car dealerships, and restaurants.[16]

Advertising agencies, like advertisers, come in all shapes and sizes. The majority are small agencies employing a handful of specialists, and many stay small by using free-lancers and suppliers as needed. Two examples are Tom Simons's Boston agency, Partners & Simons, and Charles Dozat's London agency, Advertising Planning and Management. Neither has more than a few permanent staffers: what they're offering is their expertise in hiring the right free-lance specialists and outside suppliers for each client. This allows the agencies to select from a pool of talented professionals without the burden of a large payroll or expensive offices, so clients pay less and pay only for the services they need.[17] At the other end of the spectrum are the giant international advertising agencies. The world's largest agency is the WPP Group, a London-based corporate powerhouse with yearly earnings of more than $2.6 billion (see Exhibit 2.6).[18]

Large agencies became even larger when a frenzy of mergers and acquisitions in the 1980s and again in the early 1990s created a string of globe-spanning multiagency organizations equipped to offer a full range of advertising services virtually anywhere in the world. These giant groups each own several advertising

EXHIBIT 2.6 The World's Largest Advertising Agency Organizations

The top 10 agency organizations are able to provide a complete range of advertising services for companies all over the world.

Rank	Advertising Organization, Headquarters	Worldwide Gross Income ($ millions)*
1	WPP Group, London	$2,633.6
2	Interpublic Group of Cos., New York	2,078.5
3	Omnicom Group, New York	1,876.0
4	Dentsu Inc., Tokyo	1,403.2
5	Saatchi & Saatchi Co., London	1,355.1
6	Young & Rubicam, New York	1,008.9
7	Euro RSCG, Neuilly, France	864.8
8	Grey Advertising, New York	765.7
9	Hakuhodo, Tokyo	667.8
10	Foote, Cone & Belding Communications, Chicago	633.7

*1993 data.

Reprinted with permission from the April 14, 1993 issue of *Advertising Age.* Copyright, Crain Communications Inc., 1993.

agencies; for example, Interpublic Group owns the Lowe Group and McCann-Erickson, among others. Coca-Cola is an Interpublic client, and although it also uses other agencies and suppliers, the firm enjoys the benefits of this agency's global coverage. Says David Sanderson, vice president of marketing for Coca-Cola in Toronto, "If we were to isolate ourselves from this network, we would lose the chance to tap into new ideas and marketing techniques around the world." For instance, television commercials created by McCann-Erickson for Coca-Cola in Canada have also been shown in the United States.[19]

Although the megamergers were intended to create better economies of scale and a wider range of services for international advertisers, they also caused a rash of client defections as newly combined agencies wound up handling competing products. At the same time, some large agency groups have been struggling to cut debt, slash costs, and juggle functional duplications—all the time trying not to hurt creativity or service—as they attempt to shake off the effects of the 1990s recession, which put some large advertisers into bankruptcy, squashed other advertisers' budgets, and squeezed agency profits.[20]

To compete with the global presence and buying power of these agency giants, many local agencies are joining independent agency networks. For example, to better serve advertisers that want to reach the unified European Union market, a number of local agencies have joined networks such as the Alliance International Group (based in London) and Dialogue International (based in Brussels).[21] Large or small, independent or network-affiliated, advertising agencies are important resources because of the many functions they handle for advertisers.

WHAT ADVERTISING AGENCIES DO

Advertising agencies exist for one basic purpose: to interpret for the advertiser's target audience information about the goods or services being marketed. To do this, an agency must go through a series of steps:

1. Agency people get to know the strengths and weaknesses of the product and its competitors, and analyze the product's current and potential market.

2. The agency examines all appropriate methods of distribution and sales and investigates the appropriate media for the advertiser's messages.

3. With this background, the agency prepares and executes an advertising plan, creating and producing the advertisements, buying media space and time, checking that the advertisements run, and billing the client for services and media used.

4. The agency works closely with the advertiser to be sure that the advertising is coordinated with sales and other marketing activities.[22]

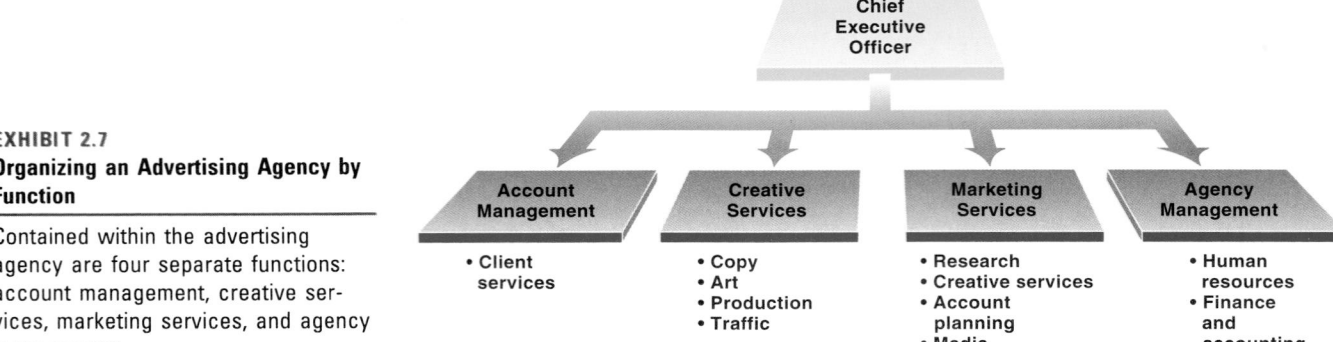

EXHIBIT 2.7

Organizing an Advertising Agency by Function

Contained within the advertising agency are four separate functions: account management, creative services, marketing services, and agency management.

A variety of functional experts (specialists in particular skills) become involved as the agency moves from understanding the product and the market to planning, creating, executing, and evaluating the advertising (see Exhibit 2.7). These specialized functions include account management, creative services, marketing services, and agency management. Although these functional areas appear to be separate, they coordinate and integrate their efforts so that they can most effectively serve each client.

Account Management

The account management function is the main link between the agency and the client. In this function, the **account executive** (known informally as the AE) serves as liaison by staying in close contact with the client and with the agency people who work on that client's account. It's a pivotal but pressured role because the AE works *for* the agency but *on behalf of* the client, so priorities sometimes conflict. The AE represents the client within the agency, marshaling agency resources; keeping ad creation, production, and placement on schedule; and pushing for the agency's best efforts. At the same time, the AE is the voice of the agency to the client, representing the agency's viewpoint and working to get approval for the agency's work.[23] In a large agency, several account executives are supervised by a *management* (or *account*) *supervisor,* who is supervised in turn by the agency's director of account management.

As an agency goes through the four steps needed to interpret the advertiser's product for its audience, the AE plays an important role. First, the account executive considers what research is needed to learn about the client's product and market. Then with research in hand, the AE works with other agency people to devise an advertising strategy, a detailed advertising plan, and a budget. Once the client has approved this plan, the AE coordinates the efforts of the people who develop and produce the ads, the agency's creative services function.

Creative Services

The second major function in advertising agencies is creative services. Think of it as an umbrella covering a collection of related creative tasks, including copywriting, art direction, and print and electronic production. The **creative director** (also known as the *director of creative services*) supervises all the activities within this function; at Deutsch, Inc., the creative director is Donny Deutsch. Under the creative director, the **copywriter** writes the **copy,** the words in the message. An agency may have many copywriters, depending on the number of clients it serves. The **art director** supervises the creation of the **art,** including such visual elements as the design, illustrations, photos, and type that appear in print ads and commercials. The art is created by the people in the **art department,** who also prepare detailed sketches to guide the filming of television commercials.

After its clients have approved the agency's creative concepts, the **production department,** supervised by the creative director, translates the art and copy into finished ads. Within this department, the **print production manager** works with outside suppliers such as printers and photographers to make the copywriter's words and the art department's design and illustrations into newspaper or magazine ads. Similarly, the **broadcast production manager** hires suppliers such as directors and musicians to work the words created by copywriters (and the art ideas developed by the art department for television commercials) into finished commercials for radio or television.

Holding together the diverse duties of all these creative departments is the **traffic department,** which works closely with each account executive to coordinate all aspects of development and production. This is a pivotal function because agencies typically work on many ads simultaneously, and the process of designing, producing, and placing each ad involves many steps. It's the job of the traffic department to see that the agency people meet their deadlines so that ads are completed and submitted to the media on time. (In some agencies, the traffic department is grouped with agency management rather than with creative services.)

Marketing Services

The third agency function is marketing services. Just as the people in creative services work with the words and the art to produce the ad or commercial in finished form, the people in marketing services figure out what audience the advertising will target, what strategies will influence that audience to act, and which media will best reach that audience. Although the marketing services function sometimes incorporates other specialties such as sales promotion, two distinct types of tasks are usually the focal point: research and media.

The **research director,** assisted by market research specialists (also known as market analysts), investigates the current and potential customers for a product, looks at what motivates these customers to act, and gives the creative services people the background they need to create effective ads for a specific product and market. Research specialists test the audience's reaction to various versions of a proposed ad, and once an ad has run, they measure the audience's response.

A growing number of agencies are adopting **account planning,** a research-based discipline that represents the consumer's viewpoint and feelings about the product and the advertising. Long practiced in Great Britain, account planning is now used by Deutsch, Inc., Chiat/Day, Goodby Berlin & Silverstein, and other U.S. agencies as a way to go underneath the research numbers to see what really makes the customer tick. Then they work with the creative experts and the media specialists to apply this knowledge when creating advertising aimed at appropriate audiences.[24]

The **media director** is responsible for finding the best media at the best price that will most effectively reach the client's target audience. Under the media director in the **media department** is the **media planner,** who decides which media to use, when to use them, and at what cost; the **media buyer,** who books the time or the space needed for a commercial or an ad; and the **media researcher,** who supports media planning and buying by analyzing the number and type of people each medium reaches. Although this function may sound simple, it isn't. Consider the problems of buying network television time in September when you don't know which new show will be a hit or who is likely to watch any particular new program; that's only one of the challenges media specialists face.

Agency Management

The fourth major function is agency management, which involves running the agency's day-to-day activities. Although this function covers a range of tasks, from ordering supplies and furniture to managing advertising databases, two of the most important tasks deal with human resources and finance.

In any business, the human resources department is responsible for hiring, firing, and training agency employees. Even when specialists are recruited directly by the agency owners or the functional heads, the human resources people coordinate their salary, their benefits, and other details.

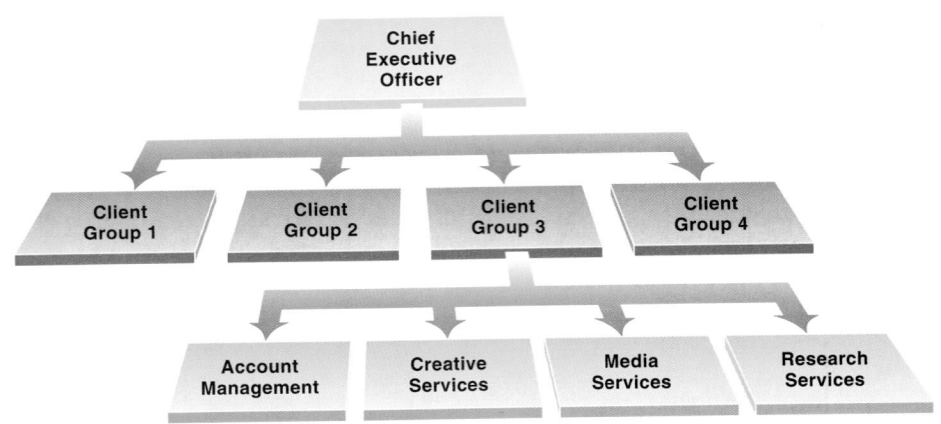

EXHIBIT 2.8
Organizing an Advertising Agency by Groups

When an ad agency uses the group system, it defines its structure in terms of self-contained groups. Each group is responsible for all the advertising functions for one major advertiser or, on occasion, several smaller advertisers.

Finance and accounting tasks involve an enormous amount of paperwork. So that the proper clients are billed, agencies must sort the mountain of media bills they receive for buying ad space and airtime. They also check on billing errors, track payments made to the agency, pay bills submitted by photographers and other suppliers, calculate and pay agency taxes, and handle the payroll. In addition, the finance department keeps a close eye on agency income and expenses and helps top management track profitability.

HOW AGENCIES ARE STRUCTURED

If you were to diagram the structure of a typical full-service advertising agency, you'd find the four basic functions mentioned earlier: account management, creative services, marketing services, and agency management. People in smaller agencies may share the work of two or even three of these functions, and when staff members don't have the time or expertise to tackle a specific function, an agency may contract with outside suppliers or temporarily hire free-lancers (who don't show up on the formal organization chart shown in Exhibit 2.7). Most large agencies have experts on staff in all four functions, but their position titles may vary somewhat. When an agency is organized according to this **departmental system,** the day-to-day work for each client is accomplished by a group of experts assigned from each function except agency management.[25]

Some agencies prefer to formalize the **group system** by using group assignments as the basis for all or part of the agency's official structure. Such an agency defines its structure as a series of formal, relatively self-contained groups (see Exhibit 2.8). A functional expert in account management, creative services, media, and perhaps research is permanently assigned to each group, which handles all the advertising functions for one major advertiser or perhaps several smaller advertisers. For example, Young & Rubicam uses permanent groups to service the U.S. Army, one of its key clients; Lintas:New York uses teams of account managers and experts in strategy, creative services, media, and marketing to service its clients.[26]

WHAT VARIOUS AGENCIES OFFER

As you've seen, advertising agencies vary widely in size from a single-person shop or a partnership of copywriter and art director to a globe-spanning agency with a staff of thousands. In addition to size, agencies vary according to their level of service or their specialty. Depending on their needs, advertisers may hire full-service, limited-service, or specialized agencies.

Full-Service Agencies

A **full-service advertising agency** is capable of providing all the services necessary to develop, create, and execute advertising for its clients. Full-service agencies may develop particular specialties, but their main focus is on advertisers that want to sell to consumers. Whether advertisers are selling shampoo, minivans,

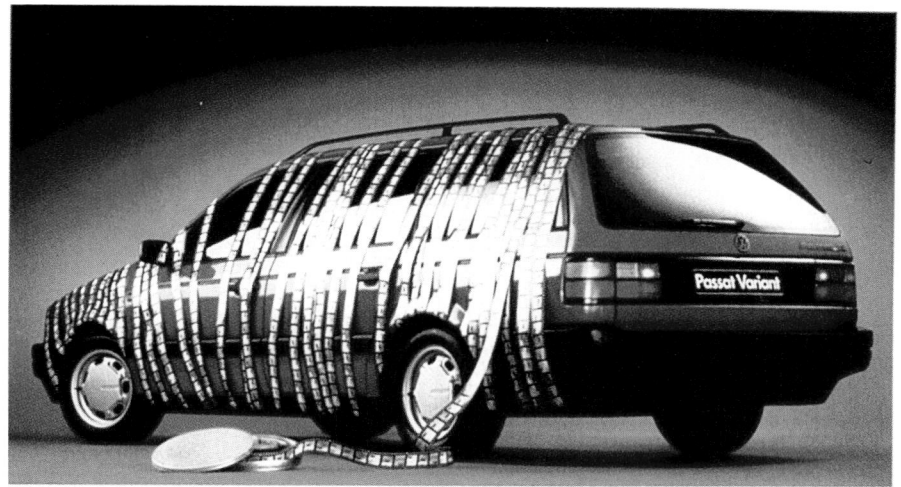

Chi ha detto che le grandi passioni si vivono solo al cinema?

Passat
Variant

Volkswagen
C è da fidarsi.

EXHIBIT 2.9
A Full-Service Agency That Knows Consumers

DDB Needham is a full-service agency with the expertise to help Volkswagen promote its cars to consumers in 25 international markets. In Italy, Verba DDB Needham created this eyecatching ad to target people who buy cars for personal use.

or cookies, the common thread is the emphasis on goods bought by consumer households (see Exhibit 2.9). Some full-service agencies even handle production and programming for movie and television shows sponsored by their clients. Lintas:Paris produced the television program *Wheel of Fortune* for Unilever in France; Hakuhodo produced the *Figaro Story,* a movie that acted as a commercial to sell Nissan's Figaro model in Japan.[27]

A recent trend among full-service agencies is to integrate a wider variety of communications specialties, including public relations, sales promotion, and others. The agency uses an integrated marketing communications approach to create, place, and coordinate the advertiser's communications so that all messages are compatible—and, of course, the agency gets more of the advertiser's business. Ryder Truck Rental signed on with Ogilvy & Mather to take advantage of the full-service agency's multifaceted range of integrated services. The agency suggests the best combination of communications for each Ryder division and then executes and coordinates all efforts to send one cohesive message. In a recent campaign to sell Ryder's used rental trucks, Ogilvy & Mather used television advertising, a toll-free number, and direct mail to reach truck buyers. The agency handled all the elements, ensuring that the campaign was properly coordinated and executed.[28]

Limited-Service Agencies

A **limited-service advertising agency** concentrates on selected advertising services. This lets an advertiser buy the services it needs on an "à la carte" basis, mixing and matching the services of several agencies. One type of limited-service agency is the **creative boutique,** an advertising agency that restricts its services to developing innovative advertising concepts and messages. Although creative boutiques don't always offer agency services such as media planning or research, many advertisers value their responsiveness and their ability to come up with fresh, exciting ideas.[29]

In a new twist on the creative boutique concept, Coca-Cola hired Michael Ovitz's powerful Hollywood talent agency, Creative Artists Agency (CAA), as a media and communications consultant for its global advertising. Providing creative strategies and services to supplement the work of Coca-Cola's full-service agencies and suppliers, CAA used Rob Reiner and other directors, actors, and writers it represents to produce a series of Coca-Cola television commercials.[30]

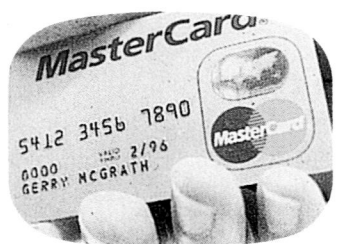  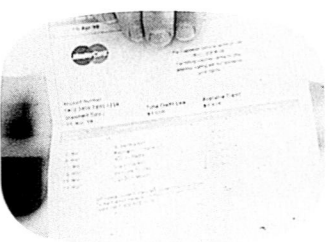 

(SFX): island instrumental music
V.O.: You know those credit card commercials where they tell you to jaunt off to some exotic paradise? This isn't one of them, OK?

(SFX): abrupt change in music
V.O.: We're taking our Master-Card to the supermarket. How's that for exotic? Actually, I guess it is kind of exotic. I mean, you've got a MasterCard; they've got tropical fruit and

crystal clear water, right? And now, no card is more accepted on the planet, including super-markets, and it's smart to use your monthly statement to keep track of your grocery spending. I mean, the supermarket isn't

exactly paradise, but at least you can drink the water.
SUPER/V.O.: MasterCard. It's more than a credit card. It's smart money.™

EXHIBIT 2.10
How MasterCard Uses a Media-Buying Service

Like an increasing number of advertisers, MasterCard uses separate agencies for the creative portion and for the media-buying portion of its advertising business. Ammirati & Puris developed this MasterCard television commercial and DeWitt Media purchased the media time.

Another type of limited-service agency is the **media-buying service,** an agency that handles only media planning, buying, and placement. The media-buying service specializes in buying print space in newspapers and magazines and airtime on radio and television, placing the ads, and handling media billing; some also manage media planning. Because they buy for many clients (and increasingly for many agencies), media-buying services can negotiate price reductions of 25 percent or more, a major savings for advertisers. These agencies are well established in Western Europe, where they handle over 75 percent of the media buys in France and nearly 50 percent in Spain. In the United States, media-buying services handle under 10 percent, but this number is growing.[31]

The media-buying field is changing as more full-service agencies, including Bozell, Jacobs, Kenyon & Eckhardt and Saatchi & Saatchi, set up departments specifically to handle media buying for advertisers and other agencies. In turn, advertisers are seeking savings by consolidating their media buying into one shop, whether it's a media-buying service or a full-service agency (see Exhibit 2.10). For example, Kodak uses the full-service agency Lintas:USA to buy its media, but it uses another agency's creative and production services for its ads and commercials.[32]

Specialized Agencies

Some advertisers sell to smaller, more specialized markets, so they hire special agencies that concentrate on the audiences they want to reach. Business-to-business, medical, and ethnic agencies are examples of *specialized advertising agencies,* firms that focus on specific markets. Specialized agencies know their markets' needs and jargon, so they can create appropriate messages and select the right media for their clients (see Exhibit 2.11). These agencies generally perform all the functions of a full-service agency, but only in their specialized field.[33]

Many full-service agencies also take on nonconsumer assignments such as business advertising; for example, McCann-Erickson Worldwide handles $2 million worth of such advertising for KnowledgeWare, a business software manufacturer. However, even companies that use full-service agencies to handle the bulk of their advertising use specialized agencies to reach certain audiences. Look at Procter & Gamble (P&G). This giant advertiser uses full-service agencies to advertise Crest, Dawn, Cover Girl, Hawaiian Punch, and its many other consumer products to the general public. P&G also hires specialized agencies to reach targeted markets in the United States. To reach Hispanic markets, P&G uses Noble & Asociados in Irvine, California, and Font & Vaamonde Associates in New York; to reach African-American markets, P&G uses Burrell Advertising in Chicago. Similarly, specialized agencies in other countries help advertisers reach particular audiences. For example, advertisers in South Africa that want to reach black markets can use Herdbuoys, a specialized agency.[34]

EXHIBIT 2.11

Specialized Agencies Target Specific Markets

DuPont calls on Rumrill-Hoyt, a specialized advertising agency in Rochester, New York, to develop ads specifically for the agricultural market.

HOW AGENCIES ARE PAID

For decades, advertising agencies made money in one simple, straightforward way: by selling space for the media. In the nineteenth century, an agency represented newspapers, and later magazines, finding advertisers to buy space in their publications. In those days, agents were paid by the newspapers and magazines according to the amount of space they sold; as part of the package, the agents would often write the ad's words and create the art. Over the years, the tasks of the agencies evolved from selling space for the media into buying space for advertisers, a subtle but important shift toward representing the advertisers' interests. Today, much of the agency's **billings,** or total revenues, still come from media commissions, but agencies also receive revenues from their clients in the form of fees, markups, and incentive-based compensation.[35]

Media Commissions

A **commission** is a payment from a media firm (such as a newspaper or radio station) to an agency that purchases advertising space or time for its clients. At the turn of the century, the commission ranged from 10 to 25 percent of the price paid for the advertising space. By the 1920s, newspapers and magazines were paying a consistent commission of 15 percent on the space sold by an agency. Most media still offer 15 percent, but when agencies sell ads for outdoor media (such as billboards) and transit media (such as buses), these media sometimes offer 16⅔ percent.[36]

Here's how the commission system works. You're an advertiser with a budget of $1,000 for a newspaper ad, and you ask your agency to buy the space, prepare the ad, and send it to the paper. Once the ad appears, the newspaper bills your agency for $1,000, and the agency bills you the same $1,000. You pay the agency the full $1,000, but by agreement with the newspaper, the agency keeps 15 percent as its commission ($150) and pays the newspaper $850. Because the agency works on commission, it tries hard to keep its own costs down so that your account is profitable. Of course, if you use an in-house agency to make media placements, you can apply the media commissions earned in-house to offset some of your advertising costs.

Advertisers seeking to lower their costs have been paying only for the services they want, chipping away at the standard 15 percent commission. In other words, although the agencies still receive 15 percent (or whatever discount the media will pay), the advertisers effectively cap the amount they reimburse the agencies for media time or space. In fact, the number of advertisers that allow agencies a 15 percent commission has dropped considerably: in 1976, 68 percent allowed 15 percent, but by 1986 that number had dropped to 43 percent, and by 1992 it had dropped again to 33 percent. Many carmakers in the United States have negotiated commission schedules of 12 percent or less. When Nissan hired Chiat/Day as its U.S. agency, it arranged to pay an average commission of 10 percent up to a certain level of media purchases and a lower commission after that point. One problem with the commission system is that some agencies may be tempted to pump up media purchases so that they can boost revenues. However, cutting an agency's commission rate may severely squeeze its profits and hobble its ability to give quality service.[37]

Markups

As they prepare an ad, agencies often buy services from outside suppliers such as photographers and video production houses. These suppliers don't normally offer an agency commission; instead, the agency adds a **markup,** an additional percentage, to the supplier's bill when it's presented to the client. The typical markup is 17.65 percent, a figure that sounds odd until you look at what it does. On a photography bill for $850, a 17.65 percent markup is $150; adding $150 to $850 allows the agency to bill its client a total of $1,000—and receive the equivalent of a 15 percent commission ($1,000 × 15% = $150). Of course, this percentage doesn't always cover the cost of supervising the suppliers, nor does it always yield the expected profit, so agencies sometimes use a higher markup.[38]

Fees

An increasingly important source of agency revenues is fees. Although many variations exist, two types of fee arrangements are common: a fee-commission

This advertisement for Burger King (created by Sosa) is targeted toward the Hispanic market in the United States. The message "Así Lo Quiero" translates as "The Way I Want It."

agency's ads for Chicco children's clothing play up the "Made in Italy" label and the company's Italian origin. Other clients include Pomi tomato products and Beltrami leather goods.

Of course, specialized ad agencies do more than merely translate an ad or a commercial from English. They also have expertise in selecting the appropriate media for a particular audience. Perhaps the major reason to hire a specialized agency is to utilize its in-depth knowledge of the needs, interests, and buying habits of the ethnic audience you want to

reach. In a world of increasing cultural diversity, that knowledge just might give you the edge you need.

Apply Your Knowledge

1. *What might prevent an advertiser from hiring a specialized ad agency to target a particular ethnic group?*
2. *Do you think full-service agencies should work with specialized agencies when their clients want to reach ethnic audiences? Or should full-service agencies hire specialists experienced in reaching those audiences? Why?* ■

combination and a retainer system. When commissions from media placements don't bring in enough revenue to profitably service an advertiser's account, the agency will often supplement commission revenue with fee revenue. This involves charging a separate fee for services such as developing advertising strategy or for services not directly related to commissionable media, such as public relations. The fee may be based on the hourly rate of the agency specialist providing the service, or it may be calculated on a project basis for specific activities. Some advertisers, such as AT&T, have eliminated media commissions altogether in favor of fee systems tied to the hourly rates of agency specialists; some agencies, such as ARM in London, bypass commissions and charge a fixed fee for each service they offer.[39]

Sometimes an advertiser and an agency will agree to a *retainer* system. Similar to the way attorneys and architects are paid, the agency receives a set fee instead of a commission, and this fee covers a set number of hours. If the agency devotes more hours to the advertiser's projects, it bills the client for that time. As an advertiser, you might put your agency on retainer when you want sales brochures and point-of-purchase materials but have no need for services that generate commission revenues. Of course, if you do advertise in commissionable media, the agency can apply any commissions it receives as a credit against the retainer fee.[40]

Incentive-Based Compensation

Another way of paying agencies is **incentive-based compensation,** also known as *performance-based compensation,* which rewards an agency according to the results its advertising achieves for the client. The theory behind incentive-based compensation is simple: if the advertising is effective, the agency will receive more money. In this age of advertising accountability, incentive-based compensation is one way to focus advertiser and agency efforts on specific goals and on measures of performance. Still, results such as higher sales can be affected by many factors, so linking agency compensation to performance can be tricky.[41]

Just as the goals and performance measures vary from advertiser to advertiser, so does the form of incentive-based compensation. For example, Unilever is phasing in a system that allows its agencies worldwide commissions on media purchases plus a 1 to 2 percent bonus for superior work. Murphy-Phoenix, which makes Murphy Oil Soap, adjusts its agency fees monthly according to product sales. As an agency, DDB Needham Worldwide offers its own incentive-based compensation program: the agency receives a bonus if it achieves the expected results, and it refunds some money if it fails. However, the agency requires that advertisers allow it considerable control over communication messages; otherwise, the results can't be guaranteed.[42] Of course, negotiating payment is only one part of the advertiser-agency relationship.

Forging the Advertiser-Agency Partnership

The relationship between advertiser and agency is a little like one plus one equals three: when the combination clicks, it can produce exciting, creative, effective advertising that goes beyond merely getting the job done. In years past, partnerships between Chiat/Day and Apple and between Ogilvy & Mather and Hathaway produced memorable advertising that catapulted product sales into orbit. Some relationships are enduring to the point of becoming legend: advertiser Lever Brothers has been with the J. Walter Thompson agency for over 90 years, and Kellogg has been with Leo Burnett for over 40 (see Exhibit 2.12).[43] However, few relationships stretch for decades, so most advertisers and agencies face the task of starting new relationships more often.

STARTING A NEW RELATIONSHIP

As an advertiser, you might be an entrepreneur readying your first product or a fast-food chain looking for a fresh advertising hook. As an agency, you could be small and eager to grow or large and staffed with enough talent to handle additional clients. No matter which side of the desk you're on, putting together a new advertiser-agency relationship can be exciting, challenging, and at times frustrating.

EXHIBIT 2.12
An Enduring Advertiser-Agency Relationship

Since 1949, Kellogg and Leo Burnett have been partners in advertising such well-known cereal brands as Frosted Flakes and Rice Krispies. In fact, the agency's creative people invented Tony the Tiger and other Kellogg spokescharacters.

Say you're an advertiser that wants to hire an agency or switch agencies. Whether your ad budget is big or small, whether your audience is consumer or business, here's an overview of what you'll look for:

- *Competence.* Does the agency do quality work? What are its capabilities? Are its ads creative? Effective?

- *Expertise.* Does the agency know your industry? Your product? Your markets? Is it experienced in solving problems like yours? If you're selling financial services, for example, you might want to consider agencies that have done work for other financial services firms (see Exhibit 2.13).

- *Reputation.* What do other advertisers—and the media—say about the agency? What image does the agency project?

- *Compatibility.* Can you communicate easily with the people who'll be working on your account? Is the agency responsive to your needs and concerns?

- *Cost consciousness.* Does the agency understand your budget and cost constraints? Is it careful with clients' money?[44]

To evaluate your current agency, you might ask questions such as those in this chapter's checklist. However, when you're considering a switch to another agency, you'll go through the formal process of an account review to evaluate your current and prospective agencies.

The Account Review

The **account review** is a formal process in which an advertiser invites selected agencies to present their credentials and their advertising ideas for a specific

CHECKLIST FOR EVALUATING YOUR AGENCY

❏ A. Evaluating account management
- Be sure that the personnel assigned to your account understand your business and its needs, goals, products, and markets.
- Consider whether agency personnel are knowledgeable about your competitors and their strengths and weaknesses.
- Confirm that agency personnel can successfully balance long- and short-term advertising issues and activities.
- Be sure that the agency maintains confidentiality and respects your need for safeguarding proprietary information.
- Confirm that agency personnel conscientiously meet all deadlines.
- Be sure that the agency is careful with your money and avoids extra charges wherever possible by planning ahead or offering less-expensive alternatives.
- Consider whether the people working on your account are professional and have the proper training and experience.
- Look for stability rather than a high rate of turnover among the agency people working on your account.

❏ B. Evaluating creative services
- Expect the agency to recommend creative strategies appropriate to your business and your situation.
- Be sure the agency develops fresh, compelling creative strategies to generate excitement and build your business.
- Consider whether all advertising materials are consistent with your organization's standards of quality and good taste.
- Confirm that the advertising materials produced by your agency meet all legal requirements and are appropriate for the regions and cultures where they will be used.
- Be sure that production costs are reasonable and within your budget.

❏ C. Evaluating media planning
- Be sure that agency personnel are knowledgeable

about all media alternatives appropriate for your advertising.
- Confirm that the agency is familiar with competitive media activity.
- Ask that media recommendations be supported with facts.
- Expect the agency to suggest media options that are innovative, effective, and cost-efficient.
- Be sure that the media budget suggested by the agency is realistic and prudent.
- Find out whether the agency maintains good controls for ensuring that the materials are sent to the media on time and that the ads run as planned.

❏ D. Evaluating research services
- Be sure that the agency's research is insightful and provides guidance for your advertising process.
- Find out whether agency research personnel are responsive to your requests.
- Confirm that research personnel are sensitive to your need for speedy and accurate but cost-efficient research to support your advertising decisions.
- Be sure that research personnel are professional and objective and understand their role in providing guidance for your advertising decisions.

❏ E. Evaluating agency management
- Be sure that you can easily reach senior agency people when you need to address urgent problems.
- Confirm that the chemistry between agency personnel and your management team is good.
- Expect agency invoices to be accurate and timely, and make sure that billing disagreements can be quickly resolved.
- Look at whether the agency understands and responds to the goals you set for its performance.
- Be sure that the agency understands how you measure its performance.
- Consider whether agency personnel are able to adjust their activities when necessary to achieve goals and whether they are open to comments for improving performance.

product. Then the advertiser selects an agency to handle that product. In an account review, you identify one or more agencies you'd consider working with (including your incumbent, if you choose) and examine their qualifications; you might ask an outside consultant to help select and evaluate the agencies. Then you invite the finalists to make a presentation about their capabilities, expertise, and ideas for advertising your products. For example, several years ago, when Club Med found its business stagnating, it started an account review, first compiling a list of 52 agencies. It narrowed the field to 4 finalists plus Ammirati & Puris, then the incumbent, which declined to participate in the account review. (It's interesting that fewer than 2 in 10 incumbents retain the account when they participate in a review.)[45]

The next step might be to ask each finalist to make a **speculative presentation,** showing the advertising approach it would use to solve a specific problem for the advertiser. Not every advertiser requests a full-blown speculative presentation with completed ads (1) because the time and cost pressures on the agencies are too great and (2) because some agencies don't want to give away their ideas before they're hired. Although some advertisers, such as MasterCard, reimburse agencies for some of their expenses, these payments usually don't cover the whole cost. Club Med asked finalists to submit rough (rather than polished) versions of suggested ads, but the contenders were eager to win this account and pulled out all the stops. Saatchi & Saatchi spent $350,000 competing for the business, and Chiat/Day spent $250,000. After considering all the presentations, Club Med awarded its business to TBWA (but recently switched agencies again).[46]

How an Agency Signs New Clients

The flip side of the advertiser's search for an agency is the agency's search for new business. If your agency wants to expand its business and profits, you'll work hard to keep current clients happy and to increase the amount of business they do with you, but you'll also pursue new clients. Some advertisers may have already noticed your work if you're among the few European and U.S. agencies that add their names to clients' print ads. Direct mail, telephone contact, and advertising are other ways you can solicit new business. You may also get leads for new clients as a result of referrals from your current clients.

Surprisingly, few agencies use advertising to attract clients, and those that do spend little, usually less than $100,000 in the course of a single campaign. However, agency giants such as J. Walter Thompson and Foote, Cone & Belding seek new business by periodically advertising in major newspapers and business magazines to attract the attention of prospective clients (see Exhibit 2.14).[47] Such ads also bolster the agency's image and reputation, which helps when you're looking for new clients. Advertisers that hear about the outstanding work of a particular agency or see the exceptional ads the agency has done for another client are more

EXHIBIT 2.14
An Agency Advertises for New Business

This print ad was designed to help J. Walter Thompson showcase its advertising expertise and attract new clients.

Agency-Client Teamwork Overcomes Crisis

When General Motors' Oldsmobile division held an account review in September 1992, incumbent agency Leo Burnett was shaken up. At stake was a $140 million account and a stable 25-year relationship. Burnett chairman Rick Fizdale hadn't expected the review because no GM brand had changed agencies since 1958. However, the world's largest carmaker was under great pressure to revive sales and profits following a $4 billion loss in 1991. At the division level, Oldsmobile's sales had skidded from more than 1,000,000 vehicles in 1986 to 416,000 in 1992, and dealers were unhappy with Burnett's proposed campaign for the 1993 models. Said John Rock, vice president and general manager of Olds, "It appeared that firing the agency and getting that behind me would create a heck of a lot better atmosphere among the dealers."

So Rock held an account review. Because dealer commitment was critical to his turnaround plan, Rock put four dealers on the eight-member agency review panel that would make the final decision. Including Burnett, which had never before participated in an existing client review, 15 agencies participated in the five-month review. Halfway through, Rock advised Burnett to drop out of the competition. Fizdale refused, saying, "No. We're your agency until you tell us we're not."

Meanwhile, Oldsmobile was being buffeted by rumors that GM was planning to close the division. Sales plunged even further, and Olds looked to Burnett for help in convincing the public that the division had a future. Olds executives and members of the review panel met with agency personnel to hatch a plan for combating the rumors. As one dealer on the review panel recalled, "At that point, it was apparent that they [Burnett] wouldn't keep the business. But they were putting their heart into it, working late into the night, and giving a 110 percent effort."

Olds general manager Rock attacked the rumors head-on by holding a news conference, which was broadcast to dealers across the country. At the same time, Burnett created a bold new series of print and television ads. One ad declared, "Oldsmobile sells more vehicles in America than Mercedes-Benz, Infiniti, Acura, BMW, Volvo, and Lexus combined. If you've heard rumors that Oldsmobile is thinking about throwing in the towel, don't believe them." Close on the heels of that campaign, the agency produced ads around the theme "Demand better" to position Olds as a responsive carmaker. Olds added a new pricing strategy, and sales started to recover.

Thanks to Burnett's hard work on the antirumor campaign and the "Demand better" ads, Oldsmobile's review panel real-

Oldsmobile Sells More Vehicles In America Than:

Mercedes-Benz
Infiniti
Acura
BMW
Volvo
and Lexus

Combined.

If you've heard rumors that Oldsmobile® is thinking about throwing in the towel, don't believe them. Why would a company stop doing business that does this much business? As you can see, this is one car company that has a lot going for it.

Buckle Up America!

OLDSMOBILE

Source: R.L. Polk & Co. Total Registrations 1992 Model Year End

Leo Burnett created this ad to convey the message that GM was not going to close the Oldsmobile division.

ized that the agency could create good advertising for Olds—as good as the ads it created for clients like United Airlines, McDonald's, Procter & Gamble, and Kellogg. In addition, the rumor crisis forced both client and agency to recognize, confront, and overcome several existing problems: the management turnover at Olds, the conflicting instructions given Burnett, and a general breakdown in communication. Working together to renew public confidence in Olds, the client and the agency wound up forging an entirely new relationship. Finally, in February 1993, the cliffhanger account review came to an end when Oldsmobile's review panel voted unanimously to retain Burnett.

Apply Your Knowledge

1. Short of holding an account review, what might an advertiser do if it believes its agency is not performing up to expectations?

2. What might Burnett's Rick Fizdale do to ensure that communication doesn't break down between his personnel and Oldsmobile executives and dealers?

likely to consider that agency when they're thinking about making a switch. Finally, you can use public relations and publicity to attract new clients by doing *pro bono* work (meaning you work for free) on a charity's advertising campaign, giving a speech to advertising students in a nearby college, or writing an article for an advertising publication. These and similar activities help an agency become better known to potential clients.

No matter how the contact was initiated, agencies generally make an introductory presentation, possibly participate in an account review, and provide the names of current clients who can serve as references. They'll put in overtime to show their best efforts, and they frequently spend a bundle on new-business pitches. It can be expensive (and demoralizing) when an agency doesn't win: the agencies in an account review by MasterCard reportedly spent $2.6 million on their presentations before the advertiser chose Ammirati & Puris. However, because growth depends on new clients as well as additional business from current clients, agencies continue to aggressively compete for new accounts.[48] Once an advertiser has hired an agency, the next step is to figure out how best to work together to create effective advertising.

WORKING WITH AN AGENCY

Every advertiser-agency relationship is unique because no two advertisers have the same needs and resources. Once an agency is hired, an advertiser must identify which advertising tasks the agency should assume. This is especially complex for advertisers like Nestlé that develop and place ads in many countries. If you have a limited-service in-house agency, you'll assign some functions to your own specialists and ask the independent agency to handle others. All advertisers retain or participate in certain tasks such as drafting strategy or creating the advertising budget.[49]

Once you've defined the roles and responsibilities for each side, you'll move into the planning stage and set specific advertising goals. During and after the advertising campaign, you'll evaluate agency performance, but not just on the basis of whether your specific advertising goals have been achieved. You'll want to look at a wide range of issues, from account management contacts and creativity to innovative media coverage and accurate billing (look again at the Checklist for Evaluating Your Agency). At the same time, you'll want feedback about how well the people in your organization work with the agency; many advertisers, including Reynolds Aluminum and Rorer Consumer Pharmaceuticals, ask the agency to rate the quality and responsiveness of the advertiser's interaction. Such two-way evaluations can reveal potential problems in the advertiser-agency relationship and can also help an advertiser become a better client.[50]

CHANGING AGENCIES

Few advertiser-agency relationships last forever. Although some deteriorating relationships can be improved by the threat of a change, either side may actually want a change. According to a recent study of advertiser-agency relations, agency pay is a major source of tension for both partners. For the agency, changes in strategy or management and disappointment with compensation are key reasons for resigning an account. Agency management may believe that the advertiser is asking for more than the agency can deliver on the revenue it earns from that account.[51]

For the advertiser, frustration with agency performance or pay, changes in strategy or management, new products, new businesses, new competition, or faltering sales may prompt a change. In some cases the advertiser expands and decides it wants a larger agency; in other cases the advertiser feels its account is too small to command the proper attention from a rapidly growing agency. At times the agency and advertiser simply don't communicate well, and their working relationship suffers, which prompts the advertiser to seek a change. Sometimes large advertisers, such as Dow Chemical and PepsiCo, have reduced the overall number of agencies they work with, a change that doesn't always reflect disappointment with agency performance but may simplify the advertising process or lower the overall cost to advertisers.[52]

Even advertisers with a successful campaign eventually want a change. Although seven years of advertising with the same agency (using *Crocodile Dundee* star Paul Hogan) raised the global profile of Australia as a tourist destination, the Australian Tourist Commission decided to change agencies. "Australia is now the first or second most desired holiday destination in five of our major markets," said

(SFX): conga music
V.O.: From Little Caesar's, 2 pizzas, 2 crazy breads, and 2 servings of Coke Classic, all for $7.98. It's enough food to make a family meal into a party, party!

managing director Jon Hutchison, but the commission wants to increase the number of people who actually visit the country. Instead of hiring one agency to craft a single worldwide theme, the commission hired a different agency in each market and asked for a campaign targeted specifically to that region—a change that Hutchison hopes will raise the number of tourists visiting Australia to 6.8 million by the end of the decade.[53]

One study of why advertisers switch agencies found that more than half the time the reason is simply *chemistry,* the way people on both sides interact with each other. For example, Little Caesar's senior executive vice president Denise Ilitch Lites says that good chemistry, as well as creativity, caused her to switch her pizza advertising to Cliff Freeman & Partners (see Exhibit 2.15).[54] Whether an agency has had an account for a few weeks or for decades, chemistry plays an important role in agency selection and in ongoing relations. When Pollenex, a Chicago firm, chose a new agency, it had a series of disagreements with agency personnel within the first few weeks. The advertiser quickly switched agencies again, finding better chemistry with Hal Riney & Partners/Chicago.[55]

Perhaps the most controversial reason for making a change in the advertiser-agency relationship is a conflict over a competing account. Generally, agencies don't work for more than one advertiser in a given product category because clients fear their confidential information might be used for the benefit of competitors. Although an agency can't legally handle advertising for a client's competitor unless the client agrees, the trend toward megamergers and corporate acquisitions has raised new questions about how to manage agency-client conflicts.[56]

For instance, before Saatchi & Saatchi bought Ted Bates, Backer & Spielvogel, and others, these independent agencies had carefully avoided account conflicts. However, once the agencies were under the same agency umbrella, some clients complained about conflicts. Although the acquired agencies voluntarily resigned several accounts because of potential conflicts, clients soon pulled a total of $358 million in media billings from Saatchi & Saatchi. However, the megamerger didn't bother everybody: during the same period, new advertisers signed on with a total of $103 million in billings.[57]

Advertisers and agencies don't always agree on the exact definition of a conflict, and the problem gets worse when advertisers work with more than one agency. A few advertisers don't want their agencies working with competitors in any product category; others outlaw only specific products or categories. McDonald's, for one, doesn't allow its agencies to work with other fast-food advertisers for at least six months after their McDonald's work ends. The agency giants argue that their structure keeps agency offices separate from each other and promotes competition within the group, so client confidentiality is properly protected under the corporate umbrella. At the same time, staying clear of conflicts can hamper an agency's quest for new business. Experts say the best way to handle perceived conflicts is (1) to

THE ALL-SEASON ATTRACTION WITH ALL SEASON TRACTION.

THE POWER TO TURN MILES INTO MILESTONES.

EXHIBIT 2.16
Two Cars Park at One Agency

Although clients usually object to sharing their agencies with others in the same industry, BMW and Rolls-Royce both decided to use Mullen Advertising. The advertisers saw no conflict because their product pricing structure and target audiences don't overlap.

hammer out an initial agreement about the types of competitors and products the agency can handle and (2) to encourage discussions between agency and advertiser to settle any potential conflicts that may arise during the relationship (see Exhibit 2.16).[58]

Summary

Advertisers and agencies are key partners in the advertising process. Few advertisers can afford to keep many advertising specialists on staff, so hiring an independent advertising agency is a cost-effective way to gain access to professionals who can enhance the advertiser's knowledge and experience. Independent agencies work with many advertisers and many industries, so they know what works, and they can be objective. They can also recruit and retain talented professionals who enjoy the excitement of working on a variety of problems and products, and they offer expertise in every aspect of advertising.

An advertiser may prefer to use an in-house agency when management wants to control all advertising functions, to keep the agency focused on its needs, to keep costs down, and to improve coordination among departments. As head of such an advertising department, an advertising manager's duties include planning and budgeting advertising, creating and producing ads (when an independent agency isn't used), handling administration tasks, and coordinating the organization's advertising efforts with internal departments and activities.

The advertising agency has four main functions: account management, which links the agency and the client; creative services, which includes copywriting, art-direction, and production tasks; marketing services, which includes research and media tasks; and agency management, which includes human-resources and financial tasks. Full-service advertising agencies offer all the services necessary to develop, create, and execute advertising for their clients. Limited-service advertising agencies offer selected advertising services such as creative support or media planning and buying. Specialized advertising agencies focus on specific markets, such as business-to-business, medical, and ethnic audiences. Advertising agencies receive revenues in four ways: media commissions, fees, markups, and incentive-based compensation.

An account review is the formal process used by an advertiser to examine the credentials and work of several agencies and to select one to handle its advertising. The advertiser looks at the qualifications of several agencies, narrows the field, and then invites finalists to explain their capabilities and make speculative presentations (which show how they would solve a specific advertising problem).

Client conflicts stem from the agreement that agencies won't work for more than one advertiser in a particular product category; clients want their information held in confidence, and they may change agencies when they see a conflict. Unless a client agrees, an agency cannot legally handle advertising for a client's competitor; however, some advertisers don't want their agencies working with competitors in any product category, and others prohibit only specific products or categories. This issue has become more pronounced as megamergers create groups of formerly independent agencies within one corporation and as more advertisers buy other firms or products.

Meeting an Advertising Challenge at Deutsch, Inc.

Donny Deutsch knew that an agency can't survive for long without taking on new business. His goal was to boost annual revenues and at the same time to make a name for Deutsch as an agency that produced unconventional and creative advertising and yet was capable of handling the diverse challenges posed by larger clients. So Deutsch started a sales effort to promote the agency like a product.

He assigned his creative team to develop an ad campaign that would captivate prospects and showcase the agency's skills. They responded with intriguing print ads specifically designed to make people curious. The first ad never mentioned the agency by name; instead, it featured a diagram of the brain and the words "For sale," followed by the agency's phone number. A later ad, designed to look like a page from the dictionary, defined the word "Deutsch" in several ways, including as a noun that means "capacity for reason."

However, Donny Deutsch wasn't relying solely on advertising to bring the growth he wanted. Large agencies often have dedicated new-business departments, but smaller agencies can rarely afford to keep such experts on staff. Despite the expense, Deutsch believed that hiring an aggressive team of salespeople to pursue prospects was the best way to engineer fast growth. Whereas most agencies start their pursuit of a new client by sending a letter accompanied by samples of their best ads, Deutsch encouraged his sales team to get their prospects' attention through less conventional tactics. For example, one salesperson sent a chainsaw to a prospective client as a symbol of how the agency is able to cut through ad clutter.

Within a year, Deutsch had landed several big accounts, but he was angling for more. He decided to flesh out the agency's account services capabilities with seasoned industry executives, reasoning that this would provide a good balance to the irreverent and creative tone of the agency. During this period, he and his top managers also revamped the account management department and the new-business department, and they brought in a new director of strategic and account planning. Bolstered by these changes, the agency was able to land a string of new accounts, including Swatch Watch USA ($8 million in annual billings), Publishers Clearing House ($22 million), Six Flags ($10 million), and Rax Restaurants ($7 million), among others.

What's more, Deutsch was invited to join the Clinton-Gore Creative Team, a group of ad executives who were responsible for developing and producing presidential campaign advertising. That highly visible work helped elevate the agency to a new level and gave it more credibility as a "serious, national agency," Deutsch said soon after the election. By now, the agency's billings had soared to nearly $160 million. Despite this success, Deutsch has not forgotten that signing new clients is only the first step; the agency has to deliver on its promises of developing results-oriented advertising to keep clients' businesses growing too.

Your Mission: Donny Deutsch has just hired you to work in the agency's new-business department. Use your understanding of advertisers and agencies to help Deutsch grow by signing new clients.

1. You're trying to get business from an international carmaker that is just about to introduce a new car in the United States. A full-blown speculative

Key Terms

account executive 36
account planning 37
account review 45
advertising manager 31
art 36
art department 36
art director 36
billings 41
brand manager 32
broadcast production
   manager 37
category manager 32
centralized advertising
   department 31
client 30
commission 41
copy 36
copywriter 36
creative boutique 39
creative director 36
decentralized advertising
   department 32

departmental system 38
full-service advertising
   agency 38
group system 38
incentive-based
   compensation 43
in-house advertising
   agency 30
limited-service advertising
   agency 39
markup 42
media buyer 37
media-buying service 40
media department 37
media director 37
media planner 37
media researcher 37
print production manager 36
production department 36
research director 37
speculative presentation 47
traffic department 37

Questions

FOR REVIEW

1. Why would an advertiser use an in-house advertising agency? An independent advertising agency?

2. How does a centralized advertising department differ from a decentralized advertising department?

3. How do advertising agencies acquire new clients?

4. Why do advertisers change agencies?

5. How does a full-service advertising agency differ from a limited-service agency? A specialized agency?

FOR ANALYSIS AND APPLICATION

6. Many agencies complain that speculative presentations waste a lot of time and money and in the end may not be representative of the work they will actually do for the advertiser. Can you suggest a more cost-effective way for advertisers to evaluate agencies?

7. Should an advertising manager be held accountable for a campaign's results if an independent agency develops the creative ideas and selects the media? Why or why not?

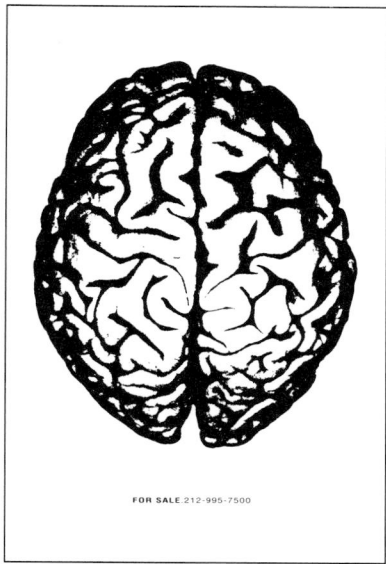

FOR SALE 212-995-7500

presentation would be impressive, but you're not sure the cost is justified. Which of these suggestions would you make to Donny Deutsch?

a. Recommend that your agency present finished print ads but only sketches of television commercials, which are more costly to prepare.

b. Rather than spend money to make new ads, take the carmaker's current ads and revamp them to show how they can be improved.

c. Sketch out several sample ads and commercials that show the creative theme without details, which can be developed later.

2. You hear that a jewelry manufacturer is holding an agency review of its $25 million account. If Deutsch pursues this account, it might face a conflict of interest because of the Swatch account. What should you do?

a. Advise Deutsch to resign the Swatch account so that he can pursue the larger jewelry account.

b. Tell the prospect that you can assign a separate creative team to each client to avoid any conflict.

c. Ask Swatch whether the jewelry maker is really a rival, and reassure Swatch of your dedication to handling its business.

3. The American Heart Association has approached you about handling advertising for a new public education program. You know that the association's budget is tight, but you're not sure the agency can do the work for free right now. Which of these options is best?

a. Agree to do the advertising for free but ask that the ads carry the agency's name in bold type.

b. Do the ads for a modest fee, but give them the same creative attention you'd give to other clients' ads (so that prospects will be impressed).

c. Recommend another agency that might be willing to handle the account.

4. One prospect, a rapidly expanding barbecue restaurant chain with a limited budget, is considering whether to hire Deutsch to handle its first national television campaign. Which of these responses would best show the prospect that the agency understands and can meet its needs?

a. Stress that the agency can shoot its own commercials, thereby saving the cost of using outside suppliers without giving up any creativity.

b. Emphasize the chemistry between Donny Deutsch and the restaurant's advertising manager, which should enhance the working relationship.

c. Prove that the agency understands the food business by showing the campaign it recently developed for a franchised doughnut chain.[59] ■

8. Why do you think few incumbents retain the account when their clients conduct account reviews?

9. How could a computer manufacturer like Apple use the services of one or more specialized agencies to increase U.S. sales?

10. Some of today's full-service advertising agencies began as limited-service agencies such as creative boutiques. Why would an agency broaden its service offerings, and how would such a change affect its structure?

Sharpen Your Advertising Skills

You're the account executive for a fast-growing industrial cleaning service that has many suburban customers but wants to serve more urban customers. This client has asked your agency to develop a campaign aimed at the downtown market. Your creative services department has prepared a concept you believe will differentiate your client from its competitors, but the client's advertising manager turned it down, saying, "It just doesn't work for me." Although the client wants to see another creative concept, the creative director believes that the concept is not only workable but distinctive and attention-getting.

Decision: As the AE, you're the liaison between the client and the creative director. Should you take the client's side and insist that the creative director work on another concept? Should you take the creative director's side and try to convince the client to reconsider? As you make your decision, keep in mind that you have to maintain a good relationship with your client and that you also need the cooperation and enthusiasm of your creative director.

Communication: Once you make your decision, you'll have to talk with both the advertising manager and the creative director. Assume you're going to call them, and prepare an outline for a brief (two- or three-minute) introduction and explanation of your decision—including what you believe the agency and advertiser should do next to make progress toward completing the campaign.

The Advertising Environment

After studying this chapter, you will be able to

1. **Outline the role of advertising in the economy**

2. **Discuss how advertising can be viewed as both helpful and harmful to society**

3. **Analyze how advertising relates to social responsibility**

4. **Differentiate between ethical dilemmas and ethical lapses**

5. **Explain how the First Amendment and the Lanham Act affect advertising**

6. **Highlight the role that the Federal Trade Commission and other federal agencies play in regulating advertising**

7. **Describe how the advertising industry regulates itself**

Facing an Advertising Challenge at Members Only

RAISING CONSCIOUSNESS AS WELL AS SALES

Ed Wachtel didn't want Members Only to be caught on the exit side of fashion's revolving door. As co-founder of Members Only, a maker of young men's casual clothing, Wachtel recognized that styles change quickly in the fast-paced world of fashion. To succeed, he had to have the looks and colors that customers wanted—and a strong brand identity that would draw customers back year after year.

Wachtel and a partner started Members Only in New York City in 1979. Among its first products was a line of men's jackets in updated, casual styles and a wide range of fashion colors. Riding a trend away from dungaree jackets, the Members Only outerwear began to fly off the racks. At the height of this sales explosion, Wachtel sold his interest in the business to the Marcade Group, but he was soon wooed back as chief executive officer to help battle a growing throng of competitors.

By 1986 Wachtel was looking for a way to differentiate Members Only from copycat rivals. However, he also had another agenda: he wanted to give something back to society. He and other Members Only executives set up a meeting with Korey, Kay and Partners, the firm's ad agency, to explore ways of building the brand while supporting an important social cause. During their discussion, a glance at the front page of that day's newspaper revealed that Len Bias, a college basketball star, had died in a drug-related incident. That's when the Members Only executives decided to invest their entire advertising budget in fighting drug abuse.

Members Only spent more than $6 million on antidrug advertising during the first year. Celebrities and athletes supported the campaign by appearing in the ads and bringing the message to young people through personal appearances in stores that sold Members Only clothing. In 1987 and 1988, the firm's advertising focused on

voter registration and then switched back to drugs in 1989 with a campaign titled "Drugs Don't Just Kill Addicts." One ad showed a badge being showered with bullets to make the point that police are also hurt in the war on drugs. Although the Members Only logo was featured in each ad, no product was ever shown or mentioned.

By 1990 Members Only had spent about $25 million on ads dealing entirely with social causes. Sales had skyrocketed, but the firm now faced stiffer competition. Moreover, styles were changing and Wachtel needed to tell his audience that Members Only was changing, too. Put yourself in Ed Wachtel's place. How would you use advertising to promote Members Only? Would you continue to advertise in support of social causes? And if so, what issues would you feature in your ads?[1] ∎

CHAPTER OVERVIEW Advertisers—and ads—do not exist in a vacuum, something that Ed Wachtel of Members Only understands all too well. In this chapter, you'll explore the environment of advertising and learn how advertisers interact with the economic, social, ethical, and regulatory elements that make up that environment. First you'll look at advertising and the economy, including how advertising relates to pricing, consumer demand, and competition. Next you'll see how advertising is viewed as both helpful and harmful to society, and you'll examine advertising in the context of social responsibility. After considering the distinction between ethical dilemmas and ethical lapses, you'll explore several key ethical questions facing contemporary advertisers. The chapter closes with a discussion of the legal and regulatory influences on advertising.

The Environment of Advertising

Advertisers, agencies, the media, and audiences are all part of a larger environment, influencing and being influenced by a network of forces that includes the economy, government, interest groups, and society at large. The general atmosphere created by these external elements is the **advertising environment.** The advertising environment is always changing, which creates both opportunities (such as new media alternatives) and threats (such as additional competition). The impact of these complex environmental elements can be positive or negative, sometimes both (see Exhibit 3.1).

As an advertiser, you can respond to your environment in two ways. When you believe you have no control over environmental elements, you'll be reactive and simply try to adjust to them. However, when you think you have some control, you'll be proactive and take steps to make changes that result in a more conducive

EXHIBIT 3.1
How New Media Changes the Advertising Environment

After Columbia Pictures draped an ad for the movie *Last Action Hero* across a NASA rocket launched from Wallops Island, Virginia (as shown in this model), some media experts hailed space as the new advertising frontier. Some U.S. lawmakers, however, had reservations, and introduced legislation to ban ads in space.

environment for your activities. For example, if you're faced with a new law banning billboard advertising, you might react by switching to another medium, or you might decide you can work to change this law through proactive measures such as lobbying the legislature. Of course, whether you're reactive or proactive will depend on each situation and on the specific elements you face. For this reason, it's important to understand the role that elements such as the economy, society, ethics, and regulation play in the advertising environment.

Advertising and the Economy

As discussed in Chapter 1, during the evolution of advertising (especially in the past 100 years), merchants, manufacturers, and the media built their businesses on the basis of advertising. Advertising today accounts for a significant part of the U.S. economy. When the economy is expanding, consumers and businesses have the money and the inclination to buy, and higher sales fire up advertisers to increase their ad budgets, which in turn fuels retail and industrial sales as well as media sales. For example, ad spending skyrocketed during the economic expansion of 1976-1988—even during the 1981-1982 recessionary dip.[2]

However, during most recessionary periods, profit pressures may cause some advertisers to cut back, despite studies suggesting that advertising during downturns can help firms increase sales and capture market share from competitors who slow or stop advertising.[3] For instance, in the recession of the early 1990s, retail bankruptcies, decreased real estate sales, and sluggish consumer spending dampened many advertising budgets. In turn, the reduced ad spending set off a chain reaction that hurt the media, advertising agencies, and suppliers.[4]

The media and advertising agencies are especially dependent on advertising, and they suffer when the economy depresses ad spending or advertisers move their budgets elsewhere. Roughly 50 percent of magazine revenues and 80 percent of newspaper revenues come from advertising, so when print ads are down, these media suffer. Nor is television exempt: during the early 1990s, the recession-battered networks reported lower profits, and both CBS and NBC discounted commercial time to drum up business. When an agency loses an advertiser's business, it can mean layoffs as well as lower billings and profits. For instance, Ingalls, Quinn & Johnson Cipolla Group had to lay off people when footwear maker Converse switched its account (worth $25 million in billings) to Houston, Effler & Partners.[5]

The link between advertising and the economy has traditionally been viewed in two ways. Some experts view advertising as a source of information for consumers, enabling them to choose among the bevy of products—and their substitutes—on the market; advertising can be especially helpful (and persuasive) when consumers want to learn more about new products. Other experts charge that the "information" view of advertising is too narrow. They see advertising as a source of power for manufacturers that want more control over distribution and pricing. They contend that a manufacturer that advertises directly to the user may be able to stimulate requests for its product, compelling wholesalers or retailers to carry the manufacturer's product and motivating the consumer to pay the manufacturer's desired price. Of course, this power is diminished when retailers demand *slotting allowances* and other payments from manufacturers eager to get new products onto crowded store shelves (see Chapter 17).[6]

The debate over advertising's ideal and actual roles in the economy continues. Economists, scholars, and practitioners are divided over advertising's influence on several economic elements, including pricing, consumer demand, and competition.

PRICING

Does advertising raise or lower the price that customers pay for products? The arguments on both sides of this complex issue are persuasive. Some argue that advertised products are priced higher because advertisers pass along their advertising costs. Moreover, when one company's advertised products draw sales away from other companies' products, its rivals may try to recover by boosting their own advertising, which sets off a new round of higher costs and higher prices. In addition, if ad budgets in a given category are usually high, newcomers may not have the financial resources to compete, so the few established firms in the market don't have to compete on price, which keeps their prices up.[7]

Others argue that advertising helps keep prices down because it allows producers to sell more, thus raising productivity. This higher productivity lowers the cost per unit, so manufacturers can price their products lower. Also, because advertising gives consumers information about products and pricing, buyers can compare information and select the brands that offer the quality they want at a price they are willing to pay. In other words, advertising allows consumers to pay a lower average price because the information in ads allows them to easily compare products, quality, and prices. In fact, members of the Federal Trade Commission and the Supreme Court successfully pushed to allow legal, medical, and other professionals to advertise because they believed that keeping these people from advertising tended to stifle competitive pricing. Regulators in the United States encourage comparative ads (which are banned or restricted in some other countries) precisely because they help consumers check pricing.[8]

CONSUMER DEMAND

Whether advertising stimulates demand is a complex question without easy answers. Demand is affected by a variety of factors, including changes in population, income, and lifestyle. For example, it's clear that advertising can stimulate demand for an entirely new product by introducing that type of product, its features, and its benefits (see Exhibit 3.2). Without advertising, Sony, Apple, and Federal Express might have taken longer to successfully establish such new products as the Walkman cassette player, the Macintosh computer, and overnight delivery service.

The keyboard
has disappeared.
The first pen computer
that accepts handwriting.
NCR Pen Computer.

EXHIBIT 3.2
Stimulating Demand for a New Product

This Japanese ad for the NCR pen computer aims to stimulate demand for a new product category by giving information about the product as well as about the brand.

PEOPLE ON THE STREETS OF CHICAGO ARE ASKED WHAT THEY THINK OF POSSIBLE DESIGNS FOR THE BEST BUY LOGO.

YOUNG MAN: To be honest with you, I think it's kind of cheesy. *WOMAN:* Make it red. *OLDER MAN WITH ACCENT:* God forbids, no red. *MAN:* Maybe red, white, and blue. Somethin' patriotic.

WOMAN: I would keep the yellow color. *V.O.:* Hey! *DUDE:* A lightnin' bolt. *YOUNG COUPLE:* Real, real flashy, slanted-type thing.

YOUNG GUY: I like the fact that it's shaped like a price tag. It means low prices. *YOUNG WOMAN:* I think it's a great logo.

EXHIBIT 3.3
Breaking into a Market

Before Best Buy opened an electronics store in Chicago, it mounted a multimedia advertising campaign to build awareness of its name and product line.

When product categories are growing (such as over-the-counter drugs), firms use advertising to get a bigger piece of that growth. However, advertising can't do much to revive the sales of a product category that's nearly obsolete (such as manual typewriters) or falling out of fashion (such as men's hats).[9] When a product is in short supply, advertising can help *dampen* demand or explain the shortages. In a static market, advertising can help defend market share or take sales from competitors. For example, the U.S. market for ground roast coffee isn't growing, so brands battle furiously over market share. When market leader Maxwell House reduced its advertising in the 1980s, rivals Nestlé and Folger's grabbed so much market share that Maxwell House had to brew up more advertising to avoid losing more sales. Soon Maxwell House's advertising had helped boost its market share to more than 33 percent, again leading the market.[10]

COMPETITION

Advertising has been said to reduce competition because few businesses have the resources to lay out millions for advertising when they enter a market where extensive advertising is the norm. Want to start a national hamburger chain? You'll be up against McDonald's $380 million annual ad budget and the image it has built over decades of advertising. It's hard to compete with that much media muscle and the customer loyalty it can generate.[11]

At the same time, some argue that advertising actually allows newcomers to gain entry to an established market where advertising plays an important role. New entrants can use their advertising as a tool to attract attention and sales for new or improved products (see Exhibit 3.3). Consider how General Motors used a heavy schedule of advertising to introduce the GM Card, its MasterCard credit card. GM was up against some strong competitors in the crowded credit card field, including AT&T and Citibank. To call attention to its new entry, GM used an extensive campaign of television ads, print ads, and direct mail.[12]

Of course, advertising alone doesn't make a product competitive. To attract customer attention, you need a reason to advertise, such as explaining how your product differs from those of competitors because of special features, sizes, colors, or other enhancements. Product enhancements and new products give people more choices and give producers something tangible to advertise. Take wristwatches, a category long dominated by Swiss watchmakers. This category started to heat up when Seiko, the Japan-based manufacturer, perfected quartz wristwatch technology and advertised its products as both accurate and stylish. In 1983, Switzerland's SMH Group fought back with the Swatch, a wristwatch jazzily advertised more as a fashion accessory than a timepiece. Spurred by strong competition, U.S.-based Timex started advertising wristwatches that combined high-tech functionality and fashion.[13]

Many of today's top brands have been market leaders for decades (see Exhibit 3.4). They're well known both because they've been well advertised and because

BUSINESSMAN: I say go with it.
VARIOUS KIDS, YOUNG
ADULTS AND SENIORS SHOW-

ING HOW THEY EAT OREOS

(SFX): rock music background

V.O.: You've got to adoreo an
Oreo.

they're good products in their own right—and have been for some time. Starting with a good product and then advertising it helps companies beat the competition: by promoting their advantages, advertisers can build the brand's reputation and market position, and ultimately build profitability over the long term.[14]

Advertising and Society

Over the years, advertising has been attacked by critics who charge that it goes beyond selling products or ideas to exert a powerful influence on society. According to this view, advertising in its many forms is so pervasive—and so persuasive—that it has the ability to shape social trends and mold personal attitudes. This influence is unwanted, intrusive, and often detrimental to society, say critics.[15] Defenders respond that, in addition to the economic benefits of improved competition, lower prices, and more product choices, advertising promotes freedom of speech, supports the media, and provides needed information about social issues as well as goods and services. Furthermore, advertising is actually influenced by society because it acts as a mirror in reflecting certain societal changes. For example, advertisers must continually adjust their language and illustrations to conform to changes in socially acceptable practices.

This ongoing debate over the proper role of advertising in society is entirely separate from the ethical issues of deceptive or fraudulent advertising (which are discussed later in the chapter), and it boils down to one basic question: Does advertising help or hurt society?

CONTRASTING VIEWS OF ADVERTISING

The question of whether advertising is good or bad for society is best examined on an issue-by-issue basis. In this section, you'll explore the arguments on both sides of five issues: the influence of advertising on language and literacy, advertising as manipulation and exploitation, stereotyping in advertising, the influence of advertising on the media, and bad taste and offensiveness in advertising. These issues are far from resolved, and as society and advertising evolve, the issues and arguments may also evolve.

Language and Literacy

It's easy to see why critics attack advertising for hurting language: advertisers sometimes twist words or change spelling and grammar to make a point. Advertising copy is accused of playing fast and loose with the rules of language, which encourages the audience to do the same. Ultimately, the constant wearing away of correct spelling, usage, and grammar can take a bite out of literacy, a problem in a country like the United States where standardized tests reveal many students already read below grade level. Some critics go further, complaining that people have less need for reading and writing because advertisers make information and entertainment readily available in the electronic media both by advertising and by sponsoring news and entertainment programs.[16]

EXHIBIT 3.4
Staying at the Top

Oreos have been the best-selling cookies for years because the product tastes good and because ads like this Canadian television commercial remind people to buy Oreos when they shop for snacks.

TEENAGE BOYS ARE SMOKING IN
THE BOYS' BATHROOM AT SCHOOL.
ONE OF THE BOYS HAS A GAS
MASK ON AND IS READING FROM A
CIGARETTE PACKAGE.
BOY WITH GAS MASK: "You know,
smoking causes a wide array of damage
to the human body. Here's just a partial
list of side effects: number one, lung
cancer; number two, heart disease; num-
ber three, emphysema. I mean, asthma,
stroke, bronchitis, pneumonia, *death*."
*ONE OF THE SMOKERS TAPS HIM
ON THE SHOULDER:* "Hey man, can I
bum a smoke?"
BOY WITH GAS MASK: "Birth defects."
BOY THROWS CIGARETTE PACKAGE
ON FLOOR AND LEAVES IN DIS-
GUST. SMOKER PICKS·IT UP
LOOKING FOR A CIGARETTE BUT
THROWS IT DOWN WHEN FINDS
NONE.

EXHIBIT 3.5
Gearing an Ad to the Teenage Market

Advertisers can reach out to the teen
market by using situations, language,
and fashions that are familiar to that
audience. This antismoking television
commercial, made for the California
Department of Health Services,
appeared on MTV.

Why do ads bend grammar and use slang? Sometimes it's to avoid sounding stilted, sometimes it's for emphasis, and sometimes it's to sound like the people you want to reach. "There's no real intent to damage the language," says Ted Sann, vice chairman and executive creative director of BBDO New York, the advertising agency that creates Pepsi-Cola ads. "You're simply reflecting the audience you're speaking to." For instance, when many advertisers want to reach teenagers, they try to adopt teenage speech patterns (see Exhibit 3.5). As a takeoff on the teen expressions used in the movie *Bill and Ted's Excellent Adventure,* a McDonald's television commercial featured a fashionably dressed young man in front of a mansion yelling, "Yo, seriously rich dudes. May we come in and see your most excellent stuff?"[17]

Although staying in tune with the vocabulary and usage of the target audience is the main reason for less-than-perfect advertising language, it's not the only one. An advertiser often uses unorthodox spelling so a word can be used as a legal part of a brand name, a **trademark** (a brand registered with the U.S. government for exclusive use by the brand owner), or a **service mark** (a trademark for a service rather than a tangible good).[18] For example, Reynolds Cut-Rite is an easy-to-remember registered trademark for wax paper that conveys the product's benefits while defending against any competitors using the same words. However, advertisers (such as Aaaaace Plumbing) that add a's to their names to appear first in their categories of yellow pages directories have lost their edge at companies like Bell-South, which says it will allow only proper names and names found in the dictionary.[19]

Manipulation and Exploitation

Does advertising manipulate people into buying what they don't need? Does it exploit people's fears to create artificial needs? Critics contend that advertising is so powerful and persuasive that people have no choice but to buy what they see advertised, regardless of their actual need for these products. You're being manipulated, say these critics, by advertisers who exploit your inadequacies, anxieties, hopes, and fears. Advertisers using psychological or emotional appeals get you to buy their products by making you feel that these products help you gain status, acceptance, even love. You're driven to buy things you don't really need, rather than buying only products that satisfy basic needs such as food and clothing.[20]

On the other side of the controversy, defenders acknowledge that the whole reason to advertise is to persuade. There's no magic or dishonesty about using the marketing mix to identify customer needs, to create an appropriate product, and to advertise that product. Defenders contend that advertising offers people the information they need to choose among products in the marketplace. Advertising can be seen as building consumption not by making people purchase what they don't need but by making the market more efficient for both consumers and producers by offering information about the product, its availability, and so on.[21]

These defenders believe that advertising can't create demand for a product no one wants. Advertising may bring people into a store to buy, but if they can't find the right size or color, or if the quality isn't acceptable, they can—and do—leave without buying.[22] No amount of advertising pressure can force people to buy something they don't want, and anyone who is persuaded by advertising to buy a bad product (or a product that doesn't meet a legitimate need) won't make that mistake again. Far from being helpless to resist advertising's persuasive power, people are able to ignore or discount advertising messages, by zapping television commercials, turning down the radio, or simply turning the page in a magazine or newspaper. Most consumers are savvy about what they see advertised, and research indicates that children as young as 8 understand and are skeptical about advertising's persuasive power.[23]

Stereotyping

Another common criticism of advertising is that it perpetuates **stereotyping,** the process of categorizing individuals by predicting their behavior based on their membership in a particular class or group. Of course, it's nearly impossible in a 30-second television commercial or a small magazine ad to reveal the people in the ad as distinct individuals, so some form of visual "shorthand" is generally used to give the audience cues about these characters. The problem, critics say, is that ads often portray entire groups of people in stereotypical ways, showing women only as homemakers and elderly people only as senile, for example. These advertising stereotypes can reinforce negative or undesirable views of these groups, and this can contribute to discrimination against them.[24]

Given the diversity of the population in the United States (and in many other countries), advertisers are realizing that stereotyping isn't acceptable because it alienates potential customers. Moreover, by presenting minorities and women more realistically, advertisers can significantly expand their markets for a wide variety of products (see Exhibit 3.6). The situation is slowly changing as minority groups protest against stereotypes, but more needs to be done. One continuing criticism is that advertising features primarily white, middle-to-upper-class characters, a portrayal that is at odds with the melting pot of ethnic and economic diversity around us. There are signs of change: one study of 2,108 ads in 10 magazines found that the percentage of African-American models used rose from 3.4 percent in 1991 to 5.2 percent in 1992. Advertisers are making changes, too: Kmart advertising uses actors of various weights, heights, ages, and ethnic backgrounds, including some actors with disabilities. Looking for ways to make ads seem more realistic, more advertising agencies are using real-life people rather than professional models or actors, including people with physical disabilities and youngsters with Down's syndrome.[25]

However, showing more women, African-Americans, Hispanics, Asians, and members of other groups is only half the answer. The other half, perhaps more difficult, is to make their portrayal realistic. Mark Green, who conducted the study of minorities in advertising as New York City's consumer affairs commissioner, also noted that the African-American models used in ads were shown as "stereotypes, as musicians, as athletes, as objects of pity in corporate philanthropy ads, rather than as consumers."[26]

Influence on the Media

The media's reliance on advertising as a source of income leads many to question how advertising influences the media. Perhaps the most serious charge is that advertisers, with the implied or actual threat of pulling their ads, can directly

EXHIBIT 3.6
Gearing an Ad to the African-American Market

The considerable buying power of the African-American market has attracted a wide range of advertisers. To promote Maybelline's Shades of You line of cosmetics for African-American women, Lintas:New York created a series of ads tailored to the specific needs and interests of that target audience.

influence media content. Major advertisers such as Coca-Cola, McDonald's, Mazda, and General Mills have, in fact, stopped advertising on certain television shows when customers protested program content such as excessive violence or complained about airing adult programs in the early evening when children might watch. After studying more than 50 cases, the nonprofit Center for the Study of Commercialism found that advertiser pressure can cause the media to suppress some stories, downplay the negative, or highlight the positive. One example cited was of a consumer reporter at WCCO-TV, a Minneapolis television station, who lost her job after local car dealers (who advertised heavily) complained about her stories on how to buy cars from rental agencies. The reporter was rehired following a wave of viewer and reporter protests.[27]

Some journalists believe that when ad revenues are at risk, the temptation to cater to advertisers can be too great. "When you write about business, the attitude tends to be one of caution," says Bill Lazarus, an investigative reporter. "And for businesses who happen to be advertisers, the caution turns frequently into timidity." Certainly, not everyone minces words to avoid offending advertisers. During a speech, *Automobile* magazine's editor criticized General Motors for closing plants and cutting jobs; GM pulled its ads from the magazine for three months.[28] Even when the media want to cover important but sensitive subjects such as AIDS or abortion, they can't always interest advertisers, who worry about customer backlash or boycotts. For example, live coverage of political conventions has become less popular with advertisers not only because the conventions are often lengthy and undramatic but because they may include discussions of controversial topics that advertisers don't want to be associated with.[29]

The other side of this argument is that in many countries advertising allows the media to exist as low-cost, nongovernment sources of news and entertainment. After all, people get local, national, and international news from the media, and by selling ads to many advertisers, the media can perform this critical role without being held hostage by a single source of financial support or by government forces. For example, before the collapse of communism in the Soviet Union, unbiased news about government crackdowns was hard to come by. However, during a crackdown in Lithuania, Moskus Echo (then the only private radio station in the U.S.S.R.) broadcast news of the conflict. How could this station stay on the air for 16 consecutive hours to broadcast the story to 6 million Muscovites? "Oddly enough, thanks to advertisements," says one owner. By accepting ads for small businesses and consumer goods, Moskus Echo receives money that "enables us to exist, to continue and to perform an important public service, in a country where democracy is just about to be born," the owner says.[30]

In some countries, the media are government supported, but proponents of freedom of the press argue that this opens the possibility of government control. Although advertiser support has its problems, media that are supported by many advertisers are less susceptible to the influence of a single advertiser. Still, when the media accept ads from many sources, they may feel pressure to avoid controversial or unpopular topics that can offend sponsors. To avoid such pressures, *Consumer Reports* magazine, the Public Broadcasting System, and other media vehicles operate without advertising support. However, banning ads from all media would mean that you'd have to pay more for magazines or newspapers (because advertising revenues usually subsidize subscription rates) and you'd even have to pay for radio and television programs.

Bad Taste and Offensiveness

A frequent criticism often launched at advertising is that it's in bad taste or, even worse, downright offensive. However, before making such a judgment, it's important to separate the product being advertised from the content, presentation, and medium: advertising products such as condoms may be offensive to some, but the advertising issues really relate to how tastefully the ads are done and where and when they're shown. Taste is personal, so what's acceptable to one person may be objectionable to another. Over time an ad that once seemed offensive

I'm spontaneous
and Secret with pH balance
always protects me.

Because you are a special woman,
trust in Secret with pH balance.

may appear less distasteful as social changes cast it in a different light (see Exhibit 3.7).[31]

What's more, ads may seem less offensive if they appear in one medium and not another. Several studies have determined that consumers find television commercials more intrusive and offensive than print ads; ads delivered over the telephone, in schools, and on videotapes are also particularly intrusive and distasteful. Because print ads can be easily ignored, consumers find them to be less offensive and less misleading than other types of ads, and more informative and entertaining.[32]

Consider sexually provocative television advertising. For more than 30 years, the ABC, CBS, and NBC television networks wouldn't air commercials showing lingerie products on live models. In the late 1980s, the networks dropped this restriction, and Playtex bras and Bali women's underwear were among the first products to appear on live models in commercials. Some groups blasted the change: both the National Federation of Decency and Women against Pornography protested, branding the ads sexual exploitation, and the Christian Broadcasting Network condemned the ads as offensive to its viewers. Despite these objections, the networks maintained their policies. Of course, advertisers generally don't intend to offend or outrage their customers, and some advertisers point out that truly offensive ads would provoke so many customer complaints that those ads would be voluntarily and quickly withdrawn.[33]

Although ads of questionable taste may generate discussion, they don't necessarily generate sales. Consider Calvin Klein, which often uses explicit sexual imagery in its advertising. In five out of six annual surveys, readers indicated that Calvin Klein magazine and newspaper ads were the most memorable print ads they had seen. Despite these memorable ads, Calvin Klein's jeans sales have been slowing.[34] Forging an image of social consciousness through advertising landed Benetton, the international knitwear manufacturer and retailer, the ninth position on the 1991 annual list of most memorable print ads. Benetton's ads have been banned and denounced because of questions of taste. One ad shows a man dying of

The last thing PaineWebber expected when it aired a radio commercial spoofing a piano recital was controversy. The commercial featured two mothers watching their children perform. One woman commented that the other woman's daughter played as though she had studied in Europe. "She did," said the second. Then came the slogan, "Thank you, PaineWebber." A few piano teachers, angry at the implication that people have to go to Europe to study piano properly, protested to PaineWebber, and the advertiser yanked the ad.

Advertisers grapple daily with the possibility that the most innocent reference might offend someone. Of course, no advertiser sets out to intentionally offend people; however, many have become cautious—perhaps overly so—rather than risk angering a particular group. In a world where advertisers often have to go to extraordinary lengths to make their ads stand out from the clutter, blandness may be a way of defending against potential protests—but it also may be bad for business.

Look what happened when the fast-food chain Roy Rogers aired an ad poking fun at school cafeteria food. The television commercial, which ran during the summer months, showed cafeteria employees dishing up platefuls of unappetizing food. Youngsters, the target audience, loved the ad, and sales climbed. However, a trade association representing school food-service employees insisted that Roy Rogers drop the ad, saying that it showed an "old fashioned, outdated view" of school cafeterias. After two weeks of pressure, the advertiser stopped the campaign, despite the sales increases.

Tiptoeing around possibly offensive words or images is only one worry. Television advertisers also worry about whether the programs they sponsor offend anyone. Complaints about excessive violence, sexual activity, or some other objectionable aspect of plot or character can kick up controversy for advertisers as well as for the media. For instance, Procter & Gamble, Kimberly-Clark, Tambrands, and McDonald's all changed their television advertising plans when threatened with boycotts by groups upset over their sponsorship of programs with sexually explicit content.

In response to these environmental forces, some firms have developed policies to guide their ad agencies in selecting programs. Other advertisers have no written policies; they rely on their agencies' discretion and deal with any protests on a case-by-case basis. When deciding whether to change an ad because of a protest or concern over offending someone, an advertiser should think about the reaction of its target audience as well as the impact of any negative publicity. After all, ads are designed for specific audiences and are not meant to appeal to everyone. For example, Bugle Boy's audience overwhelmingly liked its sexually suggestive ad campaign in *Rolling Stone* magazine.

Forced to choose between making a statement about the freedom to communicate with their target audiences and making a change to avoid disputes, most advertisers back down. As a Coca-Cola spokesperson says, "The bottom line is we are in business to make friends." But even making a change may not satisfy protesters. After Roy Rogers pulled its ads, the association went ahead and boycotted the chain's parent company. "They felt we shouldn't have run the ads in the first place and that we didn't move fast enough to pull them," explained a Roy Rogers official. So Roy Rogers couldn't satisfy everyone, no matter what it did.

Apply Your Knowledge

1. If an ad effectively reaches its audience and stimulates sales, should it be changed because of a protest by a group not in the target audience?
2. Should groups be allowed to boycott the advertisers rather than the stations (or the networks) that air programs seen as objectionable? ∎

AIDS surrounded by his family; another shows a black woman nursing a white baby. Some Benetton franchisees blame the ads for driving away much-needed business in the United States, where the company has lost money—and closed many stores. But Benetton's Oliviero Toscani, who's responsible for the ads, says, "Advertising is not just about the selling of a product. It has an equal social obligation to do something more."[35]

ADVERTISING AND SOCIAL RESPONSIBILITY

The question of exactly what obligations advertisers owe to society has been debated for years. The concept of **social responsibility** argues that every organization has obligations to society that go beyond pursuing its own goals. Many businesses, including Members Only, believe that commitments to social responsibility and profitability are not incompatible.

A large number of ad agencies donate their time and talents, and the media donate advertising space and time, for **public service announcements (PSAs),** ads by government and nonprofit groups that meet the community's needs by

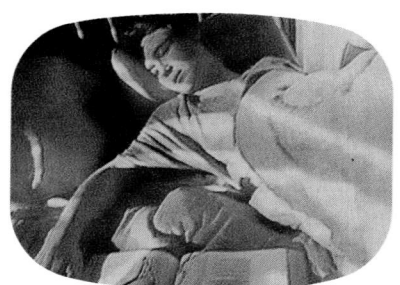

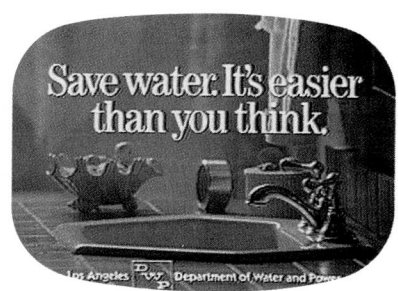

MAN SITS UP IN BED. HE IS THIRSTY. STEPS UP TO BATHROOM SINK. TURNS ON FAUCET AND NOTHING COMES OUT. ABRUPTLY THE MAN WAKES FROM HIS NIGHTMARE WITH A START. MAN WALKS INTO BATHROOM. HE

TURNS ON WATER SUCCESSFULLY. REALIZES HE'S LEFT THE WATER RUNNING. TURNS OFF WATER.
(SFX): eerie music
V.O.: Imagine how you'd feel if you couldn't get water.

(SFX): rock music
V.O.: We're suffering a serious drought and we have to change our habits now. If you're using more water than you need, wake up. Save water. It's easier than you think.

EXHIBIT 3.8
Using Public Service Announcements

Water conservation is a serious issue in many communities. The Los Angeles Department of Water and Power uses public service announcements to persuade people to save water.

addressing social issues such as drug abuse, pollution, and racial harmony. In 1992 alone, more than $300 million in media time and space was donated for antidrug PSAs.[36] Both for-profit and nonprofit organizations use advertising to back up their commitment to society by addressing a wide range of social issues such as public health and welfare, education, and human rights (see Exhibit 3.8).

Despite the good intentions of for-profit advertisers, some observers fear that firms will support only issues that are in their self-interest. "Often, messages that get on the air are not just in the public interest," says Michael Jacobson of the Center for the Study of Commercialism, pointing out that many are also in the sponsor's interest. Some experts worry that paid ads might squeeze out unpaid ads about social issues—or that only advertisers with the biggest budgets will be able to get their messages across.[37]

For example, Johnson & Johnson has sponsored a series of television commercials promoting prenatal care as part of its commitment to maternal and child health. "Johnson & Johnson has been caring for mothers and babies for over a hundred years," explained Phil Crosland, executive vice president of account services at Lintas:New York, the ad agency that created the commercials. "It's only natural Johnson & Johnson would take up a cause focusing on low birth rates." The J&J ads were introduced at the same time as another new commercial about prenatal care was completed, this one created by Grey Advertising for the Advertising Council, a nonprofit industry group that coordinates many public service campaigns. The J&J commercials were sure to be aired because the advertiser paid for the time; the Ad Council's commercials depended solely on the generosity of the stations donating the time, so they weren't guaranteed to be shown. However, David Freilicher, a senior vice president at Grey, maintained that the prominence of the paid ads by J&J might just provoke the media to donate *more* time for the Advertising Council's unpaid ads.[38]

The antidrug campaign run by Members Only is just one example of the causes supported by advertisers that buy ad space and time. For example, Benetton has underwritten the development and distribution of "A Guide to Safer Sex," a pamphlet on AIDS prevention written by the Gay Men's Health Crisis that appeared as an advertising supplement in *Spin,* a magazine aimed at readers aged 18 to 34.[39] Kraft General Foods has advertised to persuade people to donate money to Food-Patch, a nonprofit organization that distributes food to hungry children in suburban New York.[40] Another such advertiser is Z. Cavaricci, as shown in Exhibit 3.9. Nonprofit advertisers also support a broad range of issues; two examples are cancer and voting. In the United States, the National Institutes of Health has sponsored ads showing the early warning signs of cancer, and the League of Women Voters has used advertising to persuade people to register and vote.[41]

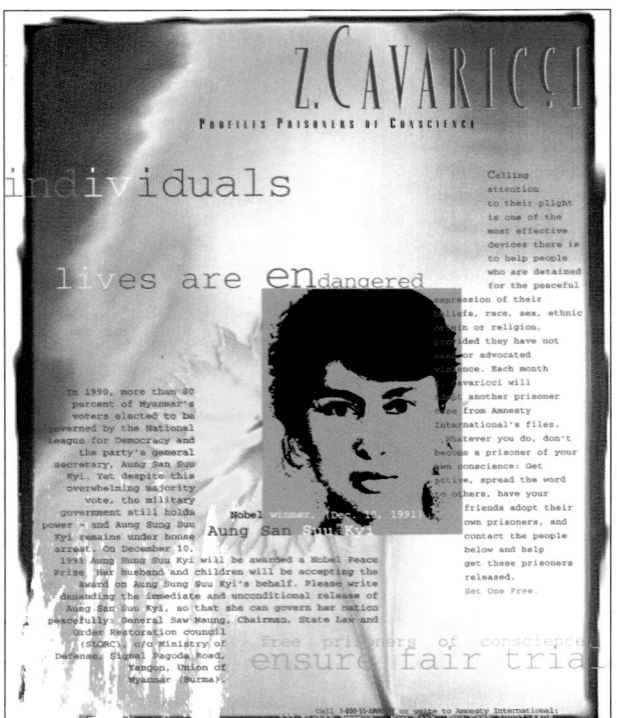

EXHIBIT 3.9
Corporate Advertising to Support Human Rights

Many corporations display their commitment to social responsibility by using ads that focus on specific societal issues. Here, apparel maker Z. Cavaricci advertises to draw attention to the international struggle for human rights.

Advertising and Ethics

Another hotly debated issue in the advertising environment is the role of ethics. The call for more ethical advertising isn't new. In the United States, fraudulent ads were already the target of public criticism—and legal action—a hundred years ago, and these problems led to many legal and regulatory reforms that today define what advertisers can and cannot do.[42] Ethical issues in advertising can be categorized as either ethical dilemmas or ethical lapses.

ETHICAL DILEMMAS AND ETHICAL LAPSES

An **ethical dilemma** is an unresolved ethical question in which each of the conflicting sides can make an arguable case. A classic ethical dilemma is whether tobacco companies should be allowed to advertise. Allowing them to do so encourages unhealthy behavior, but not allowing them to advertise could violate their freedom of speech and hamper their ability to sell a legal product. The common theme in all ethical dilemmas is the conflict between the rights of two or more important groups of people.

An **ethical lapse** occurs when normally ethical people make unethical decisions. Be careful not to confuse ethical dilemmas (which are unresolved interpretations of ethical issues) with ethical lapses (which are cases of unethical behavior). For example, a liquor company's decision to advertise a product that contributes to alcoholism reflects an ethical dilemma, but an automaker's decision to knowingly advertise advantages that its car can't live up to is an ethical lapse. When Volvo wanted to advertise the strength of its car roofs, it ran an ad showing a pickup truck with giant tires driving over the top of a row of cars. All the car roofs collapsed except for the Volvo's. When the ad was challenged, Volvo revealed that its car's roof had been reinforced by unseen braces. The company apologized for the ethical lapse and stopped running the ad; the ad agency resigned the account.[43]

How Advertisers Support Social Causes

Marketing efforts and charitable interests cross paths when an advertiser uses *cause-related marketing*, a promotional program in which the company contributes a specified amount to a social cause when customers buy a certain product. The term was coined by American Express, which is credited with popularizing the technique after its successful drive to raise funds for the restoration of the Statue of Liberty. The company raised $1.7 million to refurbish the statue by donating one cent from every American Express card purchase made during the lengthy advertising campaign.

For its part, American Express garnered free publicity, higher card usage, and a crop of new applicants. The company has since advertised more than 60 cause-related marketing campaigns, and other firms have followed its lead. Competing with American Express and Visa, MasterCard has used cause-related marketing to increase credit card use, to create a higher profile for its brand, and to raise millions of dollars for several charities.

In one recent advertising campaign, MasterCard promoted an alliance with Global ReLeaf, a group dedicated to reforesting public lands. During the yearlong promotion, MasterCard arranged to plant a tree every time consumers ordered merchandise from participating catalogs and paid with their MasterCard credit cards. As a result of this effort, hundreds of thousands of trees were planted throughout the United States. By creating a sense of involvement and promising real progress for the cause being supported, MasterCard reinforced its advertising message both to the target audience of current and prospective cardholders and to the catalog merchants who accept the credit card.

Cause-related marketing is growing because it makes financial, as well as humanitarian, sense; it's a good compromise between a company's need to earn revenue and its desire to help the community. It differs from normal corporate philanthropy because it is more than outright charity; the advertiser also makes money on the deal. Once the company has

Make A Difference In The Lives Of Seniors And Homeless Pets.

The Purina Pets For People Program helps unite homeless shelter dogs and cats with senior citizens, free of charge through participating humane shelters. And during the month of October, every time you buy Purina pet food, you are helping make possible cash donations ($1 million annually nationwide) to the program.

Studies show that seniors who own pets receive life enriching benefits such as lowered blood pressure and less stress. They make fewer visits to the doctor and have a greater sense of well-being*

Kmart wholeheartedly supports community efforts like Pets For People. And Kmart and Purina thank you for your support.

If you know a senior who would benefit from the companionship of a pet, or if you would like the name of the participating shelter nearest you, call 1-800-345-5678. And help kiss loneliness goodbye.

*Source: Delta Society®

© 1993, Purina Pets For People   ©1993 Kmart® Corporation

Kmart supported the Purina Pets for People program by placing advertisements to promote the cause.

selected a cause, it uses advertising, public relations, and other promotional tools to publicize the connection and to show how contributions will help. The association with a worthy cause boosts the advertiser's public image and its sales while the charity gains wider public exposure and needed donations (as happened in the Kmart ad for the Purina Pets for People Program).

However, critics question whether the nonprofit organizations that benefit from these programs will feel pressured to make compromises so that their activities will seem more acceptable to the advertisers. Some also question whether funding for nonprofit groups should depend on sales campaigns. Finally, should seemingly less-marketable causes such as preventing teenage pregnancy be allowed to languish? These and other issues will continue to be raised as cause-related marketing gains momentum.

Apply Your Knowledge
1. Would a cause-related marketing program be more effective if the charity or social cause being supported had a close connection to the advertiser's products or business? Why or why not?
2. Should the advertising that supports a cause-related marketing campaign stress the charity, the donation, the product, or the brand name of the advertiser? ■

ETHICAL ISSUES IN ADVERTISING

As the target audience for many advertising campaigns, you've probably been exposed to a wide variety of ethical issues in advertising. Advertising unhealthy products, advertising to children, and using puffery are among the hottest ethical topics being debated today. Here's a brief overview of the questions raised by each of these ethical advertising issues:

- *Advertising unhealthful products.* Should manufacturers be allowed to advertise harmful products? In particular, alcohol and tobacco ads have come under fire for encouraging people to use unhealthful products. Some countries (such as Canada and Finland) have banned cigarette advertising; others (such as the United States and Sweden) restrict but don't ban cigarette ads. Tobacco companies contend that as long as tobacco products can be sold legally, manufacturers should be allowed to advertise them. These advertisers say they're trying to get smokers to switch brands, not to convince nonsmokers or children to take up the habit, but critics disagree. Antismoking groups say that children are quite aware of certain tobacco ads, including those that feature Joe Camel, the cartoon character in R. J. Reynolds's Camel cigarette ads, so they may be tempted to try smoking.[44]

- *Advertising to children.* Should advertisers be allowed to aim commercials at children? One of the hottest battlegrounds for this ethical dilemma is television. For instance, more than 7 million students see Channel One, a daily program of news mixed with commercials. The school systems that show Channel One are pleased with the free television equipment provided by the program's makers, Whittle Communications, but critics charge that Channel One makes students a captive audience for commercials. Another controversy concerns the link between cartoon shows and ads. Although some children's shows support a line of toys and other products related to the shows, many say that the separation between programs and commercials is too fuzzy for youngsters to understand and that the shows themselves actually function as ads to sell products rather than as entertainment.[45] The Canadian Supreme Court recently upheld a Quebec law that forbids ads aimed directly at children, seeking to protect youngsters from being manipulated. Even so, the debate over advertising to children continues in many areas.[46]

- *Using puffery.* Should advertisers be allowed to use **puffery,** the exaggerated, subjective praise of a product without offering facts to back up the claim? A statement such as "Sleeping on a Sealy is like sleeping on a cloud" is a good example of puffery in advertising, because it's obviously impossible to make this comparison, so no one can prove or disprove the claim. Critics say puffery is misleading, but defenders say people can tell when an advertiser is simply exaggerating. Obvious puffery—puffery that doesn't really deceive customers—isn't illegal, but legal and regulatory action has made clear that advertisers can't use puffery as a license to lie.[47]

Although these ethical issues are far from being resolved, all have been examined by legal and regulatory officials. Regulation has become an important part of the advertising environment.

Advertising and Regulation

Every billboard, every television commercial, every newspaper ad, and every direct-mail letter has to comply with a web of requirements designed to protect both consumers and businesses. Advertising was free from such requirements in the United States until 1872, when the government passed the first in a series of laws following a wave of schemes that used newspaper ads to sell useless inventions, medicines, securities, and other products. Because con artists sent their products through the mail, early advertising laws focused on combating postal fraud, which duped the public out of millions of dollars each year.[48]

Today, regulation affects virtually every step in the advertising process, including protecting a product with a trademark, creating the message, showing the product in action, and announcing a special sale. Following is an overview of some of the laws, government regulations, nongovernment regulations, and industry self-regulation efforts that advertisers and agencies need to understand.

THE LAWS THAT GOVERN ADVERTISING

Freedom of expression, as defined by the First Amendment, is perhaps the most basic legal element governing advertising in the United States. For many years, free speech protection didn't include **commercial speech,** the advertising and other forms of speech that promote a commercial transaction. Then in the mid-1970s, a series of rulings indicated that commercial speech is indeed covered by the First Amendment. For example, in 1976 the Supreme Court ruled that states can't forbid companies' advertising the prices of prescription drugs, because such ads contain information that helps consumers choose between products. On the same grounds, the Court ruled in 1977 that bar associations can't forbid attorneys from advertising their services and prices (see Exhibit 3.10). (British law also changed in the 1980s to allow lawyers and other professionals to advertise.)[49]

However, the U.S. Supreme Court modified its stand on extending First Amendment rights to commercial speech in 1986 when it ruled (in *Posadas de Puerto Rico Associates v. Tourism Company of Puerto Rico*) that even though casino gambling was legal in Puerto Rico, the government could ban the advertising of gambling to residents (to lessen the harmful effects on their welfare) and still allow advertising to nonresident tourists. In a 1993 case, the Supreme Court decided that states in which lottery ads are banned can bar the broadcast media from airing ads for other states' lotteries.[50]

In allowing the government to ban advertising in cases where it also has the authority to outlaw a specific product or activity, these rulings introduced the possibility that a state can legally forbid advertising of other products seen as harmful—such as tobacco and alcohol. Since these cases, antismoking factions have called for a total ban on cigarette advertising, whereas the American Tobacco Institute, the American Civil Liberties Union, and others have argued against a ban. As you saw earlier, this dilemma is still unresolved, so advertisers and agencies that promote products viewed as harmful will have to watch for developments.[51]

In **comparative advertising,** when advertisers claim that their products are better than those of competitors, companies have to comply with the laws requiring these claims to be truthful. The Lanham Act, which is part of the Trademark Protection Act of 1946 (revised in 1988), allows a business to take legal action when it believes that its trademark has been hurt by a competitor's misrepresentations in comparative advertising.[52] For example, Coca-Cola, owner of Minute Maid orange juice, sued Tropicana Products over an ad for ready-to-serve orange juice. Tropicana implied that its juice was better than other juices because it was unprocessed. In truth, Tropicana's juice was pasteurized, which isn't the same as being unprocessed. Coca-Cola believed that Tropicana's claim would cost its own Minute Maid considerable market share, and research found that a large number of people would likely be misled by the Tropicana ad. Coca-Cola won the suit, and Tropicana had to change its ad.[53]

A case that was decided in 1992 extends the possibility of legal action against the ad agency that prepared the ad. A U.S. district court ruled that ad agency Friedman Benjamin had to share financial liability with Wilkinson Sword for damages awarded because of what the court said were false claims made in ads comparing Wilkinson Sword's Ultra Glide razors with Gillette's Atra and Atra Plus razors. (The case is being appealed.)[54] The Lanham Act's ban against deceptive advertising can also extend to celebrities. When National Video, a video rental firm, used a Woody Allen look-alike in its ads, Allen filed suit, and the court agreed that people might be confused by the look-alike.[55]

In addition to national laws such as the Lanham Act, advertisers and agencies must comply with a variety of state and local laws. These laws cover a wide range of issues, including comparative advertising, consumer protection, disclosure of restrictions, and invasion of privacy, among others. Because the laws vary, it's important to understand which state and local laws (as well as federal laws) apply to your advertising plans (see Exhibit 3.11).

FEDERAL REGULATION OF ADVERTISING

Just as advertisers must abide by the complex web of laws that govern advertising in the United States, they must also comply with rules set by many federal agencies. Virtually every advertising practice comes under the jurisdiction of the Federal Trade Commission, and depending on the advertiser's industry and product, regulations set by the Food and Drug Administration and the Federal Commu-

(SFX): music thoughout
V.O.: It's a whole new world facing today's chief executive. The economy is global. Competition is fierce. Financial pressures are unrelenting. But, there is one firm that can help CEOs make the difference between the worst of times . . . and the best of times.
(SFX): crowd applauding
V.O.: Coopers & Lybrand. Not just knowledge. Know how.

EXHIBIT 3.10
An Accounting Firm's Ad to Attract New Clients

A series of legal decisions has opened the way for professionals such as accountants, lawyers, and doctors to advertise their services. This television commercial, shown during the Super Bowl, trumpets the professional expertise of accountants Coopers & Lybrand.

KELLY: Choosing a breath mint is as easy as 1, 2, 3. One: an independent test shows Tic Tac freshens breath even better than Breath Savers. Two: there are eight calories in each Breath Savers. Three: but only 1-1/2 calories in each Tic Tac.

EXHIBIT 3.11
How Tic Tac Uses Comparative Advertising

When ad agency Altschiller/Reitzfeld made this advertisement for Tic Tac breath mints, it carefully followed all the legal rules for making claims in comparative advertising.

nications Commission may also apply. Other government agencies are also involved in advertising regulation, including the U.S. Postal Service; the Bureau of Alcohol, Tobacco, and Firearms; the Patent Office; and the Library of Congress.

The Federal Trade Commission

The **Federal Trade Commission (FTC),** created in 1914, is the U.S. government agency charged with regulating most business practices, including advertising activities. The agency's regulatory powers originally covered only unfair or uncompetitive business practices. Those powers were extended in 1936 through the Robinson-Patman Act. Under that act, the FTC forbids manufacturers from offering large retailers special pricing arrangements or promotional and advertising allowances that aren't available to small retailers. Then, in 1938, the Wheeler-Lea Amendment gave the FTC regulatory powers covering consumer protection.[56] In regulating advertisers, the FTC is concerned with two main areas: deceptive advertising and unfair advertising.

The FTC has defined **deceptive advertising** as a significant representation, omission, or practice that is likely to mislead a consumer and lead to consequences not in the consumer's favor. When the FTC examines an ad to see whether it's deceptive, it asks three questions:[57]

1. Does the ad involve a portrayal, practice, or omission likely to mislead consumers?
2. Can consumers interpret the advertising message reasonably?
3. Does the ad's portrayal lead to material consequences, such as influencing a consumer's behavior or decision relating to the product?

Adopted in 1983, this three-part test was designed to help the FTC focus its efforts on serious rather than trivial cases. Some observers say this standard makes proving deception more difficult for the FTC and may mean less protection for consumers. Despite this concern, the agency continues to successfully identify and press cases against deceptive advertising. For example, to combat deceptive ads related to environmental claims, the FTC recently issued specific guidelines for using terms such as *compostable* and *recyclable*. To use the word *compostable,* the advertiser must have proof that "all the materials in the product or package will break down into, or otherwise become part of, usable compost in a safe and timely manner." If an advertiser can't back up its claims, the FTC may find the advertising deceptive.[58]

Unfair advertising is likely to cause consumers substantial harm (in terms of economics, safety, or health) that can't reasonably be avoided. Advertising can be nondeceptive but unfair, for instance, when an ad makes claims that tend to exploit vulnerable groups such as the elderly and children. Other examples of unfair advertising include ads that make claims without having proof and ads that don't include the key information that a consumer needs to make a valid choice between products.[59]

Ads suspected of violating the regulations against deceptive or unfair advertising may be brought to the FTC's attention by consumers, competitors, or FTC staff members. When the agency examines these ads, it looks at a variety of elements, including the use of affirmative disclosure, the availability of substantiation, and the use of endorsements.

- **Affirmative disclosure** is the revelation of the specific conditions, limitations, or consequences related to the use of the advertised product. When an automaker's ad shows the Environmental Protection Agency's mileage rating for that model, it's using affirmative disclosure to announce who conducted the test and to offer a rating that consumers can compare with other cars being considered.

- **Substantiation** is the documented proof of an advertiser's claims. At one time, advertisers and agencies weren't required to have such proof, but now they must have it even before an ad runs; if they don't, the ad may be seen as unfair.

CHECKLIST OF KEY LEGAL ISSUES IN USING ENDORSEMENTS

❏ A. Be sure that the person chosen to make the endorsement is not connected with the sponsoring advertiser.

❏ B. Verify the product usage as well as the viewpoint of the person making the endorsement.
  • Be sure the ad reflects the true opinions, beliefs, findings, or experience of the person making the endorsement.
  • Check that the person making the endorsement is still using the product.
  • Check that the person making the endorsement hasn't

changed his or her view of the product before or during the time the ad is running.

❏ C. Be sure that the ad is not misleading.
  • If the ad uses models or actors posing as consumers, disclose that they are not actual consumers.
  • Check that any person making an expert endorsement has the expertise to endorse the product and has actually used that expertise in making the endorsement.
  • Verify that endorsement comments used in the ad have not been taken out of context or the meaning distorted.

For example, if an ad uses phrases such as "tests prove" or "nine out of ten doctors recommend," the advertiser must first have documents to back up its claim—and some media ask to see the substantiation before running an ad.[60]

• **Endorsement** is the implied or actual approval of a product by someone other than the advertiser, such as a celebrity, an expert, or a product user. Because an endorsement lends credibility to an advertiser's message, the FTC requires that it be substantiated.[61] See this chapter's checklist for questions advertisers and agencies should consider when using an endorsement.

If the FTC finds that an ad is unfair or deceptive, the agency can take action by pushing for a consent decree, issuing a cease-and-desist order, and, in some cases, requiring corrective advertising. A **consent decree** is a legally binding agreement that the advertiser will stop the disputed activity. If the advertiser agrees to the consent decree or negotiates some of the details but ultimately agrees, it must discontinue its deceptive or unfair advertising. However, if the advertiser doesn't agree to the consent decree, the case goes to an administrative law judge who can dismiss some or all of the charges or issue a **cease-and-desist order** to stop the advertiser from repeating the ad. An advertiser can appeal a cease-and-desist order to the federal court of appeals and, if it loses there, to the U.S. Supreme Court.[62]

Sometimes the FTC requires an advertiser whose ads have been found to be unfair or deceptive to run **corrective advertising** to disclose specific information that corrects a false impression left by previous ads. Corrective advertising is used when the FTC believes that an incorrect view created or reinforced by the disputed ad will linger even though the ad has been withdrawn or changed. For example, in 1989 Cooper Rand agreed to a consent decree regarding ads that compared its battery chargers, which operate from car lighters, with traditional battery jumper cables. Then the FTC ordered the company to run corrective advertising notifying people who had already bought the charger about its actual performance.[63]

Advertisers, agencies, the media, and their legal advisers can get copies of the FTC's Rules of Procedure and of its operating manual to see in detail how the agency functions as it investigates suspected violations and applies remedies. Other FTC materials explain specific statutes and compliance procedures to help advertisers avoid violations.

The Food and Drug Administration

The **Food and Drug Administration (FDA)** is the U.S. government agency that regulates packaging and labeling of packaged foods, drugs, cosmetics, medical devices, and hearing aids. As part of the Department of Health and Human Services, the FDA has authority over both prescription and over-the-counter drugs. The FDA's authority also extends to the copy and the graphics on product containers and wrappers, on package inserts, on warning statements, on price lists, in brochures, and in advertisements (regardless of the medium). If an advertiser violates these regulations, the FDA has the power to seize its products.[64]

Pharmaceutical ads aimed at doctors have come under closer FDA scrutiny in recent years as regulators check for substantiation of claims, full disclosure of side effects, and misleading information. For example, the FDA in 1991 accused Syntex Laboratories of false and misleading advertising for making exaggerated claims about its naprosyn arthritis drug; to settle the case, Syntex agreed to run corrective advertising. However, because the FDA rarely sees prescription drug ads before they run, the agency has also called for more vigilant industry self-regulation.[65]

The Federal Communications Commission

The **Federal Communications Commission (FCC)** was established in 1934 by the Communications Act as the U.S. government agency charged with regulating broadcast media such as radio, television, telephone, and telegraph. As part of its regulation of radio and television advertising, the FCC requires sponsorship identification for all political or commercial ads and enforces the *equal-time* section of the Communications Act, which holds that stations must make advertising time available on an equal basis (and at the lowest rate paid by any advertiser) for all political candidates. The FCC forbids fraudulent billing for broadcast commercials and prohibits the broadcast of obscene, profane, or vulgar material in programming or advertising. The agency also regulates sales activities conducted by telephone, and it is charged with enforcing federal laws such as the Telephone Consumer Protection Act, which seeks to stop people from receiving unwanted sales calls. Like the FTC, the FCC can issue cease-and-desist orders, and it can set fines or revoke the broadcasting licenses of violators.[66]

Other Federal Regulatory Agencies

Other U.S. government agencies regulate advertising in its various forms. Among the most important of these agencies are the U.S. Postal Service; the Bureau of Alcohol, Tobacco, and Firearms; the Patent Office; and the Library of Congress.

- *The U.S. Postal Service* has jurisdiction over direct-mail advertising and advertising (in any media) that involves shipping items by mail or mailing promotional materials to retail outlets.

- *The Bureau of Alcohol, Tobacco, and Firearms* is part of the Treasury Department and regulates alcoholic beverage advertising. This agency bans misleading and deceptive alcohol advertising, and it decides what information (such as warnings) must be included in alcohol ads. For example, the agency requires that liquor labels include warnings about fetal alcohol syndrome.

- *The Patent Office* supervises the registration of trademarks, brand marks, and service marks. Advertisers can use the registration symbol ® following a trademark or service mark to indicate that it's registered; if the mark hasn't yet been registered, using the trademark symbol ™ identifies that mark as the advertiser's exclusive property. Some trademarks that remain in common use for years run the risk of becoming generic terms if owners don't protect their usage (see Exhibit 3.12). For example, *zipper* and *raisin bran* were once brand names, but after years of use, the courts ruled that they had become generic terms and could no longer be used exclusively by their original owners.

- *The Library of Congress* oversees the registration of materials that receive a **copyright,** the exclusive right to print or reproduce the material during the life of the copyright owner and for 50 years after. You can copyright an ad if it contains original copy or artwork, but you can't copyright slogans and common symbols or designs. The word *Copyright,* the abbreviation *Copr.,* or the symbol © near the advertiser's name indicates that an ad has been copyrighted. A copyrighted ad can't be legally used by others without the express written consent of the copyright owner.

EXHIBIT 3.12
Advertising to Protect a Trademark

DuPont sent this direct-mail advertising package to writers and editors to remind them that Lycra is a registered trademark. This is one way DuPont protects its trademarks from passing into generic usage.

NONGOVERNMENT REGULATION

In addition to government regulation, advertising is subject to nongovernment regulation by consumer groups, business groups, and the media. Although groups such as the Consumers Union don't have the same authority as government regulators, their actions can be effective against false or deceptive advertising. Consider how consumer advocacy groups such as Action for Children's Advertising regulate advertising through a series of escalating actions. Such groups investigate consumer complaints, and if appropriate, the groups ask advertisers to stop the unfair or fraudulent practices. If the advertisers don't stop, the groups can publicize the advertisers' actions, using the weight of public opinion to pressure advertisers. Finally, they can gather evidence to submit to government regulators, and on occasion, groups may file suit against advertisers. For example, when the consumer group Public Citizen petitioned the Food and Drug Administration to require more conspicuous warnings on print ads for nicotine skin patches designed to help people quit smoking, it also took its case to the media, hoping to build support for its proposal.[67]

The most prominent business group that regulates advertising is the **Better Business Bureau (BBB),** a business-monitoring group with more than 100,000 member companies. The BBB works primarily on the local level to address consumer complaints of false or deceptive advertising and marketing practices. When a consumer lodges a complaint against an advertiser (which may or may not be a BBB member), the local BBB contacts that organization to ask for changes. Most advertisers make the requested changes; if they don't, the BBB forwards the complaint to the appropriate government regulators and cooperates with local law enforcement officials to pursue legal remedies.

The media also regulate advertising by setting standards for taste, truthfulness, and substantiation. Until 1982, the National Association of Broadcasters set and enforced standards for radio and television advertising, but after the U.S. Justice Department charged that the code of standards violated antitrust rules, the networks and stations took over the role of regulating the commercials they air. As many as 50,000 radio and television commercials are screened every year by the radio and television networks for product acceptability, method of presenting claims, good taste, and substantiation—and up to one-third of the commercials are either refused or sent back for changes. Because television commercials are expensive to produce, advertisers and agencies often ask the networks to review

EXHIBIT 3.13
Guidelines for Truthful Advertising

To guide its members in developing fair and accurate advertisements, the American Advertising Federation has developed this voluntary code of advertising principles.

"Advertising Principles of American Business"

1. **Truth**—Advertising shall tell the truth, and shall reveal significant facts, the omission of which would mislead the public.

2. **Substantiation**—Advertising claims shall be substantiated by evidence in possession of the advertiser and the advertising agency, prior to making such claims.

3. **Comparisons**—Advertising shall refrain from making false, misleading, or unsubstantiated statements or claims about a competitor or its products or services.

4. **Bait Advertising**—Advertising shall not offer products or services for sale unless such offer constitutes a bona fide effort to sell the advertised products or services and is not a device to switch consumers to other goods or services, usually higher priced.

5. **Guarantees and Warranties**—Advertising of guarantees and warranties shall be explicit, with sufficient information to apprise consumers of their principal terms and limitations or, when space or time restrictions preclude such disclosures, the advertisement shall clearly reveal where the full text of the guarantee or warranty can be examined before purchase.

6. **Price Claims**—Advertising shall avoid price claims which are false or misleading, or savings claims which do not offer provable savings.

7. **Testimonials**—Advertising containing testimonials shall be limited to those of competent witnesses who are reflecting a real and honest opinion or experience.

8. **Taste and Decency**—Advertising shall be free of statements, illustrations, or implications which are offensive to good taste or public decency.

proposed commercials before they're made, which minimizes the cost of making any needed changes.[68]

Individual media firms such as local radio stations and local newspapers can set their own standards. If they believe an ad doesn't meet their standards, they can ask the advertiser to make changes or they can simply reject the ad. What's more, the media can regulate the content as well as the form of the ads they accept. For example, some media companies refuse to accept ads for alcohol, tobacco, or firearms; the *Reader's Digest* is a case in point—it doesn't run any tobacco ads. An example of regulating the form of an ad is *The New Yorker*'s decision to stop accepting scented fragrance ads after receiving complaints from readers who were offended by or allergic to the perfume aromas.[69]

INDUSTRY SELF-REGULATION

Concerned with presenting accurate, informative ads, many advertisers and ad agencies have formal or informal guidelines they apply to their advertising. On top of those individual efforts, dozens of industries have established (through their trade associations) guidelines and codes covering fair and truthful advertising (see Exhibit 3.13). For instance, members of the National Swimming Pool Institute are expected to abide by the advertising code this industry group has developed.[70]

The Council of Better Business Bureaus, which is the parent of the local BBBs, works with national groups that represent both advertisers and agencies to develop standards and control mechanisms for industry self-regulation. In 1971 the council joined forces with the AAAA, the AAF, and the ANA to create the **National Advertising Review Council (NARC).** As the industry's most comprehensive self-regulatory mechanism, the NARC promotes truth, accuracy, social responsibility, and ethics in advertising. The **National Advertising Division (NAD)** of the Council of Better Business Bureaus and the **National Advertising Review Board (NARB)** are the NARC's two operating arms.

- *NAD activities* include monitoring the media for misleading or false advertising; reviewing complaints from consumers and consumer groups, advertisers, competitors, and agencies; contacting advertisers whose ads have provoked complaint to seek substantiation; and asking for changes or withdrawal (see Exhibit 3.14). For instance, a college student challenging an ad for ExerClimb exercise conditioners presented the NAD with statements from exercise instructors who disputed some of the ad's claims. As a result, the product's distributor agreed to cut those claims from future ads. When advertisers won't

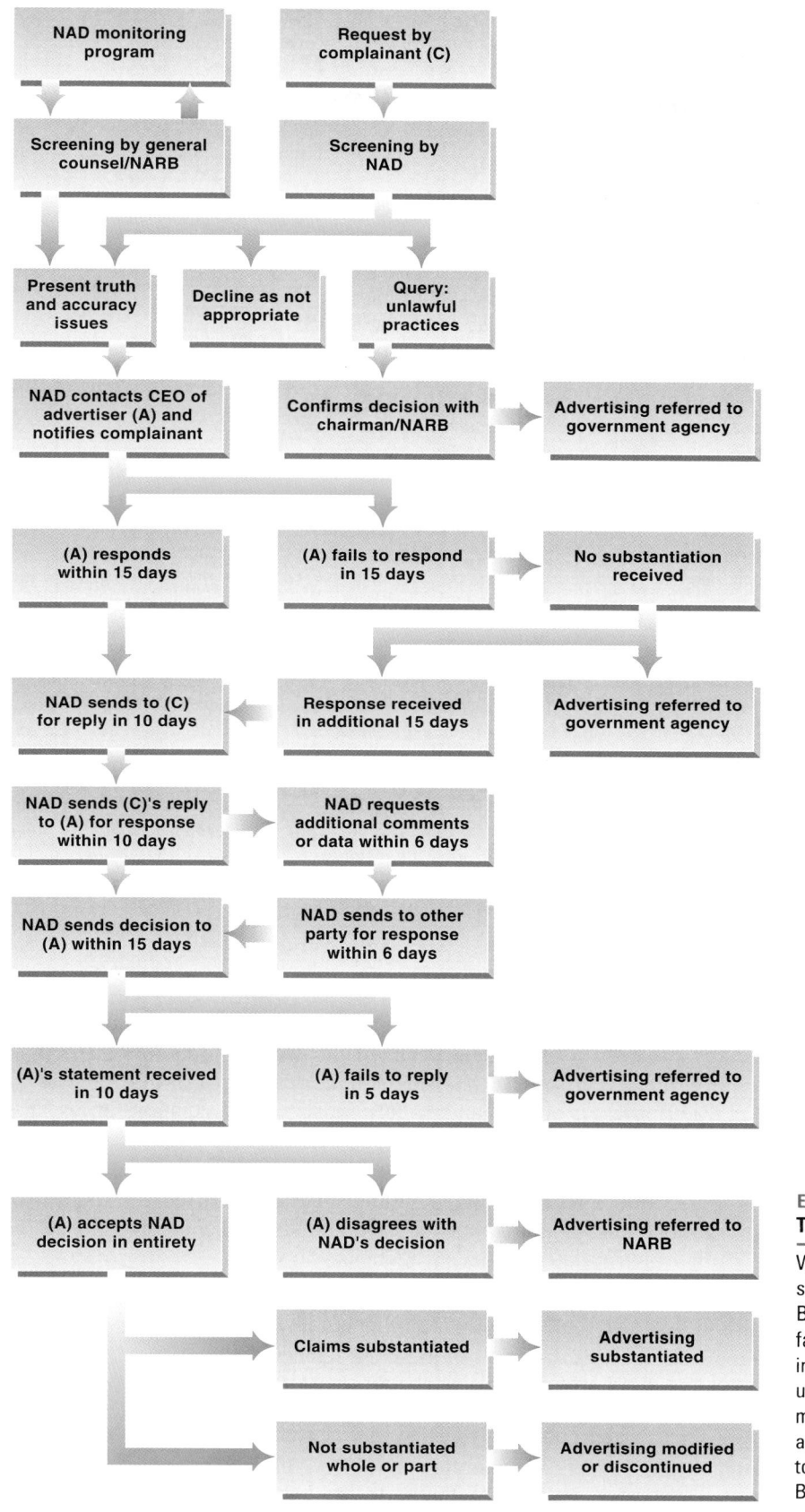

COUNCIL OF BETTER BUSINESS BUREAUS
NATIONAL ADVERTISING DIVISION RESOLUTION PROCESS

EXHIBIT 3.14

The NAD/NARB Process

When the National Advertising Division of the Council of Better Business Bureaus receives complaints about false or misleading advertising, it investigates and, if the claims are unsubstantiated, asks the advertiser to make changes. Advertisers that disagree with NAD findings can appeal to the National Advertising Review Board.

75

A CASE FOR CRITICAL THINKING

The Members Only ad campaigns against drug abuse and for voter registration did more than raise social consciousness; they also raised sales. During four years of advertising in support of social causes, sales soared 25 percent. By linking the Members Only logo to a series of powerful and caring messages, Ed Wachtel had been able to build brand awareness while establishing a bond of trust with his target audience.

By 1990, though, the environment had changed, and Members Only had to respond. In addition to changes in fashion and in consumer tastes, Wachtel was facing an economic recession that had slowed retail sales. Because the market for men's casual clothing was barely growing, Wachtel had to wrench business away from competitors if he was to keep sales strong.

After reviewing these environmental factors, Wachtel decided to temporarily suspend the cause-related advertising and turn back to basics with a campaign featuring Members Only products. To bring the products to life for the target audience, Korey, Kay and Partners produced commercials that focused on issues in the lives of three men. "We wanted the advertising to continue dealing with the real world," said Neil Leinwohl,

the agency's creative director. "We're just tackling smaller problems." In a departure from the previous social-issue ads, this new campaign featured shots of Members Only clothing as well as the brand's logo.

These ads helped Members Only hold its own during a difficult time, but Wachtel never meant to abandon the causes he supported. Within a year, he had shifted the entire ad budget back to the war on drugs, reviving the slogan "Do clothes, not drugs." In 1992 Members Only addressed the issue of voter turnout in a $3 million campaign that received the backing of retailers as well as the endorsement of the League of Women Voters, a nonprofit group dedicated to improving the U.S. political process. Throughout these social-issue campaigns, the Members Only ads got a lot more exposure than Wachtel paid for because many television and radio stations ran the commercials free as public service announcements.

After the 1992 presidential election, Wachtel put the ad spotlight back on drugs, planning to continue antidrug messages until 1995. At that point, he expects to move the ad focus to homelessness in the United States. He also wants to convince other advertisers to bankroll campaigns in support of key social issues. As Mem-

bers Only sales continue to rise and the company tackles new social issues, Wachtel can feel good about helping society as his company does well.

Your Mission: Wachtel has hired you to help plan the campaign to call attention to the problems of homeless people. You'll be looking at the advertising environment and making recommendations about how to make the campaign effective for the cause as well as for Members Only sales.

1. Some television stations refused to carry the antidrug ad showing a badge being riddled with bullets, saying it was too graphic. Now you must decide how graphic you want to be in the images and copy you will show in your ads about homeless people. Of the following options, which would best convey your message without the risk of losing airtime?

a. Carefully edit the commercial to avoid offending the media or your target audience. After all, your ultimate goal is to sell clothing.

b. Don't worry about being too graphic. You should realistically portray the plight of homeless people so that viewers will understand the magnitude and the reality of the situation.

go along with the NAD—which isn't often—the matter goes to the NARB; to date, fewer than 70 cases have reached the NARB.[72] Another part of the NAD, the Children's Advertising Review Unit (CARU), monitors truth and accuracy in print and broadcast ads aimed at children.

- *NARB activities* focus on reviewing cases being appealed from the NAD. Each case is heard by a five-person panel (three advertisers, one agency professional, and one member of the public), and the decision is binding on the NAD. If the panel asks for changes but the advertiser refuses, the NARB can publicly disclose information about the case and forward the complaint to the FTC or other appropriate regulatory agencies.

The results of monthly NAD, CARU, and NARB proceedings are made public. Although NARC activities aren't part of any governmental regulatory process, they have been an effective form of industry self-regulation.

National groups of advertisers, agencies, and media owners also encourage and reinforce industry self-regulation. The **American Association of Advertising Agencies (AAAA),** with 750 member agencies around the country, has long had a "standards of practice" statement supporting ethical, tasteful, and fair advertising; members that violate these standards can lose their membership, and nonmembers that violate them can be denied membership.[71] The **Association of National Advertisers (ANA),** whose more than 400 members represent the largest U.S.

50% VOTER TURNOUT ISN'T EXACTLY WHAT THEY HAD IN MIND.

There is no excuse not to vote.

MEMBERS ONLY.
Apparel And Other Fine Products.

A public service message provided by Members Only and The League of Women Voters.

c. Talk with the stations about their advertising standards and share your ideas before you make the commercials. This way, you'll know in advance exactly how graphic you can be and still get your commercials on the air.

2. You want to encourage other advertisers to join the fight against homelessness, but you know that many won't spend the money to make

or run special ads. What can you do to gain their support?

a. Offer to let any advertiser use your ads, free of charge. To make this offer even more enticing, produce the ads so that other advertisers can easily and inexpensively substitute their logos for the Members Only logo.

b. Donate a percentage of the profits from all Members Only clothing sold during December to a fund that will be used to buy time or space for any advertiser willing to produce an ad devoted to homelessness.

c. Ask the retailers that carry Members Only products to insist that other apparel makers spend some minimal amount of money to support the cause.

3. Two of your competitors decide to support the cause by advertising that they'll donate some of their men's clothing to shelters for homeless people. They challenge Ed Wachtel to match their clothing donations. Which of these actions would you recommend that Wachtel take in response?

a. Advertise that Members Only will match the value of any clothing donated by its competitors by buying an equivalent amount of airtime for its commercials in support of

the fight against homelessness.

b. Advertise that Wachtel will donate more than his rivals—and invite competitors to match this higher donation level.

c. Advertise that shelters choosing to accept your contributions will be required to accept donations from no company other than Members Only.

4. When you approach the national television networks to buy time for the Members Only commercial, you ask whether they will also contribute airtime to run the commercial as a public service announcement. All the networks agree except one, which says it will run the commercials free if the Members Only logo is removed. What is your best response?

a. Remove the logo. The other networks will show the commercials with the logo, so everyone will know that Members Only is responsible for the ad.

b. Leave the logo and air the commercials on the other networks. If it's the lone dissenter, this network may eventually come around.

c. Write a letter explaining why you won't remove the logo and send it to local newspapers to pressure the network into giving you free airtime.[74] ■

manufacturing and service advertisers, has a code of advertising ethics that members are expected to uphold. The **American Advertising Federation (AAF),** an association of U.S. advertising agencies, advertisers, media owners, and local advertising clubs, has a written code outlining standards for truthful and responsible advertising. Similarly, the Canadian Advertising Foundation brings together representatives of advertisers, agencies, the media, and the public to examine questions of taste, public decency, guidelines for advertising specific products, and ads aimed at vulnerable groups such as children.[73]

Summary

Advertising and the economy are closely linked. Advertising is a source of information for consumers and a source of market power for advertisers. Its economic influence on product pricing, consumer demand, and competition is still being debated. Advertising has been accused of harming society because it seems to go beyond merely selling products or ideas and can shape social trends and attitudes in powerful ways. However, advertising also helps society by improving competition, lowering prices, encouraging more product choices, promoting freedom of speech, supporting the media, and providing information. Specific issues being debated include advertising's role in language and literacy, manipulation and exploitation, stereotyping, influence on the media, and bad taste and offensive ads.

Whether advertisers have obligations to society beyond their own organizational goals is part of the debate about the ideal relationship between the organization and society. Some ad agencies donate time and talent, and the media donate advertising space and time, for public service announcements that address social issues such as drug abuse and racial harmony. Although for-profit and nonprofit organizations use advertising to address many social issues, critics fear that these groups will support only those issues that are in their self-interest.

An ethical dilemma is an unresolved ethical question in which each of the conflicting sides has an arguable case to make. In contrast, an ethical lapse occurs when someone makes an unethical decision. Advertising as a form of commercial speech has some protection under the First Amendment. However, the U.S. Supreme Court has left open the possibility that a state government can legally ban advertising for products considered harmful, such as alcohol and tobacco. The Lanham Act permits a business to take legal action when it believes that its trademark has been hurt by misrepresentations in a competitor's comparative advertising.

The Federal Trade Commission is the U.S. government agency charged with regulating most business practices, and it is concerned with both deceptive and unfair advertising. The Food and Drug Administration regulates packaging and labeling of packaged foods, drugs, cosmetics, medical devices, and hearing aids. The Federal Communications Commission regulates broadcast media such as radio, television, telephone, and telegraph. The U.S. Postal Service regulates direct-mail advertising and advertising that involves shipping goods or promotional materials by mail. The Bureau of Alcohol, Tobacco, and Firearms regulates alcoholic beverage advertising, and the Patent Office supervises the registration of trademarks, brand marks, and service marks.

The advertising industry has several forms of self-regulation. Individual advertisers and agencies regulate their own ads, and some industries have guidelines for advertising their products. In addition, industry groups such as the American Association of Advertising Agencies, the American Advertising Federation, and the Association of National Advertisers have set standards for ethical advertising. The National Advertising Review Council has two operating arms, the National Advertising Division and the National Advertising Review Board, to investigate advertising that has been challenged as misleading or false.

Key Terms

advertising environment 55
affirmative disclosure 70
American Advertising
  Federation (AAF) 76
American Association of
  Advertising Agencies
  (AAAA) 76
Association of National
  Advertisers (ANA) 76
Better Business Bureau
  (BBB) 73
cease-and-desist order 71
commercial speech 68
comparative advertising 69
consent decree 71
copyright 72
corrective advertising 71
deceptive advertising 70
endorsement 71
ethical dilemma 66
ethical lapse 66

Federal Communications
  Commission (FCC) 72
Federal Trade Commission
  (FTC) 70
Food and Drug
  Administration (FDA) 71
National Advertising
  Division (NAD) 74
National Advertising Review
  Board (NARB) 74
National Advertising Review
  Council (NARC) 74
public service
  announcements (PSAs) 64
puffery 68
service mark 60
social responsibility 64
stereotyping 60
substantiation 70
trademark 60
unfair advertising 70

Questions

FOR REVIEW

1. How do critics say advertising influences prices? How do defenders of advertising answer those charges?

2. How do ethical dilemmas differ from ethical lapses?

3. What is social responsibility, and how does it relate to profitability?

4. Why do some people think advertising is manipulative and exploitive? How do defenders of advertising answer those charges?

5. How do the NAD and NARB operate to self-regulate the advertising industry?

FOR ANALYSIS AND APPLICATION

6. What are the ethics of advertising sugary ready-to-eat cereals on television cartoon shows geared to 4-year-olds? On shows geared to 12-year-olds?

7. Why do you think the Federal Trade Commission allows advertisers to use puffery such as "soft as a cloud"? Should the FTC ban puffery?

8. You've just invented a new type of in-line roller skate with a cushioned braking system that allows skaters to gradually slow instead of stopping abruptly. How can you use advertising to break into the competitive in-line roller skate market?

9. If you were the advertising manager for DeBeers, the world's largest diamond producer, how would you answer charges that your ads encourage materialism?

10. Imagine you're an account executive meeting with your client, a truck rental firm that's trying to increase its business among consumers who rent trucks to move their own furniture. One idea that comes up is to advertise the size and rental fee for the client's truck compared with the size and fee for the leading competitor's truck. Your client suggests you make the point by having the ad show the competitor's truck as being much smaller than it actually is while showing the client's truck as being ridiculously enormous. What legal and regulatory guidelines apply to such a situation? How should you respond to your client's idea?

Sharpen Your Advertising Skills

What exactly is a best-seller? This question is an ethical issue in publishing because advertising a book as a best-seller can give sales a boost. When Doubleday released *Sam Walton: Made in America,* its ads trumpeted, "America's #1 Merchant Just Became America's #1 Best-seller." A best-seller? Not according to the lists compiled by the *New York Times* or *Publishers Weekly.* However, as the fine print in the ad noted, the book was a best-seller at Sam's Club, the discount warehouse chain founded by Sam Walton. Just about every book you can name "is on some list, somewhere," observes Deborah Aiges, vice president and creative director of Random House. "If you look at it that way, everything is a national best-seller."

Put yourself in Aiges's shoes. You're planning an ad campaign to sell a new biography of Michael Dell, the young entrepreneur who founded Dell Computers. Assume the book just hit the bookstores and it's selling quickly, especially in Dell's home state.

Decision: Should you advertise the book as a best-seller? If so, what criterion should you use—a listing in an independent source such as the *New York Times*? Store sales lists? If not, what's the best way to advertise how much interest the public is showing in the new book?

Communication: Write a two-page memo to your ad agency explaining exactly how you want to advertise the new book. If you decide to use the term *best-seller,* describe the basis for this label and indicate how it should be used. Mention any disclaimers or explanations you think your ad should include.

An Ad, Ad, Ad, Ad World?

SYNOPSIS

What is the role of advertising in contemporary society? In this video, Adam Smith and industry experts analyze advertising from a variety of perspectives. As advertising has become increasingly pervasive, some wonder whether *every* moment of human attention is seen as an opportunity to convey a sales message. Consumers are developing resistance to sales messages and are becoming cynical about advertising and about the institutions that use advertising. In turn, this cynicism brings problems for advertisers and agencies, which must struggle to get—and keep—the consumer's attention.

After taking a look at advertising messages of the 1950s, 1960s, 1970s, and 1980s, the video examines advertising trends in the 1990s. Today, more clients are demanding accountability for the money they invest in planning, producing, and placing advertisements, so agencies must be more responsive to this requirement. At the same time, advertisers and agencies continue to grapple with the problem of how to advertise products in other countries.

EXERCISES

Analysis

1. How does the pervasiveness of advertising discussed in the video affect the consumer's ability to receive and decode messages?
2. Do the music videos shown on MTV have to comply with the federal and state regulations that govern advertising? Explain.
3. Is the advertiser or the agency responsible for advertising messages in the classroom, in the movies, and in other nontraditional locations?
4. What evidence can you offer to support the idea that advertising is pushing nonadvertising messages out of public view? How can you refute this charge?
5. What does BBDO's Allen Rosenshine mean when he says, "People either filter them [ads] out or factor them in"?

Application

Are the rock videos shown on MTV entertainment or advertising? Take the advertiser's viewpoint, and examine the purpose of rock videos. Next, take the audience's viewpoint, and discuss the purpose of rock videos. If you were a rock musician, would you want your recording company to place your rock video on MTV? Why or why not?

Decision

Thanks to a series of high-energy commercials in the 1980s and early 1990s, Michael Jackson became closely identified with Pepsi soft drinks. After Jackson interrupted his 1993–1994 world tour amid controversy and medical problems, the advertiser faced a difficult decision about the celebrity's future role in Pepsi promotions. Identify Pepsi's options, and discuss how each might affect the advertiser and its relationship with consumers.

Ethics

Imagine watching television commercials that sell products you can't buy. This is the situation for many people in Eastern Europe, where television signals from other countries carry ads for fashionable clothing and other goods not locally available. Do these commercials unfairly create demand for products that viewers aren't able to buy—and that many couldn't afford even if the items were in local stores? Discuss the ethical issues.

Teamwork

Pair up with two other students, and play the roles of account executive, creative director, and client advertising manager. The advertiser wants to promote a new bubble-gum flavor to preteen boys and girls. What questions should the advertising manager ask the account executive and the creative director about a new television campaign the agency is proposing? What should the agency do to anticipate these questions and respond appropriately? Role-play a meeting in which the new campaign is presented. ■

Audience Definition, Research, and Planning

Audience Analysis and Buyer Behavior

After studying this chapter, you will be able to

1. Explain the importance of understanding an advertising audience
2. Describe the consumer and organizational markets
3. Identify the psychological influences on buyer behavior
4. List the social and interpersonal influences on buyer behavior
5. Explain the process of perception and its importance in advertising
6. Describe the rational decision-making model and list several types of nonrational purchase decisions
7. Summarize the key differences between the consumer and organizational markets

Facing an Advertising Challenge at American Express

INSIDE THE MIND OF THE TRAVELING PUBLIC

Few organizations need to understand the world's travel habits more than American Express Travel Related Services (TRS), the travel division of the nation's largest financial services company. TRS doesn't transport people to their destinations or put a roof over their heads when they arrive. It offers just about every other travel-related service you can imagine, though, and it advertises to a wide variety of travel audiences. As the travel unit's U.S. president of marketing services, Roger Ballou is in charge of advertising. Before he can initiate the advertising programs that would be most effective, he has to find out who those travel audiences are and how he can advertise his company's diverse services to them.

Travelers are a varied group; what appeals to one might be a major turn-off to another. The leisure travel market offers a vast array of options, from ultra low budget to five-star luxury. Vacationers can travel by bus, book first-class passage on an airline, or choose any of the numerous travel options in between. Travelers can sleep in a campground or in a $1,000-a-night suite at a world-class resort. Some people enjoy group activities such as cruises and luaus; others enjoy being on their own. With so many differing preferences, how can Ballou hope to gain the attention of such a wide-ranging audience?

To complicate matters for Ballou, TRS's product offering is as diverse as its advertising audience. Although American Express is best known for its green, gold, and platinum charge cards, the company provides a wide range of other goods and services. By visiting or phoning one of the more than 2,500 American Express offices worldwide, cardholders and travel customers can get help with personal emergencies, travel planning, traveler's checks, flight insurance, and such amenities as theater tickets. Through the Membership Miles program, cardholders can earn awards as basic as free airfare or as unusual* as tennis lessons from top pro Ivan Lendl. Travel & Leisure *is one of several magazines that TRS publishes, and the company engages in a variety of cooperative marketing and advertising programs with travel companies such as hotel chains, resorts, and airlines.*

For TRS and its marketing partners to be able to create truly effective advertising programs, they must get a better understanding of who their target customers are and what those people think and feel about vacation travel. If you were in Ballou's shoes, how would you approach the challenge of understanding your audience? Would you try to find something all vacationers have in common? Would you try to identify distinct groups that could be reached more effectively with specific advertising messages? How would you learn more about the attitudes and experiences of the traveling public? Finally, how would you apply what you learn to your advertising efforts?[1] ■

CHAPTER OVERVIEW Roger Ballou recognizes the importance of understanding his diverse and far-flung advertising audience. This chapter explores three essential steps in understanding your audience: discovering *who* your audience is, understanding *why* audience members buy what they buy, and recognizing *how* these people make purchases. You'll get acquainted with the various kinds of data that advertisers use to understand their audiences. (Chapter 5 continues this discussion with a look at how advertisers use these data to select particular audiences, and Chapter 6 explains the research methods advertisers use to collect the data.) The chapter discusses the importance of understanding an advertising audience and gives an overview of consumer and organizational markets. The remainder of the chapter is devoted to three vital topics: why people buy the products they buy, how they go about making these purchases, and how organizational buying differs from consumer buying. By understanding your audience and by knowing what the people in it care about, you can dramatically increase your chances of creating successful advertising messages.

Why It's Important to Understand Your Audience

For the past hundred years, some of the best minds in advertising and marketing have been struggling to understand and analyze their audiences. Although this struggle has always been important, today's environment puts additional pressure on advertising in three areas. First, advertisers are looking for a greater degree of accountability. Advertising budgets can be one of an organization's biggest

SEDUCED BY
OVER 30,000 BEACHES,
NO WONDER
ULYSSES TOOK
TEN YEARS
TO GET HOME

GREECE
Chosen by the Gods

EXHIBIT 4.1
Advertising across Borders

This ad for the Greek National Tourist Organization persuades vacationers from the United States to visit Greece. Tourism is a common example of advertising across national borders.

expenses, so managers want to see how their ad budgets are translating into increased sales. Second, markets for everything from cars to cookies are increasingly fragmented, with more product options in nearly every category, more niche markets, and more advertising and media options. Third, many organizations now face more competition than ever before, particularly with population and economic growth leveling off in many areas of the world and with competitors reaching across national borders to find new customers (see Exhibit 4.1).[2]

These powerful environmental forces give advertisers less room for error and less time to work. For each product, today's advertisers must discover which audiences are the best, where these people get information about new products, how they respond to various styles of advertising, and where they shop; then advertisers must reach them before competitors jump on the opportunity. It's a big challenge, but it's also a major opportunity for smart advertisers to move ahead of their competitors. Clear insight into your audiences gives you several key advantages:

- *Less waste.* Advertising can be expensive, and it's wasted when it's directed toward the wrong people. Audience insight helps advertisers choose their audiences with greater precision.

- *Greater effectiveness.* You've probably recognized that the better you know someone, the easier it is to make yourself understood. It's the same for advertising; improved audience insight leads to better advertising. When Reebok introduced the Blacktop basketball shoe, the ads reflected the gritty urban realities of sandlot and playground basketball. The ads clearly got through to their young audience and helped earn Reebok another 15 percent of the basketball-shoe market.[3]

- *Improved buyer-seller relationships.* Most successful advertisers try to build long-term relationships with their customers. The more they know about these customers, the more they can use advertising to foster those relationships. Keeping your current customers is usually far less expensive than getting new ones, so buyer-seller relationships are an important issue for most advertisers.

The Two Advertising Audiences

All customers can be split into two general groups: consumers and organizations. The **consumer market** is made up of individuals and households who buy goods and services for private use. The **organizational market** consists of nonprofit organizations, governments, and businesses of all sizes (advertising to this market is often referred to as *business-to-business advertising*). The ways in which the two groups respond to advertising and make purchase decisions are similar in many respects but are quite different in others.[4]

THE CONSUMER AUDIENCE

The consumer market is complex. In the United States alone, you'll find a bewildering diversity in economics, culture, lifestyle, and attitude, and the situation grows even more complicated as you move from country to country around the world. In a city such as Miami (with a population that is 42 percent Hispanic-American and 19 percent African-American), advertising to consumers is complicated enough.[5] Imagine advertising in Switzerland, which has four official languages; in Russia, where consumers are still struggling with the change to a free-market economy; or in Indonesia, where a shortage of paper limits the number of newspaper ads.[6] Even in countries that are similar in terms of economics and education levels, differences in the consumer market can be pronounced. In the United States, home ownership remains a key part of the "American dream," but in Japan, home prices are so high that three-quarters of the population have given up hope of ever owning a desirable home. On the other hand, the lack of opportunity to invest in real estate gives affluent Japanese consumers a great deal of discretionary cash for other purchases.[7]

Advertisers describe the composition of consumer markets through **demographics,** statistics that categorize people by age, occupation, income, and other external, objective variables.[8] (Chapter 5 explains how advertisers use demographic information.) In the United States, the Census Bureau is an important source of demographic data. Exhibit 4.2 shows the kinds of demographic variables collected by the Census Bureau. A number of other government bodies (such as the National Center for Health Statistics) and private research firms collect and supply important data as well.[9]

For all the valuable information it can provide, demographic analysis does have a distinct limitation: it doesn't get inside consumers' heads or hearts to tell you what they think and feel. Consumers' thoughts and feelings determine their response to advertising and their overall purchasing behavior. Demographic data provide a great framework for understanding an audience, but by themselves, they aren't all that effective in predicting or explaining consumer behavior. Of course, senior citizens rarely shop for skateboards, and desert dwellers aren't a good market for raincoats, but demographics can't tell you why one 40-year-old will drive nothing but a Ford when the 40-year-old next door, with identical income and education, will drive nothing but a Toyota. Such behavior is better explained by *psychographics,* covered later in the chapter.

THE ORGANIZATIONAL AUDIENCE

The counterpart to the consumer market is the organizational market, which consists of all groups that purchase goods and services to use in operations, to resell to others, or to use as raw materials or components for their own products. In other words, the organizational market represents all buyers other than consumers. This market is huge. In the United States alone, it employs over

EXHIBIT 4.2 **Demographic Variables Collected during a Census**

This table shows the major demographic variables collected by the U.S. Census Bureau. Advertisers often combine Census results with data from other sources to gain unique insights into consumer behavior.

Age
  Under 5, 5–12, 13–17, 18–24, 25–34, 35–44, 45–54, 55–64, 65–74, 75–84, 85+
	Educational attainment
	  Not high school graduate
	  High school graduate
	  Some college (1 to 3 years)
	  College degree
	  Advanced degree (master's degree, doctorate, etc.)

Sex Male, female	

Race/ethnicity
  White
  Black
  Asian
  Hispanic (may be of any race)
  Other (includes Native Americans)
	Employment status and occupation
	  Employed full-time
	  Employed part-time
	  Not employed
	  Retired

Household types
  Families:
    Married couple with children under age 18
    Married couple with no children under age 18
    Other family (includes single parents)
  Nonfamilies:
    Persons living alone
    Unrelated persons sharing living quarters
	If employed:
	    Professional worker, executive/administrative/managerial
	    Clerical/sales/technical
	    Craft/repair/equipment operator
	    Service worker (food service, etc.)
	    Other

Household ownership
  Single-family, owner-occupied
  Two+-family, owner-occupied
  Condominium or co-op
  Rented unit
  Mobile home or trailer
  Other (includes houseboats, etc.)
	Household income
	  Under $10,000
	  $10,000–$24,999
	  $25,000–$34,999
	  $35,000–$49,999
	  $50,000–$74,999
	  $75,000+

100 million people and buys over $5 trillion worth of goods and services every year. The organizational market includes Nike, Chemical Bank, McDonald's, the Red Cross, the Pentagon, and all other manufacturers, banks, wholesalers, retailers, restaurants, schools, police departments, federal agencies, and so on—nearly 19 million organizations in the United States. In Europe, Asia, and other parts of the world, there are millions more organizational customers; all this adds up to an enormous market.[10] Advertisers can split the organizational market into four parts:

- *The industrial/commercial market* consists of businesses that market goods and services to other businesses or to consumers. These companies spend billions of dollars a year on raw materials, equipment, machinery, component parts, supplies, and services, which makes them a major advertising audience.[11]

- *The reseller market* consists of businesses that buy finished products to resell either to other businesses or to consumers. This market includes retailers (such as department stores, specialty stores, and mail-order companies) and wholesalers (companies that distribute to retailers and to other business customers). Much of the advertising in the organizational sector is aimed at resellers, first because they are responsible for moving products on to consumers, and second because they themselves represent a major customer segment for business services, warehouse equipment, and other organizational products.

- *The government market* consists of agencies and institutions at the federal, state, and local level. Government customers in the United States spend more than $1.5 trillion every year on the machinery, equipment, facilities, supplies, and services needed by the military, schools, hospitals, law enforcement agencies, public utilities, and so on.[12] Half of all government spending is done at the federal level. Governments in other countries are also significant markets for organizational goods and services.

- *The nonprofit market* consists of organizational customers in the nongovernment, not-for-profit sector. This market includes religious institutions, private hospitals, museums, most colleges and universities, civic clubs, charities, foundations, and political parties.

The final section in the chapter explores organizational buying behavior in more detail and contrasts it with consumer behavior, the subject of the following two sections.

Why People Buy

Consumers are influenced by forces that can be separated into three groups. *Psychological influences* encompass the complex emotions, motivations, attitudes, and other internal forces that lead people to make decisions. These psychological factors are themselves influenced from the outside by the remaining groups of forces. *Social and interpersonal influences* cover a wide variety of external pressures, including families, friends, ethnic groups, and co-workers. *Situational influences* stem from the circumstances surrounding a purchase, such as the time of the year or the reason for making a particular purchase. Naturally, financial resources —both cash and available credit—affect purchase behavior to a large extent as well. Many of us have psychological forces that would love to be satisfied with a Ferrari, but few of us have the financial resources to buy one.

PSYCHOLOGICAL INFLUENCES

Age, income, and the other demographic factors can provide a starting point for understanding an advertising audience, but such factors don't explain the thoughts and feelings that motiviate customer behavior (see Exhibit 4.3). A movie star doesn't buy a Rolls-Royce because she is rich. Her enormous income provides only the means to make the purchase; it isn't the driving force that influences her decision to buy. She may buy it because it supports the image she has of herself or because it makes her feel better about herself. The study of lifestyles, attitudes, motivations, personalities, and self-concepts as they relate to buyer behavior is called **psychographics.** In particular, psychographic analysis is used to *quantify* the thoughts and feelings that motivate human behavior.[13]

As with demographics, psychographic research has its limits; its strengths are balanced by some potential weaknesses. First, psychographic data are inherently

EXHIBIT 4.3

Psychological Influences in Advertising

This Norwegian ad for a national postal service makes a direct appeal to the consumer's emotions, one of the key psychological forces in advertising.

Uansett
hva du føler
er det
plass for det
i et brev.

Skriv litt oftere

Whatever
you may be feeling,
there is
room for it
in a letter.

Write more often.

EXHIBIT 4.4
Higher-Level Motivations

The appeal of this Ebel watch goes beyond mere function; it is a piece of jewelry and a statement of personal and financial success. (This ad is written primarily in Arabic and appeared in Saudi Arabian magazines.)

imprecise. You're either measuring what people say about their thoughts and feelings (so not only is the subject of your study vague and at times irrational, but you can't even measure it directly) or trying to infer from observation and other data why people behave as they do. In either case, results are sometimes open to the interpretation of the person conducting the research. Second, buyers of competing products often exhibit similar psychographic characteristics, giving you little information about how to form a distinctive advertising message. For instance, it's hard to imagine many profound intellectual or emotional differences in the way people feel about Coke and Pepsi. Third, research has uncovered cases in which the attitudes that people have toward various brands seem largely to be the result of previous advertising (not surprising when you think about it). This helps advertisers understand where their brands have been, psychographically speaking, but it doesn't always provide much help with charting future advertising directions.[14]

However, these potential shortcomings don't diminish the value of psychographics; they simply highlight the need for careful and thorough research. The psychological factors of most interest to advertising researchers are needs and motives, attitude and lifestyle, and personality and self-concept.

Needs and Motives

All purchases are driven by **needs,** which buyers sense as gaps between their current conditions and their ideal conditions. If you're hungry, you feel a need for food. If you sense a lack of excitement in your life, you might try to fill that need by purchasing a sports car, going bungee jumping, or signing up for a class in organic chemistry. These needs create **motives,** the internal factors that guide your behavior toward satisfying those needs. Your hunger, for instance, creates a motive to acquire and consume massive amounts of food.

In some cases, the needs that will generate sales of a particular product are easy to identify. To get to work or school, you might need a car; to make shoes, Nike needs leather, rubber, and the various other components that are part of a shoe. Sometimes consumers will make a semantic distinction between a *need* and a *want,* as in "I don't really need a $150 pair of shoes; I just want them." Researchers usually describe wants as the particular choices consumers make to satisfy their needs (as in needing shoes and wanting a pair of Nike Air Maxes).

Needs go far beyond the physical, a key advertising point that influences ad designs in many industries. The buyer's motivation often reflects needs other than the most basic and obvious (see Exhibit 4.4). In the strict physical sense of supporting your feet, you don't "need" a $150 pair of basketball shoes. Your need for physical comfort and protection could be filled just as well by a pair of $75 shoes or maybe even by a pair of $25 shoes (or at least very nearly as well, depending on how convinced you are about the value of high-tech sneakers). However, the $150 shoes fulfill another need, perhaps one for self-esteem or peer acceptance. Think about it; if athletic shoes were purchased only for function, Nike and Reebok wouldn't pay millions to superstar athletes like Shaquille O'Neal and Andre Agassi. Ads would simply show the shoes' features and explain why they are good for your feet.

This shoe issue demonstrates that there are various types of needs. Psychologist Abraham Maslow proposed that people are motivated to satisfy five categories of needs, from basic to aesthetic:[15]

- *Physiological needs* are for elements that ensure basic survival, such as food and shelter.
- *Safety needs* ensure a safe, secure life that is free from harm. You probably could survive without shoes, but you'll stay healthier with them.
- *Social needs* are for belonging and social interaction; they include the need for love, affection, and acceptance. Social needs are key factors throughout the fashion industry, including $150 basketball shoes; most of us want to be

accepted by our peers, and many of us perceive that acceptance as being dependent on dress and grooming.

- *Esteem needs* are for self-respect and personal recognition. These needs go beyond our more basic need for mere acceptance, encompassing our desire to achieve special recognition from friends and other people; having the most stylish shoes on the planet is important to many people.

- *Self-actualization needs* are for whatever will help us realize our full potential and further develop our personal capabilities. Many goods and services are advertised with self-actualization in mind. The U.S. Army's long-running campaign to "Be All You Can Be" is a good example, as is Nike's "Just Do It" slogan, which encourages people to get off the couch and improve themselves.

Maslow asserted that people must satisfy the more basic needs before they can progress up the hierarchy to higher-level needs such as self-esteem. Other researchers have suggested that people can pursue two or more categories at the same time and that the needs aren't in a hierarchy. In addition, the hierarchy exhibits a distinctly western bias that may not hold true in other parts of the world.[16] These particular arguments aside, Maslow's hierarchy is an important concept for advertisers because it emphasizes the range of needs that can influence buyer behavior and because it got a lot of people thinking about the complexity of human needs. At the very least, it shows that advertisers can promote products more effectively if they know where in the hierarchy they are most likely to appeal to customers (see Exhibit 4.5).

Some buyer motives can seem downright mysterious until psychographic researchers dig around and find the needs that create these motives. The advertising agency McCann-Erickson wanted to know why women were more apt to buy Raid roach spray rather than Combat insecticide disks in some parts of the country, even though the Combat product required far less effort to use. All the women queried by the agency viewed roaches as male creatures, and their feelings toward

Godiva, the Figure of the Woman on Horseback and the Gold Ballotin are registered trademarks.

EXHIBIT 4.5
Maslow's Hierarchy in Advertising

The need for love and social approval drives many consumer purchases, a fact not lost on successful advertisers such as Godiva.

the roaches were similar to their feelings toward a lot of the men in their lives. Some went so far as to equate the roach's habit of "only coming around when he wants food" to the behavior of these men. It turns out that actively spraying roaches and watching them die fulfilled a need for power and control, unlike the disks, where the women did nothing but wait.[17] This mindset may not be shared by all women, of course, but it certainly was a strong factor for these women.

Attitude and Lifestyle

Many aspects of buyer behavior are related to **attitude,** defined as a lasting, general evaluation of products, issues, companies, people, colors, and many other elements. Attitudes show up as tendencies to respond to ads or products in positive or negative ways. This is an important topic for advertisers because attitude can make or break products and companies.[18] You may have a negative attitude about a particular car model or fast-food chain, for instance. If enough people share your attitude, that manufacturer or that restaurant chain is headed for trouble. If you have a positive attitude, the advertiser is halfway to the finish line before it even starts. Every attitude has three components:[19]

- *The affective component* involves the audience's positive and negative feelings. Burger King's research uncovered negative feelings about the relentless consistency of fast food; even if consumers wouldn't actually request modifications to their hamburgers, they were displeased by the lack of choices. Burger King responded, first with the "Have It Your Way" ad campaign and later with the "Your Way, Right Away" campaign.[20]

- *The behavioral component* involves the audience translating its beliefs and feelings into action. The behavior may be buying a product, avoiding it, using it, or recommending it to others. Of course, simply having a positive attitude toward a product doesn't mean that a person will rush out to buy it; he or she may not need it, may not be able to afford it, may have other priorities, or may have to take other household or organization members into consideration.

- *The cognitive component* encompasses the beliefs and knowledge a person has about a particular subject, product, or organization. Sometimes customers develop inaccurate beliefs, acquire incorrect knowledge, or hang onto beliefs that are no longer valid, forcing the advertiser to try to change the cognitive component (see Exhibit 4.6). In other cases, the audience has more or less correct information, but the advertiser feels compelled to provide new information in an attempt to change the audience's attitude. When Sprint entered the

EXHIBIT 4.6
Changing the Cognitive Component

Karastan, a respected maker of high-quality rugs, wants consumers to view its products as an investment, not simply as another household expense.

Activities	Interests	Opinions	Demographics
Work	Family	Themselves	Age
Hobbies	Home	Social issues	Education
Social events	Job	Politics	Income
Vacations	Community	Business	Occupation
Entertainment	Recreation	Economics	Family size
Club membership	Fashion	Education	Dwelling
Community	Food	Products	Geographic
Shopping	Media	Future	City size
Sports	Achievements	Culture	Stage of life cycle

EXHIBIT 4.7
Defining Lifestyle

These dimensions help advertising researchers define the lifestyles of an audience. Advertisers use this information in many ways, ranging from how they depict people in ads to which media they choose in order to reach potential customers.

national long-distance market, for instance, its ads emphasized the reliability and quality of its fiber optic network. The goal was to convince consumers that Sprint was as good as or better than the much more familiar supplier, AT&T.

It's easy to remember the components of attitudes by thinking ABC: *a*ffective, *b*ehavioral, and *c*ognitive.

Attitudes figure prominently in **lifestyle,** which can be defined as a person's activities, interests, opinions, and consumption patterns.[21] Exhibit 4.7 shows the variables commonly used to define lifestyles. The basic approach of this type of research is to create an individual profile of various consumer types, according to their lifestyles. Various lifestyle researchers have devised different profiles, and lifestyle has proved to be one of the more reliable predictors of consumer behavior and is an important way to select target markets (as you'll see in Chapter 5).

Personality and Self-Concept

Another psychological element that has attracted the attention of advertising researchers is **personality,** a person's characteristic and consistent patterns of behavior.[22] Over the years, personality theorists have tried to categorize people according to a discrete number of personality "types" or on the basis of specific personality "traits." However, researchers have found little relationship between such categories and buying behavior. (Ironically, a more reliable application of personality concepts may be found in developing the personalities of particular brands, rather than trying to understand the personalities of people who buy them.[23])

It's likely that purchase behavior is driven less by personality and more by **self-concept,** which is the sum of the perceptions, beliefs, and feelings people hold about themselves. Self-concept encompasses four elements: how you see yourself, how others see you, how you really are, and what you would like to be.[24] Some purchases and possessions (such as clothing, cars, furniture, and houses) are more central to self-concept than others because they become extensions of yourself.[25] Advertisers of products that contribute strongly to self-image need to assess the self-concepts of their target customers and develop brand images that maintain or enhance those self-images.

The cosmetics and fashion industries provide classic examples of advertising to self-concept (see Exhibit 4.8). Most of us need to feel that we are attractive, and that is the need on which these industries base their ads. The forces at play in their advertising become obvious when you consider cases that step over the ethical edge. For instance, cellulite (a term coined by a beauty writer, not a medical specialist) appears to be a combination of fat cells and fibrous tissue that causes dimples in the skin. No independent scientific evidence supports the cosmetic industry's claim that some mysterious "toxins" are at work. However, ads that appeal to the self-concept of women with cellulite (over 90 percent of all women)

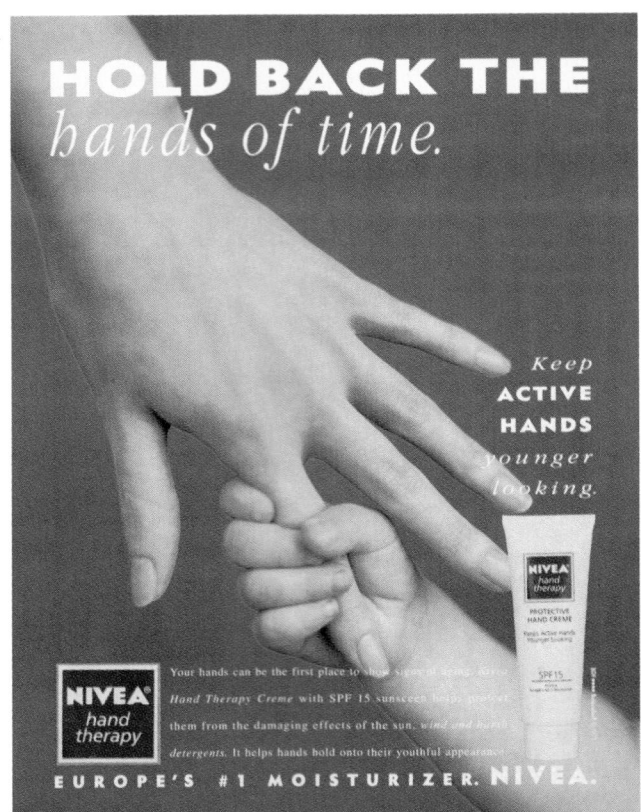

have convinced many consumers that cellulite is really a problem and that various lotions and creams can make the problem disappear. Complaints from consumer groups and government regulators have prompted these firms to back off from advertising that their products actually do very much, but that hasn't stopped the sale of $50 million worth of questionable potions every year.[26]

SOCIAL AND INTERPERSONAL INFLUENCES

Other people can be major influences on the way an individual responds to ads and on the purchase choices he or she makes. Four issues of top concern to advertisers are culture, social status, reference groups, and word-of-mouth communication. In addition, advertisers trying to reach families and other household groups need to address group buying behavior, which raises some special issues when more than one person is involved in the purchase decision.

Culture

The beliefs, values, and symbols that a society shares and passes from generation to generation constitute its **culture.** There is a French culture, a Japanese culture, and an Australian culture. Like most other countries, the United States also has many **cultural segments,** groups of people within a larger culture who share beliefs, values, and customs that differ, at least in some respects, from those of the overall society. Membership in a cultural segment (sometimes referred to as a *microculture*) can also affect buyer behavior.[27]

Chapter 8 is devoted to international and intercultural advertising, but here are some key points to consider. First, culture can influence audience and buyer behavior in ways that are obvious (e.g., the types of food that people buy) and in ways that are more subtle (e.g., responses to certain colors and images used in ads). Second, cultural mistakes can ruin an ad campaign, either by causing the ads to miss their target or by insulting or offending the audience. Third, behavioral patterns result in part from a culture's **core values,** those pervasive and enduring values shared by the people in that culture. A culture's core values define how products are used, determine whether products are seen negatively or positively, and delineate market relationships. In the United States, for example, core values include material comfort and well-being, progress, individualism, and freedom of expression and choice.[28]

Social Status

Social status is another important factor in buyer behavior. Every society has **social classes,** groups of people who share similar lifestyles, values, interests, and behaviors. Class distinctions are more pronounced in some countries than in others, but it's safe to say that class is a factor virtually all over the world. The desire to join (or stay in) a real or perceived class can affect an individual's purchase behavior regarding quality and style of clothing, homes and furniture, use of leisure time, choice of media, shopping habits and choices, and financial management patterns. As purchase behavior is affected, so is the response to advertising. An ad that appeals to living a status-conscious "good life" will strike a chord with people who have their social sights aimed upward; however, it might turn off those people who don't value status (see Exhibit 4.9).

Social class is determined primarily by occupation but is also based on income, education, possessions, personal success, social skills, community involvement, and other factors.[29] It's important to recognize that income and social class are separate influences on consumer behavior, and the two are not necessarily related.

Reference Groups

In addition to culture and social status, buyer behavior can be influenced by a **reference group,** which is one or more people who have a direct influence on the buyer's decision making.[30] There are three types of reference groups: those to

The Sulka Blazer.

For the man who knows the Concorde isn't a grape.

S   U   L   K   A

EXHIBIT 4.9
Appealing to Social Status

With the pun about people who don't know the difference between a grape and a supersonic airliner, Sulka reaches out to people who recognize and appreciate luxurious products.

BEHIND

EVERY GREAT MAN IS

A WOMAN

WHO'S ABOUT

TO PASS HIM.

Women's athletics are taking off. And with it, the sales of Nike women's shoes and apparel. Last year our sales were up nearly 20%. That's because all 369 pieces of apparel and all 171 different styles of shoes are designed not only to improve your customers' appearance, but, more importantly, their performance. Call your Nike representative now. Because women aren't following, they're taking the lead.

EXHIBIT 4.10
The Selling Power of Reference Groups

Nike uses ads like this one (this particular ad is aimed at retailers, not the general public) to appeal to women who want to be identified with performance and personal success.

which the individual belongs (such as a family, a club, or a cultural segment), those to which he or she aspires to belong, and those that he or she shuns (see Exhibit 4.10).

Reference groups influence people's decisions by providing information, by pressuring them to conform to group norms, or by offering a set of values for people to identify with and express.[31] The implication for advertisers is clear: if your customers are influenced by those groups, you'd better find a way to get those groups on your side. For example, using a celebrity in advertising assumes that the celebrity's endorsement will appeal to the target audience's desire to identify with that person.

Word-of-Mouth Communication

Sometimes a marketer's best—and worst—advertising comes from other customers. When the communication between customers and potential customers influences purchase decisions, the interaction is called **word of mouth.** This interaction can be especially influential for products that have to be experienced to be evaluated.[32] **Opinion leaders,** people who are knowledgeable about products and who command the attention and respect of other customers and potential customers, play a key role in the word-of-mouth process. You probably know someone (or you may be someone) whom people turn to when it's time to buy a computer, a car, or a vacation package. As with reference groups, advertisers should view opinion leaders as a key audience because they can increase the impact of the advertising message.

Household Buying Behavior

Buyer behavior takes on some new characteristics when a group of people in a household (whether a traditional family or some other combination) make the purchase decision. In households of two or more persons, many day-to-day purchases involve group decision making. This can be as simple as the family trying to decide where to go for dinner or something as important as what kind of car to buy or where to build a new house. Advertisers can benefit by understanding this group interaction. Research commissioned by Chrysler over 50 years ago showed that women "had significant input into the car-buying decision," and Chrysler increased its sales by modifying its ads to respond to this insight.[33] However,

Advertising is sometimes called *controlled communication* because advertisers control the timing, content, and distribution of the message. However, some of the most important communication with potential buyers is *uncontrolled communication,* messages over which advertisers have no direct control. Word of mouth is a good example.

In general, the more difficult it is for potential purchasers to evaluate a product before making a decision, the more important word of mouth can be. For instance, you can't sit through a movie at your local cinema and then decide whether or not you want to pay for it; you have to buy your ticket first. As a result, movies can get a big boost from positive word of mouth. Potential customers can relate to the experience of actual customers, particularly customers they already know and trust, which helps reduce the uncertainty of trying a new product or supplier.

Conversely, dissatisfied customers can destroy a business. Customers who aren't happy with the goods and services they purchase will also spread the word. If word gets around that people didn't like a movie, the film can fail quickly. Moreover, dissatisfied customers are likely to tell from 10 to 20 people about their bad experiences, whereas happy customers share their experiences with one-third as many people. Your ads may lose their impact for potential customers who heard from friends or neighbors that your product wasn't all it was cracked up to be.

What can you do to help ensure positive word of mouth? The possibilities fall into two categories: things that can be done through advertising and things that can't. One of the few ways that advertising can help with word of mouth is to target people whose opinions are respected by others. Product enthusiasts, people who take great interest in particular types of products, are a good example. Consumers in the market for cars, cameras, computers, and other complicated products often turn to enthusiasts for advice. A good way to reach enthusiasts with your advertising message is through specialized magazines such as *Fine Woodworking* or *Road & Track.* Enthusiasts are usually willing to read ads with long copy if the message gives them the information they want. Many of these magazines also highlight new products or product innovations that will appeal to enthusiasts. Software manufacturers such as Borland and Microsoft make a point of rushing advance copies of new program versions to computer magazines to test and review so that enthusiasts will be the first to know about the latest features.

More important than what you can do with advertising, however, is what you can't do with it. Above all else, the product must satisfy its intended market. Advertising can't overcome poor product performance or mistakes in customer service. Advertising isn't magic. The best way to get your customers to spread the good word about you is to make sure they are satisfied.

Apply Your Knowledge
1. Can you think of any ways to help satisfied customers and product enthusiasts spread your message?
2. How should you respond if your company or one of its products is suffering from negative word of mouth? Explain your answer.

somewhere in the last five decades, carmakers seem to have forgotten the role women play in car purchases, and the typical auto ad is designed to appeal largely to men. Mazda's marketing vice president Jan Thompson recognized this and sensed a marketing opportunity waiting for the company that targeted women buyers. By taking the macho edge off Mazda's advertising and using words and images that women find more appealing, she seized that opportunity and helped Mazda maintain strong sales in a weak automotive market (see Exhibit 4.11).[34]

Children also play an important role in family purchasing decisions and advertising to families and households. First, successful advertisers seek to better understand family decision making in order to develop more effective ads. Second, advertisers must be aware of the growing concern over advertising to children and the effect that such ads may have on family spending patterns. To see this issue plainly illustrated, hang around the cereal aisle at a nearby grocery store on a Saturday morning, when parents and their children are likely to be shopping together. Watch how often children demand particular brands, and determine whether those brands are linked to TV shows and whether they are heavily advertised.

SITUATIONAL INFLUENCES
The final group of influences on buyer behavior involves the circumstances surrounding the purchase. These **situational influences** can have a tremendous impact on buyer behavior, so it is important for advertisers to understand them. The situational influences affecting consumers can be grouped into five categories:

Before
There's something you should do before life hits you in the knees with ten bags

the spouse,
of groceries and the need for a garden hose. You should know how it feels to have

the house,
the sun on your head and a growl at your back as you flick through five gears

the kids,
with no more baggage than a friend. This has been known since the beginning of cars.

you get
Which is why roadsters were invented. The Mazda Miata. The roadster returned.

one chance.

mazda
IT JUST FEELS RIGHT*

The Mazda MX-5 Miata is backed by a 36-month/50,000-mile, no-deductible, bumper-to-bumper limited warranty. See dealer for details. For a free brochure: 1-800-639-1000 © 1993 Mazda Motor of America, Inc.

EXHIBIT 4.11
New Advertising Directions at Mazda

Advertising for sports cars typically adopts a man's point of view, but Mazda used a different approach here. The ad is clearly aimed at women and addresses key issues in the lives of many women.

physical surroundings, social surroundings, temporal perspective, task definition, and antecedent state:[35]

- *Physical surroundings* are the location, weather, sounds, aromas, lighting, decor, and other factors that make up the physical situation in which consumers are exposed to products, purchase them, or use them. One way advertisers can use such information is by presenting products in surroundings that are most like the consumer's real or desired surroundings. For instance, manufacturers of sport utility vehicles such as the Ford Explorer often create ads that show the vehicle being used in a beautiful mountain setting and in other places that prospective buyers would like.

- The *social surroundings* of a situation consist of the other people who are present when a product is purchased or consumed. For instance, when entertaining influential guests, consumers often buy better-quality or trendier foods than they would normally eat; an advertiser of such products would want to take this fact into account. To promote a gourmet food item, you might create an ad that shows the food being served at an elegant dinner party, for example.

- The *temporal perspective* is not only the amount of time available for consumers to learn about, shop for, or use a product; it is also the amount of time since the product was last used, the amount of time until payday, the time of day, and the time of year (see Exhibit 4.12). For example, 80 percent of all bicycle purchases are made between May and August, but many buyers make up their minds over the winter, when they have more time to consult other owners and peruse advertisements.[36] As a result, a bicycle maker armed with such information might choose to run ads in the middle of winter, when people are thinking about which brands to buy the following summer.

KID: Mom, Dad, um, I don't wanna go back to school this year.

MOM & DAD: And what do you propose to do instead, Timmy?

KID: Well, ya know how I've always liked those karate movies?

MOM & DAD: Yes, Timmy. And we've always encouraged your interest in violence.

KID: Well, instead of school, I wanna go to Tibet and study Ti Chuan Shi so someday I can kick butt in movies, while retaining foreign syndication rights.

MOM & DAD: Timmy!

KID: Okay, how 'bout Nepal. You can visit. They just got a sewerage system there, running water, the works . . .

VO: Who you kiddin'. Ya gotta go back. So go to Foot Locker and get the shoes, the shorts, the T's you want to look cool for back to school. Foot Lockers's Back to School Sale. Now that's something to look forward to.

EXHIBIT 4.12

The Element of Time in Audience Behavior

Foot Locker recognizes key shopping periods during the year, as it demonstrates in this radio ad aimed at the fall back-to-school shoppers.

- *Task definition* is the reason the buyer is seeking information about buying or using a product. For example, items chosen as gifts depend on the reason for the gift and on the relation of the recipient to the giver (a woman might buy silk pajamas for her husband but not for her boss). Such factors need to be considered when ads are designed and placed, so that you portray products in ways that fit the customer's ways of using them.

- The *antecedent state* is the consumer's state of mind before and during a purchase. Mood, for instance, can prompt on-the-spot purchase decisions, and the advertiser who has already staked out a place in the consumer's mind has the best chance of getting these impulse sales.

Even though advertising researchers have compiled extensive information about consumer behavior, it's important not to assume that purchasing is always predictable or even rational, at least in ways that are obvious to outside observers. For instance, some purchases are made on the spot with no forethought at all. Also, it's not unusual for people to make particular purchases for the sake of variety. You've probably tried a new restaurant or other retail facility just because you were bored with the places you've been frequenting.

How People Buy

Now that you have a basic grasp of why people buy, the next step is understanding *how* they buy—a process that involves perception, learning, and decision making.

PERCEPTION

The only way an audience can get your advertising message is through **perception,** the process of being *exposed* to a stimulus, paying *attention* to some degree, and then *interpreting* the received message. Success at each step is crucial to effective advertising (see Exhibit 4.13). Competitors are struggling to get their messages to the same audiences, and audiences routinely misinterpret, confuse, or ignore messages, so success is never assured.

Of course, the process must start with exposure to the message, which is why advertisers spend millions to insert messages between segments of your favorite TV show, paste ads on the sides of buses, hang billboards inside sports stadiums,

... monster suction.
Vampire 791i.

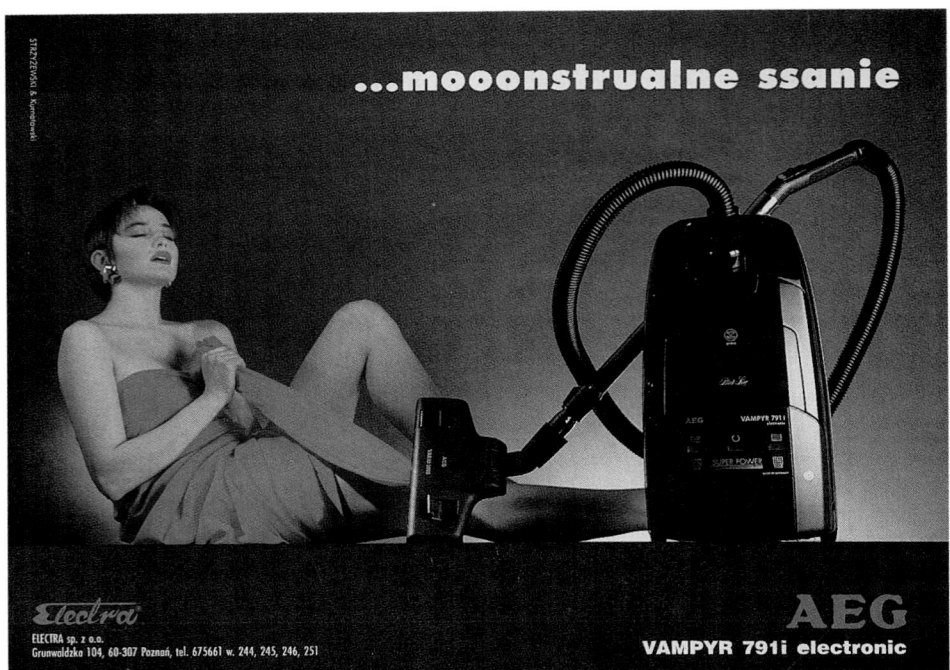

EXHIBIT 4.13
Successful Visual Stimuli in Advertising

The German manufacturer AEG provides a graphic illustration of the inhaling powers of its line of vacuum cleaners; this ad ran in Polish consumer magazines.

and have their products consumed by actors in movies. **Exposure** is the process of presenting ads to audiences, and as you'll see in Chapter 13, exposure is a key factor in media planning. Advertisers keep finding new media to carry their messages, in the hope that the right audiences will encounter them. Some media give people the option of being exposed to advertising stimuli; you can always hit the mute button on your TV remote control, for instance. Other media, such as outdoor billboards, are sometimes harder to miss, although successful exposure is influenced by weather, traffic, and other elements that the advertiser can't control.

Mere exposure to a stimulus doesn't guarantee that people will pay attention to it, however. The typical advertising audience is overloaded with messages from advertisers. This often prompts people to choose which stimuli to attend to, a behavior known as **selective perception.** Studies suggest that people notice fewer than 15 percent of the ads they are exposed to, which should give you an idea of how hard it can be to communicate an advertising message successfully.[37] To improve their odds, advertisers try various approaches, including making message stimuli particularly relevant, novel, or unexpected or making them larger, more colorful, louder, or otherwise more intense than competing stimuli (see Exhibit 4.14 on pages 100–101).

Assuming that the audience has been exposed to a message and has paid attention to it, the advertiser still has to clear the hurdle of correct interpretation. One study found that an average of 30 percent of television communications (both commercial and noncommercial) were miscomprehended.[38] In another study, the marketing research firm R. H. Bruskin Associates found that 60 percent of respondents recognized the phrase "Never let them see you sweat," but only 4 percent connected this slogan with Dry Idea deodorant, the brand in the advertising campaign.[39] In addition to the message content and the quality of presentation, interpretation is affected by the audience's needs, motives, experiences, and expectations; the context or situation in which the message is received; and the order in which related stimuli are received. Advertisers can increase their interpretation odds by keeping several key points in mind:[40]

- People tend to organize perceptions into simple patterns.
- People tend to focus on a single aspect of a situation (called the *figure*) and to treat the rest as background (called the *ground*).

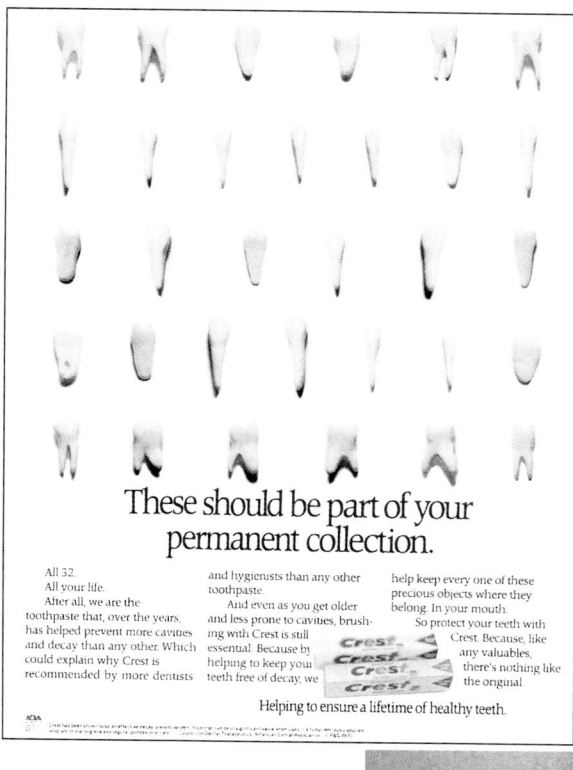

These should be part of your permanent collection.

All 32.
All your life.
After all, we are the toothpaste that, over the years, has helped prevent more cavities and decay than any other. Which could explain why Crest is recommended by more dentists and hygienists than any other toothpaste.
And even as you get older and less prone to cavities, brushing with Crest is still essential. Because by helping to keep your teeth free of decay, we help keep every one of these precious objects where they belong. In your mouth.
So protect your teeth with Crest. Because, like any valuables, there's nothing like the original.

Helping to ensure a lifetime of healthy teeth.

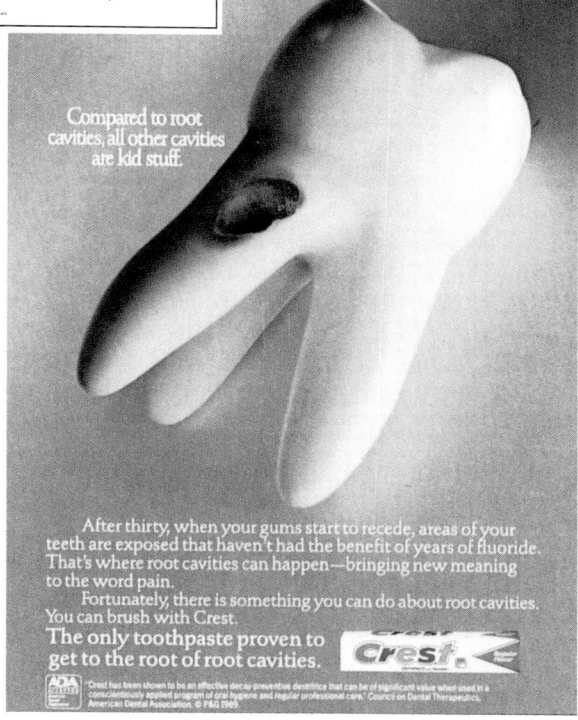

Compared to root cavities, all other cavities are kid stuff.

After thirty, when your gums start to recede, areas of your teeth are exposed that haven't had the benefit of years of fluoride. That's where root cavities can happen—bringing new meaning to the word pain.
Fortunately, there is something you can do about root cavities. You can brush with Crest.
The only toothpaste proven to get to the root of root cavities.

The Starch readership test is one of the most common ways that advertisers use to measure the effectiveness of the ads they create. Starch tests magazine ads for performance at three levels: how many people noted that the ad was in the magazine (the Noted score), how many associated the ad with the right brand/advertiser (the Associated score), and how many read most of the ad (the Read Most score). Starch also compares each ad's scores with the other ads that it tests from the same product category, so advertisers get some idea of how they stack up against competitors.

Here and in six other chapters throughout the book, you'll get to test your analysis skills against the Starch surveys and other readership tests. For the Starch tests, you'll be shown a pair of ads and asked which one you think had higher Starch Read Most scores. Your instructor has the actual Starch scores, along with some commentary on why particular ads scored the way they did.

The two Crest ads shown here take different approaches to communicating with the audience. One relies on a collection of small images and gentle copy that reminds you about the need to brush. The other uses a single dramatic picture and doesn't pull any punches when talking about pain. Based on what you've learned about audience behavior and on your own reaction to the ads, which do you think was more effective, and how do you think both compared with the average for the product category? Be prepared to explain your answers.

- People tend to relate things that are close together physically or temporally. Coca-Cola, for example, does not advertise on TV news shows for fear of associating its upbeat products with the bad news inevitable on such programs.[41]
- People tend to fill in missing parts in a stimulus, a behavior called **closure.** This can involve supplying words to fill out a phrase, images to complete a picture, or sounds to complete melodies or other patterns. Closure can help get people more involved with an advertising message because they have to think in order to supply the missing parts of the message.

CHAPTER 4
Audience Analysis and Buyer Behavior

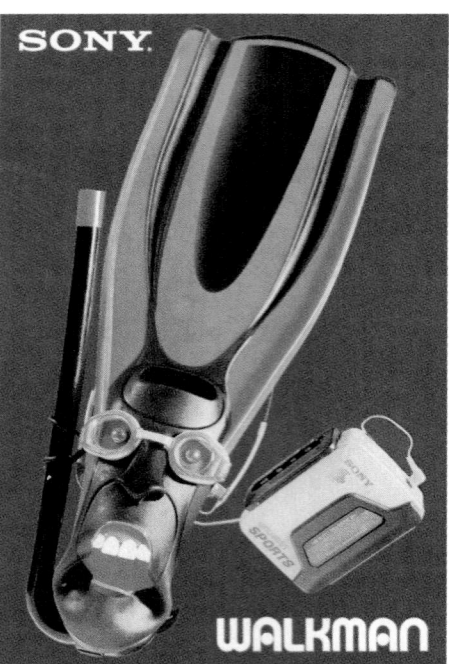

Advertisers can capitalize on all these perceptual tendencies to increase the effectiveness of their advertisements.

LEARNING

Advertisers are keenly interested in theories about human learning because learning is central to the whole idea of persuading people to change their purchase behavior. **Learning** can be formally defined as any change in the contents of a person's long-term memory or in the way those contents are organized, particularly as those changes relate to changes in behavior.[42] Two general classes of theories, cognition and conditioning, help explain how buyers respond to advertising and make purchase decisions.

- **Cognition** is learning through mental activity. According to this theory, buyers treat purchase decisions as problems to be solved. The buyers process informational inputs (advertising messages), combine these with information retrieved from memory (good and bad experiences with products and suppliers), and reach conclusions by weighing the mix of information available.[43] The fact that buyers combine information from various sources emphasizes the benefit of integrated marketing communications: the more coherent and unified your messages are, the better chance you have of leading prospects to choose your product.

- **Conditioning** is learning to respond in a certain way to a given stimulus. *Classical* conditioning theory asserts that by repeatedly associating stimulus X with stimulus Y, the advertiser can evoke the same response from X that is associated with Y.[44] This is why advertisers often incorporate popular songs (or the melodies of pop songs with new words) in TV and radio commercials; they want their products to evoke the same responses that the songs evoke. In contrast, *instrumental* conditioning is more a case of learning by trial and error. Buyers who are satisfied with one brand will tend to keep using it, whereas dissatisfaction prompts buyers to avoid brands. This highlights the importance of product quality and customer satisfaction; the cleverest ads imaginable won't convince people to keep using products that have failed them in the past.

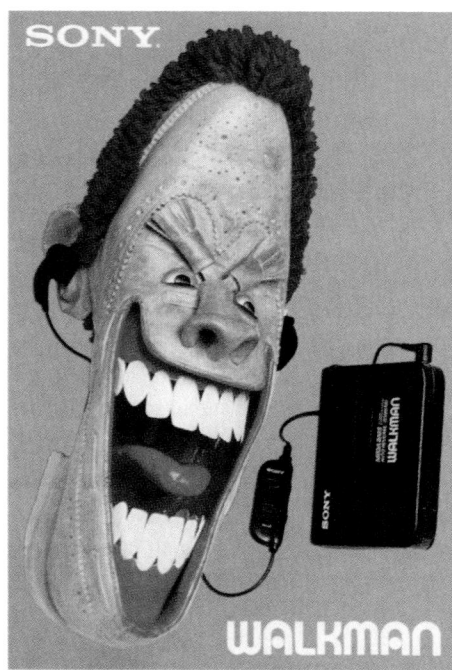
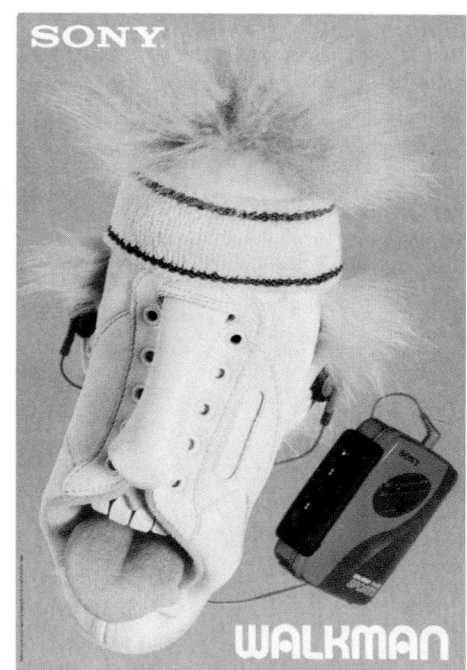

DECISION MAKING

Whether a purchase involves a new shirt or a cargo ship, both rational and nonrational elements are usually at work in the purchase decision. Cars are a good example of this. The choice you make usually involves some rational factors (such as mileage, reliability, size, cost) and some not so rational factors (such as what your friends will think or how you'll feel driving the car). Also, the more important the decision is to you, both emotionally and logically, the more involved you are likely to get in the purchase process. A homeowner might shop over a period of several weeks for a sofa or other piece of furniture, but not for fill dirt for the backyard—even though the purchase might cost roughly the same.

Some buyer perceptions, learning patterns, and decisions can be more easily understood by placing them in a purchasing model. The rational decision-making model can involve up to six major steps, although not all purchases cover all six steps. In some cases, the buyer bypasses one or more steps, for a variety of reasons. In general, the more expensive, complex, and important the product, the more time buyers spend on the purchase process.[45]

Step 1: Recognize a Need

In the rational model, a buyer's first step toward a purchase is recognizing a need, which means that the buyer perceives a discrepancy between a desired state and an actual state. This discrepancy can be as simple as craving a salad at lunchtime or realizing that your factory's paint robots aren't fast enough for your auto assembly line. Of course, the discrepancy must be significant enough to activate the decision process, or no purchase will be made.[46]

Successful advertisers know that need recognition can be triggered from two directions, either from a decline in the buyer's actual state (e.g., your car keeps breaking down) or from an increase in the buyer's desired state (e.g., you just saw an ad for a splendid new car that you simply must have). In addition, the issue of time and future conditions plays a role in recognizing a need. This is the whole idea behind insurance, for example: in anticipation of a possible future decline in your actual state, you purchase some form of insurance. An ad for Unum's disability insurance urges people to consider that "sometime in the not-too-distant future you

The Nonrational Side of Decision Making

Not all purchases are made as logically as the rational decision-making model suggests. In fact, many purchases seem downright illogical to an outside observer, and it's important to understand how these nonrational elements affect decision making and responses to advertising. Even organizational purchasing, with its specifications, procedures, and controls, isn't always completely rational. Here are some factors that can affect purchasing behavior and cause it to be less than totally logical:

- *Feeling and intuition.* Particularly when competing products are close in terms of price and quality, decisions can be swayed by how confident the buyer is in the seller. A feeling that deserves special attention is fear. For consumers, fears can range from physical safety to social acceptance. For organizational customers, fears range from peer humiliation all the way up to job security. Buyers in the computer industry often used the phrase "nobody ever got fired for buying IBM," implying that it was always a safe career move to go with a well-known supplier, even in cases where other products might be technically superior.

- *Impulse buying.* How many times have you walked out of a store with some item that you had no intention of buying when you walked in? Such is the nature of impulse buying, when the buyer sees a product and buys it on the spot. Procedures and policies tend to limit impulse buying in organizations, but consumers don't usually have such constraints.

- *Information overload.* One of the ironies of the Information Age is a decrease in the quality of decision making that sometimes occurs when people have *too much* information. Particularly in the consumer market, buyers are often bombarded with so much advertising information that they no

longer try to organize and process it all. They begin to rely on perceptions formed by bits and pieces of information they've gathered here and there, rather than relying on coherent, complete messages.

- *Postdecision rationalization.* Buyers have often made up their minds before they even begin a "buying process." They continue through the steps of collecting and evaluating information, often to confirm their initial hunches or to sell their ideas to members of the family or the organizational buying center. Sometimes an effective ad can clinch a sale immediately, even for a buyer who appears to continue to evaluate alternatives before making the purchase.

Harley-Davidson is a good example of an advertiser that recognizes the nonrational side of buyer decision making. In fact, the company's ads even play up the idea. One print ad showed a new, exquisitely polished Harley parked next to an old, tiny trailer house. The obvious conclusion was that this person spent a lot more on the Harley than on the house, not a choice that all consumers would make. The headline said it all: "It's Not a Rational Decision."

These nonrational aspects of decision making highlight the supreme importance of understanding your advertising audience. Only by knowing who the people in your audience are, why they buy what they buy, and how they reach those purchase decisions will you be successful in tomorrow's competitive markets.

Apply Your Knowledge

1. Are there advertising situations in which you should probably not use the approach in the Harley-Davidson ad? Explain your answer.
2. How might you address the issues of emotion and nonrational decision making in an ad for factory automation equipment?

---

could find yourself called upon to provide for your parents, just as they once provided for you."[47] The message here is that your financial situation may be fine now, but if you need to care for your parents later in life, you should think about adding special insurance to help.

Step 2: Collect and Analyze Information

In some cases, the buyer recognizes a need but isn't aware of all possible solutions or perhaps of any solutions. In other cases, a solution is presented before the buyer even perceives a need. Such was the case for most buyers when the personal computer first hit the market; many people didn't think they needed one. Only when people began to understand what a computer could do for them did they develop the need to have one—a case of raising the buyer's notion of the ideal state.

The buyer's next move is to gather information about potential solutions. Part of this information search is external, but part is internal, and the buyer's memory can be a key aspect of the process: First, the best advertising in the world won't win over buyers who were dissatisfied the last time they tried your product. On the

INTRODUCING THE RE-DESIGNED, RE-CALIBRATED, RE-ENGINEERED, RE-INVENTED BMW 3-SERIES.

In today's volatile economy, even people of means are asking a question that should alarm the world's automobile makers: "Just what makes this car worth the money?"

The new BMW 325i sedan, however, welcomes such scrutiny. Because not only does it embody the traditional BMW passion for driving, it offers a whole set of more practical-minded virtues—most notably safety, durability and ease of maintenance.

It represents eight years of intensive thought from every automotive discipline. An effort unlike any in BMW's history.

THE NEXT BEST THING TO A CAR THAT MAINTAINS ITSELF.

At the heart of the 325i is a new 189-hp, 24-valve engine so advanced that it requires little regular maintenance beyond the changing of oil, filters and plugs. Its sophisticated electronics incorporate a "black box" system that can play back past engine events for the BMW technician, revealing problems that might otherwise be difficult to detect. Or even describe.

THE 325i IMPACT-ACTIVATED SAFETY SYSTEM.

BMW has always held that the greatest safety feature is a car that enhances the driver's ability to avoid accidents in the first place. Thus, BMW's historic excellence in the areas of suspension, steering and advanced antilock brake technology.

But, in the event that you are unable to avoid a frontal impact, the 325i is also designed to launch an entire sequence of events to help minimize injuries.

Hydraulic bumpers absorb a part of the impact energy. A system of "crush tubes" absorbs yet more. The seat belts tighten their grip. Three sensors trigger the driver's-side airbag. Interior lights are automatically turned on and the doors are unlocked, to assist in escape or rescue.

A SAFE CAR NEEDN'T BE A BORING ONE.

The unique driving character of the original 3-Series is not only alive in the new 325i sedan, but substantially enhanced.

The rear suspension is so unlike other cars in its class, it's patented. Resulting in improved stability in hard cornering, and a better grip of the road overall.

When it comes to comfort, the 325i is now longer, taller and wider than before. It has firmly supported seats. Left and right temperature controls, to allow for individual preferences. Even a microfiltration system that removes dust, pollen and most odors from the interior air.

Of course, the 325i is also equipped with BMW's four-year/ 50,000-mile bumper-to-bumper warranty, for protection against unexpected expenses, as well as a Roadside Assistance program you can call upon any day of the year, on any road in the U.S.A.

If you would like to receive literature on the new 3-Series, or be connected directly to your nearest BMW dealer, you need only call 800-334-4BMW.

We also invite you to stop in for a test drive, so you can find out what makes the 325i sedan worth the money from the best vantage point of all: the driver's seat.

THE ULTIMATE DRIVING MACHINE.

If peer pressure has kept you from getting a Saab, get new peers.

Too bad you're a grown-up. Who'll tell you to stop doing something dumb when everybody else does it?

Please let us. "Just because your friends throw away money to strike a pose in a car, it doesn't mean you should."

There. Now you're free to get the best performance, handling and safety your money can buy, with absolutely no fear of getting beat up on by your buddies. Get yourself a Saab.

The turbocharged Saab 9000 CD shown here, for example, is quicker than most European cars near its price ($32,995*) and many cars far costlier. (Saabs are intelligently priced from $16,995 to $32,995.) The gang will be genuinely irritated to learn this.

Saabs handle with the best Europe has to offer. But front-wheel drive helps them do this in bad weather as well as good. This will irk your neighbors, when you make tracks while they make ruts.

Saabs are very safe cars. For five years running they've ranked best in their class, according to the Highway Loss Data Institute. Better than that other Swedish car. This shocks everybody.

The 9000 CD (and all 1990 Saabs) comes with driver's air bag, ABS brakes and new Roadside Assistance Program, standard. It also comes with incredible roominess. Which will amaze your cronies who ride in it.

Test drive a Saab soon. Take one home and irritate, irk, shock and amaze your peers. But who cares?

We've been doing that for years. And we're not the least bit sorry.

The most intelligent cars ever built.

*MSRP including taxes, license, freight, dealer charges and options. Prices subject to change.

WHICH AD PULLED BETTER?

Now try your hand at a pair of automobile ads. You'll notice several differences that may affect ad performance. The BMW ad is a two-page spread with significantly more copy than the Saab ad. The Saab ad, however, has a photo that some people might see as more exciting and energetic. BMW went with a lighter style of type and also broke the type up with three subheads. One ad put the copy above the picture, while the other put it below.

Which do you think was more effective, and how do you think both compared with the average for the product category? Be prepared to explain your answers.

---

other hand, satisfied buyers may need only a gentle reminder from an advertisement to make another purchase. Second, buyers aren't always ready to buy when they see ads, so an ad that sticks in the buyer's memory can keep selling long after the ad itself is gone. Third, positive memories of a particular product may keep the buyer from ever bothering to look for alternatives.

Advertising can be a major factor in the buyer's external information search, provided the advertiser understands what kind of information buyers are looking for and where they are looking for it (see Exhibit 4.15). A person looking for a mutual fund needs a different amount of information than someone looking for a new perfume. A recent ad in the upscale magazine *Travel & Leisure* promoting Yves Saint Laurent's Opium perfume contained little verbal information: only the brand name, company name, a note that it's available at Nordstrom, and the subtitle "The new eau de parfum." The ad contains powerful visual information,

EXHIBIT 4.15
Information Content in Advertising

Mitsubishi goes against the usual grain in consumer advertising by packing this ad with technical information.

however, from a close-up shot of the distinctive container to the richly decorated room in the background. Compare this with an ad in *Money* for T. Rowe Price's Equity Income Fund, which offered a full page of text packed with information about annual returns and investment strategy. (In some cases, lots of text in an ad impresses buyers, not because of any technical content but simply because so much information is presented.[48]) The luxuriously colorful Opium ad and the starkly black-and-white Equity Income Fund ad differ greatly in terms of information content, but each does a great job of delivering the right information at the right time, in a place where the right people (likely buyers) will be looking.[49]

Step 3: Evaluate Potential Solutions

With information in hand, buyers then work through the possible solutions to their need, looking for the best choice in terms of price, quality, reputation, and whatever other factors they deem important. Again, advertising plays an important role, through logical and emotional appeals. As Exhibit 4.16 shows, the advertiser has to survive three stages of evaluation and elimination. The first is simply to be known to the prospective buyer, a process of building *awareness* for a brand or company. The second is to be considered acceptable and to be remembered when the buyer is moving toward a purchase. Brands falling into this fortunate category are called the **evoked set,** those products that are "finalists" in the evaluation process. The third stage is to be selected from the evoked set; those brands that aren't chosen make up the *inert set.*[50]

If you're an advertiser and your brand wasn't chosen, you ended up in one of the four "dead-end" positions in Exhibit 4.16. Which dead end you ran into determines what you need to do to move toward winning. The tasks of making sure buyers both know about you and remember you can often be solved through advertising and other promotional efforts. The other challenges, being considered acceptable and then being considered the most attractive of the acceptable group, may require modifications to the product, lower prices, or some other change to the marketing mix, or they may require advertising that does a better job of communicating your product's strong points.

It's important to realize when buyers make their decisions. For most consumer goods, the great majority of purchases are not planned very far in advance. Studies show that 66 percent of purchasing decisions are made right in the store.[51] This highlights the importance of in-store advertising, free in-store samples, and prod-

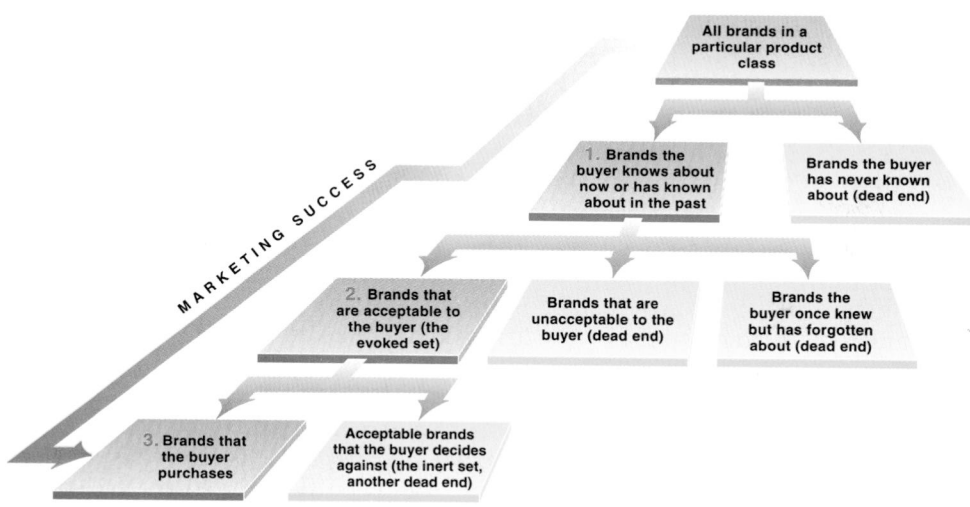

All brands in a particular product class

1. Brands the buyer knows about now or has known about in the past

Brands the buyer has never known about (dead end)

2. Brands that are acceptable to the buyer (the evoked set)

Brands that are unacceptable to the buyer (dead end)

Brands the buyer once knew but has forgotten about (dead end)

3. Brands that the buyer purchases

Acceptable brands that the buyer decides against (the inert set, another dead end)

MARKETING SUCCESS

EXHIBIT 4.16

Winning the Product Selection Contest

Advertisers have several hurdles to overcome before making a sale: being known, being acceptable, and being the most attractive of the acceptable alternatives.

uct packaging. It doesn't mean regular advertising isn't important, though; advertising messages will still be swirling through consumers' conscious and subconscious minds as they stand in the store making decisions.

Also, advertisers in many product categories frequently find themselves competing with their potential customers. This can happen whenever buyers have the option of creating the good or performing the service themselves. Buyers face a **make/buy decision** in which they evaluate the costs and benefits of doing something themselves relative to paying someone else. Homeowners, for instance, make such decisions often, particularly with services such as painting and landscaping.

Step 4: Select and Evaluate Potential Suppliers

In many product categories, the buyer has to decide not only which product to buy but also where to buy it. This is especially true in retailing, where a given product might be available from half a dozen stores inside the same mall. It's also important to realize that steps 3 and 4 in this model are often done in reverse order or even simultaneously. Instead of saying, "I want to buy a Ralph Lauren shirt; I wonder who might have one on sale," you'll often say, "I want a new shirt; let's go to Nordstrom or Parisian and see what they have."

National advertising can build demand for a particular product, but local advertising is often the key to steering buyers to particular suppliers. Say you live in Seattle and an ad in *Fortune* magazine for Pontiac's new Bonneville has caught your eye. This ad has moved you toward a Pontiac product, but you now have the additional step of selecting the supplier, in this case, the auto dealer. Looking in the auto section of *The Seattle Times,* you see an ad from a Pontiac dealer that promises discounts of up to $5,000.[52] This really catches your attention, and maybe you won't even bother to check the yellow pages to see whether there are other Pontiac dealers in your area. The one-two punch of national and local advertising led you to this dealer.

Step 5: Make the Purchase

Making the actual purchase is a simple step in some cases, not so simple in others. Particularly with large purchases, the buyer and seller must work out delivery, payment terms, installation, and so forth. Advertising can continue to play a role at this stage. For example, a significant delay between the purchase decision and the actual purchase can allow competitive advertisements to change the buyer's mind. Sometimes the buyer may have second thoughts and back away from the purchase entirely. However, if your advertising continues to provide positive input, the sale might be saved.

Step 6: Evaluate the Outcome

Whether they undertake a formal evaluation process or simply live with the product, customers evaluate the outcome of their purchases. Organizational customers such as Ford, for example, use standardized performance criteria to evaluate key suppliers. Consumers tend to be much less formal with their evaluations, but they evaluate nonetheless. In the United States, one-third of all households have had trouble with a purchase, and roughly one-quarter of all purchases result in dissatisfaction.[53] As already mentioned, dissatisfied customers are much more likely to tell others, creating negative word of mouth. Whether the object of their displeasure is a movie, a vacation destination, or a new home, word of mouth can be much more powerful than advertising. If you're an advertiser whose products are not satisfying customers, don't try to fix the problem with more advertising; fix the product first.

Buyers often experience **cognitive dissonance,** a sense of discomfort or doubt created by knowing that there were other choices and not knowing for sure whether one of the other choices might have been better. (When you started college, did you wonder whether you had chosen the right school?) Dissonance, also known as *buyer's remorse,* is more likely to occur when the decision has been important and difficult and when the outcome is difficult to change, such as choosing a college or buying a home. Advertising can help buyers overcome dissonance if it continues to reinforce the reasons for making a particular choice.

Organizational Buying Behavior

The behavior exhibited by organizations when they make purchases—and the advertising implication of that behavior—is similar in many respects to consumer buying behavior. Both types of customers have needs for a variety of products and look for ways to satisfy those needs. Exhibit 4.17 summarizes the major differ-

---

EXHIBIT 4.17   Consumer and Organizational Audiences

Consumer and organizational audiences are alike in many respects but quite different in others. There are general tendencies, but every generality has its exceptions.

Characteristic	Consumer Market	Organizational Market
Acceptable level of risk in purchase decisions	Depends on consumer	Tends to be low
Role of emotion and logic in purchase decisions	Varies, but emotion often plays a dominant role	Decisions tend to be more logical, but emotions still play a strong role in most decisions
Number of buyers for a given type of product	Varies; can run into the millions	Also varies, but number tends to be much smaller
Primary promotional method	Advertising	Personal selling
Buyer-seller relationship	Usually impersonal, though not always	Often close and personal
Nature of buying process	Tends to be flexible and casual	Tends to be structured and professional
Number of people involved in purchase decision	Often only one; several family members at most	Usually involves more than one person and can involve up to several dozen
Time spent on decisions	Tends to be rather small amount in comparison	Major decisions can take years of analysis and evaluation; impulse purchases quite rare
Motivation behind purchases	Personal satisfaction	Economics, generally speaking

ences. Although organizational buyers are sometimes characterized as logical and "businesslike," this isn't strictly true; even the most seemingly logical purchase can involve beliefs, emotions, and other psychological factors that are far from "logical."[54] To better understand organizational behavior, several important topics are examined here: organizational buying centers, derived demand, information collection and analysis, and supplier selection procedures.

ORGANIZATIONAL BUYING CENTERS

The decision-making process in an organization is performed by the **buying center,** those people within an organization who are significantly involved in the buying process for a particular good or service. The buying center is not a formalized group or location, although parts of it are permanently organized in purchasing departments, procurement offices, and other groups that specialize in buying. In its largest sense, the buying center is a communication network that sometimes varies from purchase to purchase, that sometimes even evolves during the purchasing process, and that differs from organization to organization.[55] The advertiser's challenge is to get the right message to the people in the six key buying center roles (note than one person can play more than one role at a time):

- The *initiators* identify a problem or need that could be resolved by purchasing a good or service.
- *Influencers* have input into whether a purchase is made, what will be bought, and what company it will be bought from.
- *Decision makers* make the actual yes-or-no decision about the purchase and choose or approve the product and supplier.
- *Gatekeepers,* such as receptionists and purchasing agents, control the flow of information in the buying center.
- *Purchasers,* usually called purchasing agents or buyers, actually order the product.
- *Users* ultimately use the product being purchased; at times they may be the initiators, and sometimes they have little say in the eventual decision.[56]

Identifying the roles in a customer's buying center is a key step in planning effective advertising because people in the various buying center roles have different information needs and purchase issues. When an organization buys important computer software, such as an accounting system, computer specialists (influencers) will want to know about technical capabilities and other details, while top executives (decision makers) will want to know about the potential return on the investment, the supplier's reputation, customer support, and other less technical factors.

DERIVED DEMAND

Of all the differences between consumer and organizational buyer behavior, perhaps the most important is the idea of **derived demand,** which means that the demand for product X is driven by the demand for product Y. With the exception of military products and certain other governmental purchases, the demand for all products sold to organizations is ultimately driven by demand in the consumer sector.[57] Say you work in the commercial airplane division of Boeing and you're trying to market the company's newest airliner. The harsh truth of your job is that there is basically nothing you can do to increase the level of demand from the airlines; you won't be able to sell more aircraft than the airlines think they can use to meet the demands of their passengers. You might be able to outmarket competitors to sell more planes, of course, but the total number of planes sold to the airlines isn't going to change until the airlines think passenger loads are going to increase.

On the other hand, if you work for the Hawaii Visitor's Bureau, you can use enticing advertising to convince people who would otherwise stay at home to take vacations in Hawaii. Hawaii can increase demand at the consumer level (vacation

Meeting an Advertising Challenge at American Express

A CASE FOR CRITICAL THINKING

To better understand the traveling public, American Express's Roger Ballou commissioned the Gallup Organization, a major polling and research firm, to survey more than 6,500 travelers in the United States, West Germany (the project was started before the two Germanies reunited), Japan, and the United Kingdom. Gallup uncovered five attitude segments, which it labeled Adventurers, Worriers, Dreamers, Economizers, and Indulgers. Each group has its own reasons for traveling, and each wants different things from the money it spends on traveling. Now Ballou and his colleagues at American Express have a clearer idea of who their audience is and how to advertise to the various subgroups in that audience.

Adventurers (23 percent of all travelers) want to meet new people, see new places, and try new experiences. Travel plays a key role in their lives, and they travel frequently. Twenty percent, in fact, had taken five or more trips within the previous year. They avoid group tours because they love to be independent and in control. Roughly half of German travelers are in this group.

Worriers (13 percent of all travelers) represent the opposite extreme in many respects. They lack the confidence of the Adventurers, and travel experiences aren't that important to them. They are far less likely to travel

by commercial airline, and travel in general is a source of stress and anxiety for them.

Dreamers (17 percent of all travelers) seem to get the most out of travel before actually going anywhere. In other words, they enjoy reading about and talking about travel and believe that it can add to their lives. However, their actual experiences tend to be less ambitious; their trips are usually simple and designed more for relaxation than for adventure.

Economizers (18 percent of all travelers) aren't into adventure, and they certainly don't feel it's worth paying extra to be pampered. They travel to relax, to get a break from life, not to explore or live it up. This group's behavior is not necessarily a function of household income, however. Overall, Economizers make about as much as the other groups; they just don't want to spend it on travel.

In contrast, Indulgers (29 percent of all travelers) live up to their name; they like to indulge themselves, and first-class travel is a great way to do that. Unlike Economizers, this group doesn't mind paying for special attention and pampering. Indulgers don't find travel intimidating or stressful, but they aren't looking for adventure, either. Nearly half of British travelers are in this group.

The study has provided TRS with tremendous insights into the minds and hearts of the traveling public,

revealing not only where they like to travel but also what they expect from the experience. TRS has used the knowledge in numerous efforts; for example, one ad portrays a man losing his American Express card while bungee jumping but getting it replaced in time to go skydiving—clearly an ad aimed at the newly defined Adventurer segment.

Your Mission: You're the new advertising manager at American Express Travel Related Services. Your job includes both managing promotional communications for TRS and working with TRS's marketing partners, which include hotel chains, rental car firms, and other travel service companies. Use what you know about consumer behavior to address the following scenarios.

1. You've developed a travel package aimed at Adventurers. The main feature of the package is a one-week stint as an assistant on an oceanographic research ship. Which of the following headlines would appeal most to the Adventurer segment?
a. "You've seen the four corners of the Earth; now look under the surface."
b. "You've read 20,000 Leagues under the Sea by Jules Verne; here's your chance to see what he was talking about."

travelers), but Boeing can't increase demand at the organizational level (the airlines). What Boeing can do is cement its place in the minds of customers, so that when they do have a reason to buy, they are predisposed toward Boeing.

INFORMATION COLLECTION AND ANALYSIS

Organizational buyers' approach to collecting and analyzing information is typically more rigorous and thorough than that used by consumers, but the basic concept is the same: successful advertisers put the right information in the right place at the right time. Specialized business publications and direct mail are the overwhelming favorites among business-to-business advertisers.[58] Such ads are typically more information oriented than ads for consumer products, simply because the organizational purchase is often more complex and organizational customers demand more information.

The evaluation stage can be more formal and more time consuming in organizational purchasing than in consumer purchasing. Organizations often invite suppliers to submit proposals that cover prices, support services, contract terms, warranties, and delivery schedules. These proposals sometimes require detailed

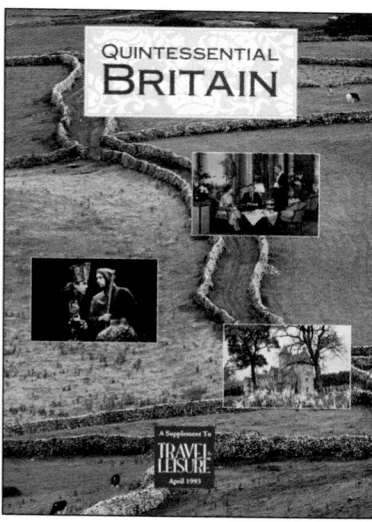

c. "Bound to be the hardest-working vacation you've ever spent."

2. The theme you communicate in your ads will reflect on the people who buy your products. If a resort is obvious about being a budget facility, its clientele will be labeled as people who don't want to spend a fortune on a vacation. Some consumers like to be known for their money-saving habits, some don't care one way or the other, and some don't want the world to know they didn't spend much money. They may want to save—they just don't want to be labeled as tight-wads. Which of the following ad headlines would be best for this "closet tightwad" segment of the market?
a. "Enjoy the luxury resort experience on a penny-pincher's budget."
b. "Stay with us this year, and you'll have enough left over for next year's vacation."
c. "We won't advertise our prices, so no one will know how little you spent."

3. Assume you're preparing a print ad with the advertising manager at the Mauna Kea, a luxury beach resort in Hawaii. Your goal is to attract more executive retreat business, in which teams of corporate executives relax and work on business problems and plans. Which of the following photo ideas would you use in the ad?
a. A conference room full of businesspeople who are dressed casually but who appear to be working and discussing intently.
b. One person relaxing on the Mauna Kea's white sandy beach, collecting his or her thoughts.
c. Several people sitting and standing next to a tennis court, smiling and laughing, obviously getting along.

4. Traveler's checks are a major business area for American Express, so the fact that Worriers and Economizers are less likely to use to them is a point of concern for you. If you were to craft a traveler's check ad for the Worrier segment, which of the following themes would you use?
a. "If traveling is more than you can handle, American Express Traveler's Cheques can help."
b. "Let's face it; traveling is a pain in the neck. American Express Traveler's Cheques, however, can make it a little less traumatic."
c. "Don't spend your vacation worrying about losing your cash; take American Express Traveler's Cheques and spend your time enjoying yourself."[60]

technical analysis, product demonstrations, or speculative projects (as frequently occurs when advertising agencies pitch new clients).

SUPPLIER SELECTION

Supplier selection is often a formal process among organizational buyers, as customers try to find the best suppliers for each type of product they need. Many organizations have "approved supplier" lists, and employees aren't allowed to purchase goods or services from anyone not on the list. This fact leads to a lot of advertising in which suppliers try to convince potential customers that they are capable and reliable sources of products.

An ad campaign from Computer Associates (CA) aimed at decision makers features photos and quotes from decision makers in organizations that have already purchased CA products. In one, a vice president from the University of Miami explains that he chooses CA products because of the company's record for quality and technical excellence.[59] Such messages help convince other organizational buyers that CA is an attractive source of software products.

Summary

The importance of understanding an advertising audience stems from the fact that the more you know about an audience, the more effective your ads will be, the more money you'll save by not advertising to the wrong people, and the better your relationship will be with your customers. Three forces in today's markets make audience analysis especially important to advertisers: increased demands for performance and accountability from the advertising budget, increased fragmentation in markets and media, and increased competition both at home and abroad.

The consumer market encompasses all the individuals and households in the world. In contrast, the organizational market is made up of businesses, nonprofit organizations, and government bodies—groups that buy goods and services to use in creating other goods and services. The key differences between consumer and organizational buying behavior are acceptable level of risk, the role of emotion and logic, the number of buyers for a given product, the primary promotional method, buyer-seller relationships, the nature of the buying process, the number of people involved in the purchase, the time spent on decisions, and purchase motivations.

The psychological, social and interpersonal, and situational forces that influence consumers explain why people buy. The psychological factors of most interest to advertising researchers are needs and motives, attitude and lifestyle, and personality and self-concept. Needs create motives, which determine buyer behavior. Attitudes are tendencies to respond to ads or products in certain ways and are composed of cognitive, affective, and behavioral components. Lifestyle is a combination of activities, interests, and opinions, and it's influenced by important demographic variables such as income. Personality is a person's characteristic and consistent pattern of behavior. Self-concept is the sum of the perceptions, beliefs, and feelings people hold about themselves.

Social and interpersonal influences include cultural forces, social status, reference groups, and word-of-mouth communication. In addition, group buying behavior is more complex than individual buying behavior and must be considered when developing advertising strategy.

Situational influences are the circumstances that surround purchases. These include physical surroundings, social surroundings, time perspective, task definition (why the buyer is looking for information about the product), and the antecedent state (what the consumer's state of mind is before making a purchase).

How people buy involves perception, learning, and decision making. Perception includes the three steps of exposure, attention, and interpretation. It's hard to overstate the importance of understanding audience perceptions; advertising works only if the right people are exposed to it, pay attention to it, and interpret it in the way the advertisers intended.

The rational decision-making model covers six steps: recognizing a need, collecting and analyzing information, evaluating potential solutions, selecting and evaluating potential suppliers, making the purchase, and evaluating the outcome. The types of nonrational purchase decisions discussed in the chapter include buying on feeling and intuition, impulse buying, acting on inadequate information, and postdecision rationalization.

An organizational buying center is made up of those people within an organization who take part in the buying process as initiators, influencers, decision makers, gatekeepers, purchasers, and users. Derived demand, which means that the demand for product X is driven by the demand for product Y, is characteristic of all organizational buying and represents the most important difference between consumer and organizational behavior.

Key Terms

attitude 90	make/buy decision 105
buying center 107	motives 88
closure 99	needs 88
cognition 100	opinion leaders 94
cognitive dissonance 106	organizational market 85
conditioning 100	perception 97
consumer market 85	personality 91
core values 92	psychographics 87
cultural segments 92	reference group 93
culture 92	selective perception 98
demographics 85	self-concept 91
derived demand 107	situational influences 95
evoked set 104	social classes 93
exposure 98	word of mouth 94
learning 100	
lifestyle 91	

Questions

FOR REVIEW

1. How can an advertiser use audience analysis to gain an advantage over its competitors?

2. How does self-concept influence purchase decisions?

3. What is derived demand, and why should advertisers understand it?

4. What are the two major types of learning?

5. Why can some purchases be considered nonrational or "illogical"?

FOR ANALYSIS AND APPLICATION

6. Computers are sold to both consumers and organizations; when the product is identical, will the purchase behavior be identical as well? Explain your answer.

7. How might a life insurance firm use demographic analysis to improve its advertising?

8. How is the household like an organizational buying center? Would it be wise to use a single ad for a product that both households and organizations use, such as personal computers? Explain your answer.

9. What cultural values might affect the purchase of cigarettes? Of bacon? Of motorcycles?

10. Should advertisers try to get buyers to act more logically when they make purchase decisions? Why or why not?

Sharpen Your Advertising Skills

Lifestyle concepts are often used in advertising to determine the words, images, and music used in an ad and to decide where the ad will be run. Magazines provide good examples of lifestyle advertising in action; in fact, many magazines are called "life-style magazines" because they appeal to people with particular activities, interests, opinions, and demographic profiles. Browse through a number of magazines and select two or three ads for products that you either own or use now or that you are likely to buy or use in the near future. Include both goods and services in your search.

Decision: For each of the ads you've selected, decide whether the words and images in the ad fit your perception of your lifestyle (using the dimensions listed in Exhibit 4.7). For instance, if people are shown in the ad, do you get the impression that these people would feel the same way you do about important issues? Also, given your lifestyle, how likely is it that you would have run across this ad in the course of your normal daily activities?

Communication: Pretend that an advertising agency has hired you to help fine-tune its ads because you represent the ideal target consumer for a particular product. Using the ad that you think least fits your lifestyle, write a one-page memo to the agency explaining how the ad needs to be changed to fit its intended audience more accurately. Also, identify where the ad should be run so that someone with a lifestyle like yours is likely to encounter it (don't restrict your choices to magazines for this part of the exercise; recommend any media option you like).

Segmentation, Targeting, and Positioning

After studying this chapter, you will be able to

1. Describe the concept of target marketing and its importance to today's advertisers
2. Explain why some advertisers are reluctant to segment their markets
3. Outline the most common ways of segmenting consumer advertising audiences
4. Contrast the approaches used to segment consumer audiences with those used to segment organizational audiences
5. Define the factors that make market segments meaningful
6. Explain why some meaningful segments are more attractive than others
7. Describe the concept of positioning and its relation to advertising

Facing an Advertising Challenge at L.A. Gear

SEARCHING FOR A FOOTHOLD IN THE CROWDED FOOTWEAR MARKET

You don't have to look far to get an idea of how big the athletic shoe market is in the United States. Just look at the feet under the desks around you; no doubt many of them are wearing shoes from Nike, Reebok, or L.A. Gear. L.A. Gear chairman and CEO Stanley Gold is looking at feet just as you are, but with a more painful perspective. He sees a lot fewer L.A. Gear shoes on those feet today than he would've seen just a few years ago.

L.A. Gear looked like an unstoppable marketing success during the late 1980s. Over the course of three or four years, the once-tiny company charged out of nowhere to carve a 12 percent slice out of the $5.8 billion U.S. athletic shoe market. Riding the fads of spangles, fringes, and other fashion features, L.A. Gear was emerging as a strong threat to market leaders Nike and Reebok. Things looked so good that L.A. Gear's foun-der Robert Greenberg boasted that his company would pass both his larger competitors by 1991.

However, 1991 didn't turn out to be anything like the chart-topper Greenberg envisioned. Problems cropped up from everywhere. Angry stockholders accused the firm of mismanagement and deceptive recordkeeping. Banks cut back on its credit, restricting marketing and advertising flexibility. Sales plunged as consumers tired of the faddish shoes and as product quality slipped. A huge investment in a Michael Jackson line of shoes was lost when the line flopped.

Gold, who along with new L.A. Gear president Mark Goldston took over the company's reins in late 1991, has his hands full, to put it mildly. Sales and financial problems continued through 1992 and well into 1993. At one point, the company was saddled with more than 12 million pairs of unsold shoes. Keds and other small competitors continue to chip away at L.A. Gear's share of the market, which dropped to around 8 percent by the end of 1992. Efforts to attract the business of serious athletes and image-conscious nonathletes have faltered, in part because these buyers view L.A. Gear as a trendy shoe for kids—an image fueled by such products as the Sun Blossom shoe for girls, which changes color in the sun.

If you were in Gold's shoes, how would you use marketing and advertising to put L.A. Gear back on track? Would you try to compete with Nike and Reebok in the performance category, or should you be more worried about Keds? What about the fashion angle—should you emphasize this or not? Finally, what about the L.A. Gear name itself—should you promote it in your ads, use it selectively, or maybe even drop it all together?[1] ■

CHAPTER OVERVIEW L.A. Gear took off in the 1980s because it identified a group of consumers who wanted high-fashion athletic shoes; unfortunately that market wasn't big enough or stable enough to fuel the company's growth forever. This chapter helps you understand how the company got into trouble and how it plans to get out. The chapter addresses three important processes in advertising: (1) segmenting a market to identify those customers who will best respond to an advertising message, (2) selecting the best segments from the ones identified, and then (3) positioning the organization or product in the audience's mind. First, you'll see why this notion of addressing specific subgroups of buyers is important. After that, you'll explore the meaning of segmentation, its importance in today's markets, and the methods most often used to segment consumer and organizational markets. Next, you'll learn about targeting—how advertisers consider all the segments in a market and then pick the ones that are most likely to respond to a given message. Then you'll have a look at the advertiser's target marketing options. Finally, you'll be introduced to positioning, one of the key concepts in defining advertising strategy.

Advertising to a Fragmented Market

It's hard to believe, when you consider today's athletic shoe market, that just a few years ago simple sneakers were the only kind of athletic shoe you could buy. You could choose between high top and low top and perhaps between black canvas and white canvas, but aside from specialized shoes for boxing, track, and a few other sports, that was about it. Nike began to offer a little more variety during the 1970s, Reebok jumped in with its aerobics shoes in the early 1980s, L. A. Gear brought a fashion emphasis a couple of years later, and the race was on to provide ever more

variety.[2] Now there are dozens and dozens of specialized shoes for every activity from aerobics to walking, with multiple variations in features, colors, and materials. Manufacturers are taking different approaches to the market, from the high-visibility celebrity endorsements of Nike and Reebok to the low-key emphasis on product performance of Wilson and K-Swiss. Furthermore, shoes aren't the only market that has exploded; you can now choose from roughly 750 different car models or nearly 100 brands of cat food.[3] These and many other markets have been fragmented on a massive scale, as buyers seek specialized solutions to their problems and sellers try to distinguish themselves with specialized marketing mixes (see Exhibit 5.1).

Selecting certain groups of customers and aiming products and advertising specifically at them is called **target marketing.** (Advertisers also use the term *niche marketing,* which refers to focusing on particular *niches* in a market. It's the same basic idea.[4]) The alternative to target marketing is **mass marketing,** or trying to reach the entire population with standardized products.[5]

Mass marketing used to be the norm: companies focused on driving their costs down by selling their basic products to as many customers as possible. Then, in the last decade or two, markets and marketing began to change dramatically. Reebok recognized this in the 1980s, first when it saw the need for a specialized aerobics shoe and later when it realized that athletic shoes were becoming fashion wear for many people.[6] Even something as seemingly basic as soup can be aimed at particular groups of buyers. Campbell breaks the United States into 22 geographic regions and formulates its soups to meet regional tastes. For example, because western and southwestern palates generally crave spicier foods than the rest of the country, Campbell puts more jalapeño peppers into the Nacho Cheese Soup it markets in these regions.[7]

For advertisers, the implications of fragmented markets are profound. You can no longer be assured of success simply by running general-purpose commercials on national television and ads in popular magazines. Customers not only have more products to choose from but also have more media options than ever before: you might have to reach some customers with commercials on prime-time television, others on a cable channel, others with personalized sales letters, and still others via a computerized information system such as Prodigy—and you might need a different message for each group. In fragmented markets, both consumers and organizational buyers have more choices than ever before, so advertisers have to choose their targets and craft their messages and media more carefully than ever before.

Being successful at target marketing involves three important stages: *segmenting* the overall market to identify the various submarkets that want specialized products, *targeting* particular segments that are the most attractive, and *positioning* yourself and your products in those target segments. Exhibit 5.2 illustrates the target marketing process, and the following sections explore each stage in more detail.

Segmentation: Identifying the Parts of a Market

The first step in the target marketing process is **segmentation,** breaking a market of varied customers into subgroups of customers that have similar needs, desired product benefits, and purchase behaviors. Each of these subgroups is considered a **market segment,** and a segment that an advertiser decides to go after is called a **target segment** (often called a *target audience*). For instance, Reebok looked at the various activities for which people wear athletic shoes, surmised that people doing aerobics would like a specialized shoe of their own, and went after that segment.

Sometimes segmentation is approached strictly from an advertising perspective, meaning that the advertiser continues to market the same product but creates

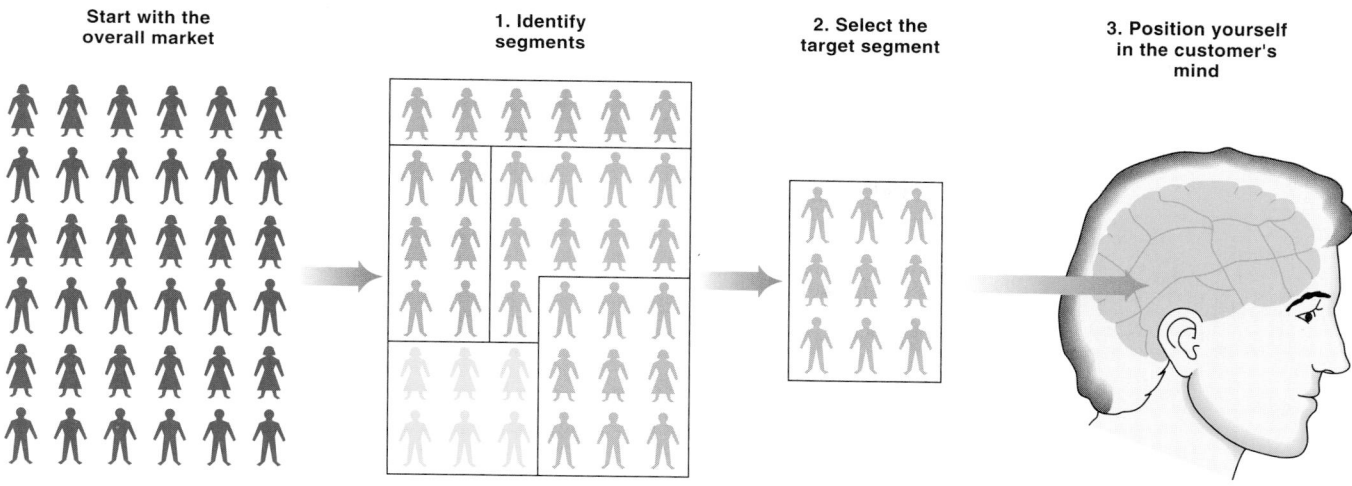

a different message or uses different media for each target segment. Coca-Cola does this for Hispanic consumers in the United States. In addition to aiming ads at Hispanic consumers, Coca-Cola sponsors Cinco de Mayo and Calle Ocho festivals to show a commitment to the Hispanic market.[8] Its advertising is specialized, but it's selling the same products it sells to other ethnic groups. Sometimes, though, segmentation involves other elements of the marketing mix, including product variations (shoes designed specifically for aerobics are a good example), pricing differences, or distribution channel changes.

WHY IS SEGMENTATION IMPORTANT?

Many advertisers don't have a choice when it comes to segmentation; if your competitors are pursuing target segments with specialized products and advertising, then you must usually do the same—or lose sales. Imagine someone introducing an "all-purpose" sports shoe and trying to market it to people involved in tennis, aerobics, basketball, and running. Even if the shoe meets the physical requirements for all four sports, people in each sport are unlikely to choose a shoe that doesn't seem optimized for their particular sport. Why pick a generic shoe when you can choose from several dozen designed just for tennis? Whether they implement segmentation strategies out of defensive pressure or out of a desire to create new opportunities, advertisers can reap three important benefits:[9]

- *More efficient use of resources.* Every advertiser has finite resources (whether it's money, time, or people), but the pressure to produce results grows every year. By defining and selecting attractive target segments, advertisers can get more from their investments because good targets, or *prospects,* are more receptive than the market as a whole (which reduces wasted advertising efforts). Bookseller Barnes & Noble has records on 750,000 customers, but within that huge customer base, the company can identify some segments as small as several hundred customers. By promoting specific selections of books to specific segments (based on their interests and buying habits), Barnes & Noble can advertise more efficiently, wasting less time and money and realizing greater returns.[10]

- *Better understanding of customer needs.* As discussed in Chapter 4, customers can be complex creatures, living in varied environments and having endless combinations of financial, legal, emotional, and physical needs: New Yorkers prefer spicier hot dogs than people elsewhere in the United States, the government of Singapore refuses to license cars with left-hand steering, and the people of Catalonia identify more with the rest of Europe than with Spain, even though Catalonia is officially an autonomous region inside Spanish borders.[11] If advertisers didn't break down their markets and examine such details in each segment, they would miss important insights into current and potential customers (see Exhibit 5.3).

EXHIBIT 5.2
The Target Marketing Process

The target marketing process involves three stages: segmenting the audience into groups of similar consumers or organizations, selecting the most attractive targets, and staking out a desirable position in each target segment.

CHAPTER 5
Segmentation, Targeting, and Positioning

EXHIBIT 5.3
Getting Close to Customers

Sberbank, a Russian financial services company, understands the mood of consumers and businesses who want to move into a new free-market economy in the former Soviet republic.

- *Better understanding of competitors.* Just as looking at the world through a segmented lens helps you understand your customers, it also helps you understand your competitors. When Family Dollar, a deep discount department store based in North Carolina, learned that Kmart was moving slightly upscale, it realized that it could worry less about that giant competitor and concentrate on Dollar General, Stuarts Department Stores, and the handful of other competitors that remain in this deep discount segment.[12]

Segmentation has a potential downside, however, and it can involve risk and organizational pain. When you choose to pursue a particular market segment as the focus of your efforts, you have automatically chosen *not* to pursue other market segments—a cause of great concern among some advertisers. You can win in a big way using a target marketing approach, but you can also lose in a big way if you define segments incorrectly, if you choose inappropriate segments, or if you don't watch for changes in the segments you've chosen and not chosen. In addition, segmentation strategies usually mean complexity—more products, more advertising choices, more distribution channels, and so on.[13] In many of today's markets, however, advertisers don't have the luxury of choosing whether to segment; customers increasingly demand narrowly focused, specialized products, and advertisers have to respond in order to be competitive.

HOW DO ADVERTISERS SEGMENT MARKETS?

You can think about segmentation from two perspectives: breaking down a whole market or building up from individual prospects. The first perspective involves starting with the total market and looking for ways to cut it into meaningful slices. Metropolitan Insurance Company, for instance, has successfully reached the growing Asian-American market with advertising appeals that are important to people in this segment (including quality, security, family, and longevity). Such cultural or ethnic segmentation takes the U.S. population and splits it along ethnic lines to produce a segment of Asian Americans.[14] The second segmentation perspective involves starting with individual customers (whether consumers or organizations) and finding other potential customers with the same characteristics to make up a segment large enough to warrant advertising attention (see Exhibit 5.4). This is the approach that entrepreneurs and inventors often use, creating solutions to problems they've personally encountered, and then looking for other customers with similar problems.

Dividing a market until you get the desired segment

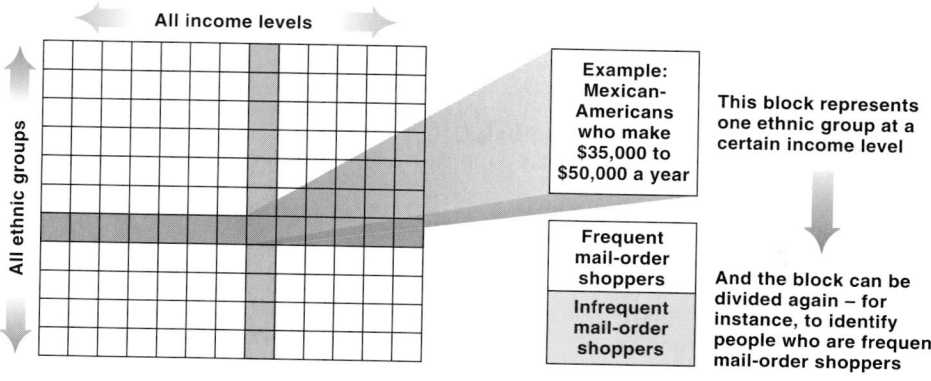

Looking for customers who fit a certain profile

EXHIBIT 5.4

Two Perspectives on Segmentation

You can view segmentation from two angles: breaking an entire market into subgroups of similar customers or starting with a single target customer and looking for enough other customers to build up a meaningful segment.

Whichever perspective advertisers take, they can choose from a wide variety of *segmentation variables,* the factors that describe and differentiate audience segments. Practically any parameter that helps distinguish probable buyers from probable nonbuyers can serve as a segmentation variable.

Segmenting Consumer Markets

Chapter 4 introduced you to the most common factors used to describe consumer audiences, including demographic, geographic, and psychographic data. Today's advertisers use all these, plus an additional category called geodemographics. You can use all four types of data, individually or in combination, to segment consumer markets.

Demographic Segmentation. Defining market segments according to demographic characteristics is called **demographic segmentation.** The audience analysis factors used most frequently in demographic analysis are age, gender, race/ethnicity, household type, home ownership, education, employment, and income. Here's a quick look at how these factors can define target markets:

- *Age.* Different age groups present different advertising challenges and opportunities. For example, the huge "baby-boom" generation (born between 1946 and 1964, when the birth rate was high) is now entering its peak earning years, making these people key targets for advertisers. The "baby-bust" generation (born between 1965 and 1976 when the birth rate was low), on the other hand, is proportionately much smaller. The "mature market" (people age 50 and over) is growing rapidly as people stay healthier and live longer.[15]

- *Gender.* Gender is a key factor in many advertising campaigns. In some cases the gender orientation is obvious, such as products for women shown in ads aimed at women. In other cases, the advertiser considers gender in a less obvious way. For instance, some evidence suggests that men and women approach information gathering differently: men tend to consult fewer information sources and rely on whatever information is most readily available,

If you've always dreamed of giving your son a good education, look into the opportunities the Army has to offer. The Army can give your son the opportunity of earning up to $30,000 through the Montgomery GI Bill plus the Army College Fund. In the Army, he'll also gain self-confidence, learn discipline, develop character, and become motivated — the basics he needs to go far in college and in life. The Army can give your son something that money can't buy — an edge on life. For more information, call 1-800-USA-ARMY today.

"The Army helped me give my son what was best for him."

ARMY. BE ALL YOU CAN BE.

EXHIBIT 5.5
Targeting Ethnic Groups

With both the models featured in this ad and the magazines in which it was placed, the U.S. Army targeted a particular ethnic segment with this promotional effort.

whereas women tend to take a more comprehensive course of action and search for more information.[16] Advertisers can respond to this potential difference by designing ads differently when they are targeting men or women.

- *Race/ethnicity.* The United States is an ethnically diverse country, and it will be even more so as time passes. Many major advertisers are trying to target their appeals toward specific ethnic groups. In some cases, advertisers have developed new products for a particular ethnic group. Maybelline perceived the frustration of many African-American women when trying to buy color-compatible cosmetics, and its new Shades of You product line aimed at this segment has been a resounding success.[17] In other cases, advertisers direct specialized ads for their basic products toward particular ethnic groups (see Exhibit 5.5). Coca-Cola, for instance, relies on Sosa & Associates in San Antonio to help it reach Hispanic audiences.[18]

- *Household type.* For advertising purposes, the basic unit in the consumer market is the **household,** defined as a housing unit (house, apartment, etc.) and the person or persons who occupy it. A household can consist of an individual, a married couple with children at home, a married couple without children at home, other family combinations such as relatives or single parents and their children sharing a dwelling, or two or more unrelated people sharing a dwelling. Colgate-Palmolive targeted large families with its Fab 1 Shot "single-serving" laundry detergent packs, but the segments who were actually buying most of the product were college students and single adults, not families. Without advertising aimed at these segments, the product eventually flopped.[19]

- *Home ownership.* When you buy your first house, you might wonder how landscapers, interior designers, home equity lenders, and others with

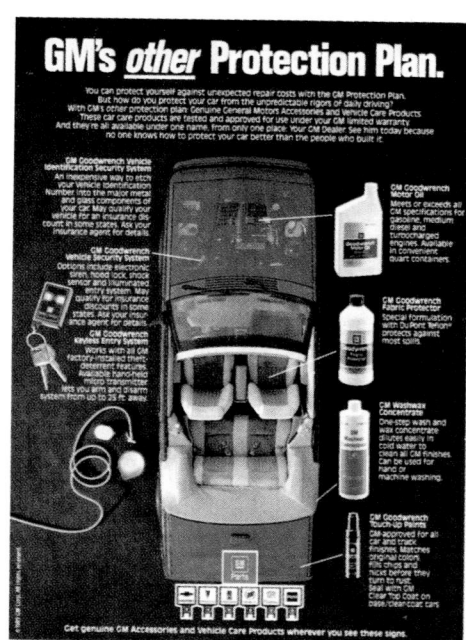

homeowner-type products are able to get direct-mail ads into your mailbox as soon as you move in. The answer is that some research company has been tracking property transfer records at the county courthouse and knows exactly when the property changed hands—just one example of how advertisers select target segments based on home ownership.

- *Education.* A consumer's educational background can also play a role in planning effective advertising. Say you want to create a feeling of camaraderie in a television commercial by having several people reminisce about their college days. Will this strike a chord among most adults? Not likely; even in the most educated segment of the U.S. population (men born between 1946 and 1955), only 30 percent have graduated from college. Among all adults, the figure is even lower.[20]

- *Employment.* Advertisers can use employment data to guide the design of products and advertisements aimed at people in particular professions. For instance, a computer manufacturer could run one version of an ad in a magazine with a high percentage of accountants as subscribers and another version in a magazine with a high percentage of engineers. Each version could be tuned to its particular market.

- *Income.* The amount of money consumers make obviously affects how they spend it. Not surprisingly, advertisers of luxury goods and leisure products are interested in the consumers who have the most discretionary income, primarily the affluent (see Exhibit 5.6). Defined as having an income of over $60,000 a year, affluent people are predominantly in the 35-to-49 age group; the affluent market is one of the fastest-growing segments, constituting a quarter of the adult population.[21] Of course, affluent people aren't the only consumers, and many advertisers focus on the middle- and lower-income groups. Everybody has to buy food, basic clothing, transportation, health care, and other fundamental goods and services, and advertisers in these markets are among the most active advertisers in the world.

Geographic Segmentation. Geographic location can also provide clues about likely purchase behavior and is therefore a key factor to consider in advertising

V.O.: (woman's voice with music): From the first moment we set foot on The Cayman

Islands, we were relaxed vacationers, not tourists.

SINGERS: The Cayman Islands!

EXHIBIT 5.6
Targeting Based on Income

Considering the expense of a vacation trip to the Cayman Islands, the country's department of tourism focuses on consumers with higher levels of disposable income.

design. **Geographic segmentation** identifies audience segments based on geographic boundaries. Some geographic differences are rather obvious, such as the market for cold-weather clothing in areas with harsh winters or the demand for water sports equipment along coasts, lakes, and rivers. Other regional differences are less obvious. For instance, many consumers in the South and Midwest prefer soft (white) bread, whereas many on the East and West coasts prefer firmer breads (rye, whole wheat, French, Italian).[22]

Geography also dictates the timing of some purchase patterns. Even though bowling doesn't have a traditional "season" like football or baseball, it tends to pick up in the fall as foul weather chases people indoors. If you were planning an advertising campaign for Brunswick, a major supplier of bowling balls, you might want to start running your ads in September, when people head for the alleys in greater numbers. However, this plan might backfire in Phoenix, because just as the bad weather is arriving up north, the ferocious Phoenix summer is starting to let up, and people leave the bowling alleys to pursue outdoor recreation.[23]

Advertisers can select from a number of geographic segmentation schemes. The most basic are those based on legal and regulatory boundaries, from postal carrier routes and ZIP codes (usually called post codes or postal codes in other countries) to various city, county, state, and national boundaries. Such boundaries don't often reflect meaningful market segments, however. Driving around any metropolitan area, for instance, you can see that business and residential areas spill over the boundaries between cities and extend beyond cities into outlying areas. San Francisco is legally separate from Oakland, San Jose, and other cities, but for many advertising purposes, all these areas constitute a single economic and social region. Of course, boundaries define more than just metropolitan areas, but cities do represent the bulk of the consumer population. Metropolitan areas make up just 16 percent of U.S. land area, yet they contain more than three-quarters of the U.S. population.[24]

In an effort to better understand metropolitan populations, the U.S. Census Bureau categorizes all U.S. urban areas into three standard types of population centers. Advertisers also benefit from these classifications, since they share the government's interest in figuring out who lives where. The three categories of population centers are used in a wide range of advertising activities, from buying ad space in local newspapers to interpreting research data (see Exhibit 5.7):

- *Metropolitan Statistical Areas (MSAs)* are geographic areas containing at least one city of 50,000 or more inhabitants *or* urbanized areas of at least 50,000 inhabitants in a region with a total population of 100,000 or more (75,000 in New England). For example, all of Midland County in Texas (including the city of Midland) is defined as the Midland, Texas, MSA.[25]

- *Primary Metropolitan Statistical Areas (PMSAs)* are metropolitan areas with 1 million or more residents that are associated with one or more urbanized

EXHIBIT 5.7
Analyzing Population Centers to Place Ads

This ad for the Discover Card, a national advertiser, used local data to identify a particular group of restaurants in the area that accept the credit card.

counties. The Seattle, Washington, PMSA consists of all of King County and all of Snohomish County, for a total of 1.86 million residents.[26]

- *Consolidated Metropolitan Statistical Areas (CMSAs)* are geographic areas containing more than one PMSA. The Seattle PMSA, for instance, is combined with the Tacoma PMSA to produce the Seattle-Tacoma CMSA, with a population of roughly 2.4 million.[27]

There are 267 MSAs and 21 CMSAs holding 73 PMSAs in the United States, counting the 4 MSAs, 1 CMSA, and 2 PMSAs in Puerto Rico.[28] Some governments in other countries have defined similar geographic segments; for example, Canada defines Census Agglomerations and Census Metropolitan Areas.[29]

Commercial researchers have implemented several other ways of segmenting along geographic lines. To help advertisers plan television campaigns, A. C. Nielsen's designated market areas (DMAs) segment geographic areas based on broadcast television coverage, rather than on political boundaries.[30] In fact, television has a habit of blurring borders. U.S. television broadcasts are regularly viewed by Canadian residents who live near border cities such as Detroit, and vice versa. Until it was recently deregulated, French television had a reputation for unexciting programs, coupled with tight restrictions on advertising. However, residents in eastern and southeastern France could pick up broadcasts from Luxembourg and Monte Carlo, respectively. These two sources provided better programming than French television and offered advertisers easier access to those residents, so Luxembourg and Monte Carlo television were more attractive media options.[31] These examples highlight the need to carefully consider geography when planning an advertising campaign; official borders and other geographic segments don't always correspond to the way the world really works.

YOU DIDN'T DIE BEFORE YOU GOT OLD. NOW WHAT?

EXHIBIT 5.8
Advertising That Addresses a Buyer Motivation

Playing on the words in a famous song by The Who ("I hope I die before I get old"), Halifax Financial Services addresses the motivation of baby boomers to prepare for financial security later in life.

Psychographic Segmentation. Defining market segments according to psychographic (psychological and behavioral) characteristics is called **psychographic segmentation.** The audience analysis factors used most frequently in psychographic segmentation are motivation, desired benefits, attitude, lifestyle, personality, consumer behavior, and brand loyalty:

- *Motivation.* The motivations that drive buyer behavior can often be useful for segmenting an advertising audience (see Exhibit 5.8). If you know why people buy—or don't buy—certain products, you can improve your advertising immensely. When instant coffee first hit the market, research pioneer Mason Haire asked shoppers whether they used instant coffee and if not, why not. Nonusers told him that they didn't like the taste, but when he probed deeper, he learned that nonusers considered using instant coffee a sign of being a lazy, inadequate wife (this was in 1950, when men rarely shopped for groceries). In other words, at least some of the people who avoided instant coffee did so not because they had problems with the taste but because they didn't want to be branded as an unworthy homemaker.[32] Even today you still don't see much emphasis on convenience in instant coffee advertising, despite contemporary consumers being much more open to the ideas of saving time and reducing effort in the kitchen.

- *Desired benefits.* An important variation of motivational segmentation is **benefit segmentation,** dividing a market according to the benefits that various buyers seek from the product in question. Wendy's founder Dave Thomas knows that in spite of increased health awareness, many people want their fast food to taste good, even if that means breaking dietary rules now and again. People don't usually come to Wendy's for low prices or low calories, two themes that often dominate today's fast-food advertising. Thomas pitches taste in the company's television advertising, and the results show the wisdom of Wendy's segmentation choice. In an era when fast-food operators are suffering from rampant price wars, Wendy's has cut out coupons and discounts almost entirely and continues to expand its sales.[33]

- *Attitude.* Attitudes toward brands and product categories can produce distinctly different consumer segments. To help Nissan craft ads for its cars, J. D. Power and Associates recently did an attitude profile of car buyers. The study grouped drivers into six attitude categories: *gearheads* enjoy driving and working on cars; *epicures* prefer stylish, elegant sports cars; *purists* like cars and enjoy driving but are skeptical about ad claims; *functionalists* want sensible, conservative cars; *road-haters* don't like driving and want safety features; and *negatives* view cars as necessary evils and don't want do be bothered.[34] It's easy to visualize how a Nissan ad strategy might change based on the particular segment it's shooting for.

- *Lifestyle.* Lifestyle segmentation is sometimes considered synonymous with psychographic segmentation. Often encompassing some of the other segmentation methods discussed in this section, lifestyle covers a range of studies and models that attempt to predict buyer behavior based on attitudes, interests, and opinions. One of the best-known approaches is VALS 2 (the second generation of the Values and Lifestyles model) from SRI International. This model attempts to profile U.S. consumers by grouping them into three "self-orientation" categories (depending on whether they are motivated primarily by principles, status, or action) and splitting these three categories again according to the resources (money, physical assets, etc.) the people have at their disposal (see Exhibit 5.9). This creates six lifestyle segments, along with special segments at the top and bottom of the resource spectrum. The *Actualizers* at the top have enough resources to indulge in any of the self-orientations (for instance, an Actualizer would have the time and money to get involved in politics or go on an African safari). The *Strugglers,* by contrast, are so urgently focused on immediate health and safety needs that self-orientation options don't really apply. A typical application of the VALS 2 model, combined with product usage data from another research supplier, showed that Actualizers are heavy users of ibuprofen pain relievers but that Nuprin (which contains ibuprofen) has relatively low sales to this lifestyle segment. If you were Nuprin's advertising agency, your next step would be to devise an improved message to do a better job of reaching this important segment.[35] Keep in mind that VALS 2 and other segmentations are models, and as such are simplified views of reality. VALS 2 doesn't claim to encompass every type of consumer or to be applicable to every product.

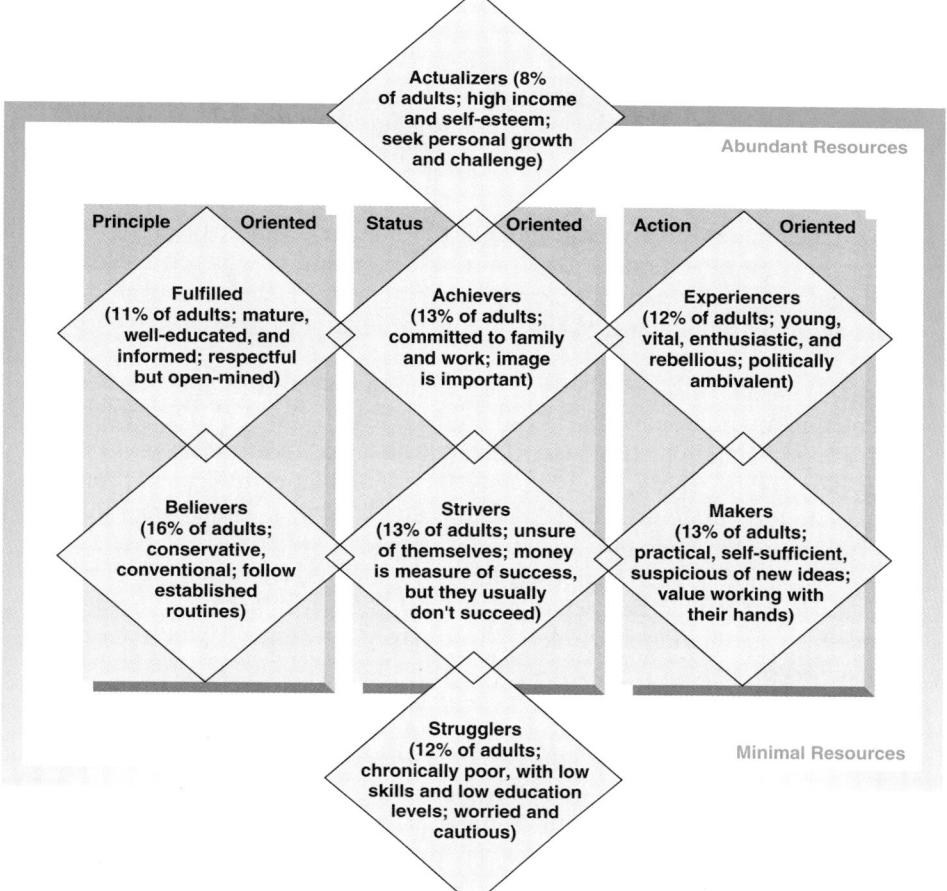

EXHIBIT 5.9
VALS 2: Segmenting by Lifestyle

The VALS 2 model segments consumers by self-orientation and resources.

- *Personality.* As discussed in Chapter 4, personality has not been a very useful factor in analyzing and segmenting audiences. There are a few exceptions, however. People who are particularly susceptible to interpersonal influence have a need to enhance their image through buying and using certain products and brands, are willing to conform to the expectations of others regarding purchase decisions, and tend to learn about products by observing others and seeking information from others.[36] Because these individuals tend to be low in self-esteem and self-confidence, they rely more on others when they have to make decisions. Another personality variable that seems to be related to buying behavior is risk taking. High risk takers, estimated to be about 25 percent of the population, have a higher than average need for stimulation, making them good prospects for advertisers of travel services, sports equipment, and similar products.[37]

- *Behavior.* The emotional and cognitive processes going on inside a consumer's head lead to particular kinds of behavior. **Behavioral segmentation** encompasses the methods used to segment audiences based on behavior. A common method of behavioral segmentation is **product-use segmentation,** grouping customers by the way they use products or by the quantities in which they buy them. Splitting a market into light and heavy users is a common tactic. Many advertisers rely on the "80/20 rule," meaning that 80 percent of sales come from 20 percent of the market—the heaviest users. Not every market exhibits this sort of behavior (and blindly following the 80/20 rule can lead to disaster), but many do, and to a surprising degree.[38] Identifying who these people are can help you define a valuable segment of the consumer audience.

- *Brand loyalty.* **Brand loyalty** is a measure of customer attachment to a particular brand. Loyalty can range from those customers who are committed through thick and thin to those customers who buy on price or convenience only and have no loyalty to any brand.[39] Harley-Davidson buyers who tattoo the product logo on their arms and who continued to purchase the bikes during a time when the motorcycles were decidedly unreliable are a good example of customers with high brand loyalty.[40] Most customers have low brand loyalty in certain product categories (e.g., many people buy gasoline from the closest or cheapest service station). Advertisers need to understand the loyalty of their own customers in order to take steps to keep them, as well as the loyalty of their competitors' customers to see what it would take to get them to switch (see Exhibit 5.10).

The development of psychographic segmentation continues to progress with new insights and new models from both academic and commercial researchers. These models usually combine several psychological factors, as well as demographic and geographic data, in the attempt to define distinct market segments.

Geodemographic Segmentation. By combining data from the first two consumer segmentation methods, advertisers can produce results that look similar to those of the third segmentation method. **Geodemographic segmentation** averages demographic data inside geographic segments; the resulting neighborhood profiles can be remarkably accurate predictors of values and lifestyles. The demographic data in each geographic segment are usually enhanced with survey data covering purchase behavior, media choices, attitudes, opinions, and other psychographic variables. Even though the results often look like psychographic segmentation, geodemographic segments are defined primarily by demographic data that are organized geographically.[41]

Geodemographic segmentation operates on the theory that people with similar demographic and psychographic profiles tend to live in clusters (in fact, geodemographic segmentation is often called *clustering*). You can get an idea of how this works by considering the neighborhood you grew up in or the one you live in now. Whether it's a rural area with scattered farmhouses or an urban center full of high-rise apartments, people within a given neighborhood usually share quite a few

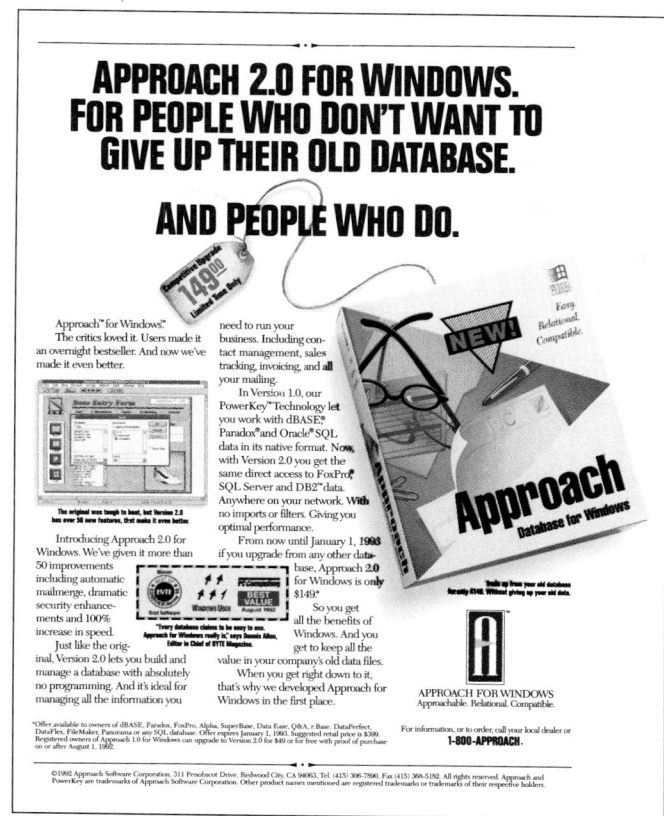

EXHIBIT 5.10

Trying to Convince Customers to Switch

Approach Software (now owned by Lotus Development), uses an increasingly common marketing tactic for the software industry—using attractively priced "competitive upgrade" offers to persuade people to switch brands.

consumer characteristics. Researchers have found similar clusters spread across the country. As one investigator put it, except for the palm trees, Fairfield, Connecticut, and Pasadena, California, are really the same place.[42] In other words, consumers in Fairfield and Pasadena behave in much the same way and are more like each other than consumers in cluster types that are physically much closer.

A look at a pioneering geodemographic system will help clarify this approach. The Potential Rating Index by Zip Markets (PRIZM) system developed by Claritas Corporation defines 40 neighborhood types that range from Blue Blood Estates, characterized by the nation's highest incomes, vacations in exotic locales, subscriptions to *Gourmet,* and so on, to Public Assistance, poor inner-city neighborhoods with poverty rates five times the national average.[43] In between are the 38 other neighborhood types, each defined by particular demographic patterns.

The National Symphony Orchestra in Washington recently profiled its subscribers, comparing the concert attendance patterns of the single adults common in Money & Brains neighborhoods with the attendance of the affluent suburban families in Furs & Station Wagons neighborhoods. The symphony discovered that four times as many Money & Brains residents attended concerts. The next promotional campaign focused on these Money & Brains neighborhoods, and subscriptions increased by 25 percent in some clusters.[44] (As you probably guessed, children are the key demographic difference between the two clusters, making it harder for Furs & Station Wagons people to attend concerts.) Major companies using geodemographic systems include American Express, Time Warner, General Motors, 3M, and Gannett.[45]

Clearly, not everyone in a "neighborhood" as large as a ZIP code area exhibits precisely the same lifestyles and consumption tendencies, but the averages that define PRIZM clusters have been extremely helpful for advertisers trying to determine target markets for media selection, store location, and other marketing tasks. To get over the generalizations inherent in any average, some researchers recommend supplementing PRIZM-type segmentation with psychological studies that probe deeper into neighborhoods.[46]

Mobay changed its name to Miles Inc. effective January 1, 1992.

With the wide variety of methods available for segmenting consumer markets, advertisers can zero in on target segments more accurately than ever. Continuing research in this area promises to yield better accuracy and new ways to identify audiences, and in the process, help reduce waste. To improve their analysis insights, advertisers often combine various segmentation approaches, such as VALS 2 and PRIZM, to pinpoint audiences as closely as possible.[47] Some of the approaches used for consumer markets also work well in organizational markets, but the organizational audience often requires some special segmentation approaches.

Segmenting Organizational Markets

Organizational advertisers run into many of the same obstacles that challenge today's consumer advertisers, from fragmented markets and increased competition to an ever-growing array of media options. Not surprisingly, segmenting organizational markets is quite similar to segmenting consumer markets, except for some obvious differences to account for the fact that organizations, and not individuals, are the targets. As you might expect, objective factors such as technology, location, and size play a bigger role in organizational segmentation than the psychographic and geodemographic factors that are so important in consumer segmentation (see Exhibit 5.11). Four of the most common segmentation approaches are demographic, geographic, operational, and behavioral. As with consumer audiences, advertisers frequently combine several approaches to pinpoint their audiences.

Demographic Segmentation. In the organizational market, demographic segmentation is the same basic concept, only with a different set of variables: sales revenues, number of employees, age of the business, business life cycle, type of business, for-profit versus nonprofit goals, and so on. AT&T, for instance, now offers more than 50 kinds of long-distance service, some focused on the needs of large organizations and others on the needs of smaller firms.[48] A demographic factor related to company size is the *concentration ratio,* the percentage of sales attributed to the biggest organizations. The four biggest U.S. car manufacturers purchase 92 percent of all car bodies made in the United States.[49] Compare this with the typical consumer market, in which even the most voracious consumer would represent a tiny fraction of overall sales. The implication for advertising is important: in consumer markets, you often have to reach thousands or millions of

Ads in *Sports Illustrated for Kids,* Channel One in the classroom, cartoon shows built around products, logo T-shirts, tie-ins between hit movies and special meal deals at McDonald's—kids are getting an earful and an eyeful of advertising. Hang out with some youngsters for a few hours and count how many advertising messages they see, hear, and wear.

Targeting kids is a multibillion-dollar business, and companies are constantly looking for new ways to reach kids through advertising. For example, *Advertising Age,* a major industry publication, recently ran one of its Special Report sections on the subject, a 24-pager called "Marketing to Kids." More than two dozen companies offered their services to advertisers trying to reach kids, from *Scholastic* magazine's promoting its ability to reach 23 million kids right in the classroom to the Smart Marketing Group's promising to put your message in front of a "captive audience" of 19.8 million kids who skate in the nation's roller-skating rinks each year. Want to put your company in front of the nation's kindergarten students? Call a toll-free number, and you can get help putting your "sponsored educational materials" into teachers' lesson plans.

All this child-focused advertising doesn't sit well with some parents, educators, and social observers. Consumers Union, publishers of *Consumer Reports* and *Zillions,* a consumer magazine for kids, said that "Educators and parents should object to promotions that exploit the inexperience and vulnerability of children or that fail to identify themselves clearly as advertising." Also on Consumers Union's hit list: the proliferation of free "educational" materials containing advertising messages that students may construe as facts.

Consumers Union is also critical of licensing deals that create kids' TV shows based on toys or that encourage children to buy products for the simple reason that they are related to a popular movie or character. Some health specialists and consumer advocates fret over ads that encourage kids to consume costly or unhealthy products and ads that use role models such as athletes and musicians to push products for their status appeal.

A fact sometimes lost in all the furor is an advertiser's legal right to conduct business and pursue profits as long as it stays within the bounds of current law. However, laws can't cover all the ethical decisions that crop up in children's advertising. Companies that are concerned about the most ethical ways to advertise to children should follow these guidelines (provided by the Council of Better Business Bureaus):

- Consider children's knowledge, sophistication, and maturity levels. Younger children often don't distinguish fact from fiction, for instance.
- Be truthful and accurate, recognizing that children may learn practices from advertising that can affect their health and well-being.
- Wherever possible, include positive social images such as kindness, justice, generosity, and respect for others.

What's Your Opinion?

1. Is it ethical to target kids? Why or why not? What about the right of advertisers to conduct business?
2. Public school teachers spend an average of $500 per year of their own money on educational materials, so some might view free materials from advertisers as a welcome relief. Should teachers accept these free educational materials? Why or why not?

potential buyers; in some organizational markets, you may have to reach only a handful.

One of the most useful organizational demographics is industry type, and a common segmentation scheme based on this factor is the U.S. government's system of **Standard Industrial Classification (SIC) codes,** which assigns numbers to industries based on various categories. Exhibit 5.12 shows how the SIC identifies those companies that rent or lease heavy construction equipment. SIC code 73 applies to all providers of business services. Adding more digits increases the level of detail: code 735 specifies equipment rental and leasing; then code 7353 narrows it further to rental and leasing of heavy construction equipment. The more digits you use, the tighter you can focus on a distinct group of companies.

In the same way that census data are used to organize information about consumers, SIC codes are used to organize information about organizational customers. A number of publications and other information sources use SIC to provide organizational advertisers with information about their audiences. For instance, an advertiser could tap into a computer database provided by Dun and Bradstreet and get the names of all the companies in the sporting goods industry, based on SIC codes.

The SIC is not an ideal solution for all advertisers, however. First, SIC categories are not updated frequently enough to reflect changes in fast-moving industries

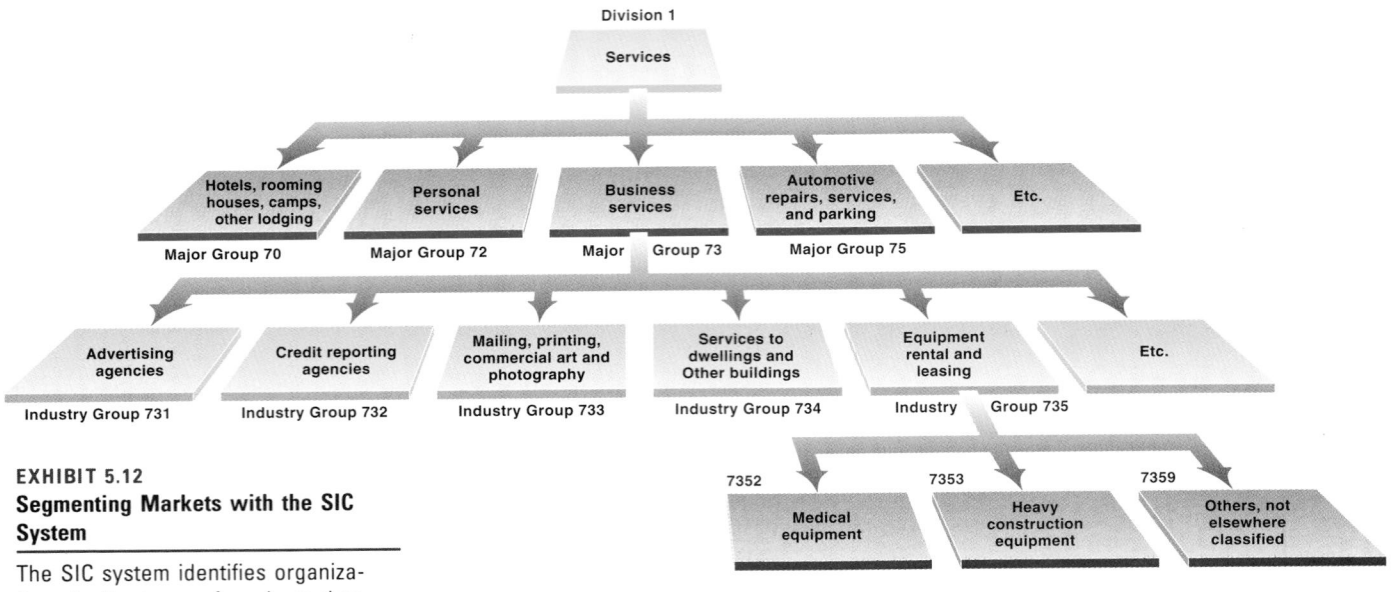

EXHIBIT 5.12

Segmenting Markets with the SIC System

The SIC system identifies organizations by the types of products they offer.

such as biomedical engineering. Second, some categories include too many types of businesses to pinpoint potential customers precisely.[50] Robot manufacturers, for instance, are included in a much broader category of factory automation equipment. Third, each company or major subsidiary is assigned one SIC code, even though it may be engaged in many different business activities. Finally, only U.S. companies are classified under the SIC system, and so it doesn't help international advertisers. To overcome these difficulties, several private research firms have developed their own classification schemes for companies in the United States and in other countries as well.

Geographic Segmentation. As in consumer markets, geography can be an important segmentation factor in organizational marketing. On a local level, organizational customers are often found in clusters, just as similar types of consumers are. Warehousing and shipping facilities are found near docks, railways, and interstate highways, for instance. On a regional level, some industries are clustered in particular spots around the country: lumber production in the United States tends be clustered in the Pacific Northwest and the Southeast; electronics and computer manufacturers have grown up in clusters such as California's Silicon Valley. Florida has more manufacturing plants than the eight-state region stretching from Idaho and Montana down to Arizona and New Mexico.[51] Geographic facts like these are important to advertisers trying to spend their media budgets most effectively.

Geographic segmentation sometimes influences advertising media selection. In most major cities, for instance, specialized newspapers or magazines cover the business community. These publications carry ads for office supply stores, computer services, import/export consultants, and other suppliers of the goods and services aimed at the organizational market.

Operational Segmentation. **Operational segmentation** identifies customers by the policies and practices they use to run their organizations. Operational factors include the kinds of technology customers employ, the products they use, the markets they pursue, and the managerial and technical capabilities they have.[52] Murata Erie North America, a supplier of electronic components, zeroed in on manufacturers of automotive subsystems who needed parts and support worldwide. One ad used the phrase "Whether you're making trip/navigation computers in Nüremburg, sensors in Seoul, or emission controls in Canada" to indicate the types of globally oriented customers Murata Erie was pursuing.[53]

But with new Microsoft Works 3.0, there's no telling where he'll go next.

In the last few years, Frank's business has come a long way. So has Microsoft* Works. Coincidence? You won't think so when you see how far new Works 3.0 can take *your* business. And this holds true whether you're working on *Star Trek: The Motion Picture* (like Frank) or something a little more down-to-earth.

That's because new Works comes with an enhanced word processor, database, spreadsheet—with charting, of course—drawing and communications tools. All of which have been redesigned to work even better together. But wait! There are still more features.

Like built-in business templates. You just plug in the information, and Works does the rest: income statements, payroll, and just about anything else you can think of. Perhaps this is the reason why Microsoft Works has been the industry's leading integrated product.

By the way, you'll even have a handy set of Avery* label forms online. When it comes to sending out flyers or bills, they make printing mailing labels just as easy as licking the stamps. And with its online Help, tutorial, and the *Getting Started* booklet, absolutely everything about Works is easy.

But don't let that fool you.

Works is powerful enough to grow with your business. To see how far, call (800) 541-1261, Department X43, for the closest Macintosh* reseller.

Microsoft
MAKING IT EASIER

FRANK SERAFINE, A MICROSOFT WORKS
USER SINCE 1986, ALSO DESIGNED SOUND EFFECTS
FOR *POLTERGEIST II: THE OTHER SIDE.*

Behavioral Segmentation. Finally, organizational customers can often be distinguished by the situations surrounding the purchase and application of the products they buy, creating an opportunity for behavioral segmentation (see Exhibit 5.13). The urgency with which orders must be filled is a good example of a situational variable that advertisers can focus on. For instance, the U.S. Postal Service pitches its Two-Day Priority Mail service to the catalog division of the Boston Museum of Fine Arts and to other organizations that need to make quick deliveries during the holiday gift-giving season.[54]

Targeting: In Search of the Ideal Audience

If your segmentation efforts have uncovered any interesting possibilities, your next move is to decide whether you want to select specific target markets (as opposed to using mass marketing) and which target segments you should select. Keep in mind also that targeting, like segmentation and positioning, is not solely an advertising issue. The targeting decision also involves questions regarding the products you have to offer, the distribution channels you'll use, the price you intend to charge, and your plans for other promotional efforts in addition to advertising. When selecting target segments, you must consider two questions: (1) What makes any segment meaningful? (2) What makes a meaningful segment attractive?

MEANINGFUL SEGMENTS

For a segment to be truly meaningful, it must be somehow different from other segments in terms of the way customers will respond to a given advertising effort or the way the segment can be approached. However, just because a group of people or organizations are somehow unique, they aren't automatically a meaningful segment for every advertiser. If you can't distinguish subgroups in a market by segmenting them according to identifiable criteria (such as geography or attitude), there is little or no value in segmenting the market (see Exhibit 5.14).

Say that you're on the staff at Rhino Records, which markets collections of hit music from the sixties and seventies. You have identified two segments: (1) recent immigrants who remember the old songs from imported movies and television

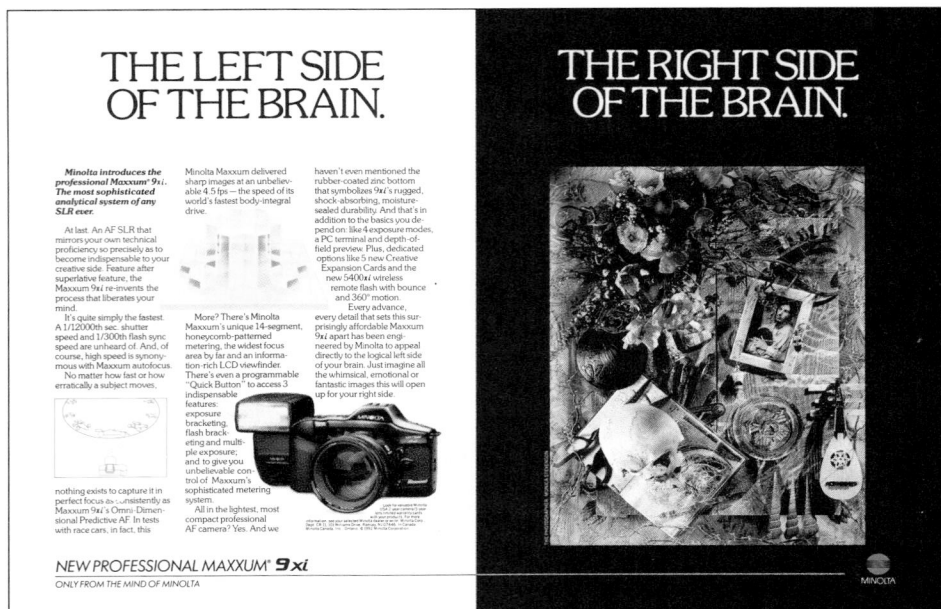

EXHIBIT 5.14
Deciding Whether to Segment

Would Minolta be as successful if it hadn't chosen to segment its market? This camera, aimed at professional photographers, would probably overwhelm many amateur photographers, as would the abundant technical information in the ad.

shows they saw in their home countries and (2) U.S. baby boomers who listened to the music here in the United States. If these two groups respond to music advertising in roughly the same way, and if you can reach them through the same media and distribution channels, then it really isn't meaningful to split them into two segments. On the other hand, if the recent immigrants view these songs as inspiring symbols of the American way of life, for instance, and the natives here view them as antiestablishment protest songs, then you might have two meaningful segments, because the two groups might respond to different advertising messages.

ATTRACTIVE SEGMENTS

An attractive segment is one that meets the criteria for being meaningful *and* that is a good fit with the advertiser's plans and available resources (time, money, and talent). Some important factors in selecting and prioritizing attractive segments include the following:[55]

- *Profitable opportunities.* You won't always be able to serve every market segment and still make a profit. Some customers demand prices that are too low relative to your production and marketing costs; other customers require too much attention and product customization. In other cases, competitors can undercut you in terms of price, leaving you to choose between being uncompetitive or being unprofitable. Of course, the segment has to be large enough to make the rewards bigger than the costs of going after them. This doesn't mean that small segments are not attractive by definition; it all depends on the individual marketer's ability to make a profit in any particular segment.

- *Growth potential.* The potential for growth in a segment isn't crucial for every advertiser in every segment, and even segments that are in fact shrinking can still be attractive targets in many cases. However, most advertisers do check to see whether a segment might be poised for growth. It is usually easier to pick up business from customers who are buying for the first time than to take customers away from competitors.

- *Acceptable risks.* Advertisers can never be sure what might happen once they choose to pursue a market segment, from new government regulations to resource shortages. On the other hand, if you can manage the risks better than your competitors can, you may have much of the segment all to yourself.

- *Acceptable entry and exit barriers.* As the terms imply, *entry barriers* are the financial, technical, political, and other obstacles that an organization must overcome before entering a market, and *exit barriers* are the constraints that keep a company from leaving a market, such as warranty commitments, customer expectations, and the investment a company makes in production facilities. For example, commercial aircraft manufacturing requires enormous sums of money for product development and production, so few firms have the resources needed to enter this market and compete with companies such as Boeing or Airbus. In fact, the costs of mounting an advertising campaign alone are sometimes enough to keep a company out of a market. Likewise, once it is selling products to a given market, a company might find it difficult to leave because of commitments to customers and distribution channels or simply because of the investment in manufacturing facilities. Advertisers should carefully consider such exit barriers before they choose a market segment, just to make sure they are committed to staying as long as they have to.

Just because you can't put your finger on every member of a segment doesn't mean the segment isn't attractive. Advertisers often rely on "segmenting through the appeal," or using a particular advertising appeal to attract the target prospects (see Exhibit 5.15). When Nike placed ads in *Tennis* magazine for its new Air Challenge Huarache tennis shoes, it was targeting a logical audience; people who read the magazine probably play tennis. However, Nike narrows its target market further. The ad copy distinguishes between serious and casual tennis players when it says, "You should try on a pair. Or you should take your wood racket and go play your niece."[56] Wood rackets are obsolete in tennis, and playing with one is a sign of being out of touch, passive, and generally not serious (or so Nike is implying). By drawing a line between the people who would wear this shoe and the people who use wood rackets, Nike is appealing to the aggressive, power-hungry players. The people in this segment would be nearly impossible to target name by name, but with an ad that appeals to their attitudes about tennis, Nike can attract them. Segmenting through the appeal is closely linked to the idea of positioning.

TARGET MARKETING OPTIONS

Target marketing presents a range of options, from not segmenting at all to making every customer a target segment. Advertisers can choose from four basic categories:[57]

Some risks are clearly visible. Others hide from sight.

The unexpected is the one thing you can always expect.

Risk. It isn't always where you expect it to be.

Suppose that overseas political upheaval thins out the flow of a raw material you can't do without. That's a risk Bankers Trust can help you contain.

Or suppose a natural disaster cripples your payments system. Again, with our merchant banking help, that risk can be dealt with.

Like every financial institution, we trade, arrange financing, close deals. But everything we do is done with an eye to helping you profit from risk.

Our greatest strength is putting all our skills to work at managing every kind of global risk.

Life can never be risk-free. Leadership isn't built on sure things. But with Bankers Trust behind you, you'll be leading from unparalleled strength.

Bankers Trust   LEAD FROM STRENGTH.

EXHIBIT 5.15
Segmenting through the Appeal

Bankers Trust has identified concern for financial risks as one of the key attributes of its target audience, but that's not a parameter the company could easily track down and measure (relative to how easily it could track down such parameters as sales volume, number of employees, or product offerings). Instead, this ad is designed to appeal most strongly to executives who are concerned about risk; those who aren't won't be as interested in or affected by the ad.

OPEN ON SHOT OF SMOGGY LOS ANGELES SKYLINE. A KNIFE CUTS OUT A BLOCK OF SMOGGY SKY. THIS BLOCK IS REPLACED WITH A CLEAR BLUE SKY BLOCK.

V.O.: Every single month people using ARCO's new EC premium unleaded and ARCO's EC-1 gasolines eliminate over 8 million pounds of air pollutants. They're doing

their part. How about you? Emission control gasolines. The pure and simple solution from ARCO.

EXHIBIT 5.16
Undifferentiated Marketing Can Still Make Sense

Other than a few obvious differences such as desire for full service and type of gasoline used, there probably isn't enough diversity in the gasoline market for differentiated marketing to make sense.

- *Undifferentiated marketing.* This is basic mass marketing, in which you sell only one product or product line and offer it to all customers in a single marketing mix. Undifferentiated marketing isn't necessarily bad, by the way, in spite of the benefits promised by target marketing strategies. Segmentation and targeting can cost more than undifferentiated marketing, so if you have no compelling reasons to employ them, undifferentiated marketing still makes the most sense (see Exhibit 5.16).

- *Differentiated marketing.* With this strategy, you target multiple groups of customers, aiming a particular marketing mix or advertising message at each one. This allows you to pursue a wide range of customers while still providing the benefits of segmentation. Coca-Cola's strategy is a good example of this approach; the company wants everyone in the world to drink Coke, but it offers a variety of product formulations served up with different advertising messages.

- *Concentrated marketing.* Both undifferentiated and differentiated marketing tackle large markets, often encompassing a number of distinct market segments. With concentrated marketing, on the other hand, you pick a single target segment and focus all your effort on it. Westfield Whip Manufacturing, for instance, makes buggy whips for harness racers; that's all the company does, so concentrated marketing to harness racers is an appropriate choice.[58] Advertisers choose concentration strategies either because their specialized markets require focused attention or because they don't have the resources to go after more than one segment at a time.

- *Individualized marketing.* This is the ultimate in target marketing: it turns every customer into a unique target segment. For the product part of the marketing mix, *individualized* can mean crafting unique products for each customer. In advertising, it can mean such things as creating unique direct-mail packages for each customer, taking into account data (such as likes and dislikes) that have been collected and analyzed in advance.

You can see that an advertiser's choice of targeting strategy depends on both the nature of the market and the advertiser's own resources. In addition, some advertisers employ more than one strategy at a time, such as combining an undifferentiated national advertising campaign with customized direct-mail letters. In any case, target marketing of one form or another is clearly the wave of the future for most advertisers.

Positioning: Moving into the Audience's Mind

Think about cheeseburgers for a minute. Who makes the very best cheeseburger you've ever eaten? Who makes the second best? Now think about sports cars, candy bars, and personal computers. In each product category that interests you, you probably have a favorite brand or supplier. This brand or store achieved the top spot in your mind through a combination of advertising, word of mouth, product performance, and other variables. The **position** that a brand occupies in your mind is the sum of your perceptions about it, relative to competing products. The process of prompting buyers to form a particular mental impression of your product relative to its competitors is called **positioning.**

How you go about achieving your desired position depends on the type of product, the competition, customer needs, and other factors. Mercedes-Benz achieved the position it occupies through years of consistent product quality, a certain style of advertising, premium prices, and upscale dealer showrooms. McDonald's achieved its position through its own combination of elements.

Marketers usually rely heavily on advertising to help them achieve their positions, but advertising is only part of the process. In some product categories, the rest of the marketing mix, particularly product and price, can affect positioning as much as or more than advertising can (see Exhibit 5.17). A television commercial that shows an economy car tooling around a posh estate isn't going to make anyone think it's a luxury car. Either you have to have a real luxury car, or you have to have an ad that supports the reality of the economy car (by showing it driving past one gas station after another, for example).

Also, it's important to realize that you don't really position your organization and your products—the market does. You can say and do whatever you want, but

EXHIBIT 5.17
Advertising's Role in Positioning

By distancing itself from high-fashion brands Armani and Versace, Harley-Davidson positions its clothing very clearly.

FASHION MAGAZINES HAVE COMMENTED THAT OUR LABEL IS NOW AS CHIC AS ARMANI AND VERSACE.

WHOEVER THEY ARE.

HARLEY-DAVIDSON OF NORTH TEXAS
1910 OLD DENTON RD. CARROLLTON (214) 620-1777

A successful positioning strategy starts with the *positioning statement*, a declaration of the position you'd like to occupy in the minds of your target customers. Whether the position you seek is "the most rugged guitar amplifiers in the universe" or "the most reliable source of industrial fasteners in the Midwest," your positioning statement serves as the guiding light and driving force behind all your advertising. You can develop positioning statements using the following steps:

- *Step 1: Recognize reality.* Start by assessing where you and your competitors stand today, even if the answer is unpleasant. If you're at the bottom, it's better to recognize that now rather than later.
- *Step 2: Make sure your business and marketing plans are clear.* Your positioning statement and the advertising that it produces need to be coordinated with all levels of strategies and plans in the organization. The place to start is by making sure that your strategic plans clearly identify which market segments the company wants to pursue and how it plans to do so.
- *Step 3: Identify what's important to customers in each target segment and what benefits they're looking for.* Before you can produce a sensible positioning goal or effective advertising, you have to know what criteria potential buyers use to pick one product over another. It might be loudness and ruggedness in the case of your guitar amplifiers. In some instances, you'll have a long list of criteria; when that's the case, comb through them to find the handful of most important ones.
- *Step 4: Understand the position of existing products.* Before you can differentiate yourself from the competition, know

who your competitors are and how they're perceived by target customers.

- *Step 5: Pick the best position.* Based on what you know about customer needs and current competitors, identify the position you want to take over. (If the best position is already taken, you have three choices: forget it and find another opportunity, try to dislodge the current occupant, or try to *reposition* the current occupant by convincing the market that the current occupant's product is no longer the best one.)
- *Step 6: Write your positioning statement.* Now you're ready to write a concise statement that describes the position you want to occupy in the market and how you'll get there. You can do this first by describing your desired position in terms of what's important to customers (the most rugged guitar amp) and then by describing the problem you're going to solve for your customers (amps get knocked around on stage, and musicians don't want equipment that can't take the abuse). Next, describe the solution you plan to offer (amps that protect their internal components with an innovative shock-absorption system) and the people who should be interested (rock and jazz musicians who perform live). Now string it all together: "This guitar amp's shock-absorption system offers live performers a new level of equipment reliability."

You can now use your positioning statement to plan an advertising campaign, develop new products, train salespeople, and perform just about any other marketing activity.

Apply Your Knowledge

1. Write a positioning statement for your college or university with high school students as the target market.
2. Can you write an effective positioning statement without first segmenting your market? Explain your answer. ∎

in the end individual customers are the ones who decide what they think about you.[59] Positioning is a lot like romance; you can influence someone's thoughts and feelings, but you can't make someone fall in love with you. In both positioning and romance, your job is to be consistent, dependable, and persuasive. If you do the right things long enough, if you've targeted the right audience, and if the competition hasn't beaten you to the punch, you should eventually achieve your goal.

THE IMPORTANCE OF POSITIONING

The more promotional communication that potential customers receive, the more important a clear position in the market becomes. In the United States and other countries with advanced free-market economies, consumers and organizational customers in many product categories often receive more communication than they can possibly absorb. A recent 200-page issue of *WindowsUser* magazine, aimed at personal computer owners, had 80 pages of product ads from 55 advertisers—and all the articles filling the other 120 pages were about computer products as well (these articles discussed more than 200 products). That's a mind-boggling amount of product information, and this was just a single issue of a single magazine. Multiply this by 12 months in a year and by the number of other computer magazines on the market, then throw in the regular stream of direct-mail ads that computer owners receive, and it's easy to see how these customers get overloaded with information.

How can any advertiser hope to stand out amid all this communication? One of the most important steps is having a clear position in the marketplace. When the customers and potential customers know who you are and what your brand name stands for, you have a much better chance of breaking through the clutter than competitors who are unknown or who haven't communicated a clear and convincing message to the market. That issue of *WindowsUser* acknowledges as much in an article about a software product called FrameMaker: "With PageMaker and Ventura Publisher, both fine programs, already solidly entrenched in the market, FrameMaker has a tough row to hoe in grabbing its share." PageMaker and Ventura have worked for years to establish their positions, making it difficult for any new product to enter this market.

POSITIONING FOR LEADERS AND FOLLOWERS

Consultants Al Ries and Jack Trout, who helped popularize the concept of positioning over the last two decades, emphasize that the best way to approach positioning depends on where you stand relative to your competitors.[60] Market leaders such as Coca-Cola, IBM, General Motors, and AT&T face a different set of challenges than smaller and newer competitors like Snapple, Zeos, Hyundai, and Sprint because they start from different positions in the market.

The issue of change is what separates the positioning strategies of market leaders and their competitors. If you have the lead position in a market, you don't want people to change their perceptions of the "pecking order." Market leader AT&T would like customers to keep thinking that it is the best provider of long-distance telephone service and that Sprint and MCI are also-rans. Conversely, Sprint and MCI are trying to change the country's mind about the pecking order; both of these newer and smaller competitors would like to be known as equal to or better than AT&T. Sprint ads talk about service quality so good that you can "hear a pin drop," an effort to convince consumers and businesses that its service is as good as and perhaps better than AT&T's, while MCI often promotes its prices relative to AT&T's. You'll learn more about positioning strategies in Chapter 7, where a number of options are discussed as part of the process of developing advertising strategies.

Summary

Target marketing is a three-stage process involving segmenting a market, targeting particular segments, and positioning your product in the minds of potential buyers. As markets have become increasingly fragmented in recent years, target marketing has become an attractive strategic option for many marketers—and a necessary choice for many others. Whether advertisers use target marketing because they choose to or because their competitors do, the process provides several potential benefits: more efficient use of resources, a better understanding of customer needs, and a better understanding of competitors. Some advertisers are reluctant to segment their markets because doing so can present significant risks, particularly if segments are misdefined or poorly chosen. Also, not everyone is comfortable with the idea of actively ignoring potential buyers in order to focus on narrowly defined segments.

The most common ways of segmenting consumer advertising audiences are based on demographic, geographic, psychographic, and geodemographic factors. Demographic factors include age, income, education, and other objective data. Geo-graphic factors center on customers' physical locations. Psycho-graphic factors include motivation, desired benefits, attitude, lifestyle, personality, consumer behavior, and brand loyalty. Geodemographic factors organize demographic data on a geographic basis, yielding segmentation models that, in many respects, seem similar to psychographic approaches. The methods used to segment organizational audiences are similar in some important ways to the methods used to segment consumer markets but different in others. In general, logical and objective factors tend to play a more important role than most of the psychographic and geodemographic factors used in consumer segmentation. The four categories discussed are based on demographic, geographic, operational, and behavioral factors.

Two factors make a market segment meaningful: the way customers respond to advertising and the way the segment can be approached. If all customers in a market respond to advertising in the same way or can be approached in the same way, there isn't much reason to segment the market. Once a segment has been designated as meaningful, several checkpoints can

Meeting an Advertising Challenge at L.A. Gear

The rise and fall (or at least temporary slide) of L.A. Gear illustrates some of the risks inherent in segmentation, targeting, and positioning. If you can attain your desired position in a healthy target segment, great. However, what if that segment stops growing or even shrinks? Worse yet, what if you become so identified with that segment that consumers in other segments are reluctant to accept you?

This is Stanley Gold's L.A. Gear dilemma in a nutshell. The company rocketed to success with faddish, wildly decorated footwear, but U.S. consumers don't seem committed to shoe fads for any length of time. Furthermore, the L.A. Gear name came to represent glitzy, inexpensively built shoes for trendy teenage girls. It's not an image that most adults or even many teens are comfortable with. As the company tried to expand into Nike's and Reebok's territory, its own name became a liability in many cases. It was a big enough liability that the Catapult basketball shoe was introduced without the L.A. Gear brand attached to it. However, Gold couldn't drop the L.A. Gear name entirely, or he'd be starting all over as a virtual nobody in terms of brand awareness.

Dropping the L.A. Gear name would also cut Gold off from the millions of customers who still buy his shoes.

So Gold decided to segment his marketing efforts in a way that reflects the major segments in the market, while still trying to take advantage of the company's presence in the market. Rather than pushing a single brand name and its associated image into every segment, L.A. Gear now splits its marketing along three lines: performance shoes, fashion shoes, and children's shoes. Gold advertises all three lines under the umbrella theme "Get in gear," but he lets each one work on its own image. For instance, the performance shoes are now marketed under the name L.A. Tech, while the children's shoes continue the search for fashion trendiness with such offerings as L.A. Lights, shoes with lights in the heel.

Gold and his management team are optimistic, but they caution that the turnaround will take several years to complete. The company's financial picture seems to be brightening somewhat, and L.A. Lights are selling well. The next few years will tell how well the new target marketing strategy is actually working.

Your Mission: You've recently joined L.A. Gear as U.S. marketing manager. Your responsibilities include segmentation, targeting, and positioning strategy, as well as the advertising programs that will support L.A. Gear's marketing strategy. In each of the following scenarios, choose the answer that will do the best job of helping L.A. Gear turn around.

1. You realize that to capture more high-end customers from Nike and Reebok, you'll need to get past the consumer perception that L.A. Gear is a brand for trendy kids. Which of the following ideas for a television commercial would do the best job of getting Nike and Reebok customers to switch without losing current L.A. Gear buyers?

a. Show teenagers and their parents together shopping for L.A. Gear; emphasize family fun and the togetherness angle.

b. Portray the comforts of L.A. Gear as a welcome relief from the daily stress of working, parenting, and so on.

c. Get rid of everything in your ads that smacks of youth and trendiness; show middle-aged consumers lounging around

---

help the advertiser select the most attractive segments, including (1) profitable opportunities, (2) growth potential, (3) acceptable levels of risk, and (4) acceptable entry and exit barriers.

Positioning is the process of prompting buyers to form particular mental impressions of a product relative to its competitors. Each buyer of a given type of product probably has a favorite brand or supplier, and he or she will compare all competitors to it. Positioning is a key part of advertising because it defines the goal that advertising should help achieve.

Key Terms

behavioral segmentation 124
benefit segmentation 122
brand loyalty 124
demographic
   segmentation 117
geodemographic
   segmentation 124
geographic
   segmentation 120
household 118
market segment 114

mass marketing 114
operational
   segmentation 128
position 133
positioning 133
product-use
   segmentation 124
psychographic
   segmentation 122
segmentation 114

Standard Industrial
   Classification (SIC)
   codes 127

target marketing 114
target segment 114

Questions

FOR REVIEW

1. Why would advertisers choose to deliberately ignore some potential customers?

2. How does mass marketing differ from target marketing?

3. What are the most common factors used to segment consumer markets, and how do these differ from the factors used to segment organizational markets?

4. How does the output of geodemographic segmentation resemble the output of psychographic segmentation?

5. What does it mean to have a position in the mind of a potential buyer?

FOR ANALYSIS AND APPLICATION

6. Would a local newspaper such as *The San Jose Mercury News* ever want to segment its market for advertising or other marketing purposes? Why or why not?

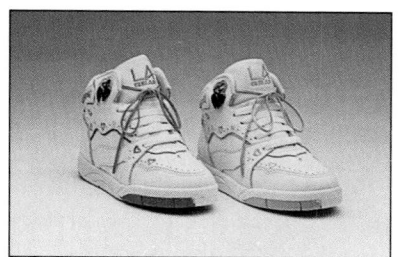

upscale resorts wearing L.A. Gear shoes.

2. Segmenting by product use is a common approach in the athletic shoe market, with shoes aimed specifically at tennis, basketball, running, walking, and so forth. This makes good sense for both consumers and shoe manufacturers, but the one big drawback is that all your competitors are following the same general strategy. You'd like to open up a market segment that no one has thought of before and establish L.A. Gear as the preferred brand in that segment. In terms of being both meaningful and attractive, how would you rate the following three segmentation ideas?

a. To capitalize on the spirit of international togetherness that the Olympic Games engender, try to create the "Olympic attitude" segment, in which people who share the Olympic spirit will be drawn toward athletic shoes that mirror this spirit. L.A. Gear's ad themes

could be linked to particular games, such as Atlanta in 1996.

b. Most ads for athletic shoes are aimed at younger audiences, so maybe you should try the other direction and target active older people. You could consider ad themes such as "For the best times of your life" or "It's time to enjoy life."

c. In addition to nearly always portraying young people, the typical athletic shoe advertising strategy revolves around healthy, active lifestyles. Not everyone is healthy and active, however, and many people have little interest in such lifestyles. Maybe these people would make a good target segment. Skip the high-energy athletic angle and focus on comfort or some other factor, with ads that say "Slow down and put your feet up . . . in shoes from L.A. Gear."

3. Assume that your positioning statement in the women's casual wear

segment is "casual shoes in understated styles for the contemporary career woman." Which of the following ad slogans proposed by your ad agency will do the best job of helping you attain that desired position? Why?

a. "High-performance casuals from L.A. Gear"

b. "Casual shoes with a contemporary touch"

c. "Very L.A. Very You."

4. Brand names play a big role in positioning, partly because they signify what the product stands for and partly because they give buyers something to identify with (such as the Air Jordan brand from Nike). Assume you're planning to launch a hiking shoe, and you want to position it as the shoe for serious hikers and backpackers. Which of these brand names would you pick and why?

a. Outdoor L.A.

b. Mountaineers

c. L.A. Mountain [61]

7. How might 7-Eleven benefit from a system like PRIZM?

8. Can you describe any possible market segments that the U.S. Army might want to avoid targeting in its advertising campaigns to recruit volunteers? What about possible segments that it should target? (You can use your imagination to describe these segments, since you don't have immediate access to all the data you would need for a serious segmentation project.)

9. Why might a builder of midrange standardized houses such as Centex Homes shy away from particular segments, even though people in those segments could afford the homes the company builds?

10. How would you describe the position(s) that your college has in the minds of the students at your old high school?

Sharpen Your Advertising Skills

Advertisers perceived some distinct changes in consumer attitudes when the buy-everything-in-sight mode of the 1980s turned into the look-for-quality-and-get-out-of-debt mode of the

1990s. In the car market, Audi went so far as to use the theme "Welcome to the '90s" in ads that talk about leaving the excesses of the 1980s behind. Mercedes-Benz took a slightly different tack with its new slogan "Sacrifice nothing," which it says reflects consumers' newfound insistence on getting their money's worth from high-quality products. It's a curious market to do business in, however; even if many consumers are no longer interested in conspicuous consumption, Audis still cost from $22,650 to $54,900 and Mercedes from $28,950 to $127,800.

Decision: Assume that you're in charge of advertising for Mercedes-Benz and that the "Sacrifice nothing" slogan doesn't exist. Decide how you'll position these very expensive products in a market that seems to focus on value these days. Come up with a slogan that reflects the position you'd like the car line to achieve in the minds of your target segment (the affluent drivers who want the best but don't want to feel like they're overindulging).

Communication: Now assume that a reporter from *The New York Times* is on the phone, asking you to explain the new slogan and how it relates to today's consumers. Explain the slogan as succinctly as you can.

Advertising Research

After studying this chapter, you will be able to

1. Differentiate between advertising research and marketing research
2. Explain why advertisers use research
3. Differentiate primary, secondary, syndicated, and single-source data
4. List the six steps in the general research process
5. Describe the three major applications of advertising research
6. Explain how research is used to measure advertising effectiveness
7. Discuss the factors that influence quality in advertising research

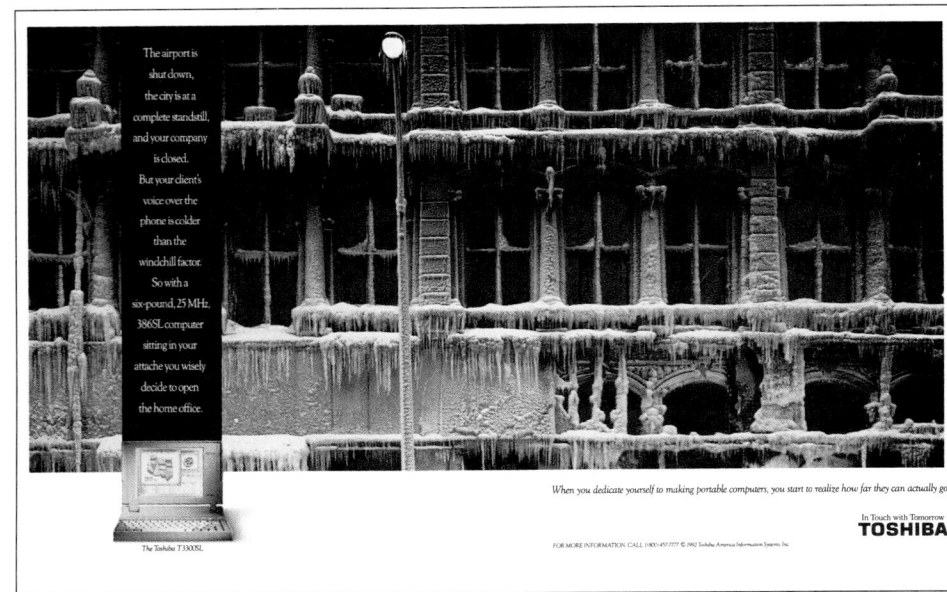

Facing an Advertising Challenge at the U.S. Postal Service

STAMPING A NEW IMAGE IN THE PUBLIC'S MIND

You wouldn't have to tell John Wargo or his colleagues at the U.S. Postal Service that they need to get more from their marketing and advertising efforts. Wargo, the assistant postmaster general in charge of marketing, describes their efforts as trying to "position ourselves as modern and caring and not necessarily as old fashioned." He knows that many consumers and businesses view the Postal Service as rather bureaucratic, impersonal, and even incompetent to a degree. His goal is to have people "walk away feeling something positive is going on in the Postal Service," and he wants advertising to play a key role in this transformation.

Image and perception are not the only issues facing the Postal Service, however. Although it has a government-mandated monopoly on the regular delivery of letters, it does face competition when it comes to overnight mail or package delivery services. This market has been cut into dramatically by hungry competi-tors, including such giants as Federal Express and United Parcel Service as well as smaller regional and local delivery and courier services. The Postal Service was the first to offer overnight express service, more than two decades ago, but even postal executives admit that Federal Express has "taken the overnight business to its heights."

Although it is a government opera-tion, the Postal Service functions like a business in many respects, including identifying new products and promot-ing them to the public. The Elvis Presley stamp, introduced on the King's birthday (January 8) in 1992, was a major commercial success. By letting the public vote on which of two versions to produce, the Postal Ser-vice not only generated a great deal of publicity but also captured the names and addresses of the 800,000 people who voted. These consumers then received direct-mail advertising for various products related to the Elvis stamp, resulting in Elvis sales to the tune of about $20 million.

Wargo also notes that beyond image, competition, and special prod-ucts, the Postal Service has an educational mission. Using the mail is no longer limited to licking a stamp and dropping your letter in the mail-box. In some cases, the educational effort is as simple as telling con-sumers when they need to mail packages in time for Christmas deliv-ery. In other cases, the story is more complex—such as helping direct mar-keters who want to send millions of odd-sized envelopes and who need to know the best way to automate the process.

What should John Wargo do to make Postal Service advertising as successful as possible? If you were in his position, what steps would you take to better understand consumers and businesses? How could you dis-cover their thoughts and feelings about the Postal Service? How would you translate such knowledge into effective advertising?[1] ■

CHAPTER OVERVIEW John Wargo realized that effective advertising research can lead to more effective advertising. In this chapter, you'll see how advertisers and their agencies use research for a variety of purposes, from defining their markets to testing the effectiveness of their ads. First you'll get a picture of why advertisers take the time and trouble to conduct research, and you'll be introduced to the basic approaches they use. Following that, you'll explore the general process of advertising research, from defining the problem at hand to presenting the results to decision makers. The next section introduces you to the most common ways advertisers use research: to assess opportunities and define goals, to develop plans and create messages, and to evaluate advertising effectiveness. Finally, you'll learn about commercial advertising research services and the factors that ensure quality in advertising research.

Understanding Research

As you've probably realized by this point, advertising involves some uncertainty and risk. Have you picked the right target markets? Do you really understand what your customers want? Will the right people watch the television shows you spon-sor? Are your ads having any effect on sales? Advertisers and their agencies face questions like these day after day. How do they find the answers to their questions? How do they make the necessary decisions? Most rely on some form of research.

The general category of this research is **marketing research,** a systematic approach to providing information and support for the entire range of marketing

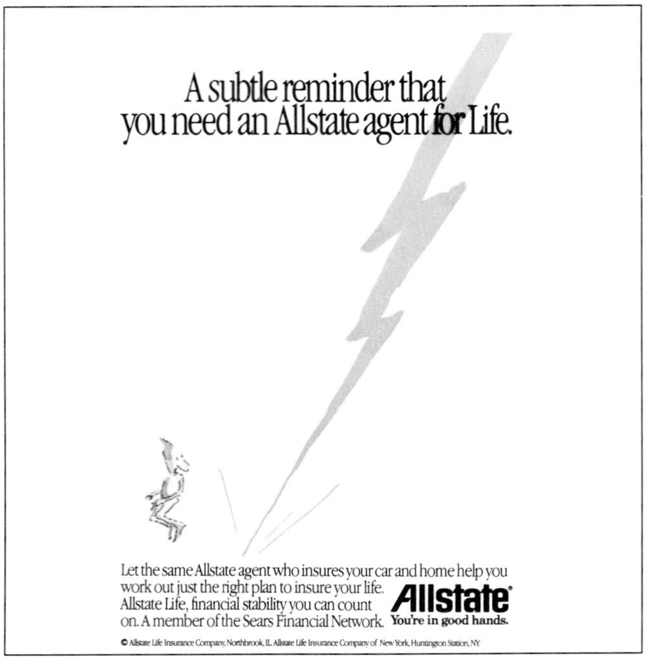

EXHIBIT 6.1
Message Research

Message research tries to measure how effectively an intended advertising message gets across to the target audience. Simple messages, such as the one portrayed in this Allstate ad, tend to communicate better than complex or obscure messages.

decisions, from sales forecasting and product development to product positioning and media selection.[2] In other words, it covers the entire marketing mix. One part of marketing research (and sometimes confused with it) is **market research,** which focuses on gathering information about a particular market. Another part of marketing research is **advertising research,** which deals with the risks, uncertainties, and decisions involved in creating and applying advertising [3] Advertising research can itself be divided in two: **Media research** concerns information about the circulation of newspapers and magazines, broadcast coverage of television and radio, and audience profiles. **Message research** addresses how effectively advertising messages are communicated to people and how well those messages influence people's behavior (see Exhibit 6.1).[4]

A recent ad campaign by Eaton Corporation's truck transmission division shows how beneficial advertising research can be, both in explaining how to create ads that customers will respond to and in helping advertisers and their agencies cast aside preconceived notions of customer needs and attitudes. Before conducting its research, Eaton ran image-based magazine ads, one showing an empty highway leading off into the horizon and one showing a truck flying over the Houston skyline. When company managers and their ad agency sat down and listened to customers, they realized that transmission buyers weren't interested in "creative imagery and intangible concepts," as one Eaton manager put it. Buyers wanted to see the transmissions up close and read about the features and the technical advantages. Clearly, Eaton needed to change its advertising strategy and it did. The company's latest ads feature close-up photos of transmissions and technically oriented copy—a direct response to the insights uncovered during research.[5]

It's important to understand that although research can help advertisers reduce the uncertainties and manage the risks associated with advertising, it cannot eliminate those risks and uncertainties. Successful advertisers rely on intuition, experience, and judgment, and they use research to support those talents. As expert advertiser and researcher John Philip Jones emphasized, research is "a disastrous substitute for judgment."[6] Effective advertising springs both from the insights that good research can produce and from the creativity and judgment of the people involved.

WHY ADVERTISERS CONDUCT RESEARCH

Advertisers conduct research primarily to increase efficiency and effectiveness, minimize risk, and improve advertising's financial accountability:

- *Make advertising more efficient and effective.* Research can help make advertising more efficient (accomplishing its goals faster and with less money) and more effective (accomplishing its goals more completely). For instance, some advertisers tried switching from 30-second to 15-second television commercials to get more commercials on the air for the same amount of money. However, researchers have shown that the 15-second commercials are sometimes too short; people can't absorb the message that quickly.[7] Such insights are enormously helpful when it's time to plan an advertising campaign.

- *Reduce risk.* Advertising involves risk, and it's more than just the risk that you'll waste money. Inappropriate advertising can alienate current customers and decrease your chances of attracting new ones. General Foods has targeted women in ads for its International Coffees ever since the brand was introduced in 1974. The company recently decided to expand its market by more actively targeting men, but the advertising team recognizes the great risk this decision involves: ads aimed more overtly at men might estrange the women who are overwhelmingly the brand's biggest consumers. General Foods is relying on advertising research to make sure it doesn't drive women away while trying to attract men.[8]

- *Make advertising more accountable.* Imagine you are in charge of the advertising budget at Procter & Gamble, which spends over $1 billion a year on advertising.[9] Wouldn't you like to know whether that mammoth investment is paying off? Advertising research can help by telling you who's getting your messages and whether or not those messages are effective.

Of course, research can't always provide the answers that advertisers are looking for, nor do all research techniques promise the same level of accuracy. However, advertising is expensive. The 100 largest advertisers in the United States collectively spend over $30 billion a year on advertising.[10] Given such enormous expenditures, advertisers are willing to consider just about any technique that will help them get more for the money they spend on agencies and media.

HOW ADVERTISERS APPROACH RESEARCH

Sometimes research is as simple as asking a group of people what's important to them in the products they use. At other times, research involves complex data-collection and -evaluation procedures that stretch out over many months and cost many thousands of dollars. To put research into perspective, look at the data sources researchers can choose from and consider the types of research methods used to gather those data.

Sources of Data

Data are basic facts, figures, ideas, and other bits and pieces that, when organized and analyzed in meaningful ways, yield **information.** The data used by advertising researchers fall into two main categories. Data being gathered first-hand for a specific purpose are considered **primary data,** which can be collected by conducting surveys, interviewing customers, observing shoppers in stores, recording checkout scanner data, and attaching devices to televisions in order to record which channels are being watched (see Exhibit 6.2).[11] Primary data can be expensive and time consuming to collect, but primary research is often the only way to successfully answer specific advertising research questions.

In contrast, data already collected for an earlier purpose and reused for a new research problem are known as **secondary data.**[12] Ranging from U.S. Census figures to reports written by stock market analysts, secondary data can be less expensive to obtain than primary data. When the advertising team at General Foods wanted to know what women thought about the coffee-drinking experience,

EXHIBIT 6.2
Collecting Primary Data

Data collected at supermarket checkout scanners is one of the consumer advertiser's most important research sources.

their researchers collected primary data, gathering answers directly from women in the target market segment. However, if these researchers had chosen to read published reports written by a coffee industry trade association or to analyze General Foods' internal sales records, they would have been collecting secondary data. Projects often involve both types of data (as you'll see later in the chapter), because researchers who are planning to collect primary data usually start by examining any available secondary data.

Each category of data has its benefits and limitations. Primary data give you an edge none of your competitors have (because they don't have the data), and you have a better chance of getting the particular data you need because you can design the research to fit your situation. The biggest limitations of primary data are the costs and the time needed to collect and process the data.[13] The benefits and limitations of secondary data are basically the reverse. Secondary data usually cost less than primary data and can often be accessed more quickly. In addition, secondary data often help advertisers do a better job of planning primary research by clarifying the key issues. Because secondary data are available to anyone who pays for them, they limit your ability to gain the competitive advantage you can get with primary data. Moreover, secondary data may not answer your specific questions, they may be too old to be accurate or useful, and you may not be able to analyze them to the same depth that you can analyze primary data.[14]

Two special categories of primary data figure prominently in many advertisers' research efforts. **Syndicated data** are collected by specialized firms for more than one client at a time. Any advertiser who wants to pay for the data can see the results. You've probably heard of the Nielsen television ratings, a good example of syndicated research.[15] **Single-source data** are the results of comparing all the advertising received and all the purchasing behavior exhibited by selected households (all the data come from a single source, hence the name). Single-source data, which are often syndicated, promise to play an interesting part in future advertising research since they offer the chance to directly measure the influence of advertising on consumer buying behavior.[16]

Types of Research

Advertisers conduct various types of research, from trying to identify who's buying what to figuring out what went wrong with a campaign. All this research can be grouped into three general categories:[17]

- *Exploratory research.* Often, the first step in advertising research is trying to get a better idea of just what you should be investigating. Research that's used to help clarify the definition of a problem and to lay the groundwork for more extensive advertising research is called **exploratory research.** This sort of research can range from simply asking experienced colleagues for their opinions and perspectives to conducting research with representative audience members.

- *Descriptive research.* Much of the research conducted by advertisers is **descriptive research,** which attempts to characterize conditions in a market, attitudes of audience members, or other factors of interest to advertisers. For instance, the U.S. Travel and Tourism Administration commissioned descriptive research to identify the characteristics of people who travel internationally for pleasure, to estimate the U.S. market share of international vacation travel, and to learn how potential travelers view the United States and its attractions relative to competing destinations. The researchers queried vacationers in Great Britain, Germany, and France to discover that people in various European countries have differing attitudes and interests. For example, French travelers rated Southern California as the most desirable destination, whereas Germans put Hawaii at the top of their lists. People from Britain find food to be a key travel experience, whereas the French place little importance on vacation eating experiences.[18] Such insights from descriptive research can be invaluable when it's time to select the words and images that go into ads.

Advertising research raises ethical questions in a couple of important areas. The first of these is privacy, which involves the issue of keeping respondents' answers secret and the issue of invading people's privacy in the pursuit of research answers. Examples of invading privacy include grocery stores that videotape shoppers to see whether they read product labels and car dealers that plant recording devices in new cars to discover what consumers say as they consider car purchases. Both examples raise important ethical concerns. In fact, California and other states have made auto showroom "bugs" and other hidden research techniques illegal.

The second area of research ethics is the use of fraudulent or deceptive research methods. One particularly troubling practice is selling (or fund-raising, in the case of nonprofit organizations) under the guise of research—a practice sometimes called "sugging," short for selling under a guise. When people agree to answer research questions, they deserve to be shielded from selling efforts. This is to the researcher's benefit, too, since people may be more inclined to open up and share personal data in a research setting than in a sales setting. In addition, ethical problems may crop up when research results are used or sold; for instance, research firms may feel pressured to please clients by making results look more positive than they really are. However, such pressures must be ignored.

Fortunately, you can avoid many ethical problems simply by applying common sense and by stopping to consider possible problems before launching research projects. Put yourself in the respondent's shoes and try to imagine how you would feel if you were divulging intimate details and you weren't sure whether the researcher would keep them secret or turn right around and use them to sell you something. Similarly, how would you feel if you discovered that your shopping habits were being recorded on video? Looking at research from the respondent's perspective goes a long way toward helping you stay on an ethical path.

In addition, a number of professional and industry associations offer their members guidelines for conducting marketing and advertising research in an ethical manner (in many cases, the associations require their members to abide by their published ethics codes). For example, the International Chamber of Commerce joined with the European Society for Opinion and Marketing Research to create the *ICC/ESOMAR International Code of Marketing and Social Research Practice.* This extensive set of guidelines addresses such important topics as protecting respondents' anonymity, interviewing children, publishing research results, and ensuring clients' rights when an outside firm is conducting the research.

What's Your Opinion?

1. *Should the practice of observing shoppers without their knowledge or permission, either live or on videotape, be banned entirely? What would you suggest as an alternative way to gather the same research data?*
2. *Successful salespeople often start by asking prospects about their wants and needs, questions that can be quite similar to the sorts of questions asked in advertising research. Is this the same problem as selling under the guise of research? Why or why not?*

- *Causal research.* The third research category is **causal research,** which identifies the factors responsible for a particular effect in the marketplace. For example, you would use causal research when you want to understand how a heavier advertising schedule might affect customer awareness of your product. Understanding such cause-and-effect relationships provides valuable information for decision making, but causal research must be used with care. It's often impossible to tell with any great certainty whether changes in audience awareness, audience attitudes, or sales resulted from changes in your advertising. Did your sales go up because you had better ads or because a major competitor stopped producing a similar product? Did customers notice your product because you increased your advertising or because a local environmental group endorsed the product as being especially safe? You cannot control every factor in the marketplace, so you must use caution when looking at the results of causal research.

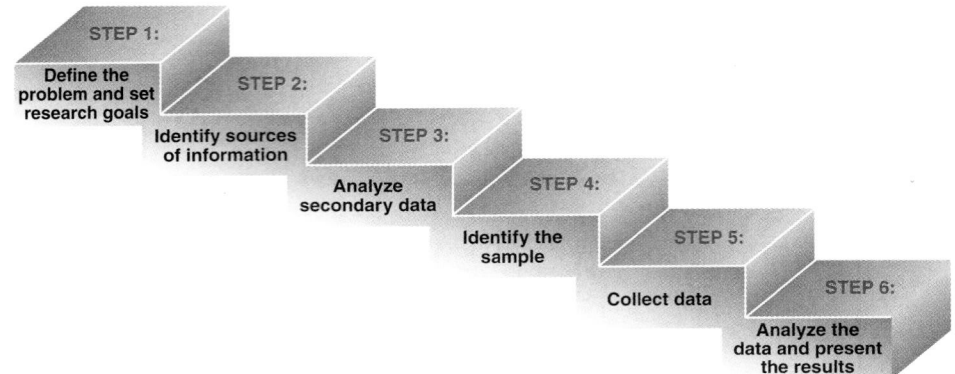

EXHIBIT 6.3
The General Research Process

The six steps shown here represent the general model for conducting marketing and advertising research.

STEP 1: Define the problem and set research goals

STEP 2: Identify sources of information

STEP 3: Analyze secondary data

STEP 4: Identify the sample

STEP 5: Collect data

STEP 6: Analyze the data and present the results

Conducting Research

Whether you're looking for new market opportunities or assessing the impact of a commercial that ran on prime-time television last night, research follows the general sequence of steps presented in Exhibit 6.3. Depending on your organizational position and responsibilities, you may be involved in all these steps or in only some of them.

STEP 1: DEFINE THE PROBLEM AND SET RESEARCH GOALS

In many advertising research projects, the problem to be investigated is quite clear. In other cases, though, the problem is difficult to define: your questions may be too vague, you may have only a hunch about what needs to be investigated, or you may recognize the symptoms of a problem without understanding the cause. One good way to help define the problem is to identify the specific advertising decision(s) that must be made as a result of the research and then focus on the pieces of information needed to make those decisions. Advertisers often use exploratory research at this stage, as they try to discover the problem, understand the questions they need to ask, and decide on the types of information to collect. It's a good idea to list the specific pieces of information you'll need, to make sure you cover all the right areas.[19] Professional researchers sometimes recommend that you write as much of the final research report as you can before starting the actual research. The logic behind this unusual advice is that writing the report forces you to focus on the problem and helps flush out additional questions that may need to be asked.

Once you've identified the information you'll need to make the necessary advertising decisions, you can establish goals for the research project. As with all business and marketing goals, the goals of advertising research should be clear and specific and should be agreed on by everyone involved before the project begins.[20] Typical research goals include the following:

- To see which of two ad concepts delivers our message most effectively
- To measure consumer attitudes regarding competitive products so that we can exploit areas of potential weakness
- To measure changes in awareness of our products from the beginning to the end of this six-month ad campaign

STEP 2: IDENTIFY SOURCES OF INFORMATION

The next step is to identify where you might be able to find the information you need. In some cases, the answers to your questions can be found among sales records, customer service reports, or other internal secondary sources. In other cases, external secondary sources may provide the information you need (see

ADVERTISING CHECKLIST FOR PLANNING RESEARCH PROJECTS

❏ A. Set realistic expectations for the research.
- Recognize the benefits and limitations of research.
- Don't expect research to provide perfect answers.

❏ B. Understand the research methods that will be used.
- Even if other people will conduct the actual research, make sure you understand the techniques they plan to use.
- Understanding the techniques used to collect and analyze research data is essential to interpreting the results correctly.

❏ C. Make sure you're not collecting more data than you need.
- Research is expensive, so don't collect data that won't affect your decision making.
- Separate "need to know" data from "nice to know" data.

❏ D. Set your research budget appropriately.
- The right amount depends on the costs and risks of the decisions for which you are doing the research.
- Expensive, high-risk decisions justify thorough research.
- Inexpensive, low-risk decisions may not justify the cost of research.

❏ E. Involve everyone who must live with the results.
- People will be more likely to accept the results if they're invited to participate in the planning.
- Involving more people may also uncover critical information needs that you haven't considered.

❏ F. Before you spend the time and money, make sure the research results will be used.
- Organizations don't always use research results, even when the results are valid and applicable.
- Resistance to change, internal politics, and shifting priorities are among the reasons for ignoring research.

Exhibit 6.4). The list of such secondary sources can be long and diverse, including databases containing everything from the names of company executives to the full text of magazine articles; periodical indexes that help you locate articles written about a particular topic; industry and professional associations, whose membership directories can identify key customers and competitors; state and federal government agencies, which provide data ranging from U.S. Census figures to specialized collections about wholesaling, retailing, and other industries; and other researchers, such as stock market analysts who examine companies and industries in search of growth potential, competitive trends, and other insights that can be valuable to someone planning an advertising campaign.

When research projects need more than secondary information, researchers collect primary data. Some advertisers choose to obtain these data themselves, others rely on the research departments in their advertising agencies, and still others hire specialized research firms to collect the data. Elrick & Lavidge is an example of a research firm that offers its clients a variety of data-collection services, including telephone interviews and personal interviews in homes, offices, stores, and shopping malls nationwide.[21] Such firms offer advertisers a trained staff, interviewing facilities, and experience with a wide range of research situations.

STEP 3: ANALYZE SECONDARY DATA

The next step is to analyze any secondary data that you were able to obtain. Even if you plan to continue with primary data collection, analyzing secondary data is a key step that shouldn't be skipped. Depending on the types of data that are relevant to your research efforts, secondary data can provide a tremendous amount of insight into both your overall advertising challenges and the particular problem you're researching at the moment.

Analyzing secondary data might involve anything from running your sales records through a computer program that searches for patterns in buying habits to reading articles in academic journals such as the *Journal of Advertising* or in trade publications such as *Advertising Age*. For instance, magazines and journals can provide information on strategies and techniques that other advertisers have tried, and learning from someone else's successes and failures is a great way to improve your advertising skills. Periodicals can also fill you in on what competitors, cus-

PTS Marketing & Advertising   File 570
    Reference Service (PTS MARS®)
Coverage: 1984 to the present   Menus: PTSMAR
Updates: Daily
Data Type: Bibliographic, Complete-text
Provider: Information Access Company, Foster City,
    CA, U.S.A.

PTS Marketing and Advertising Reference Service (PTS MARS) is a multi-industry advertising and marketing database with abstracts and full-text records on a wide variety of consumer products and services. PTS MARS is widely used by consumer products and services companies to locate market size/share information; monitor product or service introductions; evaluate markets for existing products or services; and research the marketing and advertising strategies of competitors. Advertising agencies and public relations firms use PTS MARS to research and develop new client proposals; monitor ad campaigns, budgets and target markets; locate information on products and services; and gain competitive intelligence on other agencies and public relations firms by tracking agency changes, new accounts, launch dates, contracts, and appointments. PTS MARS contains abstracts or full-text records from over 140 key source publications.

DIALINDEX Categories: FINBUS, MKTRES, MULTI-IND, NEWSDAILY, PRODUCTS, TRADENMS

U.S. prices: $2.50/connect minute; $1.20/full format online type or offline print; $.10/KWIC window; $5.00/weekly DIALOG Alert

tomers, and government regulators are up to, all of which can improve the effectiveness of your ad campaigns and help you focus your primary research. An enormous range of secondary data is available for most markets, and a few minutes with an experienced business librarian should give you plenty of avenues to pursue.

STEP 4: IDENTIFY THE SAMPLE

When research plans call for primary data, the first thing to do is choose the people who will participate. For research purposes, the entire group you want to learn more about (whether a particular group of people or a group of organizations) is called the **population,** or *universe.* If you were to ask questions of every person in the research population, you would be conducting a **census.** However, researchers rarely use the entire population; doing so would be quite expensive and time consuming in most cases. Besides, acceptably precise results can usually be obtained by questioning only a part of the population, called a **sample.** The people who participate as part of a sample are usually referred to as *subjects* or *respondents.*

Researchers measure the thoughts and attitudes of thousands or even millions of people by asking only a few hundred, and with a carefully chosen sample, such research can produce accurate results. The key is to make sure the sample represents the overall population (in terms of whatever you're researching). You can't get an accurate measure of consumer attitudes about your product by asking only the people who love it or only the people who swear they'll never buy it again (unless the entire population feels that way, of course). Both samples would give you skewed results.

With a good sample, you'll get opinions from people who love your product, from people who can't stand it, and from a whole range of people in between. Then you can project those results across the entire population. That is, you can assume that the population would respond to the research questions in the same way the sample did. For example, if 70 percent of a sample drawn from all the asthma sufferers in the country don't respond to a particular advertisement, you can project this result onto the entire population, saying that 70 percent of *all* asthma sufferers don't respond. A blood test is a good analogy. A medical specialist can test your blood by looking at only a small amount of it because the sample represents the rest of your blood.[22] If the blood in your fingertip didn't represent the blood in all parts of your body, this approach wouldn't work.

Samples fall into two basic categories. If every member (a member can be an individual consumer or an organization) of the population has a known (but not necessarily equal) chance of being included in your sample, you're dealing with a **probability sample.** The most straightforward approach of this type is the *simple random sample,* in which each member of the population has an equal chance of being included. Say that you want to research the market for dental equipment. Secondary research tells you that 174,000 dentists practice in the United States.[23] If you wanted a sample of a thousand people, you could assemble a simple random sample by selecting every 174th dentist from a list of U.S. dentists. This qualifies as a probability sample because every dentist has a known chance (1 out of 174) of being included in your sample. There are two other methods of selecting a common probability sample. For a *stratified sample,* you split the population into groups based on a relevant characteristic (such as dentists in small, medium, and large clinics) and then you select random samples from within each group. For a *cluster sample,* you isolate clusters of people that presumably reflect the overall population (such as all the dentists in Des Moines, Denver, and Sacramento) and then you select random samples from within each cluster.[24] In both cases you can still identify the probability that a given dentist will be included in your sample.

In contrast, if you are unable to determine the chances of any member of the population being selected, you would be creating a **nonprobability sample**. A common nonprobability approach is the *quota sample,* in which you specify that certain numbers of various subgroups in the population be included (for example, a sample composed of 100 college students and 100 high school students).[25] Other common types of nonprobability samples are the *judgment sample,* in which you select subjects based on whether you think they're appropriate for the study, and the *convenience sample,* which, as its name implies, involves whoever is convenient for you to question (see Exhibit 6.5).[26]

Because you can't be sure that a nonprobability sample truly reflects the composition of the entire population, you can't assume with complete confidence that the answers expressed by your sample reflect the thoughts and feelings of the entire population. Even so, nonprobability samples are the most common in commercial marketing and advertising research for several reasons. First, to ensure the true randomness that comes with a probability sample, you have to identify all the subjects in the population, which can be difficult and expensive in some cases or simply impossible in others. Imagine trying to identify all the asthma sufferers in the world or all the small businesses that need to expand their computer systems. Second, for many research tasks, the answers given by the sample are themselves adequate, and researchers don't feel the need to project the results across the entire population.[27] For instance, if you're trying to identify all your competitors by asking which products people use, it isn't necessary to project the answers; you learn what you need to know right from the people in the sample.

Selecting research samples requires a good understanding both of statistical techniques and of the population you're studying. As you'll see later in the chapter, research quality depends a great deal on the decisions you make when selecting a sample. Even if you never conduct research yourself, it's important to understand the basic principles of sampling so that you can be a more informed user of other people's research.

EXHIBIT 6.5
Nonprobability Sample

Interviewing people who happen to be walking through a mall or other public area is an example of convenience sampling.

EXHIBIT 6.6
Focus Groups

Focus group testing is a common way to explore advertising effectiveness, although researchers must take care not to assume the entire audience will respond in the same way as the focus group participants.

STEP 5: COLLECT DATA

With a sample identified, you can begin to collect data (see Exhibit 6.6). All the various techniques of data collection fall into one of two categories, qualitative or quantitative. Some research tasks involve one or the other category, and some involve both.

Qualitative Techniques

Qualitative research looks for in-depth answers that cannot be easily translated into quantitative statistics; this sort of research tries to explore respondents' attitudes, beliefs, motivations, and behaviors.[28] When you ask someone a question like "How do you feel when you go out in public wearing fashionable new clothes?" you are going to elicit very personal responses that are hard to analyze on a statistical level but that can provide great insights into buyer behavior. It's important to keep in mind that you can't project the results of qualitative research across the entire population; the thoughts and feelings of a few dozen people cannot be considered representative of the overall population.[29] Qualitative research is often exploratory and is frequently used to sound out your audience's thoughts and feelings before launching large-scale research tasks. The most common qualitative research techniques are in-depth interviews and focus groups:

- *In-depth interviews.* The **in-depth interview,** or simply *depth interview,* consists of a researcher posing questions to individuals from the sample, one at a time, in interviews that may last as long as several hours. The point of in-depth interviewing is not to have people answer lots of yes/no questions but to get them to open up and discuss their attitudes and opinions. This technique requires a great deal of skill on the interviewer's part, in terms of both conducting the interview and interpreting the results.[30]

- *Focus groups.* The **focus group** is much like an in-depth interview in that the emphasis is on probing questions and thoughtful, reflective answers; the difference is that the interview takes place with a group of respondents from the sample. The group format produces interaction among the participants that can uncover motivations and attitudes that may not surface with other kinds of research.[31] For example, advertisers interested in fashion, music, and other markets given to volatile trends conduct focus groups with teenagers and other key audiences to find out what's hot and what's not.[32] Focus groups aren't limited to consumer products, however; industrial and high-technology products are often the subject of focus group research as well.

EXHIBIT 6.7
A Projective Technique in Advertising Research

When people are asked to fill in dialog in a cartoon such as this one, they will sometimes reveal things that they wouldn't tell a researcher directly.

Both in-depth interviews and focus groups can employ two distinct types of questioning. **Direct questions** are just what they sound like; you ask subjects questions directly: "Is looking healthy important to you?" "Why did you choose a Ford over a Toyota?" In many cases, however, particularly when dealing with personal topics, direct questioning is inadequate for several reasons: subjects may be unaware of their own attitudes and motivations, they usually try to make their actions seem rational (and peoples' actions often aren't), they may not want to admit to various thoughts or actions, and they may be too polite to tell interviewers how they really feel.[33] As Paula Drillman, a vice president at the McCann Erickson agency puts it, "Rather than tell the truth, consumers say what will make them appear smarter and more discriminating."[34]

In response to these barriers, researchers can resort to **projective techniques**—vague, unstructured questions that give respondents the opportunity to rationalize their feelings by projecting them onto objects or other people.[35] For example, as a research subject, you might be reluctant to explain that you hate turkey because your family always fought at Thanksgiving, that you pretend you're Batman whenever you drive a sports car, or that you like to see children in ads because you want to have children someday. However, you'd probably be more willing to ascribe these feelings to a fictitious character. Here are some examples of the projective techniques used in advertising research:[36]

- *Sentence completion and word association tests.* Researchers ask subjects to complete sentences ("The Sony Walkman makes people feel _____ ") or to say the words that come to mind when a brand or ad is described ("What comes to mind when I say 'Burger King'?")

- *Cartoon balloons.* Researchers ask subjects to put their words into the mouths of fictitious people by filling in a blank "word balloon" in a cartoon (see Exhibit 6.7).

- *Picture drawing.* Researchers ask respondents to draw store interiors, typical users of a brand, or other representations that express how they feel about an organization or a product. When asked to draw the typical user of Pillsbury and Duncan Hines cake mixes for instance, respondents consistently drew the Pillsbury customer as a staid, stereotypical grandmotherly type and the Duncan Hines customer as fashionable and contemporary.[37] Such insights can go a long way toward evaluating advertising and planning new campaigns.

- *Thematic Apperception Test (TAT).* Researchers show subjects a collection of photos or cartoon drawings and ask them to describe what has happened or what will happen. This technique is the most common projective technique used in marketing research.[38]

As popular as some of these techniques are, advertising experts don't always agree on their usefulness. Researchers who prefer a more numerical, quantitative approach assert that direct, objective questions are better because they aren't open to an interviewer's interpretive skills.[39] In spite of such objections, however, qualitative data collection and projective techniques in particular are in common use in today's advertising business.

EXHIBIT 6.8   **Examples of Common Types of Survey Questions**

Researchers can choose from a variety of question types to collect the data they require; here are the most common forms.

Dichotomous (also called *binary* or simply *two-choice*):	**Rating**
1. Are you a member of a union? 2. Does your car take regular or premium gas?	1. Rank the following brands of pizza from most enjoyable to least enjoyable: __ Domino's __ Round Table __ Pizza Hut __ Little Caesars

Multiple choice

1. Which of the following best describes the way you feel after looking at this photograph?
   - __ Happy
   - __ Confused
   - __ Angry
   - __ Lonely
2. Which of the following soft drinks have you purchased in the last month? Check all that apply.
   - __ Coke
   - __ Pepsi
   - __ Barq's
   - __ Country Time
   - __ Koala

2. How would you respond to the following statement: "Clothes are a major factor in how I feel about myself"?
   - __ Strongly agree
   - __ Agree
   - __ Neutral
   - __ Disagree
   - __ Strongly disagree

Open-ended

1. Which brand of oven cleaner do you use?
2. How do you feel about tariffs on imported products?

Quantitative Techniques

In contrast to qualitative research, **quantitative research** tries to translate responses into numbers and statistics to reveal how many, how much, and how often.[40] The most common methods of collecting quantitative data are surveys, observation, and experiments:

- *Surveys.* You've probably participated in surveys, some that apply to marketing and advertising and some that don't. A **survey** is a method of gathering data directly from members of a sample. Surveys can be conducted through the mail, over the phone, in person, and on computer. Regardless of the form, surveys involve some sort of **questionnaire,** a document listing questions that respondents read and answer, a list of questions that telephone or in-person interviewers read to respondents, or a computer program that presents questions to someone sitting at the keyboard.[41] Exhibit 6.8 shows the most common types of questions used in surveys.

- *Observation.* Measuring audience and buyer behavior by recording what people do is called **observation.** Methods of observation can include observing consumers in their homes (with their knowledge and permission), watching shoppers in action (often without their knowledge or permission), and processing the supermarket checkout data collected by Universal Product Code (UPC) scanners. As you'll see in "Meeting an Advertising Challenge" at the end of the chapter, the U.S. Postal Service's ad agency used an observational technique to uncover attitudes toward letter carriers and then built ads based on that new knowledge.[42]

- *Experiments.* An advertising **experiment** follows the same pattern as any scientific experiment: testing a hypothesis by controlling key variables. In advertising research, these key variables might be an ad's artwork, headline, slogan, or some other element. A common experimental technique is the **split-run test,** in which a magazine or newspaper splits its circulation so that an advertiser can run a separate ad in each portion and then compare their effectiveness. Split runs are also important in developing effective direct-mail campaigns. Split runs and all other experiments that are conducted in the

How Computers Are Improving Advertising Research

Computers have invaded the world of advertising. Both desktop computers and their larger cousins can help advertising professionals be more creative and more productive. Computer power also plays an increasingly important role in advertising research.

During the data-collection phase, computers help out in two general ways. In passive data collection, computers gather data from bar code readers, checkout scanners, and other data-collection devices. In a supermarket, for instance, all those laser scanning units at the checkout counters feed data into a computer system that performs such tasks as updating inventory, analyzing sales trends, and issuing on-the-spot coupons based on what individual shoppers have purchased. Advertising researchers can use these data to find out which products are hot, where they are hot, and how well consumers are responding to coupons and other promotional efforts.

In active data collection, computers have taken the place of paper surveys in many cases. A common problem in questionnaire design is *branching,* or forcing the respondent to skip over questions that aren't relevant. For instance, you may have some questions that relate only to people who've purchased a particular product. If your first question asks whether the respondent has bought the product, you'll have to give instructions based on the response, such as "If you answered no to this question, skip ahead to question 11." Interviewing software can handle this automatically, avoiding the chance of people answering questions they shouldn't be answering.

You can establish branching based on more than one factor if need be. You might want to pose a question only to men under 30 who've bought the product, for example. On the basis of answers to questions about age, gender, and purchase history, you can route people to or away from any question in the survey. The computer not only reduces data-collection errors but allows you to route respondents through your survey in ways that would be impossibly complex on paper.

Beyond the branching issue, computers also let you ask questions that are more complex. Say that you want to know how people divide their reading time among newspapers, personal-interest magazines, professional magazines, and books. If you ask people to indicate the percentage of their time spent

in each category, chances are pretty good that some people won't get the math to work out right. A person might list percentages of 25, 30, 45, and 50, for example, adding up to an impossible total of 150 percent. Interviewing software, such as the Ci3 package published by Sawtooth Software, lets you program percent-of-total questions that take care of the arithmetic and prevent the respondent from moving on until the numbers add up to 100 percent.

These computer-based interviewing techniques can be applied in a number of ways. If you know that the respondents have computers, you can simply mail them disks that contain the surveys. Respondents run through the survey on their own computers and then mail the disks back. You can also set up telephone interviews using computers, in which the interviewers read the questions from a computer screen and type in the responses. This approach is known as computer-assisted telephone interviewing (CATI). Also, you can load the interviewing software into a portable computer and take it along for person-to-person interviews. Whatever the situation, the computer can make data collection faster and more accurate.

Apply Your Knowledge

1. *What advantages might paper questionnaires still have over computerized alternatives?*
2. *What potential risks can you picture in computer-based interviewing?*

actual marketplace are called **in-market tests.** In contrast, **laboratory tests** are conducted in a controlled setting, which can range from simulated grocery stores to actual research labs. Laboratory tests also include a wide range of physiological tests such as measuring people's eyebrow tension, eye movement, and perspiration in response to changes in emotion (see Exhibit 6.9).[43]

STEP 6: ANALYZE THE DATA AND PRESENT THE RESULTS

Data collected directly from your sample are rarely in a useful form. To draw all the research insights you need, the data must be processed, analyzed, and inter-

EXHIBIT 6.9
Laboratory Tests in Advertising Research

Using a computer to simulate store shelves, this system lets shoppers select and view products in much the same way as they would in a real store. Researchers can test packaging and other variables by observing the choices respondents make.

preted. These processes are as varied as the types of data themselves, but they all attempt to convert raw data into useful information. As you might expect, computers often play an important role in this step, sorting and tabulating data from surveys and performing other computational tasks that remove some of the burden from researchers. Sometimes, simply compiling the data, perhaps showing totals and averages, is enough for researchers to be able to interpret the information. At other times, researchers rely on sophisticated mathematical techniques and models to search for meaningful relationships in the data.

Finally, the way the research results are presented can be as important as all the other steps in the research process. The people doing the research and the people making the advertising decisions often have backgrounds and professional vocabularies that differ. Many aspects of marketing and advertising research are extremely complex and technical, and the advertisers that pay for research rarely have the detailed knowledge that researchers have. So research reports should avoid jargon and complex statistical calculations as much as possible, and researchers should provide concise, logical recommendations.

Using Research

You can use the research techniques described in this chapter for a variety of marketing and advertising purposes. A recent survey of advertisers and agencies grouped the applications of advertising research into three general stages, each answering a key question:[44]

> *What is the right thing to do?* Research can help you assess market opportunities and define appropriate goals.
>
> *What is the right way to do it?* Once you've identified your goals, you can develop and implement an advertising program to meet those goals. Research can help you put together a strong advertising plan and create effective messages.
>
> *Have we done it successfully?* After an advertising strategy has been implemented, research can help you evaluate whether or not you've achieved your goals.

Here's a closer look at how advertisers use research in each of these three stages.

STAGE 1: ASSESSING OPPORTUNITIES AND DEFINING GOALS

Before you figure out where to go, you need to understand where you are. Advertising research can help you understand your markets and audiences, analyze your current marketing position, identify opportunities, and develop goals. Research tasks can cover virtually every aspect of buyer behavior, audience analysis, segmentation, targeting, and positioning (which are discussed in Chapters 4 and 5), in addition to competitive analysis. For instance, a *market study* typically covers product usage patterns, brand and advertising awareness, buyer attitudes and perceptions, and demographic and psychographic profiles.[45] Such studies help you identify opportunities, assess competitive strengths and weaknesses, and determine ideal market positions.

Arm & Hammer's experience with its baking soda is a classic example of research uncovering an advertising opportunity. The company was searching for new product uses it could promote, so researchers talked with groups of consumers and showed some of the older print ads for the product, including one promoting baking soda as a product for cleaning the inside walls of refrigerators. As these consumers started to talk about sweetening or freshening up the refrigerator, the researchers realized that they could extend the appeal of their product by positioning baking soda as a way to keep refrigerators clean-smelling. An ad campaign was based on consumers placing an open box of baking soda in their refrigerators to absorb odors, and the campaign led to skyrocketing sales.[46]

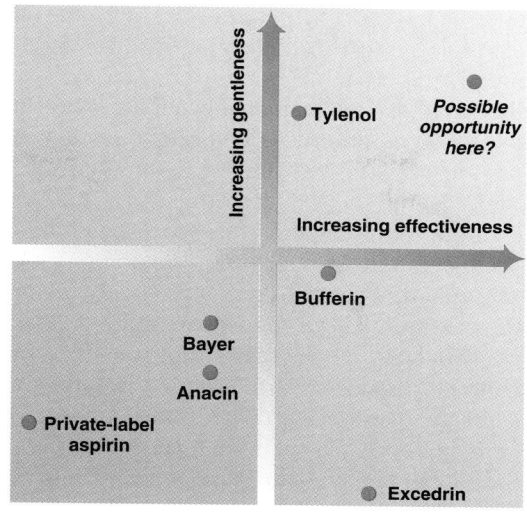

EXHIBIT 6.10
A Perceptual Map in Advertising Research

Perceptual maps help researchers understand where buyers perceive products to be relative to the competition.

A particularly useful research tool during stage 1 is the *perceptual map,* which shows how buyers perceive various products in a market, based on the most important product attributes. Exhibit 6.10 shows a perceptual map of how consumers have positioned five national pain reliever brands and private-label aspirin. The two dimensions of the map represent key product attributes, in this case gentleness and effectiveness. Judging from this map, you can see that an opportunity might exist for a product that could be positioned as both more gentle and more effective than existing products. Research like this can help you identify where you'd like to be positioned in the market and how you can use advertising to achieve that goal.

In addition to conducting their own primary research, advertisers can turn to a number of information sources during this stage, depending on their particular needs. The U.S. government is the biggest provider of secondary statistical data. Two of its largest statistical collections, the U.S. Census and the SIC system, are discussed in earlier chapters, but the government also provides directories and databases covering health, transportation, economics, and a wide variety of other topics.[47] In addition, advertisers frequently use syndicated research during the assessment stage. The section on commercial research services later in this chapter describes the services offered by the leading research firms.

STAGE 2: DEVELOPING PLANS AND CREATING MESSAGES

You've done your market analysis and positioning research, and you've set some goals. Now you need to put an advertising program together to get you where you want to be. Once again, advertising research can help in a number of ways, from identifying potential messages to suggesting how much you should spend on media.

Given the ever-increasing expense of running an advertising campaign and the growing uncertainty resulting from fragmented markets and media, advertisers and their agencies want to know whether the money they're spending is producing results, and as much as possible, they'd like to know before they invest a major portion of their budgets whether an ad campaign will be effective. The general category of research used at this point is **pretesting,** which involves testing one or more versions of an ad (often in rough format) before completing production and buying time and space in the media. You have to spend a little money to prepare possible ads to test, but the idea of pretesting is that you can then make sure you're on the right track before you invest in final production and media.[48]

An agency's creative staff usually comes up with several combinations of copy and visuals, and a variety of pretests can be performed to pick the most effective

EXHIBIT 6.11
Techniques for Pretesting

Pretesting ad samples before moving ahead with final production and media placement is one way advertisers can try to increase their chances of success.

approach (see Exhibit 6.11). The split-run tests described earlier are a good example of research that helps advertisers select the best message and overall creative approach. Focus groups, projective techniques, physiological tests, and theater tests (so named because movie theaters were traditionally used to test television commercials before groups of respondents, although research facilities often use televisions and VCRs now) are all key research techniques used during this stage.[49] The Persuasion Plus service offered by ASI Market Research is a good example of pretesting for broadcast ads. The company broadcasts a specially produced television program on an unused local cable channel along with several actual and proposed commercials. Respondents are interviewed before and after the commercials air to measure attitude changes resulting from the commercials.[50]

Not everyone is crazy about the idea of pretesting creative concepts, however. Detractors raise several issues. First, they assert that testing stifles creativity and leads to bland advertising that everyone will consider safe and predictable. A famous Coca-Cola spot that featured NFL star Mean Joe Green is considered one of the most effective television commercials ever, but it didn't score well in pretests. Second, testing is often done with just one exposure to the ad (whether it's a television, radio, or print ad), which lacks the benefit of repetition; many ads clearly need multiple exposures to build their effectiveness. Third, the ability of audiences to remember particular television ads probably depends to some degree on the surrounding programming. Research has indicated, for instance, that viewers are more apt to remember commercials aired during hit movies than those aired during other shows.

Those opposed to ad testing point out that some of the most effective ads don't score well in tests because they don't look and sound the way test audiences expect them to. Advertisers and researchers, on the other hand, often like the security of numbers and say that the expense of running ads is too great today to skip pretesting. In fact, many advertisers refuse to run ads or even proceed with final production of those ads until researchers come back with encouraging numbers on recall, likability, and other factors. The debate over pretesting promises to be around for a long time to come.[51]

STAGE 3: EVALUATING ADVERTISING EFFECTIVENESS

In contrast to pretesting, **posttesting** is conducted after the advertising program has been implemented. Posttest studies that are conducted over a period of time are called **tracking studies.** Of course, if you have a clearly measurable goal for an ad campaign, such as increased sales or increased responses to a direct-mail offer, posttesting may not be worth the time and expense—you can just look in the cash register to see whether the ads are working. However, you usually can't draw a direct link between advertising and sales, but you can use posttesting to measure the stages that lead up to sales, including communication, attitude change, and behavioral change:[52]

- *Communication effectiveness.* The two chief measures of communication are **recognition tests,** which test whether audiences can recognize the name of the brand or product that was advertised, and **recall tests,** which measure how well audiences remember particular ads. Recall tests are divided into **aided recall,** where respondents are told the name of the brand or company involved in the ad and then asked whether they remember that ad, and **unaided recall,** where subjects are asked whether they remember any ads for the type of product.[53] An example of aided recall is "Do you recall seeing a commercial for Gatorade on television last night?" An unaided version of this might be "Did you see any commercials for sports drinks on television last night?" Recall testing remains popular, especially with larger advertisers, but critics have raised several objections: Factors such as how interesting the ad is can bias the results; researchers have proved that there is no link between recall and purchase behavior; and as mentioned earlier for pretesting, recall testing is considered by some people to lead to less-creative, standardized ads designed primarily to score well on recall tests.[54]

- *Attitudinal effectiveness.* Going one step beyond communication effectiveness, advertisers like to know whether their ads produce desirable changes in audience attitudes. For example, a study conducted for a Kmart television commercial indicated that 46 percent of the respondents had a more favorable attitude toward Kmart after seeing the ad. The reasons for the positive attitude shift included the wide range of products shown and the casual, relaxed shopping environment portrayed.[55]

- *Behavioral effectiveness.* The final goal of any advertising effort is to bring about some kind of change in audience behavior, whether it's persuading people to stop smoking or convincing consumers to buy more Lay's potato chips. Research can be used to measure reported behavior (what people say they do), recorded behavior (what they actually do), and indications of sales volume (such as product flows through warehouses or retail sales recorded by supermarket scanners).

Using Commercial Advertising Research Services

Advertisers and their agencies can take advantage of a wide range of commercial research services. The firms that offer these services deal with print and broadcast formats and with messages (are the ads effective?) and media (who's watching, listening, or reading?). Some of these services are applicable to pretesting, some apply to posttesting, and some can be used for both. Some of these services are syndicated, whereas others are conducted on a custom basis for individual advertisers. Here is a sample of the leaders in advertising research and the services they offer:[56]

- *Simmons Market Research Bureau (SMRB).* SMRB's "Study of Media and Markets" is a major resource for consumer advertisers. It combines magazine and newspaper readership data, statistics on television viewing, product purchase data, demographic data, and other research results. The report helps advertisers in such tasks as profiling buyers in specific product categories and assessing the readership of a given magazine.

- *Opinion Research Corporation (ORC).* Opinion Research provides a wide range of research studies, both syndicated and private. For example, the ORC Executive Caravan study profiles the reading and travel habits of executives from the largest U.S. companies.

- *Nielsen.* A. C. Nielsen is one of the oldest, largest, and most influential research companies in the world. It is best known for its Nielsen National Television Index, which is responsible for determining the ratings that network television shows receive (and hence the ad rates that the networks can charge during those shows). Nielsen revolutionized television audience measurements with the introduction of its **people meter,** an electronic device that records the television shows watched by all members and guests in the 4,000 households that make up the U.S. market sample. The people meter (and all other audience measurement techniques and technologies, for that matter) continues to be a source of controversy in the industry, as people question just how accurate it really is. Researchers continue to look for ways to measure audience levels more accurately, so expect to see new techniques from time to time. Nielsen has a variety of other research services as well, including ScanTrack, which collects purchase data from the checkout scanners at more than 3,000 U.S. supermarkets.

- *Leading National Advertisers (LNA).* LNA tracks the amount of print advertising purchased from national advertisers, then estimates the amount each firm spends on print advertising. This is a key information resource when you want to know how much your competitors are spending on advertising. LNA also teams up with Broadcast Advertisers Reports (BAR), which tracks programming and advertising activity on broadcast and cable television, to produce the BAR/LNA Multi-Media Service. This report summarizes ad spending in all media that the two services cover.

- *ASI Market Research*. ASI offers two services for evaluating the effectiveness of television commercials. Recall Plus measures whether respondents can recall a commercial and, if so, how much detail they remember. Persuasion Plus goes a step beyond to see if the commercial changed the respondent's attitude toward the product. Both services use empty cable television channels, over which a previously unaired television show is sent along with several commercials to be evaluated.

- *Arbitron*. Arbitron produces several influential broadcast audience studies that affect advertising rates and programming. Arbitron Radio is the dominant radio audience research service, measuring audience sizes in more than 250 local markets in the United States.

- *Information Resources, Inc. (IRI)*. IRI offers InfoScan, a syndicated tracking service that measures sales in grocery stores and drugstores, and Behavior-Scan, a collection of single-source data services.

- *Starch*. Starch provides several popular services for measuring print ad effectiveness, based on interviews with more than 100,000 people every year. The Starch Readership Report measures recall and recognition at three levels: whether people remember seeing an ad, whether they can associate it with the correct brand name or advertiser, and whether they read more than half of the ad (see Exhibit 6.12). The Starch Impression Study is a qualitative effort that measures how well ads communicate their intended message. This study answers such questions as what image an ad communicates for the company and brand, how well the words and pictures work together, and whether multiple readers tend to find the same meaning in the ad.

EXHIBIT 6.12
Starch Recall Tests

The Starch Readership Report is one of the leading methods of testing print advertising. The labels on this Oshkosh ad indicate the portion of the audience that read particular parts of the ad.

In addition to these firms, a number of other companies offer specialized research services that target such segments as business executives, ethnic segments, affluent consumers, and various other slices of the market. If you advertise just about any type of widely distributed consumer or business product, chances are somebody is doing research on it.

Ensuring Quality in Advertising Research

As with advertising in general, high-quality advertising research doesn't happen without a lot of talent, good judgment, and care. Whether you end up being a researcher or a user of research, it's important to understand the issues that affect advertising quality. The fundamental components of research quality are validity and reliability.

Research exhibits **validity** to the degree that it presents an accurate picture of reality. In other words, valid research measures what you intended it to measure. (Of course, you have to make sure you're measuring the right things; a valid measurement of the wrong thing won't help much.) Research exhibits **reliability** if you or someone else can repeat the research and reach the same answer.[57] Exhibit 6.13 shows the four possible combinations of validity and reliability.[58]

Perhaps the best way to make sure research goes right is to understand how it can go wrong. The factors that cause reliability and validity problems can be divided into five categories: mistakes in preparing or implementing the study, problems with sampling, mistakes in measuring (such as not recording answers or entering them into computers incorrectly), mistakes in choosing the appropriate questions (so that they somehow distort responses), and mistakes in interpreting the answers. The term often used to describe distortion in research is **bias,** which simply means that what you measure doesn't reflect reality.[59] Some of the most common sources of bias in advertising research are preconceptions, sample problems, interviewer bias, questionnaire bias, and misinterpretation:

- *Preconceptions.* Simply having an open mind when you start a research project is one of the most important factors in research quality.[60] For all the statistics and science that researchers can employ, it's often too easy to find the answers that you hoped to find. In some cases, it's easy to select particular respondents, ask particular questions, and interpret the data in a particular way to support the conclusion that you reached before you ever started the research. To reach unbiased conclusions, you must approach the research task recognizing that you may not like the answer.

EXHIBIT 6.13
Validity and Reliability

Imagine that conducting research is like trying to hit the bull's-eye on a target. Example A represents a situation in which a researcher conducted the research a dozen times, and each time the answer was on or near the bull's-eye. These results would be highly valid because they hit the bull's-eye and highly reliable because all attempts landed in the same general area. Example B has low reliability because the answers are spread out, but it can still be considered to have high validity because the attempts center around the right answer (and would probably average out near the center of the bull's-eye). Examples C and D show the other two possibilities, low validity but high reliability (C) and low validity and low reliability (D).

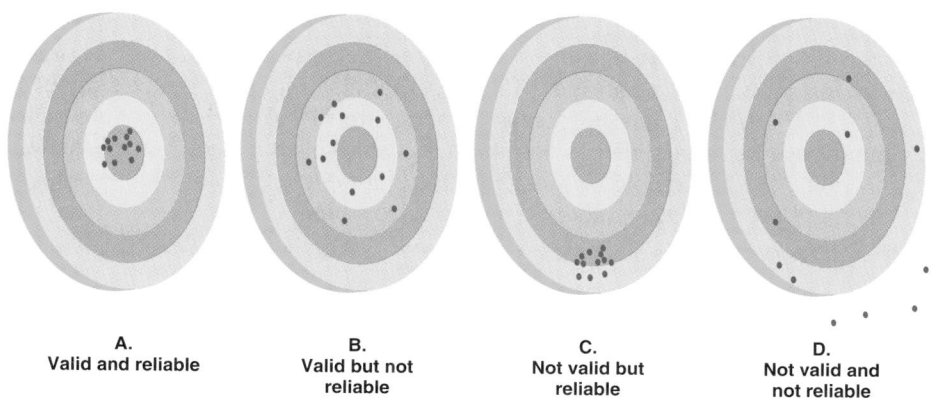

| A. | B. | C. | D. |
| Valid and reliable | Valid but not reliable | Not valid but reliable | Not valid and not reliable |

- *Sample problems.* The distortion that results when a sample does not accurately represent the target population is *sample bias.* When you hear about a survey that turns out to be wildly at odds with reality, sample bias is usually the cause.[61] For example, say that you want to know how many people saw your commercial on television last night, so you grab the phone directory and dial up 400 households at random. However, a few people don't have phones at all, some have unlisted numbers, some screen calls with answering machines, some will refuse to participate, and some won't be at home. You can't just keep calling until you reach 400 people, because the people you don't reach may not be like the people you can reach. Imagine the attitude, interest, and opinion differences among people who stay at home every evening and those who go out four or five nights a week.[62] One study has found that people get harder to reach as their incomes increase, a fact that could seriously distort surveys that don't take such criteria into account.[63]

  Not to be confused with sample bias, **sample error** reflects the differences in answers that result from the fact that you didn't query an entire population. By definition, samples don't include every member of the target population, so some error is inevitable. In one sense, sample error is easier to avoid than the other quality problems described here because the larger your sample, the lower your sample error. Sample error is expressed as a percentage margin, which means that the real answer can be above or below the measured answer by the specified number of percentage points.[64] If a survey showed that 50 percent of the respondents recall an ad that you're testing and the survey has a 5 percent error margin, then the real percentage of people who recall the ad is somewhere between 45 and 55 percent.

- *Interviewer bias.* When someone is involved in questioning a respondent, either in person (individual or focus group) or on the phone, the interviewer can bias the results. Potential problems include failing to establish rapport with the respondent (thereby keeping the respondent from opening up completely and objectively), leading the respondent with verbal or nonverbal cues, failing to reexplain questions that the respondent doesn't understand, failing to record responses accurately and completely, and failing to follow up or take good notes when the interview uncovers new areas of potential interest. Carefully selecting and training interviewers (or carefully choosing a research firm if you're hiring out the interviewing work) is the best way to avoid these biases.[65]

- *Questionnaire bias.* The questions you use in both qualitative and quantitative research can bias answers in two ways (see Exhibit 6.14). First, the type of question you use can introduce bias. For example, a study of media habits found that people reported a much higher rate of readership for various magazines if they were reminded of the names of the magazines. One group of respondents answered an open-ended question about which magazines they read, and no one listed *TV Guide.* However, when *TV Guide* appeared in a multiple-choice question given to a similar group of people, 20 percent said they read it regularly.[66] Second, the way questions are worded can introduce bias. *Leading questions* are almost sure to generate bias. If you ask a respondent, "Doesn't Brand A's 100-year tradition of quality make it a more appealing choice than Brand B or Brand C?" you'll bias the respondent in favor of Brand A by injecting a judgment about Brand A that also implies negatives about B and C. *Threatening questions* that ask a person to reveal intimate or potentially embarrassing information can bias answers because some people won't answer honestly. Also, *ambiguous, incomplete, or difficult questions* can confuse respondents and render the results invalid and unreliable.[67]

- *Misinterpretation.* It is possible for a research task to be on track right up to the point at which you interpret the results. Interpreting research data requires judgment, common sense, and in many cases a fair amount of statistical skill. A common misinterpretation is observing that some event B follows event A and then automatically assuming that A somehow *caused* B to happen. Say that

EXHIBIT 6.14 The Potential for Bias in Commonly Used Question Types

Various question types can generate bias both because of the form that each question takes and because of the way each is worded.

Question Type and Example	Example of Form Bias	Example of Content Bias
Dichotomous: "Do you own a car?"	What if the respondent leases a car and isn't sure whether to answer yes or no to this question?	Would someone who owns a minivan answer yes or no to this question?
Multiple choice: "Which of these cars is the best: Ford, Toyota, Chevrolet, or Honda?"	What if the respondent thinks the best car is a Pontiac?	Respondents can have different ideas of what "best" means—fastest, cheapest, most stylish, more reliable, etc.
Rating: "Rank these companies' ads in terms of which are most persuasive: Ford, Toyota, Chevrolet, or Honda."	What if the respondent thinks two are equally persuasive or that none is persuasive?	Is the respondent supposed to rank them from most to least or from least to most?
Open-ended: "Which brand of potato chip have you eaten the most of in the last six months, and how many bags of them have you eaten?"	What if the respondent needs to be reminded of the various brand names?	People aren't likely to remember how many bags of potato chips they've eaten in the last six months.

you're tracking consumer attitudes about fruit drinks and that you see consumers grow more positive toward your brand after you stop using a celebrity endorser in your ads. Can you conclude that consumers didn't like that celebrity or that consumers don't like celebrity endorsers in general? Absolutely not, even though it's tempting to draw such conclusions. The consumers' attitudes may have been affected by lower prices, competitors' quality problems, scientific reports praising some ingredient that happens to be in your juice, or the fact that your company's popular CEO is sick and people feel sorry for her. The point is that any number of things might be responsible for causing the change you observed; just because two things happened consecutively, you can't assume that one caused the other.

A radio station in New York City that caters largely to African-American audiences recently encountered a situation that illustrates the quality problems that researchers can encounter. In the demographic segment of men aged 45 to 49 in the station's broadcast area, Arbitron (the radio audience researcher) was able to get only 17 respondents to return their diaries, the books used to record time spent listening to various radio stations. This sample is far too small to provide meaningful results, and the low response rate among the listeners that Arbitron asked to fill out the diaries indicates that sample bias is probably present as well. To increase the response rate, Arbitron is using incentives, among other approaches.[68]

You can see that research presents quite a few opportunities for going astray. By planning your research carefully, recognizing where problems can crop up, and taking active steps to ensure quality, you stand a much better chance of producing insightful, cost-effective research.

Summary

Advertising research is one part of marketing research; whereas marketing research covers the entire marketing mix, advertising research addresses the questions, decisions, and risks specific to advertising. The primary reasons for conducting advertising research include increasing the efficiency and effectiveness of advertising, reducing the financial and perceptual risks associated with advertising, and improving advertising's financial accountability.

Primary data are gathered firsthand for a specific research task. In contrast, secondary data were previously gathered for some other purpose and are now being reused in some fashion for the current research task. Syndicated data are collected for more than one client at a time. Single-source data result from comparing the advertising received by selected households with the purchasing behavior exhibited by those households.

The six steps in the research process are (1) defining the problem and setting research goals, (2) identifying sources of information, (3) analyzing available secondary data, (4) identifying the sample to be used for primary data collection, (5) collecting the actual data, and (6) analyzing the data and presenting the results to the appropriate decision makers. The major applications of advertising research fall into three basic categories: assessing market opportunities and identifying goals, developing plans and creating messages, and evaluating advertising effectiveness.

Both pretesting and posttesting can be used to measure

In the face of a negative public image and aggressive competition, assistant postmaster general John Wargo knew his organization needed to satisfy its customers and to create effective advertising that would communicate the benefits of using the Postal Service. A research technique employed by the Postal Service's advertising agency, Young & Rubicam, uncovered an important element of customer attitude that formed the basis of much of the service's subsequent advertising.

The research technique the advertising agency used is an observational method called ethnography, which involves watching people in action and then exploring the reasons they feel and behave as they do. As Margaret Mark of Young & Rubicam explained, ethnography uncovered an interesting paradox with small-business customers. While watching businesspeople interact with their letter carriers, it became obvious to researchers that the standard notion of negative perceptions regarding the Postal Service didn't tell the whole story. Although many of these people in fact had neutral or negative feel-

ings about the Postal Service as a whole, they often had positive interpersonal relationships with their individual letter carriers. Many of the businesspeople treated their carriers as friends and neighbors.

Recognizing a great advertising opportunity, Wargo and the agency translated this important new insight into a series of television commercials that featured the individual efforts of letter carriers. One spot showed a carrier trudging through snow to deliver a graduate school acceptance notice to an elated young man. The knowledge the research yielded led to the new slogan "We Deliver," which has become the umbrella theme for all of the Postal Service's advertising.

Your Mission: You've recently joined the Postal Service as its new director of marketing research, making you responsible for all advertising research. Building on the successful research efforts that helped produce the "We Deliver" campaign, you want to continue using advertising research wherever and whenever it can help. Consider the following research situa-

tions and pick the best answer in each case.

1. In your role as the director of research, you are responsible for approving all requests for research projects submitted by various marketing staffers throughout the Postal Service. You are working with all these people to help them use research effectively and efficiently. From the following three problem definitions submitted for your approval, which one would you hold up as an example of a well-defined research problem?

a. In recognition of the time and expense that any advertising project involves, we must make sure that every new campaign is based on thorough qualitative and quantitative research.

b. We plan to identify the top three reasons for some corporate customers choosing Federal Express (or other commercial services) over the Postal Service for overnight document delivery.

c. We want to find out what people think about our current advertising

advertising effectiveness. Pretesting can help you predict whether a given ad will be effective, at least relative to the other options you have. Posttesting provides a picture of effectiveness once ads have run. Research can't always tie advertising directly to sales results, but the process can help measure the effectiveness of communication, attitude change, and behavior change.

The two key issues in research quality are validity, a measure of how accurately research measures reality, and reliability, a measure of how closely repeated attempts at measuring the same thing will yield the same answer. The major sources of error in advertising research are preconceptions, sample problems, interviewer bias, questionnaire bias, and misinterpretation.

Key Terms

Questions

FOR REVIEW

1. Given the time and expense that it can entail, why do many advertisers still choose to conduct advertising research?

2. What is the difference between primary and secondary data? What are the benefits and limitations of each type?

We deliver.
Sponsored by U.S. Postal Service.

campaign and compare this to what they thought about our previous campaign.

2. The "We Deliver" theme and its associated campaigns have been running for several years now, and you periodically check to see how well these advertising efforts are working. If you wanted to see whether the ads aimed at small businesses had prompted them to spend more with the Postal Service, which of the following 1,000-subject samples would you use?

a. The business telephone directory for your metropolitan area. It lists roughly 12,000 businesses, so you can pick every twelfth listing to get a sample of 1,000 companies.

b. The list of businesses that have purchased bulk-mail permits. You can select the 1,000 customers that have mailed the smallest volume in the last year.

c. A nationwide database. You can first select the companies that fit your definition of small businesses and then randomly select 1,000 from that list.

3. Say that earlier research has indicated that some consumers don't like the service they've received at post offices, and you want to know whether those negative experiences are hurting business. Which of the following questions would yield the most reliable information?

a. Please list all the reasons why you don't visit your local post office more often.

b. Wouldn't you conduct more business at the post office if the experience were less negative?

c. Isn't the fact that you were able to buy the goods and services you needed at your local post office more important than the way you may have been treated?

4. The Postal Service recognizes that it competes not only with Federal Express and other delivery services but with fax machines, electronic mail on computers, and even basic telephone services. Which of the following research methods would you use to find out whether increases in postage rates prompt consumers to send fewer letters and make more telephone calls? Assume that the last postal rate increase was three weeks ago.

a. Select several dozen post offices around the country and, over the course of two weeks, have clerks at those locations ask each customer whether he or she started using the telephone more after postal rates went up the last time.

b. Ask consumers the same question as in (a), but contact a nationwide sample via telephone instead.

c. Go back through the Postal Service's pricing records, looking for the date of each postage increase. Compare these data with nationwide telephone volume trends to see whether the price changes increased telephone usage (assume that you can get the data you need on telephone usage).[69] ■

3. Why is it important to consider analyzing secondary data before collecting primary data?

4. What are the major techniques used to pretest ads?

5. What can cause research results to be invalid or unreliable?

FOR ANALYSIS AND APPLICATION

6. What sort of internal secondary data do you think a retail chain such as Footlocker might have at its disposal?

7. If a client or manager said to you, a research specialist, "We need to make our ads more effective; do some research that will tell us what to do," how would you respond?

8. Assume your agency has created an ad that relies on sarcastic humor; 7 of the 12 people in a focus group said they were turned off by the sarcasm. Should you conclude that the ad shouldn't be used? Why or why not?

9. Under most circumstances, why couldn't Pizza Hut just rely on sales figures to tell whether its ads are working?

10. Say that you're researching college students' interest in various local recreational facilities and that you want to poll students as they leave a campus cafeteria. Might this approach encounter any bias problems?

Sharpen Your Advertising Skills

Bell Atlantic is taking the "infomercial" trend to a new level. These program-length commercials typically use talk-show formats or straight-ahead sales pitches to advertise products ranging from the Juicemaster to the Thighmaster. Bell Atlantic, however, is packaging its first infomercial as a situation comedy that features a family of characters called "The Ringers." The show pitches a variety of phone services, such as call forwarding and call waiting. The sitcom infomercial is being pretested in Baltimore, and if the test shows positive results, Bell Atlantic plans to move it into other markets.

Decision: Assume that you're in charge of the pretest for "The Ringers." You realize that you need to isolate the effect of the show on the company's sales, but this is hard to do for a television commercial or infomercial. Decide how you might isolate the show's contribution to sales.

Communication: In a brief memo to your colleagues, explain why it's both difficult and important to isolate the show's contribution; then describe how your idea can solve the problem.

CHAPTER 7

Objectives, Strategy, and Plans

After studying this chapter, you will be able to

1. Define the elements in a marketing plan, and explain how the plan sets the stage for the advertising effort

2. List the advertiser's positioning options

3. Describe the characteristics of effective marketing and advertising objectives

4. Define the elements in an advertising plan, and discuss how this plan relates to the marketing plan

5. Differentiate the two categories of advertising objectives, and explain why sales objectives are inappropriate for many advertising campaigns

6. Describe the concept of an advertising strategy, and relate it to advertising objectives

7. Discuss the most common methods for setting advertising budgets

Everyone needs special effects from time to time.

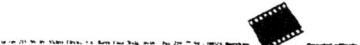

Facing an Advertising Challenge at Saturn
DRIVING INTO A NEW CHAPTER IN AUTOMOTIVE HISTORY

The challenge facing Donald Hudler must rank near the top of the difficulty scale. As vice president of sales, service, and marketing at Saturn, Hudler joined a team of like-minded innovators in what must have seemed to many observers as an impossible task: starting a new U.S. car company that could compete successfully with foreign companies. Saturn's parent, General Motors, had lost enormous chunks of the market to Honda, Toyota, and other foreign companies whose import models were considered by many consumers to be better built and more reliable than U.S. cars. Many younger buyers had sworn off U.S. cars entirely.

It wasn't always that way. In 1965 every second car in the United States was a Chevrolet, a Buick, or one of GM's other brands. At one point, in fact, some suspected the company of intentionally holding down its sales so that it wouldn't catch the eye of government antitrust regulators. However,

by the 1980s, no one thought of GM as a monopoly; the company was laying off tens of thousands of employees, shutting numerous plants, and racking up billions of dollars in losses. GM closed out 1992 with the dubious honor of announcing the largest loss ever experienced by a U.S. corporation: $23.5 billion in the red. That year saw another milestone as well. The import companies' combined share rose to the same level that GM's share had fallen to; each side finished the year with 35 percent of the market.

GM leaders tried a number of ways to get the magic back, including a massive investment in a new product line and automated factories to produce it. However, the automation and most of the other attempts proved disappointing. The most intriguing effort was launching an entirely new car company, one that would be free from the old ways of doing business. Saturn is much more than a new

brand name, though; it's a new way of approaching the automotive business. Consequently, Hudler knew that Saturn needed a new way to approach marketing and advertising as well.

Hudler and his Saturn colleagues were entering a crowded market of more than 40 brands. Although they had several billion dollars in financial backing from GM, they faced a mammoth task: build a better car and then rebuild relationships with the driving public. If you were in Donald Hudler's position at Saturn, what kind of marketing and advertising strategies would you forge? What role would advertising play in your efforts to position Saturn as a viable alternative to the imports? Would your advertising strategy focus on the car itself, the company, or some other element? How would you use advertising to communicate your positioning message and catch the attention of the driving public?[1] ∎

CHAPTER OVERVIEW This chapter represents a turning point in the course. Chapters 1 through 6 explored the advertising environment, ways to analyze an audience, and other important background information. Now it's time to formulate a plan and get ready to create some advertising. First you'll explore the connections between the objectives, strategies, and plans defined at various levels in the organization. Next you'll explore the elements of a marketing plan and examine the advertiser's positioning options. After that, you'll see how an advertising plan is related to the marketing plan. Then you'll be introduced to the challenge of defining advertising objectives and developing strategies to meet those objectives. You'll finish the chapter with a look at the process of defining an advertising budget.

Guiding the Advertising Program

Successful advertising starts with clear **objectives,** which are statements of desired future conditions. An advertising objective might entail pulling people into a retail store, prompting buyers to call a toll-free number, or changing negative perceptions about a company. Advertising objectives are vitally important because they provide direction for the entire advertising effort.

Advertising objectives are part of a larger picture, which begins with **organizational objectives,** the organization's long-range goals–generally defined in terms of return on investment or other financial measures. As Exhibit 7.1 shows, these objectives are at the top of a hierarchy in which lower-level objectives must be accomplished in order to reach higher and higher levels of objectives. Just below

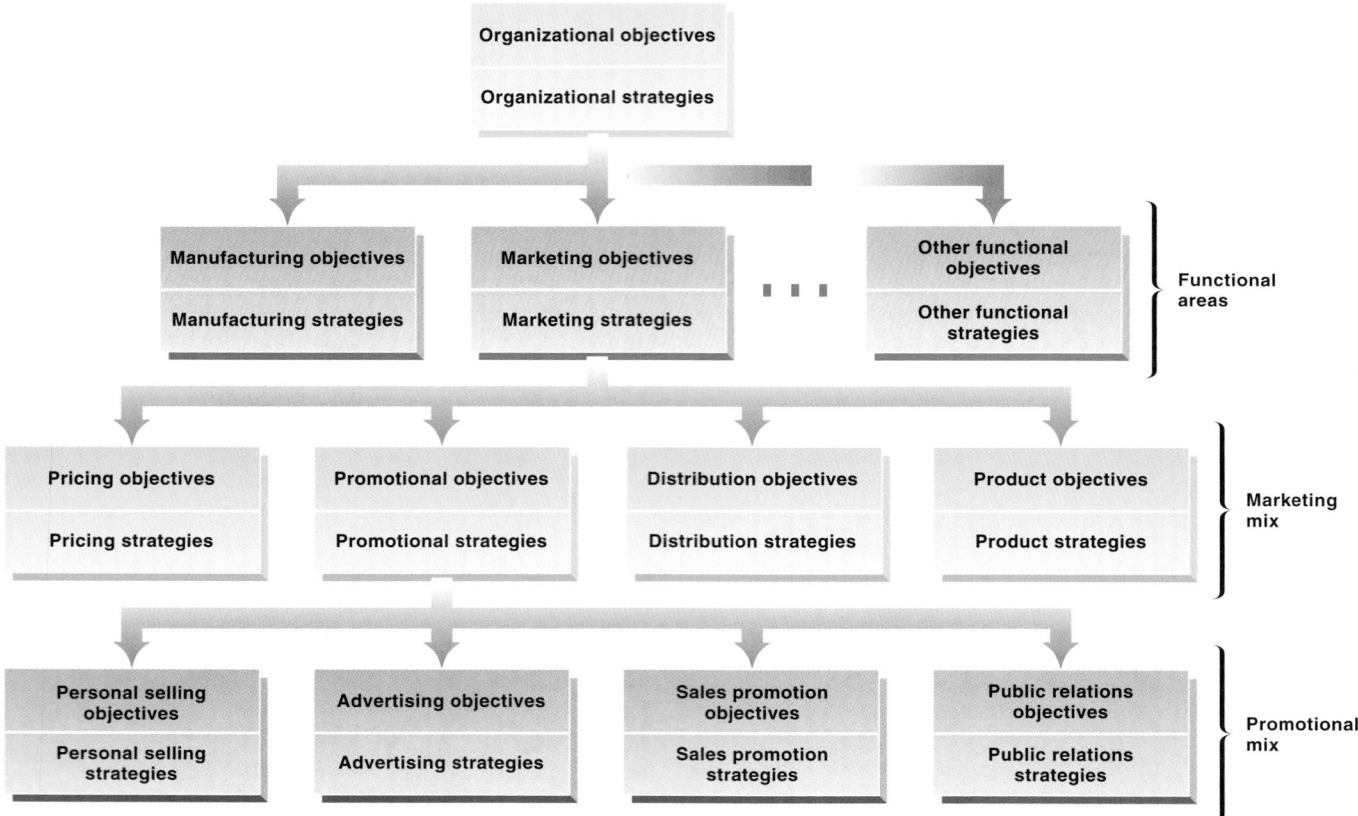

EXHIBIT 7.1
The Objectives/Strategy Hierarchy

Advertising objectives and strategies are part of a hierarchy that extends down from the organization's overall objectives and strategies.

the organizational objectives in Exhibit 7.1 are a number of *functional* objectives, which represent goals from marketing, manufacturing, and the organization's other functional areas, such as finance. The functional objectives of most interest to advertisers are the **marketing objectives,** which define targets for marketing performance, usually in terms of sales, coupled with a financial measure such as profitability.

Just as the organizational objectives are supported by a variety of functional objectives, so the marketing objectives are supported by a set of lower-level objectives (each representing a category in the marketing mix). **Promotional objectives** determine how the specific goals of personal selling, sales promotion, public relations, and advertising will help the organization meet its marketing objectives. This is the point in the hierarchy where advertising comes in. **Advertising objectives** are the desired end results of an advertising campaign (see Exhibit 7.2).

Each level of objectives is supported by a **strategy,** a statement of how those objectives will be achieved.[2] There are many definitions of strategy; the one used by aerospace and service conglomerate TRW is simple and insightful: your strategy defines *where and how you plan to compete.*[3] The **marketing strategy,** for instance, explains how the marketing function will meet its objectives by describing the target markets, the desired position in those markets, and the proposed marketing mix. Similarly, the promotional strategy defines how the promotional objectives will be met, and so on for the other levels of objectives.

The Marketing Plan: Bringing It All Together

The advertising process gets its start in the **marketing plan,** a document that contains four key blocks of information: a situation analysis, the marketing objectives, the marketing strategy, and the action plan. Individual companies and marketers may organize plans along slightly different lines, but these are the four primary classes of information you need to construct an effective marketing plan.

SITUATION ANALYSIS

A **situation analysis** is a review of past and present data that summarizes the organization's current circumstances and tries to identify trends, forces, and market conditions that might affect an organization's future prospects.[4] This involves analyzing both internal and external factors:[5]

- *Internal factors.* The two categories of internal factors are performance and strategic options. When analyzing your performance, you consider such tangible factors as profitability, market share, production costs, and new-product plans. You also consider such intangible factors as management performance and employee attitudes. Based on how you've performed in the past and how you might be able to perform in the future, you can identify a number of strategy options that take into account your financial resources, problems with your current strategies, and any other strengths and weaknesses that might affect your ability to execute a chosen strategy.

- *External factors.* The external factors in a situation analysis include such elements as customers, competitors, industries, and government regulations. The major components of customer analysis were discussed in Chapters 4 and 5, including needs, motivations, and segmentation issues. Competitive analysis involves discovering who your competitors are and determining their objectives, strategies, strengths, and weaknesses. Issues in industry analysis include growth rates, entry barriers, and distribution systems. Distribution can be a major factor in your advertising strategy; for instance, much of the

EXHIBIT 7.2
Advertising Objectives

The message in this ad for Moscow's Continent Bank is that Continent is the bank that supports businesses and protects their financial health. The objective for an ad such as this might focus on building awareness and preference among the target audience or on generating a certain number of phone calls or visits to the bank.

This is the support of business. Continent Bank.

It has occurred to us that you may want more information about Australian beef before you pick up your phone and start dialing. That's only fair. Even the gentlemen to your left would have to agree.

◆

Our facilities and methods are rigorously monitored by the USDA. It's harder on us, but easier on you this way.

◆

The land and grass of Australia are unique and make our beef naturally leaner. We call it the land's gift.

◆

We customize product to meet your individual specifications. Our beef matches your processing needs.

◆

Naturally lean and flavorful, Australian beef is in demand. So you're processing a desirable commodity.

◆

Supply is consistent and plentiful. Australian beef is available when you need it.

◆

You can call us at 1-800-874-8529* to hear more about Australian beef. But no one will mind if you'd rather just call your importer and start ordering.

◆

Either way, we'll be waiting.

*8 a.m. to 5 p.m. E.S.T.

OUR OPERATORS ARE STANDING BY TO TAKE YOUR ORDER.

AUSTRALIAN BEEF

The Land's Gift™

EXHIBIT 7.3
Advertising to the Trade

This ad from the Australian Meat and Livestock Corporation isn't intended for consumers; its goal is to persuade more wholesalers and retailers to carry Australian meat products.

advertising created by manufacturers is directed not at consumers but at the wholesalers and retailers that sell those products to consumers (see Exhibit 7.3). The major issues in government regulation are discussed fully in Chapter 2.

Advertisers often structure their situation analysis according to the acronym SWOT, which stands for strengths, weaknesses, opportunities, and threats. An organizational *strength* is an internal capability that you can exploit to achieve objectives, whereas an organizational *weakness* is an internal characteristic that may undermine your performance. An *opportunity* is an external market situation that offers potential for helping you meet your objectives. In contrast, a *threat* is an external element that can develop into a problem and potentially prevent you from achieving your goals.[6] You can use SWOT analysis to see how your strengths, weaknesses, opportunities, and threats compare with those of your competition. This chapter's Advertising Checklist shows the major issues that advertisers usually review in a situation analysis.

Procter & Gamble, whose long list of leading consumer products includes Pampers and Luvs disposable diapers, knows all too well how an external threat can force a change in organizational, marketing, and advertising strategies. Because P&G's two brands give it half the U.S. market for disposable diapers, the company became a lightning rod for public criticism when a research study slammed disposable diapers as an environmental hazard. Even though these diapers constitute only 1 to 2 percent of the country's solid waste, and even though the study was commissioned by the trade association of cloth diaper manufacturers (which of course compete with disposable diaper makers), disposables in general and P&G in particular came to represent the nation's garbage crisis in the minds of many people. The external threats to the company ranged from consumers switching to cloth diapers to government legislators and regulators considering bans on disposables.

CHECKLIST FOR CONDUCTING A SWOT ANALYSIS

❏ A. Strengths
  - Do we have a distinct competitive advantage?
  - Do we have adequate financial resources?
  - Can we do something better than any of our competitors?
  - Do buyers think well of us?
  - Are we known as a market leader?
  - Do we have proprietary technologies?
  - Can we produce and market at lower costs?
  - Does our management team have a good track record?

❏ B. Weaknesses
  - Do we lack a clear strategic direction?
  - Is our competitive position deteriorating?
  - Are our facilities obsolete?
  - Is our profitability lower than it should be?
  - Do we lack management depth and talent?
  - Are we missing any key skills?

  - Do we have internal operating problems?
  - Are we short of cash to fund current and future business efforts?
  - Do we have a weak image in the market?

❏ C. Opportunities
  - Can we enter new market segments?
  - Can we expand our product line?
  - Are competitors weak or complacent?
  - Will our markets grow?

❏ D. Threats
  - Are we likely to get new competitors?
  - Will other products be substituted for ours?
  - Will market growth slow down?
  - Will new government policies impede us?
  - Are we vulnerable to economic downturns?
  - Will buyer needs and tastes change?
  - Will demographic shifts hurt us?

The company changed a number of its strategies, both in anticipation of the public outcry and in response to it. For example, product changes included making diapers that are more absorbent (thereby requiring less material), developing packaging methods that require less outer packaging, and establishing recycling programs that collect diapers and transform them into compost (the decomposed organic matter prized by gardeners). Changes in promotion and advertising included the distribution of 30 million copies of a direct-mail brochure explaining diaper recycling, public relations activities calling attention to advances being made, and magazine ads touting the benefits of composting diapers.[7]

MARKETING OBJECTIVES

With the situation analysis in place, you have the information you need to proceed with setting objectives. As mentioned earlier, marketing objectives are usually defined in terms of sales targets, but in some cases, marketers define an objective that will in turn help meet sales targets. An example of a sales target would be "selling $10 million worth of personal-care products in the next 12 months." An example of an objective that could lead to meeting sales targets would be "increasing the number of retailers who carry our products from 150 to 200 in the next 12 months."

For nonprofit organizations and government agencies, marketing objectives aren't typically expressed in terms of sales (see Exhibit 7.4). Every four years, for instance, the Democratic and Republican national committees have the goals of getting their candidates elected to the presidency, to Congress, and to various other state and local offices.

To be most effective, objectives at any level should meet four criteria:[8]

- They are *relevant to higher-level objectives.* The key to effective organizational performance is having each level or function contribute to the organization's overall success. This means that marketing objectives, as well as promotional and advertising objectives, must support the organization's overall goals.

- They are *challenging but still attainable.* Objectives have to be set with great care because any level of performance you choose implies a level of investment in terms of time, money, and management attention. Objectives that are set unrealistically high can lead to two problems: First, they can cause you to

V.O.: This man is just one of tens of thousands of people who have been imprisoned or tortured because of the peaceful expression of their beliefs, the color of their skin,

their religion, or even their sex. Since 1961 Amnesty International has worked on behalf of over 42,000 such prisoners. (Vaclav Havel waving to crowd) By putting pressure on

governments worldwide, Amnesty members are giving prisoners like him not just hope but freedom. Raise your voice. Call 1-800-55-AMNESTY.

EXHIBIT 7.4
Objectives in Nonprofit Advertising

Amnesty International uses ads such as this to encourage more people to support its goal of freeing political prisoners and stopping human rights abuses.

spend more than you should in the pursuit of something that simply isn't attainable (if there are only 1,000 buyers of your type of product, piling on enough advertising to attract 2,000 buyers would be a waste of money). Second, unrealistically high objectives can frustrate the people working to achieve them because no amount of effort or ingenuity will allow the people to be successful. On the other hand, objectives that aren't challenging enough can also cause two problems: First, if people think the objectives will be easy to achieve, they may not be motivated by them. Second, with sales objectives in particular, if actual performance outstrips objectives, you can be left with inadequate production capacity or inventory. Hewlett-Packard, the world's top maker of laser printers, figured that it once lost out on $50 million worth of sales during a three-month period because it underestimated demand, so production couldn't keep up.[9] The challenge, naturally, is to find the midpoint between objectives that are not challenging enough and those that are not attainable.

- They are *measurable.* If objectives aren't measurable, you'll never know whether you met them. Some objectives are much easier to measure than others, of course. As discussed in the section on posttesting in Chapter 6, sales goals that can be tied directly to advertising are the easiest to measure because you simply keep track of your sales. However, since measurement is rarely as simple as adding up sales receipts, advertisers usually establish other objectives.

- They are *time specific.* Objectives can stretch out from a few weeks to several years or more, but it's always important that an objective have a deadline attached to it so that you can measure success or failure. Saying that you'll increase sales by 5 percent in the next six months means that you can come back in six months and see how you did. In some industries, the time element can be tied to holidays, seasons, or various special events. When Simon & Schuster published Mary Higgins Clark's novel *Loves Music, Loves to Dance,* it set the goal of debuting on *The New York Times* best-seller list in the number one spot. In other words, the publisher wanted the book to outsell all others in the fiction category within a week of being introduced. This led to an intense marketing program involving displays for bookstores, television ads, and a 16-city tour for the author. It was an unusual effort for the book business, but it was successful.[10]

In addition to these criteria, it is vital that goals at any level have the approval and support of managers higher up in the organization. The president or CEO of a large corporation shouldn't be involved in lower-level marketing and advertising decisions, of course, but to the extent that lower-level activities depend on and support higher-level strategic activities, top managers should be aware of them and

The Rise, Fall, and Rise of Green Marketing

Green marketing, a catchall term for advertising and marketing that uses some element of environmental responsibility as a key selling theme, has had a wild and bumpy ride during its short lifetime. At the beginning, being green seemed like a wonderful opportunity. Consumers were demanding environmentally friendly products. The technologies for cost-effective recycling, degradable packaging, and other attractive solutions were coming on line. It seemed that by merely promoting your company's commitment to protecting the planet and touting your product's environmental benefits, people would line up to buy.

For some aspiring green marketers, however, things went downhill quickly. Consumers weren't all that impressed. In a recent survey, more than a quarter of the respondents said environmental claims in advertising weren't believable, and another two-thirds said the claims were only somewhat believable.

A few green advertising attempts have drawn the ire of environmental groups and the legal attention of government regulators. New York City's consumer affairs office calls its cases "green-collar" fraud and has accused several advertisers of making environmental claims that were misleading or false. Prosecutors at the state and federal levels have slapped makers of diapers, trash bags, and aerosol products with consumer fraud lawsuits.

How did green marketing shift from a great opportunity to what one consultant called "a code word for yet another corporate hypocrisy"? Many factors no doubt contributed, but perhaps the single biggest cause was that too many companies viewed environmental responsibility as an advertising strategy, not as a comprehensive way of doing business. In other words, when the environment became a key concern among consumers, some advertisers were tempted to toss the word into their ads and onto their product labels, while doing little or nothing to actually be environmentally responsible.

Consumers remain interested in environmentally responsible products, however, and opportunities still await companies that can convince these consumers. The first step that advertisers need to take is to be more careful about what they do and say. This ranges from being more precise in advertising claims (such as pointing out how much of your recycled paper is actually from *postconsumer* waste rather than from scraps left over from producing other paper products) to worrying less about environmentally correct advertising and more about environmentally safe business practices.

Beyond that, all sides in this issue have been clamoring for some guidelines regarding advertising terminology. The Federal Trade Commission recently issued definitions for such common terms as *recyclable* and *biodegradable*. With consistent terms in place, manufacturers now have a better idea of what they can and can't say, and consumers will have a better idea of what the terms mean.

The success of those companies that have truly taken environmental concerns to heart is encouraging proof that green marketing is a productive strategy, in addition to being a responsible way to do business. Hewlett-Packard (HP), the world's leading maker of laser printers, provides a good example of how companies can demonstrate their concern and build rapport with customers. Laser printers run on replaceable cartridges of powdered toner; when the toner runs out, the customer has the problem of disposing of the empty cartridge. HP established a return program in which customers who buy new cartridges put their old cartridges in the shipping boxes in which the new cartridges arrived. The company then pays United Parcel Service to come back for the old cartridges, which can be refilled with fresh toner. Customers are relieved of the disposal burden and witness HP's environmental responsibility in action.

What's Your Opinion?

1. Does defining the ways in which certain words can be used limit an advertiser's freedom of speech? Why or why not?
2. What role do consumers play in the ongoing effort to keep green marketing and advertising free from fraud and confusion?

should be in a position to help out as needed. The cooperation necessary to pursue strategies successfully and to achieve objectives is a two-way street: Lower-level efforts must support higher-level strategies and objectives. At the same time, higher-level managers must support lower-level personnel, making sure they have the resources and freedom they need to meet their objectives.

© 1991, Ralston Purina Company

It's Not The Kind Of Fruit You Usually Find In The Cereal Aisle.

Ralston® Cranberry Walnut Muesli is a blend of five toasted grains bursting with sweet, tangy Ocean Spray® cranberries and crunchy walnuts. It's different, daring and delicious.

We've Come A Long Way Since Raisins.

EXHIBIT 7.5
Positioning by Product Difference

Ralston tries to make it clear in this ad that you won't normally find cranberries in breakfast cereals, but you will in Ralston Cranberry Walnut Muesli.

MARKETING STRATEGY

With objectives established, the advertiser can move ahead with defining a marketing strategy. As mentioned earlier, a marketing strategy identifies the target markets, the desired position in each market, and the marketing mix that will persuade those target markets to part with their money (or to exhibit whatever behavior the marketer is shooting for). Chapter 5 discussed how to use segmentation and target market selection to identify those potential customers most likely to respond to your advertising appeals, and it introduced you to the general concepts of positioning in those target segments. The following section explores specific positioning options that you can employ as part of a marketing strategy.

Positioning Options

Advertisers can choose from a number of positioning approaches, depending on what the situation analysis reveals about the strengths of their product, the needs of their customers, and the actions of their competitors.[11]

- *Positioning by product differences.* One of the strongest positioning approaches is based on some feature that your product has but that your competitors' products don't (see Exhibit 7.5). Of course, the difference must be truthful, and it must be meaningful to customers in order to have any impact. When Korg featured Genesis band members Tony Banks and Phil Collins in an ad for a new music synthesizer, it used a quote from the musicians saying that "Korg has come up with a synth that has some of the most evocative sounds we've ever heard." The instrument not only produces evocative sounds, it produces some of the *most* evocative sounds these experienced musicians have ever heard, which helps distinguish the Korg from its many competitors.[12]

- *Positioning by product attributes or benefits.* This approach identifies a product attribute or benefit that is meaningful to customers and then develops a positioning strategy around it. Robbins Sports Surfaces, which makes such products as gym floors, positions its products on the advanced design of the support structure that absorbs the shock when people jump on it.[13] Remember, too, that there's often more to a product than just its basic features. Continuum, a manufacturer of scientific lasers, created an ad about how, during a hurricane, one of its service engineers went above and beyond the call of duty to service a laser that was mounted on a lighthouse platform off the coast of Virginia. The engineer's dedication to customer satisfaction and his company's strong commitment to service are significant elements of value in the overall product that Continuum offers its customers.[14]

- *Positioning by product users.* This sounds a bit like targeting, but explicitly identifying a target market in an ad can be a good way to position a product. The Eagle Vision, one of a new line of cars introduced by Chrysler in 1992, used the theme "Not intended for the general public" in its ads. Why would someone say that a product isn't for everybody? In order to position it as something special. When you buy an Eagle Vision, part of what you get is the feeling that you're somebody unique, somebody who wouldn't buy just any old car. Of course, as *Advertising Age* columnist Bob Garfield pointed out, "95 percent of all consumers regard themselves as the 5 percent of consumers who are above the 95 percent of all consumers," so every Eagle Vision owner can feel special about the purchase.[15]

- *Positioning by product usage.* The ways a product is used can provide positioning opportunities as well. When General Foods, the makers of Jell-O, came up with the idea of Jell-O Jigglers, which are Jell-O shapes created with cookie cutters, it positioned the product as another option for holiday treats. Rather than viewing Jell-O as an everyday dessert option, people who saw the television ads and read the packaging were essentially encouraged to view Jell-O as a competitor to cookies and other traditional holiday snacks.[16]

- *Positioning against a particular competitor.* Sometimes the most effective way to move into a potential customer's mind is to compare yourself with a known competitor and try to explain why you are a better choice. In an ad for its woodworking lathe, Jet Equipment & Tools didn't pull any punches when it compared its product to the one offered by Delta, a well-established, well-known leader in the woodworking market. The ad's headline read "Why Buy Jet? Because It's Better Than Delta," and the ad featured a list comparing prices and features.[17]

- *Positioning against an entire product category.* Advertisers sometimes find themselves competing against an entire category of products, particularly when they are offering to solve a problem that customers are used to solving with other types of products. When a passenger train service such as Amtrak or British Rail advertises that it is a more attractive choice than taking an airline, for instance, it is positioning itself against the entire product category of air travel services (see Exhibit 7.6).

- *Positioning by association.* This approach involves associating your product with some other entity, in the hope that some of that entity's positive image will rub

ANNOUNCING 3 AMTRAKS DAILY TO SACRAMENTO

There's no stopping you now!

EXHIBIT 7.6
Positioning against an Entire Product Category

In this humorous billboard ad, Amtrak points out a big advantage of taking the train.

off on your product. When Nissan introduced the Altima midsize sedan in late 1992, it was entering a segment that was home to some of the most popular cars in the world, including the Toyota Camry, the Ford Taurus, and the Honda Accord, three cars that were well entrenched in the public's mind. One of the first Altima television commercials associated the car with the $45,000 Lexus luxury sedan, but at a $13,000 price tag, very competitive with the Camry, Taurus, and Accord. Nissan's agency, Chiat/Day, imitated a notable Lexus commercial in which wine glasses were stacked together on the hood of a car that ran up to 130 miles per hour in a simulated test (to demonstrate how vibration-free the Lexus is). The Altima ad showed a similar demonstration while a voice said, "You may have seen this demonstration before, but never for a $13,000 car." Nissan thus indicated that the Altima was in the same price league as the three popular cars but had some of the luxury found in a $45,000 car.[18]

- *Positioning by problem.* This is a unique approach often used by nonprofit organizations that have little or no direct competition. The goal in such cases is to position the organization by the problems it is trying to solve, rather than by the particular solutions it is offering. A nonprofit drug- and alcohol-abuse treatment program that had been positioning itself as treating addiction (i.e., offering a solution) changed its positioning to attacking the problem of addiction. This change shifted attention from curing addiction to helping people realize and admit they have a problem. Moreover, the program could reach out to friends and families, saying that it understands their problems as well. Within three months of the positioning shift, admissions to the program doubled.[19]

Keep in mind a key point brought up in Chapter 5: advertising often can't do the entire positioning job by itself, which is why positioning is addressed here with the rest of the marketing strategy. When it comes to positioning, other elements of the marketing mix can be as important as, or even more important than, advertising.

Marketing Mix

Once you've identified your target market and defined a desired position in the market, your next move is to design the marketing mix that will reach those potential buyers. Brand managers and marketing managers are involved in the whole range of the marketing mix, including such tasks as making pricing decisions, working with production engineers, and negotiating with wholesalers for distribution. As an advertising specialist, you'll most likely be given the marketing plan as a starting reference, and you'll concentrate on developing the advertising objectives and strategies to support the marketing strategy.

Because there are a number of elements in the promotion category, advertisers must also consider a **promotional mix,** which represents the particular combination of advertising, sales promotion, public relations, and personal selling that an advertiser chooses to employ for each product or business unit. Just as the marketing mix combines the best blend of product, price, distribution, and promotion, the promotional mix tries to assemble the best combination of promotional activities to achieve company objectives.

Manufacturers that sell through wholesalers and retailers have another promotional mix choice to make as well: whether to *push* products through the distribution channel or to motivate buyers to *pull* them through. With a **push strategy,** you focus your promotions on the wholesalers, or retailers if you sell directly to them, and encourage these channel members to push the products on through to final customers. In contrast, with a **pull strategy,** you create demand at the final-customer end and rely on this demand to pull products through the marketing channel as consumers ask retailers, retailers ask wholesalers, and wholesalers ask you for the product (see Exhibit 7.7). Of course, these two strategies are theoretical extremes; nearly every promotional mix has elements of both push and pull

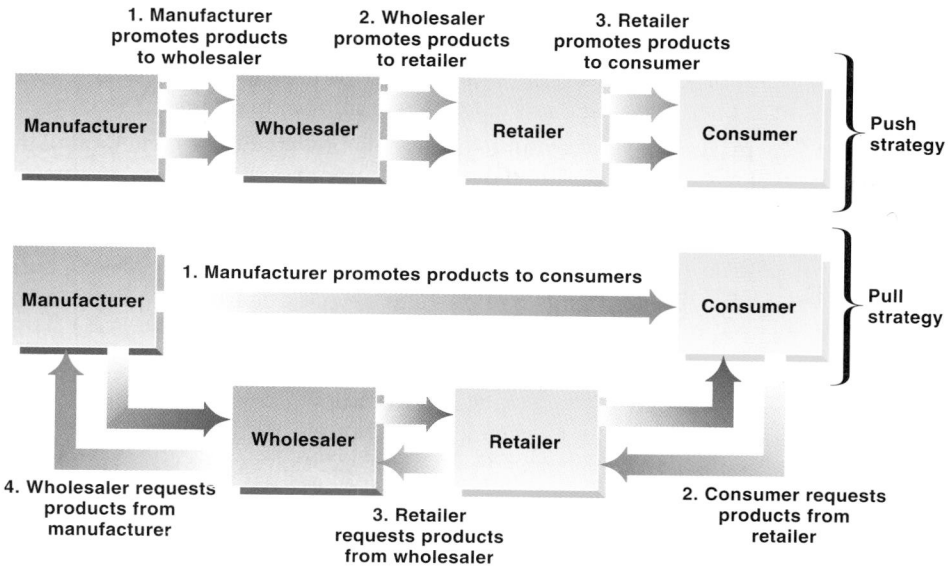

1. Manufacturer promotes products to wholesaler
2. Wholesaler promotes products to retailer
3. Retailer promotes products to consumer

Manufacturer → **Wholesaler** → **Retailer** → **Consumer** } Push strategy

1. Manufacturer promotes products to consumers

Manufacturer → **Consumer** } Pull strategy

Wholesaler **Retailer**

4. Wholesaler requests products from manufacturer
3. Retailer requests products from wholesaler
2. Consumer requests products from retailer

Information flow   Product flow

EXHIBIT 7.7
Push versus Pull Strategies

With a push strategy, the manufacturer promotes products to wholesalers, who then promote them to retailers, who then promote them to customers. In contrast, a pull strategy starts by building demand at the customer level; this demand then "pulls" products through the distribution channel.

strategies. The makers of Rogain, a medical treatment for hair loss, advertise both to doctors who might prescribe the product and to consumers who might request it from their doctors.[20]

ACTION PLAN

As part of the marketing plan, the action plan outlines what you intend to do and when and where you intend to do it. An action plan has no standard list of tasks; marketing activities vary from one advertiser to another. Even so, the basic tasks usually include activities for each element of the marketing mix, as well as for budgeting and scheduling:[21]

- *Product-related activities.* In some cases, getting a product ready for the market is fairly simple. In other cases, it can involve a vast array of decisions and tasks that can range from passing government safety tests (e.g., new medicines and aircraft), to creating packaging that meets government labeling standards (e.g., food products), to negotiating with other companies to provide all the pieces of a customer solution (e.g., a computer maker arranging to get options and software from other suppliers).

- *Pricing decisions.* Target prices are usually set early on to make sure that a product will generate acceptable profits, but fine-tuning is often needed as the product is readied for market. In addition, marketers must consider discount policies, financing, and other issues related to pricing.

- *Distribution activities.* Distribution activities vary greatly, depending on the type of organization, its position in the market, and the type of product being marketed. An unknown manufacturer with a new product can face a huge uphill battle just to get the attention of wholesalers and retailers that could help market the product. Much of its energy and marketing budget will probably be spent on just getting into the distribution channel. In contrast, a retailer, a service organization, or a manufacturer with its own sales force or retail outlets might have much less to think about in terms of distribution; the structure is already in place.

- *Promotional activities.* As you've probably surmised by now, the range of promotional activities available to today's advertisers can be overwhelming. The action plan lists the particular promotional activities you've chosen. In some cases, these activities are tied to specific events, such as the launch of an advertising campaign or a press conference to announce a major new product.

In other cases, promotional activities involve putting various elements into place for the long term, such as training salespeople or setting up a telemarketing center. In all cases, it is important to integrate your promotional efforts; doing so can decrease costs and increase communications effectiveness.

- *Budget.* The marketing budget outlines not only how much each element of the program will cost but when the money will be spent, which can affect the way you manage your finances. Just as we all do, advertisers have to make choices and compromises about how they spend their money, and the budget shows those choices. In addition, the budget section often includes a **payback analysis,** which shows such things as how much profit a marketing program will generate and how soon it will pay back all its costs and start generating that profit. The last section of this chapter discusses advertising budgets.

- *Schedule.* The schedule provides a visual overview of what will happen when. It's important to coordinate all the elements of the marketing mix so that the entire program is as effective as possible. For example, you may want to have advertising appear several weeks before salespeople start calling on customers, and you'll need products ready for those salespeople to demonstrate. The schedule helps you keep all these activities on track.

Keep in mind that the scope of a marketing plan varies from situation to situation. You might develop a "standing" plan that provides an overview of the marketing programs for all your products and supplement this with more detailed plans for each product or product line. New-product introductions require more comprehensive plans than products that are already on the market, simply because you have so many more issues to iron out. Finally, all your marketing activities may be included in a single document, or you might produce a marketing plan and an advertising plan as separate documents.

BRAND EQUITY

It's important to put marketing strategy in the context of **brand equity,** a measure of a brand's worth to both the company that markets it and the customers who buy it. Brand equity is a combination of five elements: brand loyalty, brand awareness, perceived quality, associations other than quality (such as style, excitement, or healthiness), and proprietary assets such as patents, trademarks, and relationships with retailers. Strong brand equities can lead to increased sales, protection from competitive moves, the ability to charge higher prices, and other benefits for the marketers.[22]

Brand equity has become a central concern for many marketers in recent years, as they try to design strategies that will enhance the value of their brands—and avoid strategies and tactics that chip away at their brand equity. Imagine if an upscale store such as Bloomingdale's or Neiman-Marcus thought it could get the public's attention with a silly, slapstick-style ad campaign. The effort might increase awareness, but it also might damage brand equity by tarnishing the stores' classy images. U.S. automakers have spent the last decade trying to rebuild the brand equity they lost in the 1970s and early 1980s, when Japanese and European cars began to represent higher perceived quality. Protecting and enhancing brand equity, whether it's through advertising, product design, or some other element of the marketing mix, is at the core of successful marketing and advertising strategies.

Integrated Marketing Communications Planning

As you learned in Chapter 1, integrated marketing communications (IMC) is a fundamentally different way of viewing the process of communicating with target audiences. A successful approach to planning IMC is based on four key concepts:[23]

- *IMC coordinates all customer communication.* IMC recognizes that people accumulate information over time and that this accumulated information affects their purchase behavior. In other words, when people view a commercial for Chevy trucks, they don't forget everything they've learned about the truck market and make a purchase based on that one commercial. The new information from Cheverolet connects with information the viewers have received and stored, including other information from Chevy. If Chevrolet's advertising people and salespeople have been sending conflicting messages, then consumers won't get a clear message from Chevrolet. With IMC, advertisers work to ensure that every message they send, through whatever medium, is consistent. The net result is a stronger impression left in the minds of the target audience (see Exhibit 7.8).

- *IMC starts with the customer, not the product.* Rather than starting with a product and then finding ways to communicate its benefits to target customers,

EXHIBIT 7.8
The IMC Approach to Communications Planning

In the IMC approach to planning, the advertiser starts by analyzing data about the target audience.

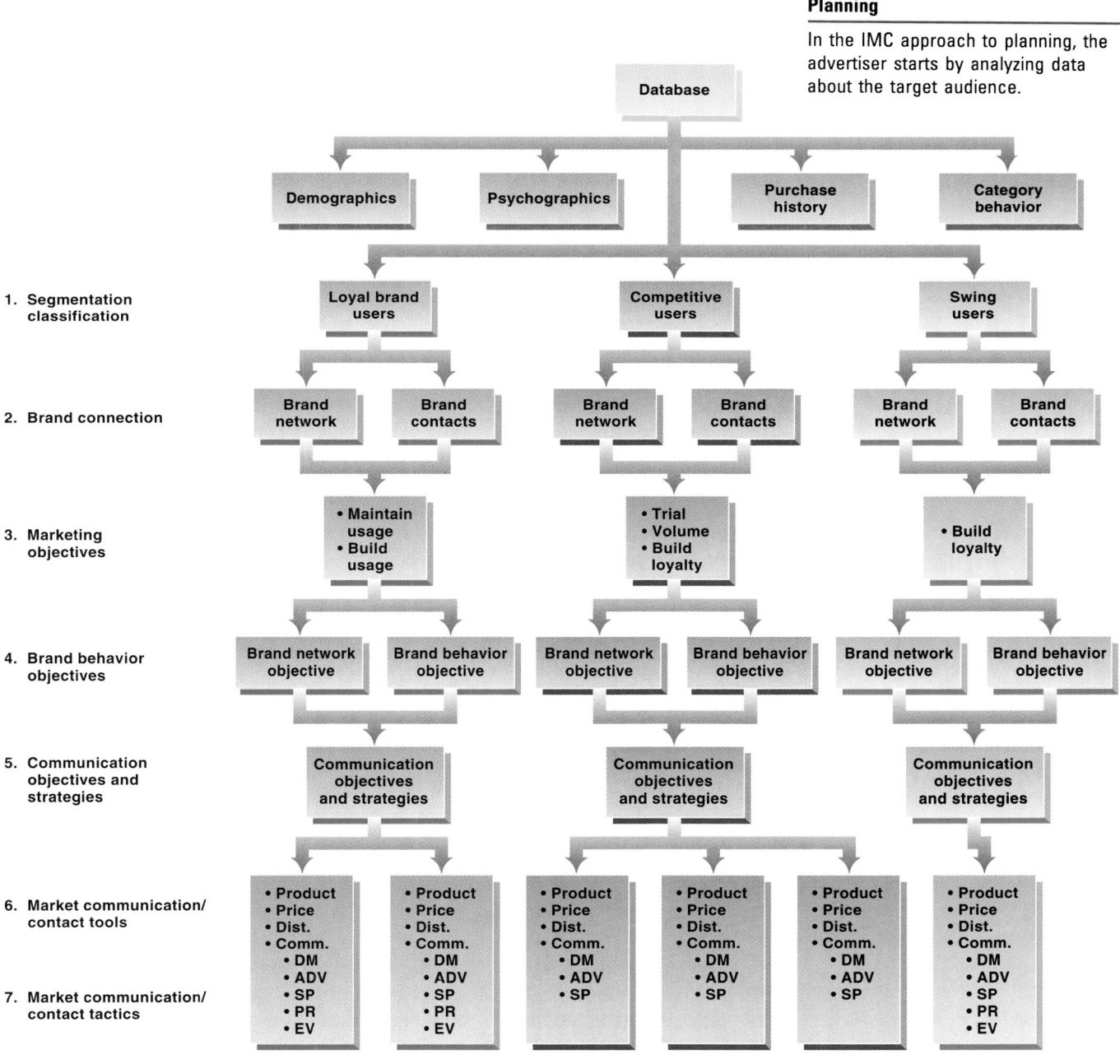

DM = Direct marketing   ADV = Advertising   SP = Sales promotion   PR = Public relations   EV = Event marketing

you start "inside the customers' heads," trying to understand what they value. Then you work backward to your product, figuring out how to structure a message that connects with the target audience.

- *IMC seeks to create one-on-one communication with customers.* A natural outgrowth of starting with the customer is recognizing that every customer is unique and will respond best to personalized communication. The seven-step process shown in Exhibit 7.8 highlights the role of computer databases in IMC. With enough information about individual customers, you can craft more effective, personalized promotional messages. From there, you can categorize your target audience into users loyal to your brand, users loyal to competitive brands, and users who can be swayed from one brand to another. The next step is a key part of IMC: determining what customers think about brands in a given product category (brand networks) and finding out how they come into contact with those brands (brand contacts). With this information, you can begin to set objectives for each category of user and then employ the most appropriate communication vehicles.

- *IMC creates two-way communication with customers.* IMC isn't just talking *to* customers but talking *with* them. In other words, you listen to what customers have to say, you create and shape your message, and then you respond. This creates a dialog that seeks to meet customers' needs.

As you'll see in the Saturn case at the end of the chapter, a vital part of the carmaker's success is a well-orchestrated IMC approach to communication. Everything (from the names of dealerships to the names of the color options on the cars) was chosen in the context of a master plan, communicating the message that Saturn is a new kind of car company. The company's ad agency, Hal Riney & Partners, didn't step in at the last minute and try to create a convincing ad campaign. Instead, it was involved from the beginning, before any cars were even built, helping coordinate every aspect of Saturn's message to consumers. The award-winning Saturn ads are only one part of an integrated communication strategy.[24]

With the help of database specialists at the Leo Burnett advertising agency, Hallmark Cards achieved IMC results that the company described as "absolutely phenomenal." In a campaign designed to increase sales to working women, Hallmark started by sorting its customer list to find its most frequent and loyal buyers. The company then began sending personalized mail to these women, based on information in its database. The direct mail included information about gift-giving, holiday entertaining, and other issues that encourage recipients to buy more Hallmark products. The direct-mail effort was coordinated with television, print, and in-store advertising, all with a personalized touch that the company equates with getting mail from your own sister.[25]

The Advertising Plan: Getting the Word Out

Just as advertising operates in the larger context of the total marketing effort, the advertising plan is developed in the context of the marketing plan. Exhibit 7.9 shows how the advertising plan is related to the marketing plan. The **advertising plan** presents an analysis of the advertising situation (more narrow than the marketing plan situation analysis, the advertising situation analysis is usually conducted to address communication issues specifically), along with a reiteration of the previously established marketing objectives and marketing strategy. It then outlines the objectives and strategy specific to advertising, along with details about messages, media plans, ties to sales promotion or special events, the advertising budget, and some sort of timeline or calendar that shows key dates in the upcoming campaign. As noted earlier, the advertising plan may stand on its own, with its

```
MARKETING PLAN                              ADVERTISING PLAN

  SITUATION ANALYSIS                          SITUATION ANALYSIS

  MARKETING OBJECTIVES                        MARKETING STRATEGY

 • Promotional objectives
 • Product objectives                         PROMOTIONAL STRATEGY
 • Pricing objectives
 • Distribution objectives                   • Personal selling strategy
                                             • Sales promotion strategy
  MARKETING STRATEGY                         • Public relations strategy
                                             • Advertising strategy
 • Promotional strategy
 • Product strategy                           ADVERTISING OBJECTIVES
 • Pricing strategy
 • Distribution strategy                     • Sales
                                             • Communications
     ACTION PLAN
                                              ADVERTISING STRATEGY
 • Promotional activities
 • Product activities                        • Creative strategy
 • Pricing decisions                         • Media plan
 • Distribution activities                   • Budget
 • Budget
 • Calendar
```

EXHIBIT 7.9
Marketing Plans and Advertising Plans

The advertising plan is an integral component of the overall marketing plan.

own activities lists, budget, and calendar, or it may be included as part of the marketing plan.

ADVERTISING OBJECTIVES

The process of setting advertising objectives is one of the most challenging in the field of advertising. Entire books have been written about just this one step. The difficulty in setting meaningful, realistic advertising objectives stems from a two-part problem. First, the effect of advertising on sales cannot always be measured, because most advertisers conduct a variety of marketing activities simultaneously, each directed toward increasing sales. For example, can you really be sure that a new ad caused an increase in sales, or was the increase due to lower prices? If you can't identify the contribution that advertising makes to your sales, it is an unfair burden on advertising to expect it to generate a certain number of sales. As a result, many advertisers set *communication objectives* for their advertising, not *sales objectives*—and this is the second part of the problem; setting communications objectives is easier said than done.

Sales Objectives

For all the emphasis in marketing and advertising on making sales, there are relatively few cases when it is reasonable to assign sales objectives to advertising. This isn't because advertising isn't effective; it's simply that sales are usually better treated as *marketing* objectives since sales are driven not only by advertising but also by pricing decisions, retailing activities, sales promotion, and other elements of the marketing mix. **Sales objectives,** in which the advertising is expected to generate a certain volume of sales within a fixed period of time, are appropriate for advertising only when one or more of the following conditions apply:[26]

- *When advertising is the only variable in your marketing equation.* In other words, you can't modify anything else in your promotional program or in your overall marketing program, such as pricing, retail availability, or the product itself, while you're trying to measure advertising's impact on sales.

- *When advertising is the dominant force in the entire marketing mix.* The role of advertising has to be significantly more important than personal selling, retailing, and other elements of the mix.

- *When the advertising is designed to solicit an immediate response.* The more time you allow for your ad to have an impact, the less reasonable it becomes to

EXHIBIT 7.10
Sales Objectives

It's much easier to measure sales performance accurately if you can tie your promotional efforts to particular audience members. Lands' End and other catalog retailers can easily measure the effectiveness of each promotional effort because they know exactly how many people see the advertising and how many place orders as a result.

assign it a sales target; other forces are likely to come into play in the meantime. For example, competitors may adjust their marketing mixes or retailers may increase or decrease their promotional efforts. Another timing issue is that advertising doesn't always have an immediate effect but may contribute to sales long after a buyer comes in contact with an ad, a phenomenon known as the **carryover effect.**

It is rare indeed that a case meets these criteria. The most obvious instances involve direct mail and direct marketing (see Chapter 16), which include direct-action advertising, or trying to solicit an immediate response from your audience (see Exhibit 7.10). As long as the direct efforts aren't heavily supplemented by other advertising or promotional efforts, you can usually isolate the impact of your advertising, so establishing a sales objective for advertising in such cases can be appropriate. In fact, the ease with which direct mail's effects can be measured is one of its most attractive aspects.

Communications Objectives

Because you can't often measure the sales impact of advertising and therefore can't assign sales objectives, your next step is to consider **communications objectives,** which define advertising performance in terms of how well a given communications goal has been achieved. Quite a number of schemes and models have been proposed for establishing communications objectives, and all start with an attempt to explain how advertising works. Most of these models operate on the notion that potential buyers move through various phases or stages; the differences between models tend to focus on how the phases are defined and in what order they function.

DAGMAR and the Hierarchy of Effects. For decades researchers have been trying to model what we know about how advertising works, and from these models they have been trying to pick meaningful communications objectives. One of the earliest

At Lufthansa, we're in the perfect position to fly to the new Europe.

With all the changes in Europe, one thing remains constant – Lufthansa's position as the best way to get your clients there. Because from Germany's central location, they can connect to any one of our 88 European destinations. That's more than three times as many destinations as American, Delta and United combined. You can also be sure that in every city Lufthansa flies to, and even in many we don't fly to, your clients will find a trained staff to help with any last minute travel arrangements and changes while they're on the road. At Lufthansa, providing you with the best service everywhere in the world isn't just our job. It's our passion.

A passion for perfection.℠   ⊙ **Lufthansa**

Schedule subject to change without notice. Lufthansa is a participant in the mileage programs of United, Delta, USAir and Continental.

We're accused of being obsessed with perfection, precision and meticulous attention to every detail. Thank you.

The little things on a flight tell you a lot about an airline. So you'll notice that at Lufthansa, your drink and meal arrive at the same time. And that your electronic headset is free even in Economy Class. Or if you don't want to eat, drink or watch movies, you can get a "Do Not Disturb" sign. Of course, the way our crew works together also adds to your flight. Things like these show our passion to make your flight enjoyable. One you feel in everyone at Lufthansa. From the wine steward who inspects every bottle to the pilot who gets you there on time. A passion for perfection that ensures you the best flying experience possible.

A passion for perfection.℠   ⊙ **Lufthansa**

Lufthansa is a participant in the mileage programs of United, Delta, USAir and Continental/Eastern. See your Travel Agent for details.

influential models was called **DAGMAR,** an acronym for *Defining Advertising Goals for Measured Advertising Results,* a book that was published in 1961. The DAGMAR model was built around four stages of communications results: awareness, comprehension, conviction, and action. DAGMAR's author, Russell Colley, pointed out that similar models have been in use in one form or another since the early days of marketing and advertising.[27] DAGMAR's premise is that you can pick the appropriate stage in the communication process and use it to define advertising objectives (e.g., making 80 percent of the target market aware of the product, or making sure that 75 percent of those who are aware of it comprehend it).

Since the publication of the DAGMAR model, more than a dozen variations and expansions have been published.[28] Each is considered a hierarchy of effects model (see Chapter 1) because it shows several phases of communication, progressing from initial awareness up to the decision to make a purchase. As you can see in

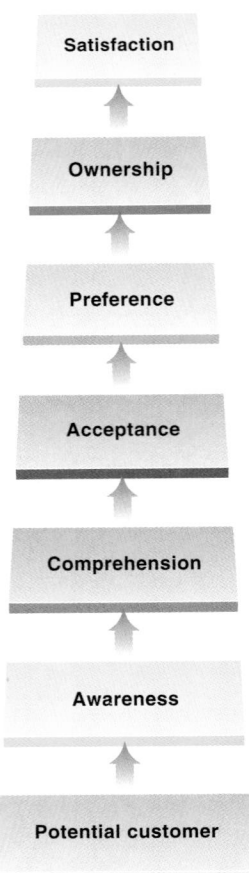

EXHIBIT 7.11
A Hierarchy of Effects Model

This is one of many variations on the hierarchy of effects model.

Exhibit 7.11, a hierarchy of effects model represents a learning process in which (in this version) a potential customer becomes aware of a product, begins to comprehend it based on what he or she has learned from the ad, begins to accept it as a potential solution, forms a preference for it over competitive products, makes the purchase, and then grows satisfied or dissatisfied with it after using or consuming it.[29] Particular advertisements can be created to pull potential buyers through each stage.

Stages in the Communication Process. Whatever the variety, a hierarchy of effects model is based on the general assumption that people first learn something from advertising, then form feelings about the product in question, and finally take action (e.g., buying product A, product B, or no product at all). This order of stages is called the *learn-feel-do* sequence. However, advertising doesn't always work in such a clear, straightforward, and logical manner.[30]

Examining your own behavior as a consumer is a good way to convince yourself of this. Say you've recently purchased a jacket. Did you learn about it through an ad, develop a positive feeling, and then decide to buy? Chances are that you didn't follow such a logical process. Maybe you saw a television star wear the jacket and figured you'd look good in one as well. Perhaps you'd never heard of the brand but saw it on sale while you were shopping and bought it because it was such a great deal—then you saw some advertising that showed what a fashionable person you are for wearing the jacket. Maybe you just bought the jacket on the spur of the moment, without thinking or feeling anything beyond the fact that you needed a jacket and this one seemed to fit the bill.

This example highlights two problems with the learn-feel-do assumption: the steps don't always occur in this order, and buyers don't always go through each step. For products that you wouldn't spend much time worrying about, such as pencils, you probably don't form feelings until after you've bought and used the product, leading to a *learn-do-feel* sequence. Advertising can make you aware of such products, but you're not going to be involved enough for that advertising to affect your emotions; instead, you generate positive or negative feelings after you try the product (if you generate any feelings at all). Another possible sequence is *feel-learn-do,* in which you first get positive feelings about a car (through advertising and other channels), then learn more about it, and then purchase it. A television commercial showing a Lexus Coupe or a Chevrolet Corvette snaking its way around a twisty mountain road might give you a positive feeling about owning such a car; then other advertisements or information sources (such as brochures from the dealer) can fill you in on the factual details. A fourth possibility is *do-feel-do,* which is probably the most common sequence according to advertising expert John Philip Jones. In such a sequence, no factual learning is going on (you know about the product because you've used it before, and you like it because it met your needs); you buy a product and like the way it works, and then advertising reinforces those feelings and prompts you to buy the same product again and again.[31]

These theoretical sequences are closely related to advertising objectives. For instance, a do-feel-do sequence contains little or no factual learning, so it wouldn't make sense to set an advertising objective of "explaining the product's benefits to 50 percent of the target audience." A better objective would be "to remind previous customers who haven't purchased in the last six months that the product is still available." In a feel-learn-do sequence, your objectives could focus on creating positive attitudes among the target audience. If your research can help you understand the steps your customers go through when making a purchase, you can pick the most appropriate sequence and then set objectives accordingly.

Other Models. As a result of all the research into the twin problems of how advertising works and how best to establish communications objectives, several other helpful models have been proposed. The Foote, Cone, and Belding (FCB) advertising agency theorized that advertising works differently depending on the type of product involved. The company's strategists devised the **FCB grid** to help

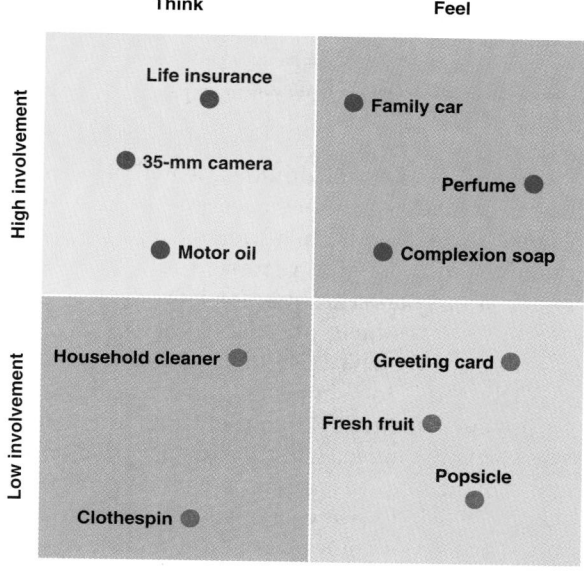

Think | Feel

High involvement

- Life insurance
- 35-mm camera
- Motor oil
- Family car
- Perfume
- Complexion soap

Low involvement

- Household cleaner
- Greeting card
- Fresh fruit
- Popsicle
- Clothespin

EXHIBIT 7.12
The FCB Grid

The FCB Grid divides advertising situations along the two dimensions of thinking versus feeling and high involvement versus low involvement.

advertisers pick the right communications model based on the type of product they're trying to advertise and the attitudes that buyers are likely to have about the product. As Exhibit 7.12 shows, the FCB grid divides advertising situations according to two dimensions: thinking versus feeling and high involvement versus low involvement. *Low-involvement* products are those that consumers don't get that wrapped up in, in either a cognitive (thinking) or an emotional (feeling) sense. In contrast, the consumer's head and heart are more engaged when dealing with *high-involvement products.* The thinking-versus-feeling distinction comes into play based on whether the purchase decision is driven primarily by logic and facts (e.g., when purchasing a professional camera) or by feelings and emotions (e.g., when buying perfume). Of course, most purchases involve a degree of both thinking and feeling, but many lean in one direction or the other.[32]

Although it is widely known, the FCB grid has not met with universal approval among advertising researchers and practitioners. John Rossiter, a professor at the Australian Graduate School of Management, and Larry Percy, the director of strategic research at Lintas:USA, have proposed an alternative grid designed to address the shortcomings they find in the FCB grid. The Rossiter-Percy grid differs in several key ways (see Exhibit 7.13). First, it includes brand awareness as

Transformational Motives
- Sensory gratification
- Intellectual stimulation
- Social approval

Informational Motives
- Problem removal
- Problem avoidance
- Incomplete satisfaction
- Mixed approach-avoidance
- Normal depletion

Low involvement (Lower Risk) | High involvement (Higher Risk)

EXHIBIT 7.13
The Rossiter-Percy Grid

The Rossiter-Percy Grid attempts to provide a more pragmatic and comprehensive view of advertising situations.

EXHIBIT 7.14
The Integrated Marketing Communications Model

The IMC model starts with the customer and works back toward the advertiser.

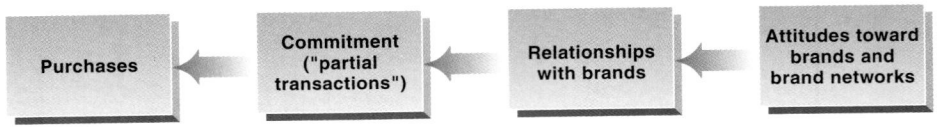

a prerequisite to brand attitude, meaning that you have to consider whether buyers have ever heard of you before worrying about what they think and feel about you. Second, it defines the involvement dimension in terms of risk. Low-involvement products are those that represent low risk; people will simply buy them and try them, rather than searching for lots of information beforehand. In contrast, high-involvement products are riskier, so buyers demand more information before making choices. Third, Rossiter and Percy assert that the think-feel dimension in the FCB grid is too simplistic to capture the various motivations that people have for buying products. The motivation dimension on their model includes five *informational* motives and three *transformational* motives. Generally speaking, the informational motives prompt buyers to remove negative elements from their lives (buying aspirin to relieve a headache or soda to quench a thirst), and the transformational motives induce them to add positive elements to their lives (buying a car that affords more social prestige).[33]

Another new attempt to define measurable advertising objectives was designed in response to the recognized shortcomings of the hierarchy of effects approach. As part of their efforts to explain integrated marketing communications, professors Don Schultz, Stanley Tannenbaum, and Robert Lauterborn devised the **integrated marketing communications model.** This model starts with purchasing rather than initial communication (see Exhibit 7.14). First you try to measure purchase behavior; if you can't do that (for the reasons discussed above), you then step back to measure a *partial transaction,* which represents some action that the potential buyer has taken that signals an intent to buy. This might be calling a toll-free number for more information or visiting a dealer, for example. If you can isolate the effects that advertising had on these actions, you can assign objectives at this level. If not, you go back another step to measure *brand relationship,* the affiliation that the potential buyer might have with your brand, such as whether the prospective buyer has seen the brand in stores. If you can't do that, you step back further to measure *the attitudes toward brands and brand networks* at the beginning of the process. Brand networks are the connections that buyers make in their minds about products and product categories. At whatever level you can isolate advertising's effects in the IMC model, that's where you can start to establish meaningful advertising objectives.[34]

Objectives and Advertising Purpose

Advertisers create ads with a variety of purposes in mind, from getting people up off the couch to call a toll-free number to simply reinforcing attitudes they already have about a product or a company. Whether you've established sales or communication objectives, they need to relate to your purpose, the job you're expecting your ads to perform. Here are six categories of advertising purpose, arranged on a continuum from most direct to most indirect:[35]

- *To prompt direct action.* Direct-action advertising is designed to motivate people to act, and the sooner the better. It involves all *direct-response advertising,* ads that try to persuade people to call a number, mail or fax an order form, or otherwise make an immediate purchase decision. Direct-action advertising also includes much retail advertising (such as the ads you see in a newspaper from local grocery stores that are trying to get you into the stores to purchase various items), in-store advertising (such as electronic kiosks or end-of-aisle displays), and package advertising (such as a sticker on the product package offering 10 percent off the regular price). Direct-action advertising is the only category for which sales objectives are appropriate, although not all types of direct-action advertising qualify. If you mail people brochures for a product that they've never seen, that they've never seen advertised, and that they can buy only through your mail offer, you can be fairly certain that almost all sales will be the direct result of your advertising. You couldn't make the same assumption for a newspaper ad run by a grocery store promoting a product that is also nationally advertised on television.

- *To encourage information search.* In some cases, it's unreasonable to expect people to make a purchase decision based only on your advertising. They'll need more information, a test drive, a demonstration, or some other form of communication before making up their minds. This is often the situation for big-ticket items, whether they're cars or computer equipment. Maxtor, a manufacturer of computer disk drives, doesn't expect its customers (computer manufacturers) to buy 10,000 or 100,000 drives after reading an advertisement. Instead, a recent Maxtor ad ended with a toll-free number and encouraged the audience to call for more information.[36] In terms of setting objectives for ads like this, if the phone number used in this ad wasn't advertised anywhere else, it would be reasonable to set an objective for the number of calls received. On the other hand, if the phone number was used on invoices, direct-mail offers, product packaging, and industry directories, Maxtor would have a hard time telling which vehicle prompted potential buyers to call. (Some companies work around this by asking callers to identify where they obtained the phone number; if this is part of the advertising plan, then an explicit objective would be reasonable to use.)

- *To relate product to needs.* A less direct form of ad, this category includes those ads that try to draw a link in the potential buyers' minds between the product and their needs. Consider the notion of evoked sets of brands (discussed in Chapter 4), in which brands can make progress from being unknown to being known to being accepted to being preferred. A key purpose of ads in this category is to get the product known and have it accepted. Sandals resorts in the Caribbean targeted people looking for romantic getaway vacations when its ads showed couples enjoying the resorts' various activities under the headline: "Sandals, Where Love Comes to Stay."[37] Objectives for such ads can be measured in terms of how effectively they convince the target audience that the product will satisfy their needs.

- *To encourage recall of past satisfactions and prompt reorders.* Ads in this category are designed to summon memories of past satisfaction and get customers to purchase your product once again. In fact, some ads of this type come right out and say things like "Remember when you had such a great time using this product?" When Toyota introduced the 1993 Corolla, it aimed ads directly at people who had bought Corollas in the past, saying "Discover Corolla. Again."[38]

- *To modify attitudes.* One of the more challenging objectives that can be assigned to an ad is to modify the target audience's attitudes. You might set an attitude modification objective if your products have gotten a bad reputation for one reason or another, if you're introducing product applications that customers have never thought of before, or if you're attempting to recapture customers who've switched to other brands (see Exhibit 7.15).

- *To reinforce attitudes.* The final category of advertising purpose seeks to reinforce attitudes that current customers already have about your products. These ads are traditionally used by market leaders that want to keep their market shares and sales volumes. Ever wonder why you continue to see so much advertising from Coke or McDonald's or other giant firms that are known to practically everyone in this and most other countries? Sometimes these advertisers are trying to perform a specific function such as introducing a new product, but often their goal is simply to keep their names in front of their loyal customers—and to make sure those customers stay loyal.

V.O.: Dean & DeLuca, are you waiting longer for overseas calls to connect? (*Music*) Latino Chicago Theatre Company, are you saving less than you'd hoped on

international calls since you left AT&T? *WE WANT YOU BACK.* AT&T PRO WATTS. Competitive prices on international calls, plus our new Favorite Nation 10 percent

discount. Switch now and get one month of long distance free. *WE WANT YOU BACK.* Call 1-800-222-0900.

EXHIBIT 7.15
Advertising to Get Customers Back

AT&T used ads such as this one to persuade former customers to give the company another try.

In addition to these general classes of objectives, advertising strategies and objectives often change as a product moves through the **product life cycle,** a general model that divides the life span of a product or product category into *introduction, growth, maturity,* and *decline* stages. For example, McDonald's has a different challenge when advertising the well-known Big Mac today than it had years ago when the sandwich was new and no one had ever heard about it. New products that are entering markets against established competitors, such as the Nissan Altima, face different challenges than products that are creating new markets.

ADVERTISING STRATEGY

As with marketing objectives and marketing strategy, once you've established advertising objectives, your next move is to develop a strategy to meet those objectives. An **advertising strategy** consists of a *creative strategy,* which describes what you're going to say and how you're going to say it, and a *media strategy,* which describes where and when you plan to say it. (Note that the term *message strategy* is sometimes used in place of *creative strategy.* Also, just to keep things interesting, some people use the term *creative strategy* in place of *advertising strategy.*)[39]

The eight chapters in Parts III and IV are devoted to these two halves of advertising strategy and their implementation. Chapters 9 through 12 show you how to put together a creative strategy and design and produce the copy and the art that make up an advertisement. Chapters 13 through 16 cover media strategy and the various media choices that you have at your disposal. Keep in mind that it's important to develop your creative strategy and your media strategy in parallel because they are interdependent. You can explore this yourself by watching a high-energy television commercial and trying to imagine how that ad would come across as a magazine, newspaper, or radio ad. In the other direction, find a detailed magazine ad that conveys a great deal of factual information and try to imagine how you'd get that message across on television. Each medium has its benefits and limitations, and the creative strategy needs to take these into account.

Advertising Budgets
Paying for It All

After setting objectives and defining strategy, you face the next advertising challenge: figuring out how to pay for it. The difficulties involved in figuring out just how well advertising works directly affect the budget-setting process. When it's hard to tell what effect advertising is having, it's hard to decide how much should be spent on it. If you can't tell how much $1 million worth of advertising will help, should you risk spending $2 million or $10 million?

Consider the experience Quaker Oats had with three new products. One product with a $6 million advertising budget reaped only $8 million in sales, just a third more than the amount spent on advertising. A second product with a $4 million ad budget garnered $28 million in sales, seven times the amount spent on advertising. The third product, with only $1.1 million in ads, earned $11 million in sales—ten times the amount spent on advertising.[40] What if the product with $11 million in sales had received the $6 million budget—would it have sold $60 million worth? Maybe, maybe not. The point is to emphasize how hard it can be to pick the right budget amounts.

THE SALES-RESPONSE FUNCTION

Quaker's experience with those products highlights the fundamental question of advertising budgeting: what is the relationship between the amount spent on advertising and the effect on sales? The model of this relationship is called the *sales-response function.* Usually, increasing the amount spent on advertising results in some increased sales (assuming it's good advertising, of course!). However, the relationship is not at all simple or straightforward.

Picture yourself at a party, trying to convince someone of something. You have to raise your voice loud enough to be heard, obviously, or your point won't get across. The more people there are talking in the room, the louder you'll have to raise your voice. Once you're loud enough to be heard, however, it becomes pointless to keep raising your voice. You'd be expending energy with no corresponding return for your effort.

The same input/output relationship holds true in advertising, as the generic sales-response curves in Exhibit 7.16 indicate. You have to spend some minimum amount just to get people's attention. As you increase spending, your sales go up in response. Then at some point, you've spent all that makes sense; budget increases start to yield smaller and smaller returns. You've hit the *saturation* level, just as you saturated the room with sound when you raised your voice at the party.

The differences between the two functions in Exhibit 7.16 are significant. In the *concave-downward function,* sales pick up quickly to start but you receive less and less return with each incremental investment. Budget increases yield proportionately smaller sales increases. In the *S-curve function,* sales pick up slowly as you increase advertising, but then rise quickly once you pass a certain budget level. For a short range, budget increases yield proportionately greater sales increases. Then at some point, the S-curve starts to behave like the concave-downward curve as you approach saturation.[41]

Advertising researchers have uncovered strong evidence of both response variations, and you can make better budget decisions if you know which function each of your products exhibits. For concave-downward products, you can spend

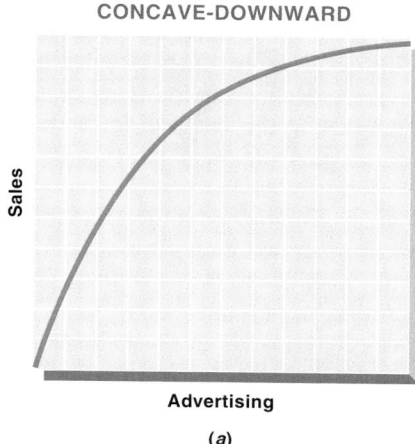

CONCAVE-DOWNWARD

Sales

Advertising

(a)

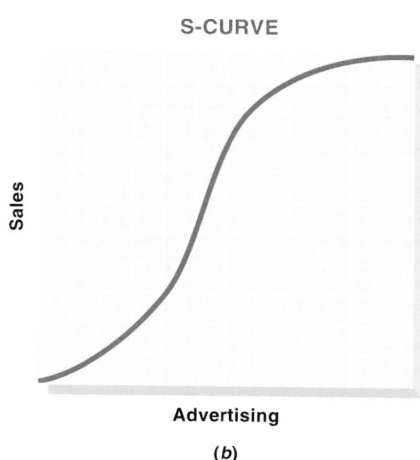

S-CURVE

Sales

Advertising

(b)

EXHIBIT 7.16
The Sales-Response Function

These two graphs model the relationship between advertising expenditure and sales; some products and industries tend to follow the concave-downward function, and others tend to follow the S-curve.

steadily over time, and sales will increase in a steady manner (although the effect of diminishing returns will apply). For S-curve products, however, you need to find the amount that puts you in the steep part of the curve right away, since you're not spending your money efficiently until you reach that level.[42]

BUDGETING METHODS

Quite a few methods and formulas for setting advertising budgets have been developed over the years, but none is adequate for all cases, and many advertisers try to employ several methods to help them arrive at the right figures. Here's a quick look at the most commonly used methods.

Affordability Method

This method provides no model or formula, but it is used often. With the **affordability method,** advertisers simply spend as much as they can afford on advertising. This is sometimes referred to as the *residual* method, because the amount spent on advertising is what's left over after everything else has been paid for (salaries, production costs, rent, etc.). This approach is certainly easy to use since there isn't any analysis or judgment involved, but it lacks any connection with competitive activity, marketplace dynamics, changes in media costs, or advertising effectiveness. Perhaps its biggest drawback is that those periods when sales are down—providing less money for advertising—are often the times when advertising is needed the most.[43] Naturally, the question of affordability has to enter any budgeting discussion at some point, but relying on it exclusively can lead to poor decisions.

Percentage-of-Sales Method

The most common of several ratio methods, the **percentage-of-sales method,** defines the ad budget as some predetermined percentage of expected sales. If you expect sales of $200 million and your advertising percentage is set at 8 percent, you budget $16 million for advertising. The primary advantage of this method is that it's simple to apply (once you've arrived at the right percentage, that is). Its disadvantages include possibly spending too much (on big sellers that may not need that much advertising) or too little (on products that could benefit from an advertising boost), failing to account for competition or for the relative effectiveness of advertising (e.g., if you could improve the effectiveness of your ads, you might not have to spend as much to get your message across), and difficulty figuring out what the actual percentage should be.[44]

Competitive Methods

Several methods use competitive spending as the key factor in setting the budget. With the **competitive parity method,** you simply match whatever your competitors are spending (see Exhibit 7.17). This approach is simple (in most markets you can readily get estimates of how much your competitors spend), and unlike percentage of sales, it does take competition into account. For instance, assume that you're budgeting the advertising for a chain of auto supply stores. You could look up this industry's advertising expenditures as a percentage of sales (the figures are available in various trade magazines) and see that the industry spends an average of 2.2 percent of sales on advertising.[45] Using this budgeting method, you would then calculate 2.2 percent of your annual sales and establish this figure as your budget.

However, the competitive parity method has several shortcomings, including the assumption that your competitors somehow know how much they should be spending, the failure to consider effectiveness, the inability to forecast what competitors might do in the future, and the possibility that your budget has no connection to your advertising objectives. You can get a sense of this last shortcoming by imagining that your objective is to become the market leader but the competitive parity method has you spending only as much as the competition does.

Another competitive method uses **market share,** your portion of the total sales in a particular market, and **share of voice,** your portion of the total advertising

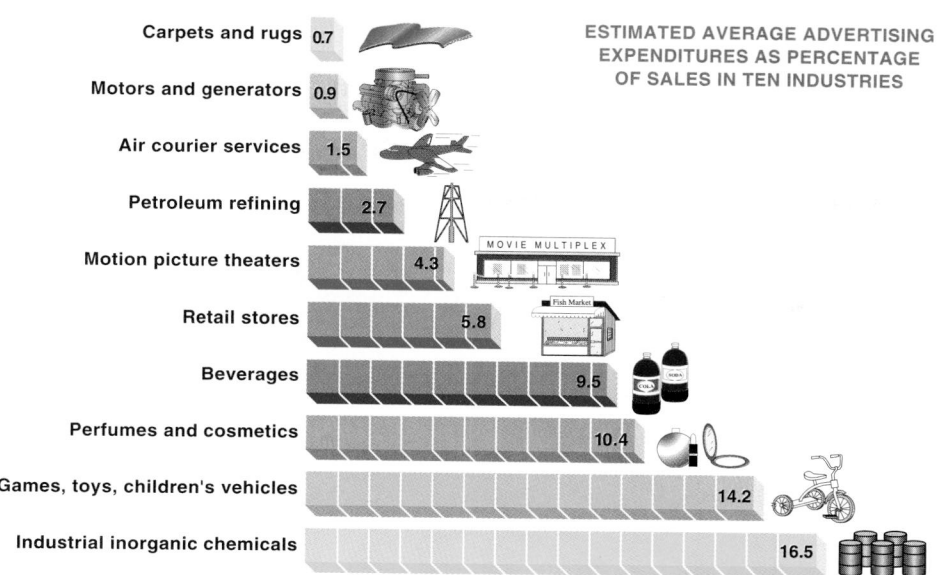

ESTIMATED AVERAGE ADVERTISING
EXPENDITURES AS PERCENTAGE
OF SALES IN TEN INDUSTRIES

Carpets and rugs 0.7
Motors and generators 0.9
Air courier services 1.5
Petroleum refining 2.7
Motion picture theaters 4.3
Retail stores 5.8
Beverages 9.5
Perfumes and cosmetics 10.4
Games, toys, children's vehicles 14.2
Industrial inorganic chemicals 16.5

EXHIBIT 7.17

Advertising-to-Sales Ratios in Various Industries

Advertisers can usually find data such as these to gauge how much money other companies in their industry are spending on advertising.

expenditure in this market. This approach is commonly called the **share-of-market/share-of-voice method.** If you were trying to increase your market share, for instance, you would probably want your share of voice to be greater than your current market share, in the hope that the increased advertising will result in increased sales. This approach is the basis of "Peckham's formula" (named for researcher James Peckham), which asserts that for a new product to reach its market-share objectives, its share of voice needs to be 1.5 times greater than the desired market share.[46] This probably makes intuitive sense to you; as a newcomer in any situation, you often have to make a little extra noise to even get noticed.

Objective and Task Method

The **objective and task method** offers attractive logic by starting with the advertising objectives, identifying the tasks that need to be accomplished to meet those objectives, figuring the cost of doing those tasks, and then totaling a budget based on those costs. Perhaps its biggest advantage is that it flows directly from your objectives; everything you plan to spend money on is in pursuit of meeting those objectives. An important effect of this method is an emphasis on accountability. With dollars flowing toward specific objectives, it's easier to measure success or failure. However, in addition to lacking a built-in check for affordability, this method's biggest drawback is the difficulty in defining meaningful advertising objectives. Naturally, the closer your objectives come to meeting the four criteria for effective objectives (listed earlier in the chapter), the easier it will be to define the tasks and therefore the budget required.[47]

Inertia

This is the "if it isn't broken, don't fix it" school of budgeting, in which you simply spend the same amount you spent last year, assuming last year's performance was satisfactory. On the plus side, this approach has the proof of performance on its side, and it's easy to administer. Its limitations include failing to account for changes in marketing objectives, advertising objectives, market forces, or media costs. A related method, called the *media inflation multiplier,* does address the media cost problem by adjusting the budget for changes in media cost from year to year.[48]

In addition to these methods, advertisers, agencies, and academic researchers have developed a variety of other approaches, including computer models that try to simulate advertising's effect in the marketplace and experiments that try to directly measure the effects of various budget levels. These specialized methods

Targeting Wasteful Advertising Expenditures

Pioneering retailer John Wanamaker framed the issue nicely when he said, "Half of my advertising is wasted; I just don't know which half." With the pressure on advertising managers and their agency counterparts to squeeze every ounce of performance out of the advertising budget, lots of people are trying to track down Wanamaker's wasted half—but where's the best place to start looking? Advertising researcher John Philip Jones suggests that sales promotion is the most likely category of waste. (Sales promotion is discussed in detail in Chapter 17.) In addition, Jones suggests four other areas of waste that bear looking into: (1) direct-action advertising, (2) global advertising, (3) advertising failed new products, and (4) overadvertising successful products.

Jones includes direct-action advertising on his list primarily because waste in this type of advertising is comparatively easy to avoid. As already mentioned, direct-action advertising is about the only category of advertising for which you can assign sales goals. Combined with the fact that you can usually test direct-action advertising with some degree of accuracy (e.g., sending out a small test mailing before going nationwide), the clear link to sales gives you a golden opportunity to find out in advance whether your advertising is going to work. Jones provides a startling example of the contrary, a case of direct mail that wasn't tested first. The Department of Health in Great Britain was trying to convince 13-year-olds to consider nursing as a career and in one instance spent the equivalent of $6.4 million on a nationwide campaign. It netted only 112 recruits, at an average cost of $57,000 each. A quick test mailing would have saved a lot of money.

Controversy rages over whether it makes more sense to run the same ad campaign worldwide or to adapt your advertising for each country (see Chapter 8). Jones acknowledges that some global campaigns have been quite successful, but he includes global campaigns on his list because the "ready possibility of disaster" is always present. Disaster comes in the form of ads created in one country that don't work in another country, leading to waste that can be substantial if you multiply the failure across a number of countries.

World's first shoe made from recycled materials

New products fail at an alarming rate. Sometimes poor advertising is a major cause of the product failure; in other cases even good advertising is unable to save a bad product. Either way, time and money are wasted. Advertisers can work to reduce the waste by planning new products more carefully and by test marketing before spending large sums on advertising.

In contrast, it is possible to spend too much on advertising for products that have succeeded in the marketplace. Once a brand has been established as a leader, with steady customers and adequate distribution, you can often trim the ad budget and rely more on nonadvertising forces to carry you along. This must be done with some care, of course, since you don't want to undo your success or lower your product's visibility, but research has shown that many successful products would stay successful even with lower ad budgets.

Apply Your Knowledge

1. Speculate on why so much money continues to be wasted on advertising, particularly in cases such as the British nursing campaign.
2. To reduce waste, would you recommend that top managers in a company simply reduce the ad budget, thus forcing the advertising manager and the agency to reduce waste? Why or why not?

usually require a great deal of technical expertise and are not used as frequently as the other methods just described.

THE BUDGETING PROCESS

Perhaps the most important point to learn about budgeting is that there is no magic formula that will deliver the right answer every time. Instead, experts recommend a logical process that can help identify minimum and maximum values. However, like most business decisions, setting the budget requires judgment and experience.[49]

The first step of the budgeting process is an extensive review and analysis of marketing and advertising objectives, current and past budgets, competitive budgets, and whatever evidence you might have about the effects advertising has had

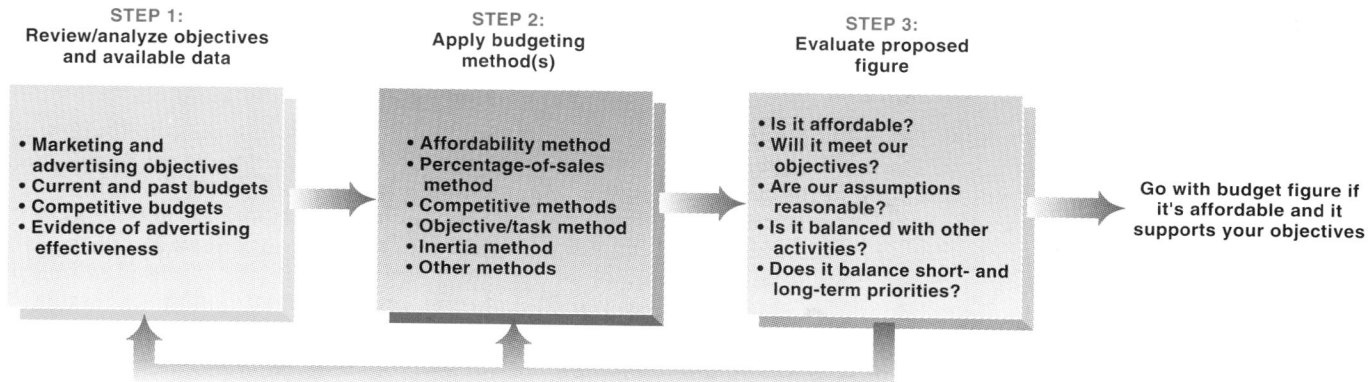

STEP 1: Review/analyze objectives and available data	STEP 2: Apply budgeting method(s)	STEP 3: Evaluate proposed figure	

• Marketing and
  advertising objectives
• Current and past budgets
• Competitive budgets
• Evidence of advertising
  effectiveness
	• Affordability method
	• Percentage-of-sales
	  method
	• Competitive methods
	• Objective/task method
	• Inertia method
	• Other methods
		• Is it affordable?
		• Will it meet our
		  objectives?
		• Are our assumptions
		  reasonable?
		• Is it balanced with other
		  activities?
		• Does it balance short- and
		  long-term priorities?
			Go with budget figure if
			it's affordable and it
			supports your objectives

Revise analysis, methods, or objectives if necessary

EXHIBIT 7.18
The Budgeting Process

This general model of the budgeting process starts with a thorough analysis of objectives, past budgets, and competitive budgets.

on your brand so far (see Exhibit 7.18). The resulting stew of data, anecdotes, and guesswork forms the basis of the budget decision.

The second step involves using several of the budgeting methods described previously to arrive at suggested budget amounts. If you use three methods, for instance, you're going to get three separate figures. Your job is to treat these as guidelines, as upper and lower boundaries, and to rely on your judgment and experience to arrive at a specific amount to spend.

The third step is the "reality check," in which you evaluate the figure arrived at in the second step. Obviously, you need to apply the affordability method, regardless of which other method(s) you used to arrive at a preliminary figure. It is also important to verify whether the amount you've identified will truly let you meet your advertising objectives (if you're using one of the methods that is based on objectives).

At this point, other important tasks include reviewing the assumptions you've made throughout the process; comparing the budget you've proposed for advertising with the budgets proposed for personal selling, sales promotion, and other marketing efforts; and balancing short-term versus long-term priorities. If the most you can possibly spend on marketing a brand is, say, $10 million, and your budgeting methods in the second step call for spending $9 million on advertising, should you really do so? Might it be better to spend several million to beef up the sales force, to offer discounts to retailers or customers, or to redesign the packaging? If things don't click at this stage (e.g., if you decide that the budget amount won't in fact allow you to meet your objectives), return to the first and second stages to review your assumptions or try other methods. If things still don't reconcile, you'll have to revise your objectives.

Granted, this process doesn't have a lot of hard-and-fast rules that you can plug numbers into and get the "right" answer; experience and common sense are the most important tools you can apply to budgeting. The ability to make these judgments is what separates successful advertisers from the rest of the pack.

Summary

The elements in a marketing plan are generally organized into four key blocks of information: the situation analysis, a list of marketing objectives, an outline of the marketing strategy (which is based on target market selection and the marketing mix), and a description of the marketing tasks, which make up the action plan.

To be most effective, marketing and advertising objectives should be relevant to higher-level objectives; challenging but attainable; measurable, so that you can track your success or failure; and time specific. Positioning options include positioning by product differences, by product attributes or benefits, by product users, by product usage, against a particular competitor, against an entire product category, by association with other products or entities, and by customer problems being solved.

An advertising plan typically contains a summary or copy of the situation analysis conducted for the marketing plan (and perhaps another analysis conducted specifically about advertising), a summary of the marketing objectives and strategy, a description of the promotional strategy, the advertising objective(s), the advertising strategy, a budget, and some sort of calendar or action plan.

The two categories of advertising objectives are sales objectives, in which the goal is to produce a certain number of sales, and communications objectives, in which some effect on the audience (such as awareness) is the goal. Sales objectives are appropriate only when one or more of these conditions exist: when advertising is the only variable being changed in the marketing mix, when advertising is the dominant force in the

Meeting an Advertising Challenge at Saturn

A CASE FOR CRITICAL THINKING

Donald Hudler and his team at Saturn put together a successful marketing and advertising program—and more. Advertising Age, the leading trade journal in the advertising industry, calls Saturn "one of the most successful new brands in marketing history." People who want to buy one of Saturn's several models often have to be content to put their name on a waiting list until a car becomes available. Saturn drivers frequently wave at each other as they pass; some even help sell cars in the showrooms. There is talk of starting an owners' club. A few owners have even driven to the factory in Spring Hill, Tennessee, to meet the people who made their cars. Saturn sold over 170,000 cars during its second year (1992) and could've sold even more cars if only it could've made more.

What kind of objectives and strategies created this remarkable success? Hudler defines Saturn's marketing objective as making Saturn "the best-liked car company in America." That's an easy thing to say, but a very difficult goal to achieve. The strategy started with building a reasonably priced car that would satisfy cus-

tomers, but it didn't stop there. Saturn's strategy involved every aspect of the business, from including employees in decision making to setting fixed prices that consumers don't have to haggle over.

Among the many things Hudler and crew did right was to make a sharp departure from traditional automotive advertising strategy. Saturn ads don't talk about technical details or show cars winding over mountain roads. They talk about real people who drive Saturns and the satisfaction those people derive from the cars. This approach not only distinguishes Saturn from the pack but also helps build a strong emotional bond between the public, the product, and the company behind the product.

A good example of Saturn's advertising strategy is a magazine ad that tells the story of New Mexico's Cheryl Silas. Silas was hit from behind while driving her Saturn coupe. The car was totaled, but she walked away unhurt. A police officer at the scene said she was lucky to be alive. The following week, Silas went back to her Saturn retailer and ordered another car. A few days later, so did the police offi-

cer. Then one of the officer's friends ordered a Saturn. So did Silas's brother. To top it off, the woman who had run into Silas came in for a test drive. This remarkable story made its way back to Hudler's office and found its way into print as another example of great Saturn advertising.

Saturn's only major stumble to date came in 1993, when the company looked at the long backlog of orders and at parent GM's continuing financial troubles and decided it would be safe to cut back on advertising for a while. Orders slowed dramatically, and Saturn was prompted to crank its ad spending back up in 1994. It may take a few years to overcome the effects of this miscalculation.

Your Mission: You've taken over Donald Hudler's job at Saturn and are now responsible for guiding the process of marketing and advertising strategy. Consider the following scenarios and pick solutions that stand the best chance of success.

1. Production slowdowns and a commitment to high-quality cars have

---

entire marketing mix, or when advertising is designed to solicit an immediate response. Otherwise, sales must be considered a marketing objective. When sales objectives are inappropriate, advertisers opt for communications objectives, which include such measures as attaining certain levels of product awareness or product preference.

An advertising strategy should flow directly from the advertising objectives and should include two key elements, the creative strategy and the media strategy. The creative strategy defines the message and describes both what will be said and how it will be said. The media strategy determines where and when the message should be delivered to the target audience.

The most common methods for setting advertising budgets include the affordability method, or spending whatever you can afford; the percentage-of-sales method, or spending a fixed percentage of sales; the various competitive methods, including both competitive parity and the share-of-market/share-of-voice approach; the objective and task method, which defines the tasks needed to meet the objectives and then determines how much they will cost to implement; and the inertia method, which simply involves spending next year what you spent this year, perhaps with inflation adjustments for rising media costs.

Key Terms

Questions

FOR REVIEW

1. Where do advertising objectives fit in an advertiser's overall hierarchy of objectives?

2. What are the basic components of a marketing plan, and how do these elements influence the advertising effort?

3. Why is it not always possible or reasonable to establish sales objectives for advertising?

CHERYL SILAS had a highway collision, was hit twice from behind, and then sold three cars for us.

When Cheryl unbuckled her shoulder harness and lap belt, it took a moment to realize her Saturn coupe was really a mess. And that, remarkably, she wasn't. That's when she decided to get another SC.

Several other people arrived at similar conclusions. A policeman at the accident scene came in soon after and ordered himself a sedan. As did a buddy of his, also on the force. Then Cheryl's brother, glad he still had a sister, bought yet another Saturn in Illinois.

Now, good referrals are important to any product. And we're always glad to have them. But we'd be more than happy if our customers found less dramatic ways to help spread the word.

A DIFFERENT KIND *OF* COMPANY. A DIFFERENT KIND *OF* CAR.

1991 Saturn Corporation. M.S.R.P. of 1992 Saturn SC shown is $12,415, including retailer prep and optional sunroof. Tax, license, transportation and other options additional. If you'd like to know more about Saturn, and our new sedans and coupe, please call us at 1-800-522-5000.

resulted in occasional product shortages. In one sense, it's nice to know people are waiting in line to buy your car, but you know you can't satisfy them until they are behind the wheel of their new Saturns. Which of the following concepts would best fit Saturn's overall marketing and advertising strategies?

a. Apologize for the delay and invite customers to call their dealers to complain.

b. Apologize for the delay but focus on Saturn's desire to make sure only top-quality cars leave the factory. Feature a Saturn buyer who says that the car is definitely worth the wait.

c. Feature a Saturn buyer who ordered early and was lucky enough to get a car within a week. The happy buyer would say, "Lucky me, I ordered early and got my Saturn before anyone else in town."

2. Assume that Saturn wants to add a sports car to its product line. Knowing what you know about Saturn's current positioning in the marketplace, which of the following cars should Saturn's sports car compete against?

a. The Chevrolet Corvette

b. The Mazda Miata

c. The Porsche 968

3. You'd like to get better data on the effectiveness of Saturn's advertising efforts. You know that the first step is to establish advertising objectives that are as measurable as possible. For the Cheryl Silas ad, which of the following objectives would be most appropriate (focus on the nature of the objectives, not the particular numbers)?

a. Increase Saturn sales by 5 percent over the next six months.

b. Prompt at least 75 percent of the people who read the ad to agree with the following statement: "Saturn is a safe car."

c. Cut into Toyota's market share by 1 percent by the end of this year.

4. Successful advertising nearly always stems from a clear statement of purpose, whether that purpose is to get current customers to buy more or to get new customers to give the brand a try. Based on the list of advertising purposes discussed in the chapter, which of the following could be Saturn's purpose for the Cheryl Silas ad? Be prepared to explain your choice.

a. To prompt direct action

b. To encourage information search

c. To encourage recall of past satisfactions and to prompt reorders[50] ■

---

4. When is it reasonable to do so?

5. What are the two main shortcomings of sequential, hierarchy of effects models?

FOR ANALYSIS AND APPLICATION

6. Would you agree with someone who said that a situation analysis isn't a terribly useful thing to do because all competitors in a given market analyze the same set of data and reach the same conclusions? Why or why not?

7. How could your college or university position itself in terms of product differences?

8. Assume that Holiday Inn wants to offer a special vacation discount for two or more families staying at the same hotel or resort (such as when people get together for family reunions). Its advertising objective is to prompt consumers to request more information on the program. What steps could the company take to measure its success in meeting this objective?

9. If Ford Motor Company met its marketing objectives this year, should it go with what worked and spend the same amount on advertising next year? Why or why not?

10. With 600 restaurants worldwide, how much should Burger King spend for its advertising? Should it spend as much as McDonald's spends for its 12,000 outlets? More? Less? Why or why not? How might percentage of sales affect this decision?

Sharpen Your Advertising Skills

Say you're an account executive, and one of your clients is a small sporting goods manufacturer that has never advertised nationally. The company sells its products to several dozen wholesalers around the country, which in turn sell to several thousand sporting goods retailers. Most of the retailers advertise locally on their own; sometimes these ads include your client's products, but sometimes they don't. You're working with the company on its first national ad campaign, and the company's management team is quite nervous about spending the $2 million it has available for the campaign. The CEO wants to make sure that the investment will have quick and measurable results.

Decision: You sympathize with the CEO's nervousness, but you know it's not always possible to assign measurable sales objectives to advertising. Decide whether you should try to figure out a way to make sales objectives work or whether you should sit down with the CEO and suggest a different sort of objective for the campaign.

Communication: You need to tell your manager, the account supervisor, which course you've decided to pursue with your client. Draft a one-page memo to your boss, describing your decision and outlining how you'll explain it to the CEO.

Intercultural and International Advertising

After studying this chapter, you will be able to

1. List the major elements of culture that influence audience response to advertising

2. Discuss the similarities and differences between intercultural advertising and international advertising

3. Describe the importance of agency networks in international markets

4. Summarize the types of restrictions placed on advertising in various countries around the world

5. Compare the global, regional, and local approaches to international advertising

6. Explain the controversy surrounding the global approach to advertising

7. Contrast geocentrism and ethnocentrism and explain the negative effect they can have on international advertising

Nouvelle Renault 19, nouvelle pour longtemps. RENAULT

Facing an Advertising Challenge at Holiday Inn Worldwide

SENDING INVITATIONS ACROSS THE GLOBE

Imagine creating an ad for a hotel that draws a mix of both vacationers and business travelers, families and individuals, men and women, and people of diverse ethnic and racial backgrounds. Now imagine creating ads for nearly 1,700 hotels in more than 50 countries and territories around the world. Such is the challenge faced by Raymond Lewis, vice president of marketing for Holiday Inn Worldwide.

Holiday Inn is an icon of the U.S. highway—its green sign, the words "Holiday Inn" written in script, and a star for emphasis—or so things used to be. Holiday Inn is now Holiday Inn Worldwide, since it was purchased in 1990 by the British conglomerate Bass plc. Business and pleasure travelers can now sleep in any one of 330,000 rooms under the global roof of the Holiday Inn chain. In fact, to keep pace with its new global image, the company is also considering changing its logo, its colors, and its signs. It's definitely changing its advertising.

Part of Lewis's job is to monitor and predict changes in the ever-evolving global market. Among the trends he has observed is the increasing similarity between the needs and desires expressed by consumers and businesses around the world, at least in certain product categories such as lodging. On the other hand, he knows that various countries and cultures approach purchases differently and that people in various cultures respond differently to advertising. So he must figure out how to satisfy both the similar and the diverse needs of his new market.

Travel patterns are another trend that help predict how Holiday Inn should conduct its business. For instance, increasing numbers of North Americans and Europeans are choosing to vacation in Japan, Thailand, Vietnam, and other Asian countries. Some of these travelers are content with traditional Asian lodging, but others have come to expect the more familiar Western-style hotels. Knowing buyer preferences such as this helps advertisers make the right choices when it comes to targeting buyers and communicating advertising messages.

If you were Raymond Lewis, how would you approach the challenge of advertising to this diverse, worldwide audience? Would you use a single strategy for all countries or develop unique strategies for individual countries? Would you use the same visual elements and copy themes? How would you handle language and other cultural issues?[1] ■

CHAPTER OVERVIEW Holiday Inn's Raymond Lewis is stepping into two of the most hotly debated subjects in advertising today: how to advertise across multiple cultures and how to plan and execute international advertising. This chapter starts with a discussion of the growing interest in intercultural advertising and gives you a look at how culture and advertising interact. Next, you'll get a feel for the growth and structure of international advertising, and you'll glimpse the major factors in the international advertising environment. After that, you'll explore both sides of the most important question in international advertising: whether to use the same ad strategy and presentation worldwide or to adapt your advertising for each country. The chapter concludes with a number of steps you can take to improve your chances of successfully planning and executing international advertising.

Intercultural Advertising

Look around at your classmates. If you're attending a typical U.S. college or university, chances are that your class represents a wide variety of cultures, ethnic backgrounds, and nationalities. Each cultural group is a potentially unique market segment, and consumers' responses to advertising (indeed, their overall purchase behavior) can largely be defined by their cultural context (see Exhibit 8.1). Therefore, identifying cultural segments and understanding their implications for advertising strategy has become both a significant challenge and a promising opportunity for many of today's advertisers.

Cultural differences are the reason some recent television commercials (which would have been perfectly acceptable in Japan, North America, or Western Europe) caused a stir when they were shown in Eastern Europe. In the former East Germany, for example, decades of government-created advertising for shoddy products made in government-owned factories had conditioned people to view television advertising almost as a signal of what *not* to buy. So when abstract,

New
33-centiliter
bottle.

Always
Coca-Cola.

EXHIBIT 8.1
Cultural Context in Advertising

People around the world are familiar with such high-profile brand names as Coca-Cola. This French ad promotes a new 33-centiliter (a little over 11 ounces) returnable bottle. You'll notice that the tagline "Always Coca-Cola" remained in English.

lifestyle-oriented commercials for Adidas and other products began to appear, some viewers became angry enough to write letters of complaint to local newspapers. From their standpoint, these Western-style ads were aggressive, and at times incomprehensible, propaganda; all these consumers wanted were the basic facts about products.[2]

Advertising that crosses cultural boundaries is called **intercultural advertising** (or *multicultural advertising*). As defined in Chapter 1, international advertising is advertising that crosses national borders. Intercultural advertising represents the same concept of crossing a border into different territory; you may end up in the same country, but you're in a different market segment nonetheless. Consultant Roger Sennott, who specializes in reaching Hispanic-American markets, refers to the challenge as "international marketing within your own borders."[3] In fact, a close relationship exists between intercultural advertising and international advertising. One of the biggest challenges in international advertising stems from *cultural* differences between countries, particularly as they relate to the encoding and decoding stages of the communication process. In other words, if you can get a handle on the intercultural issues, you're well on your way toward success in the international arena.

THE GROWING INTEREST IN INTERCULTURAL ADVERTISING

You can get plenty of practice with intercultural advertising and never leave home. Advertisers in the United States are currently stepping up their intercultural efforts for two important reasons. First, even though the country has always been home to a wide mix of cultures, it's becoming even more culturally and ethnically diverse. Between the 1980 census and the 1990 census, the U.S. population grew by roughly 10 percent. During that decade, the white population grew by just 6 percent, whereas the African-American population grew by 13 percent, the

넌 정말 스프라이트

야! 너···너··· 너도 정말 스프라이트"

함께 하면, 언제까지 즐거운 우리 그래서 더욱 나, 우린 정말 정말 스프라이트 상큼한 맛 · 새로운 느낌의 청량음료 — '스프라이트'

"Sprite"와 "스프라이트"는 The Coca-Cola Company의 상표입니다.

You are a Sprite!

EXHIBIT 8.2
Targeting Ethnic Groups

As the Asian-American population continues to grow, advertisers will increasingly target specific groups, as Coca-Cola did in this Sprite ad aimed at the Korean community in the United States.

Hispanic-American population by 53 percent, and the Asian-American population by 108 percent. By the end of this decade, white Americans will represent less than half the population in California.[4] Like any change in the advertising environment, such growing diversity represents both challenges and opportunities to advertisers.

Second, as discussed in Chapter 5, many advertisers have discovered that they need to focus on specific market segments in order to meet their customers' needs and to stay ahead of their competitors (see Exhibit 8.2). Companies such as Procter & Gamble, Bank of America, Toys "R" Us, and Coca-Cola have learned that they can increase their marketing effectiveness by targeting particular ethnic and cultural groups.[5] In fact, so many major U.S. advertisers have targeted the Hispanic-American market, in particular, that Mendoza, Dillon & Asociados, the nation's largest Hispanic-focused agency, is having trouble finding new clients. Because cultural segmentation seems to work so well, most of the big advertisers that can benefit from it are already doing so. Thus, agency president Robert Howell says that Mendoza, Dillon's future growth will have to come from existing clients.[6]

CULTURE AND ADVERTISING

Chapter 4 defines culture as the beliefs, values, and objects that a society shares and passes from generation to generation, and it points out that the population in many countries can be divided into various cultural segments. All cultures share four key attributes:[7]

1. *Culture is learned.* Children and new members of a society learn the society's cultural norms; no one is born with an innate sense of culture. Because advertising contributes to the consumers' learning, it helps shape culture.

2. *Culture is shared through social institutions.* Social institutions that share culture comprise families, religious institutions, schools, and the media (including the advertising carried in the media).

3. *Culture rewards socially gratifying behavior.* Culture makes people feel good for doing certain things, such as dressing up for a night on the town, so most people continue to do those things. Advertising that fails to take such social

factors into account is likely to be less effective. For instance, an ad that portrays a given brand's users as foul-mouthed and ill-behaved would probably not increase sales in a culture that values gentle speech and good manners.

4. *Culture changes over time.* The U.S. culture of the 1990s differs greatly from what it was in the 1890s (or even from what it was in the 1980s, in some respects). Cultures change at different rates and in different ways, however, so you can't assume that changes you see in this country will occur automatically in other cultures as well.

Success in both intercultural and international advertising requires a solid understanding both of the cultural composition of your advertising audience and of the factors that shape culture over time. Influential factors include race and nationality, language, and cultural values.

Race and Nationality

As one of the key defining elements of culture, race is an important factor in consumer advertising. Recognizing its importance is easy; figuring out how to approach the issue is far more complex. You're faced with a multitude of decisions, ranging from designing special advertising strategies for particular ethnic groups (see Exhibit 8.3) to designating the race of the actors you use in television commercials. Because skin color is one of the more visible distinctions of race, it's not surprising that cosmetics companies have been grappling with this issue in their advertising for a number of years. For example, Estée Lauder's Prescriptives Exact Color line reaches out to all major ethnic groups in the United States by including Asian, African-American, Hispanic, and white women in its ads.[8]

EXHIBIT 8.3
Race in Advertising

Would this ad be equally effective with all consumers if it featured a child of a different ethnic group? Specialists in marketing to ethnic segments usually recommend that advertisers represent the target audience in their ads.

ETHICS IN ADVERTISING

Is Targeting Ethnic Segments Ethical Advertising?

Medical specialists say smoking is directly or indirectly responsible for more than 400,000 deaths per year, more than alcohol, heroin, cocaine, suicide, homicide, car accidents, fires, and AIDS put together. Controversy has been swirling around the subject of smoking for years. One side says that people have the right to smoke if they want to; that cigarettes are a legal product, so tobacco companies have every right to advertise; and that tobacco ads are designed only to get people to switch brands, not to start smoking. The other side claims that advertising encourages people to start smoking and that, in light of the identifiable health risks, cigarette ads should be banned entirely.

Lately, critics have been raising special concerns about one particular aspect of the tobacco advertising question, and that's the targeting of specific ethnic groups with tobacco ads. They point to statistics showing that the percentage of adults who smoke is higher in several ethnic segments than it is in the overall population. For example, 29 percent of African-Americans smoke, compared with 26 percent for the total U.S. population. Cigarette marketers have wooed African-Americans using outdoor signs in black neighborhoods, ads in magazines of special interest to blacks, and sponsorship of cultural events that blacks are likely to attend. The tobacco industry defends its targeting practices as basic marketing and says that companies target all kinds of consumer segments, from inner cities to wealthy suburbs.

R. J. Reynolds Tobacco entered this controversy when it chose to target African-Americans with a brand of cigarettes called Uptown. Uptown was developed to attract black consumers, but internally, RJR faced an ethical dilemma: should it come out and say the brand was aimed at blacks, or should it be more subtle? Because it didn't want to be accused of deception, the company decided to take the straightforward approach, and it scheduled Uptown for test marketing in Philadelphia, expecting some controversy.

The company's expectations were on target. Before the first ads even hit the streets, critics took issue with the targeting.

Black community leaders spoke out, and during a speech at the University of Pennsylvania, then-secretary of Health and Human Services Louis W. Sullivan denounced RJR for "promoting a culture of cancer" among blacks. "Uptown's message is more disease, more suffering, and more death for a group already bearing more than its share of smoking-related illness and mortality," Sullivan told the audience. The very next day, RJR canceled the plans to market Uptown.

Advertising groups such as the Association of National Advertisers define cigarette advertising as a freedom-of-speech issue, saying that it's unconstitutional to limit the ways legal products can be advertised, as long as those ads meet the same regulations that all other ads must meet. Opponents define it as a public health issue, asserting that companies shouldn't be allowed to target groups that, for whatever reason, may be more inclined to purchase unhealthy products. This issue is likely to stay in the headlines for some time to come.

What's Your Opinion?
1. Do you think tobacco companies should be allowed to target ethnic minorities with their ads? Why or why not?
2. What about other products that have potential health consequences, from high-fat ice cream to fast cars? Should the government also restrict the way those products can be advertised?

■

To get an idea of the complexities that racial issues bring to advertising, assume you're hiring the cast for a McDonald's television commercial and that 10 actors will be involved. Should you use seven white actors, one Hispanic-American, one African-American, and one Asian-American, a cast that would roughly represent the country's racial makeup? If so, which Asian-American race should you use? Should your Hispanic representative have ties to the Caribbean (Cuba or Puerto Rico, for instance) or to Mexico? What about the 1.5 million Native Americans you're not including?

Maybe you should abandon the idea of a racially representative ad and create ads aimed at individual cultural segments. Assuming that you can identify and reach each segment (and that you can afford to create that many ads), you face the challenge of making each ad relevant and meaningful to its target audience. If your

CHAPTER 8
Intercultural and International Advertising

commercial for the Hispanic segment uses music, for instance, you need to make sure that the music doesn't sound too Caribbean or too Mexican, or you might limit your appeal. The Hispanic populations of New York and Miami, for example, are predominantly of Caribbean origin, whereas the populations in Los Angeles and San Antonio are predominantly of Mexican, Central American, and South American origins.[9]

Language

Language is another important cultural factor in advertising, both the words chosen and the language used. Currently, language is a hot topic among Hispanic-Americans, one of the largest cultural segments in the United States. Advertisers tend to believe that the best way to reach Hispanic-American consumers is in Spanish. The largest Spanish-language television network in the United States, Univision, cites research showing that three-quarters of all Hispanic-Americans consider Spanish their dominant language. As Douglas Darfield, Univision's research director, puts it, "Why bother to target Hispanics in English?" However, the English-language magazine *Hispanic* says that advertisers are missing out by not addressing Hispanic-Americans in English. (Keep in mind that Univision and *Hispanic* are competing for advertising dollars.) The magazine's case was bolstered when an A. C. Nielsen study in Los Angeles indicated that half of the television sets in Hispanic households were tuned to English-language stations.[10]

For both the Hispanic-American and Asian-American groups, language is also an issue in media choice. The dilemma centers on whether or not to use ethnic media at all. In other words, if you're trying to reach Chinese-Americans, should you advertise in Chinese-language media or in the mainstream English-language media? For the Hispanic-American market, advertisers overwhelmingly choose mainstream media. People of Hispanic ancestry make up 9 percent of the U.S. population, but Spanish-language media get less than 1 percent of the total amount spent on ads every year.[11]

Language issues get even more complex when you cross borders. Do you want to advertise in Spain using Spanish? Many Spanish citizens live in a region called Catalonia (which includes the major city of Barcelona), and many of these people consider Catalan their language, not Spanish. Do you want to move your ad from Spain to Mexico? The two countries don't speak the same version of Spanish. The language in most of Spain is actually called Castellano (although most people call it Spanish), and it has some major differences in pronunciation and vocabulary from the Spanish spoken in Mexico and other Latin American countries.[12] Similarly, the Portuguese spoken in Brazil varies from that spoken in Portugal. For that matter, the English spoken in the United States is quite different from the English spoken in England.

Cultural Values

You'll recall from Chapter 4 that core values are the pervasive and enduring values shared by the people in a given culture. Advertisers have to recognize a culture's values—and shifts in those values—in order to connect emotionally with their audiences. If you were to look over a selection of U.S. ads from the past half-century, you'd see some definite shifts in the cultural values expressed in advertising (see Exhibit 8.4). Take the recent series of Pepsi commercials that emphasize youth and that (not too delicately) poke fun at senior citizens—or at least at the stereotypical concepts of being older. It's unlikely that you'd see anything like this in any advertising from the 1940s or the 1950s, when patriotism, progress, family, respect for elders, and other such "wholesome" themes dominated.

In addition, countries like the United States are home to many different cultures, but what works in one of these cultural segments might not work in another. Although it's often difficult and always risky to generalize about any group of people, researchers have uncovered cultural tendencies that advertisers should take into consideration. For instance, an ad showing a mother, a father, and a couple of kids laughing at the dinner table might communicate a sense of family

Often a bridesmaid but never a bride

EDNA'S case was really a pathetic one. Like every woman, her primary ambition was to marry. Most of the girls of her set were married—or about to be. Yet not one possessed more grace or charm or loveliness than she.

And as her birthdays crept gradually toward that tragic thirty-mark, marriage seemed farther from her life than ever. She was often a bridesmaid but never a bride.

That's the insidious thing about halitosis (unpleasant breath). You, yourself, rarely know when you have it. And even your closest friends won't tell you.

EXHIBIT 8.4

Changing Cultural Values Reflected in Advertising

How effective would this Listerine ad from the 1920s be in today's society, now that the pressure on women to be married is far less intense?

unity to many U.S. residents (although even this doesn't represent the norm among families in this country), but Hispanic viewers might wonder why the grandparents or grandchildren aren't included in the ad, since Hispanic households often encompass a broader selection of family members.[13]

As with race and language, cultural values demand special attention in the international arena. For example, a U.S. ad is not likely to make jokes about death, disease, or drunkenness; any ad that did would offend large portions of the population. In Japan, however, subjects considered taboo in the United States are given humorous treatment in many ads. A good example is a television spot for Gon mothballs, which features an elderly grandfather who pretends he's dead so that he won't have to go shopping.[14]

The use of sexual appeals varies from country to country as well. The spectrum ranges from Italy, where nudity isn't at all uncommon in advertising (although there is evidence of growing public displeasure regarding this), to Islamic countries such as Saudi Arabia, where nothing of the sort is tolerated (in fact, most Arab countries don't allow women to be portrayed in ads at all, regardless of what they're wearing or doing). Islamic cultures also frown on advertising that portrays children as decision makers in the household or that relies on hero worship to make a selling point.[15]

One final issue related to values in international advertising is politics, which must be approached with great care. Business travelers to other countries are often cautioned to avoid discussing politics; the same warning applies to advertising in numerous countries. The subject is just too touchy in many countries. It might be perfectly acceptable for you as a U.S. advertiser to poke fun at the U.S. government in your U.S. ads, but don't try poking fun at other countries' political systems when you're advertising in those countries. The Swedish furniture company Ikea learned this the hard way when it ran ads that poked fun at communism in post-communist Hungary. Even though the country had ousted its communist government two years earlier, Hungarian consumers didn't appreciate an outsider making fun of their former political system. Complaints were so loud that Ikea pulled the ads.[16]

ETHNIC PERSPECTIVES

Successful intercultural advertisers recognize and respect cultural differences. People who believe their own culture to be superior to all others are said to exhibit **ethnocentrism.**[17] In advertising, it's hard to treat another culture's symbols and habits with sensitivity if you don't accept the culture as an equal.

This doesn't mean that cultural missteps in advertising are always the result of ethnocentrism, however. Lack of contact with cultural and ethnic groups, and the ignorance that can result from such isolation, is probably one of the major sources of cultural advertising error. A particular issue that troubles many in the U.S. advertising community is the shortage of African-Americans in marketing and advertising jobs. Among the 18 management categories tracked by the U.S. Department of Labor Statistics, management positions in marketing, advertising, and public relations have the lowest percentage of African-Americans. African-Americans make up 10 percent of the U.S. work force but hold only 2 percent of these positions. By one art director's personal estimate, only 60 of the 6,500 copywriters and art directors (less than 1 percent) employed by the 25 largest U.S. agencies are African-American. On the bright side, BBDO Chicago's Phil Gant, acknowledged as one of the highest-ranking African-Americans in the business, is critical of current hiring practices but is optimistic for the future. He encourages African-American students to seek careers in advertising and to be ready to demonstrate their talents.[18]

In addition to the significant issue of balanced employment levels, most experts would agree that having so few African-Americans and other minorities in advertising is simply not good business. The closer you are to your audiences, the better your advertising will be. This doesn't mean that one ethnic or cultural group can't advertise successfully to another group; it just means that having creative and management teams that reflect the composition of the audience is bound to improve the chances of success. This idea is behind the success of such agencies as Joseph Jacobs Organization in New York (specializing in Jewish markets); Sosa, Bromley, Aguilar, & Asociados in San Antonio (specializing in Hispanic-American markets); Loiminchay in New York City (specializing in Asian-American markets); and Burrell Advertising in Chicago (specializing in African-American markets). These agencies and others like them handle intercultural advertising for some of the world's largest advertisers, including Coca-Cola, Volkswagen, and MCI.[19]

Regardless of how well your own cultural and ethnic background aligns with those of your target audience, there are some general steps you can take to be a more successful intercultural advertiser. The most important is a rule that applies to any aspect of advertising: never assume your audience thinks and feels as you do.

- *Don't superimpose your own cultural values onto other cultures.* An open mind is doubly important in intercultural advertising because purchase influences can vary dramatically from one culture to another. This rule applies to any advertising professional, regardless of race or cultural status. If you're a Mexican-American trying to advertise to Chinese-Americans, or a person of Scandinavian background trying to advertise to German-Americans, it's vital that you understand how your audience's culture might differ from your own.

- *Be sensitive to cultural differences without resorting to stereotyping.* Although the line between sensitivity and stereotyping can be difficult to draw, research and common sense will solve most problems. For instance, recognizing that elderly people command a greater degree of respect in some cultures than in others is being sensitive to cultural differences. In contrast, assuming that Asian-Americans are all good at math or that African-Americans are all good at athletics is stereotyping.

- *Recognize variations in language.* For example, there are dozens of separate Asian-American market segments (the U.S. government recognizes 59 distinct Asian ethnic groups) and another 20 or so separate groups of people in the United States with a Hispanic heritage (and many more in countries around the

cuando se
sienten bien
mis pies,
se me nota
en la cara.

Dale una caricia a tus pies con estas hermosas sandalias de piel legítima, tan cómodas como nuestros precios. Rebajadas de $12.99 a... **$10.99**

¿Sandalias de piel legítima a estos precios? ¿Qué más puede una pedir? Precio regular: $9.99. Ahora en oferta por sólo... **$8.99**

La calidad de la piel se siente, se toca, se camina... y se disfruta. Sandalias de piel legítima. Antes: $14.99. Ahora: **$12.99**

¡Qué bien se siente pagar menos!
Payless ShoeSource

Oferta válida del 10/18 al 11/13, 1993

When
your feet
feel good,
it shows
on your face.
How good it feels to pay less!
Payless Shoe Source.

EXHIBIT 8.5
To Use Spanish or Not

Payless Shoe Source opted to use Spanish in this ad aimed at Hispanic-Americans.

world). Asian-American audiences obviously speak a variety of languages, but even in the Hispanic-American market you can't assume that the Spanish spoken by a recent Puerto Rican immigrant to New York is the same Spanish as that spoken by a third-generation Californian whose family came from Chile. For that matter, you can't assume that people of Hispanic ethnicity even speak Spanish; many U.S.-born Hispanic-Americans speak only English (see Exhibit 8.5).[20]

Intercultural advertising can seem a daunting challenge at times, with differences in language, religion, and all the other elements. Take heart in the fact that you can navigate through most situations by remembering two key points. First, intercultural advertising is really just another form of segmentation, which you studied in Chapter 5. The trick is to identify your audience segments and create advertising that is likely to trigger a positive response. Second, as in all dealings with customers and potential customers, common sense and respect for your audience will get you through any rough spots.

International Advertising

As already noted, international advertising is advertising that targets people in other countries. Advertisers can consider two basic approaches. Advertisers using **globalization** (also known as **standardization** or *global marketing*) develop a single strategy and implement it in multiple countries, even to the point of providing ready-to-use ads. In contrast, advertisers using **localization** (sometimes known as **adaptation** or *local marketing*) develop a unique ad or a unique variation on a generic ad for each country. Another factor that distinguishes localized advertising is that local offices (of both the advertiser and the agency) have a greater say in the advertising that runs in their countries.[21]

PepsiCo and the Anglo-Dutch conglomerate Unilever represent the two sides of this coin. Pepsi generally employs a single advertising strategy around the world, making only the minimum adaptation required, such as meeting advertising regulations in individual countries.

On the other hand, Unilever focuses on building brand success in individual countries and then tries to move successful brands around the world. In other words, the company never sets out to build a "global brand" of the sort that Pepsi and Coke represent. Unilever chairman Michael Perry minces no words when he calls much of today's thinking on global marketing "an incredible amount of pious theory." To Perry, a global brand is simply a successful local brand individually duplicated in many countries. For example, the Thomas J. Lipton unit of Unilever positions and advertises its tea products differently around the globe, simply because tea drinkers are different. British consumers like theirs hot and mixed with milk, Middle Eastern consumers like theirs with a lot of sugar, and U.S. consumers are likely to have theirs iced. Lipton is successful throughout the world, but it doesn't advertise the same way in every country. Similarly, Unilever's food products take into account different consumer perceptions about health. In the northern European countries, "healthy" means such things as low in cholesterol, whereas in southern Europe, "healthy" means fresh. Given such variations from market to market, it's easy to see why Unilever insists on giving its local operating branches control over their own advertising strategies.[22] Later in the chapter, you'll have an opportunity to explore both sides of this controversy in detail. This section takes a look at the key players in international advertising: advertisers, agencies, and their partners in the international media.

INTERNATIONAL ADVERTISERS

Roughly half of all the economic activity in the world involves transactions across borders, and this international business represents a significant challenge and opportunity for advertising. The United States currently accounts for about half of the world's advertising expenditures, but ad spending in many other countries is growing much faster than the U.S. rate. For example, the amount spent on advertising in South Africa, Saudi Arabia, Jordan, Oman, and Greece recently *doubled* in a single year.[23]

The bulk of international advertising is sponsored by **multinational corporations (MNCs),** companies with business operations in more than one country. Exhibit 8.6 shows an example of French Canadian advertising from the Anglo-Dutch company Unilever. These multinationals compete not only with each other but also with local and regional competitors, so the amounts spent on advertising in such international competition are large. For example, when McDonald's spends money to advertise in Switzerland, local restaurants spend additional money to compete with this adversary from overseas.

International advertising forces a company to address the issue of centralized versus decentralized control. In a centralized organization, decisions about everything from product research to advertising are made by a handful of people at corporate headquarters. In a decentralized organization, individual operating units make their own decisions. Although this is generally a management issue, it has a direct impact on advertising strategy because it's related to the globalization versus localization issue. The globalization strategy is most compatible with centralized organizations because a few key people can make sure that the company's advertising is consistent from country to country. In comparison, localized advertising almost requires a decentralized organization because somebody at the local level in each country has to make decisions.

As with the globalization versus localization issue, executives are split over the centralization versus decentralization issue as well. Unilever's Michael Perry says, "You can't make great advertising in corporate headquarters." This is in sharp contrast to his U.S. competitor Procter & Gamble, which tends to take a more globalized approach to advertising and a centralized approach to managing it.[24]

INTERNATIONAL AGENCIES

U.S. advertising agencies began to work internationally in 1899 when J. Walter Thompson followed some of its early clients overseas. Today, large agencies from

A pleasant
improvement.

EXHIBIT 8.6
Multinational Forces in Advertising

Unilever, the Dutch-Anglo multinational corporation that markets the Sunlight brand of detergent, is one of the world's largest advertisers. This sign in French appeared in Montreal, Canada.

all the major advertising countries are jockeying for position as strong global partners. For example, Paris-based Publicis-FCB Communications offers its clients services in 40 countries, from Austria to Australia. Only a handful of agencies have such a global reach, but many agencies can cover major regions of the world, and the quest to build global service continues.[25]

To provide international reach, many agencies have created or joined **agency networks,** which are collections of agencies connected either by ownership arrangements or by agreements to help each other implement multicountry campaigns. The British group Saatchi & Saatchi was an early network builder, and now agencies in the United States, France, Japan, and other countries are building networks. A number of well-known U.S. agencies are owned in part or in total by foreign firms. The network idea is so attractive that some of the larger firms have more than one network. The Omnicom Group, for instance, owns three agency networks: BBDO Worldwide, DDB Needham Worldwide, and the recently acquired Goodby, Berlin & Silverstein.[26] The idea behind an agency network (in contrast to a company that simply owns a number of different agencies) is that the network can serve advertisers that need multinational advertising help.

INTERNATIONAL MEDIA

Chapter 13 describes in detail the process of selecting the media you'll use in an advertising campaign. It's also helpful to understand some of the key elements of advertising media that differ around the world. First, one of the most important elements is the availability of appropriate media. Advertisers accustomed to getting their message across on television, for instance, might be in for a surprise when they try to advertise in the Middle East, where only 58 percent of the population receives television programming, or in Africa, where the figure is only 9 percent.[27]

Second, the nature of media varies from country to country. As one point of comparison, U.S. television is both more diverse and more commercialized than television in most other countries. Government-owned media are common in many

EXHIBIT 8.7
Global Media

Cable News Network is one of a small but growing number of global media outlets; MTV is another.

parts of the world. In addition, the ways advertisers can use media aren't consistent around the world. For example, as discussed in Chapter 13, one of the big challenges of television advertising is persuading the audience to stay tuned during commercials. Imagine how hard this is in Germany or Greece, where commercials aren't allowed to be aired during program breaks—all ads are broadcast together during specific blocks of time during the evening. In other words, the blocks of ads are scheduled, just as programs are, and viewers find it much easier to walk away from the set without fear of missing part of a favorite program.[28] Another international twist is **media spillover,** defined as one country receiving media from a second country. This happens to some degree in the northern United States, where consumers sometimes receive Canadian television, but it's more common in regions where countries are smaller and more numerous, such as in Europe.

Third, although advertising media have become increasingly fragmented in the United States (with cable chipping away at the once all-powerful national broadcast networks, for instance), the situation is compounded many times over with international advertising. You can reach a major portion of the U.S. audience with ads on ABC, NBC, CBS, or Fox television, but you can't reach the world nearly so easily. Only a handful of media cover a multicountry region, and only a few media are truly global. A good example of regional media is Satellite Television Asian Region (known simply as "STAR TV"), based in Hong Kong. STAR TV reaches audiences from the Middle East to Japan, carrying such channels as MTV Asia and Prime Sports. The satellite network's reach covers nearly 3 billion people, although only a small fraction currently have television sets and satellite dishes. Another barrier is strong government resistance to advertising in some countries, but progress is being made to penetrate this vast market.[29]

Three media vehicles that could be described as global are MTV, Cable News Network (CNN) (see Exhibit 8.7), and the British Broadcasting Corporation (BBC). All three are carried around the world on combinations of satellite and cable transmissions (the BBC's World Service channel and MTV Asia are carried on STAR TV in Asia, for instance). The BBC already offers translations of the news in Mandarin Chinese and plans to offer German, Portuguese, and Latin American Spanish, giving international advertisers a comprehensive vehicle for reaching a large portion of the world audience.[30]

INTERNATIONAL LAW

Regulations on advertising vary from comprehensive and strict in some countries to scant in some less-developed nations. As a U.S. advertiser, you need to recognize two general points about international advertising regulation. First, no two countries have exactly the same regulations, so you have to become familiar with the laws in each country where you plan to advertise. Second, the nature of the advertising regulations in a given country is dictated by the nature of that country's legal system. Many countries have legal systems that are quite different from the U.S. system, and these fundamental differences drive the advertising regulations you'll encounter around the world. For instance, a great contrast exists between the U.S. legal system and systems used in Islamic countries. Unlike U.S. law, Islamic law is based on religious principles and encompasses all aspects of business, social interaction, and personal behavior. The Saudi Arabian law against showing women in advertising may seem rather odd to most of the people in the United States or in other non-Muslim countries, but such a law is in keeping with traditional Islamic principles.[31]

In terms of specific regulations and legal barriers, international advertisers encounter them in four basic categories. First, some countries limit the amount of advertising that can be imported from other countries. The Australian government, for example, has decreed that 80 percent of all advertising that runs in Australia must be created by Australian companies. Second, nearly every country has a set of ideological regulations that advertisers must follow, ranging from bans on comparative advertising to content regulations on alcohol, tobacco, and medical ads. Third, many countries have consumer protection laws regarding misleading advertising, one aspect of which is unique to international advertising: language. Some governments are concerned that consumers can be more easily misled by ads that aren't in their primary language. German law addresses this in part by requiring that any product advertised in Germany that is also made there must be advertised in German. Fourth, countries have a diverse set of regulations regarding children, both as audiences and as actors in commercials. For example, France won't allow children to appear in ads without adults, Sweden bans advertising during children's television programs, and Spain and Germany don't allow ads for war-related toys.[32] Multinational agreements, such as the North American Free Trade Agreement (NAFTA) signed by Canada, Mexico, and the United States, can also affect the advertising business.

Approaches to International Advertising

If you ever want to stir up a lively argument among advertising professionals, bring up the topic of globalization versus localization. As you'll see in this section, you can find strong opinions on both sides, including strong beliefs that both sides will prevail. In most cases, the globalization/localization dilemma is likely to be an international advertiser's most important advertising decision, so you should be aware of what both sides think.

THE CASE FOR GLOBALIZATION

Globalization's most visible proponent is Theodore Levitt of Harvard (he's also on the board of directors of Saatchi & Saatchi), who helped launch the discussion in 1983 by maintaining that instead of seeking out and emphasizing differences between countries and cultures, we should look for similarities—and then advertise to those similarities.[33] This key point is sometimes lost when people consider the globalization issue (and when they criticize Levitt's position). Levitt didn't propose that advertisers disregard country-by-country differences and just bulldoze their way around the world; rather, he suggested that advertisers focus on and market to the similarities they can find—not the differences (see Exhibit 8.8).

It's also important to recognize how much global communication influences, perhaps even creates, those similarities. Coke and McDonald's are brand names known all over the world, and those names mean the same thing to consumers from one country to the next. However, the people of the world weren't born with a strong awareness of the Coke and McDonald's brands; these firms have spent years making themselves known around the globe. A teenager from Kyoto, an attorney from Miami, and a bricklayer from Lyon may not have much in common as consumers, but it's a safe bet that they all know what the red Coke swirl and the yellow McDonald's arches stand for. Global proponents say that great advertising concepts have a universal appeal and that, when those rare gems are discovered, they should be exploited fully.[34]

Proponents of globalization assert that several factors make global campaigns feasible and attractive:[35]

- *Global travel and communication.* It's often said that the world is getting smaller, that jet airliners, satellite communications, and globe-trotting businesspeople have reduced the barriers that separate countries. The people in this so-called global set, who regularly telephone and travel to points all over the world, are less likely to view the world through the narrow lens of their own countries. They're used to seeing Sony electronics, Mont Blanc pens, American Express cards, and many other high-profile global products wherever they travel (see Exhibit 8.9).
- *Regional and global media.* To show how much people in other countries view

(SFX): sound of waves in the middle of the sea and seagulls.
Rachmat: (depressed tone) We've been drifting for days and no sign of rescue . . .
Gunadi: (depressed) yeah . . . I guess that white shirt on top of the mast is not attracting attention . . .
Rachmat: I've got an idea; I'll wash it first with Superbusa.
Gunadi: SUPERBUSA?!?
(SFX): lightning.
V.O.: Only SUPERBUSA can get your white wash superwhite. SUPERBUSA for whiteness that no cream or bar can match.
(SFX): helicopter sound.
Sailor: (excited tone) Hey . . . I see something dazzling white and bright down there!
Captain: Yes . . . I can see it too, it's a boat . . . Let's go and rescue them.
(SFX): lightning.
V.O.: SUPERBUSA-SUPERCLEAN-SUPERWHITE.

EXHIBIT 8.8
Finding Similarities in Global Markets

This radio ad addresses a concern shared by consumers worldwide. If you replaced the Indonesian brand Superbusa with Tide or some other brand of laundry detergent more familiar to people in the United States, this ad would work just as well in this country.

EXHIBIT 8.9
Global Products

As these products for the Japanese market illustrate, Campbell Soup needs to take cultural context into account when it designs and promotes its products in other countries, but the cultural diversity in the United States often calls for making similar distinctions inside a single country.

and read much of the same media, supporters of globalization point to regional media (such as *The European* newspaper), global media (such as the CNN cable network), and exported programming (many U.S. television shows and movies play in other countries, for instance).

- *Converging buyer wants and needs.* A presumed result of global travel and of regional and global media is that buyers everywhere will increasingly want the same products. If fans of a popular U.S. television show wear Levi's and Ray Ban sunglasses because the star of the show does and if that program is later shown in other countries, one might theorize that demand for the two products will go up in those other countries as well (see Exhibit 8.10).

Proponents also assert that globalization offers distinct benefits:

- *Economies of scale.* An *economy of scale* is a cost saving that results from doing things in a big way. In terms of advertising production (the process of creating print or electronic ads), fans of global advertising say that global campaigns cost less than localized ones primarily because you don't have to repeat the production process for each country. With production costs running up to a million dollars or more for major television commercials, this is an attractive argument. (According to one study, however, research hasn't uncovered a great deal of evidence to support this cost savings.[36])

- *Budget reallocations.* A benefit of an economy of scale is the money that's saved—with whatever you don't spend on producing ads, you can run more ads or spend more on research to develop new products.

- *Efficiency and productivity.* As discussed in Chapters 9 through 17, the process of creating ads and putting them in front of an audience is complex and time consuming. Proponents of globalization would like to minimize the headaches and managerial overhead by not going through the process all over again for each additional country. They argue that if you don't have to spend all that time and energy adapting your ads to each country, you can spend more time selling, supporting customers, making new products, and so forth.[37]

OUR WORKFORCE

OUR PRODUCT

Golden Delicious

To turn acres of blossoms into a harvest of fruit requires a highly skilled workforce.

During the spring pollination, you see, every flower has to be individually treated. Otherwise there would be no deliciously crunchy Cape Apples rolling off our production lines in the autumn.

What's more, there are only two short weeks every year to get this crucial job done, sometimes even less. Which is why, in blossom time, our workers get busy as soon as the sun peeps over the mountains, and only knock off after it's sunk in the west.

And where do you find a workforce with all the necessary dedication and skill?

In the Cape, naturally. It's one of the reasons that make it such a perfect factory. And enable it to produce such perfect products.

MADE IN THE CAPE.
WHERE ELSE?

EXHIBIT 8.10
Trends That Span National Boundaries

This Unifruco ad from South Africa illustrates that the consumer desire for natural and healthy products spans the world.

THE CASE FOR LOCALIZATION

Critics of globalization contend that it can't work for most products, even under the best of circumstances. Even if it can, say the critics, its overstandardized products and promotions open the door for competitors offering something more closely tuned to local markets. Carl Spielvogel, chairman of advertising agency Backer Spielvogel Bates Worldwide, calls global marketing "bunk." "There are about two products that lend themselves to global marketing—" says Spielvogel, "and one of them is Coca-Cola."[38] Philip Kotler, a noted marketing professor, considers globalization a step backward to the so-called production era of business, when companies were more concerned about pumping out as many standardized products as they could, rather than worrying about satisfying customers.[39]

Nükhet Vardar, of Yaratim/FCB in Istanbul, Turkey, spent several years studying the globalization issue, and she offers a number of reasons for adapting campaigns to local or perhaps regional markets rather than trying to globalize:[40]

- *Better fit with local markets.* With a global approach, the advertiser might overlook local variations that affect buyer behavior. For instance, in the early days of its international expansion, Apple Computer decided to define advertising strategies at the local level because the degree of personal computer awareness varied from country to country.[41] In addition, although the world's consumers are becoming more similar in many respects, not all consumers in all countries are moving at the same rate. Consumers in countries with a high degree of business and cultural interaction, such as the United States and Canada, may have increasingly similar wants and needs, but the same can't be said of consumers in many developing nations around the world.[42] The average family in Pasadena or Paris may not have the same buying habits as the average family in Pakistan.

(SFX): jolly Norwegian folk music.
A MAN COMING HOME FROM WORK.
HE UNLOCKS THE DOOR OF HIS
APARTMENT. HAVING BARELY

STEPPED INTO THE HALL, HE STARTS
UNDRESSING. COMPLETELY
"STARKERS," HE HURRIES OVER TO
THE LIVING ROOM DOOR AND GAZES

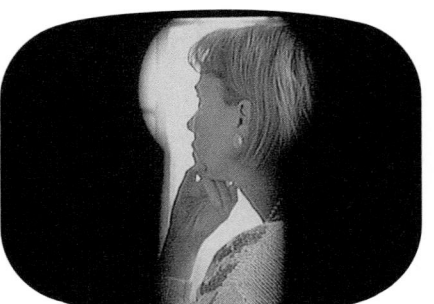

THROUGH THE KEYHOLE AT THE
OBJECT OF HIS DESIRE (HIS WIFE).
NOTHING CAN HOLD HIM BACK NOW.
HE STICKS A ROSE BETWEEN HIS

TEETH AND BURSTS INTO THE LIVING-
ROOM TO FIND HIS WIFE HAS BEEN
JOINED BY HER OUT-OF-TOWN PAR-

ENTS. HIS DRAMATIC APPEARANCE IS
GREETED BY STONY SILENCE.

Superscript: Warning: We're flying your in-
laws at half price! Braathens SAFE. The
Norwegian airline.

EXHIBIT 8.11
Different Tastes in Different Countries

This television commercial promoting
the low fare offered by the Norwegian
airline Braathens SAFE plays on a
common theme in advertising (in-
laws), but it does so in a style that
wouldn't be accepted on U.S. television (other scenes show partial
nudity).

- *Shorter response time.* As a general rule, the fewer people who have to approve decisions, the faster the decisions can be made. Some advertising situations (such as a negative newspaper article about your products or the appearance of a new competitor) sometimes demand responses within days or even hours. Requiring local managers to clear their decisions with regional or international managers in other countries can slow decisions enough so that the delay affects the company's competitiveness.

- *Local management involvement and motivation.* For both multinational corporations and their international agency networks, getting local managers and employees involved and motivated is much easier if those people have a say in the advertising decisions. People in general are more likely to support a decision or a plan if their opinions and insights were included in the decision-making process.

- *Reduced chance of cultural blunders.* Sometimes the best advertising plan imaginable can stumble over a seemingly minor cultural blunder. Even things as basic as language have tripped up otherwise well-executed marketing and advertising programs. Some errors have become classics, such as General Motors' "Body by Fisher" tagline, which translated into Flemish (one of the languages spoken in Belgium) as "Corpse by Fisher." Schweppes Tonic Water showed up in Italian advertisements as "bathroom water."[43] Obviously, having some local input would have averted both mistakes (see Exhibit 8.11).

- *Increased competitiveness.* Not surprisingly, critics of globalization believe that all the factors already mentioned culminate in increased competitiveness. If you can respond faster and more appropriately to local conditions, motivate the people responsible for carrying out marketing and advertising at the local level, and avoid cultural blunders, your advertising is almost sure to be more successful.

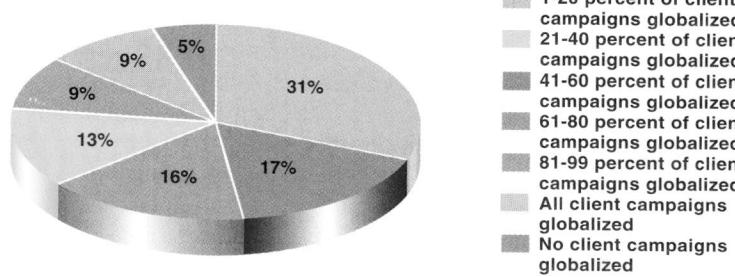

1-20 percent of client campaigns globalized
21-40 percent of client campaigns globalized
41-60 percent of client campaigns globalized
61-80 percent of client campaigns globalized
81-99 percent of client campaigns globalized
All client campaigns globalized
No client campaigns globalized

EXHIBIT 8.12

Agency Survey: Percentage of Client Campaigns that Are Globalized

As you can see from these survey results, few international advertisers practice the extremes of strictly globalized or strictly localized campaigns.

SO WHICH IS THE RIGHT APPROACH?

No single approach is always the right approach. For one thing, there's no such thing as a completely global campaign or a completely local campaign. For another, even companies committed to globalization, such as Coca-Cola and PepsiCo, must translate many of their ads into other languages, and they must make their ads conform to local standards and regulations. The German consumer-goods company Henckels explains its strategy by comparing its markets to a "highway that passes through a wide variety of terrain . . . the highway is the same throughout, but the support structures are different depending on local circumstances." In other words, Henckels's marketing and advertising strategy is the same in all countries, with minor variations made at the local level as needed.[44]

At the other extreme, a completely localized campaign could result in chaos and inefficiency. What if the U.S. arm of a major hotel chain started a joint promotion with United Airlines at the same time that the chain's U.K. office was starting a joint promotion with British Airways, one of United's strongest global competitors? At a less drastic level, what if offices in the two countries opted for the same advertising strategy and each spent $500,000 to produce nearly identical television commercials? Perhaps some coordination would have let them produce two variations of the same basic commercial for a total of only $600,000.

As a result of these two conflicting ideas, most international advertising is somewhere between the extremes of global and local. Exhibit 8.12 shows the results of a survey of 220 international advertising agencies, which were asked what percentage of their campaigns for clients were globalized. You can see that fewer than 10 percent said that their clients always go with a global approach; 5 percent never use the global approach.[45]

THE REGIONAL ALTERNATIVE

For some products in some parts of the world, a strategy of **regionalization,** in which the advertiser targets two or more countries with a single campaign, makes more sense than either globalization or localization. You get some of the benefits of globalization without all the risks, and you get some of the benefits of localization without all the costs. Bob Kingsbery of Kingsbery International, an international marketing services firm, notes that this approach is often ideal for such regions as Latin America, where the people in most countries speak Spanish in one form or another. He notes that it's possible to cover this large region with a single creative strategy and execution, if you first identify the similarities in buyer needs and purchase behaviors and avoid visual symbols or copy phrases that might be inappropriate for specific countries.[46]

The nations of the European Union are another frequently mentioned regional market. These nations share a number of links in terms of culture, geographic proximity, political history, and consumer attitudes. These attitudes and other factors are sometimes quite distinct from those in other parts of the world. A recent survey of young European women by the ad agency BBDO Europe, for instance, indicated that European women are more likely to smoke and less likely to diet or exercise than their U.S. counterparts, and that attitudes on these subjects were fairly consistent from one European country to the next.[47] You can picture how these factors might influence advertising design. For example, an ad for Nike or Reebok that shows a woman running to keep fit might play well in the United States but not so well across Europe. Conversely, showing young professional women smoking might not seem like such a big deal in Europe, but it would strike a negative chord with the majority of young U.S. women. Note that similarities in one or a few behavioral traits do not mean that European women are all alike. Rather, it implies that some traits cross national borders in Europe.

A number of advertisers are trying to craft pan-European campaigns from bits and pieces of localized campaigns, a task that is often difficult. For example, the Italian appliance manufacturer Zanussi is trying to find a single positioning strategy for Europe in the face of wildly varying consumer perceptions. English buyers tend to view Zanussi as a sophisticated and prestigious brand, but the French consider it a cheap import. If the company wanted to stick with localized ads, it could take different approaches in each country; however, a single creative concept for all Europeans would be much harder to develop.[48]

With any approach, it's important to remember that for all its complexities and distractions, international advertising, like intercultural advertising, is not unlike market segmentation in general (albeit on a giant scale). Why do you segment markets? To increase the likelihood that your message and your product offering will yield a favorable response from the target audience. Of course, segmentation is usually more expensive and more time consuming, and you always risk focusing on the wrong segments. Consequently, the best way to approach the globalization issue is to ask whether globalizing or localizing promises the best chance of a profitable return on your investment of time and money, taking into account the costs and risks associated with both approaches.

Managing International Advertising

International advertising presents a number of issues that can challenge even the best advertising managers and their agency counterparts. One of the most important is the shortage of skilled people reported by U.S. agencies operating in other countries. A survey of several hundred overseas affiliates of U.S. ad agencies exposed rather severe shortages in certain positions. For instance, a third of the affiliates in the 51 countries said they could find creative directors only rarely or never. Agencies in the Middle East reported the most severe personnel shortages, with several positions indicated as virtually unfillable. Personnel shortages aren't limited to less-developed economies, however. Denmark, Canada, and Switzerland were among those with the worst shortages.[49] Aside from personnel concerns, advertising managers need to consider several other important issues, including geocentrism and nationalism, research and planning, and creativity and production.

GEOCENTRISM AND NATIONALISM

When developing an international advertising program, it's important to watch for and minimize **geocentrism,** the tendency to view one's home country as superior to all others. Geocentrism is similar to ethnocentrism, but the emphasis is on political divisions rather than on ethnic or cultural divisions. For instance, if you flip on the television in a hotel room in Amsterdam and discover that the Netherlands has only a handful of television channels, you might compare this with the 50- or 100-channel cable television setup you have at home and conclude that U.S. entertainment technology is superior. From that mistaken conclusion it's tempting for some people to make the leap that the United States must therefore be superior. Geocentric attitudes like this not only get in the way of creating successful international advertising but also hamper the interpersonal relationships you need to establish in each country where you plan to do business.

CHECKLIST FOR CHOOSING GLOBALIZATION OR LOCALIZATION

❏ A. Are your markets homogeneous (buyers are similar) or heterogeneous (buyers are dissimilar) from country to country?

❏ B. Does your product have a universal appeal, or is its appeal more localized or regionalized?

❏ C. How is your company organized? Do you have the local staffs needed to manage localized campaigns?

❏ D. If you have local staffs or divisions, do they have decision-making authority with regard to advertising?

❏ E. Do the countries have similar degrees of economic development?

❏ F. Are legal restrictions and advertising different enough to force you to change strategies from country to country?

❏ G. Can you find similar media in each country?

❏ H. Can you find local agencies or local branches of your main agency in each country?

❏ I. Is your agency capable of handling advertising in each country?

❏ J. Which stands to increase your long-term profitability more: the short-term savings of globalization or the chance of increased advertising effectiveness through localization?

A related concept is **nationalism,** the belief that the interests of one's own country should take precedence over the interests of other countries. Nationalistic sentiments show up in advertising from time to time, usually when domestic advertisers want consumers to stop buying imported goods. For instance, you've probably seen car ads that urge you to "buy American" (see Exhibit 8.13).

Advertisers need to watch out for nationalistic themes that intentionally or unintentionally offend other countries. Recent ads running in Spain for the Italian-made Vespa scooters are a good example. Responding to the Japanese scooters that had carved out a major slice of the Spanish market, Vespa and its agency J. Walter Thompson created ads that generated official complaints from the Japanese embassy in Madrid. One ad urged consumers to "vaccinate" themselves against "a strange yellow fever," with the implication that a Vespa was the remedy and that Japanese scooters were the disease. Red circles in the ad were interpreted by the embassy as direct references to the Japanese flag. The agency said it might downplay the red circles in future ads, but it intends to continue with the same basic creative strategy.[50]

"You shouldn't buy a car just because of where it's made. Buy it because of how it's made."

What it comes down to is a car or truck you can trust not only to get you there, but also make you feel good about taking the trip. And while some people will tell you a car is just a machine, others will say it's much more than that. It's that feeling of confidence you get when you pass the last signs of civilization for 300 miles. A safe haven for preschoolers. A badge of freedom to every 16-year-old. A personal port in the storm for every weekday commuter.

Today, GM is bringing you the best vehicles we've ever built. New designs. New engines. New customer satisfaction programs. And an all-new feeling of confidence. Come see the changes we've made.

General Motors

EXHIBIT 8.13
Nationalism in Advertising

General Motors addresses the "Buy American" issue that crops up in the automobile, textile, and other markets from time to time. GM's message, however, is that you don't need to be on a "Buy American" campaign to buy a GM car; the product itself should be enough to persuade you.

INTERNATIONAL RESEARCH

As Chapter 6 points out, good research can mean the difference between success and failure in marketing and advertising. This is particularly true in international advertising, where there are more uncertainties and more variables to consider. Research can uncover powerful and often unsuspected forces at work in an international market segment. For instance, a study of quality perceptions among consumers in New Zealand showed that people tend to transfer the images they have of a particular country's automobiles to other product lines coming from that country. In other words, if you were a U.S. manufacturer of power tools starting to advertise in this market, consumers would prejudge your quality based on what they thought about the quality of U.S. cars—even though you have nothing to do with the car market. This *halo effect* from another product category can obviously have an impact on how you should design your advertising and on how effective it will be.[51]

Whatever the issue you're researching, experts emphasize several key differences in international advertising research. The first is the need to double-check at every stage in the creative process whether the developing ad will work in all its intended markets. You can't assume that once you have the strategy in place, you're all set. You have to recheck the copy, the visuals, the media selections, and every other element along the way.[52]

Second, research is often more expensive and more difficult to do in other countries, whether it's because of the unwillingness of people in other countries to share personal details with strangers or the simple lack of tools such as telephones or telephone directories. The United States has a well-developed research industry equipped to handle any project with efficiency, and while this is true in many other developed countries, it's not so true in others. Fortunately, the larger U.S. agencies and research companies can usually help their clients manage overseas research.[53]

Third, in-market testing (exposing part of your audience to an ad before sending it out to the entire audience) isn't feasible in many countries. In the United States, you can run your ads in one major city, modify them after the tests (if needed), and then run them nationally. Some countries, however, lack the local media necessary to conduct a test like this.[54]

INTERNATIONAL PLANNING

Throughout this chapter, you've already seen numerous explanations of why developing strategies and plans for international advertising is more complicated than advertising locally or nationally within one country. Budgeting, one of the key aspects of planning, provides an illustration of just how different international planning can be. As discussed in Chapter 7, budgeting for advertising is often a complex and uncertain process. It becomes even more complex when you cross national borders. You have to figure what the local and international competitors are spending in a given country, how often you need to run ads to make any impression in the midst of competitive ads, how effective various local media are, and other key data.

Budgeting practices can vary widely from country to country, based on such factors as the level of economic development and the regulation of advertising. Consider just one key budgeting variable, the advertising-to-sales (A/S) ratio (another way of looking at the percentage-of-sales method of budgeting). A study of 15 countries uncovered tremendous variations in average A/S ratios. The United States was near the low end, with an average of just 2.83 percent of sales spent on advertising. Advertisers in Australia, in contrast, spend 7.62 percent of their sales on advertising—nearly three times as much.[55] You can imagine how ineffective you might be as a U.S. advertiser trying to enter the Australian market with budgeting experience only in the United States. Advertising expenditures per capita (the total spent on advertising divided by the number of people in a country) also vary widely. Japan, for example, spends 180 times as much per capita as Indonesia does.[56] These examples highlight the need for thorough research and careful planning.

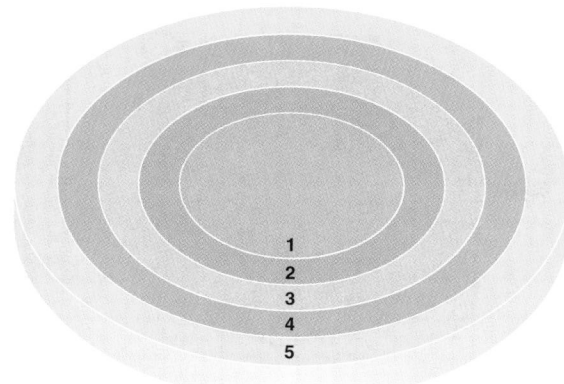

MOST LIKELY TO TRAVEL
SUCCESSFULLY

1. **Product facts and functions**

2. **Universal myths, symbols, fantasies, metaphors**

3. **Basic human emotions**

4. **News, fashions, celebrities**

5. **Cultural values, lifestyles, word usages, humor**

LEAST LIKELY TO TRAVEL
SUCCESSFULLY

EXHIBIT 8.14
How Well Will Your Advertising Idea Travel?

Some advertising concepts travel better than others; generally, the more tangible and straightforward the concept, the better it will be understood by audiences in other countries.

CREATIVITY AND PRODUCTION

The creative decisions that define your advertising must be considered carefully in the international arena. Some of the ideas that make many ads successful, such as humor and references to contemporary culture, don't travel very well. Exhibit 8.14 shows five levels of advertising ideas, from basic facts about the product in the center to cultural values in the outer ring. The closer your ideas are to the center of this model, the greater the chance they'll work internationally.[57]

The manner in which you should manage advertising creativity and production also depends on whether your strategic approach is global, localized, or somewhere in between. The Swedish agency Welinder Business Marketing represents the global approach, with local adaptations as needed. Normally, Welinder keeps the visual content the same but has the copy rewritten for specific countries. However, the agency was more extreme in the ads it created for L. M. Ericsson's Hotel-Phone System, not only using the same photographic imagery but keeping the copy in English—even though the ads ran in more than 40 countries (see Exhibit 8.15). Welinder's Scott Goodson explained that the copy was quite short, that all the words were in the vocabulary of the typical international business

"It's about communication between people. The rest is technology."

LARS RAMQVIST, President and Chief Executive Officer, Ericsson.

We expect to be able to communicate with anyone, at any time, anywhere. We want to be liberated from the constraints of time and space. Distances are shrinking. Traditional boundaries are losing their significance.

We want technology to work for us as individuals. We expect it to meet our sophisticated communications needs, but still be easy to use.

We expect technology to provide us with global freedom, and at the same time respect our privacy as individuals. It should allow us to reach others, but make ourselves available on our terms.

Today's technology makes almost anything possible. It is you and I who set the limits.

Respecting people's need for privacy is just as important in the development of new telecommunications solutions as it is in our day-to-day communications with others.

Ericsson provides innovative, flexible solutions and services for all types of telecommunications networks that are helping our customers to open up new business opportunities and supply superior service to users. We develop and maintain technologies not only for today's needs, but for tomorrow and well into the future.

70,000 Ericsson employees are active in more than 100 countries. Their combined expertise in switching, cellular, wireless and network technologies make Ericsson a world leader in telecommunications.

Ericsson North America Inc., please call (800) 835-3742.
Telefonaktiebolaget LM Ericsson, S-126 25 Stockholm, Sweden.

ERICSSON

EXHIBIT 8.15
Local Adaptations of a Global Campaign

On the reasoning that most global business travelers speak at least a little English, the Swedish company L. M. Ericsson kept this ad in English in more than 40 countries.

Successful Language for Intercultural and International Ads

Communicating an advertising message successfully is a challenge in the best of circumstances, and it only gets harder when you have to cross cultural and geographic borders. However, you can improve your chances of success by paying close attention to the way you use copy in your ads. The following guidelines will help you create print and electronic ads that get their points across more effectively.

- *Minimize the amount of copy.* The typical French style of advertising has a head start on most of the rest of the world when it comes to relying on visuals to carry the message. Since language is usually one of the biggest barriers between countries, minimizing the amount of reading or listening required will make your message that much more likely to get through to the audience.
- *Either rewrite copy for each market or backtranslate it.* Effective copywriting often relies on subtle nuances and particular word usages—elements that can be misunderstood when an ad is translated into another language. Some agencies recommend having a copywriter in each country write the copy from scratch for that particular country. Welinder, the Swedish agency, takes this approach because, as associate creative director Scott Goodson points out, "It's impossible to take an ad written in English and translate it literally into other languages." The alternative is to *backtranslate* (having the copy translated, but then having it translated back into the original language). The backtranslation gives you some idea of how well the nuances of the language survived the trip and lets you know if the original translation needs fine-tuning.
- *Keep your language simple.* Don't assume that word play, jokes, and other usages will survive an international trip. Many of the words and phrases that U.S. residents use without a second thought will draw a blank from audiences in other countries, even among those people with extensive training in English. An ad can say "We'll help your company hit a home run," and most people in the United States will get the message. However, audiences in other countries may speak English as a second language and may not get

the baseball reference at all, or if they do, they might wonder why companies are playing baseball instead of doing business.
- *Learn another language.* If you've ever tried to learn another language, you already know how difficult it can be to communicate when your grasp of a language is limited. If you haven't tried, you're in for an eye-opening experience, as you see how difficult it is to understand humor, word play, and subtle shades of meaning in another language. Gaining an appreciation of communicating in another language will help sensitize you to the difficulties your audiences face.

By recognizing the added challenges of international and intercultural advertising, you'll take the first important step to communicating successfully. Keep it simple, keep it clear, and you'll have a much better chance of getting your point across.

Apply Your Knowledge
1. *Why should you hesitate to use a copy translator who isn't also an experienced copywriter?*
2. *Assume you're adapting an English-language print ad for several other languages, but the headline relies on a subtle word play that may not survive the translation. Should you simply translate and take your chances, translate it and explain in the body copy what the headline means, or write a new headline? Explain your answer.*

executive, and that English is the preferred language of business most everywhere in the world anyway.[58]

Building an international campaign around one theme but allowing for local variations can be managed through a process known as *pattern standardization*. In this approach (used by such multinationals as Goodyear), the advertiser's head office works with the ad agency to establish the overall strategy and the way the message will be presented. Local agencies then adapt the strategy and presentation to meet particular advertising laws, languages, cultural expectations, and other local conditions. Pattern standardization works best when the advertiser uses a global agency network that has close control over the local agencies; the advertiser has to exercise some degree of control over its subsidiaries as well.[59]

In addition, it helps to understand the style of advertising most prevalent in the countries where you plan to advertise. You may or may not want to go with the creative flow in each country, but it's beneficial to understand what approach a country's advertisers tend to take. It might help to venture out into the world with the knowledge that some overseas observers view the typical U.S. ad as brash, boastful, and not particularly subtle. Ads created in England, France, and Japan (three of the world's biggest advertisers after the United States) tend to have a different look and tone than ads created in the United States. Of course, it's dangerous to generalize about something as intangible as creativity, but basic patterns can be recognized. British ads tend to be understated and mildly humorous, often with references to art, literature, or history. Japanese ads tend to be more image-oriented and less concerned with product information or overt competitive battles. Ads from Japan frequently draw blanks with viewers in the West who aren't used to abstract ads that don't seem to sell the product. Dentsu's Akira Kagami offers this explanation: Japanese consumers know so much about the products already that the key creative issue isn't what advertisers say, but how they say it. French ads are also not keen on aggressive sales pitches, taking an indirect approach and relying on imagery. Nor do they typically have much copy. Visuals are expected to carry most of the message, which leads people in the French ad industry to joke that there are only three copywriters in the entire country.[60]

Is U.S. advertising less sophisticated or less creative? Not according to John Philip Jones, a noted advertising researcher. He expects that European advertising will become more like U.S. advertising over time, as markets in those countries gradually grow more crowded with competing products. Advertisers in the United States simply can't survive with ads that sell less but entertain more; they face too much competition to have that luxury.[61] Whatever the reason for country-to-country differences, it's instructive to study advertising styles from around the world to glean new ideas.

Summary

Intercultural and international advertising are closely related, with a couple of key differences. Intercultural advertising concerns advertising across cultures, regardless of whether those cultures are in the same country or not. International advertising, on the other hand, deals strictly with advertising across borders, although there's usually a strong element of intercultural advertising involved as well.

The major elements of culture that influence audience response to advertising are race and nationality, language, and cultural values. Race and nationality raise such issues as whether to define audience segments along racial lines and whether to use models and actors of different races in your advertising. Language presents another set of challenges, including the cultural barriers that can impede the flow of communication and the dilemma of whether or not to use segmented advertising in multilingual countries. Cultural values can affect many aspects of audience behavior, from the products that people want to the way they respond to advertising. Ethnocentrism, a tendency to view one's own ethnic group or culture as superior to all others, can have negative effects on international advertising because it can blind the advertiser to changes and adaptations that are essential to success in other countries and cultures.

Agency networks play a big role in most international advertising efforts. They're particularly important with global and regional strategies; the networks help enforce the necessary standardization from country to country while still allowing for local adaptations as needed.

The restrictions placed on advertising in various countries fall into four categories: (1) limits on the amount of advertising that can be imported from other countries; (2) ideological regulations, ranging from bans on comparative advertising to content regulations on alcohol, tobacco, and medical ads; (3) consumer protection laws regarding misleading advertising, including the use of language; and (4) regulations regarding children, both as audiences and as actors in commercials.

The global and local approaches to international advertising represent two extremes. With the global approach, the advertiser tries to keep the strategy and tactics identical in every country, with necessary exceptions made for local laws and media. With the local approach, the advertiser allows its divisions or representatives in each country to design and implement their own advertising. Most international campaigns fall somewhere between these two extremes. Advertisers who opt for the regional approach strike a compromise between the efficiency of the global approach and the cost and complexity of the local approach by grouping similar countries together under a single campaign.

The controversy surrounding the global approach centers on whether audiences are really similar enough around the world to be effectively reached with a single advertising strategy. Global proponents say that advertisers should seek out and advertise to the similarities they can find. In fact, they should use advertising to shape those similarities. Opponents say there

Meeting an Advertising Challenge at Holiday Inn Worldwide

International advertising experts often use Coca-Cola as the point of reference when assessing an advertiser's choice between globalization and localization, since it's one of the best known and most committed practitioners of the global advertising strategy. The fact that even Coca-Cola executives are impressed with how far Holiday Inn has taken globalization gives you some idea of how passionately Raymond Lewis and his team have embraced the concept.

Lewis bases his globalization strategy on the idea that all travelers, regardless of where they're from or where they're going, share many of the same desires, fears, and expectations when they're traveling. They may not speak the same language or live the same lives while at home, but when they're on the road, all travelers are (1) away from home and out of their personal comfort zones, (2) in different and often unfamiliar surroundings, and (3) subject to the same hassles and hardships.

On this common base, Holiday Inn built the dual themes of "Welcome" and "Stay with somebody you know." The strategy and even the visual format of the advertising is the same around the world, although copy is translated as needed and variations are made to meet local cultural differences. For example, ads in the United States and Germany feature a businesswoman at the hotel, receiving a faxed drawing from her child. British travelers, however, didn't respond to the sentimental pitch, so the ads in England feature a friendly doorman instead.

The inspiration for this global strategy came to Lewis, not surprisingly, while he was traveling. At Dulles Airport outside Washington, D.C., he passed a group of Russian teenagers gathered around a guitar player singing "Puff the Magic Dragon," a folk song that was popularized by Peter, Paul, and Mary in the United States three decades ago. This connection between cultures helped convince Lewis that the world's people were alike in many ways, particularly in the field of pleasure and business travel.

It remains to be seen how effective Lewis's strategy will be in the long run. Holiday Inn is one of the few travel-services companies with the global reach needed to pull off such a strategy, but the company is sailing into uncharted waters. At the very least, Lewis is giving the world's advertisers a fascinating real-life study of globalization in action.

Your Mission: You've joined Holiday Inn as director of advertising, and you will be helping Ray Lewis put his global plans into action. Your responsibilities include balancing the globalization strategy with the need to adapt to local conditions. In the following scenarios, choose the solutions that will best serve Lewis and Holiday Inn.

1. You're planning a commercial for Swiss television that will reach both German-speaking and French-speaking Swiss consumers; assume that half your viewers speak both languages. You can afford only one commercial. How should you handle the language issue?
   a. Produce the commercial in one language, and rerecord the spoken words in the other language.
   b. Produce the commercial in English.
   c. Rely on visuals, rather than words, to get your message across. Use a few English words if needed.

2. The movement of women up the corporate ladder is progressing at dramatically different rates in various countries around the world. For

simply aren't that many similarities for the vast majorities of products, and that not paying attention to local audience differences leads to mistakes and ineffective advertising.

International advertising presents a number of management challenges. First, agencies report a shortage of experienced advertising professionals in many countries. Second, advertising managers need to keep geocentrism (the tendency to view one's home country as superior to all others) and nationalism (the belief that the interests of one's own country should take precedence over the interests of other countries) from diminishing the effectiveness of their advertising efforts. Third, advertising research is particularly important when moving across borders, and it is generally more difficult and more expensive to conduct outside the United States. Fourth, the planning process (and budgeting in particular) is more complex in international advertising because managers have more variables to consider (such as differences in the amount of advertising from one country to the next). Fifth, the way the creative and production processes should be managed may change in the international arena. For instance, some countries have distinctive styles of advertising, and some creative ideas travel better than others. The use of sex appeals (and nudity in particular) varies widely, and an ad that is acceptable in one country might be strongly offensive to audiences in another country.

Key Terms

adaptation 201
agency networks 203
ethnocentrism 200
geocentrism 210
globalization 201
intercultural advertising 194
localization 201

media spillover 204
multinational corporations (MNCs) 202
nationalism 211
regionalization 209
standardization 201

Questions

FOR REVIEW

1. Why is it important to recognize the behaviors that a culture rewards?

2. Given the difficulty of choosing which language (and which variety of a single language) to use when advertising to the Hispanic and Asian populations in the United States, would you just drop the language issue and advertise to everybody in English?

3. Why do proponents of global advertising say that it saves money?

WHO WOULD
KNOW BETTER HOW TO
MAKE YOU FEEL

VELCOME

IN EUROPE?

Every day, warm, attentive staff welcome guests to Holiday Inn hotels throughout Europe. To spacious and well appointed rooms. To thoughtfully prepared meals. Each Holiday Inn has meeting rooms, and provides fax machines and audio visual equipment to help you keep in touch with colleagues and clients alike. Wherever your business takes you in Europe, that's a welcoming thought.

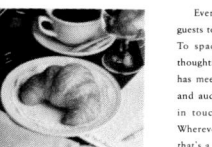

STAY WITH SOMEONE YOU KNOW.

FOR RESERVATIONS, CALL US TOLL-FREE THROUGHOUT EUROPE.
FRANCE: 05 905999   SPAIN: 900 99 31 19
GERMANY: 0130 815151   ITALY: 1678 77599   SWEDEN: 020 793 795
IRELAND: 1 800 553155   THE NETHERLANDS: 06 0221155   SWITZERLAND: 155 11 75
NORWAY: 050 11535   UNITED KINGDOM: 0800 897121
ONS FROM OTHER COUNTRIES, CALL (31)20-60 60 222 (NOT TOLL-FREE) OR ANY HOLIDAY INN HOTEL.

instance, women traveling on business is a common sight in North America, somewhat less so in Europe, fairly rare in Asia, and practically unheard of in the Islamic states of the Middle East. If you wanted to reach women business travelers in Asia without offending more conservative travelers, which of the following ad concepts would you use?

a. Although it runs counter to majority opinion elsewhere in the world, you should follow tradition in Asia and feature only businessmen in your ads.

b. The traveling businesswoman may be a rare sight in Asia, but it's on the increase. You should feature women in your ad because that will position Holiday Inn as an innovative company.

c. You can't afford to offend either group, so you should focus on the expert hotel staff in your ads, not the guests, and let potential guests of either gender decide that the hotel is for them.

3. Most other international hotel chains haven't embraced the globalization approach. Hilton Hotels, in fact, calls it "a waste of time." What should you do if one of the localized competitors starts to take market share from you in a few countries?

a. Since only a few countries are involved at the moment, study them carefully before doing anything, and then see whether some special attention in those particular markets might solve the problem.

b. If the competitor is succeeding with localization, your decision to use globalization was obviously a mistake; switch to localization.

c. Stick with your globalization strategy; it'll pay off in the end.

4. Coordinating and controlling advertising efforts around the world is always a challenge, particularly when you need the consistency required by a globalized strategy. In Holiday Inn's case, the situation is complicated by the fact that most of its hotels are franchise operations, meaning that an independent businessperson or company actually owns and manages the facility. Convincing all these people to go along with a single global strategy hasn't been easy. Which of the following managerial approaches would you recommend?

a. One of the reasons franchising works so well is that local business owners often know their environments better than outsiders; let them decide whether to accept the global campaign.

b. For a globalized strategy to work, it must have consistency. You should demand agreement and compliance from all franchisees, and in fact, make it a condition of continuing their contracts with Holiday Inn.

c. You shouldn't try to force people into agreement, nor should you ignore the corporation's strategic direction. Instead, persuade franchisees to accept the strategy by explaining that it will help them attract more international travelers.[62]

4. Why do some people disagree with the global approach?

5. Why would an advertiser choose regionalization over globalization or localization?

FOR ANALYSIS AND APPLICATION

6. If you ran a large agency such as DBD Needham, what steps could you take to ensure that the agency's work avoids cultural blunders?

7. Should Procter & Gamble and other large multinational advertisers that use the global approach design every ad to fit the media environment in every country in which they plan to run the ad?

8. Could cultural values be an international advertising issue for a company that makes only straightforward industrial products? Why or why not?

9. Would you pick a global strategy for Barq's root beer? If you're not sure, what would you need to know before you could decide?

10. Why do you suppose product features are easier to communicate internationally than cultural values are?

Sharpen Your Advertising Skills

The joy of the open road is a theme that shows up frequently in U.S. car advertising. You can picture it now: the wind in your hair as you navigate curves on a lonely mountain highway, the only car in sight. It's an attractive image for many drivers, but for most people it's not a realistic portrayal of the normal driving scenario. It's even less realistic when you move the advertising to certain other countries. Singapore, for instance, is a city that essentially covers the entire country, so you have little chance of finding a lonely stretch of road anywhere.

Decision: Assume you manage the Singapore office of a U.S. advertising agency that holds the Ford Motor account. The campaign for a new sports sedan shows it wheeling along a stretch of open highway in the Southwest. Should you keep that imagery for a commercial in Singapore? (Keep in mind why the imagery would be used in the United States.)

Communication: Draft a short memo to the U.S. office of the agency, outlining your decision on the ad along with your reasons.

Sneaker Wars

SYNOPSIS

This program traces the relatively brief but incredibly lucrative growth of the athletic shoe industry, from Nike's and Reebok's early attempts to position athletic shoes as fashionable footwear to today's multibillion-dollar global market for athletic shoes that can cost $150 or more. You'll see how the aerobics boom, technology (some of it of questionable value), and celebrity advertising fueled the market.

The video also addresses two of the most important issues facing the industry as it moves toward the turn of the century: international growth and ethical concerns over the effect that high-priced athletic shoes have on the behavior of children in general and gangs in particular. In the international arena, Nike and Reebok are working hard to unseat Adidas, which has long been the leader outside the United States. Regarding the ethical questions, some community activists say that the shoe companies should invest more money in the communities that are the source of their revenue. The shoe companies answer the criticism by saying that they do spend large amounts now and that they can't be held responsible for the country's moral conditions.

EXERCISES

Analysis

1. What role did advertising play in the growth of the athletic shoe market?
2. Given that a fairly small percentage of the people who buy athletic shoes actually use them for athletics, why are celebrity sports hero endorsers so popular in this market?
3. Do you think consumer purchase behavior is influenced by which professional athletes wear which brand of shoes?
4. Do the claims made about technological advances in athletic shoes (such as pumps and air sacs) influence consumer behavior?
5. What are the risks of relying so heavily on celebrity endorsers in this market?

Application

Brooks is a small manufacturer that focuses on running shoes. It presents a serious image as a specialist in running shoe technology. Given that its presence in the market (and its advertising budget) is so small compared with Nike and Reebok, which of the advertising purposes described in Chapter 7 would you recommend for Brooks?

Decision

The number three athletic shoe company, L.A. Gear, recently tried to stimulate consumer interest by putting flashing lights in the heels of its shoes. Let's say you work for Nike's advertising agency, and the new L.A. Gear models seem to be catching on. Should you address this issue with competitive advertising? Why or why not?

Ethics

The high price tags on popular athletic shoes has raised a difficult ethical question: Should Nike and Reebok advertise $150 shoes in a way that makes them appealing to people who can't afford them? Should the companies (1) stop selling the more expensive models, (2) stop advertising them so aggressively, or (3) change nothing in their current strategies? Explain your answer in light of the rights of everyone involved.

Teamwork

With a small group of students acting as focus-group participants and one student acting as a moderator, analyze a recent ad from Nike, another from Reebok, and another from a smaller competitor such as Brooks or K-Swiss. After recording everyone's observations about the effectiveness of each ad, work as a team to refine and improve each ad. Be prepared to present your recommendations to the class.

The Creative Process

CHARLES JOURDAN
Paris

CHAPTER 9

Creativity, Creative Strategy, and Copywriting

After studying this chapter, you will be able to

1. Explain the meaning of creativity and its contribution to advertising

2. Outline the creative process and describe the steps for generating creative ideas

3. List the three elements of a creative strategy

4. Explain the purpose and content of a copy platform

5. Differentiate the hard-sell and soft-sell styles of advertising

6. Describe the most common appeals used in advertising

7. List the major types of copy that copywriters are assigned to write

How to achieve the proper exposure when shooting with fill-flash: Take time to set the ISO 4x higher. Then read an area which is as close as possible to an 18-percent gray and slow the shutter by two full stops. This should give you the proper ambient exposure. The f-stop will determine flash-to-subject distance and setting your ISO 4x higher will underexpose the TTL flash by two stops...

Yeah, Right!

Listen carefully. That sound you hear is your heart beating. You see, the moment has finally arrived. The moment that's kept you up nights. The moment you have chased since Photography 101.

Problem is, it won't last forever. It's up to you to turn it into a picture for the rest of the world to see.

Brett Froomer experienced this feeling the other day. He only had a split second to photograph this stuntman before he became toast. Thankfully, his assistants stood by with fire extinguishers. Meaning this lucky guy was saved in more ways than one.

Mr. Froomer knew this would make a great picture. He also knew that fill-flash would make it better. Fill-flash in a situation like this, you ask?

Well, yes. Fill-flash lets the film clearly see more details in the shadows without blowing out the highlights. You get richer colors. Better pictures. But who has the time for fill-flash calculations

under tricky conditions like these?

"Excuse me, Mr. Burning Man, would you please hold still while I figure this stuff out?"

Instead, Brett put his N90 on Programmed Auto, and let the 3D Matrix Meter go to work. It analyzes the light and adjusts for all the details in the highlights. *Note the helmet on the human fireball.* It analyzes the center and background areas too. Add the SB-25 Speedlight, and further analysis from the world's first 5-segment flash sensor and you've got 3D Matrix Automatic Balanced Fill-Flash. No other camera has it. It works in milliseconds. Fast enough for you?

The Nikon N90 can mean better pictures even under the most complicated lighting conditions. See? Not only was our stuntman moving rapidly (people on fire tend to do that), but the light in the scene was changing as well.

3D Matrix Balanced Fill-Flash is harder to say than it is to use. The N90 offers more automatic fill-flash modes than any other system. It works with all exposure modes, including manual, and with all AF and AI Nikkor lenses.

When the moment you've yearned for suddenly appears, you need more than a quick eye and a fast finger to turn it into art. You need an ingenious tool. Only then will you achieve your goal. Live your dreams. Capture the moment. The N90 was made for this purpose. Are you ready for it?

The N90 System

Nikon We take the world's greatest pictures

Facing an Advertising Challenge at Apple Computer
BATTLE OVER USER FRIENDLINESS IS ANYTHING BUT FRIENDLY

Michael Markman is fighting hard to be the friendliest. As manager of Apple Computer's advertising and creative services, Markman is responsible for overseeing the creation and production of the print and electronic ads that help Apple win new customers. For the last decade, desktop-computer users have tended to fall into one of two camps: Macs or PCs. Some prefer the Macintosh series (Macs) created by Apple Computer; others favor IBM-compatible personal computers (PCs) created by hundreds of companies, large and small. The differences between the two used to be clear-cut. The Mac's graphical way of presenting information kept you away from the computer's internal complexities. If you wanted a friendly system that wouldn't force you to learn arcane computer commands, you chose the Mac. However, the nature of the Mac-versus-PC competition changed when Microsoft introduced a software product called Windows. Among other things, Windows was designed to give PCs a similarly friendly feel (so similar, in fact, that Apple took Microsoft to court over Windows). When Microsoft

introduced its improved versions of Windows and Windows-compatible products (including a word processor called Word and a spreadsheet called Excel), it used the advertising theme "Making it easier." Markman now has to battle a competitor that's trying to take over the easy-to-use position that Apple has held for years.

Apple and Microsoft are engaged in a heated competition, trying to convince buyers that each has the better solution. (Apple sells both the hardware and the friendly software; Microsoft doesn't care whose PC hardware people buy, as long as they buy Windows along with it.) From Apple's perspective, the competition boils down to several key points. First, Windows runs on top of a program called DOS, which has a reputation for being difficult to use. Apple contends that even with Windows, the user can't be completely isolated from the DOS "jungle" lurking underneath. Second, Apple asserts that expansions such as larger disk drives and better displays are easier to add on the Mac. Third, not all PCs have enough power to run Windows, and Apple points out that upgrading these older

PCs so that they can run Windows costs a lot of time and money. Fourth, Apple maintains that the Mac is easier to connect to other computers in a multi-user office environment.

Therein lies the challenge. In many advertising situations, you can pick one key attribute, wrap it up in a catchy headline, add a provocative photo, and you've got a great ad. Not so in this case. The subject matter is technical, and it's compounded by the fact that the Mac-Windows competition is neither simple nor clear-cut.

If you were Michael Markman, what kind of creative strategy would you use to get Apple's message across? Would you appeal to potential buyers through logic or through emotion? Would you try to get your message across quickly or rely on a lot of copy to make your point? Do you think a logical appeal involving technical details would be most effective, or should you concentrate on other elements? Would you confront Microsoft directly in your ads or concentrate solely on the advantages of your own products?[1] ∎

CHAPTER OVERVIEW As Michael Markman knows, the creative decisions that define and shape Apple's advertising will determine whether the ads are effective or not. This chapter begins by discussing the meaning of creativity and what makes creative people creative. You'll see how creativity contributes to the business of advertising, and you'll discover the process that advertising professionals use to generate the ideas you see in ads. The second part of the chapter shows you how to develop a creative strategy (a concept introduced in Chapter 7). The third part of the chapter covers the art of copywriting and the copywriters that produce ads.

Creativity in Advertising

One of the most important, enjoyable, and fascinating topics in advertising is **creativity,** the ability to produce original ideas or original ways of looking at existing ideas.[2] Another way to look at creativity is as the ability to draw connections between previously unrelated ideas. Creativity is too often thought of as being relevant only in the context of art and creative writing. In fact, it's an important force with much broader influence (see Exhibit 9.1). Albert Einstein was being creative when he reexamined old assumptions about the universe and pieced together the new idea of relativity. Fred Smith was creative when he took an analogy from airline travel and redefined the shipping business by introducing Federal Express. Anita Roddick created The Body Shop retail chain by combining

EXHIBIT 9.1
Creativity: It's More Than Artwork

Advertising design is an obvious example of creativity in action, but every aspect of business presents opportunities for creativity, from picking catchy new product names to figuring out new ways to distribute products.

EXHIBIT 9.2
Taking Risks in Advertising

With the implications of the man's and woman's shirts depicted in this photo, an Israeli detergent manufacturer, Nekka, risks offending some readers but does communicate the point of invitingly clean clothes in a light-hearted and low-key manner. The copy (in Hebrew) goes beyond the humor to make selling points about low cost and effectiveness.

We were a mess . . .
and we came out twice as clean.

P-2.
A better economical detergent.

business concepts and social convictions. To be sure, much of the creativity in advertising involves imaginative artwork and clever copy, but as you'll see in this chapter, a great deal of creative thinking has to occur before you ever get to the stage of dealing with words and pictures. Some of the most creative thinking in advertising happens in the planning stages, as you try to find unique connections between the market and the product you want to advertise.

CREATIVE THINKING

If creativity is the art of generating original connections between often divergent facts and concepts, how do people go about producing those connections—how do they think in a creative fashion? People who think creatively usually exhibit three qualities: a willingness to take risks, divergent thinking, and a sense of humor.[3]

The first quality of creativity, a willingness to take risks, means being willing to live with failure if things don't work out, which allows you to break away from the crowd (see Exhibit 9.2). The style of thinking taught in most other courses and used for most intellectual tasks in life is called **convergent thinking.** This process starts with the facts you've collected and immediately narrows the field, trying to weed out all possibilities except one, using rules and logic to *converge* on the one "right" solution (see Exhibit 9.3). Think about how you solve math problems. You take the facts you're given, logically apply the rules you've learned, and arrive at the right answer.

CONVERGENT THINKING ONLY

Collected facts → One "best" answer

Immediately begin eliminating possibilities in search of the one best answer.

DIVERGENT AND CONVERGENT THINKING

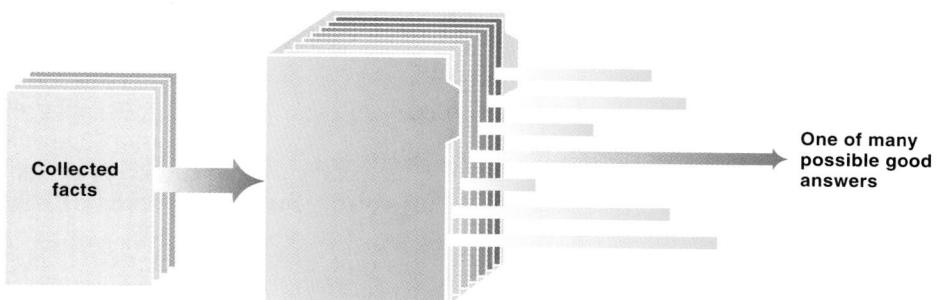

Collected facts → One of many possible good answers

First expand your realm of ideas to create as many possibilities as you can. Then begin narrowing down to reach a good answer.

EXHIBIT 9.3
Divergent and Convergent Thinking

Convergent thinking seeks to narrow the possibilities until it reaches the single "correct" answer. Divergent thinking starts in the opposite direction, by searching for even more possibilities and then selecting one good answer that may not necessarily be the only good answer.

In contrast, the second quality of creativity is **divergent thinking.** This open-ended approach to solving problems is based on the belief that some problems can be solved in more than one way and that every problem has more than one right answer. Instead of immediately narrowing the field of ideas you're dealing with, divergent thinking broadens the field, allowing you to explore ideas that are both logical and seemingly illogical and thus giving you lots of options and plenty of "thinking material" to work with. Only after you've expanded and explored all these possibilities can you apply convergent thinking to pick a good solution. Of course, you'll probably encounter more than one "correct" answer.[4]

Consider how you might demonstrate the effectiveness of the Huggies brand of diapers. You've probably seen lots of television commercials using happy babies, water absorption demonstrations, and other common approaches. Good approaches, perhaps, but with so many competitive brands advertising in the same basic manner, you might not stand out. Three employees from Ogilvy & Mather let their minds run loose and wound up with a poster displaying a mammoth dam holding back an enormous amount of water. The one word of copy on the poster, "Huggies," was written right across the top of the dam. It was a clever creative message, and one that is clearly tied to the benefits that Huggies offers consumers.[5]

To understand the need for divergent thinking in advertising, imagine what would happen if everyone applied only convergent thinking—they'd all end up with very similar advertising. It's the divergent thinking that generates fresh, *creative* advertising ideas. In fact, divergent thinking is used in any progressive activity, from artistic endeavors to the cutting edge of mathematics, theoretical physics, and other "logical" subjects. Divergent thinking lets people toss aside the old rules and look for new meanings.

When copywriter Michael Koelker of Foote, Cone & Belding was facing the task of creating a new ad concept for Levi's Dockers, he started thinking not about size and fit and material but about colors, specifically the colors in which Dockers are available. He asked himself "What if these colors walked in the door? What would they be like?" This notion allowed him to create personalities for each of the

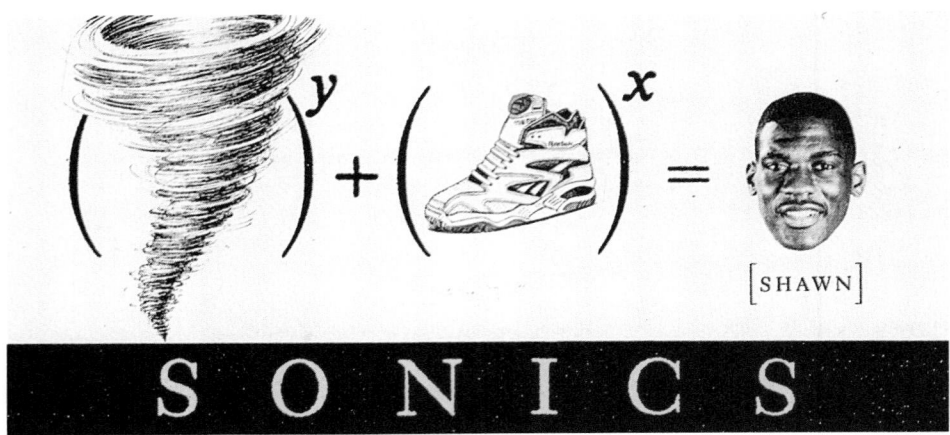

EXHIBIT 9.4
Using Humor to Make a Point

EXHIBIT 9.4
Using Humor to Make a Point

The Seattle SuperSonics used some clever humor to communicate the excitement of all-star forward Shawn Kemp's style of play.

colors; gray's personality is distinct from blue's, and so on through the range of Dockers colors. From Koelker's creative leap, FCB art director Leslie Caldwell designed television commercials to highlight each color so that each commercial was built around a color's personality.[6] Koelker's divergent thinking and creativity provided the spark for the whole campaign.

The last quality of creative thinking is a sense of humor, and along with it, a sense of intellectual and creative playfulness. The primary purpose of this humor isn't to make your job fun, although advertising can be a tremendous amount of fun; the value of humor to creativity is keeping your mind loose and open to new ideas and to new connections between old ideas. Even though most of your education and life experiences may have emphasized using convergent thinking, following the rules, and generally coloring inside the lines, being creative in advertising (or in any job) takes hard work to see beyond all the rules and to let humor help you make creative connections to solve problems on the job.[7] Humor is also used in the ads themselves; it can help make the same creative connections in the minds of your audience (see Exhibit 9.4).

Much of the creative thinking that occurs in advertising is aimed toward what professionals call the **Big Idea,** or the *creative concept.* The Big Idea is the unifying theme around which an ad or ad campaign is built. For instance, in the Dockers campaign, the Big Idea could have been defined as "creating personalities for each color in the product line and using those personalities to establish a unique market position for Dockers." An original Big Idea can go a long way toward helping an ad make its mark with today's busy, overcommunicated audiences.

THE CREATIVE CONTRIBUTION

Given all the attention that creativity receives in the advertising business, you might assume that everyone heartily endorses creativity, and the more of it the better. Not so. In fact, the contribution of creativity is one of the most hotly debated topics in the industry, centering on whether creativity actually helps sell anything. David Ogilvy calls much of today's advertising "pretentious and incomprehensible nonsense" and says it's designed only to win creative awards.[8] One might argue with the intensity of Ogilvy's criticism, but clearly, he points up an important issue: does creativity sell or doesn't it?

A look back at how advertising is supposed to work will help you put this controversy in context. The hierarchy of effects model (illustrated in Chapter 7) shows advertising moving an audience through awareness, comprehension, acceptance, and preference on the way to ownership. A similar concept is the AIDA model, which David Martin, founder of The Martin Agency and a supporter of Ogilvy's criticisms, uses to illustrate the problem with creativity. In the AIDA model, advertising moves the audience to *A*wareness, *I*nterest, *D*esire, and then *A*ction (making the purchase). Martin says that too much creative energy is being devoted to the awareness and interest stages and not enough is being focused on the desire and action stages.[9] In the defense of creativity's contribution, many agencies argue that with so much competition for attention in today's markets, they have to focus on breaking through the clutter to have anyone even notice their ads. However, Martin and Ogilvy would counter that without taking the extra step of persuading people to act, there's little point in getting their attention and building their desire for the product. Consider such recent efforts as the lavish "Uh-Huh" campaign for Diet Pepsi, in which one television commercial used 100 actors and a 70-piece band in a spoof of Congress. Over half the people in a follow-up survey could remember the "Uh-Huh" ads, but the campaign had almost no effect on sales of Diet Pepsi.[10]

The solution to the creativity controversy is to focus on what might be called *effective creativity,* or creativity that meets the objectives established for the ad. If the objective is to build awareness, then "Uh-Huh"-style campaigns are certainly valid. (The problem in Pepsi's case is that virtually everyone is already aware of Diet Pepsi, so awareness isn't a good objective.) However, if the objective is to build preference or motivate people to take action, then that's where the creative emphasis should be. The problem isn't with creative and entertaining ads; the problem is with creative and entertaining ads that don't sell effectively.

In addition, it's important never to lose sight of the fact that at the bottom of every successful advertising effort is a strong product that has something to offer customers. Good advertising can't save a bad product. As William Bernbach, co-founder of Doyle Dane Bernbach put it, "We never kid ourselves about the magic of advertising. The magic is in the product."[11] The secret is to use the creative power of advertising to communicate that product magic efficiently and effectively.

THE CREATIVE PROCESS

So how do advertising people come up with innovative ideas? It seems almost a conflict in terms to discuss the creative process, since *process* implies rules and regulations. However, many successful writers and artists do follow particular steps when trying to find creative solutions to advertising problems and opportunities. Several top creative people have shared the processes they've developed on the job. A pioneer in the study of creative thinking, Alex Osborn has defined the process in seven steps: orientation, preparation, analysis, ideation, incubation, synthesis, and evaluation.[12]

Orientation

The creative process starts when you clearly identify the problem you're trying to solve—or the opportunity you're trying to capitalize on—with your advertising. Young & Rubicam defines this as the *key fact,* the most important fact related to the advertising challenge you face.[13] Maybe the key fact is that some people in your market don't think they'll like the taste of your new diet soft drink, but they've never tried it. Your challenge is to use advertising to convince them to give it a try. Maybe the key fact is that you have an exciting new product that competitors are sure to imitate soon after you hit the market, and you need to establish your product as the leader as quickly as possible.

Preparation

Creative experts agree strongly on the need for preparation. Get as many pieces of information about the problem at hand and immerse yourself in them. The more facts and notes and anecdotes you have rattling around in your brain, the greater the chance you'll stumble across one of those unprecedented connections that define creative thought. For advertising, this means learning everything you possibly can about the product, the company, the competition, and the target customer (see Exhibit 9.5). In most cases, you'll use a combination of research you've done yourself, research provided by the client, and research gathered by others in your agency. Find out how the product is made, where the parts come from, and how it's sold. If the product is cattle feed, spend some time on a ranch and find out how

EXHIBIT 9.5
Advertising Creativity Needs Careful Preparation

Although advertising creativity seems far removed from exacting and intensive research, the most creative ads often spring from a thorough understanding of customers and competitors. It is research that provides this understanding.

EXHIBIT 9.6
Ideation and Divergent Thinking

A convergent, predictable approach to designing a perfume ad would probably lead to predictable ideas: sensual poses, luxurious rooms, romantic dinners, and so on. In contrast, opening up to every possibility leads to catchy new concepts, such as this model pouring out a huge bottle of very expensive perfume. The look is still sensual, but it now has a sense of humor and a touch of sassiness.

cows are fed. If it's a lawn-care product, spend some time in suburbia with people who are trying to make their grass grow. The creative flash might be related to any one of these elements. Former Ketchum Advertising CEO Hank Seiden once made a brand of orange juice stand apart from the competition by explaining the fact that different types of oranges are blended into the juice throughout the year. It was a small detail about the product, to be sure, but it was enough to make the product seem special.[14]

Analysis

Your next step is to break down everything you've learned in the preparation stage. Organize the facts and figures you've collected and take inventory of what you've got. Make sure you understand the technical details, market dynamics, competitive trends, and other forces that will affect the success of the advertising you're about to create. In short, become as much of an expert as you can in the time you have available.

Analysis is associated with *left-brain thinking,* which is generally assumed to encompass labeling, categorization, step-by-step processes, and the other sequential, logical thinking you do. In contrast, the next stage, ideation, involves *right-brain thinking.* Your right brain doesn't have all the hang-ups about rules and regulations and is perfectly happy to toss around bits and pieces of ideas, looking for meaningful patterns—regardless of whether those patterns fit the rules residing in your left brain.[15]

Ideation

With a head full of facts and knowledge, you're ready to generate those creative ideas that are the spark behind successful advertisements. Einstein described this as "combinatory play," meaning that you play around with the facts and thoughts, trying to find new connections.[16] This process is the divergent thinking discussed earlier, and these new connections represent creativity (see Exhibit 9.6). A common technique for generating ideas and connections between ideas is **free association,** letting your mind go and simply recording whatever thoughts come to the surface.[17] When people free associate in a group, the technique is called **brainstorming,** and the purpose is to pile up ideas one after another, with no criticism or analysis. Other good ways to get ideas flowing include using *analogies,* which are metaphors or "structural mirrors" that point out the similarities between ideas (e.g., people take a while to get up to speed in the morning, just as cars take a while to get up to speed when starting out), and using *juxtaposition,* putting two ideas side by side to see how they compare.

In addition, ad people use a variety of personal "tricks" to get ideas flowing, from exercising to horsing around the office. David Ogilvy, for instance, listened to music or read the *Oxford Dictionary of Quotations* to get creative inspiration.[18] Wieden & Kennedy copywriter Jerry Cronin, who wrote a remarkable series of print ads for Nike, says his inspirations range from the book a week he reads to "really bad sitcoms" he watches on television.[19] If you're an artist or art director used to working with images, try working with words for a while. Conversely, as a writer you might try communicating some thoughts visually. All these approaches can help the brain get into high gear.

Incubation

After the flurry of mental activity in the previous step, it's time to let ideas incubate. Give your conscious mind a break from the action, while your subconscious mind plays around with various ideas, looking for connections and insights. Getting away from the problem, even for a few hours, can help in several ways. You may have been fixated on a particular point that really isn't all that important, and some time away will help you put the point in its proper perspective. Although no one can say with much certainty how the subconscious mind works, it does seem able to wrestle with problems on its own. In addition, your subconscious is less likely to be overwhelmed by the rules and regulations that your conscious mind is always worried about, clearing the way to thinking that's more creative.

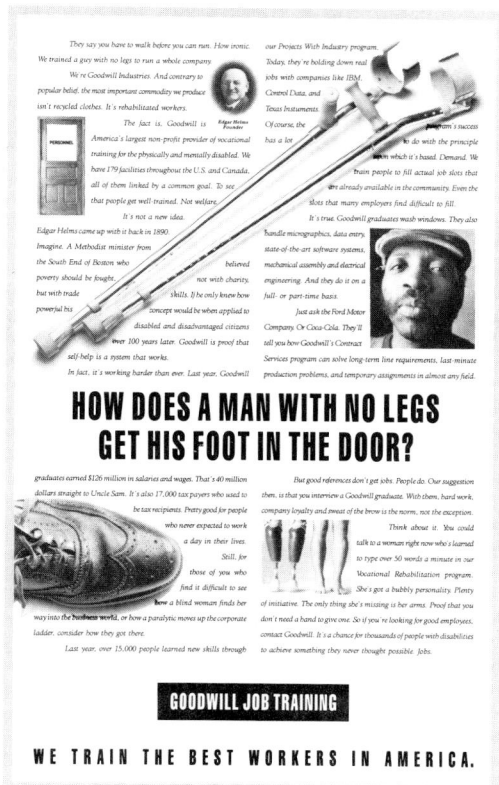

They say you have to walk before you can run. How ironic. We trained a guy with no legs to run a whole company.

We're Goodwill Industries. And contrary to popular belief, the most important commodity we produce isn't recycled clothes. It's rehabilitated workers.

The fact is, Goodwill is America's largest non-profit provider of vocational training for the physically and mentally disabled. We have 179 facilities throughout the U.S. and Canada, all of them linked by a common goal. To see that people get well-trained. Not welfare.

It's not a new idea. Edgar Helms came up with it back in 1890. Imagine. A Methodist minister from the South End of Boston who believed poverty should be fought, not with charity, but with trade skills. If he only knew how powerful his concept would be when applied to disabled and disadvantaged citizens over 100 years later. Goodwill is proof that self-help is a system that works.

In fact, it's working harder than ever. Last year, Goodwill our Projects With Industry program. Today, they're holding down real jobs with companies like IBM, Control Data, and Texas Instruments. Of course, the program's success has a lot to do with the principle upon which it's based. Demand. We train people to fill actual job slots that are already available in the community. Even the slots that many employers find difficult to fill.

It's true. Goodwill graduates wash windows. They also handle micrographics, data entry, state-of-the-art software systems, mechanical assembly and electrical engineering. And they do it on a full- or part-time basis.

Just ask the Ford Motor Company. Or Coca-Cola. They'll tell you how Goodwill's Contract Services program can solve long-term line requirements, last-minute production problems, and temporary assignments in almost any field.

HOW DOES A MAN WITH NO LEGS GET HIS FOOT IN THE DOOR?

graduates earned $126 million in salaries and wages. That's 40 million dollars straight to Uncle Sam. It's also 17,000 tax payers who used to be tax recipients. Pretty good for people who never expected to work a day in their lives. Still, for those of you who find it difficult to see how a blind woman finds her way into the business world, or how a paralytic moves up the corporate ladder, consider how they got there.

Last year, over 15,000 people learned new skills through

But good references don't get jobs. People do. Our suggestion then, is that you interview a Goodwill graduate. With them, hard work, company loyalty and sweat of the brow is the norm, not the exception.

Think about it. You could talk to a woman right now who's learned to type over 50 words a minute in our Vocational Rehabilitation program. She's got a bubbly personality. Plenty of initiative. The only thing she's missing is her arms. Proof that you don't need a hand to give one. So if you're looking for good employees, contact Goodwill. It's a chance for thousands of people with disabilities to achieve something they never thought possible. Jobs.

GOODWILL JOB TRAINING

WE TRAIN THE BEST WORKERS IN AMERICA.

EXHIBIT 9.7
Synthesizing a Creative Ad

The copy in this ad plays off the clever headline to communicate a solid customer benefit: well-trained employees.

There's no fixed rule about how long to let ideas incubate, but generally avoid thinking about the problem long enough to let your conscious mind become occupied with other thoughts and ideas, giving the subconscious enough time to get to work. With the hectic pace in advertising, your schedule will usually dictate how long you can let ideas incubate.

Synthesis

At this point in the process you probably have hundreds, perhaps thousands, of idea fragments. The next challenge is to catalog and organize your ideas, all the while trying to *synthesize* those fragments, or fit the pieces together, to create the Big Idea, the ingenious whole that makes sense out of the separate fragments (see Exhibit 9.7). You collect some thoughts into similar themes, toss out other thoughts that don't seem to fit, and always keep looking for patterns and connections. Young & Rubicam staffers in Amsterdam illustrated how synthesis works when they tried to convince more consumers to try a product called Mona Quark (something similar to yogurt). During their brainstorming session, they came up with ideas about the famous painting *Mona Lisa* (known for the subject's mysterious smile), good taste, dairy products, and Elsie (the "spokescow" for Borden dairy products in the United States). Through what they call a "lucky accident," the team synthesized the idea of their own spokescow, called Mona Lisa Quark and sporting the smile from the famous painting.[20]

Evaluation

As you begin to synthesize idea fragments, you need to start evaluating them to help separate the good ideas from those that aren't so good. Three general criteria apply here: ideas should be relevant to the context of your current advertising task, they should be original enough to generate surprise and interest, and they should be "rich" enough to generate new variations over the life of the **advertising campaign,** a series of coordinated advertisements and other promotional efforts.[21] You can see how the Mona Lisa Quark idea meets these three criteria. First, it is clearly relevant, since it combines the concept of good taste with the brand name

EXHIBIT 9.8
Creative Mindset

Experiencing life's possibilities to the fullest extent, including gritty street basketball, is an important way to generate new, creative ideas. To create an ad that feels like street basketball, as Nike and Athlete's Foot do here, it's important to know what street basketball really feels like.

and the friendly image of a cow. Second, most people probably haven't pictured the Mona Lisa smile on the face of a cow, so the idea will surprise consumers and probably catch their attention. Third, the possible situations for Mona Lisa Quark to appear in from one ad to the next are endless (e.g., shopping for groceries, visiting a dairy farm, helping a family prepare breakfast, and so on), so it's a good theme to unify multiple advertising variations.

If you sense that being creative can be a lot of hard work, you've grasped the picture exactly. In fact, when we single out people as being especially creative, the truth is often that such people simply work harder at generating creative ideas.[22]

THE CREATIVE MINDSET

In addition to these specific techniques for generating fresh ideas, some individual and organizational steps help ad professionals enhance their creative output. These involve both personal thinking habits and the organizational environment.

To improve your creativity, one of the most important habits you can cultivate is to voraciously consume ideas and experiences (see Exhibit 9.8). Ideas are to advertising what parts and supplies are to manufacturing. The French novelist Stendahl said he required "three or four cubic feet of ideas per day."[23] Ad legend David Ogilvy once said that he liked to hire people with "well-furnished minds."[24] In other words, the broader your experiences and the wider your exposure to music, literature, politics, and all the other human endeavors, the better you'll be at creating advertising. With a rich mental landscape in which to do your creative thinking, you can form analogies, find examples, look for inspiration, and draw connections between seemingly unrelated ideas—all of which leads to more creative thinking.

Your work environment also has a big effect on your creativity. Hanley Norins, for years a top creative talent at Young & Rubicam, suggests five guidelines to help advertisers and agencies build an environment that fosters and encourages creative thinking:[25]

1. Set your goals high and commit to them. The effort and enthusiasm required to meet challenging goals can stimulate creativity.

2. Cultivate an organizational culture that stimulates people toward hard work, innovation, and quality, both individually and in teams.

3. Provide incentives for creative work, which can include creative competitions, career advancement, financial rewards, and perhaps most important, an opportunity for people to have pride in their work.

4. Constantly renew the organization and its approach to advertising, keeping the best of the past while adding new thoughts and ideas.

5. Train people continuously, whether through formal seminars and classes or simply through one-on-one coaching from experienced employees and managers.

Once you recognize and practice the habits that creative professionals use, and do so in an environment that fosters creative thinking, you'll probably surprise yourself with just how creative you can be. In the following section, you'll learn how these creative concepts are put to work in developing an ad.

Creative Strategy

The **creative strategy** is the plan that defines three advertising efforts: the *art direction,* the artistic design of the ad (covered in Chapter 10); the *production values,* the various audio and visual components and stylistic touches that make up the ad (covered in Chapters 11 and 12); and the *copy platform.* The **copy platform** is essentially a checklist providing the background information that the copywriter and art director need to craft the ad (see Exhibit 9.9). The format of the copy platform varies from agency to agency, as does the name it goes by, but it generally contains some variation of the following items:[26]

EXHIBIT 9.9   **The Copy Platform**

McCann-Erickson Worldwide calls its copy platform a *creative contract*. You can see the type of information the agency looks for before it begins working on an ad, from a description of the target audience to objectives for audience behavior and attitude after exposure to the ad.

CONCEPTUAL BREAKTHROUGH

1. Describe the consumers we're most trying to motivate. (Their mindset, attitudes, psychographics, and demographics.)

2. What does this consumer look for in the category? Are there other categories the consumer can find it in?

3. What is it that makes our competitors' loyal users loyal to their brands?

4. What is it that makes our brand-loyal users loyal to our brand?

5. To build the brand, what perceptions must we change or reinforce?

6a. What action do you want people to take as a result of the advertising?

6b. Are there any issues blocking this desired behavior? (Relating to either external market factors, habit, or attitudes)

INFORMATIONAL BREAKTHROUGH

What have we uncovered about the brand that is newsworthy—or about the category that is newly relevant—that will help us build the brand?

COMMUNICATION BREAKTHROUGH

1. What do we want people to <u>think</u> about the brand?

2. What do we want people to <u>feel</u> about the brand?

- *A statement of the problem the advertising is expected to solve.* Briefly state the key fact, whatever situation, event, or problem in the market that prompted the advertiser to run the campaign. You might say something like "Younger consumers tend to think of this brand as a product for older people only," or simply "Sales have declined by 10 percent in the last year, and we need to reverse this trend."

- *The advertising objective.* Restate the objective(s) you established for the ad. Keep in mind that this statement covers only the task that *advertising* can be expected to accomplish. As discussed in Chapter 7, most advertising cannot reasonably be expected to deliver a specific number of sales, since so many other factors contribute to sales. Consider the statement, "Sales have declined by 10 percent in the last year, and we need to reverse this trend." Such a statement would be unreasonable if the cause of the sales decline is a new competitor with better performance, a problem that advertising alone probably can't solve.

- *A description of the product.* Give a quick overview of the product and its features. For many advertising tasks, the product is easy to understand and doesn't represent a major learning challenge for the copywriter and art director. In other cases, including financial services, medicine, and many high-tech areas, the people creating the advertising may need to spend a great deal of time learning about the product and its applications.

- *A profile of the target audience.* Summarize the demographic and psychographic information that describes who the target audience is and how that audience behaves (see Chapters 4 and 5).

- *An assessment of the competition.* Analyze and summarize the competition, in terms of both their advertising and their overall marketing strengths and weaknesses. This is particularly important when you plan to use comparative advertising.

- *The key customer benefit.* State the most distinctive benefit your product offers, taking customer needs and competitive strengths into consideration. You have three important points to consider: First, this must be a benefit that is important to a target customer, not just a feature of the product. Second, you should

EXHIBIT 9.10
Supporting the Key Benefit

The key benefit in this Healthy Choice ad is that consumers don't have to give up taste to get low fat. The ad supports both parts, with comparative nutritional data and with attractive visuals that represent taste.

generally resist the temptation to stuff an ad with two or more benefits—unless the key message is that your product is the only one to offer all these benefits. In nearly all cases, the simpler your message, the better its chance of registering in the minds of the audience. Third, you don't always have to be explicit about the benefits of a particular feature, as long as the audience understands the implied benefits. For instance, a recent ad for Prudential Real Estate Affiliates stresses the agents' attention to detail.[27] It doesn't say that attention to detail benefits home sellers by making sure that a house's special features are marketed properly. Most homeowners will understand the benefits of a real estate agent's attention to detail.

- *Support for the key benefit.* Make sure the key benefit and any secondary benefits spring from some aspect of the product and of the company that provides it (see Exhibit 9.10). In other words, you can't usually get away with saying that your product will make businesses more productive without explaining how you can accomplish this. For example, an ad for Stanford Graphics, a computer program for creating overhead transparencies, used the headline "Serious Presentations, Simply"—implying that it gives the user both power and ease of use.[28] The ad was careful to offer evidence to back up both parts of this claim. The best time to identify these supporting details is while developing the copy platform.

- *The selling strategy.* Clearly state the selling strategy. A number of advertising's selling strategies have been developed over the years, as advertisers and their agencies continue the search for effectiveness. One of the oldest selling strategies was identified by legendary copywriter and agency executive Rosser Reeves as the **unique selling proposition** (USP), a unique, specific benefit statement that's powerful enough on its own to motivate the customer to buy. Some years later, David Ogilvy asserted that advertisers can't expect every ad to sell on its own. He said that each ad has to contribute to the product and the company's overall *image.* Jack Trout and Al Ries claimed that by the 1970s, a flood of "me-too" ads and "me-too" products had rendered both USP and image advertising obsolete and that positioning strategies were the best way to go.[29] These approaches tend to be associated with eras, in which each new idea replaces an old strategy, but each is still useful in particular situations. The most effective ad professionals don't try to force one strategy onto every situation; they consider the circumstances and pick the best approach.

- *The selling style and the advertising appeal.* Define whether a hard-sell, soft-sell, or entertainment style of selling will be used and how the ad will appeal to the target audience. You have quite a few choices in both these areas.

THE SELLING STYLE: HARD OR SOFT

Advertisers, agencies, and individual campaigns can take on definite personalities. Leo Burnett, founder of the international agency that bears his name, described his agency's style as "straightforward without being flatfooted, warm without being mawkish." He acknowledged the enormous importance of getting noticed in a crowded marketplace but said "the art is getting noticed naturally without screaming or without tricks."[30] Contrast this with ESPN's "In Your Face" campaign or the stereotypical local television ad from an appliance retailer or car dealer screaming that "We won't be undersold!" No particular style or personality is inherently better; the choice is made according to the nature of the product, the competition, and the target audience.

Hard-sell advertising is just like it sounds, pounding at the audience with demands to "buy now!" or promises of being the best, the greatest, the most wonderful product in the world. The screaming car dealer is a great example of this style of advertising, which tends to be used when price is the buyer's most important decision criterion. However, don't confuse hard-sell ads with well-crafted ads that happen to exhibit a lot of energy and persuasive passion. The distinguishing features of hard-sell ads are the constant pressure to "buy now, buy now."

To the unsuspecting reader, the ad looked liked valuable advice from the National Mental Health Association. It listed the symptoms of clinical depression, a serious mental health condition said to affect more than 10 percent of the U.S. population. The information in the ad was fine; it was how the ad was paid for that caught critics' attention. Eli Lilly, one of the world's largest manufacturers of medicines, had shelled out between $3 million and $4 million for the advertising campaign.

The ad urges people to tell a doctor if they experience several of the symptoms for more than two weeks. (Having the symptoms for that long is usually a tipoff that you might be suffering from something more serious than just a bad case of the blues.) If you go to your regular doctor and are diagnosed with depression, chances are that your treatment will involve antidepressant medication. The number one antidepressant drug is called Prozac, and you guessed it, the company that makes Prozac is none other than Eli Lilly.

Eli Lilly contends that it is doing the public a big service, and it's hard to dispute the fact that people need to know more about clinical depression. The disorder is linked to 16,000 suicides a year and costs the country billions of dollars in treatments and reduced employee productivity. However, critics such as Dr. Sidney Wolfe of the Public Citizen Health Research Group want to know why Eli Lilly's financial backing is mentioned in the ad if the company's only interest is helping the public. Thus the dilemma: If Eli Lilly is actually trying to broaden its customer base, is it ethical to use an ad that looks like a public service announcement? However, if Eli Lilly is trying to educate the public out of concern for anyone suffering from clinical depression, doesn't the company deserve recognition for this public service?

The dilemma gets even more complicated when you consider who some of the other critics are. The American Psychiatric Association supports the ad campaign; the American Psychological Association doesn't. These two groups represent opposing approaches to treating clinical depression: antidepressant drugs and psychotherapy. Psychiatrists are medical doctors who can prescribe drugs such as Prozac. Psychologists are not medical doctors and therefore can't prescribe drugs; they rely on psychotherapy. The psychiatrists say that medical exams should be part of any program of treatment, so starting with a medical doctor is always advisable. The psychologists counter that the Eli Lilly–funded advertising will channel people to their regular family doctors and from there to psychiatrists—meaning that drugs, not therapy, will be the preferred treatment. According to this interpretation, Eli Lilly and the psychiatrists stand to benefit at the expense of the psychologists.

Eli Lilly's dilemma is just one part of the broader picture of advertising's role in health care. An issue that troubles many observers and not a few doctors is the influence that advertising might be having on a doctor's prescription decisions. With a constant stream of new drugs and other medical innovations, keeping up with all the information is a mammoth task for doctors. Critics worry that doctors who don't have the time or the inclination to read up on new drugs will rely too heavily on advertising to make their choices. This and other ethical issues in medical advertising promise to be hot debates as pharmaceutical makers try to recoup the huge development costs of new drugs and as doctors try to sort through ever-increasing numbers of maladies and cures.

What's Your Opinion?

1. *Should pharmaceutical companies be allowed to fund public service campaigns that might benefit the company financially?*
2. *What role should advertising play in the prescription drug industry?*

Soft-sell advertising is the stylistic opposite of hard sell (see Exhibit 9.11); soft sell takes a more subtle approach to persuasion and motivation in an effort to build desire for the product. Soft-sell ads don't usually demand particular audience behavior (such as the "buy now" exhortations of hard sell); indeed, such ads rarely appear to urge people to buy at all. However, that's not really the case: instead of simply making a demand, the soft-sell style tries to create a situation in the audience's mind that will lead to the desired purchase decision. Well-crafted soft-sell ads are every bit as effective as hard-sell ads in selling products—and more effective in some cases because hard-sell ads turn many people off.[31]

Circumstances in the market sometimes influence the advertiser's style choices. During downturns in the economy, for instance, glitzy appeals to a luxurious lifestyle might be toned down to avoid offending people experiencing difficult financial times. Natural disasters can also have a temporary effect on ad style. After Hurricane Andrew raged across southern Florida in 1992, some banks and insurance companies switched from a soft-sell "feel-good" style of ad to a straightforward, fact-filled ad that gave people vital information. Barnett Banks, the largest banking system in Florida, ran ads listing which of its branches were still in

EXHIBIT 9.11
Soft-Sell Advertising

With three simple words, copywriter Margaret Wilcox created a master-piece of soft-sell advertising. Consumers who've been inundated with Nike's "Bo knows . . ." series (featuring Bo Jackson in a wide variety of athletic endeavors) for the past several years will recognize the play on words that Wilcox crafted with "Keds knows bows." Not only does Keds capitalize on Nike's efforts; it positions these shoes as a gentle and feminine alternative to "jock shoes."

operation and the addresses of emergency check-cashing locations.[32] If you've just lost your house in a hurricane and the neighborhood bank is shut down, emergency information is a lot more valuable than a sales pitch.

THE APPEAL: CONNECTING WITH THE HEAD AND THE HEART

Every successful ad works because it makes an effective appeal to some need or desire in the people who view, read, or listen to it. The **advertising appeal** is an attempt to draw a connection between the product being advertised and some need or desire that the audience feels. People are motivated to close the gaps in their lives, the gaps between the way they perceive things to be and the way they'd like things to be. It is the appeal's job to stand up and say, "This is the product that will meet that need or fulfill that desire." To be successful, an advertising appeal must correspond to the target customer's buying process.

Appeals fall into two general categories: **logical appeals,** also known as *rational appeals,* aim for the buyer's head, and **emotional appeals** aim for the buyer's heart. A logical appeal tries to sell products based on performance, features, or the ability to solve problems. In contrast, an emotional appeal tries to sell products based on the satisfaction that comes from purchasing and then either owning or giving the product as a gift. Say you have two ads to create, one for diamond wedding rings and another for industrial diamonds (used to cut glass, etch steel, etc.). Clearly, an emotional appeal would probably be more effective for the wedding rings, and a logical appeal would probably be more effective for the industrial diamonds. Consider some of the tag lines used in jewelry ads from the DeBeers diamond consortium, such as "Diamonds are forever" and "Show her you'd marry her all over again." These are strong emotional appeals that draw a

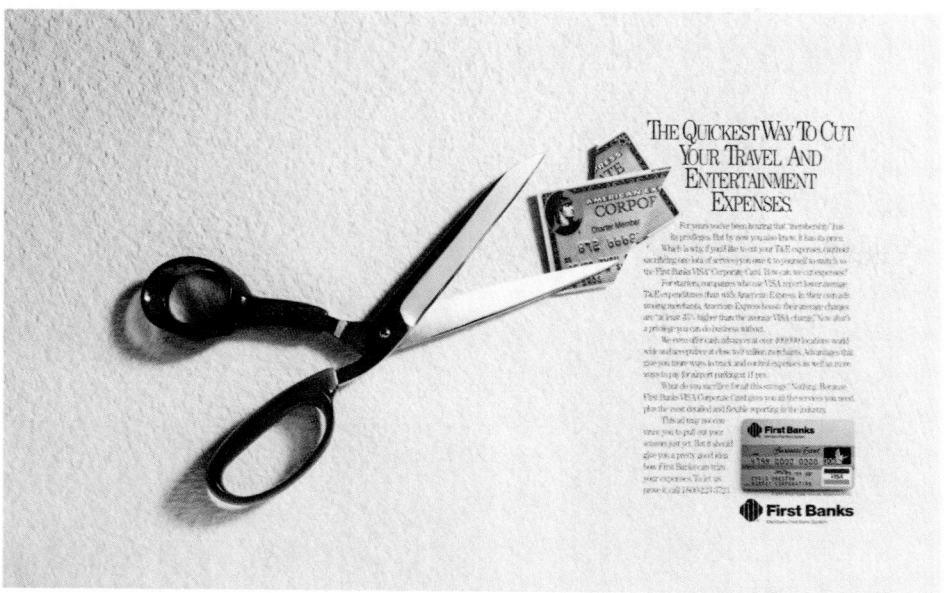

EXHIBIT 9.12
Logical and Emotional Appeals

The First Banks ad uses a simple logical appeal to businesspeople: use our card and you'll save money on travel and entertainment. The Wilson ad, in contrast, appeals to the competitiveness that many tennis players feel.

connection between the product and the need for love, commitment, and emotional security. On the other hand, your ad for industrial diamonds isn't going to talk about love and marriage. You'll want to use a logical appeal that makes a case for the performance and features of the product. The two ads shown in Exhibit 9.12 demonstrate the difference between logical and emotional appeals.

Defining appeals as either logical (thinking) or emotional (feeling) is oversimplifying the situation, however. All ads contain an element of both logic and emotion, and it's unlikely that any successful ad appeals exclusively to one or the other. For example, an ad for something as seemingly logical as a piece of office equipment can appeal to emotion. A person's decision to buy a computer or copier might be tangled up with a concern about job performance, an aversion to risk, or a fear of being ridiculed for making an illogical decision. People are people, and they all have hopes, fears, desires, and dreams, regardless of the job they have or the products they're buying. Even a highly technical ad can appeal to a buyer's emotions if the logic in the appeal leads to reduced stress on the job, increased chances of personal success, or some other satisfying emotional scenario. An ad for Canon copiers and laser printers came right out and said that the high-quality reports you could prepare with its equipment would help "get you the promotion."[33]

Conversely, as researchers Bobby Calder and Charles Gruder point out, emotional ads work only to the extent that the emotion becomes part of the buyer's

thinking process.[34] In other words, it's important that emotional appeals be tied to the product being advertised. It's not enough just to arouse feelings of friendship, security, or love; those feelings have to get connected to the purchase decision. Otherwise, the ad will be an exercise in feeling, not selling. If you're creating an ad for Hallmark Mother's Day cards, you don't want people simply to conjure up positive memories of Mom; you want them to translate those feelings into the action of buying a Hallmark card. You wouldn't say, "You sure love your mom, don't you?" You'd say, "Show Mom how much you love her by sending a Hallmark card this year."

Advertisers can employ a variety of specific appeals, most of which can be structured as logical, emotional, or a combination of the two. The most common types of appeals are based on price or value; quality; star identification; ego; fear or anger; the five senses; sex, love, and social acceptance; and novelty.[35]

Price or Value Appeals

Promising to give buyers more for their money is one of the most effective appeals you can use, particularly in terms of audience recall.[36] A value appeal can be accomplished in several ways: lowering the price and making people aware of the new price, keeping the price the same but offering more, or keeping the price and the product the same and trying to convince people that the product is worth whatever price you're charging.

Price alone, however, is rarely an effective appeal. You're not going to sell a lot of bad food or foul-smelling cologne, no matter how low the price. Only when the rest of the product offering is at least minimally acceptable will price become an effective appeal. In many cases, price is used as the extra punch in an appeal, such as when you offer high performance at a low price.

Quality Appeals

The flip side of a price appeal is an appeal to quality (see Exhibit 9.13). An ad for the Wittnauer Longlife wristwatch mentions the titanium case, the 20-year guarantee on the battery, and Wittnauer's 100-year history of quality watches. Looking at the close-up photo of the gray watch, a reader would almost think the thing is carved from a block of granite. The copy, artwork, and muted presentation of the ad speak of solidity, leaving the impression that the Wittnauer must be a high-quality product.[37]

An appeal to quality can work only if the product possesses the right level of quality, of course. Wittnauer can use this appeal because the company has been around for more than a century, because it offers a lengthy guarantee, and because its watches can effectively back up the promise made in the ad. However, consumer and organizational audiences have seen the word "quality" in ads so many times that many have grown skeptical of such claims. If you're going to use this approach, it's important to have the kind of supporting material that Wittnauer brought to its ad.

Star Appeals and Testimonials

The public's fascination with superstar athletes and entertainers is the foundation of the **celebrity endorsement ad.** Celebrity endorsements are extremely popular in Japan, particularly when they feature American stars such Sylvester Stallone, Paul Newman, and Woody Allen (all of whom have shown up in Japanese television commercials but who are generally reluctant to endorse products on U.S. television).[38] The presumed pull of the star appeal is that people like to identify with their favorite stars and will therefore be positively influenced by a star's appearance in an ad (see Exhibit 9.14). The presence of a star may also catch people's attention when they're flipping through a magazine or through television channels.

A related appeal is the **testimonial,** in which real users of the product—celebrities or not—make the sales pitch by showing the product in use, discussing

EXHIBIT 9.13
An Appeal Based on Quality

With a clever twist on the idea of trying to predict technological advancements, Mercedes-Benz makes a point in this South African ad about the lasting quality of its products. The ad could have said simply, "This car will last for 30 years," but by involving the audience in the headline payoff, the message becomes much more effective and lasting.

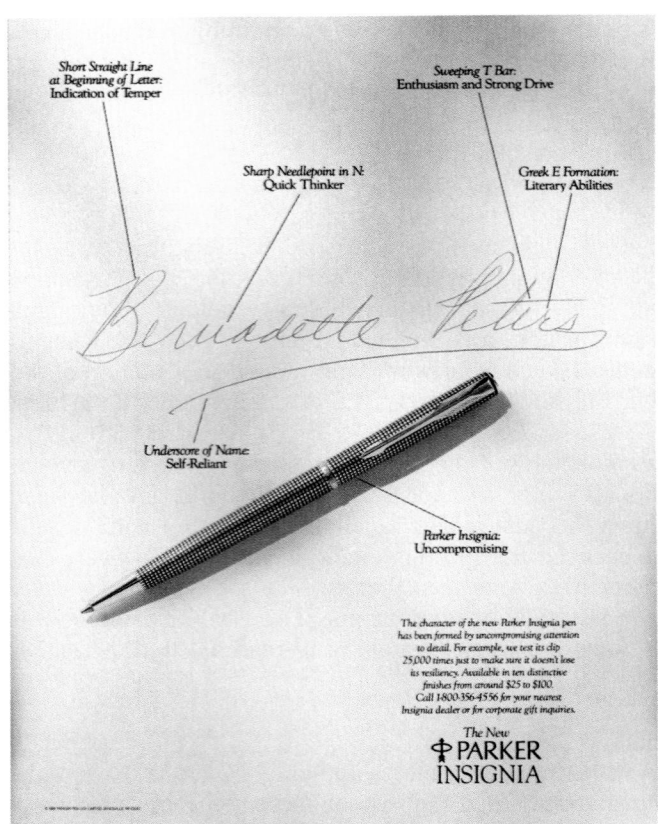

Short Straight Line
at Beginning of Letter:
Indication of Temper

Sweeping T Bar:
Enthusiasm and Strong Drive

Sharp Needlepoint in N:
Quick Thinker

Greek E Formation:
Literary Abilities

Underscore of Name:
Self-Reliant

Parker Insignia:
Uncompromising

The character of the new Parker Insignia pen
has been formed by uncompromising attention
to detail. For example, we test its clip
25,000 times just to make sure it doesn't lose
its resiliency. Available in ten distinctive
finishes from around $25 to $100.
Call 1-800-356-4556 for your nearest
Insignia dealer or for corporate gift inquiries.

The New
Φ PARKER
INSIGNIA

EXHIBIT 9.14
Celebrity Appeals

Celebrity appeals, and the effort to align a product's image with a celebrity's image, don't necessarily have to include a photo of the star.

the benefits they got from using it, or comparing it to their experiences with competitive products. As explained in Chapter 3, testimonials (endorsements) entail significant legal issues that you need to watch out for, but a skillfully executed testimonial is powerful advertising because the core message comes from satisfied customers, not the advertiser.[39]

Ego Appeals

Most consumers are open to appeals to their ego, whether the appeal relates to physical appearance, intellect, sense of humor, or any other real or imagined personal quality. The L'Oreal ads with Cybill Shepherd are a classic example of this approach. When she admits that the product may be more expensive but says, "I'm worth it," she is appealing directly to the egos of the potential buyers, urging them to think the same of themselves.

Not all ego appeals are quite so up front, however. A more subtle approach is probably more appropriate when the purchaser will be identified with the particular product for as long as he or she owns it or uses it. What might happen if you used L'Oreal's "I'm worth it" declaration to promote a car? Most likely, the car would get a reputation as a vehicle for people with big egos, and some people might be embarrassed to be seen driving a car with that reputation. L'Oreal can get away with its slogan because its customers don't have to show the world that they bought the product (usually no one knows what brand of hair-care products you're using). The ego appeal happens in private, so it works without embarrassing the audience.

Fear or Anger Appeals

Extreme cases of emotional appeals are those based on fear or anger. Fear has been used to sell a variety of products, from AT&T's phone systems (fear about losing your job if you don't buy an AT&T system) to Campbell's bean and pea soups (fear of getting cancer if you don't eat enough fiber). However, appeals to fear have to be managed carefully. Extreme appeals to fear can anger the audience

The Uncertain Appeal of Celebrity Appeals

Celebrity endorsement is a popular creative strategy in both print and electronic advertising, but it remains something of a theoretical curiosity. On the one hand, it seems like a great way to build visibility and preference for your brand: by putting your product next to the celebrity, some of the person's star appeal should rub off on your product. Experts suggest that, depending on the product, celebrity endorsement can work at three levels: (1) when the star is physically attractive, (2) when the star is trusted by the public (particularly if the star has some legitimate expertise in relation to the product), and (3) when the celebrity's image is compatible with the product (a wholesome star for a wholesome product, for instance).

On the other hand, it's hard to find a lot of evidence to support the continued and increasing use of the celebrity appeal. In one survey, consumers ranked it as the least convincing of all advertising appeals. Does this mean that it's ineffective? Not necessarily. James Patterson of the J. Walter Thompson agency argues that many people are simply too embarrassed to admit being influenced by celebrities and that, in spite of what consumers say in surveys, celebrities can indeed build emotional bonds for products. In other words, celebrities might actually persuade consumers more often than consumers would like to admit.

However strong the cases for and against celebrity endorsements, most experts agree on several points. First, it's important to match the celebrity and the product. A classic mismatch was stately actor John Houseman's appearance in a McDonald's commercial. Houseman was a great actor, of course, but it was hard for people to picture him eating at McDonald's. Another mismatch was actress Cybill Shepherd appearing in a commercial for the Beef Industry Council, when she later admitted that she rarely eats meat. Bill Cosby has been an effective endorser for some advertisers (Jell-O, Kodak, and Coca-Cola) but less effective for others (the former E. F. Hutton financial services firm).

Second, it's important to remember that celebrities are human beings with public lives outside of their advertising appearances. These public images become associated with their products' public images, so if the star gets in trouble, the brand can suffer—if not in sales, at least in public embarrassment. This is one of the reasons animated cartoon characters such as Bart Simpson are popular as "celebrity" endorsers. An executive at Fox Television, the network that airs *The Simpsons,* put it bluntly: "Bart will never get caught doing crack."

Third, it's not simply a matter of picking celebrities who are well liked by the public. A study from Total Research of Princeton, New Jersey, uncovered some interesting differences between celebrities' likability scores and their effectiveness as product endorsers. In a list of 54 celebrities, singer Paula Abdul ranked twentieth in terms of likability but ninth in terms of endorsement effectiveness. Comedian Bob Hope exhibited the reverse situation, ranking first in likability but eighth in effectiveness. However, in spite of all the confusing and sometimes contradictory evidence, the use of celebrity endorsers is a big part of the advertising business.

Apply Your Knowledge
1. *If you were planning an ad campaign for Levi's blue jeans, who would you pick as a celebrity endorser? Why?*
2. *Would you ever use a celebrity who had previously appeared in ads for one of your competitors? Explain your answer.*

or even cause them to block out the message entirely.[40] On the other hand, reducing someone's level of fear or anxiety, rather than artificially increasing it, can be effective. Perrier recognized that some people felt compelled to drink alcoholic beverages in social situations, out of fear of being rejected. To get people to start drinking Perrier in public, the company used advertising that reduced those fears of rejection and sent the message that it's acceptable not to drink alcohol.[41]

Similar to fear, anger can also be a strong emotional pull. The organization known as Handgun Control once sent out an appeal for money to fight the National Rifle Association's congressional lobbying efforts. The message on the outside of the envelope read: "Enclosed: Your first real chance to tell the National Rifle Association to go to hell!"[42] If you were mad at the NRA to start with, you probably ripped the envelope open. As a matter of fact, if you supported the NRA, you probably ripped the envelope open too.

Sensory Appeals

Many ads aim right for one or more of the five senses of taste, touch, vision, smell, and hearing (see Exhibit 9.15). When you see a close-up shot of a Wendy's hamburger in a television commercial and reach for your car keys, an appeal to your sense of taste is at work. A recent magazine ad for Sheaffer pens didn't even bother with any copy beyond the brand name and some small type with a toll-free phone number; the ad was entirely a visual appeal showing a half-dozen beautifully crafted writing instruments.[43]

EXHIBIT 9.15
Appeals to Senses Aren't Always Inviting

3M appeals to consumers' desire to protect their senses in this ad for paint stripper. Rather than evoking the aroma of great food or expensive perfume, the ad evokes the unpleasant and harmful odor of other paint strippers to make its selling point.

Advertisers often combine an appeal to one of the five senses with a supporting appeal, such as price. When you see that the tasty hamburger is on sale, the theory is that you'll be doubly motivated to go and buy one. The Sheaffer ad's visual appeal was also an appeal to the buyer's sense of quality, but there was no need to describe the product's quality in words—the photograph did all the talking.

Sex, Love, and Social Acceptance Appeals

Another common approach is the appeal that implicitly or perhaps even explicitly promises rewards from a spectrum of personal interaction that ranges from social acceptance to friendship, love, and sex. Sure antiperspirant's slogan "Raise your hands if you're sure," later replaced by the "Sure/not sure" ads, showed people whose lack of a good antiperspirant embarrassed them in social settings. The message: buy Sure and you won't be embarrassed.

Another standby in advertising is selling with sex or the implied promise of sex. Guess Jeans and Calvin Klein's Obsession perfume are well-known examples of this approach. The sex appeal has to be used with some caution, however. At its extreme, it can keep an ad from running, when print or electronic media refuse to accept it for publication or broadcast. Also, attempts to present a sexy image may cross the line and offend some readers and viewers as simply sexist, not sexy.[44]

Subliminal Advertising

You've probably heard about **subliminal advertising,** ads in which the decoding is supposed to happen subconsciously through the use of visual symbols, subaudio messages, or visual messages shown for a very brief period. A frequently cited example is a movie theater experiment in which the words "Hungry? Eat Popcorn" and "Drink Coca-Cola" were projected on the screen for one-three thousandth of a second. Supposedly, the theater's sales of both popcorn and Coke jumped during the test period, but these impressive results were concocted by the "researcher," who worked for the Subliminal Projection Company. He was trying to drum up business for his firm.[45] Nevertheless, he caused such an uproar that some states passed laws banning subliminal advertising, and the hunt for hidden persuasion was on.

Beginning in 1973 with the publication of a book called *Subliminal Seduction,* by Wilson Bryan Key, much has been made of nude figures, the word *sex,* and other such things supposedly hidden in advertising product photos and sometimes on products themselves. For example, Key claims that Ritz crackers have the word *sex* embedded on both the top and bottom of the cracker. And he says the embedded message even makes the crackers taste better. This sounds incredible, but he has been able to generate a significant amount of public mistrust of the advertising profession. Even so, no objective evidence supports this sort of trickery, and little psychological evidence suggests that it would work even if anyone were doing it.[46]

Novelty Appeals

A number of advertisers in recent years have tried to catch the audience's attention by creating ads that are really strange. Simply making an advertisement off-the-wall doesn't ensure success, however. Advertising critics and some retailers often berate the strange ads. The "Reeboks Let U.B.U." campaign from several years ago was definitely different, with a cast of characters that included a three-legged man, a fairy godmother with a briefcase, and someone vacuuming her front yard—but it left the audience out in the cold. Simply making an impression isn't enough, and getting people to remember your name doesn't mean they'll buy your product.[47]

On the other hand, given the uncertainties of what the profession knows about how advertising works, and the difficulty of getting the audience's attention in today's crowded markets, don't immediately dismiss the off-the-wall approach. Just be careful not to lose sight of your advertising message, and make sure it doesn't get buried by any strange elements in the ad.

Copywriters and Copywriting

Given the importance of copy, it comes as no surprise that copywriters are key players in the advertising process. In fact, many of the most notable leaders and voices in the industry began their careers as copywriters, including Jane Maas, David Ogilvy, Rosser Reeves, Leo Burnett, and William Bernbach. As a profession, copywriting is somewhat unusual because so many of its top practitioners have been in their jobs for years, even decades (rather than moving up the management ranks as is usual in many professions). Copywriters can either work for agencies or set themselves up as free-lancers, selling their services to agencies and advertisers. Because it presents endless opportunities to be creative, copywriting is one of those rare jobs that can be fresh and challenging year after year.

Although successful copywriters share a love of language with novelists, poets, and other writers, copywriting is first and foremost a business function, not an artistic endeavor (see Exhibit 9.16). The challenge isn't to create works of literary merit, but to meet advertising objectives. This doesn't mean that copywriting isn't an art, however; it's simply art in pursuit of a business goal. Nor is it easy. Such noted literary writers as Stephen Vincent Benét, George Bernard Shaw, and Ernest Hemingway tried to write ad copy and found themselves unable to do it effectively.[48] It's the combined requirements of language skills, business acumen, and an ability to create under the pressure of tight deadlines and format restrictions (such as the limited number of words you have to work with) that make copywriting so challenging—and so endlessly rewarding.

Copywriters have many styles and approaches to writing, but most agree on one thing: copywriting is hard work. It can involve a great deal of planning and coordinating with clients, legal staffers, account executives, researchers, and art directors. In addition, it usually entails hammering away at your copy until it's as good as it can be. David Ogilvy talked about doing 19 drafts of a single piece of copy and writing 37 headlines for a Sears ad in order to get 3 possibilities to show to the client.[49] Actually, the chance to write and rewrite that many times is a luxury that most copywriters don't have; they often must produce copy on tight schedules with unforgiving deadlines (such as magazine publication deadlines).

The task of copywriting is most often associated with the headlines and copy you see in an ad, but copywriters actually develop a wide variety of other materials, from posters to catalogs to press releases, as well as the words you hear in radio and television commercials. This section examines what copywriters write, starting with the key copy elements of print ads.

PRINT COPY

Copywriters are responsible for every word you see in print ads, whether the words are in a catchy headline or in the fine print at the bottom of the page. The three major categories of copy are headlines, body copy, and slogans.

Headlines

The **headline,** also called a *heading* or a *head,* constitutes the dominant line or lines of copy in an ad. Headlines are typically set in larger type and appear at the top of the ad, although there are no hard-and-fast rules on headline layout.[50] **Subheads** are secondary headlines, often written to move the reader from the main headline to the body copy. Even if there is a pageful of body copy and only a few words in the headline, the headline is the most important piece of copy for two reasons: First, it serves as the "come-on" to get people to stop turning the page and check out your ad (see Exhibit 9.17). Second, as much as 80 percent of your audience may not bother to read the body copy, so whatever message these nonreaders carry away from the ad will have to come from the headline.[51]

Copywriters can choose from a variety of headline types, each of which performs a particular function:[52]

- *News headlines.* News headlines present information that's new to the audi-

EXHIBIT 9.16
Creative, with a Business Purpose

It might have been tempting to talk at length about the glories of the great outdoors or the pleasures of solitude, but the copy in this ad (and the visual) works toward promoting the product. The outdoors and solitude play a role, but it's a role directed at selling a product.

ence, such as announcing a new store location, a new product, or lower prices. This approach is common because potential customers are often looking for new solutions, lower prices, and other relevant changes in the marketplace. For example, a newspaper ad from the Silo home electronics chain announced a recent sale using a news headline: "Everything on Sale! 4 Days Only! 5–20% Off Everything!"[53] Headlines like this are typical in local newspaper advertising.

- *Emotional headlines.* The emotional appeal described earlier in the chapter is represented by emotional headlines. The quotation headline "I'm sick of her ruining our lives" was used in an ad for the American Mental Health Fund to echo the frustration some parents feel when they can't understand their teenagers' behavior. Combined with a photo of a sad and withdrawn teenage girl, the headline grabs any parent who has felt such frustration, and the body copy goes on to explain that families shouldn't get mad at people with mental illnesses but should help them get treatment for their conditions.[54]

- *Benefit headlines.* The benefit headline is a statement of the key customer benefit. An ad for Quicken personal finance software used the question-form headline: "How do you know exactly where your money goes and how much you have?" followed by "It's this simple" above a photograph of the product package.[55] The customer benefit is keeping better track of your money, and Quicken is the solution offered.

- *Directive headlines.* Headlines that direct the reader to do something, or at least suggest the reader do something, can motivate consumer action. Such headlines can be a hard sell, such as "Come in now and save," or they can be something more subtle, such as "Just feel the color in these black and whites," the headline in an ad for Ensoniq keyboards.[56]

- *Offbeat and curiosity headlines.* Humor, wordplay, and mystery can be effective ways to draw readers into an ad. An ad promoting vacation travel to Spain used the headline "Si in the dark," with a photo of a lively nighttime scene. The word *Si* is catchy because it first looks like an error, until the reader reads the body copy to learn that the ad is talking about Spain (*si* is Spanish for "yes").[57]

- *Hornblowing headlines.* The hornblowing headline, called "Brag and Boast" heads by the Gallup & Robinson research organization, should be used with care. Customers have seen it all and heard it all, and "We're the greatest" headlines tend to sound arrogant and self-centered. This isn't to say that you

This time you can try your hand at a pair of business-to-business ads. These two ads promote the same product, a computer accessory that lets users process graphic images on their screens. Even without understanding the technical content of the ads, you can see the different approaches: The clown ad works with a familiar figure of speech (clowning around), whereas the "tacky dresser" ad might be more related to the benefit of color-image processing.

These two ads were tested by Readex, a research firm that specializes in testing business-to-business ads. For this exercise, you'll be interested in two figures from the Readex test: the percentage of the audience that remembered seeing the ad and the percentage that found it of interest.

Which of these two ads do you think scored higher on the "remembered seeing" test and on the "found of interest" test? Be prepared to explain your answers.

can't stress superiority; you just need to do it in a way that takes the customer's needs into account, and the headline must be honest. The headline "Neuberger & Berman Guardian Fund" followed by the subhead "#1 Performing Growth and Income Fund" blows the company's own horn but also conveys an important product benefit. Since investors look for top-performing mutual funds, the information about being number one is relevant.[58]

- *Slogan, label, or logo headlines.* Some headlines show a company's slogan, a product label, or the organization's logo. Powerful slogans like Hallmark's "When you care enough to send the very best" can make great headlines because they click with the reader's emotions. Label and logo headlines can build product and company awareness, but they must be used with care. If the label or logo doesn't make some emotional or logical connection with the reader, the ad probably won't succeed.

Headlines often have maximum impact when coupled with a well-chosen graphic element, rather than trying to carry the message with words alone. In fact, the careful combination of the two can increase the audience's involvement with the ad, especially if one of the two says something ironic or unexpected that has to be resolved by considering the other element. A magazine ad for Easter Seals had the headline "After all we did for Pete, he walked out on us." At first, you think the birth-defects organization is complaining. Then you see a photo of Pete with new artificial legs, walking away from a medical facility. It's a powerful combination that makes the reader feel good about the things Easter Seals can do for people.[59]

Jacomo.
The perfumer.

Body Copy

The second major category of copy is the **body copy,** which constitutes the words in the main body of the ad, apart from headlines, photo captions, and other blocks of text. The importance of body copy varies from ad to ad, and some ads have little or no body copy. Ads for easy-to-understand products, for instance, often rely on the headline and a visual such as a photograph to get their point across (see Exhibit 9.18). In contrast, when the selling message needs a lot of supporting detail to be convincing, an ad can be packed full of body copy. Some advertisers have the impression that long body copy should be avoided, but that isn't always the case.[60] The rule to apply here is to use the "right" number of words. You might not need many words in a perfume ad, but you might need a page or two to cover a complex industrial product.

As with headlines, body copy can be built around several different formats. **Straight-line copy** is copy that takes off from the headline and develops the selling points for the product. **Narrative copy,** in contrast, tells a story as it persuades; the same selling points may be covered, but in a different context. **Dialog/monolog copy** lets one or two characters in the ad do the selling through what they are saying (see Exhibit 9.19). **Picture-and-caption copy** relies on photographs or illustrations to tell the story, with support from their accompanying captions.[61]

Slogans

The third major category of copy includes **slogans,** or *tag lines,* memorable sayings that convey a selling message. Over the years, Coca-Cola has used such slogans as "Coke is it," "It's the real thing," and "Always Coca-Cola."[62] Slogans are sometimes used as headlines, but not always. Their importance lies in the fact they often become the most memorable result of an advertising campaign. You've probably got a few slogans stuck in your head. Ever heard of "Quality is job number 1," "Don't leave home without it," or "Melts in your mouth, not in your hand"?

Rose: The Minnesota Orchestra is putting on this opera called Falstaff—a really wonderful opera.

Todd: I would rather be dropped into a mountain of road salt. I would rather be dragged by a team of wild horses through burning hot desert sands. I am not an opera kind of person. I like to have a few beers.

Rose: So does Falstaff, Todd.

Todd: Have a few laughs.

Rose: Falstaff is very funny. Falstaff is an easy-to-love, light Italian opera about a fat, beer-swilling middle-aged guy. Who do you think that's starting to remind me of, Todd?

Announcer: Falstaff. A funny opera complete with English supertitles projected above the stage. See it Wednesday, November 7 and Friday, November 9 at Orchestra Hall. Call 371-5656 for tickets.

EXHIBIT 9.19
Dialog Copy

In this radio commercial, the Minnesota Orchestra could have tried talking directly to people in an effort to lure them into the opera, but these two characters get the message across in a more entertaining way.

The Korean automaker Hyundai recently switched back to the slogan "Cars that make sense," which is a great way of expressing its desired positioning as a lower-cost but still reliable alternative to Japanese and U.S. cars. For several years, the company had used "Hyundai. Yes, Hyundai," but "Cars that make sense" has proved to be a much more effective way to define the value it offers consumers.[63]

BROADCAST COPY

Radio and television commercials present the copywriter with unique challenges and opportunities. Although there are many similarities between print and

---

CHECKLIST FOR PRODUCING EXCELLENT COPY

❑ A. Avoid clichés.
  - Create fresh, original phrases that vividly convey your message.
  - Remember that clever wordplay based on clichés can be quite effective.

❑ B. Watch out for borrowed interest.
  - Make sure you don't use inappropriate copy or graphics since they can steal the show from your basic sales message.
  - Be sure nothing draws attention from the message.

❑ C. Don't boast.
  - Be sure the ad's purpose isn't merely to pat the advertiser on the back.
  - Tout success when you must convince nonbuyers that lots of people just like them have purchased your product; this isn't the same as shouting "We're the best!"

❑ D. Make it personal, informal, and relevant.
  - Connect with the audience in a way that is personal and comfortable. Pompous, stiff, and overly "businesslike" tends to turn people away.
  - Avoid copy that sounds like it belongs in an ad, with too many overblown adjectives and unsupported claims of superiority.

❑ E. Keep it simple, specific, and concise.
  - Make your case quickly and stick to the point. This will help you get past all the barriers and filters that people put up to help them select which things they'll pay attention to and which they'll ignore.
  - Avoid copy that's confusing, meandering, too long, or too detailed.

❑ F. Give the audience a reason to read, listen, or watch.
  - Offer a solution to your audience's problems.
  - Entertain your audience.
  - Consider any means possible to get your audience to pay attention long enough to get your sales message across.

A CASE FOR CRITICAL THINKING

Michael Markman had quite a challenge on his hands when it came to answering the "Making it easier" campaign from Microsoft. In essence, Apple's message is that adding Windows to a PC may make it look like a Macintosh, but that doesn't mean it'll work as well as a Mac. However, Markman recognized that differences between the Mac and the PC equipped with Windows revolve around some rather technical issues and that computer buyers, especially less experienced buyers, would need to hear these details to be convinced. Consequently, Markman was faced with a complex message no matter what strategy he chose. In addition, he had to decide whether to confront Microsoft's claims directly and, if so, how aggressively.

In a departure from previous Apple advertising, which had worked to build a strong, positive image for the products and the company by showing successful computer users at work, Markman and company pulled the gloves off on the new campaign. The ads confronted Microsoft and its claim of "Making it easier" by asserting that PCs equipped with Windows aren't as easy to use as Microsoft would have everyone believe. To get the point across that the Macintosh is an integrated system of hardware and software, designed together from the ground up to be easy to use, the ad created by BBDO/Los Angeles mentioned several times that "Windows is just software" and referred to Windows as "simply a party mask." It added that "even if you spend a small fortune for upgrades, you still won't have a Macintosh."

In order to communicate both the essence of the message and the supporting technical details, and to pull in elements of both logic and emotion, BBDO combined a story and a page of technical detail. In the two-page ad, the left page tells a disappointing tale from the perspective of a computer user who tried adding Windows to a PC in order to "simplify my job." The user in the story had to add new hardware components, buy new software in order to run Windows, and take the time to configure the system. Then, even after all that time and money, the performance of the new Windows setup was disappointing. BBDO summed up the user's frustration by twisting Microsoft's tag line around to create the line, "This is making it easier?"

On the second page, the ad provides technical debate to support Apple's message. The page is packed with three columns of copy, which is broken up with subheads that are set off from the body copy. A table in the middle of the page supports Apple's message that adding Windows to a PC can be an expensive proposition. The table displays the results of an independent study conducted by PC Week magazine; the study estimated that it would cost over $6,000 to upgrade each PC in an office where the PCs are connected to each other. The table not only breaks up the long columns of text, but also adds a powerful punch to a key part of Apple's message.

The competition for the hearts and minds of computer users isn't going to cool off any time in the near future, and advertising will continue to play a major role. Aggressive comparative advertising may be new for Apple, but it's becoming more common throughout the computer industry. In fact, Microsoft itself has used comparative ads in its competition with Word Perfect, another supplier of word processing software. Copywriters can expect to keep busy as these technological giants continue to pound away at each other.

Your Mission: You've joined Michael Markman's staff at Apple, and your job includes working with your counterparts at BBDO to develop effective advertising that carries the Macintosh message. The following scenarios involve creative decisions and copywriting situations that need your approval.

1. You recognize that a clear statement of the key customer benefit is a vital element in any copy platform. For an ad that will highlight a new computer's ability to run graphic-design software at higher speeds than ever

broadcast copywriting, such as the need to be clear and concise, there are some important differences as well. To start with, radio and television audiences have less control over how they participate in the communication process. They can't skip around, reading a sentence here, a sentence there, as they can with print ads, and they can't go back and reread something they didn't get the first time. Your copy is presented in a predefined order and can't be repeated. If your message doesn't get through the first time, it won't get through at all (at least not until it's heard or viewed again). With radio in particular, the fact that people are usually doing something else while they listen presents an additional barrier to breaking through the clutter and reaching the audience.

On the positive side, radio and television provide additional creative options for supporting the message. If you're trying to create a high-energy feeling in a print ad, you have to do so with the words themselves and whatever help you can get from the typography and the artwork. On radio you can add music, and on television you can add motion to help create the feeling. Sound effects and animated visual effects are key supporting tools not available in print media.

All I really wanted to do was simplify my job. So I bought Windows. I added extra RAM. I bought a bigger hard disk. I replaced my video card and monitor. I bought a half-dozen new programs, installed a mouse, configured the system, and as I sit here watching my spreadsheet crawl on my PC, I'm thinking to myself, "This is making it easier?"

Macintosh from Apple.

computer users in your company.

b. Who says the Macintosh raises office productivity? More than 300 big-league information managers, that's who.

c. Take the fear out of high-volume computer purchasing.

3. The computer industry is in the midst of brutal price competition, as small, aggressive newcomers try to make their mark by undercutting the big players such as IBM and Apple. You know you have to be careful when using the price issue in your ads because you don't want to come across as cheap or low quality. Which of the following price/value appeals sounds best?

a. You understand Macintosh quality and performance; now meet Macintosh value.

b. Here's some real news: the Macintosh is now a computer for small budgets.

c. Believe it or not, you can still afford the Macintosh.

4. Thinking back to the "This is making it easier?" ad, your research shows that some people still don't grasp the benefits of a Macintosh over a Windows-equipped PC. If you had to summarize your benefits in one sentence of copy, which of the following versions would you use?

a. Technically and financially, the Macintosh is simply a better computing solution than Windows.

b. Take a look at the technical and financial details, and you'll agree that Macintosh is a better choice.

c. The Mac is back—no question about it.[68]

before, you're mulling over three possible benefits statements. Which of these would you choose?

a. This computer boasts a processor running at 100 megahertz.

b. This computer helps designers be more productive by displaying their images faster than ever before.

c. This computer is faster than anything offered by the competition.

2. You realize that computer purchasing combines elements of both logic and emotion. When the information systems manager in a large corporation orders 5,000 desktop computers, for instance, he or she looks to fulfill a number of technical needs but also considers such issues as trust in the supplier and fear of making a bad decision. For a target audience of corporate executives such as this person, which of the following headlines for the Macintosh would do the most appropriate job of blending logical and emotional appeals?

a. Put a smile on the faces of the

Radio presents a particular challenge because it lacks the visual aspects of both print and television. Successful radio ads usually enable listeners to *visualize* the product or something related to it. In radio, your descriptive writing skills are needed to create pictures in the listener's mind, whether the message is simply the location of a retail store or the graceful lines of a new automobile.[64] Chapter 12 discusses the production aspects of broadcast advertising and provides more details on how copy works in radio and television commercials.

OTHER PROMOTIONAL COPY

As already mentioned, copywriters are often called on to produce many advertising pieces beyond the usual print and broadcast ads. This list includes sales letters, package copy, brochures, direct-mail flyers, catalogs, billboards, posters, and emerging media such as ads carried on computer disks. Each of these formats has some unique considerations, although the elements of good copywriting apply in every case. Some of these writing tasks may fall under the category of "odd jobs" that the writer is assigned to handle along with print and broadcast ads, but some of them can be rather large projects.[65]

Direct-mail copywriting is one of the most important of these additional categories, and it can in fact become a copywriter's professional specialty. If you've visited your mailbox recently, you can attest to the growth in direct-mail advertising, part of the larger world of direct-response advertising that includes infomercials and other formats designed to solicit immediate audience response. Writing for direct mail includes such key tasks as developing sales letters and product catalogs. Direct-mail copy used to take a hard-sell approach in most cases, but with the growth of such giant mail-order retailers as Lands' End and L. L. Bean has come a shift to a more sophisticated, soft-sell approach. Even with upscale, soft-sell copywriting, however, direct mail is designed for the sole purpose of generating sales, so your copy will always be expected to accomplish that.[66]

Publicity is another copywriting category that can command a great deal of time and attention. As discussed in Chapter 18, publicity covers communication both with the general public and with members of the news media. Writing assignments in this area include speeches for company executives, letters to editors, articles for newspapers or magazines, and *press releases,* short documents that provide newsworthy information to the news media in the hope that your information will be incorporated into upcoming issues or broadcasts.[67]

Summary

Creativity is the ability to produce original ideas or original ways of looking at existing ideas. The creative process, as presented in the chapter, includes seven steps: (1) orienting yourself to the problem at hand; (2) preparing by collecting all the material you can find on the product, the competition, and the target audience; (3) analyzing the material you've collected; (4) generating ideas; (5) allowing those ideas to incubate in your subconscious mind; (6) synthesizing the ideas into relevant thoughts and connected messages; and (7) evaluating the synthesized ideas to pick the best idea to drive the campaign.

The three elements of a creative strategy are the art direction (the artistic design of the ad), the production values (the various audio and visual components and stylistic touches that make up the ad), and the copy platform. The copy platform generally contains a statement of the problem the advertising is expected to solve, the advertising objective, a description of the product, a profile of the target audience, an assessment of the competition, the key customer benefit, support for the key benefit, the selling strategy, the selling style, and the advertising appeal that you plan to use.

The hard-sell style of advertising tries to pound its message home through repetition, demands that the audience do something immediately, and other attention-grabbing techniques. Soft-sell, in contrast, doesn't overtly demand anything from the audience but instead tries to create a situation in the audience's mind that will lead to the desired purchase decision.

Advertising appeals fall into the two general classes of emotion and logic. Specific appeals include price or value; quality; star identification; ego; fear or anger; the five senses; sex, love, and social acceptance; and novelty. Appeals nearly always contain a mix of both emotion and logic, and advertisers can combine two or more of the specific types of appeals in a single ad.

Copywriters are assigned to write three categories of copy: print ads, radio and television ads, and other advertising materials that include direct mail, brochures, posters, and catalogs. Copywriters are responsible for all the words in an ad, from the headline to the fine print.

Key Terms

advertising appeal 232	free association 226
advertising campaign 227	hard-sell advertising 230
Big Idea 224	headline 239
body copy 242	logical appeals 232
brainstorming 226	narrative copy 242
celebrity endorsement ad 235	picture-and-caption copy 242
convergent thinking 222	slogans 242
copy platform 228	soft-sell advertising 231
creative strategy 228	straight-line copy 242
creativity 221	subheads 239
dialog/monolog copy 242	subliminal advertising 238
divergent thinking 223	testimonial 235
emotional appeals 232	unique selling proposition (USP) 230

Questions

FOR REVIEW

1. What is effective creativity, and why is it important in advertising?

2. What is the key fact, and what role does it play in creative strategy?

3. Why is it important for creative people to have a broad background in politics, art, music, and other areas?

4. Why do copywriters and art directors bother with the additional work of writing a copy platform before starting an ad?

5. Why is price alone usually not an effective advertising appeal?

FOR ANALYSIS AND APPLICATION

6. Is it possible to produce effective advertising that isn't terribly creative? Explain your answer.

7. Using an analogy from another mode of transportation, try to describe the experience of riding a top-quality mountain bike.

8. If you were developing an ad for the Ford Taurus station wagon and planned to use a star-identification appeal, which celebrity would you pick? Why this person?

9. Are directive headlines compatible with the soft-sell style of advertising? Why or why not?

10. If you owned a flower shop and wanted to pull in business in the few days before Valentine's Day, would you use a hard-sell or a soft-sell approach? Why?

Sharpen Your Advertising Skills

Both AT&T and MCI are trying to usher in the next generation of telephones with the videophone, a specialized phone that transmits pictures along with voices. The phones are rather expensive ($500 to $1,000 or so at current prices), and both parties in a conversation have to have them, of course. On the other hand, they do provide some benefits never before available in phone service.

Decision: Put yourself in the shoes of MCI's ad agency. Pick one of the advertising appeals described in this chapter, based on how you think consumers will respond to these telephones, and explain your decision.

Communication: Write a headline that communicates the appeal you've chosen. Assume you're creating a one-page magazine ad, and you can use any photographs or illustrations you like. If the headline works in conjunction with the visuals, provide a brief description or sketch of the visuals, and explain how the two elements work together.

CHAPTER 10

Art Direction

CHAPTER OUTLINE

After studying this chapter, you will be able to

1. Explain the meaning of art direction and its role in advertising
2. Describe the elements of design
3. List the principles of good design
4. Explain the steps involved in designing print ads
5. Describe the steps involved in designing ads for television
6. List the most common formats used for television commercials
7. Discuss the audio and visual elements that make up television commercials

ADVERTISING FOR THE JET SET

Gary Hays doesn't have your garden-variety advertising challenges, to be sure. As senior vice president of marketing for Cessna Aircraft, based in Wichita, Kansas, he's in the business of using creative art direction to convince people to shell out $12 million or more for incredibly complex pieces of equipment. He and his ad agency use the same principles as other advertisers, but the rarefied atmosphere of the corporate jet industry leads to some unusual advertising challenges and results. For example, when Cessna came out with its newest jet, the top-of-the-line Citation X, Hays and his creative art director had to come up with a way to capture the attention of potential buyers—not as easy a task as you might think.

Although most manufacturers maintain deep secrecy and tight security when developing a new product, jet manufacturers often tell the world about their new products several years before production models of the jets are even built. Furthermore, unlike the vast markets for cars, potato chips, and personal computers, the market for corporate jets is measured in thousands of prospects, not millions. In the case of the Citation X, Cessna's target audience centered on the CEOs of the Fortune 1000 (the thousand largest industrial companies in the country).

Hays certainly has an impressive product on his hands, something that always makes the advertising task easier. The Citation X can fly at just under the speed of sound, making the trip from New York to Los Angeles in only four hours. The plane isn't only fast but also reliable and comfortable. Of course, this isn't a spur-of-the-moment purchase for most people. Prices start in the $12 million range, and that's without seats or any other interior appointments.

Often the hardest part of advertising to CEOs and other top executives is simply getting to them. Since they make up one of the most sought-after audiences anywhere, you can imagine how many advertisers are trying to reach these multimillion-dollar deci-sion makers. To cope with the flood of direct-mail advertising, regular business mail, magazines, and other materials sent their way, most CEOs have assistants who screen their mail. If something doesn't seem relevant, interesting, or important to the assistant, chances are the CEO will never see it. If a bit of advertising looks important, interesting, or unusual, it stands a better chance of reaching the CEO. So a big part of Hays's job is just to get Cessna's message in front of its target audience.

To get past the gatekeepers and capture the attention of the CEOs in the target audience, Hays definitely needs creative art direction on this project. Given the size and nature of the audience, what could you create that would carry the Citation X message effectively? Would you use posters, brochures, and other conventional advertising pieces, or would you try something a little different, maybe something a bit riskier?[1]

CHAPTER OVERVIEW   Gary Hays knows that visual design in advertising can make or break a campaign, quite apart from the message itself. Chapter 9 discussed how creativity is applied in advertising and how the creative strategy leads into the verbal part of advertising, the copywriting. This chapter focuses on the visual side of advertising, art direction. As an introduction, you'll learn about the elements of design (the building blocks art directors use to create ads) and the principles of design (which help art directors design more effective ads). Following that, you'll explore the two major phases of art direction in print advertising: choosing a format and designing the page. The final section of the chapter extends what you've learned about art direction to television advertising, including choosing the format, setting the style and tone, working with both the audio and visual elements in a television ad, and visualizing the ad in preparation for production. Art direction also plays a role in radio advertising, which is discussed in Chapter 12.

Art Direction: Breathing Life into Advertising

In many cases, copy is expected to shoulder most of the communications responsibility in an ad. In other cases, the visuals are just as important as copy, if not more so. However, even in ads that rely primarily on copy, it's creative art direction that attracts notice in the first place and that presents the selling message in an effective and appealing way. It's the art director's job to make sure that each ad has

Alex in Wonderland.

Vancouver's
Astounding Aquarium

*Bring your family to meet our families. We're in Stanley Park,
and we're open every day of the year. For information call (604) 682-1118.*

EXHIBIT 10.1
Art Direction

This ad for the Vancouver (British Columbia) Aquarium demonstrates the communication impact of skilled art direction. Your eye follows the graceful curve of the dolphin as you read the two parts of the headline, and the child silhouetted against the dolphin shows readers that children get to experience the wonders of the sea up close.

stopping power, the ability to make people notice and pay attention to the ad. Without this stopping power, the best copy imaginable would be of little use. It's also the art director's job to make sure that once people have noticed the ad, the message is communicated as effectively as possible.

As the copywriter's creative partner, the art director is responsible for all **visuals** appearing in an ad, that is, all the parts that aren't copy. Moreover, the graphical treatment of the copy itself (what it looks like and how it's arranged on the page or television screen) is also part of the art director's job. Thus, the art director is responsible both for the **composition** of the ad, the overall arrangement of the copy and visuals, and for the **execution** of the ad, the final result of the design process (see Exhibit 10.1).[2]

The art director leads the design effort, although he or she may not do the actual design work. **Graphic designers** are professional artists who focus on commercial artwork, such as that used in ads, brochures, posters, and other promotional pieces. A related design function is performed by **illustrators,** who create nonphotographic visuals such as technical drawings for use in ads and other materials. Art directors also work with photographers, package designers, and others who help bring the total advertising message to life. In television advertising, the art director must also work with producers, directors, and editors to create the finished commercial.

ELEMENTS OF DESIGN

When you look at an ad, you probably see copy, photographs, actors, logos, and the various other parts that make up the ad. However, the fundamentals of design start working at a level below these pieces, with the concepts of line, color, texture, shape, direction, size, sound, and space. Even if you never design an ad, it's important to understand these design elements so that you can (1) communicate with art directors and (2) make informed judgments about ad designs. Each of the following basic elements of design contributes in its own way to the overall design of an ad.[3]

A *line* can set a mood, guide the reader's eye, separate blocks of copy, and perform a multitude of other design functions crucial to the success of an ad. Lines have visual personalities; a jagged line conveys a message quite different from that communicated by a gracefully curved line. In general, vertical lines convey a sense of dignity; horizontal lines, a sense of calm; diagonal lines, a sense of vitality; and curved lines, a sense of grace.[4]

Color is one of the most powerful visual elements. It can set moods, emphasize copy points, and highlight a product. In addition, according to a study conducted by Southern Illinois University, color increases an ad's attention-getting and recall powers.[5] In magazine ads, some advertisers have reported that color ads have been as much as 15 times more effective than the same ads printed in black and white.[6] (Technically, both black and white are colors as well.) Color also carries symbolic meaning, which can complicate art direction in international and intercultural campaigns. You may think that yellow makes an ad look bright and alive, for instance, but in Mexico yellow is associated with death or disrespect.[7] Sometimes art directors decide not to use color, however, for reasons of both cost and aesthetic choice. Without the extra dimension of color, form and shape become more dominant, as art director Karen Silveira explained when she used black and white photos in ads for Marika exercise wear. "Black and white always looks more graphic and emphasizes the shape."[8]

Texture in art direction refers to both the physical and the visual. Physical texture in a print ad can include the smooth feel of glossy paper, the soft but rough feel of handmade writing paper, or the expensive feel of embossed paper with raised lettering. Physical texture is a key design decision in direct mail, where you might choose to promote an art gallery on paper that feels handmade and unusual. Visual texture is defined by patterns; the visual texture of a city street differs from that of a forest.

Another key design element is *shape,* which is formed by lines and areas of tone and color. Shapes can be realistic (the outline of a bottle of Perrier), abstract (a free-form curve that doesn't represent any particular object), or symbolic (the U.S. flag). Shape plays a big role in stopping power, especially if the shape is unexpected. To protest recent violence against foreigners in Germany, a television station commissioned an ad that showed the background of the German flag with its three horizontal stripes of black, red, and yellow—except that the red stripe in the middle was "bleeding" down on the yellow stripe at the bottom, representing the harmful effect that the violence was having on the country. The combination of expected colors with *unexpected* shapes made a stunning visual impact.[9]

Lines and shapes can imply motion or *direction* in an ad, even in a print ad that obviously has no actual motion in it. With proper planning, direction can work for you in an ad, leading the audience's eyes to focus on key visual points. Direction is a key element in *sequence,* as you'll see later in the section on design principles.

Size influences an ad's communication effectiveness, both the size of the ad and the size of its individual pieces. A headline set in huge type might appear to be screaming, whereas smaller type talks to the audience in a normal voice. In general, size implies importance; if you want the audience to notice one thing in particular, you make it bigger than the rest. This isn't an absolute rule, however. Sometimes the best way to draw the eye's attention to an item is to make it smaller than expected.

Sound in a television or radio spot can be a spoken voice, instrumental music, singing, or sound effects. The absence of sound, such as a dramatic pause, is also an element of design. Sound is vital in radio advertising, of course, since it's the only design element at your disposal.

Space plays a big role in art direction. Give a product plenty of visual "elbow room" by isolating it in the middle of a vast expanse of white or another single color, and you highlight the product, drawing observers' eyes to it. If you make the

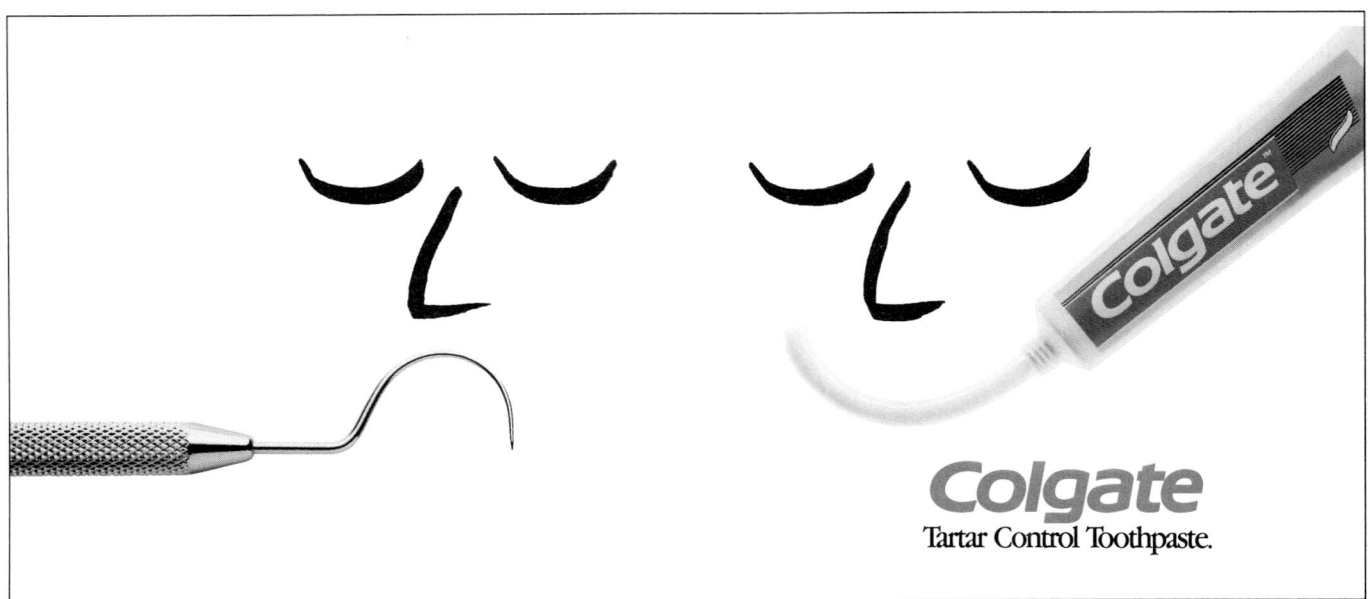

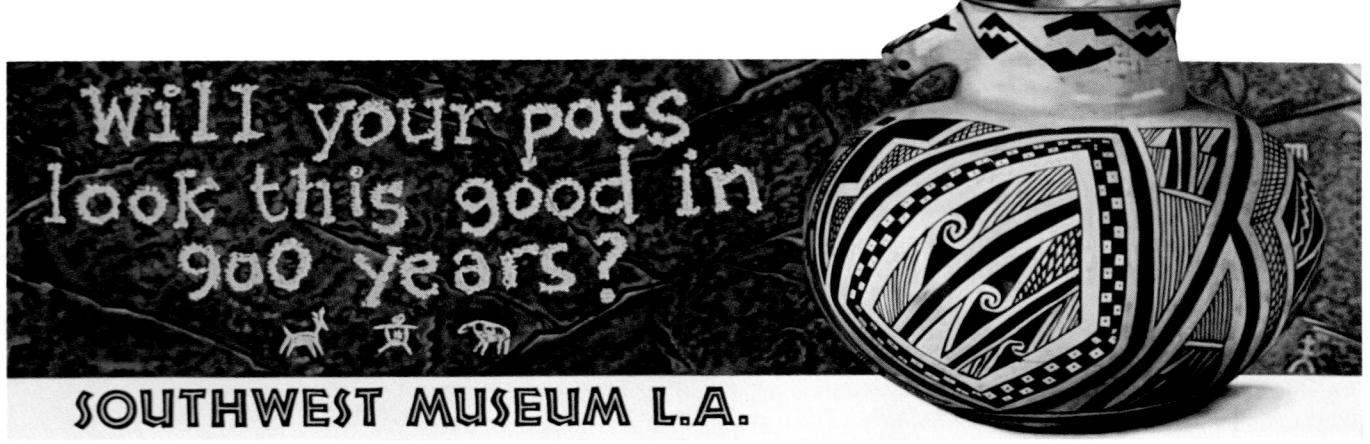

EXHIBIT 10.2
Using the Principles of Design

The Colgate ad uses very simple curves to emphasize the benefit of using the product. The Southwest Museum's billboard also uses visual simplicity to get its point across, and the three-dimensional pot catches the eye of passing motorists.

product compete for space with other elements, you'll diminish its visual importance. Regardless of the particular color it might be, any uninterrupted expanse of a single color (including black or white) is called **white space.**

Exhibit 10.2 shows a print ad and a billboard that illustrate the effective use of these design elements. To build your own design skills, get into the habit of analyzing ads, magazine covers, posters, and other visual works of art to see how artists and designers make use of the various elements of design.

PRINCIPLES OF DESIGN

As advertising professor Roy Paul Nelson puts it, design principles serve the same purpose for the designer that grammar rules serve for the copywriter.[10] These principles provide the guidelines for assembling the design elements in ways that are both pleasing to the eye and effective as advertising. Again, even if you don't design ads yourself, it's important to understand these rules so that you know what makes a design good. Design principles include balance, proportion, sequence, unity, emphasis, and the related concepts of tension and surprise.[11]

Balance

Balance is the state of equilibrium in which the parts on one side of the ad are the visual equals of the parts on the other side, and similarly from top to bottom (although the visual center of the ad from top to bottom isn't at midpoint on the

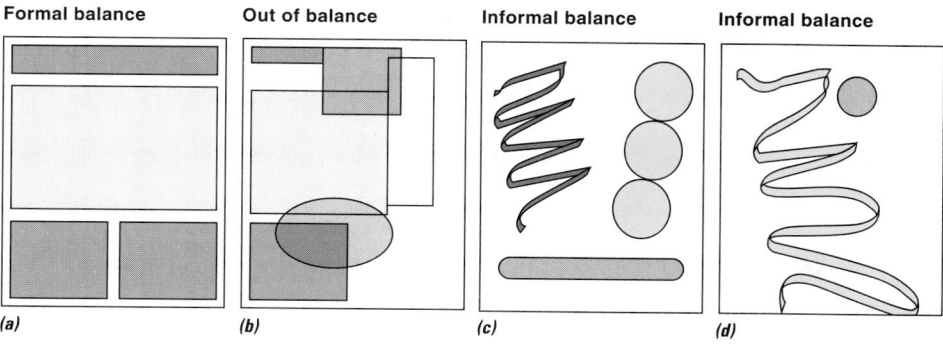

Formal balance   Out of balance   Informal balance   Informal balance

(a)   (b)   (c)   (d)

EXHIBIT 10.3
Formal and Informal Balance

Formal balance (*a*) feels solid and stable, whereas informal balance (*c* and *d*) is a more subtle arrangement that feels more alive and energetic. An unbalanced design (*b*), in contrast, looks and feels haphazard.

page, but slightly above that). Roy Paul Nelson refers to an ad that is in balance as "being at peace with itself."[12] The ad doesn't look haphazard, nor does it look like it's about to topple over. Balance is important in advertising design because, consciously or subconsciously, our sense of balance affects our reactions and judgments.[13]

To achieve *formal balance,* each item is repeated, in size and shape, on both sides of the ad. Imagine an ad that contained only two equal-length columns of copy; this is formal balance in the extreme. Formal balance gives an ad a sense of stability, dignity, and seriousness.

To achieve *informal balance,* you don't have to mirror the pieces in size and shape from side to side and top to bottom. Instead, you make sure that the sums of the *optical weights* are equal. Optical weight is an indicator of how much presence a given part of the ad has. As you might expect, the larger an element is, the more optical weight it has, but color and shape affect optical weight as well. Colors weigh more than black or white space, black space weighs more than gray, and unusual shapes weigh more than ordinary shapes. Also, the farther an element is from the center, the more weight it has.[14] Exhibit 10.3 provides some examples of formal and informal balance.

Do ads have to be in balance, either formal or informal? No, not if you *plan* them that way. Well-designed unbalanced ads can catch a reader's eye and pull it toward a specific point in the ad. However, ads that are unbalanced because the designer didn't know any better may just confuse readers or prompt them to keep turning the page or changing the channel.

Proportion

The relationship between the size of objects is **proportion,** such as the size of the human body being in proportion with the size of the head or the limbs. As art director, your concern is making ads that seem proportional (that is, the audience doesn't sense that anything is too big or too small) while at the same time avoiding the static look that comes from all parts being the same size.

For example, the most common proportion in print ads allots the top two-thirds to three-fourths of a page for a photo or other visual and the remaining one-third to one-fourth at the bottom for copy, logos, and other supporting elements. This not only creates a more lively look than a strict half-visual–half-copy page would but also forces a ratio of more visual than copy, which is good for many products.[15] However, this isn't to say that other ratios don't do well for other products. Technical products that sometimes need copy-heavy ads devote more space to the copy than to the visual.

Sequence

Sequence refers to the order in which the reader or viewer takes in the various elements in an ad. A key difference between print and broadcast ads relates to sequence: Broadcast audiences have to take in the elements in your ad in whatever order you put them because sequence is ruled by *time.* In print ads, however, sequence is ruled by *space,* and the reader is under no obligation to move through the ad in the order you intended.

EXHIBIT 10.4
Direction and Sequence

In this beautifully composed shot, photographer Michael Lupino draws your eyes to the product in the foreground, no matter where you start looking. If your eyes land on the spiral staircase at the top of the photo, they naturally flow down to the Corian countertop.

As an art director, you solve this problem by using the various design elements to lead readers from the point where you want them to start to the point where you want them to finish. So the way you use copy, lines, photos, or color leads the reader from start to finish. For instance, the eye tends to move from bright spaces to muted spaces, from big objects to small objects, and from unusual shapes to common shapes (see Exhibit 10.4). Art directors can put these phenomena to good use when designing their ads.[16]

In any case, the place to start with sequence design is with the way people are accustomed to reading a page. In the United States and other Western nations, people read from left to right and then line by line from top to bottom. That's why U.S. headlines are rarely at the bottom of a page. However, the left-right, top-bottom sequence isn't the case in all languages. Arabic, for instance, is read from right to left. Reading direction is something you probably never stop to think about, but it's a vital part of the communication process, and something that must be considered when advertising in other countries.[17]

Unity

Ads possess a sense of **unity** when all the pieces work together to form a cohesive whole.[18] Everything looks and sounds as if it belongs in the ad. Unity covers the way elements are laid out on a page (or television screen) as well as the character of the individual elements in the ad, from the personality of the type used in a headline to the background music in a radio or television commercial. You wouldn't use cartoon graphics in a serious ad, nor would you use heavy metal music in a commercial for a luxury car.

Unity presents a special kind of challenge with multipage print ads. If you're designing a two-page ad (called a *spread*) for a U.S. newspaper or magazine, you have to find some way to tie the two pages together visually. You might put a single decorative border around the spread, run the headline or a photo across the two pages, or have some visual element on the left page point to the right page. At the very least, you need to use the same color scheme and the same style of art.[19]

Emphasis

Art direction must agree with the advertising strategy on **emphasis,** the decision to highlight one element in the ad. Advertising strategy is part of this decision because the element highlighted should be chosen according to the message you're trying to deliver. Say you're designing a magazine ad for the Lexus

If it's green, we reject it.

If it's dirty, we reject it.

If it's too ripe, we reject it.

If it's just right, we squash it.

If it's bruised, we reject it.

If it's diseased, we reject it.

The tomato ketchup in a McDonald's hamburger is made only for McDonald's.

The tomatoes are, as you see, most carefully chosen. (You might think we are exaggerating, but every word is true.)

Turning them into tomato paste involves rather more than simply squashing them.

The best method is, as it happens, the most difficult and expensive.

It is the method we use.

Then we add some sugar, vinegar,

salt, cloves, chilli, bay and allspice.

We add no other flavouring, colouring, preservative or thickening, because we don't need to.

That is the amount of trouble we take over our tomato ketchup.

And this is the amount of tomato ketchup we put in a hamburger:

There's nothing quite like a McDonald's.

EXHIBIT 10.5

What Should You Emphasize in an Ad?

In this ad that ran in Great Britain, McDonald's focused on the quality of the tomatoes that go into the ketchup that goes on the company's hamburgers.

LS400 luxury sedan. Should you emphasize the headline, a line of copy listing the last day of a special sale, or a photo of the car? If you choose the photo of the car, should you emphasize the interior, the engine, or the overall body shape? These decisions must be driven by what you're trying to accomplish with your advertising. Exhibit 10.5 shows a McDonald's ad that communicates quality by emphasizing one feature of a minor supporting product.

Art directors use the design elements discussed earlier and the principles discussed here to emphasize a particular part of the ad, to make it stand apart from the rest. They can use shape, placement within the ad, size, or color, for example. Art director Robert de Roche, who creates ads for makeup and hair-care products, often shows the human model in black and white and shows the product, such as lipstick, in color.[20]

Tension and Surprise

An ad or an individual piece of art can produce a sense of tension if readers or viewers can't *resolve* what they see. In other words, if a person can't look at a magazine ad and immediately say "OK, I get the message," even at a subconscious level, the result will be tension. Most people want to resolve this tension (that is, make it go away), so they try to "solve" the ad.

Sometimes the situation can't be cleared up by studying the ad; other times it can. In either case, the art director's goal is to engage the audience, to get them involved in the ad and thinking about the message. For example, a recent Volvo ad showed a turtle and the headline "If this is what you think about Volvos, you've got another think coming." Two subheads read "The new Volvo 850 GLT" and "Coming October 24." The reader can sense that this new Volvo must be a bit sportier than earlier models, but the answer will have to wait until a future ad.[21]

In a different approach, a magazine targeting art directors ran four consecutive pages of beautifully colored drawings of insects, one insect per page. The paper used for these pages was heavier and had more texture than the rest of the magazine's pages. The first three pages said nothing. The headline finally came on the fourth page: "Sorry to keep bugging you, but as you can see, you don't need expensive paper to get great color," and then came a toll-free phone number for Weyerhauser, the paper's supplier.[22]

In the never-ending struggle to break through clutter and get an audience's attention, some advertisers try to plant little visual and verbal surprises in their ads. One method in print ads is to put part of the ad upside-down, in the hope that readers will be curious enough to flip the page upside-down and see what the rest of the ad says. DDB Needham Worldwide created a series of ads like this for Liquid-plumr drain cleaner, including putting a photo of the product upside-down. DDB's Steve Witt notes that the technique gives an advertiser another couple of seconds in front of the audience (since they have to turn the page around twice), which may be enough for the ad to make an impression.[23]

Designing Print Advertising

Designing a print ad is a process of bringing together the copy and artwork in a way that best communicates the intended advertising message. The decisions you have to make in this process include choosing a format and then designing the page itself. Much of what's covered here applies to television advertising as well, discussed later in the chapter.

CHOOSING A FORMAT

The format you choose determines how you'll structure the message. This isn't a question of how pieces are physically located on the page (that's covered in the next section under basic page design); format determines how you'll put copy and artwork together to make your point. As with most topics in advertising, you can find dozens of ways to classify print ad formats. Advertising consultant Bruce Bendinger proposes a list of six types that encompasses just about all print ad possibilities:[24]

The One-Liner

If you can get your point across with one carefully written headline and a great photo or illustration, you might choose the *one-liner* format. A big advantage of the one-liner is its conciseness and simplicity, meaning that your message can get through to the reader quickly (see Exhibit 10.6). An ad for Liz Claiborne handbags used this format nicely with the headline "Most things can be carried off with style" next to a photo of a woman with a large Liz Claiborne handbag. The dual wordplay got the message across effectively.[25] The one-liner format doesn't work well if you need to say more. In many product categories, such as financial services, business equipment, and medicine, the message needs the supporting details that come only with a fair amount of body copy.

The News

If you want to tell your audience about a great new product, compare a product with its competitors, or demonstrate how well your product works, the commonly used *news* format is most appropriate because it communicates information that you hope the target audience will find interesting and enlightening. The news format can be used with hard- or soft-sell styles, with humor or without, and with lots of copy or relatively little copy. An ad for Health-Tex baby clothes showed a hapless child struggling to put on a tight turtleneck, with the headline: "Babies tormented by their clothes. On the next Oprah." The 15 paragraphs of body copy went on to explain how Health-Tex clothes were easier for parents to put on and take off their babies.[26] The news format is great for product introductions, product demonstrations, and side-by-side comparative ads.

The Spiral

Just as a spiral staircase moves in repeating cycles while still rising upward, so the *spiral format* makes the selling point over and over again, enhancing and expanding it a little each time. You can use the spiral format when you're not sure readers will keep reading and you don't want your message to seem incomplete. The spiral layers your message, getting the point across early and then adding details as the key selling points are repeated. The longer readers stay with the ad,

the more they get out of it—but even if they bail out early, they get at least the basic message.[27]

Both copy and visuals can move the spiral along. Honda's Acura division used a spiral to convince readers that its Integra GS-R offered much of the same advanced technology found in Honda's exotic Acura NSX sports car and in its Formula One race car. In a two-page spread, the selling message was first stated in the headline along the left side of the ad, repeated in a series of photos showing the three cars, and restated several more times in the body copy along the right side of the ad. For readers who spent any time looking at the ad, it was almost impossible to miss the selling message.[28]

The Story

One of the most effective ways to get the reader involved in your ad is to tell a *story,* also called a *narrative.* Just as a well-written short story, novel, or screenplay can hold the audience's attention long enough to make a point, so too can the story format in print advertising. Testimonial appeals and "case histories" are other common applications of the story format, where customers tell their stories about using a product. The story used to be a common print format, although it's used more in television now.[29]

The Sermon

The *sermon* format is just like it sounds: the advertiser "preaching" to the audience. Sometimes this is preaching in the usual sense, but it's often more a case of *instructing* the audience.[30] You can write sermons from a formal, corporate perspective ("We at XYZ Company think the best way to . . . ") or from a friendly, one-on-one angle ("I used to be embarrassed by age spots, but no longer—and here's why . . . ").

You can use the sermon format to explain why your company's approach to life insurance is better or why customers have been so satisfied with your products. As you might expect, this is a common format for nonprofit advertising, but it's a frequent choice for commercial ads as well. The CIGNA companies used a sermon to explain why their approach to employee disability insurance was better than the approach taken by other insurers. The copy-heavy ad explained why CIGNA thought their ability to integrate several types of insurance made them the preferred choice.[31] Like the hornblowing headline (discussed in Chapter 9), the sermon format needs to be handled carefully so that you get your selling points across without sounding condescending or arrogant.

The Outline

The *outline* format communicates the key components of the selling message using brief statements in a form similar to the outlines you're used to making when you write term papers and reports. In the short-outline format, the body copy consists of a list of selling points, set off with round "bullets," check marks, or other graphical treatments. In the long-outline format, the list of selling points is replaced by a series of subheads. Blocks of body copy between the subheads provide supporting detail, but the reader can get the basic message by reading just the subheads. Long outlines can also be accomplished visually, with photos or illustrations representing the key selling points.[32]

The long-outline format is great for products whose selling message needs a lot of detail (see Exhibit 10.7). The Apple Computer ad featured in Chapter 9's "Meeting an Advertising Challenge" used this format to make the case that the Apple Macintosh was a better solution than Microsoft Windows for personal computer users. As you'll recall, the right page was packed with technical copy, but broken by seven subheads that communicated the essence of the Macintosh selling message.[33]

DESIGNING THE PAGE

Once you have a format in mind, your next step is designing the ad itself. You have three sets of decisions here: choosing a basic page design, working with the copy, and working with the visuals. After that, you're ready to lay out the page to show clients, and you can start the production process (which is covered in Chapter 11).

Choosing a Basic Design

The first step in designing the ad is to pick the basic page design. As you leaf through magazines and newspapers, you can see quite a variety of page designs, from ads that are all copy to ads that are nothing but a full-page photo and the name of the product. Each design has a unique way of communicating the selling message, and the art director chooses the design according to such factors as the nature of the product, the amount of copy required, and the reader's expectations. Naturally, there's no universal agreement on a list of basic designs, nor would all art directors agree that there are "categories" at all. Even though art directors' creative efforts can produce an infinite variety of designs, most print ads fall into one of the following categories:[34]

- *Mondrian.* Named after the Dutch painter Piet Mondrian, this design uses visible lines and bars to divide the page into two or more rectangular blocks. Each block can contain copy, a piece of artwork, or a solid color (including white). Proportion takes precedence over sequence or emphasis in this design style. An easy and effective way to construct ads, the Mondrian and other highly structured ads are usually designed with a **grid,** a matrix of horizontal and vertical lines that the designer can use to position and align the pieces of the ad (although the grid itself doesn't appear in the ad).

- *Picture window.* The picture-window design is quite common in magazine ads. It usually features one big photograph of the product (or someone using the product), a single headline, and a small amount of copy.

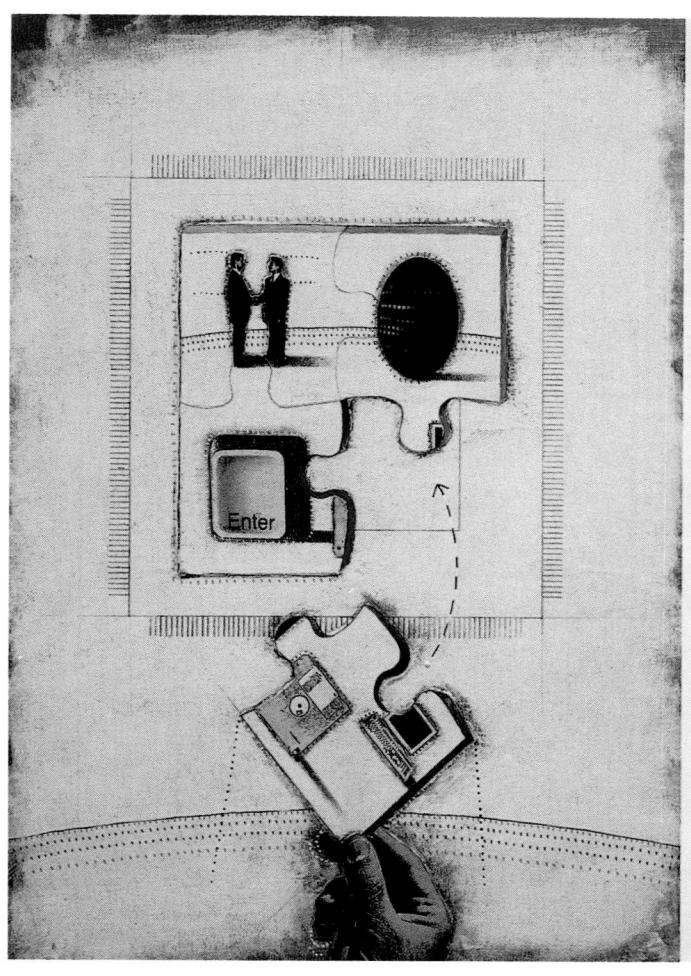

EXHIBIT 10.7
The Long-Outline Format

Texas Instruments made good use of the long-outline form in this ad. You can get the key messages by reading the subheads and all the detail by reading the body copy.

- *Copy heavy.* The copy-heavy design is just what it sounds like: an ad with a lot of copy and little or no artwork. Art directors choose copy-heavy designs when the message is long and complex or when they want the ad to stand apart visually from ads that rely on a lot of artwork.

- *Frame.* The frame design emphasizes the headline or body copy by framing it with some type of artwork. The frame may be as simple and direct as a box around the copy, or it may be a more complicated arrangement of artwork that surrounds the copy.

- *Circus.* Some designs clown around or even scream for attention, and Roy Paul Nelson refers to them as circus designs. The typical circus ad has quite a few visual elements, a bold headline, and lots of color. This is a complex design scheme, but in the hands of a skilled designer, it can impart a sense of fun and excitement to whatever product is being advertised.

- *Multipanel.* The multipanel design divides the page into numerous rectangular areas (but not with the visible lines and careful proportions found in the Mondrian). Multipanel ads can either tell a story (such as several photos showing the stages of healing achieved with a new skin medication) or simply present numerous product photos. Print ads that look like comic strips are a good example of this page design.

- *Big type.* In a big-type design, headlines set in very large type dominate the ad, and the big type serves the same attention-getting function as a piece of artwork. For instance, a recent ad for Avis Rent-A-Car used a headline that covered most of the page to say, "Hello Avis, I'm Lost." Small copy at the bottom explained that Avis has a toll-free number to help customers who need directions.[35]

These two Movado ads take different approaches in terms of displaying the product and using a headline. This pair was tested by the Starch readership test, which, as you'll recall from previous chapters, tests magazine ads for performance at three levels: how many people noted that the ad was in the magazine (the "Noted" score), how many associated the ad with the right brand/advertiser (the "Associated" score), and how many read most of the ad (the "Read Most" score). Which of these two ads do you think scored higher on the Read Most test? Be prepared to explain your answers.

- *Rebus*. You've probably seen a rebus before; it's one of those brainteasers in which pictures represent words, and you're supposed to figure out what the puzzle says by "translating" the pictures into words. The rebus ad follows the same idea, although you don't literally translate the pictures. Rather, the numerous pictures communicate the message, and copy winds around the pictures, providing supporting detail.

- *Alphabet inspired*. The final design takes its inspiration from the shapes of letters of the alphabet. The art director arranges the copy and visuals in the shape of a *T*, an *L*, an *X*, or other letter. The two big advantages of this design are the unity that comes from the underlying cohesive form of the letter and the ability to steer the reader's eye along the shape of the letter.[36]

Remember, this list of layout possibilities is a starting point for your own creativity, not a strict catalog of options.

Working with Copy

Integrating copy into the design of an ad requires a number of artistic steps, some rather obvious, others more subtle. These steps include selecting a type style that complements the design, deciding where to put the type on the page, and fitting the copy into the available space. In each step, the art director and copywriter work together to make sure that the ad projects the right image as well as the right message. The following sections provide a quick introduction to the special terminology of type and to some guidelines for choosing and using type.

The Terminology of Type. Like other areas of design, type has its own special terms. **Typeface** refers to the basic design of type, whether the letters are elegant or casual, squarish or rounded, and so on. Typefaces are usually named after their designers (or sometimes clients of the designers). Ancient Greeks and Romans began working on typefaces thousands of years ago, and art directors have hundreds to choose from today. Exhibit 10.8 presents some of the more common typefaces. As the exhibit shows, typefaces can be divided into five basic categories (although there's no general agreement on the number or names of typeface categories):[37]

- *Roman.* These typefaces trace their roots to the letters that ancient Romans carved on their buildings. All use both thick and thin strokes and feature *serifs,* small cross strokes at the end of main strokes.

- *Sans serif.* Also known as Gothic type, these typefaces are simpler and cleaner than roman, with strokes of equal width and without serifs (*sans* is French for "without"). These faces are sometimes reserved for **display copy,** which is copy in headlines and logos and everywhere else except the body. However, even though roman faces are considered easier to read in body copy, sans serif types lend such a clean and uncluttered look that they are frequently used in body copy as well.

- *Square serif.* These faces are a cross between serif and sans serif faces; they have serifs, but the serif strokes are of the same weight as the main character strokes.

- *Script.* Script fonts generally look like some form of handwriting, either cursive or calligraphic.

- *Ornamental/other.* This category covers everything else, from typefaces that look like they're made from paperclips to three-dimensional wedge-shaped type.

The vast majority of your advertising projects will be covered quite nicely with roman and sans serif faces. Square serif faces can make good headlines, but they're

---

EXHIBIT 10.8 Common Typefaces

Typefaces fall into the five general categories shown here. With the exception of ornamental/other, you can see the strong resemblance within each category.

ROMAN (SERIF)	GOTHIC (SANS SERIF)	SCRIPT
OLD-STYLE	Vag Rounded	*Brush*
Caslon	Antique Olive	*Kaufman*
Garamond	Futura	
TRANSITIONAL	Helvetica	**ORNAMENTAL/OTHER**
Baskerville	Optima	**Poster Bodoni**
Times Roman	Univers	COTTONWOOD
MODERN	**SQUARE SERIF**	Dom Casual
Benguiat	American	Broadway
Palatino	Typewriter	Auriol
	Lubalin Graph	Caslon Open Face

less common than roman or sans serif faces. Script faces aren't usually put to work in advertising, particularly in national advertising; most are fairly hard to read, and many look like unsuccessful attempts to imitate handwriting. Ornamentals are used in selected applications, but most are so distinctive and specialized that their use is limited.[38]

The vertical dimension of type is specified in **points,** usually abbreviated as "pt." One point is equal to $\frac{1}{72}$ of an inch, so 12-point type is $\frac{1}{6}$ of an inch tall. Typefaces typically range in size from 6 points ($\frac{1}{12}$ inch) to 72 points (1 inch); most of the body type you see in books, newspapers, magazines, and ads ranges from 8 or 9 points up to 11 or 12 points. The horizontal dimension of type is specified in **picas;** one pica is equal to 12 points, making it $\frac{1}{6}$ of an inch. Picas are also used to specify the length of the line; an art director might instruct the typesetter to set the body copy 21 picas, or 3.5 inches, wide.

Another important vertical dimension is the space between lines of type. You've pondered this question yourself, when you decide (or are instructed) to single-space or double-space the lines in a homework paper. The typesetter's term for the space between lines is **leading** (pronounced "ledding") or *linespacing.* Leading is measured in points. When an art director specifies "10 on 12" type, the first figure is the type size, and the second figure is the type size plus 2 points of leading. The second figure is also the baseline to baseline measurement (see Exhibit 10.9).

In addition to the typeface design and the point size, many typefaces also vary in terms of *width* and *weight.* Width can be expressed as normal, narrow, or com-

EXHIBIT 10.9
The Terminology of Type

This exhibit illustrates some of the language of type: serifs, points, leading, and picas/points/inches, as well as the parts of a typeface.

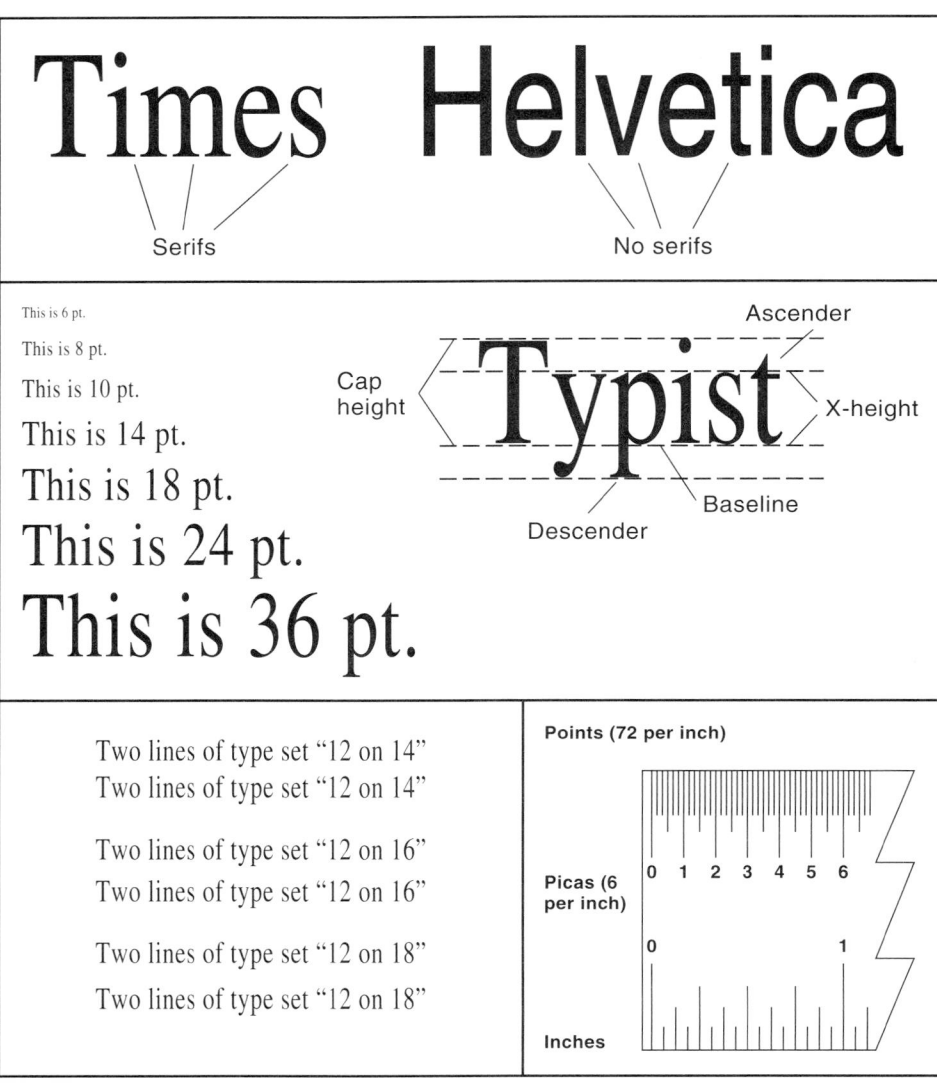

pressed, for instance. Common weights are light, normal, bold, and extra bold. (The key terms in this book are set in boldface, for example.) Also, many typefaces are available in *italics,* which are basically slanted versions of the regular upright face. Another important type term is **font,** which refers to the set of characters (roman, italic, normal, boldface, and so on) that make up one typeface in one type, size, and weight. For instance, "12-point Helvetica compressed bold" is a font. Finally, most typefaces are part of larger **type families,** which are collections of related styles. The Univers family, for example, contains fonts sized from 6 to 48 points in 20 width and weight combinations.[39] Exhibit 10.9 summarizes these key type terms, and Exhibit 10.10 shows some of the variations in a popular type family.

Choosing and Using Type. The visual, nonverbal aspects of type are a powerful communication force, quite apart from what the words themselves are trying to say. In fact, noted print designer John McWade calls type "the visible voice," meaning that the type style itself has something to say.[40] Selecting the right type is therefore a crucial part of ad design. Consider the headlines shown in Exhibit 10.11. In some of these, the type chosen clearly doesn't match the content of the message, and the result is a lack of unity, a violation of one of the key design principles discussed earlier in the chapter. In others, the "visible voice" of the type style harmonizes with the message. Another important nonverbal aspect is how typefaces work together in an ad. For instance, visually "busy" faces, such as most of the ornamentals, work best when paired with simple body type, such as a clean sans serif design.[41]

Placing type on the page and fitting the desired copy into the available space are two more design challenges for the art director. Placement on the page is usually dictated by whatever basic design you've chosen. In the picture-window design, for example, you usually get a certain amount of space at the bottom of the page in which to place the copy. Fitting the copy into that space can be a difficult task, often requiring the art director and the copywriter to work together to make the words fit the allotted space. The copywriter may have to change the wording slightly in order to get the copy to fit, or the art director may need to rethink the design. In fact, some of the more creative moments in writing and design occur when people are trying to get copy to fit.

Apart from all the technical and artistic details surrounding type, the most important point is that the type must be readable. This sounds obvious, but the decision to make copy readable is sometimes in conflict with other artistic decisions about the design of an ad. A recent ad for the Eagle Vision (Eagle is a division of Chrysler) did an aesthetically clever job of setting a collection of positive comments from car magazines to look like rain showering down on the car, playing off the headline "It's no wonder we've been showered with praise." The copy was set in white type against a dark, stormy sky, and it tilted at a steep angle to look like sheets of rain. It works well aesthetically, but the small white type is nearly swallowed by the dark background, and the slanted angle makes it even more

EXHIBIT 10.10
Varieties in One Type Family

Many type families include a number of variations that serve different design purposes.

Helvetica
Helvetica Bold
Helvetica Italic
Helvetica Bold Italic
Helvetica Condensed
Helvetica Bold Condensed
Helvetica Bold Outline

EXHIBIT 10.11   Searching for Unity with Typeface Personalities

When the typeface doesn't match the message, the result is an ad that lacks unity. Which of these typefaces match their messages, and which don't?

Exotic cuisine at everyday prices
(Arnold-Bocklin)

Global investment banking
(Hobo)

LEADING-EDGE INDUSTRIAL AUTOMATION
(Industria Solid)

Emergency Services That Could Save Your Business
(Mistral)

The Toughest Trucks on the American Highway
(Parisian)

History Tours with Dr. Jane Seybold
(Post Antiqua)

ANGELICA'S BRIDAL BOUTIQUE
(Stencil)

KEEPING YOUR INVESTMENTS SAFE AND SECURE
(Trajan)

EXHIBIT 10.12
The Difficulty of Reading Reverse Type

Most people find light type on a dark background to be more difficult to read than dark type on a light background.

Apart from all the technical and artistic details surrounding type, the most important point is that the type must be readable. This sounds obvious, but the decision to make copy readable is sometimes in conflict with other artistic decisions about the design of an ad. A recent ad for the Eagle Vision (Eagle is a division of Chrysler) did an aesthetically clever job of setting a collection of positive comments from car magazines to look like rain showering down on the car, playing off the headline "It's no wonder we've been showered with praise."	Apart from all the technical and artistic details surrounding type, the most important point is that the type must be readable. This sounds obvious, but the decision to make copy readable is sometimes in conflict with other artistic decisions about the design of an ad. A recent ad for the Eagle Vision (Eagle is a division of Chrysler) did an aesthetically clever job of setting a collection of positive comments from car magazines to look like rain showering down on the car, playing off the headline "It's no wonder we've been showered with praise."

difficult to read.[42] Light type set on a dark background is usually slower and harder to read than dark type on a light background (see Exhibit 10.12).

Working with Visuals

With the exception of the copy-heavy and big-type page designs, the visual is often the dominant element in an ad. Even when copy provides all the key selling points, the reader is often left with an image that was created by the visual. Using visuals involves two major tasks: selecting which visuals to use and then making sure they work with the copy.

Selecting Visuals. Thumb through some consumer or business magazines and you'll get an idea of the range of visual materials that art directors can use, from simple cartoon sketches to complex computer-modified photographs. Photographs can be either custom-shot for a specific ad or leased from companies that offer a wide variety of existing photos (these are known as *stock* photos). If you get the opportunity to attend an advertising photo shoot, you might be amazed at the amount of time and care that goes into getting just the right photos. The photographer may take several hundred shots of a single product or scene, from which the art director picks the one or two that do the job best.

In addition to basic photos, art directors can use a variety of illustrations or fine art. These can range from cartoons to reproductions of famous paintings. As with photos, this artwork can be created specifically for an ad, or it might come from an existing source. Computer art, both original creations and modifications to other pieces of art, is an important source of advertising visuals. Computers now give advertising artists complete creative control over visual elements. Software programs such as Aldus Gallery Effects and Adobe Photoshop allow artists to perform such drastic measures as converting a photograph to something that looks like a watercolor painting.[43] Artists can use this and other image-editing tools to produce just about any visual an art director could desire.

Coordinating Visuals with Copy. According to the design principle of unity, it's important for copy and visuals to work together in one integrated whole. This coordination involves everything from choosing a typeface and an illustration that are aesthetically compatible to making sure that the text and visual(s) don't get in each other's way. The art director's job is to make the visuals and copy work in harmony, while still trying to make a creative impact that will grab and keep the reader's attention.

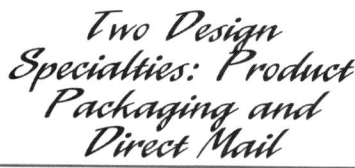

Two Design Specialties: Product Packaging and Direct Mail

Print and electronic advertising are certainly major areas of responsibility for advertising art directors, but they are far from the only tasks that these people are called on to handle. Product packaging and direct-mail pieces are important design areas as well, requiring the same level of creativity and advertising insight as their mass-media cousins.

Product packaging (including both packages that products are shipped and stored in and the labels on the products themselves) might seem like an odd thing to include on an art director's list of responsibilities, but only until you realize how important packaging is for many products. For consumer goods in particular, the product package is sometimes more important than regular advertising. The reason for this lies in the way consumers make their purchase decisions. For many consumers in many product categories, the purchase decision is made right in the store. Advertising that appeared in the mass media may still be at work in the consumer's mind, but it's no longer in front of the consumer—the product package is. All other things being equal, an attractive package with a strong promotional message will most likely outsell a package that has a weak message or doesn't look up to date.

Consider the way packaging turned sales around for Nasoya Foods, a producer of tofu-based mayonnaise and other tofu products. The company was facing one of the major hurdles that hinder small food manufacturers: simply convincing retailers to put its products on the shelf. When the company gave the packaging a more contemporary look and put a colorful and inviting label on the front, sales eventually climbed by 50 percent as the product caught the eye of both retailers and consumers.

Noted San Francisco graphic designer Primo Angeli makes an important point about food packaging in particular: if the packaging obscures the product, what the buyer sees on the packaging and the label has to carry the product message. When he designed the packaging for Capri Sun, he realized that consumers were used to buying ready-to-drink juice in see-through jars. Since Capri Sun came in an opaque foil drink pouch, Angeli compensated with a design that focuses the eye on an inviting display of fruit.

The concept of attractive product packaging is quite similar to a key design challenge in direct-mail advertising, which uses the "outsides" to sell what's on the inside. A large portion of the advertising mailed to consumers and business customers is simply tossed out unopened. As an advertiser, getting your direct-mail envelope opened is the same challenge a salesperson faces when trying to get an appointment with a prospect: you both want the chance to tell potential customers about your product. Designers choose one of two very different approaches: either they come right out and let the audience know that this is a piece of advertising, or they try to make it look like a piece of regular mail. The "this is advertising" approach tries to give the prospect a reason to open the envelope, such as promising important news, a free gift, or some other payoff for opening. The other approach tries to make the direct-mail piece look like regular mail, with no promotional copy and sometimes not even a return address.

The art designer's role is to present the package in a way that's both effective and appropriate for the product. A plain envelope suggests serious business. This is often the best choice when mailing to corporate customers or to consumers regarding important products. Flashier designs that start selling right from the outside of the envelope are often developed for consumer mailings. This flashy approach is often avoided in business mailings, because many executives instruct their assistants to screen out any mail that looks like advertising. As with everything else in advertising, the best choice is dictated by the audience and its likely response to your efforts.

Apply Your Knowledge

1. What should the relationship be between a product's package or label design and the design of its advertising?
2. Do you see any ethical problem with direct-mail envelopes that appear to contain official documents or checks or that use other tricks to get people to open the envelope? ∎

Letting your mind run loose when it comes to integrating art and type can lead to some eye-catching results. In an ad for the Mercedes 500 SL, Mike Hughs and Bill Westbrook of the Martin Agency used a clever marriage of type and photo to get their point across. At the top of the page is a blank space on the left, an equals sign in the middle, and a photo of the 500 SL model at the right. The message is of course, "Nothing equals a 500 SL," but the reader has to get involved enough with the ad to make the connection.[44] The ad communicates instantly and effectively, since copy and visuals work in harmony.

Laying Out the Page

The art director's last major step before moving into production (see Chapter 11) is laying out the ad. A **layout** is any in-progress version of the ad, from a rough sketch to something with real photos and finished type. (Some people refer to the basic design of a print ad as a layout.) Depending on their complexity, ads can move through as many as four stages in the layout process:[45]

EXHIBIT 10.13
Thumbnails, Roughs, and Comps

Ads progress through a series of design and production stages on the way from initial concept through finished piece; the six sketches on this page are thumbnails, the top two on the next page are roughs, and the final one is a comp.

- *Thumbnail.* The **thumbnail** sketch is a miniature rough draft, in which the designer sketches his or her ideas for the basic design of the ad. This stage helps identify the basic format and shape of the ad, although some designers skip this step and start with rough layouts.

- *Rough layout.* The **rough layout** is a full-size version of the sketch, showing all the elements in the ad in their basic proportions and placements. The designer may letter in the headlines and other display copy with some care or simply scribble them in, depending on how many people are going to review the rough layout.

- *Comprehensive layout.* The **comprehensive layout,** usually called the *comp,* shows all the pieces of the ad in place and drawn with some degree of care and accuracy. Exhibit 10.13 shows the progression from a thumbnail to a rough to a comp. The copy and headlines may be set with computer-generated type, and pasted-in photographs may be used to give a more realistic picture of what the final ad will look like. A key purpose of the comp is to let the advertiser see where its money is about to be spent and allow for changes before moving into final production. For brochures, flyers, and other promotional material, art directors often create a **dummy,** a mock-up that serves the same basic function that the comp serves for print ads.

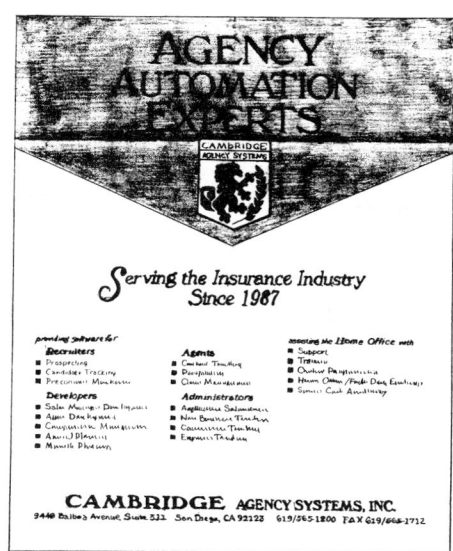

- *Mechanical.* Once the client approves the format and content of the ad, the art director moves ahead with the **mechanical.** This is the physical ad that will be reproduced as the first step in the printing process, complete with final artwork and typeset copy. Reflecting the fact that all ads used to be manually pasted together (many are now done entirely or mostly on computers), the mechanical is often referred to as the **pasteup.**

At this point, the ad is ready for production, the subject of Chapter 11. The remainder of this chapter is devoted to art direction in television ads. As mentioned earlier, many of the concepts discussed for print ads apply to television ads, although it's not surprising that television has some unique aspects.

Designing Television Advertising

The concept of sequence presented earlier in the chapter bears repeating for electronic media. In addition to reaching the audience with sound and motion, television ads also differ from print ads because they're structured in *time* (as opposed to being structured in *space*). Television ads have a beginning, middle, and end, whereas print ads happen all at once. Art directors in the electronic media still worry about line, color, texture, shape, direction, size, sound, and space; they still worry about balance, proportion, unity, emphasis, and tension and surprise. In addition, they also have to consider how things fit together over time. Not only do all the elements on the television screen have to work in harmony, but what's on the screen 20 seconds into the commercial has to work with what appeared before and what will appear after. This complexity can make art direction even more challenging, but it is what gives television ads their special ability to communicate.

Art direction in television advertising consists of four major steps: choosing a format, setting the commercial's style and tone, working with the audio and video elements you'll use, and then visualizing what the commercial will look like. Although the actual production of a television commercial is discussed in Chapter 12, the following four steps lead up to that production.

CHOOSING A FORMAT

As with print advertising, television ads tend to fall into several basic categories. Lists vary, of course, but most ads fit into problem-solution, demonstration, spokesperson-testimonial, product presentation, slice-of-life, minidrama, or musical/stage-show formats:[46]

- *Problem-solution.* The problem-solution format is quite common in television advertising. In a sense, it represents the whole idea behind marketing. The potential customer has a problem, you present a solution, the customer buys it, and the customer realizes some financial, emotional, or social satisfaction as a result.

- *Demonstration.* The demonstration format plays off a key strength of television: showing something in action (see Exhibit 10.14). When Black & Decker advertised its Heat 'n Strip paint removal tool, for instance, it could have explained in a print or radio ad how the tool removes old paint from furniture and woodwork. However, showing it strip away paint in a television close-up got the point across quickly and convincingly.

- *Spokesperson-testimonial.* The spokesperson-testimonial format uses a presenter making a sales pitch directly to the audience. The presenter can be a well-known personality or simply a user of the product. Not surprisingly, this format works best when the message is believable and the presenter fits the product, such as when home-repair expert Bob Vila talks about Sears home and garden products.

- *Product presentation.* This is sometimes called the "product as hero" format because the product is the star of the commercial. The art director and copywriter don't bother creating fictional characters, a dramatic storyline, or any other embellishments; the product is judged strong enough to carry the sales message itself.[48] This format is commonly used for cars and other products with a strong visual presence.

- *Slice of life.* The **slice-of-life** format gives the audience a look at a supposedly realistic situation in the lives of people who represent the target audience. It's essentially a problem-solution format played out by a cast of characters. You've seen this format used to advertise everything from breath mints to garbage bags. This format is so familiar, in fact, that copywriters and art directors need to take special care not to fall into ruts worn deep by countless slice-of-life ads over the years.[49]

- *Minidrama.* Unlike the slice-of-life format, the continuing-characters format creates one or more fictional characters (human or otherwise) and bases a series of ads around them. An immensely successful campaign for Nestlé's

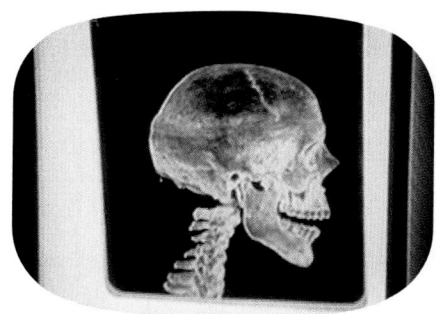
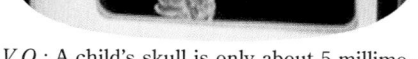
V.O.: A child's skull is only about 5 millime-

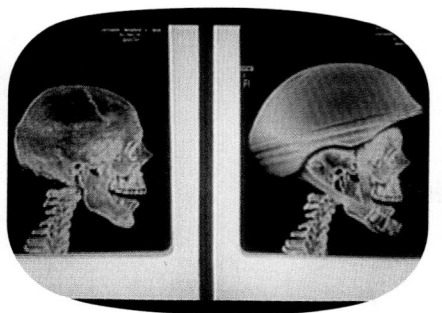

ters thick. Or, is it? Don't let your child ride

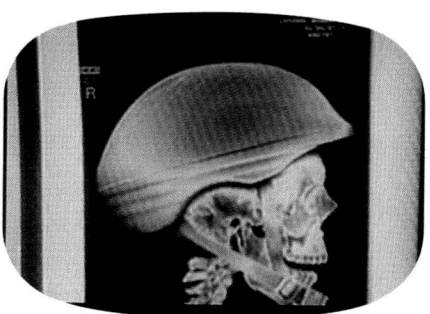
a bike without a helmet.

EXHIBIT 10.14
The Power of Demonstration

This commercial exploits the demonstration power of television to emphasize how fragile a child's skull is.

Gold Blend instant coffee has been running in Britain since 1987, showing the evolving relationship between a man and a woman brought together by a love of good coffee (a similar campaign for Nestlé's Taster's Choice coffee has been running in the United States since 1990). Gold Blend sales in Britain are up 40 percent since the campaign began, and viewers are so enthralled with the coffee couple's romance that Nestlé commissioned a novel to be written about the pair. At one point, a new twist in the couple's relationship made front-page news, getting a bigger headline than a royal wedding.[50]

- *Musical/stage show.* This format involves commercials based on songs or jingles or on more elaborate "stage shows." Soft-drink advertisers are some of the most recognizable users of the stage-show format. Pepsi's "Uh-Huh" campaign is a good example, featuring Ray Charles and a huge cast of singers, dancers, and actors.

Advertising-research pioneer William Wells divides the format possibilities for television into the two general categories of *lectures* (the problem-solution, demonstration, spokesperson-testimonial, and product-presentation formats) and *dramas* (the slice-of-life, continuing-character, and musical/stage-show formats). In the lecture format, the ad is like a speech. The speaker may be on camera or off, on location (such as in a kitchen) or not, or speaking or singing, but the flow of communication is always from the speaker to the viewing audience. In contrast, dramas communicate to the audience by letting them "overhear" the interaction between characters in the commercial.[51]

SETTING THE STYLE AND TONE

With a basic format in mind, the art director must next make a decision about the overall style and tone of the ad. Should it be rational or emotional? Serious or funny? Realistic or exaggerated? These are complex decisions that need to take both artistic concerns and overall advertising strategy into consideration (see Exhibit 10.15). Each decision should be considered on a spectrum of possibilities, from one extreme to the other. A commercial can be predominantly rational, for instance, with just enough emotional emphasis to involve the audience at an emotional level.[52]

Television commercials can range from documentary-style realism to outlandishly distorted exaggeration. Exaggeration can be quite effective in a television ad, but it can also backfire if it comes across as silly or pretentious. A commercial for the U.K.-based Barclays Bank made great use of exaggeration when it showed a hapless customer getting verbally assaulted by rude robots, being frisked by frightening humanoids, and entering a conversation with a creature who appears to be human but is revealed otherwise when the electrical cord attached to its head is shown. The exaggeration works because it highlights the frustration many people

(*SFX*): car engine
KIDS: Grandma's here.

Grandma's here.
(*SFX*): dog barks

V.O.: New York Lotto.
Hey, you never know.

EXHIBIT 10.15
Style and Tone in Television Advertising

This ad for the New York Lotto uses a humorous style to convey the benefits of winning the lottery.

shown. The exaggeration works because it highlights the frustration many people feel with computerized banking services.[53] In contrast, MCI used exaggeration in a dark and melodramatic commercial about the need for change in business telecommunications. *Advertising Age* critic Bob Garfield called it the most ominous ad of 1992 and questioned whether a decision about phone service was really as dire as MCI was trying to make it seem.[54]

WORKING WITH THE AUDIO AND VISUAL ELEMENTS

Every television commercial is constructed from various audio and visual elements. Some are simple, such as a McDonald's commercial that showed nothing but close-ups of several products while a voice was talking off-camera. Others can be extremely complex to design, such as a Diet Coke musical extravaganza or Nike's commercial in which NBA star Charles Barkley beats Godzilla at a game of one-on-one. Here's a closer look at the most frequently used audio and visual elements.

Audio Elements

The **audio** portion of a television commercial includes speaking voices, singing voices, instrumental background music, and sound effects. Copy that's read by someone off-screen during a commercial is called a **voice-over;** you've probably heard famous personalities reading voice-overs. **Jingles** are short songs that carry advertising messages; they can be either original tunes or adaptations of popular tunes. Research suggests that songs developed specifically for advertising are the most effective, that parodies of original hit songs are less effective, and that the original hit songs themselves are least effective.[55]

Sound effects have become increasingly popular in television advertising, mostly as a means to break through clutter. Scientists are still trying to pin down the effects that music and sound have on audience responses, but the uncertainty hasn't stopped a number of advertisers from experimenting. One theory is that unusual sounds, such as the buzzing sound that grows in intensity during an ad, get through the clutter because they don't get caught by the mind's conditioned filtering mechanisms. In other words, the audience is already adept at tuning out spokesmodels and jingles, but an odd sound coming from the television might break through.[56] On the other hand, if an ad sounds "like an ad," such as a musical commercial on an all-talk radio station, the audience may instantly recognize it as an ad and tune it out.

Visual Elements

The visual elements of a television commercial consist of everything that the viewer sees on the screen, whether it's film footage, an animated bunny, or simply a typed message. The art director's choice must take into account the product, the advertising strategy, the competition's strategy, and the ever-present need to break through clutter. Visual elements fall into four categories:[57]

They're Laughing, but Are They Buying?

Humor in advertising is a very serious subject indeed. Puns, slapstick, and other comic treatments show up in a significant number of print, television, and radio ads. Nearly a quarter of U.S. television commercials include a humorous element, and more than a third of British television ads do. However, humor's effect on sales isn't always clear.

Humor can range from the delicate and subtle to the "in your face" variety. A commercial for the Ikea furniture chain that some consumers call "hilarious" shows a man walking toward the television audience from off in the distance. He steps right up and presses his nose against the camera, and then he starts looking around as if the television set is a window in the viewer's home. After surveying the viewer's living quarters, the man steps back and screams, "You need some new furniture!" The commercial then shows the latest Ikea catalog as the solution to the furniture need. The humor works both because it's unusual to have someone "looking out" of your television set into your living room and because it's tied into Ikea's selling message about great new furniture.

Another advertiser that has used humor quite effectively is Alaska Airlines. Its television spots show the trials of travel on other airlines, and, in doing so, it makes a sympathetic connection with the audience. Anybody who has tried to eat an unappetizing meal off a tray table that won't lie flat, who has been sprayed by a lavatory faucet gone mad, or who has arrived exhausted and disheveled knows what the commercials are talking about.

However, humor must be used with great care, because it can backfire in several ways. First, not everyone has the same tastes and values, so what's acceptably funny to one person may be offensive to someone else. Since a great deal of general humor pokes fun at certain groups of people, it can easily cause problems. Second, if your selling message depends on people getting a joke, and they don't get the joke, they're obviously not going to get the selling message either. Many humorous messages depend on the sender and the receiver having the same cultural background and life experiences, and if these don't overlap, the joke may not get across. Third, many products and market situations are inappropriate for a humorous approach. For instance, you wouldn't want to portray a hospital with slapstick comedy; the situation is too serious for a lighthearted approach. Fourth, and perhaps most critical, humor that overshadows the selling message will be less effective than humor that supports the message.

Several years ago, Isuzu used a humorous approach in television commercials, playing up the negative perception that many people have of car dealers. The spokesman was an outrageously dishonest car salesman named Joe Isuzu who made obviously wild claims about his cars. The ads were a hit with consumers everywhere, and Joe Isuzu became something of a folk antihero. In fact, David Leisure, who played Joe in the commercials, has since gone on to a career on regular television shows. However, the ads didn't sell cars. Unlike the Ikea and Alaska Airlines spots, Isuzu humor wasn't closely linked with an advertising message. As you can see, humor can be an effective selling agent in your advertising, but it's not as likely to be helpful if it's just laughs for the sake of laughs.

Apply Your Knowledge

1. What effect would intercultural or international audiences have on your use of humorous advertising appeals?
2. Given the risks involved, would it be safer to avoid humor altogether?

- *Live action.* Live action encompasses anything shot with a television or video camera, which can include a presenter talking into a camera, a camera following actors or consumers while they use a product, or a fantasy or futuristic sequence showing people floating on clouds, flying spacecraft, or doing other things out of the ordinary.

- *Animation.* **Animation** includes essentially everything you might see in a television commercial except live action: cartoons, a series of still photos, simple copy on the screen, and so forth. For years, animated characters, often tied to Saturday morning cartoon shows, have appeared in ads aimed at children. Now animation is showing up in more and more ads aimed at adults as well. Whether it's cartoon animation (Amoco's Little Blue Engine character) or puppet-style gadgets (the Energizer bunny), audiences seem to find animated characters generally more entertaining than celebrity spokespersons and other forms of ads. The Energizer bunny seems to strike a particularly strong chord with adult viewers, since it more or less winks at some of the stereotypical ads as it goes crashing through them. The newest twist in

CHECKLIST FOR DESIGNING EXCELLENT ADS

❏ A. Print ads.
- Does the ad grab readers long enough to stop them from turning the page?
- Will the right readers know the ad is for them?
- Is the message clear at a glance?
- Do the headline and the main visual work together? Do they promise a meaningful benefit?
- Is the copy easy to read?
- Is there enough copy to support the message, but not so much as to overwhelm readers?

❏ B. Television commercials.
- Have you done something to catch the viewer's attention?

- Is there a main selling point that viewers can take away from the commercial?
- Have you given the viewer a reason (humor, mystery, etc.) to watch and listen to the entire commercial?
- Is the commercial relevant to viewers' wants and needs?
- Are the format and style compatible with your product and the market position you want to achieve or maintain?
- Is a benefit clearly stated? Will members of the target audience know that this benefit is for them?

computer animation is combining it with live action, a technique inspired by the movie *Who Framed Roger Rabbit?*[58]

- *Copy.* Copy appearing on-screen is just another form of animation, but it is becoming so common in television ads that it deserves special attention. Displayed copy is called a **super** (short for *superimpose*) when it appears on top of a visual image. Logos, brand names, and telephone numbers are common super copy.[59] More and more advertisers are turning to displayed copy to get major selling points across and to break through the clutter.[60] Displayed copy even helps get your point across when people mute commercials with their remote controls.
- *Visual effects.* Visual effects range from simple camera moves and editing tricks to advanced computer-generated illusions. Industrial Light and Magic, a special-effects company started by George Lucas of *Star Wars* fame, has turned its talents to advertising, creating such effects as buildings that bend in the wind (for a Dodge commercial).[61]

VISUALIZING THE COMMERCIAL

The final stage in designing the television commercial and getting ready for production is visualizing the commercial itself. This stage is important not only for the people directly involved in the creation of the commercial but also for the client, who will want to know what his or her money will be spent on before production begins. Production costs are hitting $1 million or more for extravagant commercials and can hit a hundred thousand dollars or more for relatively simple commercials. Consequently, the better you can visualize the commercial before production, the fewer mistakes you'll make and the less rework you'll face.

The **storyboard** in television commercials serves the same purpose as the layout in print advertising; the major difference is that the storyboard also has to illustrate the changes from scene to scene. A storyboard shows the main visual scenes, along with the voice-over copy and instructions for camera movements, sound effects, and other design elements (see Exhibit 10.16). A related design tool is the **script,** which is the copywriter's version of a storyboard, containing the copy (the spoken or sung words) and verbal descriptions of the visual elements.[62]

Agencies have developed other tools to help clients visualize ads. An **animatic** is a "filmstrip" version of the storyboard, in which sketches of the proposed visuals are filmed in sequence and linked with the audio track. A more polished version, the **photomatic,** does the same thing, only with photos instead of sketches.[63]

1. Camera opens on a shot of Luis, Christina, and Gustavo as they exit their place of business and walk towards Luis' car.
Super: BK Bug.

SFX: Door swinging open.
Christina: ¡Vamos a BURGER KING®! Lets go to BURGER KING®.

2. Same shot as we track them walking through the parking lot.

Christina: (Excited) Tienen el nuevo Everyday Value Menu. They have the the new Everyday Value Menu.

3. Same shot as they approach Luis' car.

Luis: (Excited) Sí, deliciosa comida, con precios como 99¢, $1.99, y $2.99. (Smugly) ¡Es un menú de gran Valor! (Excited) Yes, delicious food, for prices like 99¢, $1.99, and $2.99. (Smugly) It's a menu with great value!

4. Cut to a shot where the three of them look at each other from across the roof of the car.

Gustavo: (Smiling) ¿Qué... hay que ser valiente para ordenar? (Starts to laugh) (Smiling) What... you have to be brave to order? (Starts to laugh) "Valor" means value & brave in spanish.

5. Cut to a shot of Luis and Christina as they give each other a look and roll their eyes. Gustavo stops laughing and gets in the car quickly with embarrassment.

SFX: Gustavo laughing hysterically... then slowing it down to a cough.

6. Cut to a shot of patties being flame-broiled.

Anncr: En BURGER KING®, gran valor significa comida deliciosa... At BURGER KING® great value means delicious food.

7. Cut to quick shots of a WHOPPER® being built and un-built.

Anncr: Hecha a tu manera. Made your way.

8. Cut to a shot of a BURGER KING® restaurant as people walk in and out.

Anncr: En un lugar cómodo, y claro, al precio ideal. In a place that's comfortable, and of course, for an ideal price.

9. Cut to quick shots of Flame-broiling patties. We see lettuce being cut, and tomatoes being sliced.

Cut to Camera Card: Everyday Value Menu - 99¢

Anncr: Como algunas de las hamburguesas a la parrilla por 99¢... Like some of the flame-broiled burgers for 99¢...

10. Cut to shots of the CROISSAN'WICH ® being built, coffee, eggs being cooked, and of the CROISSAN'WICH® and coffee together.
Cut to Camera Card: Everyday Value Menu - $1.99

Anncr: Deliciosas combinaciones del desayuno por $1.99... Delicious breakfast combinations for $1.99...

11. Cut to shots of the WHOPPER® Combo, the Double Cheeseburger Combo, and the BK BIG FISH Combo.

Cut to Camera Card: Everyday Value Menu - $2.99

Anncr: Y "combos" que incluyen tus sandwiches favoritos a la parrilla, por sólo $2.99. And Combos that include your favorite flame-broiled sandwiches for only $2.99.

12. Cut to quick shots representing a majority of the product shots we just saw.
Super: Everyday Value Menu.

Anncr: Valor como debe de ser... What value should really be...

13. Cut to BURGER KING® tag & Logo.

Anncr: Y porque Así Lo Quiero. Because that's the way I want it.

EXHIBIT 10.16
The Television Storyboard

This storyboard for a Burger King ad shows the major scenes and accompanying dialog and sound effects that will be included in the finished commercial.

Summary

Art direction is responsible for creating ads that have stopping power and that hold the audience's attention while presenting the selling message in an effective and appealing way. In the design process, the art director is responsible for all visual elements appearing in an ad (and sound in radio and television). In short, the art director is responsible for both the composition and the execution of the ad.

The basic elements of design are line, color, texture, shape, direction, size, sound, and space. Sound, of course, isn't normally available in print ads, but it's the only element in radio ads. These elements are used in advertising according to the principles of good design, which include balance, proportion, sequence, unity, emphasis, and tension and surprise.

The two major stages of print ad design are (1) choosing a format and (2) designing the page. In the page-design stage, the art director chooses a basic page-design scheme, works with the copy to get it typeset and ready for printing, chooses and designs the visual elements, and then lays out the page. In many cases, other people do the actual work in these steps, but the art director remains responsible for the final result.

Art direction in television advertising consists of four major steps. The first is choosing the basic format, which can include problem-solution, demonstration, spokesperson-testimonial, product presentation, slice of life, minidrama, and musical/stage show. The second is setting the style and tone of the ad; the decisions here determine whether the ad will be rational or emotional, serious or funny, and realistic or exaggerated. The third step is selecting the various audio and visual elements that the commercial will be built around. Audio elements include speaking voices, singing voices, instrumental background music, and sound effects. Visual elements can be grouped into the categories of live action, animation, on-screen copy, and various visual effects. The fourth and final step is visualizing what the commercial will look like, which involves writing the storyboard and planning the overall look of the commercial.

Meeting an Advertising Challenge at Cessna Aircraft

A CASE FOR CRITICAL THINKING

The unique nature of business-jet marketing presented both challenges and opportunities to Cessna's Gary Hays. On the one hand, his product was complex and expensive and wasn't even built yet when he had to start advertising it. Moreover, his audience was largely protected by a wall of assistants just looking for reasons to toss advertising efforts into the recycling bin. On the other hand, it was no mystery who was in the target audience or where those people could be found. Cessna could easily get its hands on the names and addresses of every person in the target audience. Now Hays and his agency partners, Wichita's Sullivan Higdon & Sink, had to come up with a creative program that captured the attention of that target audience.

Realizing that a business jet represents not only an immense financial decision for buyers but a powerful emotional force as well (due to safety, reliability, image, and other such factors), Hays and company put together a direct-mail program that provided both technical information and strong emotional appeals and that was probably unusual enough to make it past most gatekeepers. Several poster-sized advertisements contained information about the jet's capabilities as well as eye-catching photography of the new model. To add to the impact, Sullivan Higdon sent the posters wrapped in large gift boxes.

Hays also knows that getting the audience involved in the advertising is one of the best ways to communicate an advertising message effectively and convincingly. He did this in several ways. First, copy on the posters proclaimed that the "New Citation is coming. And it's coming fast." This not only let the CEOs know that a new jet from Cessna was on the way; it also dropped a huge hint about the Citation X's blazing speed. Second, the posters also told the audience that, "Very soon, you'll receive some tangible reminders of that fact. Because we're about to begin sending you the components of a limited-edition, large-scale desk model of the Citation X. The three components will arrive in separate packages, several weeks apart." This injected even more anticipation into the communication process, and it served to keep Cessna and the new Citation X in front of the audience for several months in a row. Third, Hays and Sullivan Higdon fol-lowed up on these promises and delivered the parts of a sleek jet model that was sure to capture the attention of anyone with an interest in corporate jets. In fact, the design was so eye-catching that it won Business Marketing magazine's 1993 Sawyer Award for best business-to-business direct-mail campaign.

Your Mission: You've recently joined Cessna as its manager of marketing communications, reporting to marketing vice president Gary Hays. All of the company's communication activities, including advertising, are now your responsibility. In this role, you're the key contact person at Cessna for Sullivan Higdon & Sink, the company's ad agency. In the following scenarios, you'll have to choose from design alternatives that the agency's art director has submitted for your review.

1. One of the most important criteria in the purchase of a business jet is the degree to which it enables executives to work efficiently and comfortably while in the air. You've asked the agency to put together a

Key Terms

animatic 272
animation 271
audio 270
balance 252
composition 250
comprehensive layout 266
display copy 261
dummy 266
emphasis 254
execution 250
font 263
graphic designers 250
grid 258
illustrators 250
jingles 270
layout 265
leading 262
mechanical 267
pasteup 267

photomatic 272
picas 262
points 262
proportion 253
rough layout 266
script 272
sequence 253
slice of life 268
stopping power 250
storyboard 272
super 272
thumbnail 266
type families 263
typeface 261
unity 254
visuals 250
voice-over 270
white space 252

Questions

FOR REVIEW

1. What is the art director's responsibility in the design of an ad?

2. Why is it important to understand the basic elements and principles of design, even if you'll never design an ad yourself?

3. How is the decision to emphasize a particular visual point in an ad related to marketing and advertising strategy?

4. When would you use a copy-heavy ad design? Explain your answer.

5. How can humor backfire in an ad?

FOR ANALYSIS AND APPLICATION

6. Assume you were using a print ad, rather than a résumé, to promote yourself to potential employers; which format would you use and why?

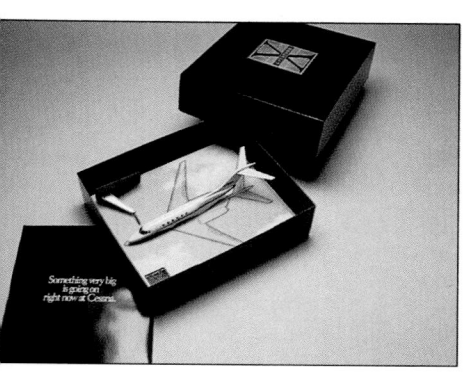

Something very big is going on right now at Cessna.

print ad that shows off a particular jet's capabilities in this regard, which include a tall center aisle for easy passage through the cabin, seat tables that are large enough to hold a laptop computer and a stack of reports, and a communications desk that includes fax machines and telephones. Which of the following photo/headline combinations would you select to include in the ad?

a. A photo of a nice, efficient-looking executive office, with the headline "Wouldn't it be great to have an office like this in the air?"

b. A composite image of photos taken inside the jet, showing a laptop computer, the fax machines, the telephones, and any other significant on-board business equipment, with the headline "You no longer have to leave your tools behind when you travel."

c. A photo taken inside the jet, showing several executives engaged in a business discussion, along with part of a computer and a fax machine or telephone; the headline reads "Put wings on your executive office suite."

2. Given the nature of the purchase decision, the product, and the potential customers, which of the following color schemes would you choose for Cessna's print advertising?

a. A color scheme that likens the jet to other business equipment; emphasize beige and gray, since most office equipment comes in such colors

b. A sleek, high-tech color scheme that features black and silver or gold

c. A colorful, eye-catching scheme that connotes energy and liveliness, relying on lots of bright yellows, reds, and other powerful colors

3. Which of the following page designs would you choose for an ad that promoted Cessna maintenance and repair services?

a. The long-outline format
b. The sermon
c. The one-liner

4. Given the extremely narrow market for corporate jets, it's unlikely that Cessna would ever advertise its aircraft on television. However, videotapes as part of a direct-mail program would make a lot of sense for such products, and many of the design concepts employed in television commercials also apply to video ads. You're considering such a videotape for the Citation X and need to decide on the overall style and tone. Which of the following statements describes the best approach for this video?

a. In keeping with the importance and expense of the purchase decision, we will project a serious, businesslike manner in the videotape.

b. Making a poor decision on something as important as the corporate jet could harm an executive's career, so we'll focus on the fear factor involved in the decision.

c. We'll highlight the Citation X's extremely high cruising speed by using humorous exaggeration related to the concepts of speed and time. Examples of the approach include showing executives traveling coast to coast in a matter of minutes, people growing to old age over the span of a 15-minute videotape, and similar visual treatments.[64] ∎

7. Could a stockbroker use the one-liner ad format effectively? Explain your answer.

8. Why do ad designers use several stages of layouts? Why not just go right to work on the final mechanical and save the time spent on preliminary stages?

9. Would the slice-of-life format be effective for a television ad promoting industrial products, such as a Fanuc manufacturing robot? Why or why not?

10. Why do art directors display copy on the screen during some television commercials, when they can just as easily have an actor or presenter say whatever needs to be said?

Sharpen Your Advertising Skills

The Leo Burnett agency recently used a creative approach to developing several low-cost television spots for its client, Oldsmobile. Each spot was designed to tie in conceptually with a certain type of television show. For game shows, an ad recreates the classic word game Hangman. The blanks gradually fill in to reveal the name of the Oldsmobile Cutlass Cierra as the answer to several question asked in the voice-over. For broadcasts of football games, the name "Oldsmobile Achieva" gets knocked around on a green background, as the voice-over talks about the Achieva winning a competition against Toyota and Honda.

Decision: Assume you're designing a television ad for the Sega Genesis video game system, and you're going to use the same game idea that Leo Burnett used for Oldsmobile. Pick whatever game you'd like to use and think about how you'd design the ad.

Communication: In a memo of no more than one page, explain your proposed design to the marketing staff at Sega.

Print Production

After studying this chapter, you will be able to

1. Describe the production process for print ads

2. Explain how print-ad mechanicals are prepared

3. Define the basic terminology of printing

4. Differentiate the four major printing processes

5. Compare the processes used to print one-color, two-color, and full-color ads

6. Explain the relationship between paper selection and choice of printing process

7. Outline the major steps that advertisers and the print media can take to control production and printing costs

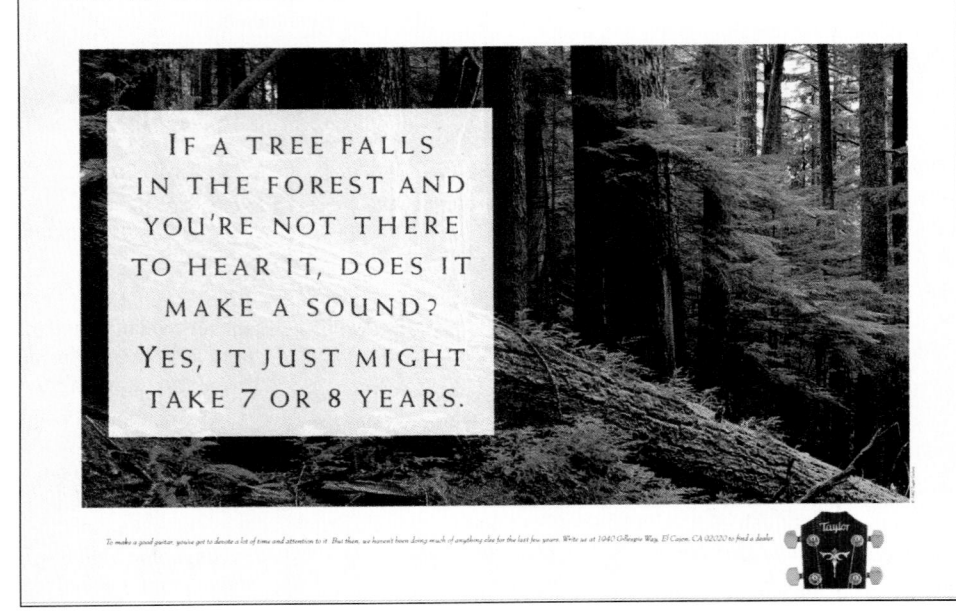

Facing an Advertising Challenge at Leo Burnett

TRAVELING ACROSS THE PACIFIC WITHOUT LEAVING CHICAGO

Imagine that you show up for work one day and get this assignment. You have to produce print ads for a product that competes in a crowded market. Because the market is so crowded, most of the obvious ideas for creative concepts and print executions have already been tried. However, the client is accustomed to having its products shown in interesting situations, and of course you need to communicate the product's benefits clearly and convincingly, so you'd better come up with something creative. Oh, by the way, you don't have a huge budget. Although you can sometimes solve print-ad production problems by throwing money at them, such a tactic won't work in this case. You'll have to think your way through this one.

That sums up the assignment that Joe Gallo and Phil Gayter of the Leo Burnett agency in Chicago recently received from Sony. The two
assistant art directors had to find a creative and compelling way to present Sony's new Digital Reference Series headphones, top-of-the-line units ranging in price from $130 to $250. They had to communicate the product's benefits to potential buyers, without running up a big bill for the client.

Gallo and Gayter started their assignment by rummaging through a pile of scrapbooks, magazines, and other materials, looking for just the right location in which to picture the headphones. They found a perfect spot, 2,300 miles out in the Pacific Ocean on the coast of Easter Island. Their creative instincts told them that the Sony headphones would look great on one of the stone statues for which Easter Island is famous. These statues, called maoi, range in height from 10 to 37 feet. All in the shape of human heads, roughly 600 of them dot
the island. Gallo and Gayter figured that four of them in a photo, with one wearing a pair of the new Sony headphones, would look just right. One small hitch was that Gallo and Gayter were in Burnett's Chicago office, and the maoi were on an island in the middle of the Pacific Ocean.

How would you respond if you were given Gallo and Gayter's production challenge? Would you forget about photography and just hire an artist to draw or paint a picture of the stone statue wearing the headphones? Then there's the issue of getting the selling point across; simply showing the statues and a pair of headphones wouldn't say much to the audience. What techniques could you use to produce a creative and compelling image without exceeding your budget?[1] ◼

CHAPTER OVERVIEW Leo Burnett's Joe Gallo and Phil Gayter met the challenge from Sony, produced a compelling ad, and demonstrated an important point: Creativity is not limited to copywriting and art direction, but extends into production techniques as well. This chapter explores the process of transforming ideas into finished print ads, from the production artist's creation of a mechanical to the various processes used for printing newspapers, magazines, and other media. As you learn about mechanicals, you'll explore methods of setting type, creating visuals, and assembling pages. Then you'll investigate printing, from the basic concepts to particular types of printing presses and the special considerations of printing in color. Following that, you'll investigate paper selection, which plays a significant role in print advertising. Finally, the chapter gives you a brief look at submitting ads to newspapers and magazines, and it wraps up with a discussion of the steps that advertisers and agencies can take to manage costs and quality in print production.

Transforming Advertising Ideas into Print

The print production process starts with the creative ideas generated by the copywriter and the art director and continues until the ad is in print, either in a publication or as a direct-mail piece or other printed item. As you can see from Exhibit 11.1, print production can involve quite a few steps. Some ads are fairly easy to create, particularly in newspapers and yellow pages, both of which will help advertisers design and lay out their ads. However, for many newspaper ads, most magazine ads, and numerous other pieces of printed advertising such as direct mail, the print production process requires a large number of individual steps, as well as the assistance of several technical specialists. In most ad agencies, the print

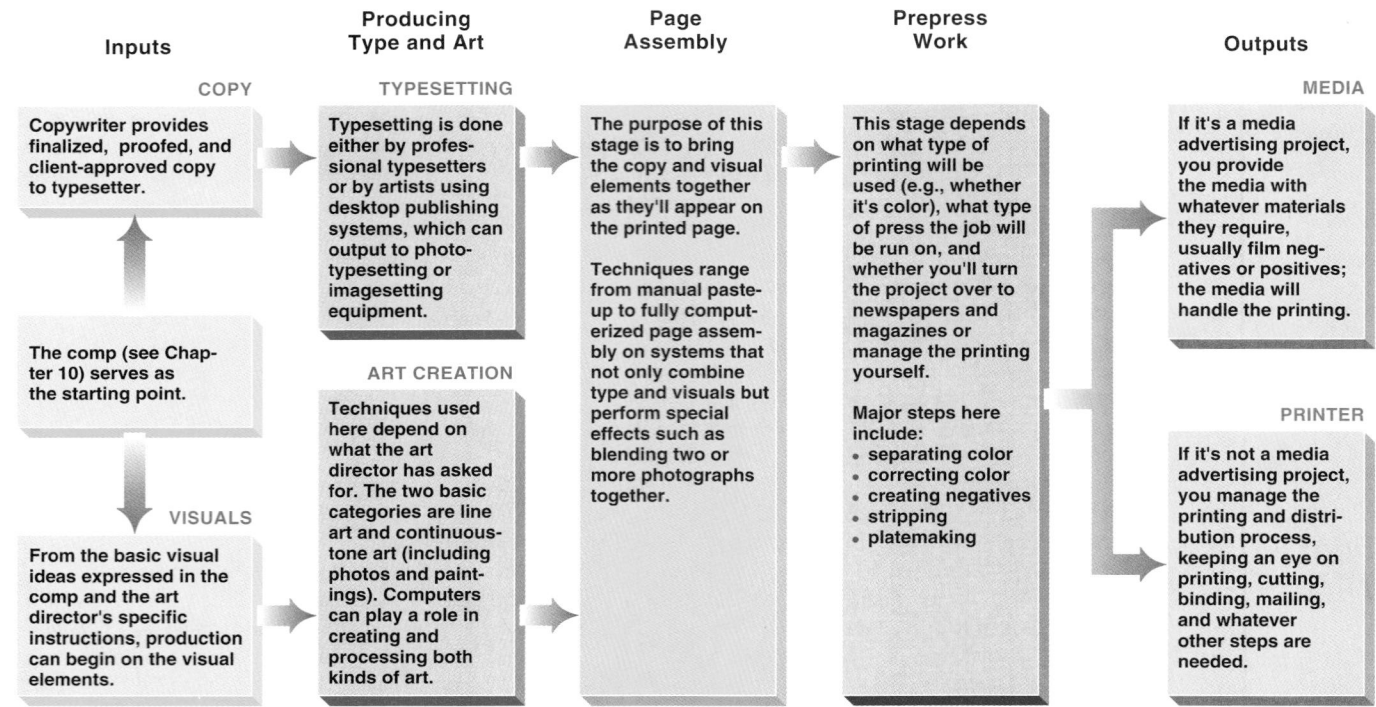

Inputs	Producing Type and Art	Page Assembly	Prepress Work	Outputs
COPY	**TYPESETTING**			**MEDIA**
Copywriter provides finalized, proofed, and client-approved copy to typesetter.	Typesetting is done either by professional typesetters or by artists using desktop publishing systems, which can output to phototypesetting or imagesetting equipment.	The purpose of this stage is to bring the copy and visual elements together as they'll appear on the printed page. Techniques range from manual paste-up to fully computerized page assembly on systems that not only combine type and visuals but perform special effects such as blending two or more photographs together.	This stage depends on what type of printing will be used (e.g., whether it's color), what type of press the job will be run on, and whether you'll turn the project over to newspapers and magazines or manage the printing yourself. Major steps here include: • separating color • correcting color • creating negatives • stripping • platemaking	If it's a media advertising project, you provide the media with whatever materials they require, usually film negatives or positives; the media will handle the printing.
The comp (see Chapter 10) serves as the starting point.	**ART CREATION**			**PRINTER**
VISUALS	Techniques used here depend on what the art director has asked for. The two basic categories are line art and continuous-tone art (including photos and paintings). Computers can play a role in creating and processing both kinds of art.			If it's not a media advertising project, you manage the printing and distribution process, keeping an eye on printing, cutting, binding, mailing, and whatever other steps are needed.
From the basic visual ideas expressed in the comp and the art director's specific instructions, production can begin on the visual elements.				

EXHIBIT 11.1
The Print Production Process

Print production requires numerous steps and a variety of specialized skills.

production manager has the responsibility of guiding ads through the production process, once the art director and copywriter have specified what the ads should say and how they should look. Regardless of the varying number of individual steps required by different kinds of printing, most ads pass through five stages in print production:

- *Inputs.* The inputs to the production process include final copy from the copywriter and graphic ideas and the overall design concept from the art director. The copywriter's role is greatly diminished after this point, but the art director stays involved throughout the process, making sure the production staffs and outside vendors implement the artistic elements in the ad as intended.

- *Typesetting and art creation.* During the type and art production phase, typesetters, photographers, and other creative personnel develop the various elements that make up the ad. In a simple, copy-heavy ad, the typesetter does most of the work. In ads that rely heavily on photography or computer-generated images, outside specialists are often called in to provide their unique services.

- *Page assembly.* During page assembly, the typeset copy and the finished or nearly finished visuals come together on the page. Assembly was traditionally a manual process, and still is in many cases, but systems based on both minicomputers and desktop personal computers can now generate finished mechanicals electronically.

- *Prepress work.* Prepress work is one of the interesting and exacting stages of the production process, where technical specialists take the mechanical and perform a variety of steps to get it ready for printing. The skills of both traditional craftspeople and advanced computer operators play a key role in making sure that the printed version accurately represents the art director's original vision.

- *Outputs.* The outputs of the production process differ, depending on whether the project involves the print media. If you're dealing with the media, your involvement in the process ends when you ship a copy of the ad to each newspaper or magazine; production staffs at the various publications will see the project through the printing phase. However, if you're printing advertising materials for brochures, direct-mail packages, or other nonmedia vehicles, you'll stay involved throughout the printing process (see Exhibit 11.2).

The remaining sections in this chapter define the specialized terms you see in Exhibit 11.1 and provide more details about the production process. Keep in mind that this discussion and Exhibit 11.1 are general models of the production process. The process will work differently in different situations, depending on the intended advertising medium, the advertiser's needs and budgets, and other factors such as whether the ad is prepared with traditional manual techniques or composed on a computer system.

EXHIBIT 11.2
Managing the Printing Process

Although printing is largely an automated process today, experts are still needed to run the complex equipment and achieve optimum results.

Creating Mechanicals

The process of creating mechanicals can range from manual pasteup through a combination of manual and computer techniques to a fully computerized creation. Regardless of how computerized or manual the process is, however, creating mechanicals always involves three basic steps: setting the type, creating the visuals, and assembling them together on a page.

CREATING TYPE

It's hard to imagine any part of the business world that has been revolutionized more by computer technology than **typesetting,** the art and science of choosing and setting type (arranging the individual letters and words on the page). Using computers, ad agencies now have the option of generating their own finished type in-house, rather than buying the services of specialized typesetting firms. This option not only gives art directors more creative freedom to try various typefaces before deciding on final font selections and page layouts, but it also reduces both the cost and the time involved.[2] With a personal computer and the right software, you can even design your own typefaces if you like, giving your ad a completely original look.

Although much of today's typesetting is done on computer-based systems that use laser beams to draw images on paper or film, a lot of the terminology and artistic direction come from the early days of typesetting. For example, the term *leading* (defined in Chapter 10 as the space between lines) used to refer to the actual strips of lead that were put between rows of metal type. Earlier generations of typesetting equipment were called *hot type* machines because molten metal was part of the typesetting process. Modern typesetting systems are called *cold type* equipment because words and graphical images are formed through photography or laser output, not with actual metal.[3]

The term **phototypesetter** applies to several generations of typesetting equipment, all of which use light in one form or another to generate images on the page. The newest machines are often called **imagesetters** because they can produce both text and graphics.[4] The Linotronic series of imagesetters, for instance, are used by many agencies, printers, and graphics designers. If you hear someone ask for "Lino output," this refers to the printout from a Linotronic imagesetter. (Although imagesetters and the laser printers you've probably seen attached to personal computers both use laser technology, imagesetters are capable of far greater *resolution,* the ability to print fine details.) A Linotronic system can accept files from personal computers, and so even if you don't have your own system, you can still do all your design work at your desk and then take the disk to a printer or graphics shop and get high-quality output.

With all this powerful technology at your fingertips, an artistic caution is in order. Typesetting and other artistic endeavors in advertising are still just that, artistic endeavors. Technology makes the mechanics of creation easier and faster, and allows you to create in ways not possible with traditional tools, but technology

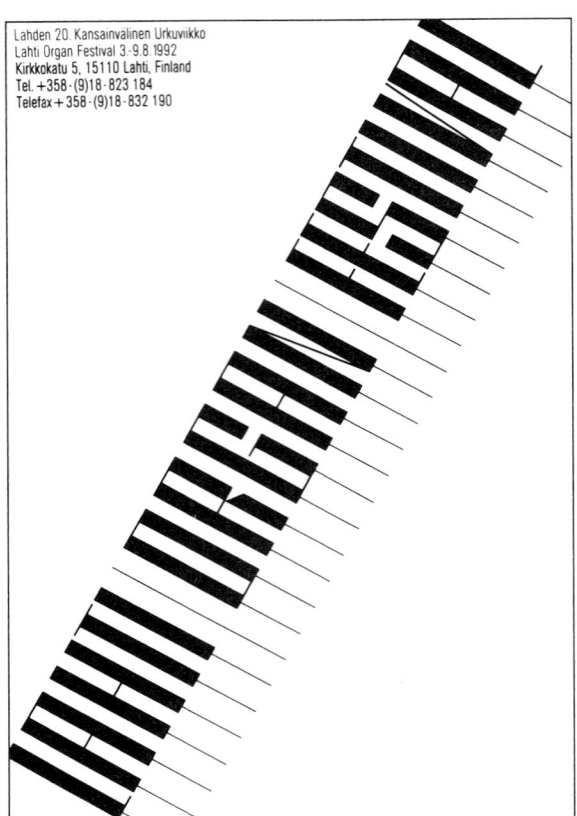

Lahden 20. Kansainvälinen Urkuviikko
Lahti Organ Festival 3.-9.8.1992
Kirkkokatu 5, 15110 Lahti, Finland
Tel. +358-(9)18-823 184
Telefax + 358-(9)18-832 190

EXHIBIT 11.3
Artistry in Typesetting

This poster for the Lahti Organ Festival in Finland shows how powerful type can be as a communication element, with the title of the festival crafted to represent the black keys on an organ.

doesn't provide any artistic ability. No matter who you are—a client buying services from an ad agency, an art director buying services from free-lancers, or a production artist—use the technology with creative care and aesthetic sensibility.[5]

Whether accomplished by the art director, a production artist, or a professional typographer, typesetting can be viewed as a series of artistic decisions (see Exhibit 11.3). **Copyfitting** is the process of making sure that the copy written for the ad will actually fit in the space allotted for it. Getting the copy to fit can involve changing the size of the type, modifying the leading between lines, adjusting the length of lines, selecting a new typeface, or even rewriting the copy itself. Sometimes the copywriter will have to step in to add or subtract a word or two. Other important typesetting decisions include hyphenating at the end of lines, arranging columns of type to flow around visuals, and managing the spaces between letters and between words to ensure easy reading.[6]

CREATING VISUALS

In nearly all print ads, typeset copy works together with one or more visual elements to communicate the advertising message. A look at just about any print ad will confirm the importance of high-quality visual elements, whether the visual is a simple company logo or some tricky special effect done on a computer. Here are the major types of visuals produced for print ads:

- *Original art.* This category includes pen-and-ink drawings, oil paintings, water-colors, and other works of art, either produced specifically for a print ad or adapted from an existing work. These images can be used in their original form, or they can be processed and modified with computer graphics techniques.

- *Clip art.* The term **clip art** applies to collections of copyright-free drawings that artists can incorporate into ads and other projects. Clip art was originally just that, art that you clipped out of a book or other publication, but much clip art is

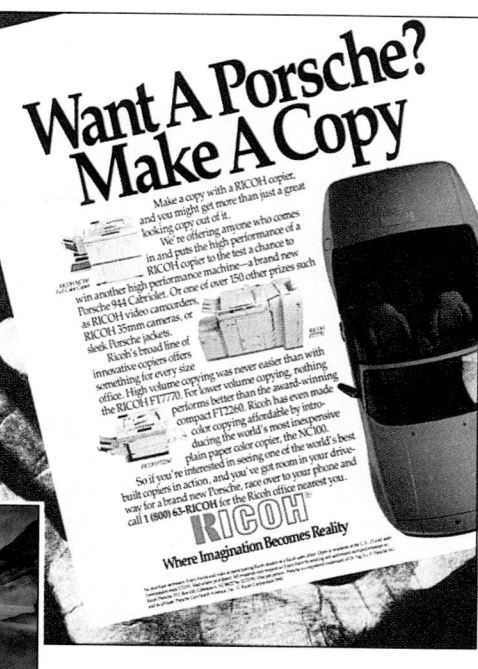

now delivered to users on computer disks. Popular graphics software packages such as CorelDRAW! now come with extensive libraries of clip art that ad designers can use or modify.

- *Photography.* Photographs are widely used in print advertising, partly because they convey a sense of realism and credibility. The types of photos you might shoot with an instant camera while on vacation are usually inadequate for advertising, however. Ad photos are either leased from a stock photo service (see Chapter 10) or taken by a professional photographer hired just for that purpose. Because the printing process generally degrades the quality of photography, it's doubly important to start with the highest-quality photos possible (see Exhibit 11.4).[7]

- *Computer-enhanced and computer-generated art.* Software packages on personal computers can both create original art and enhance art created manually. Designer John Alvin used both computer and manual techniques to instill a dark, moody look for the advertising poster he created for the movie *Batman Returns.* He imported photographs of Michael Keaton, Danny DeVito, and Michelle Pfeiffer into a program called Adobe Photoshop, where he modified

EXHIBIT 11.4
High-Quality Photos for Print Ads

To ensure top-quality photos, most agencies rely on specialists who know how to make products look attractive to the audience.

the images using the computer's drawing tools. He then hand-painted the laser-printed output to give the poster a highly original look.[8]

ASSEMBLING CAMERA-READY PAGES

With typeset copy and finished visuals in hand, the next step is to create mechanicals, or pages that are ready to be printed. The term **camera-ready** means that the ad is ready to be photographed as the first step of prepress and print activity. Before the emergence of computers, page assembly involved physically cutting the typeset copy and visuals to size with a knife and then pasting these pieces together on a backing board. This concept of "cutting and pasting" still applies, even though the work may be done entirely on a computer screen.

The term **desktop publishing (DTP)** applies to creating mechanicals using personal computers, rather than the traditional methods involving specialized typesetting equipment, manual pasteup, and so on. Software packages such as Aldus PageMaker and QuarkXPress let artists assemble type, import photographs and illustrations, add logos, and then print camera-ready mechanicals.

For more complex visual and page-assembly operations such as blending two-color photographs together (see Exhibit 11.5), *retouching* a photo to enhance some detail, or performing other special effects, art directors can use an advanced system known as a **color electronic prepress system (CEPS).** To create an ad for Toyota Canada, the Saatchi & Saatchi DFS Compton agency merged three photos into one: a shot of the car itself, a view of some Greek columns, and a picture of some marbleized flooring material. Using a CEPS, computer artists combined the photos in such a way that the final shot looked like a car sitting in a classic Greek temple.[9]

In other cases, minor enhancements are done to highlight certain details. In an ad for Procter & Gamble's Folger's coffee, the Wells, Rich, Greene agency used a CEPS to add the steam rising from the cup of coffee. The original shot used a cold cup of coffee, so no steam was in the picture. Taking another photo of just a cup of hot coffee, the agency borrowed the steam from this photo and added it to the first photo. Of course, this ability to retouch photos raises some important ethical and legal questions. Art directors have to make sure that their computer-enhanced images don't misrepresent the product or otherwise mislead the advertising audience.[10]

EXHIBIT 11.5
Visual Magic in Print Advertising

Mother Nature hasn't come up with Dalmatian cats yet, but computer technology makes it fairly easy to turn spotted dogs into spotted cats.

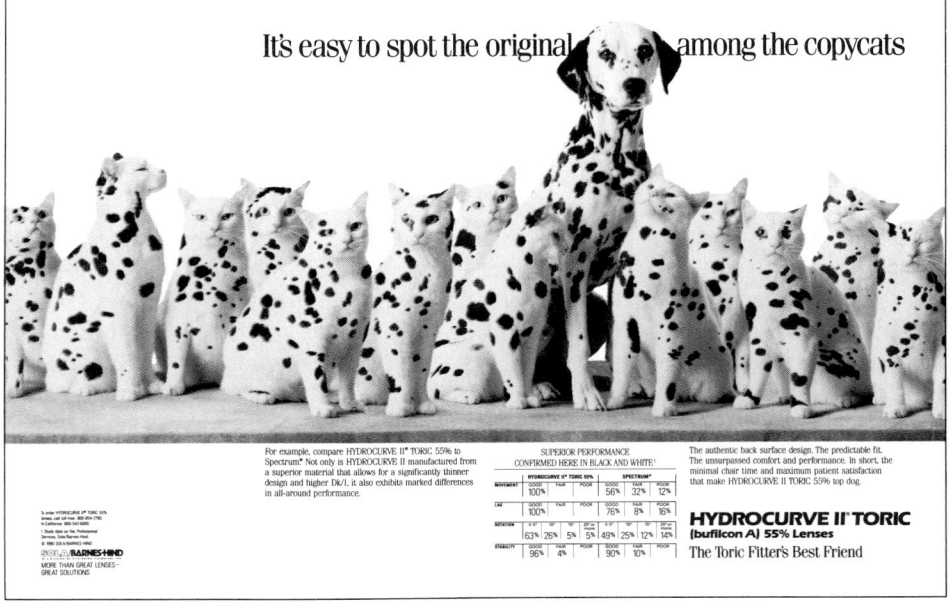

Creating interesting and effective visuals for print advertising can be a slow, expensive process. Conducting a photo shoot to get top-quality photographs can take days and cost many thousands of dollars. Hiring an artist to paint or draw visuals can also eat into your budget and schedule. Designers can always choose from a wide variety of existing photographs and fine art (from stock suppliers and sometimes from the advertisers themselves), but using these secondhand materials isn't always satisfactory. Since the visuals probably weren't created with advertising in mind, chances are good they won't have quite the right look. However, desktop technology is changing all that, producing superb advertising materials at reasonable costs.

One expert who has a good feel for life on the leading edge of computer technology is Connecticut graphics designer Paul Kazmercyk. His amazing capabilities are enhanced by his constant need to understand the technology, its benefits, and its limitations—as he demonstrated when he designed the advertising brochure for the Hotchkiss School in Lakeville, Connecticut. The 28-page brochure would've cost a fortune if Kazmercyk had tried to photograph or illustrate the many visual images included throughout. Instead, by relying on previously created or published material—and no small amount of creativity—the designer produced an award-winning piece of advertising, *and* he did it for less money than the Hotchkiss School expected.

Kazmercyk relied on a number of designing tricks and techniques for the project. A good example is the magic he worked on a photo of Hotchkiss students in a classroom. One student is standing, talking to the teacher, while several others are walking past. Kazmercyk wanted to jazz the picture up a bit, to make the scene feel more dynamic and alive. Using image-manipulation software called Photoshop, he selected the walking students and electronically blurred their images. You've seen this effect in photographs when subjects were moving while the picture was being taken. Kazmercyk accomplished the same visual result, but did so on an existing photo, saving the time and trouble of taking a new picture.

Kazmercyk's computer worked its magic on nonphotographic images as well. For a two-page spread that discussed the school's music programs, the designer wanted a stylized image of a violin. He found a drawing in a copyright-free book of old musical instruments and pulled the picture into his computer with a scanner. Playing around with a software product called Streamline, he experimented with various line weights and colors. The result is an image that looks for all the world like it was painstakingly created by a talented illustrator.

Of course, the creative freedom and productivity that the computer provides carry a price, and it's more than just the cost of the equipment. Kazmercyk not only has honed the skills of an expert designer but also has become something of a computer expert as well. To get his visions on paper, he has to know the ins and outs of the many software packages he uses, the power and limitations of the hardware he uses, and the nuances of the printing process. It's a safe bet, though, that given the enormous advantages offered by computers, designers such as Paul Kazmercyk consider the technical expertise a small price to pay.

Apply Your Knowledge

1. *What kind of training would be necessary for someone entering the world of computerized art creation?*
2. *Do you think that computers might somehow get in the way of the creative process? If so, what effect would this have on advertising production?* ■

Printing

Once the camera-ready pages are assembled, the next step is printing, which involves both *prepress work* (steps taken to get the camera-ready pages ready for printing) and *presswork* (the actual printing itself). You'll find high-speed computers, laser imaging systems, and other technological miracles in the contemporary printing plant, but some of the basic techniques of printing date back hundreds of years. Fifth-century Chinese printers carved text and pictures into wooden blocks, wet the blocks with ink, and then stamped the blocks onto sheets of paper to create multiple copies. An eighteenth-century Bavarian inventor, Alois Senefelder, devised a method of printing using flat stones. Ancient Egyptian artists used stencils to replicate designs.[11] As primitive as these methods sound, modern printing presses work on the same basic principles. This section explores the printing process, starting with an overview of how images make their way onto the printed page.

Creating Ads on Your Desktop

Desktop publishing gives you the ability to create all but the most complex print ads on your personal computer. With the right equipment, you can even produce camera-ready mechanicals for printing. The three basic classes of equipment are the computer itself, output devices (ranging from basic printers to color laser printers and imagesetters), and input devices (a desktop scanner, for instance, is often used to "read" photos and other images and place them in memory for manipulation and enhancement).

Ad designers often start with the main visual element, whether it's a photo, a sketch, a painting, or some other image. Some of these visual elements can be created right on the computer, using drawing or painting software. For instance, if you needed to show the floor plan of a house in an ad for home security systems, you could draw lines to represent the various walls in the house. Depending on the effect you're looking for, you could enhance the drawing with colors, plants, furniture, and other elements. More advanced software packages let you paint your pictures with color, using electronic "brushes" and "spray guns" that spread and spray "paint" on the screen, just as their physical counterparts do on canvas or paper.

Many of the visual elements used in print ads get started somewhere outside the computer, however. With your desktop scanner, you can pull photos, drawings, or any image on paper into your software and display it on the screen. Once it's there, you can perform simple operations (such as trimming it to size or laying text on top of it) or more complex operations (such as changing the color of an object in a photograph or erasing a skin blemish from a celebrity's face). The most advanced image manipulations are currently done on computers that are more powerful than the typical desktop machine, but given the progress of technology, it's only a matter of time before those capabilities show up on the desktop as well.

Once you have the image in place, you can use the text-handling capabilities of your desktop publishing system to add the headline, photo caption, and other bits of text. One of DTP's biggest creative advantages is the freedom it gives you to experiment. You can try a headline in 36-point Helvetica and then with a few keystrokes switch it to 18-point Versailles and compare the difference. You can also manipulate the headline and other text in ways that were difficult or impossible with traditional methods. Say you want the headline to follow the outline of a person's head that appears in the drawing. With the right software, you don't have to position each letter as you move around the person's head. Simply tell the software to fit the text to the curve, and in the blink of an eye, you've got a headline wrapped around somebody's head.

For the body copy in your ad, you can play around with the number of columns, line leading, point size, and other variables. You can place an image in the middle of a column of text and tell the software to make the text "flow" around it. Again, DTP has the ability to instantly show you the results of your decisions (in contrast to traditional methods that often made you wait hours or days to find out what a simple font change would look like). Thus DTP gives you a much greater degree of creative freedom.

If you're thinking that all this must come with some strings attached, you're right. The costs of buying the equipment, training the operators, and keeping both up to date can significantly add to the cost of starting, maintaining, and expanding an agency. Desktop publishing also presents two productivity risks: First is the risk of equipment malfunction, which in the most extreme cases can erase your work (however, simple precautionary measures can protect you from most disasters). Second is the risk of spending too much time on a project (all this creative freedom makes it easy to spend hours and hours playing with type fonts, photo manipulations, and electronic spray paints). The trick is to use all these great tools as tools, not as toys.

Apply Your Knowledge

1. *Since desktop publishing puts creative power in the hands of anyone who can afford the equipment, should advertisers handle more of their own ad production, rather than sending it to agencies?*
2. *Do you think that the continuing advances in desktop publishing reduce, increase, or have no effect on personnel training? Explain your answer.* ■

PRINTING CONCEPTS

In one sense, printing and common photocopying appear to be similar processes. You start with an original and end up with multiple copies that look more or less like that original. Actually, the two are quite different. Whereas a photocopier essentially takes a picture of your original and transfers that image to blank pieces of paper, most printing processes involve first making a physical representation of your original. This representation is called a **plate.** The plate, which can be made from metal, rubber, plastic, or paper, is then used to produce the duplicate copies. The wood blocks of the ancient Chinese and Senefelder's printing stones were the forerunners of the plates used today. Having a plate in the process opens up a new world of possibilities, including very accurate reproductions and a full range of color, as you'll see later in the section on printing methods.

(a)   (plate)   (b)   (c)

EXHIBIT 11.6
Platemaking

Photographic platemaking involves the following three steps: (*a*) The plate-maker creates a film negative of the original image. (*b*) Light passes through clear areas on the negative. (*c*) Light hardens the exposed areas on the plate; unexposed areas are washed clean.

Printing really began to take off in the late 1800s, when photographic techniques were first applied to platemaking. Photography gave printers a way to make plates without requiring artists to carve the wood blocks or etch the flat stones (which they had to carve and etch backward so that the plates would be a mirror image of the original). Moreover, wood and stone plates wore out over time, making them unsuitable for large print jobs.[12]

Photographic plates can be made either from **film negatives** (images in which normally light areas appear dark and vice versa) or from **film positives** (in which light and dark areas appear as they would in real life). For instance, to make a plate from film negatives, light is shone through the negative onto the blank plate, which is covered with light-sensitive chemicals (see Exhibit 11.6). The light that shines through the clear areas on the film negative (representing dark objects or characters) hits the chemicals covering the plate and hardens them. The light can't shine through the dark areas on the negative (representing light spaces in reality), so the chemicals remain in their original soft state. When the plate is washed in water, the hardened chemicals are left and the soft, unexposed chemicals are rinsed away. What remains is a positive image on a plate that can now be wetted with ink and used to imprint images on paper.[13] Various printing methods use different approaches to platemaking, but the basic principles apply in all cases.

Lines and Continuous Tones

One of the most important points to understand about printing is that ink is either on the printed page or not—there's no middle ground. If you're using black ink, for instance, and you want some parts of the page to print in pure black and others to print in shades of gray, you can't produce the gray areas by diluting the black ink or putting only a small amount of ink on the surface. Think about the common rubber stamp. A reverse image is formed in a block of rubber; you apply ink to the stamp and then press the stamp to the paper. You have no way of applying lighter or darker shades of the ink.

How then are various shades of gray printed using black ink? (The same situation applies to any color of ink, but black is a good way to explore how this process works.) Say that you want to print the 10 blocks shown in Exhibit 11.7. You could apply nine different shades of gray ink plus black. You'd have to either run the paper through the printing press 10 times, changing the ink each time, or build a press that can apply 10 separate inks in succession. Either approach would be extremely expensive and time consuming.

Fortunately, you can trick your audience into believing that you used 10 different inks when in fact all you've used is a single black ink. Look at the black-and-white photograph reproduced in Exhibit 11.7. Every part of the image, from the lightest shade of gray to deep black, is composed entirely of dots from a single *black* ink. As the magnified portion of the photo in Exhibit 11.7 shows, larger dots spaced closer together create an illusion of dark gray when viewed without magnification. (Your eyes are also fooled like this every time you watch television, by the way; pictures on the TV screen are also made up of dots.) To create lighter

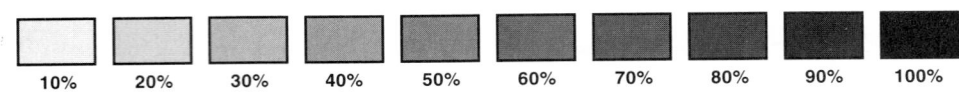

10% 20% 30% 40% 50% 60% 70% 80% 90% 100%

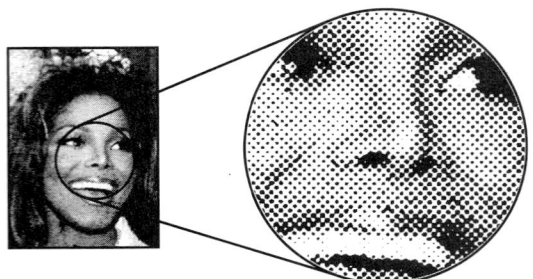

EXHIBIT 11.7
Printing in Shades of Gray Using Black Ink

By varying the density of the ink dots on the page, you can print an infinite number of different shades of gray using only black ink.

shades of gray, fewer and smaller dots are used. The 10 blocks next to the photo demonstrate this effect, as a single black ink produces increasingly darker shades of gray.

Images that consist entirely of lines and other solid areas are called **line art,** *line drawings,* or *line copy.*[14] With line art you don't have to worry about dots because every part of the image is printed the same, whether it's with black ink or any other color of ink. All the words in this paragraph are printed in the same way, since there are no variations in shade from light to dark. To reproduce such images on paper, you simply create the printing plate and you're in business. Most of the visuals in print advertising, however, can't be handled so easily. Even the simplest photograph of a product sitting on a table will have a variety of tones, from dark to light. Such images are called **continuous-tone art.** To successfully print continuous-tone images, you need to get back to the idea of dots, because dots provide the means to produce different shades with a single ink.

Halftone Screens

The secret to printing continuous-tone art lies in transforming the original image into an image composed entirely of dots so that you can get by with the ink/no-ink concept used to print line art. By photographing the original through a **halftone screen,** printers break the image down into dot patterns. The first halftone screens were made from two panes of glass; each had parallel lines etched in one surface, and the panes were turned at right angles to each other and clamped together. If you looked through one of these screens, it would look much like a common window screen. When the camera shoots through the halftone screen, it creates one dot for each hole in the screen. Black areas in the original will produce larger dots; gray areas will produce smaller dots. The type of negative that this screening process creates is called a **halftone.**

If you compare an ad printed in a newspaper with one printed in a magazine, you'll see a marked contrast in the quality of halftone reproductions. This is because halftone screens vary in terms of the number of lines per inch. The more lines per inch, the more dots you can produce per inch; the more dots per inch, the more faithfully you can reproduce the original image. Newspaper photos are traditionally shot with 55- or 65-line screens, meaning that across 1 inch of the photo, you can see 55 or 65 dots. This is rather coarse, as you might imagine, and many newspapers are moving to screens of up to 100 lines. Magazines use screens in the 110- to 150-line range, with 133 lines being a common screen in the industry. The human eye can't tell the dots apart when the screens get above 133 lines or so, which is why magazine photos look a lot more like real photos than newspaper photos do (see Exhibit 11.8). If your advertising includes the highest-quality brochures, you might use screens of 200 or even 300 lines.[15]

The most common halftone-screen methods now involve (1) *contact screens,* which are thin polyester sheets held in place directly against the film, and (2) laser

SAFARI FOR MEN
GIFT

Our "Gentlemen's Gift Edition" is yours with any 35.00 men's Safari purchase

EMPORIUM

scanners, which essentially measure the lightness or darkness of each spot on the original and generate an image for the film negative that corresponds to the measured dots. The laser scanner isn't a screen in the traditional sense, but its purpose is identical.[16]

Combination Plates

Nearly all print advertisements combine line art (which includes text for the purposes of this discussion) and continuous-tone art. You could screen the entire ad, but this would unnecessarily degrade the quality of the line-art portions. They don't need screening in order to be printed, and even a high-resolution screen will decrease their sharpness and detail. The answer is a **combination plate,** which contains both unscreened line art and continuous-tone art that has been screened to create halftones.[17]

If the line and continuous portions of the page don't overlap or touch, creating the plate is fairly straightforward. You simply photograph the two portions separately and then combine the two negatives to create the plate. **Stripping** is the process of assembling line and continuous-tone images into a single negative that is then used to create the printing plate. For instance, if you have an ad that's primarily copy with a small photo in the middle, you first make a negative of the line art (i.e., the text); next you cut a hole for the photo, which you then screen and drop into the hole. Although an actual knife can be used to cut and strip the halftone in, this step is increasingly done by computer systems that assemble the pieces electronically rather than mechanically.[18]

In many print ads, however, the copy or other line art shares the same space with the continuous-tone art. The headline in the ad shown in Exhibit 11.9, for instance, is written on top of the photograph. If you exposed the plate first to the line-art image and then to the screened halftone of the continuous-tone image, the headline would be screened as well. Printers can take one of several steps to prevent this, depending on how the art director wants the text or line art displayed.

The technique used in Exhibit 11.9 is called **surprinting,** which involves exposing the negative first to the screened halftone and then to the line image of the type. An alternative is the **dropout,** in which the line-art portion appears to be cut out of the continuous-tone image. Surprinting and dropouts are created in multistep processes that involve both film negatives and film positives.[19]

These printing details are important to understand because they affect both the cost and the quality of print-ad production. Once you understand how various images can be reproduced on the printed page, you can create advertising art that both prints well and keeps costs under control. The following section takes this discussion of the printing process a step further by comparing the printing methods in use today.

METHODS OF PRINTING

Printers employ a variety of press types and printing methods to meet the needs of their media and advertising customers. Since the particular processes used to print your advertising affect both its cost and quality, it's important to be familiar with the major printing methods. These methods can be classified according to the way the ink is deposited on the printing surface: letterpress/flexography, gravure, lithography, and silk-screen printing.[20] The following sections discuss these methods in detail, and their differences are summarized in Exhibit 11.10.

Letterpress and Flexography

In **letterpress** printing, the image you want to transfer to paper is higher than the nonimage areas on the printing plate (which is usually called a *form* in this process). Only the raised parts of the form get inked, and only those inked areas transfer the image to the paper. This is the same way a rubber stamp works.

Letterpress got its start with printing plates engraved, or carved, from wood blocks. In fact, the term *engraving* is still used to describe any type of platemaking in letterpress. To create a plate to print the letter *A,* for example, the engraver would carve down everything except the form of the letter. Even though these carving techniques were later supplanted by photographic and electronic engraving, letterpress platemaking remains a time-consuming and manually exacting process.[21]

Letterpress used to be the standard of quality for nearly all printing projects, but with one notable exception, it has been largely replaced by lithography. Lithography has proved to be more cost-effective and efficient. The exception is

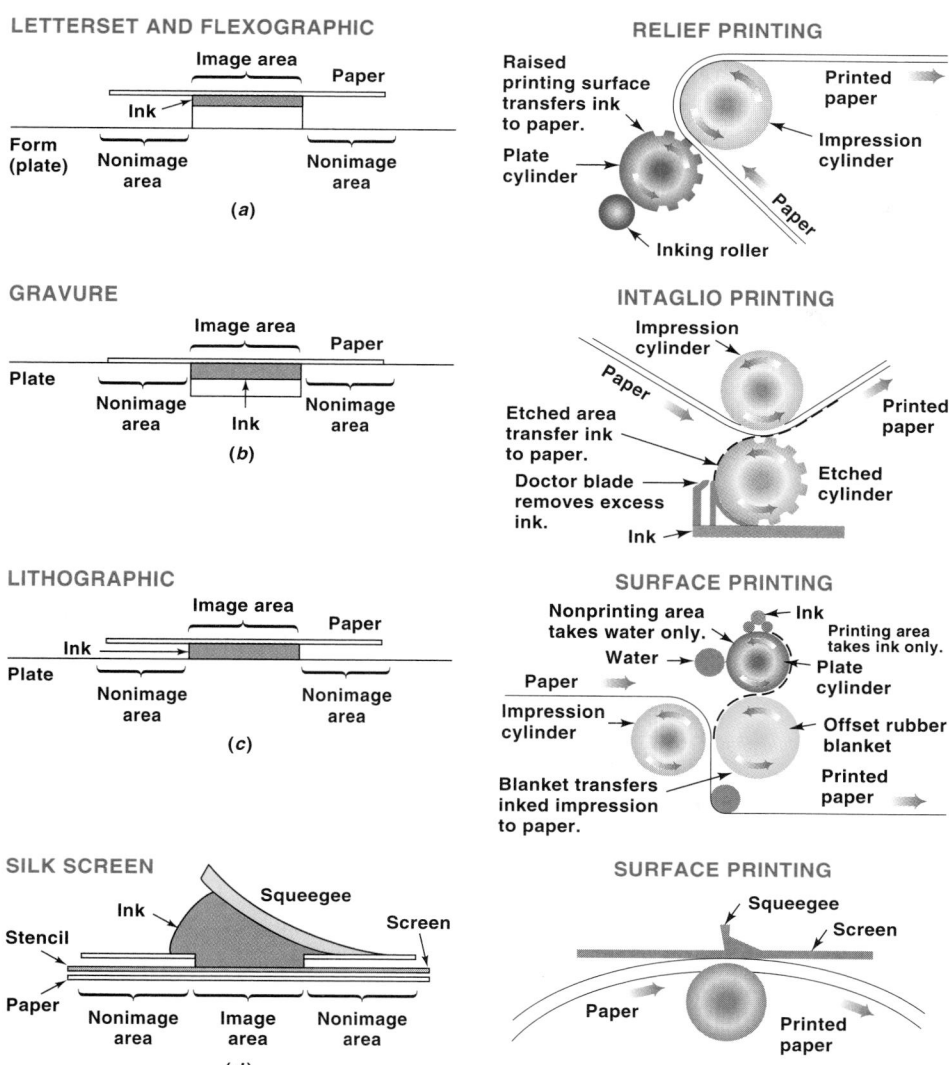

LETTERSET AND FLEXOGRAPHIC

Image area

Paper

Ink

Form (plate) — Nonimage area — Nonimage area

(a)

GRAVURE

Image area

Paper

Plate

Nonimage area — Ink — Nonimage area

(b)

LITHOGRAPHIC

Image area

Paper

Ink

Plate

Nonimage area — Nonimage area

(c)

SILK SCREEN

Ink — Squeegee — Screen

Stencil

Paper

Nonimage area — Image area — Nonimage area

(d)

RELIEF PRINTING

Raised printing surface transfers ink to paper.

Printed paper

Impression cylinder

Plate cylinder

Paper

Inking roller

INTAGLIO PRINTING

Impression cylinder

Paper

Etched area transfer ink to paper.

Printed paper

Doctor blade removes excess ink.

Etched cylinder

Ink

SURFACE PRINTING

Nonprinting area takes water only.

Ink

Printing area takes ink only.

Water

Plate cylinder

Paper

Impression cylinder

Offset rubber blanket

Printed paper

Blanket transfers inked impression to paper.

SURFACE PRINTING

Squeegee

Screen

Paper

Printed paper

NOTE: Paper is indicated as the surface to be printed in all four methods, but depending on the process, the surface may be a product package, a matchbook, a balloon, or some other surface.

EXHIBIT 11.10
Printing Methods

(*a*) In letterset and flexographic printing, the image areas are mechanically separated from the nonimage areas (i.e., they are higher). Ink comes in contact only with the image areas, and only these areas come in contact with the paper. (*b*) In gravure printing, the image areas are also mechanically separated from the nonimage areas, but in this case they are below the nonimage areas. Ink is spread across the entire plate; then the plate is wiped clean, leaving ink only in the recessed-image areas. The entire plate comes into contact with the paper, but there is no ink in the non-image areas. (*c*) In lithographic printing, the image areas are *chemically* separated from the nonimage areas. The image areas on the plate are greasy, causing the ink to adhere there. The nonimage areas are clean, so no ink adheres there. As with gravure, the entire plate comes into contact with the paper, but there is no ink in the nonimage areas. Note that the thickness of the ink is exaggerated here for clarity. (*d*) In silk-screen printing, ink is spread across the entire page area, but a stencil keeps the ink away from nonimage areas. In the image areas, the squeegee forces the ink through the screen and onto the surface being printed.

flexography, a variation of the letterpress method that uses a flexible rubber or plastic printing plate. Flexography was once dismissed as a low-quality process, but today's flexographic presses can print in full color with halftone-screen resolutions up to 150 lines.[22]

"Flexo," as it's commonly called, prints on a much wider variety of surfaces than the other methods, so it's popular for packaging, bags, cellophane, aluminum cans, and other nonpaper materials that need to carry advertising messages and product labels. If your creative advertising instincts lead you to print on unusual surfaces in large quantities, your printer will probably use a flexographic process. In addition, because the inks used in flexography don't rub off on readers' hands in the way that oily lithography ink does, flexography has been adopted by a number of newspaper publishers.[23]

Letterpress and the other printing methods can be accomplished on one of several different types of printing presses. A *platen press* transfers the image to the paper (or other material being printed) by bringing two flat surfaces in contact. In contrast, a *rotary press* feeds the paper around a drum or roller. In general terms, one roller transfers the ink to the page, and another roller keeps the paper taut and in place. (Rotary presses use either curved plates or very thin plates that can be wrapped around a roller.) Rotary presses can be either *web presses,* meaning they print page after page from huge rolls of paper called webs, or *sheet-fed presses,* meaning they print on individual sheets of paper.[24] As you can imagine, feeding a single stream of rolled paper through the press is faster than feeding individual pieces of paper. Sheet-fed presses top out at around 14,000 impressions per hour, whereas rotary presses can hit 30,000 to 40,000 impressions per hour.[25]

Gravure Printing

Gravure printing, taken from the French word for engraving, appeared at the same time as letterpress. It's like letterpress in that it relies on the mechanical separation of image and nonimage areas on the printing plate. The difference in gravure is that the image is cut into the printing plate, so the image area is below the nonimage area, and ink is held in these recessed pockets. When the paper is brought into contact with the plate, only the inked areas transfer the image. The form of gravure most widely used in commercial printing is *rotogravure,* which uses circular plates on rotary presses.

Gravure is used primarily for printing product packages (including boxes, labels, and bags) and for printing publications (including magazines, catalogs, and the full-color supplements that appear in Sunday newspapers). Gravure is better for printing color photographs than any other method. However, it allows no equivalent of a combination plate (in which line art is unscreened but continuous-tone art is screened to create halftones). Everything is screened in gravure, which can make printed copy and line art look fuzzy around the edges. To get around this problem, some art directors specify letterpress *and* gravure printing for a single project, printing copy and line art with letterpress and printing photographs and other continuous-tone art on a rotogravure press. Since gravure plates are expensive to create, gravure makes economic sense only for large print runs.[26]

Lithography

Lithography is now the most common method of printing. It has its roots in Alois Senefelder's flat stone—in fact, *lithography* means "writing from stone."[27] Stone plates are no longer used except by individual artists printing their work by hand, but the basic concept is the same as Senefelder's. The image and nonimage parts of a lithography plate are on the same level, so something must keep the ink away from the nonimage areas. The secret is in the chemical used to create image areas on a lithographic plate. This material has an oily or greasy composition to it, and when the plate is inked, the ink adheres to this oily surface, but not to the clean, nonimage areas.

The most common type of lithography is done on rotary presses and is called **offset lithography,** getting its name from an additional roller that picks up the image from the plate and then transfers it to the paper. Since other kinds of lithography don't play a significant role in commercial printing, most people refer to lithography in general simply as *offset.* One of the reasons that offset lithography is so popular is that it can print on many different surfaces without incurring the setup costs or requiring the labor intensity of letterpress.[28] Most of the print advertising you may be involved in will be printed with offset lithography.

Silk-Screen Printing

The fourth major category of printing is **silk-screen printing,** or more generally, just *screen printing.* (Screen printing isn't related to halftone screens in any way. Even though the ink is forced through the mesh created by the silk, there's no dot pattern in the printed image.) The name comes from the fact that the screens originally used in this method were actually made from silk. Silk screens are still the best ones to use for this process, although nylon and wire-mesh screens are used as well.[29]

Silk-screen printing differs from the other three methods in that it doesn't use a plate or form to transfer the image to the paper or other printed surface. Instead, ink is spread across the entire area to be printed, and a stencil keeps the ink away from the nonimage areas. The stencil is either cut by hand or created photographically. The photographic approach is similar to the general printing-plate creation shown earlier in Exhibit 11.6, except in this case the image areas are washed clean. This creates holes in the stencil where you want the ink to pass through. A squeegee, which is similar in concept to the squeegees used by window washers, pushes the ink through the holes in the stencil, through the silk below that, and onto the surface to be printed.[30]

Screen printing is particularly important in outdoor and specialty advertising, where both the bright colors and the durability of the inks involved help the advertising message get through and last longer. The presses used in screen printing vary from simple flat-frame models that are operated by hand, to rotary presses for textiles and other materials, to special-purpose presses for printing on bottles and other product packages.[31]

COLOR PRINTING

The discussion of printing up to this point has focused on **one-color printing,** using only a single color of ink—any color, including black. The only major color challenge is mixing the ink to get exactly the desired hue.[32] As you saw earlier in the chapter, however, it's possible to get various shades of one color from a single ink, using halftone screens. Advertisers use one-color ads primarily in newspapers, although some use one-color ads in magazines as well, either to save money or to make a dramatic impact (see Exhibit 11.11).

EXHIBIT 11.11
Dramatic Ads in Black and White

This Everlast ad is dramatic in simple black and white.

However, most print advertising, particularly outside of newspapers, is in two or more colors. Color is one of the most fascinating and complex subjects in all of advertising, and color printing is a technical specialty in itself. With color playing such an important role in advertising, it's essential for art directors and anyone else associated with advertising to understand how a printing press can reproduce a color image on paper. Color printing covers the simpler tasks of multicolor printing as well as the more complex tasks of full-color printing.

Multicolor Printing

Tasks in multicolor printing involve printing with two or three colors. **Two-color printing** uses two inks, whether they're black and an accent color (such as blue) or two "colorful" colors (such as red and yellow). The presence of two colors requires a change in the way negatives and plates are made and used. Because a plate can print in only one color, a second plate must be made for the second color. If the two colors don't touch each other, this can be a fairly simple process. The printer starts by creating two identical negatives. On the first negative, the printer masks out every place where the second color appears and then does the reverse on the second negative, leaving one negative that shows only the first color and one negative that shows only the second color. (Keep in mind that negatives are always black and white, even if they will be used to print colors.) From these two negatives, the printer then creates two plates. The printing press uses the two plates in succession, first printing in one color and then adding the second color.[33] The process of dividing the color components in an image into single-color "layers" is called **color separation.**

If the colors overlap, however, the situation is not so simple. In this case, the printer can't separate the colors on the identical negatives because both colors need to print where they overlap. Instead, the printer must use a **camera separation,** in which the two colors are alternately filtered out while two different

EXHIBIT 11.12
Nostalgia in Print Ads

This ad for Dunham boots creates a gentle, nostalgic feeling that sets it apart from other ads.

negatives are created. This process is based on the idea of complementary colors. To create a negative for printing red ink, for example, the printer shoots a negative using a green filter. This essentially blocks the red parts of the image from reaching the film in the camera while allowing the other color to pass through. As a result, the unexposed areas on the negative will then represent the red areas on the original.[34]

A new alternative to camera separations is available to ad designers working on computers. Popular software programs used to design ads, such as Aldus Page-Maker, allow the user to print two versions of the original, one for each color. The printer then makes a plate from a negative of each original, without the intervening step of camera separation.[35]

Printers can run two-color print jobs on two-color presses, which can handle both plates at once. They can also run two-color jobs on single-color presses, which takes more time and effort. The printer has to print the first color on all copies, change the ink and the plate, and then run everything through again to print the second color. Three-color printing is available as well.

Another variation of multicolor printing, the **duotone,** works like two-color printing but is actually used for black-and-white artwork. A second color can add richness, deepen shadows, clarify details, or change the overall tone of a picture. Printing with both black and gray inks, for example, can highlight details and intensify shadows. Adding a dark-brown tint called sepia to a black-and-white photo can make it appear older, a useful effect if you're trying to create a nostalgic feeling in an ad (see Exhibit 11.12).[36]

The colors in multicolor printing are called **spot colors,** a term for individual inks applied separately to the page. Art directors can choose from hundreds of spot colors, providing a wealth of color possibilities but also creating potential compatibility problems. To help coordinate the work of designers, printers, and others who use printed color, the PANTONE Color Matching System™ (PMS) was created (see Exhibit 11.13). Pantone licenses its color definitions (which currently include

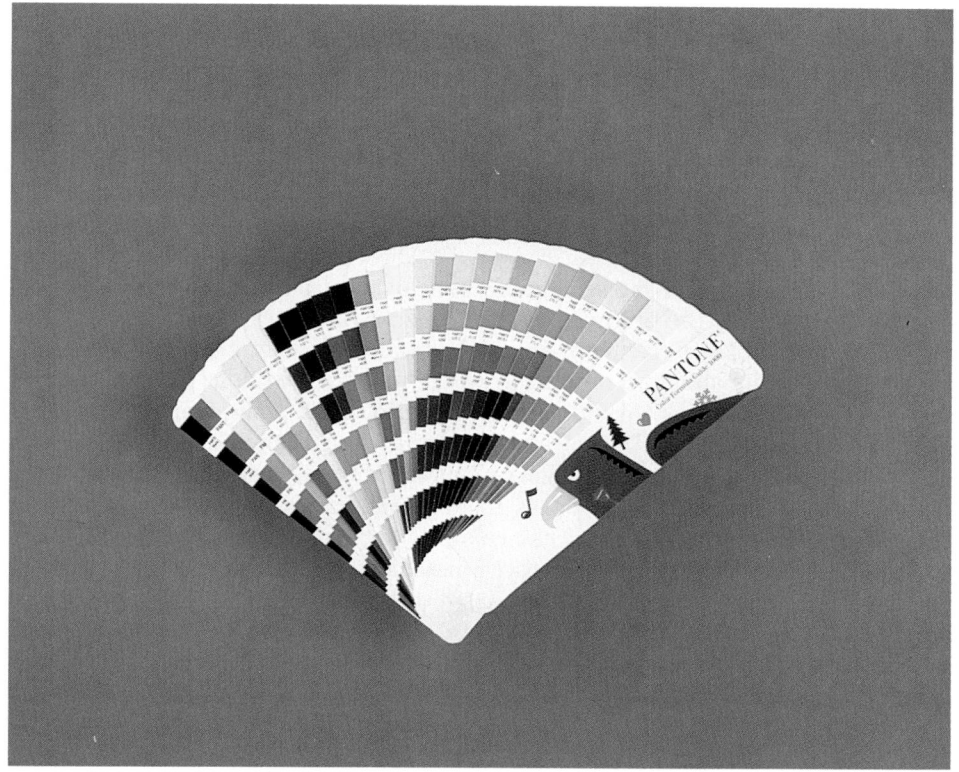

EXHIBIT 11.13
The PANTONE Color Matching System™

The PANTONE Color Matching System™ provides art specialists with a way to ensure consistent coloring across a variety of media.

more than 1,300 solid colors and 3,000 process distinct colors) to manufacturers of ink, colored pencils, marking pens, computer hardware, software, and other products used in art, advertising, interior design, industrial design, and other activities that require standardized colors. Pantone now offers a wide variety of color matching systems and standards for specific design purposes.[37]

Having a common system of identifying colors means that as an art director, you could prepare a colored sketch of a product brochure for a client using a pen labeled "PMS 485," a red with a bit of orange mixed in. You would then tell your printer to use PMS 485 ink when printing the final brochure, and the brochure would come out in the same general color that you showed to the client, avoiding any unpleasant surprises. The Pantone system also helps large, multidivisional companies maintain consistency in their advertising efforts. For example, a centralized design staff can specify that the company logo should always be printed in a certain PMS color.

Full-Color Printing

Spot colors and multicolor printing work well when you have only a handful of solid colors in your printed material, but that approach isn't practical for *full-color* photographs or for other artwork that has more than a few colors in it. (Theoretically, you could print a full-color photograph using spot colors, but the expense would be phenomenal, using a separate plate for each color in the picture.)

The method used to print full-color advertising is called **process color.** It relies not on selecting from a wide variety of particular ink colors but on mixing together just four specific colors. These colors are cyan (a medium blue), yellow, magenta (a pinkish red), and black. You'll see the abbreviation CYMK used to indicate process color, where K stands for black. **Four-color printing** refers to process color (CYMK), not to four of the PMS-type inks used in multicolor printing.

Cyan, yellow, magenta, and black are used because the first three colors can be combined to create nearly every color you'll ever need in print advertising. Black is added to increase contrast and to provide neutral tones of gray that can't always be created by mixing the other three colors.[38] The special "Behind the Scenes" section at the end of this chapter shows how process color adds up in stages to the final printed image. These intermediate steps of color combinations are called **progressive proofs,** or *progs* for short, and they allow the art director and production manager to verify the accuracy of the color reproduction before full-scale printing begins.[39]

Breaking an image down into its component colors is called color separation. The term is usually reserved for process color work, even though multicolor printing requires a similar breakdown of colors. The concept is the same. The printer uses filters to separate cyan, yellow, magenta, and black, creating four halftone negatives and four printing plates. Art directors and production managers also have the option of having separations done by electronic scanners, which use a laser beam to "read" the original and electronically separate the four colors. Two key advantages of laser scanning are its ability to correct for color deficiencies in the original and its ability to produce halftone negatives without using screens.[40]

Printing with process color doesn't necessarily mean abandoning spot colors. Designers often specify PMS colors for particular parts of their ads, even when an ad will be printed using process colors. Pantone provides a system that translates its spot-color definitions into process mixture equivalents, although not all spot colors can be recreated with process colors.[41] For example, some special colors such as silver, gold, and various other "metallics" are difficult or impossible to create with process colors and are available only as spot colors. Consequently, if you need to use one of these colors in an otherwise full-color advertisement, your ad becomes a "five-color" job. The first four cover the process inks, and the fifth applies your particular spot color. In addition, advertisers are usually quite picky

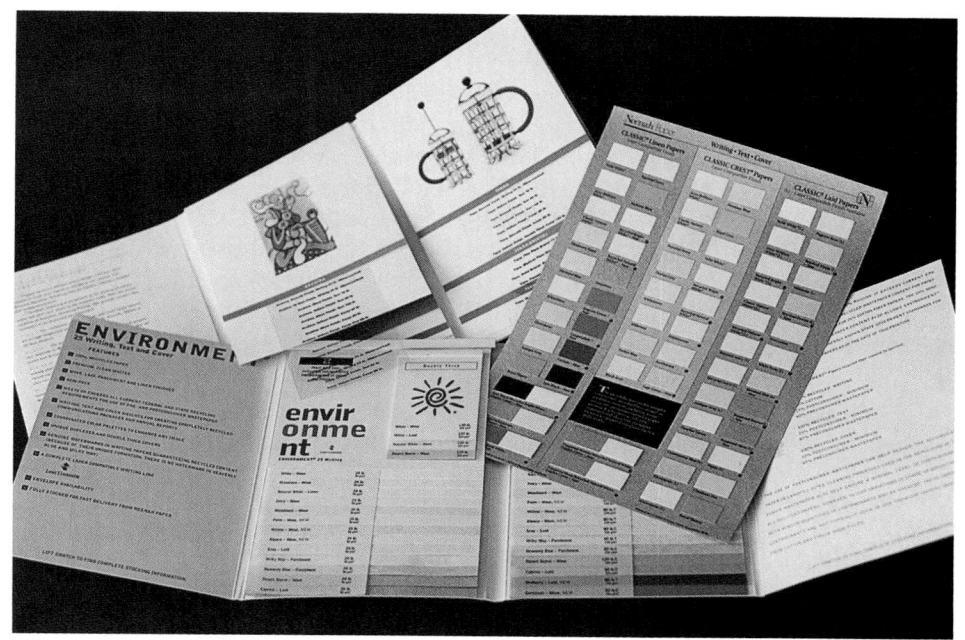

EXHIBIT 11.14
Becoming a Paper Expert

Art directors have many different
weights, textures, sizes, and colors to
choose from.

about the colors of their logos and other corporate identifiers and will often specify
a Pantone spot color to be applied in addition to the process color.

PAPER CONSIDERATIONS

Paper may seem like a small detail in the big picture of print advertising, but
paper selection plays a big role in printing, and therefore in print advertising. As
you'll see in Chapter 13, for instance, one of the drawbacks of newspaper as an
advertising medium is its lower graphical quality. In other words, if you're planning
to use newspaper, you'll need ad designs that can communicate without high-
resolution images. Even if you printed a newspaper on a top-quality press with fine
halftone screens, you still couldn't match the graphics quality of magazines. The
reason is that this sort of paper is intentionally rough and porous to absorb ink
quickly, a necessary feature to accommodate the high speeds of newspaper production. However, this means that the paper can't "hold" a high-resolution image.
The fine-dot pattern of high-resolution graphics would be lost in the rough surface
of the paper.

Paper Selection Criteria

For direct mail and other vehicles, you pick the paper, so it's especially
important to understand the basics of paper selection. In addition, even though you
don't have much influence on the paper a newspaper or a magazine uses, you need
to know what kind of paper is being used so that you can design your ads
accordingly. Because paper can have such a dramatic effect on the cost and quality
of print advertising and direct mail, the typical art director eventually becomes
something of an expert on paper (see Exhibit 11.14).[42] Here are the key factors to
consider when choosing paper:[43]

- *Cost.* Blank paper is one of the most expensive components of any printing or
  print advertising project, consuming up to half the costs in direct-mail campaigns, for instance. It's essential to reach a balance between budget constraints and the quality of appearance.

- *Proposed use.* How you intend to use the paper dictates which papers you can use. Some papers take color better than others, fold more easily, survive mail handling more readily, and so on.

- *Weight.* Various classes of paper are distinguished by weight specified in pounds, such as "20-pound bond." The weight figures are produced by weighing a certain number of pages of a certain size, such as 500 sheets of 11-by-17-inch paper. (However, the number and size of the sheets used in the calculation differ from to class to class, so comparing weights is not as simple as it might seem.) Paper weight affects the perception of quality, the thickness of multipage documents, and the cost of advertising. For example, heavier papers can give your direct-mail piece a more substantial feel in the reader's hands, but you must decide whether the effect is worth the extra postage costs.[44]

- *Surface and finish.* As you'll see in the following section on paper types, various papers have different surfaces and finishes, from porous, rough handmade papers to smooth, glossy papers used in magazines and corporate annual reports. In addition to the overall look and feel, surface and finish affect a paper's ability to reproduce color and detail. An "open-surfaced" paper that absorbs ink readily can yield duller colors because part of the ink stays on the surface and part of it is absorbed into the paper.[45] Among other things, a paper's finish determines how fine your halftone screens can be. As described earlier, rough papers can't reproduce detail as well as smooth papers can.

- *Whiteness and brightness.* A paper's "whiteness" refers to the presence or absence of other colors, which can affect color reproduction. Many "white" papers contain subtle elements of other colors. Papers with bluish tints often give yellow ink a greenish tint, for example, a fact that could upset an art director who spent hours getting just the right shade of yellow in a photograph or painting. "Brightness" refers specifically to gray content; the grayer or darker the paper, the duller the reproduced colors will be.[46]

Types of Papers

You already have a good idea of paper's diversity just from the various types of paper that you see during a typical day as a student, including the pages in this textbook, the morning newspaper, a bulletin-board poster, and handouts from your instructor. Advertisers encounter the same wide range of paper choices, most of which fall into five categories: book stock, writing stock, cover stock, newsprint, and cardboards (printers often refer to paper as *stock*).[47]

- *Book stock.* The **book stock** category covers a wide range of weights, surfaces, and finishes, all typically used in books and magazines. The two most common book stocks are *English finish,* capable of handling halftone screens up to 120 lines or so, and *coated,* capable of handling halftone screens up to 200 lines, even more in some cases.[48] In addition to its use in books and magazines, book stock is often used in direct-mail advertising, especially when color and photographs are important.

- *Writing stock.* The **writing stock** category includes stationery designed for handwriting; papers for everyday business use in typewriters, photocopiers, and computer printers; and certain specialty papers such as carbonless duplicating forms. The common varieties are *flat* (which has a smooth finish) and *bond* (which is somewhat rougher to the touch).[49] Direct-mail advertisers often choose writing stock for sales letters to avoid looking too "slick" or impersonal, which can be a problem with smoother, glossier papers.

- *Cover stock.* The **cover stock** category includes papers that are heavier and stronger than both book and writing stocks but that are often similar to book stock in terms of surface and finish. Cover stocks are available in a wide range of colors, surfaces, and finishes, from imitation leather and metallic papers to embossed papers with designs stamped into them.[50]

- *Newsprint.* The common term for the paper on which newspapers are printed is **newsprint**. It's manufactured in giant rolls for use in high-speed web presses. Newsprint is relatively cheap; it isn't usually designed to last a long time, and as mentioned previously, it isn't typically very good for reproducing color or fine detail.[51]

- *Cardboards.* The fifth category includes a variety of stocks that are made by gluing together two or more individual sheets of material. Advertisers use these cardboards (not to be confused with the corrugated cardboard you find in packing boxes) in point-of-sale displays, posters, and other signlike advertising.[52]

Although the varieties of paper are seemingly endless, these five categories cover most of the paper you'll encounter in print advertising, whether you're handling the printing yourself or relying on a media vehicle.

Submitting Ads to the Media

If your print project involves advertising in newspapers or magazines, you don't usually have to worry about all the printing steps and details. In most cases you simply provide the media with camera-ready pages or film, and the media's print managers take it from there. The exception to this is when you're providing the media with preprinted pages, in which case you need to manage the project through the printing process and then ship the pages off to the media to be inserted in newspapers or bound in magazines.

When submitting ads to the media, each publication has its own set of requirements for what you need to provide and when. *Print Media Production Data,* published by Standard Rate and Data Service (SRDS), outlines what all U.S. newspapers and business, consumer, and farm magazines require. These data include considerations such as the number of colors available, page and ad sizes, details on inserts, the dates by which the publication must receive your materials if your ad is to appear in the issue you've selected, and printing specifications. The printing specifications depend on the type of press the publication uses, since various printing methods and press types require different inputs. Here's a quick summary of what you need to provide for the major types of magazine and newspaper printing methods:[53]

- *Magazines that use lithography.* Although forms such as camera-ready pages are acceptable, magazines printing with lithography usually prefer to get film, and the SRDS manual will tell you whether the film should be halftone positives or halftone negatives, among other details.

- *Magazines that use rotogravure.* Because the gravure process involves screening all pages, these magazines require continuous-tone positives; you don't want to produce halftones because the magazines themselves will do that process.

- *Magazines that use letterpress.* Not many of these magazines are left in the United States, but those that still use letterpress require the actual plates themselves, not film.

- *Newspapers that use lithography.* These newspapers can handle a variety of forms, including film negatives and camera-ready pages.

- *Newspapers that use letterpress.* These newspapers accept camera-ready pages and a couple of other specialized formats.

You can see how a print advertising campaign that involves several media vehicles might present a considerable challenge in creating and keeping an eye on all the different formats required by the media. This is one of the valuable services an advertising agency's production department handles for clients.

Managing Costs and Quality in Print Production

Whether you're creating an ad that will be run in newspapers and magazines or managing the complete production and printing of a brochure or direct-mail flyer, production costs are always a primary concern. You can keep costs under control in two basic ways: (1) by making the most efficient use of people and equipment and (2) by minimizing errors and reworking. Given all the steps required and the number of people involved, it comes as no surprise that quite a few things can go wrong in print production. It's the art director or production manager's responsibility to manage the process in a smooth and cost-effective manner.

Not coincidentally, the steps you take to reduce cost often increase quality as well, in large part because much of the money that's wasted in print production results from mistakes and rework. So the more of these glitches you can avoid, the higher your final quality will be. Whether lower costs or higher quality is your primary goal, the following steps are some of the ways you can be more successful with print production:

- *Understand the benefits and limitations of the technology.* This is particularly true for art directors who select the vendors to produce the ad and who specify how the ad will be created and printed. For instance, if you know what a particular prepress system can and can't do, you can save time and money by not trying something that the machine wasn't designed to handle.

- *Provide high-quality inputs.* From studying this chapter, you've gotten the sense that print production is a complex, multistage process. Each person in the process provides some kind of input to the next person in the process—for example, the copywriter provides final typewritten copy to the typesetter, who then provides typeset copy to the layout artist. By giving the next person in the process the best possible material, you can cut down on the time he or she has to spend. For example, if you're a copywriter and you provide your typesetter with copy that hasn't been thoroughly proofread and cleaned up, the typesetter will have to spend extra time working through your mistakes.

- *Be a team player.* Sometimes only a handful of people get involved in the production of a print ad, such as when a small-business owner works with a newspaper's advertising department to design and create an ad. In other cases, particularly with full-color ads and direct-mail pieces, quite a few people can be involved, from photographers to color separation specialists to the agency's media buyer. The better everyone understands the overall process, the more effectively and efficiently each person can contribute, and the faster and cheaper the advertising production will be.

- *Get firm approvals as early as possible.* To avoid rework and delays, it's important that the advertiser see and approve the copy and visuals before and during the print production process (see Exhibit 11.15). This can happen at several places in the production process and should be done before any time-consuming, expensive steps are taken (such as photography). The art director's ability to communicate an ad concept to the client using mock-ups and comps is critical. The advertiser should have a good idea of what the art director wants to do before photography, typesetting, and the other production steps get under way. If a client decides that he or she doesn't like the photography (or didn't understand what the art director meant when the photography concept was first proposed), taking care of the problem can add thousands of dollars in additional expense and can delay production by days or even weeks.

- *Take advantage of specific technical tricks.* Depending on what you're working with, you can often save money by taking advantage of special technical

EXHIBIT 11.15
Getting Approvals Early and Often

To avoid costly mistakes, it's important to check each stage of the production process carefully.

knowledge. For instance, when printing in two colors, you can achieve a range of combinations of the two colors that has the effect of creating three or more colors. If your two colors are blue and green, for example, you can create bright yellow, pale yellow, and an endless variety of combinations, from a yellowish green to deep blue-greens. (The trick in this case is creating a halftone screen of each color and then stripping in combinations of the two negatives where you want the third color to appear.)[54]

- *Stay on schedule.* With so many people involved, it's important for each person to stick to his or her deadlines. Getting behind schedule can be a nuisance to others at the very least and a costly mistake at the very worst. Certain processes, such as electronic prepress work and most printing jobs, are scheduled in advance, and if the necessary materials aren't ready on time, expensive people and machinery will sit idle.

- *Check, double-check, and triple-check your work.* The most expensive errors of all are those that escape detection until after the printing is done. There are few things worse in an art director's or production manager's professional life than spending a few hundred thousand dollars to print fancy product brochures or a few million to run magazine ads, only to discover that a sentence is worded poorly or that the company logo has been left out of the ad. Taking extra care to check and recheck all the details can avert disaster and produce ads that do a great job of communicating the advertising message while keeping a lid on production costs.

Meeting an Advertising Challenge at Leo Burnett

A CASE FOR CRITICAL THINKING

Joe Gallo and Phil Gayter's work on the print ad for Sony's Digital Reference Series headphones demonstrates how a team of creative individuals can work together to produce stunning results without spending a fortune. When Leo Burnett's art buyer, Debbie Klein, joined the team, she got on the phone to several suppliers of stock photos and asked for shots of the maoi. FPG International of New York City, which boasts 5 million photos in its files, came through with a perfect image of four maoi, shot by veteran photographer Richard Harrington.

Gallo and Gayter were thrilled with the way the maoi looked in the photo, but the perfect blue sky and the patchy brown and green grass didn't provide the right effect. They went in search of a second photo of some interesting sky, with the idea that they'd replace the sky in the original photo. Chicago photographer Dan Morrill had the answer this time. In a special-effects photo he'd shot earlier but never published, he used some creative coloring techniques to create an eerie sky that ranged from lavender to teal to black. Next, photographer Laurie Rubin provided a shot of the headphones. She first created a plastic fixture to hold the headphones at exactly the same angle in which the maoi head was positioned, so that her photo could be stripped onto the statue photo.

The Easter Island statues are well known for the expressions on their faces, which range from serious to pouty. The concept Gallo and Gayter had in mind was showing one of the maoi wearing the Sony headphones—and a great, big satisfied smile. To put the pieces together and add a smile to the maoi wearing the headphones, a retoucher at Chicago's Graphic Warehouse combined Harrington's statues, Morrill's sky, and Rubin's headphones. To take care of the brown patches in the grass, the retoucher "cloned" patches of healthy green grass from other parts of Harrington's photo and replaced the brown grass with the green. To show how happy the headphones made the maoi, the retoucher copied the natural curve of a real human smile and electronically manipulated the maoi's mouth to match. The final step was adding shadows under the headset and the attached cord, completing the illusion that one of Easter Island's famous stone residents was actually wearing a pair of Sony headphones.

The results are most impressive in two important ways. First, Gallo, Gayter, and the other people involved created a striking ad for far less than the cost of constructing a giant pair of headphones and carting them off to Easter Island for a photo shoot. Second, they weren't creative just for the sake of being creative. The finished ad clearly communicates the benefits that consumers can expect from buying the Sony headphones. Any product that can make a 50-ton stone statue smile is sure to bring listening pleasure to human beings.

Your Mission: You've joined the creative team at Leo Burnett, and you've taken over from Joe Gallo and Phil Gayter (whose brilliant work for Sony led to promotions for both). Relying on the same level of ingenuity that Gallo and Gayter demonstrated, you have to shepherd your design projects through production while staying on schedule and on budget. Consider each of the following scenarios and choose the best option.

1. Imagesetting to produce print-ad mechanicals is slightly more expensive than simply printing on an office

Summary

The production process for print ads involves five stages. First, at the input stage, the copywriter submits client-approved final copy, and the art director supplies the overall design idea and instructions on visuals. Second, the typesetter sets the copy and arranges the words on the page in accordance with the design scheme, while artists create the visual elements. Third, the typeset copy and prepared visuals are assembled together on the page to create the mechanical. Fourth, during the prepress stage, the printer gets the mechanical ready to be printed, a process that involves such steps as screening continuous-tone images to create halftones and stripping negatives. The fifth stage involves either sending duplicates of the negatives to the media or managing the project through printing, depending on whether it's a media ad or a self-contained piece.

Print-ad mechanicals are prepared in three stages: creating the finished type (typesetting), creating the visuals (including photography, computer art, and fine art), and assembling the two into camera-ready pages. The page assembly can be done either by hand or by computer.

The basic terminology of printing includes many of the terms defined in the chapter. A plate is a physical representation of the original image; the plate is inked and then brought into contact with the paper. Film negatives and film positives result when the original is photographed. Both are used to transfer the image to the plate. The two categories of printed images are line art (all solid lines and areas) and continuous-tone art (varies from light to dark). The process of halftone screening creates a dot-pattern representation of continuous-tone art. The variations in the dot size and density create the effect of various shades of dark and light. The resulting negative is called a halftone.

The four major printing processes are letterpress/flexography, gravure, lithography, and silk-screen printing. Letterpress works in the same way that a rubber stamp works: The raised areas on the plate hold the image, and only these areas transfer ink to the page. Flexography is a variation of letterpress that uses flexible rubber or plastic plates. Gravure works in the opposite manner: The image area is cut into the plate, and the ink is held in these recessed pockets. Lithography differs from both letterpress and gravure in that the image and nonimage areas are at the same level on the plate; ink adheres to the image

TO YOUR HEAD.

SONY

do the best you can with the lower-quality materials.

c. Tell the clients that even subtle quality degradations can hurt a company's image, and strongly recommend that they stay with high-quality production processes.

2. Producing finished-quality type for print ads is now within the reach of anyone having access to a desktop computer and an imagesetter—which raises questions about unskilled users having too much power and skilled users costing too much. Your office now employs an experienced typesetter, but you need more type set than this person can handle alone. How would you manage the situation?

a. Have the typesetter train your designers in typesetting skills and then serve as an expert who helps the designers and who takes on the most difficult projects.

b. Hire another typesetter well versed in traditional techniques and equipment.

c. The future is here now; let the typesetter go, and make sure the designers have the equipment they need to set their own type.

3. The nature of the visuals you put in a print ad influences the way the audience responds to it. For example, splashy computer graphics convey a

tone and message different from a muted watercolor or a realistic photograph. For an ad to portray the feeling of security offered by an insurance company, which of these visuals would you choose?

a. People are most comfortable with old-fashioned family values: Use a soft-edged photo of a family sitting on the porch on a summer afternoon.

b. People relate best to parents: Use a pen-and-ink drawing of a parent with a satisfied look on his or her face.

c. People are best assured with hard facts: Skip the visual and use a copy-intensive ad that explains in full detail the benefits of buying insurance from this firm.

4. Which of the following actions would contribute the most to the quality of your print ads?

a. Tying employee compensation to mistakes; the more mistakes a person makes, the more his or her salary is reduced.

b. Establish a formal review procedure to ensure that problems are spotted early in the production process.

c. Mail your clients a checklist of points they should think about before approaching you with advertising projects.[55]

laser printer, but the quality is better. How would you respond if a couple of your clients wanted to reduce their costs by skipping the typesetting and imagesetting phases and using just the output from a regular office laser printer?

a. Refuse to do any more of their ads; you don't want your agency to be associated with lower-quality work.

b. Sympathize with their need to cut costs and assure them that you'll

---

areas because they've been treated with a chemical. Silk-screen printing works in an entirely different fashion in that it doesn't use plates at all; a stencil keeps inks away from nonimage areas.

The process used to print one-color ads is straightforward: Every part of the plate gets inked in the single color chosen for the project. Two-color printing is somewhat more complicated because two plates must be made, one for each color. This process can be relatively easy if the two colors never touch, but if they touch or overlap, some form of color separation must be used. (This applies to three- and four-color spot printing as well.) Full-color printing involves a different process, in which every color is produced by mixing cyan, yellow, magenta, and black. It involves a complete set of color separations and four plates, one for each color.

The relationship between paper selection and choice of printing process is one of physical compatibility. For example, some papers are better than others at taking and holding color, and some papers are better than others at capturing fine details.

Advertisers and the print media can take a number of steps to control production and printing costs: understand the benefits and limitations of the technology; provide high-quality inputs; be a team player; get firm approvals as early as possible; take advantage of specific technical tricks whenever possible; stay on schedule; and double-check work to keep errors from creating problems later in the process.

Key Terms

book stock 296
camera-ready 282
camera separation 292
clip art 280
color electronic prepress
  system (CEPS) 282
color separation 292
combination plate 287
continuous-tone art 286
copyfitting 280
cover stock 296
desktop publishing
  (DTP) 282
dropout 288

duotone 293
film negatives 285
film positives 285
flexography 289
four-color printing 294
halftone 286
halftone screen 286
imagesetters 279
letterpress 288
line art 286
newsprint 297
offset lithography 290
one-color printing 291
phototypesetter 279

Questions

FOR REVIEW

1. What are the two main inputs to the print production process?

2. What is the artistic risk inherent in using technology to give more people the ability to perform typesetting and create advertising artwork?

3. What is the key difference between printing and photocopying?

4. Why is it necessary to create halftone screens before printing continuous-tone images?

5. What is the most common form of commercial printing today, and why has it surpassed the other methods?

FOR ANALYSIS AND APPLICATION

6. How was the advent of computer technology able to change typesetting so dramatically?

7. If you were the one-person marketing and advertising department for a small company, would you try to handle all the print production tasks yourself? Explain your answer.

8. If someone suggests that you use sepia duotones in a print campaign for the Lexus automotive account, what points should you consider before agreeing or disagreeing with the suggestion?

9. Your company markets reproductions of nautical paintings, and its logo is a gold compass. You're producing a brochure for a new product line, which will include a color photo of each product. How will you choose between process and spot color for this printing project?

10. Your plans call for 100,000 copies of the brochure, meaning that paper costs are going to be significant. Should you consider using newsprint for the inside pages, since it's cheaper than other types of paper? Why or why not?

Sharpen Your Advertising Skills

Your job involves advertising sales and production for a small newspaper, and an advertiser has recently dropped off an ad for an automotive accessory. The ad relies on a detailed photograph of a car engine to get its point across, but the photo the advertiser submitted isn't of terribly high quality.

Decision: Decide whether you'll print the ad as it was submitted or call the client and suggest an alternative. If you want to suggest an alternative, decide what kind of visual you'll recommend.

Communication: Write down the explanation that you'll use to support your decision(s), assuming that you have to tell the client over the phone. In other words, you won't be able to draw pictures to make your point.

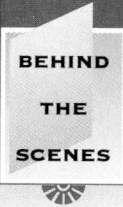

Creating a Magazine Advertisement from Concept to Production

The concept for the Compaq Computer magazine advertisement sounded simple: print a series of favorable press quotes alongside a photo of two computers sitting on a printing press; then add three crayons and two logos. However, even the simplest-sounding concept can prove a tricky production challenge, as Ammirati & Puris, Compaq's agency, discovered in the course of bringing this ad from concept to production.

MARKETING AND ADVERTISING BACKGROUND

To more effectively compete with the makers of bargain-priced personal computers (who were stealing away market share), Compaq Computer decided on a two-pronged marketing strategy. First, the company introduced a series of lower-priced computers that combined quality and performance with the engineering know-how that had built Compaq's reputation. The ProLinea line was aimed at home and business users of personal computers; the Contura line, at home and business users of laptops; and the ProSignia line, at corporate users who needed to tie together networks of personal computers. Second, the company cut prices across all lines, pricing some models lower than the budget products offered by feisty rivals such as Dell and Gateway.

In the past, Compaq had positioned itself as a technological innovator offering top quality at top prices. Now, with the new product and pricing strategies, the company had to let its target audiences know that the prices had changed but the quality and performance had not. So Compaq's ad agency, Ammirati & Puris, planned an advertising campaign to reaffirm the computer maker's position as an industry leader.

CREATIVE STRATEGY

Compaq's new product and pricing strategies were well received by the business press, and many printed favorable product reviews. To build on the excitement generated by this coverage, the agency recommended creating a full-color print ad that would highlight the best of the press comments for three target audiences: (1) information-systems managers who specify which computers their companies will buy, (2) senior executives who approve their company's computer purchases, and (3) individuals who buy computers for themselves or for their small businesses. To reach the information-systems managers, the ad was scheduled to run in computer magazines; to reach both the senior executives and the individual buyers, the ad was scheduled to run in general business magazines and (in black and white) in *The Wall Street Journal*.

Looking through a stack of complimentary press clippings, copywriter Travis Ashby and art director Curtis Melville considered how to use the best quotes in a fresh, persuasive way. Ashby came up with a headline that used wordplay to tie the quotes with Compaq's emphasis on quality and performance. Taking off on the double meaning of the phrase, "we put them through the press," Melville suggested a photograph showing Compaq computers sitting on top of a working printing press. He also planned a hand-drawn illustration of crayons to point up Compaq's more colorful computer screens. The art staff drafted a rough layout (see

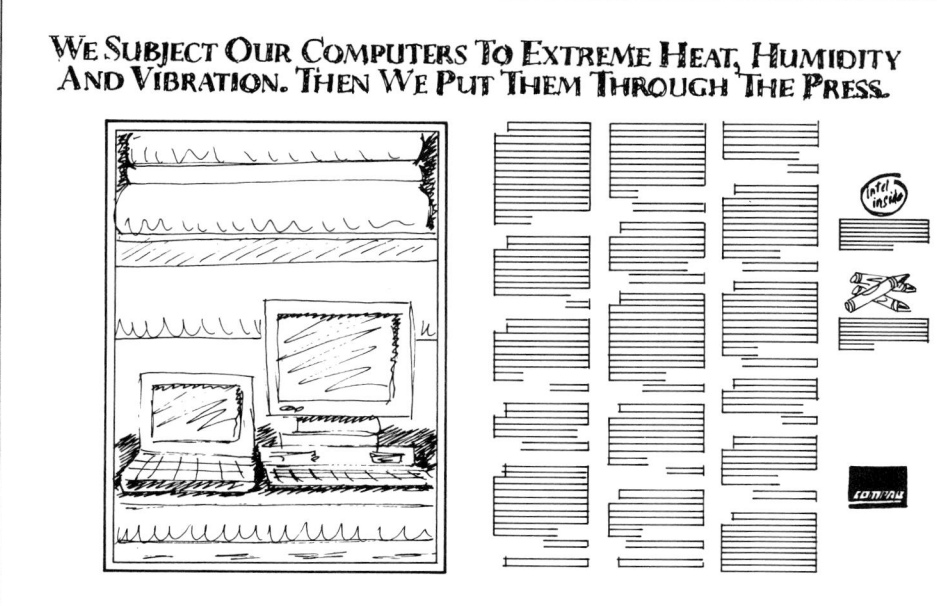

EXHIBIT 11.A A rough layout of the "quotations" ad.

EXHIBIT 11.B **A comp of the "quotations" ad.**

Exhibit 11.A) and a comp (see Exhibit 11.B) to see how the quotes would look between the photo and illustration. Once the creative strategy was approved by Mark Rosen, Compaq's director of advertising in North America, the agency went to work on the ad.

PHOTOGRAPHY AND ILLUSTRATION

Ammirati & Puris staffers started by scouting several sites to find a suitable printing press for the background in the photograph. However, the lighting and the position of these presses just didn't fit the agency's creative concept. The best alternative was to build a plywood model of a rotary press that could easily be manipulated to achieve the right effect. Once account executive Andy Berndt got the client's approval on the budget, the creative staff hired a prop house to handle the construction. Then to create a realistic look, the staff borrowed printing plates from *PC Week* and *PC Magazine* (two leading personal-computer magazines) and mounted them on the model's cardboard wheels (where plates would be located on a real rotary press).

To create the illusion of a printing press in motion, a staff member stood behind the model and slowly turned the wheels. In one shot, the photographer used a long exposure time to capture the movement of the spinning wheels (see Exhibit 11.C). In the next shot, he left the other elements as they were but reduced the lighting level to make the images on the computer screens more visible (see Exhibit 11.D). While the photography was being completed, the agency assigned an illustrator to draw the crayons. After reviewing a first-draft pencil rendering, the art director requested minor changes to make the crayons look more generic (a legal requirement to avoid infringing on Crayola's copyright) and then gave the go-ahead to create the final illustration.

EXHIBIT 11.C **Photograph of the printing press in motion.**

304

PREPRODUCTION STEPS

Next, art director Curtis Melville and production director Jay Monaco met with the supplier who would handle the color separations. Together, they reviewed the transparencies of the two photographs to determine what retouching might be needed. Because the printing-press model had been built to the agency's specifications, no major changes were needed (such as moving switches from one location to another). However, the art director did want some of the shadows removed from the model and the computers. He also wanted the separator to adjust the coloring on some parts of the press and on the spinning wheels so that more of the characters would be recognizable. In addition, he asked for color retouching on the computer screens, to make them vibrant enough to stand out prominently in the ad. Finally, he specified how the two photos should be assembled to create a single composite photo.

Meanwhile, the creative department set up the copy for the press quotes, using a Macintosh computer with QuarkXPress desktop-publishing software. A copy of the photo and a copy of

EXHIBIT 11.E Final composite photograph of computers in front of the printing press.

EXHIBIT 11.D Photograph of the computer screens in use.

the crayon line art were scanned into the computer, and the logos for "Intel Inside" and "Compaq" were retrieved from the computer's memory. All these elements were then sized and positioned to create an attractive layout. The account executive showed the layout to the client for approval before production began.

PRODUCTION

To start the production process, the separator responsible for the retouching scanned the two photographs into a computerized retouching and separation system. Then he merged the two photographs into one. Bringing each area of the photograph onto the computer screen, the separator carefully retouched the shadows and the color to achieve the look the agency wanted (see Exhibit 11.E). Next, he generated a four-color match print (which is a preliminary printout) directly from the computer output (the four-

YELLOW

MAGENTA

YELLOW AND MAGENTA

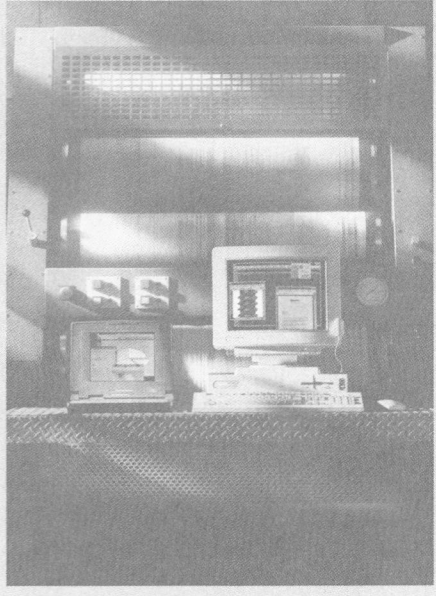

CYAN

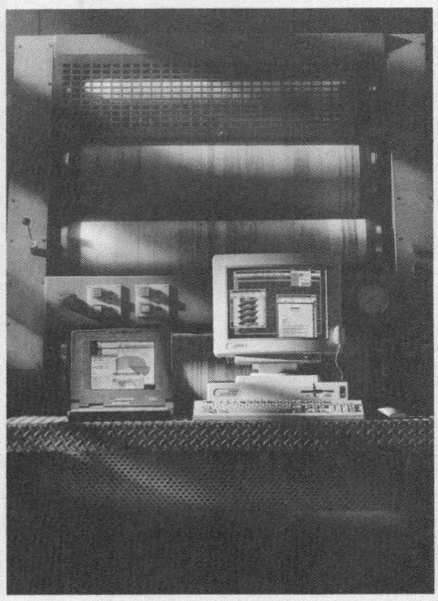

YELLOW, MAGENTA, AND CYAN

BLACK

EXHIBIT 11.F The set of progressive proofs.

color films of the retouched image). He sent this match print to the production director, who checked the changes and requested additional retouching in several areas of the image. All these changes were incorporated into the computerized image, which was then stored for later retrieval.

TYPESETTING

While the retouching process continued, the production department went ahead and ordered type for the headline. To create an overall sense of unity, one typeface was being used for all the ads in the leadership campaign. However, rather than generate type electronically from the Macintosh's desktop-publishing output, the art director specified that type should be set from a dedicated typesetting system, because the type is sharper and the agency can more easily control the spacing between letters and words. The print buyer determined the appropriate type size and spacing for this particular ad and then ordered the type from the type-setter. When the type came back, it was checked for copy errors, spacing, and other adjustments, and then it was assembled (together with the electronically retouched photo and the illustrations) to form a mechanical. Next, the account executive submitted this mechanical to Compaq for approval.

PLATES, FILM, AND PROOFS

After all corrections to art and copy were completed, the client approved the mechanical. Now the production department arranged to have the typeset copy stripped in and photographed from the mechanical. In turn, the copy was assembled with the film of the four-color artwork to create a master set of film. Then the separator made four plates from this master film (one each for cyan, yellow, magenta, and black). From these plates, the separator generated a set of press proofs (prints taken directly from a sample printing) and a set of progressive proofs so that the agency's art director and production director could review them for color, positioning, and other technical elements (see Exhibits 11.F and 11.G). The production director requested minor changes to ensure accurate color reproduction, and once the agency and the client had authorized the proofs, the production director ordered film, proofs, and progressive proofs to be sent to each publication on the media list. He also ordered additional sets of proofs and film in case the media department later lengthened

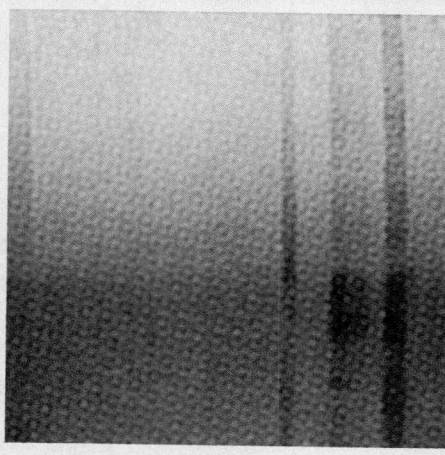

EXHIBIT 11.G An enlarged portion of the final print ad, showing how the separate colors are combined to produce continuous color tone.

the list of magazines on the media schedule. When the magazines printed the Compaq ad, they checked their color reproduction at the press by comparing their actual output with these proofs; if necessary, they made changes so that the finished ad was as faithful to the agency's specifications as possible (see Exhibit 11.H).

RESULTS

Compaq's leadership campaign (which included this press quotations ad) was designed to help raise awareness of the new product lines and the new pricing strategy. After the campaign ran for several months, the advertiser's research found that the campaign—combined with other promotional efforts—had successfully raised awareness levels among the three target audiences. The research also revealed that, compared with the period before the ads ran, more people said they were considering Compaq for their next personal-computer purchase. ∎

WE SUBJECT OUR COMPUTERS TO EXTREME HEAT, HUMIDITY AND VIBRATION. THEN WE PUT THEM THROUGH THE PRESS.

At Compaq, we put our products through some of the most brutal testing in the industry. That way we can be sure they'll withstand the toughest test of all: public opinion.

"Compaq hit the mark with 14 machines that combined low price with high performance and a most-wanted list of features."
—*InfoWorld, June 22, 1992*

"...Compaq has slashed prices without compromising quality."
—*PC Week, June 22, 1992*

"Compaq Computer Corporation has taken an aggressive pricing stance with its new ProSignia server line."
—*PC Week, October 5, 1992*

"Despite its low price, the ProSignia packs a variety of features."
—*PC Week, October 5, 1992*

"...For running Windows on the road, the Compaq LTE/25c is clearly the best notebook yet."
—*PC Laptop, October 1992*

"It is the best-looking color screen on any notebook, plain and simple."
—*PC Computing, August 1992*

"DeskPro/i...combines the traditional Compaq virtues of strong performance and technical innovation with aggressive pricing."
—*PC Week, June 22, 1992*

"Make no mistake about it: this is a strikingly energetic Compaq."
—*PC Week, June 22, 1992*

"You'd expect technical leadership from Compaq, but the Lite/25c's aggressive price took us completely by surprise."
—*PC Computing, August 1992*

"Low-cost ProLinea offers solid quality."
—*InfoWorld, October 5, 1992*

"...Compaq Contura 3/25 notebook is part of Compaq's clone-beater strategy and packs an aggressive price/performance punch..."
—*PC Magazine, August 1992*

"That's leadership."
—*PC Week, June 22, 1992*

EXHIBIT 11.H The final Compaq "quotations" print advertisement.

Electronic Production

After studying this chapter, you will be able to

1. Explain how the production of electronic advertising differs from the production of print advertising

2. List the steps required to produce a television commercial

3. Identify the key players in the production of a television commercial and describe the roles they play

4. Describe the director's role in television production

5. Explain why radio copy differs from print or television copy

6. Differentiate the two types of radio commercials in terms of production

7. List the major steps that advertisers can take to manage costs and quality in electronic production

Facing an Advertising Challenge at Fahrenheit Films

HUMAN BUNGEE JUMPING WOULD LOOK TAME BY COMPARISON

Director Rod Davis has surely heard his share of unusual television production requests, but the call he received from the McCann/SAS ad agency in Detroit stood out from all the rest. McCann/SAS client GMC Trucks, the smallest and least visible division of General Motors, needed a way to break through the television clutter and get people to notice its sports/utility truck, the Jimmy. The challenge for Davis and for Fahrenheit Films would be to pull off one of the more unusual television commercials in recent years.

One can hardly blame McCann/SAS for stretching a bit to find an original way of demonstrating truck strength, considering how many approaches had already been used in the industry. More than 25 years ago, Ford parachuted a pickup out of an airplane. Chevrolet trucks rumbled through a mud pit that the company *called the "Ditch of Doom." A recent spot for Dodge trucks showed one towing a 445-foot, 420,000-pound train from a dead stop. Ford started calling its trucks "Ford Tough" in the 1960s; Dodge followed with "Ram Tough." A few years ago, Chevy adopted the Bob Seeger song, "Like a Rock." So with all this talk of strength coming from the competition, GMC needed something different, something to stop the television audience in its tracks.*

The creative team at McCann/SAS hit on an idea that was certainly different: take the Jimmy bungee jumping. The image alone would catch almost any truck buyer's attention. Furthermore, if viewers saw the truck survive the rapid deceleration when the bungee cord snapped taut, they would know that the Jimmy could handle the stress and strain of towing a trailer. In the words of GMC's advertising manager, George Wood, *"We thought the brand needed more awareness, and this was an idea with tremendous stopping power."*

For the best effect, the McCann/SAS creative team needed a visually spectacular location to shoot and a high place to "jump" from. They selected West Virginia's New River Gorge bridge—some 876 feet above the water. The world's tallest buildings range from around 1,200 to over 1,400 feet. So imagine driving a truck out a window two-thirds the way up the Sears Tower in Chicago; that's the task McCann/SAS handed Rod Davis and his crew at Fahrenheit.

If you were Davis and in charge of filming this commercial, how would you pull it off? Could you do it with a stock truck (one that hadn't been modified or strengthened)? How would you convey the advertising message without destroying the truck or the bridge?[1] ∎

CHAPTER OVERVIEW   Rod Davis and his crew participate in one of the most interesting aspects of advertising, producing a television commercial. This chapter covers the production of both television and radio commercials, starting with a discussion of how television production and radio production compare with the print production concepts discussed in the previous chapter. After that, you'll get an overview of the television production process. Next, you'll examine each phase in more detail, from choosing between film and video to adding special effects. Then you'll get a look at radio production and the unique aspects of copywriting and creative direction in the radio environment. The chapter concludes with some advice on managing costs and quality in both television and radio production.

Comparing Print and Electronic Production

Even though they incorporate the same advertising principles, print-ad production differs markedly from electronic-ad production in six significant ways. First, television has the extra dimensions of sound and motion. These dimensions can yield powerful advertising, but they can complicate the production process. For example, when producing the copy for a television ad, you can't simply put the copywriter's words in an actor's mouth; the actor's tone of voice, facial expressions, and body language (if the actor is seen on screen) help determine whether the message gets across (see Exhibit 12.1). The situation grows even more complicated if the actor is driving a car or pouring a glass of orange juice while reciting the lines. Beyond that, you often have to work music into the scene and generally overcome numerous creative hurdles that simply don't exist in the print media.

Second, radio has the extra dimension of sound, but it has no visuals. It presents an entirely different challenge: working with sound but giving up all visual

SPORTS CAR ROARS UP TO RURAL CAFE. CINDY CRAWFORD GETS OUT OF THE CAR, BUYS A PEPSI AT THE VENDING MACHINE AND DRINKS IT WHILE TWO SMALL BOYS WATCH HER FROM BEHIND THE FENCE.

(SFX): song ("Just one look . . .")
BOY #1: Is that a great new Pepsi can or what?
V.O.: Introducing a whole new way to look at Pepsi and Diet Pepsi.

BOY #2: It's *beautiful.*
SUPERSCRIPT: New Look—Same Great Taste.

EXHIBIT 12.1
Acting Talent in Television Advertising

The two young boys in this commercial, who were more impressed with the new Pepsi can than with model Cindy Crawford or the exotic sports car she drove, needed a fair amount of acting ability to keep the ad humorous without looking silly.

communication. You can no longer use a striking photograph or artistic typography to help get your point across; the words themselves have to do the job. Naturally, you can add music or sound effects to help communicate your message, but the the words themselves (as well as how they are delivered) are paramount in radio.

Third, electronic production has rigid time constraints. Print ads are restricted by time and space to a certain degree, but not nearly as much as television and radio ads are. If the copywriter needs to add a few words or a sentence, this can often be accomplished in print with relatively little pain. You might be able to shrink a photograph just a bit or use a smaller type font. Such changes, though, are often impossible in television and radio. For instance, in a 30-second commercial, the copy is limited to 28 or 28.5 seconds to give the viewer a little breathing room between commercials. Even though technicians can electronically speed up television commercials to a point, if you're already at 28 seconds and find you need to add a sentence, you often have little choice but to cut another sentence.

Fourth, electronic ads are usually difficult to refine or revise. One of the major drawbacks of electronic media is the difficulty in fine-tuning once production is under way. To a large extent, radio and television commercials are performances that are captured on film or tape. If you're putting the finishing touches on a commercial and decide you don't like the way an actor delivered a certain line, chances are you're out of luck. You may have already spent $1 million or more getting the cast and crew together to shoot the commercial, and by now the actor could be somewhere in Africa filming a movie. In contrast, if you're on your way to the printer with your print ad and decide you don't like the typeface, you can have the typesetter run new type and you're back in business—it'll cost some time and money, but it's usually possible. As discussed later in the chapter, this lack of production flexibility is the reason successful producers of television commercials plan every detail before shooting and then film numerous *takes*—all in an attempt to avoid getting stuck with material that doesn't work.

Fifth, more people are usually involved in the electronic process than in print ads. You can produce most print ads with a handful of technical and creative specialists, but television ads can require dozens and even hundreds of people. The process can be so involved that a temporary management structure must be established (with the *producer* and *director* in charge) just to make sure all these people work together smoothly. Of course, not all television ads are this complex. Many local commercials are produced right at the television station with a small crew, and radio ads are usually produced on a small scale.

Sixth, electronic production is usually done by third parties. Most advertising agencies (and many advertisers) have the technical and creative capabilities to produce their own print ads, right up to the point of printing. This isn't the case with radio and television, however. Electronic production is nearly always performed by such third-party organizations as local television and radio stations, production companies (which have all the people and equipment needed to produce commercials), production service companies (like production companies but without on-staff directors), and even movie studios such as Paramount Pictures and Lucasfilm.[2] These organizations bring the technical and creative talents needed to translate a script and a storyboard into a finished commercial.

As you can see, electronic production, and particularly television, can be more expensive and more complex to manage overall. In addition, even though both print and electronic production are demanding, the two media require different technical and creative skills.

Exploring Television Production

The production process for television advertising breaks down into three phases (see Exhibit 12.2). The **preproduction** phase involves all the planning needed to accomplish the production task. Preproduction usually takes several weeks at a minimum, and the better the planning during this phase, the better the results: the production process will be more cost effective, and the finished advertising will be

EXHIBIT 12.2
The Television Commercial Production Process

Producing television advertising involves three phases: preproduction, production, and postproduction.

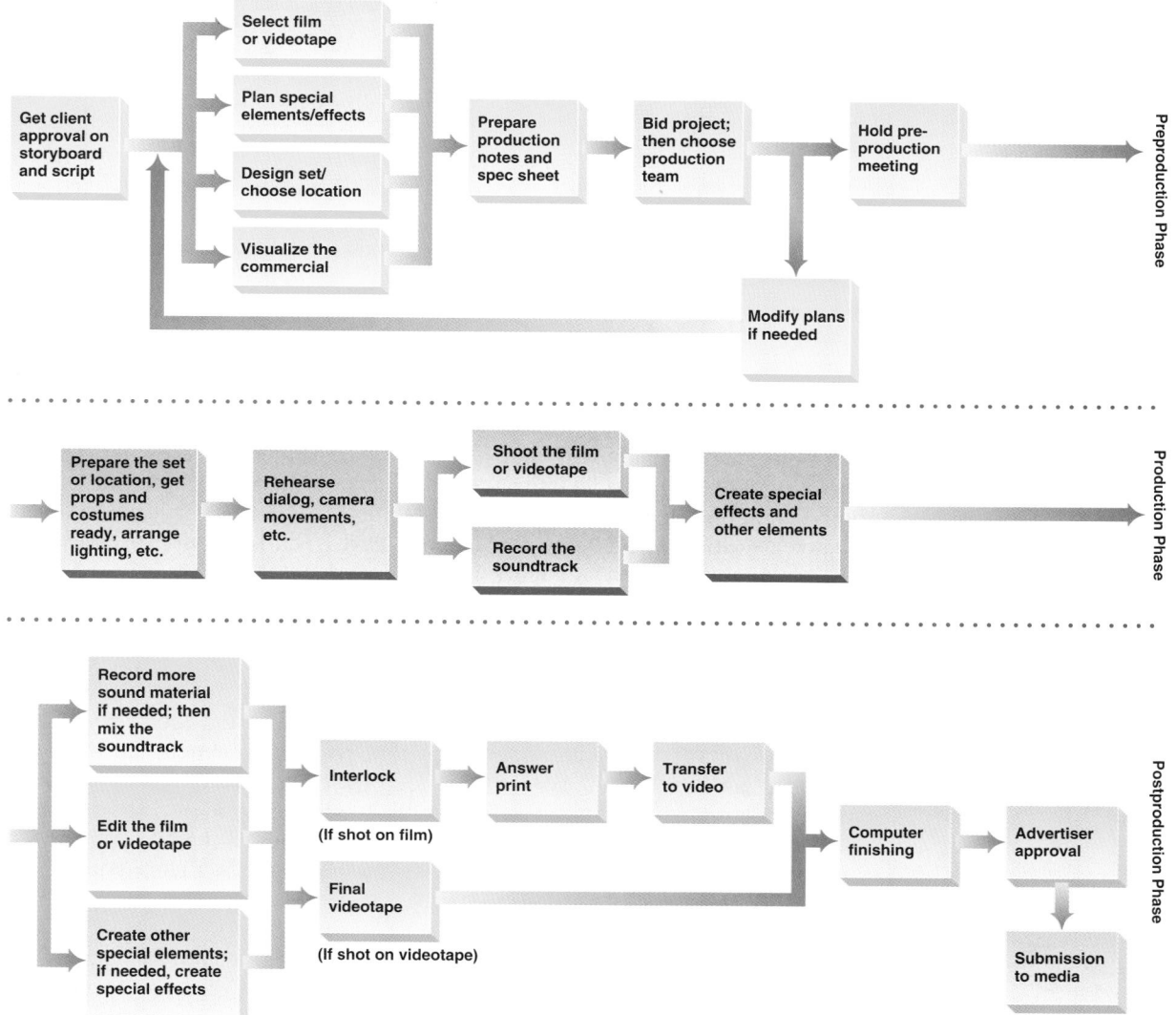

Note: For the soundtrack, special effects, and other special elements, the line between production and postproduction isn't always clear; e.g., sometimes the soundtrack will be recorded during production; other times parts or all of it will be recorded and added in postproduction.

more successful. It is during the **production** phase that the commercial is actually filmed, videotaped, programmed on computer, or drawn by artists. In the case of filmed or taped live-action commercials, production is quick, usually a day or two. However, complex commercials are an exception. A Nike spot in which basketball star Charles Barkley played one-on-one with Godzilla took two weeks to film.[3] Once the action has been captured, the **postproduction** phase begins. During this phase, editing specialists put all the pieces together, from the numerous takes of a single scene to the musical soundtrack to special effects, forming the finished commercial.

THE PREPRODUCTION PHASE

Preproduction starts when the advertiser has approved the copywriter's script (the dialog or narrative) and the art director's storyboard (the key shots from the commercial linked with the spoken or sung copy). This approval includes both the marketing and creative concepts and a legal review of such issues as competitive claims and health claims.[4] At this point, the agency's creative team and the advertiser have several important decisions to make: whether to shoot on film or on videotape, which special effects and special elements to include, whether to shoot on a set or on location, and what the commercial will essentially look like from scene to scene. With this information in hand, the agency assembles a package that includes the *production notes* and the *specification,* or "spec," sheet. This package describes what the agency would like to see in the finished commercial and then asks production companies to bid on the project. The next step is to select the production team, and then to modify the production plan if necessary. The final step in preproduction is to hold the preproduction meeting, which kicks off the production phase.

Choosing between Film and Video

A key preproduction decision is whether you want to shoot the commercial on film or on videotape. Each mode has its advantages and disadvantages, and not all production specialists handle both modes, so you need to make this decision fairly early in the process.

Film produces a softer image that many advertisers find appealing for their products (see Exhibit 12.3). For example, Hooper White, a pioneer in television commercial production (and one of the first people to shoot a commercial on videotape), thinks that the gentle imagery of film makes food look more appetizing.[5] Film is also the medium of choice when traditional animation techniques are required. In addition, film's technical qualities make it more appealing for emerging high-definition television.[6]

In contrast, videotaped commercials tend to have a sharper, more realistic edge to them. A key benefit of this feature is that it produces commercial scenes that look more like the physical scenes they represent. In addition, tape can lend a feeling of immediacy, which is important if you're going for excitement or tension in your commercial. Furthermore, unlike film, videotape doesn't have to be sent to a processing laboratory before you can view it; you can see what you've done immediately. This instant-replay capability of videotape helps the director and producer verify that they captured the intended images. This is important when the production team has limited access to a location or is shooting something of uncertain duration (such as a rainbow or a volcanic eruption). Tape's instant processing also gives the team a chance to reshoot if necessary, and it's a big plus if you need to shoot a commercial and get it on the air as quickly as possible.[7]

Planning Special Elements

Quite a few of today's commercials, especially those intended for nationwide broadcast, include special elements such as animation and special effects. All such elements need to be considered and planned for early in the preproduction phase. Some issues are relatively minor: if you want to shoot something in slow motion, for instance, you may have to alert the camera people to rent the high-speed

EXHIBIT 12.3
The Softer Edge of Film

The softer look of film is often used in food advertising.

V.O.: For the first ever straight 'A' report card . . . It was Stir-Fried Beef Fajitas.

camera motors required for slow-motion photography. Other issues have a much greater impact on costs, schedules, and the quality of the finished commercial: Visual effects that combine animation with live-action images can add weeks to the schedule, because the live-action photography must be staged and shot before the animators can go to work.[8] Whatever the magnitude of the special elements, the agency person overseeing the project must get involved early to start lining up the people and equipment required.

Visualizing the Commercial

Planning for special effects is actually only one part of a larger issue: *visualizing* the commercial, a key step in preproduction. Say that a storyboard calls for a shot looking down on a convertible as it drives along a highway. This shot is easy to describe in a storyboard, but it can be rather difficult to achieve during shooting. What is required? Can a camera operator stand in the back seat and shoot down on the driver, or do you need to arrange for a truck and boom to drive alongside so that the camera can be suspended above the car? Maybe the art director really wants an aerial shot of the car, which means that a helicopter and pilot will be needed.

The copywriter and art director communicate their vision of the commercial using some standard terminology. For instance, a scene might open with a *long shot* (also called a *wide shot*), showing the entire area in which the action will take place, and then move in to a *medium shot,* magnifying selected elements (including actors) by up to three times. A *close-up* moves in even further, making facial expressions, product packaging, and other details perceivable to the audience (see Exhibit 12.4). Other directions place the camera in a position to look over one actor's shoulder or to zoom in on an actor's eyes or on some small detail of the product.[9] The production team may suggest various ways of creating the desired action, but the copywriter and art director must provide everyone with a starting point by describing how they'd like to see the commercial come to life.

Once shooting begins, the production team needs to make sure that the shots come together in the intended fashion. A Quaker State motor oil commercial featured Burt Reynolds in an attractive horse-ranch setting, with Reynolds chatting while leaning on a fence. A nice shot overall, but the horse standing next to Reynolds faced away from the camera, making its large posterior a focus of attention in the scene.[10] Such visual glitches are hard to anticipate on a storyboard, so it's up to the production team to keep an eye out for them during filming or videotaping.

Pricing and Bidding the Project

Pricing the commercial and sending out for production bids bring financial reality down on the creative ideas of the copywriter and the art director. Special effects, large casts, elaborate sets, and exotic locations can add hundreds of thousands of dollars to the cost of production. On the other hand, simple commercials can be shot in local television studios for a few thousand dollars or less. In

EXHIBIT 12.4
Long, Medium, and Close-Up Shots

Depending on the elements to be emphasized, directors can choose from three basic shots: (*a*) the long shot, (*b*) the medium shot and (*c*) the close-up.

(a)

(b)

(c)

fact, many local advertisers bypass advertising agencies and work directly with television stations. As an example, station WXXA in Albany, New York, has three producer-directors who work with local advertisers to create commercials for as little as $150.[11]

Whatever the scale of the project, now is the time for the creative team to make sure that their ideas can be realized within the advertiser's budget. Experienced producers and technical experts can work with the writer and art director to suggest alternative ways of accomplishing creative objectives.

With the average production costs of national commercials pushing $200,000, and with many pushing $1 million and more, cost control is a hot topic in the industry.[12] Advertisers are pressuring agencies to cut costs, and the agencies are in turn pressuring production companies. Coming under close scrutiny are items such as the fees charged by star directors and the markups charged by production companies (to cover overhead expenses and profits).[13] Kimberly-Clark, a major producer of paper products, attacks its costs in four ways: by hiring consultants to monitor costs during production, by requiring its agencies to get three competitive bids for each project, by shooting outside Los Angeles and New York whenever possible (production costs are highest in those two cities), and by modifying pay arrangements to more directly reflect actual production costs.[14] If you get involved in any aspect of television production, you can expect cost concerns to be a regular part of your job.

Once the agency thinks it has a production plan that fits the range of the client's budget, the next step is to ask production companies to submit bids on the project. Standardized forms published by the Association of Independent Commercial Producers (AICP) help everyone keep track of the details so that everything is included in the bid. These forms cover all costs from wigs and set paint to crane rental and the rates that celebrities will be paid for appearing in the commercial.[15]

Choosing the Production Team

Given the costs and complexity of television production, picking the people who will be on the production team is a critical step. Talented people who can work as a team under pressure can transform a script and a storyboard into a powerful selling instrument. On the other hand, production people who don't have the right skills or the right attitude can both decrease the effectiveness of the finished commercial and increase the cost of production. When you're eating through the budget at an average of $65,000 a day during shooting, you don't want your production team to waste time or make mistakes.[16] That's why the top production people are so well known and so highly respected. Advertisers and agencies know they can count on such people to get the job done right.

Who gets involved in producing a commercial? The number of people involved in production and the roles they play vary widely, depending on such factors as the budget, the type of product, the place the commercial is being shot, and the commercial's overall design. In small projects done for local television, the art director and a handful of technical specialists from a television station may be the only people required. At the other extreme, an extravagant ad destined for national broadcast or network cable may require several dozen creative and technical specialists and 100 or more actors, dancers, and musicians. A Diet Pepsi commercial featuring singer Ray Charles had 100 actors, a 70-piece band, and a team of backup singers.[17] Most production projects fall somewhere between these two extremes. However, most of the technical and creative tasks required in a major production are also required in a small local production—there may simply be fewer people handling the work. The following sections explore the production roles played by the producer, the director, the copywriter and art director, the cast, and the crew.

The Producer. The **producer** is the person who manages the entire production process, from start to finish. In some cases, one producer represents the ad agency and manages things from that perspective, and a second producer represents the studio where the commercial is being created. It's up to the agency producer to make sure that the copywriter and art director's creative concept is transformed into a finished commercial, on time and on budget. The producer's job is part technical specialist, part manager and leader, and part referee and coordinator for the many people involved in production. It may seem odd that the copywriter and art director aren't in charge of production (since they're the ones who came up with the idea in the first place), but producers have the unique set of skills and experience needed to transform an idea into a finished commercial. This doesn't mean that one person can't handle both jobs, and in fact, art directors in some agencies double as producers.[18]

Aside from the administrative and managerial tasks, producers often need to step into creative and technical discussions and dilemmas. The scripts and storyboards that copywriters and art directors turn in for production aren't always producible as they are. If the storyboard asks for a shot that's impossible or prohibitively expensive, for instance, the producer must work with the copywriter and art director to find a more reasonable way to meet the same objective. During shooting, the producer sometimes has to balance the director's desire to create a beautiful and imaginative piece of film with the client's desire to sell the product. As you might suppose, such negotiations can require a great deal of tact and a healthy appreciation for the creative, technical, and financial aspects of production.[19]

The Director. The person who makes it all happen on shooting day is the **director.** Directors usually work for production companies (or run their own). In addition to guiding the cast members through their motions and lines of dialog during shooting, the director is responsible for managing the crew. In short, the director is in charge during the shooting (see Exhibit 12.5). It's his or her job to create the visual image that carries out the advertising task for which the commercial is being created. This can involve everything from helping the actors emphasize just the right words in their dialog to finding the best camera angle to highlight a product's unique shape. Even though other people take care of such

EXHIBIT 12.5
In Charge on the Set

From guiding the talent to giving technical personnel specific instructions, the director is in charge on the set.

creative and technical aspects as lighting and sound, a good director understands all these elements and knows how to use them to best advantage.[20]

Many of the top directors tend to have individual styles, and for each project, agencies look for a style that matches the advertising challenge. To give you a sense of how these star directors go about their work, here's a quick sample of directors and their styles:

- *Satoshi Saikusa.* Shadows and reflections are key elements in Saikusa's directing style. Born in Japan but now based in Paris, Saikusa stunned the European advertising industry with a spot for the Greek tourism agency. To illustrate the advertising theme, "In Greece, the sea is the theater of life," he used a giant mirror to reflect various images onto the rippling waters of a swimming pool. The result looked like trees and other objects dancing on the open sea.[21]

- *Tarsem Singh Dhandwar.* Tarsem, as he's known in the industry, combines mythology, offbeat humor, references to old movies, and various other elements in his work. One example is a commercial for Maxell audiotape, in which the face of a man listening to some music is grotesquely distorted by the sound blasting from the speakers. (Tarsem shot compressed air into the actor's face to illustrate him being "blown away" by the sound.)[22]

- *Joe Sedelmaier.* Sedelmaier is credited with helping to change the style of contemporary television advertising by replacing the "too-perfect mannequins" often used as characters in commercials with offbeat people who look like they belong in the real world—almost. His commercials entertain while they sell. One of his classics, a spot for the Wendy's hamburger chain, showed an elderly and slightly cranky woman hollering "Where's the beef?" when she didn't like the size of a competitive burger. The actress became a minor celebrity, and "Where's the beef" became a favorite catchphrase around the country.[23]

- *Jon Francis.* Also working in a humorous vein, but taking a more subdued approach, Francis has earned the nickname "Subtlemaier" for his style of directing. One spot for the discount grocery chain Cub Foods pokes fun at the chain's high-priced competitors by showing several managers of an imaginary Cub competitor spying on shoppers in their store. When a woman drops an exorbitantly priced piece of fruit into her shopping cart, the managers slap high-fives in celebration.[24]

- *Joe Pytka.* The high-profile Pytka is almost as well known for his forceful personality (having no qualms about ordering pampered celebrities around) as for his ability to produce great commercials in nearly any style. With a personal fee reported to run as high as $15,000 a day, Pytka doesn't come cheap—but many agency creatives jump at the chance to work with him. Pytka's recent credits include the Nike Hare Jordan spot (starring Michael Jordan and Bugs Bunny), commercials for the Gap, and all of Pepsi's recent megaproductions.[25]

Where do directors come from? There really isn't a standard career path. Joe Sedelmaier started as an agency art director. Tarsem Singh Dhandwar got his big break when he directed the video for REM's hit song "Losing My Religion" (voted the top video on MTV the year it appeared). Satoshi Saikusa started out as a hair stylist and makeup artist for fashion photographers. Jon Francis worked in various advertising and corporate communications jobs before directing his first spot. Joe Pytka got his start by making documentary films for PBS, and then he moved to commercials. It's not uncommon for directors to cross the line between commercials and television programs or movies. Such entertainment-industry stars as Rob Reiner and the late Federico Fellini have directed commercials in recent years.[26] The common thread in all cases, in spite of the differences in background and style, is that these directors know how to use the medium of television to persuade audiences.

The Copywriter and Art Director. Even though someone else usually handles the production of their commercial ideas, the copywriter and the art director still play important roles. At the very least, they need to make sure that their ideas aren't misinterpreted as the script and storyboard get transformed into a commercial. Because they're experts on the product, the target audience, and the competition, copywriters and art directors may understand nuances and points of detail that producers and directors aren't aware of. They should share these insights at the preproduction meeting, and they should be available to review the results from each day's filming or taping, to make sure that what shows up on the television screen accomplishes the advertising mission.[27]

The Cast. Just as in the movies and on television, the people who appear on-camera in a commercial are referred to as the *cast,* or as the **talent.** Some are professional actors; others are "civilians" recruited for testimonials or for the way they look and sound (see Exhibit 12.6). For slice-of-life formats, the agency and the director look for people who seem like everybody's next-door neighbors. In other cases, directors look for people who are just a little bit outside the ordinary. Joe Sedelmaier, for example, tries to find people whose faces, voices, walks, and mannerisms make them stand out from the crowd. Of course, established celebrities are used in many commercials.

The person who dreamed up the creative concept (usually the copywriter or art director) should be closely involved with the director to select actors whose on-screen appearance and overall persona mesh with the advertising strategy. As already noted, the production notes should clearly describe the type of people who the copywriter and art director envision. Because advertisers are increasingly portraying a broad cross section of society in their television commercials, they're reaching beyond the "spokesmodel" look. People with physical and mental disabilities, for instance, were a rare sight in commercials just a few years ago, but not anymore. Although casting choices from groups outside the traditional mainstream are sometimes used to tug at the viewer's heartstrings, more and more advertisers are simply trying to reflect society as a whole. Bob Thacker, marketing vice president of the Target retail chain, says his company would use a disabled person "the way we would use someone with glasses." He adds that the "Benetton shock-value approach" (such as showing scenes of urban violence or human suffering in an ad) is not Target's goal at all, stressing that "Our goal is to blend in."[28]

For help in finding just the right casts, directors can turn to casting specialists at production companies or at larger ad agencies. Firms such as PeopleFinders and Faces & Places specialize in finding "real people" who want to talk about their product experiences on-camera. These talent scouts constantly prowl shopping malls and other public areas, looking for new faces.[29]

The minimum amounts that actors earn (called *scale*) are set by the three unions to which they can belong, although celebrities can charge far more than the basic rates. Directors usually try to limit the number of cast members in an effort to keep costs down. This isn't just for the costs of paying people to show up for

OLDER MAN IS CHALLENGED TO MAKE LAWNMOWER CHANGES IN LESS THAN TEN SECONDS WHILE ANNOUNCER AND ANOTHER OLDER MAN LOOK ON.

ANNOUNCER: How fast can you change a John Deere Tricycler mower from a mulcher to a rear bagger? Then a side discharger? Under ten seconds!

OLDER MAN ONLOOKER: I think I could have done it faster.
ANNOUNCER: The Tricycler mower, from John Deere.

shooting, however. Principal cast members whose faces appear on-screen or who have speaking parts receive **residuals,** which are payments made to the actors whenever their commercials appear on the air. With a large cast and a commercial that airs dozens of times, residuals can add up quickly, sometimes to more than the original cost of production.[30]

By the way, did you ever notice how attractive the hands and feet shown in close-ups usually are? Professional hand and foot models with nicely proportioned, unblemished hands and feet are in big demand in the advertising industry. These models work hard to protect their perfect appendages, and some are paid quite handsomely to appear in commercials (and in print ads as well).

The Crew. The crew encompasses everyone else involved in the production phase of the commercial. The **cinematographer,** also called the *director of photography* or the traditional term of *cameraman,* is second in command during the shoot. Cinematographers are responsible for the look of the lighting and for camera positioning and movement. In this capacity, they have a great deal of influence over the final look of the commercial. In fact, some cinematographers also direct commercials themselves.[31]

The **script clerk** performs vital tasks, including making sure the dialog being filmed matches the script and carefully timing each scene. Since commercials have to air in very precise time slots of 15, 20, 30, or 60 seconds, scene timing is critical. Script clerks also perform the "continuity checks" to keep little visual glitches from creeping into the commercial, such as making sure that the actors' wardrobes don't change from scene to scene when they're not supposed to. With the dozens or hundreds of takes and retakes that a commercial shoot can involve, keeping track of these visual details is a demanding job.[32]

Large-scale television production is a highly unionized business, and union contracts spell out specific levels of crew staffing. Other key members of the crew include the gaffer (the head electrician), juicers (assistant electricians), grips (people who move carts and perform other manual labor), home economists or food stylists (used in food commercials to prepare food in such a way that makes it look delicious in front of the camera), prop handlers, and makeup artists. Some commercials require helicopter pilots, teacher/welfare workers (usually required when children are used as actors), teamsters to drive trucks, and so on. It's not hard to see why a single commercial can cost hundreds of thousands of dollars to shoot, especially if all these people and their equipment have to be transported to a filming location.[33]

Designing the Set/Choosing the Location. Another important preproduction decision is where you're going to shoot the commercial. You can shoot on a **set,** which is an area in a studio constructed just for the purpose of shooting, or **on location,** which refers to anything outside a studio; shooting on the Serengeti plain in Africa and shooting in your mother's real-life kitchen are both shooting on location (see Exhibit 12.7). Sets can be found at the production studios of television stations, at production companies, or at movie and television studios. Paramount and other television/movie studios are working hard to pull in advertising production business because it helps them recoup more revenue from the often enormous investments they make in building sets.

Although both options have advantages and disadvantages, some types of commercials are simply easier to shoot either on a set or on location. Food commercials, especially those showing prepared food, are nearly always better to shoot on a set. Studios used for food shots have multiple ovens that the home economist can use to prepare the many different presentations that the director may want.[34] On the other hand, if you want to show people frolicking under a waterfall while drinking your new diet soda, you'll have to go on location to find one.

Sets usually have advantages over locations when it comes to sound, lighting, crowd control, and the use of bulky equipment. If the way you've visualized a

EXHIBIT 12.7
On the Set

Shooting a TV commercial can be a complex affair involving lots of equipment and dozens of people.

commercial that takes place in a kitchen involves low-angle shots, high angles, or lots of camera movements, you're probably better off in a studio because you'll have more room to set up and move the cameras. Among the drawbacks of set shooting is the lack of authenticity often apparent in studio shots. For instance, it can be difficult, expensive, and time consuming to dress a set in a way that looks like a real, lived-in house. You can construct simple walls and move in furniture without too much expense, but adding ceilings, stairs, outdoor landscaping, and other features of a real house might be too much to ask.[35]

Shooting on location overcomes the realism issue of studio shooting but introduces some limitations of its own. Lighting can be an issue, particularly if the cinematographer wants natural lighting and the sun won't cooperate. Noise from highways or crowds, and even the crowds themselves, can pose problems.[36] In addition, cost can be a major sticking point in location shooting. Bermuda may seem like the perfect place to shoot your swimwear commercial—until you add up the cost of flying your cast, crew, and equipment there. A beach closer to home (or perhaps even a studio shot) may be the only affordable answer.

Conducting the Preproduction Meeting

With your plans more or less in place, your next move is holding the **preproduction meeting,** a checkpoint session that's your last chance to nail down all the details before shooting. Its purpose is to make sure everyone understands what the production will entail, who is responsible for which tasks, and what the commercial is going to look like. The meeting typically involves one or more people from the agency creative team, a representative from the advertiser, a director, and an agency producer (who runs the meeting).[37] Here's the agenda of a typical preproduction meeting:[38]

- Explain the advertising objective established for the commercial.
- Discuss the storyboard in detail, frame by frame.
- Play and discuss the music track, if it has been recorded prior to shooting.
- Go over the director's shot list, which describes each shot in the commercial.
- Review the videotapes taken during the casting session (the agency and the director make the final cast selections now).
- Review the production schedule.

- Approve the props, wardrobe, and other details.
- Make sure the product will be ready and that a product expert will be on hand to operate it if necessary.

This list should give you a good sense of how complex commercial production can be and how important it is to manage this process effectively. With all the details hammered out during the preproduction meeting, you're ready to shoot your commercial.

THE PRODUCTION PHASE

The agency producer is still in charge during production, but the director is the boss during shooting. He or she instructs the crew to get everything ready and then puts the actors through their paces. Shooting is definitely not a democratic process; anyone with alternative ideas or questions about how the commercial will look should bring them up at the preproduction meeting. When the cast and crew arrive, it's show time, and things need to click along according to schedule.

Preparing for the Shoot

The production team starts to work by getting the props in place, preparing the product (e.g., cooking the food if it's a food commercial), getting the cameras in place, arranging the lighting, styling the actors' hair, and performing other necessary tasks. Sometimes a shot that takes up only a few seconds during the final commercial can take several hours to set up. It's tedious work at times, but it's all necessary, and an experienced crew knows how to get it done as quickly as possible.[39]

Lighting is a tremendously complex part of setting up a shoot, and the top directors and cinematographers are all experts at it. They know which lighting techniques to use to establish an upbeat mood, an air of mystery, a somber mood, or any other feeling for the commercial. Their lighting choices fall into four categories (see Exhibit 12.8):[40]

- *Key light*. The *key light* is the main source of light in a scene. In a product shot, the key light is focused on the product itself. High-key lighting creates a cheerful mood, whereas low-key lighting makes things look mysterious or even sinister.
- *Fill lights*. As their name implies, *fill lights* fill in most of the rest of the lighting needed in a scene, both in places outside the key light's focus and in places

EXHIBIT 12.8
Lighting a Television Commercial

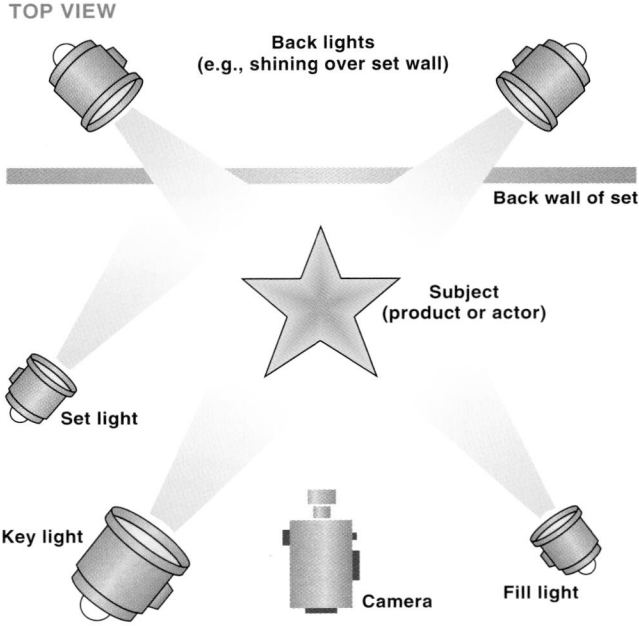

TOP VIEW

Back lights
(e.g., shining over set wall)

Back wall of set

Subject
(product or actor)

Set light

Key light

Camera

Fill light

where the key light creates shadows (such as behind the product). The proportion of fill lighting to key lighting determines the degree of contrast. More fill lighting makes the scene appear softer; the light areas aren't as harsh and the shadows aren't as dark. More key lighting increases the contrast, making the light areas brighter and the shadows darker.

- *Back lights.* To help define the outlines of a product or other object, directors use *back lights* placed behind the object. These lights help separate the object from the background.

- *Set lights.* Finally, *set lights* can be used to light up part of the set (or location). Special visual tricks can be used with set lights as well, such as shining the light through a cutout in the shape of window panes, which then casts the shadow of the panes onto the back wall of the set. This creates the illusion that sunlight is filtering through a window somewhere in front of the set.

In addition to working with these main categories of lights, the lighting specialist is often called on to solve particular problems, such as a reflection on a shiny object or light that is spilling over from the key light and visually emphasizing something the director doesn't want emphasized.[41] The lighting situation can be even more complicated if you're shooting on location and forced to deal with sunshine and clouds.

Shooting

With the set ready, the actors in wardrobe, and the lighting in place, shooting begins. Directors rarely shoot scenes in the exact order in which they will appear in the final commercials. Sometimes the director will shoot all the scenes that involve one or more of the actors, so that these people won't have to be paid for too much sitting-around time. In other cases, the director will want to shoot all the close-ups at once, or all shots requiring one style of lighting. It will be the *editor*'s job (in postproduction) to put the pieces together in the right order.[42]

The director will shoot and reshoot each scene until it looks just right and will then usually shoot a few more takes just to be sure. The editor can use these extra takes during postproduction to get just the right look and sound for each scene. Certain shots, such as of an actor taking a bite of food or pouring a beverage, can involve many takes to get them right. All of this taking and retaking can be maddeningly slow to watch and participate in, but it's necessary to produce a first-rate commercial.

If you're shooting on videotape, it's a simple matter of rewinding the tape to see whether you've gotten a take you like. Film, of course, has to be sent out to be developed. Following a day's shooting, the director, producer, and editor review these **rushes,** or **dailies,** selecting shots they like, tossing out shots they don't like, and making plans to retake particular shots if necessary.[43] It's important to make sure you've got all the tape or film you need before you tear down the set or leave the location.[44]

Recording the Soundtrack and Creating Special Effects

As already indicated in Exhibit 12.2, the line between the production phase and the postproduction phase is a little fuzzy when it comes to the soundtrack and special effects. Sometimes you'll record the sound while you're shooting the film or tape, and sometimes you'll record it after production has finished. As you can imagine, recording sound during production adds another level of details to plan and manage during shooting. Sometimes the music track is recorded before any shooting is done, and then the visual elements are assembled in a way that matches the rhythm and flow of the music. This *prescoring* is often used in animated production.

Although most special effects are added in postproduction, some must be created during production. A good example is extreme slow motion, such as flakes of cereal falling out of a box. Simply replaying regularly recorded film or video at a slower speed will result in poor picture quality. To get high-quality slow-motion

ETHICS IN ADVERTISING

When Creative Visuals Become Deceptive Visuals

Presenting the advertiser's product in a favorable and flattering manner is clearly an important aspect of television commercial production. However, at some point, creative efforts to make the product look good can cross ethical and legal lines, making the product look better than it really is. The tricky part is deciding where those ethical and legal lines lie, and then getting everyone involved to agree.

In some cases, the deception—and the intent to deceive—is obvious. Volvo and its former ad agency got into hot water several years ago when the agency admitted modifying both the Volvos and the competitors' vehicles shown in print and television ads. The ads showed a "monster truck" driving over cars. The Volvos held up nicely, but the competitive cars were crushed. A powerful demonstration, but clearly deceptive; production technicians had beefed up the frames in the Volvos with steel and wood, and they had weakened the frames in competitors' cars. In a close-up shot that showed one truck tire rolling over the Volvo, it was literally that—one tire, with no truck attached, which crew members were simply rolling across the car while the camera zoomed in. The whole affair was even presented as a real monster truck exhibition, when in fact it was staged, with 400 extras hired to simulate a crowd. When word leaked to the press about the deception, the agency resigned the account, and Volvo publicly apologized (without admitting any wrongdoing, however; the company said the cars had been modified for safety reasons).

In other cases, however, the line between creative production and deception is not so clear. Have you ever seen a commercial for hot fudge sauce and watched it being poured over scoops of vanilla ice cream? Well, it probably wasn't ice cream, which would melt under the hot lights used to illuminate the set. What you thought was ice cream was probably mashed potatoes or another durable substitute. Is this deception? Maybe, but the ad isn't selling ice cream; it's selling chocolate sauce. Referring to the ice cream/mashed potatoes issue, Rick Kurnit, an attorney specializing in advertising, sums it up this way: "The basic issue is that you can mock up only to the extent that it doesn't make for a false message about the product. But as soon as you address any product attribute of ice cream, then the visible depiction has to be an accurate and truthful depiction."

Sean Fitzpatrick of McCann-Erickson points out that just about anything is possible with today's special-effects technology, but if you depict the product doing something it can't really do, then you'd better add a disclaimer statement to the ad. To be on the safe side, his agency takes the extra step of having consulting engineers study the creative concept behind some commercials before the ideas are even presented to the clients. The engineers can tell whether the agency can execute the commercial as planned without having to pull any tricks with the product.

What's Your Opinion?

1. *Would you support a strict interpretation of truth in advertising when it comes to visuals? For instance, should the Big Mac shown in a television spot look exactly like the average Big Macs that customers get, or is it okay for a home economist or food stylist to craft a perfect burger for the commercial?*
2. *Where would you draw the line between putting the best possible face on a product and deceiving the audience?* ■

replay, you need to shoot at a faster speed and then play this film or tape back at normal replay speed.[45] Some production concepts require more elaborate planning, such as the Diet Coke commercial in which scenes from old movies were woven into footage taken just for the commercial. The result was that classic film stars such as Humphrey Bogart appeared to be in the same scenes as such contemporary figures as singer Elton John.[46] The new footage had to be planned and executed around the existing film clips, so that the two could be combined seamlessly.

Once you've shot all the film or tape you need and created the special effects and other elements that fit in the production phase of the project, your next step is to put the commercial together in postproduction. Traditionally, the director would turn the project over to the editor at this point, but increasingly directors are remaining involved and lending their special talents throughout the postproduction phase.

THE POSTPRODUCTION PHASE

Much of the audio and visual magic in a television commercial is created in the postproduction phase. Beth Stewart Morris, a vice president and executive producer at J. Walter Thompson/L.A., stresses that "Postproduction is more vital to the look of the commercial than it ever has been."[47] Think of postproduction as the same process you go through when you're getting ready to hand in a major term

CARGO PLANE PILOT IS YELLING BACK TO CREWMAN AS THEY ARE GETTING READY TO "BOMB" THE GROUND BELOW WITH TV'S PLAYING SEGA SONIC 3.
(SFX): loud engine hum, and rushing wind.
CAPTAIN: Has it got huge new zones?
CREWMAN: Check!
CAPTAIN: Twice as big as Sonic 2?

CREWMAN: Check!
CAPTAIN: New 3-D special stage!?
CREWMAN: Check!
CAPTAIN: And the new game save feature?
CREWMAN: Check!
CAPTAIN: Do it!!
THERE IS A SMALL PUFF OF SMOKE AS A TV HITS THE GROUND. SMOKE CLEARS TO REVEAL A SOOT-COVERED

SMILING WOMAN WITH THE TV SITTING IN HER SHOPPING CART. THE CLERK RINGS UP THE SALE.
(SFX): ping!
ANNOUNCER: New Sonic 3 is now available. At a store near you.
PILOT: Sega!!!
ANNOUNCER: New Sonic 3 game cartridge and Sega Genesis, sold separately.

EXHIBIT 12.9
Executing a Difficult Creative Concept

Goodby Silverstein & Partners combined animation, still photography, and live-action footage to create this commercial for Sega video games.

paper or make an important presentation to the class. From the type of report cover you use to the props you select for your presentation, the way you package your work has a great deal to do with how well your message is received. All this packaging is your version of postproduction. For a television commercial, the major tasks in postproduction are editing, recording additional sound elements (voices, sound effects, and music) as necessary and mixing them together, creating whatever special effects are required, and finally tying the audio and video elements together (see Exhibit 12.9). At that point, you're ready to make copies and send them off to local stations, national networks, or cable systems, depending on where the commercial is scheduled to run.

Editing

Imagine that you have to reduce 60 or 70 pages of rough draft material to a single-page report—that's on the same scale as the editing task of distilling the 3,000 or so feet of film shot for a typical commercial down to the 45 feet needed for a 30-second commercial. This problem is compounded by the fact that the commercial has absolutely no leeway in terms of time; it can't run long and it can't run short (although electronic time-compression techniques can squeeze more than 30 "natural" seconds into a 30-second slot by playing the commercial at higher speeds). The person responsible for this sometimes mind-boggling reduction task is the **editor,** whose job ranges from creating smooth visual transitions between scenes to piecing together film or video footage and still photographs to fit a prerecorded soundtrack. In many cases, the editor's creative decisions have as much impact on the final look of the commercial as the director's. In fact, top editors are as well known in the industry as many directors.[48]

Creative editing not only increases the effectiveness of a commercial but also covers up shooting problems and incorporates last-minute creative decisions.[49] Assume you've shot a family eating a brand of breakfast cereal. One of the actors looked into the camera while reciting the line "And it has less sugar than any leading cereal." Now assume that between the time you shot the film and the time you're editing the commercial, a new competitor starts advertising a product with even less sugar than yours. Do you have to throw out your commercial? Not at all. Just have the editor splice in a second or two of film where the camera was focused on the bowl of cereal, not on the actor's face. Then have the actor come into a sound studio and record a new line, such as "Less sugar than most leading cereals." The editor can make the visual transitions from actor to bowl and back to the actor look seamless and natural, and no one will ever know about your last-minute change.

The process of editing television commercials starts with looking at a copy of the dailies or the videotape, known as a **work print,** and selecting the best takes of the scenes that the storyboard says should be included. In some cases, the director will make a *director's cut* first, to indicate which takes he or she thinks are best and in which order they should appear. Editors use a variety of tools to cut and piece the footage together, from traditional mechanical devices (which allow editors to physically cut and splice film) to computer-based tape-editing systems such as the one shown in Exhibit 12.10 (which let editors "cut and paste" footage in much the same way you would use a word processor on a personal computer).[50]

If you shoot the commercial on videotape, the editing will be done on tape as well. If you shoot on film, however, you have the option of transferring the film to tape either before or after editing. Transferring before editing lets you take advantage of the latest computer advances in tape editing, and it speeds the editing process because you don't have to wait for an optical laboratory to process any special effects you might want to create.[51] The editing processes for film and videotape involve different steps and terminology, but the intent in either case is the same: assemble the desired visual elements in the correct order and then mix the voices, music, and sound effects with the visual elements.

The first stage of editing produces a **rough cut,** which includes the scenes in the order they'll appear in the final commercial but which doesn't include the finished soundtrack, special effects, or final editing touches.[52] The next step for film is the **interlock,** in which the editor brings the film and the soundtrack into close-to-final form. A major part of creating the interlock is adding **opticals,** the various visual effects that can be done with film cameras. These include *fades* (where a scene gradually disappears and the screen goes to black), *dissolves* (where one scene fades out but is replaced by another scene fading in), and *wipes* (where one scene is visually "pushed aside" by another scene coming on-screen). When everything is in place, the editor creates an **answer print.** This is the final version sent out for the advertiser's approval before shipment to the media.[53] After the client approves, the film is usually transferred to video, and **dupes,** or duplicate copies, are sent to the broadcast and cable systems that will run the ad.

The process for editing on videotape is usually computerized in today's leading-edge production and editing shops. Computerized editing systems can perform tasks from the simple (showing a company logo on the screen) to the complex (showing a montage of images on the screen simultaneously). Such equipment

How Computer Technology Is Revolutionizing Commercial Production

Desktop publishing revolutionized print advertising production when it gave individual designers capabilities that previously required a variety of specialized skills and equipment. Desktop video editing is now doing the same thing for television production. Computer-assisted editing has been possible for some time, but desktop video takes the process a significant step further by transferring the images from videotape to computer memory. With the images in memory, the editor can instantly access and manipulate any shot, even if the director brings in hours and hours of raw footage. The editor can then assemble the final commercial using only the images stored in computer memory, without having to fuss with the videotapes any more.

With $80,000 to $100,000 price tags, desktop systems such as the Avid/1 are far cheaper than traditional editing systems, putting them within the financial reach of more agencies and production shops. However, the attraction of desktop video goes far beyond the price tag. The ability of these systems to provide virtually instantaneous results yields an important creative advantage as well. Because editors don't have to spend time manually searching through raw footage and don't have to piece bits of footage together by hand, they can "play" with the footage much more easily. This flexibility lets them try out different shot combinations, new sequences, and other variations until they hit on the best edit.

The desktop systems also offer two appealing advantages in efficiency and cost effectiveness. First, the systems manage many of the organizing, filing, and retrieval tasks that tie up an editor's time. Alan Miller of Rebo Studio in New York described an editing project in which the director came in at the last minute and decided that the ad's complicated opening sequence should be composed entirely of close-up shots. With a tradi-

tional system, Miller would have been forced to play through all the videotapes, manually searching for and then keeping track of every close-up shot. With his Avid/1 system, however, he simply asked the computer to show him all the close-ups. A task that might have meant hours and hours of laborious searching was accomplished in a few seconds.

Second, desktop systems offer the ability to compile more commercials from the same amount of raw footage. Because the systems keep track of all the raw footage, editors can concentrate on creative possibilities, finding new ways to piece together more spots from the same material. For example, the Hollywood editing shop Straight Cut recently created 18 Skippy Premium Dog Food commercials from raw footage that was originally supposed to yield only 4 spots.

As with desktop publishing, though, some people worry that desktop video puts powerful creative tools in the hands of people who might not be ready for them. These systems can't suddenly give unskilled users the visual talent and creative instincts needed to edit videotape successfully. Others are concerned about giving editors so many creative options that the sheer number of decisions slows the process. Peter Farago of Farago Advertising likens it to giving a print designer 10,000 possible typefaces. However, similar concerns didn't stem the desktop-publishing tide, and they're not likely to hold desktop video back, either.

Apply Your Knowledge
1. What are the implications of desktop video for small businesses, nonprofit organizations, and other advertisers with small production budgets?
2. What steps could the following groups take to make sure that quality remains high when desktop video technology gives nonspecialists their own postproduction and editing capabilities: (a) advertisers, (b) agencies, (c) postproduction shops, and (d) manufacturers of desktop video equipment? ∎

---

used to be found only in the largest production facilities, but even local television stations now have access to advanced editing capabilities.[54]

Recording Additional Sound, Adding Special Effects, and Mixing

Unless you captured all the necessary voices, sound effects, and music live during production (which is unlikely for major productions), you'll need to record them in postproduction. Sometimes you'll just need to add some voice-overs or perhaps a few sound effects. In other cases, you'll record an entire musical soundtrack in postproduction, a process called *postscoring*. Postscoring can create powerful combinations of audio and video because the music is created specifically to enhance the video images you created in production. Postscoring, in fact, is one of the major quality differences between local and national television advertising.[55]

Chances are good that you'll also add some level of special effects at this point. Paul Babb of Paramount Images (Paramount's ad production division) says that three-quarters of his studio's commercial work involves some level of special effects.[56] It might be as simple as adding the company's logo in the corner of the screen or adding a *super* or a *crawl*, a line of text that runs across the screen. For

(SFX): drum roll and choral voices.
V.O.: When you are the world's largest hotel and entertainment complex, the MGM Grand, you need plenty of wide open spaces. So it's only fitting that a city of pyra-mids, palaces, and castles would be the new home of our 5000-room kingdom complete with a magical Emerald City, a 15,000-seat event center, and a 33-acre theme park. Las Vegas. Where the lion will reign supreme.

EXHIBIT 12.11
The Power of Special Effects

The MGM Grand Hotel in Las Vegas gets special morphing treatment in this commercial.

additional time and increased expense, special-effects computers can produce some eye-catching imagery. A good example is the Nike commercial that shows an athlete running past buildings on which giant images of sports legends have been projected. Normally Nike's agency, Wieden & Kennedy, could have arranged to project the images onto actual buildings and then film the jogger running past. However, some of the buildings in this commercial were skyscrapers, far too large to cover with projected images. For help, the agency turned to Planet Blue, a Hollywood postproduction shop. Planet Blue electronically blended footage of the buildings as they normally look with pictures of the sports legends and footage of the jogger running past. The merging of images was so smooth that viewers couldn't tell that the scene had been assembled by computer.[57]

The general term for visuals created on a computer system is **computer-generated imagery (CGI).** You've no doubt seen some computer magic in recent television commercials. A technique called **morphing,** for instance, allows a postproduction expert to transform an object that was captured on film or video. Chrysler used this technique to show how its new LH line of cars was different from previous models. The new cars seemed to "grow" out of the old cars. (If you saw the movie *Terminator 2,* you saw morphing in action; that's how the evil terminator kept changing form.) To viewers, morphing looks like a real object changing shape right before their eyes (see Exhibit 12.11). CGI also plays an ever-increasing role in animation. In fact, some advocates of CGI say it's only a matter of time before they can create human images that are impossible to tell apart from real people.[58]

The final step is **mixing,** combining the various audio and visual elements into one finished tape. The process for mixing the sound portion is similar to the process for mixing the music for an album: you select which elements need to be emphasized and which should play supporting roles; then you adjust their respective volumes accordingly. Although mixing, like every other aspect of postproduction, takes place on some of the best audio and video equipment available anywhere, it's a good idea to play the soundtrack through a tiny, low-quality speaker before completing the mix. Most televisions have such speakers, so this will give you a better idea of what the audience will actually hear.[59]

Exploring Radio Production

When television stormed onto the scene several decades ago, radio fell into something of a creative slump, but that trend is clearly being reversed. Some of the hottest creative people in the industry, particularly among copywriters, now spend time in radio—and some of them exclusively in radio. Two of the best known in the industry are Joy Golden of Joy Radio in New York City and Dick Orkin of the Radio Ranch in Los Angeles. Golden says she has had people tell her that they had to stop their cars while listening to her radio spots for Laughing Cow cheese—they were laughing too hard to drive. Such a personal connection with the audience is often easier to achieve in radio because listeners have to create the picture in their minds; they become more involved in a good radio commercial.[60]

WRITING GOOD RADIO COPY

Good radio advertising involves creative design and production, just as print and television ads do. However, it's obviously a different sort of creativity, since the only element you have to work with is sound. This places a greater burden on the copy and emphasizes the need for good sound effects and music.

Once relegated to junior writers as a way to hone their skills on the way up the ladder to television, radio copywriting is gaining more respect among many advertisers and agencies. Experienced radio writers point out that simply rewriting print or television copy for the radio is a mistake; radio copy needs to be created from the ground up. What makes good radio? Bob Schulberg of CBS radio says that radio writers should start by following Winston Churchill's five points of successful speechwriting: begin on a strong note, keep to a single theme, use simple language, leave a picture in the listener's mind, and finish with a dramatic ending.[61]

Although the lack of visuals is often listed as a drawback of radio, good radio writers often consider it a plus. Steve Rabonsky of Chiat/Day points out that "I can do a radio commercial that convinces you you're on Mars. On television, we're talking about big bucks for that." In other words, it's sometimes *easier* and definitely cheaper to achieve your objective when you create the picture in the listener's mind, rather than on a computer or a sound stage (see Exhibit 12.12). That doesn't mean the writing task is easy, however. In Rabonsky's opinion, radio is the hardest of all advertising copywriting jobs.[62]

CHOOSING MUSIC AND SOUND EFFECTS

The art direction in radio centers on the way you combine music and sound effects with the spoken (or sung) copy. Brent Walker, owner of a radio commercial production shop in Little Rock, Arkansas, chooses from his library of more than 60,000 sound effects to put together just the right sound for his client's commercials. In a spot for the White Castle hamburger chain, Walker wanted to create the audio illusion of sitting in a car, ordering from the White Castle drive-through. He rerecorded the actor's voice-over tape through a modified speaker that made the

EXHIBIT 12.12
Getting Inside the Listener's Mind

This radio ad does a great job of letting listeners know what to expect if they hire a cabinet company with poor artistic tastes. (This photo shows the much more refined look of a Cabinetmasters Kitchen.)

MAN'S VOICE: Walking down the street one day, you encounter a man. He is dressed in white patent leather shoes with silver side-buckles and dark brown socks. His trousers are burnt orange bell bottoms with a yellow madras pattern throughout. Wrapped provocatively around the elastic waistband is a harvest gold utility belt with a large Elvis commemorative buckle. His shirt is avocado green with the name "Lou" embroidered just above one pocket. It occurs to you this must surely be the man who designed and decorated your kitchen. You resist the impulse to confront him and instead vow to call Cabinetmasters Kitchen Showroom, where they will design and install the kitchen of your dreams no matter how large or small. Cabinetmasters. Kitchens redone, tastefully. Mockingbird at Central. Call 821-6200.

Courtesy The Richards Group

voice sound as though it were coming out of a drive-through speaker. Then he added various highway sounds, such as different types of cars driving by in both directions. Finally, using stereo recording techniques, he "placed" the actor's voice and the car sounds in such a way that gave the listener the exact audio sensation of ordering from a drive-through speaker.[63]

Not all radio spots are produced with the same effort as Walker's White Castle ad, of course. Many ads are simply read live by a **radio personality,** who can be a disk jockey, weather reporter, or other person who listeners are accustomed to hearing on the air. This is a fast and inexpensive way to get a commercial on the air, and many radio stations have writers who can put the copy together for an advertiser. Plus, a personality who believes in your product and is used to talking on the air can often sell more effectively than a recorded commercial, especially if the person is adept at improvising (linking a commercial for snow tires to the latest weather report, for instance).[64]

UNDERSTANDING THE RADIO PRODUCTION PROCESS

In terms of production complexity, radio ads fall into two basic categories: live and taped. For speed, simplicity, and low cost, it's hard to beat a live radio commercial. You can type up your copy, fax it to the station, and have your commercial read on the air according to whatever schedule you're willing to pay for. In addition to the advantages noted earlier, having a station personality read your ad live gives you a great deal of flexibility. If you need to respond to a competitor's new ad, for instance, you simply revise the copy and fax it to the station.

On the downside, live ads may not catch the listener's attention effectively enough, since the voice reading them is the same voice that has been reading the news, announcing the songs, and so forth. In some cases, you'll want to tape the spot just so that you can use a different voice. Also, you don't have exclusive rights to the personality; what if he or she is also assigned to read ads from your competitors? Making sure that your commercial's "voice" doesn't appear in other commercials is another good reason for using taped ads.[65]

Taped ads are recorded prior to broadcast, either at specialized radio production companies, at general-purpose recording studios (which may also be used for recording music, educational cassettes, and other audio products), or at the station itself (see Exhibit 12.13). In addition to the advantages just cited, taping your ads

EXHIBIT 12.13
Radio Production

Studios for recording radio commercials often have musical instruments on hand to make it easy to add music to commercials.

lets you add music, effects, multiple characters, and other sounds as required. Taping also gives you more control over how the copy is read (more dramatic, faster, slower, and so forth). Even when you're using a station personality, you may opt for taping to get this extra level of creative control.

The production process for taped ads is similar in concept to television production: it starts with a script approved by the advertiser and then moves through preproduction, production, and postproduction phases. Of course, radio production is a good deal simpler since it doesn't involve visuals. However, the process can still involve sending bids out to production companies, hiring the talent, tying down the details in a preproduction meeting, mixing in special effects and music, and then duplicating tapes for distribution to radio networks or to the stations in your target market.

Managing Costs and Quality in Electronic Production

As Chapter 11 points out for print production, you can take several steps to control costs and quality. Those steps apply to electronic production as well. In addition to staying on schedule and making the most of technology, the following points will help you control the cost and quality of electronic production:

- *Simplify the design of the commercial.* Exotic locations, elaborate sets, special equipment, and large casts are surefire ways to drive up costs.[66]

- *Keep a close eye on animation and special-effects costs.* Animation, both traditional hand-drawn animation and computer-generated imagery, presents all kinds of possibilities for cost overruns. Hooper White points out that many commercials relying heavily on special effects wind up costing more than twice the amounts originally budgeted. Planning the commercial carefully and in detail, sticking to the plan, and limiting the number of production people involved are all good ways of keeping a lid on costs.[67]

- *Reduce the complexity of editing and other postproduction activities.* The more complicated the editing and postproduction job, the more the commercial is going to cost. Steve Weber of the postproduction house Adventure Film and Tape in Los Angeles explains that the cost of the average postproduction job has recently more than doubled because of all the computer animation and tricky edits. He notes that "MTV-style" commercials, with dozens of short snippets of film or video, are much more expensive to edit because an editor has to spend time on every transition between shots.[68]

- *Reduce the amount of film or video you shoot.* Another way to drive up editing costs is to hand editors a massive amount of film or tape and ask them to edit it down to a 30- or 60-second spot. An editor at Mad River Post in Santa Monica, California, said that one client dropped off 50,000 feet of film and wanted it reduced to one commercial.[69] This is more than 500 times as much film as will fit in a 60-second spot, and more than 1,000 times the amount needed for a 30-second spot.

Summary

The production of electronic advertising differs from the production of print advertising in six ways. First, television has the extra dimensions of sound and motion, which make producing it more challenging both creatively and technically. Second, although radio has the extra dimension of sound, it has no visuals. The copy and the sound together have to carry the entire work load of getting the message across, even if you have a fairly visual message. Third, electronic production has rigid time constraints, giving you less flexibility in terms of how much you can say or show. Fourth, radio and television ads are usually more difficult to refine or revise once production has begun. Fifth, television and radio production usually involves more people. Finally, electronic production is usually done by third parties, not by the advertising agency.

The steps required to produce a television commercial fall into three phases. In the preproduction phase, the steps include

Meeting an Advertising Challenge at Fahrenheit Films

A CASE FOR CRITICAL THINKING

Foremost among the technical challenges that Rod Davis faced in the GMC bungee-jumping commercial was the question of how to stop the truck's fall. Moreover, he had to do it in a way that conveyed the advertising message. At first, Davis wanted to connect the truck to the bridge with a steel cable, but he switched to a bungee cord after GMC engineers convinced him that a cable wouldn't let the truck fall and stay in one piece. The bungee cord's elasticity would help absorb some of the shock of the fall, although just like in human bungee jumping, the object at the end of the bungee cord obviously shares in the shock.

This wasn't just any old bungee cord, however. This cord was similar to those used in military operations to drop tanks and other vehicles during troop deployments; it weighed 1,400 pounds and was 100 feet long in its unstretched state. The cord eventually stretched to about 600 feet. To demonstrate that the truck's frame could handle the stress of sudden deceleration that vehicles experience when towing heavy loads, the Fahrenheit crew attached the cord to the truck's trailer hitch (which is connected to the frame). A key aspect of this demonstration was that the truck wasn't

modified or strengthened in any way, but as a safeguard against polluting the river below, Davis did have his crew remove all the gas and oil from the truck.

With the attachment problem solved, the next challenge was getting all this on film. When you're doing something as expensive and as potentially risky as tossing a truck over a bridge, you don't have much room for mistakes or retakes. To get as many angles and perspectives on film as possible, Davis set up eight cameras—on the bridge, under the bridge, in the truck, and in a helicopter flying around inside the gorge. It took three jumps over the course of two days, but Davis got the film he needed. The editing staff spliced together shots from the various cameras, starting with a close-up from behind the truck as it started to roll and ending with a helicopter shot of the truck dangling in mid-air.

As you might expect, this wasn't an inexpensive production task. The tab came to roughly $400,000. However, as GMC's advertising manager emphasized, with so many competitors stressing the strength of their products, it was important for GMC to get the audience to notice and listen to the GMC message. Although it's

always hard to link advertising with sales success, GMC is clearly doing something right. The ads began running in 1992, and GMC posted record-setting sales for that year. Sales of the Jimmy itself increased nearly 40 percent over the previous year, and combined GMC truck sales were up nearly 20 percent.

By the way, did the truck survive? Yes, and without a hitch, so to speak. When the crane lifted it back onto the bridge after the third fall, technicians replaced the oil and gasoline, and a driver hopped in and drove away. To top it off, McCann/SAS staffers believe they've set a new world record for height and weight in a bungee jump. It wasn't your typical television production job, and surely it isn't one that Rod Davis and his team at Fahrenheit will soon forget.

Your Mission: You've recently moved up the ladder at Fahrenheit films to become Rod Davis's assistant director. In this role, you help out with many of the planning and production decisions behind the commercials that Fahrenheit shoots for its clients. Consider the four scenarios that follow, and use what you've learned in this chapter to make the best choice in each case.

---

selecting film or videotape, planning special elements, visualizing what the commercial will look like, bidding the project and selecting the production team, designing the set or choosing the location, preparing the production notes and spec sheet, and then holding the preproduction meeting. In the production phase, the steps consist of preparing the set or location (which includes costumes, lighting, food preparation, and so forth), rehearsing, shooting the film or video, recording the sound, and creating special effects or other elements. The steps in postproduction include editing the film or video, recording additional sound and creating additional special effects as needed, creating the rough cut and interlock for film and then transferring it to video, getting final approval from the advertiser, and making dupes for the media.

The key players in the production of a television commercial include the producer (who's responsible for the overall management of the process), the director (who's in charge of translating the creative idea into film or tape), the copywriter and art director (who make sure that their idea gets translated cor-

rectly), the cast (who are the actors in the commercial), the cinematographer (who sets up the camera shots and either operates the camera or supervises the camera operator), and the script clerk (who does a variety of tasks, such as monitoring dialog and timing scenes).

Radio copy differs from print and television copy most significantly in the fact that the copy has to work alone (or with music and sound effects at most). Radio presents no opportunity for using a photograph or a special visual effect to get the point across. In terms of production, radio commercials come in two types. Live ads are read by a radio personality such as the disk jockey. Taped ads are recorded before they're played on the air, in a process that's conceptually similar to television production.

Four significant steps that advertisers can take to manage costs and quality in electronic production are simplifying the design of the commercial, keeping a close eye on animation and special-effects costs, reducing the complexity of editing and other postproduction activities, and reducing the amount of film or video that's shot.

a. A professional driver wheeling the car through an obstacle course set up in a vacant lot

b. The cast of a top-rated television show sitting around the set of their show and talking about how much they like the Toyota

c. A fleet of Toyotas and stunt drivers weaving patterns on the Bonneville Salt Flats in Utah

2. McCann/SAS's art director wants to use some type of special effects to capture viewer attention in the next Jimmy commercial. Assuming the same advertising objective as the bungee-jump commercial, which of these approaches would you recommend?

a. A totally animated spot showing a cute cartoon version of the Jimmy towing a big, nasty trailer

b. A production using computer-generated imagery in which the "camera" flies in and around the chassis of the truck while the voice-over points out the engineering features responsible for the Jimmy's towing strength

c. A production combining computer-generated imagery with live action to show the Jimmy towing an entire planet

3. Step back in time to the bungee-jump commercial and imagine that GMC can't afford $400,000 for production. Which of the following less-expensive ideas would you choose to

1. Toyota's ad agency approaches you with three ideas and wants to know which one is likely to be the simplest and cheapest to produce. Think through the potential production issues and pick one of the following:

communicate the same product-strength message that the bungee shot communicated?

a. Position the Jimmy back-to-back with a large semi (such as a Peterbilt) and connect them with a 200-foot cable, temporarily coiled on the ground. Then drive the semi away as fast as possible, showing that the Jimmy can handle the stress when the cable tightens.

b. Use a steel cable to attach a Jimmy to a competitor's truck back-to-back, and have them engage in a tug-of-war.

c. Stack several competitors' trucks on top of a Jimmy.

4. You've been asked to recommend sound effects for a luxury car's radio commercial. The ad's storyline involves a professional couple on their way from work in the city to their home in the country. Which sound-design approach would you recommend?

a. Start with loud, annoying city driving sounds and end with quiet country sounds to emphasize the pleasant change that this luxury car promises.

b. Use quiet, gentle country sounds throughout to emphasize the car's quiet interior.

c. Use blaring, grating traffic noise from start to finish to emphasize that this car can isolate the driver from such unpleasantness.[70] ∎

Key Terms

Questions

FOR REVIEW

1. In what ways is copy more challenging to produce in a television ad, compared to a print ad?

2. What are the three main phases of the television commercial production process?

3. Why is the choice of director so important?

4. What are the editor's responsibilities in television commercial production?

5. In what way can the lack of a visual dimension make the radio commercial easier to design and produce, even when you're trying to communicate a visual message?

FOR ANALYSIS AND APPLICATION

6. Given that television production is generally more complex and difficult than print production, why wouldn't advertisers

want to have all the capabilities needed in-house, which would give them tighter control over the process?

7. Would you shoot a spot for L'Oreal cosmetics on film or on tape? Why?

8. Would you recommend that art directors always direct their own commercials? Why or why not?

9. If Honda wanted to film a commercial that emphasized the details of its cars, would you recommend a studio shoot or a location shoot? Why?

10. Why shouldn't you simply take the soundtrack from a television commercial and run it as a radio commercial?

Sharpen Your Advertising Skills

Manufacturers of computer software typically don't advertise on television, since that's usually not the most efficient way to reach software buyers. However, certain products, such as soft-ware for managing personal finances, do have a wide potential audience in the consumer market, making television a more attractive media option. You've been given the task of directing a television commercial for Managing Your Money, one of the leading personal finance programs. The agency art director wants to show both the computer screen (to demonstrate the product's features) and the face of a spokesperson who'll appear using the software (to let her speak directly into the camera and to show her positive emotional response to using the product).

Decision: Assuming you have 28.5 seconds to work with, divide the time into (a) shots of the screen, (b) shots of the spokeperson's face, and (c) any special shots such as the camera moving around the computer. Without worrying about the actual message, decide how many times you'll show the screen and for how long, how many times you'll cut to the spokesperson, and so on.

Communication: Once you've divided the time into however many shots you want to use, outline your plan in a page or two for the agency art director.

Creating a Television Commercial from Concept to Production

To cook up Leaf's Jolly Rancher television commercial, ad agency Ayer Chicago took two teen actors and a bowlful of computer-generated fruit, added a dash of futuristic technology, and stirred vigorously. The result: a mouth-watering taste demonstration on the screen, courtesy of virtual reality simulation, a technology that simulates actual sensory experiences. In addition to the usual challenges that pop up in the course of moving from concept to production, Ayer faced yet another challenge: integrating the output of two separate production groups, one handling live action and one handling computer animation.

MARKETING AND ADVERTISING BACKGROUND

Jolly Rancher has been waging a long-term battle with established brands such as Life Savers, Brach, Reed's, and Werther's for a larger bite of the hard-candy market. Jolly Rancher's stick candy held a good share of the preteen market, and its bags of individually wrapped candy were popular with adults. However, research showed that the brand was losing its loyal customers after age 10—and not getting them back for nearly two decades, when they had children of their own. Looking at the competitive situation, Jolly Rancher found that rivals were advertising to younger children and the baby-boom generation, but they were ignoring teenagers and young adults. Forty percent of all candy is consumed by teens, so the candy maker decided to make a Jolly Rancher roll pack (featuring small, square candies stacked inside a colorful cardboard roll) to appeal specifically to young people between 12 and 24 years old.

Next, the company and its ad agency, Ayer Chicago, had to determine how to position this new product with its target audience. Through research, Ayer learned that teens and young adults shopping for fruit-flavored candy asked for competing products by *color*; in contrast, they asked for Jolly Rancher by *flavor*. Throughout the research, subjects talked about the intensity and the authenticity of Jolly Rancher candy's taste. So Jolly Rancher and Ayer agreed to position the roll pack as the little candy with the big, fruity flavor. Now the agency had to devise an advertising campaign to launch this new product.

CREATIVE STRATEGY AND COMMERCIAL CONCEPT

Based on the product's positioning, creative director John Trusk, art director Gaab Dundee, and copywriter Jeff Holinski came up with the idea of a television commercial showing a taste demonstration. Many ads feature live product demonstrations, but the creative team believed it could go a step beyond by demonstrating the realistic taste of Jolly Rancher candy. "This is an intense, authentic taste that you can tell with your eyes closed. So we've created advertising that combines authentic flavor with an intense imagination," said Tim Prosch, Ayer Chicago's managing director of client services, when he presented the creative strategy to George Steele, Leaf's vice president of marketing.

Finding a way to make the taste demonstration come alive in a 30-second television commercial was the next challenge. The Ayer staffers quickly hit on a solution: they would dramatize a personal taste trip through the imagery of virtual reality. They knew that young people are generally intrigued by cutting-edge technology, so the commercial would capture the audience's attention by linking the exciting experience of virtual reality with the taste experience of Jolly Rancher's roll pack candy. Once the client approved the creative concept, the agency went to work on the script.

SCRIPT DEVELOPMENT

The creative team started with the idea of two teens entering the virtual reality world of flavor created by Jolly Rancher candy. Then they fleshed out the story line. The commercial would begin with a live-action sequence in which a boy and girl walked into a futuristic-looking laboratory, where they donned the special gloves and helmets needed for virtual reality. Once they popped Jolly Rancher candy into their mouths, each would step into a gyroscope and be spun head over heels during the trip into virtual reality. Inside the world of virtual reality, which would be created through computer-generated images, the teens would experience the flavor of Jolly Rancher candy by interacting with giant pieces of fruit (see storyboard in Exhibit 12.A on page 334).

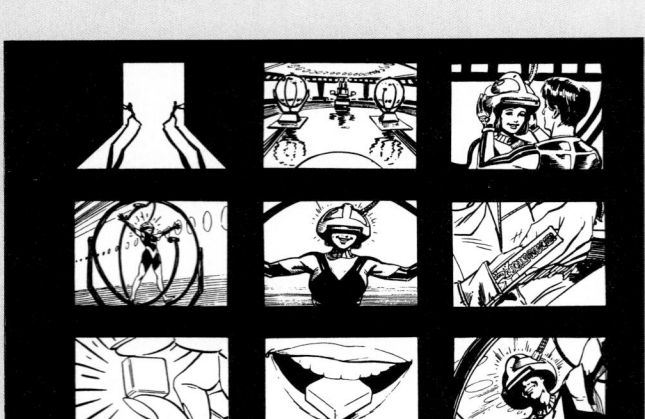

EXHIBIT 12.A **The storyboard.**

AyerChicago

515 North State Street, Chicago, Illinois 60610 • 312-644-AYER • Fax: 312-644-4123

RADIO/TV COPY

Date: May 25, 1993	**Length:** :30 TV
Client: Leaf, Inc.	**Comm. No:**
Product: Jolly Rancher Candy	**Title:** "Virtual Reality"
	Copy Option 1
Job #:	**Revision:** As Produced
Writer: JH	

MUSIC UNDER

ANNCR (VO): In reality, a Jolly Rancher candy

is 3/4ths of an inch by 3/4ths of an inch.

Square.

But, the <u>virtual</u> reality of its taste...

is immeasureable.

Jolly Rancher candy.

The great taste of fruit. Squared.

EXHIBIT 12.B **The script.**

As they developed the script, the creative staff paid close attention to the details that would make the virtual reality experience—and the taste experience—seem realistic. For example, they researched how people react as they don the virtual reality gloves and headgear for the first time. Most people immediately wiggle their fingers and glance down to see what their hands look like in the world of virtual reality. This motion became part of the action specified in the video portion of the Jolly Rancher script.

The Ayer team also considered how to incorporate one or more shots of the product into the commercial. Rather than stop the action to cut to a static product shot, the creative team decided to weave the product into the commercial more naturally by showing how it's actually used. In the video portion of the final script, the girl was to be shown pulling out a roll pack, shaking out several candies, and putting one in her mouth. For legal reasons, the video portion also called for a super disclosing that the ingredients include natural and artificial flavors.

The audio portion of the script called for computer-generated music and sound effects as well as a female voice-over (see Exhibit 12.B). By using slightly mysterious sound effects, the agency hoped to capture the viewer's attention and to reinforce the futuristic feel of the set and the virtual reality. Once the script and the storyboard were completed and approved, and once a budget was prepared and authorized, the agency moved on to pre-production.

EXHIBIT 12.C **Watching the monitor during filming to see how a particular shot looks.**

EXHIBIT 12.D **Flooding the floor of the set to reflect light and create an "other-worldly" mood.**

EXHIBIT 12.E **Looking in the camera to set up a shot.**

PREPRODUCTION

Because the commercial called for a combination of live action and computer-generated animation, which would be handled by two separate production groups, the agency took time during the preproduction stage to carefully coordinate the groups' efforts. In addition to the Ayer creative team and the agency producers, the preproduction meeting included the live-action director (David Dryer of Dryer/Taylor Productions), several specialists from Xaos (a computer-animation supplier), and Jolly Rancher executives. During this daylong meeting, the group reviewed plans for both the live-action and the computer-animated scenes. They decided on what the set should look like, what kind of talent should be hired for the live-action segment, and what the actors should look like. They also discussed the intricacies of shooting and assembling the commercial, and they worked out a plan for weaving the computer-animated scenes through the live-action scenes to simulate a virtual reality experience.

PRODUCTION

Both the set and the virtual reality gloves and headgear were created especially for the live-action portion of this commercial, which was filmed over a two-day period (see Exhibit 12.C). To achieve an eerie, other-worldly effect, the director flooded the floor of the set with water and used futuristic lighting effects as visual cues that the actors—and members of the audience—were about to enter another reality (see Exhibit 12.D). As the various scenes were filmed, the director worked closely with the teen actors to get them to respond to each other according to the script (see Exhibits 12.E and 12.F). The biggest challenge of the live-action shoot was taking care that the teens didn't get too rattled to act during the scenes when they were spinning in the gyroscopes (which required a number of takes from various camera angles—see Exhibit 12.G). Throughout the shoot, the director took time to review what had been filmed and prepare for what would be filmed next (see Exhibit 12.H).

EXHIBIT 12.F Putting makeup on one of the actors.

EXHIBIT 12.G Preparing to get a shot of the gyroscope.

EXHIBIT 12.H Reviewing scenes already shot.

Even before the live-action scenes had been filmed, Xaos set to work on the computer animation for the virtual reality scenes. Working from frame-by-frame sketches provided by Ayer, the Xaos specialists electronically created and manipulated colorful fruits (to represent the Jolly Rancher candy flavors) and two figures (to represent the teen actors). They carefully coordinated the action in the virtual reality scenes to be sure that the animated figures' movements and reactions were related to the actors' movements and reactions during the live-action scenes.

POSTPRODUCTION

At the end of every day of live-action shooting, the director and the agency producer reviewed the dailies to check for correct lighting, color, and sound. Once all filming was complete, the director cut and edited the film to reflect his idea of how the final commercial should look. He then sent it to Ayer, where the creative team reviewed the director's cut, made several additional cuts, and showed the client both the recommended cut of the film and the computer-animation output. The client's changes were

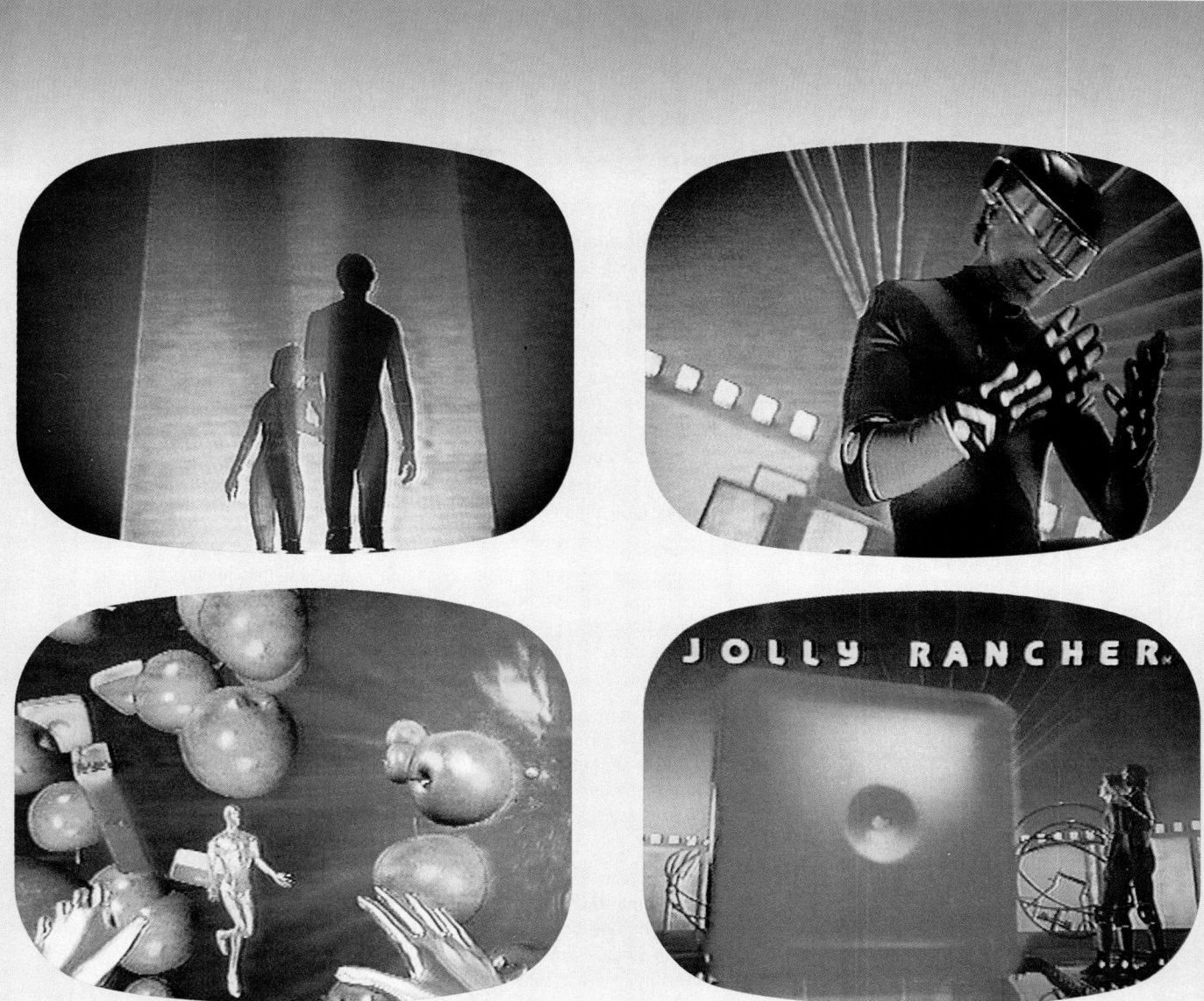

EXHIBIT 12.1 Jolly Rancher's virtual reality commercial, in its final form.

incorporated, the computer output was incorporated into the film, and both the music and the voice-over were added. At this point, the agency presented the finished commercial for client approval (see Exhibit 12.1). Once the commercial was approved, the agency transferred the commercial from film and computer output to videotape, arranging for duplicate tapes to be sent to the television networks and the individual stations on the media schedule.

RESULTS

Jolly Rancher's virtual reality commercial was part of an overall ad campaign designed to make teens and young adults aware of the new roll pack candy product. Backed by sales promotion, the campaign was also geared toward encouraging the target audience to try the new product. Even before the campaign had run its course, research showed that both awareness and trial had increased significantly—up to 25 percent over precampaign levels. ∎

An Insider's Look at Print (Jell-O) and Television (Acuvue) Advertising Production

SYNOPSIS

This program explores both print ad production and television commercial production. The print ad segment shows the planning and production steps that Kraft General Foods and its agency took to create an ad that promotes Jell-O's no-cholesterol health benefit. You'll get to watch a client presentation meeting and see how the agency and the company's marketing team interact as they search for the right way to convey a health-related message. Then you'll see the care taken during production to effectively present the visual aspects of the advertising message.

The television segment for Acuvue contact lenses also starts with the planning process, as Vistakon and its agency decide on the best approach for launching a new line of disposable contact lenses. Acuvue differs from other contact lenses in that no cleaning is required. Wearers simply sign up to receive new pairs at regular intervals and toss out each pair as they get dirty. You'll see how the commercial combines visual, verbal, and musical elements to convey a distinct message.

EXERCISES

Analysis

1. If the no-cholesterol message is so compelling, why did Jell-O decide not to use it for all of this advertising?
2. Why do you think the Jell-O advertising team places so much importance on being able to show light passing through the product?
3. Has consumer behavior changed over the years as far as health claims in food are concerned? Would the no-cholesterol message have been a reasonable choice 20 or 40 years ago? Why or why not?
4. Why do you think the Acuvue commercial is so simple visually? How does this support the advertising objective?
5. Was it worth the expense to have music composed and performed specifically for the Acuvue commercial? Vistakon could've saved a lot of money by using previously recorded material; would doing so have diminished the commercial's effectiveness? Explain your answer.

Application

Assume that the Jell-O marketing team has decided to convey the no-cholesterol message through television advertising. Design a commercial that carries the message while taking advantage of television's unique communication qualities.

Decision

The Acuvue message of doing away with messy, expensive cleaning solutions is great for experienced contact lens wearers who know how much trouble solutions can be, but what about people who are getting contacts for the first time? Since these consumers don't have firsthand experience with solutions, should Vistakon devise a different message or execution for this segment? Why or why not?

Ethics

Assume that the gingerbread man portrayed in the Jell-O print ad has some redeeming nutritional qualities, such as fiber or vitamins. Is it fair for Jell-O to use the single issue of cholesterol to portray another food choice as generally unhealthy? Why or why not?

Teamwork

With two other students, form a team that will create a print ad for Acuvue contact lenses. One of you is the art director, one is the copywriter, and one is the account executive. You can use the line "The best solution is no solution" but only as small print at the bottom of the ad; you'll need to come up with your own headline. When you're finished with a rough mock-up of the ad, present it to a fourth student who is playing the role of Vistakon's president. ■

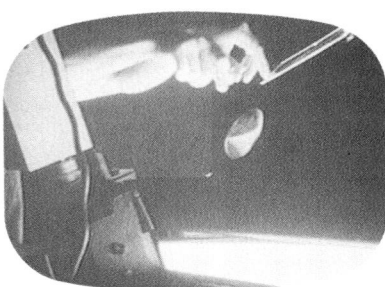

Media Choices

LACOSTE LIBERA TUTTI.

Media Objectives, Strategy, and Planning

After studying this chapter, you will be able to

1. Explain the relationship of the media plan to the marketing and advertising plans

2. Outline the ways media planning is influenced by ever-increasing media choices, audience fragmentation, and higher media costs

3. Discuss how to set objectives for targeting the audience and distributing the message

4. Explain how media planners determine geographic scope when they develop their media strategy

5. Describe how message scheduling is affected by the timing, continuity, size, length, and position of an ad

6. Discuss the advantages of checking media audiences, media environments, and competitors' media usage before selecting media

7. Outline how media planners calculate cost efficiency

Facing an Advertising Challenge at Chrysler

CHRYSLER TUNES UP ITS MEDIA STRATEGY

Arthur C. Liebler and John Damoose can tell you it's not easy to spend a $400 million yearly media budget. Not when that budget has to buy media space and time around the world. Not when you have to stretch that budget to advertise cars, minivans, sport-utility vehicles, and trucks. Not when you're coordinating the media-placement efforts of several ad agencies. Not when you're battling competitors who can outspend you by as much as $500 million.

Liebler is vice president of marketing and communications for Chrysler, the third-largest U.S. carmaker. He recently succeeded John Damoose as the executive in charge of Chrysler's advertising activities. Chrysler had strong entrants in the minivan and sport-utility-vehicle markets, but its share of the U.S. passenger car market had been dwindling since 1980. Some of the strongest competition came from popular imports, especially models made by Nissan, Honda, and

Toyota. Domestic carmakers were chasing higher sales with gigantic media budgets. General Motors, the leading U.S. automotive manufacturer, was investing more than $1 billion a year in advertising; Ford was investing more than $500 million.

On top of these competitive problems, the sluggish U.S. economy was dampening the overall pace of new-vehicle sales. The entire industry was hurting, and Chrysler found its car and truck sales skidding off the road. The manufacturer careened from a profitable 1990 to an unprofitable 1991.

When Damoose was planning 1992's advertising, he was determined to use media to help Chrysler make a U-turn into higher market share and profits. The company was investing heavily to launch the new LH family of mid-size sedans, which included the Dodge Intrepid, the Eagle Vision, and the Chrysler Concorde. Although the three cars had received advance praise from the automotive press,

Damoose knew that the right advertising to the right audience at the right time would be the key to persuading prospects to look, drive, and then buy. He also believed that the new Jeep Grand Cherokee—if backed by an effective advertising schedule—would have a good shot at helping the company regain the lead among sport-utility vehicles.

After looking at Chrysler's marketing and advertising strategies and examining how competitors advertised their products, Damoose decided to change the carmaker's approach to media. If you were steering Chrysler's advertising effort, how would you use media to reach the right target audience for your car, truck, minivan, and sport-utility products? How would you select the media for launching the LH cars and the Jeep Grand Cherokee? What would you do to ensure that your media expenditures were properly coordinated for maximum effect at minimum cost?[1] ∎

CHAPTER OVERVIEW Chrysler executives understand that effective advertising is based on more than just a compelling message; it also requires the right media to reach the target audience. This chapter examines how to use media objectives, strategy, and planning to direct an advertising message to the right audience at the right time. First, you'll explore how media planning relates to the advertising and marketing plans, and you'll examine three of the most critical challenges facing media planners today. Next, you'll learn how to develop media objectives, and you'll take a look at how to develop media strategy. The chapter concludes with a discussion of how these media decisions are implemented in a media plan to bring the advertising message to its target audience. Then you can turn to Chapters 14, 15, and 16 for a more in-depth discussion of print, electronic, and other media.

Defining Media Planning

In a world brimming with media choices—including television, radio, newspapers, magazines, billboards, and many others—you need a systematic method of determining which media to use, how to use them, when to use them, and where to use them to effectively and efficiently deliver your advertising messages. The analytical framework used to consider these decisions is **media planning,** the process of directing the advertising message to the target audience at the appropriate time and place, using the appropriate channel. Media planning helps answer such questions as: What audiences do we want to reach? When and where do we want to reach them? How many people should we reach? How often do we need to reach them? What will it cost to reach them?

EXHIBIT 13.1
Coca-Cola's Targeted Use of Media

Rather than create ads for a particular medium and then figure out which vehicles to use, Coca-Cola has started pinpointing specific media vehicles first and then developing appropriate ads for each. The campaign in which the "Polar Bears" commercial (shown here) was introduced included 26 commercials; each was aimed at the audience delivered by a specific media vehicle.

Media planners and creative specialists work closely to develop creative ad campaigns with strong media impact. Although the creative approach often sets the direction for media planning, the reverse is also true: media planning can be used to guide creative execution. For example, the creative direction for Coca-Cola's 1993 campaign was determined only after the firm had approved the media and the vehicles to be used to reach each target audience (see Exhibit 13.1). "We are going to match the message to the medium to the audience," said Peter Sealey, head of Coca-Cola's global marketing. "Media reaches diverse, segmented groups of people and this advertising is intended to take advantage of that." The company first identified the television programs that attracted its target audiences and then produced a separate commercial for each program.[2]

FROM THE MARKETING PLAN TO THE MEDIA PLAN

Just as advertising is one of the key functions of marketing, media planning is one of the key functions of advertising. As discussed in Chapter 7, the advertising plan, which is based on the situation analysis and the marketing plan, sets the advertising objectives (see Exhibit 13.2). In turn, these plans and objectives guide the development of a comprehensive **media plan** that outlines the specific media objectives, strategies, and tactics to be used in advertising a particular product or brand. The media plan also identifies each **media vehicle,** each individual program, publication, or delivery mechanism that will be used to carry your advertising message. Moreover, the media plan includes a schedule to guide buyers who purchase media time or space by specifying when and where each ad should be placed.

CHALLENGES IN MEDIA PLANNING

Although identifying the best combination of medium and message to reach the target audience has never been easy, media planning has become even more complex in recent years. A variety of elements affect contemporary media planning, but three have become particularly influential and will continue to challenge media

MARKETING PLAN
- Situation analysis
- Marketing objectives
- Marketing strategy
- Action plan

ADVERTISING PLAN
- Situation analysis
- Marketing strategy
- Promotional strategy
- Advertising objectives
  - Sales
  - Communications
- Advertising strategy
  - Creative strategy
  - Media plan
  - Budget

MEDIA PLAN
- Media objectives
- Media strategy
- Media vehicles
- Media schedule

EXHIBIT 13.2
Relating the Media-Planning Process to Marketing and Advertising

The media plan, which draws on the objectives, strategies, and tactics outlined in the advertising plan, details the specific approach an advertiser will follow when selecting media for an advertising campaign.

planners throughout the 1990s: an ever-increasing number of media choices, audience fragmentation, and higher media costs.

Ever-Increasing Media Choices

Not long ago, if you wanted to deliver your message to a large number of people, your choices were relatively straightforward. You could use newspapers, magazines, radio, television, signs, or billboards, all of which are **mass media,** communication channels that reach widespread general audiences. What's more, you had only a few choices in each medium; for example, there were only three major television networks in those days. Today, however, the number of media choices, and the number of options within each category, has multiplied—and each medium has unique characteristics (see Exhibit 13.3). Current U.S. television

EXHIBIT 13.3 **Characteristics of Advertising Media**

In the course of deciding where to place the advertiser's message, the media planner considers each medium's unique characteristics, including audience factors, creative factors, timing factors, reach and frequency factors, financial factors, and production and insertion factors.

Characteristic	Broadcast Television	Cable Television	Radio	Magazines	Newspapers	Direct Mail	Outdoor Media	Transit Media	Place-Based Media
Audience factors									
Audience selectivity	L	H	M	H	L	H	L	L	M
Geographic selectivity	L	V	H	M	H	H	M	M	V
Attention and interest	M	M	M	H	H	V	L	L	L
Intrusiveness of message	H	H	M	L	L	L	M	M	M
Availability of audience research	H	M	H	H	H	N	L	L	L
Competition from clutter	H	M	V	H	H	M	N	V	N
Creative factors									
Ability to demonstrate product	H	H	L	M	M	V	L	L	V
Creative flexibility	H	H	L	M	L	H	M	L	V
Ability to tie in with media content	M	M	H	H	M	N	N	N	N
Timing factors									
Life span of message	L	L	L	H	V	V	L	L	L
Ability to deliver long message	M	M	M	H	H	H	L	L	L
Ability to review message	L	L	L	H	H	H	L	L	L
Reach and frequency factors									
Frequency potential	H	H	H	L	M	V	H	H	M
Reach potential	H	M	H	L	L	L	H	H	L
Financial factors									
Cost to reach 1,000 people	M	L	L	M	H	H	L	L	V
Cost to create ad	V	V	L	M	L	V	M	M	V
Production and insertion factors									
Ad reproduction quality	H	H	V	H	V	H	V	V	L
Ability to place ad quickly	V	V	H	L	H	M	L	L	L
Ad schedule flexibility	H	H	H	V	V	V	L	L	V

H = high; M = medium; L = low; N = not applicable to this medium; V = varies among vehicles in this category.

options still include major networks (which now number four) but have also expanded to encompass a wide range of satellite and cable stations. Current U.S. magazine options include not only the 12,000 magazines already being published but also 500 or more new start-ups every year.[3]

In addition, new media are popping up all around. Reaching out to audiences where they live, work, play, shop, and commute, advertisers are placing ads on television screens in fitness centers, mailing ads on disks to personal-computer users at home and at work, dispensing coupons from machines clipped to grocery store shelves, and playing commercials on supermarket radio programs. These new media aren't geared to the masses: instead, they're narrowly focused, allowing advertisers to reach people exactly when and where they want. Perhaps the most directly targeted are the *private media,* magazines, newsletters, and other media produced by the advertiser exclusively for its audience (see Exhibit 13.4). American Express, for instance, publishes *Your Company,* a magazine with articles (and ads) that goes to holders of its corporate card. Using some of these new media can save advertisers from wasting money on media that reach people who aren't in their target audience.[4]

Of course, these new media can also complicate the media-planning process by forcing planners to evaluate many more alternatives and analyze the value of less-traditional media choices. For example, a Nabisco promotion in which MTV gave away rock star Jon Bon Jovi's house was hardly an everyday occurrence. So agencies such as Bozell have appointed media-strategy specialists or committees to examine the new media and to analyze how they affect clients' media plans.[5]

EXHIBIT 13.4

Using Private Media to Reach Only Your Audience

Ben & Jerry's Homemade publishes *Ben & Jerry's Chunk Mail* to tell customers about the company's new flavors, social activism, and other news. Customers can pick up a copy of the newsletter in their local Ben & Jerry's ice cream store, or they can send in a coupon to get on the company's mailing list.

Audience Fragmentation

Fragmentation of the audience for each medium and vehicle occurs when people spread their attention among many choices. Of course, the mass media still reach gigantic audiences (like the more than 135 million U.S. viewers who watch the Super Bowl network broadcast every January). However, the audiences for most programs and publications are dwindling. For example, the audiences of the three broadcast television networks are being splintered by a fourth network (Fox) and by dozens of cable networks.[6] Because the average cable household has more than 37 channels to choose from, broadcast networks are generally not drawing the huge numbers they once did. This is a challenge for media planners who want to reach large audiences.[7]

People are also moving to other media for specialized information and entertainment. They can turn to local cable channels for neighborhood news, read about leisure-time interests in specialized magazines, and listen to the headlines and weather on all-news radio stations. With all these choices, many people spend less time with each media vehicle, posing an additional challenge for media planners who try to find specific audiences and who try to be sure that these audiences are actually exposed to the ads.

To reach fragmented audiences, some media planners are taking advantage of *multimedia* (or *cross-media*) promotional packages, a kind of one-stop shopping offering convenient access to a combination of media and vehicles that repeat and reinforce the advertiser's message in more than one way. For example, to promote a line of prepared vegetables, Del Monte bought a multimedia package from Turner Broadcasting, including promotional messages on Turner's cable television stations and a commercial spliced onto the video reissue of *Citizen Kane*. Del Monte supplemented the package with newspaper and in-store advertising.[8] Most multimedia packages offer the additional benefit of reduced cost.

Higher Media Costs

Not only can it be expensive to produce television commercials (as much as $1 million for a 1-minute ad), but it can also be costly to run commercials (more than $300,000 for 30 seconds during a popular network television show). In fact, no matter what media are used, the media budget can dwarf the production budget, which makes rising media costs a major concern (see Exhibit 13.5). From 1982 to 1991, the yearly increase in the cost of reaching 1,000 people with an ad on network television, network radio, magazines, newspapers, or billboards rose faster than inflation, often growing by 6 percent or more.[9]

Sometimes the price hikes are much steeper. In one recent year, CNN, MTV, and Nickelodeon raised their rates as much as 50 percent over the previous year, reflecting advertisers' interest in these cable channels' growing audiences. The result is that media specialists are under more pressure than ever to get the most bang for their clients' media bucks. At the same time, they realize that media planning means more than keeping costs down. In the end, many organizations judge cost efficiency according to the cost per sale or per vote or whatever result is desired, not just by the price tag for reaching a certain number of people.[10]

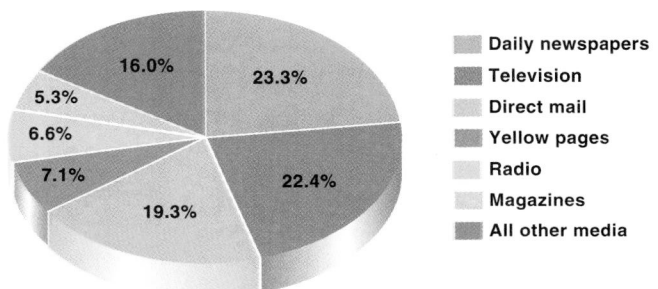

Daily newspapers
Television
Direct mail
Yellow pages
Radio
Magazines
All other media

EXHIBIT 13.5
Where U.S. Advertisers Spend Their Media Dollars

Newspapers, television, and direct-mail advertising received the largest share of the money that U.S. advertisers spent on media time and space in 1992.

345

Developing Media Objectives

The first step in the media-planning process is to set media objectives that will guide your selection and use of media. By setting these media objectives, you're outlining the goals you'll need to reach to support your marketing and advertising plans. Whether you're launching a new product, introducing a product in a new market, repositioning a product, or fending off new competitors, specific measurable objectives guide your media decisions, provide a focus for coordinating your advertising activities, and offer a clear standard for measuring performance after the ad campaign has run.

For example, when personal-care marketer Avon Products wanted to update its image, it set a specific media objective for the first month of its new campaign: to use media to reach 81 percent of all women aged 25 to 49 an average of 5.5 times during the month.[11] This objective pinpoints a clear and measurable target to be attained. You'll notice that it has two main components: a goal of reaching the target audience (women aged 25 to 49) and a goal of distributing the message (reaching 81 percent).

REACHING THE TARGET AUDIENCE

What audience should your ads be directed toward? This is the most fundamental decision involved in setting media objectives. The starting point is a look at your marketing and advertising plans, which always include a description of your target market. Target audience profiles are generally developed using demographic, psychographic, and product-usage descriptions, including age, education, income, occupation, lifestyle, and brand preference. For business advertising, you may describe your target audience in terms of the people who participate in or influence the purchase or the specification of the products needed. The more specific your description, the better you'll be able to select the media vehicles that effectively and efficiently reach your target audience, avoiding those media that reach only a few members of your target audience or that reach people who never use your type of product (see Exhibit 13.6).

Media planners use research to uncover those media vehicles that reach their target audiences. Many ad agencies conduct media research, and as Chapter 6

EXHIBIT 13.6
How W. W. Grainger Reaches Its Target Market

W. W. Grainger, a national distributor of hand tools, relies on industrial advertising in specific trade magazines to reach its audience of professionals who buy tools for use in maintenance and construction. Its agency, DFM/Tatham, chooses the magazines on the basis of the industries they cover and their readers' occupations. In addition, Grainger mails a catalog of its products to prospects and customers, which is an even more targeted way to reach its audience.

Now available in paperback.

Our biggest story in professional tools and accessories: thousands more than we've ever had.

Drill bits to drill presses. Pullers, pliers, routers and wrenches. Hammers, sockets, blades and bandsaws. Now, Grainger can be your main source for the maintenance and construction tools you need to do the job right. Right now. Because all these tools are in stock. And they're all close by.

With 335 branches nationwide, there's probably a branch only a few minutes from you or your job site. Staffed by people who are well-trained to give you great service every time. Just phone or fax your order. It'll be ready for pickup when you arrive. We can also deliver or ship the same day.

So the next time you need to get your hands on just the right tool, look in our paperback. The Grainger catalog has over 42,000 items from tools to motors, generators to gloves. For your free catalog, call: 1-800-473-3473.

GRAINGER
The Right Stuff. Right Here. Right Now.

points out, syndicated research sources such as Simmons Market Research Bureau (SMRB) and Mediamark Research, Inc. (MRI) are commonly used. These syndicated studies describe audiences for selected print and electronic media in terms of age, household size and income, education level, marital status, occupational category, race, home ownership, product and brand usage, and other factors. In addition, most media vehicles conduct their own research to show potential advertisers what audiences they reach. For example, Prime Ticket, a West Coast sports cable television network, commissioned research on its viewers' buying habits, sports preferences, and demographics. This research revealed that Prime Ticket's viewers in Palos Verdes, California, have a median household income of $75,000 and are tennis buffs—information that would be quite valuable to advertisers of upscale tennis apparel and equipment.[12]

When you apply integrated marketing communications (IMC) to coordinate and focus all marketing and promotional communications, you generally define your target audience segment by segment and then select the appropriate media vehicles for each segment. In many cases, the media you use to reach one segment will differ from the media you use to reach another segment. What won't differ, however, is the consistent and unified image and message that is conveyed through all your media choices.

DISTRIBUTING THE MESSAGE

Once you've identified your target audience, your next step is to set objectives for where, when, and how often you want to distribute your message to that audience. How many messages should you schedule? How often should you schedule them? Should you show your message at least once to everyone in your target audience, or should you repeat your message more often to a smaller percentage of the audience? To answer these questions, you need to consider how to balance reach and frequency within your overall budget and how to calculate the total message weight of your campaign.

Reach versus Frequency

Reach is a measure of how many different members (or what percentage) of the target audience are exposed at least once in a given period to a particular media vehicle (see Exhibit 13.7). Reach measures the number of audience members exposed to that medium at least once, no matter how many times they actually see or hear your ad message in that medium. Thus, if 6,000 out of a target audience of 10,000 young adults aged 13 to 18 tune in to a daily MTV program one or more times during a 4-week period, the reach is 6,000 divided by 10,000, or 60 percent.

Reach gauges exposure to a particular media vehicle, but it can't show the number of people who actually notice a specific ad. This means that your objective of reaching 60 percent of the target audience is based on who views the television

VARIOUS CRIMINALS TRYING TO BREAK DIFFERENT TYPES OF MASTER

LOCKS. LOCK IS PIERCED WITH A BULLET AND STILL DOESN'T OPEN.

(SFX): Classical music.
V.O.: Master Locks are tough under fire.

show or reads the magazine carrying your ad, regardless of whether these people pay any attention to your ad.[13] The time period you select when setting reach objectives is another important factor. Many media planners set objectives according to a traditional four-week cycle, but some researchers advise using a period that corresponds to the customer's purchasing cycle.[14] So if Chrysler is planning an ad campaign to sell the LH cars and research shows that most customers plan to buy cars in the fall when many new models are introduced, Chrysler's media objectives might measure the percentage of the target audience reached during September, October, and November.

Frequency measures the number of times people in the target audience are exposed to a media vehicle during a given period. **Average frequency** is the average number of times people or households in your target audience are exposed to the vehicle. To determine average frequency, you divide the total number of exposures by the total audience reach. If 3,000 people in your target audience watch a daily MTV program four times during a four-week period and 3,000 people watch it six times, your calculation would be

$$
\begin{aligned}
\text{Total number of exposures} &= (3{,}000 \times 4) + (3{,}000 \times 6) \\
&= 30{,}000 \\
\text{Total audience reach} &= 3{,}000 + 3{,}000 = 6{,}000 \\
\text{Average frequency} &= \frac{30{,}000}{6{,}000} = 5
\end{aligned}
$$

In this example, the average frequency for the 6,000 people you've reached is 5, meaning that those reached have been exposed an average of five times. Of course, this doesn't mean that everyone in your target audience has been exposed five times; it's only an average of the number of exposures.

Usually, one exposure isn't enough to make your audience aware of your product or to prompt them to buy it; the more often they're exposed to your ads, the more likely they are to understand and remember the message, and you often need many exposures to overcome competitive ads. So you use frequency to plan how many times you want your audience to see your message in a given medium. When you're introducing a new product, starting a new campaign, sending a complicated or long message, using small-size ads, trying to break through clutter, or battling strong competition, you may need more frequency to raise awareness and comprehension.[15] Exhibit 13.8 shows some factors to consider when determining frequency.

How much frequency is actually needed to effectively communicate with the target audience? Media planners must determine the **effective frequency,** the

---

EXHIBIT 13.8   Factors That Influence Frequency

What's the proper frequency for your advertisement? Media planners take these factors into account when determining the appropriate frequency for a particular message.

- **PURCHASE CYCLE.** The number of times the target audience sees the message during each purchase cycle is important. Match the advertising frequency to the length of the purchase cycle so that the audience members remain aware of the brand and see the message when they're ready to buy.

- **MARKET SHARE.** Brands with high market share usually enjoy high audience awareness. As a result, they generally require less frequency than brands with lower market share.

- **BRAND HISTORY.** Higher frequency levels can help establish a new brand but may not be needed for brands that are already established.

- **CLUTTER AND COMPETITIVE SHARE OF VOICE.** In an environment of advertising clutter, frequency can help one brand's advertising stand out. Similarly, when competitors have a high share of voice in the category, frequency can help call attention to one brand's ad message.

- **MESSAGE COMPLEXITY.** Frequency can be varied depending on how simple the ad message is. Use higher frequency to help audiences understand and retain complicated messages.

- **MESSAGE SIZE AND LENGTH.** Frequency can be used to enhance the impact of smaller or shorter ad messages. Small print ads or short broadcast and cable messages often need more frequency than large ads or long messages.

number of times a target audience must be exposed to a particular ad in a given medium to communicate the message and stimulate action. Although experts agree that one exposure is often not enough, they don't agree on the optimal number of exposures needed to stimulate a response.[16] So think about the minimum frequency as well as the maximum frequency you need to be effective. Providing too few exposures means that your audience may not hear or see your message often enough to be aware of what you're communicating. However, providing too many exposures wastes money, since you can use fewer repetitions to communicate your message. Too much frequency can also lead to *wearout,* which happens when your audience turns away from the ads or responds negatively after repeated exposures.[17]

When you use the concept of effective frequency to establish the minimum number of exposures needed, you can then look at **effective reach,** the number or percentage of the members in the target audience exposed to your ad some minimum number of times (or more). If you set the minimum number of exposures at three, your calculation of effective reach would show the portion of your audience that has seen the ad at least three times during the period you're measuring. This concept expands the notion of reach by adding the dimension of repetition so that you can see how many people were exposed to the ad enough times to understand and respond to it.[18]

Media planners have to juggle reach and frequency because it's difficult to stretch any media budget to reach large numbers of people and at the same time ensure that the audience sees the message enough times to act on it (see Exhibit 13.9). You must balance one against the other, but which one you emphasize depends on your product's situation, your media budget, the competitive challenges, and many other factors. Balancing reach and frequency is especially difficult when working with two or more ads or when working in two or more media, so it's useful to check the message weight of the entire media plan.

Message Weight

Message weight is the size of the combined target audiences reached by the media vehicles in a single media plan. To calculate message weight, you add all the reach numbers for each ad in the plan, ignoring any overlap or duplication. You can express message weight in terms of gross impressions or gross rating points.

Gross impressions are the sum of all possible target audience exposures to the vehicles in a media plan. To calculate gross impressions, you count each exposure to a vehicle as one impression and then combine the number of impressions for every ad in the media plan. If you advertised for four weeks on an MTV

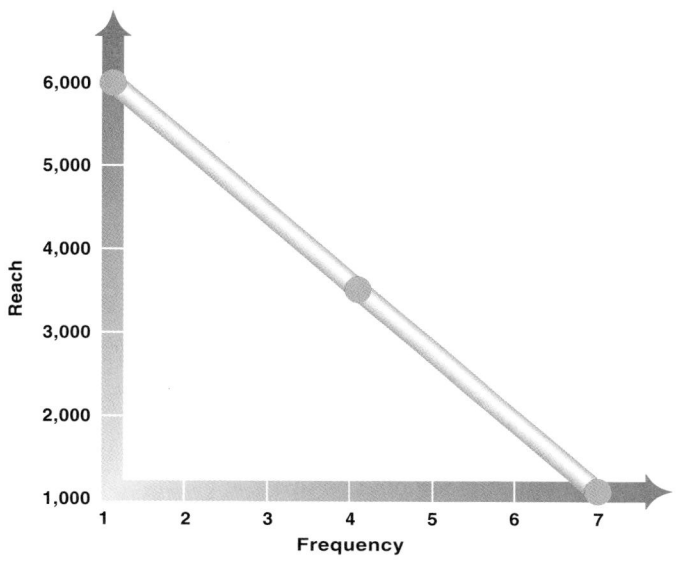

EXHIBIT 13.9
Reach versus Frequency

When you're working within a set advertising budget, you can't maximize both reach and frequency, because these two factors have an inverse relationship. In this example, you can choose to allocate the same media budget to reach 1,000 people seven times, 3,500 people four times, or 6,000 people one time.

program watched four times by 3,000 people in your target audience and six times by 3,000, and advertised during the same four weeks on a Nickelodeon program viewed four times by 2,000 in your target audience, you would calculate your gross impressions this way:

$$\text{Gross impressions} = (3,000 \times 4) + (3,000 \times 6) + (2,000 \times 4) = 38,000$$

In this example, the first group of 3,000 people receives 12,000 impressions, the second group of 3,000 receives 18,000 impressions, and the third group of 2,000 receives 8,000 impressions, for a total of 38,000 gross impressions during that four-week period. Gross impressions measure only the overall number of impressions, including any duplication among audiences when more than one vehicle is used; this is why the term *gross* is used.

When you're measuring gross impressions for mass media such as network television, the numbers can become very large. For convenience, media planners sometimes express message weight in terms of **gross rating points (GRPs),** which are the sum of the ratings of all programs in the television schedule; in the context of one media plan, GRPs measure the total target audience exposed to all the vehicles in that plan. One percent of the target audience is equivalent to one **rating point.** To calculate GRPs for the entire media plan, you multiply the proportion of the target audience reached by the average frequency. In the MTV/Nickelodeon example, out of 10,000 in your target audience, the reach was 8,000 (80 percent, expressed as 80) with an average frequency of 4.75 (38,000 ÷ 8,000), so the calculation would look like this:

$$\text{GRPs} = (80 \times 4.75) = 380$$

You can also calculate GRPs by dividing the number of gross impressions by the number of people in the target audience and multiplying the result by 100. Here's how to use this formula with a target audience of 10,000 and 38,000 gross impressions:

$$\text{GRPs} = (38,000 \div 10,000) \times 100 = 380$$

When you use electronic media, you generally calculate GRPs over a week or a month. However, when you use print media, you count the exposures for every ad in every print vehicle used during the entire campaign.

Ideally, your media objectives should represent the best balance of reach and frequency, as well as the appropriate message weight, to support your advertising and marketing plans. For example, when you're trying to combat a heavy schedule of competitive advertising, you might want to aim for greater frequency rather than more reach so your message reaches your audience over and over again, overcoming the competitors' messages. When advertising a new product, you may want to aim for more reach and message weight so a larger audience is exposed to your message. That's the route AT&T chose when it introduced its Universal Card credit card. AT&T ran three 30-second commercials during the Academy Awards on national network television; the following day, AT&T ran three consecutive pages of advertising in national newspapers such as *USA Today*. The ads reached millions in two days and prompted more than 250,000 responses within 24 hours.[19] After you've determined your media objectives, you can begin to develop your media strategy.

Developing Media Strategy

Like a road map, your **media strategy** describes the course of action you plan to follow to achieve your media objectives, including the media and the individual vehicles you'll use to deliver your messages. The right media strategy can help ads break through the competition and the clutter to reach the target audience more effectively. Media planners are continually looking for ways to use media more creatively, and the Checklist for Creative Use of Media offers some ideas to stimulate your thinking. The decisions you make as you develop media strategy revolve around four broad areas: (1) determining geographic scope, (2) scheduling the message, (3) selecting the media, and (4) calculating cost efficiency.

DETERMINING GEOGRAPHIC SCOPE

Where should you advertise? Your marketing and advertising plans can help you choose which areas are most important (see Exhibit 13.10). One consideration is product availability: you don't want to waste money advertising in areas where your product isn't available. For example, when Nestea wanted to build U.S. sales for its line of bottled ready-to-drink iced teas, it introduced the line by airing television commercials only in cities where the products were available in local stores. After the line was established, Nestea continued to advertise in some cities where the products competed with those of rival Lipton. In those cities, Nestea used advertising to counter the effects of Lipton's television advertising for its own bottled teas.[20] In addition to distribution, advertisers take into account how the other elements of the marketing mix (product, pricing, and promotion) affect sales in the geographic areas they're considering.

Because a product that sells well in one market may not sell as well in another, be sure to analyze the product's relative sales strength in various geographic areas. By comparing each market under consideration, you can pinpoint the markets that offer an opportunity for higher return. Two tools used to compare sales strength in individual markets are the brand development index and the category development index.

The Brand Development Index

The **brand development index (BDI)** is a ratio that measures the relative sales strength of a given brand in a specific area of the United States. The formula for calculating the BDI is

$$\text{BDI} = \frac{\text{percentage of brand's total U.S. sales in the market}}{\text{percentage of total U.S. population in the market}} \times 100$$

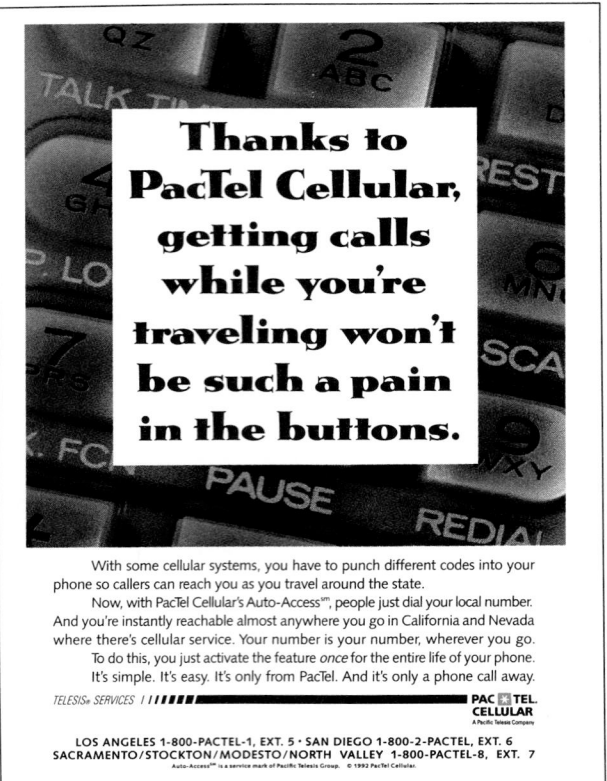

For example, if you're looking at the Cleveland market, start with the percentage of sales of your brand in that market (assume that company records show that you sell 1.4 percent of your total U.S. sales in Cleveland) and divide this number by the percentage of the total U.S. population in that market (U.S. census information says this is 1.09 percent); then multiply by 100 and round off to the nearest whole number. Your calculation would look like this:

$$\text{BDI} = \frac{1.4}{1.09} \times 100 = 128$$

This index is convenient for comparing the sales strength of your product in all markets under consideration so that you can prioritize where you'll invest your media budget. In general, the higher the BDI, the higher your brand's sales strength in that market. In this example, if Cleveland's BDI is higher than the BDI in other markets, you might give Cleveland extra attention.

The Category Development Index

Knowing your brand's strength is important, but it's also helpful to look at the overall sales potential for your category, including the potential for all competitors selling your type of product. The **category development index (CDI)** expresses the sales potential of a particular product category in a specific market in the United States. The CDI formula is similar to that for BDI:

$$\text{CDI} = \frac{\text{percentage of product category's total U.S. sales in the market}}{\text{percentage of total U.S. population in the market}} \times 100$$

To calculate the CDI for Cleveland, divide the product category's percentage of total U.S. sales in that market (assume that research using trade association figures says this is 2.54 percent) by the percentage of the U.S. population in that market (1.09 percent); then multiply by 100. Here's the CDI calculation:

$$\text{CDI} = \frac{2.54}{1.09} \times 100 = 233$$

EXHIBIT 13.11   Using BDI and CDI in Media Planning

Using both BDI and CDI can help you evaluate your product's sales strength and sales potential and yield clues about where to invest your advertising budget. However, it's important to pay attention to other factors such as the size of the population (considering larger markets even if they have lower BDI/CDI), the level of product usage (looking at markets with higher usage), and the strength of your distribution (avoiding markets where you have little or no distribution).

	High BDI	Low BDI
High CDI	Good sales strength for brand, good potential for category; your brand holds high market share. Media spending is needed to defend brand's share and to maintain awareness.	Good sales potential for category, but your brand isn't doing as well as others in category. Check the competitive situation; try adjusting your marketing mix to improve brand sales. Consider flighting; consider higher frequency during peak purchasing periods.
Low CDI	Poor sales potential for category but high market share for your brand. Be alert for brand sales decline. Media spending can be used to increase the overall frequency of purchase in the category.	Potential low for both the category and your brand. Question whether advertising can make a difference.

Taken together, the BDI and the CDI give you a good picture of your product's sales strength and potential in each market under consideration (see Exhibit 13.11). Although the BDI shows promising brand strength in Cleveland, the CDI indicates that the category sales potential is nearly twice as high, which implies that your brand may have the opportunity for much higher sales. In this case, you may want to advertise more in Cleveland to get a bigger piece of the category's sales potential. Honda recently used category sales potential to prioritize its advertising efforts in U.S. markets. The carmaker wanted to concentrate on the specific markets representing the bulk of the category sales. To reach only those areas, Honda switched from national print ads to television commercials purchased market by market.[21]

Not all media cover geography in the same way. For example, people in some markets can receive television and radio broadcasts that originate in nearby cities. Because of this broad coverage, your commercials may reach people who aren't in your target audience. On the other hand, you may find that your commercials aren't blanketing all the areas you want to reach. Similarly, newspapers are generally distributed in defined areas, which may or may not include those areas where you want to deliver your message. In addition, the geographic areas you select may be based on where the people in your target audience work or shop, not just on where they live.[22] Therefore, consider how the media cover each area you target. (Geographic coverage of individual media is discussed in Chapters 14, 15, and 16.)

SCHEDULING THE MESSAGE

The second set of decisions you face as you develop your media strategy revolve around message scheduling. When should you advertise? How long should you advertise in each medium? How long in all media? Should you schedule your ads for every day, every week, every month; or should you advertise on and off over some period? How large or how long should your ad be, and where should it be placed in the vehicle? These are examples of the three types of decisions involved in scheduling your messages: decisions about timing, continuity, and size (or length) and position.

Determining Timing

Would you advertise snowblowers to consumers in Maine during December? Of course. In July? Don't be so quick to say no—you might want to sell your stock of last year's model to make room for a new model coming out in October, or you may want to pump up enthusiasm for your new model in advance of the customer's actual purchasing decision. Depending on your objectives, you can use message timing in four ways:

1. *To reach people when they are most interested in buying your type of product.* If people generally purchase a product like yours during a particular period—such as snowblowers during cold weather or weight-control services just before the beach season—it's smart to advertise during that period so that you can get your fair share of these purchases. Blockbuster Video, for example, found that people rent more movies during periods of bad weather, especially on weekends. So the ad agency Lintas devised a media strategy in which radio commercials air only when bad weekend weather is on the way.[23]

2. *To stimulate demand during slower periods.* Even when people aren't clamoring for your product, you may want to encourage them to change their usual buying habits if you have excess stock or excess service capacity. You can use the timing and volume of your advertising to accomplish this. For instance, to convince people to eat soup throughout the year, Campbell Soup is looking at advertising all year, instead of only during the cooler months when soup traditionally sells best.[24]

3. *To avoid competitors' messages.* If everyone else advertises during a certain period, you may be able to capture your audience's attention by scheduling your ad in another period. That's what Coca-Cola did to get a jump on Pepsi-Cola's 1992 Super Bowl Sunday ad blitz. It broadcast a barrage of commercials throughout the Friday before, using CNN and MTV to reach viewers in 100 countries. Without competition from Pepsi, Coca-Cola's commercials could grab cola drinkers' full attention.[25]

4. *To reach the people in the target audience when they're receptive to the medium you use.* If you're using television to reach school-age children, you can time your ad to run when they're most likely to be watching—late on weekday afternoons, early on weekday evenings, and on Saturday mornings. Similarly, if you're using newspapers to reach the family food shopper, you can schedule your ad to appear on "food day" when coupon-clippers check their papers for bargains and savings.

To time your ad correctly, study the marketing and media research for clues to the audience's behavior patterns. You can analyze product and media trends to understand the influence of various seasons, holidays, days of the week, and times of the day. With this information, you can determine the best timing for your ad messages as well as choose the media that are best suited to delivering the messages during those periods. For example, research by Dutch Boy Paints revealed that customers plan their painting projects around the weather, so the firm began sponsoring "Weekend Weather Outlook" reports on cable television's Weather Channel. After checking the weather report (and seeing commercials for Dutch Boy), people decide whether to paint—and which brand to buy.[26]

Determining Continuity

Once you know when to advertise, your next step is to decide whether to run your message consistently throughout the campaign or concentrate the message at regular intervals.[27] The pattern of message repetition you choose determines the **continuity** of your media schedule. When you schedule your message to run consistently over a long period, without gaps, you're using **continuity scheduling,** also known as *continuous advertising* (see Exhibit 13.12). In a continuity schedule, ads run consistently every day, every week, or every month. Continuity schedules are used to advertise food items, soap, and other products that are in demand all year, serving as a constant reminder of your brand's availability.

Not everyone needs—or can afford—to advertise continuously. One alternative to continuity scheduling is **flighting,** an intermittent schedule with periods when your advertising runs and gaps when it doesn't. You can use flighting to schedule

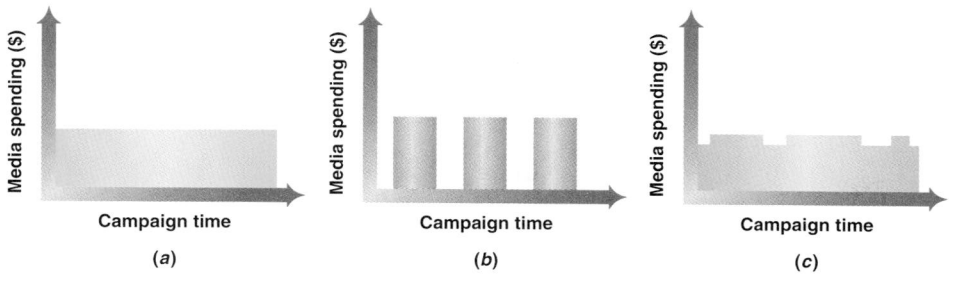

EXHIBIT 13.12
Media Continuity Options

Depending on your budget, the seasonality of your product, the diversity of media and vehicles in your media plan, and other factors, you can choose among continuity (*a*), flighting (*b*), or pulsing (*c*) schedules.

your messages at peak purchasing periods or during times when your audience is most receptive, allowing intervals between each *flight.* This approach is useful for products that aren't in strong demand all year, such as skis and suntan lotion. For example, Hasbro uses flighting to advertise its toys and games during November and December. During the preholiday advertising flight in 1992, Hasbro used a variety of media, including 30-second commercials on movie screens in major markets, multiple-page ads in 40 Marvel Comics issues, and television commercials. The seasonal television flight began on the day after Thanksgiving, when Hasbro sponsored a 14-hour block of cartoons on three Turner Broadcasting stations.[28]

If you use more than one medium or vehicle, you can achieve continuity by scheduling alternating flights in various media, media vehicles, areas, or periods. For instance, you might alternate a television flight with a magazine flight, a flight on news radio with a flight on oldies radio, a national medium flight with a local medium flight, or an early-morning television flight with a late-evening television flight. This continuous schedule with alternating flights lets you balance reach and frequency and maneuver around competitive advertising.[29]

Another option is to use **pulsing,** which combines a steady pattern of continuity with periods of more intense advertising activity. In pulsing, you maintain a consistent, relatively low level of advertising throughout the year and add *pulses* to make a heavier schedule during peak periods or to answer competitive challenges. For example, auto manufacturers advertise year-round, but they increase their schedules when they introduce new models and at other key times. When Chrysler launched the Jeep Grand Cherokee, it scheduled a pulse of print and electronic ads to run even before the model was available in local dealerships. After weeks of intense television, radio, newspaper, and magazine advertising following the new-model launch, the carmaker dropped back to a lower but consistent level of advertising for this product.[30]

If you use television advertising, you can try additional scheduling techniques to stretch your budget. During peak periods, you might use **bursting,** scheduling one ad to run repeatedly on the same station, which works well if you're selling a complex or expensive product or if you need to reinforce your message repeatedly during a short period. This ensures that the audience receives the message and has time to catch all the details.

Another technique is **roadblocking,** scheduling the same ad on several major television networks at the same time. Roadblocking lets you snare viewers who are watching any of those channels for maximum reach in a short period, and also gives the impression (to people who are switching channels) that you're advertising heavily. Chrysler used roadblocking when it introduced the Jeep Grand Cherokee, running television commercials on ABC, CBS, NBC, Fox, and 15 cable networks to kick off a $40 million, six-week ad campaign.[31] Still another choice is **gridlocking,** scheduling your commercial on one network while you schedule the same (or another) commercial immediately before and after on other networks. Like roadblocking, this technique maximizes your reach during the period and helps you catch viewers who switch channels.[32] However, as the number of networks multiplies, such techniques are likely to become obsolete—for most advertisers, buying time on all networks would be prohibitively expensive.

EXHIBIT 13.13
The Impact of a Full-Page Magazine Ad

Jincheng Motorcycle of Nanjing, China, uses full-page color magazine advertising to highlight the styling and features of the motorcycles it manufactures.

Determining Size/Length and Position

When scheduling your ad, also take into consideration its size or length and its position in the media vehicle. If you use print media, determine how large your ad will be; your size options vary widely, ranging from a tiny fraction of a page to several pages (see Exhibit 13.13). If you use broadcast media, determine how long your commercial will run; again, your choices are wide, ranging from a 10-second commercial to a 30- or 60-minute infomercial. You face the same questions when using other media. How long should your direct-mail letter be? How large should your outdoor sign be? The answers depend greatly on your objectives, your creative strategy, your ad budget, and your reach and frequency requirements.

The price of a full-page magazine or newspaper ad is usually less than double the price of a half-page ad, so if you choose the half page, you won't be able to buy two ads for the price of one full-page ad. In addition, although you save some money by buying a smaller space (or less time in electronic media), you may sacrifice some audience attention. However, if your creative strategy depends on repeated exposures, you may be willing to give up size or time in exchange for greater frequency. Of course, depending on your creative approach and your budget, even small ads can incorporate color, art, and other elements to grab audience attention.

Another consideration is the position of your ad within each medium. Because they're looking for extra impact, some print advertisers prefer the inside front and inside back covers of a vehicle; some broadcast advertisers ask for the first commercial slot during a sports event. For many years, Campbell Soup asked that magazines place its ads on the first right-hand page following the main editorial section, which eventually became known as the "Campbell's Soup position."[33] Media usually charge more when you specify a position, so you must weigh the potential benefits of such positions against the costs, especially if you're on a limited ad budget.

IN A VERY GREEN TOPIARY GARDEN, A SHAGGY BUSH IS BEING CLIPPED INTO THE SHAPE OF A NEON CAR.
(SFX): classical music and the sound of clipping.

V.O.: Many of its plastic parts have been labeled for the day they can be recycled. It's painted with a new technology that reduces factory emissions and its air conditioning refrigerant won't deplete the ozone.

No matter which color Neon you choose, we've done our darnedest to make it green. Say hello to Neon. $8975 for starters. $12,500 nicely loaded.

IT'S ONE OF THE FRIENDLIEST CARS ON EARTH.

EXHIBIT 13.14
One Message, Two Media

When Chrysler wanted to demonstrate how environmentally friendly its Neon car could be, it used both television and print advertising. Using two media enabled the advertiser to extend its reach, boost its frequency, and reinforce its advertising message.

SELECTING THE MEDIA

The third set of decisions you face when developing a media strategy relates to the selection of the media you use to meet your objectives. You might use only one medium to reach your target audience when you believe that this concentration will give you special impact, giving the impression that your brand dominates that medium. Using one medium also allows you to negotiate for a better price and special add-ons such as additional research or promotional assistance. In addition, focusing your efforts on one medium might allow you to make more of an impact than if you stretched your message across more media. Moreover, you generally pay lower creative and production costs when you place ads in one medium.[34]

On the other hand, you might reach your target audience by building a **media mix** of two or more media. A media mix makes sense when a single medium won't reach your target audience in sufficient numbers or with sufficient impact to achieve your media objectives. It also makes sense when you have segmented your market to create a series of target audiences and when you can identify a medium that's most effective for each. With a media mix, you can enhance your creative execution by varying it according to each medium's capabilities, such as using music on radio or animation on television. In addition, you can use one medium to reinforce your message in another or to break through clutter for more impact (see Exhibit 13.14).[35] In fact, research suggests that a combination of print and television is more effective than either medium alone.[36]

Choosing the Right Media Mix for a Product Launch

Few advertising challenges are as exciting as the launch of a new product. However, regardless of the type of product you're launching—a crunchy chocolate bar, a high-tech telephone service, or a low-cost color copier—your target audience won't learn much about it until you start to promote your breakthrough. That's why you need a carefully selected media mix and a balance of reach and frequency to introduce the product's features and benefits. Even so, when consumer and business advertisers launch their new-product campaigns, their approaches to using media often differ.

For example, when national advertisers such as PepsiCo and Procter & Gamble launch new consumer products, they typically start with a media mix that emphasizes television supported by print media. Television helps them reach a large number of people quickly and efficiently to build product awareness and to stimulate product trial. When PepsiCo introduced Crystal Pepsi and Diet Crystal Pepsi throughout the United States, it ran network television commercials to persuade soft-drink fans to try the new beverages. One of the kickoff commercials aired during the 1993 Super Bowl, bringing that product message to a national audience of more than 135 million. Television's wide reach gave both products a boost, and a reformulation in 1994 was promoted with another round of television advertising.

When Procter & Gamble introduced Cheer with Advanced Color Guard, it started with a heavy television schedule to maximize reach. Then, after the commercials had aired for several weeks, P&G ran print ads to reinforce the new-product message through increased frequency and to reach additional members of the target audience. "Our goal is for over 90 percent of U.S. households to be aware of the new product quickly," explained A. G. Lafley, P&G USA's president of laundry and cleaning products. This concentrated media schedule positioned the new Cheer product for a fast shot at a good-sized chunk of the $2 billion powdered detergent business.

On the other hand, when national advertisers such as Hewlett-Packard launch business products, they often choose magazines for the reach and the targeted audiences those magazines can deliver. When Hewlett-Packard introduced its Apollo 7000 workstation computers, it targeted two audiences: (1) top managers who approved workstation purchases but who weren't familiar with HP and (2) information systems managers who knew HP's reputation but who weren't aware of the new product line. Buying space in news, business, and technical

For obvious reasons, the cotton industry believes in Cheer with Advanced Color Guard.

Print ad used to launch Cheer with Advanced Color Guard.

magazines, Hewlett-Packard initially repeated a series of quarter-page teaser ads that stirred interest by showing the workstations' performance capabilities and price—but not the company name. After two weeks, the company switched to two-page spreads that reinforced the performance-and-price message and included the company name. These spreads drew over 5,000 inquiries, and within four months, HP workstation sales were up 40 percent.

By itself, advertising can't *guarantee* the success of a new product. However, as these advertisers know, the right media mix and the balanced blend of reach and frequency can go a long way toward bringing the new-product message to the right audience at the right time.

Apply Your Knowledge

1. If Hewlett-Packard were to introduce a portable personal computer targeted to college students, would you suggest using television, magazines, or both? Why?
2. Why would business advertisers tend to avoid television for new-product introductions? ■

A thoughtful media mix is the key for advertising Barq's root beer, whose annual media budget (usually under $10 million) is less than 10 percent of Coca-Cola's ($150 million) or Pepsi-Cola's ($139 million). "We're never going to outspend Coke or Pepsi, yet we have to push our message across to our target group, males 12-24," says vice president of national marketing Rick Hill. He puts most of his budget into television, including MTV's *Headbanger's Ball,* NBC's *Friday Night,* Fox's *In Living Color,* and wrestling programs on cable. The remainder goes to magazines (including *Rolling Stone*), to radio (including the syndicated *King Biscuit Flour Hour*), and to special promotions (including a tie-in to the movie *Freddy's Dead: The Final Nightmare*). Barq's creative execution and media choices increase impact by garnering millions of dollars' worth of free publicity when reporters, intrigued by the firm's unusual themes and contests, discuss (and show) its ads in media news stories.[37]

For Barq's, as for other advertisers, the media mix is a carefully crafted combination in which each medium complements and enhances the overall effect to produce **synergy,** a whole that is greater than the sum of its individual parts, a media mix that yields a total communication effect greater than the response measured from any individual medium.[38] Thus, if your radio commercial is effective in reminding the audience members about the newspaper coupon they saw for your product, you may see more sales than if you ran either ad alone. Whether you decide to concentrate your ads in one medium or to build a media mix, you need to understand (1) which media attract the audience you're targeting, (2) what kind of environment each medium creates for your message, and (3) what level of advertising competition you face in each.

Understanding Media Audiences

When you advertise in any medium, you have no way of knowing exactly who or how many people will be exposed to that ad. Instead, you're buying time or space on the basis of estimates of the general size and characteristics of the medium's usual audience. That's why it's important to use market and media research (including syndicated sources, information compiled by individual vehicles, and agency studies) to learn about the audience that each medium and vehicle attracts (see Exhibit 13.15). Only then can you select the media that reach the specific group of people you're targeting.

Media research can tell you, for instance, that people in France spend more time with radio than with any other medium throughout the day and that people in

EXHIBIT 13.15
What *USA Weekend* Knows about Its Audience

USA Weekend, a Sunday magazine published by Gannett, advertises in advertising industry publications to show media planners the demographic and behavioral characteristics of its audience.

the Netherlands spend more time with television. You can also find out the time of day each country's audience is most likely to use each of these media.[39] These data help you evaluate how and when the electronic media reach your target audiences. If you're considering newer media, such as television channels that air only in airport terminals, you'll have far less data to work with, although Nielsen is starting to measure audience exposure to more of these media.[40]

If you want to reach Hispanic audiences in the major U.S. markets, you have an increasing number of media options, as discovered by advertisers like Sears and Best Foods. Newspaper choices include *El Diario* (based in New York City), *La Opinión* (based in Los Angeles), *El Extra* (based in Chicago), *El Nuevo Herald,* and *El Diario de las Americas* (both based in Miami). Spanish-language television choices include Univision and Galavision, radio choices number more than 200, and Hispanic magazines and journals total more than 1,500.[41]

Multimedia opportunities to reach Hispanic audiences in the United States are also growing. For example, Gannett Outdoor and Caballero Spanish Media have teamed up to create Vista Sonido (Sight and Sound), a program of outdoor and radio ads backed by direct-mail distribution of coupons for advertised products. Testing Vista Sonido, Sears found that this media mix reached a segment of the target audience who had not previously been exposed to the store's commercials on Spanish-language television.[42]

Reach is important, but you have to go behind the exposure numbers to understand how the audience actually interacts with each medium. This means gauging both the attention value and the motivation value for your product's audience in each medium. **Attention value** refers to the degree of attention an audience pays to ads in a particular medium. Attention value isn't determined by the medium alone; the message and its creative execution are also important influences.

For example, television has relatively high attention value for many products and many audiences. Its characteristics of sound, color, and moving images capture audience attention by convincingly bringing a product to life; moreover, the use of music, words, tone, and attitude contributes to the high attention value.[43] In addition, when an audience is highly involved with a program, the effect of advertising shown during that program may be heightened.[44] Similarly, business advertisers selling technical products generally find an attentive audience in specialized magazines, which are avidly read by people who work in the field. If you're considering advertising in *Engineered Systems,* you'll find that the magazine's audience consists of people who buy, install, and service commercial heating and ventilation systems. Thus, it's natural to assume that ads for related products such as air-conditioner filters are likely to enjoy high attention value in this medium.

However, audience attention is only one part of the equation; to achieve your media objectives, you also need audience response. **Motivation value** is the degree to which a medium stimulates its audience to respond. Newspapers have high motivation value for many product categories, because their audiences often seek out ads in that medium when they're ready to buy cars, homes, and a host of other consumer and business products. Given the nature of newspapers, you can use long copy and illustrations to educate your target audience about the product and category; readers can take as much time as they need to review your message and decide on a purchase, which also contributes to motivation value.[45] The motivation value for specialized magazines such as *Engineered Systems* is high because readers browse the magazine for ideas about improving their operations or about new technology, so they're more responsive to messages from advertisers of related products.

Understanding Media Environments

Closely related to the need for understanding media audiences is the need to understand the **media environment,** or the context for advertising reception, which includes the content surrounding the ad and the look that the media create for ad messages. As you might imagine, when a medium's environment is compatible with the desired audience mood as well as the product and its benefits, you're more likely to get a good audience response than if the environment is incompatible. If you're advertising Good and Plenty candy to adults, for example, you'll find that the media environment of the Nickelodeon cable network differs from that of *The Wall Street Journal,* so the audiences' moods and their responses to your message are likely to differ. Nickelodeon's look is light and humorous; *The Wall Street Journal*'s look is staid and businesslike. Nickelodeon provokes laughter; *The Wall Street Journal* provokes serious thought. So an ad for Good and Plenty candy might fit the environment created by Nick but seem out of place in the environment of *The Wall Street Journal.*

The mood created by each medium (and by individual vehicles) can enhance the advertising message. For instance, Quaker Oats knew that its target audience was most interested in hot cereals during cold weather. Its agency decided to take advantage of the cold-weather mood created by the environment of the Weather Channel by requesting that Quaker Oats commercials be aired only when the mercury dipped below 40 degrees.[46] However, mood can sometimes work against a product. Most airlines don't allow their television commercials to air during news reports of plane crashes because they know that the context works against a message promoting air travel.

Advertisers can also benefit from the environment of respectability that an authoritative media vehicle lends to a message. Look at the environment created by *Good Housekeeping* magazine. Readers know that the magazine awards its Seal of Approval only to products of proven quality. Motorola used that association to good advantage during a recent consumer campaign for its pager products. To counter the "drug dealer" image of pagers that many adults have, Motorola set a more wholesome tone by prominently displaying the *Good Housekeeping* seal in its print ads.[47] Even if an advertiser hasn't earned that seal, readers may believe that the message has more credibility simply because it's contained in a magazine they respect.

Another consideration is the combination and position of editorial material and ads in a given vehicle. If your ad is buried in the clutter of numerous ads broadcast during a station break, or if it's embedded in pages of ads slipped into the back of a newspaper or magazine, the media environment may distract your audience and keep them from noticing and acting on your message. To stand out, you may have to change position, vehicles, media, schedules, creative execution, or other elements.[48]

Understanding Competitors' Use of Media

Despite the variety and abundance of media, advertising time and space aren't unlimited. Even though all advertisers compete with one another as each tries to lock in the most desirable media placements, direct competitors in your product category present a special challenge because they're rivals for your target audience's attention. However, if you understand your competitors' media budgets, mixes, and share of voice, you can construct a more effective media strategy that takes advantage of the weaknesses in competitors' media plans or of the strengths in your own media plans. Depending on your situation, you might meet rivals head on, avoid them in a medium, or vary your media mix, geographic scope, or activity.[49]

As discussed in Chapter 6, syndicated research sources such as Leading National Advertisers and A. C. Nielsen track media expenditures by product and brand for many national brands. You can use this research to analyze competitors' media expenditures and compare their spending patterns with your own. You can also compare the media mix, media schedule, and geographic scope of each competitor. It's often helpful to analyze competitors' share of voice in each medium (see Exhibit 13.16).[50] The formula for calculating one brand's share of voice in a specific medium is

$$\text{Share of voice} = \frac{\text{brand expenditures}}{\text{total-category expenditures}}$$

	LEADING NATIONAL ADVERTISERS 1993 BRAND DETAIL REPORT AS OF OCTOBER 31							

TRANSPORTATION - AGRICULTURE

PUB #	YEAR-TO-DATE NEQ PG $(000)	JANUARY SPACE $(000)	FEBRUARY SPACE $(000)	MARCH SPACE $(000)	APRIL SPACE $(000)	MAY SPACE $(000)	JUNE SPACE $(000)	JULY SPACE $(000)
TOYOTA MOTOR CORP					LEXUS GS300			
FORBES 2	4.00 205.8			2.00 4S 102.9	2.00 4S 102.9			
FORTUNE 2	6.00 337.6		2.00 4S 112.5	2.00 4S 112.5	2.00 4S 112.5			
GOLF MAG	2.00 109.4				2.00 4S 109.4			
GOLF DGST	2.00 149.2				2.00 4S 149.2			
GOURMET	2.00 69.8			2.00 4S 69.8				
LEARS	4.00 99.7				2.00 4S 49.8	2.00 4S 49.8		
MIRABELLA	4.00 149.6				2.00 4S 74.8	2.00 4S 74.8		
MONEY	2.00 166.4				2.00 4S 166.4			
MTR TREND	4.00 239.3				2.00 FS 123.5	2.00 4S 115.9		
NY MAGAZN3	4.00 128.4			2.00 4S 64.2	2.00 4S 64.2			
NEW YORKR1	......		2.00 4S 82.1					
NEW YORKR2	......			2.00 4S 82.1				
NEW YORKR4	6.00 254.6				2.00 FS 90.3			
NEWSWEEK 2	......			2.00 04S 102.9				
NEWSWEEK 3	1.45 308.7		2.00 04S 102.9		2.00 04S 102.9			
RD & TRCK	2.00 97.6					2.00 4S 97.6		
STHRN ACC	2.00 35.0					2.00 FS 35.0		
STHRN LVG	2.00 134.6				2.00 FS 134.6			
SPORTS IL2	......			2.00 04S 120.6				
SPORTS IL4	2.63 433.5		2.00 4S 312.8					
SUNSET	2.00 87.0				2.00 4S 87.0			
TENNIS	2.00 92.7				2.00 FS 92.7			
TIME 2	1.30 336.8		2.00 04S 168.4	2.00 04S 168.4				
US NEWS 2	......		2.00 04S 102.6					
US NEWS 4	1.40 205.2			2.00 04S 102.6	2.00 4S 94.3			
NY TM MAG1	......							
NY TM MAG2	4.00 188.6		2.00 FS 94.3					
TOT DOL		0.0	1,117.3	1,143.5	1,834.4	548.6	0.0	0.0
TOT NEQ PGS		0.00	11.83	16.47	37.48	16.00	0.00	0.00
				10$ 2,260.9			20$ 2,383.0	
Y-T-D$	4,643.9			10P 28.30			20P 53.48	
Y-T-D P	81.78							

EXHIBIT 13.16
Checking Competitive Share of Voice

Research by Leading National Advertisers can help you determine how much rivals spent in print media. This report shows that Toyota bought space in a variety of magazines, including the second *Forbes* issue of the month (Forbes 2), from January to June, 1993. The total amount of space bought in *Forbes* was 4 NEQ PG or 4 *national equivalence pages*, a measurement based on ad size and on the percentage of the publication's total circulation that is reached by the ad. Toyota spent $205,800 advertising in *Forbes*: In March and again in April, the carmaker used 2 advertising pages in a four-color spread (4S) costing $102,900 per insertion.

Suppose that Kellogg's All-Bran spent $13,631,700 to advertise on network television last year. If network television spending for all ready-to-eat bran cereals was $58,905,400, share of voice would be calculated like this:

$$\text{Share of voice} = 13{,}631{,}700 \div 58{,}905{,}400 = .231 = 23.1\%$$

In this illustration, All-Bran had a 23.1 percent share of voice in the category. If you were the media planner for the General Mills cereal that competes with All-Bran and you found that your brand had a lower share of voice in network television, you might suggest matching or exceeding All-Bran's ad expenditures to gain more audience attention, or you might suggest using another medium in which you could develop a larger share of voice.

Consider how Porsche crafted a competitive media strategy. The carmaker wanted to harness the excitement of the *Twentieth Anniversary of Monday Night Football* television special to advertise its new models, but it couldn't buy national network time during the program because ABC had exclusive ad contracts with competitors. So it bought commercial time on local stations in the carmaker's top 16 markets during the opening game of the season, which aired the same evening. In the Eastern and Central time zones, where the special was scheduled to run before the game, Porsche bought the entire first commercial break in the game, to take advantage of the audience that watched the special and stayed tuned to the game; in the Mountain and Pacific time zones, where the special ran after the game, it bought the game's last commercial break, to take advantage of the audience that stayed tuned to watch the special. Porsche aired 90-second commercials in those breaks, thus avoiding clutter and competition from rivals' commercials.[51]

CALCULATING COST EFFICIENCY

Even advertisers with huge budgets need to analyze the cost of using various media to reach people in their target audiences. By evaluating the cost and comparing the cost efficiency of each medium, of each vehicle, and of each media plan under consideration, advertisers can determine the combination of media, vehicles, and schedules that best meets their objectives.[52] One calculation used to

How much are your rivals spending on advertising? The question's not a new one—advertisers have been checking up on competitors for decades—but today checking up on your competitors is much easier because you don't have to spend time counting magazine ads or watching television commercials. Instead, you can buy the data you need in a convenient form from research firms that monitor ad expenditures.

However, not all forms of advertising are tracked by the various research services. Generally, you can get information only on *measured media,* which includes ad expenditures in newspapers, magazines and Sunday supplements, outdoor media, radio, and television. One service looks at business advertising in business magazines, but most of the available research covers consumer advertising. It's harder to find information on *unmeasured media,* which includes spending on direct mail, catalogs, sales promotion, cooperative advertising, most business and farm publications, and special events.

Here's an overview of some of the tools you can use to track competitive share of voice in 10 measured media:

- *Newspapers.* Leading National Advertisers (LNA) reports on ad space in newspapers published in 88 U.S. cities. The Advertising Checking Bureau (ACB) monitors national advertising expenditures in every U.S. daily and Sunday newspaper (and many weeklies).
- *Magazines and Sunday supplements.* Leading National Advertisers/Publishers Information Bureau (LNA/PIB) reports ad spending in more than 175 consumer magazines and Sunday supplements. LNA Business-to-Business tracks business advertising in 700 magazines serving 85 industries.
- *Outdoor.* LNA Outdoor measures expenditures on poster and billboard ads placed with more than 200 outdoor firms.

- *Network television.* Arbitron's MediaWatch tracks commercials broadcast on ABC, CBS, and NBC network programs; Nielsen's Monitor-Plus covers ads on ABC, CBS, NBC, and Fox networks.
- *Spot television.* Nielsen's Monitor-Plus checks spot television advertising in 50 top U.S. markets; Arbitron's MediaWatch collects data on spot television advertising in the largest 75 U.S. markets.
- *Syndicated television.* Nielsen's Monitor-Plus covers ads on more than 100 syndicated programs.
- *Cable television networks.* Nielsen's Monitor-Plus checks ad spending on 17 cable networks; Arbitron's MediaWatch reports ad spending on 6 cable television networks.
- *Network radio.* Arbitron's MediaWatch monitors commercials airing on 17 radio networks.
- *Spot radio.* LNA National Spot Radio checks commercials airing on 2,500 radio stations in more than 200 U.S. markets.

In addition, the Advertising Checking Bureau collects data on consumer sales promotions in the print media and on point-of-purchase consumer sales promotions. Armed with these tools, you can measure your share of voice, compare your advertising and sales promotion expenditures with your competitors', and create an appropriate media plan to meet your objectives.

Apply Your Knowledge

1. Why do you think research firms can't measure direct-mail advertising expenditures? What are the implications for media planners?
2. Is it helpful to check competitors' expenditures in all media, even when you plan to advertise only in print media? Explain your answer. ■

compare media cost is **cost per thousand (CPM),** the cost of reaching 1,000 people in a medium's audience. The basic formula for CPM is

$$\text{Cost per thousand} = \frac{\text{cost of media unit}}{\text{gross impressions}} \times 1,000$$

This formula reflects the cost of reaching the medium's entire audience. However, cost efficiency is determined by calculating how much you spend to reach only your *target audience.* For example, if you place a full-page color ad in *Student Travels* magazine at a cost of $11,590 to target 300,000 of the publication's 500,000 circulation, your CPM would look like this:

$$\text{Cost per thousand} = \frac{\$11,590}{300,000} \times 1,000 = \$38.63$$

Although CPM can help you compare the cost efficiency of reaching your target audience through various media, it's important to remember that cost comparisons don't take into account variations in creative execution, media audience, media environment, or competitive media usage. Because media planning is both an art and a science, media planners make judgments based on more than CPM calculations. CPM can be a handy yardstick to support media selection, but it can't predict how *your* target audience will react to a particular medium or which media mix will work best for *your* product. Thus, CPM may be a good way to measure cost, but it doesn't measure effectiveness.[53]

Using Computers in Media Planning

Especially when media planners must juggle numerous markets, media, and scheduling alternatives, computers can be valuable tools for storing, manipulating, and reporting the vast reservoir of data involved. Today, virtually every ad agency and media-buying service relies on computers to handle many aspects of the media-planning process. Computers generally support the media-planning process in three ways: (1) to analyze the market, the audience, and the media; (2) to develop media strategies; and (3) to buy media and construct media schedules.

- *Analyzing the market, the audience, and the media.* Media planners use computers to manipulate a mountain of details about markets, competitors, brands and categories, target audiences, and all the media under consideration. Some computer programs (such as Conquest) are specifically designed to help pinpoint the target audience by analyzing a range of geodemographic data. In addition, most syndicated research services, including SMRB, MRI, and single-source suppliers, make data available in computerized form so that media planners can select only what they need. Then the planners use various computer models to sort and combine these data in a search for patterns to help them set and meet media objectives. For example, DDB Needham/Chicago has created a Personal Media Network computer program that identifies the loyal audience of people for a particular media vehicle; this helps the media planners understand who they're reaching when they buy space or time in that vehicle.[54]

- *Developing media strategies.* Given the proliferation of media and vehicles—as well as increased audience fragmentation—media planners have more choices and combinations to consider than ever before. Using computer programs such as Marketron, AdWare, and Tapscan streamlines the process of assembling several media strategies that fit the advertiser's budget and then calculating and comparing the reach, frequency, and cost efficiency of each (see Exhibit 13.17). Computers also help media planners prepare alternative media strategies for possible use in case some major change (such as a massive increase in a competitor's ad spending) threatens the effectiveness of the current media strategy.[55]

EXHIBIT 13.17

Media Planning via Computer

Many agencies now use computer software to prepare media schedules, evaluate reach and frequency, and calculate the cost efficiency of a particular media plan. This screen from Stone House Systems summarizes the broadcast television component of a media plan targeting men 25 to 54 years old.

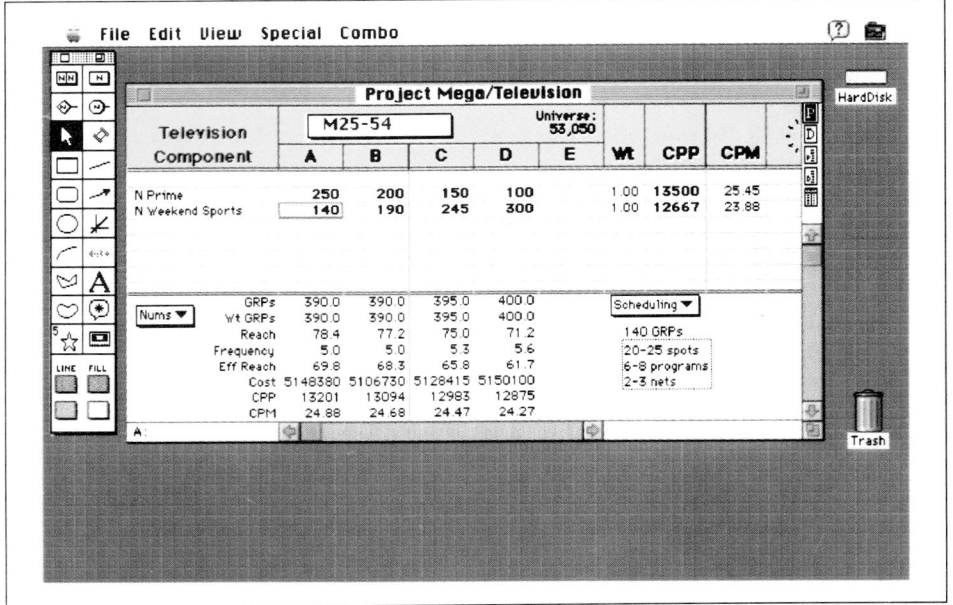

- *Buying media and constructing media schedules.* A recent survey found that 69 percent of the responding agencies use computers for media buying and scheduling. Media planners can use computer programs such as Media Management Plus and Donovan Data Systems to build, change, and print *media schedules* (also known as *flowcharts*) showing the exact timing and media placement of every ad.[56] Because media planners can mix and match the timing of ads in each vehicle to create a virtually endless variety of possible schedules, using such programs eases the burden of preparing and comparing schedules that both meet the objectives and fit the budget. Once a schedule has been chosen, these programs can print out the details to guide media buyers as they reserve the media time and space needed—sometimes using computers.[57]

However, as fast and efficient as a computer may be for supporting media planning, it's only one of the tools in a media planner's tool kit. Just as media planners can't reduce all media decisions to a simple comparison of CPM, they can't use computer programs as a substitute for experience and good judgment. Computers can't judge which medium or environment is most suitable for a particular message or when one medium should be substituted for another. At best, computers provide the background data and the computational power to support media planners as they use their personal knowledge of the situation to scan computer-generated alternatives and choose the one that best meets their brands' objectives.[58]

Implementing the Media Plan

Once the media strategy has been approved by both the agency and the advertiser, the next step is to prepare and implement the media plan. Although the exact order and detail level of each component varies from agency to agency, media plans

EXHIBIT 13.18
A Six-Month Media Schedule for GMC Trucks

The media planners at GMC Truck's ad agency, McCann/SAS, constructed this media schedule to guide its media buyers as they negotiated for advertising time and space in selected media vehicles. It also provided GMC Truck with an overview of where and when advertising messages would appear.

GMC Truck Media Plan
January – June 1993
Magazines

Week(s) →	Jan 1	2	3	4	Feb 1	2	3	4	Mar 1	2	3	4	5	Apr 1	2	3	4	May 1	2	3	4	5	June 1	2	3	4
Automotive																										
Business/finance																										
Epicurean																										
Men's journals																										
Newsweeklies																										
Science/technology																										
Special appeal																										
Sports																										

Network/Cable Television

Week(s) →	Jan 1	2	3	4	Feb 1	2	3	4	Mar 1	2	3	4	5	Apr 1	2	3	4	May 1	2	3	4	5	June 1	2	3	4
A&E																										
CNN																										
CNBC																										
Discovery																										
Turner Broadcasting																										

Several months of the year show five weeks instead of four.
The shaded portions of the media charts indicate the weeks GMC Truck was advertising.

Meeting an Advertising Challenge at Chrysler

A CASE FOR CRITICAL THINKING

In a world in which his company was being outspent by domestic rivals that advertised more heavily—and squeezed by the continued popularity of imports—Chrysler's John Damoose was searching for effective and efficient ways to bring product messages to his target audiences. At the start of 1992, he had two big new stories to tell: he was launching both the LH family of cars and the Jeep Grand Cherokee. His media budget allocated at least $200 million for the LH family introduction and roughly $40 million for the Jeep Grand Cherokee introduction.

For the LH cars, Damoose worked closely with his four agency partners (BBDO Worldwide, Bozell, CME-KHBB, and Ross Roy Group) to research the media habits of the target audience, baby-boomer adults. This research laid the groundwork for the LH product positioning and for the creative direction of the advertising campaign. It also gave Damoose valuable insight into how to spend the media budget to reach this audience most effectively. For example, the study found that many in the target audience were heavy readers; as a result, Damoose realized that he could reach this segment through print.

Even before the LH models rolled into showrooms, Damoose approved a media plan of magazine and television ads to whet the boomers' appetite for the new cars. The magazine schedule (intended to plant an image in con-sumers' minds) included a steady stream of ads in Time, Fortune, Sports Illustrated, National Geographic, Car and Driver, and seven other publications. The television schedule (intended to encourage people to visit local dealers) kicked off with national network commercials and continued with commercials shown in selected local markets. Ads reinforced the message being delivered in all other media. Boosted by the ad blitz, LH car sales accelerated, and Chrysler passed Toyota and Honda to take the number three slot in the U.S. market.

For the Jeep Grand Cherokee, Damoose approved a media plan of television, radio, and magazine ads designed to build awareness of the new model and to recapture sales momentum lost to the market leader, the Ford Explorer. Two months before the new Jeeps were due in show-rooms, 15-second teaser ads on network television during the Winter Olympics started to build audience interest and curiosity by mentioning—but not showing—the new product. One month before the Jeeps were due in showrooms, television commercials that actually showed the new product whipped up more audience excitement and anticipation. Damoose supported the launch with radio ads and an extensive schedule of magazine ads in Time, Business Week, Esquire, Sailing, Motor Trend, and more than a dozen other publications. The magazine ads touted the product's advantages, including antilock brakes as a standard feature. Within a year, the Cherokee was outselling the Explorer.

Damoose was also convinced that Chrysler could save money by revamping the way its agencies bought media space and time. After discussing the problem with other Chrysler executives and reviewing agency proposals, he decided to place all media planning and buying with PentaCom, a new BBDO subsidiary formed for this purpose.

Even more media decisions are ahead for Arthur C. (Bud) Liebler, who now supervises Chrysler's advertising function. By 1996 Chrysler will have replaced virtually every model with an entirely new one or a refurbished version of the existing model. So Bud Liebler can't take his eyes off the road just yet.

Your Mission: As Chrysler's manager of advertising, you supervise the media strategies and plans developed for all company products. You've taken a special interest in the Jeep line. Using your knowledge of media planning, choose the best alternative in each of the following situations.

1. You're drafting the media objective that will guide the agency's development of a media plan for the Jeep Grand Cherokee in the United States.

generally include (1) a statement of media objectives, (2) a summary of the situation analysis, (3) a description of the media strategy, and (4) a complete set of media schedules and expenditures (see Exhibit 13.18 on page 365). Other components sometimes included are (1) a brief overview of the entire plan (intended to help the advertiser and agency executives understand its scope) and (2) one or more alternative media plans (to be implemented if any change in strategy is needed).

The media plan guides the implementation of the media strategy. With the media plan in place, it's time to negotiate for the time and space specified in the media schedule. When an advertiser uses several agencies, media buying is usually assigned to the **agency of record,** which purchases time and space for all the agencies that serve a particular advertiser. When the advertiser uses a media-buying service, its specialists handle the negotiations. For example, MasterCard and Reebok use specialists at DeWitt Media in New York to manage their media buying.[59] Some advertising agencies, such as Young & Rubicam and Hal Riney & Partners, handle their own media services, and they separate media buying from media planning to allow each group to focus on its specialty. Other ad agencies,

Which of these objectives would be most helpful?

a. Use media to raise brand awareness among men aged 21 to 45 by 50 percent above current levels within 6 months.

b. Use media to raise brand awareness among men aged 21 to 45 during May.

c. Use media to reach all men aged 21 to 45 at least four times.

2. You're reviewing plans for network television advertising for the Jeep Grand Cherokee. Knowing your budget limitations, the agency has presented several continuity alternatives. Which of these proposals should you accept?

a. Use continuity scheduling to reach your target audience every day. Even if you buy only one 15-second commercial a day, you need to advertise continuously because you're up against rivals with much bigger budgets.

b. Use flighting to schedule commercials only in the months when Jeep sales tend to be strongest and in the regions where Jeeps sell best. You won't waste money advertising when or where people aren't interested in Jeeps.

c. Use pulsing to combine a low level of weekly Jeep advertising during slow periods with a higher level of weekly Jeep advertising during periods of peak sales or audience interest. That way you can support the Jeep name all year but advertise more aggressively during peak periods.

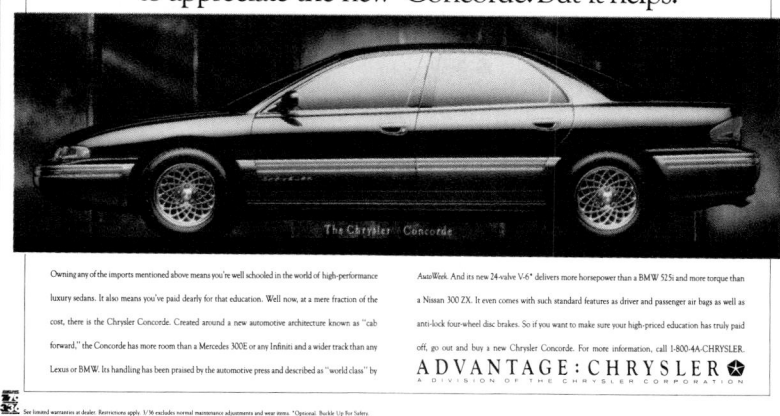

You don't have to own a Mercedes, Lexus or BMW to appreciate the new Concorde. But it helps.

The Chrysler Concorde

Owning any of the imports mentioned above means you're well schooled in the world of high-performance luxury sedans. It also means you've paid dearly for that education. Well now, at a mere fraction of the cost, there is the Chrysler Concorde. Created around a new automotive architecture known as "cab forward," the Concorde has more room than a Mercedes 300E or any Infiniti and a wider track than any Lexus or BMW. Its handling has been praised by the automotive press and described as "world class" by *AutoWeek.* And its new 24-valve V-6* delivers more horsepower than a BMW 525i and more torque than a Nissan 300 ZX. It even comes with such standard features as driver and passenger air bags as well as anti-lock four-wheel disc brakes. So if you want to make sure your high-priced education has truly paid off, go out and buy a new Chrysler Concorde. For more information, call 1-800-4A-CHRYSLER.

ADVANTAGE: CHRYSLER
A DIVISION OF THE CHRYSLER CORPORATION

See limited warranties at dealer. Restrictions apply. 3/36 excludes normal maintenance adjustments and wear items. *Optional. Buckle Up For Safety.

3. You're considering nontraditional media for the Jeep Grand Cherokee media mix. You want to physically display the product and present its benefits in a credible way. On the basis of appropriate target audience, good media environment, and lack of competitive clutter, which idea would you recommend?

a. Sponsor the U.S. tour of the hit show Will Rogers Follies. Display the Jeep in each theater, and arrange for the lead character to discuss product benefits onstage in an amusing but positive way.

b. Sponsor the next U.S. tour of Madonna as she promotes her latest album. Arrange for her to drive the Jeep onstage during every performance.

c. Sponsor the U.S. tour of the Indianapolis 500 race vehicles and drivers. Invite local media representatives to sit in the Jeep and in the race cars.

4. You're considering three other ideas for nontraditional media to reach your audience. Which one would you recommend for the Jeep Grand Cherokee?

a. A commercial spliced on the video release of Jurassic Park would reach adventurous consumers and counter the movie's use of Ford Explorers.

b. A yearly customer newsletter that goes only to Jeep owners would reinforce the Jeep name and highlight product benefits.

c. A test-drive video mailed to people who bought competing vehicles three or more years ago would showcase the Jeep driving experience.[62] ■

such as Lintas, use teams of media generalists devoted to individual media (such as electronic and print) to handle both planning and buying so that team members develop experience in making both strategic and tactical media-buying decisions.[60]

When media buyers negotiate with each media vehicle, they look at the audience, the rate, and the position the ad will be given within the vehicle. They also consider any special add-ons such as media-sponsored contests that involve the audience in the advertiser's message. To stay within the advertiser's budget— and to stretch limited dollars—media buyers work hard to negotiate the best combination of space or time, position, add-ons, and rates. Sometimes media vehicles accept advertisers' merchandise or services instead of cash as payment for time or space. Such *barter* arrangements have helped Dole, Konica, Nestlé, and other advertisers exchange products for media services.[61]

After the ads run, media buyers are responsible for checking that they ran correctly and that the vehicles delivered the promised reach. If an ad wasn't run properly, or if a vehicle delivered a smaller audience than expected, the media buyer negotiates for an appropriate adjustment. An adjustment may take the form of a price cut or a promise to repeat the ad.

Summary

Media planning is a part of advertising, which is in turn a part of marketing. The information from the situation analysis, marketing plan, and advertising plan guides the development of a comprehensive media plan that includes specific media objectives, strategies, and tactics to be used in advertising a particular product or brand. Contemporary media planning has become more complex because planners must evaluate an increasing number of media options. With more media choices, the audience for each is fragmented, so planners have more difficulty reaching specific groups. In addition, higher costs put more pressure on advertisers to use the media more cost-effectively.

Media planners need to set specific, measurable objectives using a description of the target audience and a description of the reach, frequency, and total message weight of the ad campaign. These objectives clarify the description of the people the ads should be directed to and help planners select the media vehicles that will reach these people most efficiently and effectively. Reach indicates how many different members of the target audience are exposed to the media vehicle during a given period, and it must be balanced with frequency, the number of times people are exposed to the message during that period. Message weight is the size of the combined target audiences reached by all media used in a media plan; it's expressed in terms of gross impressions or gross rating points.

To determine the geographic scope of their media strategy, media planners check the product distribution and the sales potential in various markets. Two tools to evaluate sales strength and potential are the brand development index and the category development index. Message scheduling is affected by the timing, continuity, size (or length), and position of an ad. Message timing can help advertisers reach people when they're most interested in a product, stimulate demand during slow periods, avoid competitors' messages, and reach people when they're most receptive to the medium being used. With continuity scheduling, ads run consistently over a long period without gaps; with flighting, ads run intermittently; and with pulsing, ads run continuously with periods of more intense advertising activity. Balancing an ad's size (or length) and its position depends on the media objectives, the budget, and the reach and frequency requirements.

To develop an effective media strategy, media planners must understand the target audience attracted by each medium, the environment each medium creates for the message, and the level of advertising competition that exists in each medium. To compare the cost efficiency of various media, media planners calculate the cost per thousand, the cost of reaching 1,000 people in the audience. Cost per thousand is calculated by dividing the cost of a media unit by the gross impressions in that medium and then multiplying the result by 1,000. Computers are used to support media planning in three ways: (1) to analyze the market, the audience, and the media; (2) to develop media strategies; and (3) to construct media schedules. The final step is to prepare and implement the media plan.

Key Terms

agency of record 366
attention value 360
average frequency to
category development index
(CDI) 352
continuity 354
continuity scheduling 354
cost per thousand
(CPM) 363
effective frequency 348
effective reach 349
flighting 354
frequency 348
gridlocking 355
gross impressions 349
gross rating points
(GRPs) 350
brand development index
(BDI) 351
bursting 355
mass media 343
media environment 360
media mix 357
media plan 342
media planning 341
media strategy 350
media vehicle 342
message weight 349
motivation value 360
pulsing 355
rating point 350
reach 347
roadblocking 355
synergy 359

Questions

FOR REVIEW

1. What is media planning, and how does it relate to marketing and advertising?

2. What factors do media planners have to consider when striking the appropriate balance between reach and frequency in a particular advertising campaign?

3. How does an understanding of media audiences help media planners select the appropriate media?

4. When does it make sense to build a media mix?

5. How do timing and continuity scheduling affect message scheduling?

FOR ANALYSIS AND APPLICATION

6. How can an advertiser compare the environments of two dissimilar media such as television and magazines?

7. By analyzing the competitive share of voice of a giant cookie competitor such as Nabisco, what might a relatively small firm such as Frookies learn about placing advertising for cookies sweetened with fruit juice?

8. What target audience might Steelcase, a maker of office furniture, direct its advertising to? Which media and vehicles would be likely to reach this target audience most effectively?

9. How might a chocolate manufacturer such as Whitman's use flighting to schedule advertising for gift-boxed assortments to consumers?

10. What might Revlon do if it were threatened by a perfume competitor with a higher share of voice in magazines, a key medium for this category?

Sharpen Your Advertising Skills

Congratulations! You've just opened a new Subway sandwich franchise one block from your campus, and you're ready to promote your menu to a target audience of hungry students. You decide to run ads in the college newspaper in late August to catch students when they first return to school. Although this is a good first step toward introducing your new sandwich shop, you also want to plan your full advertising schedule for the next 12 months.

Decision: Which continuity pattern should you use for your newspaper advertising? Should you use continuity scheduling, flighting, or pulsing, or a combination? As you consider your decision, don't forget to look at the school year and its impact on student buying patterns.

Communication: Prepare a one-year media schedule covering the period from August of this year to July of next year. Show the continuity patterns you plan to use for newspaper advertising, and include a one- to two-paragraph explanation of why this pattern is appropriate.

Print Media

After studying this chapter, you will be able to

1. Classify the types of newspapers and the types of newspaper advertising

2. Outline the advantages and limitations of newspaper advertising

3. Explain the measures of newspaper circulation and readership

4. Discuss the structure of newspaper advertising rates

5. Describe how magazines can be categorized according to the three broad audiences they serve

6. Identify the advantages and limitations of magazine advertising

7. Describe the structure of magazine advertising rates and differentiate among cover, on-sale, and closing dates

Facing an Advertising Challenge at Lexmark International

BIDDING A GRACEFUL GOOD-BYE TO A FAMILIAR BRAND NAME

What happens when you spend millions of dollars over the course of many decades to build a reputable brand name—and then have to switch to a new brand name? That's the challenge faced by Marvin Mann. As chairman and chief executive of Lexmark International, which makes typewriters, keyboards, printers, and printing supplies, Mann has only a short time to use, and then phase out, one of the world's best-known brand names: !BM. Along with the changeover comes the task of creating a powerful brand image that will help sell its products once the Lexmark nameplate replaces the IBM nameplate.

Originally, Lexmark was an IBM division, manufacturing high-quality electric typewriters that became office legends for their durability and innovation. Once IBM introduced the personal computer, the division also began to turn out keyboards and printers. Then IBM decided to reorga-

nize and get out of the typewriter and printer business. An investment firm acquired the subsidiary in 1991, along with the right to use the IBM brand name on its products until 1996.

Mann was plucked out of IBM's executive ranks to head the newly independent company. His first order of business was to select a new company name. "We wanted a name that had some punch to it, but something that also had some relationship to what we do," he said. From a list of 200 possible names, he and his managers decided on Lexmark. The lex is reminiscent of lexicon, referring to a dictionary or a particular vocabulary. The mark derives from the idea of making a mark on paper, which Lexmark products have been specifically designed to do.

Only a few months after separating from IBM, the company embarked on an ambitious new-product program. The firm revamped its existing printers and came up with a new line of laser

printers, which competed head-on with products made by market leader Hewlett-Packard. Labeled with the IBM brand, Lexmark's laser printers quickly caught the attention of computer magazines, which praised the products' simplicity, reliability, and print quality.

Although Mann and his marketing staff had a lot riding on the product introductions, they also had to consider how to raise awareness of the Lexmark brand. Some $20 million was earmarked for advertising in the coming year, of which $5 million would be spent on building Lexmark's brand image. If you were Lexmark's chairman, how would you use print advertising to help build sales in the short term while supporting the name change in the long term? Where would you advertise Lexmark products? How would you use the advantages of print to showcase the benefits of Lexmark products?[1] ∎

CHAPTER OVERVIEW The print media can help an advertiser make a powerful impact, as Lexmark is discovering. This chapter examines the use of the two main print media, newspapers and magazines. Starting with a discussion of newspapers, the older of the two, you'll explore the various types of newspapers, the types of newspaper advertising, the advantages and limitations of newspaper advertising, and the future of newspaper advertising. Then you'll see how to plan newspaper advertising through an understanding of circulation and readership, advertising rates, ad placement, and special services. You'll follow a similar path as you explore magazines, including the types of magazines, the advantages and limitations of magazine advertising, the future of magazine advertising, and the factors to consider when planning magazine advertising.

Advertising in the Print Media

In the years before radio and television, newspapers (and later magazines) were important channels of communication. In addition to providing a tangible record of the news of the day, the print media also carried advertisers' messages far and wide. Radio, followed by television, siphoned a lot of advertising dollars away from both newspapers and magazines; however, print remains an important part of many advertisers' campaigns because of the way people interact with these media. In fact, print is the primary—often the only—medium for many business advertisers.

Why is print the preferred medium for some advertisers? The answer lies in the way audiences receive messages through those media. Watching television and listening to the radio are passive activities, but people have to pick up, open, and read a newspaper or a magazine to receive any message. Readers are actively

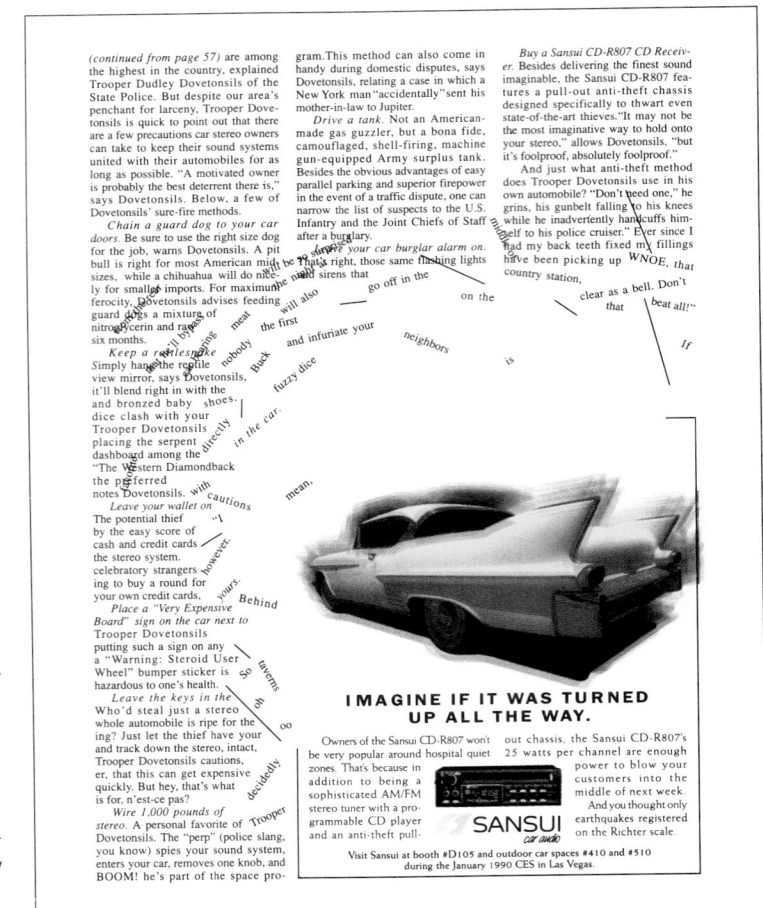

EXHIBIT 14.1
Using Print Advertising to Best Advantage

To demonstrate the capabilities of Sansui car-audio systems, ad agency Kirshenbaum & Bond created an eye-catching magazine ad in which the sound seemed to blast the type right off the printed page. The "article" surrounding the ad was actually a parody of a "how-to" story showing how to protect car stereos from being stolen.

involved with the print media, and *they* control how long or short a time they spend looking at editorial and advertising material. This makes print media ideal for explaining complicated product features. Some print media can also be used to visually portray product benefits and features (see Exhibit 14.1). Lexmark chose print media because print offered an excellent way to showcase the special capabilities of the company's laser printers.

Moreover, by choosing the print media that interest them, people automatically count themselves a part of the readership these publications serve. This makes it easier for you as the advertiser to find people who are part of your target audience and to craft a message that appeals to their needs. Think of your own experience: you're more likely to notice ads in publications you read, because the messages are specifically geared to the target audience you belong to.[2]

The power of print was the key to an innovative media plan developed by Lintas:New York to make its client Van Heusen the biggest seller of men's dress shirts in the United States. Lintas found that over 60 percent of men's dress shirt purchases are made by women, so the agency decided to target women as the primary audience and men as the secondary audience. Instead of using television, which was Van Heusen's usual choice, Lintas suggested that the audiences could be reached more efficiently and effectively through magazines, specifically those with an editorial content in tune with the shirtmaker's style and quality message. To reach women, Van Heusen's ads ran in women's beauty and fashion magazines; to reach both women and men, the ads ran in large-circulation magazines such as *People*; and to reach men, the ads ran in business and men's fashion magazines. This campaign helped Van Heusen overtake arch rival Arrow for the first time in the company's 111-year history.[3]

Advertising in Newspapers

Despite vigorous competition from magazines (since the late 1800s), radio (since the 1920s), and television (since the 1950s), newspapers have traditionally attracted the largest share of advertising dollars in the United States. Local advertisers, especially retailers, spend the bulk of their advertising budgets on newspapers, and this spending is one reason daily newspapers enjoy 23 percent of all ad expenditures, compared with television at 22 percent and direct mail at 19 percent. However, the volume of newspaper advertising often fluctuates, depending on economic conditions. In the early 1990s, retailers such as Sears, Bloomingdale's, and Saks Fifth Avenue were hit hard by recession and industry changes, so they slashed their newspaper ad budgets, which hurt newspaper ad revenues. Of $30.7 billion in annual U.S. newspaper ad volume, local advertising accounts for $26.9 billion and national advertising accounts for the remaining $3.8 billion (see Exhibit 14.2).[4]

In an increasing number of cities, advertisers have fewer newspapers to choose from. At the start of the 1980s, over 150 U.S. cities supported two or more competing weekday newspapers; a decade later, only 81 cities had two or more.[5] Adults of all ages continue to read newspapers, but the overall percentage of people in the United States who read newspapers has been dropping. Roughly 63 percent of all adults now read a weekday newspaper, compared with nearly 78 percent in 1970. However, when you consider that 63 percent of adults translates into more than 115 million readers, you can see that newspapers still reach a large audience.[6]

TYPES OF NEWSPAPERS

As you know from your own experience, no two newspapers are exactly the same. That's why successful advertisers consider how various types of newspapers can help them reach their audiences. Newspapers can be classified according to frequency of publication, page size, audience, and market.

Frequency of Publication

Advertisers can choose between newspapers that are published daily and those that are published weekly. In the United States, 1,570 newspapers are *dailies,* published Monday through Friday. Two-thirds of these are evening newspapers, which are distributed starting in the afternoon. However, a growing number of dailies (such as *The Free Press* of Mankato, Minnesota) are switching to morning editions, which are distributed in the early morning.[7]

In addition to their weekday publishing schedules, an increasing number of U.S. dailies publish Sunday editions. During the 1980s, 99 new Sunday editions

EXHIBIT 14.2 **The Top 10 National and Top 10 Local U.S. Newspaper Advertisers**

The total amount spent by the top 10 national U.S. newspaper advertisers is dwarfed by the total amount spent by the top 10 local U.S. newspaper advertisers. The local-newspaper-advertisers category is dominated by large retail organizations, for which local advertising is a major portion of the overall promotional budget.

Rank	National Advertiser	National Newspaper Spending	Rank	Local Advertiser	Local Newspaper Spending
1	Fidelity Investment Cos.	$29.7	1	May Department Stores Co.	$303.5
2	General Motors Corp.	28.7	2	Circuit City Stores	186.9
3	Dreyfus Corp.	18.1	3	Federated Department Stores	175.7
4	IBM Corp.	17.6	4	R.H. Macy & Co.	171.3
5	AT&T Co.	16.9	5	Sears, Roebuck & Co.	165.9
6	American Express Co.	15.0	6	Kmart Corp.	129.0
7	Ford Motor Co.	14.7	7	Dayton Hudson Corp.	120.2
8	Dow Jones & Co.	14.6	8	Dillard Department Stores	117.0
9	Toyota Motor Corp.	14.5	9	Montgomery Ward & Co.	107.6
10	Hewlett-Packard Co.	13.2	10	Carter Hawley Hale Stores	106.4

Note: Dollars are in millions. 1992 data.

were launched, and today, nearly 900 newspapers produce Sunday editions. Anyone who's recently hefted a Sunday newspaper knows that they bulge with news, features, and ads; moreover, the average reader spends more time with the Sunday edition than with any weekday edition. That's good news for advertisers, especially for retailers that do business on Sundays (see Exhibit 14.3). Kmart's newspaper advertising schedule stresses Sunday editions because "research tells us Sunday is the one day of the week consumers have the time to read the paper, which means it's the day of the week consumers have the most time to read various Kmart ads and inserts," says Michael Moors, Kmart's director of advertising media.[8]

You can also buy space in the **Sunday supplement,** a full-color magazine distributed within the Sunday newspaper. Because the Sunday supplement is printed on higher-quality paper than the newsprint used for other sections, color reproductions are of higher quality, which attracts national advertisers such as Kraft General Foods. A newspaper may publish its own Sunday supplement, such as the *Bethlehem Sunday Magazine* put out by the *The Morning Call* in Allentown, Pennsylvania. Or it may distribute a syndicated supplement such as *Parade* (published by Advance Publications and delivered in more than 350 newspapers) or *USA Weekend* (published by Gannett and delivered in more than 380 newspapers).[9] Because of competition from syndicated Sunday supplements—and vastly improved newspaper color—fewer than 50 newspapers now publish their own supplements; the syndicated supplements have weekly audiences in the millions, which attracts national advertisers.[10]

Weekly newspapers (known as *weeklies*) are published once a week and generally serve smaller cities, towns, suburbs, and communities within large metropolitan centers. Weeklies concentrate on local news, sports, and personalities, and they often offer detailed entertainment and shopping listings. The number of weekly newspapers has dropped from 8,174 in 1960 to just over 7,400 today, but the number of people who receive weeklies has grown to more than 55 million.[11] Many people hold on to the weekly paper for several days to check the movie listings or to find restaurant ideas, so local retailers, restaurants, and movie advertisers are the mainstays of the weeklies' ad revenues. On the other hand, national advertisers rarely use weeklies: the cost of reaching 1,000 readers (CPM) is usually higher for weeklies than for dailies, and advertisers find that the two readerships tend to overlap.

Page Size

A second way to classify newspapers is according to page size. Newspapers are typically published in one of two sizes, broadsheet or tabloid. A **broadsheet** newspaper (also known as a *standard-size* newspaper) has a page size of about 22 inches deep by 13 inches wide, and each page is divided into six columns. Most daily newspapers in the United States are broadsheet newspapers; the *Detroit News* and the *Chicago Tribune* are two examples. In contrast, a **tabloid** newspaper has a page size of about 14 inches deep by 11 inches wide. National tabloid newspapers such as the *National Enquirer* and the *Globe,* which are sold at the supermarket checkout, are published in this tabloid page size. Many people think only of these newspapers when they hear the word "tabloid," but the term applies to any newspaper of this size, such as New York City's *Newsday,* which has a slightly narrower page.

In decades past, when advertisers wanted to buy space in more than one newspaper, they were frustrated by the variations in page size, ad size, and column format that often forced them to create a separate ad for each paper. These headaches evaporated in 1984 when most newspapers adopted the **standard advertising unit (SAU) system,** a consistent industrywide method of defining ad size (see Exhibit 14.4). In the SAU system, each column is 2 1/16 inches wide, and ad space is measured in terms of the **column inch,** a unit that's one inch deep by one column wide. Now advertisers can create materials in any of the 57 SAU sizes and know that their ads will fit any newspaper using the system.

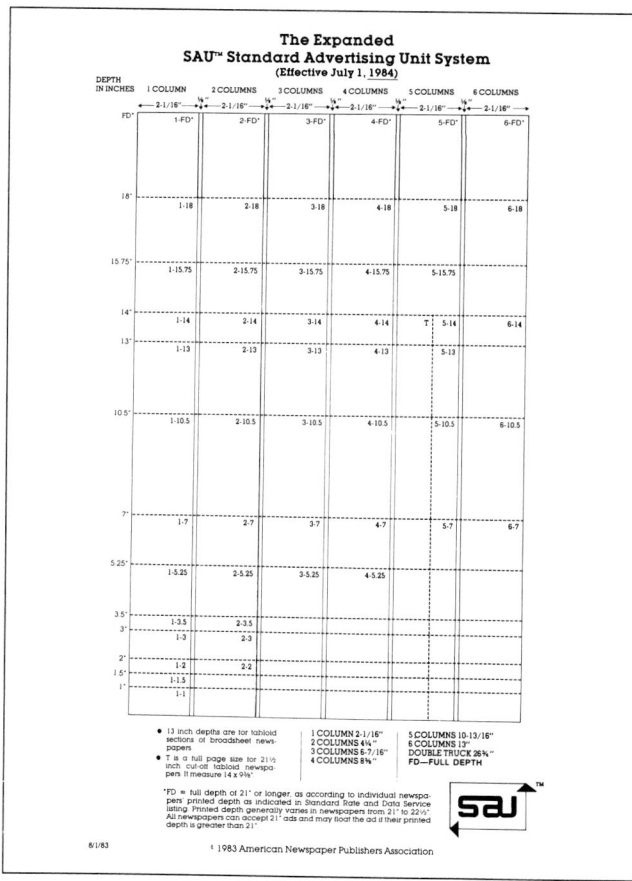

EXHIBIT 14.4
Describing Standard Newspaper Ad Sizes

The SAU grid gives advertisers and newspapers a common language for planning and accepting ads. By using the grid as a guide to size and shape, advertisers can be sure that the ads they design will fit in any newspaper that has adopted the system.

Audience

A third way to classify newspapers is in terms of the audiences they serve. Most newspapers report information of interest to the general population, so their audiences are broad, cutting across social, economic, and cultural lines. However, some newspapers serve specialized audiences, which makes them particularly good media vehicles for advertisers that target those groups. Special interest audiences range from businesspeople and military personnel to members of ethnic groups. For example, *The Wall Street Journal* (in the United States) and the *Nihon Keizai Shimbun* (in Japan) are avidly read by members of the business and financial community. *The Benning Patriot* is a military-oriented tabloid that reports on news of interest to active and retired military personnel who live near Fort Benning in Georgia.[12]

The number of ethnic newspapers published in the United States continues to expand as the minority population boom gains momentum. Approximately 200 U.S. newspapers, most of them weeklies, report news of interest to African-Americans; among the largest of these are the *New York Amsterdam News,* the *Michigan Chronicle,* and the *L. A. Sentinel.* More than 350 U.S. newspapers serve the Hispanic community, including dailies such as *El Diario de las Americas* in Miami and weeklies such as *Tu Mundo* in Costa Mesa, California.[13] In addition, newspapers now serve the Asian, Armenian, and Filipino populations in some cities. Although local stores, travel agents, and restaurants place most of the ads in these papers, a small but growing number of national advertisers have discovered that ethnic newspapers can reach specific target audiences cost effectively. For example, AT&T uses African-American, Asian, and Hispanic newspapers to promote local corporate events.[14]

Market

A fourth way to classify newspapers is according to the markets in which they're distributed. In the United States, most newspapers are distributed in only one town, city, or metropolitan area (see Exhibit 14.5). Examples of newspapers

EXHIBIT 14.5
Newspapers Reach Specific Geographic Markets

Newspaper advertising helps Citibank reach members of its target audience who live or work in particular markets. This ad, which appeared in the *New York Amsterdam News*, promotes a lending program available to housing developers who plan to build in certain sections of New York City.

We help finance affordable housing so a lot can be turned into so much more.

Thanks to developers committed to affordable housing, thousands of low and moderate income families have a place to call home. A dinner table to gather around and talk about their day – a room to tuck the kids in with a bedtime story.

At Citibank, we're committed to helping build better lives for more people. That's why we created CitiBuilders,™ a lending program that's been dedicated to helping rebuild the community for over 20 years. CitiBuilders offers a variety of financing options designed to work in conjunction with government financing.

Our loans can help developers purchase, construct or renovate low and moderate income multi-family housing units. CitiBuilders will help an empty lot reach it's full potential.

1-800-328-CITI

For more information about financing starting at $250,000, call 1-800-328-CITI, ext. 2212.

The CitiBuilders program is only offered through the Citibank Economic Development Banking Center.

CitiBuilders

©1993 Citibank, N.A. Member FDIC.

that reach local audiences are the *Greenville News* in South Carolina and the *Akron Beacon Journal* in Ohio. Although a few U.S. dailies, including *USA Today* and *The New York Times,* are distributed nationwide to an audience of millions, other countries have a stronger tradition of national newspapers. For example, the *Asahi Shimbun* is one of several daily newspapers read by millions throughout Japan, the *Frankfurter Allgemeine Zeitung* circulates throughout Germany, and the *News of the World* is a Sunday-only newspaper distributed across the United Kingdom.[15]

TYPES OF NEWSPAPER ADVERTISING

Various types of ads appear in newspapers, and just as newspapers can be categorized, these ads can also be categorized. The major types of newspaper ads are display advertising, classified advertising, and preprinted inserts.

Display Advertising

Display advertising consists of headline and body copy, illustrations, and other visual elements that set the message apart from the editorial material surrounding it. Large or small, in black and white or in color, display ads are designed to grab the reader's attention, and they may appear almost anywhere in the newspaper except on the editorial page (some newspapers don't run display ads on the front page or in other selected locations). As the name implies, *general display advertising,* also known as *national display advertising,* is placed by national advertisers to support brands available in local markets. *Local display advertising* is placed by retailers and local businesses, and it accounts for more than half of a newspaper's ad revenues (see Exhibit 14.6). Sometimes a local display ad is supported by a **cooperative advertising program,** popularly known as *co-op advertising,* in which a manufacturer pays part of the bill when a local-store ad features its brand; newspapers often have specialists available to help coordinate co-op advertising arrangements between manufacturers and retailers. See Chapter 17 for more details on co-op advertising.[16]

EXHIBIT 14.6
Local Display Advertising

Revenues from local display ads placed by retailers, businesses, and institutions such as the University of Phoenix typically account for more than half of a newspaper's advertising revenues.

Most of the time, newspapers charge a lower rate for local display advertising than for general display advertising, creating a rate differential that national advertisers complain is burdensome. In a recent survey, large general display ads were found to cost 75 percent more on average than the same-size local display ads. Newspapers defend the cost difference by pointing to the higher costs of servicing national advertisers and the 15 percent commission paid to their ad agencies. Gannett, for example, operates its own national sales office to sell national and regional advertising, and some newspapers hire media representatives to call on national advertisers and agencies; these costs are not incurred to sell local display advertising. Although most newspapers offer volume discounts when advertisers buy more display space, national advertisers contend that these price breaks don't go far enough. The Newspaper Association of America, a U.S. trade group, is working on a simplified cost-per-thousand pricing formula for national advertisers.[17]

Classified Advertising

In contrast to display advertising, which can include illustrations and other attention-getting visual devices, **classified advertising** consists of an all-text message positioned in the newspaper (or magazine) according to categories such as employment, automotive, and real estate. Classified ads typically account for about 35 percent of a newspaper's ad revenues and are used by individuals as well as by real estate firms, automobile dealers, employment agencies, and other businesses. Whereas regular classified advertising runs in small, uniform type, many newspapers also accept **classified display advertising,** which includes illustrations, borders, and other visual elements as a way of setting the ads apart from other ads in the classified section.

In recent years, classified ads have branched out beyond the traditional categories, advertisers, and methods. For example, *The Milwaukee Journal/Sentinel* in Wisconsin has created a special section called the Classified Ad-Venture in which children can place inexpensive ads to buy, trade, and sell baseball cards, video games, toys, and other items, or simply send a message to family and friends.[18] Also, more newspapers are inviting people in search of romance to answer "personal ads" in the classified section by telephoning their messages into a voice mailbox; the advertisers dial in later to hear the responses.[19]

Preprinted Inserts

A **preprinted insert** is an advertisement that's printed in advance and enclosed within the newspaper. Advertisers or their agencies can print any type of advertising material—brochures, catalogs, or postcards, in black and white or in color—and ship them to the publisher, where they are folded into the newspaper for delivery to readers. This distribution method generally costs advertisers less than using mail or door-to-door delivery. In many cases, advertisers can have their inserts delivered within a specified area to reach only the target audience.

A special form of preprinted insert is the **free-standing insert (FSI),** an insert containing cents-off coupons for a variety of products (see Exhibit 14.7). Many people habitually check and clip coupons from these ads in newspapers (and magazines); more than 80 percent of all coupons are distributed through FSIs. Food- and household-product manufacturers such as Kraft General Foods, Scott Paper, and Ralston Purina frequently use FSIs, especially on Sundays.[20] Chapter 17 discusses coupons in more detail.

ADVANTAGES OF NEWSPAPER ADVERTISING

Despite competition from other media, newspapers have remained a popular advertising medium because they offer advertisers a variety of advantages. These include market penetration, geographic selectivity, responsive timing, creative flexibility, and audience interest.

- *Market penetration.* Newspapers generally offer good market penetration

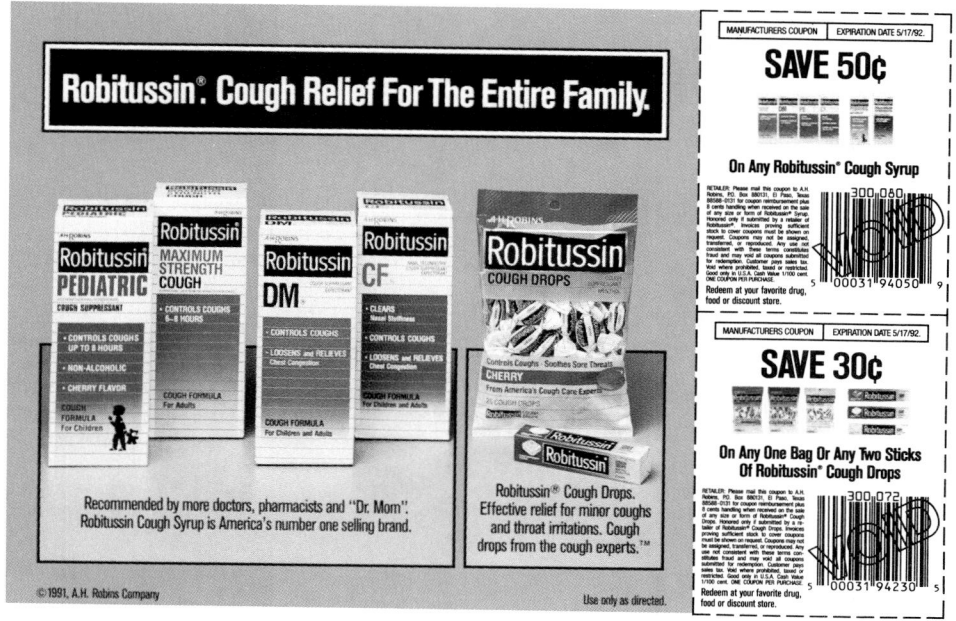

because their readership cuts across economic, social, and cultural lines. In two-newspaper markets, advertisers can penetrate virtually the entire market by advertising in both newspapers. Another way advertisers can improve penetration is to have the newspaper deliver the entire paper (or just the section with the ad) to local households that don't subscribe, a service known as *total market coverage.*[21]

- *Geographic selectivity.* Advertisers can target narrowly defined areas by running ads in the newspaper's *zoned editions* or *zoned sections* that are distributed only in specific parts of the market. For example, *The Sun,* a daily newspaper in San Bernardino County, California, publishes zoned sections that allow advertisers to select the best geographic areas for their messages. To avoid the expense and the waste of reaching people who won't travel far to shop, Gerrards, a two-store supermarket chain, now runs a weekly full-page ad in *The Sun*'s zoned food section, reaching only the area surrounding its stores.[22]

- *Responsive timing.* Daily newspapers have daily ad deadlines, so if you need to place or change an ad right away, you don't have to wait more than a day or two. (Preprinted inserts, special sections, and Sunday editions require a little more advance planning.) Furthermore, you can quickly gauge audience reaction to your ad. When the Sharper Image, an upscale gadget retailer, started using newspaper ads in Kansas City, Missouri, and in Buffalo, New York, it could tell right away that its ads were successful when store sales rose more than 80 percent during the week after the ads ran.[23]

- *Creative flexibility.* Newspapers offer many creative options for print advertisers, whether ads are large or small, all-text or illustrated, in black and white or in color (see Exhibit 14.8). Since *USA Today's* colorful debut in 1982, an increasing number of newspapers have adopted color printing technology; nearly 97 percent now print some news pages in color.[24] Among the last to move to color were *The New York Times* and *The Philadelphia Inquirer.* Now some newspaper advertisers will run only color ads. For example, Kraft General Foods used four-color newspaper ads to introduce its Fat Free salad dressings, bypassing black-and-white newspapers altogether.[25] However, the creative possibilities do not include sound or motion.

- *Audience interest.* Readers are interested in what they read in the newspaper, and this medium is the main source of information when people want to rent or buy a home, find a new job, or shop for a car. What's more, advertisers seeking

To see what a weekend at Residence Inn can do for the average couple, fold here.

Our Weekend Getaway is bound to bring the two of you closer together. Because here at Residence Inn everything you need is nearby. Free continental breakfast, a full kitchen, swimming pool, Jacuzzi™ And most important, each other. Just call 800-331-3131 or your travel agent for reservations at special low rates.

Weekend Getaway, $49-$79 a night.

EXHIBIT 14.8
Newspaper Advertisers Have Flexibility

Martin Agency, which created this striking full-page newspaper ad for Residence Inn, used both color and clever copy to involve readers in the ad message. Of course, the headline makes sense only in a print medium. Moreover, by surrounding the copy and color illustrations with a lot of white space, the agency ensured that the ad would stand out from other newspaper ads and editorial material.

specific target audiences can advertise only in the sections likely to be read by those targets. For instance, 84 percent of all male readers scan the sports section, so many advertisers see it as a good place to advertise products geared toward men.[26]

LIMITATIONS OF NEWSPAPER ADVERTISING

Although newspapers offer advertisers many advantages, they (like other media) also have limitations. Among these are reproduction constraints, limited targeting capabilities, short life span, and clutter.

- *Reproduction constraints.* Because of the coarse paper stock, the color printing process, and the fast turnaround time, the reproduction quality of most newspaper ads is limited. Even with the improved color reproduction possible with today's sophisticated printing processes, color newspaper ads do not look as good as they would in magazines. If color quality is a concern, newspaper advertisers can choose to use the Sunday supplements or supply preprinted inserts, but these options require more time and more expense.

- *Limited targeting capabilities.* As one of the mass media, newspapers can reach broad audiences, but they're not effective at isolating specific market segments. To counter this limitation, many newspapers now publish sections that appeal to specific audiences such as children, women, and ethnic groups. These special sections help advertisers build readership and therefore reach target audiences more effectively. For example, Superior Coffee & Foods advertises its Kayo children's chocolate drink in the *Chicago Tribune's* weekly KidNews section. This special section is geared to young readers aged 9 to 13, Kayo's target market, and it's distributed in neighborhoods where the product can be purchased.[27]

- *Short life span.* Most readers spend relatively little time with newspapers before putting them aside. The average reader spends 45 minutes reading one or more dailies during the day (62 minutes on Sunday); after clipping a coupon or tearing out an article, he or she has no further use for that day's newspaper.[28] As a result, newspaper ads have only a short life span. One way newspapers try to overcome this limitation is by creating special interest sections that readers save for later use. For instance, although separate television guides are commonly distributed by U.S. newspapers, *The Sun*, a London daily, only recently decided to include one with its Saturday edition. Because readers open these guides throughout the week, the ads may be seen more than once.[29]

- *Clutter.* Newspapers are filled with articles, photos, ads, and inserts, so an individual ad competes with a lot of clutter. More than 55 percent of the daily paper is devoted to advertising—more than 65 percent on Sunday. Using color, white space, and an eye-catching creative design can help cut through the clutter to grab the reader's attention.[30]

NEWSPAPERS TODAY AND TOMORROW

Contemporary newspapers are being challenged by other media on two fronts: audience interest and advertiser interest. As mentioned earlier, the percentage of adults who read daily newspapers has dropped, which is a source of concern for advertisers seeking to reach a large audience (see Exhibit 14.9). Whereas newspapers were once the public's only source of news and information, other media such as all-news radio and cable television now offer more immediate coverage of local, national, and international events. On the other hand, newspapers have both the space and the resources to report community news such as zoning-board meetings, two advantages that draw new readers and keep current readers involved.[31]

A key priority for many newspapers is building readership among adults aged 18 to 34. Although this age group reads newspapers less than any other age group, it's a prime target audience for many advertisers, so newspapers are looking for ways to attract this group. For example, to draw college-age readers, the *Knoxville News-Sentinel* has started *Campus Detours,* a free monthly newspaper distributed to 24,000 University of Tennessee students. Some newspapers court even younger readers: the *Chicago Tribune's* Spots section gives preteen children a special section of their own to enjoy, helping to build the newspaper audience of the future.[32]

EXHIBIT 14.9

Trends in U.S. Newspaper Readership and Advertising

Although weekday readership of U.S. newspapers has been dropping, weekend readership has rebounded in recent years, which is a positive trend for the many advertisers that place display ads or preprinted inserts in Sunday newspapers. At the same time, both national and retail newspaper advertising expenditures have fallen since their peak levels in 1991, reflecting nationwide economic problems as well as competition from cable television and other media seeking a larger piece of advertisers' budgets.

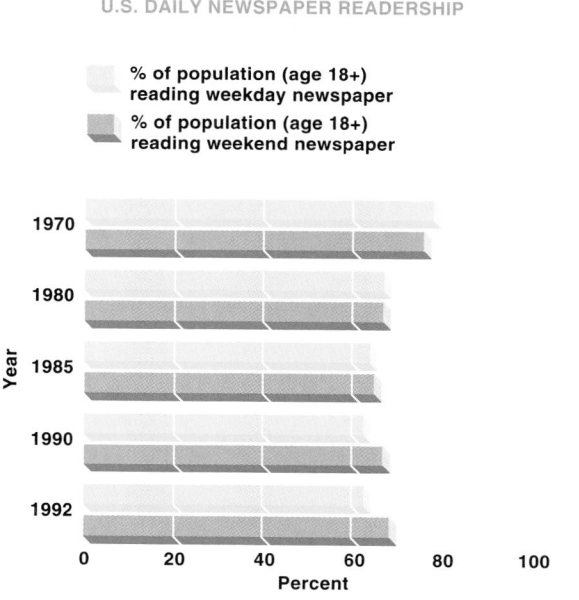

U.S. DAILY NEWSPAPER READERSHIP

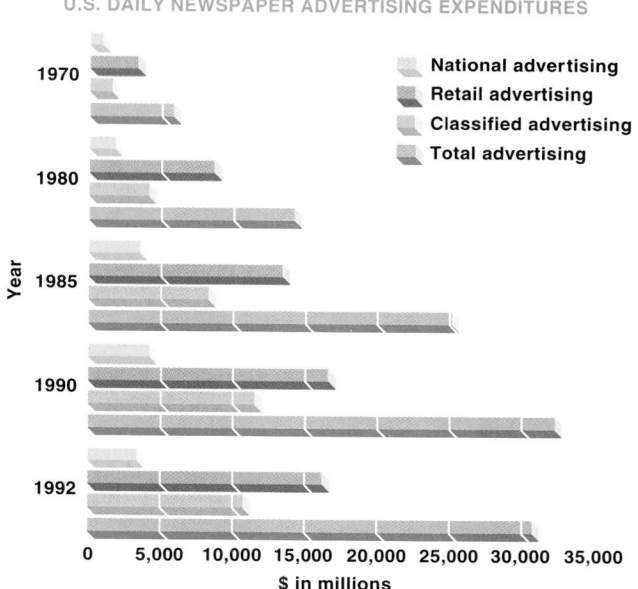

U.S. DAILY NEWSPAPER ADVERTISING EXPENDITURES

Strange as it may seem, another way newspapers are fighting for audience interest is by delivering news and advertising in another medium. Some newspapers have experimented with delivering news text via television and facsimile machines; more than 500 have set up pay-per-call telephone systems that readers can call for updated sports, weather, and other information. One alternative receiving a lot of attention is the electronic newspaper, accessed through a personal computer. For example, more than 4,000 subscribers now read Denver's *Rocky Mountain News* on their home computers, including text and color charts showing local, national, and business news as well as sports. Subscribers also get an advance peek at the following day's classified ads, and they can look through a library of articles on travel destinations and movie reviews. Electronic delivery looks so promising that *USA Today* has joined with Prodigy, the computer-based information service, to provide a national classified advertising service accessible to all Prodigy subscribers.[33]

In their quest for increased advertiser interest, newspapers are building new alliances. *The Washington Post* (in Washington, D.C.) has teamed up with *The New York Times* (in New York City) and the *International Herald Tribune* (which is distributed outside the United States) to allow advertisers to buy an ad in all three with one order. *The Washington Post* and *Newsweek,* both part of the Washington Post Company, now allow advertisers to buy space in both publications at a lower price than if the ads were placed separately in each publication.[34]

To draw more national advertising, many newspapers have joined newspaper networks that make it easier and often cheaper for advertisers to place ads in many markets. More than 100 such networks have been formed, including the Northwest Newspaper Network (in the Pacific Northwest) and Newspapers First (based in New York). These networks work closely with advertisers and agencies to tailor ad placements. For example, when General Motors launched the Saturn model, its agency, Hal Riney & Partners, bought $20 million worth of newspaper ads in more than 140 newspapers across the country through the Newspaper National Network, and the agency keyed the timing of the ads to the car's availability in each market.[35]

Finally, newspapers are introducing services to better compete with other media, especially media such as direct mail, which advertisers can use to reach audiences with pinpoint precision. One increasingly popular service is doorstep delivery of product samples (such as detergent, shampoo, cereal, or coffee) along with the newspaper. After Procter & Gamble tested the *Cincinnati Enquirer*'s door-to-door delivery service to distribute 250,000 samples of Vidal Sassoon shampoo one Sunday morning, it went on to use a national newspaper network to deliver 18 million samples of Pantene shampoo across the country in a single weekend. All samples arrive on the same day (which is a help when planning for expected response), and advertisers can run ads or coupons in the newspapers that carry the samples, another benefit.[36] In addition, more newspapers are developing computerized databases that contain extensive details about demographic, lifestyle, and other audience factors so that advertisers can analyze and target specific newspaper audiences.[37]

Planning Newspaper Advertising

Important elements to consider when planning and purchasing newspaper advertising include (1) how circulation and readership are measured, (2) how newspaper ad rates work, (3) how the mechanics of placing an ad operate, and (4) how to use the special services many newspapers offer.

MEASURING CIRCULATION AND READERSHIP

When you plan newspaper advertising, it's important to understand who will see your ad. One measure of a newspaper's reach is its **circulation,** the number of

Los Angeles Times

Times-Mirror Square, 130 S. Broadway, Los Angeles, CA 90053.
Phone 213-237-3000, 1-800-528-4637, TWX, 910-321-2460.

 ABC

Location ID: 1 NSNL CA   **Mid** 016171-000
Member: ABC Coupon Distribution Verification Service; ACB, Inc., NAA
MORNING, SATURDAY AND SUNDAY MORNING.
SHIPPING INSTRUCTIONS
Send address materals to Los Angeles Times, 130 S. Broadway, Los Angeles, CA 90012.
1. PERSONNEL
Pub/CEO—David Laventhol.
Exec VP Mktg—Lawrence M. Higby.
Dir Display Adv—Janis Heaphy.
Asst Dir Display Adv—Len Pomerantz.

9. SPLIT RUN
Non-commissionable mechanical charge of 390.00 for black and white and 780.00 mechanical charge plus color premium for black and 1 color. Ads must be of same size dimension and products.
25 inch minimum for black and white, 55 inch minimum for black and 1 color. Both ads must be same dimension.

11. SPECIAL DAYS/PAGES/FEATURES
Best Food Day: Thursday.

12. R.O.P. DEPTH REQUIREMENTS
Ads over 18 inches deep charged full col.

14. CLOSING TIME
Published Morning, Saturday and Sunday.

Day	Time	Closes	Day	Time	Closes
Mon	11 am	Fri	Fri	12 n	Wed
Tue	9 am	Mon	Sat	12 n	Thu
Wed	12 n	Mon	Sun	12 n	Thu
Thu	12 n	Tue			

SPECIAL SECTIONS

Day		Time	Closes
Calendar, View, Travel, Real Estate (Sun)		11 am	Tue
Main News, Financial, Sports		12 n	Thu
Food Section (Thu)		10 am	Mon

CLOSING TIMES
Camera-ready copy deadline 10 days preceding publication. 20 days for color. Reservations: 19 days subject to availability. Allow 9 days extra if typesetting required. No cancellation accepted after 17 days prior to publication.

MECHANICAL MEASUREMENTS
PRINTING PROCESS: Offset.
Type page size 8" wide x 10" deep.
5 cols. to page. 50 col. inches to page, each col. 10 inches.
Colors available: B/w 1 c; b/w 2 c, b/w 3 c.
Send copy and reservations to Magazine Advertising Division, TV Times, 6th Floor, Times Mirror Bldg., Los Angeles, CA 90053.

20. CIRCULATION
Established 1881. Per copy, daily .25; Sunday 1.00.
Net Paid—A.B.C. 9-30-93 (Newspaper Form)

NEWSPAPER DESIGNATED MARKET

	Total	NDM	Outside
MxSat	1,089,690	900,474	189,216
SatM	1,012,880	828,195	184,685
Sun	1,488,484	1,207,925	280,559

---

issues distributed each day (or each week, for a weekly publication). **Paid circulation** refers to the number of copies purchased through subscriptions and at stores and newsstands. In contrast, **controlled circulation** refers to the number of copies distributed free, whether by mail to selected audiences or in stores and on sidewalk racks. Circulation changes constantly as subscribers sign on or cancel and as newsstand or store purchases fluctuate. Newspapers must reassure advertisers who want to reach a certain number of people that the circulation figures are accurate. That's why many newspapers join independent auditing groups such as the Audit Bureau of Circulations (ABC), which verifies and analyzes its members' circulation.

Of course, any newspaper's audience is larger than its circulation, because each copy may be read by more than one person. Industry figures show that an average of 2.28 people read each of the daily newspapers sold in the United States; services such as Scarborough-Simmons Syndicated Research Associates investigate the number of readers per copy and the readership profile of specific publications.[38] By multiplying the average number of readers per copy by the circulation, you can estimate the **readership,** the total number of people who read a print vehicle. For newspapers (and magazines), the concept of readership is the same as audience; therefore, readership can be used to determine the number of people who see the publication in which an ad appears.

UNDERSTANDING NEWSPAPER AD RATES

Once you understand the newspaper's circulation and readership, the next step in planning an ad is to examine its rates. Every newspaper has a **rate card,** a printed schedule of its advertising rates, production specifications, advertising deadlines, and other details (see Exhibit 14.10). When you're considering more than one newspaper, you can use rate cards to compare ad rates and readership and to calculate the best use of your budget. You can also refer to the Standard Rate and Data Service publication *Newspaper Rates and Data* for a summary of rates, circulation, and other information. When a newspaper offers no discount for buying one or more ads, it's charging a **flat rate.** However, many newspapers offer a **volume discount** by charging less per ad when advertisers buy space repeatedly. In this case, an **open rate,** the highest rate for running a single ad, applies until more ad space is purchased and the advertiser qualifies for a discount. You pay less when you arrange a **contract rate** or an *earned rate,* a discount based on a a contract that indicates how many ads or how much space will be purchased during a period. However, if you don't buy as much space as your contract specifies, the publisher will bill you an additional charge, known as the **short rate.**

A newspaper's basic advertising rates cover only **run of paper (ROP),** also known as *run of press,* which means your ad can appear anywhere on any page. However, as you saw in Chapter 13, many media allow advertisers to request a

EXHIBIT 14.10
Looking Up Newspaper Advertising Rates

Advertisers that are considering adding the *Los Angeles Times* to their media schedules can consult the newspaper's rate card or Standard Rate and Data Service publications to determine ad rates, preferred positions, deadlines, and all the other information they need to place their ads.

special position—for which they pay more. Some newspapers charge a higher rate for ensuring that an ad will be placed in a **preferred position** specified by the advertiser, such as in a particular section. For an additional charge, advertisers can request a **full position,** a preferred position in which the ad is surrounded by editorial material on both sides or is placed near the top of the page. In addition, newspapers charge more for color ads than for black-and-white ads, another element to take into consideration.

Advertisers often have the opportunity to buy space in more than one newspaper at a **combination rate,** which is lower than the charge for buying space in each individual newspaper. Combination rates may be offered by a publisher that owns two newspapers in the same city, by a chain that operates newspapers in several cities, or by newspapers that belong to a network. By signing on for a combination rate, you can save money and extend the reach or frequency of your advertising, depending on the arrangement. Another consideration is the availability of a split run; as mentioned in Chapter 6, a newspaper can split its circulation so that an advertiser can test two or more variations of an ad in the same day's newspaper (or magazine) to see which is more effective. Many advertisers are willing to pay extra for the ability to see how a change in headline, body copy, or art can affect audience response.

PLACING NEWSPAPER ADS

When you place a newspaper ad, you fill in an **insertion order,** a form that specifies the date(s) you want the ad to run, the size the ad should be, any preferred position you require, the rate you'll be charged, and any production details the newspaper needs to prepare for the ad. Most national advertisers provide newspapers with ad materials in finished form, but local advertisers may ask newspapers to create their ads from information they supply. In such cases, the newspaper creates a **proof,** a trial print that's sent to the advertiser so the accuracy of the ad can be checked before it's scheduled to run. After the ad runs, the newspaper sends the advertiser or the agency a **tear sheet,** the actual page torn from that day's newspaper in which the ad appeared. The tear sheet serves as proof that the ad ran as agreed; if the advertiser or agency finds an error in the ad's position or reproduction (or any other error on the part of the newspaper), it asks for a rate adjustment or a free insertion.

National advertisers that advertise in many newspapers often have a hard time juggling multiple insertion orders and handling multiple bills after the ads have run. The Newspaper Association of America is implementing a one-order–one-bill system that simplifies the process for advertisers that buy space in many newspapers. This system may help newspapers win a larger piece of the national advertising pie.[39]

USING SPECIAL NEWSPAPER SERVICES

Nearly every big-city daily—and many smaller newspapers—offers a variety of special services to support advertisers' efforts. One common service is providing information about the newspaper's readers and about the community the paper serves. Typically, this information includes reader demographics such as sex, age, education, household income, and occupation; some publications also commission studies of reader purchasing patterns, neighborhood shopping habits, and other elements of interest to advertisers. The *Miami Herald* and other major dailies combine marketing information from outside sources with data about their subscribers to help advertisers determine the area where their best prospects live and the demographic profile of these people.[40]

Another special service gaining favor is the use of *loyalty marketing programs* that more closely link subscribers and advertisers. These programs provide subscribers with a card entitling them to discounts at area stores and businesses. "Advertisers just love it because it drives business into their stores," explains Larry Martin, circulation director for *The Arizona Daily Star* and the *Tucson Citizen,* two newspapers that jointly operate a loyalty marketing program dubbed "The Extra!

Card." More than 700 advertisers participate in this program, and subscriptions have jumped since its inception in 1990.[41]

Advertising in Magazines

Although magazines have been published in the United States since the late 1700s, they initially carried few ads. Their power as a national advertising medium grew after the Postal Act of 1879 granted magazines low-cost second-class mailing privileges. Thanks to this lower cost of distribution, magazines quickly built a national audience, which in turn attracted the interest of advertisers. By the turn of the century, magazines had become a major advertising medium for all types of products.[42]

Today, automotive, food, and household products are among the largest magazine advertisers (see Exhibit 14.11).[43] These advertisers find that magazines offer many creative possibilities in terms of color, space, and text. Just as important, they find magazines an effective medium for zeroing in on their target audiences, one of the key benefits this medium offers.

TYPES OF MAGAZINES

Like newspapers, magazines are so diverse that it's helpful to classify the various types. Magazines are commonly categorized by the three broad audiences they serve: (1) consumer, (2) business, and (3) farm.

Consumer Magazines

As the name implies, a **consumer magazine** offers information and entertainment for the general public, people who buy products for personal or family use (see Exhibit 14.12). Sold by subscription, on newsstands, and in stores, consumer magazines can be further categorized according to their editorial appeal. Some common editorial categories include general interest magazines (such as *Reader's Digest* and *People*), women's magazines (such as *Redbook* and *Glamour*), special-interest magazines (such as *Backpacker* and *Horse & Rider*), news magazines (such as *Time* and *Newsweek*), and shelter magazines (such as *Better Homes & Gardens* and *House Beautiful*).

Business Magazines

A **business magazine** contains information useful to people responsible for buying business products. Under this classification are three subcategories: the *trade publication,* which is edited for retailers, wholesalers, or other distributors;

EXHIBIT 14.11 The Top Magazine Advertisers in the United States

General Motors, the world's largest automaker, is also the largest user of U.S. magazine advertising. Magazine advertising helps GM reach a variety of target audiences with ad messages promoting individual products and product lines, including cars, trucks, and vans.

Rank	Advertiser	Magazine Spending
1	General Motors Corp.	$238.3
2	Philip Morris Cos.	219.2
3	Procter & Gamble Co.	164.7
4	Ford Motor Co.	161.7
5	Chrysler Corp.	151.5
6	Nestlé SA	118.3
7	Toyota Motor Corp.	107.6
8	Unilever	86.4
9	Nissan Motor Co.	76.3
10	Johnson & Johnson	68.2

Note: Dollars are in millions. 1992 data.

Your very own worldwide Citibank.

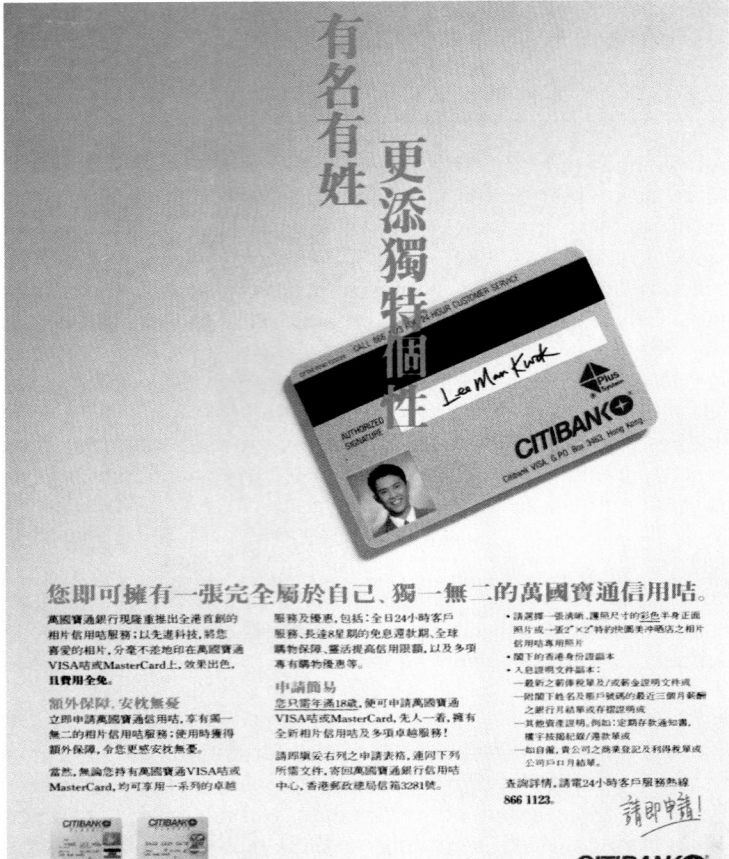

the *industrial magazine,* which is edited for manufacturers; and the *professional magazine,* which is edited for dentists, lawyers, physicians, or other professionals. When a business magazine is a **vertical publication,** it covers all aspects of a single industry; one example is *Computerworld,* which reports on the information-systems industry. In contrast, a **horizontal publication** covers a particular job function that exists in many industries; one example is *Information Executive,* which covers news of interest to computer-systems managers in any business. Ads in horizontal publications helped Lexmark reach its target audience of computer-systems executives who specify which printers their firms will purchase.

Farm Magazines

A **farm magazine** is published for farmers and for businesses that make or sell agricultural products. Most farm magazines offer business tips, review new agricultural goods and services, and discuss regulatory developments; some also cover issues related to farm life. *Progressive Farmer* and *New Farm* are two national farm magazines; *Pennsylvania Farmer* and *Niagara Farmers' Monthly* are two local farm magazines. Farm magazines can be further divided into classifications that reflect agricultural specialties; for example, greenhouse operators might read *Greenhouse Grower,* and soybean growers might read *Soybean Digest.*

ADVANTAGES OF MAGAZINE ADVERTISING

Although newspapers and magazines are both print media, the advantages they offer advertisers are not identical. Magazines are particularly powerful advertising vehicles because of their geographic selectivity, audience selectivity, creative flexibility, long life span, and audience interest.

- *Geographic selectivity.* Some magazines target relatively confined market areas, such as one region (*Southern Living*), one state (*South Carolina Farmer*), or

BETTER HOMES AND GARDENS TOP MARKETS

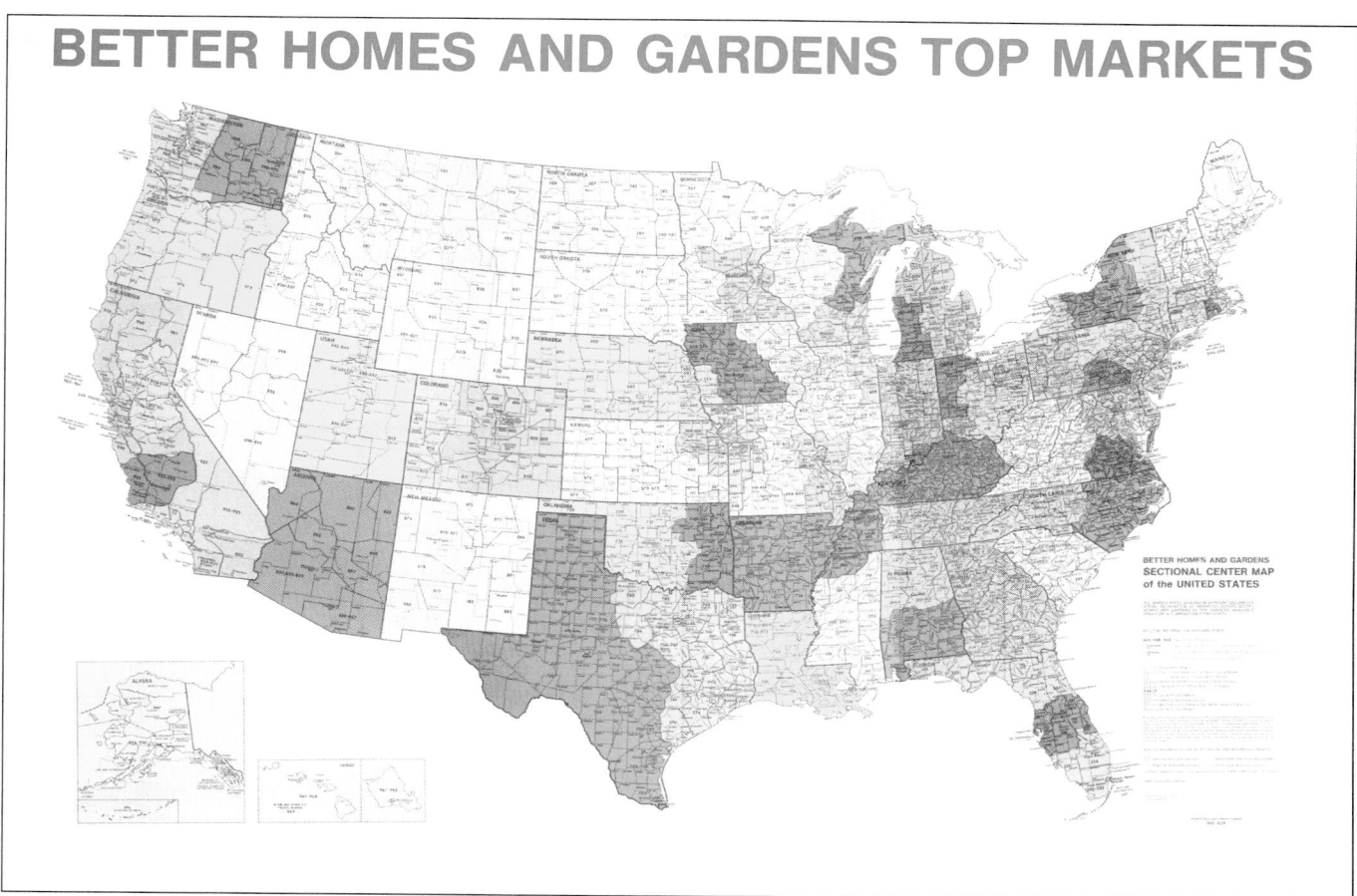

BETTER HOMES AND GARDENS
SECTIONAL CENTER MAP
of the UNITED STATES

one city (*Toronto Business*). This allows advertisers to easily reach target markets with little waste. However, most consumer magazines are national; to let advertisers target specific geographic areas, more than 250 of these magazines have developed a variety of regional editions (see Exhibit 14.13). For example, *Time* offers a choice of 11 regional editions, 50 state editions, and 50 city editions.[44]

- *Audience selectivity.* In the same way they offer geographic selectivity, many national magazines offer audience selectivity. *Time* slices its circulation into editions that reach people in specific age and income groups as well as people with certain behavioral characteristics such as a tendency to buy products by mail. Moreover, special-interest magazines allow advertisers to reach a specialized audience, sometimes with demographic selectivity. An example is *Prevention,* which covers personal health issues; advertisers selling health-related products—or those that simply want to reach an audience of health-conscious consumers—can buy space in the Family Edition (mailed to subscribers under 55 years old) or the Masters Edition (mailed to subscribers over 55 years old)—or both.[45]

- *Creative flexibility.* In addition to the same creative options newspapers provide, magazines offer superior color reproduction and the ability to use special paper for added effect. They can also help advertisers grab attention through *pop-up ads,* which expand into three dimensions, and ads with strings or tabs that reveal a logo or a creative element (see Exhibit 14.14). Further, magazines can bind in small product samples as well as scent and makeup samples, an especially handy way to introduce readers to new products. Ralph Lauren (among many others) finds scented ads effective for selling perfume. (However, some readers are allergic to or object to fragrance samples, so a few publications no longer accept scented ads.) Another option is the **outsert,** a

EXHIBIT 14.13
**The Geographic Selectivity
of Magazines**

Better Homes & Gardens offers advertisers the opportunity to reach 85 specific markets in the United States, one at a time or in any combination. This allows advertisers to buy space only in editions that reach the markets they're interested in.

EXHIBIT 14.14
Advertising in Three Dimensions

Cost Plus World Market placed this eye-catching ad in *San Diego Magazine* to reach local consumers who were interested in a wide variety of Easter items.

preprinted multipage ad that's enclosed in a plastic bag along with the magazine. For example, Revlon used a 68-page outsert delivered with the October 1992 issue of *Vogue* to reach fashion-conscious young women.[46]

- *Long life span.* Unlike newspapers, which are read and tossed out relatively quickly, magazines are around for a longer period. On average, people spend 61 minutes reading a magazine, and they frequently keep magazines on hand for future reference. People open *TV Guide* throughout the week to check television listings, and they often file publications such as *Gourmet* for future use. This means that your ad has more than one chance to get the audience's attention.

- *Audience interest.* Readers choose magazines on the basis of content, whether it's information about a favorite hobby or about business and finance. Whereas newspapers might cover a topic in one story or a few pages in a special section, readers seek out magazines because they can contain one or more longer articles (or even an entire issue) on the topic. Further, more than 80 percent of all readers find magazine ads to be informative, appealing, and helpful buying guides. And because magazines contain a mix of about 52 percent editorial and 48 percent advertising material, there's less clutter than in newspapers.[47]

LIMITATIONS OF MAGAZINE ADVERTISING

Despite the many advantages of magazines as advertising vehicles, the medium has several limitations. Among these are limited reach and frequency, long lead time for ad planning, and lack of sound and motion.

- *Limited reach and frequency.* The flip side of the ability to use magazines for pinpoint targeting is the lack of reach. *Reader's Digest* has a circulation of 17 million and is one of the largest in the United States, but the magazine reaches only a fraction of all U.S. households. Obviously, magazines aren't as mass market a medium as, say, television; if you want to reach a broad audience, you have to buy a lot of magazine space. What's more, most magazines are published monthly (some weekly), so you can't easily build frequency through one magazine. To overcome this limitation, advertisers may add more magazines or other media to their ad schedules.

- *Long lead time.* Because magazine printing processes require considerable preparation, advertisers have to submit materials well in advance of the publication date. The lead time for placing an ad can be as long as 90 days before a specific issue; once that deadline has passed, advertisers are locked in and can't change their ads, even if they need to respond to competitive shifts or other marketplace changes. To address this limitation, more magazines are shrinking the lead time and accepting ad materials as late as the day the issue goes to the printer.[48]

- *Lack of sound and motion.* Despite the creative advantages of good-quality color reproduction and the ability to use long copy, illustrations, and other options, magazine advertising (like newspaper advertising) relies primarily on visual techniques to communicate. Ordinarily, a magazine ad can't use sound (like radio) or motion (like television) to attract and maintain the audience's attention. However, some advertisers have experimented with tiny sound-making chips embedded in their ads. Also, technologies such as holography can add the illusion of movement to a magazine ad. For example, L.A. Gear has used hologram magazine ads to demonstrate the structural design of its athletic shoes.[49]

MAGAZINES TODAY AND TOMORROW

In this multimedia age, magazines must, like all other media, battle for audience and advertiser interest. Unlike newspapers, magazines draw their heaviest readership from people under the age of 44, and they appeal to a more educated, more affluent audience than television, which are advantages for advertisers that target those groups. However, many magazines have suffered because their audiences are being fragmented by an ever-growing number of media and vehicles. In addition to the 12,000 magazines already available, every year brings at least 500 new publications, which means stiff competition for the reader's interest. The competition has hurt the circulation of many general interest magazines.[50]

At the same time, many special-interest and lifestyle magazines, which are more targeted than general interest publications, have gained ground, and those that further strengthen their physical and editorial appeal are thriving. For example, the formerly low-budget *Workbasket* craft magazine upgraded to glossy paper stock and used more exciting, better photographed covers to entice new readers. The magazine kept printing its basic how-to instructions, and circulation (and advertising) surged, despite a price increase. Some specialized magazines, though, have stumbled by trying to broaden their appeal to attract more readers and advertisers. *Organic Gardening,* for instance, tried to expand its audience by moving beyond coverage of chemical-free gardening. This change alienated loyal readers and longtime advertisers, so the magazine recently returned to its original, narrower editorial emphasis, which is helping to woo back readers and advertisers.[51]

Like newspapers, magazines are exploring alternative methods of delivering information to readers. Some magazines, such as *PC Magazine, New York,* and *The New Republic,* offer articles through on-line computer services. Another delivery method is via CD-ROM (compact-disk read-only memory), which allows readers to retrieve text, pictures, and sound from a compact disk inserted into a special device attached to a personal computer. Among the publishers experimenting with CD-ROM delivery are the National Geographic Society, Reader's Digest, and Time Warner. For example, *Time* has produced special single-topic CD-ROM issues on such subjects as Desert Storm and the Olympics.[52]

To better compete with the electronic media, many magazines are harnessing technology to allow advertisers to do things they can't do in television or radio. One technology being applied is *ink-jet printing,* which enables a magazine to personalize advertising messages seen by individual subscribers (see Exhibit 14.15). Not long ago, Isuzu aimed customized ads in *Time, People,* and *Sports Illustrated* for selected subscribers in the carmaker's target audience. Ink-jet printing was used to print each person's name in the Isuzu ad in his or her issue. The ad prompted many to visit local car dealerships and test-drive Isuzu cars. Although ink-jet printing can add 35 percent or more to the cost of a four-color magazine ad, the novelty and higher impact may justify the extra expense.[53]

EXHIBIT 14.15
Taking Advantage of Ink-Jet Technology

Cargill used personalized ads in the *Farm Journal* to offer products geared to the specific needs of each subscriber whose name was incorproated into the ad using ink-jet printing.

In addition, more magazines are offering **selective binding,** a publication process in which the selection of editorial and advertising matter included in each issue can be customized for individual subscribers. *Farm Journal, Time, Child, American Baby,* and other magazines equipped to handle selective binding can analyze their subscriber databases to pick out segments that are attractive to advertisers and then assemble a magazine that includes articles and ads that are geared to each segment. For example, selective binding allowed Cadillac to reach specific audiences within the same magazine database with separate messages: ads aimed at young, affluent buyers promoted the Allante model, and ads aimed at mature buyers promoted the Fleetwood model. Selective binding gives advertisers the benefit of better targeting and subscribers the benefit of reading a magazine that more closely fits their needs and interests.[54]

Moreover, many magazines are forging relationships with other print vehicles and with other media to offer ad packages that help advertisers boost both reach and frequency at a lower cost. For example, Newsweek has arranged with Meredith (the publisher of women's magazines such as *Better Homes & Gardens*) and with Times Mirror (the publisher of men's magazines such as *Field & Stream*) to give discounts to advertisers that buy a minimum amount of space in two of the three companies' magazines. Kmart has taken advantage of this alliance by booking space in all three companies' magazines.[55] Going beyond print, research in seven countries (commissioned by magazine publishers) found that a combination of magazine and television advertising works better than television alone.[56] Thus, multimedia deals that include magazines may help boost the overall effectiveness of an ad campaign.

Finally, more magazines are moving into *custom publishing,* an arrangement in which a publisher develops a magazine specifically for a particular advertiser or group of advertisers. The advertiser's ad messages are interspersed with editorial copy geared to the particular interests and needs of that advertiser's audience. As a result, the media environment is ideal for the advertiser's message—and there's no competitive clutter. One example is *Sony Style,* which is published by Hachette Filipacchi for Sony. This twice-yearly guide to Sony products is sold on the

Few magazines (agricultural or otherwise) can match the pinpoint-targeting ability of *Farm Journal*, a monthly magazine that offers advertisers 451 ways to reach operators and owners of commercial farms and ranches in the United States. Through selective binding, the magazine offers a choice of 7 national and regional editions, 26 state editions, 8 crop-market editions, 5 special editions for larger producers, and 405 combinations of demographic factors such as crops, acreage, livestock, and degree of business involvement. That adds up to maximum targeting flexibility for advertisers—and an individualized issue for every reader.

Farm Journal's use of selective binding began in 1982, but its seeds were sown in 1953, when the magazine started printing regional editions. This innovation meant that Iowa farmers weren't forced to leaf through articles on farming in Georgia, and it had the additional advantage of allowing advertisers to reach regional audiences rather than sending their messages to the entire national readership. In 1962 *Farm Journal* added the ability to segment according to agricultural specialty when it introduced a special edition for hog producers; soon after, the magazine started special editions for beef, dairy, and cotton producers, as well as an edition geared to top-producing farms and ranches.

However, assembling each issue to meet the interests of individual readers and the needs of individual advertisers wasn't practical until *Farm Journal*'s printer, R. R. Donnelley & Sons, patented its computerized selective binding system. Here's how the process works. Depending on the reader's agricultural specialty and other details in *Farm Journal*'s database, Donnelley's system puts together a collection of articles, ads, and inserts for each subscriber. The equipment checks each issue to be sure that it's been assembled correctly for each subscriber; if it's incorrect, the system scraps it and assembles another. Then, using ink-jet printing, the equipment finishes the job by addressing each magazine and adding any personalized advertising or editorial messages.

Donnelley's system prints and assembles more than 700,000 issues of *Farm Journal* every month, entirely without human intervention. One month, the printer assembled 8,896 different versions of the same issue (counting the various combinations of advertising material, editorial material, and renewal messages to readers whose subscriptions were expiring). Indeed, because of this individualized approach, two farmers living across from each other might receive magazines that differ in size by as much as 50 pages and that contain different articles and ads.

Using *Farm Journal*'s selective binding capability allows advertisers to efficiently and accurately communicate with only their most likely prospects. For example, the magazine has helped Mobay Chemical reach wheat farmers throughout the United States—leaving out Florida, Alabama, Georgia, and the Carolinas—and it's helped Sperry New Holland target only the largest dairy, hay, and beef producers. As *Farm Journal* continues to expand its subscriber database, advertisers will find even more ways of using selective binding to reach their target audiences.

Apply Your Knowledge

1. *Readers sometimes ask* Farm Journal *to include articles and ads unrelated to their specialty. Should the magazine grant these requests?*
2. *How might a local Ford dealer use* Farm Journal *'s selective binding capabilities to advertise a new truck model?* ∎

---

newsstand like any other magazine. Similarly, Capital C Communications publishes *Pop Life* for Pepsi-Cola Canada, which mails the magazine to 250,000 Canadian teens twice a year.[57]

Planning Magazine Advertising

Just as in planning and buying newspaper ads, the essential elements in planning and purchasing magazine advertising include an understanding of circulation and readership, knowledge of the structure of magazine ad rates, familiarity with the mechanics of placing magazine ads, and awareness of the special services many magazines offer.

MEASURING CIRCULATION AND READERSHIP

Who will see your magazine ad? Circulation fluctuates from issue to issue as subscribers come and go or as retail sales go up or down, so many magazines base their advertising rates on **guaranteed circulation,** the minimum number of copies of a particular issue that will be delivered (see Exhibit 14.16). This assures advertisers that their ads will reach a certain number of people—and assures them

EXHIBIT 14.16   **The Circulation and Rates of Top U.S. Magazines**

Modern Maturity, a magazine published by the American Association of Retired Persons for its members (who are aged 50 and over), has by far the largest circulation of any U.S. magazine. Not surprisingly, its one-time rate for a four-color ad is considerably higher than rates for magazines with smaller circulations.

Magazine Rank	Magazine Name	Total Circulation	One-Time Four-Color Page Rate
1	*Modern Maturity*	22,879,886	$229,970
2	*Reader's Digest*	16,258,476	$153,600
3	*TV Guide*	14,498,341	$119,500
4	*National Geographic*	9,708,254	$142,915
5	*Better Homes and Gardens*	8,002,585	$143,000
6	*Family Circle*	5,283,660	$105,000
7	*Good Housekeeping*	5,139,355	$133,875
8	*Ladies' Home Journal*	5,041,143	$99,400
9	*Woman's Day*	4,810,445	$92,500
10	*McCall's*	4,704,772	$83,315

of a rebate if the ads don't. Magazines try to promise conservative guaranteed circulation figures; that way they lessen their chances of having to rebate money to advertisers. For example, during its second year of publication, *First for Women* spotted a rising sales trend, so it promised a guaranteed circulation of 3 million. However, the delivered circulation was only 2.6 million. The magazine worked out price adjustments for its advertisers—and lowered its guaranteed circulation.[58]

Recently, several major magazines such as *TV Guide, Redbook,* and *Time* have lowered their guaranteed circulation figures. This action runs contrary to the usual push toward higher guaranteed circulation as a way of raising ad rates and offering advertisers more reach. These voluntary decreases reflect a renewed focus on the core of loyal readers rather than on sheer numbers, and the emphasis on quality over quantity is starting to win support. "We at DDB Needham are now evaluating magazine audiences strictly on the basis of what we call core readers: people who really look forward to each issue," says Michael White, the ad agency's executive vice president.[59] Because these readers have a long-term bond with their magazines, they're likely to pay closer attention to (and have more confidence in) the ads.

A magazine's actual purchasers or subscribers make up its **primary readership.** In contrast, its **secondary readership,** also known as *pass-along readership,* reflects the number of people other than the original purchaser or subscriber who read the same copy. Readership research is used to gauge the size of a magazine's secondary readership, which can be many times the size of its circulation. For example, in addition to offering individuals paid subscriptions, *Health* distributes 125,000 copies of each issue to physicians and dentists for patients to read in waiting rooms. Over time, many patients will pick up those copies of *Health;* the number of people who read each issue makes up the magazine's secondary readership.[60]

In the same way that many newspapers belong to independent auditing organizations that verify their circulation statistics for the benefit of advertisers, magazines can join such services as the ABC and the Business Publications Audit of Circulation (BPA). For controlled-circulation magazines, which are distributed free, the auditing organization can also spot-check to see whether the recipients have completed questionnaires that show they're qualified to get the publication. This verification is important for advertisers that are paying to reach people in specific industries or job titles through targeted special-interest magazines.

UNDERSTANDING MAGAZINE AD RATES

Magazines prepare rate cards that show not only their ad rates but also their production specifications, policy on agency commissions, and other information needed to place an ad (see Exhibit 14.17). In addition, you can look up magazine

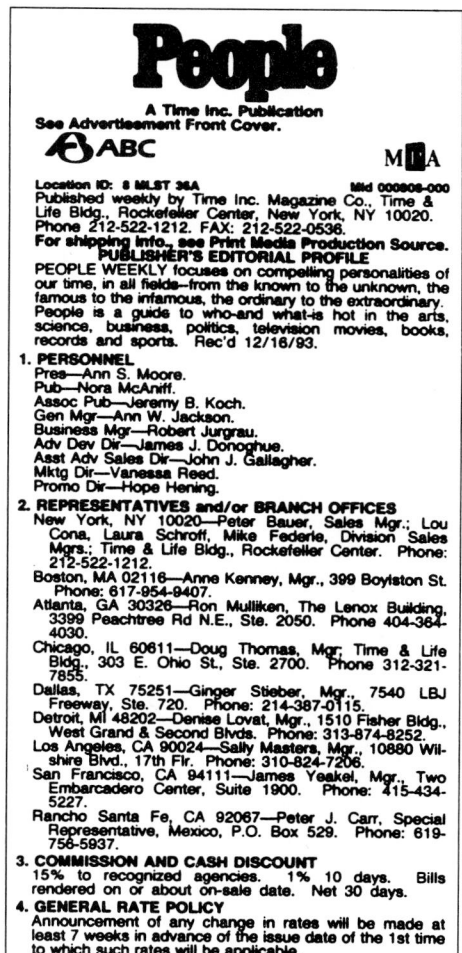

People

A Time Inc. Publication
See Advertisement Front Cover.

Ⓐ ABC   M🅱A

Location ID: 8 MLST 36A   Mid 000908-000
Published weekly by Time Inc. Magazine Co., Time & Life Bldg., Rockefeller Center, New York, NY 10020. Phone 212-522-1212. FAX: 212-522-0536.
For shipping info., see Print Media Production Source.

PUBLISHER'S EDITORIAL PROFILE
PEOPLE WEEKLY focuses on compelling personalities of our time, in all fields—from the known to the unknown, the famous to the infamous, the ordinary to the extraordinary. People is a guide to who-and what-is hot in the arts, science, business, politics, television movies, books, records and sports. Rec'd 12/16/93.

1. PERSONNEL
Pres—Ann S. Moore.
Pub—Nora McAniff.
Assoc Pub—Jeremy B. Koch.
Gen Mgr—Ann W. Jackson.
Business Mgr—Robert Jurgrau.
Adv Dev Dir—James J. Donoghue.
Asst Adv Sales Dir—John J. Gallagher.
Mktg Dir—Vanessa Reed.
Promo Dir—Hope Hening.

2. REPRESENTATIVES and/or BRANCH OFFICES
New York, NY 10020—Peter Bauer, Sales Mgr.; Lou Cona, Laura Schroff, Mike Federle, Division Sales Mgrs.; Time & Life Bldg., Rockefeller Center. Phone: 212-522-1212.
Boston, MA 02116—Anne Kenney, Mgr., 399 Boylston St. Phone: 617-954-9407.
Atlanta, GA 30326—Ron Mulliken, The Lenox Building, 3399 Peachtree Rd N.E., Ste. 2050. Phone 404-364-4030.
Chicago, IL 60611—Doug Thomas, Mgr; Time & Life Bldg., 303 E. Ohio St., Ste. 2700. Phone 312-321-7855.
Dallas, TX 75251—Ginger Stieber, Mgr., 7540 LBJ Freeway, Ste. 720. Phone: 214-387-0115.
Detroit, MI 48202—Denise Lovat, Mgr., 1510 Fisher Bldg., West Grand & Second Blvds. Phone: 313-874-8252.
Los Angeles, CA 90024—Sally Masters, Mgr., 10880 Wilshire Blvd., 17th Flr. Phone: 310-824-7206.
San Francisco, CA 94111—James Yeakel, Mgr., Two Embarcadero Center, Suite 1900. Phone: 415-434-5227.
Rancho Santa Fe, CA 92067—Peter J. Carr, Special Representative, Mexico, P.O. Box 529. Phone: 619-756-5937.

3. COMMISSION AND CASH DISCOUNT
15% to recognized agencies. 1% 10 days. Bills rendered on or about on-sale date. Net 30 days.

4. GENERAL RATE POLICY
Announcement of any change in rates will be made at least 7 weeks in advance of the issue date of the 1st time to which such rates will be applicable.

6. COLOR RATES

	Natl. Iss	Spec. Iss	Year-End Dbl. Iss
2-Color:			
1 page	106,500.	122,000.	144,000.
2 cols	92,500.	105,500.	124,500.
1/2 page	72,500.	83,000.	98,000.
1 col	50,000.	57,000.	67,000.
1/2 col	25,500.	29,000.	34,500.
	Natl. Iss	Spec. Iss	Year-End Dbl. Iss
4-Color:			
1 page	106,500.	122,000.	144,000.
2 col	92,500.	105,500.	124,500.

7. COVERS

	Natl. Iss	Spec. Iss	Year-End Dbl. Iss
4-Color:			
4th cover	138,500.	158,500.	187,000.

2nd & 3rd covers are charged at the 4/C full page rate.

8. INSERTS
Available.

9. BLEED

	Natl	Spec iss	Yr end dbl
BLACK AND WHITE:			
1 page	95,450.	108,675.	128,225.
2 col	76,475.	87,400.	102,925.
1/2 page	60,950.	69,000.	81,650.
1 col	40,825.	46,000.	54,625.
1/2 col	23,000.	25,875.	30,475.
COLOR RATES:			
2-Color:			
1 page	122,475.	140,300.	165,600.
2 col	106,375.	121,325.	143,175.
1/2 page	83,375.	95,450.	112,700.
1 col	57,500.	65,550.	77,050.
1/2 col	29,325.	33,350.	39,675.
4-Color:			
1 page	122,475.	140,300.	165,600.
2 col	106,375.	121,325.	143,175.
1/2 page	83,375.	95,450.	112,700.
1 col	57,500.	65,550.	77,050.
1/2 col	29,325.	33,350.	39,675.
COVERS:			
4th cover	159,275.	182,275.	215,050.
PEOPLE 1,575:			
B/W Page	52,900.	60,375.	71,300.
2-C Page	67,850.	77,625.	91,425.
4-C page	67,850.	77,625.	91,425.
Other bleed, extra			15%

12. SPLIT-RUN

PEOPLE 1,575
Advertisers can purchase 1/2 of People's circulation -a perfect A/B split- so that every other national copy contains their message. People 1,575 is limited to full size run-of-book pages in all 1993 issues.

	(*)	(†)	(**)
BLACK AND WHITE RATES:			
1 page	46,000.	52,500.	62,000.
COLOR RATES:			
2-Color:			
1 page	59,000.	67,500.	79,500.
4-Color:			
1 page	59,000.	67,500.	79,500.

EXHIBIT 14.17
Checking Magazine Rates

Advertisers can look up information about a magazine's current ad rates, production specifications, preferred positions, and other details in the rate card or in the appropriate Standard Rate and Data Service publication.

rates in two Standard Rate and Data Service publications, *Consumer Magazine and Agri-Media Rates and Data* and *Business Publication Rates and Data.* However, rate cutting has become more common in recent years as magazines compete more vigorously for ad dollars, so rate cards are sometimes seen merely as a starting point for negotiation. In the bridal magazine category, for example, competition has prompted magazines such as *Brides, Your New Home, Bridal Guide,* and *Elegant Bride* to book ads at rates significantly lower than those on their rate cards, offering deep discounts in exchange for more volume. Similar rivalries among other magazines have led to rate cutting in other categories.[61]

Like newspaper rates, magazine rates differ depending on the frequency of insertions, the use of color, and the size of the ad. Magazines have separate rates for four-color printing, metallic inks, and other uses of color that add zing. Many offer the option of using a **bleed page,** in which the background color of the ad runs all the way to the edge of the page. There's usually an extra charge for this option, but it can help an ad stand out more than a white border (see Exhibit 14.18). Ad size is also an effective way to attract attention; common magazine ad sizes include the two-page spread (which takes up facing pages) and full-page, half-page, third-page, and quarter-page ads. Some advertisers buy full-page or fractional-page ads in special combinations designed to catch the reader's eye.[62] Another option is the **gatefold,** an extra-wide page folded inward that opens like a gate to present the ad. Despite the extra cost, many advertisers use gatefolds because of their added impact; for example, Ford used a gatefold on the inside front cover of *People* and in other magazines to introduce the Probe GT.

Run-of-press ads can appear anywhere in the magazine, so they cost less than preferred positions. Preferred magazine positions include the front cover, known as the *first cover;* the front inside cover, known as the *second cover;* the inside back

Discover your complexion.

Dévoilez votre teint.

Trois effets magiques, issus de l'alliance du soin et du maquillage
pour mettre votre teint en lumière.
Hydratant, le nouveau fond de teint Estompe Givenchy Beauté
améliore la cohésion inter-cellulaire.
Lissant, il gomme les imperfections de l'épiderme et exerce
une action tenseur instantanée.
Matifiant, il assure au maquillage un fini très doux et une tenue
longue durée. Votre teint est aussitôt éclatant de naturel.
Les teints Estompe existent en six nuances:
porcelaine, lumière, vanille, sable, soleil ou épice.

LES TEINTS ESTOMPE

GIVENCHY

EXHIBIT 14.18
The Impact of a Bleed Page

The stunning color in this Givenchy magazine ad stretches to the edge of the page because the advertiser specified the use of a bleed page.

cover, known as the *third cover;* and the outside back cover, known as the *fourth cover.* Few U.S. publications sell space on the first cover; an exception is *Publishers Weekly,* a trade magazine for the book publishing industry. Research suggests that ads placed in cover positions may gain more attention than ads on inside pages, so some advertisers sign long-term contracts (and pay premium rates) to keep such positions. Another preferred position that grabs reader attention is opposite the table of contents or adjacent to one of the more popular editorial features.[63] Despite the higher rates, creative use of position, size, and space can help a magazine ad really stand out (see Exhibit 14.19).

PLACING MAGAZINE ADS

When you place magazine ads, keep in mind three key dates: the cover, the on-sale, and the closing dates. The **cover date** is the date that appears on the magazine's cover; you identify which issue you want to advertise in by referring to this date. The cover date is often later than the **on-sale date,** which is the date the magazine goes on sale in stores. The on-sale date may be the first day a magazine appears on the newsstand, or it may reflect a range of dates such as the week a magazine is to be sold. By referring to the on-sale date, you can determine exactly when readers will see a specific issue. The earliest date you have to worry about is the **closing date,** the deadline for submitting advertising materials for a particular issue. The closing date can be anywhere from a few days to a few weeks before the on-sale date.

When you prepare your ad, be sure it fits the page size of the magazines you use. The basic magazine page measures approximately 8 by 11 inches; *Newsweek* appears in this size, as do many popular magazines. Pages in larger magazines measure about 11 by 14.5 inches or even larger; *Advertising Age* is printed in this size. Pages in the small or digest-size magazine measure about 5 by 7 inches; *Reader's Digest* is published in this size. Although it's rare, magazines do change page sizes to keep up with competitors or to accommodate advertisers. For

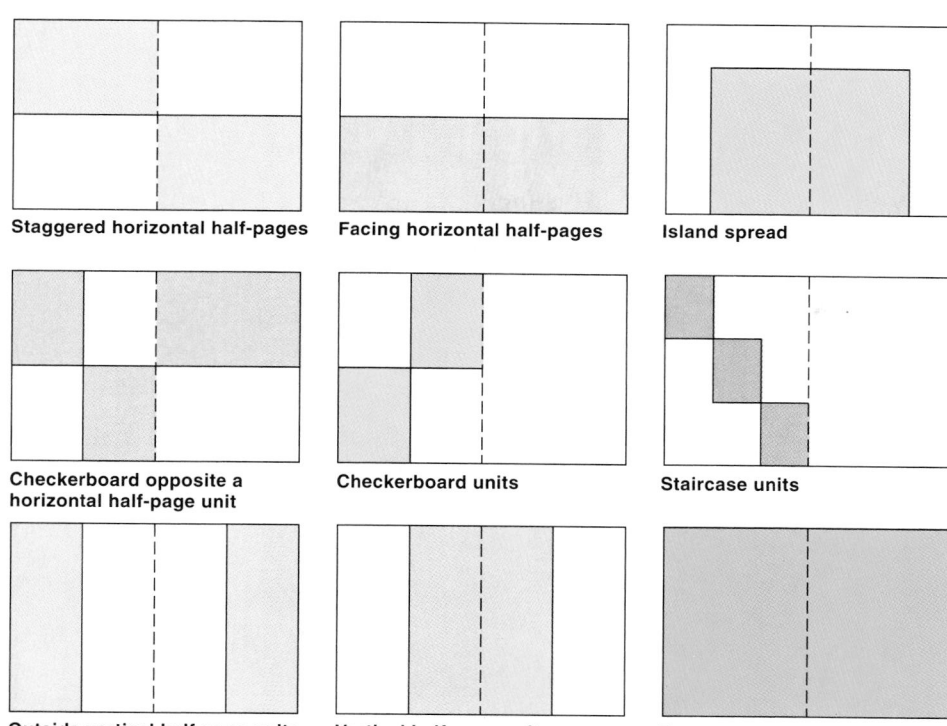

Staggered horizontal half-pages

Facing horizontal half-pages

Island spread

Checkerboard opposite a horizontal half-page unit

Checkerboard units

Staircase units

Outside vertical half-page units on a spread

Vertical half-page units across the gutter on a spread

Two-page spread

EXHIBIT 14.19

Using Size and Space in Magazine Ads

Depending on your creative approach, your budget, and the options offered by individual magazines, you can use ad size and shape in a variety of ways. Checkerboard and staircase units, for example, are used less frequently than many other combinations, so they tend to attract reader attention. On the other hand, a two-page or island spread can dominate the layout, drawing the reader's attention because of its size and position.

example, after 25 years in digest size, *Expecting* changed to a basic size of 7⅞ by 10⅕ inches in 1993. The change helped the magazine compete more effectively with its rivals (all basic size), and it offered new creative options for advertisers.[64]

As with newspapers, you use an insertion order to reserve your magazine ad and to set out details such as size, color, and preferred position. Once the ad has been created, the ad agency will show you a proof before your ad runs. After your ad runs, the magazine will send a tear sheet to prove that the ad ran exactly as scheduled.

USING SPECIAL MAGAZINE SERVICES

Like newspapers, nearly every major magazine (and many smaller magazines) offers detailed information to help advertisers and agencies evaluate the potential match between their target audiences and the magazine's readers. (In addition, as discussed in Chapter 6, you can buy syndicated studies from SMRB, MRI, and other research firms that collect and analyze data about the demographics, lifestyle, and product usage of the readers of many larger magazines.) Some magazines also conduct research that helps advertisers learn how readers perceive their ads or how a particular combination of editorial and advertising is likely to be perceived.[65]

Many magazines offer advertisers the opportunity to buy space in an **advertorial,** a special advertising section within the magazine in which ads are interspersed with related editorial material on a single theme. Advertorials focus reader attention on one topic to create a good editorial environment for related ads. For example, *Reader's Digest* periodically runs an advertorial called *Food Digest,* filled with food and appliance ads and featuring recipes using advertisers' brands. Ralston Purina, Black & Decker, and the National Dairy Board are just some of the advertisers that have bought space in this section.[66]

Another service many magazines provide is merchandising support. This service helps tie a magazine advertising campaign to the wholesalers and retailers that sell the product. For example, a magazine may provide stores with countertop displays featuring a copy of the manufacturer's ad; this reinforces the ad message and links the magazine's credibility with the product in a tangible way. Magazines

Advertorials have become a way of life for many magazines. Originally used to lure advertisers that ordinarily didn't buy space in a particular magazine, advertorials have evolved into a service to keep long-term advertisers happy, help ads stand out amid the clutter, and give advertising messages the boost of a friendly, editorial-like setting. Advertorials have become so popular that advertisers buy nearly 7,000 advertorial ad pages every year. However, critics say the use of advertorials raises two ethical issues. First, critics fear readers may be fooled into thinking they're reading regular editorial material. Second, critics object to the influence a sponsoring advertiser may wield over an advertorial's content.

As an advertising technique, the advertorial is little more than a decade old. In the beginning, magazines used advertorials to sign new advertisers. For instance, women's magazines developed advertorials on family cars to attract auto manufacturers that didn't usually buy space in those magazines. The magazines hoped to convince these new advertisers to switch from a one-time test to a longer-term commitment.

For their part, advertisers have come to see advertorials as hooks to draw attention to their messages within a supportive editorial environment. For example, readers of *Snow Country* are likely to enjoy an advertorial on ski vacations and to react positively to the adjacent ads placed by ski resorts. Further, when an advertiser sponsors an entire advertorial section, it buys the right to all the ads in that section and the freedom to place the ads anywhere in the section. This eliminates competition from other ad messages.

The advertorial is controversial because it's designed to blend with the magazine design, so it may be mistaken for regular editorial matter rather than material written specifically as a background for advertising. As a result, some worry that these sections may fool readers into thinking that the featured products are being discussed objectively. To address this concern, industry guidelines call for advertorials to have a distinctive look that can be distinguished from the rest of the magazine; they also require that an advertorial be clearly marked "Special Advertising Section," "Special Advertising Supplement," or a similar title.

Of course, a sponsor buying an entire advertorial would probably expect to decide the section's focus and theme. This leads directly to the second ethical question: How much control

This advertorial about investing in mutual funds appeared in *Time*.

should an advertiser have over the material in an advertorial? Should the advertiser have the right to see and approve the editorial matter that surrounds its ads? Some experts argue that giving advertisers editorial control violates the traditional separation of editorial and advertising functions and may ultimately compromise the magazine's integrity in the eyes of its audience.

The Magazine Publishers of America and the American Society of Magazine Editors, two trade groups, have established voluntary guidelines to help magazines come to grips with these ethical questions. However, as advertisers continue to push for special services—and as advertorials continue to show up in every type of magazine, from *Sesame Street Magazine Parent's Guide* to *Newsweek*—these issues are likely to be debated for some time.

What's Your Opinion?
1. *Should magazines disclose any advertiser involvement in the development of the editorial matter in an advertorial section? Why or why not?*
2. *Do you think readers have become so accustomed to seeing advertorials that they dismiss them as nothing more than lengthy advertisements? Explain.* ■

also create special events such as contests and entertainment to more directly involve readers with the advertiser and its product (see Exhibit 14.20).

For example, *Rolling Stone* enticed snack maker Frito-Lay to buy an extensive ad schedule after the magazine developed a national package of comedy shows titled *The Rolling Stone/Doritos Cool Ranch Flavor Tortilla Chips Cool Comedy Nights*. The Doritos brand was featured at each performance around the country and in a special comedy issue of the magazine. Frito-Lay's message reached all 1.2 million *Rolling Stone* subscribers as well as the estimated 20 million people exposed through the extensive publicity.[67]

Summary

Newspapers and magazines are the two main print media. Newspapers can be classified in four ways: (1) according to their frequency of publication, which can be daily or weekly and which can include a Sunday edition and a Sunday supplement; (2) according to page size, which can be either broadsheet or tabloid; (3) according to audience, which can be general interest or special interest; and (4) according to where they're distributed, which can be local or national. Newspaper advertisements can be classified into three broad categories: display advertising, classified advertising, and preprinted inserts.

Among the advantages of newspaper advertising are good market penetration, geographic selectivity, responsive timing, creative flexibility, and audience interest. However, newspaper advertising has limitations, which include reproduction constraints, limited targeting capabilities, short life span, and clutter. Newspaper circulation is measured according to the number of issues that are distributed each day or during the period covered by a single issue. Paid circulation measures the number of copies purchased through subscriptions and at stores and newsstands; controlled circulation measures the number of copies that are distributed free. A newspaper's readership can be estimated by multiplying the average number of readers per copy by the circulation.

A newspaper rate card shows advertising rates, production specifications, deadlines, and other details. When a newspaper offers no discount for buying more than one ad, it's charging a flat rate; if it offers a volume discount, it charges less per ad for repeat purchases. An open rate, the highest rate for running one ad, applies until the advertiser qualifies for a volume discount. Advertisers pay less when they arrange a contract rate, a discount based on a contract for purchasing a set number of ads or a set amount of space. Basic advertising rates cover run of paper, in which the ad can appear anywhere on any page; some newspapers charge more for placing ads in preferred positions such as in particular sections. A full position, which usually costs more, is a preferred position in which the ad is surrounded by editorial material on both sides or is placed near the top of the page. When an advertiser buys space in more than one newspaper, it may receive a combination rate that's lower than the rate each individual newspaper would charge.

Magazines can be categorized according to the three broad audiences they serve: (1) consumer, (2) business, and (3) farm. Among the advantages of magazine advertising are geographic selectivity, audience selectivity, creative flexibility, long life span, and audience interest. Magazine advertising has some limitations, including limited reach and frequency, long lead time for ad planning, and lack of sound and motion. Magazine rate cutting has become more prevalent; ad rates can vary depending on the frequency of insertions, the use of color, the size of the ad, and the ad's position—whether run of press or preferred. The cover date is the date that appears on the magazine's cover, the on-sale date is the date the magazine goes on sale, and the closing date is the deadline for submitting ads for a given issue.

Key Terms

advertorial 395
bleed page 393
broadsheet 375
business magazine 385
circulation 382
classified advertising 378
classified display
    advertising 378
closing date 394
column inch 375

combination rate 384
consumer magazine 385
contract rate 383
controlled circulation 383
cooperative advertising
    program 377
cover date 394
display advertising 377
farm magazine 386
flat rate 383

Meeting an Advertising Challenge at Lexmark International

A CASE FOR CRITICAL THINKING

When Lexmark International ventured out on its own after years in the IBM family, chairman Marvin Mann faced a double advertising challenge. First, he wanted to boost sales of Lexmark's products, including a new line of laser printers that competed with Hewlett-Packard's market-dominating models. Second, he had to build awareness of the Lexmark brand name and prepare his target audience for the phaseout of the respected IBM brand name.

To explain the features and benefits of the new products, Lexmark would need lots of copy and perhaps the opportunity to show samples of the printers' output. Moreover, because the company was targeting businesspeople rather than consumers, it needed vehicles that reached this specialized audience. The ad agency, Lintas:New York, recommended the use of business magazines (such as Business Week), computer magazines (such as Computer World), and a few newspapers that reach national business audiences (such as The Wall Street Journal).

The agency developed full-page ads that showed the products and provided details about their performance. By discussing specific features and benefits of Lexmark laser printers, the ads helped build brand awareness and differentiate the models from competing products. In addition, the ads established credibility by including a sentence or two in the body copy about Lexmark's evolution from an IBM division to an independent company.

The advertiser and its agency also looked ahead to replacing the IBM brand name with the Lexmark brand name. They devised a four-stage process for phasing in the Lexmark name in all product advertising. In stage 1, the IBM brand name would appear alone; in stage 2, the IBM name would loom large but would be accompanied by the phrase " . . . by Lexmark"; in stage 3, the IBM name would be dwarfed by the phrase " . . . by Lexmark"; and in stage 4, only the Lexmark name would appear.

Supported by a series of copy-intense print campaigns, Lexmark's sales and profits have grown in the years since it spun off from IBM. To see whether the advertising is building awareness of the Lexmark brand name, Mann is commissioning yearly audience surveys. By comparing each year's level of brand-name awareness with the previous year's level and with the level measured during Lexmark's first year of independence, Mann will be able to see just how effective his print advertising really is.

Your Mission: You've joined the staff of Lintas:New York as a print media specialist. Use what you've learned about the print media to select the best answer to the following questions posed by Marvin Mann.

1. In addition to making laser printers, Lexmark makes printer supplies (such as toner cartridges). Mann wants your suggestion about the best way to use magazine advertising to encourage purchases of Lexmark printer supplies.
   a. Buy ads in three nationwide, monthly office administration magazines to reach office managers, secretaries, and other users of Lexmark printers. Run the same ad in all three magazines during the same month. That way, the members of your target audience are likely to be exposed to your ad message no matter which magazine they open that month.
   b. Place the ad two weeks in a row in three weekly business magazines that reach purchasing

Questions

FOR REVIEW

1. How do broadsheet newspapers differ from tabloids?

2. What is run-of-paper advertising, and what alternatives do newspaper advertisers have?

3. How can magazine advertisers benefit from selective binding and ink-jet printing?

4. What are the functions of the insertion order, the proof, and the tear sheet?

5. How do vertical publications differ from horizontal publications?

FOR ANALYSIS AND APPLICATION

6. If you were a media planner at Maybelline's ad agency and you wanted to use the lifestyle section of major-city newspapers to introduce a new line of women's cosmetics, how would you suggest overcoming the limitations of reproduction constraints and clutter?

7. Should newspapers charge national advertisers higher rates than local advertisers? Why or why not?

8. As the advertising manager at Lenox China (which makes dinnerware and fine china), would you buy space in two bridal magazines that consistently contain more ads than editorial material? Why or why not?

Our Idea Of A Perfect Ten.

10

At Lexmark, we take a close look at every aspect of character generation to make sure your IBM equipment delivers maximum performance.

A zero-defect zone. Even at this extreme point size there's no edge blurring or semi-softer startstepping to bring you down.

This is the one. Dark and bold, even and uniform at every turn.

IBM printer toners by Lexmark cover your characters are permanently fixed to the page. No smudges here.

There are a number of reasons to use Lexmark original replacement toner in your IBM printer. This number is just one of them.

Lexmark is constantly testing and improving our toners to make sure they consistently produce the finest quality characters and the highest possible yield.

For the pinnacle in laser printing, insist on original IBM toners by Lexmark. Our toners will never do a number on you.

To order, to locate the dealer nearest you, or to receive your free catalog, call 1-800-438-2468, ext. 80. (In Canada, call 1-800-663-7662.)

Lexmark International, a former subsidiary of IBM, is an independent, worldwide company that develops, manufactures, and markets IBM personal printers, IBM typewriters, related supplies and keyboards.

IBM Supplies by
LEXMARK.
Make Your Mark

IBM is a registered trademark of International Business Machines Corporation in the United States and/or other countries and is used under license. Lexmark is a trademark of Lexmark International, Inc. © 1992 Lexmark International, Inc.

managers and financial managers. Wait three weeks, and then repeat the insertion for another two weeks. This will give you some frequency and at the same time will help avoid message wearout.
c. Buy ads in three monthly national business magazines to reach purchasing managers and financial managers who approve purchases of printer equipment and supplies. Stagger the placement so that only one of the three magazines carries the ad each month, thus stretching your budget.

2. Lexmark is introducing a new color printer that prints on both sides of a single sheet. Mann wants to promote the product to information-systems executives who buy for their corporations. Which one of these ideas about preferred positions in computer magazines would you not recommend?
a. Buy space opposite the first page of the magazines' regularly scheduled sections on printers to reach people who want to know about the latest breakthroughs in printer technology.
b. Buy space opposite the section in which printers are advertised. When readers want to find a particular printer, they'll turn to that section and notice your ad before they see any others.
c. Stick to run-of-press space. You can't predict which features your target audience will read, and the computer magazines run a varied collection of articles, so readers browse through the entire publication anyway.

3. Mann wants to use magazine advertising to support a new-product launch scheduled for September 15. However, he doesn't want any advertising to appear before the product has been officially launched. What should you do?
a. Buy space in magazines whose on-sale dates are September 16 or later so readers won't be able to see the ad before the product is launched.
b. Buy space in magazines whose cover dates are September 16 or later, so the ads will be officially dated after the new-product release date.
c. Buy space in magazines with closing dates of September 16 or later so no advertising will appear until after the new product is released.

4. Lexmark is sponsoring an advertorial section on office automation in Crain's Chicago Business, a weekly business magazine. Mann doesn't want to overwhelm readers with too many Lexmark ads, but he does want readers to associate Lexmark with innovative office technology. What would be the best way to position Lexmark ads in this advertorial?
a. Instead of an ad on the second cover, position a letter from Mann welcoming all readers to this special advertorial. Then put full-page Lexmark ads on the advertorial's third and fourth covers.
b. Put a half-page Lexmark ad on the advertorial's cover. Then put a full-page ad opposite the table of contents and a full-page ad on the back cover.
c. End the advertorial with a third-cover gatefold ad featuring all Lexmark products. Don't add any other identifying tags because that would remind readers that the section wasn't an objective series of articles.[68]

■

9. If you owned a local Domino's pizza franchise, would you use newspapers or magazines to advertise your grand opening? Briefly describe how you would make the best use of the print medium you prefer.

10. From an integrated marketing communications perspective, what special magazine services might Gerber Products ask for when buying space in 12 consecutive issues of *Parenting*? Be as specific as possible.

Sharpen Your Advertising Skills

How can a fast-growing manufacturer of technical software make its ads stand out in magazines crowded with competing ads? National Instruments, which makes instrument-control, measurement, and medical-analysis software for personal computers, faced just this problem. Specialized magazines read by the company's target audiences (including medical technicians, scientists, and other technical specialists) were full of ads for technical software. John Graff, corporate marketing manager, wanted to creatively use size and position to grab his audience's attention. He had a healthy advertising budget (about 6 percent of annual sales, unusually high for that industry) and was prepared to pay a premium for special positions in trade magazines such as *NASA Tech Briefs, Electronic Design,* and *Electronic Products.*

Decision: Imagine Graff has just hired your ad agency to handle his magazine advertising. Which preferred positions and size/placement combinations would you recommend that Graff request in the specialized magazines? (Keep in mind the principles of creativity and print production discussed in Chapters 9, 10, and 11.)

Communication: Draft a brief (one- to two-page) memo to Graff, outlining the positions you recommend and explaining why each would be likely to capture the attention of National Instruments' target audience. Be as specific as possible in describing the size and positions you propose, including the impact on creating and producing the ad. If you want to go to the library and research which magazines reach Graff's target audience, you might also include the titles you recommend in your memo.

Electronic Media

After studying this chapter, you will be able to

1. List the three ways that television reaches viewers and the three forms of television advertising

2. Discuss the advantages and limitations of broadcast television advertising

3. Describe the advantages and limitations of cable television advertising

4. Explain how television ratings and audience share are calculated

5. Outline how radio reaches listeners and list the types of radio advertising

6. Identify the advantages and limitations of radio advertising

7. Discuss how radio audiences can be measured using average quarter-hour and cume calculations

MUSIC: Throughout.
ANNOUNCER: SEGA!!!
SUPER: SONIC 2 IS COMING NOVEMBER 24.
(SFX): car horns, traffic noise

(SFX): crash, the doorbell
SUPER: SO REMEMBER TO LEAVE A DOOR OPEN.
SUPER: WELCOME TO THE NEXT LEVEL.
SUPER: GENESIS AND GAME GEAR.

Facing an Advertising Challenge at Colgate-Palmolive

SELLING PERSONAL CARE, UP CLOSE AND PERSONAL

Selling $9 billion worth of toothpaste, soap, and cleanser in 165 countries in one year is a tall order. That was the challenge Colgate-Palmolive's William S. Shanahan faced in 1991. At the end of the 1980s, annual sales were hovering around $5 billion, and in 1991 top management set a bold five-year plan to spark significantly higher sales. As the chief operating officer and the executive in charge of global sales of household and personal-care products, Shanahan was charged with ringing up $9 billion in annual sales by 1995. He had a sizable advertising budget and a factory full of powerhouse brands—including Ajax, Colgate, Fab, Palmolive, Plax, and Mennen. Now he had to figure out the best way to reach the right consumers in each country so that he could reach his ambitious goals.

Global advertising is nothing new for Colgate-Palmolive, which has been selling internationally for well over 50 years. In fact, more than 60 percent of the advertiser's sales come from outside the United States and Canada. What's more, the company leads the market in many parts of the world. For instance, out of the 18 categories in which Colgate-Palmolive competes in Mexico, its products are number one or number two in 16; out of the 16 product categories the company offers in Malaysia, its products are number one or number two in 11.

Despite a long history of international sales, the venerable Colgate-Palmolive brands have yet to establish themselves in some countries. For instance, as many as 300 million customers in Eastern Europe, Russia, and Ukraine are just starting to find the advertiser's products on local store shelves. Nigeria, Chile, and South Korea are only three of the many countries outside Europe that Colgate-Palmolive is also targeting for increased sales growth.

Shanahan was drawing on a beefed-up yearly advertising budget of roughly $500 million (nearly twice the size of the 1985 ad budget) to reach out to Colgate-Palmolive's worldwide target audience. He knew that one of the fastest and most economical ways of bringing ad messages to large numbers of people across many lands is to use television advertising. Now put yourself behind Shanahan's desk. How would you use television to promote Colgate's brands in each country? Would you approach your television advertising strategy from a global or a local perspective? How would you ensure that your media schedules are appropriate for audiences in each country?[1] ■

CHAPTER OVERVIEW Colgate-Palmolive's William Shanahan wanted to tune into sales success by using television to reach his global target audience. This chapter gives you a close look at television and radio, the two main electronic media. First you'll learn about television delivery systems and the types of television advertising. Next, you'll explore the advantages and limitations of television advertising, the key trends in television, and the elements involved in planning television advertising. You'll get an in-depth view of the various radio delivery systems as well as the types of radio advertising. After examining the advantages and limitations of radio advertising and considering the medium's future, you'll learn how to plan and purchase radio advertising.

Advertising in the Electronic Media

Although the electronic media are among the youngest of the major media— television came of age in the 1950s and radio in the 1920s—they're available virtually everywhere. In the United States, 99 percent of all households have radio, and 98 percent of all households have television. (In fact, the average household has five radios and two televisions.) Radio is a take-along medium, keeping listeners company anywhere and everywhere—at home, in the car, on the beach. Even television, which was once confined to the home, has become a more mobile medium as both the size and the price of portable sets continue to shrink. Adults in the United States now spend considerably more time with the electronic media (88 percent) than they do with the print media (12 percent). Given this attractive combination of audience reach and interest, it's not surprising that the electronic media are highly popular with advertisers.[2]

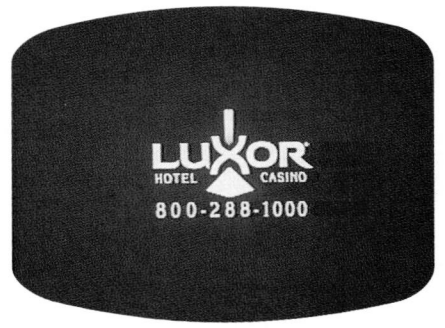

A BRILLIANT WHITE LIGHT SHOOTS SKYWARD FROM THE GRAND CANYON, THEN STONEHENGE, NIAGARA FALLS, THE GREAT WALL OF CHINA, THE TAJ

MAHAL, AND THE GREAT PYRAMIDS AT GIZA. THE SAME WHITE LIGHT BURSTS FROM THE LUXOR HOTEL.

V.O.: There is a new wonder in the world and it will change the way you see Las Vegas. Luxor Hotel & Casino.

EXHIBIT 15.1

How Luxor Combines Television and Radio

To promote the opening of the Luxor Hotel & Casino in Las Vegas, the company used the sight, sound, and motion of television advertising as well as the vivid words and images evoked by radio advertising. This combination allowed the hotel to build awareness on the national and local levels by making the best use of each medium's particular characteristics.

(SFX): exotic, mysterious music
V.O.: It is one of the greatest undertakings the world has ever seen.
(SFX): giant crowd, rhythmic "heave ho" sound
V.O.: A mighty empire, building a monumental pyramid in the sand of a vast desert. It is the pinnacle of design . . .
(SFX): echoing vault doors shut
V.O.: . . . and the ultimate resting place for the select few. Introducing Luxor, Las Vegas.
(SFX): music becomes very fast paced and orchestral
V.O.: A 30-story pyramid-shaped hotel, casino, and entertainment complex. Enter, and journey through time on three dazzling adventures created by Douglas Trumbull, the visionary Hollywood film maker.
(SFX): jet pass-by and whooosh!
V.O.: Search for treasure in a glittering subterranean casino.
(SFX): sparkling sounds (a "rain tree" instrument)
V.O.: And rejuvenate your spirit in our pool and health spa.

When you advertise in the print media, you buy space, and readers can absorb your message at their own pace. However, when you advertise in the electronic media, you buy time, as little as a few seconds or as much as 30 to 60 minutes. The people in your audience have no control over the speed at which they receive your message, nor can they review it (unless they record the commercial for later playback). This means you have only a short time to communicate your ideas before the commercial disappears.

Although many advertisers use either television or radio to promote national products throughout the United States, some use a combination of television and radio to create a national voice supplemented by a local presence (see Exhibit 15.1). For example, even though Pepsi blankets the country with television commercials featuring such well-known stars as Ray Charles, the company's local radio commercials feature hometown bands.[3] As Pepsi's advertising experts know, each of the two electronic media has unique characteristics, advantages, and limitations. In the next section, you'll learn more about television's characteristics and how the medium operates.

Advertising on Television

In more than four decades of television advertising, advertisers and agencies have proved over and over that the immediacy of television's sight, sound, and motion offers endless creative opportunities to reach viewers' hearts and minds. Because of this medium's power, the makers of soap, cereal, candy, fast food, toys, soft drinks, coffee, and cold and pain relievers typically spend a high percentage of

EXHIBIT 15.2   **The Top U.S. Television Advertisers**

Procter & Gamble, the largest advertiser in the United States, invested more than $2 billion in advertising during 1992. About 45 percent of that total—nearly $1 billion—was spent in all forms of television advertising, which enabled the advertiser to efficiently reach a large audience for its food and household products.

Top 5 network TV advertisers			Top 5 spot TV advertisers		
Rank	Advertiser	Network TV Spending	Rank	Advertiser	Spot TV Spending
1	Procter & Gamble Co.	$535.3	1	Procter & Gamble Co.	$236.4
2	General Motors Corp.	449.5	2	PepsiCo	223.4
3	Philip Morris Cos.	410.3	3	General Mills	222.8
4	PepsiCo	279.6	4	Philip Morris Cos.	185.1
5	Kellogg Co.	254.1	5	Chrysler Corp.	171.6

Top 5 cable TV network advertisers			Top 5 syndicated TV advertisers		
Rank	Advertiser	Cable TV Network Spending	Rank	Advertiser	Syndicated TV Spending
1	Procter & Gamble Co.	$112.0	1	Philip Morris Cos.	$133.8
2	General Motors Corp.	41.9	2	Procter & Gamble Co.	94.1
3	Anheuser-Busch Cos.	37.7	3	Kellogg Co.	52.5
4	Philip Morris Cos.	36.9	4	Unilever	44.1
5	General Mills	33.5	5	Warner-Lambert Co.	28.3

Note: Dollars are in millions; 1992 data.

their ad budgets on television (see Exhibit 15.2).[4] These advertisers are attracted by the efficiency of broadcast television's mass-market reach. However, in recent years, advertisers have also learned how to exploit the narrower reach of cable television, which is growing fast and diversifying to target audience niches that include highly prized segments such as working women and upscale families.[5]

BROADCAST TELEVISION

Television reaches viewers in a variety of ways. At first, television was only a *broadcast* medium, transmitting signals through the air. No special cables, wires, or decoding devices were needed to pick up the electronic signals; anyone in the range of those signals who had a television set could tune in for free. Today, broadcast television in the United States operates on 82 channels. Channels 2 through 13 are carried on the *very high frequency (VHF)* band, and channels 14 through 83 are carried on the *ultrahigh frequency (UHF)* band.[6] Because VHF stations can broadcast farther than UHF stations, many UHF stations connect with cable delivery services to extend their coverage. Broadcast television consists of two main players: network television and local television.

Network Television

As you saw in Chapter 1, a network links stations in diverse locations by beaming a single set of programs and commercials to a series of **affiliates,** individual stations that have contracted to broadcast the network's material to local viewers or listeners. This allows advertisers that buy time during network programs to conveniently reach many people in many markets at one time. The four major U.S. broadcast television networks are the American Broadcasting Company (ABC), the Columbia Broadcasting System (CBS), the National Broadcasting Company (NBC), and Fox Broadcasting (Fox). ABC, CBS, and NBC each have more than 200 affiliates; Fox has more than 135. Another network, the Public Broadcasting System (PBS), provides programming to nonprofit affiliates but doesn't sell commercial time (although program sponsors receive on-air recognition).

Local Television

Many broadcast television stations in local markets are affiliated with one of the four major networks. ABC, CBS, and NBC each offer about 90 hours of weekly programming (Fox offers less but has been increasing its offerings), so local affiliates broadcast a mix of network-provided and locally produced programming and commercials.[7] Some local stations are independent, and they air movies, children's programs, local news and sports, and other nonnetwork programs. Although much of the commercial time is sold by the network, affiliates can sell a portion of the time before, during, and after network programming. Some local stations show programs geared to specific ethnic or religious groups, and they attract a variety of advertisers that want to reach those target audiences.

CABLE TELEVISION

Cable television relies on wires (cables) to carry signals to viewers. Originally known as community antenna television (CATV), cable television began in the 1940s as a way to bring television to remote or mountainous areas of the United States that couldn't receive broadcast television signals. This form of television has grown rapidly in the past 20 years, fueled by the wiring of major cities and by interest in the expanded number of channels available through satellite transmission. In 1975 only 10 million households (13 percent of all U.S. households with television sets) subscribed to cable systems, but by the early 1990s more than 60 million households (65 percent) subscribed.[8]

Subscribers served by one of the roughly 10,000 cable-system operators in the United States pay a monthly fee to receive an average of 37 channels featuring diverse programming such as news, movies, music, weather, and sports. Although some local cable operators develop their own programming, most comes from other sources and carries commercials; suppliers include national and regional cable networks, syndicators, local affiliates of broadcast television networks, and independent stations.[9]

There are more than 60 cable networks, including the Nashville Network, Arts & Entertainment, and CNN; more narrowly focused channels include the Black Entertainment Channel (targeted to African-American viewers) and Lifetime (targeted to women viewers). A large independent broadcast station such as WTBS in Atlanta may operate as a **superstation,** sending signals via satellite to cable systems throughout the country; only a handful of such superstations are in operation. For an additional fee, subscribers can receive ad-free cable channels such as Showtime, and they may order *pay-per-view (PPV)* programming by paying for selected concerts, shows, or sports events.[10]

TELEVISION SYNDICATION

Broadcast and cable stations are always looking for programs that attract audiences and advertisers, and two forms of television syndication have become increasingly popular in recent years as alternatives to network programming (see Exhibit 15.3). In **off-network syndication,** individual stations rerun established programs that originally appeared on network television, such as *The Cosby Show.* In **first-run syndication,** stations air new programs that are produced specifically for syndication, such as *Star Trek: The Next Generation.*

Another fast-growing trend in syndication is **barter syndication,** in which a local station pays less (or nothing) for a first-run or off-network program in

EXHIBIT 15.3
Turning on Syndicated Television

Syndicated television programming, which generates more than $4 billion in revenues a year, is purchased through cash payments by cable stations, independent stations, and network affiliates and through the use of barter.

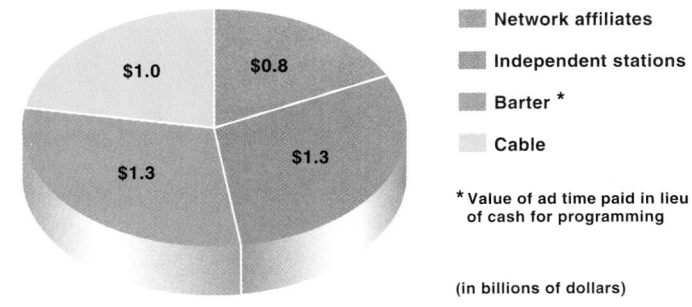

$1.0 $0.8

$1.3 $1.3

▮ Network affiliates
▮ Independent stations
▮ Barter *
▮ Cable

* Value of ad time paid in lieu of cash for programming

(in billions of dollars)

syndication that comes with a percentage of its commercials presold to national advertisers. In essence, the station exchanges (barters) some of its commercial time for programming; part of its commercial time must be used to air a certain number of national ads during that show, and then any remaining time can be sold to local advertisers. Off-network syndication hits such as *Roseanne* usually command a high price, but they're sometimes offered through barter syndication when local stations are strapped for cash or when the syndicators need to build an audience for national advertisers.[11]

TYPES OF TELEVISION ADVERTISING

Which type of television advertising should you buy? In general, the answer depends on your budget and your need to control the program as well as the timing and placement of commercials. Your choices include sponsorship, participation, and spot announcement.

Sponsorship

When an advertiser chooses a **sponsorship** arrangement, it assumes responsibility for producing a program and enjoys the exclusive right to air commercials during the show. In television's early days, national advertisers such as Texaco sponsored shows that bore their names (*Texaco Star Theater*), taking charge of the program content as well as all commercials. Gradually, the networks and a growing stable of independent producers took over program production, so sponsorships dwindled. Procter & Gamble, Hallmark, and other major advertisers continue their longtime use of sponsorships, and others have begun new sponsorship traditions. For example, Sears has sponsored the broadcast of the movie *E.T.: The Extraterrestrial* on Thanksgiving Day for several years.[12]

Although expensive, sponsorship has two main advantages. First, a sponsor can link its products with a high-quality program, gaining prestige from the public's perception of the show. For example, public television viewers see the sponsor's name, logo, and a brief message before and after the sponsored programs, and the sponsors often promote this connection in other media; Mobil Oil, a longtime sponsor of *Mystery!* on PBS, runs print ads promoting the program. Second, a sponsor has complete control over the placement and content of its commercials (except on PBS), which can be shown at any time during the sponsored program and which can be any length, providing they meet network and station regulations (see Exhibit 15.4). However, being the sole sponsor of a program is costly, so many

EXHIBIT 15.4
Co-Sponsoring a Television Special

When Chrysler Jeep Eagle co-sponsored the *Queen of the Elephants* on The Discovery Channel, the advertiser also received recognition in print ads promoting the special.

advertisers become *co-sponsors,* sharing the costs and the commercial time with others. Another alternative is to sponsor just a segment of a program, the way AT&T has sponsored "Science & Technology Today" segments on CNN.[13]

Participation

An advertiser that doesn't want the expense or responsibility of sponsorship can choose **participation,** in which various advertisers buy commercial time during a specific program. Advertisers can participate in a program regularly or only sporadically, and they may buy one or more commercials during each program, depending on their budgets. For example, Hyundai participated in network, syndicated, and cable programs to reach young adults aged 18 to 34 for its "Cars That Make Sense" campaign. Participation allowed the carmaker to stretch its ad dollars by zeroing in on programs viewed by its target audience.[14] Such flexibility is an advantage, especially for smaller advertisers with limited budgets. However, advertisers have no control over program content or broadcast schedules; moreover, participations may not be available during popular time periods or programs.

Spot Announcement

A less costly alternative to sponsorship is the **spot announcement,** a segment of commercial time purchased from a local station. For broadcast and cable television, this is known as **spot television.** Sponsorships and participations often fill nearly all the commercial time during network-provided programs, but you can buy an **adjacency,** some commercial time just before or just after a network program, or you can buy time during a *station break,* when the network releases time to its local affiliates. However, when affiliates or independent stations run their own programming, they can sell spot announcements at any point during or between programs. A **national spot** is commercial time purchased by a national advertiser from a local station; a **local spot** is purchased by a local advertiser from a local station (see Exhibit 15.5).[15]

By buying spot announcements, advertisers can reach specific markets without a lot of waste, or they can emphasize particular markets where they see more sales potential (or where they need to combat competitive activity). For example, Pacific Bell Information Services bought a series of local spot announcements on cable systems in Southern California to reach only those communities in the utility's service area. You can also buy spot announcements when you want to research audience reaction to a new product or to a new television ad. The New England, an insurance firm, bought spot television in six markets to test the effectiveness of two new television commercials. In addition, spot announcements can be used to support the introduction of new products market by market, and local retailers

EXHIBIT 15.5
Using Spot Television

Six Flags Magic Mountain in Southern California used local spot television advertising to introduce Batman The Ride, promising viewers "the ride of your life."

BATMAN INSIGNIA IN NIGHT SKY WITH ACTION SHOTS OF PEOPLE RIDING ON THE BATMAN ROLLER COASTER.
ANNOUNCER: This year at Six Flags Magic Mountain . . . Answer the call to Batman The Ride. Imagine, the air below . . . The sky above. As you fly through a zero gravity roll . . . On the world's greatest suspended outside looping, nothing like it on earth experience. Answer the call to Batman The Ride. Only at Six Flags Magic Mountain. Come for the ride of your life.

often buy spot announcements under cooperative advertising programs offered by the national advertisers whose products they carry (see Chapter 17).[16]

Keep in mind, however, that buying spot time in many markets can be complex; you must contact every station and juggle a variety of pricing, scheduling, and billing details. Christina Mantoulides, an ad agency executive with CME-KHBB, describes national spot advertising as "a paperwork nightmare." One way to reduce the complexity is to deal with station representatives who sell time on a number of broadcast or cable stations. To cut down on the paper logjam, Ogilvy & Mather and several other ad agencies have moved to electronic invoicing. With cable, you can work through **interconnects,** groups of system operators that sell time on any or all of their linked systems; Urban Contemporary Interconnect is one such group selling spot time on cable systems in 14 markets.[17]

ADVANTAGES AND LIMITATIONS OF BROADCAST TELEVISION ADVERTISING

Although broadcast television can be a powerful and effective medium for many advertisers, it can have limitations. As an advertiser, you have to determine whether television advertising is right for you. The following sections examine the advantages and limitations of broadcast television.

Advantages

Television's advantages as an advertising medium have long made it a popular medium for consumer advertising. Now business advertisers are also discovering the benefits of television advertising. The advantages of broadcast television include creative flexibility, coverage of mass markets, and cost efficiency.

- *Creative flexibility.* Television offers countless possibilities for using sight, sound, color, and motion to communicate an ad message. As discussed in Chapter 10, you can use animation, music, and a variety of other techniques to grab the viewer's attention. To tell your story, you can make your commercial short or long, and you can build credibility by demonstrating your product (see Exhibit 15.6). For instance, when Puma USA introduced a no-lace athletic shoe, it used television commercials to demonstrate the ease of turning a dial to tighten the shoes.[18]

- *Coverage of mass markets.* It's hard to beat broadcast television for reaching huge numbers of people quickly, in the United States or abroad. Virtually every U.S. household owns a television set (a potential audience of more than 94 million households), and those sets are used, on average, more than 7 hours a day. To reach its global markets, Colgate-Palmolive maintains a heavy U.S. television schedule as well as extensive television schedules in many other

EXHIBIT 15.6

Taking Advantage of Television's Sight and Sound

To demonstrate the freshness of foods served by Chevys Mexican Restaurants, ad agency Goodby Berlin & Silverstein/San Francisco filmed a new television commercial every day, focusing on that day's fresh produce, fish, tamales, or other specialties. Each commercial incorporated sight or sound elements proving that the ad, like the food being shown, was made that day.

TV CAMERA CREW AND REPORTER IN A PASTURE ATTEMPTING TO INTERVIEW THE COWS.
(SFX): Mexican folk music
REPORTER: Ladies (addressing the cows), can you tell me the date today? (holding the newspaper in front of a cow and pointing to

the date) Here's a hint, it's Wednesday. Can you read the weather? Morning low clouds . . .
V.O.: We made this commercial today. We call this "Fresh TV." At Chevys we make our food fresh every day using 100% real cheese. We call this "Fresh Mex." Real

cheese from real cows, cows outstanding in their field. Sure, we could pay more, but we pass the savings on to you.
REPORTER: Did you hear *Thirtysomething* was cancelled? (low moos) What a bummer, huh?

countries. Similarly, to more efficiently reach its U.S. audience, the eyewear retail chain Pearle Vision recently increased its network broadcast television advertising. "With the nature of [our] market being just about everyone in the United States, network TV is attractive," says Bob Nance, vice president of marketing services.[19]

- *Cost efficiency.* Although the cost of airing a 30-second commercial during a popular program can be more than $300,000, this is a relatively low price tag for reaching a huge audience. The cost per thousand (CPM) for an early-evening 30-second commercial on network broadcast television in the United States was less than $10 in the early 1990s; the CPM for a daytime 30-second commercial was under $3. During the same period, the CPM for prime-time television ads was under $12 in Italy, under $7 in the United Kingdom, and under $5 in Japan. For Colgate-Palmolive and many other global advertisers, such CPM figures are relatively modest compared with the national audiences that can be reached.[20]

Limitations

As beneficial as television can be for many advertisers, it also has limitations, including limited selectivity, audience erosion, relatively high entry cost, clutter, brevity, and limited viewer attention.

- *Limited selectivity.* Broadcast television isn't geared to precise demographic or geographic targeting. Of course, you can make broad audience distinctions, such as using cartoon programs to reach children and sports events to reach men, but it's difficult to be much more specific than that. Even if you choose spot television in a certain market, you may reach people outside your desired area.

- *Audience erosion.* Network broadcast television viewers have slowly but steadily been changing channels, with many defecting to cable stations. Fewer viewers (especially those aged 18 to 49) are turning on ABC, CBS, and NBC programs during the peak evening hours, which means smaller audiences for advertisers that buy network time during that period. Although special events such as the Olympics help slow the erosion, broadcast television is in danger of losing the massive audience desired by some national advertisers.[21] Fox is drawing young adults, but overall broadcast network viewership continues to slide, which may cause more advertisers to move toward both cable and syndicated television advertising, where viewer numbers are starting to rise.

- *Relatively high entry cost.* Despite the cost efficiency of broadcast television, it can take a big chunk out of an advertiser's budget. Aside from the cost of talent (which can be high for well-known celebrities) and production (which may cost hundreds of thousands of dollars for an elaborate commercial), airing ads during desirable shows and time periods is costly. High cost is one reason why some advertisers are turning to 15-second ads (see Exhibit 15.7).[22]

- *Clutter.* Breaking through clutter has become a major challenge because viewers see more ads than ever. Twenty years ago most commercials were 60 seconds long, but today most are 30 seconds, so that more fill the same time slot. Network viewers may see an average of 20 commercials per hour on weeknights and 31 on weekday afternoons. It's not surprising that four out of five people can't remember a commercial the day after it airs.[23] However, if you're one of the few in your industry to use television, you may stand out. That's why Sharp Electronics uses television to advertise its office products. Says Daniel J. Infanti, general manager of corporate communications: "One reason we've been effective is because there are so few [business-to-business] advertisers on TV."[24]

- *Brevity.* It's not easy to make a strong impression in a minute or less, and once your commercial has aired, there's nothing physical to keep your message alive. Although research shows that 15-second commercials have more than

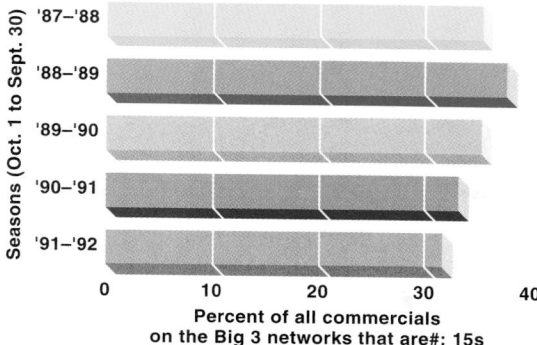

EXHIBIT 15.7
Trends in Television Commercial Length

Introduced in 1983, 15-second commercials quickly gained popularity among cost-conscious advertisers. However, 15-second commercials have become less popular in recent years as more advertisers return to 30-second commercials, which now account for nearly 63 percent of all television advertising.

half the persuasion and recall of 30-second commercials, trying to cram too much message into a few seconds can hurt the effectiveness. One way to counterbalance a short life span is to carefully match the commercial length to the advertising objective. According to one study, 15-second ads may be effective reminders for people who are familiar with a product, but longer ads are more effective when launching a new product.[25]

- *Limited viewer attention.* Television competes with other media as well as with everything else going on around the viewer. During an ad, viewers may turn away or leave the room, they may mute the volume (easy for the three-quarters of the viewers who use a remote-control device), or they may resort to **zapping,** using the remote control to change channels. Many indulge in **grazing,** using their remote controls to quickly scan a lot of channels as they search for something interesting to watch. What's more, many people who use video-cassette recorders fast-forward through the ads on recorded programs, a practice called **zipping.** To combat these challenges, advertisers are using sophisticated production techniques, humor, and music to hold viewers' interest.[26]

ADVANTAGES AND LIMITATIONS OF CABLE TELEVISION ADVERTISING

Cable television advertising shares many of the characteristics of broadcast television advertising. In addition, it has its own unique set of advantages and limitations.

Advantages

Cable television's advertising revenues are smaller than those of broadcast television. However, they've been growing as more advertisers discover the benefits of using cable. Compared with broadcast television, cable offers three advantages: increased selectivity, lower entry costs, and increased flexibility.

- *Increased selectivity.* Cable television is built around **narrowcasting,** the ability to deliver specialized programming to highly targeted audiences. There's a cable vehicle to reach almost any target audience (see Exhibit 15.8). For example, Citibank recently aired a Vietnamese-language commercial on the International Channel Network (which draws Asian-American viewers) to promote a money-transfer service between Vietnam and the United States. Cable viewers tend to be younger, better educated, and more affluent than broadcast viewers, a plus for advertisers seeking those demographics. Moreover, cable offers a high degree of geographic selectivity. Consider how BSN Groupe uses cable to reach into the upscale areas most likely to buy its Evian bottled water. In Miami, for instance, the cable system sends Evian commercials only to wealthier neighborhoods like Key Biscayne.[27]

- *Lower entry costs.* Cable television advertising generally costs less than broadcast. At the Lifetime channel, the CPM for reaching women ages 18 to 49 is half that of broadcast networks. At New York 1 News, a New York City cable

EXHIBIT 15.8

Using Cable Television to Reach a Targeted Audience

This cable television commercial brought Citibank's advertising message to Asian-American viewers of the International Channel Network in New York City. By using cable rather than broadcast television, the advertiser was able to reach a highly targeted audience.

ANNOUNCER: Citibank announces a new service where you can send money safely and conveniently to your families in Vietnam. We are offering this service at selected branches in New York and, in the next few months, in California. For more information contact us in New York at 212-559-1379. Citibank sincerely wishes our customers a Happy and Prosperous New Year.

channel, a 30-second commercial costs as little as $200, but during a newscast on the local ABC-owned broadcast station, a 30-second commercial costs as much as $11,000. Moreover, sponsoring a series on cable can be cheaper than buying a single broadcast commercial spot—and the advertiser gains program control. National advertisers such as Procter & Gamble are using cable sponsorships, as are local advertisers.[28]

- *Increased flexibility.* Cable television advertisers aren't locked into the 15-, 30-, or 60-second commercial time slots usually offered by broadcast television. Commercial length on cable is much more flexible and can be as long as 30 or 60 minutes. For example, Club Med has used 30-minute infomercials on the Arts & Entertainment cable network to show viewers footage of its vacation resorts. Some cable stations link advertisers more closely with programming, which adds emphasis to the message. Domino's message got a boost when the announcers on a Home Team Sports basketball game were shown on-screen calling for a Domino's pizza and digging in hungrily when the pie arrived.[29]

Limitations

Many advertisers have found cable television a highly effective medium. Despite its advantages, though, it also has three distinct limitations: limited reach, audience fragmentation, and limited research.

- *Limited reach.* As you saw earlier, cable systems don't yet reach as many people as broadcast television. The good news is that nearly 90 percent of the U.S. households equipped with television have access to cable television; the bad news is that only 65 percent subscribe, and some small percentage of households drop the service every year. However, despite this subscriber turnover and rising subscription costs, cable's reach is expanding by as many as 2 million households every year.[30]

- *Audience fragmentation.* With dozens of channels competing for the subscriber's attention and more on the way, it's difficult for any one channel to build a sizable audience, so advertisers have to build a patchwork of vehicles to reach their target audiences. However, some stations are trying to attract and keep viewers by presenting higher-quality programs. For example, ESPN is building a following through expanded baseball coverage and sports specials; USA Network is putting more emphasis on developing original series and movies. As these programs attract larger audiences, they'll also attract more ad dollars.[31]

- *Limited research.* Although some research is available, advertisers and agencies want more detail to better understand cable audiences. One challenge is

Interactive Television: Coming Soon to a Screen Near You

Interactive television—linking the visual power of television with the two-way communication capability of the computer—lets viewers participate in programs, request product or banking information, buy products, and complete banking transactions. This futuristic medium is already a reality in some areas. In Australia, the In-Touch Interactive System is available to families in Adelaide; in Canada, ACTV serves more than 80,000 homes in Montreal; and in the United States, 36 interactive television projects are under way, involving the Interactive Network, EON, GTE's Main Street, and other organizations. By the year 2002, consultants project that 40 million U.S. viewers will be interactive television subscribers.

What's appealing about interactive television from the advertiser's viewpoint is the ability to communicate with a target audience and be able to receive direct and immediate feedback. For example, most interactive television projects take home-shopping programs a step further by eliminating the need to use telephones when ordering merchandise; viewers simply use a keypad, a joystick, or another device attached to the television set to make their selection and then indicate how they'll pay. As a result, advertisers see immediately which products are selling, and they can get details about buyers and their behavior because customer feedback (whether inquiry or purchase) is recorded and ready for analysis more quickly.

Interactive television can also help advertisers quickly gauge reaction to specific commercials. For instance, Pepsi-Cola worked with the Interactive Network to run a contest built around the advertiser's soft-drink commercials aired during the 1993 Super Bowl. More than 700 viewers earned prizes by responding to multiple-choice questions such as "What's the name of Pepsi's new clear cola? All Clear, Geyser, Crystal Pepsi, or Mountain Pepsi?" By examining the answers, Pepsi-Cola determined whether viewers had noticed and remembered its Super Bowl commercials.

Pepsi-Cola, Sony, BMW, Domino's Pizza, and J.C. Penney are just a few of the growing number of advertisers that are testing ad messages on interactive television. One question these tests are trying to answer is how best to exploit the interactive tech-

Interactive television allows fans to get directly involved with sports programs.

nology to capture viewers' attention. A second question is how to persuade viewers to actively participate in interactive ads and—ultimately—to place orders. A third question deals with the size of the audience for interactive television and its ads.

Of course, advertisers can't reach the audiences they need if viewers don't subscribe. Subscribers must plunk down a one-time charge (as high as $500) for the interactive unit, and they also have to pay a monthly connection charge of about $15. Skeptics argue that viewers aren't clamoring for the opportunity to participate in programs or buy products with the flick of a keypad. Although the medium is technically feasible, no one knows whether viewers will pay for the privilege of pointing a gadget at the screen to order a pepperoni pizza. That's why, for the next few years, advertisers will be watching the size and composition of subscriber audiences and experimenting with ways of involving viewers in their interactive advertisements.

Apply Your Knowledge

1. What types of products might most effectively be sold on interactive television? Why?
2. How would the interactive nature of the medium affect an advertiser's creative strategy?

measuring the size and composition of local cable audiences; another is measuring the buying behavior of cable audiences. More and better research will lead to more effective media plans.[32]

TELEVISION TODAY AND TOMORROW

As technology advances and television finds new ways to reach viewers, channel choices will multiply and advertisers will be able to choose among even more options. For instance, regional telephone companies are interested in building digital delivery systems to bring cable programming to their subscribers. Another technology that offers many channel options is **direct broadcast satellite (DBS),** a delivery system in which television or radio signals are transmitted directly from a satellite to homes equipped with a small receiving satellite dish. SkyPix, introduced in 1991, uses DBS to offer 80 channels and 200 movies.[33]

SkyPix is one of a growing number of cable-system operators that offer many channels by using *digital compression,* a technique that reduces the size of the television signals before they're transmitted and allows them to be decompressed at the receiving end. This technology can be used to offer cable subscribers hundreds or even thousands of channel choices, including the choice of seeing a program in more than one format or at various times. On the horizon is a digital compression service that will let an advertiser submit a commercial simultaneously to many cable systems.[34]

In areas not wired for cable, television signals can be delivered by a **multipoint distribution system (MDS),** which uses very high frequency microwaves to transmit many channels to viewers. The use of microwaves is expanding: In 1992 the Federal Communications Commission approved a new microwave technology that can deliver up to 49 channels. Cellular Vision, which developed this technology, equips subscribers with a 6-inch antenna that picks up the several dozen channels it offers. On the receiving end, high-definition television may soon make commercials look clearer and more colorful than they do on existing television sets.[35]

In its infancy is **interactive television,** a two-way communication technique in which viewers interact with programs and commercials through a joystick or keypad. Although today viewers of the home-shopping network QVC call up to buy merchandise, they'll soon be able to order by pointing a remote-control device or touching a keypad. Interactive television is just one example of the growing interest in multimedia marriages between television, video, audio, and computer technologies. Such alliances will allow advertisers to reach consumers through an ever-wider array of home-based vehicles in the coming years.[36] These developments mean that, more than ever, reaching consumers through television takes careful planning.

Planning Television Advertising

Understanding how audiences are measured and how television time periods are defined is essential to planning and purchasing broadcast and cable television advertising. The process also involves knowing how television commercial rates operate, how a commercial is placed, and what special services are available to advertisers.

MEASURING TELEVISION AUDIENCES

Looking at audience size and audience composition in a particular market helps you determine whether a specific television vehicle fits your media plan. Audience research can be purchased from A. C. Nielsen, which collects data on national television viewership from a sample of households and which tracks local station viewership in hundreds of U.S. markets.

For more than 30 years, Nielsen relied on the **audimeter,** a device attached to the television that recorded when the set was on and which stations were watched; the firm gleaned information on who was watching from diaries kept by household members. In 1987, Nielsen switched to the people meter, a device on the television set connected to a handheld unit that viewers use to indicate what they're watching. Critics charge that people meters don't take the full measure of television audiences because viewers tire of punching buttons to record their viewing choices; they're also skeptical about whether children consistently and accurately indicate what they watch. One answer may be the passive people meters that Nielsen is testing, which automatically record who is in the room and what channel is on (see Exhibit 15.9).[37]

Although Nielsen continues to develop new techniques for measuring the viewing habits of television audiences, advertisers and agencies are raising questions about how the research takes into account the number of people who mute the volume during commercials, change channels to watch several programs during a given period, or tape shows for later viewing.[38] Another research issue is the size and composition of the out-of-home television audience. One Nielsen study found that about 28 million adults watch nearly 6 hours of television when they're away from home during the week at work, at college, and in hotels. If networks add these viewers to the at-home audience, they can show higher program ratings and may be able to raise ad rates. However, many advertisers and agencies argue that out-of-home viewers are distracted by their surroundings and are therefore less attentive, so higher ratings and rates aren't justified.[39]

Ratings and Audience Share

Once the researchers have gathered the data from their sample, they can estimate the size of a program's audience by calculating its **program rating,** the percentage of all households with a television in a specific market tuned into that program. To make this calculation, they start with the number of households tuned to the program being rated and divide this figure by the total number of **television households (TVHH),** those households in the market equipped with television. The formula is

$$\text{Program rating} = \frac{\text{households tuned to the program}}{\text{total television households in the market}}$$

Program ratings are usually expressed without the percent sign, and they can be calculated for specific audience segments. If a televised sports event attracts an audience of 5,142,250 men aged 18 to 34, and 36,630,000 men in that age group are in TVHH in that market, the program rating would be calculated this way:

$$\text{Program rating} = \frac{5,142,250}{36,630,000} = .14 = 14$$

Networks and stations gauge the popularity of their programs by comparing the ratings for their programs with those of competing programs; higher-rated shows reach larger audiences and therefore command higher advertising rates. Another key audience measure is **share of audience** (usually shortened to *share*), which reflects the audience of a particular program as a percentage of the total audience viewing television at that time. To calculate share, the researchers start with the number of households that are watching the program. They divide this by the number of households that are watching any television program during that period, a figure known as **households using television (HUT)** (or *sets in use*). The formula for share of audience in a particular market is

$$\text{Share of audience} = \frac{\text{households tuned to the program}}{\text{households using television}}$$

Like program ratings, share is expressed without the percent sign. If 60 households in a market are watching a given program, and 300 households are using television at that time, the program's share is 20. A program's share is always higher than its rating because share compares how many of the households actually watching television are tuned to that program, whereas the rating covers all households that own televisions, even though some of these households may not be watching television at all. Share can be a useful way of determining a program's relative audience appeal when the ratings of all the programs in a time slot are somewhat low. It's also a way of assessing the popularity of programs during various times of the day, days of the week, or seasons of the year, because it takes into account fluctuations in the number of households using television.[40]

Television Markets

When you plan to buy time on local television stations, you have to understand not only the audience size and composition, but also the geographic boundaries of each local market. To avoid overlap in the definition of local markets, Nielson assigns every U.S. county to a **designated market area (DMA),** a discrete geographic area in which the local television stations attract the most viewing

EXHIBIT 15.9
The Technology of Measuring Television Audiences

To more accurately measure the size and composition of television audiences at home, Nielsen is introducing passive people meters that automatically take note of which viewers are in the room and which channels are switched on.

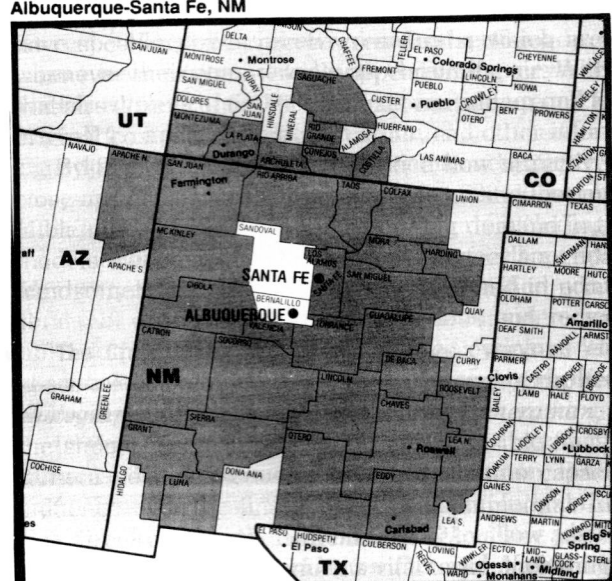

Albuquerque-Santa Fe, NM

EXHIBIT 15.10
The Albuquerque-Santa Fe DMA

Advertisers who want to reach consumers in and around Albuquerque and Santa Fe can check the designated market area established by Nielsen to see which television stations reach specific counties in New Mexico.

hours (see Exhibit 15.10). Nielsen also ranks local markets in terms of the number of TVHH, which is useful if you're buying spot television advertising and you want to show commercials in only the largest markets.

SELECTING TIME PERIODS

A second consideration when you're planning to buy television time is selecting which time of day your commercial should air. If you choose **run of station,** the station can run your commercial at any time during the day. However, if you specify a particular time, you'll pay more. The size (and composition) of the television audience changes during various times of the day, which affects the cost of commercial time. Time periods can be categorized according to **daypart,** a defined segment of the 24-hour television or radio day (see Exhibit 15.11).

As you might imagine, **prime time,** which stretches from 8 P.M. to 11 P.M., is the daypart with the highest viewing level, so you'll pay more to advertise during those hours. In fact, demand for network prime-time commercial slots has been so strong that the number of commercials grew by 11 percent from 1986 to 1991. In particular, Sunday prime time draws more viewers than other evenings.[41]

Certain dayparts tend to attract specific audiences. For example, daytime and early fringe (between 9 A.M. and 7 P.M.) have traditionally drawn a high number of women viewers, so soap manufacturers and others that want to reach this audience

EXHIBIT 15.11   **Television Dayparts**

Although daypart definitions may vary at individual stations and in other time zones, this chart shows how dayparts are commonly defined in Eastern Standard Time.

Daypart	Time Period	
Early morning	6:00 A.M.–9:00 A.M	
Daytime	9:00 A.M.–4:00 P.M.	
Early fringe	4:00 P.M.–7:00 P.M.	
Prime-time access	7:00 P.M.–8:00 P.M.	(6:00 P.M.–7:00 P.M. on Sundays)
Prime-time	8:00 P.M.–11:00 P.M.	(7:00 P.M.–11:00 P.M. on Sundays)
Late news	11:00 P.M.–11:30 P.M.	
Late fringe	11:30 P.M.–1:00 A.M.	

often schedule more ads during these periods. However, when Unilever introduced the deodorant and beauty soap Lever 2000, it targeted men as well as women, which affected its choice of dayparts. The company ran some daytime commercials but emphasized prime time, late news, and late fringe to reach both men and women, including the high proportion of young men who watch after 11 P.M.[42]

UNDERSTANDING TELEVISION AD RATES

As mentioned earlier, networks and stations generally base their ad rates on the ad length and the size of each program's audience, which is measured by the program rating. To compare the cost efficiency of reaching your target audience through commercials on various programs, you can calculate the **cost per rating point (CPP),** which shows how much you're spending to reach 1 percent (one rating point) of the audience. The CPP formula is

$$\text{Cost per rating point} = \frac{\text{cost of commercial time}}{\text{program rating}}$$

For example, if an early-morning 30-second commercial on a local station in Hartford, Connecticut, costs $300 and has a rating of 10 among adult women, the CPP would be $300 ÷ 10 = $30. According to this calculation, you'd be paying $30 to reach 1 percent of this target audience, a figure you can compare with those for other programs. The lower the CPP, the more cost-efficient the program is in reaching that audience.

Individual television stations issue rate cards (see Exhibit 15.12). However, network and syndication ad rates are negotiated rather than purchased according to a fixed rate card. Advertisers interested in buying time during the upcoming television season (which begins every fall) often start negotiating with the networks and syndicators in the *up-front market,* the spring and summer before the new schedules air. Buying up-front allows you the best opportunity to buy time during highly rated programs. You might get some price concessions as well as the flexibility to cancel some of your purchases if your needs change. Also, advertisers that buy up-front may obtain program rating guarantees, which are similar to the circulation guarantees offered by the print media. If the rating doesn't meet the guarantee, the network must offer a **makegood,** free commercial time to compensate for the ratings shortfall or for any mistakes in airing the ad.[43]

Once the up-front market has ended and the fall season is nearly under way, you can buy network time in the *scatter market,* during which any leftover time is

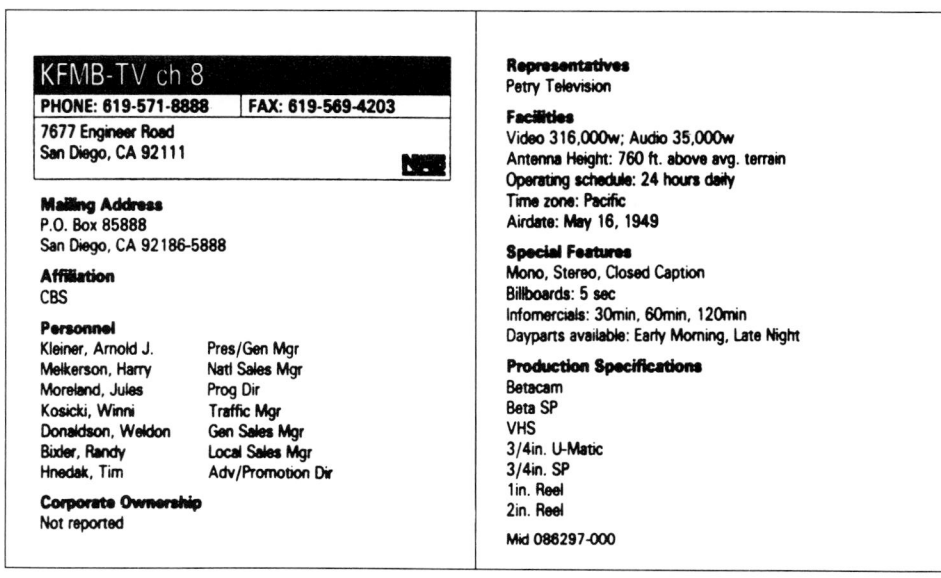

KFMB-TV ch 8

PHONE: 619-571-8888	FAX: 619-569-4203

7677 Engineer Road
San Diego, CA 92111

Mailing Address
P.O. Box 85888
San Diego, CA 92186-5888

Affiliation
CBS

Personnel
Kleiner, Arnold J. — Pres/Gen Mgr
Melkerson, Harry — Natl Sales Mgr
Moreland, Jules — Prog Dir
Kosicki, Winni — Traffic Mgr
Donaldson, Weldon — Gen Sales Mgr
Bixler, Randy — Local Sales Mgr
Hnedak, Tim — Adv/Promotion Dir

Corporate Ownership
Not reported

Representatives
Petry Television

Facilities
Video 316,000w; Audio 35,000w
Antenna Height: 760 ft. above avg. terrain
Operating schedule: 24 hours daily
Time zone: Pacific
Airdate: May 16, 1949

Special Features
Mono, Stereo, Closed Caption
Billboards: 5 sec
Infomercials: 30min, 60min, 120min
Dayparts available: Early Morning, Late Night

Production Specifications
Betacam
Beta SP
VHS
3/4in. U-Matic
3/4in. SP
1in. Reel
2in. Reel

Mid 086297-000

EXHIBIT 15.12
Buying Spot Television Time from KFMB-TV

When media planners buy spot television time from local stations, they check the rate cards or the listings in the Standard Rate and Data Service publications for information about production specifications and other details.

sold. Typically, you can't cancel time that you buy in the scatter market, and you may or may not enjoy ratings guarantees. Prices vary depending on how much time is left over and how heavy the demand is, so you may get a discount or you may pay more than on an up-front buy. Quintessence, a Chicago-based fragrance manufacturer, waited until the up-front market ended, after which its media-buying service was able to bargain for pre-Christmas time slots. This scatter buy allowed the firm to cost-effectively promote three fragrances during prime time and on sports events.[44]

PLACING TELEVISION ADS

To buy commercial time, you first check with the networks, stations, or media representatives for a list of **avails** (short for *availabilities*), time slots that are available to be purchased, plus their prices and ratings. Then you start negotiating for price and schedule. You may accept a run-of-station position, which allows the station the flexibility of running your commercial at any time. If you're willing to let the station reserve your slot and simultaneously look for an advertiser willing to pay more, you could pay the **preemption rate,** so called because your slot may be preempted by a higher-paying advertiser.

Alternatively, your media strategy may call for placing a commercial on a particular program at a particular time and, in some cases, in certain positions on the program. For example, Mennen bought two ads on *Saturday Night Live* for its Teen Spirit deodorant, scheduling one directly before each of the two appearances of Nirvana, who played their hit song "Smells Like Teen Spirit."[45] Perhaps you may try to negotiate a particular slot within the **commercial pod,** the group of ads scheduled to run during a particular program break. When Ogilvy & Mather/L.A., the agency for software giant Microsoft, bought network television time to tout the Windows product, it reserved the first and last ads in each pod because it hoped these positions would boost viewer retention of the message.[46]

Once you've selected the programs and negotiated prices, you submit an insertion order that gives the network or station the details on when and where to run your ad. After the commercial runs, the station will provide an **affidavit of performance,** a sworn statement confirming that an ad ran as scheduled.

USING SPECIAL TELEVISION SERVICES

Like other media, television often offers special services that add value to the basic buy. In addition to audience research, networks and stations may promise advertisers product exclusivity, merchandising support, contests, or other special services. For example, General Motors has signed two multimillion-dollar, multi-year deals with CBS that lock up coveted spots during popular programming such as major league baseball and NCAA basketball broadcasts. In exchange, GM will be the only domestic carmaker allowed to advertise during those network-televised sports events.

Newer networks such as cable's Sci-Fi Channel often offer special services because they need to build an advertiser base and they have no lengthy ratings history to show advertisers. When it was launched, the Sci-Fi Channel created promotional commercials that hyped the channel but also featured the products of major advertisers. One commercial showed a twenty-first-century alien discovering a Snickers bar. Such ads gave Mars and other advertisers additional exposure for their money.[47]

Advertising on Radio

Since the early days, radio commercials have painted word and sound pictures that bring to life the products they promote (see Exhibit 15.13). Of course, radio may look like little more than a viable low-cost fallback for times when a tiny budget rules out television, but savvy advertisers know that radio is a personal medium that can help build brand awareness.[48]

Tom's of Maine is one advertiser that has taken advantage of radio's ability to talk one-to-one with its audience, at reasonable expense. Up against Colgate-Palmolive and other big-budget rivals, Tom's promoted its toothpaste by using radio ads that feature founder Tom Chappel discussing his commitment to natural ingredients. This personal approach to radio advertising has helped Tom's increase sales 20 percent annually in a competitive category.[49]

Advertisers also use radio to reach people when they're about to make a purchase. When people are in their cars driving to a store or a restaurant, the last medium they're exposed to before they get to their destination is the car radio. For example, McDonald's found that 40 percent of its customers decide to eat at McDonald's within 2 minutes before they arrive at the restaurant, and 85 percent travel by car. Knowing that radio can reach these fast-food customers before they decide which restaurant to visit, McDonald's runs commercials before and during mealtimes.[50]

In the United States today, more than 9,300 commercial (for-profit) radio stations are on the air: 4,987 are AM and 4,392 are FM. In addition, 1,400 noncommercial stations (including educational stations) operate, mainly on the FM band. The Federal Communications Commission (FCC) assigns each station to a specific spot on the AM or FM band to ensure that its signals don't interfere with those of other stations. A station's audience is determined by the type of programming format the station chooses (see Exhibit 15.14). Unlike television viewers who are loyal to programs regardless of station, radio listeners tend to be loyal to specific stations.[51]

HOW RADIO REACHES LISTENERS

Both radio programming and advertising messages reach listeners through four methods: AM, FM, network, and syndication.

- *AM radio.* AM stations transmit signals using the *amplitude modulation* (AM) system, and they occupy positions on the AM dial ranging from 540 to 1600. Although more listeners tune to FM stations, AM retains a sizable audience, especially among adults 35 to 64. AM stereo is available, but the sound quality doesn't match that of FM. Both sound quality and an understanding of listener needs have lead many AM stations to use nonmusic formats. For example, Boston's WMEX-AM switched to an all-business news format because station

EXHIBIT 15.13
Radio Advertising Harnesses the Power of Sound

To motivate listeners across the United States to buy apples grown in Washington state, the Washington Apple Commission airs radio commercials that vividly portray the experience of taking a bite from the sweet, crunchy apples.

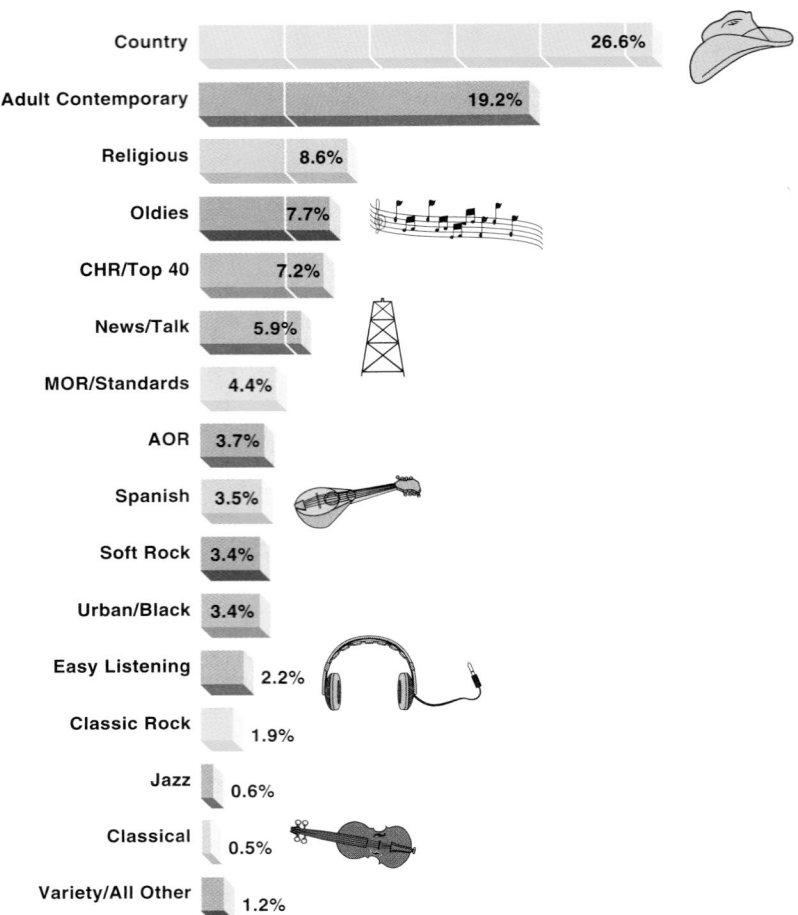

Country	26.6%
Adult Contemporary	19.2%
Religious	8.6%
Oldies	7.7%
CHR/Top 40	7.2%
News/Talk	5.9%
MOR/Standards	4.4%
AOR	3.7%
Spanish	3.5%
Soft Rock	3.4%
Urban/Black	3.4%
Easy Listening	2.2%
Classic Rock	1.9%
Jazz	0.6%
Classical	0.5%
Variety/All Other	1.2%

EXHIBIT 15.14

U.S. Radio Programming Formats

Listeners are attracted to particular stations by the type of programming they offer. That's why station programming is an important consideration when buying radio advertising time.

manager Peter Smyth believed listeners needed more financial and business information.[52]

- *FM radio.* FM stations use the *frequency modulation* (FM) transmission method. The first FCC-licensed FM stations began broadcasting in 1941, and despite AM's head start, the number of FM listeners now vastly overshadows the number of AM listeners. In 1972, 25 percent of the radio audience listened to FM stations; by 1990, 77 percent of the listeners were tuned to FM. FM has better sound quality than AM, so most FM stations offer music programming, including the increasingly popular classic rock format that appeals to 25- to 54-year-olds, an audience that many advertisers target.[53]

- *Networks.* Network radio began in 1923 when AT&T used telephone lines to relay signals to affiliates; today most networks deliver their programming via satellites. Networks provide affiliates with newscasts, sports reports, business news, short features, and some longer programs. A few network features have huge audiences: ABC network news star Paul Harvey draws nearly 6 million listeners, who also hear the network commercials. Procter & Gamble and other major advertisers use network radio to reach national audiences.[54]

- *Syndication.* Radio syndicators provide full-length programming to individual stations across the country. Many networks also offer syndicated programs, blurring the distinction between these two methods of reaching listeners. Westwood One, for instance, is a network that syndicates more than 30 programs, including Casey Kasem's top 40 rock music countdown; in all, nearly 3,800 stations air one or more Westwood One syndicated programs. As in television, radio syndicators package commercials with their programs, which benefits advertisers seeking large audiences.[55]

TYPES OF RADIO ADVERTISING

Radio advertising can be classified as network (including syndicated) or spot radio. Network radio is the smallest slice of radio's ad pie. Even when you add in syndicated radio, network contributes only 5 percent of all radio ad revenues. As with television, the radio network transmits both the program and the commercials to its affiliates, so the advertiser's message reaches many markets at one time. For example, when MediaAmerica beamed live network coverage of Bob Dylan's thirtieth anniversary concert from New York's Madison Square Garden, the 200 station affiliates also carried network commercials from Butterfinger, AT&T, Tri-Star Pictures, and others. Network radio is convenient and relatively low priced for advertisers seeking regional or national audiences. However, with network you can't control the number or the type of stations your commercials reach, so your message may reach people and areas outside your target audience.[56]

You can use **spot radio** to advertise in selected markets by buying commercial time directly from local stations. With spot radio advertising, you can add as many markets (and as many stations in each) as you need to reach your target audience with the required frequency. John Sortino, the founder of the Vermont Teddy Bear in Shelburne, Vermont, uses spot radio ads to build sales for made-in-America stuffed toys. He tried a small schedule of spot radio ads featuring folksy scripts read by local announcers, and when telephone orders jumped by 300 percent, he increased to 40 stations in six markets. Fueled by spot radio, sales have surged from $2 million to $12 million in just three years.[57]

National spot radio advertising makes up about 20 percent of all radio ad revenues, and it's growing as multimarket advertisers discover its benefits (see Exhibit 15.15). For instance, American Express spends more than $4 million each year on national spot radio.[58] As flexible as spot radio time can be, it's also complex and time consuming to buy because of differing station forms, rules, and rates. That's why you may want to buy spot time through reps who sell time for a number of stations.

Local spot radio time, which brings in about 75 percent of all radio ad revenues, is purchased by advertisers such as car dealers, department stores, banks, restaurants, and other local businesses (see Exhibit 15.16). Consider how New York's Metro-North Commuter Railroad uses local spot radio to reach people when they're in the right area and the right frame of mind to think about commuting by train. The Metro-North commercials run on city and suburban New York City stations during the morning and evening rush hours, when many drivers listen to their car radios while stuck in traffic. The ads contrast the problems of commuting by car with the convenience of using the railroad. By using only stations within the

EXHIBIT 15.15 The Top U.S. Network and Spot Radio Advertisers

The top 10 spot radio advertisers are able to select the specific markets where their advertising messages will be broadcast. In contrast, the top 10 network radio advertisers enjoy the benefit of reaching many markets across the country with one advertising message at one time.

	Top 10 network radio advertisers			Top 10 spot radio advertisers	
Rank	Advertiser	Network Radio Spending	Rank	Advertiser	Spot Radio Spending
1	Sears, Roebuck & Co.	$59.2	1	Philip Morris Cos.	$24.9
2	American Home Products Corp.	28.2	2	Anheuser-Busch Cos.	18.7
3	AT&T Co.	26.6	3	News Corp.	15.8
4	Himmel Group	17.9	4	Kmart Corp.	15.6
5	Accor SA	14.9	5	General Motors Corp.	15.2
6	Procter & Gamble Co.	13.6	6	Southland Corp.	14.8
7	U.S. government	13.4	7	PepsiCo	13.9
8	Warner-Lambert Co.	13.1	8	American Stores Co.	11.6
9	Gateway Educational Products	13.0	9	Grand Metropolitan	10.5
			10	BellSouth Corp.	10.3
10	Dow Jones & Co.	12.8			

Notes: Dollars are in millions; 1992 data.

EXHIBIT 15.16

EXHIBIT 15.16
Promoting Jiffy Lube on Local Spot Radio

Jiffy Lube in Baltimore, Maryland, uses local spot radio to reach people who need fast oil-change services. Its ad agency, Gary Kirk/Van Sant, creates the commercials and buys spot time on stations that reach audiences in Jiffy Lube's local market.

ANNOUNCER: Jiffy Lube presents the way things are, Part 2: Today's most commonly used customer service phrases.
MECHANIC: No. We can't do that.
CUSTOMER 1: Excuse me.
MECHANIC: I'm sorry but we're very busy.
CUSTOMER 2: I tried to call you.
CUSTOMER 1: Excuse me.
MECHANIC: I only have two hands.
CUSTOMER 2: What was your name again?

MECHANIC: I have to wait 'til the driver calls in.
MECHANIC: It looks OK to me.
MECHANIC: That's extra.
MECHANIC: I don't know who you talked to.
(list continues under announcer)
ANNOUNCER: In a world where good service is the exception rather than the rule, isn't it nice to know you can get your car's oil changed, get complete 14-point service at a low price with a guarantee, by professionals who know what they're doing and are actually polite? Jiffy Lube. A job well done in minutes. There's still hope.
MECHANIC: I'll have to get the manager. The manager's not here.

railroad's service area and advertising when drivers are trapped in traffic, Metro-North can deliver its message to the people most likely to hop its trains.[59]

ADVANTAGES AND LIMITATIONS OF RADIO ADVERTISING

Metro-North and other radio advertisers understand that to use radio advertising most effectively, they need to consider not only its advantages but also its limitations. In this way, they can make the most of radio's unique characteristics and try to minimize its limitations. This section takes an in-depth look at both.

Advantages

Among radio's many advantages for advertisers are its cost and efficiency, wide exposure, audience selectivity, flexibility, and potential for powerful imagery (see Exhibit 15.17).

EXHIBIT 15.17
Using Radio to Evoke Imagery

This radio script (created and produced by ad agency Hal Riney & Partners) invites listeners to imagine the rich tapestry of color that Fuji Film can capture.

ANNOUNCER: What's the difference between Fujicolor and regular color? Well, what do you think of when you think of "Yellow?" A traffic sign or a banana, right? That's regular yellow. Fujicolor yellow is more like a bunch of kids wearing bright yellow raincoats and getting into a bright yellow school bus, and they've all got shiny yellow umbrellas and slick yellow galoshes and they're holding yellow roses for their teacher who is racing by in her new yellow sportscar. Not *that's* Fujicolor yellow. See the difference?
2nd ANNOUNCER: Fujicolor Super HG 100, 200, and 400 film. It's a new way of seeing things.

- *Cost and efficiency.* Radio's cost per thousand is among the lowest of any medium. The CPM to reach adults via network radio averages about $4.50; spot radio costs in large markets average slightly more, still a good buy compared with television or the print media. This means you can afford to build reach and frequency through radio, even on a modest budget. The production cost for radio commercials is also quite low, and it's almost nothing if you hand the radio announcer a script to read on the air.

- *Wide exposure.* Radio reaches virtually everyone in the United States. As mentioned early in this chapter, 99 percent of all U.S. households own a radio, and the average household has five or more. Radio reaches its vast audience all day long, at work, in the car, in stores, at the beach, or on the streets. Every day, radio reaches 77 percent of the population aged 12 and older (and it reaches nearly 80 percent of teens 12 to 17 on a daily basis).[60]

- *Audience selectivity.* Radio also has the ability to reach audiences selectively. This is because each station's programming format and geographic coverage attract a specific audience segment. No matter who you want to reach or where they are, you can find a radio station that's aimed at your target. For instance, when candy maker Leaf wanted to advertise Jolly Rancher hard candy to teens, it created hip and humorous commercials that aired on rock music stations in 25 top U.S. markets.[61]

- *Flexibility.* If you need to delete, change, or insert ad copy, radio lets you do that almost instantly. It's as fast as substituting a new script or sending the station a new tape. This flexibility in what you run and when allows you to adjust quickly to changing market conditions. Such flexibility has been a plus for LoJack, which uses radio advertising to build awareness for a tracking device that locates stolen cars. Every time a LoJack system is used to find a stolen car, the firm writes a script about the case and faxes it to local stations. The announcers or disk jockeys not only read the script but also chat about it, another aspect of radio's flexibility that adds a personal touch to the message.[62]

- *Potential for powerful imagery.* Because radio has no visual component, you supply the voices, sound effects, or music, and the listener has to supply the mental picture. By inviting—or challenging—listeners to use their imaginations, you may evoke feelings and reactions more powerful than those created by ads in other media.[63]

Limitations

Although many advertisers appreciate radio's advantages, they also recognize that it has a number of limitations. Drawbacks of radio include lack of visuals, short life span, audience fragmentation, and clutter.

- *Lack of visuals.* When you use radio, your creativity is limited to sound. You can't demonstrate or even show your product, and you can't use color, movement, or any visual images to communicate your message.

- *Short life span.* As with television commercials, radio commercials are broadcast only for a few seconds and then disappear. What compounds this fleeting life span is the tendency of some people to leave radio on in the background as they work, drive, read, or do something else. These listeners aren't giving the broadcast their full attention, so they're likely to miss some or all of your brief message.

- *Audience fragmentation.* With thousands of U.S. radio stations and a wide choice of program formats, a single station or network can capture only a tiny fraction of the total listening audience. In a sprawling market such as Chicago, more than 50 radio stations crowd the airwaves, each drawing its own small but loyal band of listeners. Advertisers that need to reach large numbers in one market or in many are therefore forced to buy time on several stations or

Reaching Teens through Radio

It's no surprise that teenagers and young adults are a large and lucrative target audience that many U.S. advertisers want to reach. Teens are estimated to spend more than $20 billion every year (estimates range as high as $80 billion), and they're savvy consumers of everything from food and clothing to books and entertainment products. Exactly how can advertisers zero in on this attractive audience? For many advertisers, the most cost-efficient and direct way of reaching teens on the local level is through radio.

Each week, radio reaches nearly 99 percent of the 20 million U.S. teens who are between the ages of 12 and 17. What's more, over 90 percent of these teens listen to radio each weekday. The favorite radio format of this age group is contemporary hit radio, followed by hard rock and album-oriented rock. That's why many radio advertisers choose local stations with those formats when they want to reach teenagers.

For example, Gillette had two goals in mind when it began a radio campaign aimed at teens in the St. Louis area. First, it wanted to boost sales of its Right Guard and Soft & Dri deodorants. Second, the firm wanted to reach young people when they're just starting to use deodorants, as a way of encouraging brand loyalty at an early age. Gillette found the answer working with station KSHE-FM in St. Louis, which plays album-oriented rock. The advertiser agreed to sponsor a program titled "High School Athlete of the Week" to associate Right Guard and Soft & Dri with high school sports.

The 60-second program honored the outstanding high school athlete chosen every week by a local newspaper, and it included a testimonial explaining why the athletes like Gillette deodorant products. The spot also told listeners where to buy the product by touting savings at Grandpa's, a local discount chain. As a result of this radio campaign, Gillette significantly increased deodorant sales and laid a solid foundation for long-term brand loyalty.

Unlike Gillette's goals, which were both short- and long-term, Faces Model Agency in New Orleans had a short-term goal in mind when it targeted teens through radio. The agency wanted

Gillette used radio advertising to promote Right Guard deodorant to a teen audience.

a quick and cost-efficient ad campaign that would bring 300 teenagers to a one-day talent search. Working with sister stations WEZB and WMXZ in New Orleans, both of which use a contemporary hit radio format and hold an audience of 12- to 24-year-olds, the advertiser created a 60-second radio commercial with the message "This is your chance to be discovered."

The commercial explained the rules and requirements of the talent search, and it aired 29 times a day on each station, during every daypart, to whip up excitement and interest on the five days before the event. The agency also advertised in the local newspaper during the week before the event. The result? Faces' hard-driving radio campaign succeeded in attracting 570 participants. For Faces Model Agency, as for Gillette, radio proved to be an effective medium to reach an attractive audience.

Apply Your Knowledge

1. Which dayparts do you think would be most effective for Gillette to use in reaching teens to sell deodorant products?
2. How might the Faces Model Agency use its one-time local newspaper ad to support the radio ad campaign? ■

---

networks, which can be both cumbersome and costly. To address this limitation, most networks have restructured their affiliate lineups and added stations to build a larger total audience that's more attractive to regional and national advertisers.[64]

- *Clutter.* Unfortunately, clutter is as much a part of the radio environment as it is for any other medium. In the wee hours of the morning, radio stations carry an average of 9.7 minutes of advertising every hour, and during the morning rush hour, the hourly commercial load may swell to 12 minutes or more.[65] It's even worse in some other countries; most radio stations in Mexico, for instance, carry 24 minutes of commercials per hour.[66] To combat this clutter, advertisers need to devise creative commercials that capture audience attention, and they can also try sponsorships or adjacencies to features such as weather or sports reports that carry only a limited number of commercials.

RADIO TODAY AND TOMORROW

Radio is entering a new era of improved technology. One development is digital cable radio, which provides cable television subscribers with high-quality, commercial-free music for an additional monthly fee. Direct broadcast satellite audio is another development starting to take hold because of its superior sound quality. Like DBS television, DBS audio subscribers use a small dish to receive programming in homes, offices, cars, and trucks. Another technology used in Europe and proposed for the U.S. market is digital audio broadcasting, a system that avoids many of the interference and quality problems of AM and FM broadcasting.[67]

Technology isn't the only force shaping the radio industry today and tomorrow. In the late 1980s, when many recession-weary advertisers trimmed their radio ad budgets, some stations under pressure to survive entered into local marketing agreements, pacts in which two or more stations merge their sales and management operations—and sometimes their programming—to reduce costs. In a few instances, two strong stations have joined forces to offer advertisers wider geographic coverage and a larger total audience. For example, WHK-AM and WMMS-FM in Cleveland have hooked up with Legacy Broadcasting's WMJI-FM to sell time on all three stations. Although such combinations create larger audiences and therefore extend the stations' reach, advertisers sometimes find that they're paying more to reach people or areas they don't necessarily want.[68]

Planning Radio Advertising

As with other media, planning radio advertising involves a number of elements. One is understanding how to measure radio audiences. Another is understanding how to select time periods and how to approach radio ad rates. When you're ready to reserve commercial time, be sure you know how to place radio ads and how to use the special services networks or stations may offer.

MEASURING RADIO AUDIENCES

Just as you would when you buy television time, you can check audience research when you buy radio time. As you look into the size and composition of radio audiences, you'll be most concerned with who and how many listeners tune to a particular station at a particular time. The major firm in radio audience research is Arbitron, which depends on diaries maintained by listeners who record when they listen and what they listen to every week (see Exhibit 15.18).

Arbitron compiles information on several key measurements. One is the **average quarter-hour persons,** a measure of the average number of listeners tuned to a station for at least 5 minutes during a particular 15-minute interval of a daypart. The average quarter-hour persons is used to determine the **average quarter-hour share,** the percentage of the total radio audience that listens to a particular station during a given quarter-hour in a daypart. The formula is

$$\text{Average quarter-hour share} = \frac{\text{average quarter-hour persons for a station}}{\text{average quarter-hour persons for all stations}}$$

Another measure is the **average quarter-hour rating,** which expresses the number of listeners during a quarter-hour in a daypart as a percentage of the area population (or of the target audience population). Like television ratings, this calculation helps you compare various stations' audiences and popularity (on which ad rates are based).

When you run a radio campaign, determine how many people are likely to hear the ad at least once. To estimate this reach potential of a radio commercial, figure out the **cume persons,** also known as the *cume audience,* or the number of

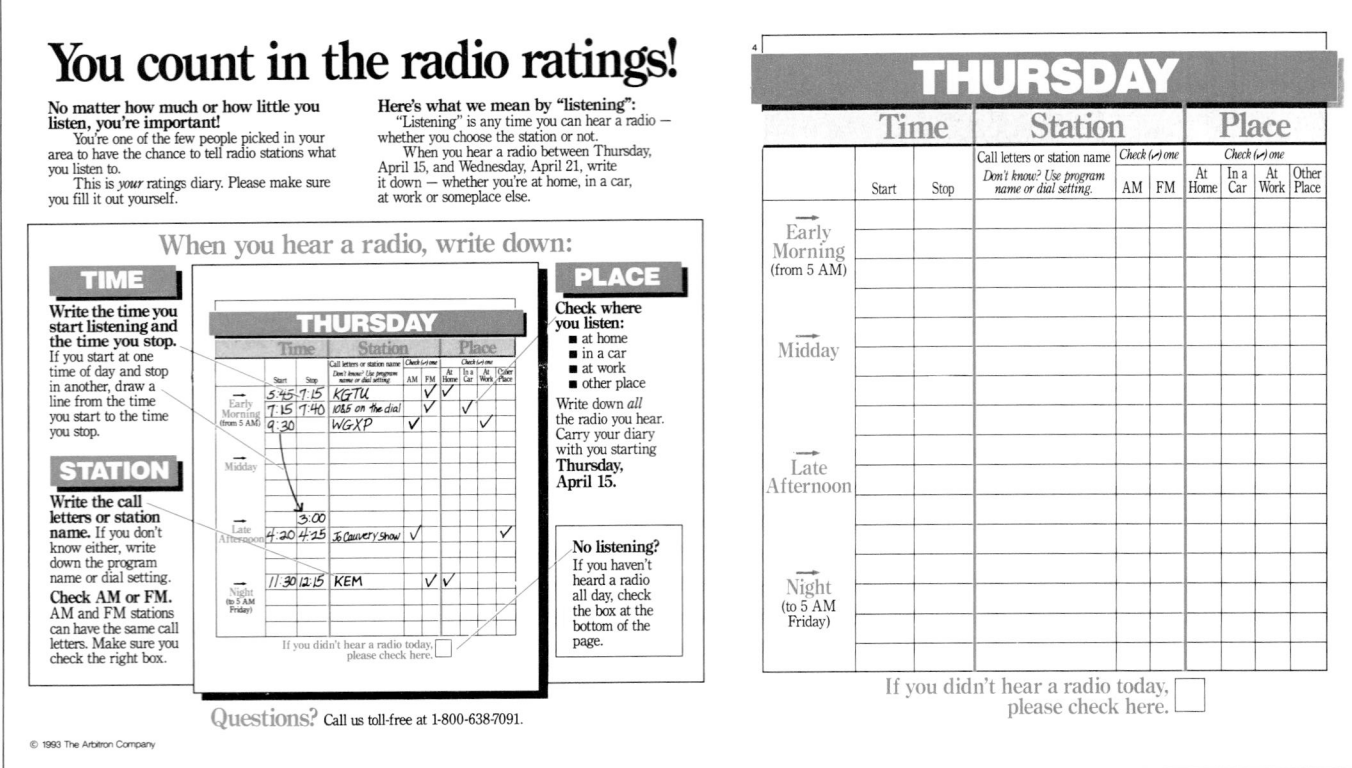

EXHIBIT 15.18
Arbitron's Radio Diary

Participants in Arbitron's radio research panel fill out diaries indicating which radio stations they heard during the day and how long they listened. Using this diary information, Arbitron can estimate the audience size and composition for each station in the market.

different people who listen to a specific station for at least 5 minutes in a given daypart. The cume-persons figure shows the potential audience for a commercial on a particular station (much like readership shows the potential audience for an ad in a magazine or newspaper), because each listener is counted only once, no matter how many times he or she tunes in during that period. The cume-persons figure is used to calculate the **cume rating,** the percentage of different people within a population or target audience who listened to a station for at least 5 minutes during a given period. The cume rating measures the cumulative (*cume*) audience during that period. The formula is

$$\text{Cume rating} = \frac{\text{cume persons}}{\text{population}}$$

Cume ratings are expressed without the percent sign. Like television ratings, cume ratings reflect audience size and are used by stations to set rates; advertisers use them to compare stations' reach (see Exhibit 15.19).

SELECTING TIME PERIODS

As you know from your own experience, people tune in and turn off the radio frequently, which means that the radio audience swells and shrinks throughout the day. So to plan your ad schedule, find out the size of the audience and the price of the ad during the various radio dayparts. The five weekday radio dayparts are:

Morning drivetime (6 A.M.–10 A.M.)

Daytime (10 A.M.–3 P.M.)

Afternoon drivetime (3 P.M.–7 P.M.)

Nighttime (7 P.M.–12 midnight)

Overnight (12 midnight–6 A.M.).

In addition, many stations lump Saturday and Sunday into a single weekend daypart. Radio draws its largest audiences during the morning and afternoon drivetime periods when people are listening as they start the day, commute to and

Specific Audience
MONDAY - FRIDAY   3PM - 7PM

			Persons 12+	Persons 18+	Men 18+	Men 18-24	Men 25-34	Men 35-44	Men 45-54	Men 55-64	Women 18+	Women 18-24	Women 25-34	Women 35-44	Women 45-54	Women 55-64	Teens 12-17
KABC																	
MET	AQH	PER(00)	519	512	266	19	17	40	52	64	246	6	11	57	59	24	7
MET	AQH	RATING	.5	.6	.6	.3	.1	.4	.8	1.6	.6	.1	.1	.6	.9	.6	.1
MET	AQH	SHARE	2.6	2.8	2.8	1.3	1.1	1.8	3.8	8.0	2.8	.4	.4	2.9	4.3	3.6	.4
MET	CUME	PER(00)	3836	3778	2152	105	219	543	412	452	1626	58	79	269	374	231	58
MET	CUME	RATING	4.0	4.4	5.0	1.4	1.9	5.9	6.7	11.4	3.7	.9	.8	2.9	5.9	5.3	.6
TSA	AQH	PER(00)	588	581	313	21	18	64	63	69	268	6	19	63	61	27	7
TSA	CUME	PER(00)	4358	4300	2497	121	235	712	486	481	1803	61	95	325	398	258	58

EXHIBIT 15.19
Using Radio Audience Research

How many listeners can your radio commercial reach during a particular time slot on a given station? You can answer this question by checking research estimates of the station's cume persons and average quarter-hour persons during each daypart. This Arbitron report indicates the estimated audience size and composition for KABC in Los Angeles.

from work or school, and wind down from the day. Because of the larger audiences, you'll probably pay higher rates during those hours.

Selecting time periods means more than just counting the number of people tuned in. It also means considering which dayparts reach people when they're most receptive to your product. For example, Heinz advertises Ore-Ida french-fried potatoes on radio only during afternoon drivetime, when people are making dinner plans as they come home from work. Similarly, Volkswagen uses drivetime radio to catch people when they're in their cars. "Many commuters hate driving," says Robert Mancini, senior vice president and media director at DDB Needham Worldwide (VW's agency), "but our research shows Volkswagen prospects really enjoy it. Advertising to them during drivetime is like pitching skis to people while they're skiing."[69]

UNDERSTANDING RADIO AD RATES

Radio ad rates, like television ad rates, vary according to the amount of time and dayparts purchased. Individual stations issue rate cards, but these rates are often negotiable (see Exhibit 15.20). As with television, run-of-station ads are usually less costly than ads scheduled during specific dayparts. Of course, network rates are higher than individual station rates because network commercials let you reach a larger audience; in fact, a network commercial costs roughly the same as buying spot time in 15 to 20 markets. However, network advertisers may pay only 50 percent of the price of a 60-second commercial to buy a 30-second commercial, whereas local and national spot advertisers may pay as much as 80 percent of the

EXHIBIT 15.20
Checking Station Facilities, Formats, and Rates

When you're buying local spot radio advertising, it's important to check each station's facilities, format, and other details. You can get this data from the local station's rate card or from its listing in Standard Rate and Data Service publications.

KRFX-FM
1961
DENVER
COUNTY:

Location ID: 4 RLST CO
Jacor Communications, Inc.
1380 Lawrence St., Ste. 1300, Denver, CO 80204. Phone 303-893-0103.
FORMAT DESCRIPTION
KRFX-FM: MUSIC: Classic Rock with AIR PERSONALITIES, traffic, special entertainment features, news, information and sports. Contact Representative for further details. Rec'd 2/10/92.
1. **PERSONNEL**
Gen Mgr—Don Howe.
Oper Mgr—Jack Evans.
Gen Sales Mgr—Mark Remington.
2. **REPRESENTATIVES**
Eastman Radio, Inc.
4. **NETWORK/GROUP AFFILIATION**
Affiliated with Eastman Radio Network.
5. **FACILITIES**
ERP 100,000 w. (horiz), 100,000 w. (vert.); 103.5 mhz. Stereo.
Antenna ht.: 1,061 ft. above average terrain.
Operating schedule: 24 hours daily. MST.
6. **AGENCY COMMISSION**
15/0.
7. **GENERAL ADVERTISING REGULATIONS**
AM facilities: KOA.
TIME RATES
Rates not submitted.

Meeting an Advertising Challenge at Colgate-Palmolive

A CASE FOR CRITICAL THINKING

Facing a 1995 deadline for growing annual sales to $9 billion, William S. Shanahan needed to bring some persuasive advertising messages to a lot of people around the world. He realized that Colgate-Palmolive's products fulfilled fairly universal needs, which meant he could use a mass-market rather than a highly targeted medium. Although Shanahan had a $500 million advertising budget, he needed to stretch those dollars across many markets where the company's products were sold.

Given these considerations, Shanahan and one of the firm's two ad agencies, Young & Rubicam, decided to emphasize television advertising. Although Colgate-Palmolive had previously pursued a global advertising approach, the effort hadn't saved as much time and money as top management had hoped. As a result, the executives and agency in each country now tailored both the media and the creative strategy to local market needs.

In Poland, for instance, Young & Rubicam's Warsaw office adapted existing commercials from other countries and created new ones geared to local tastes. At the same time, the media planners were careful to avoid the kind of ad blitz that Polish viewers associated with communist propaganda. Instead of bombarding viewers

with ads during the start of a new-product campaign, they scheduled only 12 commercials during the first week.

In England, Young & Rubicam's media planners came up with a clever scheduling idea to promote Actibrush mouthwash, an idea that could easily be transported across national lines. A well-dressed gentleman started the viewers' television day by explaining Actibrush's long-lasting effects during a 30-second commercial. Then the spokesman popped up in 10-second commercials during the next 12 hours with the reminder that "it's still working."

Sharing media and creative strategies across national borders and adapting to local market conditions are methods that have strengthened Colgate-Palmolive's push for higher sales. Shanahan, of course, plans to stay tuned for the 1995 results.

Your Mission: You've been appointed director of advertising for all Colgate-Palmolive products in Europe and North America. Use your knowledge of television advertising to choose the best option in each of the following situations, bearing in mind what you learned in Chapter 8 about intercultural differences in audiences and media.

1. Colgate Plax holds nearly 30 percent of the international mouthwash market, but you know that there's plenty of room for sales growth in Europe. You're planning a television ad campaign to tap this potential. Which of the following ideas would be the most cost-effective way to test the campaign?

a. Buy spot time to test one commercial on one cable station in one market. Depending on the results, you can adapt the commercial and try it country by country on other stations. You want to reach people throughout Europe, so don't worry about media spillover—in fact, you should check sales in neighboring markets to see whether spillover has had an impact.

b. Test a pan-European commercial by buying spot time on international cable television channels such as CNN and MTV. These cable channels reach upscale audiences in nearly every European country, so you'll avoid wasting media dollars on audiences and areas you don't want to reach.

c. Sponsor a Christmas concert that's carried live on cable television throughout the continent. That way you can test an entire set of commercials during one program that reaches audiences all over Europe.

60-second price for 30 seconds.[70] For this reason, network radio can be cost effective for national advertisers seeking to reach many markets.

PLACING RADIO ADS

When you place radio ads, you start by identifying the stations or networks that attract your target audience, determining which dayparts offer the greatest number of potential customers; then you check station or network rates and avails. However, buying radio time doesn't involve the same scramble to lock up time in the up-front market as buying television entails. Some advertisers, such as Campbell Soup, make up-front deals during the summer for commercials that run in the fall and winter, but others prefer to buy according to the calendar year or their companies' fiscal years. One reason to buy early is to try for exclusivity, shutting out competitors; another is to arrange better prices or special services that stretch your ad dollars. However, when you buy up-front, you run the risk that a station may change formats before your ads run, which means your message might be heard by an entirely different audience than you'd originally planned.[71]

#1 Around the World!

2. To encourage first-time purchases of a new fabric softener being launched in Canada, your agency has created two 30-second commercials. Which of these scheduling options would be most appropriate?

a. Fabric softener is a big enough mass-market product that it doesn't matter when or where your ads air. You should buy run-of-station time only.

b. Buy 30 seconds at the beginning and 30 seconds at the end of one commercial pod in the middle of programs that draw a large share of viewers in your target audience. This way, you grab viewers as the program winds down for the commercial break as well as just before the program resumes—without annoying the audience by showing the same ad twice.

c. Use the idea in option b, but buy time only during the highest-rated programs on each station. This helps you maximize your reach and gives you the prestige of advertising during popular shows that viewers watch and discuss.

3. Colgate-Palmolive is planning to introduce a combination shower gel-and-lotion product in the southern United States, following a successful European launch. The target audience is women 18 to 49. Which of these ideas will help you build awareness among the target audience?

a. Use sponsorship to link this product with the highest-ranking, longest-running daytime soap opera shown on television. This way, your message will be seen every day—and will be received positively—by loyal viewers, and you'll retain control over the commercial schedule.

b. Buy spot television time on afternoon and early-evening programs in markets where the new product will be available. Where possible, buy adjacencies rather than station breaks, so you can catch viewers who are waiting for the next show or who are lingering after the previous one.

c. Rotate commercials for the new product into participations that you've already arranged for other products. This way, you can take advantage of time you've already purchased.

4. You're meeting with the media planners from Young & Rubicam, who are working on a media plan for introducing Mennen Crystal Clear deodorant in Great Britain. They want to use the same kind of scheduling technique that was used for Actibrush mouthwash. Which of the following three proposals should you approve?

a. Use a 60-second commercial during the first commercial pod of the first morning newscast to introduce the product and explain its long-lasting deodorant action. Then buy the first 15-second slot during news programs in all other dayparts to remind viewers that the product is still working.

b. Buy the first and last minute of commercial time during every weekend sports program. Use the first 60-second commercial to let viewers know that the product works all day, and mention that it will work until the last Mennen commercial airs later that night. Reinforce the benefits of all-day protection during the second 60 seconds.

c. Use a series of live 15-second commercials to follow an athlete as he puts on Mennen deodorant in the morning and goes through his rigorous daily routine, odor-free. Air the first commercial at 7 A.M. and then air subsequent commercials every three hours until 1 A.M.[73] ∎

USING SPECIAL RADIO SERVICES

With radio advertising, you have the opportunity to take advantage of special services such as detailed audience research, merchandising support, and product exclusivity in certain dayparts. In addition, because advertisers can get involved with the station and its air personalities, radio ads often take on an extra bit of local color that appeals to the local target audience.

For example, when Campbell Soup worked with Dallas's WBAP and its sister station KSCS to promote Campbell's Ranch Style Beans, the stations asked listeners to send in their favorite barbecue recipes, and then they staged a Labor Day weekend cookoff at a local store; winners received a grocery-shopping spree. Stations KIXZ and KMML in Amarillo, Texas, cooked up a different promotion: they gave away samples at live broadcasts before Labor Day and arranged with local supermarkets to create in-store displays so that people could find the beans they had sampled. To encourage stores to participate, the Amarillo stations gave prizes to those with the best displays. By letting local stations develop unique promotions for their audiences, Campbell localized the appeal of its product.[72]

Summary

Television and radio have become an integral part of everyday life. Television programs and commercials reach viewers through broadcast, cable, and syndication. The three forms of television advertising are sponsorships, participations, and spot announcements. Broadcast television has a number of advantages, including creative flexibility, coverage of mass markets, and cost efficiency. Among its limitations are limited selectivity, audience erosion, relatively high entry cost, clutter, brevity, and limited viewer attention. Compared with broadcast television, cable offers three advantages: increased selectivity, lower entry costs, and increased flexibility. Its limitations include limited reach, audience fragmentation, and limited research.

Nielsen estimates the size of a program's audience by calculating its program rating, the percentage of all households with a television in a specific market tuned into that program. To make this calculation, Nielson divides the number of households tuned to the program by the total number of television households (the number of households in that market equipped with television). Share reflects the audience for a program as a percentage of the total audience viewing television at that time. Share is calculated by dividing the number of households viewing a program by the number of households using television at that time.

Radio programs and commercials reach listeners through four methods: AM, FM, network, and syndication. Radio advertising can be classified as network (which usually includes syndicated advertising) or spot radio. Local and national spot radio account for 95 percent of all radio advertising revenues; network radio (including syndicated advertising) accounts for 5 percent. The advantages of radio advertising are its cost and efficiency, wide exposure, audience selectivity, flexibility, and potential for powerful imagery. Radio's limitations include the lack of visuals, the short life span, audience fragmentation, and clutter.

One key measurement of radio audiences is average quarter-hour persons, a measure of the average number of listeners tuned to a station for at least 5 minutes during a particular 15-minute interval of a daypart. The average quarter-hour persons is used to determine the average quarter-hour share, the percentage of the radio audience listening to a particular station during a given quarter-hour in a daypart. The average quarter-hour rating expresses the number of listeners during a quarter-hour in a daypart as a percentage of the population (or of the target audience). To estimate the reach of a radio commercial, figure out the number of cume persons, the number of different people who listen to a certain station for at least 5 minutes in a given daypart. The cume-persons figure is used to calculate the cume rating, the percentage of different people within a population who listen to a station for at least 5 minutes during a given period.

Key Terms

adjacency 406
affidavit of performance 416
affiliates 403
audimeter 412
avails 416
average quarter-hour
  persons 423
average quarter-hour
  rating 423
average quarter-hour
  share 423
barter syndication 404
cable television 404
commercial pod 416
cost per rating point
  (CPP) 414
cume persons 423
cume rating 424
daypart 414
designated market area
  (DMA) 413
direct broadcast satellite
  (DBS) 411
first-run syndication 404
grazing 409
households using television
  (HUT) 413
interactive television 412
interconnects 407
local spot 406
makegood 415
multipoint distribution
  system (MDS) 412
narrowcasting 409
national spot 406
off-network syndication 404
participation 406
preemption rate 416
prime time 414
program rating 413
run of station 414
share of audience 413
sponsorship 405
spot announcement 406
spot radio 419
spot television 406
superstation 404
television households
  (TVHH) 413
zapping 409
zipping 409

Questions

FOR REVIEW

1. What is a daypart, and how are dayparts defined in television and radio?

2. How is cost per rating point calculated?

3. What are the advantages and limitations of broadcast television advertising?

4. How does television sponsorship differ from participation and spot announcements?

5. How does the fragmentation of radio audiences work for and against the advertiser?

FOR ANALYSIS AND APPLICATION

6. If the networks reduce clutter by capping the number of commercials or the total number of commercial minutes broadcast every hour, what are the implications for television advertisers?

7. What challenges do grazing and zapping pose for researchers who measure audiences by asking viewers to keep a diary of their viewing habits? How would advertisers and agencies be likely to react to the use of technology such as passive people meters that record every channel change?

8. What radio formats and dayparts might Kraft choose to reach a target audience of working women with commercial messages about its Macaroni and Cheese Dinner?

9. If you were the agency media planner for a local Midas Muffler franchise in Anchorage, Alaska (where roughly 53 percent of the TVHH have cable), would you recommend that your client buy spot announcements on broadcast or on cable television? Why?

10. How might a business advertiser such as Federal Express use sponsorship of a segment of a television show to cost effectively reach a target audience of small-business owners who buy next-day shipping services?

Sharpen Your Advertising Skills

One of Barry Kinsey's favorite sayings is "Let them eat little cakes!" As vice president and associate media director at CME-KHBB, Minneapolis, Kinsey handles media for Interstate Bakeries' Dolly Madison snack cakes, and he believes that men 18 to 34 who buy single-serving snack cakes in convenience stores are an attractive target audience. This is a big change from the previous strategy, which called for Dolly Madison to reach mothers aged 24–54 through primary sponsorship of "Charlie Brown" television specials.

Kinsey has a limited media budget and a target audience where there's little share-of-voice competition but lower brand awareness, so he wants more frequency. He's developed a fictional character called the "Snackin' Dude" who goes to great lengths to seek out Dolly Madison and her snack cakes. Now he has to decide how to stimulate young men to make a snacking stop at the local convenience store before or after work or school.

Decision: Should Kinsey use spot television or radio? Think about the advantages and limitations of each and decide which makes the most sense for Dolly Madison. You can also look back at Chapter 13 to refresh your memory about media schedules.

Communication: Write a brief (one- to two-page) memo to the client proposing a media schedule based on the decision to use television or radio. Although you don't need to suggest specific television or radio stations or programs, you should mention the dayparts you prefer, the type of television or radio programs you want your spots to appear in or adjacent to, and the rationale for choosing the medium you're recommending.

Direct Marketing and Out-of-Home Advertising

After studying this chapter, you will be able to

1. Distinguish among direct marketing, direct-response advertising, and direct-mail advertising

2. Discuss the purpose of database marketing

3. Explain how to use direct mail, catalogs, print media, electronic media, and telemarketing as direct-marketing media

4. Outline the advantages and limitations of direct marketing

5. List the various types of outdoor advertising and describe their advantages and limitations

6. Identify the types of transit advertising and highlight the advantages and disadvantages of such advertising

7. Describe other types of out-of-home advertising and discuss the audience measurement issues associated with these advertising approaches

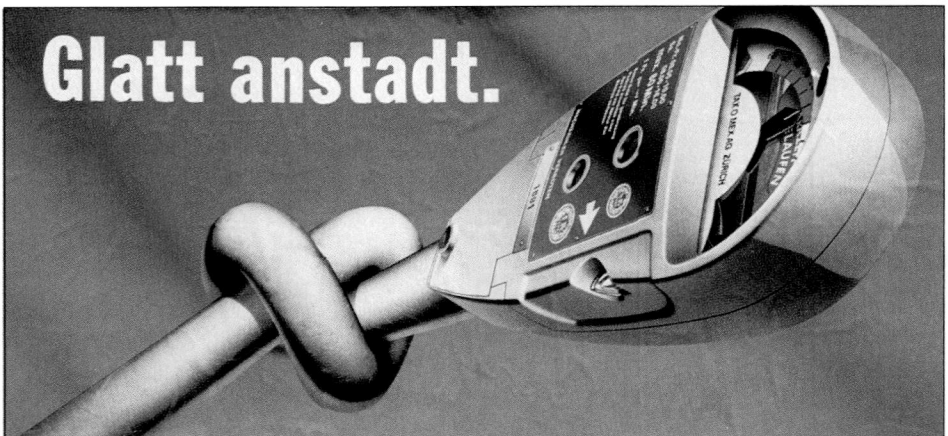

Facing an Advertising Challenge at MCI Communications

BELLS ARE RINGING FOR MCI'S FRIENDS & FAMILY

How do you compete with a rival whose name is practically synonymous with your product? Ask Angela L. Dunlap. When she was senior vice president of product marketing and communication for MCI Communications, she faced the formidable name recognition of AT&T, which had held the long-distance telephone monopoly in the United States for many decades. It was Dunlap's job to persuade consumers to choose MCI as their long-distance telephone carrier; once they became customers, it was her job to persuade them to stay with MCI.

MCI's advertising duel with AT&T began in earnest after legal challenges opened the long-distance business to competition in the 1970s. Staking out a position as a low-cost provider, MCI targeted price-conscious consumers with an intense campaign that helped boost its market share to number two. At the start of 1990, MCI held nearly 14 percent of the U.S. market, and market leader

AT&T held 71 percent, but by year's-end MCI's share had dropped to 13 percent. As AT&T and others bombarded consumers with ad messages about the quality and cost of their long-distance services, MCI's revenue growth slowed.

Faced with this onslaught of competitive pressure, MCI knew just who to call: friends and family. Aptly named, MCI's innovative Friends & Family program was designed to expand its customer base and encourage long-term loyalty by offering a 20 percent discount on calls made to as many as 12 other households. The mechanics were simple: customers gave MCI the names and phone numbers of people in their own "Calling Circle," the 12 friends, family members, and others they called most often. In turn, MCI contacted these people to offer its long-distance services and the added benefit of a 20 percent discount on calls made to 12 of their friends and family.

Friends & Family, launched in 1991,

was an immediate hit. Moreover, it differentiated MCI from other low-rate rivals by giving it a "good-guy" image. In 1992, MCI added more Friends & Family benefits (increasing the Calling Circle size to 20, doubling the discount for a limited time, and offering other goodies). Now Angela Dunlap was ready to mount an ad campaign to explain these new benefits and to convince more customers to join or use the Friends & Family program. Given MCI's detailed list of customer names and addresses, Dunlap knew she could reach this target audience directly—through the mail.

Imagine yourself in Dunlap's position. How would you use direct mail to deliver the message? Could you use the information in MCI's files to personalize the message for each person in the target audience? What could you do to encourage recipients to read what you send? How would you encourage fast response, and what would make it easier for customers to respond?[1] ■

CHAPTER OVERVIEW Going directly to the target audience has become one of MCI Communications's most effective methods of increasing its market share. This chapter explores how direct marketing and out-of-home advertising are used to achieve a variety of advertising goals. First you'll look at the many direct-marketing approaches you can use, and you'll learn how database marketing operates. Next you'll examine the major types of direct-marketing media, including direct mail, catalogs, print media, electronic media, telemarketing, and billboards. Then you'll explore direct marketing's advantages and limitations. Finally, you'll learn about out-of-home advertising, including outdoor advertising, transit advertising, and other methods.

Direct Marketing

As mentioned in Chapters 13, 14, and 15, one of the biggest trends in advertising is the push toward media that can reach narrowly defined target audiences. Ultimately, advertisers want to be able to communicate with individuals—one at a time, rather than as part of an anonymous group. After all, it isn't the target audience that buys (or votes or donates money); it's the individual who takes action.

In their quest to reach out to specific individuals, more advertisers are using **direct marketing** to communicate directly with individuals in their target audiences and to sell products without going through intermediaries such as retailers or wholesalers. You can use direct marketing to establish direct two-way communi-

cation between your organization and your customers and prospects, without the distractions, interruptions, or inefficiencies of working through intermediaries.

However, direct marketing is not an advertising technique; it's an umbrella term covering various ways in which advertisers directly approach their target audiences to make a sale (or to accomplish some other objective) (see Exhibit 16.1). One form of direct marketing is **direct-response advertising,** which supports a direct-marketing effort by asking the target audience to respond, to take immediate action. Exactly what response you ask for depends on what you're selling and how you're selling it. If your product is inexpensive and simple to explain, you may make the offer and ask for the order in one step. However, if your product is more expensive or complicated to explain, you may prefer to use a two-step approach. In the first step, you introduce your product and invite prospects to call or write for more information or to get a small sample. The actual sale comes in the second step: After prospects have seen the additional information or the sample, or met with a salesperson, they can call or write to place their orders.

For example, Florida Fruit Shippers advertises its grapefruit and oranges in *CompuServe Magazine* and includes the price and a telephone number for immediate (one-step) ordering. In contrast, North Carolina Discount Furniture Sales sells its fine furniture by mail in a two-step process. The firm advertises (in *The New York Times Magazine* and other publications) to encourage prospects to call for a list of brands and prices. Once prospects have seen the list and compared prices with those in local outlets, they can call or write to order any item.[2]

Another form of direct marketing is **direct-mail advertising,** which refers to any advertising that's delivered directly to the target audience by mail (or by a private delivery service). When you both sell and deliver merchandise by mail, you're using the traditional technique of **mail order,** a method some retailers have used for over one hundred years. Of course, mail order is no longer the only way to sell products outside a store. Today you can encourage customers to order by telephone, by fax, or even by computer (through Prodigy, CompuServe, or other computer services, discussed in Chapter 17). These newer ordering methods don't depend on the mail to deliver the message, but they're still considered part of the mail-order industry when the products are delivered by mail.

Direct marketing has become a way of life for many advertisers. Advertisers can use almost any medium for direct marketing, and it's not uncommon to use a combination of, say, direct mail and telemarketing or some other media mix to reach the targeted audience several times and in several ways. For example, AT&T wanted to defend its share against other carriers (including MCI and Sprint) that had wooed small businesses with promises of lower long-distance telephone rates and more responsive service. AT&T kicked off its "We want you back" campaign with network television, print media, and billboard advertising. Each ad included a toll-free number for small-business owners to call for more information. When a prospect called, a representative assessed the firm's needs and offered the appropriate promotional package. The prospect received a direct-mail piece with further details, and AT&T salespeople followed up by telephone to close the sale.

The campaign was only beginning. After building awareness through six weeks of media advertising, AT&T started a direct-mail, telephone, and personal sales blitz that continued the theme "We want you back." Using lists of small-business customers, AT&T segmented the market according to the size of each prospect's monthly long-distance bill and carefully created a special offer for each segment. When the results were in, this multimedia direct-marketing campaign had helped stop AT&T's market-share loss.[3]

USING DATABASE MARKETING

It's impossible to use direct-marketing techniques if you don't know who the members of your target audience are, what they buy, or how you can reach them. An increasing number of advertisers base their direct-marketing programs on a **database,** a comprehensive and continually updated file of information about individuals in the target audience. Many advertisers use databases to turn prospects into customers, and an increasing number of advertisers are using databases to cultivate long-term relationships with existing customers. It's cheaper to get repeat business from customers than it is to attract new customers, so keeping customer information on a database can help boost sales as well as profits.[4]

With specialized computer systems, you can develop a database of the names, addresses, and buying patterns of your customers, using details gleaned from subscriptions, invoices, inquiries, warranty cards, and other sources. MCI's database consists of names, addresses, phone numbers, and other details about customers that use its long-distance telephone services. Similarly, Toyota Motors' U.S. unit maintains a 7-million-customer database that includes names, addresses, and dates of purchase.[5]

Building a customer database can take time, especially if you don't sell by mail or if you don't generally record your customers' names and addresses, but it's the only way to know exactly who does business with you. Pizza Hut, Walt Disney, and Nintendo are just three of the many companies that are developing databases so that they can communicate directly with their customers. For example, Pizza Hut has offered a Value Card as one way of gathering information about customers. In exchange for receiving a card that entitles them to discounts, customers are asked to provide basic personal data (such as name and address).[6] You can enhance your customer files by **overlaying,** or adding information purchased from market research firms, credit-reporting agencies, the U.S. Census, and other sources. With these extra data, you can get a well-rounded picture of your customers' lifestyles, interests, and habits.

In turn, this comprehensive file becomes the foundation for **database marketing,** a form of direct marketing in which advertisers use a database to define the best target audience for a given offer at a particular time. Unlike traditional direct marketing, which relies on market segmentation techniques to target groups of people (see Chapter 5), database marketing is an updated technique that helps you target individuals more accurately. By analyzing each person's situation, purchasing patterns, and needs, you can determine the likelihood that he or she will buy or

EXHIBIT 16.2
Cross-Selling to Customers via Database Marketing

Time Life marketers know that once a prospect becomes a customer, he or she is often the best prospect for the sale of a related product. By using the firm's computerized database to analyze customer buying patterns and interests, Time Life marketers can more effectively target the individuals most appropriate for a particular offer.

use your product, vote for a particular candidate, or donate money to your cause. This allows you to assemble the target audience for each offer—one name at a time.[7]

For instance, for a promotion to sell new trucks, Madrid-based Mercedes-Benz España went into its database of current truck owners. It singled out people whose trucks were aging (and who would therefore be likely to want a replacement) and people who had bought a lower-priced model (and who might be interested in upgrading to a better model). Because Mercedes-Benz could identify its target market on an individual level, the firm was able to reach only those people most interested in the promotion.[8]

If you're introducing a new product, you might start by doing research to learn about the people most likely to buy the product. Once you know the profile of these people (their demographics, their buying behavior, and so on), you can identify your target market by searching through other databases for individuals with those characteristics.[9] Database marketing also lets you identify the most promising prospects by looking at your best customers. To do this, you first determine the common characteristics of those who donate the most money or buy your most profitable products. Then you choose your target audience by combing prospect databases for more people with the same characteristics.

Database marketing is well suited to *cross-selling,* selling a related product to a customer who bought some other product (see Exhibit 16.2). MCI did this when it sifted through its customer lists to find prospects for Friends & Family. Time Life is a big believer in cross-selling, too. To find prospects for related products, its personnel regularly scour the Time Warner database of 44 million customers (people who subscribe to its magazines or buy its records, books, or videos). Not long ago, it analyzed the database of book buyers to assemble a target audience for its videocassette of *Land of the Eagle,* a documentary about history and nature in the American West. After weighing the kinds of interests that a prospective buyer

Database Marketing and the Law

Database marketing has become a priority for advertisers who are searching for ways to target their audiences efficiently and effectively. However, as the number of databases grows, and as computerization makes data collection and interchange faster and easier, government officials and consumer advocates are voicing concerns about the impact on privacy. Consumers don't always know who's seeing their personal data—or exactly what's in any particular database. That's what troubles people. In a recent survey, 80 percent of the respondents said that companies shouldn't share personal information.

These concerns are being heard and discussed by both government and business leaders. "I think privacy is going to be the issue of the 1990s," comments Bonnie Jansen of the U.S. Office of Consumer Affairs. "We have to address consumer expectations and consumer concerns." Jonah Gitlitz, president of the Direct Marketing Association, says, "Consumers want to be satisfied that we're sensitive to their needs, that some of the information they're providing should be considered confidential."

In response to these concerns, Congress has established or proposed a variety of rules for U.S. advertisers to follow in ensuring consumer privacy. On the federal level, advertisers that use databases must comply with at least five major privacy laws. Four separate laws govern the collection and dissemination of consumer credit information, government data, banking information, and videotape rental records, and a fifth lays out the rules for computerized matching of government information.

Advertisers also have to comply with the laws and regulations in each state where they operate. Since the rules vary from state to state, it's important to carefully research exactly what can and can't be done in a particular state. For example, in Virginia, retailers that provide customer information to other companies must post signs so that consumers are aware of this practice. Even though Virginia stores can build customer databases, they can't avoid letting consumers know that personal data may be exchanged with others. In New York, stores can't ask a customer to write his or her address or phone number on a credit card slip; this means that the stores have to find another way to gather this information for their databases.

As straightforward as these laws may seem, advertisers that mail to people in more than one state may spend a good deal of time and money understanding and complying with all the states' rules. Moreover, some proposals could, as a by-product, create operational nightmares for advertisers. For instance, one recently defeated California measure would have forced direct marketers to notify consumers each time a list that included their name was sold or rented. If the law had passed, advertisers that rent their databases often (or that have large databases for rent) would have faced a lot of letter writing—and a large bill for postage.

Still being considered in various states are proposals (1) to require advertisers to act when consumers ask that their names be removed from databases, (2) to strengthen safeguards against the unauthorized disclosure of credit information, and (3) to restrict the use of motor vehicle records for marketing purposes. So for the foreseeable future, advertisers may have to comply with even stronger measures to ensure consumer privacy.

Apply Your Knowledge

1. How much should database marketers be required by law to tell consumers about the collection and interchange of personal information?
2. How might a catalog merchant reassure customers that their privacy is being protected?

---

of this video might have, the company sent mailings to customers who had bought books about the old West, about nature, and about life under the ocean.[10]

For businesses that rely on *direct selling,* in which the seller and the buyer meet face to face, database marketing can efficiently generate more and better leads. For example, when Polaroid launched a new camera to photograph employees or students for identification tags, it mailed letters to business customers in its database who had purchased the previous model. This approach generated more than twice the number of leads of a nondatabase promotion, and it slashed the cost of each lead by 70 percent.[11]

As the Polaroid example shows, database marketing reduces advertising waste by helping you concentrate your efforts on only those most likely to respond. In turn, as you learn more about each person in the database, you can more precisely target your offers and your media. Also, because you know enough about the individuals in your target audience to understand what they're likely to buy—and what they don't need or want—you can forge an ongoing relationship with your customers that transcends any one purchase.[12]

Advertisers can reach out directly to customers and prospects in many ways. In the following sections, you'll take a closer look at the major direct-marketing media, including direct mail, catalogs, print and electronic media, telemarketing, and billboards.

USING DIRECT MAIL

As you might expect, direct mail is the most common medium for direct marketing, and it's truly big business. Every year, advertisers spend $25 billion to send postcards, letters, and other direct-mail pieces to businesses and consumers. What's more, despite periodic postal rate increases, the volume of direct mail continues to grow. In 1986, 55 billion pieces of direct-mail advertising were sent out, but by 1991, the number had ballooned to 62.4 billion. Direct-mail advertising now represents fully half of all the mail delivered to U.S. households.[13] When you use direct mail, you need to be concerned about your format and your lists.

Choosing Direct-Mail Advertising Formats

Direct-mail advertising can take many forms. A **self-mailer** is a postcard, brochure, or other printed material that's delivered without an envelope. The recipient's name and address are printed directly on the outside of the self-mailer, which may be stapled or sealed shut for mailing. Postcards do get their messages across: in one study for the U.S. Postal Service, researchers found that postcards were more likely to be read than other forms of direct-mail advertising.[14]

If you put your message into an envelope, your first task is to get the recipient to actually open the piece. So your envelope might dazzle the reader with color, with graphics, or with important benefits; it might impress the reader with its importance; or it might tease the reader to arouse curiosity (see Exhibit 16.3).[15] Another way to encourage people to read your message is to put it inside an intriguing three-dimensional package. To reach managers of group pension plans, Phoenix Mutual Life Insurance used a box with teaser copy reading "There's more than one way to make a name for yourself." Inside was a tangle of puzzle pieces that, when assembled, formed the prospect's name. Ten days later, the insurance company sent the same prospects a service bell with a message reading, "You won't need a bell this big to get our attention. We're into serving our clients." The results? Even though group pension sales are usually slow to complete, Phoenix completed a $10 million pension deal within three months of the first mailing.[16]

The letter, which may be computer-generated, typewritten, or typeset and printed, is the main ingredient in most direct-mail packages. Although some letters may be as brief as a single page, most run two to four pages or longer—as long as necessary to fully explain the offer, the benefits, and the call to action. Ending the letter with a strong appeal in the postscript (P.S.) is a practice that experts say can help close the sale or at least entice readers to read through the letter.[17]

A letter rarely rides alone. It's often accompanied by a brochure, a leaflet, or a **broadside** (also known as a *broadsheet*), a folded sheet of paper, printed on one or both sides, that opens into a large ad. In addition, many mailings include reply cards on which customers can note their orders or their donations. To make things even easier for your customers, you can include a **business reply envelope,** a postage-paid envelope that the customer can use to respond. All the customer has to do is insert the reply card, seal the envelope, and mail it.

Potential donors to the Potato Project, a nonprofit group that distributes potatoes and other produce to local food-bank groups, received a direct-mail envelope that contained (1) a four-page letter asking for a cash contribution (signed by a farmer who had donated hundreds of pounds of potatoes), (2) a two-part reply card (one part to be returned with the donation and the other to be retained as a receipt), and (3) a postage-paid business reply envelope for the donor's convenience.[18]

Other forms of direct-mail advertising include the **statement stuffer,** a small printed ad designed to be inserted into a customer invoice; a **reprint,** a copy of an ad, an article, or some other material that has appeared elsewhere but may be of interest to customers or prospects; and a **house organ,** a publication produced by a business or a nonprofit group to keep customers, contributors, dealers, investors, and others informed. Increasingly, advertisers are turning to house organs such as newsletters or magazines to help build customer loyalty and to convert prospects into customers.

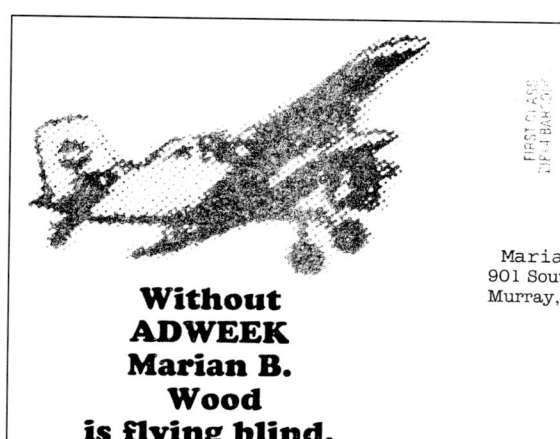

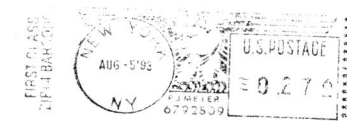

FIRST CLASS ZIP+4 BARCODE
NEW YORK NY
AUG -5'93
U.S.POSTAGE
Marian B. Wood
901 South Street
Murray, UT 84107-2157
Without ADWEEK Marian B. Wood is flying blind.

EXHIBIT 16.3

The Envelope, Please

One way to stimulate interest in what's inside is to splash eye-catching color illustrations over the envelope—and offer something free (see envelope below). Another way is to personalize the envelope with a slightly cryptic message that arouses curiosity (see envelope on left).

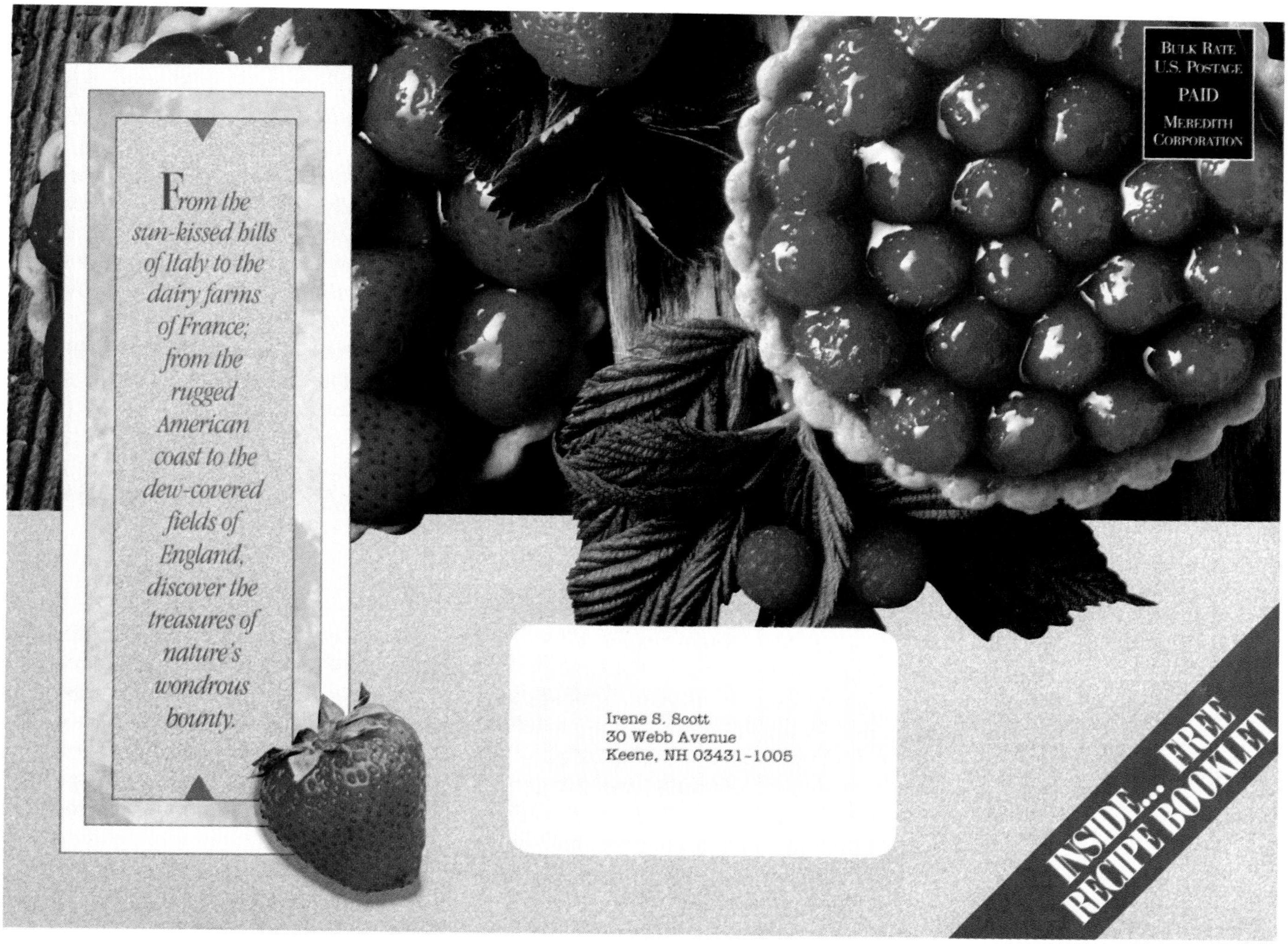
BULK RATE
U.S. POSTAGE
PAID
MEREDITH CORPORATION
From the sun-kissed hills of Italy to the dairy farms of France; from the rugged American coast to the dew-covered fields of England, discover the treasures of nature's wondrous bounty.
Irene S. Scott
30 Webb Avenue
Keene, NH 03431-1005
INSIDE... FREE RECIPE BOOKLET

For example, the Barn Nursery & Landscape Center in Cary, Illinois, sends a newsletter to more than 2,000 customers. The newsletter provides gardening tips that most customers can't get from discount or self-serve nursery chains, which gives them a reason to stay with Barn Nursery. On the other hand, Scientific Information Services of Fort Worth, Texas, uses its monthly newsletter to attract new customers who need the firm's expertise in hazardous-waste regulations; as a result of leads generated by the newsletter, the firm gains six or more new accounts every month.[19]

Doubleday Book Club

Doubleday List Marketing

Location ID: 10 DCLS 564   Mid 019984-000
Member: D.M.A.
Participant D.M.A. Mail Preference Service.
Doubleday Mailing Lists.
501 Franklin Ave., Garden City, NY 11530. Phone 516-
873-4477. Fax: 516-873-4774.
Specific list selections are located in each
appropriate classification in their normal alphabetical
sequence.
1. **PERSONNEL**
   Manager, List Marketing—Diane Silverman.
   Assistant Manager, List Mktg.—Liz Maletta.
   List Mktg. Coordinator—Linda Jackson.
   Broker and/or Authorized Agent
   All recognized brokers.
2. **DESCRIPTION**
   Doubleday Book Club members.
   ZIP Coded in numerical sequence 100%.
3. **LIST SOURCE**
   Direct mail and space ads.
4. **QUANTITY AND RENTAL RATES**
                     Rec'd Mar. 8, 1990.

	Total Number	Price per/M
Members	900,000	75.00
Hotline	479,000	80.00
Completers (1989-90)	433,000	40.00
Age-coded names	2,130,000	80.00

   Selections: enrollment date, 5.00/M extra; dollar select,
   6.00/M extra; Mr./Mrs./Miss/Ms., sex, 3.00/M extra;
   state, SCF, ZIP tape, 4.00/M extra.
5. **COMMISSION, CREDIT POLICY**
   20% commission to all recognized brokers. Payments
   due 30 days after billing.
6. **METHOD OF ADDRESSING**
   4/5-up Cheshire labels. 4-up pressure sensitive labels,
   5.00/M extra. Magnetic tape (9T 1600/6250 BPI).
7. **DELIVERY SCHEDULE**
   Ten working days.
8. **RESTRICTIONS**
   Sample mailing piece required for approval.
9. **TEST ARRANGEMENT**
   Minimum 10,000.
11. **MAINTENANCE**
   Cleaned and updated quarterly.

EXHIBIT 16.4
Selecting Mailing Lists

One of the most important steps in planning any direct-mail advertising program is selecting the right mailing list. You can check the size, composition, and cost of many consumer and business lists in the Standard Rate and Data Service *Direct Mail List Rates and Data.*

Selecting Mailing Lists

Just as a television show's viewership or a magazine's readership determines who will see your commercial or magazine ad, the mailing list defines the target audience that will receive your direct-mail piece. By selecting mailing lists according to the specific characteristics you require, you can reach highly targeted market segments (see Exhibit 16.4). Depending on its source, a list may include not only name and address but also demographic details (such as occupation and family status) or behavioral information (such as purchasing habits and brand preferences). In general, you can use three types of mailing lists: house lists, response lists, and compiled lists.

A **house list** is a list of customers (and sometimes prospects) that's maintained by your organization. No list is more valuable, because (1) customers who have established a relationship with you are the most likely to purchase (or donate) again, and (2) people who have asked for information in the past are better prospects than people who have never expressed interest in you or your product. Businesses and retailers that send invoices to their customers can also use their billing lists for advertising new products or selling additional services. Organizations without a house list can encourage customers and prospects to sign up by offering prizes, information, discounts, or other incentives.[20]

A **response list** is a mailing list of people who have responded to direct-mail offers for products that are similar or related to your own. The prospects on such lists can be valuable because they're interested in mail-order offers and, more important, they're proven direct-mail customers of goods or services much like your own. For example, Barnes & Noble, which sells $30 million worth of books by mail every year, reaches prospects through a number of response lists. Its best results come from the lists of the Book-of-the-Month Club and the Quality Paperback Book Club, but response lists from Time Life Books, Laissez-Faire Books, and Knowledge Products also perform well.[21]

A **compiled list** is one that has been assembled by an outside firm from directories, public records, and other readily available sources. Such lists don't indicate whether the people have ever responded to direct-mail offers, so they're not as valuable as response lists. However, you can use compiled lists to identify prospects in specific market segments such as new home owners, corporate purchasing agents, small-business owners, and others. American Business Information, a source for compiled lists of businesses, puts its lists together from yellow page directories, government data, annual reports, and other sources. In addition to the name and address of the business and the name of the owner or manager, its lists show the number of employees and the type of business.[22]

You can obtain response lists and compiled lists (both of which are rented for one-time use) from a **list broker,** an individual or a business that arranges for one organization to use the lists of others. List brokers are aware of the wide variety of lists available, so they can help select the most appropriate lists for your campaign. When you use more than one list, you should eliminate any duplication through a computerized **merge and purge** process that puts the lists together (merge) and deletes the duplicates (purge). Thus, each person on the combined list receives only one copy of your mailing.

USING CATALOGS

A **catalog** is a direct-mail booklet that shows pictures, gives descriptions, and quotes prices of merchandise for sale. More than 13 billion catalogs are mailed in the United States every year by retailers, wholesalers, manufacturers, and nonprofit organizations seeking a piece of this $35 billion industry. J. Crew, L.L. Bean, Fingerhut, and Woodworker's Supply are just some of the millions of catalogs mailed to U.S. consumers. In fact, so many catalogs are landing in consumer mailboxes that the increased competition for attention and sales dollars has put some catalog merchants out of business and changed the way others operate.[23]

Sears, for instance, has shut down its giant catalog, but rival J.C. Penney hasn't stopped mailing its jumbo catalog. Instead, Penney's has started to produce an

CHECKLIST FOR SELECTING RESPONSE LISTS

❏ A. Understand exactly what response the listed prospects have given.

❏ B. Understand exactly when the listed prospects made their response.

❏ C. Understand exactly when the names and addresses of listed prospects were last updated.

❏ D. Look for specific clues when evaluating response lists.
- Look for a recent interest in buying by mail and, depending on the list, in buying your type of product.
  1. Make sure listed individuals have taken some definite action (such as buying or donating).
  2. Make sure they have taken action within the past twelve months.
- Look for an active interest in direct-response advertising and for addresses that are as current as possible.
  1. Make sure listed individuals have responded to a direct-response ad.
  2. Make sure they responded in the past three months.
  3. Make sure the names and addresses were updated no longer than six months ago.
  4. Check whether the addresses were recently updated by using the U.S. Postal Service's National Change of Address Service.
- Be careful of lists of individuals who have only inquired about a product; if these people haven't actually made a purchase, the list may not be as valuable as a list of buyers.
- Look for listed individuals who have bought more than once; multiple buyers are generally better prospects than one-time buyers.
- Look carefully at lists of former buyers who have purchased products within the past twelve months.
  1. Keep in mind that they may have no further need for a particular type of product.
  2. Be aware that their addresses may be out of date.
- Track listed individuals who make purchases using major credit cards; if you don't honor credit cards, a list of credit card users won't help you.
- To promote your product before major gift-giving periods such as Christmas and Mother's Day, look for lists of individuals who have bought a good or service for someone else.
- Know what medium the listed prospects responded to in the past—catalogs, magazines, newspapers, television offers—so that you can match the list to the media you use.
- As a fund-raiser for a nonprofit organization, look for listed individuals who have contributed in the past to charities or causes similar to yours.

additional series of specialized catalogs geared to narrowly focused target audiences, such as an apparel catalog for women with arthritis and an apparel catalog for tall women. However, finding mailing lists for such audiences isn't always easy, which is why Penney's also promotes the specialized catalogs in its stores.[24]

Some catalog advertisers have cut back on their use of the medium, citing the high cost of postage and printing. At the same time, advertisers who traditionally used other media have begun testing catalog sales. Look at the personal-computer market, where more than 20 percent of all sales are made via direct-marketing channels. To compete more effectively with Dell, Gateway, and other rivals that sell direct to consumers, IBM recently mailed 1 million copies of an 80-page, four-color catalog of all the products in its personal-computer line. Similarly, Apple Computer has moved more heavily into catalogs and now mails more than 4 million every year.[25]

Nonprofit organizations use catalogs in a variety of ways. For instance, Volunteer: The National Center, in Arlington, Virginia, mails a catalog of gift items to other nonprofit organizations that buy gifts, which they either sell or give to their own volunteers. The nonprofit Jesus Project takes a different approach. Its catalog describes specific items that the ministry needs and asks contributors to donate money for these gifts, which range from a $25 projector bulb to a $20,000 translation of an evangelical movie. In this way, donors know exactly how their contributions will be used.[26]

USING PRINT AND ELECTRONIC MEDIA

Newspapers, magazines, television, and radio can be used as direct-marketing media. With print advertising, you can simultaneously reinforce brand awareness

Cruising Rover

車を走るたび、車の中は、東境がかれば遠くにいるまだ。わが家に着いたローバー400のしなやかな車。車のシートに身を沈めた私は、やっとそのことに気づいた。「こんなとき、遠かい、もう一つのリビングが出来たみたいなわけです。ウォールナットの木目を得てるそうなから、薄かつやびいた、後らの床で。

この車には、ちょうど良い時の流れがある。クルージング・ローバー。

ROVER JAPAN
LAND-ROVER · ROVER
〒153 東京都目黒区青葉台4-7-1

カタログのご請求及び販売店のご案内は、お気軽にフリーダイヤルでどうぞ。

ROVER CALL 0120-00-6832
全国どこからでも無料でご利用いただけます。受付時間：10：00～20：00

EXHIBIT 16.5
Using Print Media for Direct Marketing

Rover Japan includes a toll-free telephone number in its magazine advertising to encourage the target audience to call for a catalog with more information about Rover vehicles.

or describe product benefits while offering more information, a product sample, or the product itself through a direct-response mechanism such as a coupon or a phone number (see Exhibit 16.5). To make it easy for prospects to respond, you can have reply cards bound into a magazine or inserted between the pages of a newspaper or magazine. Although you can use the print media to reach mass-market audiences, you can also promote products geared toward highly targeted audiences if you use special-interest magazines or newspapers.

Consider how AT&T promoted its "Call Me" card to military recruits who wanted to call home but needed to have their families pay for the call. AT&T's direct-marketing agency created ads for on-base newspapers that described how the "Call Me" card works and asked recruits to call AT&T with their families' names and addresses. The families received a packet of information and a letter explaining that their son or daughter had asked that AT&T send the material. After reading AT&T's material, a whopping 40 percent of the families decided to use the service.[27]

Direct-response advertising on broadcast and cable television is used to promote a wide variety of products from cosmetics and kitchen gadgets to cars and cruises. Television advertisers not only use picture and sound to communicate product benefits but also repeat the telephone number or the address for ordering by using both voice-overs and on-screen displays. To convey more complex messages, an increasing number of television advertisers are testing longer infomercials. As explained in Chapter 1, infomercials combine a programlike format with a sales pitch. Despite the controversy over whether such ads mislead viewers who believe they're watching unbiased programs, the 30-minute commercial is becoming popular with more advertisers.

For example, Club Med airs infomercials that promote the company's full range of vacation packages, because "when people make vacation decisions, they need more than a 30-second or 60-second commercial to get them interested," says Anthony Salerno, director of advertising and sales promotion. Club Med commercials feature brief vignettes showing vacationers enjoying themselves at two resorts, interspersed with frequent sales pitches mentioning the toll-free number to call for more information. More than 20,000 viewers responded in the first eight months the infomercial was shown.[28]

Another form of direct-response advertising is television home shopping, which functions like a televised retail catalog to promote a variety of products. QVC, one of several television home-shopping networks on the air in the United States, invites viewers to order any featured merchandise via toll-free telephone. Housewares, fashion clothing, and jewelry are among the most popular products sold through television home-shopping shows, which ring up over $2 billion in annual sales. In fact, advertisers can test products on television home-shopping shows to determine which copy points work and whether it's necessary to use a lengthy infomercial to sell the product.[29]

Television isn't the only electronic medium that drives direct response. Radio audiences have also been known to respond to commercials urging them to "Call now. Operators are standing by!" Radio ads can be a good way to persuade the audience to take the first step in a two-step sales approach. Once your prospect has requested a brochure about your product (the first step), you can send order or dealer information or you can call to ask for the order (which leads to the second step, an actual sale). You can also use radio to build awareness and anticipation before or during a direct-mail blitz so that people will be primed to watch their mailboxes and respond quickly.

USING TELEMARKETING

Telemarketing is the promotion of goods and services via telephone contact with businesses or consumers. As a cost-effective alternative to personal sales calls, telemarketing lets you reach more customers in less time to sell anything from office products and magazine subscriptions to investment services and computer systems. Business and industrial advertisers find telemarketing an efficient way to reach both prospects and customers. Nonprofit organizations are also heavy users of telemarketing to solicit donations or to sell fund-raising products. What makes telemarketing so effective is the personal contact through a two-way conversation and the ability to understand the customer's needs and to respond immediately to questions or requests. Hewlett-Packard, Citibank, and IBM are just three of the growing number of advertisers that use some combination of direct-mail advertising and telemarketing to dramatically improve their chances of making a sale.[30]

Using Outbound Telemarketing

When you use *outbound telemarketing,* you're taking the initiative to call customers or prospects (see Exhibit 16.6). J. Fegeley & Son, an industrial supplies distributor in Pennsylvania, signed up 2,000 new customers solely through the use of outbound telemarketing. Most of the accounts ranged in size from $4,000 to $12,000, but one account bought supplies worth $60,000 by phone. These customers are small-machine-shop owners who would rather buy by phone than take the time to meet with salespeople in person.[31]

Outbound telemarketing is a convenience for some people. However, it's a nuisance for others, and they complain about the intrusiveness. To answer such complaints and to protect consumers against fraud, many states have passed strict laws governing telemarketing contacts. Telemarketers must also comply with federal legislation and regulation. The Federal Communications Commission's 16-point Telephone Consumer Protection Act of 1991, for instance, allows calls to consumers only between 8 A.M. and 9 P.M. and requires that telemarketers strictly honor the requests of consumers who ask not to be called.[32] Considering local and long-distance telephone charges, as well as the cost of hiring and training knowledgeable telephone representatives, outbound telemarketing can be costly, but it's still less expensive than sending a representative to make a personal sales call.

Using Inbound Telemarketing

With *inbound telemarketing,* you set up incoming phone lines so that customers can call you to place orders or to ask for further information. With a toll-free 800 number, you pay for the call, not the customer, which means that customers from hundreds or even thousands of miles away won't hesitate to call. This is a highly

EXHIBIT 16.6

Scripting an Outbound Telemarketing Call

Advertisers that use outbound telemarketing generally develop a standard script to guide their telemarketers through the call. When telemarketers for KPBS Public Radio and Television used this script to call people whose memberships recently expired, they were able to present the message the same way in each call.

popular method of communicating with customers and prospects: by one estimate, more than 16 billion calls are made to 800-number call centers every year.[33]

Diagraph, a St. Louis–based maker of industrial labeling and marking equipment, prints its toll-free telephone number in its catalog. Although customers can mail their orders in, most find it faster to call. When they do, Diagraph's telephone salespeople ask about their future buying plans, the kinds of products they're interested in, who will make the final decision to buy, and so on. The answers are stored in a computerized database so the firm can decide when and how to follow up for additional sales.[34]

The customer pays for calling 900 and 976 numbers, and the list of pay-per-call offerings is quite diverse (see Exhibit 16.7). Even the Vatican has a 900 number that allows callers to hear a taped message from the Pope—for $1.95 per minute. In the past, some pay-per-call advertisers defrauded customers or offered sleazy programs and merchandise. However, stricter legislation and regulation is weeding out unscrupulous operators and cleaning up the image of pay-per-call adver-

EXHIBIT 16.7

The Diverse World of Pay-per-Call Services

In recent years, the use of 900 and 976 phone numbers for inbound telemarketing has increased dramatically. The most prevalent forms of pay-per-call services are those that entertain the caller and those that invite the caller to talk directly with other callers or with a consultant.

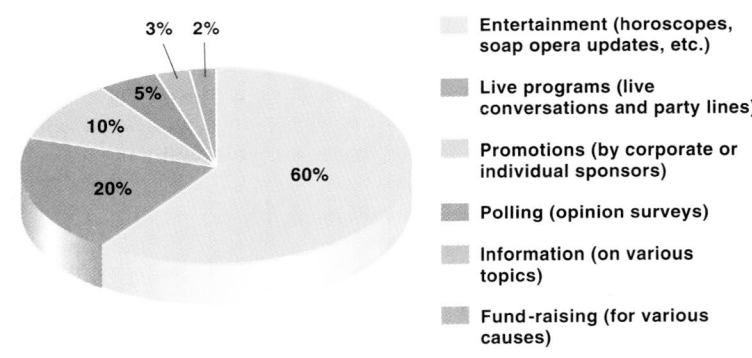

- 3%
- 2%
- 5%
- 10%
- 20%
- 60%

- Entertainment (horoscopes, soap opera updates, etc.)
- Live programs (live conversations and party lines)
- Promotions (by corporate or individual sponsors)
- Polling (opinion surveys)
- Information (on various topics)
- Fund-raising (for various causes)

tisers. The media are also helping to police such ads; for instance, ABC network television refuses all 900-number ads. (Exempted from ABC's ban are ads from the Red Cross and other public welfare organizations that encourage donations via 900-phone lines.)[35]

An increasing number of advertisers are automating their inbound telemarketing programs and inviting callers to choose from a prerecorded menu of options. Known as *interactive telephone,* this approach leaves an advertiser's operators free to talk with other customers and, at the same time, allows callers to listen only to offers that interest them. For example, an American Express program called Privileges On Call allows customers to call up and use their telephone buttons to navigate through a menu offering descriptions of various leisure-time activities and travel offers. A caller can place an order and charge it on American Express without talking to a human being—although operators are available if needed.[36]

USING BILLBOARDS

Another way to make a sale is to post your message and a toll-free number on a **billboard,** a large, flat sign structure erected outdoors away from the place of business. When automaker Suzuki put its toll-free number on billboards across the United States, it received 12,000 calls a month asking for more information—and 20 percent of the callers bought the Suzuki Samurai shown in the ad. What's more, Suzuki's billboard ads provoked more calls than its direct-response television or print ads.[37]

A similar success story is told by 800-Flowers, a 24-hour floral telemarketer that delivers anywhere in the country (see Exhibit 16.8). Its initial billboard campaign drew 2,000 calls the first week, and the calls kept coming. To encourage response, make your telephone number easy to remember, and relate it to your product: for instance, 800-Flowers is the company's name as well as its phone number.[38] The selling power of direct-response billboards has also been boosted by the growing number of car phones, which allow drivers to call when they see an interesting offer.

UNDERSTANDING THE ADVANTAGES AND LIMITATIONS OF DIRECT MARKETING

As you know by now, direct marketing has the potential of being both powerful and persuasive. To use it effectively, though, you have to understand its limitations as well as its advantages. Direct marketing offers advantages such as audience selectivity, flexibility, personalization, and the ability to measure results.

- *Audience selectivity.* Whether you're aiming for a large, diverse audience or a small, selected group, direct marketing can give you the reach you need. By using newspapers, radio, or television, you can put your message in front of large audiences; by selecting your lists carefully, you can use direct mail to reach selected audience segments; and by using special-interest magazines, you can tell your story only to those most interested in your product. For instance, Gateway 2000 has built a $600 million mail-order personal-computer

EXHIBIT 16.8
How 800-Flowers Uses Billboards for Direct Marketing

Joining a growing number of direct-response advertisers who use outdoor advertising, 800-Flowers keeps its message simple and includes a toll-free telephone number that's easy to remember.

business by advertising in computer magazines and taking orders on its toll-free telephone line.

- *Flexibility.* You can plan and implement a direct-mail advertising campaign relatively quickly, which gives you the flexibility to respond to changing market conditions. Moreover, depending on the direct-marketing medium you use, you have almost unlimited creative flexibility. With direct-mail advertising, you can vary the size, color, paper, copy, type, illustrations, inserts, and other creative elements, and you can use all the creative possibilities of the electronic and print media. When you use a variety of direct-marketing media, you can tailor the creative elements to the individual medium. For example, to sell porcelain dolls to collectors, the Hamilton Collection in Florida uses one sales message and a variety of creative approaches: for magazines, Hamilton prepares a full-page ad with a coupon; for direct mail, the company prepares a colorful mailer with a letter and a business reply card.[39]

- *Personalization.* One of direct marketing's strongest points is the degree to which you can personalize the message. Of course, with telemarketing and direct-mail advertising, you can address individuals in your target audience by name. You can also tailor your approach to each person's situation. For example, letters sent by the nonprofit organization Disabled American Veterans to prospective members use the prospect's name two or three times in the letter. The organization also refers to the prospect's home state, the number of disabled veterans in the prospect's home state and city, the name of the nearest chapter, and the exact amount of dues (which varies from chapter to chapter). As a result of this extensive personalization, responses to the Disabled American Veterans' direct-mail programs have tripled.[40]

- *Ability to measure results.* Although it's often difficult to measure the exact results of a particular advertising campaign, you can easily measure your direct-marketing results by counting the number of coupons, order forms, or telephone responses you receive. To determine the **cost per order,** which shows how much you spent to make each sale, you divide the total cost of the direct marketing effort by the number of orders received. This calculation also lets you compare the cost efficiency of two or more campaigns: the lower the number, the more cost efficient the campaign.

Just as direct marketing offers a number of advantages, it also carries some important limitations. Before committing to a direct-marketing campaign, consider the potential problems of questionable accuracy, public criticism, and a lack of content support.

- *Questionable accuracy.* Although direct marketing can help you pinpoint your target audience, your accuracy is only as good as the list you use for direct-mail advertising or outbound telemarketing. If the names, addresses, or telephone numbers aren't correct or current, or if some names on the list have been mistakenly included, your offer won't reach its intended audience. For this reason, it's important to ask how old the mailing list is and what percentage of mail sent to people on the list may be returned because the post office can't deliver it. In contrast, when you use broadcast and print media—even targeted media such as cable television or special-interest magazines—you may reach people who aren't right for your offer.

- *Public criticism.* It's a cliché to call unwanted direct-mail advertising "junk mail," but many people are annoyed about the flood of catalogs, letters, and brochures they receive. They're also irritated by what they perceive to be "junk phone calls" and, in this age of office automation, "junk faxes." Some of the criticism stems from a distrust of buying by mail, some from the tidal wave of inappropriate offers, and some from a rising concern over the environment and the waste of paper and packing materials used in direct marketing. In response to environmental criticisms, more advertisers are using recycled materials and cutting down on the number and size of their mailings. Responding to the interests of consumers who don't like receiving unwanted ads, the Direct Marketing Association has established a code of ethics and set up a system by which consumers can ask to have their names removed from mailing lists.[41] Although some consumers may avoid doing business with direct marketers under any circumstances, those that do are protected by a variety of laws and regulations outlawing questionable or fraudulent direct-marketing practices.

- *Lack of content support.* When you advertise in the print or the electronic media, your ads are interspersed with entertainment or information, which can help set a mood or put the ads into a context. This also gives people a reason to be paying attention in the first place. In contrast, some forms of direct marketing (such as direct mail, direct-response billboard advertising, and telemarketing) stand alone without the support of any editorial or programming material. Also, if you use direct mail, your envelope has to compete with every other piece of mail the target audience receives that day—which is why yours must be enticing enough for people to open and read.

Out-of-Home Advertising

Advertising that reaches the target audience away from home is called **out-of-home advertising.** To reach people out of their homes, you can position ad messages outdoors, on or in trains and buses, and in a variety of other places. Since being banned from the electronic media, tobacco advertisers have relied on out-of-home advertising to communicate their messages. Now other advertisers are finding that the creative approaches possible in out-of-home advertising can help grab audience attention in unexpected ways and in unusual places. As an alternative to the mass media, out-of-home advertising is often a cost-effective way to quickly reach large areas or local communities.[42]

USING OUTDOOR ADVERTISING

On your campus, in your town, in the mall, and on nearby roads and highways, you're likely to see some evidence of **outdoor advertising,** messages displayed on posters, billboards, and other outdoor surfaces. As discussed in Chapter 1, outdoor advertising has been in use for thousands of years; today, a growing number of advertisers around the world are discovering its benefits (see Exhibit 16.9). Although outdoor advertising is increasingly popular, it accounts for less than 1 percent of all annual U.S. ad expenditures, just under $1 billion; in Europe, outdoor ad revenues are about $3.5 billion, or just over 5 percent of ad spending.[43]

Types of Outdoor Advertising

Outdoor advertising can take a variety of forms, but the three types most commonly available are poster panels, painted bulletins, and spectaculars. Both

EXHIBIT 16.9 The Top 10 U.S. Outdoor Advertisers

The two largest users of outdoor advertising in the United States are Philip Morris and RJR Nabisco, legally barred from promoting their tobacco products on television. However, such advertisers have reduced their use of outdoor advertising in recent years, freeing up prime poster space for advertisers such as McDonald's.

Rank	Advertiser	Outdoor Spending	Rank	Advertiser	Outdoor Spending
1	Philip Morris Cos.	$59.9	6	Anheuser-Busch Cos.	$10.9
2	RJR Nabisco	29.1	7	B.A.T. Industries	10.5
3	Loews Corp.	26.4	8	Grand Metropolitan	5.7
4	McDonald's Corp.	12.5	9	Seagram Co.	5.2
5	American Brands	11.7	10	BankAmerica Corp.	5.1

Note: Dollars are in millions; 1992 data.

poster panels and painted bulletins are types of billboards, and they're differentiated by their standardized sizes. In contrast, spectaculars are larger outdoor ad displays that are generally customized for individual advertisers.

Poster Panels. A **poster panel** is the smaller of the standardized billboard sizes. It carries a preprinted message and may be mounted on the top or the side of a building or may stand alongside a street or highway (see Exhibit 16.10). Traditionally, the basic poster size of 12 feet high by 24 feet wide was called a *24-sheet poster* because it required 24 large printed sheets of advertising to cover its surface. The size of the sheets has changed in recent years, as have the standardized sizes, but the custom of referring to the number of sheets has remained. Now the *30-sheet poster* (a 9-foot 7-inch by 21-foot 7-inch surface), the *bleed poster* (a 10-foot 5-inch by 22-foot 8-inch surface), and the *junior panel,* or *8-sheet panel* (with a 6-foot by 12-foot surface), have become standard. The messages mounted on poster panels are usually printed using silk screen or lithography. Then the strips are prepasted, packaged, and brought to the site, where they're smoothed into position on the billboard.

Painted Bulletins. A **painted bulletin** is the larger of the two standardized sizes of billboards, typically measuring 14 feet by 48 feet. Occasionally, painted bulletins are painted directly on the billboard, but most often they're painted in sections in the studio and then brought to the display site to be hung on the billboard. In addition, some suppliers offer computerized printing services that improve reproduction quality and consistency.[44] To prevent message wearout and to expand exposure, many suppliers offer a **rotary plan** in which a bulletin is moved to another location in the same market every 30, 60, or 90 days; however, if you specify particular locations, you may have to pay a premium. Of course, if the locations you want are already reserved for other advertisers, you'll have to wait—or select others.

EXHIBIT 16.11

Spectaculars Light Up the Ginza

Spectaculars brighten the Tokyo night to deliver the advertiser's message through vivid color and, increasingly, impressive graphics. A spectacular is usually only one part of an advertising campaign designed to enhance the prestige of a major corporation.

Spectaculars. An extremely large outdoor display that incorporates special electrical or mechanical devices is called a **spectacular.** Spectaculars such as huge neon or electronic signs are expensive to produce, but because they're glitzy and colorful and often include moving text or graphics, they have a visual impact that commands attention. These impressive ads are often used in corporate image campaigns, and they tend to be mounted in major cities such as New York and Tokyo (see Exhibit 16.11).

Advantages and Limitations of Outdoor Advertising

Outdoor ads have little time to capture the audience's attention, so they can't communicate a complex message. However, they can be used to support advertising in other media, and they're a good way to build awareness in a new market or to remind people about your brand. Among the advantages of outdoor advertising are the opportunity for reach and frequency, creative flexibility, and audience impact.

- *Reach and frequency.* An outdoor message is on display 24 hours, so it can gain wide and repeated exposure if it's in the proper location; moreover, its position can be fixed, or it can be rotated through a market to reach all geographic sections. The intensity of the market coverage is reflected in the **showings,** the percentage of the area population exposed to the message daily. Showings are equivalent to gross rating points, so a billboard buy that offers 300,000 daily exposures in a market of 600,000 would be measured as a #50 showing or 50 GRPs, covering half the market's population; the total monthly showings would exceed 1,500 GRPs (see Exhibit 16.12). Carl's Jr. took advantage of outdoor's reach by blitzing Southern California with 2,500 billboard ads when it introduced its turkey club sandwich. The billboard buy had a potential daily reach of over 28 million people.[45]

- *Flexibility.* The creative choices for billboards and other outdoor ads are almost endless. Color, typeface, size, and shape can be varied, and you can use three-dimensional elements, inflatables, lights, and other attention-getting techniques (see Exhibit 16.13). What's more, you have the flexibility of targeting your audience by street or neighborhood and of putting your ad next to a specific store—or near a competitor. Tops Appliance City in Hawthorne, New York, used this technique when promoting its discount prices by buying billboard space just yards from a major rival's storefront.

EXHIBIT 16.12

The Cost to Rent Eight-Sheet Poster Panels in Selected U.S. Cities

Monthly rental rates for eight-sheet poster panels vary from city to city. The rates shown here are only for monthly billboard rental space yielding a #50 showing, and they don't include production costs.

Market Location	Cost per Month for a #50 Showing	Number of Panels for a #50 Showing
Los Angeles	$105,000	500
New York City	$40,500	300
Chicago	$35,000	200
Philadelphia	$35,000	200
Detroit	$21,700	140

EXHIBIT 16.13
Using Outdoor Advertising Creatively

Tausche Martin Londsorf, the advertising agency for the Task Force for the Homeless in Atlanta, Georgia, used the creative properties of outdoor advertising to call attention to the deteriorating conditions facing homeless people.

- *Audience impact.* Outdoor ads are larger than life, so they have a tremendous impact; moreover, that impact goes on and on because the ads can't be turned off like a television or thrown away like a newspaper (see Exhibit 16.14). For example, for an outdoor ad for the Museum of Flight in Seattle, a model of an old-time airplane was positioned to protrude from the billboard. The plane looked like it had crashed through the sign, and the pilot (a dummy) was seated at the bottom of the billboard amid the debris. It's hard to ignore this type of ad, and frequent passersby can't resist another peek.[46]

Like any advertising technique, outdoor advertising also has disadvantages. Before committing to an outdoor campaign, be sure to balance the advantages against such limitations as limited audience measurement, limited message communication, message wearout, and public criticism.

- *Limited audience measurement.* Although the suppliers can estimate how many people are exposed to an outdoor vehicle, more specific measurement is difficult. New measurement packages that overlay census data and other variables with local traffic counts help to more precisely define the outdoor audience, but no one knows when or if people actually see a particular billboard or poster—or if they notice its message.[47]

- *Limited message communication.* How much of a message can be absorbed by a driver passing a billboard at 55 miles per hour? Obviously, an outdoor message has to be short and simple to register quickly; some experts recommend limiting the message to no more than seven words. For example, a billboard for Levi's 501 jeans showed three elements: the open button-front fly, the Levi's 501 name, and a one-word headline: "Ouchless." Though the copy was extremely brief, the picture helped put the message across.[48]

EXHIBIT 16.14
Outdoor Advertising that Stops Traffic

It's hard to imagine motorists *not* slowing down as they passed this unique outdoor advertisement for Reno Air. Ad agency Goldberg Moser O'Neill was able to capture audience attention by positioning the replica of a local police car directly below the billboard.

- *Message wearout.* After an outdoor ad has been up awhile, people may become indifferent to the ad or tire of the message; to avoid this, you need to periodically change the message or its execution. Frequent change was more difficult in the past, when suppliers offered billboard space by the month, but some suppliers now offer space by the week. Consider how Garcia's Irish Pub in Buffalo, New York, used a 9-week series of slightly mysterious billboard ads to keep public interest high. The first ad read, "Angel in Red: Saw you at Garcia's Irish Pub. Love to meet you. William." Each week a new message was posted, and passersby as well as local television, radio, and newspaper reporters followed the romance up to the happy ending: "Angel: Thanks for Friday at Garcia's. I'm in heaven. Love, William."[49]

- *Public criticism.* Some people call billboards "litter on a stick" and want them banned or at least their number and size reduced. On the national level, the Highway Beautification Act of 1965 regulates the use of billboards along federally subsidized highways. In addition, four states (Alaska, Vermont, Hawaii, and Maine) ban billboards, and U.S. legislators have debated various federal proposals to ban them or to further restrict their size and number. Outdoor ads for liquor and tobacco have also drawn fire, as protesters in Baltimore and other U.S. cities battle to remove them from poor and minority neighborhoods and from areas where children may see them. In response, the industry has set a voluntary ban on such billboard advertising near schools, places of worship, and hospitals. To date, more than 20,000 billboards have been designated as off-limits for products such as tobacco and liquor.[50]

Despite these limitations, the use of outdoor advertising has grown in recent years. Some advertisers that never used it are now taking the plunge. Revlon, McDonald's, and Paramount Pictures are among the U.S. advertisers that now use outdoor advertising to supplement other media. In Japan, where spectaculars featuring liquid-crystal displays and other high-tech innovations are becoming commonplace, Toshiba and other advertisers use outdoor ads to efficiently reach large numbers of people in Tokyo and other major cities.[51]

USING TRANSIT ADVERTISING

Transit advertising is placed inside or outside public transportation vehicles, in train or bus stations and on platforms, and in airport terminals. You can buy some form of transit advertising in virtually every metropolitan area, from San

EXHIBIT 16.15
Transit Advertising in Phoenix

Transit advertising helps advertisers reach commuters as well as local residents who use mass transit in urban areas. This striking ad for the Phoenix Suns basketball team attracts attention all along the bus's route.

Francisco's trolleys and London's underground to New York City's taxicabs and Moscow's buses (see Exhibit 16.15). The list of transit advertisers is long and varied, from local businesses and professional firms to movie studios, telephone companies, and charities.

Types of Transit Advertising

As with all out-of-home advertising, transit advertising includes several types. You can choose from among the three most common: inside cards, outside posters, and terminal posters. In addition, you can choose a variation on transit advertising, a mobile billboard.

Inside Cards. An **inside card** is an advertising panel displayed on the interior of a transportation vehicle such as a bus or train. Inside cards are horizontal and may be mounted on the walls above the windows or doors, on larger spaces next to the doors, or at either end of the vehicle. Card sizes vary slightly from market to market, depending on the vehicles in use.

What makes inside cards so attractive to advertisers is the captive audience of riders who often have little to do but read the ads—sometimes when commuting both to and from work or school. In fact, the average bus or subway ride is 22 minutes long. This means the audience has time to absorb a lengthy list of copy points or a complicated message, unlike the fast-moving audiences for outdoor advertising who have time only for a brief, simple message.[52] Moreover, you can make an inside card into a direct-response ad by adding a telephone number, a pad of coupons or business reply cards known as **tear-offs,** or a pocket to hold brochures or business reply cards known as **take ones.** You can also dominate the audience's attention by buying all the inside space on a group of buses, an approach known as **basic bus.** With basic bus, riders see your message no matter which bus they board.

The Massachusetts Department of Environmental Protection recently used inside cards on Boston subways and buses to publicize a hotline to report environmental polluters. Before the transit campaign, the hotline was getting 8 to 10 calls per week; after the campaign began, calls jumped to 30 to 40 per day. As a result of this advertising, the department was able to investigate hundreds of cases for possible prosecution.[53]

Outside Posters. You can also rent advertising space on the exterior of mass-transit vehicles. An **outside poster** is an advertising panel attached to the side, front, rear, or roof of a bus, train, subway, trolley, or taxi. You might want to be the only advertiser on a particular bus by making a **total bus** buy, which gives you all the exterior ad space to tell your story. That's the route PepsiCo took when it contracted for all the outside space on 10 buses in four cities to advertise Crystal Pepsi for a year.[54] Another way to make a big impact is to buy a **bus-o-rama,** a large roof-mounted sign with a backlighted transparency that stretches the length of the bus.

Many buses (and trains) travel through suburban and downtown shopping areas, which makes outside posters a good way to remind shoppers about a particular brand just before they make a purchase. Outside posters also attract attention from riders waiting to board as well as from people passing on foot or in cars, which means that outside posters offer a lot of reach and frequency for the money. As a result, an increasing number of movie studios, recording companies, and other entertainment advertisers are using outside posters to build awareness at a reasonable cost.[55]

For example, Mercury Records used outside posters to promote John Mellencamp's "Whenever We Wanted" album. At the time, Mellencamp hadn't released a record or toured the United States in more than two years, and the record company wanted to reestablish his name in markets where his previous records had sold well. Mercury put outside posters on public buses in 12 markets, which it estimated reached 90 percent of the target audience 10 to 15 times a month during the four-month campaign.[56] As Mercury Records realized, outside posters are large and visible, but they have only a few seconds to communicate their message before they roll out of view. Outside posters therefore must have simple messages; Mercury Records' posters read "John Mellencamp. Whenever We Wanted." and featured a photo of the performer.

Terminal Posters. In addition to advertising on or in mass-transit vehicles, you can buy ad space inside and outside the terminals and stations and on the platforms. A **terminal poster** is an advertising panel mounted inside a bus, subway, train, or trolley station; on a transit platform; in a bus-stop shelter; or in an airline terminal. For instance, Bugle Boy uses terminal posters in New York City train and subway stations and at bus-stop shelters to promote its trendy line of young men's casual apparel.[57]

Some terminal posters are printed onto cardboard stock and then mounted in wall brackets, so they look much like small versions of poster panels. Terminal posters may also be produced as transparencies and placed in backlighted frames so that their images are illuminated from behind. These backlighted ads shine out at the audience night and day and in any weather.[58] In addition, you can rent terminal floor space for a special product display, arrange for your message to appear on an electronic sign inside the terminal, or place your ad on or around a terminal clock.

Mobile Billboards. A variation of transit advertising is the *mobile billboard,* a type of rolling advertisement in which a poster is mounted on the side of a flatbed, a van, or a tractor-trailer. Small flatbeds are a manageable way to tow mobile billboards through the narrow streets of many urban areas, whereas tractor-trailers or vans with ads posted on their sides can spread the message along highways. For example, Applebee's Neighborhood Grill in Cincinnati reached rush-hour travelers by advertising on a 33-foot-long van that drove up and down a nearby highway.[59] In addition, in many cities, you can buy ad space on the trunk or roof of taxis to send your message throughout the metropolitan area. Another type of rolling advertisement is used by Oscar Mayer, which sends its Wienermobiles (vehicles in the shape of a hotdog on a bun) to state fairs, food shows, and other events to promote the brand and to offer samples. The Wienermobile's shape—and the aroma and taste of hot dogs—makes a real impression on the audience.[60]

EXHIBIT 16.16
Reaching Local Audiences through Transit Advertising

The Ontario Science Centre in Toronto, Canada, uses transit advertising to put its message in front of local audiences who live and work in specific geographic areas surrounding the museum.

Advantages and Limitations of Transit Advertising

Although mobile billboards attract attention, critics say they compound traffic and pollution problems. Yet the various forms of transit advertising offer several advantages that should be weighed against the potential problems. Among the advantages are cost efficiency, high frequency, geographic coverage, and long exposure.

- *Cost efficiency.* Transit advertising is one of the least expensive ways to reach an audience. Not only is the cost per thousand low, but the production costs are low also.

- *High frequency.* People who follow the same route to and from work or school are exposed to your ad day after day. Transit ads are usually displayed for at least 30 days and sometimes as long as a year, which gives them high frequency rates (but which may lead to message wearout).

- *Geographic coverage.* With transit advertising, you can blanket an entire city or reach just the section in which your target audience lives or works (see Exhibit 16.16). For instance, to reach college students, you might put ads on or in the buses serving the local campus. You can also put ads on buses or trains that pass by stores where the product is sold.

- *Long exposure.* As long as riders stand or sit in a bus, train, or trolley, they have the opportunity to see your ad inside the vehicle. When it's a long trip—or when they have nothing else to read—your ad may be studied quite carefully. If you have a complex message, transit advertising gives the audience time to read and understand each point.

Of course, transit advertising has some limitations that must be weighed against the advantages. These limitations include limited selectivity, limited creative flexibility, limited reach, and poor public perception.

- *Limited selectivity.* Although transit advertising allows you to send your message to specific geographic areas, your ad may still reach audiences you're not targeting. Mass transit serves a large and diverse population, so it's difficult to use transit advertising to pinpoint specific audience segments. Also, buses and train cars may be rotated throughout the system from time to time, bringing your ad to areas you hadn't intended.

- *Limited creative flexibility.* Unlike billboard ads, which can incorporate three-dimensional gadgets and other attention-getting elements, transit posters must be flat. They may feature eye-catching photography or gimmicky graphics, but they're essentially a piece of cardboard or a transparency mounted in a frame. Although inside cards can carry more copy than outside posters or terminal posters, all three types of transit ads have to be easy to read as the vehicles (and the riders) bounce along.

- *Limited reach.* Although transit ads may be seen by a large daily audience, their reach is somewhat limited; for example, they don't reach people who live or work outside the city. People who commute by car won't see terminal posters or inside cards, and their route may not take them past buses with outside posters, so you risk missing an entire segment of your market unless you supplement transit ads with other media advertising.

- *Poor public perception.* Although transit advertising can be a diversion for many mass-transit riders, it's generally not seen as being as prestigious as ads in the electronic or print media. What's more, when buses, trains, or stations are dirty (or ads are covered with graffiti), the audience may have difficulty separating your product from its advertising environment.

USING OTHER OUT-OF-HOME ADVERTISING

Although outdoor and transit ads are commonplace, they aren't the only ways to reach people when they're away from home. Aerial advertising has been available for more than 60 years, and on-screen ads in movie theaters have taken hold across the United States. A third type is electronic place-based advertising, which includes out-of-home television, radio advertising, and interactive kiosks.

Aerial Advertising

Advertising that is displayed on the side of a blimp or a hot-air balloon, that trails from a small plane, or that is created by skywriting is considered **aerial advertising.** Aerial advertising reaches audiences when they're outdoors or when they're looking outside (see Exhibit 16.17). It can be expensive, but it also tends to gather a lot of attention that usually translates into free publicity. You can use aerial advertising to cover specific areas or to reach large crowds gathered for events such as sports contests. British Petroleum, Jaguar, and Agfa use hot-air balloons to reinforce brand awareness among European audiences; Metropolitan Life, Fuji Film, Sea World, and Goodyear use blimps to reinforce brand names among U.S. audiences. Goodyear was one of the earliest users of aerial advertising. The tire maker launched its first blimp in 1925, and now has three crisscrossing the country bearing the message "Goodyear, #1 in Tires."[61]

On-Screen Theater Advertising

If you've been to a movie lately, you know that some theaters flash colorful still ads for local businesses before the movie starts—and follow those ads with filmed previews for other movies and with filmed ads for snacks sold at the food concession. Some theaters run several filmed or animated commercials before each movie, promoting products by Coca-Cola, Reebok, Trident, and other advertisers. Advertising on the big screen is also big business in Great Britain, where theater chains air up to 20 minutes of commercials before the main feature. However, after studies revealed that movie audiences found these ads irritating, Walt Disney and Warner Brothers announced bans on ads in U.S. theaters where their motion pictures play. To avoid audience backlash, American Express has taken a different approach. Instead of using made-for-television commercials or other obvious advertising messages, the firm produces short, entertaining film features that show the Amex logo only at the beginning and at the end.[62]

Electronic Place-Based Advertising

Electronic place-based advertising is an umbrella term for radio, television, and computer ads that are aimed at audiences when they're not in their own homes. This type of advertising can be used to target audiences when and where they can't avoid being exposed to your message; the captive audience of people watching monitors in an airport lounge or a doctor's office can't change channels and therefore must sit through the ads as well as the programs. One example of electronic place-based advertising is the Medical News Network, a network that beams medical news and ads to televisions in thousands of U.S. doctors' offices. Another example is *USA Today*'s Sky Radio, which offers a mix of news and commercials on certain airline flights (see Exhibit 16.18).[63]

Electronic place-based advertising can be especially effective when the products being promoted have a logical link to the advertising environment. Turner Broadcasting's Airport Channel, which is seen at airline gates in Atlanta, Chicago,

EXHIBIT 16.18
Using Electronic Place-Based Advertising

Advertisers are increasingly interested in how electronic place-based advertising through media such as Sky Radio can deliver messages to highly targeted audiences. One unanswered question, however, is whether audiences will pay attention to such advertising; another unanswered question is whether the public will resent it.

"...the 3-2 pitch from the tall lefty...there's a towering fly ball to deep center field. Way back. He's not even going to chase this one, folks. It's outta here..."

—Sky Radio, 9:17 p.m.

Introducing Sky Radio. The business traveler's only live connection to the world below.

With USA TODAY Sky Radio up-to-the-minute news, weather, business and sports including Major League Baseball updates are delivered live via satellite to the airline passenger's audio headset. It's the only live in-flight medium to capture this audience. Now on select United and Delta flights. Call 1-800-SKY-2300. Commercial inventory is limited.

SKY RADIO

Chris Whittle just couldn't ignore a captive audience with $250 billion in spending power. He's the founder of Channel One, a network that gives schools free television sets in exchange for showing a daily 12-minute program mix of entertainment, news, and commercials in the classroom. On the air as a pilot project since 1989, Channel One provides 194 school days of programming, reaching millions of students and claiming a teen audience nearly twice the size of the hit television series *Beverly Hills 90210*. However, since its inception, Channel One has been surrounded by the controversy over the ethics of bringing commercials into the classroom.

For schools, Channel One looks like an easy, almost painless way to get television equipment they can use for a variety of educational functions. The offer of free equipment is no small consideration for financially strapped school systems, and many cite this as the main reason they sign up with Channel One. For advertisers, Channel One provides a direct, nearly clutter-free pipeline to the lucrative student market. Advertising in the school environment has traditionally consisted of textbook covers with brand logos and curriculum handouts adorned with company names. That means that commercials on Channel One, from advertisers such as Quaker Oats, Procter & Gamble, and PepsiCo, face little classroom competition from other advertisers.

However, critics are upset that advertising is being invited into the classroom. Gordon Cawelti of the Association for Supervision and Curriculum Development, an education association, believes that Channel One goes too far. "There is nothing wrong with a company taking credit for what it is doing in the classroom," he says, "but when a foot like Whittle's gets in the door,

you begin to see a dangerous shift to advertising, which ought not be a part of instructional materials in the schools." Moreover, research shows that students who watch advertising in school are likely to think that the schools endorse the advertised products, a misconception that alarms many.

Another troubling aspect is the trade-off of equipment for audiences. "You're selling the children to the advertisers. You might as well auction them off to the highest bidder," says Peggy Charren, a lobbyist who has long fought for quality children's television. Finally, concerns have been raised over the educational value of Channel One. A study (commissioned by Whittle) found that Channel One had little effect on the measured current events knowledge of the average student viewer. This rankles some educators, who see the study as more evidence that Channel One is completely commercial.

Whittle responds by pointing to the value of the equipment he gives the schools. "The critics say that there should never be commercials in class. In an ideal world, they're right. But we don't live in an ideal world. Education is an underfunded area," he says. Despite the controversy—and some groups' boycotts of advertisers' products—he has no plans to pull the plug, and only a few advertisers have pulled out. Advertising time is still selling, and annual ad revenues top $100 million. However, even as Whittle signs up more schools, the ethical debate rages on, and in the end, advertiser support will probably be the single most important factor that determines Channel One's future.

What's Your Opinion?

1. *Should Channel One be required to air a disclaimer indicating that the advertised products aren't endorsed by any schools?*

2. *Should schools be forbidden by law to accept anything of value (including television equipment) in exchange for bringing ads into the classroom?*

Channel One programming includes news and current events, entertainment, and commercials.

Dallas, and other airports, carries weather and entertainment interspersed with a variety of travel-related ads from AT&T, GTE, and American Express, among others. The companies are able to reach their target audiences when and where they're most interested in the advertised products, and the travelers may appreciate being distracted by the Airport Channel while waiting for their flights.[64]

Meeting an Advertising Challenge at MCI Communications

Up against the name recognition and huge market share of AT&T, MCI used its Friends & Family program to regain momentum in the long-distance telephone market. When MCI added five new benefits for Friends & Family participants, Angela Dunlap needed to mount an advertising campaign that would promote these improvements. Her objectives were (1) to sign more Friends & Family customers, (2) to expand current customers' usage of the program, (3) to reinforce customers' choice of MCI, and (4) to enhance the ongoing relationship with MCI customers.

With such a complex story to tell, she needed a lot of copy to explain the benefits. The target audience was the 9 million long-distance customers already in MCI's database, which showed customer names, addresses, and phone numbers as well as the names and phone numbers of the people in each Calling Circle. Dunlap decided to tap this database to mail each customer an advertising message tailored to his or her own needs.

To capture the audience's attention, Devon Direct Marketing and Advertising (MCI's direct-marketing agency) created an oversize, multipage self-mailer filled with friendly faces. Because the colorful piece looked dramatically different, it stood out in the mailbox. To entice recipients to open the piece, the outside cover displayed intriguing teaser copy:

"Friends & Family: Five Free New Benefits For '92! Come inside and see . . ."

The agency also had to solve the creative problem of how to present the details of the benefits in an exciting yet clear and logical way. The solution: put an easy-to-read summary of the plan on the second cover, and then devote one inside page to each of the five benefits. To make it easy for customers to respond, the agency printed MCI's toll-free number on every page.

In addition, the agency folded into the self-mailer a combination letter and response form. The letter (on eye-catching orange stationery) briefly outlined the program's benefits and urged customers to sign up right away by calling the toll-free number. The agency used MCI's database to vary the message on the letter and response form, depending on whether a customer had never joined Friends & Family, had joined but never suggested people for the Calling Circle, or had joined and named only a few people for the Calling Circle. The response form was personalized with the customer's name and address and the names and phone numbers of Calling Circle members, if any.

Rather than mail the ad to all 9 million customers at once—and take the risk that customers might get a busy signal when they called to respond—the agency mailed no more

than 500,000 pieces a day. Soon MCI's phones began ringing: over 1 million customers responded. The promotion, which cost just over $4 million, racked up $19 million in long-distance revenues. Boosted by this and other Friends & Family promotions, MCI's market share jumped to 17 percent by 1993—and AT&T's share shrank to under 66 percent.

Your Mission: *Before Angela Dunlap was promoted to president of MCI's consumer business, she hired you to head MCI's worldwide direct-marketing efforts. Using what you know about direct marketing and database marketing, select the best response in each of the following situations.*

1. To persuade more customers to join Friends & Family right after they sign up for MCI long-distance services, you decide to insert an ad with the letters you send to welcome new customers. Which of these ideas would most effectively encourage customers to read the ad and respond quickly?
a. A reprint of a recent MCI newspaper ad trumpeting the low cost and advantages of Friends & Family. Print a sign-up coupon on the bottom of the reprint for customer convenience.

Advertisers spend less than $1 billion a year on electronic place-based advertising, but the figure is growing steadily as more options appear and more companies test the waters. In particular, in-store television and radio vehicles are making a big play for customer attention. Muzak beams in-store audio ads to Winn-Dixie and other retail chains at a cost of roughly 40 cents per 1,000 people reached, an attractive price tag for many advertisers. Stopwatch Entertainment sends out programs and ads to television sets on display in appliance and electronics stores, and POP Radio plays a mix of information and ads in grocery stores.[65]

Interactive kiosks are freestanding machines equipped with a computer, a touch-sensitive screen or a keyboard, and a monitor that can display advertising, offer product information, and sometimes sell the products they feature. Nearly 90,000 interactive kiosks have already been installed in stores, malls, and other locations around the United States by a wide variety of advertisers. For example, the Minnesota Twins baseball team has placed 30 interactive kiosks in Minneapolis-area grocery and discount stores. These units advertise team merchandise and show the view that fans can enjoy from various seat locations. They

FRIENDS & FAMILY
ONLY FROM MCI!

AT&T doesn't have it! Sprint doesn't have it! Only MCI customers can invite friends and family members to share in the unprecedented 20% extra savings when you call each other.

Over 5 million Americans have already joined Friends & Family and are entitled to the fabulous 20% in extra savings. That's in addition to MCI's already low rates ...with no restrictions on when you call and with no fees or monthly charges. Now we've added five exciting FREE benefits to make Friends & Family more valuable than ever to every member.

- 40% off all Friends & Family calls in May!
- Circle size increased to 20!
- Friends & Family calling cards with special new features!
- Include a special member overseas!
- 20% extra off calls to the U.S. from abroad!

Plus—Your own personal Friends & Family 800 number.

Find out how these benefits can help you save more and get much more value from MCI. Then call our Friends & Family Benefits Advisor toll free to take advantage of all these free benefits today. **1-800-678-1580.**

b. A colorful self-addressed, stamped postcard that includes a quick and simple sign-up form for joining Friends & Family.
c. A colorful flyer that summarizes the same copy points as the Friends & Family self-mailer but in a smaller two-sided format. Print the toll-free number on both sides.

2. Your boss wants you to design a new computerized database to be used for both direct-mail and telemarketing efforts to current customers. In addition to name, address, and telephone number, which one of the following sets of data do you think would be most useful for cross-selling other MCI services?
a. The amount spent on long-distance services each month, the states and countries most frequently called, and the MCI services used by each household.
b. The date the customer started using MCI, the states and countries most frequently called, and the number of telephones in the household.
c. The date the customer started using MCI, the way the customer first learned about MCI's services, and the number of people in the household.

3. You're planning a new ad campaign to target people who left MCI and signed up with AT&T. Which one of these ideas would be most appropriate?
a. Start with a television commercial asking people who left MCI for AT&T to watch their mailboxes for an exciting new offer. After two weeks, mail packages to these former MCI customers. Then wait a week to start a new television commercial that encourages people to open the packages and respond.
b. Start with a radio commercial asking people who left MCI for AT&T to watch their mailboxes for an exciting new offer. After two weeks, air a television commercial that explains the new offer. Wait two more weeks, and then mail the actual packages and wait for the responses.
c. Start with a television ad discussing MCI's competitive advantages over AT&T and announcing that an exciting new offer is on the way. One week later, mail the package to people who left MCI for AT&T. After a week, follow up with a postcard reminding the audience that there's still time to sign up and save.

4. You're starting an outbound telemarketing campaign to offer small-business owners discounts on business and personal long-distance calls. Which one of these lists would be most appropriate for this telemarketing effort?
a. A response list of small businesses that ordered new telephone systems from mail-order suppliers in the past year (because they would be likely to respond to telemarketing offers)
b. A compiled list of all the new businesses established in the previous 12 months (because they're all young, so by definition they'll be small)
c. A response list of all the owner-operated small businesses that have joined a discount membership club in the past six months (because such businesses are more likely to be interested in low-cost telephone services)[68] ■

also sell game tickets, which are printed at the kiosk for the customer's convenience.[66]

Though these out-of-home approaches appear promising, questions linger about cost, audience measurement, and audience interest. Advertisers and agencies are uncertain about the size and composition of the audiences exposed to such advertising. Moreover, it's not yet clear whether captive audiences welcome, tolerate, or loathe out-of-home radio and television, so advertisers and agencies are concerned about consumer backlash over the bombardment of ads that follows them nearly everywhere they go. For example, patrons of the Vertical Club in New York City protested the installation of monitors to show commercials inside the health club, forcing management to remove most of the monitors. Another question being debated is the ethics of targeting children with such electronic out-of-home systems as Channel One, which beams programs and ads to 12,000 U.S. high schools in exchange for providing the schools with free television equipment.[67] These questions will continue to be debated as electronic place-based advertising comes into its own.

Summary

Advertisers use various forms of direct marketing to communicate directly with their target audiences and sell products without going through intermediaries such as retailers or wholesalers. One form of direct marketing is direct-response advertising, advertising that supports a direct-marketing effort by asking the target audience to take immediate action. Another form is direct-mail advertising, which refers to any advertising that's delivered directly to the target audience by mail or by a private delivery service. Database marketing helps advertisers get a better picture of who their target audience members are, what they buy, and how and when they can be reached. By building a database and overlaying information from outside sources, advertisers can better understand the habits, lifestyles, and interests of customers and prospects.

Direct mail is the most common medium for direct marketing. The two key concerns in using direct mail are format and lists. A catalog is a direct-mail booklet that shows pictures, gives descriptions, and quotes prices of merchandise for sale; it can be used by a retailer, a wholesaler, a manufacturer, or a nonprofit organization. Advertisers using both newspapers and magazines can simultaneously reinforce brand awareness or describe product benefits while offering more information, a product sample, or the product itself through a direct-response mechanism such as a coupon or a phone number.

Using television, advertisers can repeat the telephone number or ordering address as well as display or demonstrate the product. Television home-shopping programs act like televised retail catalogs to promote various products. Radio ads can be a good way to persuade the audience to take the first step in a two-step sales approach; they can also be used to build awareness before or during a direct-mail campaign. Telemarketing is a fast and convenient way to reach many people to promote products or raise funds via direct telephone contact with businesses or consumers. Direct marketing's advantages include audience selectivity, flexibility, personalization, and the ability to measure results. However, it also has limitations, which include questionable accuracy, public criticism, and a lack of content support.

The three most common forms of outdoor advertising are poster panels, painted bulletins, and spectaculars. Outdoor advertising offers advantages such as the opportunity for reach and frequency, creative flexibility, and audience impact. On the other hand, outdoor advertising also has limitations. These include limited audience measurement, limited message communication, message wearout, and public criticism.

Transit advertising is placed inside or outside public transportation vehicles, in train or bus stations and on platforms, or in airport terminals. The three basic types of transit advertising are inside cards, outside posters, and terminal posters; in addition, mobile billboards are a variation available to advertisers. Users of transit advertising gain the advantages of cost efficiency, high frequency, geographic coverage, and long exposure. At the same time, they need to consider drawbacks such as limited selectivity, limited creative flexibility, limited reach, and poor public perception.

Other types of out-of-home advertising include aerial advertising, on-screen theater advertising, and electronic place-based advertising, which includes out-of-home television, radio, and computer advertising. However, advertisers and agencies are uncertain about the size and composition of audiences being exposed to such advertising. They are also unsure about the level of audience acceptance and interest.

Key Terms

aerial advertising 453	merge and purge 438
basic bus 450	out-of-home advertising 445
billboard 443	outdoor advertising 445
broadside 436	outside poster 451
bus-o-rama 451	overlaying 433
business reply envelope 436	painted bulletin 446
catalog 438	poster panel 446
compiled list 438	reprint 436
cost per order 444	response list 438
database 433	rotary plan 446
database marketing 433	self-mailer 436
direct-mail advertising 432	showings 447
direct marketing 431	spectacular 447
direct-response advertising 432	statement stuffer 436
house list 438	take ones 450
house organ 436	tear-offs 450
inside card 450	telemarketing 441
interactive kiosks 456	terminal poster 451
list broker 438	total bus 451
mail order 432	transit advertising 449

Questions

FOR REVIEW

1. What is electronic place-based advertising, and what questions does it raise for advertisers and consumers?

2. What are the advantages and limitations of transit advertising?

3. How do direct-response advertising and direct-mail advertising differ?

4. What role do lists play in direct-mail advertising?

5. What are the three main types of outdoor advertising?

FOR ANALYSIS AND APPLICATION

6. How might a local photography studio starting a direct-response advertising program encourage prospects to add their names to its house list?

7. If you were in charge of regulating roadside signs on your state's highways, what size, shape, or other guidelines would you propose that advertisers follow to ensure that billboards aren't seen as visual pollution?

8. How might a TCBY frozen yogurt store use aerial advertising during the summer to promote its low-calorie desserts?

9. If you were organizing a student committee to call alumni and ask for donations to a college scholarship fund, what calling guidelines would you recommend to avoid irritating potential contributors?

10. In what locations (other than its own restaurants) might McDonald's use electronic place-based advertising to reach people hungry for a quick meal?

Sharpen Your Advertising Skills

Get in the holiday gift-giving mood and try sitting behind the desk of W. Howard Lester, chairman of Williams-Sonoma. His San Francisco–based retail chain and mail-order business operates five catalogs: the Catalog for Cooks (kitchen items), Pottery Barn (dishes and household accessories), Hold Everything (closet accessories), Gardener's Eden (gardening supplies), and Chambers (mirrors and other household items).

Imagine that Lester wants to build year-end holiday sales by mailing a new catalog filled with all-natural soaps, shampoos, and other personal-care products for environmentally aware men and women throughout the United States. The first place he'll look for prospects will be his house list of 4.5 million customers. He'll also want to place direct-response ads in the print and electronic media to develop a house list of prospects for future editions of this new catalog.

Decision: Where do you suggest that Lester place ads inviting prospects to send for a free copy of this catalog? Think about the target audience and the media and vehicles they're likely to be exposed to.

Communication: Write a brief (one- to two-page) memo to Lester explaining your media-buying recommendations. Remember that he'll give this memo to the ad agency that actually handles the media buying, so be as specific as possible about your choices.

Reaching the Few and the Proud

SYNOPSIS

The cold war is over, but the peacekeeping role of the U.S. military is far from over. In 1993 the U.S. Marine Corps needed to recruit 40,768 young men and women—10 percent more than the number recruited in 1992. The Marine Corps also set three specific advertising objectives: (1) to attract more high-quality recruits, (2) to encourage more people in the target audience to consider enlisting, and (3) to improve both awareness of Marine Corps advertising and consideration to enlist in a cost-efficient way.

This video shows how the Marine Corps worked with its ad agency, J. Walter Thompson/Atlanta, to reach the target audience, high school seniors who have a strong desire to excel. Realizing that no single medium could effectively reach this audience of "media surfers," the agency used a media mix that included television, radio, consumer magazine, newspaper, direct-mail, out-of-home, and point-of-purchase advertising. This integrated campaign helped the Marine Corps achieve all its objectives.

EXERCISES

Analysis

1. Why would the Marine Corps use direct mail in addition to the mass media when reaching out to potential recruits?
2. How can public service announcements improve the cost-efficiency of the overall campaign?
3. Identify any geographic limitations that J. Walter Thompson had to consider when buying media time and space for the ads in this campaign.
4. How does the "Chess" commercial use television's capabilities (sight, sound, and moving images) to enhance the ad's attention value?
5. Why would the Marine Corps want to reach teachers, counselors, and advisers by distributing the *Educator's Guide*?

Application

Imagine that J. Walter Thompson bought commercial time to show the Marine Corps commercials during four consecutive weekly sporting events on network television. Through research, the agency learned that 1 million people in the target audience tuned in during all four weeks, 2 million tuned in during two of the four weeks, and 1.5 million tuned in once during the four weeks. Calculate the gross impressions for this four-week period.

Decision

Should J. Walter Thompson use local or network radio advertising to extend the reach of the media schedule? Explain your answer.

Ethics

What should the Marine Corps tell prospective recruits about the rigors of its training program? List at least three questions you think the advertising should answer so that people in the target audience can get a fair and balanced view of the challenges they would face as Marines.

Teamwork

Working with a classmate, draft a letter asking a local radio station to play one of the public service announcements prepared by J. Walter Thompson. What does the station need to know about the PSA? What do you want to emphasize? Compare your letter with those drafted by others in the class. Which is the most persuasive? Why?

Putting the Campaign Together

Sales Promotion and Supplementary Media

After studying this chapter, you will be able to

1. Define sales promotion and describe its relationship to advertising
2. Explain the objectives of consumer and trade sales promotion
3. Outline the reasons for and concerns about shifting to a sales promotion emphasis
4. Describe the various sales promotion techniques used to target the consumer
5. Identify the various sales promotion techniques used to target the trade
6. Explain how advertisers can use yellow pages advertising and specialty advertising to reach their target audiences
7. Describe the four forms of supplementary media used to reach people who have video-cassette recorders and personal computers

"COME OUT WITH YOUR EARS UP!"

What's up, in digital colour technology? What's up is that for the very first time you can connect your PC directly to the Canon Color Laser Copier 500. This totally unique system now lets you get more out of your PC. Everything that's up on your screen, or up in your head, can be captured on paper. With the Color Laser Copier 500, nothing escapes you. You now have the perfect outlet for getting everything out of your system. Let us make your day. Contact Canon Europa N.V., Copier Division, P.O. Box 2262, 1180 EG Amstelveen, the Netherlands.

Canon
THE CREATOR OF DIGITAL COLOUR

Facing an Advertising Challenge at Kellogg

FEEDING AN APPETITE FOR MORE MARKET SHARE

In a big-stakes industry where one percentage point in U.S. market share means $70 million in sales, longtime leader Kellogg was stumbling. The company that created the ready-to-eat cereal business still dominated the industry. However, its share had been declining for more than a decade, and hungry challengers such as General Foods, Quaker Oats, General Mills, and Ralston Purina were gaining ground. To reverse the market-share slide—and to keep profits up—Carlos M. Gutierrez, executive vice president of sales and marketing for Kellogg U.S.A., knew he had to take a long, hard look at the way his cereals were promoted.

Kellogg cereals have been poured into breakfast bowls for 100 years, starting with Wheat Flakes (created in 1894) and Corn Flakes (1898). In fact, Kellogg launched ready-to-eat cereal in the United States, where today more than 20 billion bowls are served

every year. However, despite a proliferation of products, Kellogg wasn't getting the share it wanted of this huge market: from over 42 percent in 1976, the advertiser's share had dropped to under 35 percent by 1989.

One reason for this slide was a shift in adult eating habits away from sugary breakfast foods and toward healthier fare. When news reports touted the health advantages of oat fiber, consumers jumped for oat cereals, which Kellogg lacked. By the time Kellogg could crank out a line of oat-based cereals, adults had already started buying rival products. However, the company was able to attract many health-conscious consumers when it launched a variety of new adult-oriented cereals (some low fat, some low sugar, and some high fiber).

A second reason for the slide was a steady increase in prices. For example, Kellogg's Corn Flakes had long been the top seller, but annual 7 per-

cent price increases to cover rising costs had finally pushed the price to twice the level of competing brands. Kellogg halted the price hikes for a time to keep the cereal competitive and then increased prices again a short time later. A third reason was pressure from the many store-brand cereals, which were lower-priced than Kellogg cereals and therefore more appealing to budget-conscious buyers.

Faced with the need to boost market share while maintaining profitability, Gutierrez had to consider how he might most effectively promote Kellogg cereals to U.S. consumers. If you were Gutierrez, how would you encourage adults and children to try new Kellogg cereals? What would you do to persuade them to buy these cereals again? How would you respond to the threat posed by competing national brands and store brands?[1]

CHAPTER OVERVIEW   In the race for market share—a race that never ends—Kellogg managers know that sales promotion and advertising can be a powerful combination. This chapter closely examines sales promotion techniques and the use of supplementary media to round out an advertising program. First you'll learn about the connections between sales promotion and advertising, and you'll explore the objectives of consumer sales promotion and trade sales promotion. After examining the shift toward sales promotion and the concerns about this shift, you'll look at common techniques for consumer and trade sales promotion. Finally, you'll explore the role of supplementary media in the overall ad campaign, including yellow pages and specialty advertising.

The Partnership between Sales Promotion and Advertising

In today's highly competitive environment, the promotion part of the marketing mix plays a vital role in helping advertisers stay in touch with prospects and customers. Within promotion, advertising is especially important when you're introducing new products and reminding your target audience about the benefits of existing products. At the same time, consumers faced with many choices sometimes need an extra incentive to buy a particular product, and retailers sometimes need a special inducement to carry the product. You can provide that extra incentive by using **sales promotion,** an offer of direct inducements that enhance the basic value of a product for a limited time to stimulate immediate distributor commitment, sales force effectiveness, and consumer purchasing (see Exhibit 17.1).[2]

Hours: Always open.

Attire: Black leather to black tie.

Entertainment: Jazz pianist (daily).

Motto: "Bureaucrats are the meatloaf of humanity."

Ketchup: The slow one.

4 out of 5 restaurants serve America's favorite ketchup. Heinz.

YOUNG MAN COMES INTO DINER AND ORDERS HAMBURGER.
(SFX): diner noises, clatter of dishes and chatter of people, background music
YOUNG MAN: The usual.
COOK: Comin' up.

YOUNG MAN: Mind passing the Heinz?
WAITRESS: Sure.
(SFX): Heinz bottle sliding on counter and hitting the palm of young man's hand
YOUNG MAN GETS HIS HAMBURGER AND IS WAITING FOR THE THICK

KETCHUP TO COME OUT OF THE BOT-TLE.
V.O.: When you've got something this rich, this thick, why waste time with anything else? Heinz Ketchup. The best things come to those who wait.

EXHIBIT 17.1
Using Sales Promotion and Advertising

One way advertisers such as H. J. Heinz can enhance the basic value of their products is by supporting their advertising campaigns with coordinated consumer and trade sales promotion activities to reach distributors, salespeople, and consumers.

As you can see from this definition, sales promotion works by using direct inducements to boost the basic product value that advertising has established in the minds of distributors, salespeople, and consumers. One inducement might be offering a lower price, which makes the product seem like a better value for the money; another might be offering a free item, which makes the product seem like more value for the same money. Whatever the incentive, it's offered only for a short period, so the target audience must act quickly before the offer expires.

One important difference between advertising and sales promotion is the type of appeal used. Advertising often relies on emotional appeals to create a product image and to encourage purchasing, whereas sales promotion typically relies on rational appeals to show tangible reasons for buying right now. Reasons for buying immediately may be price cuts, prizes, or any of a wide range of incentives

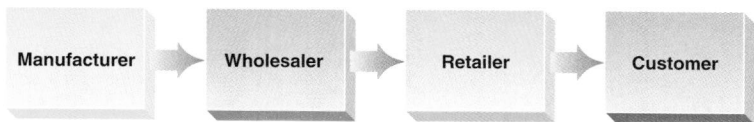

| Manufacturer | → | Wholesaler | → | Retailer | → | Customer |

EXHIBIT 17.2
The Distribution Channel

Distribution channels move goods and services from manufacturers and producers to customers. In a typical distribution channel, shown here, products pass through the hands of both wholesaler and retailer on their journey from manufacturer to customer.

attractive to consumers or to salespeople or other intermediaries in the distribution channel that links manufacturers to consumers. The intermediaries separating the producer and the consumer include wholesalers, dealers, retailers, and others responsible for bringing the product from the manufacturer to the place where consumers can obtain it (see Exhibit 17.2). By influencing the short-term buying behavior of consumers or of any or all of the intermediaries, you can speed the movement of your product through the channel.

Consider how Calgon combined the power of advertising with the incentives of sales promotion to reach both consumers and distributors. The company created a campaign to introduce and build awareness of all the items in the Calgon Bath Collection, encouraging consumers to try these products and to make repeat purchases and encouraging retailers to carry the whole line. The campaign revolved around an insert in *Mademoiselle, Self,* and other magazines targeted to women aged 25 to 49. The ad on the front of the insert featured lifestyle images of working women and a message about relaxing with Calgon bath products (emotional appeal). The sales promotion incentive on the back included scratch-and-sniff fragrance samples and a limited-time "buy one, get one free" offer (rational appeal). What's more, shoppers were buying not one but two items of the Calgon line, so retailers felt obliged to carry the entire line to avoid disappointing customers.[3]

Calgon created a sense of urgency and excitement by using **consumer sales promotion,** a set of promotional incentives aimed directly at the ultimate product purchaser. An advertiser such as Microsoft can use consumer promotions to boost sales of computer software to individuals who are making purchases for their own use and, at the same time, step up sales to people who are buying for business use. A recent study found that 28 percent of all promotional dollars is spent on consumer sales promotion activities (such as coupons and samples). These activities support pull strategies by increasing short-term consumer demand. Consumers ask retailers for a product, and retailers ask their wholesalers or distributors for the product. This demand pulls the product through the distribution system to the ultimate buyer.[4]

In contrast, **trade sales promotion** is a set of promotional inducements targeted toward wholesalers, retailers, and other intermediaries in the distribution channel responsible for bringing products to the consumer. According to the same study, trade sales promotion accounts for 45 percent of all promotional dollars (and advertising accounts for the remaining 27 percent). Such activities, including trade deals and trade contests, support push strategies to propel the product through the distribution system by offering incentives to the next link in the marketing chain to get the product onto store shelves or to dealers that sell to consumers.[5]

CONSUMER PROMOTION OBJECTIVES

You can harness the power of consumer promotion to achieve a variety of specific objectives. The most common objectives for consumer sales promotion are:

1. *To persuade consumers to try (and rebuy) a new product.* This is one of the most common uses of sales promotion, and it's not hard to see why: Out of the more than 13,000 new products launched every year, 80 percent fail, in part because too few people try or buy again. With that kind of competition, it's absolutely vital to get your target audience's attention, give them a reason to try your new offering—and convince them to continue buying; sales promotion is one way to do this quickly and effectively.[6] For example, when Weyerhaeuser introduced a glare-free paper stock that featured good color reproduction, its managers

SANTA CLAUS IS POSING AND LEAPING IN FRONT OF THE CAMERA IN THE STYLE OF A FASHION MODEL
(SFX): background music for runway model
PHOTOGRAPHER: All right, Santa, work for me, work to the camera.

(SFX): camera shutter clicking, female voice singing "Santa Claus, Santa Claus"
V.O.: We had to work real hard to get just the right look for our Carvel Santa Claus

ice cream cake. Buy one now and get 4 little elves for only $4 more. Carvel, the ice cream bakery. *Everything* should be made of ice cream.

EXHIBIT 17.3
Using Consumer Sales Promotion to Sell Companion Products

To convince consumers to buy two products at once, Carvel advertised a sales promotion in which consumers who purchased a Santa Claus ice cream cake could buy companion products at a special price.

reasoned that magazine publishers would want to carefully examine the new stock before placing an order. So Weyerhaeuser offered free samples to publishers.[7] After you've established your product, you can also use sales promotion to win over customers of rival products.

2. *To convince consumers to stay with a brand.* Once you've persuaded customers to try and buy, you face a new challenge. Now you have to keep them from switching to a rival product. Because competitors are always trying to woo away your customers, this is an ongoing sales promotion objective for many advertisers.

3. *To increase product purchase and usage.* In addition to keeping your customers, you may also want to use sales promotion to persuade customers to load up on your brand. In this way, you can effectively take them out of the market for similar products—and lock out competitors for as long as it takes customers to use up what they bought. For example, when consumers buy Kodak's 3-pack of film—which includes 12 extra exposures—they're won't need more film until they use up all 3 rolls.[8] In addition, stores will buy more of your product to replace the stock they've sold.

4. *To encourage consumers to buy your other products.* When you sell more than one product, you can use sales promotion to persuade customers to buy the companion products in your line (see Exhibit 17.3). For instance, Bausch & Lomb recently offered one free container of Sensitive Eyes saline solution when consumers bought two other items in the Sensitive Eyes line.[9] You may also encourage your customers to trade up to a more expensive (and possibly more profitable) version of the item they now use.

5. *To reinforce advertising and marketing efforts for more immediate results.* When used skillfully and tastefully, sales promotion can enhance your advertising message, your product image, and your overall marketing plan to speed up the sales process. Integrated with your marketing communications program, it acts as an additional way to emphasize your product benefits and competitive advantages, and its more urgent call to action drives your target audience to quickly take the next step—and buy. For instance, when Hershey began using the tag line "Hershey's . . . Now That's Chocolatese," the company offered a "Hershey's Chocolatese Cowculator" (topped by a smiling cow) to consumers who sent in two proofs of purchase and $5.99. The offer linked a giveaway (the calculator) that enhanced the product image, and it echoed the tag line to support the brand's advertising. Also, the offer included a coupon to encourage an immediate purchase, thus speeding up the sales process. Moreover, by requiring two proofs of purchase, this promotion sparked multiple purchases.[10]

To make sales promotion as powerful and as effective as possible, it's important to coordinate these objectives with your marketing and advertising objectives.

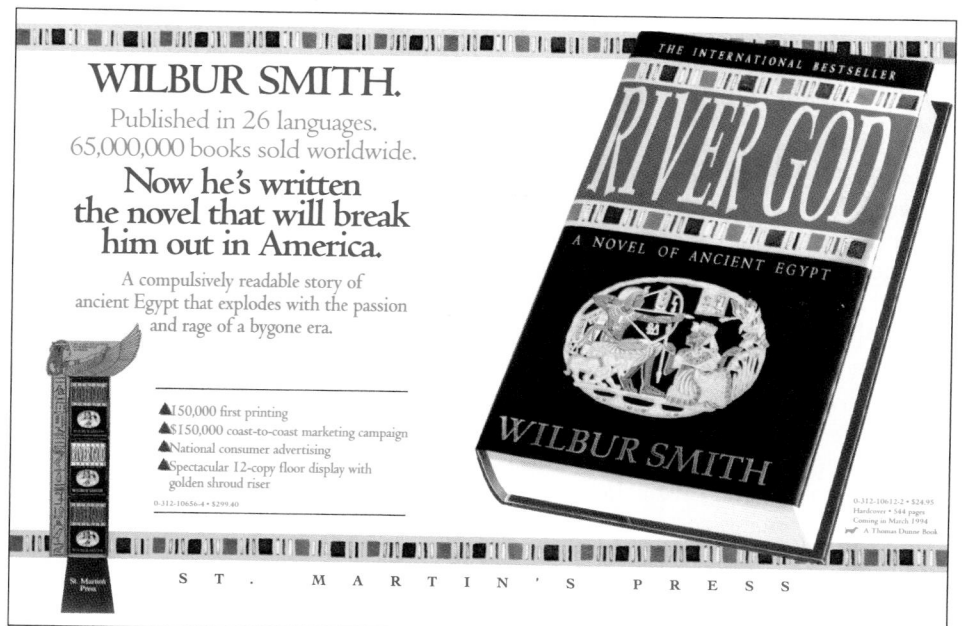

EXHIBIT 17.4
Using Trade Sales Promotion to Launch a New Product

When St. Martin's Press announced the publication of *River God*, it offered trade promotions (such as eye-catching point-of-purchase displays) and extensive consumer advertising support to induce retailers to order the book in quantity.

Moreover, like all marketing and advertising objectives, your sales promotion objectives must also be measurable, time specific, challenging, and attainable.

TRADE PROMOTION OBJECTIVES

You often have to sell to the trade before you can sell to the consumer. Although each advertiser's objectives will vary, depending on its unique situation and its own marketing and advertising goals, trade sales promotion may be started to achieve one or more of four objectives:

1. *To gain distribution.* It's not enough to create a product; you also have to get it onto store shelves where consumers can buy it. Whether you're introducing a new product, expanding an existing product into new markets, or putting the product into an entirely different type of store, you can use sales promotion to win over the wholesalers and retailers that sell the product (see Exhibit 17.4). Manufacturers often pay a fee to have their products placed on store shelves, but new firms can't always afford this approach. For instance, when Richard S. Worth founded R. W. Frookies, he couldn't afford to pay for shelf space, and he knew that stores would be reluctant to take space away from established brands to display his fruit-juice-sweetened cookies. He solved the problem with a two-pronged trade promotion program. First he developed colorful free-standing displays to hold boxes of Frookies so that retailers wouldn't lose any shelf space. Then he staged special events that brought customers into the stores to buy Frookies and, with any luck, other grocery items as well.[11]

2. *To encourage support for a consumer product or a consumer sales promotion.* Getting the product onto the shelf is just the first step; next, you have to get distributors excited about your product or about a consumer sales promotion you've planned. Consider how General Foods stirred up retailer excitement for Country Time drink mix in the Southeast by using a trade promotion linked to stock-car racing. Country Time sponsored a stock car in national races, and both car and driver would visit any retailer that ordered 100 cases of Country Time drink mix. A pedal-car replica of the race car went to retailers ordering 50 cases of Country Time, and various racing items (such as caps) went to other retailers as incentives to order. A related consumer trade promotion invited consumers to win a pedal car or to send for racing items in exchange for proofs of purchase.[12]

3. *To stimulate distributors to raise or lower their inventory levels.* When you have lots of stock in your warehouse, you may want to use trade sales promotion to persuade wholesalers or retailers to order higher quantities. Toshiba America used this approach when it wanted to sell off its six-month supply of the BD-5110 copier. As a sales promotion, Toshiba offered dealers a free copier and a four-day cruise for two to the Bahamas for every 12 BD-5110 copiers they ordered; the cruise could be used in a push strategy as an incentive for dealer employees, or it could be used in a pull strategy as a consumer incentive. In just one month, Toshiba came close to selling out of this model.[13] Trade sales promotions can also be used to stimulate distributors to lower their inventory levels (by motivating them to sell more to make space for a new model).

4. *To strengthen relationships with distributors and salespeople.* Once you have an effective distribution network, it's important to keep competitors out of the picture by staying on good terms with your wholesalers and retailers and their salespeople. Trade sales promotion can help strengthen these relationships and at the same time give salespeople the tools they need to sell your product. In fact, many manufacturers now tailor specific promotional programs to meet the needs of their key retail customers.[14]

THE SHIFT TOWARD SALES PROMOTION

Over the past two decades, a definite shift has occurred in the promotion end of the marketing mix. Most advertisers have taken money from advertising to beef up the amount spent on sales promotion activities (see Exhibit 17.5). In the 1970s, advertising accounted for up to 70 percent of an advertiser's promotion budget; today, sales promotion takes up 73 percent of the budget while advertising accounts for only 27 percent.[15] Moreover, company increases in spending for sales promotion have outpaced increases in spending for advertising. This adds up to a major shift toward sales promotion at the expense of advertising.

Reasons for the Shift

Why are advertisers putting more emphasis on sales promotion? The shift has been prompted by a variety of factors. Among them are the focus on short-term results, the need for accountability, the growth in retailer power, the proliferation of products, and the changing behavior of buyers.

EXHIBIT 17.5
The Shift toward Sales Promotion

For over a decade, U.S. advertisers have allocated more of their promotional budgets to sales promotion than to advertising. This is a reversal of the budget allocations that were common during the 1970s, when advertising accounted for more than two-thirds of the promotional budget.

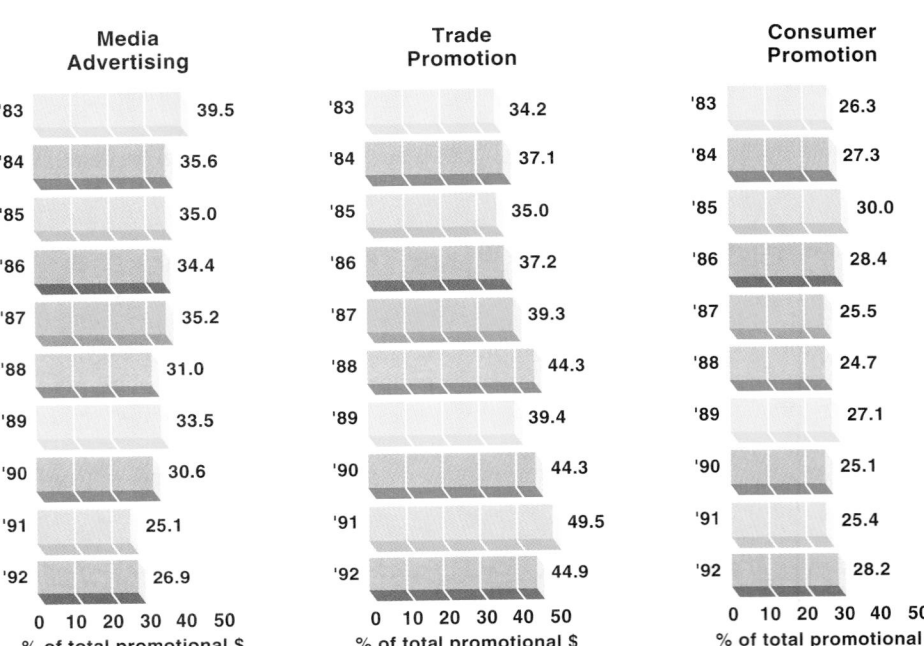

	Media Advertising	Trade Promotion	Consumer Promotion
'83	39.5	34.2	26.3
'84	35.6	37.1	27.3
'85	35.0	35.0	30.0
'86	34.4	37.2	28.4
'87	35.2	39.3	25.5
'88	31.0	44.3	24.7
'89	33.5	39.4	27.1
'90	30.6	44.3	25.1
'91	25.1	49.5	25.4
'92	26.9	44.9	28.2

0 10 20 30 40 50 % of total promotional $

0 10 20 30 40 50 % of total promotional $

0 10 20 30 40 50 % of total promotional $

- *Short-term results.* For many U.S. advertisers, success is measured by the inch rather than by the yard. Under pressure to achieve weekly, monthly, quarterly, and yearly sales quotas, managers may look to sales promotion as an immediate antidote for slow sales. What's more, the way marketing, advertising, and sales personnel are rewarded can contribute to this short-term mentality. In some companies, bonuses or salary increases are tied directly to sales results, so sales promotions that yield a quick payoff may seem more inviting than image advertising or other types of advertising that can take a long time to show results.

- *Accountability.* Not only are companies under pressure to show short-term sales results, they're also increasingly concerned about measuring the results of promotion investments. Although it's difficult to measure the results of any given advertisement, it's fairly easy to see whether a particular sales promotion achieved the desired results. If you use coupons, you can count how many were turned in; if you temporarily lower your wholesale price, you can see how many cases are sold. For this reason, some managers see sales promotion as the most convenient way to satisfy the demand for accountability, a trend discussed in Chapter 1. In fact, a growing number of manufacturers are using the level of store sales to determine how much trade promotion support to give retailers.[16]

- *Retailer power.* In years past, manufacturers with giant advertising budgets and high brand recognition were seen as more powerful than retailers. They could use their muscle to create a level of consumer demand that virtually forced stores to carry their products or risk losing sales. However, the balance of power has now shifted to retailers. First, thanks to computerized checkout systems, more retailers have detailed information about consumer purchasing patterns, so they can quickly determine which products are selling, to whom, how quickly, and at what profit levels. Retailers now have the data to know whether a product is selling as the manufacturer promised, and they can ask for incentives on the basis of actual sales. Second, consolidation in the retail industry has left fewer but larger retailers such as Wal-Mart and Toys "R" Us with more clout to seek incentives in return for stocking and selling products.[17]

- *Product proliferation.* It's a new-product jungle out there, and there seems to be no letup in the rate of product launches. Advertising alone may not get a new product onto store shelves and then into consumers' shopping carts, but trade and consumer sales promotion can give new-product sales a head start. Store shelves are overflowing, leaving little room for new products or for any increase in the stock of current best-sellers. To make matters worse, the market for many products is stagnant, and when sales stall, any increase in market share (or store shelf space) comes at the expense of other products— preferably competitors' products. So to combat competitive challenges from new products, many advertisers turn to fast-working sales promotions that defend market share and lift sales levels.

- *Buyer behavior.* Consumers are becoming less loyal to brands and more interested in comparing factors such as price, value, convenience, and service when evaluating competing products. Although many new products are brought out every year, few are truly novel or offer distinct advantages over competing products, so consumers have come to rely on price as one key way of differentiating among products they perceive to be essentially the same. Some consumers have become so conditioned to choosing on the basis of price incentives offered by frequent sales promotions that they buy only during promotions. Moreover, for consumers who have little time to shop, it's easier to buy whichever acceptable product is being promoted.[18]

These factors have fueled a distinct and measurable shift in marketing budgets toward the sales promotion side. However, as the next section shows, the continuing emphasis on sales promotion also raises real concerns that advertisers must take into consideration.

Concerns about the Shift

No one denies that sales promotion can give market share and sales volume a short-term shot in the arm. However, ongoing reliance on such techniques can pose potential problems. One concern is whether consumer sales promotion hurts long-term brand loyalty, a disadvantage to advertisers that have invested in developing a brand image and in advertising specific benefits to give the product a competitive edge. As just mentioned, buyer behavior is changing, and over time, continual sales promotion may condition consumers to choose among competing brands on the basis of promotions rather than quality or other elements.[19]

During recessionary periods, brand loyalty may dip even more, and advertisers that use promotions to defend market share or to boost sales may only encourage more promotion-consciousness. Even when advertisers mount sales promotions to attract new customers to existing products, they often draw either current customers who would buy anyway or people with little loyalty who tend to buy the brand that offers the best promotion. Thus, rather than building a steady stream of sales on the basis of real product differences and competitive advantages, frequent or continual promotions can undermine the brand image and loyalty that advertising has worked to instill. This can lead to an erratic sales pattern in which consumers buy when they get incentives and then wait until a new promotion starts—or switch to a brand offering a promotion.[20]

However, promotion experts say that integrating sales promotions into the overall advertising program can effectively build on and extend brand loyalty. As a result, many advertisers are now looking beyond one-time or quick-fix programs and using integrated marketing communications to coordinate sales promotion with advertising efforts. This helps them enhance brand image, reward long-term brand loyalty, and encourage repeat purchases.[21] One example is Camp Hyatt, an attempt to build long-term loyalty by advertising that Hyatt offers parents a safe, supervised place for their children to play when the family vacations at more than 100 Hyatt hotels and resorts (see Exhibit 17.6). This program is also a good way to introduce the next generation of travelers to Hyatt's facilities and services, another long-term benefit.[22]

EXHIBIT 17.6

Camp Hyatt Encourages Long-Term Loyalty

Targeting family vacationers, the Camp Hyatt program promotes Hyatt hotels and resorts as secure and fun destinations for both parents and children. By integrating this promotion with a carefully crafted advertising campaign, Hyatt is working to strengthen customer loyalty over the long term.

Another concern is the impact that sales promotions can have on profitability. In some cases, mounting a sales promotion can be so costly that the advertiser must sell an extraordinarily large amount of product (or raise prices considerably) to make back the profits lost from offering discounts or other incentives. If the profit margin is small to begin with, the advertiser has little or no chance of making the kind of profit that it would have earned if it hadn't offered the promotions. Also bear in mind that few competitors will sit idly by while your promotion lures customers away. Rivals often respond by raising the promotional stakes even higher, which can spiral into a never-ending profit-sapping cycle.[23]

The airline industry learned this lesson the hard way. For years, American Airlines, United Airlines, and most other carriers competed to see which could offer the most and best free trips to keep frequent travelers loyal. Soon the airlines found that they could squeeze fewer and fewer paying customers onto flights that were increasingly filled with travelers collecting on their free trips. When American Airlines tried to change the rules and increase the number of miles needed to win a free trip to Hawaii, its frequent fliers yelled so loudly that the change was dropped. United Airlines tried the same change, and its frequent flyers actually filed a lawsuit against the airline. Now the airlines have started offering nonflight prizes that rivals can't easily imitate, and they have tightened up the free-flight rules to reward only their best customers.[24]

Just as a steady diet of promotions can condition consumers to expect more and larger incentives, the trade can also come to expect incentives on a regular basis—and to want more control over where, when, and how any promotional dollars are spent. A growing number of retailers are developing programs to reinforce shopper loyalty, and they want to use the incentives offered during trade promotions to benefit their stores as well as the advertised brands. Responding to this trend, more advertisers are working closely with retailers to create promotions that meet the stores' needs and effectively sell the promoted product. Dannon, the yogurt maker, now plans promotions keyed to the sales and profitability of each retail account. After some early successes, including a joint promotion with Von's supermarkets to sponsor the Los Angeles marathon, Dannon is doing more and more promotions with retail partners.[25]

Types of Consumer Promotion

As you know from your own experience, manufacturers, service firms, and even nonprofit organizations use a variety of sales promotion techniques to target the consumer. Among the most commonly used are samples, coupons, price promotions and price packs, money-back offers, contests and sweepstakes, premiums, frequency programs, and point-of-purchase displays. Advertisers may use any or all of these techniques, depending on the objectives they want to achieve.

SAMPLES

One of the most effective but costly methods of encouraging consumers to try a product is through **sampling,** the practice of offering a small quantity of your product free or at an extremely low price. Whether you're introducing a new product or seeking higher market share for an existing product, you can use sampling to showcase your product's benefits and encourage the target audience to switch from competing products. A successful sampling program depends on the product's ability to quickly demonstrate its competitive advantages; if consumers can't see, feel, or find the product's superiority, they won't buy it. For this reason, sampling is widely used for health and beauty products and food, which have specific selling points (such as fragrance or taste) that are best conveyed by a brief trial rather than by advertising.

You can use many techniques to get samples to your target audience. You can send samples through the mail, hire a firm to deliver door-to-door, bundle samples

For several years, manufacturers of breakfast cereals and foods have issued more coupons than manufacturers in any other product category. Among nonfood products, the makers of hair-care products and household cleaners have used coupons more aggressively in recent years.

1	Cereals & breakfast foods
2	Medications, remedies, health aids
3	Pet food
4	Household cleaners
5	Condiments, gravies, sauces
6	Prepared foods
7	Cough & cold remedies
8	Detergents
9	Hair-care products
10	Bread & baked goods

with magazines and newspapers, give away samples in the store, or distribute them almost anywhere your target audience is likely to be. For example, when Christian Dior launched Dune, a women's fragrance, the firm used direct-mail sampling to reach department store customers; when Elizabeth Arden introduced Chloe's Narcisse, it distributed perfume samples in magazines and at department store beauty counters. In a unique twist on a sampling technique used by car companies, Apple advertised the "Macintosh Test Drive" and invited prospects to take a Macintosh computer home overnight. More than 200,000 people nationwide sampled the Macintosh, and this exposure helped boost sales.[26]

The popularity of sampling is growing as the price of trial-size containers and of sample distribution continues to decline. Advertisers are also finding that sampling is a good way to build word of mouth about a product. Unconventional sampling techniques helped Smartfood's cheese-coated popcorn sales jump to $12 million in only three years. Targeting young adults, the firm used people costumed in giant popcorn bags to give away samples at ski resorts and other recreation areas. "Our efforts have given us exposure and notoriety, which translates into interest, curiosity and eventually sales," says Smartfood president Ken Meyers.[27]

COUPONS

A **coupon** is a certificate good for a specific price reduction when a particular product is purchased. Coupons are by far the most popular—and the most effective—sales promotion technique in the United States, and their use is growing in Canada as well as Italy and several other European countries. Manufacturers in the United States distribute more than 300 billion coupons every year; the largest issuers of coupons are makers of breakfast foods and cereals, such as Kellogg and General Mills (see Exhibit 17.7). However, less than 3 percent of all manufacturers' coupons are redeemed, in part because of competition from retailers' coupons (redeemable only in the issuer's stores) and in part because of the clutter caused by the blizzard of coupons.[28]

Coupons can help you launch a new product, build market share, and convert customers of competing brands. In a recent survey, more than 70 percent of the respondents said that a coupon encouraged them to try a product they'd never used before. Coupons can also keep sales strong during difficult economic times, when consumers would otherwise buy less frequently or switch to lower-priced store brands to save money. Despite these advantages, coupons are one of the sales promotion techniques that have been accused of shaping changes in buyer behavior by instilling a bargain-hunting mentality in many consumers. Another concern is the wasted advertising and the lost profits resulting from delivering coupons to people who would buy the product anyway: one study revealed that 90 percent of the consumers polled use coupons for the brands they usually buy.[29]

You can distribute coupons in any number of ways. The most popular method (used by Kellogg and other major manufacturers) is through free-standing inserts (FSIs) in newspapers. These inserts, which contain coupons for a variety of products, carry more than 80 percent of all manufacturers' coupons. You can also use direct mail, print ads, product packages, and even yellow pages directories. Perhaps the fastest growing method is in-store distribution, which gets coupons to shoppers when they're making their buying decisions. An increasing number of grocery and drugstores are being outfitted with on-shelf dispensers to distribute coupons for nearby products.[30]

Also growing is the use of **electronic couponing,** a computerized system of issuing coupons or price reductions in response to specific in-store buying patterns (see Exhibit 17.8). Thousands of stores are equipped with scanner systems to read the Universal Product Code (UPC), the machine-readable bar codes printed on product packages. As the scanner reads the UPC bar code, the system triggers a printer next to the cash register to issue a particular coupon when a consumer buys a competing brand or a companion product that's scanned through the checkout. For instance, ConAgra used this system to put coupons for Healthy Choice frozen meals into the hands of people who buy Weight Watchers frozen entrees.[31]

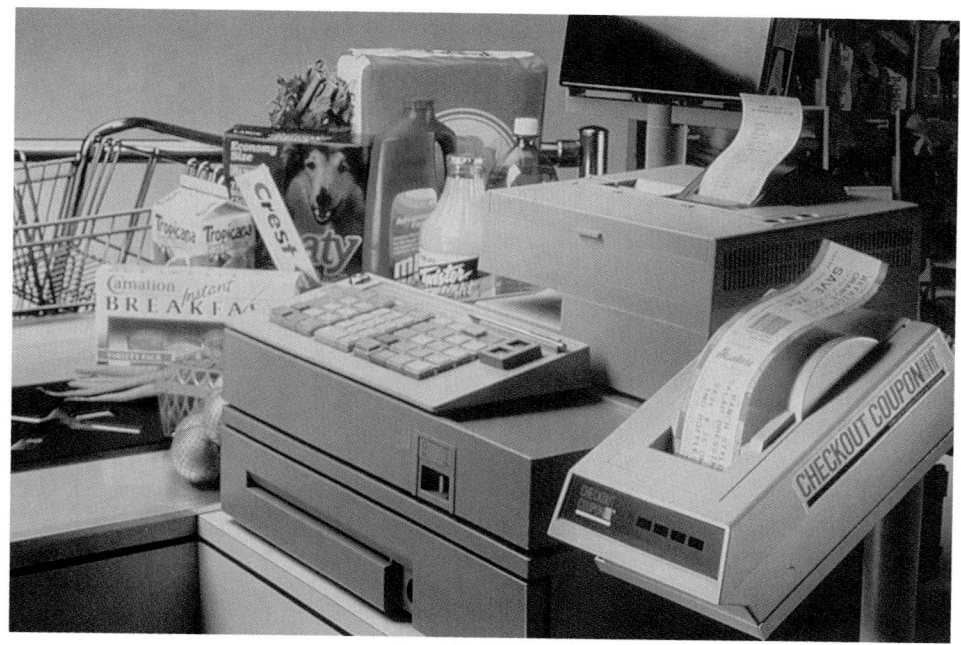

EXHIBIT 17.8
Electronic Couponing

An advertiser that signs up with an electronic couponing program such as Catalina's Checkout Coupon can control exactly who gets its coupons. Generally, participating advertisers arrange to issue coupons at the checkout counter to shoppers who purchase particular companion products or competitors' products.

Other systems do away with paper coupons and offer shoppers couponlike price reductions at the cash register when they present a special card. Shoppers like electronic couponing because it's simpler and easier than traditional coupon methods; manufacturers like it because they can target specific consumers and buying patterns; retailers like it because the coupons are redeemable only in the issuing store or chain, which builds store loyalty. However, some manufacturers believe that the price (as much as 7 cents per coupon delivered electronically, compared with less than 1 cent per coupon delivered through FSIs) is difficult to justify.[32]

PRICE PROMOTIONS AND PRICE PACKS

In contrast to a coupon, which is only valid when the certificate is presented at the cash register, a **price promotion** is a short-term price reduction that's available to everyone who purchases the product during the promotional period. Some price promotions decrease the selling price by a specific amount (50 cents or $50); others reduce the price by a certain percentage (20 percent or 50 percent). Price promotions can encourage consumers to try new products, buy more of a product, buy a product more frequently, or switch from a competing brand.

Rather than taking money off the purchase price, you can give the consumer more value for the same money by offering a **price pack,** which bundles something extra with the product package. This is a good way to reward current customers while encouraging all customers and prospects to stock up so that they'll be less interested in rival offers. One type of price pack is a *bonus pack,* which contains more than the usual quantity of the product at the regular price. For instance, Vidal Sassoon has offered a bonus pack of 20 percent more shampoo, or 13.2 ounces, for the price of the regular 11-ounce size. A second type of price pack is the *banded pack,* in which two or more units of a product are sold together at a lower price than if purchased separately. An example is a recent Gillette promotion in which two cans of Gillette Foamy shaving cream were wrapped together in plastic and advertised as "Buy one can, get one free!"

MONEY-BACK OFFERS

Many advertisers use money-back offers to reward current customers, to remove the risk from trying a new product, to encourage multiple purchases, and to persuade consumers to buy now rather than later. A **refund** is a money-back offer to return a specific amount of money after a particular product (or combina-

Sales Promotion Campaigns: Solo versus Team Efforts

Most of the ads you see are for one advertiser's product or product line. In contrast, consumer sales promotions aren't always solo affairs. Although many are developed by one advertiser, a good number represent joint efforts of 2, 3, even up to 10 partners. The decision to go solo or to team with other advertisers to plan and produce a consumer promotion depends on your specific objectives, your need for control, and the amount of time and money you want to invest.

In a solo consumer sales promotion, you're in complete control of all creative elements, and you can choose the media and the timing as you wish. You can also decide how much you want to spend. Because you don't have to consult any partners, you can make changes whenever and wherever you want, even after the promotion has begun. By going solo, you also keep the spotlight firmly on your own product and brand name, which tends to maximize the promotional impact and minimize any distractions.

For example, in Australia, Coca-Cola Amatil Samboy Chips decided on a solo consumer sales promotion to keep the focus squarely on two new flavors of snack chips it introduced. Starting with television commercials to create a hip image and to build awareness, Samboy added a sales promotion to encourage teens to try the new products. The heart of the promotion was an electronic game that challenged players' strength; to play, teens had to present an empty Samboy Chips pack. Samboy brought the game to shopping centers in Brisbane and other Australian cities, and it drew at each location hundreds of players who competed for compact disk players, Samboy caps, and other prizes. No other products were featured in the promotion, so participants thought only of Samboy when they played the game or saw the ads. Thanks to this solo promotion, the new Samboy Chips flavors moved off store shelves.

On the other hand, you can spread the work load and the expenses—and widen your exposure—by linking with other advertisers for a joint sales promotion program. For instance, Gatorade recently sought out Foot Locker as its partner for a national promotion to build summertime sales. During July and August, Gatorade drinks carried special $10-off certificates redeemable at any Foot Locker store when customers bought merchandise at Foot Locker worth $50 or more. Why did Gatorade choose Foot Locker? Margaret Dyer, vice president of marketing for Gatorade, explains, "They have essentially the same target market as Gatorade, and both brands have 'athletic' personalities."

Gatorade and Foot Locker teamed up for a joint sales promotion campaign.

Another reason to do a joint promotion: competitors can't easily steal your idea by duplicating what you do, simply because they can't copy your partner. For instance, when Kellogg joined with major league baseball and Walt Disney, the cereal maker knew that rivals would be locked out of using well-known Disney characters and baseball stars in their own promotions.

Finally, the combined clout of several major advertisers may spark more excitement than a solo promotion. When Domino's Pizza teamed with video-game powerhouse Nintendo for a recent year-end holiday promotion, the take-out chain enjoyed its best sales week of the year. As a result, Domino's is looking to work with more category leaders like Nintendo, and it plans to use these partnerships to develop even more aggressive and memorable promotions. In the end, that extra spark may make the difference between an average promotion and a great one.

Apply Your Knowledge

1. What might Walt Disney gain from a joint promotion with Kellogg?
2. If Samboy wanted to do a joint promotion to introduce its line of chip flavors in the United States, what partners might be most appropriate? Why?

tion of products) is purchased. Unlike price promotions, which are immediately available to all purchasers, refunds are offered to all but are sent only to purchasers who actually file the refund forms. However, filling out forms and waiting for cash back can seem troublesome, so many people don't bother to send for their refunds.[33]

In the past decade, automobile manufacturers have popularized the *rebate*, which is essentially the same as a refund but has come to refer to money-back offers on expensive products such as cars, trucks, and appliances. One example is Okidata's offer of a $50 rebate to consumers or businesses that buy any of four laser-printer models. Like most money-back offers, this promotion lasted for only a limited time, a restriction designed to create a sense of urgency about making the purchase.[34]

CONTESTS AND SWEEPSTAKES

Some of the most exciting consumer sales promotions are built around contests and sweepstakes. In a **contest,** participants use their skills or abilities to compete for prizes. For example, a Tropicana Twister Holiday Drink Recipe Contest offered a grand prize of $10,000 for the best punch or drink recipe using a Twister beverage. However, no skill or ability is needed to win a **sweepstakes,** in which prizes are awarded based on a random drawing or on some other method of selection by chance. It's easy to qualify (by completing a form with name and address and sometimes other information, such as a dealer name), so more people enter sweepstakes than contests. For instance, Pepsi-Cola has been reaching out to a Hispanic target audience since 1986 with an annual sweepstakes offering a $100,000 top prize to buy the "casa de sus sueños" (house of your dreams); more than 1.5 million entries are received every year. Contests and sweepstakes can boost interest in your product because they involve consumers in the promotion and link the product to an attractive prize, but studies show that for getting consumers to change their buying behavior, sweepstakes are less effective than coupons or money-back offers.[35]

Another way to involve consumers is through a **game,** a type of sweepstakes that incorporates the usual elements of chance but continues for a longer period. Games are popular with fast-food chains, hotels, and gasoline retailers because they draw customers back again and again in search of a particular game piece or some other winning element. Duracell recently used an instant-win game to battle Eveready for battery sales in the United Kingdom. The winning symbol was revealed when consumers used the battery tester on the Duracell package—a clever way to play up one of the brand's unique features.[36] A national contest, sweepstakes, or game can cost $5 million or more and requires compliance with a variety of federal and state laws. Despite these issues, advertisers such as Exxon and RCA have found that these promotions generate a high level of enthusiasm both among consumers and in the trade; however, games can be complicated to create and manage—and experts question their long-term effect on sales.[37]

PREMIUMS

To reward consumers for visiting a dealer, trying a new product, or continuing to buy your brand, you can offer a **premium,** an item provided free (or at a greatly reduced price) as an incentive to try or buy. Of course, to effectively change buyer behavior, the premium must be attractive and valuable to the target audience. For example, when Canon promoted its Canofile 250 computerized document-storage system to small businesses, the premium was two free optical disks with every purchase, a $460 value that started buyers off with storage space for 26,000 documents. Premiums are also used by nonprofit organizations to reward contributors or to encourage larger donations; for instance, Mothers Against Drunk Driving sends each donor a free cookbook as a gesture of thanks.[38]

Four methods of distributing premiums in the store can encourage purchases of your product. They include offering (1) merchandise (or certificates for goods or services) at the cash register, (2) *in-pack premiums* that are put into the package at the factory, (3) *on-pack premiums* that are attached to the outside of the package by the manufacturer, and (4) *container premiums,* in which case the decorative or commemorative container holding the product is the actual premium. For example, Crayola recently used a container premium and an in-pack premium in a holiday promotion that featured crayons packaged with a free Christmas ornament in a special tin container.[39] To encourage repeat purchases, you can offer premiums by mail in exchange for box tops or other proof of purchase; some advertisers print a

premium catalog and encourage consumers to save proofs of purchase for the premiums they choose.

Another way to reward customers is to offer a **self-liquidating premium,** a more substantial premium that, rather than being free, is partly or completely paid for by the consumer (see Exhibit 17.9). Although consumers have to send some proof of purchase and a small payment to cover the item's cost and shipping, they can get a desirable premium such as a tote bag or a sports jacket at a bargain price. Advertisers don't usually make a profit on these premiums; the point is to generate goodwill and reinforce brand loyalty. Oscar Mayer is a good example, offering a toy version of its Wienermobile (a car shaped like a wiener on a bun) as a self-liquidating premium that can be purchased for $2.99 plus 2 proofs of purchase; the toy is free with 10 proofs of purchase.[40] A variation used by retailers is the *continuity premium,* in which regular customers qualify to buy a different premium every week if they spend a preset amount on other merchandise. To complete the set of dishes, encyclopedias, or whatever premiums are offered, customers must shop at that store week after week.

FREQUENCY PROGRAMS

Closely related to the continuity premium is the **frequency program,** also known as a *frequent-buyer* or *loyalty program,* an ongoing offer of free merchandise or services designed to encourage purchasing more of a product or purchasing a product more frequently. Unlike self-liquidating and continuity premiums, which are discontinued after some period, frequency programs are relatively permanent, so they're more effective in building long-term customer loyalty. Customers can typically earn more valuable rewards when they buy more frequently or when they accumulate many proofs of purchase. Hotels (Marriott and Hilton), airlines (American Airlines, Delta Air Lines), fast-food chains (Burger King, Arby's), and makers of food and household products (Procter & Gamble, Nabisco) are just some of the advertisers using frequency programs (see Exhibit 17.10).[41]

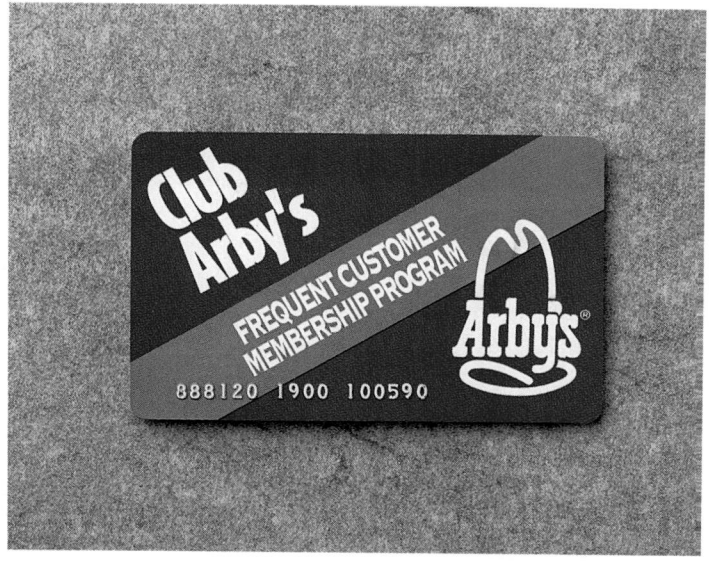

EXHIBIT 17.10
Arby's Encourages Return Visits

Recognizing that hungry consumers have many fast-food choices, Arby's created the Club Arby's frequency program to keep customers coming back. Purchases are tracked electronically, and repeat customers receive food prizes when they present their Club Arby's cards.

As these advertisers have found, frequency programs can change consumer purchasing patterns: once consumers start buying specific products in anticipation of the rewards they want, they're less likely to switch to competing products. As part of an integrated marketing communications program, frequency programs can help you gain a competitive edge in a category where consumers see few real differences between brands. However, both the rewards and the administration can be costly, and as discussed earlier in the chapter, after you've started a frequency program, you may have difficulty ending it without alienating your customers.[42]

POINT-OF-PURCHASE DISPLAYS

A good way to reach people at the moment they're ready to buy is through **point-of-purchase (POP) displays,** in-store materials designed to influence the purchase of a particular product. POP displays include special merchandise racks, banners, signs, and other items arranged inside (or in front of) a retail outlet. In recent years, electronic POP displays have become more common. For example, Kraft is one of a growing roster of manufacturers that flash messages on electronic signs straddling grocery aisles. In some supermarkets, advertisers can also promote products through the **product information center,** a video display terminal programmed to flash brief commercials and community news items.[43]

Research shows that nearly 70 percent of all buying decisions are made when consumers are already in the store, so POP displays can help you put your message in the right place at the right time. Using POP, you can encourage consumers to try new products, switch from one brand to another, or make unplanned purchases (see Exhibit 17.11). However, so many advertisers are now vying for consumer attention at the point of purchase that many stores are virtually swimming in POP displays, creating a clutter problem for retailers and shoppers. That's why some stores are refusing some displays or are charging for the space that displays occupy.[44]

Types of Trade Promotions

Promoting to consumers is only half the sales promotion equation; the other half is promoting to the members of the distribution channel. Whether you deal directly with each store or go through other intermediaries to get your products to the outlets where consumers buy them, you can use a variety of trade sales promotion

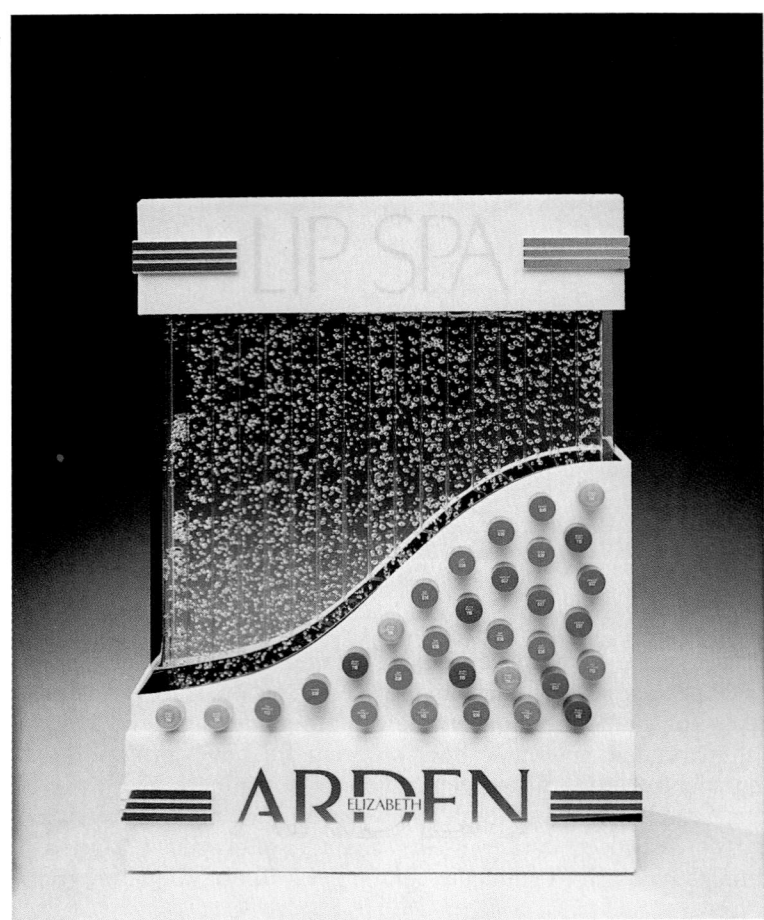

EXHIBIT 17.11
Using Point-of-Purchase Displays

Elizabeth Arden's eye-catching point-of-purchase display was designed to visually portray the most important benefit of its Lip Spa line of lipsticks—moisturizing action.

techniques to gain the commitment and support of people throughout the distribution channel. These techniques include trade deals, trade contests and incentives, trade shows, and sales support. In addition, you can use a cooperative advertising program to support the efforts of your distributors.

TRADE DEALS

A **trade deal** is a short-term arrangement in which wholesalers and retailers are encouraged to stock and promote products in exchange for special discounts, payments, or additional merchandise. Trade deals can be used to persuade distributors to stock a product for the first time, prominently display a product, offer promotions that attract consumers, or buy more of a product. Three common types of trade deals are buying allowances, display allowances, and slotting allowances.

A **buying allowance** is a payment or discount offered to a distributor to encourage the purchase of a certain amount of merchandise during a specified period. These trade deals are often coupled with consumer sales promotions to more quickly move the product through the distribution channel. For instance, a manufacturer might offer dealers 10 cases for the price of 8 just before printing a coupon in the newspaper. However, one unintended result is that many distributors will order more than they need and hold the extra stock to sell (at the regular price) after the consumer promotion is over, a practice known as *forward buying*.[45]

A **display allowance** is a fee paid (or a discount offered) by the manufacturer to the retailer in exchange for a desirable shelf location, an end-of-aisle display, or some space for a POP display. Generally, a display allowance is used to support an established product. A new product is often supported by a **slotting allowance,** a fee paid by the manufacturer to the retailer in exchange for a "slot," or position, on

ETHICS IN ADVERTISING

Are Slotting Allowances Justified?

In recent years, retailer demands for slotting allowances have ignited considerable controversy. On the one hand, retailers obviously want to stock products that people want to buy. On the other, they have only a limited amount of shelf space and they can't afford to waste it on poorly conceived products. At the same time, advertisers know that new products can't succeed if they're not stocked in enough stores. Advertisers also need the support and enthusiasm of retailers if they're to properly display and promote their products—and receive the feedback they need to stay on target with customer needs. The clash of these competing viewpoints has raised several ethical issues.

Advertisers question whether it's ethical for stores to demand slotting allowances for doing nothing more than what they ordinarily do, which is to put products on the shelf. After all, a store can't stay in business without products to sell, and a constant stream of new products can keep customers coming back to try new items and to buy their favorites. The advertisers also say that slotting allowances are inflated, and they assert that paying these fees results in much higher retail prices, which ultimately hurts consumers.

Finally, they question the ethics of permitting slotting allowances so high that only large or established firms can afford to pay. Does this discriminate against small businesses, which may not have the money to launch their new products? Will consumers lose out because potentially useful products developed by small firms may never reach store shelves?

Retailers deny that slotting allowances are unethical. They say they can't afford to display every one of the growing number of new products on their crowded store shelves. Moreover, they're concerned about the risk of lost profitability when a new product—which has taken space from an established product—doesn't sell. In fact, the demand for shelf space is so great that some retailers now feel justified in charging a *failure allowance* if a new product doesn't meet some preset minimum sales level

Selsun Gold avoided slotting allowances by offering in-depth sales training and consumer promotion support.

by the end of a specified period. That way, the store earns profits if the new item sells, but it can't lose if the item doesn't sell.

So far, the ethical dilemmas surrounding slotting allowances are unresolved. Major retailers still have the clout to ask for—and get—slotting allowances, and most advertisers have reluctantly learned to factor these fees into the overall cost of introducing new products. However, despite retailer pressure, some advertisers have successfully sidestepped slotting allowances. For example, Ross Laboratories recently got Selsun Gold for Women shampoo into stores by offering in-depth sales training for store employees, demonstrating the product's unique benefits, and providing strong consumer promotion support. Even so, for many advertisers, slotting allowances remain an expensive (and ethically questionable) fact of life.

What's Your Opinion?
1. Should retailers be allowed to charge slotting allowances for every new product, regardless of the manufacturer's ability to pay?
2. Should consumers be expected to pick up the tab for slotting allowances in the form of higher retail prices? ∎

the store shelf. Stores that charge slotting allowances require manufacturers to pay for every item in a new product line; for instance, a manufacturer would pay for three slots if a new yogurt product was offered in three flavors. Although many supermarket chains insist on slotting allowances, advertisers object to paying these fees, which have become controversial.

Manufacturers expect stores to pass along to consumers some of the savings on products discounted in trade deals, but the stores frequently don't. Studies show that up to 75 percent of grocery distributors' profits come from keeping trade dollars instead of lowering retail prices or offering other consumer incentives. In recent years, concern about the high cost and possible retail abuse has led some manufacturers to revise or reduce their use of trade deals. Procter & Gamble, for example, now considers each retailer's payment and sales history when allocating trade promotion money. The company has also adopted a policy of **everyday low pricing (EDLP),** in which the number of special pricing deals is reduced or eliminated in favor of lower year-round prices. To wean the trade (and consumers) from expensive promotions, P&G has lowered the price of Tide and Cheer laundry detergents by 9 percent, eliminated trade allowances, and gradually reduced the frequency and value of coupons issued for those products. Other advertisers, including Kraft General Foods, are also reevaluating and, in many cases, cutting back on trade deals.[46]

TRADE CONTESTS AND INCENTIVES

Once you get your product into the hands of wholesalers and retailers, the next step is to give them an incentive to sell it. One way is to develop a sales contest that rewards distributors for meeting—or exceeding—sales goals. For example, General Motors-Holden in Australia offered its car dealers the chance to win 24 prizes ranging from scuba gear to home security systems when they met or exceeded their sales goals. The contest was so successful that sales skyrocketed 33 percent over the target, in spite of a weak economy.[47] To encourage retail salespeople to sell more, you might offer **push money,** the payment of a set amount (such as $1 or $10) to a salesperson every time a particular item is sold. However, unless they're carefully designed, trade contests and push money programs can backfire if salespeople try to win by insisting that customers buy what they don't need or by applying so much pressure that they drive customers away.

When your goal is to gain more shelf space or to encourage the use of a special POP display, you can use incentives to reward distributors for performing the needed tasks. Say you ship appliance retailers a fancy POP display for a new air conditioner, and the display includes a demonstration unit. As a reward for assembling the display and putting it in a prominent place, you might give the demonstration units to the store managers after the promotion ends. Or you might award a prize to the store manager who sends in a photo of the most imaginative POP display.

TRADE SHOWS

Another way to reach out to the trade is through a **trade show,** an event where manufacturers display and sell their products to current and potential distributors. For example, at the annual BookPub World trade show, printers and graphic arts firms rent exhibit space and put out samples to show book publishers. You can meet many customers and prospects in a short period during a trade show, so it's a good place to take orders and set up appointments for future sales calls (see Exhibit 17.12). For instance, when Omron Electronics displayed new products at an industrial trade show, it received 169 requests for sales calls and 1,248 leads on prospective buyers, a good head start on its year's sales activities. A trade show is also a good place to see what your competitors are offering.[48]

SALES SUPPORT

No matter what your product, it's important to support the efforts of your own sales force and those of your distributors by providing product information and training programs. That's why Nestlé and many other advertisers demonstrate new products, discuss sales strategies, and offer sales tips at periodic sales and dealer meetings. Scheduled just before the biggest selling season or before a new product line is to be introduced, these meetings help build sales and trade commitment while giving salespeople the tools necessary to meet customer needs. For example, to support the launch of Contadina Fresh Pizzas, Nestlé staged a sales meeting for independent food brokers and used a Star Trek theme to dramatize the product's selling points.[49]

In between sales meetings, you can continue dealer training by conducting seminars, distributing training materials, and working with your dealers on joint sales calls. Selling expensive or sophisticated goods or services often requires additional sales support in the form of **collateral sales material**—brochures, videotapes, slides, and other items that show detailed product information. Prepared by the advertiser for dealer use, this collateral can be presented during a

EXHIBIT 17.12
Meeting the Trade

Wholesalers and retailers attending COMDEX, an international trade show featuring computer hardware and software marketers, walk through more than 2.1 million square feet of exhibit space. One way exhibitors like Microsoft can attract and keep the attention of attendees is to offer product demonstrations and detailed product literature.

sales call, displayed at the point of purchase, or exhibited at trade shows so that customers and prospects can review product specifications and features before buying.

COOPERATIVE ADVERTISING

In addition to building product awareness through national or regional advertising, you have to let your target audience know where the product is available in each market. One tool for associating a national product with a local distributor is a cooperative advertising program, in which the manufacturer pays part of the bill when a local store ad features its product or when a local store uses the manufacturer's prepared ad in print, electronic, or out-of-home media. For example, Frigidaire, Panasonic, and Apple are just some of the manufacturers that pay part of the cost when local retailers buy billboard space.[50] As discussed in Chapter 14, newspapers and other media often have experts on staff who can help retailers plan co-op ads that meet the manufacturers' guidelines for size, timing, and wording. To receive payment, the retailer must send a tear sheet or some other proof to the manufacturer after the ad has run.

Typically manufacturers link the level of co-op reimbursement to the level of the retailer's purchases, so the more a retailer buys, the more co-op ad dollars are made available. The North American Van Lines co-op program is a good example. The firm reimburses up to 35 percent of its agents' ad costs using a sliding scale based on each agent's previous year's sales.[51] In addition, manufacturers can vary the percentage of reimbursement offered to emphasize particular products. Also, co-op ads placed in newspapers save the manufacturer money, because retailers and other local advertisers usually pay a lower rate than national advertisers do.

Supplementary Media

Sales promotion is one way to augment a traditional media advertising campaign. However, given the fragmentation of media audiences and the rising costs of mass-media vehicles, many advertisers are looking for additional methods of bringing their messages to the target audiences. Additional approaches to enhancing your main media campaign include yellow pages and specialty advertising, along with ads in other supplementary media.

YELLOW PAGES ADVERTISING

For many local and national advertisers, an ad in the yellow pages telephone directory is an effective way to bridge the gap between product awareness and product purchase. Once consumers see your product on a television commercial or read about its benefits in a magazine ad, they need to know where they can buy it. That's where yellow pages advertising comes in. People who are ready to buy check the yellow pages for the name of a nearby store or dealer, and to grab the attention of these prospects, U.S. advertisers spend nearly $10 billion a year on yellow pages ads. Of all yellow pages ads, more than 85 percent are booked by local businesses—sometimes with cooperative advertising support from national advertisers. For example, Wisconsin-based American Family Insurance Group pays 50 percent of the cost of display ads placed by local agents in the yellow pages.[52]

Over 6,400 separate yellow pages directories are published in the United States. These directories are put out by telephone companies, associations, professional organizations, and other groups. As a result, you have many choices for reaching your target audience through yellow pages advertising. You can advertise in a directory geared to consumers or in a directory geared to businesses. You can advertise in a neighborhood directory that serves a small area or in a regional directory that covers several communities. You can advertise in specialized directories such as the *Hispanic Yellow Pages,* the *Korean Business Directory,* or the *Yellow Pages of Golf.* Of course, the variety of options can really complicate media planning; for example, in Los Angeles you can buy space in more than 120 neighborhood, regional, consumer, and business directories.[53] Any or all of these books can carry the yellow pages title and walking-fingers logo, which aren't protected by copyright.

CHECKLIST FOR USING YELLOW PAGES ADVERTISING

❑ A. Match your choice of directory to the area and the audience(s) you want to reach.
  - See how the geographic scope of each directory under consideration fits with the area you want to reach.
  - Check whether you should be in the business-to-business directory, the consumer directory, or both.
  - Find out how many people each directory reaches and how many directories are distributed in each area.
  - Determine whether specialized directories can help you reach a narrow audience niche such as professionals in a particular occupation or alumni of a certain college.
  - If you haven't previously advertised in a particular directory, ask other advertisers what results they have seen from their ads.
  - Ask to see any available audience research for each directory under consideration so that you can check the audience and its usage patterns.

❑ B. Consider which heading or headings are appropriate for your product and your target audience.

❑ C. Decide whether to offer or to take advantage of cooperative advertising allowances.

❑ D. Compare prices for various space, size, and color combinations in the books under consideration.
  - Note that ads within the alphabetical listing under each directory heading can help reach current customers, who will be searching for you by name.
  - Keep in mind that display ads can attract new customers who browse through your heading and try to decide where to buy the product they need.
  - Check to see whether color or photo reproduction is available, and consider whether these creative elements are worth the extra expense.

❑ E. Check out competitors' yellow pages ads and design yours to stand out.

❑ F. Wherever possible, use your yellow pages ad to reinforce or to echo advertising in other media as a way of building on awareness you have already created in the minds of your audience.

❑ G. Track all responses to your yellow pages ads to determine which directories and which headings yield the best results.

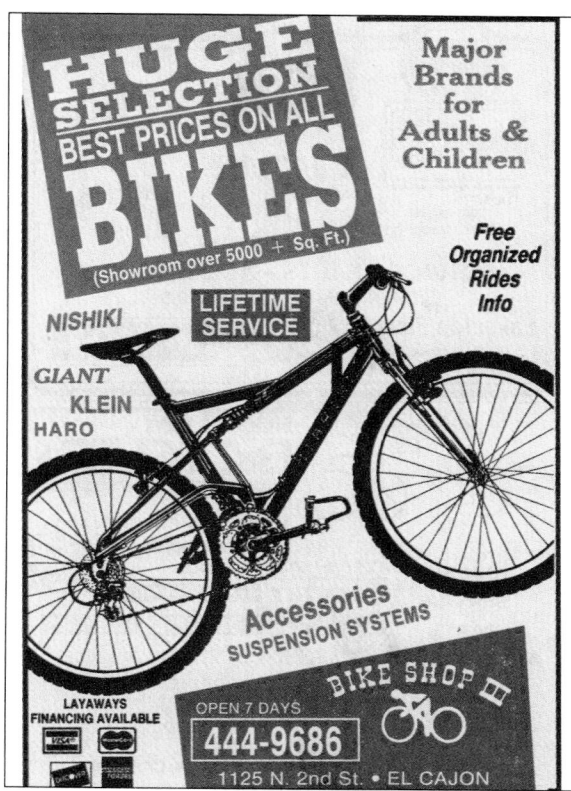

Despite the difficulties of selecting the right directory, the yellow pages can be an important medium. Because these directories are convenient and available 24 hours a day, roughly 60 percent of all U.S. adults consult a directory during the week—on average, more than twice a week—and nearly half make a purchase afterward. When you use yellow pages advertising together with newspaper, television, or radio advertising, you have the ability to reach and influence many more prospects, especially those who have decided to make a purchase. What's more, your creative options are getting wider as more yellow pages publishers offer the capability of printing four-color ads, full-color photographs, and other eye-catching elements (see Exhibit 17.13). For example, Sunkel & Sons Plumbing and Repair in Bloomington, Illinois, saw business boom after it placed a 5-by-6-inch four-color ad in a local directory.[54]

The traditional printed yellow pages is the starting point for several new developments. One is the *Talking Yellow Pages,* a service that allows consumers to look up a number and then dial in to hear a prerecorded ad message or to access information such as a weather report accompanied by a brief ad. Another development is the electronic yellow pages, a directory that operates on compact disk interactive (CD-I) technology. Users can view listings and product details on their television screens when they insert a compact disk into the CD-I player hooked up to their sets.[55]

Even though yellow pages advertising has many advantages, you have to consider several limitations. The directories are usually distributed only once a year, so any corrections or changes in address, telephone number, rates, or business operations that are made during the year won't appear until the new edition comes out. The Rib Trader restaurant in southern California uses a copy of its menu as a yellow pages display ad, but because the book comes out only once a year, it can't include prices. Another limitation is the scarcity of audience research, needed by advertisers and agencies to evaluate reach, audience composition, and usage. Syndicated audience research is available in some markets, but not all. As an alternative (or to enhance this information), some publishers subscribe to

EXHIBIT 17.14
Using Specialty Advertising

Specialty advertising can help an advertiser such as SAIC keep its name in front of the target audience over a long period. Every time people use specialty items featuring SAIC's name or logo, they can't help but be reminded of the advertiser and its offerings.

circulation auditing services that confirm directory delivery, much like the audits used by newspaper and magazine vehicles. To overcome skepticism about the effectiveness of yellow pages advertising, more publishers are guaranteeing results—and offering rate cuts if responses don't live up to expectations.[56]

SPECIALTY ADVERTISING

What do pens, calendars, and baseball caps have in common? They're all used for **specialty advertising,** a form of advertising in which the advertiser's name, message, or logo is imprinted on useful items to be given away. Coffee mugs, flashlights, coasters, T-shirts, and key rings are only a few of the *advertising specialties* that advertisers distribute to promote their companies or products to consumers or to the trade. These small items add up to big business: U.S. advertisers spend more than $5 billion on specialty advertising every year. Nearly 20 percent of the items given away are wearable, such as T-shirts and hats. However, even a small item can open the door for a later sale, boost brand-name recognition, or reinforce the company name (see Exhibit 17.14).[57]

In contrast to premiums, which are given away or sold only when people take some action such as buying a product or visiting a booth at a trade show, advertising specialties are free. Advertisers don't expect customers and prospects to send proofs of purchase or money in exchange for advertising specialties. Instead, these items are handed out (or mailed) without charge as another way to get the advertising message to the target audience. Every time prospects drink from mugs printed with your telephone number or use stadium seats emblazoned with your logo, they're exposed to your ad. Thus, it's important to choose a gift that's attractive and appealing to your target audience so that it can serve as a continuous and tangible reminder of your organization's image and products.

However, choosing the right item can be tricky; if it's cheap or flimsy, it may not present the right image for an upscale product; and if it's extravagant or luxurious, it may be seen as an attempt at bribery. You want something that's small enough to make prospects feel they should listen to your sales pitch but not so large that they feel suspicious of your motives. Studies show that with the right item, specialty advertising can boost both response and sales.[58]

Specialty advertising can be especially effective when used with other advertising or promotional programs. For example, to reach a target audience of information-services and data-processing managers responsible for purchasing printing systems, Xerox put together a series of direct-mail packages with an advertising specialty in each mailing. The campaign was intended to show how Xerox could orchestrate a printing system to meet the buyer's needs. One mailing pictured an orchestra conductor and included a conductor's baton; prospects who mailed back a response card received a classical recording as a premium. Another mailing included an imprinted pencil that was tucked into a package shaped like a record album. Xerox received a high response: over one-third of the target audience responded, setting the stage for months of sales calls.[59]

OTHER SUPPLEMENTARY MEDIA

The list of ways to reach your target audience isn't complete without a look at some of the newer options that take advantage of the equipment and technology available in the consumer's home or office. For instance, growth in the use of videocassette recorders (VCRs), personal computers, and facsimile (fax) machines hasn't gone unnoticed by advertisers. In recent years, more advertisers have experimented with ads spliced onto videotaped movies, ads distributed on videocassette, ads sent by fax, ads offered on computer disk, and ads delivered through computer-based information services.

- *Ads spliced onto videotaped movies.* As the popularity of videotaped movies soars—more than 3 billion movies are rented every year—a growing number of national advertisers see this as an attractive medium for their commercial messages. One of the earliest examples is the Pepsi-Cola commercial spliced onto the beginning of *Top Gun.* Since then, many other advertisers, including Schweppes and General Motors, have paid to put their ads at the start of videotaped movies. However, many consumers are annoyed by such ads, and a good number fast-forward directly to the movie.[60]

- *Ads on videocassette.* It's one thing to reach a captive audience of people who pay to see a movie rather than an ad, and quite another to send a commercial on videocassette to your most interested prospects. Like any television commercial, an ad distributed on videotape can demonstrate your product in use and visually prove its benefits (see Exhibit 17.15). Also, people can view the tape at their convenience at home or at the office, whenever they're likely to be most responsive to your message. Both consumer and business advertisers are using videotaped ads. Polymer Plastics, which sells components to circuit-board makers, doubled the sales of one line after it sent video catalogs to 1,000 prospects; Hartmarx Specialty Stores boosted retail sales by sending a videotaped fashion show to 150,000 of its best customers just before Christmas.[61]

- *Ads by fax.* Many advertisers find that advertising by fax is a fast and efficient way to get product information and order forms to businesses and consumers. In addition, advertisers often encourage customers to fax their orders for

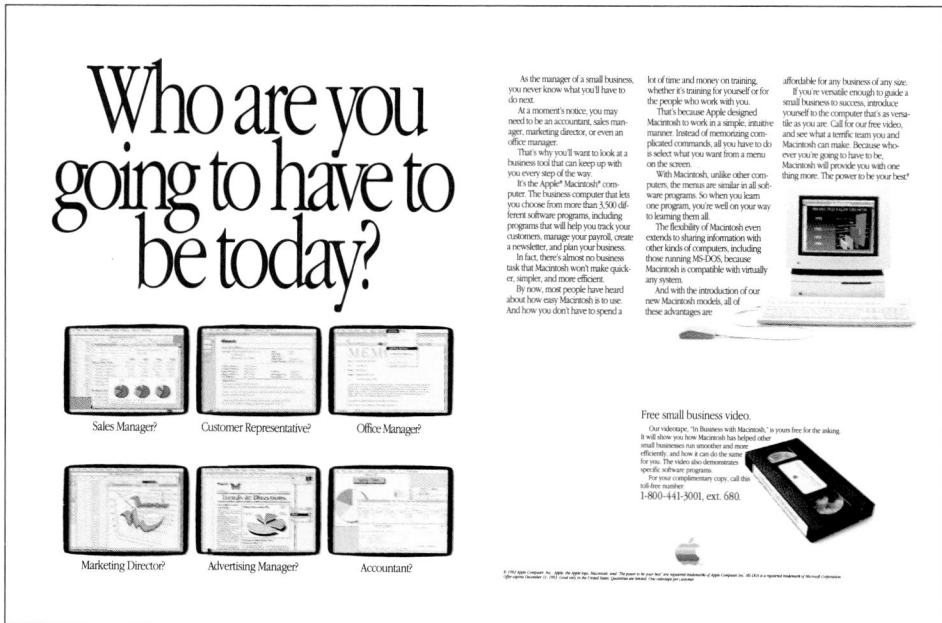

EXHIBIT 17.15
Videocassette Ads Keep on Selling

Apple offers a free copy of its *In Business with Macintosh* videotape to small-business owners, one important target audience for its Macintosh line of personal computers. Prospects watch the videotape at their leisure to see how the Macintosh can solve a variety of problems commonly faced by small businesses.

Meeting an Advertising Challenge at Kellogg

A CASE FOR CRITICAL THINKING

Kellogg's share of the ready-to-eat cereal market had been dwindling for more than a dozen years. It was eaten away by lower-priced store brands as well as by name-brand advertisers such as Quaker and General Mills, whose newer products included such health-related features as lower sugar and higher fiber. Carlos Gutierrez knew that Kellogg's products were still selling well, but he'd also seen more rivals crowding the store shelves over the past few years, a development that turned up the competitive heat.

During the mid-1980s, 27 brands accounted for two-thirds of all ready-to-eat cereal sales in the United States. By the early 1990s, however, 40 brands were sharing the same two-thirds of the country's sales. Now Kellogg would have to fight harder just to stop the market-share slide, let alone to build share. Responding to this double challenge, the advertiser unveiled a series of consumer promotions. Although samples, premiums, and point-of-purchase displays were used, coupons were the centerpiece of most of the promotions, which supported selected new cereals and some older favorites.

To launch Rice Krispies Treats cereal, Kellogg ran only two separate coupon ads—and rang up $5.3 million in sales in just 12 weeks. In another coupon promotion, Kellogg invited adults to return to Kellogg's Frosted Flakes, which was touted as having "The taste adults have grown to love." A coupon for Kellogg's Corn Flakes acted as an inducement for adults to enjoy "The Original and Best" brand of corn flakes. All three promotions aimed at adults who had eaten Kellogg cereals as children as well as adults who had switched to other brands in recent years. To tempt the taste buds of younger cereal-lovers, Kellogg ads showcased cartoon spokescharacters (such as Coco the chimp) and described mouth-watering flavors. Of course, their parents appreciated the coupons in these advertisements.

In all, Kellogg distributed more coupons in 1991 and 1992 than any other cereal maker. However, the value of these coupons was generally lower than that of competitors' coupons, a deliberate step to avoid severely draining profits. Coupled with television and print ads reinforcing brand names and product benefits, these coupon promotions helped reverse Kellogg's market-share slide.

By 1992, the advertiser's share of the cereal market had rebounded past 37 percent, although store brands were still gaining share. By continuing to use cost-efficient yet effective consumer promotions, Gutierrez remains determined to keep Kellogg's share moving even higher.

Your Mission: *Gutierrez has asked you to chair a special committee that will come up with ways to use consumer and trade promotions to boost Kellogg's share among the cereals sold in supermarkets. Consider the following situations and decide which answer you'll recommend to Gutierrez in each case.*

1. Supermarket sales of the low-fat version of Quaker 100% Natural cereal are starting to edge out sales of your own Low-Fat Granola cereal. You need a trade promotion that will encourage stores to put a stronger push behind Kellogg cereals. Which of the following would you suggest to Gutierrez?
a. Offer the supermarkets a substantial one-year buying allowance so they support the Kellogg cereal over the long term.

---

speedier service. Advertising by fax can take the form of a personalized letter or memo when the customer or product is known by name. Another method is to send catalog pages, product specification sheets, and order forms on request. For example, Software Developers of Hingham, Massachusetts, invites its target audience, computer programmers, to dial a special fax number and receive product descriptions by fax.[62]

- *Ads on computer disk.* When you know your prospect has a personal computer, sending an ad on a disk can be a novel way to get your message across. Ads on computer disk are more effective if they entertain, inform, and invite participation. For example, the U.S. Army's ads on computer disk helped potential enlistees calculate the value of the benefits they would receive if they signed up. This feature enticed twice as many people to request the disks as usually ask for the Army's printed material. Similarly, the Netherlands Foreign Investment Agency designed an ad touting the economic benefits of doing business in Holland and sent it on computer disk to executives of high-tech companies considering European locations. The disk allowed prospects to compare costs in the Netherlands with costs in other European countries; 85 percent of the recipients reviewed the disk and more than 10 percent requested more information.[63]

- *Ads on computer-based information services.* Another way to reach millions of computer users is through computer-based information services such as Prod-

NEW...THE TASTE OF KRISPIES TREATS' IN A CEREAL.

b. Pay store managers a $50 bonus for every shelf of the Quaker cereals they replace with a shelf of the Kellogg cereals.
c. Start a contest to see which supermarkets can sell the most cases of Low-Fat Granola during the next six months. Reward every employee in the top 3 supermarkets with a $50 gift certificate from a local department store.

2. Another way to compete with Quaker is by encouraging consumers to stock up on Kellogg's Low-Fat Granola cereal. Your committee has come up with three consumer promotion ideas to spark multiple purchasing. Which of these would most effectively influence long-term consumer behavior?
a. Devise a frequent-buyer promotion with a catalog partner who's asso-

ciated with healthful outdoor activities (such as Eddie Bauer). This will encourage consumers to save Low-Fat Granola proofs of purchase to exchange for discounts on merchandise.
b. Offer a cereal storage canister with the Kellogg logo in exchange for Low-Fat Granola proofs of purchase. Every time consumers use this premium, they'll be reminded of your cereals.
c. Offer a self-liquidating premium such as a sporty fanny pack with a Kellogg logo in exchange for five proofs of purchase and a small shipping fee. Consumers will associate the fanny pack (and the cereal) with active sports and outdoor activities.

3. Kellogg wants to reemphasize perennial favorites such as Frosted Flakes. One audience you want to target is baby-boomer adults, who ate these cereals when they were young. Which of these consumer promotions would you recommend?
a. Offer coupons only on the older cereals, so consumers will save only when they buy those cereals.
b. Use a price pack to include a trial size of each of the older Kellogg cereals with the newer adult-oriented cereals. This will invite baby-boomer adults to rediscover their childhood favorites.

c. Offer nostalgic premiums such as 1950s-style radios when consumers send proofs of purchase from the cereals you're promoting. This will rekindle memories of the Kellogg cereals that baby boomers enjoyed as children.

4. Your committee wants to encourage supermarkets to more heavily promote Kellogg's sweetened cereals for youngsters. Which one of these cooperative advertising ideas would you recommend to Gutierrez?
a. Base each supermarket's cooperative advertising allowance on the increase in sales of the promoted cereals over the next six months. The higher the increase, the higher the reimbursement.
b. Prepare ads showing special promotional pricing for the featured cereals. The supermarkets can add their names and logos and send the ads to the media to receive reimbursement under the regular cooperative advertising plan.
c. Base the cooperative advertising allowance on last year's cereal sales. Stores that sold a lot of the promoted cereals last year will earn a higher reimbursement.[67] ■

igy, CompuServe, GEnie Information Services, America Online, Delphi, and Internet. For a fee, a consumer with a personal computer and a modem (a gadget that connects the computer to the telephone line) can tap into Prodigy, for example, and browse files of news and entertainment as well as product offerings from 160 advertisers including Nissan, Coca-Cola, and Fidelity Investments. More than 2 million people subscribe to Prodigy, and advertisers receive a detailed report of the demographic profile of every subscriber who views an ad. To satisfy advertisers' requests for more audience research, Prodigy has invited the Audit Bureau of Circulations to review and analyze its subscriber base.[64]

Advertisers who use the Prodigy system can buy a specific number of "screens" (the electronic equivalent of pages in a printed magazine) for their advertising messages. Both CompuServe and GEnie sponsor an "electronic mall" where subscribers can buy goods and services through participating businesses. All services allow users to post messages in on-line classified advertising sections, often for a fee. Internet also allows commercial advertising, but only within strict guidelines. However, the service already has 15 million subscribers, and it's looking increasingly attractive as a computer-based advertising medium as the subscriber base continues to grow at the astounding rate of 20 percent per month.[65]

One way to promote merchandise or services using a computer-based information service is to provide valuable product data on-line and include a subtle advertising message relating to the product. For instance, a free-lance advertising copywriter might post a message with information about how to create an effective direct-mail package on a tight budget. The copywriter could discuss successful campaigns he's written and include his name and address (or electronic mail address). This invites people who want more details to respond.[66]

This list may be only the beginning, as advertisers explore other supplementary media in their quest for direct and uncluttered channels of communication. In time, the combination of new technology and lower costs is likely to encourage more advertisers to bolster their main media choices with new types of supplementary media.

Summary

Sales promotion is an offer of direct inducements that enhance the basic value of a product for a limited time to stimulate immediate distributor commitment, sales force effectiveness, and consumer purchasing. Advertising is an effective way of introducing new products and of reminding target audiences about the benefits of established products; in contrast, sales promotion offers a special short-term inducement to encourage consumers to buy a particular product or retailers to make room for a specific product.

Consumer sales promotion can be used to (1) persuade consumers to try and rebuy a new product, (2) convince consumers to stay with a brand, (3) increase product purchase and usage, (4) encourage consumers to buy related products, and (5) reinforce advertising and marketing efforts for more immediate results. Trade sales promotion can be used to (1) gain distribution, (2) encourage support for a product or a sales promotion, (3) stimulate distributors to raise or lower their inventory levels, and (4) strengthen relationships with the trade and with salespeople.

Many advertisers have shifted their promotional budgets to emphasize sales promotion. This shift has come about because of the emphasis on short-term results, the need for accountability, the growth in retailer power, the proliferation of products, and the changing behavior of buyers. However, continual reliance on sales promotion can pose potential problems. Among these are the impact on long-term brand loyalty, the possibility that consumers will become conditioned to buy only when promotions are offered, the influence on profitability, and the response of retailers.

A variety of sales promotion techniques can be used to target the consumer. Among the most commonly used are samples, coupons, price promotions and price packs, money-back offers, contests and sweepstakes, premiums, frequency programs, and point-of-purchase displays. To gain the commitment and support of salespeople and the trade, you can use trade sales promotion techniques such as trade deals, trade contests and incentives, trade shows, sales support, and cooperative advertising.

Yellow pages advertising can bridge the gap between product awareness and product purchase. Once advertising in other media has made the audience aware of a product, yellow pages advertising shows where the product can be purchased. Specialty advertising is a form of advertising in which the advertiser's name, message, or logo is imprinted on useful items to be given away to the target audience. Advertising specialties generally supplement advertising in other media as another way to get the message to the consumer or the trade. Also, growth in the use of videocassette recorders and personal computers in homes and offices hasn't gone unnoticed by advertisers. More advertisers are experimenting with ads spliced onto videotaped movies, ads distributed on videocassette, ads sent by fax, ads offered on computer disk, and ads delivered through computer-based information services.

Key Terms

buying allowance 478
collateral sales material 480
consumer sales promotion 465
contest 475
coupon 472
display allowance 478
electronic couponing 472
everyday low pricing (EDLP) 479
frequency program 476
game 475
point-of-purchase (POP) displays 477
premium 475

price pack 473
price promotion 473
product information center 477
push money 480
refund 473
sales promotion 463
sampling 471
self-liquidating premium 476
slotting allowance 478
specialty advertising 484
sweepstakes 475
trade deal 478
trade sales promotion 465
trade show 480

Questions

FOR REVIEW

1. Why do advertisers use trade sales promotions?

2. How can sampling help launch a new product?

3. What is specialty advertising and how is it used?

4. What concerns have been raised about the long-term effects of relying on sales promotion techniques?

5. What are buying allowances and how are they used?

FOR ANALYSIS AND APPLICATION

6. How might Baskin-Robbins use a frequency program to boost its sales of ice cream cakes?

7. What potential problems should an advertiser consider when moving away from the use of trade deals to everyday low pricing?

8. What kind of sales contest might American Express design to encourage banks to sell more of its traveler's checks?

9. Compaq sells computers to individuals as well as busi-

nesses; what are the arguments for and against this advertiser placing ads in both the consumer and the business versions of local yellow pages directories?

10. Thinking about movies that have recently been released on videocassettes for home viewing, which would you recommend as good advertising vehicles for Eskimo Pies ice cream novelties? Why?

Sharpen Your Advertising Skills

How do you develop top-of-mind awareness for a product that's underfoot? That was the problem Du Pont faced in introducing its Stainmaster carpet, a carpet specially treated to resist dirt. The television commercial that Du Pont used to launch this product was both inspired and memorable: a toddler sitting in a highchair plays with the food in his airplane-shaped dish until the announcer clears him for take off. The boy launches his plane full of food into the air—and onto the carpet. Of course, the carpet recovers perfectly because it's Stainmaster.

As soon as the commercial aired, Du Pont started receiving letters from parents whose children also liked to throw their food on the floor. Because of the strong response, Du Pont managers decided to create a consumer sales promotion to reinforce the commercial's theme and message as well as Stainmaster's brand name. They've approached you, an expert in sales promotion, and asked for your recommendations.

Decision: Would you recommend that Du Pont use samples, coupons, or premiums to achieve its sales promotion goals? Choose one technique, bearing in mind the effect it may have on the consumer's perception of Stainmaster quality and its unique benefits. Then think up at least one specific idea for a sales promotion based on the recommended technique.

Communication: You're meeting with Du Pont executives tomorrow afternoon to present your ideas. In preparation for your discussion, write a few notes to summarize the major points you want to make. Be sure to explain which technique you're recommending and why. Also, describe how the specific sales promotion you suggest will achieve Du Pont's objectives.

Public Relations and Special Communication

After studying this chapter, you will be able to

1. Define public relations and explain how it differs from advertising
2. Identify the most common objectives of public relations
3. Outline the five steps in the public relations process
4. Identify the six major publics addressed by public relations
5. Describe the three primary vehicles for carrying a public relations message
6. Explain the three factors required for successful crisis communication
7. Define product placement, cause-related marketing, public service announcements, and advocacy advertising

IMAGINE HAVING TO IMAGINE IT.

PLEASE RECYCLE/PRINTED ON RECYCLED PAPER

PHOTOGRAPHY MARIA BUENO © KCMXC: THE IMAGE BANK · DESIGN WALSH AND ASSOCIATES INC · PRINTING S & S PRINTING · COLOR SEPARATIONS COLOR CONTROL · COPYWRITING KEVIN BUEHLE

Facing an Advertising Challenge at Starbucks Coffee

POURING ON THE PR FOR SUCCESSFUL MARKET ENTRIES

To most people in this country, a cup of coffee is just a cup of coffee, nothing very special. It comes out of a pot, maybe you add cream and sugar, and you down a few cups on the way to work. To Howard Schultz, however, coffee is an all-consuming passion. From tramping through Central American jungles in search of just the right coffee beans to finding precisely the right brewing equipment, Schultz overlooks nothing on the way to a perfect cup of coffee.

Schultz's interest in great coffee extends beyond his personal palate, however. As president and CEO of Seattle-based Starbucks Coffee, Schultz wants everyone to crave premium coffee as much as he does. In Seattle, Portland, and a few other coffee-crazed cities with Starbucks retail stores, people line up every morning to get their favorites, from simple espresso to exotic chocolate concoctions. Schultz isn't content to let Starbucks be a regional brand,

however. He views the whole country as his target market and public relations as his key marketing tool.

With more than a decade of coffee retailing experience, Schultz knows that once people get a taste of Starbucks and other premium coffees, they often resist going back to regular coffee. Aficionados think the preground coffee sold in tin cans at the grocery store tastes weak and bitter compared with premium coffees. The key is to get people's attention and interest long enough to give Starbucks a try.

In addition to the taste benefits, premium coffee is a lifestyle issue for many people. Coffee shops and "coffee bars" have replaced traditional bars and taverns for these people, offering patrons all the social benefits of going out with friends and meeting new people without the health and safety risks associated with alcoholic beverages. Caffeine concerns some coffee drinkers, of course, but a wide

selection of decaffeinated products allows these people to enjoy coffee without the jittery side effects.

With these trends in mind, Schultz is active in his nationwide expansion, moving both down the West Coast and across to the East Coast. With its millions of inhabitants, Los Angeles represents a key market for just about every consumer product, coffee included. If you were Howard Schultz and wanted to build a strong Starbucks presence in L.A. without spending a fortune on advertising, what communication options would you take advantage of? How would you involve the news media to help spread your message? Would you take advantage of the show business aspects of life and business in L.A.? What steps would you take to make people feel good about adding premium coffee to their diets and their lifestyles?[1] ∎

CHAPTER OVERVIEW As the head of a small firm trying to break into new markets without spending a fortune on marketing, Howard Schultz realizes that he has to use every available means to build awareness for Starbucks and its products. Public relations is among the most effective tools that organizations have to further their corporate and marketing goals. This chapter explores the nature of public relations, its relationship to advertising, and its role in the marketing mix. You'll discover the many audiences that public relations professionals address and the vehicles they use to convey their messages. You'll also learn about two special functions in public relations, crisis communication and event sponsorship. The chapter concludes with a look at three related issues: product placement in movies and television shows, cause-related marketing, and public service and advocacy advertising.

Public Relations

Of all the business and organizational functions that the public can observe, public relations is perhaps one of the most misunderstood. When we see a politician's assistant addressing the news media after a speech, explaining what the politician said or meant to say, and when we hear a corporate spokesperson describing a company's actions in response to an oil spill or other catastrophe, we recognize two of the more visible PR roles. However, these roles represent only a tiny part of what the function encompasses. Public relations professionals also work with the media to provide facts and information about the company and its products, respond to questions from community activists, explain to investors why the company is a good investment, and make sure government officials understand the impact of regulations on the company and its industry. Public relations includes virtually all

EXHIBIT 18.1
The Diversity of Public Relations

Sponsoring a sporting event and getting a public personality booked on a talk show are two of the many activities that fall in the field of public relations.

communication activities outside of advertising and personal selling (see Exhibit 18.1).

Public relations activities change so often that the field has been difficult to define. When a team of experts from the Foundation for Public Relations Research and Education sat down to hammer out a single definition, they started with the *472* definitions people have been using over the years. James Dowling, CEO of Burston-Marsteller, a leading PR agency, no longer even tries to define public relations because it covers so many diverse activities.[2] Expanding on the definition provided in Chapter 1, **public relations (PR)** is the process of understanding public attitudes on relevant issues, interpreting those attitudes for senior management, and then working either to align the organization's policies and practices with those attitudes or to modify the attitudes themselves.[3] The term **publicity** has sometimes been confused with public relations, but it's actually only one part of the field, limited to generating media coverage about an organization and its products.

Four important points will help you grasp the essence of public relations and understand how it differs from advertising:

- *Public relations lacks total control over the final message.* When you run an ad, it says just what you want it to. You created it, and you bought the media time or space to run it in, so your message is presented as you wish. In public relations, you don't always have that level of control; the news media often stand between you and your intended audience. When Ford introduces a new car model and invites reporters in to see it, Ford's executives and PR people can tell them all about the car and why it's such a great product. However, these reporters are under no obligation to pass that message on to the general public. So if a magazine reporter isn't impressed with the car, the magazine's readers will get the reporter's negative message—not Ford's original one. In fact, you have no guarantee that you'll receive media coverage *at all*.

- *Public relations addresses a variety of audiences.* Advertising is usually aimed at consumers, wholesalers, and retailers. Public relations targets these audiences and quite a few others, including investors, the news media, activists (environmental groups, for example), local communities, legislative bodies, and government agencies.

- *Public relations involves no direct media costs.* Like advertising, public relations is a communications activity; unlike advertising, it doesn't involve the purchase of any time or space in the media. So PR budgets are usually much smaller than ad budgets.

- *Public relations addresses important aspects outside the realm of marketing.* Public relations is used to increase sales, but it's also used to stimulate the interest of investors, engage the cooperation and esteem of local communities, respond to and work with activist groups, and so on. **Marketing public relations** attempts to increase sales, both short term and long term, so it's a part of the promotional mix. **Corporate public relations** operates outside the product-marketing effort, focusing primarily on all the organization's audiences other than its customers and potential customers.[4] However, efforts on both sides are closely related. For example, if you held a press conference to introduce your company's latest product to the news media (a marketing PR activity), and if the media representatives give your product coverage so that sales take off, then investors (an audience targeted by corporate public relations) might consider investing in your company. Marketing public relations has caught on in recent years as companies look for new and cheaper ways to promote products, but it's important not to cut corners on corporate public relations. Labor relations, community involvement, government relations, and a host of other issues not directly related to marketing fall under corporate public relations, and organizations that focus too heavily on marketing public relations risk managing these other issues inadequately.[5]

MANAGING THE PUBLIC RELATIONS PROCESS

What do public relations people do? These professionals can do anything from coordinating a company-sponsored golf tournament to giving newspaper reporters a tour of a new factory. Public relations reaches its wide range of audiences by using any number of vehicles to carry its messages. The PR process involves five basic steps.

Setting Your Objectives

Just as successful organizations identify clear objectives for advertising, personal selling, and all other business functions, they also identify clear objectives for public relations. Even though you will have multiple ways of sending PR messages to your audiences, most of your PR activities will focus on one of the following objectives:

- *Keeping management in touch with public sentiments.* One of the distinguishing characteristics of public relations is that it works in both directions. You can think of PR people as interpreters. In one direction, they interpret the organization's positions and policies for the public; in the other direction, they interpret public attitudes and beliefs for the organization's management (see Exhibit 18.2). Top managers expect their PR people to keep them informed honestly and objectively. As Robert Cushman, chairman and CEO of the Norton Company, puts it, he wants his PR people to "talk straight to members of management. We want advisors who will advocate, debate, and defend their thinking and proposals."[6]

- *Aligning the organization with public attitudes.* This is one of the most important, but also one of the trickiest, objectives of PR. Consider an example that appears often in today's headlines. Concern for the natural environment is a strong sentiment for many people in the general public, nonprofit organiza-

tions, and government. Understandably, most companies would like to be perceived as being in line with public opinion on this issue; in other words, they want to be seen as firms that are friendly to the environment. The tricky part is making sure the promoted image matches reality.

- *Correcting or updating public perceptions.* Just as there are times when you want to bring your company in line with public attitudes, there are times when public perceptions are either incorrect or out of date. Jan Lachenmaier, who served as the PR manager for a hazardous-waste treatment facility in California, can offer many stories of the struggles she had trying to bring objective facts to the public discussion of her company's operations. In one case, the news media focused on a man who said he had to move because the dump operated by Lachenmaier's company smelled so horrible. In fact, the man's landlord evicted him because he hadn't paid his rent in nine months.[7] Correcting public perceptions can be a big part of the PR manager's job, especially for companies in high-profile industries such as waste management.

- *Promoting goods and services.* This is the most direct application of marketing public relations. Your goal is to use nonadvertising communication to create sales. Techniques used to accomplish this objective range from telling the news media about your products (in the hope that they'll tell the public) to sponsoring festivals and other special events. For example, Toyota dealers from New York City and Philadelphia banded together to sponsor the Toyota Comedy Festivals as a way to help promote Toyota's lines of cars and trucks.[8] The sponsorship both increases the company's exposure to its audience and links the Toyota name with an enjoyable consumer activity.

- *Adding value to brands.* All other things being equal, brands from well-known companies are considered more valuable than brands from unknown companies. Public relations adds value because it boosts a brand's credibility.[9] Say you're considering buying one of two cars. Both are well engineered and well built, with similar price tags. One is from Chevrolet, and the other is from Michigan Motors. You just watched the Indy 500 car race and noticed that Chevy is a major supplier of racing engines; you've never heard of Michigan Motors. Which car will you buy? Chances are you'll go with the Chevy, and knowing that Indy race teams like Chevy engines might play a big part in your decision. The fact that you know about Chevy's racing connection is largely a function of public relations (see Exhibit 18.3).

- *Responding to crisis situations.* Things can go wrong, even at the best-managed organizations. One of PR's key roles is managing the dialog between the organization and the outside world during times of crisis. From natural disasters to financial problems, the PR spokesperson is the key link in the communication process.

One useful way to sum up these objectives is to say that public relations helps an organization manage its *reputation.* Companies with good reputations can market their products more efficiently, attract better employees, and hang on to customers more effectively (see Exhibit 18.4). A good reputation also paves the way for new-product introductions, fosters relationships with communities, and builds goodwill among all the people that interact with the organization.[10] Public relations professionals use a variety of techniques and talents to meet specific objectives and build positive reputations for their organizations.

Conducting Preliminary Research

As you saw in Chapter 6, research plays a key role in advertising, and it does the same in public relations. Before you can try to align your organization with public attitudes or influence public perceptions, you have to understand those attitudes and perceptions. In addition to the research techniques you've already explored, PR managers and agencies often rely on a *communication audit.* This special research program compares real messages with perceived ones. For instance, managers may *think* they've clearly explained the company's position on an issue, but the point may not be getting through to community groups. A communication audit uncovers such discrepancies and helps you formulate necessary PR solutions.[11]

Of course, public relations has an objective that advertising doesn't—interpreting public attitudes for management. This aspect of the PR function requires the usual formal research techniques, as well as less formal ones. When you're in public relations, you spend a lot of time interacting with community and government leaders, customers, and other key audiences. That puts you in a position to pick up bits and pieces of information that can provide your company with valuable clues about public attitudes.

Developing a Plan and Taking Action

The next step in the process is to develop a plan to meet your objective and take the actions necessary to implement your plan. The action you take is defined by the objectives you set. In some cases, no specific action is required, so you proceed directly to communicating your message. If a newspaper article questions your environmental practices when in fact your practices are responsible and environmentally sensitive, you don't have to change what you're doing—you only have to communicate more effectively so people know what's really going on inside your organization.

EXHIBIT 18.3
Building Brand Value

All of the companies involved in this racing effort, from the manufacturer of the car and the engine to the sponsoring organizations whose names appear on the car, build brand awareness with fans and television audiences.

EXHIBIT 18.4   **The Top 10 Most Admired Corporations in America**

A positive reputation gives you an edge in many activities, from marketing products to attracting employees; a recent survey identified these 10 companies as the most admired in the United States.

Rank	Company	Primary Business
1	Rubbermaid	Rubber & plastics products
2	Home Depot	Specialist retailing
3	Coca-Cola	Beverages
3	Microsoft	Software
5	3M	Scientific & photo equipment
6	Walt Disney	Entertainment
6	Motorola	Electronics
8	J.P. Morgan	Commercial banking
8	Procter & Gamble	Soaps, cosmetics
10	United Parcel Service	Transportation/delivery

CHAPTER 18
Public Relations/Special Communication

In other cases, you have to take some action before you can communicate successfully. When PepsiCo began to hear reports of people finding syringes and other dangerous objects in cans of Diet Pepsi during the summer of 1993, the company first determined that it was virtually impossible for the syringes to get into the cans in its bottling facilities or for outsiders to tamper with the cans in the store. It then worked with the Food and Drug Administration to follow up on reports that the syringe stories may have in fact been hoaxes. After taking these actions, PepsiCo president Craig Weatherup took to the airwaves on news programs and talk shows to explain the investigations that the company had conducted. PepsiCo integrated this PR effort with an ad that ran in major newspapers after the investigations, explaining that the company had been the victim of publicity and litigation seekers who had faked their claims (see Exhibit 18.5).[12]

In a far less dramatic but no less important case of taking action, Baskin-Robbins, the ice cream chain of 31 flavors fame, found itself stuck in the 1990s with a 1970s image. As marketing director Carol Kirby put it, "We had become dated." Research showed that people had good memories of eating there but that the stores looked and felt old. Offbeat, 1970s-style flavors like Lunar Cheesecake didn't exactly fit the new world of frozen yogurt and low-fat ice cream, either. Still, Kirby knew that updating public perceptions would take more than a good PR campaign. She initiated new products, introduced new flavors, and redesigned store interiors *before* going out to convince the public that Baskin-Robbins was in tune with the times.[13]

EXHIBIT 18.5
PepsiCo Responds to a Crisis

PepsiCo used ads such as this one to restore public confidence after false reports surfaced of syringes in cans of Diet Pepsi.

Pepsi is pleased to announce...

...nothing.

As America now knows, those stories about Diet Pepsi were a hoax. Plain and simple, not true. Hundreds of investigators have found no evidence to support a single claim.

As for the many, many thousands of people who work at Pepsi-Cola, we feel great that it's over. And we're ready to get on with making and bringing you what we believe is the best-tasting diet cola in America.

There's not much more we can say. Except that most importantly, we won't let this hoax change our exciting plans for this summer.

We've set up special offers so you can enjoy our great quality products at prices that will save you money all summer long. It all starts on July 4th weekend and we hope you'll stock up with a little extra, just to make up for what you might have missed last week.

That's it. Just one last word of thanks to the millions of you who have stood with us.

**Drink All The Diet Pepsi You Want.
Uh Huh.**

This message is brought to you by the Pepsi Cola Bottling Company of San Diego.

How Computers Are Aiding Public Relations

Computers haven't yet advanced on public relations to the extent they have invaded advertising and other marketing functions, but they are definitely making some inroads. New software products can help PR specialists manage media relations and the overall PR process more efficiently and effectively. Not only can computer tools let you get more done in less time, they can also help you do a thorough job.

For most organizations, media relations involves a great deal of paperwork and recordkeeping, in addition to mailing or faxing press releases and working with other tools of the trade. Media relations software can shoulder some of this work load by offering computerized media directories (which contain names and addresses of important contacts), clipping trackers (which record and keep track of articles that have appeared about the organization), and paperless fax generators (which can send out faxes to hundreds of media contacts automatically). SpinWare, a new product in this category, can perform such tasks as automatically faxing press releases to all environmental journalists within 100 miles of a particular factory. SpinMaster's clipping tracker could then follow up by keeping tabs on how much publicity you get and how much of it is positive or negative.

Issues management is another vital PR activity where software can lend a hand. Communication with the media, employees, and other publics often focuses on issues that are important to both the organization and the public. The larger an organization gets, the more difficult it becomes to ensure that all the people who address a public on an issue say the same thing. Imagine the task General Motors faces during a labor conflict: financial analysts, union leaders, employees, and the news media will all be interested in whatever the company has to say on this issue. Of course, any number of managers might be called on to address one or more publics during the course of the conflict, so you want to be sure they all "speak with one voice." Issues-management software can be loaded with approved answers to all likely questions; managers can simply check their computers to see what should be said.

The numerous tasks involved in running a PR agency represent another great opportunity for computerized solutions. Products in this category can help you stay on top of everything from records of phone calls to profit analyses for each client and project. Keeping close track of the time each person spends on a project is a key part of keeping an agency profitable.

These software tools join a few workhorses that some PR specialists have grown to rely on, particularly programs for database management, word processing, and on-line literature searching. Say you work for Quaker Oats and would like to send a press release to all newspapers and magazines that have run articles on oat bran in the last year. You can access an on-line service such as Dialog, type in "oat bran" and the year in question, and, within a few minutes, get a complete list of the article and publication titles you're interested in. Research tools such as this cut the time required to launch a PR campaign and also help ensure that you've covered all possible bases. Together with the new generation of software for media relations, issues management, and agency management, these tools give PR professionals a way to bring public relations into the computer age.

Apply Your Knowledge

1. Based on what you know about the public relations process, how can the software described here enhance the communication process?
2. How might computerized public relations make a company more competitive?

Communicating with Your Audience

Every PR initiative involves communication of some sort. It may be as modest as making a phone call to a newspaper reporter or as complex as sponsoring a major international sporting event such as the Olympics. Some of this communication is planned and prepared (such as press releases and speeches); some of it is less controlled, even impromptu (such as interviews and community meetings), in response to requests from various people. Such communication is more interactive, so you're unable to manage the message quite as closely.

For PR professionals, communication involves a lot of unplanned, interpersonal contact with members of the press, community activists, and other people interested in or affected by an organization's activities. Reporters frequently ask large corporations and government agencies questions on a variety of subjects ranging from specific news about the organization to general industry trends. These requests are great opportunities for presenting the organization's messages and furthering its interests, but they must be handled carefully (see Exhibit 18.6). Most organizations restrict media access to a few employees who are well versed in what's going on inside the organization and who know how to work with reporters. Chase Manhattan Bank, for example, requires all interview requests to go through its public relations department, and only trained media specialists and executives from the vice president level and up are usually allowed to speak with the press.[14]

Such restrictions aren't designed to keep the press or other outsiders in the dark, only to make sure that communication with the outside world is managed carefully and that the organization speaks with one voice.

Conducting Evaluative Research

As with any business effort, it's important to measure the success of your PR efforts. The traditional means of measuring PR effectiveness involves counting the number of column inches or broadcast mentions that you receive (see Exhibit 18.7). You'll immediately notice two key problems with this approach. First, it applies only to media relations campaigns, which is only one segment of public relations. Second, counting the number of times you're mentioned in the press

CameraMan Turns Screen Into Movies

AN INTERFACE CARD FROM New Media Graphics makes it easy to record a VGA display on videotape or any S-VHS device.

TapeIT! uses proprietary flicker-reduction algorithms to capture video output without the problems that are often encountered in making videotapes of computer screens. TapeIT! outputs VGA, S-VHS, and composite NTSC/PAL, allowing a user to simultaneously view a presentation on a VGA screen while recording it to a VCR. The board fits in an 8- or 16-bit ISA slot.

LIST PRICE *TapeIT!, $499. New Media Graphics, 780 Boston Rd., Billerica, MA 01821-5925; 508-663-0666; fax, 508-663-6678.*

CIRCLE 170 ON READER SERVICE CARD

doesn't tell you whether your message made it through the media, how many people got the message, or whether getting the message had the desired effect on their behavior.[15]

As with advertising, the best measure of effectiveness is whether or not your efforts resulted in desired audience behavior (buying a product, voting for a certain cause, and so on). The sales-versus-communication issue presented in Chapter 7 applies to public relations as well: if you have a sales objective and can isolate the effects of public relations, then you can use sales figures to evaluate your PR program. MathSoft, a Massachusetts software company, tracks the sales leads that come to it from people who have read articles about its products in technical magazines. The articles are the result of efforts by the company's PR agency, so MathSoft can tell whether a given sale was initially generated by its PR programs.[16]

If you can't trace sales or leads to specific PR efforts (or if the PR effort isn't directed toward sales), the alternative is measuring communications effectiveness. The best way to evaluate communication is to measure attitudes or behaviors before the PR effort and again afterward, to see whether the effort had an impact. The research techniques used here are many of the same ones you read about in Chapter 6, including surveys, interviews, and focus groups.[17] An additional complication to watch for when measuring PR effectiveness is time frame; PR activities can often take much longer than advertising activities to show results.

DEFINING PUBLIC RELATIONS AUDIENCES

The audience in public relations is usually referred to as a *public*. The term is one you're already familiar with, meaning everybody in the population at large. However, in public relations, the term refers to a particular group of people, such as investors, employees, customers, or regulators (see Exhibit 18.8). Each of these groups is a public, and when referring to all of an organization's audiences, it's proper to use the plural, *publics*. This section examines the major publics encountered in public relations.

Media

Media relations is the part of public relations that handles communication with the news media. The media and PR professionals have a unique relationship because both groups need each other to be successful. The media are often PR's most important public because of the reach and influence they possess. Public relations people need the media to reach a wide audience, which can include customers, community leaders, investors, and other publics. On the other hand, reporters, columnists, and editors (particularly those in the business media) rely on PR people for information about companies and industries.

One example illustrates this unique relationship. In recent years, the collapse of numerous U.S. banks and savings and loan institutions has made many people nervous about the stability of their checking and savings accounts. Consumers aren't always sure whether their banks are solid or teetering on the edge of collapse. To address this situation, a healthy bank in the Midwest decided to publish a series of educational pamphlets, giving consumers the information they would need to determine whether their banks were healthy. The local newspaper recognized this as a story that would interest most consumers, so it published an article about the bank's efforts. Unfortunately, many readers misinterpreted the article and flooded the bank with calls, asking whether it was in financial trouble. Some people even pulled their money out of the bank. To set the public straight, the bank's PR people sat down with the paper's business editor and supplied information for a second article. Without such close ties to the media, the bank could have had a PR fiasco on its hands. The bank needed the paper to get exposure, and the paper needed the bank to get information; the close relationship benefited both parties.[18]

The media's wide reach isn't the only benefit for public relations people, however. *Objective endorsement* is just as important. If you say in an ad that your new Panther sports sedan is the best-handling sedan on the road, many consumers

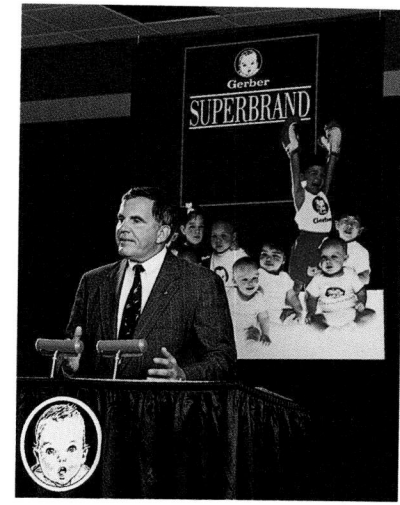

EXHIBIT 18.8
Publics in Public Relations

Stockholders are a key public for corporate public relations; the CEO of Gerber is shown here addressing the company's annual stockholders meeting.

will react with understandable skepticism for such a hard-to-prove claim. However, if *Road & Track* magazine evaluates the Panther and tells its readers the very thing you said in your ad, people will be more receptive because the endorsement came from an objective source. Readers know that the magazine's professional drivers have driven just about every car made (and so can make meaningful comparisons), and they expect *Road & Track* to be truthful (see Exhibit 18.9).

Customers

Advertising isn't the only way to reach current and potential customers; marketing public relations can communicate with this public quite effectively. Using marketing public relations to reach customers varies from launching new products to providing information that supports the advertising message (see Exhibit 18.10).

The programs established by Campbell Soup are a good example of how marketing PR can be effectively integrated with the rest of the marketing effort. Starting with the marketing objective of increasing the amount of soup that the average consumer eats, Campbell set its PR objective as giving consumers new reasons to eat soup. From this objective came two PR strategies: (1) publicizing scientific research on soup and (2) aligning soup with healthy lifestyles. For the first strategy, Campbell's PR department told the media and consumers about research showing that people who eat soup for lunch tend to consume fewer calories per day and that, calorie for calorie, soup offers more nutrients than many other foods. For the second strategy, Campbell took such steps as creating a series of lifestyle workshops for health-care professionals and sponsoring figure-skating competitions and other events with trim-and-fit images.[19]

Employees

Not all of PR's publics are outside the organization; employees are an important audience as well. The information that employees need covers a wide range, from

EXHIBIT 18.11
Vehicles for Employee Communications

Hewlett-Packard is one of a growing number of organizations that use videoconferencing to help managers and employees to communicate.

learning about individual jobs, to plans for future growth, to the organization's role in the community. Conversely, the management team in any organization needs to hear from employees, who have firsthand information about customers, competitors, and other important areas. This internal communication process encompasses numerous channels, including company magazines and newsletters, executive speeches, bulletin boards, meetings, and technological innovations such as electronic mail and videoconferencing (see Exhibit 18.11).

Although employee relations in general are the responsibility of individual managers and the company's personnel department, the PR function contributes to employee communication in several ways. First, in the same way that the PR department helps inform outside publics, it can inform managers inside the company, who can then communicate with their employees. Studies show that employees value face-to-face talks with their managers, and by ensuring that those managers are kept informed, PR specialists can foster effective communication throughout the organization. Second, PR departments often produce in-house newsletters, magazines, and videotape programs to keep employees up to date on relevant issues both inside and outside the organization. Third, as advocates for good communication, PR specialists can work to convince and remind company management that keeping employees well informed and listening to employee input are practices that are good for business.[20]

Communities

Organizations and the communities they're in are mutually dependent. Communities look to local organizations for such benefits as tax revenues and jobs; organizations look to their communities for employees, permission to build facilities, raw materials, investment, and other elements. Organizations can affect the quality of life in the community, and communities can help or hinder an organization, depending on whether community leaders support its actions.

Monsanto, a multinational producer of chemicals and related products, represents the sort of companies that are especially dependent on positive community relations. Because some of its products and processes can pose health concerns, people in the communities where Monsanto operates are understandably interested in the company's safety policies. After a tragic gas leak at a Union Carbide chemical plant in Bhopal, India, all major chemical producers realized they were vulnerable to increased government regulation, public scrutiny, boycotts, and other potential restrictions and hurdles. Monsanto took the initiative to educate the public about its safety controls and emergency plans. In Springfield, Massachusetts, for instance, the company's PR efforts have led to measured increases in the public's acceptance of new Monsanto plants, in awareness of the company's emergency procedures, and in agreement that Monsanto is a positive force in the community.[21]

Governments

Public relations is a major force in the relationship between industry and government and between government agencies and their constituents. From industry's perspective, government leaders, legislators, and regulators present significant PR challenges and opportunities. The challenges include making sure that laws and regulations don't unfairly impede the ability to conduct business. The opportunities include the access that PR professionals have to people in the government. The U.S. Congress alone has more than 200 subcommittees, many of which conduct investigations and develop legislation that affects business.[22]

The PR experts who communicate with government bodies on behalf of corporations and other organizations are called **lobbyists** (see Exhibit 18.12). Larger companies usually have their own lobbyists, and industry associations often send lobbyists to Washington, D.C., and other government centers. To the general public, lobbyists are often portrayed as people trying to gain special government favors for their employers, but their true role is much broader. Collecting information and sending it back to management is a key function, for instance, as is supporting a company's efforts to sell products to government agencies.[23]

Investors

People who invest in a corporation have an obvious interest in the company's affairs and prospects. Current investors want to know whether to keep the stocks and bonds they own, and potential investors want to know whether the company has a promising future. **Investor relations** is the subset of corporate public relations that involves communicating with current investors, potential investors, financial analysts, and government financial regulators. Because it requires extensive knowledge of corporate finances, financial markets, and government regulations, it's one of the most specialized fields in public relations.[24] Given the significance of outside investment in the financial health of most corporations, investor relations is also one of the most important PR functions. In many com-

EXHIBIT 18.12
Public Relations in Washington, D.C.

The Ruder-Finn public relations firm arranged this meeting between members of the U.S. Congress and Croatian president Franjo Tudjman (*right*). The meeting was part of an integrated campaign the firm created to educate the U.S. public and U.S. government officials.

panies the investor relations specialist is considered a member of the senior management team.[25]

Investor relations began as a way to "hype stock," according to Larry Rand of Kekst & Company. In other words, it was largely a selling function, trying to convince people that a company's stock was a good investment. In recent years, however, investor relations has emphasized research and analysis, both to provide management with information about stockholders and financial markets and to provide stockholders with the information they need to make buy and sell decisions. This shift hasn't decreased the importance of the communication function at all, but rather has increased the importance of the financial aspects of investor relations.[26]

In a sense, the primary objective of investor relations is to bring the company's actual value and its perceived value as close together as possible.[27] For instance, if your company is worth $50 a share, based on its earnings, assets, and other factors, you'd like to see the stock selling for around $50 a share. If it's selling below that, investors won't be able to realize the full value of their investments, and the company won't be able to raise as much money through the sale of stock as it should be able to. It's up to investor relations to explain why the company's stock is worth more than it's currently selling for.

On the other hand, if the stock is selling for more than its real value of $50 a share, the company could be setting itself up for a public relations calamity. Sometimes a company's stock prices will increase beyond a level that the company's performance really justifies, so at some point, those prices will have to come down. When they do, investors can get angry, sometimes even to the point of filing lawsuits against the company for not being truthful about its real performance. When a stock gets inflated in this manner, it's the job of investor relations to help bring the perceived value back in line with the real value. Even though such issues seem far removed from marketing and advertising, external financial forces can make or break a company, so investors deserve as much attention as customers and other key publics.

SELECTING PUBLIC RELATIONS VEHICLES

To reach these various publics, PR specialists can take advantage of an ever-growing array of *vehicles* to carry their messages. In fact, part of the challenge and intrigue of the profession is dreaming up new ways to communicate with your publics, whether you're providing the scorekeeping computers for a tennis tournament or beaming a videotaped message to employees in Asia or Europe (see Exhibit 18.13). The list of options continues to expand, but the bulk of PR commu-

EXHIBIT 18.13
Creative Public Relations

The marketers of the Ultra Slim-Fast weight-loss program capitalized on the town name of Pound, Wisconsin, to stage a townwide diet, complete with media events.

nication is carried by a handful of major vehicles: press releases, press conferences, and special events. In addition to these, public relations specialists create magazines, newsletters, annual reports, speeches, and other tools. Your choices are limited only by time, talent, and budget.

Press Releases

The workhorse of public relations, the **press release,** or **news release,** is a short document given to the media to provide information about the organization, its people, or its products. Releases are often distributed in *press kits,* packages that may also include product samples, publication-ready photos, background information on products and markets, and other elements that can help get the message across. Organizations send out releases when they hire new executives, open new factories, launch new products, or disclose financial results—whenever they do or experience something they'd like to tell one or more external publics about (see Exhibit 18.14). In some cases, particularly with smaller publications, an editor will use a press release as is, printing it just as the PR person submitted it. In most cases, however, the press release serves as a starting point for an article written by a member of the periodical's reporting staff or a story reported by the television or radio newscaster.

As already mentioned, PR people have a unique relationship with the media because both sides need the other to do their jobs. Reporters may rely on information from companies and organizations (the degree of this reliance varying from one media vehicle to the next), but ultimately they're in business to provide news to their readers, not to serve as publicity conduits for PR people. In other words, the relationship works best when PR people have something *newsworthy* to share with the media. You can promote your cause in a press release, to be sure, but it has to be understated and it must be of interest to the media's audiences.

The volume of press releases sent to the media is staggering. PRNewswire, a computer service that accepts press releases from PR people and makes them

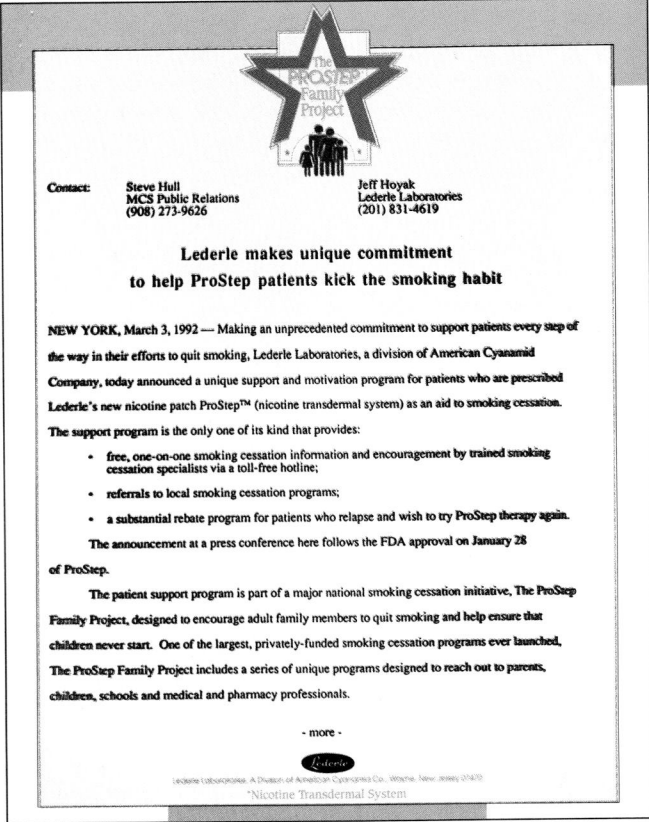

EXHIBIT 18.14
An Effective Press Release

Lederle Laboratories used this press release to inform the media about the company's efforts to help people stop smoking.

The news stories you read in the paper, hear on the radio, and see on television are written and produced by professional, unbiased journalists, right? Well, not always. In some cases the words and images come straight from public relations specialists. The practice raises some important ethical questions: Should the media use any organization's public relations material as news material? If so, should it be identified as such so that readers, listeners, and viewers know who's behind the news?

Because of the technologies involved, the situation with video news releases differs from the situation with written releases. When editors receive written releases, they can use the information provided as background for a story, rather than using the information as is. Even if editors use most of a press release intact, they can still edit it to tone down promotional claims, make it relevant to the audience, and so on. However, that's not the case with VNRs, because video footage is much harder to edit than written press releases. Unless a major story is involved, no television reporting team is likely to reshoot footage in the same way that print media editors can rewrite a news story, for instance. A print editor can alter the tone of an article with a few word and sentence changes, but an editor at a television station can't modify video footage (beyond simple changes such as cutting out parts of it).

This isn't to say that editors never use written press releases as is or with few modifications. In fact, the practice is not unusual, especially with smaller newspapers and trade journals (magazines aimed at people in particular industries). Companies known as "mat services" take press releases from clients and format them using the type styles and page designs of various newspapers. The newspapers can then drop the ready-to-print material right into their papers. Trade journals often have new-product departments that announce products of interest to readers, and the copy in these sections is sometimes taken in whole or in part from press releases.

Regardless of the media involved, journalistic ethics and a concern for quality can provide most of the answers to ethical dilemmas. No reputable news provider wants to be known as a "PR accomplice," simply relaying the promotional material it receives from PR staffers. If the story doesn't contain meaningful and relevant news, the media shouldn't treat it as such, and good editors don't.

Even with good journalistic decisions, however, the questions of VNR footage and disclaimers still exist. To address these issues, groups in the VNR business have begun suggesting ethical guidelines to ensure that viewers are not misled. Medialink, a leading distributor of VNR materials, developed a code of ethics that includes the suggestion that the producer and sponsor of all video PR materials be identified in the video material itself. The guidelines established by VNR-1, a production company, go a step further and suggest that television stations should identify VNR footage as such when they use it in newscasts. If the stations add a disclaimer that the footage is supplied courtesy of the sponsoring organization, viewers will be less likely to view it as regular news reporting. VNR-1's president, Jack Trammell, adds that the disclaimer gives the sponsoring organization additional exposure and shouldn't decrease the attractiveness of the VNR concept.

What's Your Opinion?

1. Do you think the mat service concept is ethical? Is this the same thing as running VNR footage without disclaimers?
2. How do you think viewers would respond to VNR-1's suggested disclaimers during news programs?

available to reporters and editors, receives over 100,000 releases a year.[28] Successful PR writers know what it takes to get noticed amid this paper flood and avoid a quick trip to the editor's recycling bin:[29]

- *Follow the format that reporters and editors expect to see.* Look back at Exhibit 18.14 for some of the formatting details. For instance, the release is double-spaced, has wide margins, and contains the notation "more" to indicate additional pages. Experts also recommend that you don't put your release on fancy corporate stationery; plain white paper is preferred.

- *Write in a journalistic style.* Filling a press release with advertising slogans is the surest way to get your release tossed out. Promoting your cause without making it seem like "advertising hype" can be a subtle distinction. The key is to make sure that what you have to say is new and important to readers. If your company has just introduced a water heater that consumes half as much energy as anything else on the market, you would certainly want to promote that message through advertising. You would also want to get the message to the press because it's news that cost- and energy-conscious homeowners would certainly want to read about. To have the greatest impact, good press releases are written to read like good news stories.

EXHIBIT 18.15
Video News Release

A key component in the ProStep PR program (explained in Exhibit 18.14) was this video news release, which contained various timed segments that television news producers could work into their broadcasts.

- *Write a strong lead and follow the inverted pyramid.* If you compare a newspaper or magazine article with a section of this textbook or an article in an academic journal, you'll see a distinctly different approach to writing. Journalists start with a strong *lead,* which is an opening sentence that summarizes the key points of the story. The article then proceeds from the most important to the least important details, a structure called the *inverted pyramid.* If your release doesn't have this same structure, you won't be terribly successful with editors.

The **video news release (VNR)** is the videotaped equivalent of the written press release. Some of the coverage you see on news programs and other information shows is produced by PR specialists and sent to networks and individual stations, just as printed press releases are sent to newspapers and magazines. VNRs are especially popular with local television stations, which sometimes struggle to fill up their airtime (see Exhibit 18.15). Three-quarters of the local stations in the United States use VNRs regularly. The practice is far less common in other parts of the world, however.[30]

Press Conferences

When you have significant news and reporters are likely to have questions for you, you'll probably want to go beyond simply issuing press releases and stage a **press conference.** This is a meeting between the media and the media representatives and executives of an organization. You've no doubt seen press conferences on television, when the president or other political leaders entertain questions from the press. A business press conference proceeds in the same manner, although the topic of conversation is a new product, a key industry development, news about a company crisis, a major management change, and so forth (see Exhibit 18.16). A related technique is the presentation to financial analysts, a common tool for financial PR specialists.

The number one reason for holding a press conference (as opposed to relying on press releases or other PR vehicles) is to allow the media to ask questions that the organization's representatives will answer. Other key reasons are to demonstrate products that are otherwise difficult to explain and to foster the idea that something major is happening with the company. Naturally, the media won't show up if they don't think there's a news story or if they can get the information they need in a less time-consuming manner. If they do show up and get lots of boastful self-promotion but no story, they're likely to turn a deaf ear the next time you're looking for some media attention.[31]

A press conference kicks off with an opening statement either from a member of the organization's PR staff or from a key executive. Following that, reporters take turns asking questions while photographers and camera operators (if television coverage is involved) collect pictures to accompany the news stories. Combining the interaction with reporters and the visual elements of photography and television cameras makes the press conference unique: in a sense, it's a *performance* for the media and indirectly for the media's readers and viewers. In other words, how you say what you have to say can be as important as the message. Good reporters

EXHIBIT 18.16
Performing for the Press

Actress Lauren Bacall played a role in the ProStep PR program as well; she is shown here at a press conference sponsored by Lederle.

look for clues such as a nervous or evasive spokesperson, particularly during emergencies and times when they want more information than the organization is able or willing to provide.

Special Events

These days it's hard to find a sporting, cultural, or social event that doesn't have a corporate affiliation of some sort. **Event sponsorship** is the part of public relations concerned with tying an advertiser's name to a public event. The basic model of event sponsorship is the advertiser providing financial support in exchange for having its name or products linked to the event. The benefits of sponsorship include being associated with something that your target audience enjoys and reaching what can add up to millions of people (see Exhibit 18.17). The bowl games at the end of the college football season are a good example, when millions of television viewers tune in and see the names and logos of USF&G, Mobil, John Hancock, Sunkist, Thrifty Rent-A-Car, and other corporations that pay to be associated with particular bowl games.[32] It's no longer just the Fiesta Bowl, for instance—it's the *Sunkist* Fiesta Bowl. The fans in the stands and the millions watching on television see and hear Sunkist's name and logo over and over again.

To sponsor an event, you can either arrange to have your organization aligned with an existing event or create your own event. For example, Bausch & Lomb, Coca-Cola, Pontiac, and other advertisers have signed up to sponsor the Professional Surfing Association of America's surfing contests.[33] Not only do these companies gain exposure to surfing fans, but some of the surfing image rubs off on them as well. Similar "image borrowing" happens when companies sponsor comedy festivals, rock concerts, operas, and other events.

Creating its own event, Rand McNally, a leading producer of atlases and maps, found an imaginative way to promote the sixty-seventh edition of *U.S. Road Atlas.* One of the company's marketing objectives was to draw consumer attention to the changes that went into the new edition, thereby encouraging people to replace their obsolete atlases. The company's PR agency, Ketchum Public Relations in Chicago, was intrigued by a letter from a 10-year-old boy who had written Rand

EXHIBIT 18.17
Communicating through Special Events

Peugeot sponsors ski races as part of its effort to keep the brand name in front of potential buyers.

McNally with the request that his grandparents' town (Parrott, Virginia, population 700) be added to the atlas. The town was added, and Ketchum worked with the citizens of Parrott to organize a day of celebration in honor of the boy's successful efforts and the town's new-found "fame." The agency then offered an *exclusive* on the story to *ABC Nightly News, People* magazine, and the Associated Press. From this starting point, the story generated 97 million *media impressions,* the number of times it was seen in print or heard on television. As pointed out earlier, this is an incomplete measure of PR effectiveness, but all the stories were positive, and most emphasized that Rand McNally's maps are continually updated.[34]

MANAGING CRISIS COMMUNICATION

The PR professional's job isn't all new-product launches, grand openings, financial news, and other business-related issues. Sometimes a crisis hits the organization, and it's during these emergencies that the PR staff's contribution becomes especially valuable to the organization. **Crisis communication** is the branch of public relations that concerns communicating (primarily with the media) during accidents, natural disasters, strikes, and other important events. Crisis specialist Mary Woodell of the consulting firm Arthur D. Little notes that corporations face two kinds of crises: catastrophic crises (explosions, fires, floods, etc.) and management crises (hostile takeovers, labor unrest, executive fraud, etc.).[35]

The most visible role of public relations during a crisis is serving as the organization's voice. When a crisis occurs, media from across the country, perhaps even from around the world, will be on your doorstep, demanding information. Experienced communicators know that PR people should be involved long before any crisis strikes. Furthermore, the process of planning what you will say to the media in the event of a crisis can lead to changes that will help you avoid the crisis in the first place.[36]

Successful crisis management involves three elements. First and most important, the organization must have a real interest in the welfare of employees, customers, stockholders, and the surrounding community. More than anything else, simply operating in a decent and caring manner will keep you out of most crises and help you through the ones you can't avoid. Moreover, the growth of news media in recent years has created a skeptical populace. You can't manage in an irresponsible manner and then try to gloss over it with good PR communication when tragedy hits. People are too smart for that. Second, you need a plan in place before the crisis occurs. The plan needs to cover a variety of issues, from the names and phone numbers of key local media to a list of which executives are authorized to speak for the organization. Third, you need to act decisively during the crisis, providing as much information as possible. It's crucial for top executives to be visible during this period, both to take control of the situation and to show the public that they acknowledge the seriousness of the crisis and their responsibility for setting things right.[37] Company reputations that have been carefully nurtured over many decades are on the line during a crisis, and effective communication can determine whether the organization recovers from the crisis.

A comparison of two recent oil spills illustrates the impact of crisis communication. When the Exxon *Valdez* ran aground, dumping 10 million gallons of oil in Alaska's Prince William Sound, Exxon had a major PR problem on its hands. The information provided by the company during the days following the spill was inadequate and sometimes contradictory. CEO Lawrence Rawl was quiet for six days, and when he did speak he blamed other parties for the slow cleanup. An Exxon executive later said that the company's management couldn't be blamed for the mistakes of a single tanker captain.[38] Public relations experts soundly criticized the way Exxon handled the affair, and the company's reputation suffered greatly.[39]

In contrast, when Ashland Oil spilled a million gallons of diesel fuel in the Monongahela River, CEO John Hall was immediately visible and on the scene. He took responsibility for the company's mistakes and offered to pay for damages. Ashland emerged from its crisis with the respect of some observers, who appreciated the company's willingness to accept responsibility and to do whatever it could to clean up the mess.[40] Ashland received high marks from PR experts for its handling of the crisis.

Special Communication

In addition to public relations, organizations sometimes engage in other communication efforts to meet their marketing and business goals. The four techniques discussed here—product placement, cause-related marketing, public service announcements, and advocacy advertising—are often used in conjunction with public relations and advertising. While they're not strictly part of the public relations function, they represent another set of communication tools that can help you reach your target audiences.

PRODUCT PLACEMENT

Did you ever notice how often characters in movies, television programs, and music videos use or consume brand-name products? In some cases, this is an artistic decision, such as when the production team decides that a character should drive a certain model of car. Moreover, many producers say that today's audiences are too sophisticated to accept fake brand names.[41] In other cases, the company behind the brand name paid to have its product used on-screen (or simply provided products free of charge), a practice known as **product placement.** Putting your product in the hands of a popular star or even in the vicinity might imply endorsement, and presumably some of the star's image might rub off on the product as well. PepsiCo, Quaker Oats, and BMW are among the many well-known advertisers whose products have been placed in movies and shows.[42]

The increase in product placements in recent years has sparked two controversies. The first revolves around the question of whether it's fair to subject members of the audience to what is essentially advertising when they have paid for commercial-free entertainment. Many believe such practices are deceptive. Opponents have gone so far as to request that the Federal Trade Commission require producers to list the placed products at the beginning of the movie, alerting viewers that advertisers paid to have their products included. (Some even support flashing the word *advertising* on the screen when the product appears). However, the FTC recently declined to institute such a ban, saying that it couldn't find a pattern of deception.[43] (Paid placements on television are already illegal unless accompanied by a disclosure, which is why television placements usually involve only free products.[44])

The second controversy involves the ban on tobacco advertising on U.S. television. You can't run a television ad for cigarettes, but you can pay a movie producer to use your cigarettes in a movie. Philip Morris, for instance, paid $42,000 to have Superman demolish a Marlboro truck (one of the company's brands) in the movie *Superman II.*[45] When that movie was later shown on television (after its run in theaters was over), the company had in a sense circumvented the ban on television advertising. Although product placement isn't as explicit as an ad, it is paid promotion, and it often involves a popular celebrity, with all the presumed persuasiveness of celebrity appeal. However, in spite of the controversies, product placement is already a big part of the entertainment business, and it shows no signs of diminishing.

CAUSE-RELATED MARKETING

Philanthropy and advertising strategy meet head-on in the fairly recent development of **cause-related marketing (CRM)** (introduced in Chapter 3). Programs vary in some respects, but the basic idea of CRM is for an advertiser to donate money to a nonprofit organization in exchange for using the organization's name in connection with a promotional campaign. The money can be either a fixed sum or a per-transaction fee paid each time consumers redeem a coupon, make a purchase, sign up for or use a credit card, and so forth. The connection between corporation and cause is played up in the advertising, attempting to link purchases to charitable contributions in the customer's mind. It becomes a "painless" way for people to give to charity; they pay the regular price, and the company gives money to the charity.[46]

Kimberly-Clark, maker of Kleenex, Huggies, and other leading products, has run a number of CRM campaigns linked to such nonprofit organizations as the Make-a-Wish Foundation and the Reading Is Fundamental program. The company's director of advertising and promotion, Dennis Lahey, notes that coupon redemption rates are nearly always higher when a CRM element is involved. American Express is another fan of CRM; the company staged one of the first major campaigns with a program tied to the restoration of the Statue of Liberty.[47]

On the surface, CRM looks like the ideal marriage of marketing strategy and charitable contribution. Everybody wins: the advertiser gets the positive exposure from being associated with a good cause, the nonprofit organization gets money from the deal, and consumers get to contribute without actually spending any of their own money. However, the people who've been successful at CRM emphasize that it's first and foremost a marketing strategy. American Express's Warner Canto, who manages the company's CRM efforts, puts it rather bluntly: "It's not meant to be philanthropy. Its objective is to make money for your business."[48] Not that CRM isn't a good deal for the nonprofit organization—it's just that if your primary goal is to donate to the cause, the experts say it's a lot less complicated simply to write a check.

In a sense, the charity or cause functions almost like a celebrity appeal in a CRM campaign. Rather than linking your product to Whitney Houston or Candice Bergen, you link it to restoring the Statue of Liberty or helping sick children. Consumers feel good about supporting a worthy cause, and they feel good about your company for providing the funds. A successful CRM campaign can be a win for everyone involved.

PUBLIC SERVICE AND ADVOCACY ADVERTISING

Causes and public issues also play a part in two other special categories of advertising. Chapter 3 defined public service ads as ads sponsored by government and nonprofit groups that address social issues such as drug abuse, pollution, and racial harmony. Agencies often donate the time and talent to create the ads, and the media set aside a certain amount of time and space to run them at no charge. Public service ads remain one of the most important communication tools available to nonprofit advertisers. The public service ads that appear on television and radio are often referred to as public service announcements (PSAs).

The Federal Communications Commission once required television and radio stations to provide time for PSAs. Even though that requirement no longer exists, stations are usually willing to provide time for PSAs on issues that concern their audiences. Drunk driving, health, education, and crime prevention are among the most common national issues covered in PSAs. Focusing on local interests is important to the stations as well—56 percent of the PSAs in one recent survey dealt with local, rather than national, organizations and issues.[49]

Advocacy advertising is advertising that communicates an organization's position on public issues. Traditionally, advocacy advertising has addressed topics that relate directly to an organization's line of business.[50] It differs from public service advertising in that the advertiser both pays for the media and has a direct stake in the issue, whether it's public attitudes, regulatory policy, social trends, or some other topic. A Philip Morris campaign in which the company advocated free speech and adherence to the Bill of Rights is a good example; the company has a direct interest in efforts to limit commercial freedom of speech as it applies to cigarette advertising.[51] W. R. Grace, a diversified Florida-based corporation, has run ads warning the public and pressuring government leaders about the growing federal budget deficit. Mobil Oil, a longtime user of advocacy advertising, has shared its opinions on a variety of business and economic issues. When gasoline prices jumped up after Iraq invaded Kuwait in 1990, people were quick to criticize oil companies for squeezing them for excessive profits (presumably using the situation in the Middle East as an excuse to raise prices). Mobil was equally quick to respond, with an ad that listed price trends over the previous months and that showed how the company had actually raised its prices less than its own costs had gone up. The ad wasn't an attempt to sell more gasoline; its purpose was to set the record straight on an issue of great importance to both the company and the general public.[52]

Advocacy advertising has recently expanded beyond issues in which the organization has a stake. Some companies now use advocacy advertising that doesn't directly benefit their business; for example, companies use it to project opinions and attitudes that support those of their target audiences. As mentioned in Chapter 3, clothing manufacturer Members Only has at times devoted its entire advertising budget to antidrug and voter registration advertising.[53] This sort of advertising ties into one of the primary objectives of public relations: aligning the organization with public attitudes.

Summary

Public relations is the process of understanding public attitudes on relevant issues, interpreting those attitudes for management, and then taking steps either to identify the organization with those attitudes or to modify the public attitudes. This is a broad definition that necessarily encompasses a diversity of activities. Public relations differs from advertising in four key ways: Public relations (1) lacks total control over the final message, (2) addresses a wide variety of audiences, including groups not usually targeted with advertising, (3) involves no direct media costs, and (4) addresses important aspects that are outside the realm of marketing.

The most common objectives of public relations are (1) keeping management in touch with public sentiment, (2) aligning the organization with public attitudes, (3) correcting or updating public perceptions of the organization, (4) promoting products, (5) adding value to brands by building the company's reputation, and (6) responding to crisis situations.

The five steps in the public relations process are setting objectives, conducting research, defining a plan and taking action, communicating with your audience, and evaluating the results. The six major publics addressed by public relations are the media, customers, employees, communities, governments, and investors.

The three primary vehicles for carrying a public relations message are press releases, press conferences, and special events. A press release is a short document given to the press in the hope that reporters will write favorable articles about the organization, its people, or its products. Organizations send out releases when they have news of interest to one or more external audiences. A press conference is a meeting between an organization (represented by both PR people and key executives) and the news media. Organizations invite reporters to press conferences when the situation calls for interaction (questions and answers) with the media. Event sponsorship covers a wide range of activities, from linking the organization's name to an existing event (such as an annual golf tournament) to creating one-time or recurring events just for the company's PR purposes.

Successful crisis communication requires three key factors. First, the organization must operate with genuine concern for its employees, customers, communities, and shareholders. An uncaring organization that stumbles into a crisis won't be able to redeem itself with persuasive communication. Second, the organization must plan how communication will proceed once a crisis hits, from how to reach the media to which executives are authorized to speak on the organization's behalf. Third, the organization must take decisive action and must disclose to the public as much information as possible. In crises that involve one or more segments of the general population, the news media will need to report the news; the more facts they get from the organization itself, the better the organization's chances of being portrayed accurately.

Product placement is the practice of paying a fee or providing products free in exchange for having products used and displayed in movies, television programs, and music videos. Cause-related marketing is a marriage of philanthropy and advertising strategy, in which the advertiser promises to donate money to a nonprofit organization in exchange for using its name in connection with the promotion. Public service announcements are television and radio ads used in public service advertising, taking advantage of donated airtime. Advocacy advertising communicates an organization's position on public issues that may or may not be related to that organization's line of business but on which the organization has distinct opinions.

Key Terms

advocacy advertising 510
cause-related marketing (CRM) 509
corporate public relations 493
crisis communication 508
event sponsorship 507
investor relations 502
lobbyists 502
marketing public relations 493
media relations 499

news release 504
press conference 506
press release 504
product placement 509
public relations (PR) 492
publicity 492
video news release (VNR) 506

Meeting an Advertising Challenge at Starbucks Coffee

A CASE FOR CRITICAL THINKING

To ensure a successful entry into the Los Angeles coffee market, Howard Schultz and his team at Starbucks utilized an array of public relations vehicles aimed at several key publics. With the help of its PR agency, Berkhemer-Kline Golin/Harris, Starbucks created a plan for moving into Los Angeles using no initial advertising at all. The plan had four key elements. First, the PR would be closely integrated with the rest of the marketing program. Second, the initial audience would be trendsetters, people in the area who tended to be among the first to pick up new fashions, new products, and so on. Third, education would be an important part of the PR program, reaching out to chefs and food reporters in the media. Fourth, Starbucks would continue to support and identify itself with social and charitable causes important to its target audience.

Integration with the rest of the marketing program was a vital issue because Schultz wanted to build awareness for the products in stages. The first stage involved establishing small Starbucks kiosks in selected area supermarkets. These began to appear in conjunction with the initial PR efforts. Then as awareness and word of mouth began to build in the next three to six months, Starbucks began the next stage, opening its own retail stores, which sell coffee-making equipment and coffee beans, in addition to a wide variety of ready-to-drink coffee beverages.

The trendsetters Schultz wanted to reach are the people who dine out frequently and seek a wide range of cultural and culinary experiences. Two special events were central to this effort. The first was a preview party for the 2,000 members of the singles group associated with the Museum of Contemporary Art. These people, who were likely to tell others about new tastes and trends, got to sample the product and learn more about premium coffee. The second event was an appearance at Taste of the Nation, a fund-raising event that drew other "foodies" and showcased Starbucks alongside the city's finest restaurants and food providers.

Taste of the Nation and other media events and food tastings also played a role in the second element of the PR plan, forging ties with and educating chefs and food editors at local media. Schultz wanted to get these groups on his side early, since they influence the buying behavior of many more people. He also wanted to teach them about the difference between the coffee they were used to and the premium products Starbucks would be offering. Moreover, the company's reputation had been built in large part on its quality products, and getting the endorsements of third parties such as chefs is a key part of building a reputation for quality. The events led to numerous stories in local media, and several chefs expressed interest in serving Starbucks in their restaurants.

Since its founding, Starbucks has been an active contributor to and participant in social causes and charitable programs. The company is one of the biggest corporate supporters of CARE, an international relief organization. Through CARE, Starbucks fulfills its commitment to giving something back to the international communities from which it buys coffee beans. The company has funded such CARE projects as a literacy program in Kenya and a health-care program in Guatemala. The news media pick up on these contributions and help position Starbucks as a caring corporation, thereby identifying it with a theme

Questions

FOR REVIEW

1. How does corporate public relations differ from marketing public relations?

2. Why are PR specialists well positioned to provide top management with feedback and analysis concerning public attitudes?

3. What are the benefits of sponsoring a sporting event such as the Fiesta Bowl?

4. Why is it important for top managers to stay visible to the media and the public, even if they aren't the experts who can best solve the problem at hand?

5. Why would Members Only decide to spend all its advertising budget on antidrug messages?

FOR ANALYSIS AND APPLICATION

6. Why do specialists in the field have such a difficult time defining public relations?

7. Knowing that you can't control the final message when you communicate through the news media, what steps could you take to reduce the chance of miscommunication or negative communication?

8. Should a manufacturer of complex products such as semiconductor production equipment use the media for public relations? Considering how complex these products are, is the risk of miscommunication through the media too high? Why or why not?

9. How can public relations add to the value of the brand name of a highly regarded business school?

10. Should ConAgra (the company behind such brands as Healthy Choice frozen dinners) stage a press conference to announce a new addition to its line of frozen foods? Why or why not?

Sharpen Your Advertising Skills

Airline companies have struggled through a number of labor battles in recent years, as price wars force them to find ways to

512

that's important to many consumers in the premium coffee market. On a local level in Los Angeles, Starbucks participated in such events as "Backlot Blowout," a fund-raising party held every summer by the AIDS Project of Los Angeles. Not only is this support consistent with its corporate philosophy, but it helps identify the firm with causes that its target audience cares about as well.

The PR program, which continues with special events and other efforts, helped Schultz build a solid foundation in Los Angeles. The L.A. Times recently referred to Starbucks as a "role model for budding coffee merchants" and as the "Michael Jordan of the coffee business." Overall, the company's sales have risen ninefold in the past five years. Thoughtful and

creative use of public relations continues to be the driving force behind this rapid growth.

Your Mission: *You're now in charge of the public relations effort at Starbucks. It's a double challenge: not only have your successful predecessors left some big shoes to fill, but public relations remains the cornerstone of the company's marketing plans. Consider the following situations, and make the choices that will best support Starbucks' long-range goal of being the dominant premium coffee producer in the country.*

1. *Several store managers have suggested that a videotape on making the perfect cup of coffee would be a good PR tool. What should the primary objective of such a tape be?*
a. *To update public perceptions about coffee, explaining what a great cup of premium coffee is all about and how it's made*
b. *To promote sales of Starbucks coffees and coffee-making equipment*
c. *To add value to the brand by making it more visible*

2. *From what you've learned about Starbucks so far, which of the following would be the best slogan to use with respect to community relations efforts? How would you address cynical consumers who've heard one too*

many claims about "companies that care"?
a. *"Coffee and caring"*
b. *"Starbucks cares"*
c. *"Premium coffee for a quality lifestyle"*

3. *If you wanted to demonstrate the taste of Starbucks to some 100 food editors scattered across 15 or 20 states, which of the following would be most sensible to include in a press kit?*
a. *A videotape of customers at a Starbucks store, enjoying the coffee*
b. *A coffee-making kit, complete with a low-cost French press (a type of coffee maker) and a selection of Starbucks coffees*
c. *A selection of clippings from newspapers and magazines that have praised Starbucks' taste*

4. *Starbucks seems like a natural for product placement, since its coffee can be worked unobtrusively into a variety of situations. Which of the following movies would be the best choice for Starbucks?*
a. *A thoughtful and classy film on the meaning of life, shot in French with English subtitles*
b. *A romantic comedy based on a best-selling novel*
c. *A blockbuster action-adventure film*[54] ∎

cut costs. Employees, understandably, are often reluctant to accept wage cuts and to make other concessions. The result can be disruptive and embarrassing strikes, during which labor unions take their case to the public by picketing airports. You work in public relations for Seattle-based Alaska Airlines, which found itself in this situation in 1993.

Decision: Assume that the company and its unions were able to reach an agreement that helped the company lower its costs without inflicting too much financial pain on the work force. Should you hold a press conference to tell the media that you've solved your problems or simply get back to business as

usual in a quiet way? Keep in mind that people who didn't need to fly during the strike may not have known that you were having troubles, but announcing your return to the air will let everybody know you are, or at least were, in financial trouble.

Communication: If you decide not to hold a press conference, write a one-page memo to all employees, expressing the company's pleasure and relief at resolving the strike and top management's hopes for smooth operations for everyone involved. If you decide in favor of the press conference, write a two-minute announcement to open the proceedings with the media.

Local Advertising

After studying this chapter, you will be able to

1. Explain why local advertising is important

2. Describe three common objectives and six common formats used in local retail advertising

3. Contrast supplier-controlled and customer-controlled cooperative advertising programs for retailers

4. Identify four common objectives for local business advertising

5. Discuss the challenges involved in creating local business advertising for both technical and nontechnical audiences

6. Highlight the two basic objectives of political advertising

7. Discuss the use of local media for local advertising

Tired of the sartorial sameness of it all, Arthur dares to make his own fashion statement.

T O P A N G A   P L A Z A

If it feels good, wear it.

More than 150 ways to honor Dad's one-of-a-kind style with great stores like Array, Bachrach, Cignal and Structure. Plus Crate & Barrel, Nordstrom, Robinsons-May, The Broadway, Montgomery Ward and more stores you love to shop. Victory and Topanga Canyon Boulevard in Warner Center.

Facing an Advertising Challenge at Ikea

OPENING THE DOOR TO SALES ON TWO COASTS

What's yellow and blue, as large as seven football fields, and filled from floor to ceiling with furniture? The answer, as millions of shoppers from Budapest to Burbank have learned, is an Ikea store. Based in Denmark, Ikea now operates some 119 warehouse-sized furniture stores in 24 countries, including 12 in the United States. The retailer opens between 5 and 10 outlets every year, and no two grand-opening advertising campaigns are exactly alike, because no two markets and no two audiences are exactly alike. So when the chain planned a new U.S. store on the East Coast followed by a new West Coast store only a few months later, Ikea president Anders Moberg knew that the grand-opening ad campaigns had to be distinctly different.

Ikea's international success has been anything but an overnight phenomenon. Founder Ingvar Kamprad came up with the company name in 1943 by combining his initials with the first letter of his farm, Elmtaryd, and the first letter of his native parish, Agunnaryd (similar to a county in the United States). His first furniture showroom, in southern Sweden, featured bargain prices and simple but stylishly functional designs. However, it wasn't until he opened his Stockholm store, in 1965, that Kamprad put into practice the marketing concepts that now distinguish Ikea from its competitors: moderate prices, quality products, and a pleasant shopping environment.

Going to an Ikea store is like entering a home-furnishings paradise. Customers are invited to wander through each model room and measure, touch, even sit or lie on any of the hundreds of furniture samples inside each 200,000-square-foot outlet. What's more, hungry shoppers can snack at the in-store cafe, and harried parents can leave their children at the in-store play area while shopping. Prices are low because customers select their own items and carry them home in flat-pack cartons, where they assemble the pieces using simple tools included with every purchase.

Ikea opened its first U.S. store outside Philadelphia in 1985 and soon plunged into other U.S. markets. Moberg's 1990 plan was to open stores on both coasts: the Elizabeth, New Jersey, store would open in May, and the Burbank, California, store would open in November. To enter two separate markets, he knew that the stores would need completely different ad campaigns. If you were Moberg, how would you use advertising to introduce Ikea to the target audiences in Burbank and Elizabeth? What creative and media strategies would you use to develop ads that would attract customers? How would you measure the results of your grand-opening advertising campaigns?[1]

CHAPTER OVERVIEW Although Ikea wants to introduce its name and products to its target audience, the chain also needs to convince people to visit its stores and buy furniture. Motivating people in a particular geographic area to take action is the role of local advertising, which is examined in detail in this chapter. The chapter begins with a discussion of the scope and immediacy of local advertising. You'll explore local retail, local business, and local political advertising, and you'll see how these three types of advertising are used to stimulate action at the local level. Finally, you'll examine the selection and use of local media to create a coordinated program of integrated marketing communications.

Local Advertising for Local Results

Browse through any newspaper or flip around the television dial, and you'll see a mixture of national, regional, and local advertising, each level pursuing its own goals with its own message emphasis. For example, Cadillac puts glossy, colorful ads in national magazines and makes eye-catching commercials for network television. Its national advertising has three goals: (1) to build brand awareness, (2) to polish its upscale image, and (3) to introduce new car models. As a result, the messages in these national Cadillac ads generally tout the quality, styling, and comfort of a particular model.

Building on the higher awareness and positive attitude fostered by Cadillac's national advertising, the San Diego Cadillac Dealers (a group of dealers in San Diego, California) also advertise. Their regional goal is to make car buyers aware (through newspaper, magazine, and television advertising) of the superior offer-

A CAMEL IS WALKING ACROSS THE BARREN DESERT FOLLOWED BY A CADILLAC SEVILLE DRIVING ALONE ACROSS THE DESERT.
(SFX): desert nomad music
ANNOUNCER: This camel's system is so adaptive it can travel 50 miles in desert heat without taking fluid, making it one of the world's most dependable animals. This automobile's system is so adaptive that if necessary for your safety it is engineered to travel 50 miles in desert heat without a single drop of coolant, which might also tell you something about ITS dependability. The Seville STS with the Northstar system by Cadillac. Creating a higher standard.

EXHIBIT 19.1

Using National, Regional, and Local Advertising

National television advertising from Cadillac works together with regional print advertising from the San Diego County Cadillac Dealers to communicate Cadillac's position and image. In contrast, local advertising placed by Bob Baker Cadillac is geared toward making the sale by drawing people to that dealer.

ings and services of area dealers. That's why their messages concentrate on option and price packages and the availability of quality repair services.

Both the national and regional ads are important ways of giving potential buyers a perception of Cadillac as a classy, quality product and of Cadillac dealers as attentive to customer needs. However, the sale is actually made on the local level, where dealers like Bob Baker Cadillac advertise in the print and electronic media with the goal of bringing car buyers into *their* showrooms to buy the models featured in national or regional Cadillac advertising (see Exhibit 19.1). Bob Baker Cadillac's ads stress not only the model and the price but also the dealership's selection, financing options, and services.[2] Obviously, the national and regional ads have to be more general because they aren't able to address the selection, the hours, or the parking situation at every dealership that sells Cadillacs. In contrast, Bob Baker Cadillac's local ad can effectively highlight the unique elements that might encourage consumers to choose that dealership over others in San Diego County.

Local advertising is the key to local results, whether your objective is to make the cash register ring, bring in votes, or solicit donations. If you're affiliated with national or regional organizations, you can use local advertising to interpret the national or regional advertising message for the target audience in one city or in one town. Local advertising messages are geared to the local audience, so they often differ, sometimes subtly, from the messages in national or regional advertising. In many cases, local ads focus on specific products and ask for a specific, usually immediate, audience response. This product orientation and direct-action focus tends to be missing from national ads because they concentrate on molding a positive attitude toward a brand name or an advertiser. What's more, local ads tend to have longer copy, offering specific incentives for action, because they must give consumers a reason to buy from one advertiser rather than another.

Even if your goods or services aren't supported by national or regional advertising, you can use local advertising to generate community interest and to suggest to your audience where (and when) to buy, to vote, or to make a contribution. Of course, such local ads must work a little harder; without national and regional advertising, they not only need to introduce the advertiser and build credibility but also need to discuss the product and ask the audience to take action. However, many local advertisers can't afford to hire an ad agency. These advertisers either design their own ads or seek help from the media in developing ads. For instance, when a local advertiser buys airtime at WXXA/Channel 23 in Albany, New York, the station will produce a 30-second commercial for as little as $150, depending on the production requirements.[3]

Some local organizations are too small to advertise on anything other than a shoestring, whereas others devote thousands of dollars to a year-round calendar of multimedia advertising. As a whole, spending by local advertisers makes up more than 40 percent of all U.S. advertising expenditures. Although this figure includes all types of local advertising, the majority can be classified according to three categories: **Local retail advertising** is used by retail outlets to reach consumers in a defined target market who buy for their personal use. **Local business advertising** is used by organizations or individuals to promote goods and services to businesses in the local area. Finally, **local political advertising** is used by politicians, interest groups, and individuals who want to influence the political process in a particular local area.

As you might imagine, these three categories differ in terms of their target audiences, their advertising objectives, and their creative approaches. As you read through the following sections and learn about these differences, bear in mind that all local advertisers need to avoid such common mistakes as paying too little attention to the advertising effort, not knowing what to advertise, and assigning unqualified people to handle the advertising (see Exhibit 19.2 on page 518).

Local Retail Advertising

In every medium, you can find a wide variety of ads promoting outlets that want to sell to consumers in your neighborhood, your town, or your city. The world of local retail advertising is colorful, creative, and diverse, in part because of the wide variety of businesses that retail goods and services. Here's a sampling of the types of organizations that use local retail advertising to reach consumer audiences:

- *Dealerships* such as Ford automotive dealers, John Deere lawn equipment dealers, and Exxon gasoline stations
- *Local branches of large retail chains* such as Ikea furniture stores, J.C. Penney department stores, and A&P supermarkets
- *Locally owned stores* such as hardware stores, shoe stores, and record stores
- *Franchised retail businesses* such as Midas muffler shops, Domino's Pizza outlets, and Blockbuster Video stores
- *Restaurants* such as Taco Bell, Sizzler steak houses, and local take-out places
- *Service businesses* such as banks, travel agencies, and dental clinics

EXHIBIT 19.2 **Mistakes that Local Advertisers Commonly Make**

In many cases, local businesses that lack advertising expertise tend to make mistakes that can undermine the effectiveness of the advertising function. This list describes some of the common but avoidable errors often made by local advertisers.

Mistake	Description
Paying too little attention to the advertising function	**Local advertisers may devote too little time or effort to advertising because of distractions caused by business problems or a lack of interest or ability in advertising.**
Delegating advertising to unqualified personnel	**Especially in smaller organizations, people who are asked to manage advertising programs may not have the right skills to plan, produce, and evaluate the ads.**
Having too much ego involvement	**Sometimes local advertisers get carried away by the thought of appearing in their own ads (or featuring their friends and family). However, not every business owner can be a truly effective spokesperson.**
Trying to use advertising to counteract other mistakes	**No amount of advertising can make up for an inconvenient location, poorly trained personnel, excessively high prices, or other business mistakes.**
Having too little inventory to cover demand	**If a local advertiser has too little stock to meet the demand produced by an ad, it loses sales, generates ill will among customers, and wastes the money spent on advertising.**
Not knowing what to advertise	**Some local advertisers want to advertise, but they're unsure of which products to feature. Local advertisers with limited budgets may do well by featuring popular products that have already established their brand names through national advertising.**
Not coordinating advertising with other functions	**Local advertisers may forget to coordinate product purchasing, employee training, and supplementary promotional efforts with the approach and timing of their ad campaigns.**

- *Entertainment and cultural destinations* such as movie theaters, theme parks, and museums

Look just at retail stores, and you'll find that two-thirds of the establishments in the United States are independent one-unit operations, the kind that use only local advertising because their target audiences are small, well defined, and concentrated in a particular geographic area. These independents, the backbone of U.S. retailing, ring up more than $780 billion in sales every year. However, with more than 1 million stores around the country—and new malls and shopping strips everywhere—retail competition has never been fiercer.[4]

In recent years, the retail industry has been dramatically influenced by a failing economy and a rash of mergers and acquisitions. Retailers suffered through a recessionary economy in the late 1980s and early 1990s that slowed consumer spending, hurt sales and profits, and ultimately put some outlets out of business. In 1991 alone, 17,000 retailers (large and small) filed for bankruptcy. In addition, because of the myriad mergers and acquisitions during the 1980s, retail ownership was consolidated in the hands of a few giants. Now these large merchants, such as Federated Department Stores, wield considerable clout, so they can buy the brands they want in the quantities they need, and they can lease the best locations. The giants can also afford to advertise more heavily and more often than small independent store owners. This puts pressure on small stores to target their audiences more accurately and to use their ad budgets efficiently yet creatively in order to better compete.[5]

Regardless of size, all stores follow the same advertising planning steps as they learn about their target audiences, research what motivates audience members to buy, and gain an in-depth knowledge of the strengths and weaknesses of the competition. On the local level, store owners or store managers are typically responsible for the advertising planning process. Once they've conducted any needed research, segmented their markets, and staked out their positions, the next step in the advertising planning process is to decide on campaign objectives.

SETTING LOCAL RETAIL ADVERTISING OBJECTIVES

Like all advertisers, local retailers need to set specific and measurable sales and communication objectives for their ad programs. Most national and regional advertisers usually can't isolate the effects of a particular ad or campaign. Local retailers, however, can more easily measure and compare their results to the advertising objectives they've set; their objectives generally relate to sales and to the number of customers who come into the store (known as *store traffic*). Of course, traffic and sales are also affected by elements other than advertising, but retailers can often detect a strong connection between sales or traffic increases and advertising. Here's a brief list of the three most common objectives of local retail advertising and how each can be measured:

- *To sell a particular item or product line.* Local retail advertising is a good way to sell more of a highly profitable product, a product that's in oversupply in the advertiser's inventory, a product that will soon be out of season, or a product that's particularly likely to attract your target audience. To measure your results, you simply compare that product's sales before and after the ad. For example, Wegmans Food Markets of Rochester, New York, used an aggressive campaign of local television commercials, T-shirt giveaways, and point-of-purchase displays to launch W POP cola, a store brand with higher profit margins than nationally advertised brands. As a result of this campaign, W POP sales skyrocketed, becoming the chain's best-selling cola brand within five weeks.[6]

- *To stimulate store traffic.* Throughout the year—even during peak purchasing periods—local retail advertisers such as Ikea need to bring people into their stores. Advertisers may want to set objectives for building traffic during non-peak periods as well as during less busy times of the day and slower days of the week. To plan and space promotional efforts, many local retailers use a **monthly promotional calendar,** a monthly schedule of sales, in-store appearances, and other promotional events. This calendar helps retailers build and maintain customer traffic throughout the year. By counting the number of shoppers during a particular period, they can see whether their goals have been achieved.

- *To support a new-store opening.* Just opening the front door on the first day of business isn't enough to bring people in. When you open a new retail business, you usually need to advertise to let people know the location, the hours, the product assortment, and other details. If you're opening in a new market, you may have to introduce your store or business name as well as your merchandise or services (see Exhibit 19.3). Most local retail advertisers set both sales and traffic objectives for new-store openings and then check the cash register and count the number of shoppers to see how their results stack up. Once local retailers have introduced their new stores to the community, the emphasis switches to building loyalty and increasing the average sales amount.

For example, when First Wisconsin Bank opened a branch in Appleton, Wisconsin, it set goals for bringing in potential depositors (similar to the traffic objectives set by retailers) and for acquiring deposits (similar to sales objectives). John F. Rankin, the president of the bank, used integrated marketing communications to reinforce the grand-opening message in radio and newspaper advertising as well as in direct mail and flyers. Then he tracked the number of people who attended each of the special events held during the 13-day grand-opening celebration. At least 7,500 people came through the bank's doors during the 13-day period, and another 10,000 attended the final day's fete. Although many people opened savings and checking accounts during the grand opening, Rankin knew that establishing the bank's name in a new market would take time. When he measured the results of the grand-opening ad campaign at the end of the first three months, he found that the bank had more than met its goals by pulling in $8 million in deposits since opening its doors.[7]

EXHIBIT 19.3
Advertising a Grand Opening

Wal-Mart supported the opening of its Santee, California, store with a colorful newspaper insert featuring price promotions and a photo of the People Greeter who worked in that store.

BUDGETING FOR LOCAL RETAIL ADVERTISING

After you've set your objectives, you're ready to determine your advertising budget. One common way is to base it on a specific percentage of annual sales (see Exhibit 19.4). You can check the percentage that stores in your industry typically spend by looking at reports issued by U.S. government agencies, Dun & Bradstreet, Robert Morris Associates, and other sources. Of course, you don't have to budget the same percentage of sales as others in your industry. The amount you invest will depend on your local market, local competition, and other challenges and opportunities you identify when you conduct your situation analysis.

Another budgeting method is to set aside a fixed sum for each unit sold. For example, if you know from experience that you have to spend $2 in advertising to sell each $100 car stereo, you would multiply $2 by the number of units you plan to sell to come up with a budget. A third method you can use is to set advertising objectives and then calculate how much advertising support is needed to achieve those objectives.[8] (Budgeting is discussed in more detail in Chapter 7.)

Regardless of how they set their budgets, many local stores have so little to spend that they can't afford to work with an established ad agency, so they hire free-lance copywriters and artists to create the ads, and they rely on the media to manage the production tasks. Small stores with more money to spend often prefer to hire local ad agencies to develop and produce their ads. For example, Radio Play in Los Angeles produces radio commercials for such local retailers as the American Tool Exchange, a one-store operation in North Hollywood.[9] Multiunit retailers and stores with larger budgets usually hire an agency, or if they're quite large and have a busy advertising schedule, they may have experts on staff to create ads in-house.

EXHIBIT 19.4   Budgeting for Local Retail Advertising

To calculate the advertising budget using the percent-of-sales method, a local retailer would follow these procedures.

Procedure	Purpose	Profit Pointers
Establish your sales goals.	Relate the amount you spend in advertising to the sales you expect to make.	When setting sales goals, think about these factors: • Last year's sales • Local population, income, employment levels • New and enlarged departments or stores • Competitive pressures • New sales or growth strategies
Calculate the percentage of sales you'll set aside for advertising.	Set a budget that will help you meet your sales goals.	Check the percentage of sales that other stores about your size in your industry spend, on average. Consider increasing this figure in the following situations: • You plan to expand. • You have many competitors. • Your strategy stresses price. • Co-op advertising funds are available. • You can take advantage of market opportunities. • Extra sales generated by advertising will be more profitable. • Your location is less favorable.
Determine what you'll advertise.	This decision guides the creative process.	Think about how to relate what you advertise to the sales goals you've set. Some items to consider: • Products that have sold well in each department • Seasonal products to be sold during certain periods • Discontinued products and other items to be cleared from stock • Co-op advertising support available for particular products or lines • New items that show signs of becoming best-sellers
Spread your ad budget through the year.	By doing this, you determine when is the best time to advertise.	Using your monthly promotional calendar as a guide, decide exactly when to place ads. Some tasks to do: • Research national, regional, and local events that offer tie-in potential, such as holidays or sidewalk sales. • Check your store's records to determine heaviest traffic periods. • Time your ads to support new-store or new-department openings. • Find out when major firms typically distribute their payroll to employees.

CREATING LOCAL RETAIL ADVERTISING

Whether your budget allows you to hire free-lancers, use an agency, or develop your ads in-house, the next step is to decide on the creative approach. Not all local retail ads are alike, but you may have noticed that these ads are often geared toward solving similar problems or trying to achieve similar objectives. That's why, if you look closely, you'll start to recognize particular formats in the local retail advertising you see. The next section looks at the most common local retail advertising formats.

Using Local Retail Advertising Formats

Depending on the products they offer and the specific objectives they set, local retail advertisers tend to rely on six types of advertising formats. The first is the *promotional format,* in which the focus is on reduced-price merchandise. Many stores use the promotional format in weekly circulars distributed with local newspapers or through the mail; consumers check these circulars to comparison shop and to make buying decisions.[10] The second type is the *semipromotional format,* in which reduced-price items are featured along with regular-price merchandise. This is perhaps the most commonly used format, as you can see by checking newspaper, radio, or television ads from department stores, grocery chains, and other retail outlets. The semipromotional format helps the advertiser build demand for both sale and nonsale merchandise, whereas the promotional format whets the consumer's appetite for sale items alone. Of course, a promotional format also gets customers into the store, where they may buy nonsale items as well.

The third format is the *nonpromotional format,* which highlights nonprice benefits such as customer service and product quality. This is the format that Jacadi, a store in Arlington, Virginia, uses to highlight the quality of its European-made children's clothing and furniture. The fourth format is the *assortment format,* which showcases the advertiser's in-depth or broad selection of products for sale.

How can a local store break through ad clutter to make an impression on its target audience? Competitive clutter is a particular problem for local merchants, who compete daily with a blizzard of ads from smaller stores as well as splashy campaigns backed by big-name retailers with megabuck budgets. The problem is compounded for local advertisers that need to build awareness—and store traffic—on a limited ad budget.

In response to the clutter challenge, some retailers try to attract notice by hiring celebrities to appear in or narrate their local ads. By linking its name to the right celebrity, a local retailer can capture the audience's attention, build credibility, and boost retention of the store name and ad message. Often, the celebrity is a local athlete or a local television or radio personality whose perceived glamour, accomplishments, and public image fit with the store's merchandise or name. If the retailer operates in Los Angeles or in another area where celebrities live, it's sometimes possible to sign a more widely known star.

For example, Morrie Dym, president of $5 Clothing Stores, wanted to use advertising to grab the attention of young women, the target audience for his California chain of low-priced apparel outlets. His answer was to hire a television actor well known to this audience. Dym's first choice was Johnny Depp, who appeared in the television series *21 Jump Street,* but Depp's rate was too high. So Dym hired Scott Baio, who starred in *Happy Days, Charles in Charge,* and other programs. Although Baio charged more than a no-name actor would, Dym believed that the celebrity's reputation among the target audience was well worth the extra investment.

The store ads capitalized on Baio's star status and added a touch of fantasy to set off a wave of word-of-mouth advertising. In one commercial, a teenage girl says to a friend, "Clothes for $5? What are you, crazy? Yeah, and Scott Baio's going to ask me for a date!" Just then, Baio strolls out of a nearby elevator, leaving the two teens awestruck. At the end, the first teen runs into Baio again—and this time they go off together in a limousine. "Believe it!" says the girl as the commercial closes.

Another way to break through competitive clutter is to make local retail ads so outrageous that the audience can't help but remember the store. You can probably name the local dealer known for smashing car windshields or the local store whose owner brandishes a sword as he slashes prices. The trick, however, is to harness the hijinks without turning tasteless or getting into hot water. For instance, a sarcastic print ad promoting fresh milk at the Oak Tree Farm Dairy in Long Island, New York, was calculated to provoke laughter—but it wound up irritating officials in a neighboring state. The ad, which poked fun at milk produced in New Jersey, showed a cow grazing next to a highway, right in front of a petrochemical plant. The headline asked, "Ever wonder why milk from New Jersey doesn't taste as fresh as ours?" It's not difficult to understand why New Jersey state officials weren't amused. However, as a way of breaking through clutter to draw attention to the dairy and its products, the ad was a big success.

Apply Your Knowledge

1. What two creative possibilities can you envision to make the most of hiring a nonsports celebrity spokesperson for a local sporting goods store?

2. Should a local retailer purposely develop provocative ads that irritate the public but call attention to the store? Why or why not? ∎

For instance, The Patchworks, a quilting supply store in Bozeman, Montana, uses the assortment format to advertise its extensive collection of more than 440 classic fabric reproductions.[11]

The fifth format is the *omnibus format,* which centers on numerous items but, unlike the assortment format, does not emphasize the range of available products. The sixth format is the *institutional format,* in which the advertiser itself is the star (see Exhibit 19.5). To establish and maintain a positive public image, the store uses this format to highlight its unique history, philosophy, or position in the community.

However, as appealing as the promotional and semipromotional formats may be for drumming up business, it's important to avoid misleading consumers about sale prices or products. One illegal tactic is the use of **bait-and-switch advertising,** in which a store promotes a low-priced product, one that it doesn't want to sell, as the *bait* to lure customers, who are then *switched* to higher-priced or higher-profit products. Burned by bait-and-switch tactics, exaggerated product claims, false promises of reduced prices, and similar rip-offs, many shoppers are skeptical about local retail and sale ads.[12] Local retail advertising has to overcome this skepticism to inspire confidence and trust in addition to promoting the store and its goods and services.

When local retailers such as supermarkets use promotional or semipromotional ad formats on a regular basis, they have to avoid confusing the target audience or

DOG OWNER COMES OUT OF STORE TO TELL HIS DOG THAT HE HAD TO TAKE A RAIN CHECK FOR THE DOG FOOD. DOG DRIVES OFF IN CAR WITH OWNER RUNNING BEHIND.
DOG OWNER: I went into the market to

get that dog food that was on sale. But they were sold out. They gave me this rain check. Uh, we have to come back again. (Dog growls.) Spike, I know you're disappointed, but . . . (dog rolls up window and drives away).

V.O.: Cub. If we're out of an advertised item you won't get a rain check. You'll get something bigger or better for the same price. Cub. What service should be.

EXHIBIT 19.5
The Store as the Star

One way Cub Foods differentiates itself from competitors is by promoting its commitment to customer service and satisfaction. In this television commercial, the store demonstrates what *won't* happen when shoppers try to buy sale items that have sold out.

busting the budget. To meet this challenge, many develop a distinctive advertising look or sound that can be used for a long period but that's adaptable for individual ads. In print ads, this distinctive look may be created by repeatedly using a particular color, typeface, layout, and page size for every ad, changing the featured products only as needed. In electronic ads, this distinctive look and sound may be created by opening and closing with the same logo or music or by using the same spokesperson in all ads.

Using Cooperative Advertising

As discussed in Chapter 17, many suppliers offer cooperative (co-op) advertising programs in which they share the cost when particular products or product lines are advertised by local retailers. In fact, an estimated $15 billion is made available for local retailer advertising by manufacturers and distributors. Despite the many supplier offers, local retailers haven't always taken advantage of such programs because of the difficulty in tracking the innumerable details involved in planning and evaluating these ads. More recently, however, suppliers, retailers, and the media have turned to computerized systems to more easily track co-op expenditures and reimbursements.[13]

Co-op ad programs can be organized in two ways. In a **supplier-controlled cooperative advertising program,** the manufacturer or distributor creates and places ads that are customized with one or more retailers' names.[14] These co-op ads may run in the print media, with space allocated for the local retailer's name, address, and phone number, or they may run in the electronic media with a **dealer tag,** an identifier mentioning the local retailer's name at the end. As part of their co-op programs, many manufacturers make available a series of **ad slicks,** also known as *ad mats,* professionally developed camera-ready ads that local retailers can use when featuring particular products in their print ads. All the local advertiser has to do is drop in the store name and address or have the newspaper or magazine insert that information (see Exhibit 19.6 on page 524). For example, furniture maker Ethan Allen prepares ad slicks that local outlets can personalize and place in their local print media.[15] (Outside of co-op ad programs, national retailers send ad slicks to their local outlets for use in local advertising.)

Another creative approach used in a supplier-controlled cooperative advertising program is to run an ad listing many dealer names. For instance, Pixall uses a dealer listing alongside its ads to let farmers know where to buy the firm's knife-roll attachments for farm equipment. Also, the supplier can insert a toll-free number that consumers can call to find the name of the nearest store. General Electric uses this method and also supplies the stores with callers' names and addresses.[16]

In a **customer-controlled cooperative advertising program,** the supplier reimburses its customer (the retailer) for all or some of the cost when the retailer

EXHIBIT 19.6
Using a Manufacturer's Ad Slick

From the local advertiser's viewpoint, ad slicks such as this one from Technics reduce the cost of creating an attractive ad for a particular manufacturer's products. From the manufacturer's viewpoint, ad slicks ensure that the local ads for particular products are both consistent and accurate.

advertises certain products. For example, Cigna, a major insurance firm, pays 50 percent of the production and media costs when agents who exclusively offer Cigna policies create brochures or place ads in the major media. However, like many suppliers, Cigna puts a cap on the amount of local ad expenses it will repay. Cigna limits its reimbursement to no more than one-half of 1 percent of each

---

 CHECKLIST FOR USING COOPERATIVE ADVERTISING

❏ A. Determine whether the products you want to promote are backed by a supplier's cooperative ad program.

❏ B. Understand any minimum purchasing requirements that must be met to be eligible for the co-op program.

❏ C. Examine the advertising guidelines set by the manufacturer or distributor.

   • Check whether you must advertise the entire product line or whether you can highlight only certain models.
   • Understand how and where the brand name or trademark must be shown, what size the ad or the featured product must be, and whether model names or numbers must be included in the ad.
   • Be sure you know whether the product's price can or can't be mentioned.
   • Check for restrictions on when the ad may appear.
      1. Note whether you're required to advertise during periods that coincide with special manufacturer or distributor promotions.

      2. Note whether you'll be refused reimbursement for advertising during certain periods.
   • Look for restrictions on where the ad may appear.
      1. Check whether certain media are excluded from the program.
      2. Look for any limitations on the geographic area in which the ad can appear.
   • Ask about any creative materials such as ad slicks that may be supplied to local retailers for personalization and insertion into local media.

❏ D. Determine the rate of reimbursement (which may vary according to the products featured and the media used).

❏ E. Be sure you know what materials (such as tear sheets or media invoices) must be submitted to receive reimbursement.

❏ F. Observe any deadlines for submitting proof for reimbursement after an ad has run.

agent's insurance premium volume during the previous year. This means that as agents produce more premium volume, they're entitled to more co-op ad support.[17]

Most co-op advertising is customer-controlled, which is popular with local retailers because they aren't obligated to use the supplier's ready-made ad. Instead, they create their own ads, so they have some leeway in terms of product selection, timing, media selection, and ad copy—as long as they stay within the supplier's guidelines (see the Checklist for Using Cooperative Advertising). Because the retailers know their local markets and target audiences better than their suppliers do, they can enhance their co-op ads with local flavor to capture shoppers' attention.[18]

Local Business Advertising

In contrast to local retail advertising, which directs messages to consumers, local business advertising directs messages toward people who buy or use products in businesses, nonprofit organizations, and government agencies. As explained in Chapter 1, business advertising is a broad category that contains four classifications, each with its own distinct target audience:

- **Industrial advertising** targets people who buy or use the materials and services needed to conduct business or to manufacture other products.
- **Trade advertising** targets intermediaries such as wholesalers and retailers that buy goods for resale to customers.
- **Professional advertising** targets licensed professional practitioners such as accountants, doctors, dentists, and engineers.
- **Agricultural advertising** targets farmers and agricultural businesses.

Much of the time, the target audience in each of these classifications is one individual, either the person responsible for buying or the person responsible for using the product you sell. However, in many cases a number of people play a role in deciding what to purchase and from whom. Then you have to target your local business advertising toward the buying center, the group of individuals within an organization who make the buying decision or influence the buying process for a particular product.[19]

Of course, just as in local retail advertising, you need to follow the various steps in the advertising planning process. This means that you should understand your target audience, research its buying behavior, and analyze your current situation. Then you're ready to set objectives for your local business advertising.

SETTING LOCAL BUSINESS ADVERTISING OBJECTIVES

Local businesses have to set both communication and sales objectives for their advertising, especially when they're targeting a number of individuals in the buying center of a business, a nonprofit organization, or a government agency (see Chapter 4). Rarely will every member of the buying center have the same image of the advertiser, the same attitude toward its products, and the same inclination to buy. Thus, to reach buying-center members and to set the stage for a sale, the owners or managers of local businesses commonly set four kinds of advertising objectives:

- *To build awareness.* It's difficult to make a sale when the prospect has never heard of you, your reputation, your product, or its benefits. So first and foremost, local business advertising has to make the prospect aware of who you are and what you have to offer. To set and measure objectives, you can conduct audience research to determine the level of awareness before and after an ad campaign. Awareness paves the way for your salesperson to get in the door—and ultimately to make the sale. However, it's important to remember that an awareness campaign won't automatically lead to higher sales.[20] At the same time, a good awareness campaign can provide a solid foundation for the business's sales campaign.

- *To provide technical product information.* When deciding between competing products or considering a new product, business buyers often need a lot more information about performance, maintenance, costs, and so on. Local business advertising, especially print ads, can provide a great deal of technical product information in a format that's easy for the prospect to review and save.

- *To generate sales leads.* By offering to send detailed information about products, guarantees, and so on, you can encourage people to respond, which identifies them as good sales prospects. This is especially important when you're targeting a buying center, because you don't always know exactly who you must sell and what they want to know. It's equally important when you're targeting audience segments that are difficult to reach, such as home-based businesses. For instance, Colucci Insurance, an agency in Stamford, Connecticut, poses six questions in its print ads for home-office insurance. Home-based business owners are invited to take this brief quiz and then call for a professional insurance audit if they answered no to any of the questions in the ad; each response is a good sales lead.[21]

- *To support distribution-channel members.* Whether you need to widen your distribution, let your wholesalers or dealers know about new products, or boost your distributors' sales efforts, you can use local business advertising to support channel members. After all, your salespeople can't be everywhere at once, so a local business ad can serve as a reminder or an update for distributors who need to know about your product, its availability, its profitability, and your support services.

CREATING LOCAL BUSINESS ADVERTISING

Once you've established your objectives, you're ready to set a budget and then create and place the advertising. Because business buyers are generally quite busy, with many forms of communication competing for their attention, you have to make your message as clear as possible. That's easy when you're communicating straightforward concepts such as dependable service, low price, wide distribution, and broad product assortment. However, trying to communicate technical information or other complex details can be more complicated. When you want to convey technical information to a nontechnical audience (for example, to people who approve purchases but who don't actually run the equipment or to people who are new to the field), you run the risk of becoming dull, overwhelming your audience, or losing their attention. For such an audience, you may want to tone down the technical language, use headlines to summarize the important facts about your product, and play up key product benefits.[22]

On the other hand, when you're targeting a technical audience that's experienced in buying or using products in your category, you need to offer more technical details to explain your product's features or to prove its superiority. Thus your copy will often be lengthy, and in the case of industrial products, you'll need diagrams, tables, or charts that directly relate to the message and that support the ad's claims (see Exhibit 19.7). Using the information in your ad, technical experts such as engineers can evaluate product claims, compare your product's specifications and performance with those of rival products, and then decide which one they want.[23]

Despite the need to tailor the message to each target audience, many local business advertisers have only a limited ad budget. They can't afford to create a separate ad for technical and nontechnical audiences, so they want to use a single ad to reach both. One creative approach to this dilemma is to gear the ad to a nontechnical audience and offer to send more detailed information on request. This reduces advertising space or time, allows you to slant the additional information to the specific needs of the respondents, and helps you build a prospect database.

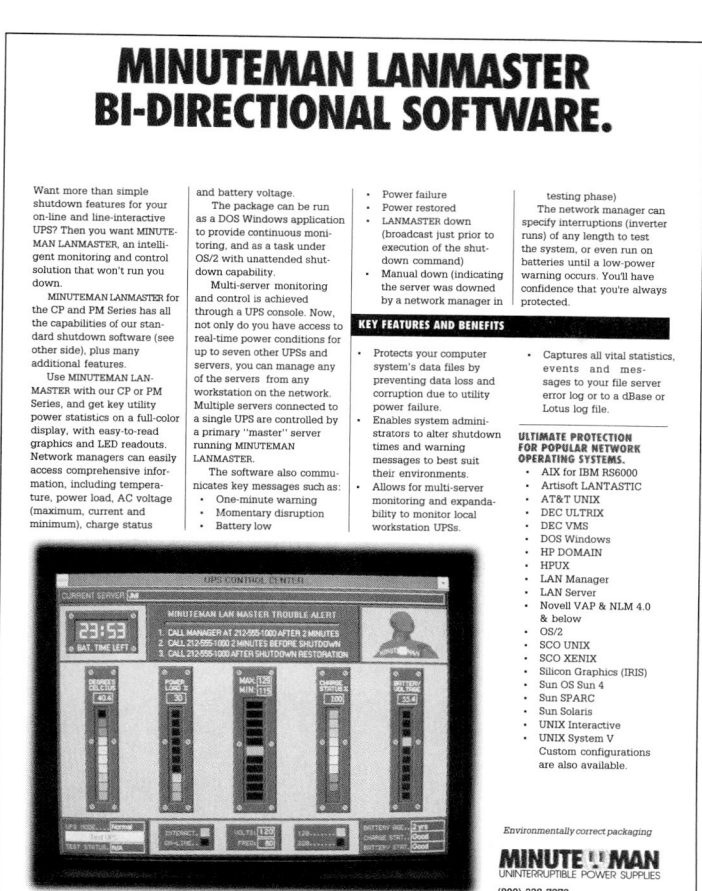

EXHIBIT 19.7

Industrial Buyers Need Technical Information

Local businesses generally need a considerable amount of technical information before they decide to buy or specify a particular product. Minuteman's direct-mail ad, distributed by local software stores, explains in detail how its computer power supply products will benefit local business users.

Another approach is to use a foldout page in your print advertising or in brochures that can be inserted in the local newspaper or mailed to prospects. Nontechnical material would appear on the front, and technical material would be hidden under the fold where it's readily available for those who need the details. A third approach is to use large headlines to concisely convey key benefits or features and to print supporting details in smaller type. This approach allows nontechnical audiences to quickly get the message while encouraging technical audiences to continue reading.[24]

Finally, like local retail advertisers, local business advertisers may be eligible for co-op advertising funds. Of the $10 billion spent annually on co-op advertising, as much as 10 percent goes for business co-op ads. In addition to covering print and electronic ads, business co-op programs often encompass activities that retail co-op programs don't, such as sales seminars, telemarketing, trade shows, and direct mail.[25]

Local Political Advertising

Local advertising has become integrated into the political process throughout the United States and, increasingly, around the world. Candidates for local office use advertising to share their views, qualifications, and plans; officials and groups at odds over governmental problems can use advertising to present their arguments (see Exhibit 19.8). Although no political questions have been resolved (and no candidates elected) solely on the basis of advertising, it's clear that ads play an important role in alerting local audiences to important political issues, informing them about the candidates, and persuading them to take action (such as voting for a candidate or phoning their legislators).

On June 7th, vote as if *y<u>our neighborhood</u>* depends on the result — someday it just might!

"Yes on G"

Paid for by Yellow Ribbon Committee - Yes on "G"
1504 California St.
Oceanside, CA 92054

Bulk Rate
U.S. Postage
P A I D
S.M.I.

EXHIBIT 19.8
Local Political Advertising Can Address Local Issues

Local political advertising plays an important role in raising public consciousness and arousing citizens to take action about local issues. This direct-mail ad encouraged voters in Oceanside, California, to vote yes on a zoning issue that would prevent certain businesses from opening in their neighborhood.

Any and all media can be used in local political advertising, from huge roadside billboards and full-page newspaper ads to brief radio commercials and inexpensive flyers. (Political advertisers have to pay for media time and space in advance or their ads won't run.) However, television's ability to bring the candidate's message to life—and its ability to help the viewing public connect a face and a voice with the message—has made it one of the most popular media for political advertising of any sort. Television was first used during a national election when the legendary ad agency executive Rosser Reeves produced commercials to support Dwight D. Eisenhower's successful run for the U.S. presidency.[26] Since then, television has been part of every U.S. presidential election as well as a growing number of regional and local races, from statewide senatorial and gubernatorial campaigns to local campaigns for mayor and for other offices.

Cable television is also a common choice for local political advertisers who need a cost-effective way of bringing their personal messages to audiences in specific local markets. For example, Barney Frank started using local cable television during the 1980s when he successfully challenged a popular incumbent from Fall River, Massachusetts, for a seat in the U.S. House of Representatives. His cable campaign kicked off with three half-hour programs produced at a local Fall River station, in which representatives from each of the district's key constituencies questioned Frank about local issues. Then he aired cable commercials that consisted of excerpts from each of the three programs, following up with commercials that featured local residents offering their endorsements. In total, Frank paid less than $10,000 for production expenses and commercial time to reach Fall River voters via cable television advertising.[27]

In addition, direct-mail advertising and telemarketing continue to be popular methods for reaching local voters. Consider how political newcomer Maurice Williamson used both during his campaign for a legislative seat in Pakaranga, New Zealand. At the start of the campaign, Williamson's volunteers asked 35,000 local voters about their concerns. After entering this information into a database, the candidate began a highly targeted direct-mail program. As Williamson wrote to voters, he customized his letters to reflect his position only on the issues that mattered to each voter. Then, on election day, volunteers pulled phone numbers from the database and called to ask whether voters had any questions for the candidate, who was standing by to answer. As a result of this database-driven campaign, Williamson triumphed over a well-known and popular incumbent.[28]

Like other forms of advertising, local political advertising is developed and implemented according to the advertising planning process. To start, you need to look at your overall situation, understand your target audience, and research competitors' positions. Only then are you ready to set specific objectives for your local political ads.

SETTING LOCAL POLITICAL ADVERTISING OBJECTIVES

Local political advertising is usually geared to two basic objectives. The first is to raise public awareness of some candidate or some issue. The second is to persuade people to take action. Although a campaign will sometimes aim to fulfill only one of these objectives, local political ads often seek both to raise awareness and to persuade.

Raising the Audience's Awareness

Before they ask their audiences to take action, candidates as well as officials, interest groups, and others involved in the local political process usually set goals for raising public awareness of key issues. Whether the advertising centers on a local zoning struggle, a race for public office, or a tax problem, advertising is one of the few ways to directly control the transmission of the message from the advertiser to the receiver. For that reason, it's a good way to convey information without the disruptions or potential distortions associated with personal appearances, debates, and media interviews.[29]

For instance, John T. Grant, the county executive in Rockland, New York, advertised in the local newspaper to explain the county's viewpoint after salary negotiations with its largest union had become sticky. The ad provided information about the county's salary offer and its financial pressures. The ad also explained the efforts Grant and other county managers were making to resolve the impasse with the 2,100-member union.[30]

Persuading the Audience to Act

Once local audiences have been made aware of the issues, the candidates' records, and other pertinent information, advertisers usually move to the second objective, which is to convince people to take a specific action (see Exhibit 19.9). The action may be to vote for (or against) an issue on the ballot, to support or protest a specific cause by contacting local legislators and officials, or to vote for a particular candidate.

Several years ago, when Glenda Hood was seeking the Democratic nomination for mayor of Orlando, Florida, she successfully used advertising to convince Democrats to vote for her in the primary election. In addition to advertising before primary day, she got a little last-minute exposure on primary day by arranging for an ad to appear on the outside of the plastic bag in which the local newspaper was delivered. (Hood won the primary—and went on to be elected mayor.)[31]

CREATING LOCAL POLITICAL ADVERTISING

Whichever objective you set, you plan and create local political advertising to promote a candidate or an issue in much the same way that you promote any good or service. That means starting with research to find out about your audience and its perceptions of your candidate or your cause and then designing a campaign to get your message across as effectively and efficiently as possible. By careful planning, you can match the message, the creative approach, and the media strategy to the needs and interests of the audience.

The San Diego Police Officers Association is proud to endorse the following candidates.

These candidates have been listening to your concerns and understand the need to provide law and order. They will work to increase the number of officers on the streets and make your safety their number one priority.

The Deputy Sheriffs Association of San Diego County supports the endorsements of the San Diego Police Officers Association.

THE PUBLIC SAFETY CANDIDATES

 HARRY MATHIS
Council District One

 CHRIS KEHOE
Council District Three

 BARBARA WARDEN
Council District Five

YES **YES ON PROPOSITION 172**

Paid political advertisement. Paid for by San Diego Police Officers Association PAC
619 Kettner Blvd., San Diego, CA 92101, ID # 831267
An independent expenditure not authorized by or coordinated with any campaign or candidate.

EXHIBIT 19.9
Persuading Local Residents to Take Action

This ad from the San Diego Police Officers Association encouraged voters to take action by electing three City Council candidates and approving a specific proposition on the ballot.

Is negative political advertising unethical? In many local, statewide, and national elections, candidates use advertising not to explain their own achievements and credentials, but to attack their opponents' qualifications and promises. In effect, such advertising is a twist on traditional comparative advertising. Whereas comparative ads try to show the audience why a competing brand isn't as good as the advertised brand, political ads sometimes don't even bother to say why the advertised candidate is better than his or her opponent. Instead, the ads simply create doubt about an opponent's background or capabilities and encourage voters to vote *against* the opponent (which means a vote for the advertiser).

From the candidates' viewpoint, attack ads gain the audience's attention by cutting through clutter and delivering a clear (but negative) message. Considering the volume of political ads that are aimed at voters during any election period, standing out from the clutter is a real consideration for any politician. However, experts worry that attack ads may alienate voters and cause them to question not only the candidates' ability to govern but also the entire democratic process.

Negative political advertising isn't new; it's been a standard tactic for decades, especially in presidential elections. However, since the 1980s, the use of attack ads has accelerated and spread to nearly every political race in the United States. Furthermore, when one candidate goes on the attack, opponents may have no choice but to respond.

For example, California candidate Bruce Herschensohn used advertising to bash his rival for the Republican nomination for the U.S. Senate in 1992. In one television commercial, he pointed only to his opponent's record as a state legislator and never mentioned his own qualifications: "I'm Bruce Herschensohn. My opponent, Tom Campbell, was the only Republican Congressman opposing the 1990 anti-crime bill. He's liberal and wrong." In reply, Campbell aired a commercial that said, "Bruce Herschensohn is lying. Tom Campbell voted to extend the death penalty to 27 crimes, and was named 'Legislator of the Year' by the California Fraternal Order of Police." Did this advertising work? Herschensohn received the Republican nomination, but he was defeated in the end by Democrat Barbara Boxer.

In response to charges that political attack advertising can stretch the truth and mislead the public, concerned groups have called for a renewed emphasis on ethics in political advertising. The American Association of Political Consultants has a code of ethics that outlaws the use of false or misleading information, and the American Association of Advertising Agencies has joined with the League of Women Voters in Project Run Fair, a mechanism for protesting unfair or misleading political ad messages. However, these voluntary programs aren't backed by the force of government regulation, so observers doubt that the programs have the muscle to curb abuses. What has helped derail unethical attacks in recent campaigns is the vigilance of television and newspaper reporters, who review political ads and publicly expose any distortions they find. However, political reporters can't be expected to police every race in every area, so the question remains: Should political attack advertising be allowed?

What's Your Opinion?

1. *Who do you think is responsible for negative political ads: politicians, ad agencies, or the media? Why?*
2. *Would you vote for a local candidate whose ads attacked opponents rather than presenting answers to community problems?*

For example, the Straphangers Campaign (a public interest group concerned about proposed mass-transit fare increases in New York City) used an aggressive advertising program to encourage public protest against a planned hike. Its ad agency, Robett & Rosenthal, created nearly 6,000 transit posters to be placed in the city's subway cars; this allowed the group to reach as many mass-transit riders as possible. The message was conveyed succinctly but dramatically by the headline "$1.50 subway fare? Maybe it's not just this train that's taking you for a ride" and by copy that urged riders to call city and state officials (whose phone numbers were included). Although the ads offered information to raise awareness, their main objective was to generate action. As Gene Russianoff, staff attorney for the Straphangers Campaign, explained, "If riders don't want to pay a quarter more for each trip—and if they want better and safer subway service—then they should spend a quarter on a call to Governor Cuomo and Mayor Dinkins."[32]

Of course, it's important to coordinate your creative strategy with the medium you use. The Straphangers Campaign knew that mass-transit riders would have a lot of time to read their ads, so they used a generous amount of body copy. When you use billboards or other outdoor advertising vehicles, you have much less time to make an impression on your audience, so you need to say and show less. Consider how two nonprofit groups in Chicago used outdoor advertising to raise public consciousness and generate support for their causes. One group, protesting immigration rules that require proficiency in English, put up a billboard that read "Ningún Humano Es Illegal" ("No Human Is Illegal"). Another group used a billboard to respond to a city-funded educational ad about AIDS that showed a well-off white male saying, "I will not get AIDS. No matter what it takes." The billboard put up by the AIDS Coalition to Unleash Power (ACT UP) pictured people of various ages, genders, and races, and included copy that read: "AIDS doesn't discriminate. We demand AIDS treatment, education and support. No matter what it takes."[33]

Even though local political advertising is widely used, many people are concerned about its role in informing voters about candidates and issues. One concern is that voters will decide who to vote for on the basis of superficial or emotional messages that candidates can convey in 10 or 30 seconds, rather than on the basis of a careful and deliberate review of the candidates' records and qualifications. Another concern, addressed in this chapter's Ethics in Advertising box, is that the negative approach used by some local political advertisers will alienate voters. The governmental agencies that regulate product advertising have no control over political advertising, which is protected by the First Amendment of the U.S. Constitution. A move to ban or even regulate political advertising (no matter how misleading or dishonest the ads) would violate the Constitution. In the end, advertising has become so much a part of the political process that it's likely to remain a key if somewhat controversial tool for years.[34]

Local Media for Local Impact

Whether you're using local retail, local business, or local political advertising, you have a wide range of media options. For an integrated marketing communications approach in a multimedia campaign, it's important to be sure that the message in each medium is consistent with that in the other media. As you develop and implement a media strategy, your decisions will often depend on how much you can spend; however, as discussed in Chapter 13, cost isn't the only factor you should consider. Other factors include the ability to reach your target audience, the geographic coverage, the lead time for placing and changing ads, and any special services that will enhance your ad or streamline its production. In the following sections, you'll build on material presented in Chapters 14, 15, and 16 to see how local advertisers can best take advantage of print, electronic, and other media.

PRINT MEDIA

Many local advertisers use the print media (newspapers in particular are a favorite choice of retail advertisers) for several reasons. First, residents depend on the newspaper as the most trusted source for local news, so the editorial environment is a good match for ads about local stores and businesses (see Exhibit 19.10). Second, many people expect to check newspaper ads for local store sales or to get information about local political issues. Third, newspaper ads can be inserted or changed with only a few days' lead time, which means advertisers can act quickly when necessary. Fourth, a local advertiser can target its audience by placing ads in the zoned editions distributed within its local market (or the store's trading area) or in the appropriate newspaper sections. Little wonder that May Department Stores invested over $300 million in newspaper advertising in 1992.[35]

The Chicago branch of upscale toy retailer F.A.O. Schwarz is another believer in newspaper advertising, which it sees as a good way to reach both adults and children. During peak gift-giving seasons, the store advertises in the news section and other sections of the *Chicago Tribune* to reach adults who buy toys for children. In addition, to reach a target audience of youngsters aged 9 to 13, the store advertises in the KidNews section, a 12-page section that appears every Tuesday.[36]

EXHIBIT 19.10
Using Newspaper Advertising to Reach a Local Audience

Accountant Robert Felsenfeld used newspaper advertising to reach taxpayers in Southern California before the tax-filing deadline of April 15.

Local advertisers, especially local merchants, can also use *shoppers,* ad-filled publications that are distributed free, usually once a week, to residents throughout the local market. Although shoppers typically contain a few articles of general interest, they serve mainly as vehicles for classified and display advertising. Examples include local editions of the *PennySaver* guide, published in urban and suburban areas around the country, and *Little Nickel Want Ads,* a weekly shopper distributed in Snohomish County, Washington.

Magazines are an important part of the media mix for some local advertisers. Using the geographic and demographic selectivity of national magazines can help local advertisers reach local audiences with a colorful message in the right editorial environment. For example, local advertisers might choose from among *Time*'s 50 metropolitan editions as well as the magazine's 50 state editions.[37] Magazines with a local or regional focus, such as *Dallas Child* and *Chesapeake Bay Magazine,* are good vehicles for local retail advertisers seeking to reach local or specialized audiences. However, the lead time for magazine advertising is much longer than for newspapers or shoppers, so when local retailers use magazines, it's often for nonproduct or nonpromotional advertising.

In particular, advertising in specialized magazines can be a cost-efficient way for business advertisers (local and nonlocal) to reach their targets (see Exhibit 19.11). Because of the relatively low cost per exposure, the pinpoint accuracy in reaching the exact audience, and the creative flexibility, most business advertisers invest a lot of their ad budgets in specialized magazines, including the trade publications that serve their industry.

EXHIBIT 19.11
Comparing the Cost per Exposure to Reach Business Buyers

Of the many media that local advertisers can use to expose their audiences to promotional messages, specialized magazines offer the lowest cost.

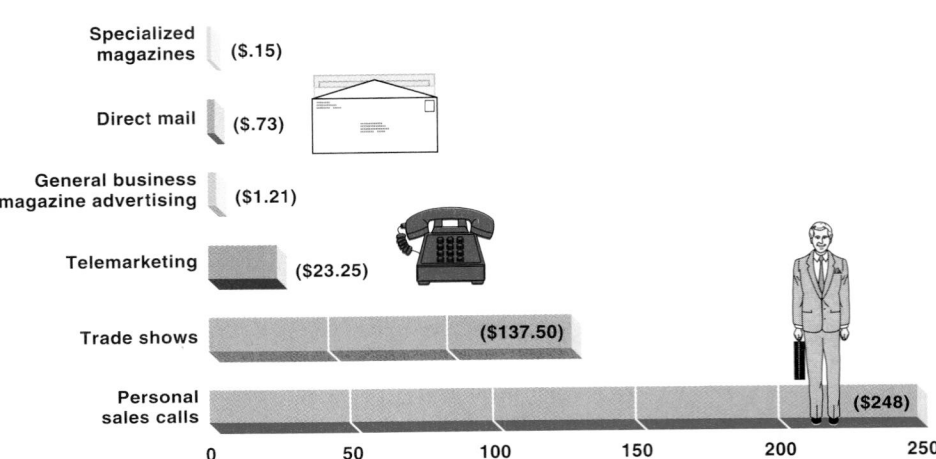

Specialized magazines	($.15)
Direct mail	($.73)
General business magazine advertising	($1.21)
Telemarketing	($23.25)
Trade shows	($137.50)
Personal sales calls	($248)

0   50   100   150   200   250

ELECTRONIC MEDIA

Both television and radio can be effective media for reaching local audiences. Commercial time on local television is relatively affordable (compared with national network rates), and local advertisers can reach a lot of people throughout their target markets by advertising on local stations or on local network affiliates. Television is usually used for consumer rather than business advertising, so its use for local business advertising may impress prospects (as well as current customers). For example, airing commercials during local news programs can help local businesses dazzle out-of-town buyers attending local trade shows.

Of course, television may not make sense for every local advertiser. Local businesses that need to reach a small or select target audience, for instance, may find television expensive and inefficient. "If only 15 percent to 20 percent of the viewers of a program are decision-makers, that's incredible waste," says Bruce Cashbaugh, senior vice president at Juhl Marketing Communications, an Indiana-based business advertising agency.[38]

However, the narrowcasting capabilities of cable television are providing new and effective avenues for local advertisers to reach particular audiences or geographic areas. When Keating Ford of Stratford, Connecticut, tried a single truck commercial on Southern Connecticut Cablevision, it quickly tripled its truck sales. The dealership added a second commercial that featured vans and cars, and bought more airtime. Within months, new car and truck sales skyrocketed (87 percent over the same period in the previous year), and vans sold out. The only change in Keating Ford's advertising schedule for the year was the addition of cable.[39]

Radio has been one of the mainstays of local advertising since its inception (see Exhibit 19.12). Radio time is extremely affordable, and ad production costs are much lower than those for television. What's more, local advertisers have more flexibility to make changes or add or pull commercials at the last minute because radio requires less lead time than television. Using local radio, local advertisers can target audiences not only by geographic location but also by lifestyle and interest.

EXHIBIT 19.12

Using Radio Advertising to Reach a Local Audience

Round Table Pizza uses local radio advertising to reach pizza lovers in Northern California. Appropriate sound effects work together with a humorous script in this good example of local radio advertising.

(SFX): chattering teeth
ANNOUNCER: Today's Round Table discussion comes to us from a Mrs. Susan Berry of Weaverville. She knows, like millions of others, that Round Table uses fresh dough instead of frozen dough. But she writes, simply, "Why?"—a fair question. Clearly, the only possible way on earth for me to illustrate this is to float around Antartica on an iceberg.

So here I am on an iceberg. And my teeth are chattering. I said my teeth are chattering. Brrrr. It's cold. These are roughly the temperatures other pizza places freeze their dough. In other words, their dough is frozen, this iceberg is frozen, thus their pizza must taste like this iceberg. So I'll just press my tongue against this iceberg. There, now which would you rather have, Mrs. Berry? A pizza made with dough that's frozen like this iceberg I'm stuck to . . .
(SFX): suction pop sound
ANNOUNCER: Ouch! That really hurts when you pull your tongue off an iceberg like that . . . or a hot and steamy Round Table Pizza made with fresh dough. Get real. Get Round Table. Get me off this iceberg!

In particular, many local business advertisers find they can reach a target audience of business managers by advertising on radio stations with all-news formats. Accountants Overload, a Los Angeles-based placement company that provides temporary and permanent financial service employees to local businesses, has been reaching its target audience of top executives, financial managers, and personnel managers since 1977 by advertising 52 weeks per year on KNX, the local all-news radio station. Similarly, many local businesses trying to reach buyers in the automotive industry reserve commercial time on WWJ, the Detroit all-news radio station. In addition, they often buy time during the evening news on WJR, a local music station. This program includes a 15-minute feature titled "Automotive Reports," which is especially popular with auto industry managers.[40]

OTHER MEDIA

As you're aware, local advertisers can use a variety of other media to get their messages to local audiences. No matter who their target audience or what their budget, local retailers, businesses, and political candidates should examine their media mix to add vehicles that can effectively communicate their message. In addition to the print and electronic media, other media commonly used by local advertisers are yellow pages directories, direct mail, and various out-of-home vehicles.

Yellow Pages Advertising

Few media are as local as the yellow pages, which can cover as small an area as a single neighborhood. In fact, a listing or a display ad in the local yellow pages is the only type of advertising that some small retailers and businesses use. With the wider availability of creative options such as two-, three-, and four-color printing, local advertisers are better able to grab the attention of people looking for nearby sources for goods and services. Most manufacturers and franchisors offer ad slicks or creative guidelines to help local advertisers design effective yellow pages ads (see Exhibit 19.13). However, as mentioned in Chapter 16, both the number and the diversity of directories have increased; in addition to more directories serving the same area, specialized directories such as business-to-business yellow pages are now available in many markets, which complicates the media buy.

Direct-Mail Advertising

Thanks to personal computers and good-quality printers, even local advertisers on a skinny budget can afford to reach their target audiences using direct mail. You don't have to have a gigantic budget to buy a suitable mailing list—or to request your customers' names and addresses so that you can notify them of sales and other promotions. If you aren't equipped to handle the mailings yourself, you can hire an outside firm. For example, Stan Golomb specializes in producing and mailing direct-mail pieces for more than 600 dry cleaners across the United States. At an average cost of 70 cents per envelope, these mailings have helped participating stores build customer loyalty and find new customers.[41] Alternatively, you can use *shared mail*, a direct-mail approach in which two or more local advertisers insert their messages in a single mailing that goes to selected ZIP codes in the local area. Advo Systems, one of the largest shared-mail vendors in the United States, specializes in teaming local advertisers with compatible (rather than competitive) partners for local shared-mail efforts.

Large local advertisers, like Von's (a California supermarket chain) and Dominick's Finer Foods (a Chicago food chain), have developed regular mailing schedules that allow them to tailor their direct-mail message to specific audiences. What's more, although most food retailers invest heavily in newspaper advertising, Dominick's has gone the other way, moving completely out of newspapers and into direct mail. "Direct-mail advertising is very effective in getting our sales message out to customer homes," says Rich Simpson, Dominick's director of public affairs.[42]

EXHIBIT 19.13
Local Retail Advertisers Find It in the Yellow Pages

Yellow pages advertising is one of the best ways of directing the local audience's attention to a particular source for goods or services. This ad for a shoe retailer prominently features the Birkenstock brand name and an illustration of one Birkenstock sandal. It also offers two reasons to visit the store and lets readers know the store hours, location, and phone number.

Out-of-Home Advertising

One of the simplest but most effective forms of out-of-home advertising for a local advertiser is signage. Local retailers, businesses, and political party or candidate headquarters can put signs over the door, in the window, on the roof, on an awning, or in other locations to catch the attention of passersby. In-store signs at Ikea and other retail establishments can be hung from the ceiling, mounted on the walls, propped on top of fixtures, or placed in sign holders near high-traffic locations to direct attention to particular departments, certain products, or special promotions (see Exhibit 19.14). In addition, local advertisers located in office buildings can use lobby signs to showcase their names and products.

When you need to act quickly, a low-cost way of getting your message to a local target audience is through the use of **handbills,** printed flyers or circulars that can be tacked up on community bulletin boards, distributed on the street, left on car windshields, or delivered door-to-door. Graphics and color can help your handbill stand out, but even the simplest flyer distributed at the right time in the right place can be effective; for example, you might advertise a one-day sale on a handbill that's distributed to shoppers as they enter the shopping center parking lot. Handbills can be printed and distributed in a short time if you're in a hurry to get a message out, such as announcing a candidate's position on some hot topic or responding to a competitor's price reduction. However, because the reproduction quality is generally poor, handbills are seen as throwaways by many recipients, so they may not be appropriate for advertising upscale goods and services—and some localities are moving to restrict or ban certain handbill distribution methods.

EXHIBIT 19.14
Store Signage

Out-of-home advertising such as store signage is useful for calling attention to particular products. This window sign invites PayLess Drug Store customers to visit the camera department to buy prepaid long-distance telephone cards.

Summary

Local advertising is important because it's the key to local results. Local retail, political, and business advertisers often use product-oriented and direct-action advertising to encourage an immediate and specific audience response. The copy in local ads tends to be longer and tends to include more specific incentives for action, mainly to give consumers a reason to select one advertiser over another. In contrast, the goal of national ads is to create a positive image for the brand name or for the advertiser.

Local retail advertisers commonly set three types of objectives: (1) to sell a particular item or product line, (2) to stimulate store traffic, or (3) to support a new-store opening. Local retail advertising relies on six formats, including (1) promotional, (2) semipromotional, (3) nonpromotional, (4) assortment, (5) omnibus, and (6) institutional. Cooperative ad programs used by local retail advertisers can be organized in two ways. In a supplier-controlled cooperative advertising program, the manufacturer or distributor creates ads that are customized with one or more retailers' names and places them in local media. In a customer-controlled cooperative advertising program, the supplier reimburses its customer (the retailer) for all or part of the retailers' advertising expenditures on certain products. Retailers like customer-controlled co-op programs because suppliers aren't forcing them to use ready-made ads.

Local business advertising is generally used to accomplish one or more of four specific objectives: (1) to build awareness, (2) to provide technical product information, (3) to generate sales leads, and (4) to support distribution-channel members. Creating local business advertising for technical as well as nontechnical audiences can be tricky. This is because technical audiences (such as engineers) need a lot of technical information to evaluate a product, whereas nontechnical audiences (such as people who are new to the field or managers who approve purchases but don't actually run the equipment) may find technical data dull, may be overwhelmed by the details, and

may therefore stop paying attention. For nontechnical audiences, business advertisers may have to minimize the technical language and use headlines to summarize the product's features and to play up key benefits.

Local political advertising is generally geared to two basic objectives: (1) to raise public awareness of some candidate or some issue and (2) to persuade people to take action. Although a campaign will sometimes aim to fulfill only one of these objectives, local political ads often seek both to raise awareness and to persuade. Local retail, business, and political advertisers can choose among a wide range of media options to reach their target audiences. The print media, including newspapers, shoppers, and magazines, are often used by local advertisers to reach local audiences. Among the electronic media, local advertisers usually choose local cable television, local broadcast television, and local radio. In addition to the print and electronic media, other media commonly used by local advertisers are yellow pages directories, direct mail, and various out-of-home media vehicles.

Key Terms

ad slicks 523
agricultural advertising 525
bait-and-switch advertising 522
customer-controlled cooperative advertising program 523
dealer tag 523
handbills 535
industrial advertising 525
local business advertising 517
local political advertising 517
local retail advertising 517
monthly promotional calendar 519
professional advertising 525
supplier-controlled cooperative advertising program 523
trade advertising 525

Meeting an Advertising Challenge at Ikea

A CASE FOR CRITICAL THINKING

Introducing Ikea to two entirely different markets—several months and 3,000 miles apart—was the advertising challenge that Anders Moberg faced in 1990. Despite the success of the chain's first four U.S. outlets, Moberg knew that the grand openings in Elizabeth, New Jersey, and Burbank, California, were important stepping-stones to the heavily populated New York and Los Angeles metropolitan areas. The advertising had to build awareness of the store name and the retailing concept as well as attract store traffic. The Ikea president also realized that the two grand-opening campaigns couldn't be clones; each had to be carefully tailored to its local audience.

The first store opening, in Elizabeth, was scheduled for May 23. To reach a target audience of young adults and families, the retailer launched an integrated marketing communications campaign of print, television, billboard, transit, and direct-mail advertising before the store opened. For instance, billboards on the New Jersey Turnpike teased motorists with cryptic messages. One billboard read, "On May 23, find a place to crash on the Jersey Turnpike." Print ads used lots of copy to explain the headline "Why thousands will spend their Memorial Day vacation on the Jersey Turnpike." Topping off the ad blitz, Ikea mailed more than 1 million copies of its 200-page cata-

log to households within 40 miles of the new store.

While the preopening hoopla was going on, Ikea also kicked off a television campaign to support the chain's overall image. The commercials poked fun at the irritations of shopping at traditional furniture stores, such as high prices and delivery hassles. Still, the campaign didn't take itself too seriously; its tag line was "It's a big country. Someone's got to furnish it." The two campaigns started people talking about Ikea, and they helped bring people—by the thousands—to the store on opening day. During the first hour the Elizabeth store was open, 3,000 people surged through the doors; by the end of the first day, 25,000 had visited the store.

Once the Elizabeth store was open, Moberg could concentrate on the Burbank store opening, which was set for November 7. Sticking with a tongue-in-cheek creative approach, the retailer adjusted the media to the local market by relying more heavily on outdoor media, because Southern California is car country. So for six weeks before the new-store opening, slightly irreverent teaser ads appeared on 1,600 billboards, buses, and transit shelters around Los Angeles. These intriguing outdoor ads were designed to start people talking about the campaign. Passersby might look at one poster, for example, and wonder what could possibly have "more mass

appeal" than the Pope.

The suspense ended two weeks before the Burbank store opened, when Ikea added its store name and opening date to the posters. In addition to mailing catalogs to homes within an hour's drive, the retailer also used radio, television, newspaper, and magazine advertising to give more detail about the outlet's products, services, and location. Once again, a brief but intense preopening campaign brought results: the Burbank store's first day was another blockbuster. Despite the results of these new-store openings—which were grand by any standard—Moberg isn't about to take the U.S. market for granted. After all, it's a big country. Somebody's got to furnish it, and Anders Moberg is determined to see that Ikea gets the job.

Your Mission: *Cynthia Neiman, the marketing manager of Ikea West, has hired you to work on local advertising campaigns at the Burbank outlet. Your assignment is to battle competitors, to build store traffic, and to sell selected products. Use what you've learned about local retail advertising to choose the best option in each situation.*

1. Pier 1 Imports, a major competitor, recently started advertising its wide variety of international products. You

Questions

FOR REVIEW

1. How do supplier-controlled cooperative advertising programs operate? Customer-controlled cooperative advertising programs?

2. What six common formats can local retail advertisers choose among?

3. How do buying centers affect local business advertising?

4. What concerns have been raised about the use of local political advertising?

5. What factors should local advertisers consider when selecting local media?

FOR ANALYSIS AND APPLICATION

6. As a small one-store operation, would you want to be

included in a nationwide dealer list that's incorporated into a supplier-controlled cooperative advertisement? Why or why not?

7. What objectives might a campus club interested in putting a recycling referendum on the local ballot set for its local political advertising?

8. If you were opening a branch of a pet hospital in a neighboring town, how would you use local retail advertising to introduce the new branch to pet owners in the new market?

9. How might an accountant use local business advertising to generate sales leads for a tax preparation service?

10. What local media would you recommend a neighborhood Mail Boxes Etc. franchise use to reach local businesses that might use its packing, mailing, and copying services?

wonder whether your audience will be tempted to try Pier 1 because it sells items from many countries, whereas Ikea sells mainly Scandinavian-inspired items. Which retail advertising format would best help you combat this competitive threat?

a. Use the semipromotional format so you can show that Ikea offers good prices and a mix of sale and nonsale merchandise every day.

b. Use the nonpromotional format to stress Ikea's superior product quality and customer service.

c. Use the assortment format to emphasize your wide selection of products and the depth of choice in each product category.

2. After years of trying to sell European-sized beds, the chain recently switched to beds in standard U.S. sizes. Which headline do you think would play off the tone of Ikea's image advertising and entice people to the Burbank store to look at the new line of Swedish-style beds?

a. "Now you can sleep with a Swedish king (or a queen, full, or twin)."

b. "Now you can sleep in a bed designed in the land of the midnight sun."

c. "Come see Ikea's new line of Swedish-style beds, the best of the Old World available in the New World."

3. Stor, another competitor, also offers a huge product selection and provides many of the same amenities as Ikea. Watching a television talk show, you notice a commercial inviting viewers to the grand reopening of the newly enlarged Stor outlet near your Burbank location. What should you do?

a. Do nothing; Stor isn't advertising special prices or special products, so you don't have to, either. You can save your ad budget for other things.

b. Double the number of times your existing television ads run during the next four weeks, when Stor is likely to be advertising most heavily. This will cost-effectively keep the Ikea name in front of the target audience.

c. Create new commercials showing how Ikea is superior to Stor in terms of prices, assortment, and customer service. This is more costly than (b), but it's a good way to position Ikea as the market leader once and for all.

4. The average sale at the Burbank store isn't as high as at other Ikea outlets. How can you use advertising to increase the average sales amount?

a. Show complete rooms of home furnishings rather than isolated pieces in your print ads. This will encourage customers to buy more than one of the items they see pictured so they can get the same "finished" look at home.

b. Advertise large assortments of lower-priced accessories. Because the items aren't expensive, shoppers will be encouraged to buy several.

c. Show only expensive furniture in your ads. This will entice customers to buy those items, increasing the average sale amount.[43]

Sharpen Your Advertising Skills

Groceries, electronics, office supplies, and more—all under one roof and all at wholesale prices—that's the Pace warehouse-membership formula for retail success. More than 250 product categories can be found in the typical (and cavernous) Pace outlet, which looks more like a warehouse than a standard discount store. To be eligible for Pace's low prices, local businesses and consumers must become members, which means paying either a small annual fee or a surcharge on purchases. Although individuals do join, people who work for local businesses make up the bulk of Pace's membership. That's why the chain's promotional activities emphasize a target audience of local business owners and employees.

You're the Pace account executive at the firm's ad agency. Pace is opening a new outlet in Southern California. You have several objectives: you want to make local businesses aware that Pace is opening in their neighborhood, you want to explain the warehouse-membership concept, and you want to persuade both owners and employees to become members and shop at Pace. The grand-opening budget is limited, so you can't waste your ad dollars on media that have large nonlocal and nonbusiness audiences. At the same time, you must be able to explain your concept and the price breaks to people who aren't familiar with warehouse-membership retailing.

Decision: Which media should you use to reach local business owners? Consider the budget, the targeting capabilities, and the ability to explain the Pace concept. Recommend two or three media (not vehicles) to be used.

Communication: Write a two-page memo to Pace's advertising manager to suggest media for the grand-opening campaign. Explain why each medium is appropriate for reaching the target audience at the local level.

From Plan to Results: The Complete Campaign

After studying this chapter, you will be able to

1. Explain how situation analysis helps advertisers and agencies identify problems to be solved by the advertising campaign

2. Describe how to coordinate the communications objectives of national, regional, and local ad campaigns to pull the target audience through the buying process

3. Outline how an ad agency's creative director uses the situation analysis and the advertising objectives to draft a creative strategy

4. Explain how an agency develops a media plan to reach the target audience while staying within budget constraints

5. Discuss the role of advertising research in developing effective advertising messages

6. Show how an advertiser applies the concept of integrated marketing communications in a complete advertising campaign

7. Discuss how an advertiser evaluates the effectiveness of its ad campaign

Facing an Advertising Challenge at GMC Truck

STEERING TOWARD A STRONGER BRAND IMAGE

Do you have a Safari, Sierra, Sonoma, or Suburban in your garage? How about a Jimmy, Rally, Typhoon, or Yukon? If not, Eddie Messenger and George Wood want to park one there. Messenger is consumer influence manager and Wood is advertising manager for GMC Truck. Together, they're responsible for persuading people to buy utility trucks, sport-utility trucks, pickup trucks, truck wagons, and vans from GMC Truck dealers all over the United States.

GMC Truck is the smallest division of General Motors, the world's largest maker of automotive products. However, despite the global reach and reputation of its parent, the GMC Truck brand wasn't widely known among noncustomers. One challenge facing Wood and Messenger was to make more people aware that the company had been making trucks for more than 90 years. Founded as the Grabowsky Motor Vehicle Company in 1902, the firm was acquired by GM in 1909. Over the years, it has developed considerable expertise in the design and manufacture of trucks and utility vehicles. During World War I, the company built ambulances, troop carriers, and cargo haulers for the U.S. Army. During World War II, it built two vehicles for the U.S. military, including a 6 × 6 (six-wheel drive) cargo truck that was informally known as the "Jimmy." After phasing out these wartime models, the company began making trucks and vans for business and personal use.

A second challenge facing Messenger and Wood was the question of how to take advantage of the changing purchasing patterns of car, truck, and van buyers. One trend influencing buyers was a growing interest in off-road excursions; a second trend was a growing appetite for cargo and passenger space. People who would have chosen traditional passenger cars in the past were now considering roomier, more rugged alternatives. As a result, trucks and vans that were once seen only in rural settings or on construction sites started to accelerate into the mainstream of city and suburban life. Individual buyers liked these vehicles' outdoorsy looks and go-everywhere capabilities; family buyers liked their strength and spacious interiors.

In addition to low brand awareness and marketplace changes, Messenger and Wood faced another major challenge: competition from such high-profile rivals as Ford, Chrysler, and Toyota. If you were Messenger and Wood, what steps would you take to analyze the competition and understand your products' strengths and weaknesses? Who would you select as your target audience, and how would you position your products? How would you mount an advertising campaign to raise audience awareness of the GMC Truck brand? Where would you place ad messages to most effectively communicate with your audience?[1]

CHAPTER OVERVIEW As the marketing and advertising professionals at GMC Truck know, bringing a product line to the attention of potential buyers through a coordinated set of advertising messages in many media isn't an overnight process. Planning, implementing, and evaluating a complete advertising campaign can take months and sometimes years from start to finish—with adjustments in between to keep up with market changes. In this chapter, you'll see how GMC Truck and its advertising agency, McCann/SAS, worked together to develop a new advertising campaign. The client and agency started with two key planning steps: analyzing the current situation and understanding the competition. Next, they set the campaign strategy, including establishing the brand position, selecting audience segments, defining advertising objectives, determining the creative and the media strategies, and using research to assess the audience's reaction to the campaign. After producing all advertisements, sales promotion items, and public relations materials, the partners stepped back to evaluate the campaign. Start to finish, the process required more than a year and a multimillion-dollar investment. The results were well worth the effort.

Planning the Complete Advertising Campaign

An advertiser and its agency rarely concentrate on stand-alone ad messages. Instead, like GMC Truck and McCann/SAS, they prepare a complete campaign, a program of related ads designed to promote a specific product or brand during a particular period (see Exhibit 20.1). A small campaign—for a local advertiser or a

"As a matter of fact, I do own the road."

Seeing it suddenly advancing in the rearview mirror, drivers of lesser vehicles instinctively feel about and surrender the passing lane.

Eighteen feet long, with five tons of towing power,* three available V8 choices, a 42-gallon fuel tank, 4-wheel ABS and an interior equally comfortable and expansive, the GMC Suburban is an uncompromisingly capable presence on any terrain, a vehicle that is equal parts enlightened engineering and sheer, unbounded practicality. And the epitome of a truck company's way of looking at the world.

A call to 1-800-GMC-TRUCK (1-800-462-8782) will bring you a catalog of the indomitable Suburban. Your change of attitude awaits you.

*When properly equipped including trailer, passenger, cargo and equipment.

GMC, GMC Truck and Suburban are registered trademarks of General Motors Corp. © 1992 GM Corp. All Rights Reserved. Buckle up, America!

GMC TRUCK

THE STRENGTH OF EXPERIENCE

EXHIBIT 20.1
The GMC Truck Campaign

The print component of the GMC Truck campaign featured in this chapter included five advertisements. Although each focused on a different model, all included the distinctive red GMC Truck logo and the tagline "The Strength of Experience" in the lower righthand corner.

nonprofit organization—may include only a few ads run in one medium; in many cases, a campaign includes a series of ads placed in several media over the course of weeks, months, or even years. By coordinating these ads with other tools such as public relations and sales promotion, companies such as GMC Truck can create a solid foundation of integrated marketing communications to bring the ad message to every target audience they need to reach.

Depending on the advertiser's objectives, a campaign may use one medium or several media; it may run for only a few days or for several years. As mentioned in Chapter 15, the Faces Model Agency of New Orleans used a short-term campaign in two media to achieve a short-term objective. The agency wanted to bring 300 contestants to a one-day talent search, so it created one newspaper ad and one radio commercial with the theme "This is your chance to be discovered." These ads ran only during the week before the contest, but they helped the advertiser exceed its objective. On the day of the talent search, 570 people showed up.[2]

On the other hand, when an advertiser's objective is long term rather than short term, its campaign is likely to run far longer. Look at the "Do you know me?" campaign for American Express, which ran on television for 11 years. This campaign was designed to reinforce the prestige of the American Express Card and to encourage people to apply for it. The various commercials in the campaign featured people who were famous in their own industries but weren't necessarily recognized when they visited hotels and restaurants—which is why they used the American Express Card.[3]

However, American Express research showed that consumers' values were changing. To stay in tune with this change, American Express and its agency, Ogilvy & Mather, launched another lengthy campaign. In this campaign, titled "Membership has its privileges," the long-term objective of conveying the card's prestige was modified to include the idea that personal values and achievements are important. The print component of this campaign (known as "Portraits"), which ran for years in the United States, Germany, and other countries, included photographic portraits of celebrities such as Mary Steenburgen and Yo Yo Ma, American Express cardholders who were famous for their achievements. While it ran, this campaign outperformed all the objectives that American Express set for increasing awareness, building public perception of the product, and increasing card applications.[4]

Of course, no two campaigns are alike, simply because no two advertisers find themselves in the same situation. In addition, as American Express's experience demonstrates, even a successful campaign may need to be modified or replaced after a time. That's why an advertiser must look carefully at the current situation when developing a marketing plan, which in turn is used to guide the new ad campaign. In the following sections, you'll see how GMC Truck and its agency developed a new advertising campaign.

ANALYZING THE CURRENT SITUATION

The first step was to take stock of the current situation and the competitive environment through a situation analysis. When advertisers such as GMC Truck conduct an analysis to understand their current situation, they carefully examine a variety of internal factors, including the organization's capabilities, resources, profitability, and track record. In addition, no situation analysis would be complete without a look at the external factors that can affect performance. These include product image, market growth, competitive pressures, and changes in buyer needs and tastes. As discussed in Chapter 7, a situation analysis can be organized by following the SWOT structure of strengths, weaknesses, opportunities, and threats. Strengths and weaknesses arise from internal factors, whereas opportunities and threats arise from external factors.

As they conducted the situation analysis, marketers at GMC Truck and their counterparts at McCann/SAS looked at internal and external factors for every product. They also examined the company's overall situation to understand the strengths, weaknesses, opportunities, and threats that would influence the direction of the new ad campaign and all product advertising under the umbrella of the campaign theme.

The analysis of GMC Truck's internal capabilities pointed out four key strengths. One was its 90 years' experience in the design and manufacture of trucks. GMC Truck's record of making *only* trucks and vans for nine decades was unrivaled in the industry. In fact, the company's singular focus was a second important strength. It reflected the company's long-term commitment to truck and van products, which was in contrast to competitors that had to spread their resources across car, van, and truck lines. A third strength was, quite literally, the physical strength of GMC Truck products. With its background in engineering and production, GMC Truck had learned how to make a truck that would stand up to its customers' toughest requirements. A fourth strength was the firm's new product offerings. Typhoon, Yukon, and other new models incorporated state-of-the-art features as well as stylish exteriors, comfortable interiors, and outstanding performance.

GMC Truck also had several weaknesses. First, marketing research showed that many truck buyers didn't even know that GMC Truck existed. This posed a real problem, because prospects who weren't aware of the brand wouldn't consider it when planning a purchase. Second, the advertiser had gone through a series of relatively short-lived campaigns. In fact, GMC Truck ads had featured nine separate themes in 11 years. As a result of this rapid change, the advertiser had been unable to establish a strong brand image, so customers and prospects who were aware of GMC Truck were confused about what the brand stood for.[5] Moreover, General Motors, the parent company, finished 1990 and 1991 with heavy losses; this led to plant closings and personnel changes as well as a squeeze on the resources available to the GMC Truck division.[6]

At the same time, GMC Truck could take advantage of some exciting opportunities. The public's growing interest in off-road exploration—and its demand for more cargo and passenger space—made sport-utility trucks, light trucks, and vans attractive alternatives to conventional cars. Sales of trucks, minivans, and sport-utility vehicles had jumped from roughly 20 percent of all the vehicles sold in the United States in 1981 to nearly 35 percent by 1991. Singles and families alike were now considering trucks and trucklike vehicles for everyday use. Sales of extended-cab pickups (with expanded passenger seating) and compact sport-utility trucks were steadily rising, creating an opportunity for GMC Truck to make more sales in those categories.[7]

However, several threats had to be considered. One was the negative publicity generated by product liability suits, government investigations, and media coverage related to allegations about the safety of the fuel tanks on older GMC Truck pickups. Although the design of the fuel tanks had long since been changed, continuing litigation was keeping the issue in front of the public. Coupled with the possibility of plunging resale values for GMC Truck pickups, this threat had the potential of damaging the brand's reputation with customers and prospects alike.[8] Another threat to consider was the competitive pressure being applied by domestic and international rivals.

UNDERSTANDING THE COMPETITION

Apart from Chevrolet (another GMC division), GMC Truck faced a number of tough competitors in the truck and van market, including Ford, Chrysler, and Toyota. Of the three, Ford was the most formidable opponent, largely because its market share in 1991 was more than three times that of GMC Truck. Whereas GMC Truck's unit sales totaled just over 300,000 units during the 1991 model year, Ford's unit sales were considerably higher: In pickup trucks alone, it sold nearly 700,000 units during the 1991 model year. Ford's F Series pickups, its Bronco sport-utility vehicle, and its Ranger compact pickup were consistent market leaders. In addition, in the fiercely competitive category of compact sport-utility vehicles, the Ford Explorer's 1991 share of the market was 27 percent, way ahead of models made by GMC Truck, Chrysler, and eight other competitors. In fact, the Ford Explorer was the first sport-utility vehicle to make the top 10 list of best-selling vehicles in the United States.[9]

What's more, Ford's $100 million annual advertising budget for trucks and vans was far more than GMC Truck's advertising budget. Calling its trucks "Ford Tough," the firm had exposed its audience to nearly three decades of torture-test advertising designed to demonstrate the toughness of Ford trucks. In one memorable commercial, Ford sent a truck parachuting out of a plane toward the desert floor; right after the vehicle hit the ground, a driver stepped in, started the engine, and drove away.[10] Although Ford had come out of 1991 reporting huge losses, its market share and advertising clout kept the firm a potent competitive force (see Exhibit 20.2).

GMC Truck was also feeling competitive heat from Chrysler, which had all but created the minivan market. Despite its large losses in 1991 (on top of losses in 1990), Chrysler had invested $160 million to advertise vans and trucks during that year. In particular, the company was looking to regain ground in the market for sport-utility vehicles. Chrysler's Jeep Cherokee had once dominated that market; over time, however, the Cherokee had lost ground to Ford's Explorer. By 1991 the Cherokee's share of market was slightly less than half the share that the Explorer enjoyed. Hoping to reclaim the market, Chrysler had spent $40 million in 1992 to advertise the upscale Jeep Grand Cherokee. In addition, the company raised the level of competition in full-size pickups when it launched its redesigned Dodge Ram with a $40 million multimedia ad blitz in 1993.[11]

Toyota, GMC Truck's third major competitor, was financially stronger than its domestic counterparts, and it maintained a sizable ad budget. During 1991, Toyota had spent more than $78 million promoting its light trucks and vans. Its U.S. sales of pickup trucks trailed way behind those of Ford but were close to the unit sales of GMC Truck and Chrysler during the 1991 model year. In the sport-utility market,

YOUNG COUPLE DRESSING ON A SATURDAY MORNING.

MAN: So, what are we doing today?

WOMAN: I'd like to go . . . buy some flowers. (She visualizes loading flowers into the back of the Explorer at the flower mart.)

MAN: Oh, I know a place we can . . . go by some flowers. (He visualizes driving the Explorer through fields of wildflowers.)

WOMAN: Great, then maybe the theatre . . . to catch something? (She visualizes

arriving at the curb in front of the theatre in the Explorer.)

MAN: Yeah . . . catch something. (He visualizes fishing in a stream.)

WOMAN: And then I thought a nice candle-light dinner. (She visualizes romantic dinner.)

MAN: Yeah . . . candlelight dinner. (He visualizes the two of them roasting hot dogs over the campfire.)

V.O.: Ford Explorer. The world's just too big to be left unexplored.

EXHIBIT 20.2
How Ford Advertises the Explorer

Ford's Explorer model is the sales leader among compact sport-utility vehicles. During the 1993 model year, when this television commercial appeared, Ford held a 28.8 percent share of the truck and van market, compared with GMC Truck's share of 7.3 percent.

the Toyota 4-Runner, the Jimmy and other GMC truck models, the Jeep Cherokee, and the Ford Explorer were all contenders in the race for sales.[12]

Setting the Campaign Strategy

After the situation analysis is complete, the next step is to develop the campaign strategy, which builds on the information gathered in the situation analysis and on both the marketing objectives and the marketing strategy. GMC Truck's marketing objectives included market-share goals that, in turn, guided manufacturing plans and advertising efforts for the brand overall and for individual models. To meet these objectives, the GMC Truck marketers determined their overall approach to positioning and then expanded on the positioning statement as necessary for each audience segment and for each model in the line.

BRAND POSITION

As GMC Truck and McCann/SAS looked at the results of their situation analysis and reviewed their competitors' positions, they realized that the experience gained from the company's specialization in trucks differentiated the advertiser from its rivals. They decided to use this experience as the basis for positioning GMC Truck as a brand name that truck and van buyers can trust.

At the same time, GMC Truck wanted to emphasize its expertise in making strong products. Strength was a meaningful attribute to truck and van buyers, who wanted a tough product that could stand up to off-road use and heavy cargo loads. The "tough" positioning wasn't new; other brands had positioned themselves as tough by using phrases such as "Ford Tough" and by airing ads that showed their products performing under torturous conditions. However, by linking its years of experience with the idea that its products were virtually invincible, GMC Truck could occupy a unique position in the minds of its target audience.

Once potential buyers started to think of GMC Truck as an experienced maker of strong products, they still needed a reason to choose GMC Truck over competing brands. The advertiser and agency decided to use advertising to convey the package of value that buyers gained by choosing GMC Truck products. Ideally, buyers would perceive GMC Truck as offering exceptional value for the money, based on the company's many years of experience as well as the specific quality, design, engineering, and packaging attributes that its products offered.

AUDIENCE SEGMENTS

As a result of what they'd learned in the situation analysis, GMC Truck and McCann/SAS decided to target two main audience segments. The first segment was traditional truck buyers. Using the PRIZM geodemographic system (described in Chapter 5), the agency targeted groups of people who fit the profile of a traditional truck buyer by focusing on neighborhoods such as Young Suburbia, Agri-business, and Blue Chip Blues. Some of these people were loyal GMC Truck customers who knew and trusted the brand. However, many in the segment didn't know the brand or what it stands for, so when these people were ready to make a purchase, they didn't consider GMC Truck.

The second segment consisted of upscale buyers, primarily people in their mid-forties, who have the money to live distinctive lifestyles. These people want (and are willing to pay for) quality, and they tend to be attracted to powerful vehicles. When they make a purchase, they evaluate their alternatives logically and thoroughly; they often favor imported over domestic vehicles. These buyers were identified by the PRIZM system as people who tended to be clustered in neighborhoods such as Furs & Station Wagons. In reaching out to these consumer segments, GMC Truck was looking to expand its customer base and take advantage of the market opportunities uncovered in the situation analysis.[13]

What GMC Truck and its agency *didn't* want, however, was to alienate traditional buyers as they pursued upscale buyers. Both audience segments were important as the advertiser geared up for higher sales. In particular, the upscale buyers were important prospects for compact sport-utility vehicles. In this fast-growing market, GMC Truck's Jimmy competed for a share of sales expected to reach 800,000 units annually by the year 2000.

To better address the specific needs of buyers in this market, GMC Truck targeted two specific audience segments. The first, dubbed the "Go Anywhere Personal Sporty" segment, was more interested in styling. This group wanted a fun-to-drive truck with a distinctive look and sporty styling. The second, which the marketers called the "Go Anywhere Family Fun" segment, cared more about convenience. These potential buyers wanted more passenger and cargo room. They were also interested in off-road recreation for family fun.

ADVERTISING OBJECTIVES

As you saw in Chapter 7, the advertising objectives for a particular campaign are derived from the marketing objectives. To support the overall marketing objective of increasing market share, GMC Truck and McCann/SAS agreed on the communication objective for the national advertising campaign: to increase awareness of the brand (rather than individual products) among members of the target audience. Once people became aware of GMC Truck and were more familiar with what the brand stands for and what products are being offered, they would be more likely to put it on the list of brands they consider when planning a purchase.

Like all automotive advertisers, GMC Truck communicated with its target audience through three levels of advertising. At the national level, the company advertised to build overall awareness, familiarity, and consideration. At the regional level, dealer groups advertised to increase consideration and to get the brand onto consumer shopping lists through preference. At the local level, individual dealers advertised to motivate consumers to take action and buy *now*. GMC Truck's national agency, McCann/SAS, was also responsible for the advertising placed by 18 of the 170 regional dealer ad groups.[14] By coordinating the advertising objectives, strategies, and tactics on all three levels, GMC Truck and its dealers could present a seamless program of integrated marketing communications to more effectively move consumers through the six stages from awareness to purchase.

CREATIVE STRATEGY

Armed with the client's advertising objectives, McCann/SAS was ready to formulate its creative strategy for the new national campaign. First, agency executives developed a comprehensive copy platform (which McCann-Erickson refers to as the "Creative Contract") to guide its creative staff. This document outlined relevant information about the brand, the target audience, buyer behavior, brand loyalty, and consumer perceptions of the GMC Truck brand. It also detailed what specific action the advertiser wanted the audience to take as a result of the advertising—and any issues that might block this desired behavior, such as external market factors, habit, or attitudes. Finally, the copy platform indicated what the agency wanted people to *think* and *feel* about the brand.

Taking into consideration both the copy platform and the brand's positioning, the agency proposed the theme "Strength of Experience" to guide the campaign's creative direction and to serve as a foundation for all ongoing promotional activities. This theme, which ultimately became the name of the campaign as well as its tag line, reflected GMC Truck's heritage as a truck manufacturer, the strength of GMC Truck's vehicles, and the value of buying from a company with nine decades of experience. Research showed that truck strength was more important to consumers than truck experience, so the agency set as its creative objective the need to communicate truck strength.

At the same time, McCann/SAS knew that GMC Truck wasn't a prominent brand. To capture and maintain the attention of the target audience, the brand's advertising would have to be especially memorable, incorporating the kind of creativity that people would remember and talk about. Agency executives also believed that the creative approach would need both a sense of wit and an air of intelligence to reach the upscale audience segment. In short, GMC Truck advertising couldn't appear to be like the ads created by its competitors, because it had to differentiate the GMC Truck brand and invite the audience to participate in the message communication.

MEDIA STRATEGY

Media strategy is no less important than creative strategy. As you saw in Chapter 13, media strategy is usually developed at the same time as creative strategy. In more and more cases, the media strategy comes first, as a way of identifying how and when to reach the audience most effectively. The choice of media then determines the direction of the creative strategy. Of course, the size of the advertising budget is also a consideration. If the client can't afford to foot the bill for producing and airing commercials, it's a waste of time to include television in the media strategy.

For GMC Truck, McCann/SAS proposed using both television and print ads to communicate the campaign theme "Strength of Experience." The creative approach would take advantage of the unique qualities of each medium. On television, the theme would be exemplified through dramatic demonstrations of truck strength and capabilities. No other medium could capture the excitement and authenticity of such demonstrations—or have the needed stopping power that television's sound, motion, and color could lend to GMC Truck's advertising. In line with the campaign theme, each commercial would include the tag line "The Strength of Experience."

In print, the theme would be communicated more subtly, through ads focusing on particular elements that relate to the performance, strength, and value of individual GMC Truck models. To attract the reader's attention, the headlines would dominate the ads; both headline and copy would use language with an *attitude,* reflecting what truck and van owners think and feel about driving their vehicles. Although each ad would feature a different model, all would include the GMC Truck logo and the tag line "The Strength of Experience" to unify the ads as a series and to tie the print portion of the campaign to the television commercials.

In preparing the media schedule for GMC Truck advertising, the media planners at McCann/SAS considered the timing of new-model introductions, peak buying periods, and the media habits of the audience segments being targeted. In their search for specific media vehicles that members of the target audience are exposed to, agency personnel were able to identify more than 35 magazines that reach the upscale audience segment (see Exhibit 20.3). They arranged to rotate

	Jan				Feb				Mar					Apr				May					June			
Monday Dates	28	4	11	18	25	1	8	15	22	1	8	15	22	29	5	12	19	26	3	10	17	24	31	7	14	21
PRINT SCHEDULE																										
Time									SUB						YUK						SAF					
Newsweek								JIM					SUB					SAF							YUK	
U.S. News & World Report						SAF							YUK								SUB					
Natural History											SAF									JIM						
Travel & Leisure							JIM								SUB										SAF	
Architectural Digest												JIM								SUB						
The New Yorker									YUK						SAF						SUB					
Rolling Stone									JIM					YUK							SAF					
Bon Appetit											JIM									YUK						
Food & Wine							JIM								SUB										YUK	
Smithsonian											JIM									SUB						
Discover						SAF									JIM									SUB		
Scientific American											JIM													SUB		
Omni		JIM									SAF									SUB						
Ski		SAF					JIM				SAF															
Skiing		SAF					JIM																			
Golf							SAF								YUK									SUB		
Tennis		JIM													YUK											
Golf Digest											JIM									SUB					YUK	
Motor Boating & Sailing							SAF																			
Inc.											JIM									YUK					SAF	
Kiplinger's Personal Finance						SAF									SUB											
Money											JIM									YUK						
Forbes									SUB					YUK				SAF				YUK		SUB		SAF
Fortune								JIM			SAF												YUK			

JIM - Jimmy Spread 4/CB   SAF - Safari Spread 4/CB   SUB - Suburban Spread 4/CB   YUK - Yukon Spread 4/CB   SIE - Sierra Spread 4/CB

EXHIBIT 20.3
GMC Truck's Media Plan

In the media plan that McCann/SAS developed for GMC Truck, a continuity schedule kept GMC Truck advertisements in front of the target audience throughout the year. This six-month segment of the 1993 plan shows that at least one GMC Truck ad ran every week, in magazines or on television or in both media.

the model ads placed in the magazines they selected, which included *Architectural Digest, Ski,* and *Business Week.* So the *Ski* reader who saw the Safari ad in the January issue would see the Jimmy ad in the February issue. All the print ads would be similar in look, attitude, and copy, so they would be able to convey their individual messages and at the same time contribute to the unity of the overall campaign.

GMC Truck's advertising budget was relatively modest, so the agency bypassed the broadcast networks and booked time for the commercials to air on four cable networks (A&E, CNN, CNBC, and Discovery). The media experts also arranged for GMC Truck to participate in sponsoring the *Jimmy Rogers Show* and *Truckin' USA,* two cable television programs. Finally, they reserved participation for NBA and NFL sports events as well as other sports programs airing on the Turner Broadcasting System.

ADVERTISING RESEARCH

In the course of planning the GMC Truck campaign, McCann/SAS conducted advertising research to determine how people from the two targeted audience segments reacted to proposed messages, specific copy points, and creative approaches. First, the agency tested three proposed campaign concepts in a series of focus groups. The participants, drawn from samples of traditional truck buyers and upscale buyers, were shown three sets of storyboards and asked to react to the

	Jan				Feb				Mar					Apr				May					June			
Monday Dates	28	4	11	18	25	1	8	15	22	1	8	15	22	29	5	12	19	26	3	10	17	24	31	7	14	21
PRINT SCHEDULE																										
Financial World										SUB				JIM								SAF				
Esquire						JIM														YUK				SUB		
Men's Journal												JIM									YUK					
Car & Driver		JIM																							YUK	
Car & Driver 1993 Truck Guide																			SAF							
Road & Track										JIM																
RT Track & Van Buyers Guide																			SUB							
Automobile						SAF					JIM									YUK						
Motor Trend						JIM									SUB											
MT Truck & Van Buyers Guide																			SIE							
Autoweek		SAF				YUK															YUK		YUK			
NETWORK/CABLE																										
A&E																										
CNN																										
CNBC																										
Discovery																										
Turner Golf																										
Turner NBA/NFL																										
Truckin' USA																										
TCI																										
Jimmy Rogers																										

JIM - Jimmy Spread 4/CB   SAF - Safari Spread 4/CB   SUB - Suburban Spread 4/CB   YUK - Yukon Spread 4/CB   SIE - Sierra Spread 4/CB

messages and the way they were conveyed. Of the three campaigns, "Strength of Experience" was judged the strongest. Participants liked the way this campaign expressed the physical strength of the trucks and the manufacturer's integrity and support. They also liked the humor in the storyboards they were shown.

One of the storyboards being tested was a proposed commercial showing the Jimmy running off a cliff and being suspended in air by a cable attached to the truck's trailer hitch. Participants found that this ad conveyed a sense of adventure in a fresh, dramatic, and creative way. They told research personnel that the ad did a good job of communicating the Jimmy's frame strength. However, some wondered whether the body would withstand the impact along with the frame—and some questioned the practical implications for the message they perceived the ad to be delivering.

Next, the agency conducted a series of focus groups to pretest animatics of three proposed television campaigns. As before, half the participants were traditional truck buyers and half were upscale buyers. The researchers wanted to study how well each campaign communicated the brand image of "a name you can trust" and "good value." In addition, they wanted to test each campaign's attention-getting power and check that the commercials were attractive to upscale buyers without alienating traditional buyers. The results of this research helped McCann/SAS and GMC Truck make final decisions about the campaign's content and planned media weight.

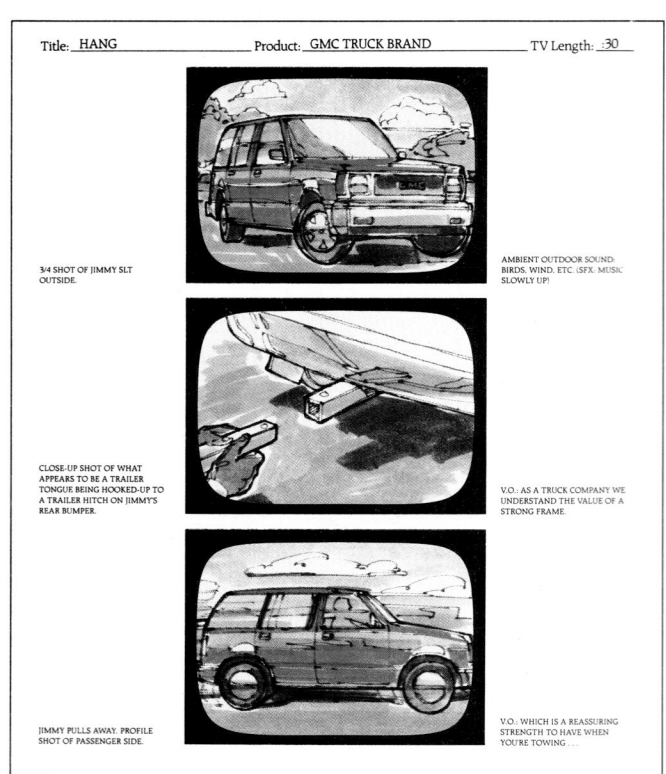

EXHIBIT 20.4
The "Hang" Storyboard

Before McCann/SAS could produce the "Hang" commercial, GMC Truck officials had to review and approve this storyboard showing the creative approach to be used.

Producing the Complete Advertising Campaign

With the advertising research completed, the agency was ready to produce final versions of two commercials and five print ads. This was also the time to arrange sales promotion materials for the new campaign and to prepare ads that dealer groups or individual dealers could place in supplementary media.

ELECTRONIC MEDIA

McCann/SAS produced two 30-second commercials for the "Strength of Experience" campaign. One was the commercial (called "Hang") in which the Jimmy was sent bungee jumping from the New River Gorge Bridge to demonstrate the vehicle's frame strength. As discussed in Chapter 12, producing this commercial was anything but routine. From preproduction to postproduction took about four months.

At the outset, GMC Truck had to approve the budget and sign off on the storyboard (see Exhibit 20.4). During preproduction, McCann/SAS and Fahrenheit Films consulted with GMC Truck engineers about the Jimmy's ability to survive a bungee jump, about the effects on the bridge of such a stunt, and about the construction of the bungee cord. The agency and the production company conducted drop tests to determine exactly what to expect when they dropped the truck from the bridge, and they built in safeguards that would protect the bridge in the unlikely event of a problem.

Scouting a location took time, as well. The agency selected the New River Gorge Bridge because of the look of the bridge and the scenery around it. Before filming, agency personnel had to get permission from officials in the state of West Virginia, who had questions about possible safety problems and bridge damage. The agency also provided proof that the Jimmy was a standard model and hadn't been altered in any way (with the exception of draining all fluids for environmental

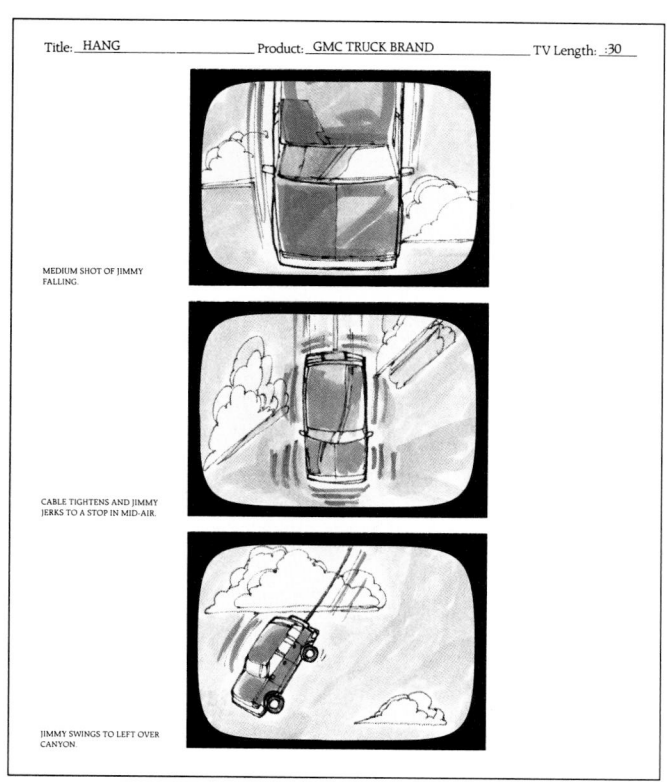

Title: __HANG__   Product: __GMC TRUCK BRAND__   TV Length: __:30__

MEDIUM SHOT OF JIMMY FALLING.

CABLE TIGHTENS AND JIMMY JERKS TO A STOP IN MID-AIR.

JIMMY SWINGS TO LEFT OVER CANYON.

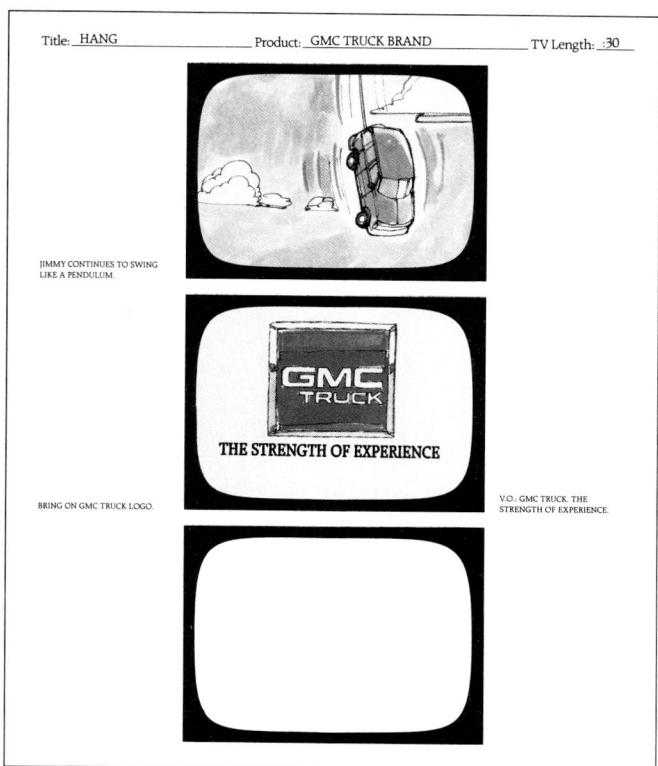

Title: __HANG__   Product: __GMC TRUCK BRAND__   TV Length: __:30__

JIMMY CONTINUES TO SWING LIKE A PENDULUM.

THE STRENGTH OF EXPERIENCE

BRING ON GMC TRUCK LOGO.

V.O.: GMC TRUCK. THE STRENGTH OF EXPERIENCE.

safety reasons). Following the script approved by GMC Truck (see Exhibit 20.5), the Fahrenheit Films crew set up on location in West Virginia and filmed the bungee-jumping sequence.

During postproduction, McCann/SAS added a rock music track and sound effects. One reason for the sound effects was to intrigue viewers and people who

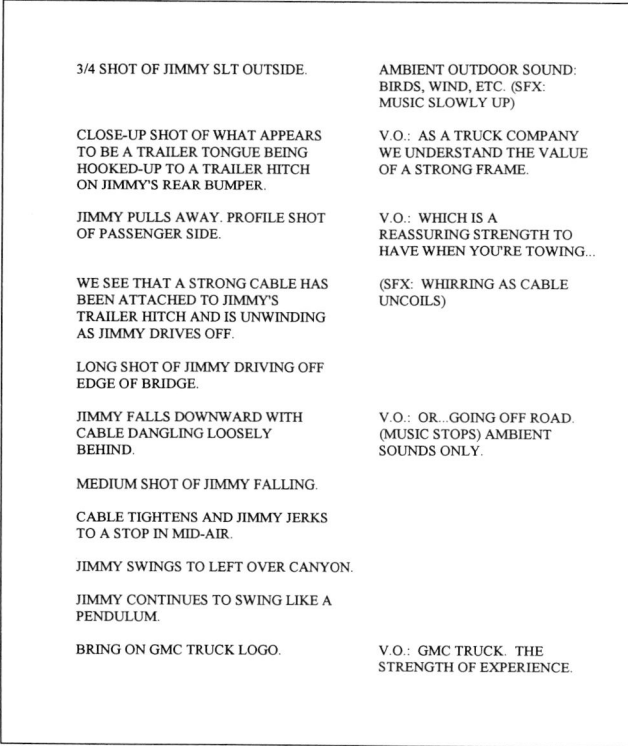

EXHIBIT 20.5
The "Hang" Script

After GMC Truck management approved the "Hang" storyboard, McCann/SAS developed this script (also approved by GMC Truck) to guide the production of the commercial.

3/4 SHOT OF JIMMY SLT OUTSIDE.	AMBIENT OUTDOOR SOUND: BIRDS, WIND, ETC. (SFX: MUSIC SLOWLY UP)
CLOSE-UP SHOT OF WHAT APPEARS TO BE A TRAILER TONGUE BEING HOOKED-UP TO A TRAILER HITCH ON JIMMY'S REAR BUMPER.	V.O.: AS A TRUCK COMPANY WE UNDERSTAND THE VALUE OF A STRONG FRAME.
JIMMY PULLS AWAY. PROFILE SHOT OF PASSENGER SIDE.	V.O.: WHICH IS A REASSURING STRENGTH TO HAVE WHEN YOU'RE TOWING...
WE SEE THAT A STRONG CABLE HAS BEEN ATTACHED TO JIMMY'S TRAILER HITCH AND IS UNWINDING AS JIMMY DRIVES OFF.	(SFX: WHIRRING AS CABLE UNCOILS)
LONG SHOT OF JIMMY DRIVING OFF EDGE OF BRIDGE.	
JIMMY FALLS DOWNWARD WITH CABLE DANGLING LOOSELY BEHIND.	V.O.: OR...GOING OFF ROAD. (MUSIC STOPS) AMBIENT SOUNDS ONLY.
MEDIUM SHOT OF JIMMY FALLING.	
CABLE TIGHTENS AND JIMMY JERKS TO A STOP IN MID-AIR.	
JIMMY SWINGS TO LEFT OVER CANYON.	
JIMMY CONTINUES TO SWING LIKE A PENDULUM.	
BRING ON GMC TRUCK LOGO.	V.O.: GMC TRUCK. THE STRENGTH OF EXPERIENCE.

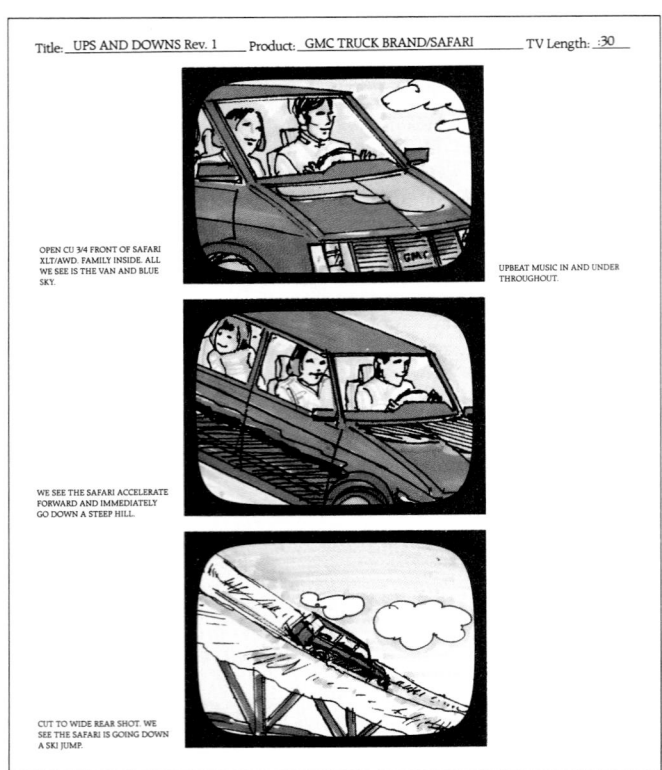

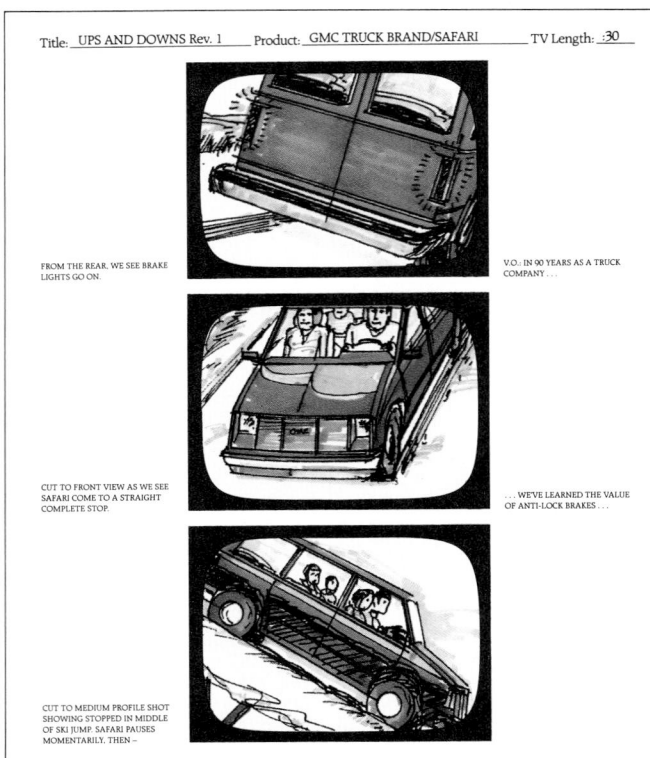

EXHIBIT 20.6
The "Ups and Downs" Storyboard

As they had with the "Hang" commercial, GMC Truck management reviewed and approved the "Ups and Downs" storyboard and projected budget before McCann/SAS started production.

weren't watching but could hear the commercial. The agency used an echoing sound at the start and end of the commercial to help break through the clutter, to capture the audience's attention, and to keep people interested in the ad all the way to the end. A synthesized jet airplane sound helped build excitement as the Jimmy was sent hurtling from the bridge.

The second commercial, called "Ups and Downs," featured the Safari rolling down—and backing up—a snow-covered ski jump to demonstrate its antilock brakes and all-wheel drive system. Once again, the client had to approve the budget and the storyboard before production (see Exhibit 20.6). GMC Truck engineers consulted with the agency and with Fahrenheit Films, the production company, about the Safari's handling on incline slopes and its surface traction capabilities. In addition, the agency conducted preliminary tests to determine the maximum incline and stopping distances that could be accommodated.

With an approved script in hand (see Exhibit 20.7), McCann/SAS started searching for a suitable location. Because this commercial was scheduled to run in the winter, the agency had to find a location likely to have snow early in the season when the ad would need to be filmed. The best choice was Lake Louise, a ski area in a national park high in the Canadian Rockies. With the permission of Canadian officials, the Fahrenheit Films crew constructed a ski jump and covered it with snow. Then they started filming as a stunt driver drove the Safari down the incline, applied the brakes, and shifted into reverse to back up to the top.

During the postproduction period, McCann/SAS added original music to accompany the "Ups and Downs" commercial. Through careful editing, shots of the snow-covered Rockies helped establish the cold and icy conditions under which the Safari was being driven. This reinforced the commercial's all-weather safety and handling message.

The client approved the edited versions of both commercials, and the agency added a super at the end of each ad showing the GMC Truck logo and the tag line "The Strength of Experience" (see Exhibit 20.8). The final versions of "Hang" and "Ups and Downs" also included space for a dealer name or dealer-group name to be superimposed next to the GMC Truck logo.

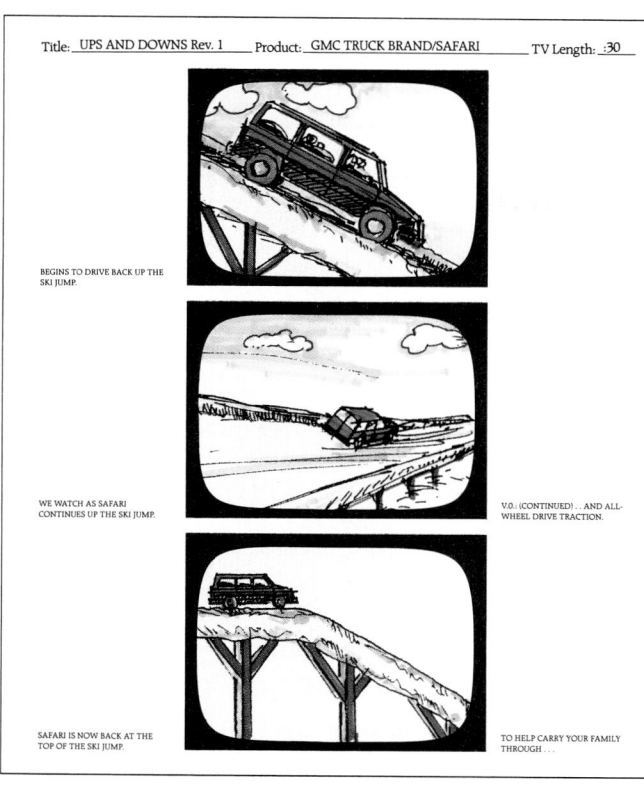

Title: UPS AND DOWNS Rev. 1   Product: GMC TRUCK BRAND/SAFARI   TV Length: :30

BEGINS TO DRIVE BACK UP THE SKI JUMP.

WE WATCH AS SAFARI CONTINUES UP THE SKI JUMP.

V.O.: (CONTINUED) . . . AND ALL-WHEEL DRIVE TRACTION.

SAFARI IS NOW BACK AT THE TOP OF THE SKI JUMP.

TO HELP CARRY YOUR FAMILY THROUGH . . .

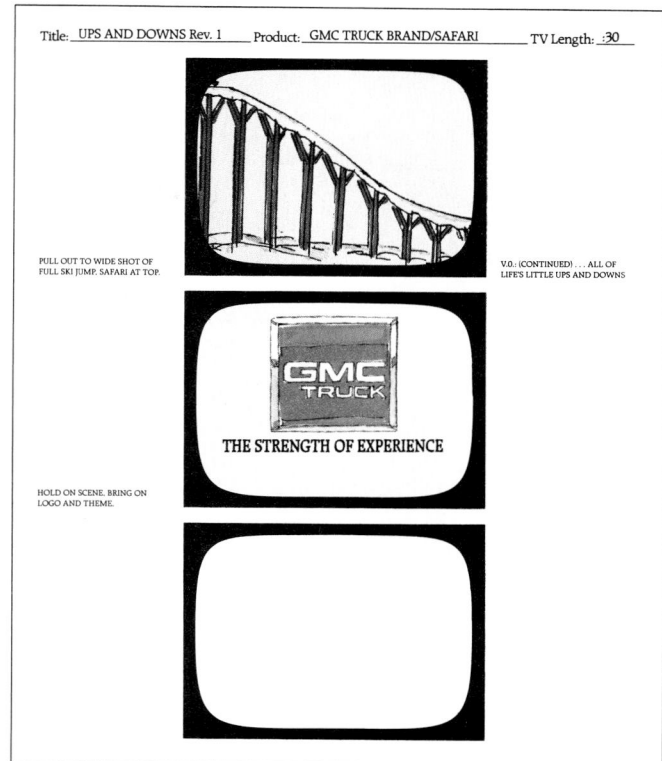

Title: UPS AND DOWNS Rev. 1   Product: GMC TRUCK BRAND/SAFARI   TV Length: :30

PULL OUT TO WIDE SHOT OF FULL SKI JUMP. SAFARI AT TOP.

V.O.: (CONTINUED) . . . ALL OF LIFE'S LITTLE UPS AND DOWNS

GMC TRUCK

THE STRENGTH OF EXPERIENCE

HOLD ON SCENE, BRING ON LOGO AND THEME.

PRINT MEDIA

McCann/SAS produced five print ads for the "Strength" campaign. The copy in all five echoed the distinctive attitude of adventure and self-confidence that permeated the television commercials. Drawing on what it learned from the focus-group

---

OPEN CU 3/4 FRONT OF SAFARI XLT/AWD. FAMILY INSIDE. ALL WE SEE IS THE VAN AND BLUE SKY.

WE SEE THE SAFARI ACCELERATE FORWARD AND IMMEDIATELY GO DOWN A STEEP HILL.

CUT TO WIDE REAR SHOT. WE SEE THE SAFARI IS GOING DOWN A SKI JUMP.

FROM THE REAR. WE SEE BRAKE LIGHTS GO ON.

CUT TO FRONT VIEW AS WE SEE SAFARI COME TO A STRAIGHT COMPLETE STOP.

CUT TO MEDIUM PROFILE SHOT SHOWING STOPPED IN MIDDLE OF SKI JUMP. SAFARI PAUSES MOMENTARILY, THEN-

BEGINS TO DRIVE BACK UP THE SKI JUMP.

WE WATCH AS SAFARI CONTINUES UP THE SKI JUMP.

SAFARI IS NOW BACK AT THE TOP OF THE SKI JUMP.

PULL OUT TO WIDE SHOT OF FULL SKI JUMP, SAFARI AT TOP.

HOLD ON SCENE, BRING ON LOGO AND THEME.

UPBEAT MUSIC IN AND UNDER THROUGHOUT.

V.O.: IN 90 YEARS AS A TRUCK COMPANY...

...WE'VE LEARNED THE VALUE OF ANTI-LOCK BRAKES...

V.O.: (continued)...AND ALL-WHEEL DRIVE TRACTION.

TO HELP CARRY YOUR FAMILY THROUGH...

V.O.: (continued)...ALL OF LIFE'S LITTLE UPS AND DOWNS.

EXHIBIT 20.7
The "Ups and Downs" Script

McCann/SAS hired Fahrenheit Films to shoot the "Ups and Downs" commercial using this script (as approved by GMC Truck prior to production).

(SFX): echoing sounds,

hook clangs down in hitch,

clang of control being pushed

and the echoing of a ratchet mechanism

V.O.: As a truck company for 90 years we understand the value of a strong frame. A reassuring strength for towing . . . whether you're on road or . . . off-road.

(SFX): synthesized jet rip followed by rock music

V.O.: GMC Truck.

(SFX): deep echo

V.O.: The Strength of Experience.

EXHIBIT 20.8
The "Hang" Commercial

Only with a television commercial could McCann/SAS use the combination of sight, sound, and motion to convey truck frame strength so vividly.

research, the agency chose as headlines quotes that consumers might use to describe their thoughts and feelings about driving trucks and sport-utility vehicles:

"As a matter of fact, I do own the road."

"The salesman starts talking resale value. I said, 'Buddy, I'm gonna drive this truck into the ground.'"

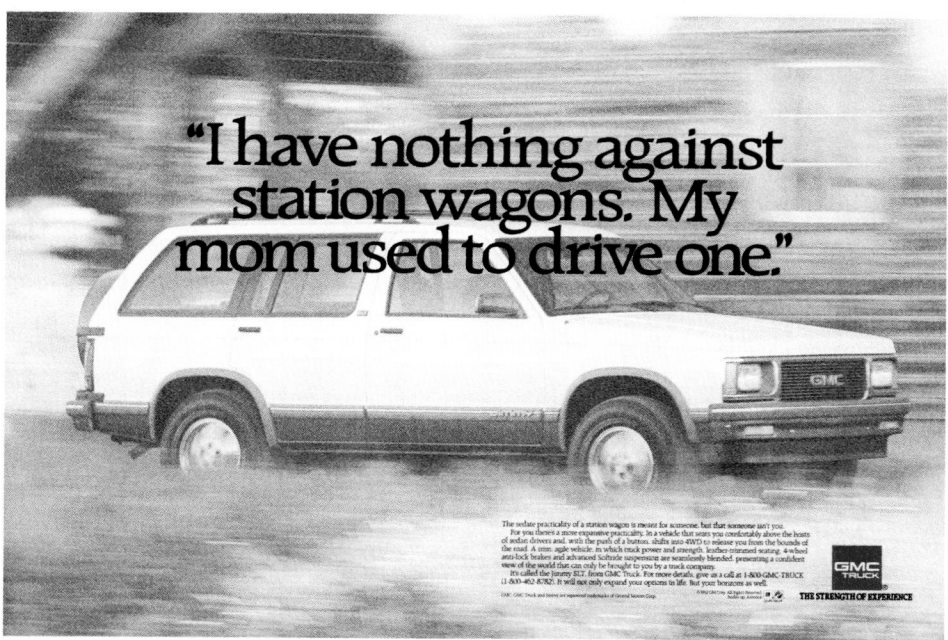

EXHIBIT 20.9
Advertising the Sierra and the Jimmy in Print

The print ads for GMC Truck's Jimmy and Sierra models reinforced the overall message of strength and experience using a creative approach entirely different from that used in the television commercials.

"I have nothing against station wagons. My mom used to drive one."

"Great. Now I can get a bigger boat."

"I had a car once. It was nice. Blue, I think."

To allow these headlines to attract the reader's attention, the product photos were produced in a "ghosted" technique that mutes the color intensity but maintains the details (see Exhibit 20.9). The body copy built on the subtle wit and attitude of each ad's headline to expand on the unique benefits of each model and, at the same time, reinforce the overall image of GMC Truck as an experienced, knowledgeable truck manufacturer. The bright-red GMC Truck logo and the tag line "The Strength of Experience" were shown in the lower right of each ad, which helped tie the ads together and to the rest of the campaign. The ads also invited consumers to call a toll-free number for more information about the advertised models.

CHAPTER 20
The Complete Campaign

553

EXHIBIT 20.10
Consumer Sales Promotion Reinforces Advertising

People who attended the major U.S. auto shows couldn't help but notice this impressive display, which echoed the look of the "Hang" commercial to reinforce the main message of GMC Truck's television advertising.

SALES PROMOTION AND SUPPLEMENTARY MEDIA

GMC Truck's national advertising was designed to convey brand image and to increase awareness, familiarity, and consideration of the brand. However, to more effectively pull the consumer through the buying process, the company and its agency envisioned "Strength of Experience" as the theme for an integrated marketing communications program. Using multiple media and many communication vehicles, the various elements of the program would work in tandem to consistently convey the brand image and the exceptional value that buyers receive when they buy a GMC Truck product.

EXHIBIT 20.11
Dealers Can Dangle the Jimmy

To further reinforce the message in GMC Truck's national advertisements, dealers could order a point-of-purchase display that, when assembled, dangled a cardboard model of the Jimmy from a miniature color mural of the New River Gorge Bridge.

Revving Up Multimedia Deals

One target audience, many media: that's the idea behind GMC Truck's recent multimedia contracts. Three separate deals were made involving championship soccer, country music, and voting issues. However, they had one thing in common: they helped GMC Truck reach its target audience across the United States both more effectively and at a lower cost than if the company had made individual purchases of media time and space.

In one deal, GMC Truck sponsored a cable television show that focused on environmental voting issues. The show aired on ESPN Saturday mornings before the fall 1992 election. Several Times Mirror publications promoted the show, giving GMC Truck exposure in print as well as on cable. This sponsorship offered GMC Truck an important opportunity to communicate with the target audience in multiple media without the noise caused by clutter from competing messages.

GMC Truck also arranged a yearlong multimedia deal with Group W Satellite Communications, this time booking a package of pay-per-view television, cable television, radio, and magazine advertising. The sponsorship arrangement included the telecast of a star-studded 1992 country music concert featuring the Highwaymen. Initially, the concert was offered as a pay-per-view event, and it later ran as a special on the Nashville Network. In addition to preconcert promotions, GMC Truck participated in promotions and advertising on the Nashville Network, on Country Music Television, on the Nashville Network Radio, and in *Country America* magazine.

The advantage of this country music package was that all the media vehicles reached a similar audience—the target audience that GMC Truck wanted to reach. So audience members were likely to be exposed to the brand-image message more than once. What's more, the ad messages in one vehicle were consistent with (and helped to reinforce) the ad messages in others.

A third deal was negotiated by General Motors (GMC Truck's parent) and named GM the exclusive automotive sponsor of the 1994 World Cup soccer championship matches. GMC Truck advertising was featured in the United States, and GM divisions in other countries tailored their advertising messages for their local markets. The package included magazine and television advertising exposure both before and during the 52 soccer matches, which aired on the ABC broadcast television network and the ESPN cable television network.

Because GM used its huge purchasing power to negotiate on behalf of all its divisions, it bought the World Cup sponsorship at an extremely attractive rate. However, that wasn't the only advantage. Because this was the first time the soccer championship had been played in the United States, advance promotion built audience anticipation, giving GM (and GMC Truck) the added advantage of being the only automotive sponsor of an eagerly awaited sports series that received wide media coverage in the United States and around the world.

Apply Your Knowledge

1. If GMC Truck agreed to sponsor radio and television coverage of the America's Cup sailing championship, what kinds of point-of-purchase displays might it offer its dealers to tie in with the media advertising?

2. What consumer and trade sales promotions would you suggest that GMC Truck develop to support the multimedia deal in question 1?

A key element in this program was using consumer sales promotion to reinforce the company's advertising and marketing efforts. Playing off the Jimmy "Hang" commercial, GMC Truck sent an attention-getting display to major U.S. auto shows in Detroit, Chicago, Los Angeles, and other cities. The display included an actual Jimmy dangling in front of a wall-length mural of the New River Gorge Bridge (see Exhibit 20.10). GMC Truck vehicles were parked in front of the mural and a television monitor played a videotape of the making of the "Hang" commercial continuously during show hours. Attendees who were drawn by the suspended Jimmy would be likely to watch all or part of the videotape and examine the vehicles before moving on.

To support advertising efforts by dealer groups and individual dealers, GMC Truck and McCann/SAS developed a series of consumer sales promotion tools, including point-of-purchase displays and sales support materials. One POP package offered to dealers included a brief Jimmy "Hang" video, a colorful poster of the Jimmy bouncing on the bungee cord, and a three-dimensional cardboard mobile of a Jimmy hanging from the bridge (see Exhibit 20.11).

In addition, dealers received a catalog of sales support materials they could use in their showrooms. Among the items that GMC Truck provided was a product information display (showing full-color product photos, vehicle specifications, lists of features and equipment, and warranty details) and a commercial vehicle capability chart (showing the capabilities of the light truck commercial vehicles in the GMC Truck product line). For a fee, dealers could order optional items such as a literature display rack, window displays, logo banners, and truck window decals.

GMC TRUCK LOGO FLAGS
A set of four 3-1/2' by 3-1/2' nylon flags for use indoors or outdoors.
Item 05 $75.50/set of four

GMC TRUCK THEME BANNER
Present your "Strength of Experience" at special showings, on outside lots, or over service entranceways as well as identifying yourself as a GMC Truck dealer. This impressive 4' by 20' banner is fully hemmed, grommeted and complete with rope extensions for easy placement.
Item 06 $43.97 each

GMC TRUCK LOGO BANNER
Use indoors or outdoors to call attention to all of your trucks on display. This 3' by 10' heavy duty banner is color-coordinated with the GMC Truck flags. Grommeted with rope extensions for easy hanging.
Item 07 $23.90 each

GMC TRUCK LICENSE PLATES
Promote the GMC Truck name on all of your products with this set of six plates. Removable and reusable throughout the year.
Item 08 $31.50/set of six

FRAMES ONLY FOR TRUCK PICTURE INSERTS AND LIGHT DUTY COMMERCIAL VOCATIONAL CHART
Use this set of three frames to prominently display the full color truck inserts and Light Duty Commercial Vocational Chart you will receive as part of the 1993 On-Going Merchandising and Promotion Program. Unused pictures self-store behind the photo being featured. Order several sets to complete your presentation of the 1993 GMC Trucks.
Item 09 $84.37/set of three

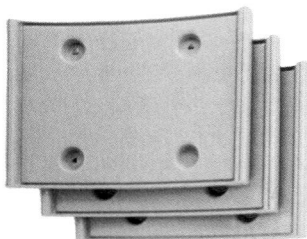

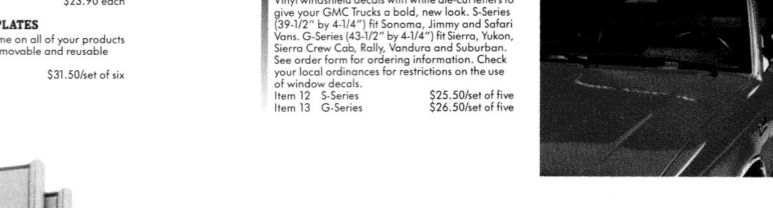

PENNANT STRINGS
Set of nine bright, festive red and silver pennant strings available in 50' lengths including rope extensions for easy hanging.
Item 10 $140.00/set of nine

TRUCK ANTENNA FLAGS
Use and reuse. Easy to apply sleeve color blends with pennant strings. Set of twenty-five.
Item 11 $56.75/set of twenty-five

TRUCK WINDOW DECALS
Vinyl windshield decals with white die-cut letters to give your GMC Trucks a bold, new look. S-Series (39-1/2" by 4-1/4") fit Sonoma, Jimmy and Safari Vans. G-Series (43-1/2" by 4-1/4") fit Sierra, Yukon, Sierra Crew Cab, Rally, Vandura and Suburban. See order form for ordering information. Check your local ordinances for restrictions on the use of window decals.
Item 12   S-Series $25.50/set of five
Item 13   G-Series $26.50/set of five

PROGRAM INFORMATION

BILLING INFORMATION

If you are enrolled in the On-Going Merchandising and Promotion Program, you will automatically receive the 1993 Announcement materials, and subsequent model year materials and be billed $695.00 on your GMC Truck Open Account on a yearly basis. The $695.00 charge per year includes all freight.

TOLL-FREE TELEPHONE NUMBER
1-800-833-7611

EXHIBIT 20.12
Sales Support Materials Echo the Campaign Look

Sales support materials such as a product information center and updated product photos helped GMC Truck dealers bring the look and message of the "Strength of Experience" campaign into their own showrooms.

The design of these sales support materials echoed the look of the overall campaign (see Exhibit 20.12).

Supplementary media such as outdoor advertising linked local advertising efforts with the national campaign. GMC Truck arranged for attention-getting outdoor advertising materials that could be customized with dealer name, logo, address, and other information. Each dealer received a catalog offering seven billboard designs with space for dealer tags. GMC Truck paid for the bleed posters; dealers paid for the outdoor board media space, shipping costs, and other expenses. The posters displayed the GMC Truck logo and the campaign tag line, which helped tie them to the overall campaign (see Exhibit 20.13).

EXHIBIT 20.13
Outdoor Advertising for Dealers

This poster, one of a series offered by GMC Truck to its dealers, was designed to be customized for local audiences by including the name, address, and logo of individual dealers.

However, GMC Truck didn't stop there. Its public relations experts issued a series of press releases discussing the new ad campaign and the individual models featured in the ads. In addition, they took advantage of the publicity value of sending the Jimmy hurtling hundreds of feet off a high bridge by arranging to send video news releases of the event to television stations across the country. Through Medialink, a monitoring service, GMC Truck learned that within days of the VNR's release, 11 stations had aired clips during their news broadcasts. More than a million viewers saw the Jimmy bounce on the end of the bungee cord and heard the GMC Truck and Jimmy names during these VNR broadcasts, reinforcing the effects of the electronic and print advertising.

Evaluating Advertising Results

Once the campaign started, GMC Truck and McCann/SAS tracked progress toward the advertising objectives that were set. As you recall, the campaign's primary communication objective was to improve awareness of the brand. After the campaign had been running for several months, the agency arranged for posttest studies to measure the awareness among members of the two audience segments.

Results indicated that awareness of the GMC Truck brand within the target audience had increased 21 percent within three months. This was a substantial increase considering that the advertiser had boosted neither media spending nor media weight compared with previous campaigns. More important, higher awareness meant a more solid foundation for the advertising and promotion efforts mounted by dealer groups and individual dealers, who were ultimately responsible for making the sale.

The "Strength of Experience" campaign helped GMC Truck to a record-setting sales year in 1992. Overall, GMC Truck's market share rose from 6.9 percent in 1991 to 7.3 percent in 1992. Not only that, but the momentum carried over as advertising for the 1993 model year kept awareness, familiarity, and consideration strong.

Summary

In the course of planning a complete advertising campaign, GMC Truck and McCann/SAS started by using a situation analysis to look at the internal and external factors that can affect performance. By examining the results of this analysis, they uncovered specific problems (such as low brand awareness) to be addressed in an advertising campaign. At the same time, the situation analysis provided insight into the market, the audience, and the competition, important ingredients in the development of both the creative and the media strategies.

By coordinating the communications objectives of national, regional, and local ad campaigns, GMC Truck and McCann/SAS more effectively pulled the target audience through the buying process. They did this by gearing the objectives of each campaign toward a particular step in the process. The national campaign was geared toward building awareness, familiarity, and consideration; the regional advertising campaigns were geared to increasing consideration and building preference; and the local advertising campaigns were geared to persuading the target audience to shop for—and buy—GMC Truck products.

The situation analysis offered clues to consumer perceptions of brand, buyer behavior, brand loyalty, and market opportunities, which can be exploited when creating advertising. The analysis also uncovered competitive problems to watch for when developing a creative strategy to set the brand apart from its rivals. McCann/SAS developed the media strategy by considering the unique qualities of each medium, the timing of product introductions, peak buying periods, and the media habits of the target audience. Because GMC Truck was on a limited budget, the agency chose cable rather than broadcast television, used a lot of print advertising, and arranged participation rather than sponsorship of television programs.

GMC Truck and McCann/SAS used advertising research to determine how people from their target audience would react to proposed messages, specific copy points, and creative approaches. After pretesting advertising campaigns and individual commercials, the companies were in a better position to make final decisions about the message content, creative alternatives, and planned media weight. Using multiple media and communication vehicles, GMC Truck coordinated the various elements of its integrated marketing communications program to convey brand image and its specific advertising messages consistently and cost-effectively. After the campaign started running, GMC Truck and McCann/SAS evaluated its effectiveness by using posttest research to measure progress toward their advertising objectives.

Meeting an Advertising Challenge at GMC Truck

Eddie Messenger and George Wood faced an advertising challenge that was almost as tough as backing a Safari up a snow-covered ski ramp. They set out to raise awareness of the GMC Truck brand among two target audiences, traditional truck buyers and upscale buyers who were thinking of switching from cars to trucks or sport-utility vehicles. To do this, they had to differentiate GMC Truck from its competitors by positioning it as the brand with strength, experience, and exceptional value. They also had to spark audience interest by making the brand's advertising both distinctive and memorable compared with all other automotive advertisements. Moreover, they had to do all this on a limited advertising budget.

The "Strength of Experience" campaign met all these requirements—and then some. In addition to boosting overall brand awareness, the campaign provided a foundation for regional and local promotional efforts mounted by dealer groups and individual dealers. Midway through the model year, GMC Truck's sales were outpacing the previous year's sales by 24 percent.

A look at the 1992 results shows that sales of the Jimmy (featured in "Hang") jumped nearly 38 percent over the previous year; sales of the Safari (featured in "Ups and Downs") increased nearly 18 percent. Sales of the Yukon, which was featured in a print ad, soared more than 150 percent, and sales of the Suburban, also shown in a print ad, grew nearly 42 percent.

Despite this strong showing, Messenger and Wood aren't ready to take their eyes off the road just yet. To keep brand awareness high, they'll be holding the campaign throttle wide open and continuing to measure how well GMC Truck advertising communicates with the two audience segments they've targeted.

Your Mission: As the newly hired assistant to GMC Truck's advertising director, George Wood, you've been asked to work with McCann/SAS on a new campaign for the Jimmy. Choose the best option in each of these situations, using your knowledge of how to develop a complete advertising campaign.

1. You've been told that the Jimmy will be completely redesigned next year. The new model will be less expensive than the current model; it will also have attractive new features, such as passenger-side airbags, which you can promote. According to the guidelines for good objectives, which of these objectives and purposes would be best for the new-model campaign? Why?
a. Sell two-thirds of the manufacturing output of the new model in the first year by using direct-action advertising.
b. Persuade one-third of the target audience to either request a videotape of a test drive or go to a local dealer for an actual test drive by developing ads intended to encourage information search.
c. By using ads designed to encourage recall of past satisfaction with the brand, bring half of the people who own Jimmy models that are four or more years old into local showrooms to see the new models in the first six months of the campaign.

2. Your situation analysis reveals that both Ford and Toyota have just introduced new "loaded" models with more standard features and higher suggested prices than most of the competing vehicles. The new Jimmy, to be introduced six months from now, will offer many of these features as options, and when options are added to the vehicle's base price, the "loaded" Jimmy will cost less than the new Ford or Toyota models. Which of

these short-term campaigns do you think would be most effective in persuading the "Go Anywhere Personal Sporty" audience segment to postpone buying until the new Jimmy becomes available? Be prepared to defend your choice.
a. Using the theme "U-Turn for Savings," create television and newspaper ads featuring young men and women going in and quickly coming out of a revolving door at Toyota dealerships and Ford showrooms. The copy should stress that the new Jimmy model will offer features and savings worth waiting for. Replace this with a new-product campaign a month before the new Jimmy is introduced.
b. Create a campaign around the theme "Worth the Wait." In television and print ads, show a new Jimmy covered up so only the sticker price and option listing can be seen. The copy should discuss the new features and compare the price with the new competitive models. Include the sound of a cash register ringing in the background of the television commercials; in the print ads, show an adding machine tape with the savings circled. Replace this campaign the week before the new Jimmy is introduced with your new-product campaign.
c. Use the theme "Brake for Better Value." In television commercials, show young people running, skating, and biking past GMC Truck showrooms, where a "Brake for Better Value" poster is displayed. The people's movement stops and then is reversed and speeded up as they return in the direction they originally came from. The voice-over explains that the new loaded Jimmy will be a better value than any competing vehicle. Print ads should show the people seeming to

go backward after reading the poster in the showroom windows and should include copy about the new features and improved value. Replace this campaign 6 weeks before the new Jimmy is introduced with a new-product campaign.

3. Once the new Jimmy comes out, you'll need to change the message you used in question 2 to one that shows your product as a better value than competing products. Which of the following campaigns most effectively communicates better value to budget-conscious young men 18–34? Explain your answer.

a. In print and television ads, show a loaded Jimmy next to similarly configured Ford and Toyota models. Under each vehicle, print the price in large type, underlining the Jimmy's price. The Jimmy could be shown hauling a race car. Use the tag line "Strength and Value." Create posters of this three-vehicle comparison and send them to GMC Truck dealers, who can display them in showroom windows and inside the showroom. Put this ad on billboards located within 10 miles of the GMC Truck dealerships that sell the most Jimmy models.

b. In print ads, show a photo of the loaded Jimmy in a showroom. Superimposed over the vehicle, show a bulleted list of every Jimmy option, its price, and then the total price of the Jimmy loaded to match the new Toyota and Ford models. The headline could read "The Best Value for Your Money." Television ads could show the Jimmy hauling a piece of heavy machinery; the voice-over could list the options and their prices and then compare the total with the higher prices of the Toyota and Ford models. End with the super "The Best Value for Your Money." Put up billboards near Ford and Toyota dealerships, showing the Ford and Toyota models small— and their prices large—while the

Jimmy is shown larger, along with its fully loaded "small" price. Include the location of the nearest GMC Truck dealership.

c. In major-city newspapers, run weekly ads with the headline "Which Is the Best Value?" Illustrate by showing price tags below the Ford and Toyota models in the background; then show the Jimmy model in the foreground with its price on a smaller price tag. Place this ad in the sports section of the Sunday newspaper. Reprint the ad for use as a direct-mail piece going to young owners of Ford and Toyota sport-utility vehicles; reproduce the ad for bus-shelter and train-terminal advertising.

4. Although Jimmy advertising is placed primarily in the print media and on television, you want to test the use of radio commercials. You're targeting the "Go Anywhere Family Fun" audience segment for the new Jimmy model. How can you use radio to communicate with this segment and to reinforce an overall campaign theme of "Strong and Sporty"?

a. Sponsor daily family recreation reports on local radio stations with country music and oldies formats. Create one 30-second commercial to air immediately before the report. This commercial will introduce the Jimmy's new features and include the tag line "Strong and Sporty." Create another 30-second commercial to air immediately after the report. In this

commercial, let the audience eavesdrop on a father and son sitting in the Jimmy, talking about the fun they have together riding where cars can't go. With outdoor noises in the background, the father asks the son to jump out and unhook the trailer so they can launch the boat. The commercial ends by repeating the tag line and suggesting that listeners visit local showrooms to test-drive the new Jimmy.

b. Sponsor the evening news reports on network radio. Create one 30-second commercial to air during the first commercial break and another 30-second commercial to air at the end of the report. The first commercial could mention the new functional features of the latest Jimmy model, ending with the tag line "The new Jimmy. Now even stronger." The second commercial could discuss the new trim packages and new body and upholstery colors, ending with the tag line "The new Jimmy. Now even sportier."

c. Sponsor the early-morning national sports news on network radio. Record one 50-second commercial, to air immediately before the sports news, that compares the new Jimmy with last year's Jimmy. At the end, 10 seconds of copy will be read by a live announcer, who reminds listeners to test-drive the new model at local showrooms. End with the tag line "Still Strong and Sporty."[15]

Questions

FOR REVIEW

1. What can a situation analysis tell you about your current circumstances that will help you plan a more effective advertising campaign?

2. How is the creative strategy affected by brand positioning and targeted audience segments?

3. What can pretesting tell you about a proposed advertisement or campaign?

4. What role should a theme or tag line play in a multimedia ad campaign?

5. How does the concept of integrated marketing communications apply to a complete advertising campaign?

FOR ANALYSIS AND APPLICATION

6. Potential donors are often exposed to two types of United Way advertising: a national campaign planned by the national organization and local campaigns planned by state or local chapters. How can these two levels of advertising be coordinated into an integrated marketing communications program that has more impact than either campaign alone?

7. How can Walt Disney use sales promotion materials in Disney Stores to reinforce the message being communicated by an ad campaign that uses only television to promote the video release of a new Disney movie?

8. Imagine that Coca-Cola is releasing a new television campaign created by using a technologically advanced animation system. What might it show on a video news release to capture the attention of the news media? To whom might Coca-Cola send the VNR?

9. How might a local dental office use a newspaper ad campaign to communicate its position as a specialist in children's dental care?

10. What might a manufacturer like Progresso learn about Campbell Soup (an important competitor in the soup category) that would affect the strategy for a campaign to promote a new line of soups?

Sharpen Your Advertising Skills

Who cares about safety? Perhaps the most concerned are parents, who want to know just how well the vehicles they buy will protect youngsters in the event of an accident. To reach this target audience, automotive advertisers have spent many millions of dollars touting the safety advantages of antilock brakes, passenger airbags, and other features.

Suppose that GMC Truck introduced a new pickup with an extended cab that provides bucket seats in front and bench seating for three behind. One of its competitors is the Ford Ranger, which has bucket seats in front and two side-facing jump seats behind. Benches can legally be equipped with child safety seats, but some state laws forbid the use of child safety seats on jump seats that face sideways.

As GMC Truck's advertising manager, consider how you might promote the safety features of your new vehicle to capture the attention of families who might be attracted to the Ranger.

Decision: Should you use comparative advertising as the basis of a campaign in which the GMC Truck pickup's safety features are compared with those of the Ranger? (You'll be sure that the campaign meets legal and regulatory guidelines for comparative advertising.) If you do decide to compare the Ranger's sideways jump seats (which aren't allowed to hold child safety seats) with your own bench seats (which are allowed to hold child safety seats), how do you think Ford will respond? If you don't want to use comparative advertising, what approach would you prefer?

Communication: Write a brief (one-to-two-page) memo to your ad agency outlining the approach you want to take. If you decide to use comparative advertising, explain how you think Ford will respond.

Advertising Worldwide Savings

SYNOPSIS

Finding a convenient way to save money on telephone calls from the United States to other countries isn't easy. Both AT&T and MCI offer international calling programs, but customers generally have to say in advance which country or telephone numbers they will call before they can receive discounts. Sprint saw an opportunity to increase its international calling volume by introducing "The Most WORLDWIDE," a plan that simplified calling rates and offered discounts even if customers changed the telephone numbers or countries they called.

This video shows how Sprint and its ad agency, J. Walter Thompson/ West, developed an ad campaign to support the new plan. The target audience was people who moved to the United States from other countries and wanted to call friends and relatives back home. The creative strategy was to illustrate the plan's convenience. The media strategy was to reach the target audience using television, newspapers, radio, magazines, and special events. The results: an impressive increase in Sprint's international calling volume.

EXERCISES

Analysis

1. Are the Sprint print ads an example of direct-action or indirect-action advertising? How do you know?
2. Does the "Castles" commercial use an emotional or a logical appeal? Explain your answer.
3. Why would J. Walter Thompson suggest holding 12 block parties on one day?
4. Sprint's "Blah Blah Blah" radio commercial was produced in four languages and aired on selected ethnic radio stations in the United States. As an example of intercultural advertising, does this represent the globalization or the localization approach? Why?
5. Why would Sprint use a different toll-free phone number in each print ad?

Application

How can J. Walter Thompson find out where Sprint rivals AT&T and MCI are advertising their international calling programs and how much they are spending in each medium or vehicle? Why is this information important?

Decision

When Sprint incorporates a consumer sales promotion technique such as offering $50 worth of Sprint long-distance coupons for signing up now, should it set sales or communication objectives for its ads? How can the results be measured?

Ethics

The Sprint ads allude to other international calling plans but don't mention competitors by name, so the target audience may be unable to make direct comparisons. Outline the ethical issues involved.

Teamwork

Working with another classmate, role-play a conversation in which a Sprint representative tries to convince a Tianguis supermarket manager to allow Sprint to set up a free calling booth inside the store during the next promotion. What benefits would the store gain from this arrangement? Why would the manager be reluctant to agree? Summarize the points for both sides during a class discussion following the role play. ■

Situation Analysis
Marketing Objectives
Marketing Strategy
Target Markets
Positioning
Marketing Mix
Action Plan

Sample Marketing Plan

Music by Mail (MBM), based in Boise, Idaho, is a hypothetical supplier of music compact disks. The company buys CDs from a variety of music distribution companies and resells the disks by mail to consumers across North America. It specializes in four music segments that are difficult for most consumers to find in mainstream music stores or through other CD clubs: blues, jazz, early music (instrumental and vocal music written before the classical period, such as Gregorian chants), and Celtic (traditional and modern Scottish and Irish music). This appendix shows a plan that MBM's marketing manager might have put together. The plan presented here is shorter and contains less detail than a typical marketing plan, but it illustrates the key points a marketing plan needs to address. Also, keep in mind that companies use a variety of formats and terms in their marketing plans. The companion advertising plan is presented in Appendix B. All figures in this plan are fictional.

Situation Analysis

We've enjoyed several years of rapid growth, and we closed 1994 with sales of $1,838,000. This represents 105,000 CDs at an average price of $17.50 each. Exhibit A.1 shows our revenue growth over the last four years and our projections for the next three years. Exhibit A.2 shows how these sales split into our four music lines: approximately 36,750 in European jazz, 31,500 in blues, 21,000 in Celtic, and 15,750 in early music. In total, our sales represent under 2 percent of the 6 million CDs sold in the United States in these four categories every year.

Our customer base is demographically diverse, covering practically every category of age, income, education, household status, employment, and geographic location. In terms of lifestyles and other psychographic variables, however, our research shows several strong common threads. The majority of our customers express an inter-

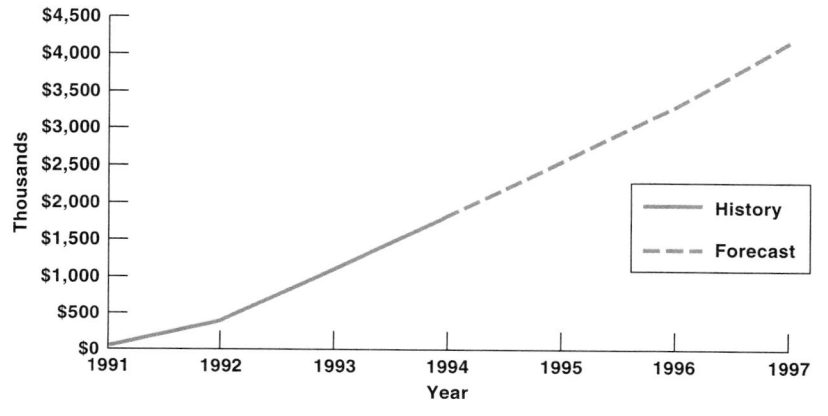

EXHIBIT A.1
Sales History and Forecast

Here is our sales performance over the last four years along with our forecast for the next three.

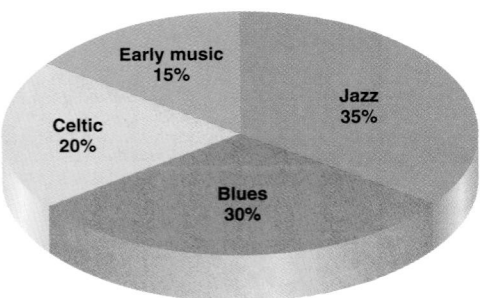

EXHIBIT A.2
Sales by Product Category

Here is how our sales break down by music category.

EXHIBIT A.3 Customer Groups

Although Group A is the smallest in terms of number of customers, it is the most important group in terms of sales volume.

Group	Number of Customers in Group	Average Number of CDs Purchased in 1994	Group's Total in 1994	Group's Percent of Sales
A	2,689	22.7	61,040	58%
B	4,225	7.2	30,420	29%
C	7,126	1.9	13,540	13%
	14,040		105,000	100%

est in politics and current social issues, and nearly all attend concerts and music festivals regularly. Customers outside the major metropolitan areas express frustration with the poor selection of their favorite musical genres found in typical music stores. Many who do live near large retailers with good selections aren't happy with the quality of service they receive at those stores (the two biggest complaints are clerks who don't know enough about the music and clerks who have unpleasant attitudes). Most of our customers consider music to be an important part of their lives, and they're generally interested in learning more about the music they listen to and the performers they hear.

Three types of companies compete to serve the same markets that we serve. The first group is composed of traditional mass-market music retailers, from single-store independents to regional and national chains such as Tower Records. The second group comprises the mainstream, mass-market mail-order clubs such as Columbia and BMG. The third consists of specialty retailers who offer deep selections and knowledgeable sales assistance. Virtually all of these sales are in the jazz category, although most of these companies carry extensive selections of blues titles as well. We're not aware of any stores that specialize in early music or Celtic, although most stores that carry classical music also carry a limited selection of early music. Celtic music is very much a hit-or-miss situation, depending largely on individual store owners' tastes.

Viewing our situation in terms of a SWOT analysis, we have three competitive strengths that apply in different combinations to each group of competitors: (1) we usually have the widest selection of CDs in each of the four music categories, (2) we give customers outside metropolitan areas a way to buy products they can't find in local stores, and (3) our staff of experts can provide customers with detailed information on music and performers.

Our primary weakness is our small size relative to the big names in music distribution. However, we've been fairly successful so far in turning this to our advantage by convincing the informed buyer that since we don't need to worry about moving millions of copies of the latest pop hits, we can concentrate on the unique music that's our specialty.

We see three opportunities for sales growth. First, we can continue to serve the needs of our Group A customers, those who are active, regular purchasers. These people buy an average of nearly 23 CDs per year, and they're always open to new recordings. The secret here is to present them with an ever-expanding list of products to choose from. Second, we can try to build sales among our Group B and Group C customers, who now average 7.2 and 1.9 CDs per year, respectively. We think that by introducing them to new artists and new styles, we can prompt them to buy more. (Exhibit A.3 shows how the sales of the three groups compared in 1994.) Third, we can find new customers.

The biggest threat we perceive at this point is that one of the larger distributors might be attracted by our growing success and make plans to focus on our markets. The best thing we can do to protect ourselves is to build strong relationships with customers and stay healthy financially, in case we have to increase promotions dramatically or lower prices.

Marketing Objectives

Based on our research into the number of people who would buy more of our types of music if only they could find it, we believe it will be possible to sell $2.625 million next year, or a total of about 150,000 CDs. Reaching this goal will require aggressive marketing, to be sure. We'll support that sales goal by striving to meet the following objectives in the marketing mix:

- *Product objectives.* Our overriding product objective is to provide our Group A customers with products they either can't find anywhere else or can't buy conveniently anywhere else.

- *Distribution objectives.* The number one distribution objective is to meet customer expectations in terms of speed, accuracy, and reasonable cost of delivery. We strive for 100 percent accuracy and offer two delivery options: overnight for $3 per disk or regular UPS for $1.50 a disk.

- *Pricing objectives.* Because our customers are less price-sensitive than the general music-buying public, offering the lowest possible prices isn't an absolute must. We'll strive to maintain a 10 percent profit margin while always keeping customer prices below $20 per CD.
- *Promotional objectives.* Promotions is the area where we'll devote most of our attention in the next year. Exhibit A.4 shows one scenario for meeting the goal of 150,000 CDs in 1995. If we increase the size of each customer group by 25 percent and then sell 15 percent more on average to each customer, we can break the 150,000-unit barrier. In terms of promotions, experience shows that we average one new customer for every 120 we contact, so to add 1,782 customers to Group C, for instance, we'll need to reach around 214,000 people.

Marketing Strategy

We developed our 1995 marketing strategy by considering three elements: our target markets, the position we'd like to achieve in those target markets, and the marketing mix we'll employ to meet our sales objectives.

TARGET MARKETS

We can divide our target markets in two key ways: by type of music and by volume of purchasing. The four music-type segments correspond to the four product categories we offer. We have some customers in more than one segment, of course, but it makes sense to treat each type of music as a separate segment so that we can focus our marketing efforts on each one. In terms of purchasing volume, we group customers into heavy, medium, and light purchasers. The heavy purchasers, Group A, are those who buy 15 or more CDs per year. The medium purchasers, Group B, buy 5 to 14 CDs per year and currently average 7.2 CDs per year per customer. The light purchasers, Group C, are those who buy 1 to 4 CDs per year and now average 1.9 units per year. At present, nearly all our customers are in the United States, but we may consider international expansion at some point.

POSITIONING

We want customers and potential customers to view us as the most comprehensive and most authoritative source for CDs in the four music categories we cover. As a secondary positioning theme, we also want these people to view us as a convenient and reasonably cost-effective source of these specialized CDs.

MARKETING MIX

We've broken the definition of our marketing mix into product strategy, distribution strategy, pricing strategy, and promotional strategy. This section presents a quick overview of each component.

Product Strategy

We rely on our industry connections to get the right products from the record labels, independent producers,

EXHIBIT A.4 Reaching Sales of 150,000 CDs

Here is one scenario for reaching sales of 150,000 units in 1995: First try to increase the size of each group by 25 percent. Then try to increase average sales to customers in each group by 15 percent.

Group	Number of Customers in Group	Average Number of CDs Purchased in 1994	Group's Total in 1994	Group's Percent of Sales
A	2,689	22.7	61,040	58%
B	4,225	7.2	30,420	29%
C	7,126	1.9	13,540	13%
	14,040		105,000	100%

Increasing Group Sizes by 25% Each

Group	Target Number of Customers in Group	Average Number of CDs Purchased in 1994	Group's Total in 1994	Group's Percent of Sales
A	3,361	22.7	76,300	58%
B	5,281	7.2	38,025	29%
C	8,908	1.9	16,925	13%
	17,550		131,250	100%

Increasing Sales to Each Group by 15%

Group	Target Number of Customers in Group	Average Number of CDs Purchased in 1994	Group's Total in 1994	Group's Percent of Sales
A	3,361	26.1	87,745	58%
B	5,281	8.3	43,729	29%
C	8,908	2.2	19,463	13%
	17,550		150,937	100%

and small distributors who specialize in our four types of music. By providing artists with an effective outlet for their musical products, we also help ensure the vitality of the specialized music market, which leads to an even greater supply of products for our customers.

Distribution Strategy

Convenience is the primary concern of our distribution efforts, followed by cost. Most of our customers recognize the value we provide by delivering products right to their doorstep. They don't have to fight traffic or take time to visit stores that may or may not have the right music in stock. As long as we keep our costs in line with efficient warehousing and shipping tactics, we can provide a high level of convenience at a price that won't scare too many people away. We'll continue to offer two levels of distribution speed: regular UPS and overnight delivery by either UPS or Federal Express.

Pricing Strategy

As just mentioned, price is a secondary concern for most of our members, at least as it relates to getting the right product in a convenient manner. We believe that $20 is the highest we could charge for any single CD, even with special ordering and music advisory services. Retail stores sell popular CDs at $14 to $16, and sometimes as low as $10 to $12 on sale. However, tests we've conducted show that our nonprice-competitive issues (such as selection and convenience) are worth at least $2 to our average customer. We therefore price most of our CDs in the $18 range, not including shipping charges.

Promotional Strategy

Every aspect of our promotional strategy is shaped by two factors: Our audience represents a small fraction of the overall universe of people who buy music, and our promotional budget is minuscule compared with that of other music suppliers. Consequently, we must focus to make the most of our effort and investment.

This need for focus means that our promotions center on our customer/prospect database. This house list contains names, addresses, and purchase-related information for people who've done business with us in the past or who appear to be good prospects for our products.

Our promotional strategy is divided into two phases (often conducted in parallel): developing our house list and selling to the house list. Developing our house list means finding new names, people who haven't purchased from us before but who might be willing to do so if informed of our offerings. Finding new names is often an expensive, risky venture, but other than word of mouth through our existing customers, it's the only way to expand our cus-

tomer base and meet the goal of increasing the size of Groups A, B, and C by 25 percent each.

Selling to the house list is a much more focused operation since we've already captured the names, addresses, and at least some supporting information that help us target our promotions more effectively. When the Tannahill Weavers come out with a new album, for instance, we can pitch it in a direct-mail offering to people who've either purchased the group's music before or purchased other music in the Celtic category. Similarly, if we bundle a set of Lightnin' Hopkins albums, we can direct a promotion to people who've shown an interest in the blues category.

Action Plan

The accompanying advertising plan highlights the programs we'll put in place to both develop the house list and sell to the people already on the list. It contains a list of planned activities and events, a budget, and a schedule/calendar.

Apply Your Knowledge

1. Why does MBM divide its promotional efforts into two phases?

2. Other CD clubs advertise in national magazines and in newspaper inserts distributed nationwide. Should MBM take this approach as well?

3. Does MBM's "house list" represent a key strength for the company? Why or why not?

4. How might changes in technology affect MBM's success?

Sample Advertising Plan

The advertising plan for Music by Mail (MBM) presents an analysis of the advertising situation (more narrow than the marketing plan situation, the advertising situation analysis is usually conducted to address communication issues specifically), along with a reiteration of the previously established marketing objectives and marketing strategy. It then outlines the objectives and strategy specific to advertising, along with details about messages, media plans, ties to sales promotion or special events, the advertising budget, and some sort of time line or calendar that shows key dates in the upcoming campaign. The advertising plan may stand on its own, with its own activities lists, budget, and calendar, or it may be included as part of the marketing plan. In addition, a plan might cover an entire campaign or just a single ad.

As was noted for the marketing plan in Appendix A, this advertising plan does not contain the same level of detail you should expect to see in a real plan. In addition, the real world isn't as nice and tidy as this plan would indicate; the budget numbers don't always work out, expenses can be impossible to predict, and advertisers don't always have the information they'd like to make the decisions they need to make. The purpose of this sample plan is to highlight the elements typically included in a plan and to show you how the major pieces fit together. View the content and organization of this plan as a representative example; the specific plans created by individual advertisers and agencies vary widely.

Situation Analysis

As detailed in our marketing plan, our market situation looks quite positive as we move into 1995. We sold 105,000 CDs in 1994, continuing a strong upward trend since we got started back in 1991. Here's a quick over-

view of our major strengths, weaknesses, opportunities, and threats:

- *Strengths.* (1) We usually have the widest selection of CDs in each of the four music categories, (2) we give customers outside metropolitan areas a way to buy products they can't find in local stores, and (3) our staff of experts can provide customers with detailed information on music and performers. Serious listeners know they can get the information they need and the music they want from us.

- *Weaknesses.* Our major weakness is size; we are a tiny player in an industry dominated by giant production and distribution companies. However, our customers aren't in the market for the latest top 40 hits. We focus on four specialized areas, and we do a good job of satisfying customer needs in those particular areas.

- *Opportunities.* Our three opportunities for sales growth are (1) keeping our top customers (Group A) satisfied and presenting them with an ever-expanding selection of products, (2) converting some of our mid-range customers (Group B) and infrequent buyers (Group C) into more frequent buyers, and (3) adding to our customer base in all three groups. Experience has shown that giving fans of specialized music an easy way to get the CDs they want usually leads to increased sales.

- *Threats.* Our biggest worry is that one of the major CD clubs might be attracted by our success in this market and be tempted to aim its massive promotion and distribution machines at our customers. We're confident that by continuing to build strong relationships with our customers (through personalized service and lots of valuable information), we'll hang on to them in the event of a major competitive move.

Marketing Strategy

To achieve our 1995 goal of selling 150,000 CDs, we plan to continue expanding our customer base using the same fundamental marketing strategy that has carried us to success so far. Here's an overview of the three elements of that strategy:

- *Target market.* Our target market consists of people who are serious fans of jazz, blues, early music, or Celtic music. Most of our customers live outside major metropolitan areas in the United States (since they have fewer opportunities to visit well-stocked retailers), although quite a few metro area residents buy from us for our selection and convenience. We also segment in terms of purchasing volume, with Group A customers being the most frequent buyers and Group C being the least frequent.

- *Positioning.* For this target market, we strive to be known as the most attractive music source in terms of product selection and service. We aren't always the cheapest source of particular CDs, but our customers value the personalized service and detailed information we provide.

- *Marketing mix.* Our product strategy centers on building the most comprehensive selection of products in our four specialized market areas. Our distribution strategy is based on convenience first, with cost as a secondary (although still important) factor. Our pricing strategy reflects the desires of our customers; they would rather have us provide products and information they can't get anywhere else than to shave a few cents off the price of our CDs. Therefore, while we always keep prices reasonable, we don't try to compete on price. Our promotional strategy is built around the dual challenge of selling more products to our existing customers and expanding our customer base. The rest of this plan provides more details on the promotional strategy.

Promotional Strategy

We plan to utilize all four elements of the promotional mix this year. In public relations, we'll produce a sampler CD to be sent to music writers at magazines and newspapers nationwide. In personal selling, we'll add an in-bound telemarketer who can help customers make product selections. In sales promotion, we'll run a simple "buy three, get one free" offer to pull in new customers. In advertising, where we'll put the bulk of our resources, we've designed a two-part program. One part, composed of media advertising, is designed to pull in new customers. The other, our ongoing direct-mail effort, is aimed at existing customers and consists of our bimonthly catalog program. The following sections provide the details.

PUBLIC RELATIONS

Over the past few years, a handful of newspaper and magazine writers and editors have been in contact after hearing about us from customers. Several small articles have been written as a result. This year, we'd like to be more proactive in this regard and launch a press relations initiative. In an effort to highlight the company and introduce people in the press to the selection of music we offer, we plan to produce a sampler CD that provides three short pieces from each of our four product lines. We'll complement the CD with an informative booklet that describes the background of each style of music we carry.

PERSONAL SELLING

One of the key features that distinguishes us from the competition is the amount of information we provide about artists, recordings, and music history. To boost our strength in this area even more, we plan to hire a full-time inbound telemarketer to answer questions from customers. We'll mention this service in all communication with current and potential customers and emphasize it as a way to discover new musical pleasures and to make sure people get the music they really want. As an example of how telemarketing can help both the customer and us, a person might call in and say that he or she enjoys the music of the Celtic band Silly Wizard. The telemarketer could then suggest recordings by Battlefield Band, the Tannahill Weavers, and other bands who play music in the same vein.

SALES PROMOTION

This is an experiment for us this year. We'd like to conduct a simple sales promotion to see if it might bring new customers into the fold. Our plan is to offer a discount deal in which any first-time customer who orders three CDs gets a fourth one free. As an initial test, we'll mention the offer in our magazine and television advertising during April and May. In order to judge the true costs of the sales promotion, we've calculated the lost revenue from the free CDs as a promotional expense. It's hard to predict how many people will respond, but we've budgeted for up to 1,000 CDs, or $17,500 at our current average price.

ADVERTISING

As mentioned earlier, our advertising needs to fill two purposes: maintaining/expanding sales to our house list and expanding the house list by pulling in new customers. This section outlines our specific objectives in these two areas and then details the strategy we'll implement to meet the objectives.

Advertising Objectives

Our advertising objectives support the twin marketing objectives of (1) increasing the size of our customer base by 25 percent and (2) increasing sales by an average of 15 percent across the customer base. These goals require both a communications objective and a sales objective:

- *Communications objective.* Expanding our house list by 25 percent means adding roughly 3,500 new customers to our active list of 14,040 buyers. As shown later in our media-planning worksheet, we need to make 700,000 gross impressions through television, 187,500 through radio, and 375,000 through print. Our goals are to have 20,000 television viewers, 7,500 radio listeners, and 7,500 magazine readers call to ask for a catalog. Based on last year's data, we've determined that roughly 10 percent of the people who request a catalog become active customers. This leads to the new-customer goals of 2,000 (through television), 750 (through radio), and 750 (through magazines).

- *Sales objectives.* The sales objective addresses people on our house list, including new customers who've just made their first purchase from us. With a sales goal of 150,000 for the year, we need to average 25,000 units sold from each of our six bimonthly catalogs. Since we'll be building the list as we go through the year, however, we're estimating that bimonthly sales will grow from our current 17,500 per catalog to 32,500 or so by the last issue of the year.

Advertising Strategy

Our advertising strategy contains two key parts. The creative strategy outlines what we'll say and how we'll say it. The media strategy explains where we'll place the message so that our target audience is exposed to it.

Creative Strategy. The creative strategy defines three key blocks of information: the art direction plan, the production values for each ad, and the copy platform, which outlines the message we'll present.

Art Direction and Production Values. Our small advertising budget limits how fancy we can get with any of our advertising efforts, but this isn't a major shortcoming in terms of production value. Our customers are looking for information and the feeling they're making a connection with the artists who create the music they enjoy. Here's a description of how our ads will look and sound:

- *The televison ad.* The televison ad, aimed at our jazz audience, will feature one of our top jazz performers, who will be taped in his or her own house. Some of the performer's music will be playing in the background as he or she explains that MBM is a great source of jazz music. A personal anecdote, outlining how we helped the performer find a long-lost recording (we've done this for dozens of musicians), will personalize the message and highlight our service.

- *The radio ad.* The radio spot, which will run only on a blues-oriented program, will feature snippets of music with voice-over provided by several of the blues artists we sell.

- *The magazine ad.* The magazine ad will feature one of our Celtic artists and one of our early-music artists, shot at the actual house of one or the other. Like the televison and radio ads, the copy will explain how these artists also rely on MBM to supply the music they enjoy.

- *The catalog.* Unlike catalogs from the big CD clubs, ours features far more information and is far less glossy. It's heavy on the copy, with occasional photographs of performers or new CDs. It's meant to inform first and foremost, but it's also entertaining and gently persuasive. Printed on regular bond paper in two colors, it looks more like a newsletter than a traditional retail catalog.

Copy Platform. We'll use the same key customer benefit, support points, selling strategy, selling style, and advertising appeal for all three ads (and our bimonthly customer catalog, as appropriate):

- *The key customer benefit.* The benefit we offer that no one else can claim is comprehensive selection of recordings in each of the four areas we cover, backed by a staff of people who know what they're talking about. When people call us or read the catalog, they know we can get virtually any recording that has ever been made in our specialty areas.

- *Support for the key benefit.* We have three points of solid support for our benefit claim: (1) we have connections to virtually every record label of interest, including independents that release only a few disks every year; (2) we have an expert staff of people who have years of experience in the music business; and (3) we can provide helpful and often unique bits of information about the music and the artists who create it, enabling our customers to make better choices and to get more enjoyment from their purchases.

- *The selling strategy.* Our selling strategy is based on our desired market position as the best source of jazz, blues, Celtic music, or early music for the serious listener. The strategy is straightforward: Tell people we're the best source and then provide support for that claim.

- *Selling style and the advertising appeal.* Our customers are serious listeners, and music plays a central role in their daily lives. This is definitely not an MTV/top 40 type of audience. Most of our customers don't know and don't really care who's on top of the popular music pile from week to week. Our style, then, is one of respect for the customer's need for information. Our communication is as much education as it is persuasion. The razzle-dazzle element in our advertising comes from the artists themselves. Various artists whose music we sell have agreed to appear in our ads, explaining that they love the music as much as our customers do and that MBM is also their favorite

EXHIBIT B.1 Media-Planning Worksheet

This worksheet shows the computations we made in order to derive media budget requirements.

Television Audience

Goal:	2,000	new customers
Conversion ratio:	350	gross impressions needed to yield one new customer
Gross impressions needed:	700,000	(goal × conversion ratio)
Reach:	35,000	average viewership of *Jazz Tonight*
Required frequency:	20	(gross impressions/reach)
Cost per broadcast:	$10,000	estimated cost to air the spot one time
Media cost–TV:	$200,000	(cost per broadcast × frequency)
Cost per customer:	$100	(media cost/new-customer goal)

Radio Audience

Goal:	750	new customers
Conversion ratio:	250	gross impressions needed to yield one new customer
Gross impressions needed:	187,500	(goal × conversion ratio)
Reach:	2,500	average listenership of *Blues Beat*
Required frequency:	75	(gross impressions/reach)
Cost per broadcast:	$1,000	estimated cost to air the spot one time
Media cost–radio:	$75,000	(cost per broadcast × frequency)
Cost per customer:	$100	(media cost/new-customer goal)

Print Audience

Goal:	750	new customers
Conversion ratio:	500	gross impressions needed to yield one new customer
Gross impressions needed:	375,000	(goal × conversion ratio)
Reach:	9,000	average readership of *Music Review*
Required frequency:	42	(gross impressions/reach)
Cost per insertion:	$1,200	estimated cost to run the ad one time
Media cost–print:	$50,000	(cost per insertion × frequency)
Cost per customer:	$67	(media cost/new-customer goal)

source for CDs. With the tag line "From our house to yours," these artists will be taped (for the televison ad) or photographed (for the magazine ad) in their own homes, with their own CD collections.

Media Strategy. A company as small as ours obviously has to make advertising choices with great care. We don't have much money to spend, so we must spend it wisely. For television advertising, we've chosen the program *Jazz Tonight*, which runs nationwide on the American Arts cable channel. For radio, a local Chicago radio program called *Blues Beat* is going to be syndicated nationwide later this year, and when it is, we'll be one of its primary sponsors. To address potential customers in our other two music areas, we'll run ads in the weekly magazine *Music Review*. This magazine covers lots of different music styles, but it's the only one in national circulation that covers both Celtic and early music. The budget section that follows outlines how much money we plan to spend on each of the three media vehicles.

Budget

Our budgeting task involves two stages. The first is to identify expenses that we know we'll encounter throughout the year, more or less independent of how much or how little we advertise. For instance, the decision to have a musical expert on the phone full time leads to an identi-

EXHIBIT B.2 1995 Promotion Budget

Here is our 1995 budget, based on the media planning worksheet and other known expenses.

Public relations		
Producing sampler CD	10,000	
Printing press kit	2,000	
Mailing press kit	500	
Total public relations		$12,500
Advertising		
Production—TV	26,000	
Production—radio	5,000	
Production—print	5,000	
Media buy—TV	200,000	
Media buy—radio	75,000	
Media buy—print	50,000	
Production—catalogs	44,000	
Mailing—catalogs	16,000	
Total advertising		$421,000
Personal selling		
Telemarketer salary	40,000	
Toll-free phone service	8,000	
Total personal selling		$48,000
Sales promotion		
Cost to modify ads	1,000	
Discount cost of free CDs	17,500	
Total sales promotion		$18,500
Total promotion budget		$500,000

fiable expense that we know we'll have to cover all year. Similarly, we know every customer needs one of our bimonthly catalogs, so that's a predictable expense as well.

The second stage involves looking at our advertising objectives and working back to find how much money we'll need to spend to reach those objectives. Exhibit B.1 is the worksheet we used to estimate the media budget we'll need in order to pull in the 3,500 new customers called for by our marketing objective. Based on our advertising experience in 1993 and 1994, we estimate that we need to buy 350 gross impressions on television to yield one new customer, 250 on radio, and 500 in magazines. This figure is called the conversion ratio in Exhibit B.1.

We used the objective and task budgeting technique, starting with a rough prediction of the number of new customers we could gain through each medium. We multiplied the new-customer goal by the conversion ratio to find the total number of gross impressions needed in each medium: 700,000 for television, 187,500 for radio, and 375,000 for print. We then estimated reach based on

audience data for the selected advertising vehicles. Since we are targeting virtually everyone in the *Jazz Tonight* and *Blues Beat* audiences, we simply used the average audience for these two programs. For *Music Review* magazine, however, only 25 percent of the magazine's 36,000 subscribers are interested in Celtic or early music, so we used 9,000 as the average readership figure.

The next step was to find frequency by dividing the number of gross impressions by the average reach. This worked out to 20 times for television, 75 times for radio, and 42 times for print. With the frequency numbers in hand, we could then calculate budget requirements for each medium.

Exhibit B.2 shows the results of the two budgeting stages. Obviously, $500,000 is a significant expenditure for a company our size, but we view it as an investment since we'll be building our house list along the way.

Schedule and Media Calendar

Exhibit B.3 is a combined activities schedule and media calendar. The PR, personal selling, and sales promotion activities are shown first, followed by a production

EXHIBIT B.3   Schedule and Media Calendar

This calendar indicates when each of our promotional activities will take place through 1995.

1995	Jan	Feb	Mar	Apr	May	June	July	Aug	Sept	Oct	Nov	Dec
PUBLIC RELATIONS												
Producing sampler CD		▓	▓									
Printing press kit			▓									
Mailing press kit				▓								
PERSONAL SELLING												
Hire telemarketer	▓											
Train telemarketer		▓										
Telemarketer on-line			▓	▓	▓	▓	▓	▓	▓	▓	▓	▓
SALES PROMOTION												
Design promo		▓										
Modify ads as needed			▓									
Promo in progress				▓	▓							
ADVERTISING												
Produce TV spot	▓											
Broadcast TV spot		▓	▓	▓	▓	▓	▓	▓				
Produce radio spot						▓						
Broadcast radio spot							▓	▓	▓	▓	▓	▓
Produce magazine ad	▓											
Run magazine ad		▓	▓	▓	▓	▓	▓	▓	▓	▓	▓	▓
Distribute catalogs	▓		▓		▓		▓		▓		▓	

and media calendar for the advertising program. The television ad will run once during *Jazz Tonight* each week from February through June, a total of 20 times. We'll switch to radio ads in the second half of the year, when *Blues Beat* goes national. We'll run 15 times a month during that five-month period, for a total of 75 times. The magazine ad will run in 42 issues of *Music Review* between February and December. We're trying to negotiate a deal with the magazine's publisher for six more weeks of advertising in return for inserting information about the magazine in our bimonthly catalog mailings. If this comes through, we'll be able to cover every issue from February through December.

Apply Your Knowledge

1. This plan doesn't have any provisions for testing the effectiveness of the advertising effort. What steps might MBM take to test the effectiveness of its particular bimonthly catalog format relative to the format used by the larger CD clubs?

2. The "From our house to yours" ads are a form of celebrity advertising. Do you think they'll be effective with this audience? Why or why not?

3. How might MBM take advantage of changes in technology to advertise its products?

4. How does the catalog help counter the threat of a major distributor moving into MBM's markets?

Career Planning and Development in Advertising

Exploring Advertising Careers

If you'd like to be part of a stimulating aspect of business that will present plenty of challenges and opportunities in the coming decades, advertising is the career for you. As discussed often in this book, the advertising function encompasses a wide variety of activities, each making an important contribution to the success of the organization. As more companies, nonprofit organizations, and government agencies around the world use advertising to communicate with their target audiences, you can expect the number of job opportunities to expand.

This appendix will help you sort out your options in advertising careers and map some of the steps you can take toward landing a job in the exciting, ever-changing world of advertising. This section also reviews the skills required for an advertising career, outlines what life is like for people who work in advertising, and then talks about career paths. In the second section, you get a closer look at specific advertising functions and jobs with advertisers, agencies, the media, and suppliers. The third section is all about how to market yourself to prospective employers. The closing section includes sources with further information about advertising careers.

A VARIETY OF EMPLOYERS

In the private sector, virtually every company, large or small, uses some form of advertising. From the tiniest all-text classified ad to the most lavish television commercial, advertising provides an essential link between businesses and customers in the global marketplace. In small concerns, the president may be responsible for advertising, but even these companies hire advertising agencies, research suppliers, and other specialists to handle specific tasks. In some larger companies, staff experts create and place the advertising materials; in other companies, managers supervise outside specialists who develop and place the advertising materials for their clients.

In addition, advertising has become an important method of reaching goals for many government agencies and nonprofit organizations. For example, during peacetime, the U.S. armed services mount intensive advertising campaigns designed to enhance their image and attract qualified recruits. The U.S. Mint has become increasingly sophisticated about advertising coin sets and collectibles via direct mail. Similarly, the National Audubon Society and many other nonprofit organizations now use advertising to raise money, recruit volunteers, and attract clients or patients to serve.

On the agency side, you can work for a full-service agency, a limited-service agency, or a specialized agency. These three types of agencies (described in Chapter 2) serve the advertising and promotion needs of advertisers in the public and the private sectors. Among the fast-growing specialized agencies are those serving health-care and technology clients. Inside each agency are a variety of departments that work interdependently to apply their specific areas of expertise to solving the client's problems.

Media firms and suppliers are also vital to the advertising process. Within the wide world of media are jobs in publishing, radio and television, direct mail, and the many supplementary and emerging in-home and out-of-home media. Suppliers range from small businesses to multinational corporations offering photography, typesetting, or other services that advertisers need to bring their messages from concept to production.

To narrow your focus and choose among these organizations, consider your own background and interests. When deciding what type of organization to work for, remember that you can often transfer the skills you learn in one type of organization to positions in other types of organizations, so don't feel limited by your initial selection. In fact, people frequently move from the agency side to the advertiser side (and vice versa), and movement among suppliers, agencies, and the media is a common way of gaining additional responsibilities while honing specific skills.

A VARIETY OF JOBS

Another choice you face as you plan your career is deciding which type of job to pursue. In general, the world of advertising includes seven broad job categories: (1) creative jobs such as copywriter, (2) production and traffic jobs such as film editor, (3) media jobs such as media planner, (4) account management jobs such as account executive, (5) research jobs such as market research analyst, (6) public relations jobs such as publicist, and (7) sales and management jobs such as broadcast media sales. Of course, not every organization has job openings in every category. On the other hand, you'll find a concentration of jobs in a particular category at agencies or suppliers that specialize in that category. For instance, if you're trying to break into public relations, you might apply to public relations firms, which handle assignments from many clients.

Remember that much of the upward movement you can expect in your career will be within your chosen job category. Although you can move between organizations fairly easily, moving between job categories—say, from account management to copywriting or from research to media planning—is less common, because of the differing skills needed for each category. An entry-level creative job (as an illustrator, for instance) can ultimately lead to the position of art director. So as you set your five-year goals, try to settle on a job and category that will be exciting and fulfilling over the long term.

A VARIETY OF SKILLS

What does it take to break into advertising? Depending on your specific job objective, you'll need technical skills such as artistic ability or analytical expertise. Beyond these technical skills, however, you'll also need the following:

- *Creativity.* In copywriting or art direction, creativity is the ability to come up with an exciting concept and translate it into a campaign or an ad that really communicates with the target audience. However, creativity isn't limited to the people who work in creative services; everyone in the advertising process needs creativity. Researchers seeking insights into buyer behavior have to ask questions that no one has asked before; media planners have to come up with new ways of using media to reach the target audience at the right time and place. No matter what advertising job you choose, you'll challenge your imagination and generate new ideas every day.

- *Good communication skills.* Successful copywriters are able to write well; effective account executives are able to speak well. Beyond the communication skills needed to develop and produce ads, advertising people are in constant contact with colleagues, clients, media personnel, suppliers, and many others. Daily communication challenges range from oral presentations and telephone interviews to letters and written reports. Successful advertising people are also able to work well with others. Collaboration and cooperation are an integral part of the advertising process—especially when completing difficult assignments or coping with tight deadlines.

- *Flexibility.* Advertising professionals at all levels need the ability to adapt to frequent and sudden changes brought on by competition, market shifts, and other unforeseen forces. To succeed in an industry that never stands still, you'll have to be flexible and willing to learn.

- *Interest in the world around you.* Are you a curious person? Do you tend to analyze whatever you're involved in? You never know when some tidbit of information or some unexpected insight will turn out to be the key to a new campaign or a new way of approaching the target audience. Follow your inclination to dig deeper, and you'll be on your way to establishing a solid foundation of knowledge and analytical prowess that will serve you well throughout your advertising career.

- *Persistence and dedication.* Every ad and every campaign is the result of countless changes and refinements. With persistence, you'll be able to keep your eye on the goal and stick with your projects until completion, no matter how many detours you face. Advertising isn't a 9-to-5 industry; sometimes people work late or on weekends to get the job done. It takes a special kind of dedication to adapt to these pressures.

Remember that advertising is both an art and a science. In every organization and in every job, business ability is as much a requirement as creative and analytical skills.

Examining Your Career Options

Do you want to work for an advertiser, an advertising agency, the media, or a supplier? You have a wide range of job choices. This section describes many of the individual positions you might consider among the seven categories of jobs in the advertising industry.

CREATIVE JOBS

The top creative job in advertising is creative director (or director of creative services). This position involves supervising a number of related creative tasks, including copywriting, art direction, and print and electronic production. You generally reach this level by rising through either art or copywriting.

The art director is responsible for all visual aspects of an ad. Art directors create or, in large departments, supervise the creation of designs, layouts, illustrations, storyboards, and other visual elements in print and electronic advertising. Lower-level positions that can lead to art director include graphic artist, illustrator, and assistant (or junior) art director.

Generally, a copywriter is responsible for the headlines and copy in print ads, the scripts used to produce radio and television commercials, letters and brochures used in direct-mail packages, and all copy for related promotional materials. A typical entry-level position for a copywriter is assistant (or junior) copywriter, and an experienced copywriter can advance to senior copywriter or copy supervisor.

Of course, agencies and advertisers use the services of many creative people, including photographers, jingle writers, package designers, and type designers, to name a few. If you're interested in pursuing these creative jobs, you may work for suppliers, you may work on your own as a freelancer, or you may join the staff of an advertiser or agency.

PRODUCTION AND TRAFFIC JOBS

An agency's or advertiser's production activities are managed by the production manager, who supervises both print and broadcast production. The print production manager is responsible for completing all newspaper and magazine ads by coordinating typesetting, color separation, printing, and related activities. You might start in this department as a production assistant. Similarly, the broadcast production manager supervises the making of radio and television commercials by hiring directors and film crews, casting the commercials, and handling all other related duties. For this department, the entry-level position is also production assistant.

A key position that spans the creative and production categories is traffic manager. In this role, your duties would include scheduling and overseeing the work flow so that print and broadcast ads are produced and sent to the media on time. The entry-level position is traffic assistant, from which you could move up to traffic coordinator for either print or broadcast media.

MEDIA JOBS

The most senior media job in an agency is media director. In this role, you'd be responsible for choosing the right media and negotiating the best price to reach the target audience. Reporting to the media director is the media planner, who decides which media to use and chooses among the many media vehicles. The media buyer, who negotiates the price and books advertising time or space, also reports to the media director. You'd probably start out as a media trainee with the opportunity to advance to assistant media buyer or assistant media planner.

ACCOUNT MANAGEMENT JOBS

The account executive (AE) is the vital link between the client and the advertising agency. The AE is responsible for building and maintaining a good working partnership between the agency and the advertiser. He or she coordinates the activities of all the agency personnel who work on a particular account. At the same time, the AE serves as the voice of the agency when meeting with a client. Your first step on this career ladder would be assistant account executive. In this role, you might handle administrative tasks and analyze the advertising activities of your clients' competitors. Experienced AEs can advance to become account supervisors, who are responsible for groups of accounts.

RESEARCH JOBS

The top research job in advertising is research director. In this position, you'd conduct secondary and primary research to understand customer needs, wants, values, and concerns. You'd also test the effectiveness of various advertising concepts and approaches to find the best way of communicating with your target audience. A market researcher reporting to the research director would be responsible for all research activities needed to serve a few clients (or one major client). The entry-level position for this job category is research assistant (or assistant project manager), who gathers secondary data and helps more senior researchers summarize and interpret them. Some agencies also hire account planners, research specialists with an in-depth understanding of consumer interests and attitudes. Account planners represent the "voice of the consumer" during agency discussions of advertising strategy.

PUBLIC RELATIONS JOBS

The public relations director is responsible for all aspects of an advertiser's public relations strategy. Duties include developing or supervising the development of press releases, annual reports, internal and external newsletters, and company brochures. An entry-level position for this career path is trainee or writer (for a particular newsletter or another communication vehicle).

A publicist, who reports to the public relations director, has a narrower focus, responsible only for generating media coverage about advertisers and their products. The special-events coordinator also reports to the public relations director and specializes in developing and managing promotional events. Some special events are aimed at prospects and customers, some are geared toward boosting employee morale, and some are designed to attract media coverage. You might start as a special-events assistant and ultimately work your way up to head the public relations department.

The trade show coordinator handles an advertiser's convention activities, including arranging for exhibit space and staffing the booth with company representatives or product demonstrators. In some organizations, the trade show coordinator reports to the public relations director; in others, this position reports to the marketing director. Often, the entry-level job in this field is trade show representative, a position in which you would attend conventions and trade shows to market your firm and its products to attendees.

SALES AND MANAGEMENT JOBS

If you're interested in a sales career, advertising can offer a lot of opportunity. All media vehicles need sales representatives to sell time or space to advertisers and agencies. No matter which medium you choose—television, radio, newspapers, magazines, transit advertising, or any other—you can look forward to a challenging career. Expect to start as a sales assistant handling administrative tasks; with experience, you can move up the career ladder to be sales manager for a particular media vehicle.

Agency management is another career option. All agencies need people with finance and accounting expertise to manage the payroll, bill clients, and pay invoices from suppliers and the media. On the other hand, you might choose a position in human resources. At the very top of the management ladder is the chief executive officer, who oversees the agency's operations and monitors agency profitability and performance.

Entering the Advertising World

You've decided that advertising is the career for you. Now you're faced with the most important marketing job of all: marketing yourself. This textbook includes marketing and advertising techniques you can use in your own job search. Just put yourself in the dual role of marketer and product, and you'll be well on your way. The following sections show you how to start the job-search process by considering your skills and your goals, targeting organizations where you'd like to work, and positioning yourself for the jobs you want. Once you're on the job, you have opportunities for further development, and you can be thinking ahead to your next step up the career ladder.

TAKING INVENTORY OF YOUR SKILLS AND GOALS

The best place to start your job search is by assessing your own talents and setting personal and professional goals. Many excellent books on self-assessment are available to guide you in taking stock of your abilities and interests and to help you match them to your objectives. (See the list of resources at the end of this appendix.) Consider your educational background and the skills you've gained in college and on the job. Also think about your strengths and weaknesses and track the kinds of tasks you love (and hate) to do. Look back at the jobs you've held and determine why some were exciting or challenging while others seemed dull or monotonous. By evaluating your talents and interests and by understanding why you liked or disliked jobs you've held, you're on your way to narrowing down the world of advertising careers to a handful that make sense and that fit your background.

If your abilities don't match up to the careers you're interested in, you can take some additional courses, look for an internship to gain new skills, or find a job (full-time, part-time, or summer) that gives you more experience. Of course for some positions, a master's degree or a doctorate is desirable, if not necessary. For instance, marketing research positions are typically filled by people with advanced degrees. Remember, you're the product, so you want to make yourself as marketable as possible.

Next, take the time to think about what you want out of life, personally and professionally. Do you want fame or fortune? Do you want to help society or save the environment? Where do you want to live and work? What are your salary expectations? What position would you like to hold in five years? Although it sounds premature to worry about the future before you even have your first advertising job, setting a career objective with a definite job in mind will help guide you when selecting among organizations and jobs.

TARGETING ORGANIZATIONS AND POSITIONS

In this phase of the job search, use your targeting skills to review the market, eliminate inappropriate or uninteresting options, and focus on those you'd really like

Victoria Holland
14014 Oak Boulevard
Philadelphia, PA 19126
(215) 747-4295

OBJECTIVE

A research position that requires research design and statistical analysis skills

RESEARCH DESIGN

* Improved research design by developing moderator discussion guides for 14 focus groups conducted at the Opinions Unlimited research center, Harrisburg, Pennsylvania
* Created an effective focus-group discussion guide for researching student reactions to proposed advertising concepts promoting student bank accounts
* Developed and tested a telephone questionnaire for a survey about attitudes toward electric heat and gas heat

RESEARCH ANALYSIS

* Summarized and interpreted results of focus group interviews to pretest creative concepts, presented findings to the client, and recommended changes to the proposed commercials that resulted in higher recall scores
* Tabulated and analyzed results of telephone interviews using SAS computer software

SECONDARY RESEARCH

* Used electronic database services to research scholarship funding issues for Temple University dean's office and develop a listing of scholarship sources for student use
* Conducted periodicals research for graduate students writing theses on advertising topics

EDUCATION

* Temple University, Philadelphia, September 1991--May 1995
* B.A. Marketing (3.7 GPA on 4.0 scale)
* Advanced workshops included: advertising concept testing; personal interview techniques; and research interpretation

EXPERIENCE

* September 1994--May 1995, Research Assistant, Temple University Library, Philadelphia, Pennsylvania
* June 1994--August 1994, Evening Supervisor, Opinions Unlimited, Harrisburg, Pennsylvania
* June 1993--August 1993, Research Intern, Opinions Unlimited, Harrisburg, Pennsylvania

REFERENCES

Available on request

EXHIBIT C.1

Sample Résumé for a Research Position

If you're seeking an entry-level position right after graduation, prepare a functional résumé that emphasizes your areas of competence. Organize the résumé around a list of accomplishments, and then identify your employers and academic experiences in the appropriate sections.

to pursue. The sources listed at the end of this appendix can help you investigate the advertising areas you'd like to consider. Look for information about the job market in those fields, read about what professionals do on the job, and see how the career paths match up to your five-year goal. If your interest is piqued, make a note of any organizations or people mentioned in these sources so that you can follow up later.

The trade journals and industry associations of the advertising specialties you're investigating can provide valuable information about trends and careers. Some associations have student memberships, giving you a chance to attend professional meetings and mingle with people who work in the field. Ask the staff at your college placement office or your library about the *Occupational Outlook Handbook*, on-campus recruiting, and other help. Also check one or two of the many excellent career guides for college students. Scan the want ads in the Sunday newspaper and in industry publications to get a feel for job descriptions, locations, and salaries and to find the names of companies or employment agencies you can contact. Also call your state employment office to check on any appropriate job listings.

Talk with people you know who work in advertising; ask about the organizations they work for, what they do on the job, and whether they know of job opportunities in advertising. Perhaps some of the people you know can help arrange an "information interview" with their employers. This type of interview gives you the opportunity to learn more about advertising and the operations

14014 Oak Boulevard
Philadelphia, PA 19126
September 5, 1995

Mr. Leon Kotowski
Vice President, Marketing Services
Three Rivers Advertising
6458 River Road
Pittsburgh, PA 15237

Dear Mr. Kotowski:

During Temple University's recent Northeast Business symposium, I met your assistant, Isabel Anderson, who mentioned that you wanted to hire two research analysts. After talking with Ms. Anderson about the role of research at Three Rivers Advertising, I believe that my experience in questionnaire design and concept testing would be an asset to your agency.

In addition to my undergraduate coursework in research theory and applications, I have successfully completed a series of five advanced workshops in advertising research taught by local practitioners. I am also thoroughly familiar with the latest statistical analysis programs.

To apply this knowledge, I selected as my senior project an in-depth analysis of bank advertising aimed at the student market in Philadelphia. To date, two members of the Philadelphia Bank Association have used the results of my study to develop new ad campaigns aimed at college students in the area.

Please see the enclosed résumé for more information about my experience in research design, research analysis, and secondary research. Elinor Weinstein, director of Opinions Unlimited, will be happy to conform my accomplishments and answer any questions you have about my research skills.

Given my background and interest in advertising research, I would appreciate the opportunity to meet with you to learn more about your department and to discuss my qualifications in more detail. I can be reached at (215) 747-4295; I'll be available any day next week to meet with you at your convenience.

Sincerely,

Victoria Holland

Victoria Holland

Enclosure

EXHIBIT C.2
Sample Cover Letter Requesting an Interview

Once you've compiled a list of organizations to target, send a letter like this one to ask for an interview and further information.

of the firm. Even if there's no job immediately available, you'll have a contact if an opening should arise. However, information interviews may not be an accepted practice in your area, so don't overlook other opportunities to get information about your job category of choice. You have a wider network than you might think: relatives, friends, classmates, professors, and former employers may be able to help you meet with people who work in advertising. More often, you'll get your big break through your network rather than through a classified ad. Build a file of organizations you want to contact in your job search, and use this as your target market.

POSITIONING AND ADVERTISING YOURSELF

You've defined your target market; how can you position and advertise yourself to your audience? Your tools include a résumé, cover letter, interview skills, and follow-up communications. Most of the time, you'll start by sending a résumé and a cover letter to the contact names on your list. (See the sample résumé in Exhibit C.1 and the cover letter in Exhibit C.2.) Your résumé typically consists of a heading, including your name and address; an objective (optional); your educational background, including relevant courses you've taken; your employment experience, including any part-time or volunteer work; any activities, achievements, special language skills or computer skills; and references (optional).

Your cover letter is designed to catch the reader's attention and to be so convincing about your qualifications that you get an interview for the job you're seeking. In most cases, you'll create a slightly different version of your cover letter as a way of positioning your background and qualifications for various employers and fields. For example, if you're targeting advertising agencies for a copywriting job, you may want to emphasize your work on the college newspaper. However, if you're targeting a

CHECKLIST FOR ASSEMBLING AN ADVERTISING PORTFOLIO

❏ A. Include ads for a variety of goods and services.
  • Demonstrate your versatility by including ads you've created for a range of products.
  • Be sure to include ads that are aimed at various target audiences and that use a variety of advertising appeals.
  • Where possible, choose products for your hypothetical ads that you're familiar with so you can readily identify the target audiences and the benefits.
  • Instead of creating hypothetical ads for high-profile products that are renowned for their excellent advertising, choose products that are difficult to advertise. This will give you the opportunity to display your creativity and imagination.

❏ B. Include at least one complete campaign (more if possible).
  • Prove your abilities by carrying through a creative idea and a campaign theme for one product in multiple media.
  • Show how well you work within the limitations and advantages of each medium by including a number of ads (generally one in each of the main media) focusing on the same benefit of a single product.

❏ C. Include a variety of ads in each medium.
  • Present ads that portray various approaches to the challenges posed by limitations on media time and space, as well as various approaches to using the creative possibilities of each medium. Consider including some of the following:
    1. Newspaper ads in various sizes, including full-page, half-page, and smaller space ads; a range of black-and-white, two-color, three-color, and four-color ads
    2. Four-color magazine ads in various sizes, including two-page spreads, full-page ads, half-page ads, and other size and space combinations
    3. Scripts for 30-second and 60-second radio commercials.
    4. Storyboards for 15-second and 30-second commercials.

    5. Plans for outdoor posters or painted bulletins
    6. Ads for various positions in transit advertising
    7. Direct-mail packages such as letters and catalog spreads
  • Avoid including ads that suggest needless expense; this shows that you understand realistic budget constraints.

❏ D. Limit the number of ads you include.
  • Quality is more important than quantity, so edit your selections to show only the best.
  • Aim for at least 10 and at most 20 ads.
  • Update your portfolio as you complete additional class assignments and gain more proficiency.
  • Change and add samples as you progress in your career and create more and better ads and campaigns.

❏ E. Include ads that demonstrate a fresh approach and a clear strategy.
  • Ideas are generally more important to potential employers than finished art or copy, so infuse your work with original concepts.
  • Avoid imitating other ads or campaigns.
  • Take a chance and try some unconventional concepts.
  • Be sure that your ads follow through on a meaningful creative strategy geared to the appropriate audience.

❏ F. Include ads that offer evidence of good craftsmanship.
  • Professionalism counts, so execute your sample ads with care.
  • Remember that neatness isn't as important as creativity, but sloppy ads are likely to detract from the ideas you're trying to communicate and the impression you want to make.
  • Check your spelling, grammar, and punctuation to avoid embarrassing errors.
  • When your ads effectively sell the product, they also sell your abilities, so don't let your copy or your art obscure the message.

research supplier for an analytical job, you may want to emphasize the research project you completed for a statistics course. Of course, the opening of your letter will vary, depending on whether you're answering an ad, requesting an information interview, or asking for a job interview.

For a creative job in art or copywriting, you'll need to prepare a portfolio (also known as a "book") to bring to your interviews. A beginning copywriter or aspiring art director can fill a portfolio by using ads created for class

assignments and adding hypothetical ads and campaigns for a variety of products. The portfolio shows your target audience the kind of work you're capable of doing, so second best simply won't do: include only your best ads. Aim for good craftsmanship as well as original ideas, and you'll be on your way to putting together a portfolio that opens doors. See the Checklist for Assembling an Advertising Portfolio for some general guidelines.

If you've done a good job of positioning yourself, matching your skills and interests to the needs of the organizations in your target audience, you stand a good chance of landing a job interview. It's on the basis of the interview process that prospective employers make their decisions about candidates, so read up on interviews and hone your skills. Come to interviews prepared with background information about the organization and some questions for the interviewer about the job and the firm. Be prepared to answer standard questions interviewers ask, such as "Why did you choose our company?" and "Why do you want to be in this field?" However, don't memorize your answers or you'll sound overrehearsed. If you can, have yourself videotaped in a mock interview so that you can see yourself in action and can pinpoint areas for improvement.

Once you've been interviewed, it's important to follow up and write a thank-you letter. Not only is this good manners, but it also gives you another opportunity to sell yourself. Whether you're thanking someone for an information interview, a job interview, or a referral to another person or firm, say how much you appreciate the interviewer's time and interest. This letter needn't be long, but it should be sent soon after your meeting. If you happen to run across any items of interest—such as an article from the campus newspaper about your interviewer's company or area of expertise—you can keep the dialog going by sending the clipping with a brief personal note. By being personable yet professional, you'll stay on your interviewers' list of active candidates and, in time, land the job of your choice.

ON THE JOB

Congratulations! You've successfully launched your career in advertising. Don't stop now—it's never too soon to start thinking about the five-year career objectives you set when you were taking inventory of your skills. Watch for opportunities to learn new skills and make professional connections that will prepare you for the next rung on your career ladder. Your employer may offer to send you to a professional training course or technical seminar to introduce you to a new procedure, or you may be asked to assist a senior executive who's presenting a paper at an industry meeting. Take every opportunity to learn about the latest trends and technology and to exchange ideas with people from other organizations, industries, or disciplines.

Of course, the more skills you gain, the more valuable you are to your organization and the broader your perspective is. However, to make your next move up the ladder, you may find that you need additional qualifications, such as graduate courses or a certificate in a specialized field. If you've identified your five-year career goals in advance, you're better able to anticipate what you'll need to stay in the race. The more you learn about your chosen area of advertising expertise, the better you'll be able to pinpoint the specific direction you want your career to take. So it's a good idea to review and revise your five-year goals from time to time to see where you are and to determine whether you want to shift to a different career path. Welcome to the dynamic world of advertising.

Researching Career Options

The following sections list selected sources where you can get additional information about the advertising industry and about career planning.

PROFESSIONAL AND TRADE ASSOCIATIONS
Advertising Research Foundation
3 East 54th Street
New York, NY 10022
(212) 751-5656

Advertising Women of New York
153 East 57th Street
New York, NY 10022
(212) 593-1950

American Advertising Federation
1400 K Street N.W., Suite 1000
Washington, DC 20005
(202) 898-0089

American Association of Advertising Agencies
666 Third Avenue, 13th Floor
New York, NY 10017
(212) 682-2500

American Marketing Association
250 South Wacker Drive, Suite 200
Chicago, IL 60606
(312) 648-0536

Association of National Advertisers
144 East 44th Street
New York, NY 10017
(212) 697-5950

Cable Television Advertising Bureau
767 Third Avenue
New York, NY 10017
(212) 751-7770

Direct Marketing Association
6 East 43rd Street
New York, NY 10017
(212) 689-4977

International Advertising Association
342 Madison Avenue, 20th Floor
New York, NY 10017
(212) 557-1133

Magazine Publishers of America
575 Lexington Avenue, Suite 540
New York, NY 10022
(212) 752-0055

Marketing Research Association
111 East Wacker Drive, Suite 600
Chicago, IL 60601
(312) 644-6610

Newspaper Association of America
The Newspaper Center
11600 Sunrise Valley Drive
Reston, VA 22091
(703) 648-1000

Outdoor Advertising Association of America
1212 New York Avenue, N.W., Suite 1210
Washington, DC 20005
(202) 371-5566

Point-of-Purchase Advertising Institute
66 North Van Brunt Street
Englewood, NJ 07631
(201) 894-8899

Public Relations Society of America
33 Irving Place, 3rd Floor
New York, NY 10003
(212) 995-2230

Radio Advertising Bureau, Inc.
304 Park Avenue South
New York, NY 10010
(212) 254-4800

Sales and Marketing Executives International
Statler Office Tower, No. 458
Cleveland, OH 44115
(216) 771-6650

Specialty Advertising Association International
3125 Skyway Circle North
Irving, TX 75038
(214) 252-0404

Television Bureau of Advertising
477 Madison Avenue
New York, NY 10022
(212) 486-1111

Women in Advertising and Marketing
4200 Wisconsin Avenue N.W., Suite 106-238
Washington, DC 20016
(202) 369-7400

INDUSTRY PUBLICATIONS
Admap
7-11 St. John's Hill
London SW11 1TE
England

Advertising Age
Crain Communications, Inc.
740 North Rush Street
Chicago, IL 60611
(312) 649-5200

Advertising Age's Creativity
Crain Communications, Inc.
740 North Rush Street
Chicago, IL 60611
(312) 649-5200

Adweek
1515 Broadway
New York, NY 10036
(212) 536-5336

Art Direction
10 East 39th Street, 6th Floor
New York, NY 10016
(212) 889-6500

Asian Advertising & Marketing
Zindra Limited
31/F Citicorp Centre
18 Whitfield Road
Causeway Bay, Hong Kong

Brandweek
1515 Broadway
New York, NY 10036
(212) 536-5336

Business Marketing
Crain Communications, Inc.
740 North Rush Street
Chicago, IL 60611
(312) 649-5200

Catalog Age
PO Box 4949
Stamford, CT 06907
(203) 358-9900

Communication Arts
410 Sherman Avenue
Palo Alto, CA 94303
(415) 326-6040

Direct Marketing
224 Seventh Street
Garden City, NY 11530
(516) 746-6700

DM News: The Newspaper of Direct Marketing
Mill Hollow Corporation
19 West 21st Street, 8th Floor
New York, NY 10010
(212) 741-2095

Inside PR
235 West 48th Street, Suite 34A
New York, NY 10036
(212) 245-8680

International Archive
American Showcase
915 Broadway, 14th Floor
New York, NY 10010
(212) 673-6600

Journal of Advertising Research
Advertising Research Foundation
3 East 54th Street, 15th Floor
New York, NY 10022
(212) 751-5656

Journal of Business & Industrial Marketing
108 Loma Media Road
Santa Barbara, CA 93103

Journal of Business-to-Business Marketing
10 Alice Street
Binghamton, NY 13904

Journal of Consumer Marketing
108 Loma Media Road
Santa Barbara, CA 93103

Journal of Direct Marketing
605 Third Avenue
New York, NY 10022
(212) 850-6000

Journal of Global Marketing
10 Alice Street
Binghamton, NY 13904

Journal of International Consumer Marketing
10 Alice Street
Binghamton, NY 13904

Journal of Marketing
American Marketing Association
250 South Wacker Drive, Suite 200
Chicago, IL 60606
(312) 648-0536

Journal of Marketing Research
American Marketing Association
250 South Wacker Drive, Suite 200
Chicago, IL 60606
(312) 648-0536

Journal of Promotion Management
10 Alice Street
Binghamton, NY 13904

Marketing
777 Bay Street
Toronto, ON M5W 1A7
Canada
(416) 596-5858

Marketing News
American Marketing Association
250 South Wacker Drive, Suite 200
Chicago, IL 60606
(312) 648-0536

Mediaweek
1515 Broadway
New York, NY 10036
(212) 536-5336

PR News
127 East 80th Street
New York, NY 10021
(212) 879-7090

Promo
47 Old Ridgefield Road
Wilton, CT 06897
(203) 778-4007

Public Relations Journal
Public Relations Society of America
33 Irving Place, 3rd Floor
New York, NY 10003
(212) 995-2230

Quirk's Marketing Research
Box 23536
Minneapolis, MN 55423
(612) 861-8051

Sales & Marketing Management
633 Third Avenue
New York, NY 10017
(212) 986-4800

Sales & Marketing Management in Canada
3500 Dufferin Street, 402
Downsview, ON M3K 1N2
Canada
(416) 633-2020

Sports Marketing News
Technical Marketing Group
1460 Post Road East
Westport, CT 06880

Target Marketing
North American Publishing Company
401 North Broad Street
Philadelphia, PA 19108
(215) 238-5300

Telemarketing
Technology Marketing Corp.
One Technology Plaza
Norwalk, CT 06854
(203) 852-6800

CAREER PLANNING

Bolles, Richard N., *What Color Is Your Parachute? A Practical Manual for Job Hunters and Career Changers* (Berkeley, Calif.: Ten Speed Press, 1994).

Dumphy, Philip W., ed., *Career Development for the College Student*, 5th ed. (Cranston, R.I.: Carroll Press, 1981).

Fox, Maria, *Put Your Degree to Work: The New Professional's Guide to Career Planning and Job Hunting,* 2d ed. (New York: Wiley, 1988).

Henze, Geraldine, *Winning Career Moves: A Guide to Improving Your Work Life* (Homewood, Ill.: Business One Irwin, 1992).

CAREER GUIDES

The Career Choices Encyclopedia: A Guide to Entry-Level Jobs (New York: Walker, 1986).

Field, Shelly, *Career Opportunities in Advertising and Public Relations* (New York: Facts on File, 1990).

Greenberg, Jan, *Advertising Careers: The Business and the People* (New York: Henry Holt, 1987).

Laskin, David, *Getting into Advertising: A Career Guide* (New York: Ballantine Books, 1986).

Lewis, William, and Nancy Schuman, *Fast-Track Careers: A Guide to the Highest-Paying Jobs* (New York: Wiley, 1987).

Lidz, Richard, and Linda Perrin, eds., *Career Information Center,* 3d ed., 13 vols. (New York: Macmillan, 1987).

Paetro, Maxine, *How to Put Your Book Together and Get a Job in Advertising,* new improved edition (Chicago: The Copy Workshop, 1990).

Pattis, S. William, *Careers in Advertising* (Lincolnwood, Ill.: VGM Career Horizons, 1990).

Porterfield, Jim, *Business Career Planning Guide* (Cincinnati: South-Western, 1993).

Rosenthal, David W., and Michael A. Powell, *Careers in Marketing* (Englewood Cliffs, N.J.: Prentice-Hall, 1984).

U.S. Bureau of Labor Statistics, *Occupational Outlook Handbook* (Washington, D.C.: GPO, 1994).

DIRECTORIES FOR CAREER PLANNING

Fry, Ronald W., ed., *Advertising Career Directory* (Hawthorne, N.J.: Career Press, 1990).

Fry, Ronald W., ed. *Marketing & Sales Career Directory,* 3d ed. (Hawthorne, N.J.: Career Press, 1990).

Fry, Ronald W., ed., *Public Relations Career Directory* (Hawthorne, N.J.: Career Press, 1990).

JOB HUNTING

Beatty, Richard H., *The Complete Job Search Book* (New York: Wiley, 1988).

Beatty, Richard H., *The Perfect Cover Letter* (New York: Wiley, 1989).

Harkavy, Michael David, and The Philip Lief Group, *The 100 Best Companies to Sell For* (New York: Wiley, 1989).

Irish, Richard K., *Go Hire Yourself an Employer,* 3d ed. (Garden City, N.Y.: Doubleday/Anchor Press, 1987).

RÉSUMÉ PREPARATION

Brett, Pat, *Résumé Writing for Results: A Workbook* (Belmont, Calif.: Wadsworth, 1992).

Corwen, Leonard, *Your Résumé: Key to a Better Job* (Englewood Cliffs, N.J.: Prentice-Hall, 1993).

Eyler, David R., *Résumés That Mean Business* (New York: Random House, 1993).

Jackson, Tom, *Tom Jackson's Résumé Express: The Fastest Way to Write a Winning Résumé* (New York: Random House, 1993).

Smith, Michael H., *The Résumé Writer's Handbook: A Comprehensive, Step-by-Step Writing Guide and Reference Manual for Every Job Seeker* (New York: HarperCollins, 1993).

INTERVIEWING

Allen, Jeffrey G., *The Complete Q & A Job Interview Book* (New York: Wiley, 1988).

Allen, Jeffrey G., *The Five Hundred Interview Questions and How to Answer Them* (New York: Wiley, 1988).

Medley, H. Anthony, *Sweaty Palms: The Neglected Art of Being Interviewed* (Berkeley, Calif.: Ten Speed Press, 1992).

Shingleton, John, *Successful Interviewing for College Seniors* (Lincolnwood, Ill.: NTC, 1992).

Washington, Tom, *What Now? Interviewing Techniques for Winning in the 90's* (Everett, Wash.: MeyCor Research Institute, 1993). (Video/audio program)

INTERNSHIPS

Fry, Ronald W., ed., *Internships,* 2 vols. (Hawthorne, N.J.: Career Press, 1990).

The National Directory of Internships (Raleigh, N.C.: National Society for Internships and Experimental Education, 1989).

Renetzky, Alvin, ed., *Directory of Internships, Work Experience Programs, and On-the-Job Training Opportunities* (Santa Monica, Calif.: Ready Reference Press, 1986).

References

Notes

CHAPTER 1

1. Maryellen Gordon, "Jeans Jam the Airwaves," *Women's Wear Daily,* 11 September 1992, 10; Cathy Taylor, "Jeans Genies," *Adweek,* 14 October 1991, 44, 48; Stuart Elliott, "Can Levi Strauss Extend Its Success with Dockers?" *New York Times,* 24 February 1992, D10; Stuart Elliott, "Levi's Two New Campaigns Aim at Who Fits the Jeans," *New York Times,* 27 July 1992, D7; Marcy Magiera, "Levi's Dockers Looks for Younger, Upscale Men with Authentics," *Advertising Age,* 18 January 1993, 4; Cyndee Miller, "Jeans Marketers Look for Good Fit with Older Men and Women," *Marketing News,* 16 September 1992, 1, 6; Cyndee Miller, "Jeans Marketers Loosen Up, Adjust to Expanding Market," *Marketing News,* 31 August 1992, 6, 7; Marcy Magiera, "Levi's Boosts Ads; Hispanic Budget 'Right up There,' " *Advertising Age,* 15 April 1991, 17.

2. William Leiss, Stephen Kline, and Sut Jhally, *Social Communication in Advertising: Persons, Products, and Images of Well-Being* (New York: Routledge, 1990), 5, 15, 25.

3. "100 Leading National Advertisers: Nike Inc.," *Advertising Age,* 23 September 1992, 4–50; John Micklethwait, "Assault on the Heartland," *The Economist,* 9 June 1990, 5–7.

4. James Sterngold, "The Awakening Chinese Consumer," *New York Times,* 11 October 1992, sec. 3, 1, 6.

5. David W. Stewart, "Is Business-to-Business Advertising Really Different?" in *Proceedings of the 1991 Conference of the American Academy of Advertising,* edited by Rebecca Holman (New York: American Academy of Advertising, 1991), 199.

6. Kenneth Roman and Jane Maas, *The New How to Advertise* (New York: St. Martin's Press, 1992), 115.

7. Jane Rippeteau, "Where's Ft. Wayne When You Need It?" *The Marketer,* July–August 1990, 46–49.

8. Leo Bogart, *Strategy in Advertising: Matching Media and Messages to Markets and Motivations,* 2d ed. (Lincolnwood, Ill.: NTC Business Books, 1990), 122.

9. *The National Directory of Magazines, 1992* (New York: Oxbridge Communications, 1991), 558.

10. "AMA Board Approves New Marketing Definition," *Marketing News,* 1 March 1985, 1.

11. William E. Souder, "Managing Relations between R&D and Marketing in New Product Development Projects," *Journal of Product Innovation Management,* March 1988, 6–19.

12. John A. Howard, "Marketing Theory of the Firm," *Journal of Marketing,* Fall 1983, 90–100.

13. Tom Eisenhart, "Eaton: Clearing the Clutter," *Business Marketing,* January 1989, 36–38; Courtland L. Bovée and John V. Thill, *Marketing* (New York: McGraw-Hill, 1992), 623.

14. Don E. Schultz, Stanley I. Tannenbaum, and Robert F. Lauterborn, *Integrated Marketing Communications: Pulling It All Together and Making It Work* (Lincolnwood, Ill.: NTC Business Books, 1993), 59–63.

15. Schultz, Tannenbaum, and Lauterborn, *Integrated Marketing Communications,* 157–172.

16. Scott Hume, "Integrated Marketing: Who's in Charge Here?" *Advertising Age,* 22 March 1993, 3, 52.

17. Daniel Pope, *The Making of Modern Advertising* (New York: Basic Books, 1983), 3, 31; Stephen Fox, *The Mirror Makers* (New York: William Morrow, 1984), 66.

18. Frank Presbrey, *The History and Development of Advertising* (Garden City, N.Y.: Doubleday, Doran, 1929), 4, 14–16, 25; James Playsted Wood, *The Story of Advertising* (New York: Ronald Press, 1958), 18–24.

19. Wood, *The Story of Advertising,* 27–28; Presbrey, *The History and Development of Advertising,* 14–16.

20. Presbrey, *The History and Development of Advertising,* 14–16, 492–491; Wood, *The Story of Advertising,* 27–28.

21. Neil H. Borden, *The Economic Effects of Advertising* (Chicago: Irwin, 1942), 25, 27.

22. Borden, *The Economic Effects of Advertising,* 17–26, 49–50; Kathleen Hall Jamieson and Karlyn Kohrs Campbell, *The Interplay of Influence: News, Advertising, Politics, and the Mass Media,* 3d ed. (Belmont, Calif.: Wadsworth Publishing, 1992), 126–127.

23. Presbrey, *The History and Development of Advertising,* 62–68, 75, 132–136, 244–250; Wood, *The Story of Advertising,* 30–51; Leiss, Kline, and Jhally, *Social Communication in Advertising,* 97–99.

24. Presbrey, *The History and Development of Advertising,* 261–263; Wood, *The Story of Advertising,* 136–142; Leiss, Kline, and Jhally, *Social Communication in Advertising,* 131–133.

25. Wood, *The Story of Advertising,* 231–234; Fox, *The Mirror Makers,* 40–43; "U.S. Media Billings by Category," *Advertising Age,* 13 April 1992, S-41; Borden, *The Economic Effects of Advertising,* 126–133.

26. Fox, *The Mirror Makers,* 28–35, 40–43; Wood, *The Story of Advertising,* 193–202; Leiss, Kline, and Jhally,

Social Communication in Advertising, 100–101; Presbrey, *The History and Development of Advertising,* 456–458.

27. Wood, *The Story of Advertising,* 193–202; Leiss, Kline, and Jhally, *Social Communication in Advertising,* 100–101; Fox, *The Mirror Makers,* 28–35.

28. Fox, *The Mirror Makers,* 28–39, 64–65; Presbrey, *The History and Development of Advertising,* 590–591.

29. Sherilyn K. Zeigler and Herbert H. Howard, *Broadcast Advertising,* 3d ed. (Ames, Ia.: Iowa State University Press, 1991), 10.

30. Bob Schulberg, *Radio Advertising: The Authoritative Handbook* (Lincolnwood, Ill.: NTC Business Books, 1989), 12–14; Zeigler and Howard, *Broadcast Advertising,* 4–6; Wood, *The Story of Advertising,* 403–405; Fox, *The Mirror Makers,* 150–153.

31. Schulberg, *Radio Advertising: The Authoritative Handbook,* 14–16; Barton C. White and N. Doyle Satterthwaite, *But First, These Messages . . . The Selling of Broadcast Advertising* (Boston: Allyn and Bacon, 1989), 21; Presbrey, *The History and Development of Advertising,* 591.

32. Wood, *The Story of Advertising,* 407; Schulberg, *Radio Advertising,* 16–17; Fox, *The Mirror Makers,* 153–155; Leiss, Kline, and Jhally, *Social Communication in Advertising,* 103–104.

33. Schulberg, *Radio Advertising,* xv, 2–9; White and Satterthwaite, *But First, These Messages,* 36–37; Zeigler and Howard, *Broadcast Advertising,* 7; Leiss, Kline, and Jhally, *Social Communication in Advertising,* 107–109.

34. Zeigler and Howard, *Broadcast Advertising,* 9, 24; White and Satterthwaite, *But First, These Messages,* 22; Stephen B. Weinstein, *Getting the Picture* (New York: IEEE Press, 1986), 1.

35. Ed Papazian, ed., *TV Dimensions '92* (New York: Media Dynamics, n.d.), 3–5; William Phillips, "A Century of Modern Advertising: From Fin de Siècle to Nervous Nineties," *Admap,* July–August 1992, 11–16.

36. Weinstein, *Getting the Picture,* 2; Papazian, ed., *TV Dimensions '92,* 4–12, 18; Weinstein, *Getting the Picture,* 2; Zeigler and Howard, *Broadcast Advertising,* 9, 12–14; Dana Wechsler Linden and Vicki Contavespi, "Media Wars," *Forbes,* 19 August 1991, 38–40; Jack Z. Sissors and Lincoln Bumba, *Advertising Media Planning,* 3d ed. (Lincolnwood, Ill.: NTC Business Books, 1990), 396; Donald W. Jugenheimer, Arnold M. Barban, and Peter B. Turk, *Advertising Media: Strategy* *and Tactics* (Dubuque, Ia.: WCB Brown & Benchmark, 1992), 43–44, 324–329.

37. Jugenheimer, Barban, and Turk, *Advertising Media,* 156–157; Papazian, ed., *TV Dimensions '92,* 4–12, 18.

38. Kevin J. Clancy and Robert S. Shulman, *The Marketing Revolution* (New York: HarperBusiness, 1991), 260–261, 263–264, 266–279; Richard Kostyra, "Communications in the Future," *Vital Speeches,* 15 October 1990, 21–24; Bruce Horovitz, "The Future of Advertising," *Los Angeles Times,* 6 October 1991, D1, D18; Larry Light, "The Changing Advertising World," *Journal of Advertising Research,* February–March 1990, 30–35; "Roundtable Discussion: A Creative Exploration of the Future," *Journal of Advertising Research,* February–March 1990, 11–24.

39. Mark Landler, "The Media Get the Message—and It's Grim," *Business Week,* 23 September 1991, 70–71.

40. Bovée and Thill, *Marketing,* 18.

41. Stewart Brand, *The Media Lab* (New York: Viking, 1987), 25; Marc Doyle, *The Future of Television* (Lincolnwood, Ill.: NTC Business Books, 1992), 161–165.

42. Anthony Vagnoni, "The Agency of the Future," *Advertising Age's Creativity,* 13 January 1992, 16C–18C, 20C; Brand, *The Media Lab,* 28–29; Kostyra, "Communications in the Future," 21–24.

43. John P. Cortez, "Media Pioneers Try to Corral On-the-Go Consumers," *Advertising Age,* 17 August 1992, 25; Linden and Contavespi, "Media Wars," 38–4; Martin Mayer, *Whatever Happened to Madison Avenue? Advertising in the '90s* (Boston: Little, Brown, 1991), 227–228.

44. "David Ogilvy's Hard Advice," *New York Times,* 30 October 1991, D21.

45. Jay McNamara, *Advertising Agency Management* (Homewood, Ill.: Dow Jones-Irwin, 1990), 158–159; Laura Jereski, "Can Paul Fireman Put the Bounce Back in Reebok?" *Business Week,* 18 June 1990, 181–182; Nancy Giges, "Europeans Buy Outside Goods, but Like Local Ads," *Advertising Age International,* 27 April 1992, I-1, I-26.

46. See note 1.

CHAPTER 2

1. Noreen O'Leary, "The Donnybrook," *Adweek,* 18 January 1993, 25–27; Stuart Elliott, "Portrait of an Adman on a Hot Streak," *New York Times,* 14 October 1992, C1, C8; "Adweek's East Coast Creative Team All-Stars," *Adweek,* 14 June 1993, 41; Melanie Wells, "Deutsch Shares Bright Spotlight," *Advertising Age,* 16 November 1992, 4; Stuart Elliott, "By Design, Deutsch Chooses a Non-Madcap President," *Advertising Age,* 18 July 1991, C1; Kim Foltz, "Agency Uses Brain Power to Lure Prospective Clients," *New York Times,* 16 April 1990, D8; Bernice Kanner, "The D-Team," *New York Magazine,* 1 June 1992, 22+.

2. Donald W. Jugenheimer, Arnold M. Barban, and Peter B. Turk, *Advertising Media: Strategy and Tactics* (Dubuque, Ia.: WCB Brown & Benchmark, 1992), 435; David Laskin, *Getting into Advertising: A Career Guide* (New York: Ballantine Books, 1986), 260; ad for National Register Publishing, *Advertising Age,* 4 January 1993, 13.

3. William F. Gloede and Scott Hume, "More Advertisers Call: Come In-House," in Esther Thorson, comp., *Advertising Age: The Principles of Advertising at Work* (Lincolnwood, Ill.: NTC Business Books, 1989), 43–45; Ralph S. Blois, "Do You Really Need an Agency?" *Sales & Marketing Management,* October 1988, 120–122; William M. Weilbacher, *Choosing & Working with Your Advertising Agency* (Lincolnwood, Ill.: NTC Business Books, 1991), 2.

4. Weilbacher, *Choosing & Working with Your Advertising Agency,* 2; Blois, "Do You Really Need an Agency?" 120–122.

5. Charles B. Jones, *Advertising Services: Full Service Agency, A La Carte, or In-House?* (New York: Associa-

tion of National Advertisers, 1991), 25, 29; Gloede and Hume, "More Advertisers Call: Come In-House," 43–45; Nancy L. Salz, *How to Get the Best Advertising from Your Agency,* 2d ed. (Homewood, Ill.: Dow Jones-Irwin, 1988), 5; Richard H. Stansfield, *The Dartnell Advertising Manager's Handbook,* 3d ed. (Chicago: Dartnell, 1982), 27.

6. Gloede and Hume, "More Advertisers Call: Come In-House," 43–45; Blois, "Do You Really Need an Agency?" 120–122.

7. John P. Cortez, "Chinese Domino's," *Advertising Age,* 11 May 1992, 20; Shepherd Ogden, "Do-It-Yourself Marketing," *Inc.,* November 1991, 52–55, 60, 63, 65–66.

8. Gloede and Hume, "More Advertisers Call: Come In-House," 43–45; George Swisshelm, "Media Services Enter New Era," *Television/Radio Age,* 20 February 1989, 32–34; B. G. Yovovich, "Two European Giants Bear Offspring," *Business Marketing,* January 1992, 17–18.

9. Jay R. Galbraith, *Organization Design* (Reading, Mass.: Addison-Wesley, 1977), 17–18; Henry Mintzberg, *The Structuring of Organizations* (Englewood Cliffs, N.J.: Prentice-Hall, 1979), 181–186.

10. David Laskin, *Getting into Advertising,* 211–213.

11. Brian Dumaine, "P&G Rewrites the Marketing Rules," *Fortune,* 6 November 1989, 35–48; Robert E. Levinson, *The Decentralized Company* (New York: Amacom, 1983), 13–17; Peter Drucker, *Management: Tasks, Responsibilities, Practices* (New York: Harper & Row, 1974), 572–580; Jugenheimer, Barban, and Turk, *Advertising Media: Strategy and Tactics,* 25–26.

12. Raymond Serafin, "Guarascio Moves Closer to GM Units," *Advertising Age,* 20 July 1992, 4, 41; Fara Warner, "GM's Driving Cohesive Strategies," *Brandweek,* 20 July 1992, 5.

13. William M. Weilbacher, *Managing Agency Relations* (New York: Association of National Advertisers, 1991), 46, 48.

14. Weilbacher, *Managing Agency Relations,* xiii, 1.

15. Mark Landler, "Madison Avenue Is Getting a Lot Less Madcap," *Business Week,* 29 October 1990, 78, 82.

16. *Advertising Agencies: What They Are, What They Do, How They Do It* (1991; reprint, New York: American Association of Advertising Agencies, 1987), 6; Andrew Geddes and Laurel Wentz, "Agencies Flock to China as Market 'Explodes,' " *Advertising Age,* 31 August 1992, 12.

17. Thomas Vannah, "Simons Says," *New England Business,* February 1992, 25–28; John Tylee, "Advertising on the Cheap," *Campaign,* 6 September 1991, 24–27.

18. "Who's on Top in 1992 Gross Income," *Advertising Age,* 14 April 1993, 1.

19. Stuart Elliott, "Big Changes Are Announced by Saatchi and Euro RSCG," *New York Times,* 10 September 1992, C5; Mark Lander, "Martin Sorrell's Whip Has Madison Avenue Wincing," *Business Week,* 19 August 1991, 78–79; "The Flight of Icarus," *The Economist,* 16 March 1991, 65–66, 70; Andy Zipser, "Mad as in Madison Avenue," *Barron's,* 3 December 1990, 12–13; Bernice Kanner, "Riding the Roller Coaster," *New York,* 13 May 1991, 24–25; Jan Matthews and Greg Boyd, " The Hardest Sell," *Canadian Business,* April 1991, 60–65.

20. "The Flight of Icarus," 65–66, 70; Charles F. Frazer, "How the Top 100 Advertisers Feel about Agency Mergers," in *Proceedings of the 1988 Conference of the American Academy of Advertising,* edited by John D. Leckenby (Austin, Tex.: American Academy of Advertising, 1988), RC-103–RC-111.

21. "Independent Shops Weave Nets across Continent," *Advertising Age,* 14 April 1993, 21.

22. *Advertising Agencies: What They Are, What They Do, How They Do It,* 6–11.

23. Len Gross, John Stirling, and Jeff Saperstein, *How to Be a More Effective Account Manager* (Alameda, Calif.: Kentwood Publications, 1989), 1.

24. Warren Berger, " The British Reinvasion," *Creativity,* June 1993, 36–37; Shelly Garcia, "The Knights of New Business," *Adweek,* 20 July 1992, 21–22, 24, 26–27.

25. Jay McNamara, *Advertising Agency Management* (Homewood, Ill.: Dow Jones-Irwin, 1990), 31–32.

26. Irvin Graham, *Encyclopedia of Advertising,* 2d ed.(New York: Fairchild Publications, 1969), 13–14; Weilbacher, *Choosing & Working with Your Advertising Agency,* 33; Jon Lafayette, "Accountable Media," *Inside Media,* 9 September 1992, 40; Melanie Wells, "Lintas Is Ready to Take on the Little Guys," *Advertising Age,* 12 October 1992, 4.

27. Jones, *Advertising Services,* 11; David Kilburn, "New Roles in Movies," *Advertising Age,* 27 April 1992, I-28; Jim Forkan, "Multinational Ad Agencies Mulling Coproductions, Barter," *Television/Radio Age,* 15 May 1989, 18–19.

28. Randall Rothenberg, "Selling the Concept of Integration," *New York Times,* 8 March 1990, D21; David Kalish, "The New Advertising," *Agency,* Fall 1990, 28–33; Bernice Kanner, "The Best of Times, the Worst of Times," *New York,* 15 July 1991, 13–15.

29. Jones, *Advertising Services,* 14–15; Weilbacher, *Choosing & Working with Your Advertising Agency,* 8–9; Gordon E. Miracle, "An Historical Analysis to Explain the Evolution of Advertising Agency Services," *Journal of Advertising,* 1977, 24–28.

30. Betsy Sharkey, "The Players," *Adweek,* 8 February 1993, 38–40; "Coke's 'Non-Agency' Taps Big-Name Adman," *Advertising Age,* 4 May 1992, 2; Alison Fahey, "Coca-Cola: Creative Artists Moves in Major for Ads," *Brandweek,* 12 October 1992, 3.

31. Joanne Lipman, "Media-Buying Firms Specialize in Sales to Edge Out Agencies," *New York Times,* 12 September 1991, B4; Joe Mandese, "Holt's Billion-Dollar Baby Puts Spotlight on Emergence of Independent Shops," *Advertising Age,* 20 July 1992, S-28; "Media Buying: Time Out," *The Economist,* 29 June 1991, 60–61; Stuart Elliott, "Advertising," *New York Times,* 21 January 1993, C18.

32. Joe Mandese, "Introducing the Media Group Built for the 1990s," *Advertising Age,* 20 July 1992, S-2, S-31; John H. Taylor, "Running Scared," *Forbes,* 28 May 1990, 146–148.

33. B. G. Yovovich and Edmund O. Lawler, "Big Agency—Small Agency: Which One Is Right for Your Business?" *Business Marketing,* May 1991, 13–16, 18; Weilbacher, *Choosing & Working with Your Advertising Agency,* 8.

34. Jennifer Lawrence and Christy Fisher, "P&G Rethinks Target Marketing," *Advertising Age,* 20 July 1992, 8; Richard W. Stevenson, "Price of Success for a Top Hispanic Ad Agency," *New York Times,* 25 May 1992, 21; Judith D. Schwartz, "Writing Ads to Usher in a New Era in South Africa," *New York Times,* 24 May 1992, sec. 3, 3.

35. Martin Mayer, *Whatever Happened to Madison Avenue? Advertising in the '90s* (Boston: Little, Brown, 1991), 64–65; Miracle, "An Historical Analysis to Explain the Evolution of Advertising Agency Services," 10, 24–28.

36. Herbert S. Gardner, Jr., *The Advertising Agency Business* (Lincolnwood, Ill.: NTC Business Books, 1989), 50; Weilbacher, *Choosing & Working with Your Advertising Agency,* 117–118; Riccardo A. Davis, "Outdoor Ad Giants Trim Pay to Agencies," *Advertising Age,* 54.

37. Weilbacher, *Managing Agency Relations,* 73; Gary Levin, "ANA Looks at Agency Pay," *Advertising Age,* 11 May 1992, 26; *Trends in Agency Compensation: 1992* (New York: Association of National Advertisers, 1992), 7; "Cut the Ribbon," *The Economist,* 9 June 1990, 16–17; Alan Mitchell, "In Pursuit of a Fair Agency Fee," *Marketing,* 1 August 1991, 12; "Big Issue for '88: Compensation," in Esther Thorson, comp., *Advertising Age: The Principles of Advertising at Work* (Lincolnwood, Ill.: NTC Business Books, 1989), 46–48;

Suzanne Snowden, "The Remuneration Squeeze," *Admap,* January 1993, 26–28.

38. Gardner, *The Advertising Agency Business,* 50–52.

39. Charles B. Jones, *Agency Compensation: A Guidebook* (New York: Association of National Advertisers, 1989), 39; Joe Marconi, *Getting the Best from Your Ad Agency* (Chicago: Probus, 1991), 208; Adrienne Ward, "How Agencies Tighten Belts," *Advertising Age,* 7 September 1992, 31; Levin, "ANA Looks at Agency Pay," 26; Leslie Savan, "In for Repairs: Ayer's Image," *New York Times Magazine, Part II,* 10 June 1990, 44–45, 60–61; "Relationships," *Admap,* April 1992, 17–18.

40. Gardner, *The Advertising Agency Business,* 52–57; Weilbacher, *Choosing & Working with Your Advertising Agency,* 118–119, 135–138.

41. Weilbacher, *Managing Agency Relations,* 79–81; Mayer, *Whatever Happened to Madison Avenue?* 74; Jones, *Agency Compensation,* 53–56; Mark Bergen, Shantanu Dutta, and Orville C. Walker, Jr., "Agency Relationships in Marketing: A Review of the Implications and Applications of Agency and Related Theories," *Journal of Marketing* 56 (July 1992): 1–24; David Byles, "The Future of the Full Service Ad Agency," *Admap,* May 1992, 35–43.

42. Gary Levin, "Return of DDB 'Guarantee,'" *Advertising Age,* 22 June 1992, 2; Robert Springer, "Cost Control/Agency Compensation," in *A.N.A. Advertising Management Conference, February 24–26, 1991* (New York: Association of National Advertisers, 1991), 61–69; Laurel Wentz, "Unilever Adopts Agency Incentives," *Advertising Age,* 28 September 1992, 1, 46; Tom Eisenhart, "'Guaranteed Results' Plan May Suit Business Marketers," *Business Marketing,* July 1990, 32.

43. Joanne Lipman, "Study Shows Clients Jump Ship Quickly," *Wall Street Journal,* 21 May 1992, B6; Joseph Crump, "Top Guns," *Chicago,* August 1991, 70–75, 104–105.

44. Andy Allen, "The 12 Most Important Qualities Clients Want from an Advertising Agency," *Opinion,* Spring 1992, 18–22; Weilbacher, *Choosing & Working with Your Advertising Agency,* 55–58, 110–111.

45. Robert H. Lundin, *Selecting An Advertising Agency—Factors to Consider, Steps to Take* (New York: Association of National Advertisers, n.d.), 10–16; Noreen O'Leary, "The Reviewer's View," *Adweek,* 11 May 1992, 24–26, 30–32; Joshua Levine, "You've Got to be Perfect, But Not Plastic Perfect," *Forbes,* 30 September 1991, 152, 154; Janice Castro, "Feeling a Little Jumpy," *Time,* 8 July 1991, 42–44; Richard Morgan, "In Tough Times, Ammirati's Best Lines," *Adweek,* 2 November 1992, 70.

46. Lundin, *Selecting an Advertising Agency,* 16–18; Tibor Taraba, "The Madison Ave. Experience: How to Work with an Ad Agency," *Management Review,* October 1991, 51–53; Levine, "You've Got to Be Perfect," 152, 154; Debra Goldman, "Wild Pitch," *Adweek,* 28 September 1992, 24–27, 30–32; Bruce Crumley, "Publicist Nabs $40M Club Med Account," *Advertising Age,* 13 July 1992, 2; "Club Med Cries Uncle," *Adweek,* 21 June 1993, 3.

47. Laura Bird, "Agencies Are Returning to Self-Promotion," *New York Times,* 27 May 1992, B8; Gardner, *The Advertising Agency Business,* 177–179; McNamara, *Advertising Agency Management,* 118–120; Joanne Lipman, "Agencies Seek Visibility by Signing Ads," *Wall Street Journal,* 18 October 1991, B8.

48. Fara Warner, "Should You Nuke Your Ad Agency?" *Brandweek,* 12 October 1992, 12–14, 18, 20–21; Warren Berger, "There's No Business Like New Business," *Advertising Age,* 2 March 1992, 18C–21C.

49. Lundin, *Selecting an Advertising Agency,* 2–3; Weilbacher, *Managing Agency Relations,* 9–11.

50. Herbert Zeltner, *Evaluating Agency Performance* (New York: Association of National Advertisers, 1991), 7–9, 38–39, 41; Weilbacher, *Managing Agency Relations,* 85–91; Stephen W. Rutledge, "The Value of Evaluating Agency Performance," *The Advertiser,* Fall 1991, 53–54, 56.

51. Stuart Elliott, "Agency-Client Study Shows a Marriage on the Rocks," *New York Times,* 1 June 1992, D10.

52. Warner, "Should You Nuke Your Ad Agency?" 12–14, 18, 20–21; Elliott, "Agency-Client Study Shows a Marriage on the Rocks," D10; Weilbacher, *Choosing & Working with Your Advertising Agency,* 13–16, 26; Lipman, "Study Shows Clients Jump Ship Quickly," B6.

53. Geoffrey Lee Martin, "Australia Wants Sophisticated Image in Post-Hogan Advertising," *Advertising Age,* 28 September 1992, I-26.

54. Wayne Kirchmann and Richard F. Beltramini, "Strategic Advertising Agency-Client Service Relationships," in *Proceedings of the 1988 Conference of the American Academy of Advertising,* edited by John D. Leckenby (Austin, Tex.: American Academy of Advertising, 1988), RC-99–RC-101; Stuart Elliott, "Consolidating Agencies: Now It's the Clients' Turn," *New York Times,* 8 July 1991, D7; John P. Cortez, "Denise Ilitch Lites: Little Caesars," *Advertising Age,* 5 July 1992, S-10.

55. "Account Activity: Pollenex Corp.," *Adweek's Marketing Week,* 8 June 1992, 14.

56. Steven A. Meyerowitz, "Ad Agency Client Conflicts: The Law and Common Sense," *Business Marketing,* June 1987, 16; Herbert Zeltner, "Conflict Issue Still a Problem," *Advertising Age,* 16 June 1986, 3, 24, 28, 30, 31, 32.

57. Kirchmann and Beltramini, "Strategic Advertising Agency-Client Service Relationships," RC-99–RC-101; Philip Kleinman, *Saatchi & Saatchi: The Inside Story* (Lincolnwood, Ill.: NTC Business Books, 1989), 78–80.

58. Zeltner, "Conflict Issue Still a Problem," 3, 24, 28, 30, 31, 32; Lauren Ames, "The Great Conflict Conflict," *Madison Avenue,* June 1985, 66–69; McNamara, *Advertising Agency Management,* 80–81.

59. See note 1.

CHAPTER 3

1. John Maines, "Fighting Drugs to Get Sales High," *American Demographics,*" August 1992, 10; Howard Schlossberg, "Members Only to Include Homeless in Cause Marketing," *Marketing News,* 20 July 1992, 6; Eben Shapiro, "Members Only Offers New Anti-Drug Drive," *New York Times,* 29 September 1989, C15; Kim Foltz, "Campaign for Members Only Shifts Emphasis to Clothes," *New York Times,* 9 November 1990, C17; "Members Only Ads to Get Out the Vote," *Advertising Age,* 27 April 1992, 17; Elizabeth Barr, "Members Votes 'Democratic,'" *Daily News Record,* 12 October 1992, 6; "Getting Out the Vote," *Business Ethics,* September–October 1992, 31.

2. Mark Landler, "What Happened to Advertising?" *Business Week,* 23 September 1991, 66–71; Robert Jacobson and Franco M. Nicosia, "Advertising and Public Policy: The Macroeconomic Effects of Advertising," in *Advertising in Society: Classic and Contemporary Readings on Advertising's Role in Society,* edited by Roxanne Hovland and Gary B. Wilcox (Lincolnwood, Ill.: NTC Business Books, 1990), 277–297.

3. Courtney Crandall, "It Pays to Advertise," *New England Business,* May 1991, 35; Horst Stipp, "Crisis in Advertising?" *Marketing Research,* March 1992, 39–45.

4. Robert J. Samuelson, "The End of Advertising?" *Newsweek,* 19 August 1991, 40; Landler, "What Happened to Advertising?" 66–71; Neil H. Borden, *The Economic Effects of Advertising* (Chicago: Richard D. Irwin, 1942), 734–735; Mark Landler, "Fear of Flying in Ad Land," *Business Week,* 19 November 1990, 100, 105.

5. Borden, *The Economic Effects of Advertising,* 734–735; Landler, "What Happened to Advertising?" 66–71; Alan Radding, "What's Ahead for Ingalls after $25M Converse Loss," *Advertising Age,* 13 July 1992, 33.

6. Kim B. Rotzoll, James E. Haefner, and Charles H. Sandage, *Advertising in Contemporary Society,* 2d ed. (Cincinnati, Ohio: South-Western, 1990), 85–86; Jules Backman, "Is Advertising Wasteful?" *Journal of Marketing* 32 (January 1968): 2–8; Vincent P. Norris, "Advertising History—According to the Textbooks," *Journal of Advertising* 9, no. 3 (1980): 3–10; Stipp, "Crisis in Advertising?" 39–45; Landler, "What Happened to Advertising?" 66–71.

7. Backman, "Is Advertising Wasteful?" 2–8; Robert L. Steiner, "Does Advertising Lower Consumer Prices?" *Journal of Marketing* 37 (October 1973): 19–26.

8. Paul W. Farris and Mark S. Albion, "The Impact of Advertising on the Price of Consumer Products," *Journal of Marketing,* 44 (Summer 1980): 17–35; James M. Ferguson, "Comments on 'The Impact of Advertising on the Price of Consumer Products,'" *Journal of Marketing,* 46 (Winter 1982): 102–105; Backman, "Is Advertising Wasteful?" 2–8; Robert B. Ekelund, Jr., and David S. Saurman, *Advertising and the Market Process* (San Francisco: Pacific Research Institute for Public Policy, 1988), 138–145.

9. Michael Schudson, *Advertising, The Uneasy Persuasion* (New York: Basic Books, 1984), 39–40.

10. David Kiley, "OTC Drugs: Lessons in the Art of Leveraging," *Superbrands 1992,* 94–96; "Looking for a Man with a Dog," *The Economist,* 9 June 1990, 15; Alison Fahey, "Beverages: Thirsting for Something New," *Superbrands 1992,* 53–56.

11. Michael E. Porter, *Competitive Strategy: Techniques for Analyzing Industries and Competitors* (New York: Free Press, 1980), 9–10; Matthew Grimm, "Fast Food: Could This Actually Be the End of the Price Wars?" *Superbrands 1992,* 72–73; Robert E. McAuliffe, *Advertising, Competition, and Public Policy* (Lexington, Mass.: Lexington Books, 1987), 20–21.

12. Julian L. Simon and Johan Arndt, "The Shape of the Advertising Response Function," in Hovland and Wilcox, eds., *Advertising in Society,* 385–416; Ekelund and Saurman, *Advertising and the Market Process,* 43; Fara Warner, "GM Card Gives All Units Credit," *Brandweek,* 14 September 1992, 4.

13. Stewart Alter, "A Crisis of Confidence," *Adweek,* 12 March 1990, RC4–RC5; Thomas R. Horton, *"What Works for Me"* (New York: Amacom, 1989), 326–329; Peter Fuhrman, "Jewelry for the Wrist," *Forbes,* 23 November 1992, 173–174, 176, 178; Alison Fahey, "A Watch with a New Techno-Twist," *Brandweek,* 14 September 1992, 1, 6.

14. Peter Kim, "Does Advertising Work: A Review of the Evidence," *The Journal of Consumer Marketing* 9, no. 4 (Fall 1992): 5–21.

15. Richard W. Pollay, "The Distorted Mirror: Reflections on the Unintended Consequences of Advertising," *Journal of Marketing,* April 1986, 18–36.

16. Anne Tolstoi Wallach, "The Enemy Is Wrongness," in *Advertising Age: The Principles of Advertising at Work,* compiled by Esther Thorson (Lincolnwood, Ill.: NTC Business Books, 1989), 70–71; Sid Bernstein, "Does Advertising Harm Literacy?" *Advertising Age,* 20 January 1992, 22.

17. Stuart Elliott, "More Campaigns Are Taking a Less-Than-Perfect Tone," *New York Times,* 6 March 1992, C5; Stuart Elliott, "Hey, Dude, Big Agencies Want You," *New York Times,* 10 May 1991, C1, C15.

18. Wallach, "The Enemy Is Wrongness," 70–71.

19. Lucy Howard and Ned Zeman, "Aaaaa Great Idea," *Newsweek,* 26 October 1992, 8.

20. Schudson, *Advertising, The Uneasy Persuasion,* 8–9, 11, 235; Leo Bogart, "American Media and Commercial Culture," *Society,* September-October 1991, 62–73; Burt Neuborne, *Free Speech—Free Markets—Free Choice* (New York: Association of National Advertisers, 1987), 15.

21. William Leiss, Stephen Kline, and Sut Jhally, *Social Communication in Advertising: Persons, Products, and Images of Well-Being* (New York: Routledge,

1990), 34-39; Bogart, "American Media and Commercial Culture," 62-73.

22. Leo Bogart, *Strategy in Advertising*, 2d ed. (Lincolnwood, Ill.: NTC Business Books, 1990), 361.

23. Bogart, "American Media and Commercial Culture," 62-73; Anthony Pratkanis and Elliot Aronson, *Age of Propaganda: The Everyday Use and Abuse of Persuasion* (New York: Freeman, 1992), 206-209.

24. Kathleen Hall Jamieson and Karlyn Kohrs Campbell, *The Interplay of Influence: News, Advertising, Politics, and the Mass Media*, 3d ed. (Belmont, Calif.: Wadsworth, 1992), 173-174; Leiss, Kline, and Jhally, *Social Communication in Advertising*, 380-381.

25. Martha T. Moore, "Study: Ads Improve Little in Diversity," *USA Today*, 29 August 1992, B1; Leiss, Kline, and Jhally, *Social Communication in Advertising*, 379-380; Martha T. Moore, "More Ads Reflect Everyday Disabilities," *USA Today*, 13 May 1992, 6B.

26. Moore, "Study: Ads Improve Little in Diversity," B1.

27. Ken Wells, "Advertisers' Censorship," *Wall Street Journal*, 11 March 1992, B6; G. Pascal Zachary, "All the News? Many Journalists See a Growing Reluctance to Criticize Advertisers," *Wall Street Journal*, 6 February 1992, A1, A9; Jamieson and Campbell, *The Interplay of Influence*, 243; "The Fireproof Reporter," *Adweek's Marketing Week*, 13 May 1991, 18.

28. Zachary, "All the News? Many Journalists See a Growing Reluctance to Criticize Advertisers," A1, A9; Debra Gersh, "Study Asserts That Ad Pressure Censors Media," *Editor & Publisher*, 21 March 1992, 17, 42; Neuborne, *Free Speech—Free Markets—Free Choice*, 21; Doron P. Levin, "When Car Makers Retaliate against Critical Magazines," *New York Times*, 26 June 1992, C9.

29. Stuart Elliott, "Little Commercial Interest on G.O.P. Convention Floor," *New York Times*, 14 August 1992, C15.

30. Roger Neill, "The Vital Role of Advertising in Successful Economies," *Vital Speeches of the Day*, 15 March 1992, 336-340.

31. Joanne Lipman, "Controversy Propels a Few Ads to Top 10 List of 1991," *Wall Street Journal*, 28 May 1992, B6.

32. Lipman, "Controversy Propels a Few Ads to Top 10 List of 1991," B6; Kevin Kerr, "Where Should Advertising Be?" *Adweek's Marketing Week*, 6 May 1991, 26-27.

33. Leiss, Kline, and Jhally, *Social Communication in Advertising*, 378; "Advertising and the Problem of Taste," in Thorson, comp., *Advertising Age*, 72; Pat Sloan, "Nets Strip Undie Ad Policy," in Thorson, comp., *Advertising Age*, 72-73.

34. Noreen O'Leary, "Benetton's True Colors," *Adweek*, 24 August 1992, 27-31; Lipman, "Controversy Propels a Few Ads to Top 10 List of 1991," B6.

35. O'Leary, "Benetton's True Colors," 27-31; "Image Advertising: Can You Be Too Progressive?" *Business Ethics*, September-October 1992, 11.

36. Jamieson and Campbell, *The Interplay of Influence*, 165, 167-168; Kevin Goldman, "TV Starts to 'Just Say No' to Antidrug Ads," *Wall Street Journal*, 30 April 1993, B3.

37. Stuart Elliott, "Ad Campaign Urges Prenatal Care," *New York Times*, 11 May 1992, C1, C6; "Social Critiques and Concerns with Advertising," in Thorson, comp., *Advertising Age*, 65-66.

38. Elliott, "Ad Campaign Urges Prenatal Care," C1, C6.

39. Stuart Elliott, "Brochure on AIDS Is the Latest Departure from Benetton," *New York Times*, 29 April 1992, C19.

40. Ad in *Spotlight*, November 1992, 64.

41. Jamieson and Campbell, *The Interplay of Influence*, 167.

42. Stephen Fox, *The Mirror Makers* (New York: William Morrow, 1984), 67-68.

43. Krystal Miller and Jacqueline Mitchell, "Car Marketers Test Gray Area of Truth in Advertising," *Wall Street Journal*, 19 November 1990, B1, B6.

44. Michael G. Gartner, *Advertising and the First Amendment* (New York: Priority Press, 1989), 38-39; Leiss, Kline, and Jhally, *Social Communication in Advertising*, 370; "Cool Camel under Fire," *USA Today*, 26 December 1991, 4B; Adam Bryant, "Advertising: Antismoking Effort: Convince Joe Camel," *New York Times*, 16 March 1993, D20.

45. Shelly Garcia, "Waiting for a Verdict on Channel One," *Adweek*, 22 June 1992, 9; Stuart Elliott, "Commercial Cartoon Furor Grows," *New York Times*, 5 March 1992, D1, D21; Steven W. Colford, "Feds Urge Another Look at Toy/Program Linkups," in Thorson, comp., *Advertising Age*, 81-82; Leiss, Kline, and Jhally, *Social Communication in Advertising*, 365-366, 375-376.

46. Leiss, Kline, and Jhally, *Social Communication in Advertising*, 365-366, 375-376.

47. David C. Hjelmfelt, *Executive's Guide to Marketing, Sales & Advertising Law* (Englewood Cliffs, N.J.: Prentice-Hall, 1990), 155-156; Dean Keith Fueroghne, *"But the People in Legal Said . . ." A Guide to Current Legal Issues in Advertising* (Homewood, Ill.: Dow Jones-Irwin, 1989), 39-41; Jef I. Richards, "A 'New and Improved' View of Puffery," *Journal of Public Policy and Marketing* 9 (1990): 73-84.

48. Fueroghne, *"But the People in Legal Said . . .",* 2.

49. Dwight L. Teeter, Jr., Gary B. Wilcox, and Roxanne Hovland, "Commercial Speech and the First Amendment: The Constitutional Stepchild," in Hovland and Wilcox, eds., *Advertising in Society*, 202-219; Hjelmfelt, *Executive's Guide to Marketing, Sales & Advertising Law*, 152-153; Julia Thrift, "Services for Sale," *Management Today*, September 1990, 97.

50. Kenneth Plevan and Miriam Siroky, *Advertising Compliance Handbook* (New York: Practising Law Institute, 1991), 439-440; Gartner, *Advertising and the First Amendment*, 16-17; Steven W. Colford, "High Court Hits Commercial Speech Hard," *Advertising Age*, 28 June 1993, 1, 49.

51. Teeter, Wilcox, and Hovland, "Commercial Speech and the First Amendment," 202-219; Colford, "High Court Hits Commercial Speech Hard," 1, 49.

52. Plevan and Siroky, *Advertising Compliance Handbook*, 3; Fueroghne, *"But the People in Legal Said . . .",* 172-175.

53. Fueroghne, *"But the People in Legal Said . . .",* 182-183.

54. Steven W. Colford, "Agencies Feel More Heat on Comparative Claims," *Advertising Age*, 31 August 1992, 39.

55. Fueroghne, *"But the People in Legal Said . . .",* 86-96, 194-197; Andrew J. Sherman, "Watch Out for Unfair-Competition Laws," *D&B Reports*, March-April 1992, 44.

56. Mary Ellen Zuckerman, "The Federal Trade Commission in Historical Perspective: The First Fifty Years," in *Marketing and Advertising Regulation: The Federal Trade Commission in the 1990s*, edited by Patrick E. Murphy and William L. Wilkie (Notre Dame, Ind.: University of Notre Dame Press, 1990), 169-198; Hjelmfelt, *Executive's Guide to Marketing, Sales & Advertising Law*, 11-12.

57. Plevan and Siroky, *Advertising Compliance Handbook*, 137-140.

58. Keith Schneider, "Guides on Environmental Ad Claims," *New York Times*, 29 July 1992, C3; Jeanne Saddler, "FTC Issues a 'Green-Marketing' Guide to Help Prevent Deceptive-Ad Charges," *Wall Street Journal*, 29 July 1992, B5.

59. Fueroghne, *"But the People in Legal Said . . .",* 14.

60. Hjelmfelt, *Executive's Guide to Marketing, Sales & Advertising Law*, 167-168.

61. Hjelmfelt, *Executive's Guide to Marketing, Sales &*

Advertising Law, 161-163; Plevan and Siroky, *Advertising Compliance Handbook*, 201-202.

62. Jamieson and Campbell, *The Interplay of Influence* 210-212; Plevan and Siroky, *Advertising Compliance Handbook*, 203-207.

63. Plevan and Siroky, *Advertising Compliance Handbook*, 228-229.

64. Fueroghne, *"But the People in Legal Said . . .",* 277; Plevan and Siroky, *Advertising Compliance Handbook*, 313-331.

65. Joanne Lipman, "Drug Ads Rife with Errors, Study Claims," *Wall Street Journal*, 1 June 1992, B1, B6; Lawrence K. Altman, "Report Says Ads for Drugs Are Often Misleading," *New York Times*, 1 June 1992, A1, A12.

66. Sherilyn K. Zeigler and Herbert H. Howard, *Broadcast Advertising*, 3d ed. (Ames: Iowa State University Press, 1991), 77-81; William M. Bulkeley, " 'Cure' for Junk Calls Faces Skeptical FCC," *Wall Street Journal*, 19 May 1992, B6.

67. Robert Woessner, "Smoking Patch Ads Called Misleading," *USA Today*, 1 May 1992, 1D; Joseph Weber and John Carey, "Drug Ads: A Prescription for Controversy," *Business Week*, 18 January 1993, 58, 60.

68. Zeigler and Howard, *Broadcast Advertising*, 82-85.

69. Stuart Elliott, "New Yorker Goes Scentless after Readers Hold Noses," *New York Times*, 27 October 1992, D23.

70. Rotzoll, Haefner, and Sandage, *Advertising in Contemporary Society*, 169.

71. *Inside the AAAA* (New York: American Association of Advertising Agencies, 1990), 39-41.

72. Michael Wilke, "Paintmaker Bristles at NAD Decision," *Advertising Age*, 31 August 1992, 17; "NAD Reviews 65 Challenges to National Advertising in 1992; Total Cases Resolved Reaches 3,000 Mark," *Advertising Topics*, January-February 1993, 4.

73. J. J. Boddewyn, *Advertising Self-Regulation and Outside Participation: A Multinational Comparison* (New York: Quorum Books, 1988), 102-120.

74. See note 1.

CHAPTER 4

1. *American Express Global Travel Survey: A Typology of the Traveling Public Conducted in the United States, West Germany, United Kingdom, and Japan*, undated, published by The Gallup Organization, Princeton, N.J.; Rebecca Piirto, *Beyond Mind Games: The Marketing Power of Psychographics* (New York: American Demographics Books, 1991), 197-198; Gary Hoover, Alta Campbell, and Patrick J. Spain, *Hoover's Handbook of American Business* (Austin, Tex.: The Reference Press, 1991), 96; Leah Nathans Spiro and Mark Landler, "Less-Than-Fantastic Plastic," *Business Week*, 9 November 1992, 100-101; "American Express Study Identifies Five Types of Vacationers Worldwide," *PR Newswire*, 25 September 1989; "American Express Survey Reveals New International Travel Data," *PR Newswire*, 27 July 1989; Stuart Elliott, "American Express in Global Campaign," *New York Times*, 26 August 1992, sec. c, 17.

2. Peter Francese and Rebecca Piirto, *Capturing Customers* (New York: American Demographics Books, 1990), 6-19.

3. "Work That Works," *Adweek's Marketing Week*, 15 June 1992, 3, 4.

4. Paul Sherlock, *Rethinking Business to Business Marketing* (New York: Free Press, 1991), 19-22.

5. Francese and Piirto, *Capturing Customers*, 19.

6. Philip R. Cateora, *International Marketing*, (Homewood, Ill.: Irwin, 1990), 478.

7. Dentsu, Inc., *Japan 1991 Marketing and Advertising Handbook* (Tokyo: Dentsu, 1990), 86, 89.

8. Laurence Urdang, ed., *The Dictionary of Advertising* (Lincolnwood, Ill.: NTC Business Books, 1986), 48.

9. Francese and Piirto, *Capturing Customers*, 49.

10. U.S. Bureau of the Census, *Statistical Abstract of the United States: 1989* (Washington, D.C.: GPO, 1989), 266, 293, 517, 627; "1988 Survey of Industrial and Commercial Buying Power," *Sales & Marketing Management,* 25 April 1988, 79.

11. *Statistical Abstract of the United States: 1989,* 726.

12. *Statistical Abstract of the United States: 1989,* 268.

13. Piirto, *Beyond Mind Games,* 52-57.

14. John Philip Jones, *What's in a Name? Advertising and the Concept of Brands* (Lexington, Mass.: Lexington Books, 1986), 175; Piirto, *Beyond Mind Games,* 17.

15. A. H. Maslow, "A Theory of Human Motivation," in *Readings in Managerial Psychology,* 3d ed., edited by Harold J. Leavitt, Louis R. Pondy, and David M. Boje (Chicago: University of Chicago Press, 1980), 5-22; Herbert L. Petri, *Motivation: Theory, Research, and Applications,* 3d ed. (Belmont, Calif.: Wadsworth, 1991), 322-326.

16. Michael R. Solomon, *Consumer Behavior* (Needham Heights, Mass.: Allyn & Bacon, 1992), 78; Abraham H. Maslow, "A Theory of Human Motivation," *Psychological Review* 50 (1943): 370-396; Mahmoud A. Wahba and Lawrence G. Bridwell, "Maslow Reconsidered: A Review of Research on the Need Hierarchy Theory," *Organizational Behavior and Human Performance* 15 (1976): 212-240; David J. Cherrington, "Need Theories of Motivation," in *Motivation and Work Behavior,* 5th ed., edited by Richard M. Steers and Lyman W. Porter (New York: McGraw-Hill, 1991), 37-39; J. D. Dunn and Elvis C. Stephens, *Management of Personnel: Manpower Management and Organizational Behavior* (New York: McGraw-Hill, 1972), 167-169.

17. Rebecca Piirto, "Beyond Mind Games," *American Demographics,* December 1991, 52-57.

18. Leon G. Shiffman and Leslie Lazar Kanuk, *Consumer Behavior* (Englewood Cliffs, N.J.: Prentice-Hall, 1987), 270.

19. Courtland L. Bovée and John V. Thill, *Marketing* (New York: McGraw-Hill, 1992), 158-160.

20. Robert B. Settle and Pamela L. Alreck, *Why They Buy* (New York: Wiley, 1989), 121.

21. Piirto, *Beyond Mind Games,* 24-25.

22. Wayne Weiten, *Psychology Applied to Modern Life,* 2d ed. (Belmont, Calif.: Brooks/Cole, 1986), 19.

23. James F. Engel, Roger D. Blackwell, and Paul W. Miniard, *Consumer Behavior,* 6th ed. (Chicago: Dryden, 1990), 332-333.

24. M. Joseph Sirgy, "Self-Concept in Consumer Behavior: A Critical Review," *Journal of Consumer Research,* 9 (December 1982): 287-300.

25. Russell W. Belk, "Possessions and the Extended Self," *Journal of Consumer Research* 15 (September 1988): 139-165.

26. Nina Darnton, "The Battle of the Bulges," *Newsweek,* 2 March 1992, 70.

27. Engel, Blackwell, and Miniard, *Consumer Behavior,* 65-66.

28. Engel, Blackwell, and Miniard, *Consumer Behavior,* 67.

29. Richard P. Coleman, "The Continuing Significance of Social Class to Marketing," *Journal of Consumer Research,* December 1983, 265-280.

30. Engel, Blackwell, and Miniard, *Consumer Behavior,* 146-155.

31. William O. Bearden and Michael J. Etzel, "Reference Group Influences on Product and Brand Purchase Decisions," *Journal of Consumer Research,* 9 (September 1982): 183-194.

32. William H. Davidow and Bro Uttal, *Total Customer Service: The Ultimate Weapon* (New York: Harper & Row, 1989), 34-35.

33. Piirto, *Beyond Mind Games,* 13-14.

34. Larry Armstrong, "Woman Power at Mazda," *Business Week,* 21 September 1992, 84.

35. Russell W. Belk, "Situational Variables and Consumer Behavior," *Journal of Consumer Research* 2 (December 1975): 157-164.

36. Judith Waldrop, *The Seasons of Business: The Marketer's Guide to Consumer Behavior* (New York: American Demographics Books, 1992), 208-209.

37. "Shelter Ads Can Help Deliver 'Big Ideas,' " *Marketing News,* 23 November 1984, 13.

38. J. Jacoby and W. D. Hoyer, "Viewer Miscomprehension of Televised Communication," *Journal of Marketing,* Fall 1982, 12-31.

39. "The Slogan's Familiar, but What's the Brand?" *Wall Street Journal,* 8 January 1988, 21.

40. Bovée and Thill, *Marketing,* 155.

41. Manager of public relations, Coca-Cola Company, personal communication, 28 June 1990.

42. Solomon, *Consumer Behavior,* 42; Del I. Hawkins, Roger J. Best, and Kenneth A. Coney, *Consumer Behavior: Implications for Marketing Strategy* (Homewood, Ill.: BPI Irwin, 1989), 317.

43. Shiffman and Kanuk, *Consumer Behavior,* 246-252.

44. Brian Mullen and Craig Johnson, *The Psychology of Consumer Behavior* (Hillsdale, N.J.: Lawrence Erlbaum Associates, 1990), 63.

45. Engel, Blackwell, and Miniard, *Consumer Behavior,* 30.

46. Hawkins, Best, and Coney, *Consumer Behavior,* 536.

47. Ad appeared in *Fortune,* 26 July 1993, 68-69.

48. John Philip Jones, *Does It Pay to Advertise?* (Lexington, Mass.: Lexington Books, 1989), 231.

49. Ads appeared in *Travel & Leisure,* October 1992, 6; *Money,* October 1992, 49.

50. Shiffman and Kanuk, *Consumer Behavior,* 209.

51. "The 189 Most Important Trends for the 1990s," *Research Alert,* 22 December 1989, 26.

52. Ads appeared in *Fortune,* 5 October 1992, 56-57; *Seattle Times,* 4 October 1992, sec. h, 10.

53. "Consumer Complaint Handling in America: An Update Study" (Washington, D.C.: Technical Assistance Research Programs, 1986), Executive Summary, 2.

54. Sherlock, *Rethinking Business to Business Marketing,* 19-22.

55. Gary L. Lilien and M. Anthony Wong, "An Exploratory Investigation of the Structure of the Buying Center in the Metalworking Industry," *Journal of Marketing Research,* February 1984, 1-11.

56. Thomas V. Bonoma, "Major Sales: Who *Really* Does the Buying?" *Harvard Business Review,* May-June 1982, 111-119.

57. Paul Sherrington, "What Communicators Must Know about Business Marketing," in Charles H. Patti, Steven W. Hartley, and Susan L. Kennedy, *Business-to-Business Marketing: A Marketing Management Approach* (Lincolnwood, Ill.: NTC Business Books, 1991), 16-27.

58. Tom Eisenhart, "What's Right, What's Wrong with Each Medium," in Patti, Hartley, and Kennedy, eds., *Business-to-Business Marketing,* 193-198.

59. Ad appeared in *Software,* July 1993, 2.

60. See note 1.

CHAPTER 5

1. "L.A. Gear Reports Financial Results for Fourth Quarter and Fiscal Year," *PR Newswire,* 19 February 1993; Robert McAllister, "L.A. Gear 2nd Qtr. Loss Deepens," *Footwear News,* 13 July 1992, 17; Robert McAllister, Nancy Eieger, Ellen Rooney, Mark Tedeschi, and Jack Wessling, "Athletics Drive 1st Quarter Pickup," *Footwear News,* 13 April 1992, 18; Robert McAllister, "L.A. Gear Holders Told 1st Half May Be Rough," *Footwear News,* 16 March 1992, 30; Robert McAllister, "L.A. Gear Posts Record Loss in '91," *Footwear News,* 2 March 1992, 2-3; Robert McAllister, "L.A. Gear to Segment Casuals from Athletics," *Footwear News,* 10 February 1992, 2-3; Marcy Magiera, "Small Rivals Leap as L.A. Gear Stumbles," *Advertising Age,* 8 June 1992, 12; Kathleen Kerwin, "L.A. Gear Calls in a Cobbler," *Business Week,* 16 September 1991, 78, 82; Marcy Magiera, "L.A. Gear's Comeback Plan," *Advertising Age,* 29 June 1992, 12; Leslie Bayor, "Shoe Marketers Prep for Workout," *Advertising Age,* 11 March 1991, 12; Kathleen Kerwin and Mark Landler, "L.A. Gear Is Tripping over Its Shoelaces," *Business Week,* 20 August 1990, 39; Sharon Lee, Robert McAllister, Ellen Rooney, and Mark Tedeschi, "Basketball Look on the Rebound," *Footwear News,* 22 July 1991, 64, 66; Kathy Brown, "L.A. Gear Steps up with a 'Hipper' Show," *Adweek,* 13 May 1991, 6; Michael E. Raynor, "The Pitfalls of Niche Marketing," *Journal of Business Strategy,* March-April 1992, 29-32; David J. Jefferson, "Fashion Victim? L.A. Gear, Highflier in Sneakers, Discovers Perils of Shifting Fads," *Wall Street Journal,* 8 December 1989, A1, A4; David J. Jefferson, "Reebok Primes the Pump while Rivals Stress Value," *Wall Street Journal,* 3 February 1992, B1, B6; Christy Fisher, "No Amazing Feet: Dropouts Mar Athletic-Shoe Expectations," *Advertising Age,* 4 February 1991, 31-32.

2. "Evolution: The Athletic Shoe Tree," *Sports Illustrated Classic,* Fall 1992, 10-11.

3. David A. Aaker, *Managing Brand Equity: Capitalizing on the Value of a Brand Name* (New York: Free Press, 1991), 8.

4. Robert E. Linneman and John L. Stanton, Jr., *Making Niche Marketing Work* (New York: McGraw-Hill, 1991), xi.

5. Mark N. Clemente, *The Marketing Glossary* (New York: Amacom, 1992), 211, 345.

6. Frank Deford, "Running Man," *Vanity Fair,* August 1993, 52-72.

7. Alix M. Freedman, "National Firms Find That Selling to Local Tastes Is Costly, Complex," *Wall Street Journal,* 9 February 1987, 17.

8. Jon Berry, "Help Wanted," *Adweek's Marketing Week,* 9 July 1990, 28-30, 34.

9. Art Weinstein, *Market Segmentation: Using Niche Marketing to Exploit New Markets* (Chicago: Probus, 1987), 11.

10. Stan Rapp and Tom Collins, *The Great Marketing Turnaround* (Englewood Cliffs, N.J.: Prentice-Hall, 1990), 106-107.

11. "Barcelona, Capital of Cataluña," *Market: Europe,* September 1991, 11; "Where Cars Go, Security Alarms and Radio Follow," *Market: Asia Pacific,* 15 January 1992, 6; Cynthia Rigg, "Frankly, Meat Packer Relishes Challenge," *Crain's New York Business,* 13 May 1991, 38.

12. Hank Gilman, "Selling to the Poor: Retailers That Target Low-Income Shoppers Are Growing Rapidly," *Wall Street Journal,* 24 June 1985, 1, 12.

13. Linneman and Stanton, *Making Niche Marketing Work,* 137.

14. Chester A. Swenson, *Selling to a Segmented Market* (Lincolnwood, Ill.: NTC Business Books, 1990), 137-138.

15. "The 189 Most Important Trends for the 1990s," *Research Alert,* 22 December 1989, 4.

16. Joan Meyers-Levy, "Gender Differences in Information Processing: A Selectivity Interpretation," in *Cognitive and Affective Responses to Advertising,* edited by Patricia Cafferata and Alice M. Tybout (Lexington, Mass.: Lexington Books, 1989), 219-260.

17. "Work That Works," *Adweek's Marketing Week,* 15 June 1992, 19.

18. Berry, "Help Wanted," 28-30, 34.

19. Cara Appelbaum, "Targeting the Wrong Demographic," *Adweek's Marketing Week,* 5 November 1990, 20.

20. Margaret Ambry and Cheryl Russell, *The Official Guide to the American Marketplace* (Ithaca, N.Y.: New Strategist Publications and Consulting, 1992), 324.

21. "The 189 Most Important Trends for the 1990s," 17-18.

22. Leon G. Shiffman and Leslie Lazar Kanuk, *Consumer Behavior* (Englewood Cliffs, N.J.: Prentice-Hall, 1987), 519.

23. Joe Schwartz, "Climate-Controlled Customers," *American Demographics,* March 1992, 24-32.

24. U.S. Bureau of the Census, *Statistical Abstract of the United States: 1989* (Washington, D.C.: GPO, 1989), 892.

25. *Statistical Abstract of the United States: 1990,* 908, 909, 914, 910.

26. *Statistical Abstract of the United States: 1990,* 908, 916.

27. *Statistical Abstract of the United States: 1989,* 899.

28. *Statistical Abstract of the United States: 1990,* 908, 914.

29. Laurence Urdang, ed., *The Dictionary of Advertising* (Lincolnwood, Ill.: NTC Business Books, 1986), 27.

30. Weinstein, *Market Segmentation,* 69.

31. William Phillips, "Tele de Grandeur: How France Fouled It Up," *Admap,* September 1991, 8-13.

32. Rebecca Piirto, *Beyond Mind Games: The Marketing Power of Psychographics* (New York: American Demographics Books, 1991), 127-128.

33. Matthew Grimm, "Fatter Than Ever, Wendy's Bounces Back," *Adweek's Marketing Week,* 22 July 1991, 4-5.

34. Marc B. Rubner, "The Hearts of New-Car Buyers," *American Demographics,* August 1991, 14-15.

35. Piirto, *Beyond Mind Games,* 79-90.

36. William O. Beardon, Richard G. Netemeyer, and Jesse E. Teel, "Measurement of Consumer Susceptibility to Interpersonal Influences," *Journal of Consumer Research* 15 (March 1989): 473-481.

37. Frank Farley, "The Big T in Personality," *Psychology Today* 20 (May 1986): 44.

38. Weinstein, *Market Segmentation,* 8.

39. Aaker, *Managing Brand Equity,* 39-40.

40. Courtland L. Bovée, John V. Thill, Marian B. Wood, and George P. Dovel, *Management* (New York: McGraw-Hill, 1993), 637.

41. Piirto, *Beyond Mind Games,* 232-233; Michael J. Weiss, *The Clustering of America* (New York: Harper & Row, 1988), 10-15.

42. Weiss, *The Clustering of America,* 10-15.

43. Weiss, *The Clustering of America,* 269, 389.

44. Weiss, *The Clustering of America,* 15, 269.

45. Piirto, *Beyond Mind Games,* 235.

46. Piirto, *Beyond Mind Games,* 237.

47. Piirto, *Beyond Mind Games,* 92.

48. Stephen Barr, "Big Business Thinks Small," *Adweek,* 8 June 1992, 34, 36.

49. *Statistical Abstract of the United States: 1989,* 725.

50. U.S. Bureau of the Census, *Guide to the 1987 Economic Census and Related Statistics* (Washington, D.C.: GPO, 1990), 7, 9; Weinstein, *Market Segmentation,* 152.

51. *Statistical Abstract of the United States: 1989,* 726.

52. Benson P. Shapiro and Thomas V. Bonoma, "How to Segment Industrial Markets," *Harvard Business Review,* May-June 1984, 104-110.

53. Ad appeared in *Electronic Business,* August 1992, 11.

54. Ad appeared in *Fortune,* 2 November 1992, 55.

55. Adapted in part from Marian B. Wood and Evelyn Ehrlich, "Segmentation: Five Steps to More Effective Business-to-Business Marketing," *Sales & Marketing Management,* April 1991, 59-62.

56. Ad appeared in *Tennis,* October 1992, 20.

57. Clemente, *The Marketing Glossary,* 345-346.

58. Jack Willoughby, "The Last Iceman," *Forbes,* 13 July 1987, 183, 186-188, 190-191, 194, 196, 198, 200, 202, 204.

59. George P. Dovel, "Stake It Out: Positioning Success, Step-by-Step," *Business Marketing,* July 1990, 43-51.

60. Al Ries and Jack Trout, "Positioning: The Battle for Your Mind" (New York: McGraw-Hill, 1986), 53.

61. See note 1.

CHAPTER 6

1. Cyndee Miller, "U.S. Postal Service Discovers the Merits of Marketing," *Marketing News,* 1 February 1993, 9, 18; Rebecca Piirto, *Beyond Mind Games: The Marketing Power of Psychographics* (New York: American Demographics Books, 1991), 135-138; Paul Farhi, "Postal Service Delivers New TV Ad in Campaign to Improve Its Image," *Washington Post,* 28 November 1988, sec. f, 5; Bill McAllister, "Marketing a Public Image: From Mail Delivery to Mining Law, Postal Service Adopts Olympic Theme in Drive for 'Pride and Profit,'" *Washington Post,* 25 March 1991, sec. a, 9.

2. Thomas C. Kinnear and James R. Taylor, *Marketing Research: An Applied Approach,* 3d ed. (New York: McGraw-Hill, 1987), 18.

3. Alan D. Fletcher and Thomas A. Bowers, *Fundamentals of Advertising Research,* 4th ed. (Belmont, Calif.: Wadsworth, 1991), 8-9.

4. Jack Haskins and Alice Kendrick, *Successful Advertising Research Methods* (Lincolnwood, Ill.: NTC Business Books, 1993), 5, 11.

5. Sandra Pesmen, "Give Customers What They Want," *Business Marketing,* January 1992, 30-31.

6. John Philip Jones, *Does It Pay to Advertise?* (New York: Lexington Books, 1989), 17.

7. Michael J. McCarthy, "Mind Probe," *New York Times,* 22 March 1991, sec. b, 3.

8. Bernice Kanner, "The Secret Life of the Female Consumer," *Working Woman,* December 1990, 69-71.

9. R. Craig Endicott, "Top 100 Take It on the Chin, Feel Biggest Drop in 4 Decades," *Advertising Age,* 23 September 1992, 1.

10. Endicott, "Top 100 Take It on the Chin," 1.

11. Robert A. Peterson, *Marketing Research* (Plano, Tex.: Business Publications, 1982), 144-168.

12. Kinnear and Taylor, *Marketing Research: An Applied Approach,* 139.

13. William R. Dillon, Thomas J. Madden, and Neil H. Firtle, *Marketing Research in a Marketing Environment* (St. Louis: Times Mirror/Mosby College Publishing, 1987), 76-77.

14. Dillon, Madden, and Firtle, *Marketing Research in a Marketing Environment,* 77.

15. Fletcher and Bowers, *Fundamentals of Advertising Research,* 285-286.

16. John Philip Jones, *How Much Is Enough: Getting the Most from Your Advertising Dollar* (New York: Lexington Books, 1992), 220; Jeffrey L. Seglin, "The New Era of Ad Measurement," *Adweek's Marketing Week,* 23 January 1989, 22-25.

17. Courtland L. Bovée and John V. Thill, *Marketing* (New York: McGraw-Hill, 1992), 122-123.

18. Jack J. Honomichl, *Honomichl on Marketing Research* (Lincolnwood, Ill.: NTC Business Books, 1986), 74-84.

19. Kinnear and Taylor, *Marketing Research: An Applied Approach,* 20-21; Fletcher and Bowers, *Fundamentals of Advertising Research,* 40-41.

20. Fletcher and Bowers, *Fundamentals of Advertising Research,* 50.

21. From an advertisement appearing in *Marketing News,* 14 September 1992, IR-15.

22. Fletcher and Bowers, *Fundamentals of Advertising Research,* 82-83.

23. Margaret Ambry and Cheryl Russell, *The Official Guide to the American Marketplace* (Ithaca, N.Y.: New Strategist Publications and Consulting, 1992), 314.

24. Bovée and Thill, *Marketing,* 127-128.

25. Martin Collins, "Sampling," in *Consumer Market Research Handbook,* 3d ed., edited by Robert Worcester and John Downham (London: McGraw-Hill, 1986), 103.

26. Bovée and Thill, *Marketing,* 128.

27. Dillon, Madden, and Firtle, *Marketing Research in a Marketing Environment,* 234.

28. Haskins and Kendrick, *Successful Advertising Research Methods,* 102.

29. Thomas L. Greenbaum, *The Practical Handbook and Guide to Focus Group Research* (Lexington, Mass.: Lexington Books, 1987), ix.

30. Peter M. Chisnall, *Marketing Research,* 3d ed. (London: McGraw-Hill, 1986), 148.

31. Jane Farley Templeton, *Focus Groups: A Guide for Marketing and Advertising Professionals* (Chicago: Probus, 1987), 3-8.

32. Cyndee Miller, "Focus Groups: A Useful Crystal Ball for Helping to Spot Trends," *Marketing News,* 27 May 1991, 2.

33. Peter Sampson, "Qualitative and Motivation Research," in Worcester and Downham, eds., *Consumer Market Research Handbook,* 29-55.

34. Bernice Kanner, "Mind Games," *New York,* 8 May 1989, 34-40.

35. Sampson, "Qualitative and Motivation Research," 29-55.

36. Haskins and Kendrick, *Successful Advertising Research Methods,* 103-107; Sampson, "Qualitative and Motivation Research," 29-55.

37. Annetta Miller and Dody Tsiantar, "Psyching Out Consumers," *Newsweek,* 27 February 1989, 46-47.

38. Kinnear and Taylor, *Marketing Research: An Applied Approach,* 386-387.

39. Sampson, "Qualitative and Motivation Research," 29-55.

40. Kinnear and Taylor, *Marketing Research: An Applied Approach,* 135.

41. Bovée and Thill, *Marketing,* 129-133.

42. Gary Levin, "Anthropologists in Adland: Researchers Now Studying Cultural Meaning of Brands," *Advertising Age,* 24 February 1992, 3; Kim Foltz, "New Species for Study: Consumers in Action," *New York Times,* 18 December 1989, sec. a, 1.

43. James Rothman, "Experimental Designs and Models," in Worcester and Downham, eds., *Consumer Market Research Handbook,* 57-83; Mark Lovell, "Advertising Research," in Worcester and Downham, eds., *Consumer Market Research Handbook,* 471-512.

44. Haskins and Kendrick, *Successful Advertising Research Methods,* 56.

45. Dillon, Madden, and Firtle, *Marketing Research in a Marketing Environment,* 577-578.

46. Honomichl, *Honomichl on Marketing Research,* 119-121.

47. Kinnear and Taylor, *Marketing Research: An Applied Approach,* 169-183.

48. Fletcher and Bowers, *Fundamentals of Advertising Research,* 28-29.

49. Philip Ward Burton, *Advertising Copywriting,* 6th ed. (Lincolnwood, Ill.: NTC Business Books, 1990), 264-276.

50. Fletcher and Bowers, *Fundamentals of Advertising Research,* 225.

51. Kim Foltz, "Creativity's Big Test: Surviving Research," *New York Times,* 21 May 1990, sec. d, 4; Fletcher and Bowers, *Fundamentals of Advertising Research,* 206-207.

52. Haskins and Kendrick, *Successful Advertising Research Methods,* 343-349.

53. Dillon, Madden, and Firtle, *Marketing Research in a Marketing Environment,* 647-648.

54. Jones, *How Much Is Enough,* 222-223.

55. Fletcher and Bowers, *Fundamentals of Advertising Research,* 232-237.

56. Information on research firms compiled from the following sources: company brochure, Opinion Research Corporation, 1991; *The Wall Street Journal Directory of Research Sources,* undated; *1993 Honomichl Business Report on the Marketing Research Industry,* supplement to *Marketing News,* 7 June 1993;

Fletcher and Bowers, *Fundamentals of Advertising Research,* 222-308; *Guide to Media Research* (New York: American Association of Advertising Agencies, 1991), 34, 36-40.

57. Fletcher and Bowers, *Fundamentals of Advertising Research,* 52-56.

58. Based on an example from Fletcher and Bowers, *Fundamentals of Advertising Research,* 56.

59. Donald R. Lehmann, *Market Research and Analysis,* 3d ed. (Homewood, Ill.: Irwin, 1989), 229-237.

60. Lehmann, *Market Research and Analysis,* 231.

61. Collins, "Sampling," 85-110; Fletcher and Bowers, *Fundamentals of Advertising Research,* 128.

62. Collins, "Sampling," 94.

63. Kinnear and Taylor, *Marketing Research,* 394-395.

64. Fletcher and Bowers, *Fundamentals of Advertising Research,* 90-91.

65. Kinnear and Taylor, *Marketing Research,* 430-431; Fletcher and Bowers, *Fundamentals of Advertising Research,* 126-127.

66. Fletcher and Bowers, *Fundamentals of Advertising Research,* 110.

67. Fletcher and Bowers, *Fundamentals of Advertising Research,* 111-114.

68. Laura Bird, "Black-Oriented Radio Station Airs Complaint against Arbitron Data," *Wall Street Journal,* 19 August 1992, B4.

69. See note 1.

CHAPTER 7

1. Carol J. Loomis, "Dinosaurs?" *Fortune,* 3 May 1993, 36-42; Raymond Serafin, "The Saturn Story," *Advertising Age,* 16 November 1992, 1, 8, 13, 16; Fara Warner, "The Marketer of the Year: Donald Hudler," *Brandweek,* 16 November 1992, 21; "Saturn Gears Up Another Blockbuster Ad," *Adweek,* 4 January 1993, 8.

2. Peter D. Bennett, *Dictionary of Marketing Terms* (Chicago: American Marketing Association, 1988), 118-119, 195-196.

3. R. L. Erickson, "Marketing Planning: There Is No Magic," *Journal of Business and Industrial Marketing,* Fall 1986, 61-67.

4. Bennett, *Dictionary of Marketing Terms,* 186.

5. David A. Aaker, *Strategic Marketing Management,* 2d ed. (New York: Wiley, 1988), 23.

6. Dale D. McConkey, *How to Manage by Results* (New York: Amacom, 1983), 110-111.

7. Laurie Freeman, "The Green Revolution: Procter & Gamble," *Advertising Age,* 29 January 1992, 16, 34.

8. Roman G. Hiebing, Jr., and Scott W. Cooper, *How to Write a Successful Marketing Plan* (Lincolnwood, Ill.: NTC Business Books, 1990), 80-82.

9. Robert D. Hof, "Hewlett-Packard's Promises Are Starting to Sound Hollow," *Business Week,* 3 September 1990, 36.

10. Meg Cox, " To Make Their Big Books Even Bigger, Firms Are Spending the Biggest Bucks," *Wall Street Journal,* 19 June 1991, B1.

11. Hiebing and Cooper, *How to Write a Successful Marketing Plan,* 119-122.

12. Ad appeared in *Keyboard,* October 1992, 1.

13. "Copy Chasers: Dressed for Success," *Business Marketing,* June 1992, 42-46.

14. "Copy Chasers: Best of Southern California," *Business Marketing,* November 1992, 76-77.

15. Bob Garfield, "Ad Review: Chrysler Agencies Work to Match Ads to Cars," *Advertising Age,* 26 October 1992, 53.

16. Product usage suggestion appeared on Jell-O packaging.

17. Ad appeared in *Fine Woodworking,* May-June 1992, 15.

18. Cleveland Horton, "Nissan Enjoys Luxury of Record Altima Sales," *Advertising Age,* 30 November 1992, 52.

19. Hiebing and Cooper, *How to Write a Successful Marketing Plan,* 122.

20. Rogain advertising, 1993.

21. Hiebing and Cooper, *How to Write a Successful Marketing Plan,* 133-240.

22. David A. Aaker, *Managing Brand Equity* (New York: Free Press, 1991), 15-21.

23. Don. E. Schultz, Stanley I. Tannenbaum, and Robert F. Lauterborn, *Integrated Marketing Communications: Pulling It All Together and Making It Work* (Lincolnwood, Ill.: NTC Business Books, 1993), 42-63.

24. Alice Z. Cuneo and Raymond Serafin, "With Saturn, Riney Rings Up a Winner," *Advertising Age,* 14 April 1993, 2-3.

25. Kate Fitzgerald, "In Line for Integrated Hall of Fame," *Advertising Age,* 10 October 1993, S-12.

26. Russell H. Colley, *Defining Advertising Goals for Measured Advertising Results* (New York: Association of National Advertisers, 1961, reprinted 1984), 12.

27. Colley, *Defining Advertising Goals for Measured Advertising Results,* 38.

28. John Philip Jones, *What's in a Name: Advertising and the Concept of Brands* (New York: Lexington Books, 1986), 141.

29. Courtland L. Bovée and John V. Thill, *Marketing* (New York: McGraw-Hill, 1992), 529-530.

30. Jones, *What's in a Name,* 145-147.

31. Jones, *What's in a Name,* 148-149.

32. John R. Rossiter, Larry Percy, and Robert J. Donovan, "A Better Advertising Planning Grid," *Journal of Advertising Research,* October-November 1991, 11-21.

33. Rossiter, Percy, and Donovan, "A Better Advertising Planning Grid," 11-21.

34. Schultz, Tannenbaum, and Lauterborn, *Integrated Marketing Communications,* 107-122.

35. John Philip Jones, *How Much Is Enough: Getting the Most from Your Advertising Dollar* (New York: Lexington Books, 1992), 172-175.

36. Ad appeared in *Electronic Business,* November 1992, 65-72.

37. Ad appeared in *Travel & Leisure,* December 1992, 32.

38. Toyota advertising, 1993.

39. Don E. Schultz and Stanley I. Tannenbaum, *Essentials of Advertising Strategy,* 2d ed. (Lincolnwood, Ill.: NTC Business Books, 1988), 4.

40. Leo Bogart, *Strategy in Advertising,* 2d ed. (Lincolnwood, Ill.: NTC Business Books, 1990), 43.

41. Jones, *How Much Is Enough,* 237-239.

42. Jones, *How Much Is Enough,* 237-239.

43. Simon Broadbent, *The Advertiser's Handbook for Budget Determination* (Lexington, Mass.: Lexington Books, 1988), 95-96.

44. Broadbent, *The Advertiser's Handbook for Budget Determination,* 78-79.

45. Sue Kapp, "Finally, Some Good News on the Ad Front," *Business Marketing,* November 1991, 112-113.

46. Bogart, *Strategy in Advertising,* 46.

47. Broadbent, *The Advertiser's Handbook for Budget Determination,* 88-90.

48. Broadbent, *The Advertiser's Handbook for Budget Determination,* 84-85.

49. Broadbent, *The Advertiser's Handbook for Budget Determination,* 5.

50. See note 1.

CHAPTER 8

1. Elaine Underwood, "Innkeeper to the World," *Brandweek,* 9 November 1992, 14-19; "Holiday Inn Worldwide Brings Emmy Award-Winning Children's Game Show to Atlanta Halloween Weekend," *PR Newswire,* 9 October 1992; "Holiday Inn Worldwide Announces Management Changes," *PR Newswire,* 20 April 1992; "Holiday Inn Worldwide Brand Portfolio Strategy," *PR Newswire,* 10 March 1992; Megan Rowe, "Asia's Allure," *Lodging Hospitality,* October 1992, 51-52; Megan Rowe, "Holiday Inn: Fat and Sassy to Lean and Mean," *Lodging Hospitality,* July 1992, 24-26.

2. Elena Bowes, Milan Ruzicka, and Dagmar Mussey, "Lifestyle Ads Irk East Europeans," *Advertising Age,* 8 October 1990, 56.

3. Richard W. Stevenson, "Catering to Consumers' Ethnic Needs," *New York Times,* 23 January 1993, sec. c, 1, 2.

4. Margaret Ambry and Cheryl Russell, *The Official Guide to the American Marketplace* (Ithaca, N.Y.: New Strategist Publications, 1992), 3; Stevenson, "Catering to Consumers' Ethnic Needs," sec. c, 1, 2.

5. Stevenson, "Catering to Consumers' Ethnic Needs," sec. c, 1, 2; Dan Koeppel, "P&G Tests Foreign Brands in L.A.," *Adweek's Marketing Week,* 24 June 1991, 4.

6. Richard W. Stevenson, "Price of Success for a Top Hispanic Ad Agency," *New York Times,* 25 May 1992, 21.

7. James F. Engel, Roger D. Blackwell, and Paul W. Miniard, *Consumer Behavior,* 6th ed. (Chicago: Dryden, 1990), 65-66.

8. Christy Fisher, "Ethnics Gain Marketing Clout," *Advertising Age,* 5 August 1991, 3, 12.

9. Antonio Guernica and Irene Kasperuk, *Reaching the Hispanic Market Effectively: The Media, the Market, the Methods* (New York: McGraw-Hill, 1982), 89-99, 133-136; Marilyn Kern-Foxworth, "'Colorizing Advertising': What Ad Clubs Can Do to Make the Business More Inclusive," *American Advertising,* Winter 1991-1992, 26-28; Cyndee Miller, "Marketers Say Budgets Hinder Targeting of Asian-Americans," *Marketing News,* 30 March 1992, 2, 15.

10. Leon W. Wynter, "Choose Your Language for Reaching Hispanics," *Wall Street Journal,* 22 November 1991, B1.

11. M. L. Stein, "Advertisers Still Ignoring Hispanic Media," *Editor & Publisher,* 21 March 1992, 20, 42.

12. Eric Speno, "In Spain, Don't Overlook Regional Media," *Market: Europe,* January 1992, 6-7; Nina Streitfeld, "How to Communicate in Other Cultures," *Public Relations Journal,* February 1986, 34-35.

13. Guernica and Kasperuk, *Reaching the Hispanic Market Effectively,* 130-131.

14. C. Anthony de Benedetto, Mariko Tamate, and Rajan Chandran, "Developing Creative Strategy for the Japanese Marketplace," *Journal of Advertising Research,* January-February 1992, 39-48.

15. Jennifer Clark, "Basta Bare Bottoms in Blurbs, Say Italos," *Variety,* 18 February 1991, 20, 51; Barbara Sundberg Baudot, *International Advertising Handbook* (Boston: Lexington, 1989), 219-222.

16. Ken Kasriel, "Ikea Is Getting Poor Marx for Hungarian Ads," *Advertising Age International,* 22 June 1992, I-20.

17. *The American Heritage Dictionary,* 2d college ed. (Boston: Houghton Mifflin, 1985), 467.

18. Joseph M. Winski, "The Ad Industry's 'Dirty Little Secret,' " *Advertising Age,* 15 June 1992, 16, 38; Joseph M. Winksi, "BBDO's Gant Encourages Blacks to Seek Ad Career," *Advertising Age,* 15 June 1992, 38.

19. Miller, "Marketers Say Budgets Hinder Targeting of Asian-Americans," 2; Jon Berry, "Help Wanted," *Adweek's Marketing Week,* 9 July 1990, 28-34; Stuart Elliott, "Retailers Reach Out to Minorities," *New York Times,* 31 December 1991, sec. c, 1.

20. Judy Yu, "Ethnic Marketing: Asian American Customers," *Women & Minorities Inc.* (Supplement to *Puget Sound Business Journal*), 23 October 1992, 5A; Chester A. Swenson, *Selling to a Segmented Market* (Lincolnwood, Ill.: NTC Business Books, 1990), 88-91.

21. Nükhet Vardar, *Global Advertising: Rhyme or Reason?* (London: Paul Chapman Publishing, 1992), 6.

22. Noreen O'Leary, "Hand on the Lever," *Adweek,* 14 December 1992, 23-27.

23. Vardar, *Global Advertising,* 35, 37, 42.

24. O'Leary, "Hand on the Lever," 23-27.

25. Philip H. Geier, Jr., "Opportunities and Problems Facing the Global Advertising Business—A Personal View," *International Advertiser,* June 1990, 6-8; Alan T. Shao and John S. Hill, "Executing Transnational Advertising Campaigns: Do U.S. Agencies Have the Overseas Talent?" *Journal of Advertising Research,* January-February 1992, 49-58; Undated promotional materials from Publicis-FCB Communications.

26. Stuart Elliott, "Omnicom Group to Acquire Goodby, Berlin," *New York Times,* 24 January 1992, sec. c, 1, 5; Stewart Toy and Mark Landler, "And Now, Rue de Madison?" *Business Week,* 21 May 1990, 74-75.

27. Mark Rudolph, "World TV Audiences," *Admap,* December 1991, 15-17.

28. Armand Mattelart and Michael Palmer, "Advertising in Europe: Promises, Pressures and Pitfalls," *Media, Culture and Society* 13 (1991): 535-556.

29. Andrew Tanzer, "The Asian Village," *Forbes,* 11 November 1991, 58-60.

30. Jane Harlen, "A New Global Ad Medium?" *Admap,* September 1992, 31-34; Michael Lev, "Advertisers Seek Global Messages," *New York Times,* 18 November 1991, sec. c, 7.

31. Baudot, *International Advertising Handbook,* 54-55.

32. Paul J. Vaccaro and Joseph P. Vaccaro, "Evaluating Cross-Cultural Advertising: An International Approach," *Journal of Promotion Management* 1, no. 3 (1992): 59-74.

33. Keith H. Hammonds, "Ted Levitt Is Back in the Trenches," *Business Week,* 9 April 1990, 82, 84; Theodore Levitt, "The Globalization of Markets," in *Global Marketing Perspectives* (Cincinnati, South-Western Publishing, 1989), 2-16.

34. Vardar, *Global Advertising,* 15.

35. Vardar, *Global Advertising,* 14-21.

36. Vardar, *Global Advertising,* 14.

37. Vardar, *Global Advertising,* 15.

38. Joanne Lipman, "Marketers Turn Sour On Global Sales Pitch Harvard Guru Makes," *Wall Street Journal,* 1 February 1988, 1, 13.

39. Vardar, *Global Advertising,* 14.

40. Vardar, *Global Advertising,* 20-26.

41. Vardar, *Global Advertising,* 24.

42. Vardar, *Global Advertising,* 15-17.

43. Herschel Peak, "Conquering Cross-Cultural Challenges," *Business Marketing,* October 1985, 138-146.

44. Vardar, *Global Advertising,* 16.

45. Alan T. Shao, Lawrence P. Shao, and Dale H. Shao, "Are Global Markets with Standardized Advertising Campaigns Feasible?" *Journal of International Consumer Marketing* 4, no. 3 (1992): 5-17.

46. Personal communication with Bob Kingsbery of Kingsbery International, 25 March 1992.

47. Cyndee Miller, "No Exercise, and They Like to Smoke," *Marketing News,* 17 August 1992, 13.

48. Elena Bowes, "From Cookies to Appliances, Pan-Euro Efforts Build," *Advertising Age International,* 22 June 1992, I-1, I-22.

49. Shao and Hill, "Executing Transnational Advertising Campaigns," 49-58.

50. John Pollack, "Vespa Scooters Collide with Anti-Japan Charge," *Advertising Age International,* 22 June 1992, I-4.

51. Donald G. Howard and Brian Block, "New Zealand Consumers' Attitudes toward Imported Products," *Journal of International Consumer Marketing* 4, no. 3 (1992): 17-33.

52. Dean M. Peebles and John K. Ryans, Jr., *Management of International Advertising: A Marketing Approach* (Newton, Mass.: Allyn and Bacon, 1984), 146.

53. Peebles and Ryans, *Management of International Advertising,* 147.

54. Peebles and Ryans, *Management of International Advertising,* 147.

55. Charles F. Keown, Nicolaos E. Synodinos, Laurence W. Jacobs, and Reginald Worthley, "Transnational Advertising-to-Sales Ratios: Do They Follow the Rules?" *International Journal of Advertising* 8, no. 4 (1989): 375-382.

56. "Asian Advertising Review 91/92," *Asian Advertising & Marketing,* April 1992, 24-67.

57. Judie Lannon, "Developing Brand Strategies Across Borders," *Marketing and Research Today,* August 1991, 160-168.

58. Edmund O. Lawler, "Ads That Know No Boundaries," *Business Marketing,* December 1992, 38-39.

59. Vardar, *Global Advertising,* 27.

60. Jyotika Ramaprasad and Kazumi Hasegawa, "Creative Strategies in American and Japanese TV Commercials: A Comparison," *Journal of Advertising Research,* January-February 1992, 59-67; Debra Goldman, "The French Style of Advertising," *Adweek,* 16 December 1991, 12; Martha T. Moore, "Japanese Ads: Abstract Sells," *USA Today,* 25 June 1992, 2B; Makiko Shinohara, "Ads That Compare Rival Products Stir Debate in Japan," *Christian Science Monitor,* 26 March 1992, 8; Stuart Elliott, "British Ads Inform Viewers without Patronizing Them," *New York Times,* 6 July 1992, sec. c, 7.

61. John Philip Jones, "Why European Ads Are More Amusing," *New York Times,* 7 October 1990, sec. f, 13.

62. See note 1.

CHAPTER 9

1. Lawrence M. Fisher, "Apple Finds a New Arena for Its Fight with Microsoft," *New York Times,* 16 June 1992, sec. c, 17; Apple ad appearing in *The Wall Street Journal,* 23 June 1992, A6-A7; "Corporate Catfights: Apple Takes Bite Out of Microsoft's Hide," *Business Marketing,* October 1992, 163; Bradley Johnson, "Macintosh Gets Tough with Windows," *Advertising Age,* 15 June 1992, 4; Andrew B. Cohen, "BBDO/L.A. Plans Global Bite of Apple," *Adweek,* 15 June 1992, 2; Robert Goldrich, "Apple Computer: Video to Print," *Back Stage/Shoot,* 26 July 1991, 73; Bradley Johnson, "Can Apple Top Windows?" *Advertising Age,* 13 May 1991, 39.

2. Milan D. Meeske and R. C. Norris, *Copywriting for the Electronic Media,* 2d ed. (Belmont, Calif.: Wadsworth, 1992), 14.

3. A. Jerome Jewlet, *Creative Strategy in Advertising,* 4th ed. (Belmont, Calif.: Wadsworth, 1992), 37-41.

4. Robert Fearon, *Advertising That Works* (Chicago: Probus, 1991), 59.

5. Stuart Elliott, "Awarding Prizes to Remove Boredom from Billboards," *New York Times,* 3 September 1992, sec. c, 7.

6. Betsy Sharkey, "Adweek's National Creative All-Star Team: Michael Koelker," *Adweek,* 15 June 1992, 46.

7. Jewlet, *Creative Strategy in Advertising,* 41.

8. Joanne Lipman, "David Ogilvy Says 'Nonsense' to Modern Ads," *Wall Street Journal,* 29 October 1991, B1, B6.

9. David N. Martin, *Romancing the Brand: The Power of Advertising and How to Use It* (New York: Amacom, 1989), 5-6.

10. Laura Bird, "Study Questions the Value of Ad Dazzle," *Wall Street Journal,* 19 May 1992, B10.

11. Denis Higgins, *The Art of Advertising: Conversations with Masters of the Craft* (Lincolnwood, Ill.: NTC Business Books, 1989), 24.

12. Hanley Norins, *The Young & Rubicam Traveling Creative Workshop* (Englewood Cliffs, N.J.: Prentice-Hall, 1990), 45.

13. Norins, *The Young & Rubicam Traveling Creative Workshop,* 23.

14. Hank Seiden, *Advertising Pure and Simple,* 2d ed. (New York: Amacom, 1990), 25.

15. Fearon, *Advertising That Works,* 59-60.

16. Norins, *The Young & Rubicam Traveling Creative Workshop,* 47.

17. Wayne Weiten, *Psychology Applied to Modern Life,* 2d ed. (Belmont, Calif.: Wadsworth, 1986), 484.

18. Higgins, *The Art of Advertising,* 75.

19. Stephen Battaglio, "Adweek's National All-Stars: Jerry Cronin," *Adweek,* 4 February 1991, 7.

20. Norins, *The Young & Rubicam Traveling Creative Workshop,* 60.

21. Laurence Urdang, ed., *The Dictionary of Advertising* (Lincolnwood, Ill.: NTC Business Books, 1986), 25.

22. Meeske and Norris, *Copywriting for the Electronic Media,* 14.

23. Norins, *The Young & Rubicam Traveling Creative Workshop,* 47.

24. Norins, *The Young & Rubicam Traveling Creative Workshop,* xiii.

25. Norins, *The Young & Rubicam Traveling Creative Workshop,* 1-19.

26. Don E. Schultz and Stanley I. Tannenbaum, *Essentials of Advertising Strategy,* 2d ed. (Lincolnwood, Ill.: NTC Business Books, 1988), 53-74; Albert C. Book and C. Dennis Schick, *Fundamentals of Copy & Layout,* 2d ed. (Lincolnwood, Ill.: NTC Business Books, 1991), 23-25.

27. Ad appeared in *Forbes,* 7 December 1992, 85.

28. Ad appeared in *WindowsUser,* February 1993, 41.

29. Book and Schick, *Fundamentals of Copy & Layout,* 6-9.

30. Higgins, *The Art of Advertising,* 44.

31. William L. Hagerman, *Broadcast Advertising Copywriting* (Boston: Focal Press, 1990), 17-18.

32. Stuart Elliott, "Good Taste Survives the Storm in Print and TV Messages," *New York Times,* 4 September 1992, sec. c, 4.

33. "Canon's Descent into Incomprehensibility," *Business Marketing,* December 1992, 44.

34. Bobby J. Calder and Charles L. Gruder, "Emotional Advertising Appeals," in *Cognitive and Affective Responses to Advertising,* edited by Patricia Cafferata and Alice Tybout (Lexington, Mass.: Lexington Books, 1989), 277-285.

35. Meeske and Norris, *Copywriting for the Electronic Media,* 109-121.

36. Thomas R. King, "Pitches on Value Stick in Consumers' Minds," *Wall Street Journal,* 4 June 1990, B1.

37. Ad appeared in *Forbes,* 7 December 1992, 69.

38. Joanne Lipman, "Ads of the '80s: The Loved and the Losers," *Wall Street Journal,* 28 December 1989, B1, B4; Cyndee Miller, "Hey Dudes: Fox TV May Have a Cash Cow in Its Licensing Deals," *Marketing News,* 11 June 1990, 1; Joanne Lipman, "Name Two U.S. Stars Reluctant to Appear in TV Ads in Japan," *Wall Street Journal,* 4 November 1987, 1, 19.

39. Miner Raymond, *Advertising That Sells: A Primer for Product Managers* (Cincinnati: Black Rose Publishing, 1989), 39.

40. Paul Duke, Jr., and Ronald Alsop, "Advertisers Beginning to Play Off Worker Concern over Job Security," *Wall Street Journal,* 1 April 1988, 11; Ronald Alsop, "More Food Advertising Plays on Cancer and Cardiac Fears," *Wall Street Journal,* 8 October 1987, 33; George E. Belch and Michael A. Belch, *Introduction to Advertising and Promotion Management,* (Homewood, Ill.: Irwin, 1990), 186.

41. "Emotions Important for Successful Advertising," *Marketing News,* 12 April 1985, 18.

42. Courtland L. Bovée and John V. Thill, *Marketing* (New York: McGraw-Hill, 1992), 562.

43. Ad appeared in *Forbes,* 7 December 1992, 56.

44. Joshua Levine, "Fantasy, Not Flesh," *Forbes,* 22 January 1990, 118-120.

45. Mark Crispin Miller, "Hollywood: The Ad," *Atlantic,* April 1990, 41-45, 48-50, 52-54.

46. Timothy E. Moore, "Subliminal Advertising: What You See Is What You Get," *Journal of Marketing,*

Spring 1982, 38-47; Jack Haberstroh, "Can't Ignore Subliminal Ad Charges," *Advertising Age,* 17 September 1984, 3, 42, 44.

47. James Cox, "Infiniti's Epiphany," *USA Today,* 15 January 1990, 6B; Lipman, "Ads of the '80s: The Loved and the Losers," B1, B4; Ronald Alsop, "Surreal Ads Startle—But Do They Sell?" *Wall Street Journal,* 20 October 1988, B1.

48. Higgins, *The Art of Advertising,* 72.

49. Higgins, *The Art of Advertising,* 92.

50. Philip Ward Burton, *Advertising Copywriting,* 6th ed. (Lincolnwood, Ill.: NTC Business Books, 1990), 11.

51. Kenneth Roman and Jane Maas, *How to Advertise* (New York: St. Martin's Press, 1976), 32.

52. Burton, *Advertising Copywriting,* 52-69.

53. Ad appeared in *The Herald* (Everett, Wash.), 15 January 1993, 4A.

54. Burton, *Advertising Copywriting,* 57.

55. Ad appeared in *Money,* Forecast 1993 issue, 103.

56. Ad appeared in *Keyboard,* August 1992, 39.

57. Ad appeared in *Travel & Leisure,* January 1993, 47.

58. Ad appeared in *Money,* Forecast 1993 issue, 112.

59. Ad appeared in *Brandweek,* 7 December 1992, 26.

60. Roman and Maas, *How to Advertise,* 34-35.

61. Burton, *Advertising Copywriting,* 74.

62. Joanne Lipman, "Coca-Cola Is Close to Picking New Slogan," *Wall Street Journal,* 28 September 1992, B5.

63. "Hyundai, Again, Finds a Position That Makes Sense," *Brandweek,* 4 January 1993, 24.

64. Burton, *Advertising Copywriting,* 210-211.

65. Burton, *Advertising Copywriting,* 99.

66. Burton, *Advertising Copywriting,* 134-145.

67. Burton, *Advertising Copywriting,* 99-102.

68. See note 1.

CHAPTER 10

1. "Cessna Lands on CEO's Desks: A Big, Bold, Beautiful Campaign," *Business Marketing,* January 1993, 42; Gilbert Sedbon, "Cessna Citation X Aims for Europe," *Flight International,* 12 June 1991, 34; Edward H. Phillips, "CitationJet Nears Certification; Prototype Citation 10 to Fly Next Year," *Aviation Week & Space Technology,* 21 September 1992, 45-48; Edward H. Phillips, "Stormy Future in Business Flying," *Aviation Week & Space Technology,* 21 September 1992, 40-45.

2. Laurence Urdang, ed., *The Dictionary of Advertising* (Lincolnwood, Ill.: NTC Business Books, 1986), 35, 60.

3. Roy Paul Nelson, *The Design of Advertising,* 6th ed. (Dubuque, Iowa: WCB, 1989), 54.

4. Nelson, *The Design of Advertising,* 54.

5. Matthew D. Shank and Raymond LaGarce, "Study: Color Makes Any Message More Effective," *Marketing News,* 6 August 1990, 12.

6. Nelson, *The Design of Advertising,* 232-235.

7. Courtland L. Bovée and John V. Thill, *Marketing* (New York: McGraw-Hill, 1992), 265.

8. "Basic Black & White Goes with Everything," *Art Direction,* March 1992, 44-48.

9. Global Gallery, *Advertising Age International,* 28 September 1992, I-10.

10. Nelson, *The Design of Advertising,* 54.

11. Nelson, *The Design of Advertising,* 54-66.

12. Nelson, *The Design of Advertising,* 56.

13. Bob Dahlquist, "Equilibrium," *Before & After,* June 1992, 4.

14. Nelson, *The Design of Advertising,* 56.

15. John McWade, "How to Lay Out a Good Advertisement," *Before & After,* June 1992, 6-7.

16. Nelson, *The Design of Advertising,* 59.

17. Lennie Copeland and Lewis Griggs, *Going International* (New York: Random House, 1985), 117.

18. Nelson, *The Design of Advertising,* 59.

19. Nelson, *The Design of Advertising,* 63-64.

20. "Basic Black & White Goes with Everything," 44-48.

21. Martha T. Moore, "'90s Ads Opt for Mystery," *USA Today,* 19 October 1992, 1B.

22. Ad insert appeared in *HOW,* November-December 1992, following page 8.

23. Stuart Elliott, "When Up Is Down, Does It Sell?" *New York Times,* 21 February 1992, C1, C5.

24. Bruce Bendinger, *The Copy Workshop Workbook* (Chicago: The Copy Workshop, 1988), 180.

25. Ad appeared in *Vanity Fair,* September 1992, 157.

26. Anthony Vagnoni, "Two Heads Are Better Than One," *Advertising Age Creativity,* 4 January 1993, 18-25.

27. Bendinger, *The Copy Workshop Workbook,* 196.

28. Ad appeared in *Vanity Fair,* September 1992, 174-175.

29. Bendinger, *The Copy Workshop Workbook,* 199.

30. Bendinger, *The Copy Workshop Workbook,* 204.

31. Ad appeared on the back cover of *Business Week,* 25 January 1993.

32. Bendinger, *The Copy Workshop Workbook,* 210.

33. Ad appeared in *Wall Street Journal,* 23 June 1992, A6-A7.

34. Nelson, *The Design of Advertising,* 89-103.

35. Nelson, *The Design of Advertising,* 100.

36. Nelson, *The Design of Advertising,* 101-103.

37. Daniel Will-Harris, *Desktop Publishing with Style* (South Bend, Ind.: And Books, 1987), 33-37; Nelson, *The Design of Advertising,* 173-177.

38. Nelson, *The Design of Advertising,* 173-177.

39. Nelson, *The Design of Advertising,* 178.

40. John McWade, "Type: The Visible Voice," *Before & After,* April 1990, 4-5

41. Laura Lamar, "Type Combinations," *Before & After,* June 1992, 13.

42. Ad appeared in *Forbes,* 1 February 1993, 61.

43. MicroWarehouse Catalog, Volume 10, 1993, 3z.

44. Vagoni, "Two Heads Are Better Than One," 18-25.

45. Albert C. Book and C. Dennis Schick, *Fundamentals of Copy & Layout,* 2d ed. (Lincolnwood, Ill.: NTC Business Books, 1991), 93-97.

46. Milan D. Meeske and R. C. Norris, *Copywriting for the Electronic Media,* 2d ed. (Belmont, Calif.: Wadsworth, 1992), 254-267; Huntley Baldwin, *How to Create Effective TV Commercials,* 2d ed. (Lincolnwood, Ill.: NTC Business Books, 1989), 95-121.

47. Meeske and Norris, *Copywriting for the Electronic Media,* 258-259.

48. Baldwin, *How to Create Effective TV Commercials,* 96.

49. Baldwin, *How to Create Effective TV Commercials,* 102-104.

50. Elena Bowes, "Coffee Couple's Story to Percolate in Book," *Advertising Age,* 14 December 1992, 6.

51. William D. Wells, "Lectures and Dramas," in *Cognitive and Affective Responses to Advertising,* edited by Patricia Cafferata and Alice Tybout (Lexington, Mass.: Lexington Books, 1989), 13-20.

52. Baldwin, *How to Create Effective TV Commercials,* 82-93.

53. Baldwin, *How to Create Effective TV Commercials,* 92.

54. Bob Garfield, "MCI Fails to Connect with Melodramatic Ad," *Advertising Age,* 16 November 1992, 46.

55. Gail Tom, "Marketing with Music," *Journal of Consumer Marketing* 7, no. 2 (Spring 1990): 49-53.

56. Sana Siwolop, "You Can't (Hum) Ignore (Hum) That Ad," *Business Week,* 21 September 1987, 56.

57. Baldwin, *How to Create Effective TV Commercials,* 128-137.

58. Elaine Underwood, "Animation Goes Adult," *Adweek's Marketing Week,* 7 October 1991, 34-35; Cyndee Miller, "Agencies Agog about Animation,"

Marketing News, 6 August 1990, 1-2; Joanne Lipman, "When It's Commercial Time, TV Viewers Prefer Cartoons to Celebrities Any Day," *Wall Street Journal,* 16 February 1990, B1, B3; Stuart Elliott, "Energizer's E. B. Parades into Ad History," *USA Today,* 26 January 1990, 1B-2B.

59. William L. Hagerman, *Broadcast Advertising Copywriting* (Boston: Focal Press, 1990), 170.

60. David Kalish, *Marketing & Media Decisions,* June 1990, 16-17.

61. Hal Stucker, "Sleight of Hand," *HOW,* June 1992, 62-67.

62. Baldwin, *How to Create Effective TV Commercials,* 143-148.

63. Urdang, *The Dictionary of Advertising,* 8, 131.

64. See note 1.

CHAPTER 11

1. Rona Gindin, "Making Exotic Landscapes More Exotic," *Photo District News,* May 1992, 74-76; "Sony Unveils 5 Headphones; New High-Tech Items Will Bring SKUs to over 60," *HFD—The Weekly Home Furnishings Newspaper,* 2 January 1989, 88, 113; Gary A. Klee, "Easter Island," *Academic American Encyclopedia,* accessed on Prodigy Interactive Personal Service.

2. Peter Farago, "Darwin's Guide to Typesetting," *Advertising Age Creativity,* 14 January 1991, 33.

3. Richard M. Schlemmer, *Handbook of Advertising Art Production,* 4th ed. (Englewood Cliffs, N.J.: Prentice-Hall, 1990), 146-150.

4. Schlemmer, *Handbook of Advertising Art Production,* 152-157.

5. "Digital Typography: Bane or Boon?" *HOW,* September 1991, 102-107.

6. Amy Inouye, "Step-by-Step Copyfitting Methods," in *Designer's Guide to Print Production,* edited by Nancy Aldrich-Ruenzel (New York: Watson-Guptill Publications, 1990), 17-18; Amy Inouye, "Clear Copy Mark-Up for Designers," in Aldrich-Ruenzel, ed., *Designer's Guide to Print Production,* 19-20.

7. Schlemmer, *Handbook of Advertising Art Production,* 202-203.

8. Randy Pate, "Adrift in a High-Tech Sea, Artists Learn the Mac Stroke," *Art Direction,* September 1992, 68-69.

9. Melene Follert, "Color Electronic Prepress Systems," in Aldrich-Ruenzel, ed., *Designer's Guide to Print Production,* 88-94.

10. Follert, "Color Electronic Prepress Systems," 88-94.

11. Schlemmer, *Handbook of Advertising Art Production,* 15, 36, 70.

12. Schlemmer, *Handbook of Advertising Art Production,* 16-17.

13. Schlemmer, *Handbook of Advertising Art Production,* 45-46.

14. Schlemmer, *Handbook of Advertising Art Production,* 191-201; George A. Stevenson and William A. Pakan, *Graphic Arts Encyclopedia,* 3d ed. (New York: McGraw-Hill, 1992), 285.

15. Daniel Dejan, "Understanding Halftone Reproduction," in Aldrich-Ruenzel, ed., *Designer's Guide to Print Production,* 45-49; Schlemmer, *Handbook of Advertising Art Production,* 18-21.

16. Dejan, "Understanding Halftone Reproduction," 45-49.

17. Schlemmer, *Handbook of Advertising Art Production,* 22.

18. Schlemmer, *Handbook of Advertising Art Production,* 38-39.

19. Schlemmer, *Handbook of Advertising Art Production,* 22-24.

20. Stevenson and Pakan, *Graphic Arts Encyclopedia,* 404.

21. Schlemmer, *Handbook of Advertising Art Production,* 26-29.

22. Schlemmer, *Handbook of Advertising Art Produc-*

tion, 34-35, 66-69; Stevenson and Pakan, *Graphic Arts Encyclopedia*, 404-406.

23. Roy Paul Nelson, *The Design of Advertising*, 6th ed. (Dubuque, Iowa: W. C. Brown, 1989), 274; Schlemmer, *Handbook of Advertising Art Production*, 66-69.

24. Stevenson and Pakan, *Graphic Arts Encyclopedia*, 394, 438, 547.

25. Daniel Dejan, "Troubleshooting Press Problems," in Aldrich-Ruenzel, ed., *Designer's Guide to Print Production*, 129-131.

26. Schlemmer, *Handbook of Advertising Art Production*, 63-65.

27. Stevenson and Pakan, *Graphic Arts Encyclopedia*, 338.

28. Schlemmer, *Handbook of Advertising Art Production*, 36-52.

29. Schlemmer, *Handbook of Advertising Art Production*, 70-79.

30. Schlemmer, *Handbook of Advertising Art Production*, 70-79.

31. Stevenson and Pakan, *Graphic Arts Encyclopedia*, 449-453.

32. Schlemmer, *Handbook of Advertising Art Production*, 125.

33. Schlemmer, *Handbook of Advertising Art Production*, 125-126.

34. Schlemmer, *Handbook of Advertising Art Production*, 126-128.

35. Jess Berst, Stephen Roth, Olav Martin Kvern, and Scott Dunn, *Real World PageMaker 4: Industrial Strength Techniques*, Windows edition (New York: Bantam Computer Book, 1991), 376-377.

36. "Color Halftones and Duotones," in Aldrich-Ruenzel, ed., *Designer's Guide to Print Production*, 50-54.

37. Ellen Pinto, Pantone, Inc., personal communication, 11 February 1994; Lisa Herbert, Pantone, Inc., personal communication, 6 December 1993; Jack Siderman, "The Pantone Matching System," in Aldrich-Ruenzel, ed., *Designer's Guide to Print Production*, 86; Chris Dickman, *Mastering CorelDRAW*, 2d ed. (Berkeley, Calif.: Peachpit Press, 1991), 156-157.

38. Schlemmer, *Handbook of Advertising Art Production*, 133-136.

39. "Guide to Prepress Proofs," in Aldrich-Ruenzel, ed., *Designer's Guide to Print Production*, 82-83.

40. Andy Perni, "Basic Color Separation Methods," in Aldrich-Ruenzel, ed., *Designer's Guide to Print Production*, 74-78.

41. "Dispelling Color Matching Myths," in Aldrich-Ruenzel, ed., *Designer's Guide to Print Production*, 84-87.

42. Nelson, *The Design of Advertising*, 118.

43. Schlemmer, *Handbook of Advertising Art Production*, 297.

44. Personal communication with Mel Simpson of Evergreen Printing & Graphics, Everett, Wash., 1 March 1993; Stevenson and Pakan, *Graphic Arts Encyclopedia*, 30-31.

45. Aldrich-Ruenzel, ed., *Designer's Guide to Print Production*, 128.

46. Aldrich-Ruenzel, *Designer's Guide to Print Production*, 127.

47. Nelson, *The Design of Advertising*, 118-119.

48. Schlemmer, *Handbook of Advertising Art Production*, 290-292.

49. Schlemmer, *Handbook of Advertising Art Production*, 292-293.

50. Schlemmer, *Handbook of Advertising Art Production*, 293.

51. Stevenson and Pakan, *Graphic Arts Encyclopedia*, 327; Schlemmer, *Handbook of Advertising Art Production*, 293-295.

52. Stevenson and Pakan, *Graphic Arts Encyclopedia*, 68; Schlemmer, *Handbook of Advertising Art Production*, 294.

53. Schlemmer, *Handbook of Advertising Art Production*, 269-270.

54. Schlemmer, *Handbook of Advertising Art Production*, 128-129.

55. See note 1.

CHAPTER 12

1. "GMC Truck Announces Record-Setting Sales Performance," *PRNewswire*, 6 January 1993; "GMC's Jimmy SLT Truck: The Ultimate Bungee Jump," *Adweek*, 12 October 1992, 40; Mary Connelly, "GMC Aims for Affluent, Professional Buyers," *Automotive News*, 12 October 1992, 41; Raymond Serafin, "GMC Jimmy Takes 700-Foot Plunge to Boost Visibility," *Advertising Age*, 12 October 1992, 3; Bruce Horovitz, "'Torture Test' TV Ads Rack Up Truck Sales," *Los Angeles Times*, 13 October 1992, sec. d, 6.

2. "So You Want to Direct," *Art Direction*, March 1992, 54-58; Joanne Lipman, "Movie Studios Turn Bright Lights to Producing TV Commercials," *Wall Street Journal*, 10 August 1989, B1, B4.

3. Alice Z. Cuneo, "It's a Whole New Godzilla," *Advertising Age*, 14 September 1992, 58.

4. *What Every Account Executive Should Know about Broadcast Business Affairs* (New York: American Association of Advertising Agencies, 1990), 5.

5. Hooper White, *How to Produce Effective TV Commercials*, 2d ed. (Lincolnwood, Ill.: NTC Business Books, 1989), 74, 163.

6. White, *How to Produce Effective TV Commercials*, 74, 163-167; Sherilyn K. Zeigler and Herbert H. Howard, *Broadcast Advertising*, 3d ed. (Ames: Iowa State University Press, 1991), 202-204.

7. White, *How to Produce Effective TV Commercials*, 74, 163-167; Zeigler and Howard, *Broadcast Advertising*, 202-204; Kenneth Roman and Jane Maas, *How to Advertise* (New York: St. Martin's, 1976), 90-92.

8. White, *How to Produce Effective TV Commercials*, 229.

9. Wiliam L. Hagerman, *Broadcast Advertising Copywriting* (Boston: Focal Press, 1990), 166-168.

10. Bob Garfield, "Quaker State Sputters in 1st Ad with Reynolds," *Advertising Age*, 4 May 1992, 54.

11. Amy Poe, "TV Stations Write, Produce Low-Cost Commercials," *Capital District Business Review*, 30 September 1991, 16-17.

12. "For the Record," *Advertising Age*, 17 June 1991, 45.

13. Robert Goldrich, "At AICP National Board Meeting Markups, Payrolls Take Center Stage," *Back Stage/Shoot*, 8 June 1990, 1, 40.

14. Janet Meyers and Laurie Freeman, "Marketers Police TV Commercial Costs," *Advertising Age*, 3 April 1989, 51.

15. White, *How to Produce Effective TV Commercials*, 273.

16. Robert Goldrich and Arden Dale, "Calif. Prod'n $, Days on the Rise, but N.Y., Fla. Data Hard to Find," *Back Stage/Shoot*, 23 February 1990, 1, 43.

17. Laura Bird, "Study Questions the Value of Ad Dazzle," *Wall Street Journal*, 19 May 1992, B10.

18. Huntley Baldwin, *How to Create Effective TV Commercials*, 2d ed. (Lincolnwood, Ill.: NTC Business Books, 1989), 219-220.

19. Baldwin, *How to Create Effective TV Commercials*, 219-220, 227.

20. White, *How to Produce Effective TV Commercials*, 82-84.

21. Debbie Seaman, "Mirror Man: East Reflects West in the Work of Paris-Based, Nagasaki-Born Director Satoshi Saikusa," *Advertising Age*, 13 January 1992, 28C-30C.

22. Terry Kattleman, "Winged Victory," *Advertising Age*, 13 January 1992, 8C-10C, 21C.

23. Stuart Elliott, "Advertising: The Director Who Started a Revolution," *New York Times*, 25 March 1992, C6.

24. Julia Miller, "Comedy with a Human Face," *Advertising Age*, 13 January 1992, 12C, 14C.

25. "I Have No Charm," *Forbes*, 7 December 1992, 220-221; Kathy Tyrer, "Back to Basics," *Adweek*, 9

November 1992, 1, 5; Bob Garfield, "Nike Leads Way to Super Bowl," *Advertising Age*, 20 January 1992, 1, 60.

26. "Fellini: Making Ads 'Is a Fun Experience,'" *Advertising Age*, 28 September 1992, I-3; Seaman, "Mirror Man," 28C-30C; Kattleman, "Winged Victory," 8C-10C, 21C; Miller, "Comedy with a Human Face," 12C, 14C; Elliott, "Advertising: The Director Who Started a Revolution," C6; Carolyn T. Geer, "Sensible and Chic," *Forbes*, 7 December 1992, 222.

27. White, *How to Produce Effective TV Commercials*, 74, 103.

28. Bernice Kanner, "On Madison Avenue: Equal-Opportunity Advertising," *New York*, 25 May 1992, 22, 25.

29. Laurie Kretchmar, "She Gets Your Customers on TV," *Fortune*, 10 February 1992, 142; Bruce Horovitz, "Finding 'Real' People for Ads Takes Real Effort," *New York Times*, 20 June 1989, sec. IV, 6.

30. Baldwin, *How to Create Effective TV Commercials*, 223.

31. Baldwin, *How to Create Effective TV Commercials*, 226-230; White, *How to Produce Effective TV Commercials*, 82-95; *What Every Account Executive Should Know*, 13-14.

32. White, *How to Produce Effective TV Commercials*, 82-95; *What Every Account Executive Should Know*, 88-89.

33. Baldwin, *How to Create Effective TV Commercials*, 226-230; White, *How to Produce Effective TV Commercials*, 82-95; *What Every Account Executive Should Know*, 13-14.

34. White, *How to Produce Effective TV Commercials*, 173-174.

35. White, *How to Produce Effective TV Commercials*, 174-175.

36. White, *How to Produce Effective TV Commercials*, 177-179.

37. Roman and Maas, *How to Advertise*, 81-83; White, *How to Produce Effective TV Commercials*, 74-77.

38. White, *How to Produce Effective TV Commercials*, 78-79.

39. Albert C. Book, Norman D. Cary, and Stanley I. Tannenbaum, *The Radio & Television Commercial*, 2d ed. (Lincolnwood, Ill.: NTC Business Books, 1989), 194; Baldwin, *How to Create Effective TV Commercials*, 230-231.

40. Baldwin, *How to Create Effective TV Commercials*, 231-232.

41. Baldwin, *How to Create Effective TV Commercials*, 232.

42. Baldwin, *How to Create Effective TV Commercials*, 230-231.

43. Baldwin, *How to Create Effective TV Commercials*, 238.

44. White, *How to Produce Effective TV Commercials*, 104.

45. White, *How to Produce Effective TV Commercials*, 84-85.

46. *International Advertising Awards*, vol. 2 (New York: The New York Festivals, 1993), 18.

47. Kathy Brown, "Why Postproduction Is Just the Beginning Now," *Adweek*, 12 March 1990, 6.

48. White, *How to Produce Effective TV Commercials*, 108.

49. Roman and Maas, *How to Advertise*, 86-88.

50. White, *How to Produce Effective TV Commercials*, 109-115.

51. White, *How to Produce Effective TV Commercials*, 112-115.

52. Laurence Urdang, ed., *The Dictionary of Advertising* (Lincolnwood, Ill.: NTC Business Books, 1986), 159.

53. White, *How to Produce Effective TV Commercials*, 135-136.

54. White, *How to Produce Effective TV Commercials*, 249.

55. Walt Woodward, *An Insider's Guide to Advertising*

Music (New York: Art Direction Book Company, 1982), 63, 94–97.

56. Robert Goldrich, "Combo Work Becoming More Prevalent, Says AICP Panel," *Back Stage/Shoot,* 21 December 1990, 8.

57. Anthony Vagnoni, "Mondo Combo," *Advertising Age Creativity,* 1 April 1991, 24C–25C.

58. Cardona Tarquin, "Computer Graphics: Dreaming on the Z Axis," *Advertising Age,* 3 September 1990, S30–S34.

59. White, *How to Produce Effective TV Commercials,* 129–130.

60. Comer Brooke, "Radio's Renegades," *Back Stage/Shoot,* 9 November 1990, 38.

61. Bob Schulberg, *Radio Advertising: The Authoritative Handbook* (Lincolnwood, Ill.: NTC Business Books, 1990), 110.

62. Tom Soter, "Talk Radio," *Back Stage/Shoot,* 9 November 1990, 35.

63. C. R. Hartmann, "Sound Radio Advertising," *D&B Report,* May–June 1992, 56.

64. Roman and Maas, *How to Advertise,* 44–45.

65. Philip Ward Burton, *Advertising Copywriting,* 6th ed. (Lincolnwood, Ill.: NTC Business Books, 1990), 222–223.

66. Roman and Maas, *How to Advertise,* 78–81.

67. White, *How to Produce Effective TV Commercials,* 236–240.

68. Brown, "Why Postproduction Is Just the Beginning Now," 6.

69. Brown, "Why Postproduction Is Just the Beginning Now," 6.

70. See note 1.

CHAPTER 13

1. Raymond Serafin, "Arthur Liebler: 'Staring Death in Face,' Living Well at Chyrysler," *Advertising Age,* 6 December 1993, 36; Richard Brunelli, "Martin to Head BBDO Chrysler Unit," *Adweek,* 14 June 1993, 9; Raymond Serafin, "Larry Baker: Jeep Grand Cherokee," *Advertising Age,* 5 July 1993, S-26; Raymond Serafin, "John Damoose: Chrysler LH Cars," *Advertising Age,* 5 July 1993, S-18; "Media Market Intelligence Report: Domestic Autos," *Mediaweek,* 4 January 1993, 20–21, 24; "100 Leading National Advertisers: Chrysler Corp.," *Advertising Age,* 23 September 1992, 20–21; Raymond Serafin, "Chrysler Looks to Centralize $400M-Plus Media Buying," *Advertising Age,* 21 September 1992, 3; Raymond Serafin, "Chrysler May Switch Off Prime Time Ads," *Advertising Age,* 23 March 1992, 1, 44; Fara Warner, "Chrysler Treads Off-Road Media," *Brandweek,* 22 March 1993, 4; Raymond Serafin, "Chrysler Calls for Ad Strategy Overhaul," *Advertising Age,* 27 July 1992, 37; Richard Brunelli, "BBDO Gets Bonanza," *Adweek,* 10 May 1993, 1, 6; David Kiley, "Chrysler's Risky Ride," *Adweek,* 17 August 1992, 18–27; "For the Record," *Advertising Age,* 18 May 1992, 55; Richard Brunelli, "Big Chrysler Ad Blitz Will Put $12M into Magazines," *Mediaweek,* 16 March 1992, 1+; Jacqueline Mitchell, "New Jeep to Roll out with 'Teaser' Ads," *Wall Street Journal,* 6 February 1992, B6.

2. Gary Levin, " 'Meddling' in Creative More Welcome," *Advertising Age,* 9 April 1990, S-4, S-8; Joe Mandese, "Think Again," *Marketing & Media Decisions,* November 1990, 33–35; Laureen Miles and Alison Fahey, "Coke's Chuck Fruit Blazes New Trail as Ad Messages Are Tailored to Medium," *Adweek,* 15 February 1993, 3.

3. Donald W. Jugenheimer, Arnold M. Barban, and Peter B. Turk, *Advertising Media: Strategy and Tactics* (Dubuque, Iowa: WCB Brown & Benchmark, 1992), 304; Dana Wechsler Linden and Vicki Contavespi, "Media Wars," *Forbes,* 19 August 1991, 38–40; Laura Loro, "Heavy Hitters Gamble on Launches," *Advertising Age,* 19 October 1992, S-13, S-14.

4. Cathy Taylor, "Other Media," *Adweek,* 1 October 1990, M.O. 42–46; John P. Cortez, "Place-Based: Growing Pains Can't Stop the New Kid on the Ad Block," *Advertising Age,* 12 October 1992, S-28, S-30; Richard Cross and Janet Smith, "Staying in Touch with Private Media," *Direct Marketing,* June 1992, 28–32.

5. Joe Mandese, "Media Seers," *Marketing & Media Decisions,* November 1989, 28–30, 32; Joe Mandese, "Decoding the Deal," *Marketing & Media Decisions,* September 1989, 33–34, 38–39.

6. Marc Doyle, *The Future of Television* (Lincolnwood, Ill.: NTC Business Books, 1992), 2–3; Richard J. Kostyra, "Why Advertisers Still Need Mass Media," *USA Today,* July 1990, 65–66.

7. Stephen Battaglio, "Broadcast TV," *Adweek Western Advertising News,* 11 September 1989, 152, 154, 156.

8. Alison Fahey, " Turner Forges Multimedia Packages," *Advertising Age,* 16 September 1991, 48; Lorne Manly, "Multimagazine Mania Will Force Small Publishers to Align," *Adweek's Marketing Week,* 7 October 1991, 14–15.

9. Stuart Elliott, "60 Seconds of Persuasion Isn't Cheap," *New York Times,* 4 June 1992, C17; Jugenheimer, Barban, and Turk, *Advertising Media,* 117.

10. Joe Mandese, "With 60% Price Hikes, Some Advertisers Walk Away," *Advertising Age,* 12 October 1992, S-22, S-30; Dennis J. Donlin, "Are Your Media Buyers in the Dark?" *Marketing & Media Decisions,* July 1990, 58–59.

11. Stuart Elliott, "Advertising," *New York Times,* 27 April 1993, C17.

12. Lisa Marie Petersen, "New Research Tells Cable Ops What Their Subscribers Buy," *Mediaweek,* 29 June 1992, 4.

13. Jack Z. Sissors and Lincoln Bumba, *Advertising Media Planning,* 3d ed. (Lincolnwood, Ill.: NTC Business Books, 1990), 26, 80.

14. Sissors and Bumba, *Advertising Media Planning,* 98.

15. Kent M. Lancaster and Helen E. Katz, *Strategic Media Planning* (Lincolnwood, Ill.: NTC Business Books, 1990), 20; Ron Kaatz, *Advertising & Marketing Checklists* (Lincolnwood, Ill.: NTC Business Books, 1992), 127–128.

16. Michael J. Naples, *Effective Frequency: The Relationship between Frequency and Advertising Effectiveness* (New York: Association of National Advertisers, 1979), 63; Leo Bogart, *Strategy in Advertising,* 2d ed. (Lincolnwood, Ill.: NTC Business Books, 1990), 213.

17. Jim Surmanek, *Media Planning: A Practical Guide* (Lincolnwood, Ill.: NTC Business Books, 1986), 43–44; Sissors and Bumba, *Advertising Media Planning,* 89–96; Laura Bird, "Overusing TV Ads Exhausts Viewers, Researchers Say," *Wall Street Journal,* 3 January 1992, B3.

18. Peter R. Dickson, "GRP: A Case of Mistaken Identity," *Journal of Advertising Research,* February–March 1991, 55–59; Lancaster and Katz, *Strategic Media Planning,* 21.

19. Richard Brunelli, " The New Math of New Brands," *Mediaweek,* 9 March 1992, 12–15.

20. M. H. Moore, "Boston Tea Party," *Mediaweek,* 12 October 1992, 14–18.

21. Jack Feuer, "Asian Automakers Switch Gears," *Inside Media,* 23 September 1992, 25–26.

22. Bogart, *Strategy in Advertising,* 131.

23. Cheryl Heuton, "Best Plan: Campaign $1M or Less Spending," *Mediaweek,* 14 June 1993, 24.

24. Kevin Goldman, "Campbell Soup Swaps Backer for BBDO," *Wall Street Journal,* 30 June 1993, B7.

25. Richard Brunelli and Alan Goldsand, "Coca-Cola Ambushes Pepsi with Global Cable TV Buy," *Mediaweek,* 27 January 1992, 3.

26. Brian Bagot, "Lookin' Good," *Marketing & Media Decisions,* March 1990, 67–69.

27. Andrew Green, "Death of the Full-Service Ad Agency?" *Admap,* January 1992, 21–24.

28. Mike Reynolds, "Hasbro Toys with New Media," *Inside Media,* 7 October 1992, 30; Kate Fitzgerald and Marcy Magiera, "Hasbro, Mattel Serve Up 'Toons after Turkey Day," *Advertising Age,* 23 November 1992, 4.

29. Surmanek, *Media Planning,* 127.

30. "Speaking with Authority: The Big Breakout," *Advertising Age,* 22 January 1990, S-12; Raymond Serafin, "Chrysler Strategy Takes Jeep Grand Cherokee Anywhere on the Map," *Advertising Age,* 20 April 1992, 43; Brunelli, "Big Chrysler Ad Blitz Will Put $12M into Magazines," 1+.

31. Andrea Rothman, "Timing Techniques Can Make Small Ad Budgets Seem Bigger," *Wall Street Journal,* 3 February 1989, B4; Raymond Serafin, "Blasting Through Ad Clutter," *Advertising Age,* 22 January 1990, S-1, S-8; Richard Brunelli, "Ford Will Heavy Up in 4X4 Ad Battle," *Mediaweek,* 20 April 1992, 4.

32. Kaatz, *Advertising & Marketing Checklists,* 65; Elliott, "Advertising," C3.

33. R. Terry Ellmore, *NTC's Mass Media Dictionary* (Lincolnwood, Ill.: NTC Business Books, 1991), 92.

34. Bogart, *Strategy in Advertising,* 147; Jugenheimer, Barban, and Turk, *Advertising Media,* 224–226.

35. Wally Wood, " The Print-Plus Payoff," *Marketing & Media Decisions,* March 1990, 90; Sissors and Bumba, *Advertising Media Planning,* 206–207; Surmanek, *Media Planning,* 24.

36. Marian G. Confer and Donald McGlathery, " THE Research Study: ' The Advertising Impact of Magazines in Conjunction with Television,'" *Journal of Advertising Research,* February–March 1991, RC-2–RC-5; Marian G. Confer, " The Media Multiplier: Nine Studies Conducted in Seven Countries," *Journal of Advertising Research,* January–February 1992, RC-4–RC-10.

37. Patricia Winters, "Rick Hill, Barq's," *Advertising Age,* 5 July 1993, S-23; Mike Reynolds, "Smaller Budget, Bigger Bite," *Inside Media,* 29 April–12 May, 1992, 34; Alison Fahey, "Beverages: Thirsting for Something New," *Superbrands 1992,* 53–54, 56.

38. Jugenheimer, Barban, and Turk, *Advertising Media,* 227.

39. "Datawatch," *Advertising Age,* 26 October 1992, I-10.

40. Lynda Dexheimer, "Air Nielsen," *Inside Media,* 12 May 1993, 21.

41. José de Cordoba, "Hot Copy: One Newspaper Finds Way to Lure Readers: Publish in Spanish," *Wall Street Journal,* 23 April 1992, A1, A5; Tim Golden, "Hispanic Paper Defies the Ad Slump," *New York Times,* 22 April 1992, C1, C6; Fred Pfaff, "Hispanic Multimedia," *Inside Media,* 9 September 1992, 26; Lynda Dexheimer, "Hispanic Mags Try New Tactics," *Inside Media,* 14 July–10 August 1993, 20, 43.

42. Eva Pomice, "It's a Whole Nuevo Mundo Out There," *U.S. News & World Report,* 15 May 1989, 45–46.

43. Catherine R. Bendall, "Action Power," *Marketing & Media Decisions,* January 1990, 72, 74–75.

44. David W. Lloyd and Kevin J. Clancy, "CPMs versus CPMIs: Implications for Media Planning," *Journal of Advertising Research,* August–September 1991, 34–44.

45. Bendall, "Action Power," 72, 74–75; Joseph F. McKenna, "Trade Mags Get Good Marks," *Industry Week,* 6 December 1993, 43; Sissors and Bumba, *Advertising Media Planning,* 190–196, 207–208.

46. Bogart, *Strategy in Advertising,* 167.

47. Lois Therrien, "The Rage to Page Has Motorola's Mouth Watering," *Business Week,* 30 August 1993, 72–73.

48. Jugenheimer, Barban, and Turk, *Advertising Media,* 113–114.

49. Sissors and Bumba, *Advertising Media Planning,* 115–116, 126.

50. Lancaster and Katz, *Strategic Media Planning,* 43–50.

51. Tammie Smith, "Computers and Beyond," *Marketing & Media Decisions,* June 1990, 54, 56, 58.

52. Bogart, *Strategy in Advertising,* 320.

53. Ed Papazian, "CPM: Friend or Foe?" *Marketing & Media Decisions,* June 1990, 53-54; Karen Ritchie, "Media Accountability: An Innovative Idea," *Marketing & Media Decisions,* March 1990, 81-82; Kenneth Roman and Jane Maas, *The New How to Advertise* (New York: St. Martin's Press, 1992), 87.

54. Richard Brunelli, "Reality Check Planning," *Mediaweek,* 7 September 1992, 20-21, 24-25.

55. Jugenheimer, Barban, and Turk, *Advertising Media,* 242-243, 254-255.

56. Jon Berry, "Playing for Keeps," *Adweek,* 6 August 1990, 24-26, 28.

57. Cathy Madison, "Media Buyers Plug into Electronic Deal-Making," *Adweek,* 30 April 1990, 27.

58. Smith, "Computers and Beyond," 54, 56, 58; Bogart, *Strategy in Advertising,* 350; Sissors and Bumba, *Advertising Media Planning,* 382-383.

59. Richard Brunelli, "The Brave New World of Agency Media," *Mediaweek,* 8 March 1993, 18-23.

60. Joe Mandese, "Split Personalities," *Marketing & Media Decisions,* July 1990, 24-25; Joe Mandese, "Career View: Break-through . . . Media?" *Agency,* May-June 1991, 16, 18.

61. Bernice Kanner, "Let's Make a Deal," *New York,* 16 November 1992, 32-33.

62. See note 1.

CHAPTER 14

1. "Lexmark: The Writing on the Wall," *The Economist,* 3 October 1992, 74-75; Peter H. Lewis, "Can I.B.M. Learn from a Unit It Freed?" *New York Times,* 22 December 1991, sec. 3, 8; Stuart Elliott, "Another Remarkable Story of the Brand-Name Lexicon," *New York Times,* 13 August 1992, C7 (N).

2. Jerry Goodbody, "Finally, a Good Word for Print," *Adweek's Marketing Week,* 20 May 1991, 23.

3. Donna Campanella, "Truly Tailored Media," *Inside Media,* 9 September 1992, 54.

4. Christy Fisher, "Newspapers of Future Look to Go High-Tech as Experiments Abound," *Advertising Age,* 5 October 1992, S-1, S-8; Walt Potter, "Amid Uncertainty, Forecasters Look for Signs of Recovery," *Presstime,* January 1992, 18-24; Patrick M. Reilly, "New York Papers a Daily Struggle," *Wall Street Journal,* 10 September 1990, B1, B8; "Newspaper News," *Inside Media,* 31 March-13 April 1993, 40; Robert J. Coen, "Ad Gains Could Exceed 6% This Year," *Advertising Age,* 3 May 1993, 4.

5. Jennifer Ferranit, "Dallas' 1-Paper Challenge: Marketing with Humility," *Ideas,* January 1992, 8-9.

6. Hanna Liebman, "Reading Arithmetic," *Mediaweek,* 25 January 1993, 11; William Glaberson, "Press Notes: 'Yes, Kent, Profits Are Up. But about That Raise . . . ,'" *New York Times,* 4 January 1993, D12; Newspaper Association of America, *Facts about Newspapers 92* (Reston, Va.: Newspaper Association of America, 1992), 5.

7. Newspaper Association of America, *Facts about Newspapers 93* (Reston, Va.: Newspaper Association of America, 1993), 4; "New p.m.-to-a.m. Changes," *Presstime,* January 1992, 59.

8. Newspaper Association of America, *Facts about Newspapers 93,* 2; "News Notes," *Adweek,* 6 May 1991, N. 3; Jon Berry, "These Are the Good Old Days," *Adweek Supplement,* 23 April 1990, 6-8, 10-11; Patrick Reilly, "Publishers Proudly Trot Out Their Sunday Best," *Advertising Age,* 6 March 1989, S-1, S-2.

9. Christy Fisher, "Sunday Magazines Sing '92's Praises," *Advertising Age,* 26 April 1993, 36; Scott Donaton, "Sunday Magazines Stand Tall above Pack," *Advertising Age,* 27 April 1992, 47; Times Mirror 1991 Annual Report, 8.

10. Mark Fitzgerald, "Ironic Victims of Newspaper Color," *Editor & Publisher,* 23 September 1991, 8C, 9C, 34C.

11. Newspaper Association of America, *Facts about Newspapers 93,* 21.

12. "Ledger-Enquirer Launches New Military-Oriented Tab," *Ideas,* January 1992, 25.

13. John Wagner, "Black Papers Are Fighting for Survival," *Wall Street Journal,* 4 October 1990, B1, B5; Octavio Nuiry, "Hispanic Print Media More Competitive than Ever," *Marketing News,* 24 June 1991, 2.

14. Christine Larson, "Ethnic Issues," *Adweek,* 6 May 1991, N. 3.

15. *Japan 1991 Marketing and Advertising Yearbook* (Tokyo: Dentsu, 1990), 327-328; Noel Wickland, "The Germans and Their Newspapers," *Admap,* January 1993, 29, 31, 33-35.

16. Edward C. Crimmins, *Cooperative Advertising* (New York: Gene Wolfe, 1984), 128-129.

17. Judith A. Biltekoff, "'One Voice in the Wilderness,'" *Advertising Age,* 19 February 1990, S-12, S-13; Christy Fisher, "Hemorrhaging Halted, So Status Quo a Relief," *Advertising Age,* 12 October 1992, S-14, S-18; Warren Berger, "What Have You Done for Me Lately?" *Adweek,* 23 April 1990, 12-14, 18; Hanna Liebman, "Newspaper Execs Reconsider Ad Rates," *Adweek,* 14 December 1992, 8B.

18. "Milwaukee Kids Take a 'Classified Adventure,'" *Ideas,* January 1992, 27.

19. Fleming Meeks, "Dating for Dollars," *Forbes,* 7 January 1991, 296.

20. Donald W. Jugenheimer, Arnold M. Barban, and Peter B. Turk, *Advertising Media: Strategy and Tactics* (Dubuque, Ia.: WCB Brown & Benchmark, 1992), 288-289; Scott Hume, "Coupons Set Record, but Pace Slows," *Advertising Age,* 1 February 1993, 25.

21. Newspaper Association of America, *Facts about Newspapers 92,* 6.

22. Gannett 1991 Annual Report, 7.

23. Stephanie Strom, "Sharper Image Begins Its First Campaign in Newspapers," *New York Times,* 28 February 1992, C3.

24. William Glaberson, "Newspapers' Adoption of Color Nearly Complete," *New York Times,* 31 May 1993, 25.

25. Laura Loro, "Recalcitrant Papers Join Color Parade," *Advertising Age,* 5 October 1992, S-2, S-10.

26. Newspaper Association of America, *Facts about Newspapers 93,* 9.

27. Scott Hume and Ira Teinowitz, "KidNews Gets 'A' from Young Set," *Advertising Age,* 5 October 1992, S-6, S-7.

28. Newspaper Association of America, *Facts about Newspapers 92,* 24.

29. The News Corporation Limited 1992 Annual Report, 14.

30. Newspaper Association of America, *Facts about Newspapers 93,* 12.

31. Gary Hoenig, "Newspapers," *Adweek Supplement,* 1 September 1989, 176, 178, 180.

32. Joshua Hammer, "Pages and Pages of Pain," *Newsweek,* 27 May 1991, 39, 41; Dennis Cauchon, "Caught in Ad Squeeze, Newspapers Cut Corners," *USA Today,* 6 September 1990, 4B; Tribune Company 1991 Annual Report, 10.

33. Meryl Davids, "Electronic Newspapers: Newspapers via Computers Aren't Just Coming; They're Here," *Adweek,* 6 May 1991, N. 12-N. 13; David Shaw, "Inventing the 'Paper' of Future," *Los Angeles Times,* 2 June 1991, A1, A26, A27; Fisher, "Hemorrhaging Halted, So Status Quo a Relief," S-14, S-18.

34. Tom Weisend, "Cross-Media Buys: Two Washington Post Co. Publications Join Forces to Attract Ads," *Adweek,* 6 May 1991, N. 8.

35. Pat Hinsberg, "National Advertising: Newspapers Band Together to Sell Advertisers on the Viability of National Buys," *Adweek,* 6 May 1991, N. 10, N. 12; Cathleen Black, "Are You Being Served?" *A.N.A./The Advertiser,* Summer 1993, 62, 64, 66.

36. Eben Shapiro, "More Than Words Alone, Papers Now Include Samples," *New York Times,* 22 May 1992, C17.

37. Lisa Benenson, "The Data Chase," *Adweek,* 4 May 1992, N. 6-N. 7; James Cox, "Decline in Readership, Revenue Forces Innovation," *USA Today,* 23 December 1991, 5B.

38. Newspaper Association of America, *Facts about Newspapers 92,* 24.

39. Fisher, "Hemorrhaging Halted, So Status Quo a Relief," S-14, S-18; Liebman, "Newspapers Execs Reconsider Ad Rates," 8B.

40. Eric Weissenstein, "Papers Tap Census," *Advertising Age,* 27 May 1991, 12.

41. Michael Wilke, "Newspaper Perks," *Inside Media,* 14 July-10 August 1993, 19; Christy Fisher, "At Some Papers, Loyalty Pays," *Advertising Age,* 12 August 1991, S-2.

42. Jugenheimer, Barban, and Turk, *Advertising Media,* 303-304.

43. Scott Donaton, "Publishers Ring in '93 with Ad Gains," *Advertising Age,* 22 February 1993, 26; "Drugs, Remedies Hike Spending in Magazines Almost 40%," *Advertising Age,* 19 October 1992, S-17.

44. Jugenheimer, Barban, and Turk, *Advertising Media,* 307.

45. "From the Publisher," *Time,* 14 January 1992, 4; "*Prevention* Boasts Healthy Ad Rates," *Magazine Week,* 19 October 1992, 37.

46. Gary Strauss, "New Ads Don't Have to Make Scents," *USA Today,* 8 October 1992, 9B; Stephen Williams, "A Little Whiff Makes Big Scratch," *Magazine Week,* 30 November 1992, 14, 16, 22; Joanne Lipman, "Revlon Really Puts Itself in Vogue with a Big Look-Alike 'Outsert,'" *Wall Street Journal,* 17 September 1992, B6.

47. *The 1990-1991 Magazine Handbook* (New York: Magazine Publishers of America, n.d.), 8, 14-15; *The 1992-1993 Magazine Handbook* (New York: Magazine Publishers of America, n.d.), 18.

48. Scott Donaton, "While Not Cocky, Publishers Feel Relief," *Advertising Age,* 12 October 1992, S-10, S-18.

49. *Guide to Consumer Magazines* (New York: American Association of Advertising Agencies, 1988), 7; Junu Bryan Kim, "Cracking the Barrier of Two Dimensions," *Advertising Age,* 6 October 1991, 32, 34.

50. *The 1990-1991 Magazine Handbook,* 32-40; Pat Guy, "Circulations Drop; Shakeout Possible," *USA Today,* 28 August 1990, 4B.

51. Patrick M. Reilly, "Three Small Magazine Firms Make It Big," *Wall Street Journal,* 19 October 1992, B1, B6; Donaton, "While Not Cocky, Publishers Feel Relief," S-10, S-18.

52. Deirdre Carmody, "For Magazines, a Multimedia Wonderland, *New York Times,* 11 October 1993, C1, C6; Lisa I. Fried, "Mags Get Wired for Sound," *Magazine Week,* 2 November 1992, 47, 48; Lisa I. Fried, "Mags Venture toward CD-ROM," *Magazine Week,* 30 November 1992, 21; Adrienne Ward, "Plugging Along," *Advertising Age,* 6 October 1991, 28.

53. Stuart Elliott, "Advertisers Make Their Pitches Personal," *USA Today,* 8 January 1990, 5B; Patrick M. Reilly, "*Newsweek* Personalizes Magazines," *Wall Street Journal,* 25 May 1990, B1, B9.

54. Tracy Shields, "Up to Speed with Selective Binding," *Publishing & Production Executive,* June 1993, 23-24; Scott Donaton, "The Personal Touch," *Advertising Age,* 6 October 1991, 22; Iris Cohen Selinger, "Advertisers Slow to Accept Target Ads," *Adweek,* 16 July 1990, 17; Patricia Strand, "New Cars Make Magazines Tempting for Detroit," *Advertising Age,* 19 October 1992, S-2, S-17.

55. Joe Mandese, "Strong Roots for Cross-Media," *Advertising Age,* 6 October 1991, 34-35; Joanne Lipman, "*Time, Newsweek* Concoct Package Deals," *Wall Street Journal,* 8 March 1991, B4.

56. Marian G. Confer, "The Media Multiplier," paper

presented at the Media Research Workshop, New York City, 1 May 1991.

57. Fred Pfaff, "The Magazine Shoppe," *Inside Media,* 14 July-10 August 1993, 1, 32-34; Gerry Khermouch, "Pepsi Canada Mails New Magazine, *Pop Life,* to 250,000 Teenagers in Great White North," *Mediaweek,* 31 May 1993, 3.

58. Geraldine Fabrikant, "Many Readers, Few Ads for Bauer," *New York Times,* 22 May 1991, C1, C6.

59. Deirdre Carmody, "Magazines Rebuild Advertising Ties," *New York Times,* 15 June 1992, C7; Lorne Manly, "No Gains, No Pain," *Adweek,* 17 February 1992, C.M. 27.

60. John Klingel, "Having It All: Paid and Controlled," *Folio,* April 1991, 91-92; Patrick M. Reilly, "Gauge of Magazine Readers Is Criticized," *Wall Street Journal,* 20 October 1992, B9.

61. Lisa I. Fried, "Rate Discounting Common at *Bride's,*" *Magazine Week,* 19 October 1992, 3.

62. *The 1992-1993 Magazine Handbook,* 26-30.

63. *The 1992-1993 Magazine Handbook,* 24-25.

64. Richard Thau, "*Expecting* Delivers a Full-Size Magazine," *Magazine Week,* 2 November 1992, 30.

65. Cynthia Crossen, "Magazines Offer 'Extras' in Battle for Ads," *Wall Street Journal,* 4 January 1989, B1.

66. Scott Donaton, "Advertorials 'Are Like a Drug,' " *Advertising Age,* 9 March 1992, S-16; *Food Digest* special advertising section appeared in *Reader's Digest,* December 1992, 165-192.

67. Crossen, "Magazines Offer 'Extras,' " B1.

68. See note 1.

CHAPTER 15

1. Gail E. Schares, "Colgate-Palmolive Is Really Cleaning Up in Poland," *Business Week,* 15 March 1993, 54, 56; Riccardo A. Davis, "Setting the Pace on Colgate's New Path," *Advertising Age,* 23 September 1992, 4, 45; Judann Dagnoli, "Colgate Swells Spending, Rollouts," *Advertising Age,* 11 May 1992, 4; Laurie Freeman, "Colgate Axes Global Ads; Thinks Local," *Advertising Age,* 26 November 1990, 1; Mark Jones, "U.K.: Media Week Verdict—Young and Rubicam's Latest Advertising Campaign for Colgate-Palmolive," *Media Week,* 19 July 1991, 26; Colgate-Palmolive 1991 Annual Report.

2. Radio Advertising Bureau, *Radio Facts for Advertisers 1990* (New York: Radio Advertising Bureau, 1990), 3; Television Bureau of Advertising, *TV Basics 1990-1991* (New York: Television Bureau of Advertising, n.d.), 2.

3. Ed Shane, "Playing the Local Song," *American Demographics,* September 1989, 51-53.

4. Ed Papazian, ed., *TV Dimensions '92* (New York: Media Dynamics, n.d.), 11.

5. Lisa Marie Petersen, "Cable: Targeted Audiences Help Break New Categories," *Mediaweek,* 14 September 1992, 50, 52.

6. Sherilyn K. Zeigler and Herbert H. Howard, *Broadcast Advertising,* 3d ed. (Ames: Iowa State University Press, 1991), 27.

7. Zeigler and Howard, *Broadcast Advertising,* 120.

8. Ronald B. Kaatz, *Cable Advertiser's Handbook,* 2d ed. (Lincolnwood, Ill.: Crain Books, 1985), 3-4; Cabletelevision Advertising Bureau, *1991 Cable TV Facts* (New York: Cabletelevision Advertising Bureau, n.d.), 4; "Cable Penetration Reaches 65% of All Television Homes," *Advertising Age,* 22 February 1993, C-4; Susan Hornik, "Basically, Cable Hits a Hot Spot," *Advertising Age,* 8 April 1991, 41; "Cable 'Threat' to Home Video Increases as Penetration in TV Households Rises," *Video Marketing News,* 1 July 1991, 3.

9. Alison Fahey, "Cable's Seeing Double—or More," *Advertising Age,* 6 April 1992, S-8; National Cable Television Association, *Cable Television Developments* (Washington, D.C.: National Cable Television Association, 1991), 4-A.

10. National Cable Television Association, *A Cable Television Primer* (Washington, D.C.: National Cable Television Association, n.d.), 9-13; Geraldine Fabrikant, "Fighting for Visibility in a Proliferating Industry," *New York Times,* 4 February 1990, sec. 3, 10.

11. Eric Schmuckler, "Syndicated TV: The Primetime Assault Is Paying Off," *Mediaweek,* 14 September 1992, 56; Jane Weaver, "Beating the Cash Crunch," *Mediaweek,* 25 May 1992, B.T.V. 22; Lisa Marie Petersen, "Family Channel Goes for Barter," *Mediaweek,* 7 September 1992, 2.

12. Stephen Fox, *The Mirror Makers* (New York: Morrow, 1984), 211; Deirdre Fanning, "The Return of 'the Sponsor,' " *Forbes,* 17 April 1989, 136; Richard Brunelli, "Sears' Hoch Sees Stability in $800M Ad Budget," *Mediaweek,* 10 August 1992, 4; Joe Mandese, "Cable's Ad Allure Strong Despite Some Budget Cuts," *Advertising Age,* 9 December 1991, 28.

13. David Samuel Barr, *Advertising on Cable: A Practical Guide for Advertisers* (Englewood Cliffs, N.J.: Prentice-Hall, 1985), 67-74.

14. Chuck Ross, "New Hyundai Plan Shatters Buying Model," *Inside Media,* 7-20 October 1992, 1, 52.

15. Papazian, ed., *TV Dimensions '92,* 18.

16. Mark Robichaux, "Cable Operators Refine 'Micro-Marketing,' " *Wall Street Journal,* 16 April 1992, B10; Milo Geyelin, "Corporate Firm Takes Plunge into TV Ads," *Wall Street Journal,* 6 August 1992, B1, B4; Thomas M. Maher, "The New England Ventures into TV Advertising," *National Underwriter,* 11 April 1988, 13, 14.

17. Laureen Miles, "The Paperless Chase," *Mediaweek,* 24 May 1993, 20; Cabletelevision Advertising Bureau, *1991 Cable TV Facts,* 44; Robichaux, "Cable Operators Refine 'Micro-Marketing,' " B10.

18. Bradley Johnson, "Puma's Got a Sight for Sore Eyelets," *Advertising Age,* 15 June 1992, 3, 51.

19. Richard Brunelli, "Pearle Vision Assigns DMB&B AOR for Network and Cable," *Mediaweek,* 24 August 1992, 3.

20. Papazian, ed., *TV Dimensions '92,* 28; Jeff Jensen, "TV Is Advertisers' Big Pick in Europe," *Advertising Age,* 21 June 1993, I-19; "USA Snapshots: Ad Dollars Pour In," *USA Today,* 16 September 1993, 1B.

21. Elizabeth Kolbert, "TV's Sweeps Results Are in and, Well, Don't Ask," *New York Times,* 14 December 1992, C8; Kevin Goldman, "NBC, Aiming to Rebuild, Falls into Cellar as Viewers Reject Most of Its New Shows," *Wall Street Journal,* 16 October 1992, B1, B5; Joanne Lipman, "Fall Season at Networks Has Tough Start," *Wall Street Journal,* 7 October 1992, B6.

22. Stuart Elliott, "Advertising," *New York Times,* 27 January 1993, C2.

23. Stuart Elliott, "Commercial Clutter Up on Big Three Networks," *New York Times,* 4 October 1991, D1, D5; Joe Mandese, "TV Clutter: Who Has the Most, Who's Hurt the Worst," *Advertising Age,* 4 May 1992, 18; Papazian, ed., *TV Dimensions '92,* 27; Kenneth Roman and Jane Maas, *The New How to Advertise* (New York: St. Martin's Press, 1992), 13.

24. Jan Jaben, "TV Gives Sharp Name Recognition," *Business Marketing,* July 1992, 41.

25. "ANA on 15's: Advertising's Vietnam, or . . . ?" *The Marketing Pulse,* 20 May 1991, 1-3; Roman and Maas, *The New How to Advertise,* 17-19.

26. Scotty Dupree, "Agencies: Taping and Zipping Practice," *Mediaweek,* 10 February 1992, 13; R. Terry Ellmore, ed., *NTC's Mass Media Dictionary* (Lincolnwood, Ill.: NTC Business Books, 1991), 262; Andrew Marton, "Ad Makers Zap Back," *Channels,* September 1989, 30-31.

27. Marcy Magiera, "Cable Network Tunes in Ad Sales after Slow Start," *Advertising Age,* 27 April 1992, 12; Cabletelevision Advertising Bureau, *1991 Cable TV Facts,* 28; Robichaux, "Cable Operators Refine 'Micro-Marketing,' " B10.

28. Kathy Wussler, "Lifetime's Pipeline: Women Day & Night," *Mediaweek,* 9 March 1992, 2; Stuart Elliott, "One Channel Says Crime Doesn't Pay," *New York Times,* 1 September 1992, C1, C16; Barr, *Advertising on Cable,* 67-71.

29. Mark Landler, "The Infomercial Inches toward Respectability," *Business Week,* 4 May 1992, 175; Howard Schlossberg, "Once Fodder and Filler, Infomercials Now Attract Mainstream Advertisers," *Marketing News,* 20 January 1992, 1, 6-7; Dennis Kneale, "Regional Sports Cable Networks Score Big Gains," *Wall Street Journal,* 24 September 1990, B1, B6.

30. Cabletelevision Advertising Bureau, *1991 Cable TV Facts,* 4; Steve Weinstein, "Cable Crossroads," *Advertising Age,* 2 April 1990, S-1, S-12; Ronald Grover and Mark Landler, "Plenty of Courtroom Drama," *Business Week,* 11 January 1993, 99.

31. Robert Sobel, "Baseball Throws ESPN a Curve," *Advertising Age,* 8 April 1991, 43; Robert Sobel, "USA to Build via Sponsored Specials," *Advertising Age,* 8 April 1991, 43-44; John McManus, "Growing Pains," *Adweek,* 2 April 1990, 24-25.

32. Dean M. Krugman, "The Television Viewing Environment: Implications of Audience Change," in *Cable TV Advertising: In Search of the Right Formula,* edited by Rajeev Batra and Rashi Glazer (New York: Quorum, 1989), 75-94; Seymour Sudman, "Collecting Ratings Data for Cable Channels," in Batra and Glazer, eds., *Cable TV Advertising,* 95-114; David H. Harkness, Jack Hill, and Jonathan B. Sims, "Discussion on Chapters 5 and 6," in Batra and Glazer, eds., *Cable TV Advertising,* 115-122.

33. Mark Landler and Bart Ziegler, "The Roadbed Has Been Laid for the Digital Superhighway," *Business Week,* 6 September 1993, 25; Guy Stephens, "Will SkyPix Click?" *Satellite Communications,* April 1991, 16-18; Chuck Ross, "Broadcast Dish," *Inside Media,* 31 March-13 April 1993, 37.

34. Philip Elmer-Dewitt, "Take a Trip into the Future on the Electronic Superhighway," *Time,* 12 April 1993, 50-58; "Digital Compression: Cable Ad Insertion's Enabling Technology," *Broadcasting,* 6 April 1992, 52-55; Rich Brown, "Cable Moving to Digital Ad Inserts," *Broadcasting,* 6 April 1992, 52-53; Laurie Freeman, "As Panorama of Choice Unfolds, Buyers' Nerves Fray," *Advertising Age,* 9 December 1991, 32.

35. National Cable Television Association, *A Cable Television Primer,* 51; Edmund L. Andrews, "A New Microwave System Poses Threat to Cable TV," *New York Times,* 11 December 1992, A1, D2; Rebecca Piirto, "Terms of Interaction," *American Demographics,* May 1993, 40-41.

36. Rachel Kaplan, "Video on Demand," *American Demographics,* June 1992, 38-43; Katy Kelly, "Ex-Fox Chief Thinks Future Is in TV Sales," *USA Today,* 7 June 1993, 1D, 2D; Gary Levin, "New Medium Could Be Huge for Ads—If Public Takes to It," *Advertising Age,* 30 November 1992, 16; Gary Levin, "Interactive TV Rivals Poised for Battle," *Advertising Age,* 30 November 1992, 3, 16; Christy Fisher, "Marketers Answer Interactive TV Call," *Advertising Age,* 30 March 1992, 36.

37. Joe Mandese, "Hey Kids! Sit Still for a Minute," *Advertising Age,* 13 May 1991, S-34; Dennis Kneale, "Fuzzy Picture: TV's Nielsen Ratings, Long Unquestioned, Faces Tough Challenges," *Wall Street Journal,* 19 July 1990, A1, A4; Elizabeth Jensen, "Nielsen Rival to Unveil New 'Peoplemeter,' " *Wall Street Journal,* 4 December 1992, B4; Peter Danaher and Terence Beed, "Peoplemeters: Do They Really Measure What People Watch?" *Admap,* March 1992, 42-44.

38. Walter Goodman, "The How, Why and Junk of the Ratings Game," *New York Times,* 18 February 1992, B1, B2; Joe Mandese, "Video Technology Foils Measurement," *Advertising Age,* 9 March 1992, 30; Eric Schmuckler, "New Arbitron Passive People Described as 'Affordable,' " *Mediaweek,* 14 December 1992, 3.

39. Elizabeth Kolbert, "Networks Press Nielsen to

Count the Barfly, Too," *New York Times,* 15 March 1993, C1, C6; Lynda Dexheimer, "Found: 28 Million TV Viewers," *Inside Media,* 17 March 1993, 8, 45.

40. Jack Z. Sissors and Lincoln Bumba, *Advertising Media Planning,* 3d ed. (Lincolnwood, Ill.: NTC Business Books, 1990), 49-51.

41. Scotty Dupree, "Perception vs. Reality," *Mediaweek,* 10 February 1992, 12.

42. Scotty Dupree, "The Numbers," *Mediaweek,* 24 February 1992, 16-17; M. H. Moore, "Media Plan," *Mediaweek,* 13 July 1992, 11-12.

43. Geraldine Fabrikant, "Tepid Recovery in TV's Up-Front Market," *New York Times,* 7 August 1992, C2; Joe Mandese, "The Cry Grows Louder: Why Buy Upfront?" *Advertising Age,* 13 May 1991, S-8, S-12.

44. "A Midsummer Night's Lull," *Adweek,* 7 June 1993, T.V. 10-T.V. 12; Richard Brunelli, "Chicago Perfume Seller Plans on Big 4th Quarter Spending Boost," *Mediaweek,* 14 September 1992, 3.

45. Lorien Boyar, "National Broadcast," *Mediaweek,* 20 January 1992, 37.

46. Richard Brunelli and Mary Huhn, "Computer Comeback," *Mediaweek,* 11 May 1992, 16-19.

47. Lisa Marie Petersen, "Frito-Lay and Sony Blast Off with Sci-Fi," *Mediaweek,* 21 September 1992, 5.

48. Dave Martin, "Lunch with Dave Martin," *Mediaweek,* 16 March 1992, 12.

49. Terry Lefton, "Katie Shisler, Tom's of Maine," *Mediaweek,* 16 November 1992, 32, 34.

50. Bob Schulberg, *Radio Advertising: The Authoritative Handbook* (Lincolnwood, Ill.: NTC Business Books, 1990), 145-146.

51. Radio Advertising Bureau, *Radio Marketing Guide and Fact Book for Advertisers* (New York: Radio Advertising Bureau, 1992), 7, 8.

52. Schulberg, *Radio Advertising,* 23-25; Geraldine Fabrikant, "Struggling Stations in Search of a Niche," *New York Times,* 20 May 1990, sec. 3, 10.

53. National Association of Broadcasters, *RadiOutlook II: New Forces Shaping the Industry* (Washington, D.C.: National Association of Broadcasters, 1991), 65-66; Schulberg, *Radio Advertising,* 15; Zeigler and Howard, *Broadcast Advertising,* 29; National Association of Broadcasters, *RadiOutlook II,* 64-65; Kevin Goldman, "Radio Stations Luring Boomers with Old Songs," *Wall Street Journal,* 24 April 1990, B1, B5.

54. Danny Flamberg, "The Four Horsemen of Network Radio," *Mediaweek,* 23 November 1992, 15-19; Mark Schone, "Radio Free Europe," *Mediaweek,* 2 November 1992, 16-17; Wayne Walley, "Spectrum, Paul Harvey in Catbird Seat," *Advertising Age,* 10 September 1990, S-8; Wayne Walley, "Shifting Season," *Advertising Age,* 10 September 1990, S-10.

55. Schulberg, *Radio Advertising,* 59-60; Peter Viles, "Syndicators Head for the Niches," *Broadcasting,* 18 May 1992, 28, 30, 31.

56. "Dylan's Doings," *Inside Media,* 7 October 1992, 8; National Association of Broadcasters, *RadiOutlook II,* 123-124; Flamberg, "The Four Horsemen of Network Radio," 15-19.

57. Jenny C. McCune, "Inside Track: Switch on the Radio," *Success,* April 1992, 23.

58. Russell Shaw, "Fragmentation," *Mediaweek,* 3 May 1993, 16-18, 22, 24.

59. National Association of Broadcasters, *RadiOutlook II,* 123-125; Radio Advertising Bureau, "Metro-North: Driving the Point Home with Radio," *America on Radio* (New York: Radio Advertising Bureau, December 1989), 4.

60. Radio Advertising Bureau, *Radio Marketing Guide,* 3, 9.

61. "At Deadline," *Mediaweek,* 30 March 1992, 25.

62. Warren Berger, "LoJack's 'Bug' Fights a Stolen Car Epidemic," *Adweek's Marketing Week,* 2 April 1990, 17.

63. Paul Mulcahy, "Maximizing the Value of Radio in the Marketing Mix," in *Radio Advertising Workshop*

(New York: Association of National Advertisers and Radio Advertising Bureau, 5 June 1990), 13-17.

64. Stephen Battaglio, "Restructuring Makes Radio an Easier Buy," *Adweek,* 27 August 1990, 17.

65. Radio Advertising Bureau, *Radio Marketing Guide,* 7.

66. Courtland L. Bovée and John V. Thill, *Marketing* (New York: McGraw-Hill, 1992), 539.

67. Michael Wilke, "The Digital Dial," *Inside Media,* 14 July-10 August 1993, 36-38; National Association of Broadcasters, *RadiOutlook II,* 46-53.

68. Daniel Flamberg, "Loopholes, Lifeboats or Larceny?" *Mediaweek,* 17 February 1992, 20-22, 26, 28.

69. Joshua Levine, "Drive Time," *Forbes,* 19 March 1990, 144, 146.

70. Schulberg, *Radio Advertising,* 61.

71. Wayne Walley, "Upfront Sales Seen Static; Nets Upbeat," *Advertising Age,* 10 September 1990, S-10.

72. Shane, "Playing the Local Song," 51-53.

73. See note 1.

CHAPTER 16

1. Mark Lewyn, "MCI Is Coming through Loud and Clear," *Business Week,* 25 January 1993, 84, 88; "Trendsetters," *Direct Marketing,* November 1992, 40; Kevin Goldman, "AT&T-MCI Negative Ad Volleys Are Long-Distance Risk for Both," *Wall Street Journal,* 14 April 1993, B8; Milton Moskowitz, Robert Levering, and Michael Katz, *Everybody's Business* (New York: Doubleday Currency, 1990), 626-630; Ronald D. Greene, managing director, Devon Direct Marketing and Advertising, personal communication, 21 June 1993; Anthony Ramirez, "Battle Is Fierce on the Phone Front," *New York Times,* 27 November 1993, 13, 15.

2. Florida Fruit Shippers ad in *CompuServe Magazine,* February 1993, 52; North Carolina Discount Furniture Sales ad in *New York Times Magazine,* 18 October 1992, 74.

3. Tom Eisenhart, "Direct Marketing: AT&T Uses Highly Integrated Campaign to Take Direct Aim at Recapturing Small Businesses," *Business Marketing,* August 1992, 37-39.

4. Kenneth Wylie, "Direct Response: Database Development Shows Strong Growth as Shops Gain 16.9% in U.S.," *Advertising Age,* 12 July 1993, S-1, S-8; William M. Bulkeley, "Marketers Mine Their Corporate Databases," *Wall Street Journal,* 14 June 1993, B7.

5. Bulkeley, "Marketers Mine Their Corporate Databases," B7.

6. Scott Hume, "Pizza Hut Hungry for Data," *Advertising Age,* 22 June 1992, 4; Laura Loro, "Data Bases Seen as 'Driving Force,'" *Advertising Age,* 18 March 1991, 39.

7. David Shepard Associates, *The New Direct Marketing: How to Implement a Profit-Driven Database Marketing Strategy* (Homewood, Ill.: Business One Irwin, 1990), 254-255.

8. "Echo Winners," *DM News,* 4 November 1991, 42.

9. Kevin J. Clancy and Robert S. Shulman, *The Marketing Revolution* (New York: HarperBusiness, 1991), 79, 270-273.

10. Joshua Levine, "Smarter Boob Tube?" *Forbes,* 16 September 1991, 159, 162.

11. David Churbuck, "Smart Mail," *Forbes,* 22 January 1990, 107-108.

12. Kenneth Roman and Jane Maas, *The New How to Advertise* (New York: St. Martin's Press, 1992), 66-67; Gary Levin, "DMA Speakers Caution Use of Databases," *Advertising Age,* 5 April 1993, 37.

13. Harry J. Buckel, "Economics, Efficiency Spur Shift to Ad Mail," *Advertising Age,* Special Advertising Section, M-3-M-4; John R. Wargo and Jean Li Rogers, "USPS: A Marketing and Sales Partner," *Advertising Age,* Special Advertising Section, M-6-M-7.

14. Wargo and Rogers, "USPS: A Marketing and Sales Partner," M-6-M-7.

15. Bob Stone, *Successful Direct Marketing Methods,*

3d ed. (Lincolnwood, Ill.: NTC Business Books, 1987), 265-267.

16. Tracy E. Benson, "Marketing Enters Another Dimension," *Industry Week,* 22 January 1990, 32-33.

17. Stone, *Successful Direct Marketing Methods,* 279, 284.

18. Jerrold Ballinger, "Potato Project That Feeds Homeless Raises Money through Direct Mail," *DM News,* 10 June 1991, 2.

19. Anne Murphy, "The Best Newsletters in America," *Inc.,* June 1992, 70-72, 76, 78.

20. Susan K. Jones, *Creative Strategy in Direct Marketing* (Lincolnwood, Ill.: NTC Business Books, 1991), 384; Rhonda M. Abrams, "Direct Mail a Worthwhile Investment," *Rockland Journal–News,* 25 April 1993, E3.

21. Larry Jaffee, "Barnes & Noble Sees $30-Million in Catalog Sales for Fiscal 1992," *DM News,* 2 December 1991, 2.

22. American Business Information ad in *DM News,* 4 November 1991, 18.

23. "USA Snapshots: More Catalogs in the Mail," *USA Today,* December 19, 1990, 1B.

24. Hubert B. Herring, "Business Diary: What Next? Pave the Prairie?" *New York Times,* 31 January 1993, sec. 3, 2; Cyndee Miller, "Sears, Penney Revamp Catalogues to Compete with Specialty Books," *Marketing News,* 1 April 1991, 1, 6; Kevin Helliker, "Penney's Catalog Division, Long a Star, Risks Losing Its Luster as Sales Slacken," *Wall Street Journal,* 24 December 1990, 9, 11.

25. Gerry Khermouch, "IBM Readies Major Direct Mail Effort," *Adweek,* 31 May 1993, 10.

26. "Nonprofits Respond to Competition," *Nonprofit World,* September-October 1990, 11-12; Larry Buck and Fred West, "Want over 9:1 ROI? Listen Up," *Fund Raising Management,* November 1988, 48-50, 52, 54-55, 95.

27. Albert Haas Jr., "How to Sell Almost Anything by Direct Mail," *Across the Board,* November 1986, 45-53.

28. Mark Landler, "The Infomercial Inches toward Respectability," *Business Week,* 4 May 1992, 175; "Club Med Guests Star in Its 'Paradise Found,'" *Advertising Age,* Special Advertising Section, 25 January 1993, M-9.

29. Kathy Haley, "The Infomercial Begins a New Era as a Marketing Tool for Top Brands," *Advertising Age,* Special Advertising Section, 25 January 1993, M-3-M-4.

30. Ernan Roman, "More for Your Money," *Inc.,* September 1992, 113-114, 116.

31. Steve Zurier, "Dialing for Dollars at J. Fegely," *Industrial Distribution,* May 1988, 105, 107.

32. Lambeth Hochwald, "Telemarketing Rewired," *Folio,* 1 February 1992, 58-59, 104; Jack Namer, "Support Legislation over Telemarketing," *DM News,* 8 July 1991, 23, 36; Jones, *Creative Strategy in Direct Marketing,* 60-61.

33. Larry Jaffee, "16.2 Billion Called 800 Nos. in 1991: Study," *DM News,* 8 June 1992, 13.

34. Paul B. Brown, "Opportunity Rings Once," *Inc.,* November 1990, 152, 154, 156.

35. Richard D. Hylton, "For 900 Numbers, the Racy Gives Way to the Respectable," *New York Times,* 1 March 1992, sec. 3, 8; Dave Martin, "Lunch with Dave Martin," *Mediaweek,* 22 June 1992, 10; Namer, "Support Legislation over Telemarketing," 23, 36.

36. Mary Unkel, "American Express: 'Privileges On Call,'" *Telemarketing Magazine,* November 1992, 58-60.

37. Alison Fahey, "Quick Response: Direct Marketers Head for Outdoors," *Advertising Age,* 19 February 1990, 51.

38. Fahey, "Quick Response," 51; Roman and Maas, *The New How to Advertise,* 56-57.

39. Jones, *Creative Strategy in Direct Marketing,* 54-55.

40. Thomas K. Keller, "Getting Personal with Donors, Members, and Clients," *Nonprofit World,* September-October 1992, 20-23.

41. Anthony Pratkanis and Elliot Aronson, *Age of Propaganda: The Everyday Use and Abuse of Persuasion* (New York: Freeman, 1992), 238-239.

42. Lisa Marie Petersen, "Outside Chance," *Mediaweek,* 23 November 1992, 20-23.

43. Riccardo A. Davis, "New Advertisers Limit Outdoor Loss," *Advertising Age,* 15 March 1993, 6; Outdoor Advertising Association of America, *Billboard Basics: A Primer for Outdoor Advertising* (Washington, D.C.: Outdoor Advertising Association of America, n.d.), 12; "National Ad Spending by Media," *Advertising Age,* 23 September 1992, 69; "Outdoor Advertising: Boarding Up Europe," *Economist,* 12 October 1991, 71-72.

44. Riccardo A. Davis, "More Advertisers Go Outdoors," *Advertising Age,* 9 November 1992, 36.

45. Lawrence S. Dietz, "Carl's Gobbles Up Calif. Billboard Space," *Adweek,* 27 April 1992, 1, 5.

46. Stuart Elliott, "'Extension' Billboard Ads Get Their Due at Obie Awards," *New York Times,* 7 May 1992, C6.

47. Russel Shaw, "Outdoors: New Ways to Measure It Mean New Clients," *Mediaweek,* 14 September 1992, 66-67.

48. Outdoor Advertising Association of America, *1991 Obie Awards* (New York: Outdoor Advertising Association of America, n.d.).

49. Scott Hume, "Buffaloed into Believing," *Advertising Age,* 9 October 1989, S-2; Riccardo Davis, "Gannett Offers Clients Weekly Outdoor Ads," *Advertising Age,* 23 November 1992, 3, 34.

50. Cyndee Miller, "Outdoor Advertising Weathers Repeated Attempts to Kill It," *Marketing News,* 16 March 1992, 1, 9; "Billboard Ban? Try a 19-Foot Genie!" *New York Times,* 16 January 1991, A12; Philip Chalk, "Adversaries Take Roadside Stands," *Insight,* 18 June 1990, 22-23; Alison Fahey, "Outdoor Ads Coming Down," *Advertising Age,* 27 August 1990, 3; Outdoor Advertising Association of America, *Billboard Basics,* 20.

51. Davis, "More Advertisers Go Outdoors," 36; Steve McClure, "High-Tech Dominates Japan's Outdoor Scene," *Asian Advertising & Marketing,* May 1992, 33-34.

52. Roman and Maas, *The New How to Advertise,* 54.

53. Larry Jaffee, "Ryder Wins 2nd Straight Diamond Echo," *DM News,* 4 November 1991, 1, 56.

54. Keith H. Hammonds, "Now, It's Pepsi-Cola, the Bus," *Business Week,* 15 March 1993, 41.

55. Marcy Magiera, "Movie Rides on Transit Ads," *Advertising Age,* 29 April 1991, 14.

56. Catherine Silverman, "The Medium Is the Message," *Mass Transit,* January-February 1992, 20-21, 26-27.

57. Howard Ruben, "Bugle Boy's Guerrilla Tactics," *Adweek's Marketing Week,* 11 June 1990, 22.

58. Hanna Liebman, "New Subway Posters Light Up the Tunnels to Attract Upscale Ads," *Mediaweek,* 8 February 1993, 4.

59. Michelle B. Howard, "Messages That Move," *Cincinnati Business Courier,* 26 August-1 September 1991, 2.

60. Kevin Maney, "Hot-Rod Hot Dog: Wienermobile To Roll," *USA Today,* 28 September 1992, B1.

61. Graham Warwick, "Balloons as a Business," *Flight International,* 1 May 1991, 46-48; M. P. Dunleavey, "It's a Bird. A Plane! A Blimp?" *New York Times,* 1 September 1991, sec. 3, 5; Jonathan P. Hicks, "A New Blimp for the 90's," *New York Times,* 9 August 1992, sec. 3, 4.

62. Melanie Warner, "After the Lights Dim, Ads," *Inside Media,* 23 June-13 July 1993, 22; Kevin Goldman, "Moviegoers React to Ads on the Big Screen," *Wall Street Journal,* 18 February 1993, B10; Stuart Elliott, "In-Theater Ads to Be Cloaked in Shorts," *USA Today,* 8 October 1990, 5B; Martha T. Moore, "Movie Theaters Take Commercial Break," *USA Today,* 5 October 1992, 2B.

63. Laurie M. Grossman, "Turner Aims to Line Up Captive Audience," *Wall Street Journal,* 21 June 1991, B1, B3; John P. Cortez, "Media Pioneers Try to Corral On-the-Go Consumers," *Advertising Age,* 17 August 1992, 25.

64. Kathy Wussler, "Turner Creating First Underground Network," *Mediaweek,* 13 January 1992, 2; "Television Advertising: No Place to Hide," *The Economist,* 13 July 1991, 72.

65. Dori Jones Yang, "Hear the Muzak, Buy the Ketchup," *Business Week,* 28 June 1993, 70, 72; Eben Shapiro, "TV Commercials Chase Supermarket Shoppers," *New York Times,* 25 May 1992, 19, 21.

66. Debra Aho, "Kiosks: The Good, Bad & Ugly," *Advertising Age,* 17 January 1994, 13, 16.

67. Craig T. Gugel, "TV Is Moving Out," *Mediaweek,* 26 October 1992, 20, 22; Cortez, "Media Pioneers Try to Corral On-the-Go Consumers," 25; Joanne Lipman, "Consumers Rebel against Becoming a Captive Audience," *Wall Street Journal,* 13 September 1991, B1; Laura Bird, "TV Spots at Health Spas Slip down Drain," *Wall Street Journal,* 26 August 1992, B5.

68. See note 1.

CHAPTER 17

1. Scott Hume, "Kellogg Tops Cents-Off Derby," *Advertising Age,* 1 February 1993, 25; Julie Liesse, "Kellogg Sees Return of 40% Share as Core Brands Rise," *Advertising Age,* 15 June 1992, 1, 54; Laura Klepacki, "A New Bowl Game," *Supermarket News,* 13 January 1992, 15-16; "Cartoon Setting Helps Kellogg's Cocoa Krispies Deliver a Disney Tie-In," *Sales Pro,* January 1993, 24-25; "Innovative Premium Targets Teens for Kellogg's Corn Flakes," *Sales Pro,* January 1993, 26-27; "'Tony the Tiger' Lends Support to the United Negro College Fund," *Sales Pro,* January 1993, 28-29; "Kellogg Targets Upscale Health-Conscious Adults," *Sales Pro,* November 1992, 24-25; Betsy Spethmann, "Snack Time? Give Me My Cereal Bowl!" *Brandweek,* 3 May 1993, 24, 26; Julie Liesse, "Cereal Giants Get Crunched," *Advertising Age,* 19 July 1993, 3, 16; Julie Liesse, "Gen. Mills 1, Kellogg 0," *Advertising Age,* 20 September 1993, 2, 62.

2. John J. Burnett, *Promotion Management* (Boston: Houghton Mifflin, 1993), 7.

3. "Ad Synergizes Media," *Sales and Marketing Strategies & News,* November-December 1992, 45; "Calgon Seeks Working Women," *Promo,* October 1992, 1, 17.

4. Scott Hume, "Trade Promotion $ Share Dips in '92," *Advertising Age,* 5 April 1993, 3, 43; Donnelley Marketing, *15th Annual Survey of Promotional Practices* (Stamford, Conn.: Donnelley Marketing, 1993), 6-7.

5. Donnelley Marketing, *15th Annual Survey of Promotional Practices,* 6-7; Hume, "Trade Promotion $ Share Dips in '92," 3, 43.

6. Kevin J. Clancy and Robert S. Shulman, *The Marketing Revolution* (New York: HarperBusiness, 1991), 6.

7. Weyerhaeuser Coventry ad in *Folio,* 1 February 1993, 39-46.

8. Don E. Schultz and William A. Robinson, *Sales Promotion Management* (Lincolnwood, Ill.: NTC Business Books, 1988), 150-151; Kodak Gold 200 three-pack offer in Caldor insert, 28 February 1993.

9. Bausch & Lomb Sensitive Eyes Saline ad in free-standing insert, 8 February 1993.

10. Hershey's ad in free-standing insert, 8 February 1993.

11. Jenny C. McCune, "Cooking Up a Sales Strategy," *Success,* May 1990, 27.

12. "Country Time's Local Strategy," *Adweek,* 8 January 1990, P16-P17.

13. "Where's the Beef and Other Case Histories," advertisement in *Sales & Marketing Management,* September 1990.

14. Donnelley Marketing, *15th Annual Survey of Promotional Practices,* 44-45.

15. Michael McCarthy, "Getting Tough on Trade," *Adweek,* 13 April 1992, 20-22, 26, 28, 30; Donnelley Marketing, *15th Annual Survey of Promotional Practices,* 16-17.

16. Ira Teinowitz, "Grocery Trade Deals Set to Enter New Era," *Advertising Age,* 17 May 1993, 3, 43.

17. A.C. Nielsen, "Sales Promotion and the Information Revolution," *Admap,* January 1993, 80, 82-83, 85.

18. Robert C. Buzzell, John A. Quelch, and Walter J. Salmon, "The Costly Bargain of Trade Promotion," *Harvard Business Review,* March-April 1990, 141-149; "Advertising Executive Stresses the Need for Measuring Brand Value," *Promo,* October 1992, 14, 31.

19. Laurie Petersen, "The Pavlovian Syndrome," *Adweek's Marketing Week,* "Promote" supplement, 9 April 1990, P6-P7.

20. Magid M. Abraham and Leonard M. Lodish, "Getting the Most Out of Advertising and Promotion," *Harvard Business Review,* May-June 1990, 50-60.

21. Betsy Spethmann, "Money and Power," *Brandweek,* 15 March 1993, 21; Betsy Spethmann, "Budget Shifts Due in Drive to Become No. 1," *Brandweek,* 22 March 1993, 2; Scott Hume, "Redefining Promotion Role," *Advertising Age,* 13 August 1990, 54.

22. Laurie Petersen, "Catering to the Littlest Hotel Guests with 'Camp Hyatt,'" *Adweek's Marketing Week,* 2 July 1990, 17.

23. Philip Jones, "The Double Jeopardy of Sales Promotions," *Harvard Business Review,* September-October 1990, 145-152; Abraham and Lodish, "Getting the Most Out of Advertising and Promotion," 50-60; Thomas Exter, "Advertising and Promotion: The One-Two Punch," *American Demographics,* March 1990, 18, 20-21; Denise Gellene, "Promotions May Be Why Cereal Prices Have Risen," *Los Angeles Times,* 3 June 1992, D3.

24. Ariane Sains, "Perils of Perpetual Promotion," *Adweek's Marketing Week,* "Promote" supplement, 6 November 1989, P10-11, 20.

25. Nancy Zimmerman, "Today's Retailer: The New Power in Promotion," *Incentive,* October 1990, 42-44, 220; R. Craig MacClaren, "Trade Marketing vs. Trade Spending: The New Marketing Chic," *Promo,* November 1992, 56; Julie Liesse, "Dannon Acquires a Taste for Promotion Field Work," *Advertising Age,* 10 May 1993, S-8.

26. Glenn Heitsmith, "Try It, You'll Like It," *Promo,* September 1992, 6-7, 27, 34, 40; "Co-op Sampling Options," *Promo,* September 1992, 32-33; Pat Sloan and Scott Donaton, "Sampling Smells Sweet for Scent Biz," *Advertising Age,* 3 August 1992, 17; William A. Robinson, "Promotion Creativity," *Potentials in Marketing,* July 1991, 23-24.

27. Judith D. Schwartz, "Smartfood's Expansion Hasn't Diminished Its Sense of Whimsy," *Adweek's Marketing Week,* 29 January 1990, 34-35; Heitsmith, "Try It, You'll Like It," 6-7, 27, 34, 40.

28. Donnelley Marketing, *15th Annual Survey of Promotional Practices,* 24-25; Scott Hume, "Coupons Set Record, but Pace Slows," *Advertising Age,* 1 February 1993, 25; "Putting Hard Numbers to the Coupon Phenomenon," *Adweek,* 31 May 1993, 19; "Study: Some Promotions Change Consumer Behavior," *Marketing News,* 15 October 1990, 12.

29. "Recession Feeds the Coupon Habit," *Wall Street Journal,* 20 February 1991, B1; "Study: Some Promotions Change Consumer Behavior," 12; Scott Hume, "Coupons: Are They Too Popular?" *Advertising Age,* 15 February 1993, 32.

30. Leslie Jay, "Alternative Media: The Experiments Continue to Produce Results," *Mediaweek,* 14 September 1992, 68, 70; Lorne Manly, "Selling in the Stores of the Future," *Adweek,* 20 January 1992, 12; Michael

Bürgi, "The Next Phase in Coupons," *Mediaweek,* 12 July 1993, 9.

31. Ronald Grover, Laura Zinn, and Irene Recio, "Big Brother Is Grocery Shopping with You," *Business Week,* 29 March 1993, 60; "Smart Coupons: Step by Step, Here They Come," *Promo,* June 1992, 14-15; Laurie Petersen, "The Checkout Kings," *Adweek's Marketing Week,* 21 October 1991, 22-23; Calvin Sims, "In Coupons, It's Catalina at the Checkout," *New York Times,* 29 August 1993, sec. 3, 6.

32. Grover, Zinn, and Recio, "Big Brother Is Grocery Shopping with You," 60.

33. Thomas R. King, "Many Consumers View Rebates as a Bother," *Wall Street Journal,* 13 April 1989, B1.

34. Okidata ad in *New York Times,* 10 January 1993, sec. 3, 21.

35. Official rules for Tropicana Twister Holiday Drink Recipe Contest, 1992; Stuart Elliott, "Sales Prize of Contests Entices Big Advertisers," *New York Times,* 5 August 1991, C6; "Study: Some Promotions Change Consumer Behavior," 12.

36. "The International Beat," *Promo,* October 1992, 50-51.

37. Elliott, "Sales Prize of Contests Entices Big Advertisers," C6.

38. Canon ad in *Inc.,* September 1992, 8.

39. Crayola ad in *Better Homes and Gardens,* December 1992, 105.

40. "The Top 10 Premium Promotions of the Past Ten Years," *Promo,* April 1992, 10-11, 36.

41. Stuart Elliott, "Advertising," *New York Times,* 4 May 1993, C16; Philip S. Gutis, "After a Decade of Growth, Far Too Much Room at the Inn," *New York Times,* 8 April 1990, sec. 3, 8; Michael J. McCarthy, "Rewarding 'Frequent Buyer' for Loyalty: Companies Lock Consumers In by Giving Prizes," *Wall Street Journal,* 21 June 1989, B1.

42. Gary Levin, "Marketers Flock to Loyalty Offers," *Advertising Age,* 24 May 1993, 13; Edwin McDowell, "The Hotel Industry Is Roiled by Frequent-Guest Awards," *New York Times,* 4 May 1993, C1.

43. Richard Brunelli, "Store Wars," *Mediaweek,* 30 March 1992, 18-20, 22-23; Kathy Wussler, "Alternative Media," *Mediaweek,* 17 February 1992, 34.

44. Jonathan Rabinovitz, "Influencing Shoppers during the Moment of Decision," *New York Times,* 18 August 1991, sec. 3, 4.

45. Buzzell, Quelch, and Salmon, "The Costly Bargain of Trade Promotion," 141-149.

46. MacClaren, "Trade Marketing vs. Trade Spending," 56; Judith S. Riddle, "Procter Rewrites Trade Allowance Rule Manual," *Brandweek,* 10 May 1993, 1, 6; Jennifer Lawrence, "Tide, Cheer Join P&G 'Value Pricing' Plan," *Advertising Age,* 15 February 1993, 59; McCarthy, "Getting Tough on Trade," 20-22, 26, 28, 30.

47. "Holden's Incentive Down Under Drives Sales over the Top," *Promo,* October 1992, 65.

48. Jenny C. McCune, "On with the Show!" *Management Review,* May 1993, 37-42; Kaarina Bergstrom, "Trade Shows Rise from the Marketing Mix," *Sales and Marketing Strategies & News,* September-October 1992, 1, 6, 62; Sondra Brewer, "On the Floor, Attitude Sells," *Sales and Marketing Strategies & News,* November-December 1992, 51-52.

49. Julie Johnson McKee, "High Tech Instructs and Inspires," *Sales and Marketing Strategies & News,* September-October 1992, 9, 12.

50. Edward C. Crimmins, *Cooperative Advertising* (New York: Gene Wolfe, 1984), 136.

51. "Where Do More Than 160 Million People Shop?" Advertisement by the Yellow Pages Publishing Association, 1991.

52. Stuart Elliott, "Yellow Pages Are Getting a Nudge," *New York Times,* 23 October 1991, C17 (N); Yellow Pages Publishers Association, *Yellow Pages Industry Facts Booklet* (Troy, Mich.: Yellow Pages Publishers Association, 1991), 18-19; "Where Do More Than 160 Million People Shop?" advertisement.

53. Marvine Howe, "From Chinese to Farsi, It's in the Yellow Pages," *New York Times,* 13 April 1992, C9; William B. Beggs, Jr., "Some Soar, Some Sink," *Link,* May 1993, 9-10, 24-25; John P. Cortez, "Researcher NYPM Takes Challenge," *Advertising Age,* 16 March 1992, S-1-S-2.

54. "Industry in Brief Sidelines," *Link,* September 1992, 6; Yellow Pages Publishers Association, *Yellow Pages Industry Facts Booklet,* 16; John P. Cortez, "No Textbook for This Sort of Lab Work," *Advertising Age,* 18 March 1991, S-10-S-11.

55. John P. Cortez, "Yellow Pages Seek Audiotex Rules," *Advertising Age,* 30 September 1991, 39; "Yellow Pages: The Next Generation," *Link,* November-December 1992, 26.

56. Stuart Elliott, "Yellow Pages Are Offering Menu Ads," *New York Times,* 10 October 1991, C17 (N); Cortez, "Researcher NYPM Takes Challenge," S-1-S-2; "Canvass: What You Get Is What They See," *Link,* October 1992, 40; Doug Kaufman, " 'Risk Free' Yellow Pages Advertising: Publishers Offer a Guarantee in Shaky Economic Times," *Link,* November-December 1992, 17-20.

57. Joshua Levine, "Stirring Story," *Forbes,* 12 November 1990, 308, 310; "Consumer Promotion Spending Reached $59.4 Billion in 1991," *Promo,* D28; Rhonda M. Abrams, "Specialty Ads Send Subtle Promos," *Rockland Journal-News,* 18 July 1993, E3.

58. G. A. Marken, "Ad Specialties Enhance Marketing," *Sales and Marketing Strategies & News,* September-October 1992, 44-45; Avraham Shama and Jack K. Thompson, "Promotion Gifts: Help or Hindrance?" *Mortgage Banking,* February 1989, 49-51; Martin Everett, "This One's for You," *Sales & Marketing Management,* June 1992, 119-122, 124, 126.

59. Terence A. Shimp, *Promotion Management & Marketing Communications,* 3d ed. (Fort Worth, Tex.: Dryden Press, 1993), 482-483.

60. David Allen Shaw, "Communiqué," *Video Store Magazine,* 1 February 1993, 10; Joanne Lipman, "Studios Infuriated by Local Ads in Videos," *Wall Street Journal,* 2 August 1989, B8; Scott Hume, "Consumers Pan Ads on Video Movies," *Advertising Age,* 28 May 1990, 8.

61. "Mail Sights and Sounds," *Business Marketing,* August 1990, 24; "Hartmarx to Mail 12-Minute Video to Customers as Traffic-Builder," *DM News,* 21 October 1991, 7.

62. Cecil C. Hoge, Sr., *The Electronic Marketing Manual* (New York: McGraw-Hill, 1993), 181-182.

63. Cynthia Rigg, "Putting Message on a Disk Lets Marketers Target Niche," *Crain's New York Business,* 7 October 1991, 5; "Enticing Them with Interactive Diskettes," *Business Marketing,* August 1990, 25, 28.

64. Hanna Liebman, "The Microchip Is the Message," *Mediaweek,* 2 November 1992, 22-23, 25-26, 29; Jay, "Alternative Media: The Experiments Continue to Produce Results," 68, 70; Hanna Liebman, "Alternative: The Future Is Nearly Now," *Adweek,* 13 September 1993, 58-59.

65. Nancy Nelson Melin and John Gabriel, "Moving from Mystique to Money: Flaming the Internet," *Information Today,* January 1994, 11-12; Rick Tetzeli, "The Internet and Your Business," *Fortune,* 7 March 1994, 86-96; Liebman, "The Microchip Is the Message," 22-23, 25-26, 29; Hanna Liebman, "Alternative: The Future Is Nearly Now," *Adweek,* 13 September 1993, 58-59.

66. Library, CompuServe, 11 April 1994.

67. See note 1.

CHAPTER 18

1. Denise Gellene, "Designer Coffee Is Hot Stuff," *Los Angeles Times,* 14 April 1993, sec. a, 1; "Cool Beans: A Coffee Company with No Bitter Aftertaste Comes to L.A.," *Inside PR,* June 1992, 28-29; Ingrid Abramovitch, "Miracles of Marketing," *Success,* April 1993, 24-27; Debra Prinzing, "Schultz: Grand Designs for Filling Tall Order," *Puget Sound Business Journal,* 25 December 1992, 8; Charles McCoy, "Entrepreneur Smells Aroma of Success in Coffee Bars," *Wall Street Journal,* 8 January 1993, B2; Matt Rothman, "Into the Black," *Inc.,* January 1993, 59-65.

2. Thomas L. Harris, *The Marketer's Guide to Public Relations* (New York: Wiley, 1991), 11.

3. Fraser P. Seitel, *The Practice of Public Relations,* 5th ed. (New York: Macmillan, 1992), 8-9

4. Harris, *The Marketer's Guide to Public Relations,* 43.

5. William N. Curry, "PR Isn't Marketing," *Ad Age,* 16 December 1991, 18.

6. Seitel, *The Practice of Public Relations,* 63.

7. Jan Lachenmaier, "Sticks & Stones: When Even the Best PR Didn't Work," *IABC Communication World,* February 1991, 20-25.

8. "Toyota Dealers Plan Comedy Festivals," *New York Times,* 27 January 1993, sec. c, 2.

9. Harris, *The Marketer's Guide to Public Relations,* 44-45.

10. Susan Caminiti, "The Payoff from a Good Reputation," *Fortune,* 10 February 1992, 74-77.

11. Seitel, *The Practice of Public Relations,* 142.

12. Gerry Khermouch, "Pepsi Flack Attack Nips Hoax in the Bud," *Brandweek,* 21 June 1993.

13. Carol Kirby, "When Your Image Is Frozen in Time," *Working Women,* October 1990, 53-56.

14. Seitel, *The Practice of Public Relations,* 376-377.

15. Tom Watson, "Evaluating PR Effect," *Admap,* June 1992, 28-30; "Moving the Needle, Proving the Value," *Inside PR,* April 1992, 13-21.

16. "Public Relations: Putting a Value on PR," *Inc.,* March 1992, 95.

17. Seitel, *The Practice of Public Relations,* 140-160.

18. Adam Shell, "Bankers Use Public Relations as Survival Strategy," *Public Relations Journal,* September 1991, 7-13.

19. Thomas L. Harris, "Marketing Communications," in *Experts in Action,* 2d ed., edited by Bill Cantor and Chester Burger (White Plains, N.Y.: Longman, 1989), 28-44.

20. Robert D'Aprix, "Employee Communications," in Cantor and Burger, eds., *Experts in Action,* 70-79.

21. John F. Hussey, "Community Relations," in Cantor and Burger, eds., *Experts in Action,* 115-125.

22. "Juice: The Future of Power and Influence in Washington," *Inside PR,* May 1992, 15-17.

23. Seitel, *The Practice of Public Relations,* 420-421.

24. Seitel, *The Practice of Public Relations,* 484-485.

25. Robert D. Ferris and Richard M. Newman, "Building Better Financial Communications: IR Specialists Cooperate with Others in Corporate Structure," *Public Relations Journal,* October 1991, 18-25.

26. "Investor Relations: From Art to Science?" *Inside PR,* August 1991, 13-15.

27. "Investor Relations: From Art to Science?" 13-15.

28. *PR Newswire,* 4 June 1993.

29. David R. Yale, *The Publicity Handbook: How to Maximize Publicity for Products, Services & Organizations* (Lincolnwood, Ill.: NTC Business Books, 1992), 94-104.

30. "Will Europe Be the Next Frontier for VNRs?" *Public Relations Journal,* December 1991, 10-28; Harris, *The Marketer's Guide to Public Relations,* 91.

31. Yale, *The Publicity Handbook,* 259-262.

32. Julie Cohen Mason, "Corporate Sponsorships Help Target the Right Audience," *Management Review,* November 1992, 58-61.

33. Robert Barker, "Tubular Marketing, Dude," *Business Week,* 22 April 1991, 106.

34. "Creativity in Public Relations Awards," *Inside PR,* April 1992, 23-24.

35. "Core Values, Culture & Crisis," *Inside PR,* June 1991, 10-14.

36. "Core Values, Culture & Crisis," 10-14.

37. Courtland L. Bovée, John V. Thill, Marian B. Wood, and George P. Dovel, *Management* (New York: McGraw-Hill, 1993), 547-548.

38. Stuart Elliott, "Public Angry at Slow Action on Oil Spill," *USA Today,* 21 April 1989, B1-B2; E. Bruce Harrison and Tom Prugh, "Assessing the Damage: Practitioner Perspectives on the Valdez," *Public Relations Journal,* October 1989, 40-45; Allanna Sullivan and Amanda Bennett, "Critics Fault Chief Executive of Exxon on Handling of Recent Alaskan Oil Spill," *Wall Street Journal,* 31 March 1989, B1; Tom Eisenhart, "The King of Public Relations Talks Damage Control," *Business Marketing,* September 1990, 86-88; Ben Yagoda, "Cleaning Up a Dirty Image," *Business Month,* April 1990, 48-51.

39. Clare Ansberry, "Oil Spill in the Midwest Provides Case Study in Crisis Management," *Wall Street Journal,* 8 January 1988, 21; Jay Stuller, "When the Crisis Doctor Calls," *Across the Board,* May 1988, 45-51.

40. Ansberry, "Oil Spill in the Midwest Provides Case Study in Crisis Management," 21; Stuller, "When the Crisis Doctor Calls," 45-51.

41. Will Tusher, "Producer Assails Product Placements," *Variety,* 10 September 1990, 79.

42. Joanne Lipman, "Brand Name Products Are Popping Up in TV Shows," *Wall Street Journal,* 19 February 1991, B1, B5.

43. "Product Placement," *New York Times,* 21 December 1992, sec. c, 17; Stuart Elliott, "Product Placement Is under New Attack," *New York Times,* 2 September 1992, sec. c, 4.

44. Lipman, "Brand Name Products Are Popping Up in TV Shows," B1, B5.

45. Joanne Lipman, "Outcry over Product Placement Worries Movie, Ad Executives," *Wall Street Journal,* 7 April 1989, B6.

46. John K. Ross III, Mary Ann Stutts, and Larry Patterson, "Tactical Considerations for the Effective Use of Cause-Related Marketing," *Journal of Applied Business Research,* Spring 1990-1991, 58-65.

47. Bill Kelley, "Cause-Related Marketing: Doing Well While Doing Good," *Sales & Marketing Management,* March 1991, 60-65.

48. Kelley, "Cause-Related Marketing," 60-65.

49. Philip Kotler and Alan R. Andreasen, *Strategic Marketing for Nonprofit Organizations,* 3d ed. (Englewood Cliffs, N.J.: Prentice-Hall, 1987), 587.

50. *Advocacy Advertising: A Statement by the Board of Directors, American Association of Advertising Agencies* (New York: AAAA, 1980).

51. Richard W. Pollay, "Propaganda, Puffing and the Public Interest," *Public Relations Review* 16, no. 3 (Fall 1990): 39-55.

52. Seitel, *The Practice of Public Relations,* 310-311.

53. "Not for Members Only," *Marketing Management* 1, no. 4 (1993): 6-7; Herb Goldsmith, "Members Only Fashions a Unique Selling Strategy," *Journal of Business Strategy,* May-June 1989, 8-11.

54. See note 1.

CHAPTER 19

1. Richard W. Stevenson, "Ikea's New Realities: Recession and Aging Consumers," *New York Times,* 25 April 1993, sec. 3, 4; "Ikea Blasts into L.A. Marketplace with Record-Bashing Outdoor Blitz," *Adweek Western Advertising News,* 22 October 1990, 1, 4; Cara Appelbaum, "How Ikea Blitzes a Market," *Adweek's Marketing Week,* 11 June 1990, 18-19; Michael Winerip, "Shopping Siren Sings This Song: Ikea! Ikea!" *New York Times,* 25 May 1990, B1 (L); Judith Newman, "Swede Deal," *Adweek,* 20 July 1992, 16; Randall Rothenberg, "Deutsch's Campaign for Ikea Furniture," *New York Times,* 4 May 1990, D 17 (L); Mary Krienke, "Ikea's Anders Moberg," *Stores,* January 1992, 98-100, 102.

2. San Diego County Cadillac Dealers ad, 1994; Bob Baker Cadillac ad, 1994.

3. Amy Poe, " TV Stations Write, Produce Low-Cost Commercials," *Capital District Business Review,* September-October 1991, 16+.

4. Mike McDermott, "The Revenge of the Little Guy," *Adweek's Marketing Week,* 17 September 1990, 21, 24, 26-27.

5. Isadore Barmash, "The Future of Retailing," *Adweek,* 10 February 1992, 20-25.

6. Gerry Khermouch, "Wegmans Builds Its Local Base with Private Label," *Brandweek,* 8 March 1993, 23.

7. James Rubenstein, "A G-r-a-n-d Opening," *Bank Marketing,* January 1989, 28-30.

8. Stewart Henderson Britt, "Plan Your Advertising Budget—A U.S. Small Business Administration Guide," in Barry Maher, *Getting the Most from Your Yellow Pages Advertising* (New York: American Management Association, 1988), 225-231.

9. Thomas R. King, "In Hollywood, Stars Come Out in Local Ads," *Wall Street Journal,* 25 July 1990, B1, B4.

10. "A Shopper's Reading," *Adweek,* 3 May 1993, 20.

11. Jacadi ad in *Spotlight,* March 1993, 41; The Patchworks ad in *Quilter's Newsletter Magazine,* March 1993, 66.

12. Kate Fitzgerald, "Better Watch Out," *Advertising Age,* 19 November 1990, 12; David C. Hjelmfelt, *Executive's Guide to Marketing, Sales, and Advertising Law* (Englewood Cliffs, N.J.: Prentice-Hall, 1990), 159-160.

13. William Panczak, "Co-Op Advertising: Cutting through the Confusion," *Discount Store News,* 21 October 1991, 10, 14; Ed Crimmins, "Automation: Co-Op's Secret Weapon," *Sales & Marketing Management,* May 1990, 100-102.

14. Edward C. Crimmins, *Cooperative Advertising* (New York: Gene Wolfe, 1984), 41.

15. "The Concept Is Retail," *Art Direction,* June 1992, 56-59.

16. John Masterton, "Testimonials Put Ag Product in the Field," *Business Marketing,* Special Supplement, October 1992, A6, A8; Wally Wood, "Co-Op Advertising: The More Things Change . . . ," *Sales & Marketing Management,* May 1990, 94+.

17. Thomas A. McCoy, "Your Company as a Marketing Partner," *Rough Notes,* January 1989, 10-11.

18. Crimmins, *Cooperative Advertising,* 43.

19. Frederick E. Webster, Jr., and Yoram Wind, "A General Model for Understanding Buying Behavior," in *Business to Business Advertising,* edited by Charles H. Patti, Steven W. Hartley, and Susan L. Kennedy (Lincolnwood, Ill.: NTC Business Books, 1991), 43-52.

20. Bill Kelley, "Advertising on a Shoestring," *Sales & Marketing Management,* July 1992, 92-93, 96.

21. Colucci Insurance ad in *Connecticut Home Office,* December 1992, 7.

22. Charles H. Patti, Steven W. Hartley, and Susan L. Kennedy, eds., *Business to Business Advertising* (Lincolnwood, Ill.: NTC Business Books, 1991), 159.

23. Joseph A. Bellizzi and Robert E. Hite, "Improving Industrial Advertising Copy," in Patti, Hartley, and Kennedy, eds., *Business to Business Advertising,* 170-174.

24. Bellizzi and Hite, "Improving Industrial Advertising Copy," 170-174.

25. Miles David, "Business to Business Is a Co-Op Bright Spot," *Sales & Marketing Management,* May 1992, 44.

26. Stephen Fox, *The Mirror Makers* (New York: Morrow, 1984), 309-310.

27. David Samuel Barr, *Advertising on Cable: A Practical Guide for Advertisers* (Englewood Cliffs, N.J.: Prentice-Hall, 1985), 120.

28. Drayton Bird, "Database Politics from Down Under," *Direct,* May 1993, 39-42.

29. Steven Fradkin, "The Politics of Ads: Good versus Evil," *Adweek,* 10 February 1992, 54.

30. Rockland County ad in *Rockland Journal-News,* 15 March 1993, B4.

31. Steven W. Colford, "Papers Go on the Stump for Political Ad Dollars," *Advertising Age,* 5 October 1992, S-9-S-10.

32. Marvine Howe, "Group Warns of Transit Fare Increase," *New York Times,* 5 March 1993, B6.

33. Heather Rhoads, "Old Medium, New Messages," *The Progressive,* July 1991, 14-15.

34. Ronald Paul Hill, "An Exploration of Voter Responses to Political Advertisements," *Journal of Advertising* 18, no. 4 (1989): 14-22; Joanne Lipman, "Candidates Consider Airing Longer Ads," *Wall Street Journal,* 4 June 1992, B4; Tom Dworetzky, "Original Spin: Has Reality Been Entirely Banished from Politics?" *Omni,* May 1992, 18; Richard M. Perloff and Dennis Kinsey, "Political Advertising as Seen by Consultants and Journalists," *Journal of Advertising Research,* May-June 1992, 53-60; David Ogilvy, "What's Wrong with Advertising?" in *Advertising in Society: Classic and Contemporary Readings on Advertising's Role in Society,* edited by Roxanne Hovland and Gary B. Wilcox (Lincolnwood, Ill.: NTC Business Books, 1990), 477-485.

35. Gerry Khermouch, "In Need of a Shopping Spree," *Brandweek,* 26 April 1993, 29-30, 32, 34.

36. Scott Hume and Ira Teinowitz, "KidNews Gets 'A' from Young Set," *Advertising Age,* 5 October 1992, S-6-S-7.

37. Donald W. Jugenheimer, Arnold M. Barban, and Peter B. Turk, *Advertising Media: Strategy and Tactics* (Dubuque, Iowa: WCB Brown & Benchmark, 1992), 307.

38. Jan Jaben, "Finding a Happy Medium," *Business Marketing,* July 1992, 40-41.

39. Steve Kaufman, "Cable TV Captures Advertisers," *Washington Post,* 14 July 1991, H1, H4; Barr, *Advertising on Cable,* 43.

40. Bob Schulberg, *Radio Advertising: The Authoritative Handbook* (Lincolnwood, Ill.: NTC Business Books, 1990), 139; William H. Dunlap, "Staying Tuned to Business/Industrial Radio Advertising: Who's Doing It, and Why," *Business Marketing,* October 1985, 104, 106, 108, 110-111, 114.

41. Murray Raphel, "Where's the Retail Direct Mail Revolution?" *Direct Marketing,* November 1992, 23-26.

42. Raphel, "Where's the Retail Direct Mail Revolution?" 23-26.

43. See note 1.

CHAPTER 20

1. Arlena Sawyers and Jack Keebler, "Rota Sees Value-Leader Jimmy in '95," *Automotive News,* 11 January 1993, 48-49; Julie Edelson Halpert, "Pickups: From the Barn to the Carport," *New York Times,* 18 July 1993, sec. 3, 8; Arlena Sawyers, "Automakers Mining Niches for Sales, Image," *Automotive News,* 6 January 1992, 14; information on GMC Truck and McCann/SAS and their work on the "Strength of Experience" campaign is drawn from materials provided by the advertiser and the agency.

2. "570 Attend Model Agency Event," *Radio Success Stories: A Reference Book,* vol. 2 (New York: The Interep Radio Store, 1992), 57.

3. Kenneth Roman and Jane Maas, *The New How to Advertise* (New York: St. Martin's Press, 1992), 76.

4. Judith Graham, "Amex 'Portraits' Stresses Values," *Advertising Age,* 1 January 1990, 12, 38.

5. L. Keith Stentz, Director of Creative Services, McCann/SAS, personal communication, 8 July 1993.

6. "100 Leading National Advertisers: General Motors Corp.," *Advertising Age,* 23 September 1992, 29-30.

7. Halpert, "Pickups: From the Barn to the Carport," 8; Doron P. Levin, "The Cars That Are Hot Are Not," *New York Times,* 24 August 1993, C1, C6.

8. James B. Treece, "Now, the Court of Public Opinion Has GM Worried," *Business Week,* 22 February 1993, 38–39.

9. "GMC Truck Announces Record-Setting Sales Performance," *PR Newswire,* 6 January 1993; "100 Leading National Advertisers: Ford Motor Co.," *Advertising Age,* 23 September 1992, 29; Halpert, "Pickups: From the Barn to the Carport," 8; Jacqueline Mitchell, "New Jeep to Roll Out with 'Teaser' Ads," *Wall Street Journal,* 6 February 1992, B6.

10. Bruce Horovitz, " 'Torture Test' TV Ads Rack Up Truck Sales," *Los Angeles Times,* 13 October 1992, D6; "100 Leading National Advertisers: Ford Motor Co.," 29.

11. "100 Leading National Advertisers: Chrysler Corp.," *Advertising Age,* 23 September 1992, 20-21; Mitchell, "New Jeep to Roll Out with 'Teaser' Ads," B6; Fara Warner, "Automotive: Ripe for a Rebound," *Superbrands 1992,* 44–46, 48; David Woodruff, "This Ram Can Go Head to Head with Anyone," *Business Week,* 23 August 1993, 46.

12. "100 Leading National Advertisers: Toyota Motor Corp.," *Advertising Age,* 23 September 1992, 62; Halpert, "Pickups: From the Barn to the Carport," 8.

13. Mary Connelly, "GMC Aims for Affluent, Professional Buyers," *Automotive News,* 12 October 1992, 41.

14. Raymond Serafin, "GM Opens Up $700M in Ads to Big Agencies," *Advertising Age,* 20 September 1993, 3, 57.

15. See note 1.

Illustration and Text Credits

CHAPTER 1

9 Based on information from Stuart Elliott, "Marketing a Hockey Team as a New, Improved Product," *New York Times*, 18 August 1992, C7; Gary Levin, "Baseball's Opening Pitch: Winning Over New Fans," *Advertising Age*, 5 April 1993, 1, 42.

21 Based on information from Stuart Elliott, "Some Big Marketers Join Audience for Infomercials," *New York Times*, 5 June 1992, C9; Pat Sloan, "Avon Looks beyond Direct Sales," *Advertising Age*, 22 February 1993, 32; Stephen Winzenburg, "Infomercials Flowering on Cable TV," *Advertising Age*, 22 February 1993, 18; Mark Landler, "The Infomercial Inches toward Respectability," *Business Week*, 4 May 1992, 175; Howard Schlossberg, "Once Fodder and Filler, Infomercials Now Attract Mainstream Advertisers," *Marketing News*, 20 January 1992, 1, 6–7; Kenneth A. Plevan and Miriam L. Siroky, *Advertising Compliance Handbook*, 2d ed. (New York: Practising Law Institute, 1991), 283–284; Joe Flint, "More Infomercial Identification Sought," *Broadcasting*, 13 January 1992, 89–90.

27 Based on information from Karen Benezra, "Digest Acts to Increase Global Ads," *Gannett Suburban Newspapers*, 27 September 1992, H1–H2.

CHAPTER 2

42 Based on information from Cyndee Miller, "Marketers Say Budgets Hinder Targeting of Asian-Americans," *Marketing News*, 30 March 1992, 2, 15; Isabel Fonseca, "Top Agencies Feel the Heat," *Hispanic Business*, December 1992, 10–11; Gary Levin, "Shops Make the Most of Ethnic Niches," *Advertising Age*, 17 September 1990, 29; Richard W. Stevenson, "Price of Success for a Top Hispanic Ad Agency," *New York Times*, 25 May 1992, 37; W. F. Joseph, "Marketing to Blacks: Promotions Play Well with Blacks," *Advertising Age*, 14 December 1987, S1–S2; Gary Levin and Jon Lafayette, "How Hispanic Fits Big Shops' Schemes," *Advertising Age*, 16 October 1989, S2–S4, S16; Kate Ballen, "How America Will Change over the Next 30 Years," *Fortune*, 17 June 1991, 12.

46 Adapted from Herbert Zeltner, *Evaluating Agency Performance* (New York: Association of National Advertisers, 1991), 10–19. Used by permission.

48 Based on information from Raymond Serafin and Scott Hume, "Olds Win: How Burnett Rallied Back," *Advertising Age*, 8 February 1993, 1, 46; David Kiley and Jim Kirk, "For Olds, It Was Burnett Once Again," *Adweek*, 8 February 1993, 6; Fara Warner, "GM Shocker: Agency Reviews Loom," *Brandweek*, 21 September 1992, 1, 6; Raymond Serafin, "GM's Troubled Olds Unit Reviews $140M Account," *Advertising Age*, 21 September 1992, 1, 54; Jacqueline Mitchell, "Oldsmobile Ads Try to Counter Rumors," *Wall Street Journal*, 16 November 1992, B6; Joanne Lipman, "GM Puts Its Oldsmobile Account Up for Review, Stunning Burnett," *Wall Street Journal*, 21 September 1992, B6.

CHAPTER 3

64 Based on information from Jon Berry, "Think Bland," *Adweek's Marketing Week*, 11 November 1991, 22–24; Alix M. Freedman, "Never Have So Few Scared So Many Television Sponsors," *Wall Street Journal*, 20 March 1989, B4; Ronald Paul Hill and Andrea L. Beaver, "Advocacy Groups and Television Advertisers," *Journal of Advertising* 20, no. 1 (1991): 18–27.

67 Based on information from "MasterCard 'Hotline' to Help Plant Trees," *Promo*, November 1992, 58; Emily DeNitto, "Marketing with a Conscience," *Marketing Communications*, May 1989, 42–46; P. Rajan Varadarajan and Anil Menon, "Cause-Related Marketing: A Coalignment of Marketing Strategy and Corporate Philanthropy," *Journal of Marketing*, July 1988, 58–74; Joshua Levine, "I Gave at the Supermarket," *Business Week*, 25 December 1989, 138, 140.

71 Adapted from David C. Hjelmfelt, *Executive's Guide to Marketing, Sales & Advertising Law* (Englewood Cliffs, N.J.: Prentice-Hall, 1990, 164; Robert J. Posch, Jr., *What Every Manager Needs to Know about Marketing and the Law* (New York: McGraw-Hill, 1984), 255–260.

74 Exhibit 3.13, courtesy of American Advertising Federation.

75 Exhibit 3.14, reprinted with permission from Council of Better Business Bureaus Inc.: National Advertising Division, Children's Advertising Review Unit & National Advertising Review Board Procedures, November 1, 1993.

78 Based on information from Joanne Lipman, "The Making of a Best-Seller Is a Mighty Serious Business," *Wall Street Journal*, 21 July 1992, B1, B6.

CHAPTER 4

86 Exhibit 4.2, from *Capturing Customers* by Peter Francese and Rebecca Piirto, p. 49. Copyright © 1990. Used by permission of American Demographics.

91 Exhibit 4.7, from *Beyond Mind Games: The Marketing Power of Psychographics* by Rebecca Piirto, p. 27. Copyright © 1991. Used by permission of American Demographics.

95 Based on information from Courtland L. Bovée and John V. Thill, *Marketing* (New York: McGraw-Hill, 1992), 160–161; William H. Davidow and Bro Uttal, *Total Customer Service: The Ultimate Weapon* (New York: Harper & Row, 1989), 34–35.

99 *Starch Tested Copy*, March 1992.

102 Based on information from Don Schultz, Stanley Tannenbaum, and Robert Lauterborn, "Why People Ignore Facts in Buying Decisions," *Advertising Age*, 4 May 1992, 22; Paul Sherlock, *Rethinking Business to Business Marketing* (New York: Free Press, 1991), 27–30.

103 *Starck Tested Copy*, December 1992.

105 Exhibit 4.16, Shiffman/Kanuk, *Consumer Behavior*, 3/e, © 1987, p. 209. Adapted by permission of Prentice-Hall Inc., Englewood Cliffs, N.J.

106 Exhibit 4.17, based on information from Courtland I. Bovée and John V. Thill, *Marketing* (New York: McGraw-Hill, 1992), 196–199; Charles H. Patti, Steven W. Hartley, and Susan I. Kennedy, *Business-to-Business Marketing: A Marketing Management Approach* (Lincolnwood, Ill.: NTC Business Books, 1991), 9–13; Frank G. Bingham, Jr., and Barney T. Raffield III, *Business-to-Business Marketing Management* (Homewood, Ill.: Irwin, 1990), 6–15.

CHAPTER 5

119 *Starch Tested Copy*, December 1992.

123 Exhibit 5.9, based on information from *Beyond Mind Games: The Marketing Power of Psychographics* by Rebecca Piirto. Reprinted by permission of American Demographics, 1991.

127 "Marketing to Kids," Special Report section, *Advertising Age*, 8 February 1993, S1–S24; "Food Makers Hunger for Younger Market," *Insight*, 18 June 1990, 43; Patricia Sellers, "The ABC's of Marketing to Kids," *Fortune*, 8 May 1989, 114–116, 120; David J. Morrow, "Picking Junior's Pocket," *The Marketer*, May 1990, 20–25; Kim Foltz, "Kids as Consumers: Teaching Our Children Well," *Adweek*, 30 November 1987, 40; Noreen O'Leary, "Study Portrays Children as Complex, Savvy Media Mavens," *Adweek*, 30 November 1987, 42; "Selling to Children," *Consumer Reports*, August 1990, 518–521; Susan Dillingham, "The Classroom as a Marketing Tool," *Insight*, 24 September 1990, 40–41.

128 Exhibit 5.12, from *Marketing* by Courtland L. Bovée and John V. Thill, copyright © 1992, p. 194. Reproduced with permission of the publisher, McGraw-Hill, Inc.

134 Adapted from George P. Dovel, "Stake It Out: Positioning Success, Step-by-Step," *Business Marketing*, July 1990, 43–51. Used by permission of *Business Marketing Magazine*.

137 Based on information from Stuart Elliott, "Marketers Still Struggling to Appeal to 90's Consumers," *New York Times*, August 1992, sec. c, 7; car prices obtained from CompuServe, 20 October 1992.

CHAPTER 6

143 Based on information from "ICC/ESOMAR International Code of Marketing and Social Research Practice," in *Consumer Market Research Handbook*, 3d ed., edited by Robert Worcester and John Downham (London: McGraw-Hill, 1986), 813–826; Robert A. Peterson, *Marketing Research* (Plano, Tex.: Business Publications, 1982), 154.

150 Exhibit 6.8, based on information from A. B. Blankenship and George Edward Breen, *State of the Art Marketing Research* (Lincolnwood, Ill.: NTC Business Books, 1993), 204–211.

157 Exhibit 6.13, from Earl Babbie, *The Practice of Social Research*, copyright 1989 in *Fundamentals of Advertising Research*, 4/e by Alan D. Fletcher and Thomas A. Bowers, copyright 1991, p. 56. Used by permission of Wadsworth Publishing Co.

161 Based on information from Steven W. Colford, "Bell Atlantic Weds Sitcom, Infomercial," *Advertising Age*, 9 November 1992, 8.

CHAPTER 7

167 From *Management* by Courtland L. Bovée, John V. Thill, Marian Burk Wood, and George P. Dovel, p. 243. Copyright © 1993. Reproduced with permission of the publisher, McGraw-Hill, Inc.

169 Based on information from Melanie Rigney, "Matter of Semantics—or of Survival?" *Advertising Age*, 29 June 1992, S-2, S-9; Dennis Chase and Therese Kauchak Smith, "Consumers Keep on Green but Marketers Don't Deliver," *Advertising Age*, 29 June 1992, S-2, S-4; Debra Aho, "Be Precise; Don't Overstate Claims," *Advertising Age*, 29 June 1992, S-6; Monte Williams, "Environmentally Safe . . . Can Enhance Sales," *Advertising Age*, 29 June 1992, S-8; Stuart R. Taylor, "Green Management: The Next Management Weapon," *Futures*, September 1992, 669–680; Michael Parrish, "FTC Issues Guidelines for Green Marketing," *Los Angeles Times*, 29 July 1992, sec. d, 1; Kathleen A. O'Brien, "Green Marketing: Can It Be Harmful to Your Health?" *Industry Week*, 20 April 1992, 56–60; "Research Group Says Some Green Marketers Are Only Pretending," *Marketing News*, 20 January 1992, 3.

179 *Starch Tested Copy*, August 1992.

181 Exhibit 7.13, adapted with permission from "A Better Advertising Planning Grid," by John R. Rossiter, Larry Percy, and Robert J. Donovan, *Journal of Advertising Research*, October-November 1991, pp. 11–22.

185 Exhibit 7.16, reprinted with the permission of Lexington Books, an imprint of Macmillan Publishing Company, from *How Much Is Enough: Getting the Most From Your Advertising Dollar* by John Phillip Jones. Copyright © 1992 by Lexington Books.

187 Exhibit 7.17, adapted from Schonfeld & Associates, "Advertising Ratios and Budgets," as reported in "Ratios Indicate Hikes in Ad Levels," *Advertising Age*, 13 November 1989, 32.

188 Reprinted with the permission of Lexington Books, an imprint of Macmillan Publishing Company from *How Much Is Enough: Getting the Most From Your Advertising Dollar* by John Phillip Jones. Copyright © 1992 by Lexington Books.

CHAPTER 8

197 Based on information from "Smoking Is up among Blacks and Women," *Seattle Times,* 2 April 1993, sec. c, 1; Courtland L. Bovée and John V. Thill, *Marketing* (New York: McGraw-Hill, 1992), 234-235.

203 Exhibit 8.6, reprinted with permission from the April 14, 1993 issue of *Advertising Age.* Copyright, Crain Communications Inc., 1993.

209 Exhibit 8.12, © By The Haworth Press, Inc. All rights reserved. Reprinted with permission. For copies of the complete work, contact Marianne Arnold at The Haworth Document Delivery Service (Telephone 1-800-3-HAWORTH, 10 Alice Street, Binghamton, N.Y. 13904). For other Questions concerning rights and permissions contact Wanda Latour at the above address.

211 Adapted from *Global Advertising: Rhyme or Reason?* by Nükhet Vardar, pp. 27-28. Copyright 1992 by Paul Chapman Publishing. Used by permission of the publisher.

213 Exhibit 8.15, adapted from "Developing Brand Strategies Across Borders," by Judie Lonnan, *Marketing and Research Today,* August 1991, pp. 160-168. Used by permission of Elsevier Science Publishers B.V., Academic Publishing Division.

214 Based on information from Edmund O. Lawler, "Ads That Know No Boundaries," *Business Marketing,* December 1992, 38-39; Nina Streitfeld, "How to Communicate in Other Cultures," *Public Relations Journal,* February 1986, 34-35; Roger E. Axtell, ed., *Do's and Taboo's around the World* (Elmsford, N.Y.: Benjamin, 1985), 140-141.

CHAPTER 9

223 Exhibit 9.3, adapted from Robert Fearon, *Advertising That Works.* Copyright © 1991. Used by permission of Probus Publishing.

231 Based on information from Elyse Tanouye, "Critics See Self-Interest in Lilly's Funding of Ads Telling the Depressed to Get Help," *Wall Street Journal,* 15 April 1993, B1, B6; Ron Winslow, "U.S. Agency Urges Early Diagnosis of Depression," *Wall Street Journal,* 15 April 1993, B1, B6; Howard M. Spiro, "Speaking Out: A Physician Looks at Direct-to-Consumer Advertising," *Medical Marketing & Media,* November 1992, 24-28; Joseph M. Winski, "Nasty Side Effects Plague Some Prescription Drug Ads," *Advertising Age,* 3 August 1992, 18, 20.

234 Philip Ward Burton and Scott C. Purvis, *Which Ad Pulled Best?* (Lincolnwood, Ill.: NTC Business Books, 1993), 53.

237 Based on information from Grant McCracken, "Who Is the Celebrity Endorser? Cultural Foundations of the Endorsement Process," *Journal of Consumer Research* 16, no. 3 (December 1989): 310-321; Mary Walker, Lynn Langmeyer, and Daniel Langmeyer, "Celebrity Endorsers: Do You Get What You Pay For?" *Journal of Consumer Marketing* 9, no. 2 (1992): 69-76; Cara Appelbaum, "Signing On: Celebrity Popularity Is No Guaranteed Endorsement," *Adweek's Marketing Week,* 21 October 1991, 6; "USA Snapshots: Ads We Find Least Convincing," *USA Today,* 9 March 1988, 1D; Alix Freedman, "Marriages between Celebrity Spokesmen and Their Firms Can Be Risky Ventures," *Wall Street Journal,* 22 January 1988, 23; Christian Ryssel and Erich Stamminger, "Sponsoring World-Class Tennis Players," *European Research,* May 1988, 110-116; Joanne Lipman, "Celebrity Pitchmen Are Popular Again," *Wall Street Journal,* 4 September 1991, B5.

241 Philip Ward Burton and Scott C. Purvis, *Which Ad Pulled Best?* (Lincolnwood, Ill.: NTC Business Books, 1993), 141.

247 Based on information from Kate Fitzgerald, "MCI Fights AT&T over VideoPhone," *Advertising Age,* 11 January 1993, 3.

CHAPTER 10

260 Philip Ward Burton and Scott C. Purvis, *Which Ad Pulled Best?* (Lincolnwood, Ill.: NTC Business Books, 1993), 53.

261 Exhibit 10.8, from Daniel Will-Harris, *Desktop Publishing with Style* (South Bend, Ind.: And Books, 1987), 33-37; Roy Paul Nelson, *The Design of Advertising,* 6th ed. (Dubuque, Iowa: WCB, 1989), 173-177.

265 Primo Angeli, *Designs for Marketing, No. 1* (Rockport, Mass.: Rockport Publishers, 1989), 70-74; Paul B. Brown, "Sitting Pretty," *Inc.,* September 1990, 148, 164.

271 Based on information from Bradley Johnson, "Ikea Snorts: Your Digs Stink," *Advertising Age,* 7 September 1992, 3; Marc G. Weinberger and Leland Campbell, "The Use and Impact of Humor in Radio Advertising," *Journal of Advertising Research,* December 1990-January 1991, 44-52.

272 Adapted from Ron Kaatz, *Advertising & Marketing Checklists* (Lincolnwood, Ill.: NTC Business Books, 1990), 22-27.

275 Based on information from Raymond Serafin, "Ads Help Olds Move Closer to Saturn," *Advertising Age,* 14 December 1992, 43.

CHAPTER 11

281 *Starch Tested Copy,* December 1992.

283 Reprinted with permission of *Step-by-Step Graphic,* magazine, © 1992, Vol. 8, No. 4, 6000 N. Forest Park Dr., Peoria, IL 61614-3592; 800/255-8800.

285 Exhibit 11.6, based on information from Richard M. Schlemmer, *Handbook of Advertising Art Production,* 4th ed. (Englewood Cliffs, N.J.: Prentice-Hall, 1990), 45.

289 Exhibit 11.10, based on information from George A. Stevenson and William A. Pakan, *Graphic Arts Encyclopedia,* 3d ed. (New York: McGraw-Hill, 1992), 404-408.

303 Information on Compaq and Ammirati & Puris and their work on the "Leadership" campaign is drawn from materials provided by the advertiser and the agency.

CHAPTER 12

311 Exhibit 12.2, based on information from *What Every Account Executive Should Know about Television Commercial Production* (New York: American Association of Advertising Agencies, 1989), 6-13; Hooper White, *How to Produce Effective TV Commercials,* 2d ed. (Lincolnwood, Ill.: NTC Business Books, 1989), 107-140.

320 Exhibit 12.8, based on information from *How to Create Effective TV Commercials,* 2/e by Huntley Baldwin, p. 233. Copyright © 1989. Used by permission of NTC Business Books.

322 Based on information from Jon Lafayette, "Scandal Puts Focus on Ad Visuals," *Advertising Age,* 26 November 1990, 62; Jennifer Lawrence, "How Volvo's Ad Collided with the Truth," *Advertising Age,* 12 November 1990, 76; David Kiley, "Candid Camera: Volvo and the Art of Deception," *Adweek's Marketing Week,* 12 November 1990, 4.

325 Based on information from Robert Goldrich, "Desktop Video Editing Hits West Coast," *Back Stage,* 4 May 1990, 1, 30; Cathy Madison, "Desktop Video Editing Has Ad Makers Clicking," *Adweek,* 11 March 1991, 46.

333 Adapted from Kate Fitzgerald, "Jolly Rancher Takes Taste Message to New Level," *Advertising Age,* 15 March 1993, 44; Margot Nightingale, "Get Real!" *Screen,* 8 March 1993, 30; information on Jolly Rancher and Ayer and their work on the "virtual reality" commercial is drawn from materials provided by the advertiser and the agency.

CHAPTER 13

343 Exhibit 13.3, based on information from Jim Surmanek, *Media Planning: A Practical Guide* (Lincolnwood, Ill.: NTC Business Books, 1986), 3; Jack Z. Sissors and Lincoln Bumba, *Advertising Media Planning,* 3d ed. (Lincolnwood, Ill.: NTC Business Books, 1990), 190-201; Ron Kaatz, *Advertising & Marketing Checklists* (Lincolnwood, Ill.: NTC Business Books, 1992), 52-58.

345 Exhibit 13.5, adapted from Newspaper Association of America, *Facts About Newspapers 93* (Reston, Va: Newspaper Association of America, 1993), 11, which in turn quotes McCann-Erickson Inc. and its own NAA studies as the source.

348 Exhibit 13.8, based on information from Michael J. Naples, *Effective Frequency: The Relationship between Frequency and Advertising Effectiveness* (New York: Association of National Advertisers, 1979), 63-78.

351 Adapted from Ron Kaatz, *Advertising & Marketing Checklists.* Copyright © 1992. Used by permission of NTC Publishing Group.

353 Exhibit 13.11, adapted from Jack Z. Sissors and Lincoln Bumba, *Advertising Media Planning,* 3d ed. (Lincolnwood, Ill.: NTC Business Books, 1990), 155; Don E. Schultz, *Strategic Advertising Campaigns,* 3d ed. (Lincolnwood, Ill.: NTC Business Books, 1991), 394; Robert W. Hall, *Media Math* (Lincolnwood, Ill.: NTC Business Books, 1991), 49-50.

358 Based on information from Laura Zinn, "Does Pepsi Have Too Many Products?" *Business Week,* 14 February 1994, 64-65, 66; Jennifer Lawrence, "Cheer Sews Up Link to Cotton, Inc.," *Advertising Age,* 15 March 1993, 16; Patricia Winters, "Fast Break for Crystal Pepsi," *Advertising Age,* 12 April 1993, 10; Magazine Publishers of America, "Marketing Success Stories: Our Magazine Ads for HP Workstations Helped Send Sales Up 40%," *52 More* (New York: Magazine Publishers of America, n.d.), 46-47.

363 Adapted from "Methodology for Ranking the 100 Top Advertisers," *Advertising Age,* 23 September 1992, 72. Also based on information from Maureen Goldstein, "Nielsen's Monitor-Plus Questioned," *Inside Media,* 13 May 1992, 18, 61; "A Unique Resource for Advertisers," brochure from the Advertising Checking Bureau; *LNA Business-to-Business,* brochure from Leading National Advertisers; "First with More," brochure from Nielsen's Monitor-Plus Service.

365 Exhibit 13.18, adapted from GMC Truck Media Plan for 1993 Calendar Year, provided by McCann/SAS.

CHAPTER 14

373 Exhibit 14.2, adapted from "Top 25 National Newspaper Advertisers," *Advertising Age,* 29 September 1993, 36; "Top 25 Local Newspaper Advertisers," *Advertising Age,* 29 September 1993, 34.

381 Exhibit 14.9, adapted with permission from *Facts about Newspapers 93,* Newspaper Association of America, 1993, 7, 10-11.

385 Exhibit 14.11, adapted from "Top 25 Magazine Advertisers," *Advertising Age,* 29 September 1993, 40.

391 Based on information from Patricia W. Hamilton, "Farm Journal Feels Its Oats," *D&B Reports,* July-August 1988, 22+; *Farm Journal* Rate Card No. 140, January 1993; Dale E. Smith, "Database Harvest," *Direct Marketing,* October 1986, 64+; "Down on the Farm: Planning a Magazine Publishing Revolution," *Marketing Communications,* March 1985, 18+; Ray E. Evans, Manager, Direct Marketing Sales, Farm Journal Publishing, personal communication, 5 February 1993.

392 Exhibit 14.16, adapted from "MPA Top 100 ABC Magazines, Average Paid Combined Circulation Per Issue, Second Six Months of 1992," Magazine Publishers of America, in Adweek, *Marketer's Guide to Media,* Spring-Summer 1993, pp. 108-111. Used by permission.

396 Based on information from Lorne Manly, "Can Anyone Police Integrity?" *Folio,* 1 August 1993, 20; Scott Donaton, "Advertorials 'Are Like a Drug,'" *Advertising Age,* 9 March 1992, S-16; Deirdre Carmody, "New Guidelines Established for Magazine Advertising," *New York Times,* 21 October 1992, C17.

399 Based on information from John Masterton, "Positioning Helps Software Maker Measure Up," *Business Marketing,* October 1992, A20, A22.

CHAPTER 15

403 Exhibit 15.2, adapted from "Top 25 Network TV Advertisers," *Advertising Age,* 29 September 1993, 44; "Top 25 Spot TV Advertisers," *Advertising Age,* 29 September 1993, 46; "Top 25 Syndicated TV Advertisers," *Advertising Age,* 29 September 1993, 48; "Top 25 Cable TV Network Advertisers," *Advertising Age,* 29 September 1993, 50.

404 Exhibit 15.3, from Elizabeth Jensen, "Networks Gain in Syndication Dispute, but Many See Rerun of Battles Ahead," *Wall Street Journal,* 9 November 1992, B1, B5. Reprinted by permission of *Wall Street Journal* © 1992 Dow Jones & Company, Inc. All Rights Reserved Worldwide.

409 Exhibit 15.7, from Stuart Elliott, "Advertising," *New York Times,* 27 January 1993, C2. Copyright © 1993 by *The New York Times Company.* Reprinted by permission.

411 Based on information from Gary Levin, "Interactive Network Draws Advertisers to Test New Media," *Advertising Age,* 15 March 1993, 8; "Pepsi Pleased with Interactive Ad Test," *Broadcasting,* 15 February 1993, 23; Gary Levin, "Interactive TV Rivals Poised for Battle," *Advertising Age,* 30 November 1992, 3, 16; "Two-Way Systems Break Out," *Adweek Western Advertising News Superbrands 1991,* 23 September 1991, 129; "Australia's Seven Network Hooks up with Interactive TV," *Variety,* 21 September 1992, 36; Michael Antonoff, "Interactive Television," *Popular Science,* November 1992, 92-95, 124, 126, 128; "Newsline," *Advertising Age,* 17 August 1992, 8.

415 Exhibit 15.11, from *Advertising Media: Strategy and Tactics* by Donald W. Jugenheimer, Arnold M. Barban, and Peter B. Turk, p. 332. Copyright © 1992 by Wm. C. Brown Communications, Inc.

419 Exhibit 15.15, adapted from "Top 25 Spot Radio Advertisers," *Advertising Age,* 29 September 1993, 38; "Top 25 Network Radio Advertisers," *Advertising Age,* 29 September 1993, 52.

422 Based on information from "Getting Hip to Free-Spending Teens," *Adweek,* 15 June 1992, 70-71; "The Numbers: The Teen Beat," *Mediaweek,* 29 July 1991, 26-27; "Gillette Product Sales Increase by $47,000," *Radio Success Stories: A Reference Book,* Vol. 2 (New York: The Interep Radio Store, 1992), 109; "570 Attend Model Agency Event," *Radio Success Stories: A Reference Book,* Vol. 2 (New York: The Interep Radio Store, 1992), 57.

429 Based on information from Barry Kinsey, "Let Them Eat Little Cakes!" *Inside Media,* 4 December 1992, 46.

CHAPTER 16

435 Based on information from Deborah L. Jacobs, "Consumers Learn to Battle Rising Volume of Junk Mail," *San Diego Union-Tribune,* 13 March 1994, I-2, I-4; Steven W. Colford, "States Take the Lead from Congress on Privacy," *Advertising Age,* 15 February 1993, 36; Dan Fost, "Privacy Concerns Threaten Database Marketing," *American Demographics,* May 1990, 18, 20-21; Gary Levin, "Learning Where to Draw the Line on Privacy Issue," *Advertising Age,* 15 February 1993, 35-36.

439 Based on information from Chuck Orlowski, "Mail-Order Lists," in Edward L. Nash, *The Direct Marketing Handbook* (New York: McGraw-Hill, 1984), 225-234.

442 Exhibit 16.7, reprinted from *Telemarketing®* magazine, Volume 10, Number 5 dated November 1991, published by Technology Marketing Corporation, One Technology Plaza, Norwalk, CT 06854 USA Copyright © 1991 Technology Marketing Corporation, all rights reserved. Subscriptions: $49.00 domestic, $69.00 Canada, $85.00 foreign. To order, call toll-free 800-243-6002, or 203-852-6800.

445 Exhibit 16.9, adapted from "Top 25 Outdoor Advertisers," *Advertising Age,* 29 September 1993, 54.

447 Exhibit 16.12, based on information from Adweek, *Marketer's Guide to Media,* Spring-Summer 1993 (New York: Adweek, 1993), 88-89.

455 Based on information from Thomas Toch, "Homeroom Sweepstakes," *U.S. News & World Report,* 9 November 1992, 86-89; Susan Dillingham, "The Classroom as a Marketing Tool," *Insight,* 24 September 1990, 40-41; Scott Donaton, "More Turbulence for 'Channel One,'" *Advertising Age,* 18 May 1992, 48; Joanne Lipman, "Criticism of TV Show with Ads for Schools Is Scaring Sponsors," *Wall Street Journal,* 2 March 1989, B6.

CHAPTER 17

465 Exhibit 17.2, from *Marketing* by Courtland L. Bovée and John V. Thill, copyright © 1992, p. 23. Reproduced with permission of the publisher, McGraw-Hill, Inc.

468 Exhibit 17.5, adapted from Donnelley Marketing, *15th Annual Survey of Promotional Practices* (Stamford, Conn.: Donnelley Marketing, 1993), 17.

472 Exhibit 17.7, NCH PROMOTIONAL SERVICES, 1994, *Worldwide Coupon Distribution and Redemption Trends Volume XXVII, 1993* (Chicago: NCH Promotional Services, 1993), 7.

474 Based on information from Ron Melk, "Samboy Chip Promotion Is an Aussie Hit," *Promo,* August 1992, 51; Glenn Heitsmith, "Back to School Tie-In Pairs Gatorade with Foot Locker for Fall Promotion," *Promo,* August 1992, 8; Betsy Spethmann, "Kellogg Steps into the Box with Baseball, Disney," *Brandweek,* 5 April 1993, 3; John P. Cortez, "New Direction for Domino's," *Advertising Age,* 4 January 1993, 3, 34-35.

479 Based on information from Leonard M. Rudy, "Slotting Fees Do Little to Stem New-Item Intros," *Promo,* July 1992, 83; Jeffrey K. McElnea, "Retailers: Skip the Quick Fix," *Sales and Marketing Strategies & News,* September-October 1992, 62; "No Slotting for Selsun Intro," *Promo,* September 1992, 1, 53.

481 Exhibit 17.12, based on information from Jenny C. McCune, "On with the Show!" *Management Review,* May 1993, 37.

484 Based on information from Alan D. Fletcher, *Yellow Pages Advertising* (Chesterfield, Mo.: American Association of Yellow Pages Publishers, 1987), 15-22; Yellow Pages Publishers Association, *Yellow Pages Industry Facts Booklet* (Troy, Mich.: Yellow Pages Publishers Association, 1991), 29-41; Barry Maher, *Getting the Most from Your Yellow Pages Advertising* (New York: American Management Association, 1988), 91-123.

489 Based on information from Ronald Alsop, "Don Rickles and Devilish Kid Bring Dull Carpet Ads to Life," *Wall Street Journal,* 9 July 1987, 31.

CHAPTER 18

495 Exhibit 18.4, from Tricia Welsh, "Best and Worst Corporate Reputations," *Fortune,* 7 February 1994, 58-62. FORTUNE, © 1994 Time Inc. All rights reserved.

497 Based on information from "Soft News," *Inside PR,* April 1993, 74.

505 Based on information from David R. Yale, *The Publicity Handbook: How to Maximize Publicity for Products, Services & Organizations* (Lincolnwood, Ill.: NTC Business Books, 1992), 309-310; "VNR Production: An Ethical Guide," *Inside PR,* July 1992, 22.

CHAPTER 19

518 Exhibit 19.2, adapted from materials produced by the Newspaper Advertising Bureau.

521 Exhibit 19.4, based on information provided by the Newspaper Advertising Bureau.

522 Based on information from Thomas R. King, "In Hollywood, Stars Come Out in Local Ads," *Wall Street Journal,* 25 July 1990, B1, B4; Ann Cooper, "For Big or Small, Image Is Everything," *Adweek,* 8 March 1993, 28-32.

524 Based on information from Edward C. Crimmins, *Cooperative Advertising* (New York: Gene Wolfe, 1984), 32, 35-38, 43-76; William Panczak, "Co-Op Advertising: Cutting through the Confusion," *Discount Store News,* 21 October 1991, 10, 14.

531 Based on information from "Do Negative Ads Affect Elections?" *USA Today,* August 1992, 16; Elizabeth Kolbert, "Low Tolerance for Political Commercials? Just Count to 10," *New York Times,* 30 May 1992, 9; Ronald Paul Hill, "An Exploration of Voter Responses to Political Advertisements," *Journal of Advertising* 18, no. 4 (1989): 14-22; Tony Schwartz, "The Pot Calling the Kettle Black," *Media Industry Newsletter,* 29 May 1991, 7; Stuart Elliott, "Four A's Effort Takes Aim at Negative Campaign Ads," *New York Times,* 4 February 1992, C19; Gary Levin, "Negative Ads Win on Election Day '90," *Advertising Age,* 12 November 1990, 3, 78.

532 Exhibit 19.11, based on an American Business Press study quoted by Richard R. Szathmary, "Media Outlook: The Byword Is 'Flexibility,'" *Sales & Marketing Management,* January 1992, 62-64, 66, 68.

537 Based on information from "Keeping Up the Pace," *Direct Marketing,* November 1992, 37.

CHAPTER 20

555 Based on information from Kevin Goldman, "World Cup Sponsors Roll Ads for Soccer," *Wall Street Journal,* 23 March 1993, B10; Jim Henry, "GM to Tailor Cup Ads to Local Markets," *Automotive News,* 20 July 1992, 25; James McBride, "Magazines in Motion," *Mediaweek,* 1 February 1993, 18-21, 24; Joe Mandese, "GMC Truck Signs Solo Cross-Media Sponsorship," *Automotive News,* 2 March 1992, 35.

560 Based on information from Julie Edelson Halpert, "Pickups: From the Barn to the Carport," *New York Times,* 18 July 1993, sec. 3, 8.

APPENDIX C

C-7 Based on information from Maxine Paetro, *How to Put Your Book Together and Get a Job in Advertising,* new improved edition (Chicago: The Copy Workshop, 1990); Ann Marie Barry, *The Advertising Portfolio: Creating an Effective Presentation of Your Work* (Lincolnwood, Ill.: NTC Business Books, 1990).

C-8–C-11 Based on information from American Advertising Federation, *Careers in Advertising* (Washington, D.C.: American Advertising Federation, n.d.); American Association of Advertising Agencies, *Go For It: A Guide to Careers in Advertising* (New York: American Association of Advertising Agencies, 1989); Shelly Field, *Career Opportunities in Advertising and Public Relations* (New York: Facts on File, 1990); Maxine Paetro, *How to Put Your Book Together and Get a Job in Advertising,* new improved edition (Chicago: The Copy Workshop, 1990); Beth Heitzman, "Finally . . . an Ad Sector That's Hiring," *Adweek,* 4 October 1993, 14.

Photo Credits

208 Courtesy of Braathens SAFE and Leo Burnett, Oslo
210 Courtesy of New York Telephone
211 Courtesy of General Motors
213 Courtesy of Ericsson
214 Courtesy of Procter & Gamble
217 Courtesy of Holiday Inn Worldwide/photograph (upper right) Image Bank
218 "Adam Smith's Money World" produced by WNET and Alvin H. Perlmutter, Inc.

CHAPTER 9

220 Courtesy of Nikon and Bernstein & Andriulli
222 **top** AP/Wide World
222 **bottom** Courtesy of Nekka
224 Courtesy of Seattle Supersonics
225 Bob Daemmrich/Image Works
226 Courtesy of Chanel
227 Courtesy of Goodwill Industries and Earle Palmer Brown
228 Courtesy of Nike
230 Courtesy of ConAgra Frozen Foods
232 Courtesy of Leonard Monahan Lubars & Kelly
233 **top** Courtesy of Martin Williams Advertising
233 **bottom** Courtesy of Wilson Racquet Sports
234 **top** Courtesy of Samsonite
234 **bottom** Courtesy of LA Gear
235 Courtesy of D'Arcy Masius Benton & Bowles S.A. Ltd., Johannesburg
236 Courtesy of Parker Pen Company
238 Courtesy of 3M Corporation
239 Courtesy of Toyota of America
240 Courtesy of Glamour Magazine
241 Courtesy of Data Translation
242 Courtesy of Waked Internacional S.A.
243 **left** Courtesy of Minnesota Orchestra
243 **right** Ron Scherl/Bettmann Archive
245 Courtesy of Apple Computer

CHAPTER 10

248 Courtesy of Young & Rubicam, Vienna
250 Courtesy of Vancouver Aquarium
252 **top** Courtesy of Colgate-Palmolive
252 **bottom** Courtesy of Southwest Museum and Livingston & Co.
254 Courtesy of DuPont Company, photography by Michael Luppino
255 Courtesy of Leo Burnett Ltd., London
257 Courtesy of Neutrogena
259 Courtesy of Texas Instruments
260 Courtesy of North American Watch Company/ Movado Watch Company
266–267 Courtesy of Cheryl Solheid
269 Courtesy of St. Mary's Hospital, Richmond
270 © New York Lottery 1993. Reproduced by permission.
273 Courtesy of Burger King Corporation and Sosa Bromley Aguilar & Associates
275 Courtesy of Cessna Aircraft Co.

CHAPTER 11

276 © 1992 Taylor Guitars
279 Jim McCrary/Tony Stone Worldwide
280 Courtesy of Lahti Organ Festival, Finland
281 **top** Courtesy of Ricoh
281 **bottom** Courtesy of Minolta Corporation
282 **top** Donald Dietz/Stock, Boston
282 **bottom** Photography Bybee Studios, San Francisco
287 Courtesy of Emporium, San Francisco
288 Courtesy of Sony Electronics
291 Courtesy of Everlast World's Boxing Headquarters Corporation
292 Courtesy of Doyle Advertising
293 Courtesy of Pantone
295 Courtesy of Zellerbach
299 George Haling/Photo Researchers

391 Courtesy of Sony Electronics
303–307 Courtesy of Ammirati & Puris and Compaq

CHAPTER 12

308 Courtesy of Deere & Company and Sedelmaier Films
310 Courtesy of Pepsi Cola Co.
312 Courtesy of Beef Industry Council
315 Barry Fitzsimmons/San Diego Union-Tribune
317 Courtesy of Deere & Company and Sedelmaier Films
319 Don Smetzer/Tony Stone Images
323 © Goodby, Silverstein & Partners, 1993. All Rights Reserved.
324 Courtesy of Avid
326 Courtesy of MGM Grand Hotel
327 **left** Courtesy of The Richards Group
327 **left** Courtesy of Cabinetmasters
328 Mark Burnett/Photo Researchers
331 Courtesy of GMC Truck and McCann/SAS
334–337 Courtesy of Ayer Chicago and Jolly Rancher
338 **right** "Behind the Scenes: The Advertising Process at Work" made possible by the Advertising Educational Foundation, Inc.

CHAPTER 13

340 Courtesy of Alberta Economic Development and Tourism
342 Courtesy of Coca-Cola USA
344 Courtesy of Ben & Jerry's Homemade
346 Courtesy of Grainger Division, W. W. Grainger
347 Courtesy of Master Lock Company
352 © PacTel Cellular
356 Courtesy of China Jincheng Motorcycle Group
357 Courtesy of Chrysler/Plymouth and BBDO Detroit
358 Courtesy of Procter & Gamble
359 Courtesy of USA Weekend
362 Courtesy of Competitive Media
364 Courtesy of Stone House Systems
367 Courtesy of Chrysler

CHAPTER 14

370 Courtesy of J. Walter Thompson, London
372 Courtesy of Sansui USA
374 Courtesy of J.C. Penney
375 Courtesy of Newspaper Association of America
376 © 1993 Citibank
377 Courtesy of University of Phoenix and Castle Advertising
379 Courtesy of A. H. Robins
380 Courtesy of Residence Inn by Marriott
383 Newspaper Advertising Source, May 1994 edition, published by SRDS, Wilmette, IL
386 Courtesy of Citibank Hong Kong
387 Courtesy of Better Homes & Gardens
388 Courtesy of Cost Plus World Market
390 Courtesy of Farm Journal Publishing
393 Consumer Magazine and Media Source, May 1994 edition, published by SRDS, Wilmette, IL
394 Courtesy of Givenchy, Paris
396 © 1994 Time Inc.
397 Courtesy of Sports Illustrated, Comedy Central, Nike, NFL Films and Martin Mull
399 Courtesy of Lexmark International

CHAPTER 15

400 Courtesy of Sega of America
402 © 1993 Circus Circus Enterprises
404 Courtesy of The Discovery Channel
406 © 1994 Six Flags Theme Parks, Inc. BATMAN and all related elements are the property of DC Comics, TM & © 1994.
407 Courtesy of Chevy's Mexican Restaurant
410 Courtesy of Dr. Hieu Tri Nguyen
411 Courtesy of Interactive Network
413 Courtesy of Nielsen Media Research

414 Courtesy of Nielsen Media Research
415 TV and Cable Source, March 1994 edition, published by SRDS, Wilmette, IL
417 Courtesy of McCann-Erickson Seattle
420 **top** Courtesy of Gray Kirk VanSant
420 **bottom** Courtesy of Fuji Photo Film USA
422 Robin Landholm
424 Courtesy of The Arbitron Company
425 **top** Courtesy of The Arbitron Company
425 **bottom** Radio Advertising Source, April 1994 edition, published by SRDS, Wilmette, IL
427 Courtesy of Young & Rubicam and Colgate Palmolive

CHAPTER 16

430 Courtesy of Ruedi Wyler, Zurich
432 © 1994 American Express Travel Related Services Company, Inc.
434 © 1993 Time Life Inc.
437 **top** Courtesy of Adweek
437 **bottom** Courtesy of Meredith Corporation
438 Direct Mail List Rates and Data, May 1994 edition, published by SRDS, Wilmette, IL
440 Courtesy of Rover Japan
442 Courtesy of KPBS
443 Courtesy of McCann Erickson
446 Robert Simko
447 Charles Gupton/Stock, Boston
448 Courtesy of Tausche Martin Lonsdorf
449 Courtesy of Goldberg Moser O'Neill
450 Courtesy of TDI and SRO Communications
452 Courtesy of Mediacom
453 David Wells/Image Works
454 Courtesy of USA Today Sky Radio/Gannett and The Martin Agency, Richmond
455 Courtesy of Whittle Communications
457 Courtesy of MCI and Devon Direct Marketing & Advertising
460 Marine Corps materials courtesy of the U.S. Government, as represented by the Secretary of the Navy

CHAPTER 17

462 Courtesy of Canon Europa N.V.
464 Courtesy of Heinz USA
466 TBWA Advertising
467 *River God*, Wilbur Smith, St. Martin's Press, Inc., New York, NY. Ad created by The Mesa Group, Inc. Art Director: Aldo Coppelli for the book *River God* by Wilbur Smith. Reprinted with permission from St. Martin's Press, Inc., New York, NY.
470 Courtesy of Hyatt Hotels
473 Courtesy of Catalina Marketing
474 Courtesy of Quaker Oats
476 Courtesy of Goya Foods
477 Courtesy of Arby's
478 Courtesy of Elizabeth Arden
479 Robin Landholm
481 Courtesy of Las Vegas Convention & Visitors Authority
484 Courtesy of Logo Communications
485 Courtesy of Apple Computer
487 TM, ® Kellogg Company; © 1993 Kellogg Company

CHAPTER 18

490 Courtesy of Walsh & Associates; photographer Harald Sund, designer Miriam Lisco, copywriter Kevin Burrus
492 **left** © 1994 Delta Air Lines
492 AP/Wide World
494 UPI/Bettmann
495 Timo Salonen/Agence Vandystadt/Photo Researchers
496 Courtesy of Pepsi Cola Bottling Company of San Diego. DIET PEPSI and UH-HUH are registered trademarks of PepsiCo, Inc.

Glossary

A

account executive The person in the advertising agency who serves as liaison between the client and the agency.

account planning A research-based discipline within the advertising agency that represents the consumer's viewpoint and feelings about the product and the advertising.

account review A formal process in which an advertiser invites selected agencies to present their credentials and their advertising ideas for a specific product or brand.

ad slicks Professionally developed camera-ready ads prepared by manufacturers or distributors for local advertisers to use when featuring particular products in print ads.

adaptation Another term for *localization*.

adjacency The commercial time just before or after a network program or during a station break, when the network releases time to its local affiliates.

advertisers People or organizations that seek to sell products or influence people through advertising.

advertising The paid, nonpersonal communication of information about products or ideas by an identified sponsor through the mass media in an effort to persuade or influence behavior.

advertising agencies Independent organizations that specialize in developing and implementing advertising on behalf of advertisers.

advertising appeal An attempt, through some combination of emotion and logic, to draw a connection between the product being advertised and some need or desire that the audience feels.

advertising campaign A series of coordinated advertisements and other promotional efforts.

advertising environment The general atmosphere in which advertisers operate, created by forces (such as the economy, the government, and society at large) with the potential to influence advertising.

advertising manager In an advertiser's organization, the head of the advertising department.

advertising objectives The desired end results of advertising efforts.

advertising plan A document that guides the implementation of the advertising program.

advertising research A part of marketing research that focuses on the risks, uncertainties, and decisions involved in creating and applying advertising.

advertising strategy A statement that consists of a creative strategy (what you're going to say and how you're going to say it) and a media strategy (where and when you plan to say it).

advertorial A special magazine advertising section in which ads are interspersed with related editorial material focusing on a single theme.

advocacy advertising Advertising that communicates an organization's position on public issues that may or may not relate to that organization's line of business.

aerial advertising Advertising that is displayed on the side of a blimp, appears on a hot-air balloon, trails from a small plane, or is created by skywriting.

affidavit of performance A sworn statement provided by a radio or television station to confirm that an ad ran as scheduled.

affiliates Individual radio or television stations that have contracted to broadcast the network's material to local viewers or listeners.

affirmative disclosure The advertiser's disclosure of specific conditions, limitations, or consequences related to the use of the advertised product.

affordability method A budgeting approach in which the advertiser simply spends as much as it can afford on advertising.

agency networks International collections of agencies connected either by ownership arrangements or by agreements to help each other implement multicountry campaigns.

agency of record The agency designated to purchase media time and space for all the agencies that serve a particular advertiser.

agricultural advertising Advertising that targets the agricultural industry.

aided recall Recall tests in which respondents are told the name of the brand or company involved in the ad and then asked whether they remember the ad.

American Advertising Federation (AAF) A national association of U.S. advertising agencies, advertisers, media owners, and local advertising clubs.

American Association of Advertising Agencies (AAAA) A

national association of 750 member agencies around the United States.

animatic A moving version of the storyboard, in which sketches of the proposed visuals are filmed in sequence and linked with the audio track.

animation Moving visual elements in a television commercial other than live action; includes cartoons, series of still photos, copy on the screen, and so forth.

answer print The final version of a commercial sent out for the advertiser's approval before distribution to the media.

art Visual elements such as the design, illustrations, photos, and type that appear in ads and commercials.

art department The department in an advertising agency that creates the illustrations, designs, and sketches for ads and commercials.

art director The manager in the advertising agency who supervises the creation of art for ads and commercials.

Association of National Advertisers (ANA) A national association of more than 400 members representing the largest U.S. manufacturing and service advertisers.

attention value The degree of attention an audience pays to ads in a particular medium.

attitudes Lasting, general evaluations of products, issues, companies, people, colors, and so on; a learned tendency made up of cognitive, affective, and behavioral components.

audimeter A device attached to the television that records when the set is on and which stations are watched; used in television viewer research.

audio The portion of a television commercial that includes speaking voices, singing voices, instrumental background music, and sound effects.

avails Short for *availabilities*, a listing of television time slots that are available to be purchased.

average frequency The average number of times people or households are exposed to a media vehicle.

average quarter-hour persons The average number of listeners tuned to a radio station for at least 5 minutes during a particular 15-minute interval of a daypart.

average quarter-hour rating The number of radio listeners during a quarter-hour in a daypart as a percentage of the area population, calculated by dividing the average quarter-hour persons listening to one station by the area population or the target audience.

average quarter-hour share The percentage of the total radio audience listening to a particular station during a given quarter-hour in a daypart, calculated by dividing the average quarter-hour persons listening to one station by the average quarter-hour persons listening to all stations.

B

bait-and-switch advertising An illegal form of advertising in which a store promotes a low-priced product (the bait) in order to lure in customers, who are then switched to higher-priced or higher-profit products.

balance A state of equilibrium in a design, in which the parts on one side are the visual equals of the parts on the other side.

barter syndication A method of delivering television programs in which a local station pays less (or nothing) for a first-run or off-network program that comes with a percentage of its commercials presold to national advertisers by the syndicator.

basic bus The purchase of all the inside ad space on a group of buses.

behavioral segmentation Segmentation that uses buyer behavior as the distinguishing factor between groups of customers.

benefit segmentation The categorization of customers according to the benefits they seek from products.

Better Business Bureau (BBB) A business-monitoring group that works on the local level to protect consumers against false and deceptive advertising.

bias Distortion in research; it means that what you measure doesn't reflect reality.

Big Idea The creative spark or unifying theme around which an ad or ad campaign is structured; also called the *creative concept*.

billboard A large, flat sign structure erected outdoors away from the place of business.

billings An advertising agency's total revenues.

bleed page An ad in which the background color runs all the way to the edge, eliminating any white border.

body copy The words in the main body of the ad, apart from headlines, photo captions, and other blocks of text.

book stock A paper category that covers a wide range of weights, surfaces, and finishes, all typically used in books and magazines.

brainstorming Free association in a group setting, with no initial criticism or analysis of the ideas generated.

brand A name, word, phrase, symbol, or any combination of these elements that distinguishes one product from another.

brand development index (BDI) A ratio that measures the relative sales strength of a given brand in a specific area of the United States.

brand equity The measure of a brand's worth to the company that markets it and to the customers who buy it.

brand loyalty The degree to which buyers are committed to a brand, which can range from complete commitment under any circumstances to no commitment at all.

brand manager A manager in the advertiser's organization who is responsible for marketing a specific brand or product.

brand mark The portion of a brand that can't be expressed verbally, such as a graphic design or symbol.

brand name The portion of a brand that can be expressed verbally, including letters, words, or numbers.

broadcast production manager The individual in the advertising agency who translates the words and art into a finished commercial for electronic media.

broadsheet A newspaper with pages measuring about 22 inches deep by 13 inches wide and six columns on each page; also known as a *standard-size newspaper*.

broadside Also known as a *broadsheet*, a folded sheet of paper, printed on one or both sides, that opens into a large advertisement.

bursting A message schedule in which one ad runs repeatedly and frequently on the same television station.

bus-o-rama A large roof-mounted ad sign with a backlighted transparency that stretches the length of the bus.

business advertising Advertising directed toward people who buy or use products in businesses, nonprofit organizations, and government agencies.

business magazine A magazine that contains information useful to people who buy business products.

business reply envelope A postage-paid envelope that the customer can use to respond.

buying allowance   A payment or discount offered to a wholesaler or retailer to encourage the purchase of a certain amount of merchandise during a specified period.

buying center   The people within an organization who are significantly involved in a purchase.

C

cable television   A television delivery system that relies on wires (cables) to carry signals to viewers.

call to action   In advertising, the element that urges the audience to take action.

camera-ready   A general term that means an ad is ready for the platemaking process.

camera separation   A color separation process in which the two colors are alternately filtered out while two different negatives are created.

carryover effect   A phenomenon in advertising in which the advertising continues to exert influence in the market after the ad campaign is finished.

catalog   A direct-mail booklet that shows the pictures, descriptions, and prices of merchandise for sale.

category development index (CDI)   A ratio that expresses the sales potential of a particular product category in a specific area of the United States.

category manager   A manager in the advertiser's organization who coordinates the efforts of all the brand managers handling a related group of products.

causal research   Research that identifies the factors responsible for a particular effect in the marketplace.

cause-related marketing (CRM)   Promotional programs in which the advertiser promises to donate money to a nonprofit organization in exchange for using its name in connection with the promotion.

cease-and-desist order   A legal order obtained by the FTC to stop an advertiser from repeating a disputed ad.

celebrity endorsement ad   The use of a well-known entertainer, athlete, or other public person as a spokesperson in an ad.

census   A research approach in which you ask questions of every person in the population.

centralized advertising department   A way of organizing advertising activities so that one group plans, controls, and coordinates all advertising efforts for every unit and product of that organization.

cinematographer   The person responsible for the look of the lighting and for camera positioning and movement in filming a commercial; also called the *director of photography* or simply the *cameraman*.

circulation   The number of newspaper or magazine issues distributed each day or during a publication's normal distribution period.

classified advertising   All-text advertising positioned in a newspaper or magazine according to categories such as employment, automotive, and real estate.

classified display advertising   Classified advertising that includes illustrations, borders, and other visual elements as a way of setting ads apart from all-text ads.

client   An advertiser that has signed up to use the services of an advertising agency.

clip art   Collections of printed and computerized drawings that artists can incorporate into ads and other projects without worrying about copyrights.

closing date   The deadline for submitting advertising materials for a particular magazine issue.

closure   The tendency to want to fill in the missing parts of a phrase, picture, melody, or other recognizable pattern.

clutter   The overall number of ads competing for audience attention.

cognition   Learning that involves processing inputs, combining these inputs with information retrieved from memory, and reaching conclusions.

cognitive dissonance   Also known as *buyer's remorse*; a sense of discomfort or doubt after a purchase when buyers know that they could have made a different choice and wonder whether another choice might have been better.

collateral sales material   Brochures, videotapes, slides, and other items that show detailed product information.

color electronic prepress system (CEPS)   A sophisticated print production system that can perform such tasks as blending two-color photographs, retouching photos, and assembling pages.

color separation   Breaking an image down into its component colors; the term is usually reserved for process color work.

column inch   A measure of advertising size in which a single unit is one inch deep by one column wide.

combination plate   A printing plate that contains both unscreened line art and continuous-tone art that has been screened to create halftones.

combination rate   The rate that applies when advertisers buy space in more than one newspaper; usually lower than the rate for buying space in individual newspapers.

commercial pod   The group of television ads scheduled to run during a particular program break.

commercial speech   Advertising and other forms of speech used to promote commercial transactions.

commission   A payment from a media firm to an advertising agency that has purchased advertising space or time for its clients.

communication objectives   Advertising objectives expressed in terms of how well a given communication goal will be achieved.

comparative advertising   A type of ad in which the advertiser claims its product is better than a competing product.

competitive parity method   A budgeting approach in which the advertiser simply matches whatever its competitors are spending.

compiled list   A mailing list assembled by an outside firm from directories, public records, and other readily available sources.

composition   The overall arrangement of the copy and visuals in an ad.

comprehensive layout   Usually called the *comp*, this stage of the layout shows all the pieces of the ad in their more or less final positions.

computer-generated imagery (CGI)   A general term for visuals created on a computer system.

conditioning   Learning to respond in a certain way to a given stimulus; classical conditioning transfers the response normally associated with one stimulus to another stimulus, and instrumental conditioning is learning by reward and punishment.

consent decree   A legally binding agreement between an advertiser and the FTC stating that the advertiser won't repeat a disputed activity.

consumer advertising Advertising aimed at people who buy products for personal use.

consumer magazine A magazine that offers information and entertainment for people who buy products for personal or family use.

consumer market All individuals and households that buy goods and services for private use.

consumer sales promotion A set of promotional incentives aimed directly at the ultimate product purchaser.

consumers Individuals and families who buy goods and services for personal or family use.

contest A promotion in which participants use their skills or abilities to compete for prizes.

continuity The pattern of message repetition used in a media schedule.

continuity scheduling A message schedule in which ads run consistently over a long period without gaps.

continuous-tone art Images such as photographs that have a variety of tones, from dark to light.

contract rate A discounted ad rate based on a contract that states how many ads or how much space will be purchased during a given period.

controlled circulation The number of magazine or newspaper copies distributed free by mail to selected audiences or to the public through store and sidewalk racks.

convergent thinking Thinking that starts with available facts and tries to weed out all possibilities except one, converging on the one right solution.

cooperative advertising program An ad program in which a manufacturer pays part of the bill when a local store ad features its brand; often referred to as *co-op advertising*.

copy The words in an advertising message.

copy platform A checklist of the background information needed to craft an ad; generally contains a statement of the problem the advertising is expected to solve, the advertising objectives, a description of the product, a profile of the target audience, an assessment of the competition, the key customer benefit, support for the key benefit, the selling strategy, the selling style, and the advertising appeal that will be used.

copyfitting The process of making sure that copy will fit the space allotted for it.

copyright The exclusive right to print or reproduce material during the life of the copyright owner and for 50 years after.

copywriter The person within the advertising agency who writes the words for clients' advertising messages.

core values The values shared by people in a given culture; values that tend to be sustained from generation to generation.

corporate public relations The PR activities that don't include marketing PR; in other words, communicating with all the organization's audiences other than its customers and potential customers.

corrective advertising Advertising ordered by the FTC that requires an advertiser to disclose information to correct a false impression left by previous ads.

cost per order A method of measuring direct-marketing results that shows how much was spent to make each sale by dividing the total cost of the direct-marketing effort by the number of orders received.

cost per rating point (CPP) The cost to reach 1 percent (one rating point) of the targeted television or radio audience.

cost per thousand (CPM) The cost of reaching 1,000 people in a medium's audience.

coupon A certificate good for a specific price reduction when a particular product is purchased.

cover date The date that appears on a magazine's cover.

cover stock Papers that are usually heavier and stronger than both book and writing stocks.

crawl A line of text that runs across a television screen, usually along the bottom.

creative boutique A limited-service advertising agency that focuses on developing innovative advertising concepts and messages.

creative director The manager in the advertising agency who supervises the activities of the creative services function.

creative strategy The plan that defines a particular advertising effort, made up of the art direction, production values, and copy platform.

creativity The ability to produce new and original ideas or original ways of looking at existing ideas.

crisis communication The branch of PR that concerns communicating during accidents, natural disasters, strikes, and other serious events.

cultural segments Groups within a larger culture whose beliefs, values, and customs differ from those of the larger society while still being part of the larger society.

culture A society's beliefs, values, and symbols.

cume persons The number of different people who listen to a radio station for at least 5 minutes in a given daypart; also known as *cume audience*.

cume rating The percentage of different people within a population who listen to a radio station for at least 5 minutes during a given period, calculated by dividing the cumepersons figure by the area population.

customer-controlled cooperative advertising program A cooperative advertising program in which the supplier reimburses its customer (the retailer) for all or part of the cost of advertising certain products.

customers The people or organizations that purchase a company's products.

D

DAGMAR An acronym for the title of a book, *Defining Advertising Goals for Measured Advertising Results*, that proposes a four-stage model of communications results: awareness, comprehension, conviction, and action.

dailies Another term for rushes.

data Basic facts, figures, and ideas about a subject, not yet organized to form meaningful patterns.

database A comprehensive and continually updated file of information about individuals in the target audience.

database marketing A form of direct marketing in which advertisers use a database to define the best target audience for a given offer at a particular time.

daypart A defined segment of the television or radio day.

dealer tag An identifier that mentions the local retailer's name and that's inserted at the end of a supplier-controlled cooperative ad.

decentralized advertising department A way of organizing advertising activities so that each division or product group has a department to handle its own advertising.

deceptive advertising A representation, omission, or practice that's likely to mislead, leading to consequences not in the consumer's favor.

demographic segmentation Market segmentation based on demographic characteristics such as age and income (in the consumer market) or company size and industry group (in the organizational market).

demographics A collection of external, objective variables such as income, age, and occupation that describe a population.

departmental system A method of organizing an advertising agency's activities according to functional departments.

derived demand The nature of organizational demand, in which all demand for the product in question is driven by demand for another product.

descriptive research Research that characterizes conditions in a market, attitudes of audience members, or other factors of interest to advertisers.

designated market area (DMA) A market definition used by Nielsen to designate the boundaries of a geographic area in which the local television stations attract the most viewing hours.

desktop publishing The process of using personal computers and specialized software to create camera-ready pages.

dialog/monolog copy Copy that lets one or two characters in an ad do the selling through what they say.

direct broadcast satellite (DBS) A delivery system in which television or radio signals are transmitted directly from a satellite to homes equipped with a small receiving satellite dish.

direct-mail advertising Advertising that's delivered directly to the target audience by mail or by a private delivery service.

direct marketing Communicating directly with the target audience to sell products without going through intermediaries such as retailers or wholesalers.

direct questions Questions that request answers explicitly, such as "How old are you?"

direct-response advertising Advertising that supports a direct-marketing effort by asking the target audience to respond by taking immediate action.

director The person responsible for creating the commercial during the production phase, from composing the shots to directing the cast and crew.

display advertising Print advertising that consists of headline and body copy, illustrations, and other visual elements that set the message apart from editorial material.

display allowance A fee paid (or a discount offered) by the manufacturer to the retailer in exchange for a desirable shelf location, an end-of-aisle display, or some space for a POP display.

display copy Copy in headlines, in logos, and everywhere else except the body; generally refers to larger sizes of type in an ad.

distribution The process of moving products from the producer to the customer.

divergent thinking Open-ended thinking that expands the field of ideas and then converges on one of the many possible good solutions.

dropout An alternative to surprinting; the line-art portion appears to be cut out of the continuous-tone image.

dummy A mock-up for brochures, flyers, and other promotional material that serves the same basic function that the comp serves for print ads.

duotone A type of halftone in which black-and-white artwork is printed with two colors of ink to add richness, deepen shadows, clarify details, or change the overall tone.

dupes Duplicate copies of a finished commercial that are sent to the media.

E

editor The person responsible for converting raw footage into a finished commercial.

effective frequency The number of times a target audience must be exposed to a particular ad in a given medium to communicate the message and stimulate a response.

effective reach The number or percentage of the target audience members exposed to an ad some minimum number of times.

electronic couponing A computerized system of issuing coupons or price reductions in response to specific in-store consumer behavior patterns.

emotional appeals Appeals that try to sell products based on the emotional satisfaction that comes from purchasing and then either owning the product or giving it as a gift.

emphasis The condition of one element in an ad being highlighted relative to the other elements.

endorsement The implied or actual approval of a product by someone other than the advertiser, such as a celebrity, an expert, or a product user.

ethical dilemma An unresolved ethical question in which each of the conflicting sides has an arguable case to make.

ethical lapse A situation in which a normally ethical person makes an unethical decision.

ethnocentrism A cultural perspective in which a person believes that his or her own culture is superior to all others.

event sponsorship The branch of public relations concerned with tying an advertiser's name to a public event, which can be either an existing event or one created specifically for PR purposes.

everyday low pricing (EDLP) A policy in which the number of price promotions is reduced or eliminated in favor of lower year-round prices.

evoked set The group of products from which the buyer makes the final purchase decision; all the products in the evoked set are acceptable, but one usually stands out from the pack.

execution A finished ad, the final result of the design process.

experiment A research technique that follows the same pattern as any scientific experiment; testing a hypothesis by controlling key variables.

exploratory research Research that helps clarify the definition of a problem and lay the groundwork for more extensive research.

exposure The process of presenting ads to audiences.

F

farm magazine A type of magazine published for farmers and for businesses that make or sell agricultural products.

FCB grid A planning tool that divides advertising challenges by the type of product being advertised and the attitudes buyers are likely to have about the product; uses the two dimensions of thinking versus feeling and high involvement versus low involvement.

Federal Communications Commission (FCC) The U.S. government agency that regulates broadcast media such as radio, television, telephone, and telegraph.

Federal Trade Commission (FTC) The U.S. government agency that regulates most business practices, including advertising and marketing activities.

film negatives Film images in which normally light areas appear as dark areas and vice versa.

film positives Film images in which light and dark areas appear as they would in real life.

first-run syndication A method of delivering television programs in which the syndicator makes available to individual stations new programs that are produced specifically for syndication.

flat rate The undiscounted rate for buying one or more ads in a print vehicle.

flexography A variety of letterpress printing that uses a flexible rubber or plastic printing plate.

flighting An intermittent message schedule alternating periods when advertising runs with gaps when it doesn't run.

focus group A research process similar to in-depth interviews; the difference is that focus-group research involves a group of respondents.

font All the characters that make up one typeface in one type, size, and weight, such as 12-point Helvetica bold.

Food and Drug Administration (FDA) The U.S. government agency that regulates packaging and labeling (including advertising) of packaged foods, drugs, cosmetics, medical devices, and hearing aids.

four-color printing Printing using process color.

free association A technique for generating ideas by letting your mind go and simply recording whatever thoughts come to the surface.

free-standing insert (FSI) A preprinted insert devoted to cents-off coupons for a variety of products.

frequency A measure of the number of times people in the target audience are exposed to a media vehicle during a specified period.

frequency program An ongoing offer of free merchandise or services designed to encourage purchasing more of a product or purchasing it more frequently; also known as a *frequent-buyer program* or *loyalty program.*

full position A preferred print ad position in which the ad is surrounded by editorial material on both sides or is placed near the top of the page.

full-service advertising agency An agency capable of providing all the services necessary to develop, create, and execute advertising.

G

game A type of sweepstakes that incorporates the elements of chance but continues for a longer period.

gatefold An extra-wide page that is folded inward and opens like a gate to present an ad.

geocentrism The tendency to view one's home country as superior to all others.

geodemographic segmentation A research method that yields data functionally similar to psychographic data but derived by averaging demographic data inside geographic segments.

geographic segmentation The identification of audience segments based on geographic boundaries or other geographic spaces.

globalization Advertising in which a single strategy and execution are used for every country.

goods Tangible products that can be physically examined.

graphic designers Artists who focus on commercial artwork, such as that used in ads.

grazing Using a remote control to quickly scan a lot of television channels in search of something interesting to watch.

grid A matrix of horizontal and vertical lines that a designer can use to position and align the pieces of an ad; the grid itself doesn't appear in the finished ad.

gridlocking Scheduling a commercial on one television network while the same (or another) commercial is scheduled immediately before and after it on other networks.

gross impressions The sum of all possible target audience exposures to the vehicles in a media plan, calculated by counting each exposure as one impression.

gross rating points (GRPs) The sum of the ratings of all programs in a television schedule; in the context of one media plan, GRPs measure the total target audience exposed to all the vehicles in the plan.

group system A method of organizing an advertising agency's activities according to a series of formal, relatively self-contained groups, each of which is responsible for one or more clients' work.

guaranteed circulation The minimum number of copies of a particular issue of a periodical that will be delivered.

H

halftone A negative produced with the halftone-screening process.

halftone screen Prepress accessories that break an image down into dot patterns.

handbills Printed flyers or circulars that can be put up on community bulletin boards, distributed on the street, left on car windshields, or delivered door-to-door.

hard-sell advertising An advertising style that more or less pounds at the audience with demands to buy or to take some action.

headline The dominant line or lines of copy in an ad, usually but not always set in larger type and placed at the top of the ad; also called a *heading* or a *head.*

hierarchy of effects model A continuum of stages through which an audience passes as it reacts to advertising.

horizontal publication A type of magazine that covers a particular job function that exists in many industries.

house list A list of customers (and sometimes prospects) maintained by the advertiser.

house organ A publication produced by a business or a nonprofit group to keep customers, contributors, dealers, investors, and others informed.

household A housing unit and the person or persons who occupy it, which can include an individual, a married couple with children at home, a married couple without children at home, single parents and their children, other relatives sharing a dwelling, or unrelated people sharing a dwelling.

households using television (HUT) Also known as *sets in use,* the number of households in a market that are watching any television program during a given period.

I

illustrators Artists who create nonphotographic visuals such as technical drawings.

imagesetters Laser-based phototypesetters that can produce both text and graphics.

in-depth interview A research process in which a researcher poses questions to individual respondents.

in-house advertising agency An advertising agency owned and operated by the advertiser.

in-market tests Experiments conducted in the actual marketplace, as opposed to a laboratory.

incentive-based compensation A payment method that rewards an agency according to the results its advertising achieves for the client.

industrial advertising Advertising that targets people who buy or use the materials and services needed to conduct business or to manufacture other products.

infomercial A longer commercial that mixes information, entertainment, and a sales pitch in a programlike format.

information The useful and meaningful result of organizing and analyzing data.

insertion order A form that specifies the date(s) a print ad is to run, the size it should be, any preferred positions, the rate to be charged, and other production details.

inside card Advertising displayed on the interior of a transportation vehicle such as a bus or train.

integrated marketing communications (IMC) A strategy of coordinating and integrating all of a company's marketing efforts and promotional communications to convey a consistent, unified message and image.

integrated marketing communications model A model that examines communications effectiveness starting with the purchase and working back through the communications stages.

interactive kiosks Freestanding machines equipped with a computer, a touch-sensitive screen or a keyboard, and a monitor that can display advertising, offer product information, and sometimes sell the products they feature.

interactive television A two-way communication technique in which television viewers interact with programs and commercials through a joystick or keypad.

interconnects Groups of cable-system operators that sell advertising time on any or all of their linked systems.

intercultural advertising Any advertising that crosses cultural boundaries; the cultures can be in a single country or in multiple countries.

interlock For film editing, the next step after the rough cut, in which the editor brings the film and the soundtrack into close-to-final form.

international advertising Advertising that targets people in other countries.

investor relations The part of corporate PR that involves communicating with investors, financial analysts, and government financial regulators.

J

jingles Short songs that carry advertising messages; can be either original tunes or adaptations of popular tunes.

L

laboratory tests Experiments that are conducted in a controlled setting, as opposed to the actual market.

layout Any in-progress version of an ad, from a rough sketch to a finished mechanical with real photos and final type; some people refer to a print ad's basic design as its layout.

learning Changes to the contents or organization of a person's long-term memory.

letterpress A method of printing in which the image areas are higher than the nonimage areas on the printing plate, meaning that only the image areas get inked.

lifestyle A person's activities, interests, opinions, and consumption patterns.

limited-service advertising agency An agency that concentrates on selected advertising services such as creative concepts or media buying.

line art Images that consist entirely of lines and other solid areas; also known as *line drawings* or *line copy*.

list broker An individual or a business that arranges for one organization to use the mailing lists of others.

lobbyists PR specialists who communicate with government bodies on behalf of organizations.

local advertising Advertising that concentrates on a narrow area such as a city.

local business advertising Advertising used by individuals and businesses to promote goods and services to businesses in the local area.

local political advertising Advertising used by politicians, interest groups, and individuals who want to influence the political process in a particular area.

local retail advertising Advertising used by retail outlets in a narrowly defined target market to reach consumers who buy for their personal use.

local spot Commercial time purchased by a local advertiser from a local station.

localization The strategy of developing a unique ad or a unique variation on a generic ad for each country, rather than using a single strategy for the entire world.

logical appeals Appeals that try to sell products based on their performance, features, or ability to solve problems; also known as *rational appeals*.

M

mail order A form of direct marketing in which merchandise is sold and delivered by mail.

make/buy decision A decision customers make when they have a choice between creating a good or performing a service themselves and paying someone else to provide the product.

makegood Commercial time made available free to advertisers to compensate for a ratings shortfall or for any mistakes in airing the ad.

market research A subset of marketing research that focuses on gathering information about a particular market.

market segment A subgroup of buyers in a market, distinguished from other buyers by unique needs and responses to advertising.

market share One advertiser's portion of the total sales in a particular market.

marketing The conception, pricing, promotion, and distribution of ideas, goods, and services to satisfy the needs of individuals and organizations.

marketing communication The process of sending promotional messages to a target audience.

marketing concept The idea of focusing on meeting customer needs and integrating marketing with every part of the organization while working for long-term profits.

marketing mix The most effective combination of four elements (product, price, distribution, and promotion) that forms the basis of a marketing strategy aimed at satisfying customer needs.

marketing objectives Objectives that define targets for marketing performance.

marketing plan A document used to guide the implementation of the marketing strategy; contains a situation analysis, marketing objectives, marketing strategy, and an action plan.

marketing public relations   The use of PR to increase product sales.

marketing research   A systematic approach to providing information and support for the entire range of marketing decisions.

marketing strategy   A statement of how the marketing function will meet its objectives; describes target markets, the position desired in those markets, and the planned marketing mix.

markup   The additional percentage an advertising agency adds to a supplier's bill.

mass marketing   The alternative to target marketing; in mass marketing the advertiser tries to reach the entire market with a single marketing mix.

mass media   Channels that reach a widespread general audience.

mechanical   The finished physical ad that will be reproduced as the first step in the printing process; often referred to as the *pasteup*.

media   The channels through which advertisers' messages are carried to their intended audiences.

media buyer   The person inside the advertising agency who books the time or space needed for a commercial or an ad.

media-buying service   A limited-service advertising agency that handles only media planning, buying, and placement.

media department   The department in an advertising agency that develops plans for how to use media to reach the target audience and buys the time or space for the client's advertisements.

media director   The manager inside the advertising agency who is responsible for finding the best media at the best price to most effectively reach the client's audience.

media environment   The circumstances surrounding advertising reception, including the content and look that the media create for the messages they deliver.

media mix   The use of two or more media in a media plan.

media plan   A comprehensive outline of the specific media objectives, strategy, and tactics to be used for advertising a particular product or brand.

media planner   The person inside the advertising agency who decides which media to use, when to use them, and at what cost.

media planning   The process of directing the advertising message to the target audience at the appropriate time and place, using the appropriate channel.

media relations   The branch of PR that communicates with the news media.

media research   One of the two halves of advertising research; media research concerns information about the circulation of newspapers and magazines, broadcast coverage of television and radio, and audience profiles.

media researcher   The person inside the advertising agency who supports media planning and buying by analyzing the number and type of people each medium reaches.

media spillover   A situation in which one region receives media from a second region.

media strategy   The course of action planned to achieve an advertiser's media objectives.

media vehicle   The individual program, publication, or delivery mechanism that is used to carry an advertising message.

medium   A single channel that carries the advertiser's message to the intended audience.

merge and purge   A process of combining mailing lists to eliminate duplicate names and addresses.

message research   The other half of advertising research; addresses how effectively advertising messages are communicated to people and how well these messages influence people's behavior.

message weight   The size of the combined target audiences reached by all the media vehicles used in a media plan.

mixing   Refers to both audio mixing, which combines the various elements of sound (dialog, music, etc.), and final mixing, which combines the audio and visual elements into one finished tape.

monthly promotional calendar   A monthly schedule of sales, in-store appearances, and other promotional events that retailers prepare to plan and space their advertising efforts throughout the year.

morphing   A computer graphics technique for transforming the shape of an object on-screen.

motivation value   The degree to which a medium stimulates its audience to respond.

motives   The internal factors, created by needs, that guide behavior toward meeting those needs.

multinational corporations (MNCs)   Companies with business operations in more than one country.

multipoint distribution system (MDS)   A television delivery system that uses very high frequency microwaves to transmit many channels to viewers.

N

narrative copy   Copy that tells a story as it persuades.

narrowcasting   Cable television's ability to deliver specialized programming to highly targeted audiences.

national advertising   Advertising in more than one region of a country.

National Advertising Division (NAD)   The operating arm of the National Advertising Review Council that investigates questionable advertising practices.

National Advertising Review Board (NARB)   The operating arm of the National Advertising Review Council that investigates disputed decisions of the NAD.

National Advertising Review Council (NARC)   An association established by the Council of Better Business Bureaus, the AAAA, the ANA, and the AAF to promote truth, accuracy, social responsibility, and ethics in advertising.

national spot   Commercial time purchased by a national advertiser from a local station.

nationalism   The belief that the interests of one's own country should take precedence over the interests of other countries; it sometimes surfaces in advertising in appeals to buy products from a particular country.

needs   Perceived gaps between current conditions and ideal conditions.

network   A group of radio or television stations that simultaneously broadcast in many markets.

news release   Another term for *press release*.

newsprint   The paper on which newspapers are printed.

nonprobability sample   A sample in which you cannot determine the chances of any member of the population being selected.

nonproduct advertising   Advertising that stresses image or ideas rather than products.

O

objective and task method   A budgeting approach that starts with the advertising objectives, identifies the tasks that need to be accomplished to meet those objectives, figures the cost of doing those tasks, and then totals a budget based on those costs.

objectives Goal statements that identify desired future levels of performance.

observation A method of measuring audience and buyer behavior by recording what people actually do, as opposed to what they say they do.

off-network syndication A method of delivering television programs in which the syndicator makes available to individual stations established programs that originally appeared on network television.

offset lithography The most common type of lithography done on a rotary press; uses an additional roller to pick up the image from the plate and then transfers it to the paper.

on location Being at any shooting site away from the studio.

on-sale date The date a magazine goes on sale.

one-color printing Print jobs done with a single ink (whether black or any other color).

open rate The highest rate for running a single print ad, which applies until more space is purchased and the advertiser qualifies for a volume discount.

operational segmentation The segmentation of organizational customers by the technology they use, the products they buy, the managerial and technical capabilities they have, and other policies and practices they use in the operation of their organizations.

opinion leaders People whose knowledge of product classes commands the attention and respect of other buyers.

opticals Special effects done with film cameras.

organizational market Businesses, nonprofit organizations, and government agencies that buy goods and services in order to produce other goods and services.

organizational objectives Long-range goals for the organization as a whole, usually defined in financial terms.

out-of-home advertising Advertising that reaches the target audience away from home.

outdoor advertising Advertising messages displayed on posters, billboards, and other outdoor surfaces.

outsert A preprinted, multipage ad enclosed in a plastic bag along with a magazine.

outside poster An advertising panel attached to the side, front, rear, or roof of a bus, train, subway, trolley, or taxi.

overlaying Enhancing data in customer files by adding information purchased from outside sources such as market research firms, credit-reporting agencies, and the U.S. Census.

P

paid circulation The number of newspaper or magazine copies purchased through subscriptions and at stores and newsstands.

painted bulletin The larger of the two standardized sizes of billboards, carrying a preprinted ad message.

participation A type of advertising in which various advertisers buy commercial time during a specific program without the responsibilities of sponsorship.

payback analysis A way of analyzing a marketing or advertising budget to see how much profit a marketing program will generate and how soon it will pay back all its costs.

people meter An electronic device introduced by Nielsen that records the television usage of all household members and guests.

percentage-of-sales method A budgeting approach that defines the ad budget as some predetermined percentage of expected sales.

perception The three-part process of exposure to a stimulus, attention to the stimulus, and then interpretation of the stimulus.

personal selling Face-to-face sales contact in which a salesperson tries to persuade someone to buy a product.

personality The characteristic and consistent patterns of behavior that a person exhibits.

photomatic A moving version of the storyboard that's similar to an animatic but uses photos instead of sketches.

phototypesetter Several generations of typesetting equipment that use light in one form or another to generate images on the page.

pica The unit of measurement for the horizontal dimension of type (and most other parts of a design); 1 pica equals ⅙ of an inch, or 12 points.

picture-and-caption copy A body-copy approach that relies on photographs or illustrations, with support from their accompanying captions.

place-based advertising Out-of-home advertising that reaches the target audience where and when that audience will notice it.

plate A physical representation of an original pasteup or piece of film; the plate transfers the image onto the printed page.

point-of-purchase (POP) displays In-store materials designed to influence the purchase of a particular product.

points The units of measurement for the vertical dimension of type; 1 point equals 1/72 of an inch.

population The entire group you want to learn more about in a research project; also called the *universe*.

position The place a brand occupies in the mind of a potential buyer, relative to competing products.

positioning The process of achieving a desired position in the mind of potential buyers.

poster panel The smaller of the two standardized billboard sizes, carrying a preprinted ad message.

postproduction The third and final phase of the television production process, when editing specialists put all the pieces together to form the finished commercial.

posttesting Research conducted after the advertising program has been implemented.

preemption rate The lower spot advertising rate a television station may offer in exchange for the right to resell the commercial time at a higher rate to another advertiser.

preferred position An ad position specifically requested by the advertiser.

premium An item offered free (or at an extremely low price) as an incentive to try or buy a product.

preprinted insert Advertising material printed in advance and distributed through enclosure in a newspaper.

preproduction The first phase of the television production process; involves all the planning needed to accomplish the production.

preproduction meeting In filming a commercial, a checkpoint session used to make sure that all the details are taken care of before shooting.

press conference A meeting designed to allow reporters to ask questions and interact with an organization's executives and media representatives.

press release A short document given to the media to share information about an organization, its people, or its products.

pretesting Research that involves testing one or more versions of an ad before completing production and buying media.

price The value, usually monetary, that sellers ask for in exchange for their products.

price pack A promotional technique in which something extra is bundled with the product package.

price promotion A short-term price reduction available to everyone who purchases a product during the promotion period.

primary data Data gathered firsthand for a specific purpose; can be collected by conducting surveys, interviewing customers, observing shoppers in stores, recording checkout scanner data, and attaching devices to televisions.

primary readership The actual purchasers of or subscribers to a print vehicle.

prime time The television daypart that stretches from 8 P.M. to 11 P.M. (Eastern Standard Time); the daypart with the highest viewing level.

print production manager The individual in the advertising agency who translates the copywriter's words and the art director's design into a finished ad for newspapers or magazines.

probability sample A sample in which every member of the population has a known (but not necessarily equal) chance of being included.

process color The method used to print full-color advertising; relies on mixtures of cyan, yellow, magenta, and black.

producer The person who manages the production process for a television commercial; usually refers to a person from the ad agency but can also be someone representing the studio.

product A good or service for which customers will exchange something of value, usually money.

product advertising Advertising that sells the advertiser's goods or services.

product information center An in-store video display terminal programmed to flash brief commercials and community news items.

product life cycle A model that divides the life span of a product or product category into the introduction, growth, maturity, and decline phases.

product placement The practice of paying a fee (or providing products free) in exchange for having products used and displayed in movies, television programs, and music videos.

product-use segmentation The segmentation of markets based on the way buyers use products or on the quantities they purchase.

production The second phase of the television production process, during which the commercial is actually filmed, videotaped, programmed on computer, or drawn by artists.

production department The department in an advertising agency that translates the art and copy into finished ads.

professional advertising Advertising directed toward licensed professionals such as lawyers, accountants, doctors, dentists, and teachers.

program rating The percentage of all households with television (or radio) in a specific market tuned into a particular program.

progressive proofs The intermediate steps of color combinations in process color printing.

projective techniques Vague, unstructured questions that request answers implicitly; they give respondents the opportunity to project their feelings onto objects or other people.

promotion The variety of techniques an advertiser uses to communicate with current and potential customers.

promotional mix The particular combination of advertising, sales promotion, public relations, and personal selling that an advertiser chooses to employ.

promotional objectives Objectives that show how promotional activities will support the attainment of marketing objectives.

proof A trial print sent to the advertiser so that the accuracy of the ad can be checked before it's scheduled to run.

proportion The relationship between the size of elements in a design; a design is in proportion when the sizes of the various elements make sense relative to one another.

psychographic segmentation The segmentation of markets using psychological or behavioral factors, including motivation, desired benefits, attitude, lifestyle, personality, consumer behavior, and brand loyalty.

psychographics The study of motivations, attitudes, lifestyles, personalities, and self-concepts as they relate to buyer behavior, particularly the efforts to quantify the thoughts and feelings that drive human behavior.

public relations (PR) The relationship between a business and the media, including press conferences to announce political candidates, media announcements to support fund-raising events, and press releases to bolster a company's image; this communication process involves understanding public attitudes, interpreting those attitudes for management, and then taking steps either to identify the organization with those attitudes or to modify the public attitudes.

public service announcements (PSAs) Ads by government and nonprofit groups that meet the community's needs by addressing social issues such as drug abuse and pollution.

publicity A part of public relations that involves generating media coverage about an organization and its products.

puffery The exaggerated praise of a product by its advertiser without offering facts to back up the claim.

pull strategy A promotional strategy that creates demand at the final-customer level and relies on this demand to pull products through the marketing channel.

pulsing A message schedule that combines the steady pattern of continuity with intermittent periods of more intense advertising activity.

push money The payment of a set amount of money by the advertiser to a salesperson every time a particular item is sold.

push strategy A promotional strategy that focuses on the next link in the marketing chain and encourages whoever makes up that link to push products on through to final customers.

Q

qualitative research Research that looks for in-depth answers that cannot be easily translated into quantitative statistics.

quantitative research Research that tries to translate responses into statistical results.

questionnaire A list of questions that respondents read and answer, a list of questions that telephone or in-person interviewers read to respondents, or a computer program that presents questions to someone sitting at the keyboard.

R

radio personality A disk jockey or other radio performer.

rate card A printed schedule of a newspaper's or magazine's advertising rates, production specifications, advertising deadlines, and other details.

rating point A measure equivalent to 1 percent of the target audience.

reach A measure of how many different members of the target audience are exposed to the media vehicle at least once during a specified period, usually four weeks.

readership The total number of people who read a print vehicle.

recall test A test of how well audiences remember particular ads.

recognition test A test of whether audiences can recognize the name of the brand or product that was advertised.

reference group People who influence a buyer's decisions; a buyer belongs to some reference groups, would like to belong to others, and shuns some other reference groups.

refund A money-back offer that returns to the consumer a specific amount of money after a particular product is purchased.

regional advertising Advertising in a specific region within a country.

regionalization An international advertising approach in which the advertiser targets two or more countries with a single campaign. This offers some of the benefits of globalization, without all the risk, as well as some of the benefits of localization, without all the cost.

reliability The degree to which the original researcher or someone else can repeat the research and arrive at the same answer.

reprint A copy of an ad, an article, or some other material that has appeared elsewhere but may be of interest to customers or prospects.

research director The manager in the advertising agency who investigates the current and potential customers for a product, looks at what motivates these customers to act, and gives the creative services people the background they need to create effective ads.

residuals Payments made to the actors whenever their commercials appear on the air.

response list A mailing list of people who have responded to other advertisers' direct-mail offers for similar or related products.

retail advertising Advertising placed by retailers, such as supermarkets and department stores, that want to reach consumers.

roadblocking A message schedule in which the same ad appears on three or four major television networks at the same time.

rotary plan A plan that entails moving an outdoor bulletin to another location in the same market every 30, 60, or 90 days.

rough cut The output from the first stage of editing a commercial; includes the scenes in the order in which they'll appear in the final commercial but doesn't include the finished soundtrack, special effects, or final editing touches.

rough layout A full-size version of the thumbnail sketch of an ad, showing all the elements in their basic proportions and placements.

run of paper (ROP) Positioning an ad anywhere on any page within the print medium.

run of station The placement of a commercial to air, at the discretion of the station, during any time of the day.

rushes The film or videotape from a day's shooting, used by a commercial's director and producer to see if they captured what they wanted to capture.

S

sales objectives Advertising objectives expressed in specific levels of sales within a fixed period of time; they are appropriate for advertising only under certain conditions.

sales promotion An offer of direct inducements that enhance the basic value of a product for a limited time to stimulate immediate distributor commitment, sales force effectiveness, and consumer purchasing.

sample A subset of the research population, selected to represent the overall population.

sample error An error in research that reflects the differences in answers resulting from the fact that researchers didn't query an entire population; all sample surveys have some level of sample error.

sampling The practice of offering a small quantity of a product free or at an extremely low cost to the consumer.

script The copywriter's version of a storyboard, containing the copy (the spoken or sung words) and verbal descriptions of the visual elements.

script clerk The person on the set of a commercial who performs such key tasks as verifying that the dialog being filmed matches the script, timing each scene, and checking for continuity from scene to scene.

secondary data Data already collected and used for an earlier purpose that are reused for a new research problem.

secondary readership The number of people other than the original purchaser or subscriber who read the same copy of a print vehicle.

segmentation The process of breaking a market of varied customers into subgroups of similar customers, as defined by their needs and purchase behaviors.

selective binding A publication process in which the selection of editorial and advertising matter included in each issue can be customized for individual subscribers.

selective perception The phenomenon of choosing which messages to pay attention to and acknowledge.

self-concept A person's perceptions, beliefs, and feelings about himself or herself.

self-liquidating premium A more substantial premium that's partly or completely paid for by the consumer rather than given away free.

self-mailer A postcard, a brochure, or other printed material that's delivered without an envelope.

sequence The order in which the reader or viewer takes in the various elements in an ad or other piece of design.

service mark A trademark for a service rather than for a tangible good.

services Intangible products that offer financial, legal, medical, recreational, or other customer benefits.

set An area in a studio constructed just for the purpose of shooting.

share of audience The percentage of the total audience viewing television at a given time that is watching a particular program.

share-of-market/share-of-voice method An advertising budgeting method in which the advertiser defines its budget after considering the market share it hopes to achieve and the share of voice it will need for achieving that market share.

share of voice One advertiser's portion of the total advertising expenditure in a particular market.

short rate An additional charge levied by publishers when advertisers that have signed for a contract rate buy less space than agreed on.

showings A measure (percentage) of the area population exposed to an outdoor message each day.

silk-screen printing Printing in which ink is spread across the entire area to be printed; a stencil keeps ink away from the nonimage areas.

single-source data Collections of data about the advertising reception and purchasing behavior exhibited by households.

situation analysis A review of past and present data with the goal of summarizing an organization's current circumstances and identifying relevant trends, forces, and market conditions.

situational influences Circumstances surrounding a purchase, such as time of year or reason for buying, that influence purchase behavior.

slice of life A television format that gives the audience a look at a supposedly realistic situation in the lives of people who represent the target audience.

slogans Memorable sayings that convey a selling message; also called tag lines.

slotting allowance A fee paid by the manufacturer to the retailer in exchange for a "slot," or position, on the store shelf.

social classes Levels in a society defined by similar values, lifestyles, interests, and behaviors.

social responsibility The concept that every organization has obligations to society that go beyond pursuing its own goals.

soft-sell advertising An advertising style that takes a more subtle approach to persuading and motivating consumers to act without actually demanding a particular audience behavior.

specialty advertising A form of advertising in which the advertiser's name, message, or logo is imprinted on useful items to be given away.

spectacular An extremely large outdoor display that incorporates special electrical or mechanical devices.

speculative presentation An agency's presentation of the advertising approach it would use, if hired, to solve a specific problem for the advertiser.

split-run test A common experimental technique in which a magazine or newspaper splits its circulation so that an advertiser can run a separate ad in each portion and then compare their effectiveness; also vital in developing effective direct-mail campaigns.

sponsorship A type of advertising in which the advertiser assumes responsibility for producing a program and in exchange enjoys the exclusive right to air commercials during that program.

spot announcement A type of advertising in which a segment of commercial time is purchased from a local station.

spot colors The colors used in multicolor printing (as opposed to full-color printing).

spot radio Radio time purchased from local stations.

spot television Television time purchased from local broadcast and cable television stations.

standard advertising unit (SAU) system A consistent industrywide method of defining newspaper ad size.

Standard Industrial Classification (SIC) codes A U.S. government system of categorizing industries by the types of goods and services they produce.

standardization A synonym for *globalization*.

statement stuffer A small printed ad designed to be delivered with a customer invoice.

stereotyping The process of trying to categorize individuals by predicting their behavior based on their membership in a particular class or group.

stopping power An ad's ability to catch the audience's attention.

storyboard A planning document that shows the main visual scenes in a television commercial, along with the voice-over copy and instructions for camera movements, sound effects, and other design elements.

straight-line copy Copy that starts where the headline leaves off and begins developing the selling points for the product in a straightforward fashion.

strategy A statement of how objectives will be achieved.

stripping The process of assembling line and continuous-tone images into a single negative.

subheads Secondary headlines, often written as transitions from the headline to the body copy.

substantiation The availability of documented proof of an advertiser's claims.

Sunday supplement A full-color magazine distributed inside the Sunday newspaper.

super Copy displayed on the television screen; short for *superimpose.*

superstation A large independent broadcast station that sends its signals via satellite to cable systems throughout the country.

supplier-controlled cooperative advertising program A cooperative advertising program in which the manufacturer or distributor creates and places ads that are customized with one or more retailers' names.

suppliers Individuals or organizations that provide the specialized services (such as photography) needed in the process of creating and executing advertising.

surprinting Superimposing copy or other line art on top of a half-screened photograph or other visual image.

survey A method of gathering data directly from members of a sample.

sweepstakes A promotion in which prizes are awarded based on a random drawing or some other chance-selection method.

syndicated data Data collected by specialized firms for more than one client at a time; any advertiser that wants to pay for the data can see the results.

synergy The creation of a combination of media in which each medium complements and enhances the overall effect to produce a whole that is greater than the sum of its individual parts.

T

tabloid A newspaper with a page size of about 14 inches deep by 11 inches wide.

take ones Brochures or business reply cards held in a pocket attached to a piece of advertising.

talent The cast or actors in a television commercial.

target audience The specific group of people an ad is aimed at.

target marketing Marketing to selected target segments rather than to the entire market.

target segment A market segment that an advertiser decides to focus on with a particular marketing mix.

tear-offs A pad of coupons or business reply cards attached to a piece of advertising.

tear sheet The actual page, torn from the newspaper or magazine in which an ad appeared, sent to an advertiser or agency to prove that an ad ran as planned.

telemarketing The promotion of goods and services via telephone contact with businesses or consumers.

television households (TVHH) The number of households in a market that are equipped with television.

terminal poster An advertising panel mounted inside a bus, subway, train, or trolley station; on a transit platform; in a bus-stop shelter; or in an airline terminal.

testimonial An appeal in which real users of a product—they may be celebrities, but they don't have to be—make the sales pitch.

thumbnail A miniature rough sketch used by designers to try out design ideas.

total bus The purchase of all exterior ad space on a bus.

tracking studies Posttest studies conducted over a period of time after an ad campaign has begun.

trade advertising Advertising that targets intermediaries such as the wholesalers and retailers that buy products for resale to customers.

trade deal A short-term arrangement in which wholesalers and retailers are encouraged to stock and promote products in exchange for special discounts, payments, or additional merchandise.

trade sales promotion A set of promotional inducements targeted toward wholesalers, retailers, and other intermediaries in the distribution channel.

trade show An event in which manufacturers display and sell their products to current and potential distributors.

trademark A brand of a tangible good registered with the U.S. government for exclusive use by the brand owner.

traffic department The department in the advertising agency that coordinates all aspects of creative development and production to ensure that ads are submitted to the media on schedule.

transit advertising Advertising placed inside or outside public transportation vehicles, in train or bus stations and on platforms, or in airport terminals.

two-color printing Print jobs done with two inks (one of which can be black).

type families Collections of related type styles, such as the Univers family.

typeface The basic design of type, such as letters that are elegant or casual, that have a classic or modern feel, and so on.

typesetting The process of setting typefaces and arranging letters and words on the page.

U

unaided recall A test of how well subjects remember any ads for the type of product being advertised.

unfair advertising Advertising likely to cause consumers substantial harm (in economic, safety, or health terms) that can't reasonably be avoided.

unique selling proposition (USP) A unique, specific benefit statement that's powerful enough on its own to motivate customers to buy.

unity A design state that occurs when all the pieces work together to form a cohesive whole.

V

validity The degree to which research results present an accurate picture of reality.

vertical publication A type of magazine that covers all aspects of a single industry.

video All the elements of a commercial that the viewer sees on the television screen; includes live action, animation, displayed copy, and visual effects.

video news release (VNR) The television equivalent of the written press release; a short piece of video created to convey a PR message.

visuals All the noncopy elements in an ad, although the graphic treatment of the copy can be considered a visual element as well.

voice-over Copy in a television ad that is read by someone off-screen.

volume discount A schedule of lower charges that applies when advertisers buy space repeatedly.

W

white space Any uninterrupted expanse of a single color, including black or white.

word of mouth Information about products and suppliers that is passed from customer to customer, rather than from advertiser to customer.

work print A copy of the dailies or of the videotape for a commercial, from which the editor (and sometimes the director) starts to assemble the finished product.

writing stock Paper that includes stationery designed for handwriting as well as papers for everyday business use in typewriters, photocopiers, and computer printers.

zapping Using a remote control to change television channels, especially during commercials.

zipping Fast-forwarding through the commercials on programs that have been taped using a videocassette recorder.

Author Index

Name/Organization/Company/Brand Index

Subject Index